OXFORD PAPERBACK REFERENCE

The Concise Oxford Chronology of English Literature

Michael Cox was formerly Senior Commissioning Editor for Reference Books at Oxford University Press. His previous books include the *Oxford Book of English Ghost Stories* and the *Oxford Book of Victorian Ghost Stories* (both with R. A. Gilbert); *Victorian Detective Stories: An Oxford Anthology*; and the *Oxford Book of Twentieth-Century Ghost Stories*.

Oxford Paperback Reference

The most authoritative and up-to-date reference books for both students and the general reader.

ABC of Music
Accounting
Allusions
Animal Behaviour*
Archaeology
Architecture
Art and Artists
Art Terms
Astronomy
Better Wordpower
Bible
Biology
British History
British Place-Names
Buddhism
Business
Card Games
Catchphrases
Celtic Mythology
Chemistry
Christian Art
Christian Church
Chronology of English Literature
Classical Literature
Classical Myth and Religion
Computing
Contemporary World History
Countries of the World
Dance
Dates
Dynasties of the World
Earth Sciences
Ecology
Economics
Encyclopedia
Engineering*
English Etymology
English Folklore
English Grammar
English Language
English Literature
Euphemisms
Everyday Grammar
Finance and Banking
First Names
Food and Drink
Food and Nutrition
Foreign Words and Phrases
Geography
Humorous Quotations
Idioms
Internet
Islam
Kings and Queens of Britain
Language Toolkit
Law
Linguistics
Literary Quotations
Literary Terms
Local and Family History
London Place-Names
Mathematics
Medical
Medicinal Drugs
Modern Design*
Modern Slang
Music
Musical Terms
Musical Works
Nicknames*
Nursing
Ologies and Isms
Philosophy
Phrase and Fable
Physics
Plant Sciences
Plays*
Pocket Fowler's Modern English Usage
Political Quotations
Politics
Popes
Proverbs
Psychology
Quotations
Quotations by Subject
Reverse Dictionary
Rhyming Slang
Saints
Science
Shakespeare
Slang
Sociology
Space Exploration*
Statistics
Synonyms and Antonyms
Weather
Weights, Measures, and Units
Word Games*
Word Histories
world History
World Mythology
World Place-Names*
World Religions
Zoology

**forthcoming*

The Concise Oxford Chronology of English Literature

Edited by
Michael Cox

OXFORD UNIVERSITY PRESS

OXFORD
UNIVERSITY PRESS

Great Clarendon Street, Oxford OX2 6DP

Oxford University Press is a department of the University of Oxford.
It furthers the University's objective of excellence in research, scholarship,
and education by publishing worldwide in

Oxford New York
Auckland Cape Town Dar es Salaam Hong Kong Karachi
Kuala Lumpur Madrid Melbourne Mexico City Nairobi
New Delhi Shanghai Taipei Toronto

With offices in
Argentina Austria Brazil Chile Czech Republic France Greece
Guatemala Hungary Italy Japan Poland Portugal Singapore
South Korea Switzerland Thailand Turkey Ukraine Vietnam

Published in the United States
by Oxford University Press Inc., New York

First published 2004

Reissued with updated material 2005

British Library Cataloguing in Publication Data

Data available

Library of Congress Cataloging in Publication Data

ISBN 0-19-861054-8

1

Typeset in Pondicherry, India, by
Alliance Interactive Technology
Printed in Great Britain by
Clays Ltd, St Ives plc

Contents

Introduction vii

Editorial Team x

Using the Concise Chronology xii

Abbreviations xiv

The Concise Oxford Chronology of English Literature 1

Author Index 615

Index of Anonymous Titles 819

Index of Periodicals 822

Introduction

THIS book is derived from *The Oxford Chronology of English Literature* (*OCEL*, 2002), which listed nearly 30,000 works by just over 4,000 authors. The present reduction contains roughly half the number of works by nearly 3,000 authors.

Like the parent work—and, indeed, like its original impetus, the *Annals of English Literature*, first published by OUP in 1935—this compilation aims to show, at a glance, the main literary output of a given year, beginning in 1474 and ending in 2001. The purpose has been to present a generous sampling of printed publications in time and in relation to other contemporaneous works. Its focus is literature written in English by British and Irish authors or by authors born elsewhere, such as Henry James or V.S. Naipaul, who have made Britain their home. Some authors of the colonial period (mainly Australians) who published principally with British publishing houses have also been admitted. Though, regrettably, no attempt has been made to chronicle the full range of post-colonial anglophone writing, several non-British authors whose work has achieved recognition and influence in Britain (e.g. R.K. Narayan) do find a place. Selected translations of classical and European works are also included. Overall, works of the imagination—poetry, novels, short stories, plays—predominate; but examples of other literary forms (biographies, memoirs, critical works, historical scholarship, philosophical and religious texts) also find a place.

As far as possible, the range of authors and works offered by *OCEL* has been preserved. Highbrow, lowbrow, and middlebrow tastes are all represented in a view of British literary culture that is, I hope, both wide and deep. Works of indisputable greatness will thus be found alongside others whose very ephemerality exemplifies the taste of the moment. Works of high intellectual purpose rub shoulders with the frankly trivial, or with publications that have contributed to the development of a popular genre such as the detective story. There are provincial, as well as metropolitan, writers, and many works that reflect popular rather than elite interests.

The list of authors and titles contained in *OCEL*, of which this book is an edited selection, was of course only one of many possible lists; but it was the result of considered critical review by the editor and his team of advisers rather than a random assemblage. The grounds of choice were both specific and general. They included: inevitability (i.e. those works of universal stature, such as *King Lear*, whose absence would have been nonsensical); the importance of a work in the career of a particular writer; topicality; resonance with the broad literary character of the period, or with specific forms or genres; popular success; and contributory importance to contemporary debate. Throughout the chronological range, works were occasionally selected for their intrinsic interest, originality, or curiosity. In all cases, however, the works selected were felt to have left some mark, however slight, on the fabric of time that is worthy of remark or remembrance.

As the list moved closer to the present, the choices became harder and the element of arbitrariness greater. Without the benefit of historical distance, judgements—not only on what may prove to be enduringly significant, but also on what may truly be said to represent contemporary literary culture at all levels—become acutely difficult and contentious. It must be stressed that the list of works representing the immediate past lays no claim to completeness; the aim has simply been to provide a broadly representative view of the recent literary landscape. The primary function of the book as a whole—as it was for *OCEL*—is to provide a historical view of British literature.

So what can a chronological listing like this provide? At its most basic, it tells you what was being published, when, and by whom, and who an author's chronological neighbours were when a particular work was first published. These simple facts and proximities can often be useful, even revealing. For example, in 1921, the year the Irish Free State is established, Arnold Bennett, in his mid-fifties, publishes the first series of *Things That Have Interested Me*, whilst his exact contemporary E.F. Benson publishes his third novel, *Dodo*. In this year John Buchan's *The Path of the King* is published; Agatha Christie's *The Mysterious Affair at Styles* appears, along with Somerset Maugham's comedy *To Let*, Lytton Strachey's biography of Queen Victoria, and George Bernard Shaw's *Back to Methuselah*. The younger generation is represented in this year by Aldous Huxley (*Chrome Yellow*) and D.H. Lawrence (*Women in Love*), as well as by works by Robert Graves, Vita Sackville-West, and Virginia Woolf; but some eminent Victorians are also active in 1921, amongst them Sir Henry Rider Haggard (now aged 65) and Sir Arthur Conan Doyle.

Similar résumés could be written for each year list, which together present a series of windows in time through which can be seen, not the complete, unmediated output of a given year, but a constructed view of representative elements. The familiar giants of the forest are all there—*Le Morte DArthur*, *Hamlet*, *Gulliver's Travels*, *David Copperfield*, *Lady Chatterley's Lover*, *Ulysses*, *Four Quartets*. But lapping round their feet are hundreds of less familiar works, all of which, in their own way, offer authentic glimpses of the *Zeitgeist*—whether it be Jacob Bauthumley's *The Light and Dark Sides of God* (1650), Grant Allen's *The Woman Who Did* (1895), or Marjorie Firminger's *roman-à-clef*, *Jam To-Day* (1930). By means of the chronological view one becomes aware of relationships, sometimes unsuspected or forgotten; of reactions and counter-reactions; of the birth of new literary species and hybrids; alliances and antagonisms; conformities and dissidence. And, time and again, one sees how the taste of the moment is so often at odds with the settled judgements of posterity, and also how artificial our notions of 'period' are as we watch the generations rise, fall, and commingle.

Perhaps most useful of all, the chronological view provides a corrective to the way we tend to judge or characterize a particular period of literary history by the output of a limited number of writers. Widening our frame of reference to include more than the canonical elite, or the academically fashionable, reveals that the samples on which we base our literary estimates can be startlingly small. Charles Dickens, W.M. Thackeray, George Eliot, Anthony Trollope, and Thomas Hardy are all great writers; but they do not define Victorian fiction in its totality. To see such luminaries in their proper chronological context, surrounded by a wide and representative company of lesser artists and jostled by the good, the bad, and the indifferent, is to see them and their achievements in a different light and unencumbered by hindsight. We see them, for a moment, as their contemporaries saw them.

Not every author we now consider to be 'great' was regarded as such by their contemporaries; conversely, many writers who have been consigned to obscurity or worse have enjoyed their fifteen minutes of fame. Yet these brief moments of celebrity, or perhaps notoriety, can provide insights into how people thought, wrote, and read at a particular moment in time. Again, such examples underline how the authentic tone of a literary period can often be more accurately characterized by the collective contributions of the ephemeral many rather than by the exceptional work of the iconic few.

It may be deduced from the foregoing that the inclusion of a work in the present selection does not necessarily imply the possession of aesthetic or intellectual value. It could therefore reasonably be asked: even if one had unlimited time and inclination, are all the works listed here worth reading? The answer would have to be: most definitely not. But are they worth the acquaintance and remembrance of posterity, as historical or cultural signifiers, or as a contextual canvas against which 'great works' may be viewed and measured? That is a different question, and one which I hope users of this book, as well as of its parent, will answer in the affirmative.

For this concise version of *OCEL*, though the general character of the parent has been retained, a great many minor titles have been omitted, along with other works that were included to give representation in depth. Within each title entry, information has been reduced to the author's name and life dates; the main title of the work; a category code for each work (see p. xiv); and, in many cases, a brief gloss.

Unlike *OCEL*, each year sequence in this concise version begins with some select items of information on key historical and cultural events, as well as listing important literary and other figures who were born or who died in the year in question. The main focus of the historical information is on British affairs, though this widens considerably from the late nineteenth century. The aim has been to provide some outward points of reference for the main literary information, whether this be the Battle of Trafalgar or the release of the film *Shakespeare in Love*. It need hardly be said that extreme selectivity has been necessary in the compilation of this supplementary feature.

Finally, I must state the obvious. The information provided throughout the text has been checked and rechecked, but inevitably some errors may have escaped the process. Where this is the case, I take responsibility for them and apologize in advance. I would also like to thank again the team of advisers (listed on p. x), in particular *OCEL*'s Consultant Editor, Dr Michael Suarez, who worked with me on the selection and compilation of the data on which this book is based.

MICHAEL COX

June 2002

Editorial Team

John Sloan
Lecturer, English Faculty, University of Oxford
Poetry 1890–1914

David Bradshaw
Hawthornden Fellow and Tutor in English Literature, Worcester College, Oxford
1918–1939

Valentine Cunningham
Professor of English Language and Literature, University of Oxford, and Tutor in English Literature, Corpus Christi College, Oxford
1939–1975

Claire Squires
Senior Lecturer in Publishing, Oxford Brookes University
1975–2000

Meic Stephens
Professor of Welsh Writing in English, University of Glamorgan, Wales
Welsh authors 1900–2000

Other Advisers
Dr Tony Bareham
Owen Dudley Edwards *Yeats*
Professor Stephen Gill *Wordsworth*
Professor Peter Holland *Shakespeare*
Professor Neil Keeble *Baxter, Bunyan*
Professor John Pilling *Beckett*
Professor Angus Ross *Swift*
Dr Felicity Rosslyn *Pope*
Dr Paul Schlicke *Dickens*

Renewed thanks are also due to Jeremy Noel-Tod for his verification work on *The Oxford Chronology of English Literature*, and to all the other people who helped to produce the database of information on which the present work is based.

Using the Concise Chronology

TITLES are arranged year by year according to date of publication. Title-page dates can be deliberately, or inadvertently, misleading, or they may not appear at all. In particular, the common practice of post-dating—when books published at the end of one year were given the date of the succeeding year—means that works are listed here according to the *actual* year of publication, rather than the deliberately amended post-dated year of the imprint. Thus the first two volumes of Samuel Richardson's *Pamela* will be found under 1740, the year in which they were actually published, rather than 1741, the date given on the title-page. Occasionally a work may be pre-dated—for example, Edmund Blunden's *Poems 1930–1940* was published in 1941, though dated 1940. If a well-known work cannot be found in the expected year, the reason is probably due to post- or pre-dating (usually the former). In all cases, locating the work under the author's name in the author index will supply the year to which it has been assigned.

For works published serially in more than one volume, the date of the first volume(s), rather than the last, has been taken as the year locator. Undated works for which a year of publication is definitely known, or which can be inferred with a high degree of certainty, are located under that known or inferred year. Undated works for which no publication year can be assigned (applying particularly to the early years of printing) have been given a consensual location and appear in the author index with a question mark following the date.

Up to the reform of the calendar in 1752, many English books were dated taking the Feast of the Annunciation ('Lady Day', 25 March) as the starting-point of the year. This meant that a book published between, say, 1 January and 24 March 1640 might be dated 1639 (as was the case with William Davenant's masque *Salmacia Spoila*). In the *Concise Chronology*, all year dates are given according to modern, post-1752 reckoning which took 1 January as the start of the year. Thus Davenant's masque will be found under 1640 rather than under the imprint date of 1639. Again, the author index will supply the year in which the work is listed.

Within each year, works are ordered alphabetically by author surname, and then alphabetically by title if there is more than one work by the same author. Occasionally this ordering has been intentionally amended to take account of the actual sequence of publication. Anonymous works, including periodicals, are listed at the beginning of the year in question, ordered alphabetically by title.

Each entry opens with the author's name, followed by his or her life dates (or *floruit* dates). The use of a pseudonym is indicated by a name appearing in single quotation marks followed by the author's real name in square brackets—for example, 'F. Anstey' [Thomas Anstey Guthrie (1856–1934)]. Victorian women writers who were formerly referred to by their husbands' Christian names appear under their own first names, with any other designation by which they were known appearing in square brackets—for example, Ellen Wood [Mrs Henry Wood] (1814–87).

Following the title of each work is an abbreviation denoting the broad category (e.g. Fiction, Verse, Drama) to which it belongs. (A full list of the abbreviations used will be found on p. xiv.) For the titles of works, original spellings and punctuation are usually retained, except where standardized titles have been substituted for the original—as in the case of John Skelton's *The Bouge of Court*, the original 'title' of which was the incipit *Here begynneth a lytell treatyse named the bowge of courte*.

Many of the listed works have brief glosses. Most commonly these contain information on authorship or attribution issues; dating; whether a work was published anonymously or under the formula 'By the author of' (indicated in the notes by the contraction 'bao'); first performances of dramatic works; original sources of translated works; serialization details; topical relevance and miscellaneous points of interest; illustrators and editors; and cross-references.

The author index is organized alphabetically by author surname and contains three elements: the author's full name, life or *floruit* dates, and brief description; a short-title list of his/her works in chronological order; and the date under which the work appears in the main listing.

Abbreviations

Categories of works

ANTH	Anthology
BIB	Bible
DICT	Dictionary
D	Drama
EDN	Edition
F	Fiction
MISC	Miscellaneous
NF	Non-Fiction
OP	Opera
PER	Periodical
PS	Prose Satire
V	Verse
VMUS	Verse with Music
WKS	Works

General

attrib.	attributed
b.	born
bao	by the author of
c.	*circa*: about
d.	died
ed.	editor
fl.	*floruit*: flourished
jun.	junior
n.d.	no date
q.v.	*quod vide*: which see (singular)
qq.v.	*quae vide*: which see (plural)
ser.	series
tr.	translator
USA/US	United States of America/American

1400

1474

- EDWARD IV (1442–83; reigns 1461–83)
- Gavin Douglas born?

William Caxton (1422?–91) (tr.)
The Recuyell of the Historyes of Troye F
Publication date conjectural (late 1473 or early 1474). The first book printed by Caxton in English. Translated from the French of Raoul Le Fèvre, with prologue, interpolations, and epilogue by Caxton.

William Caxton (1422?–91) (tr.)
The Game and Playe of the Chesse NF
Translated from Jean de Vignay's French version (*c.*1350) of Jacques de Cessolis, *Libre de ludo scachorum* (*c.*1300), with prologue, interpolations, and epilogue by Caxton

1475

- Edward IV invades France (July)
  Peace of Picquigny between England and France (Aug.)
- Alexander Barclay born
  John Rastell born?

1476

- Caxton sets up a printing-press at Westminster
- Henry Parker, 8th Baron Morley, born

Benet Burgh (*d.* 1483) (tr.)
Parvus Cato; Magnus Cato V
A collection of maxims written *c.*1440 (attributed to Dionysius Cato) widely used as an elementary textbook. Latin and English.

John Lydgate (1370?–1449)
The Chorle and the Birde V
Anonymous. Written *c.*1400 and circulated widely in manuscript form.

John Lydgate (1370?–1449)
The Horse, the Goose, and the Sheep V
Anonymous. Publication date conjectural. Probably written soon after 1436.

John Lydgate (1370?–1449)
Stans Puer ad Mensam V
Publication date conjectural. The most popular version of this medieval 'courtesy' book, instructing young boys how to behave at table.

1477

- Defeat and death of Charles the Bold of Burgundy

William Caxton (1422?–91) (tr.)
History of Jason F
Publication date conjectural. Translated from the French of Raoul Le Fèvre, *Les frais et prouesses de Jason* (*c.*1460), with prologue and epilogue by Caxton.

Geoffrey Chaucer (1340?–1400)
Anelida and Arcite V
Anonymous. Publication date conjectural. Contains other Chaucerian short poems.

Geoffrey Chaucer (1340?–1400)
Canterbury Tales V
See also *Canterbury Tales* 1526

Geoffrey Chaucer (1340?–1400)
The Parliament of Fowls V
Anonymous. Publication date conjectural. Contains other short Chaucerian poems.

John Lydgate (1370?–1449)
The Temple of Glas V
Anonymous. Publication date conjectural. Written *c.*1403.

Anthony Woodville, Earl Rivers (1422?–83) (tr.)
Dicts or Saying of the Philosophers NF
Translated from the French version of the Latin original by G. de Tignonville. Epilogue by Caxton.

1478

- The Pazzi conspiracy
  Papal attack on the Medici in Florence
- Sir Thomas More born

Geoffrey Chaucer (1340?–1400) (tr.)
The Consolation of Philosophy NF

Publication date conjectural. Translated from Boethius (*c.*470–*c.*525) *c.*1380, using Jean de Meun's French version, collated against the Latin.

Anthony Woodville, Earl Rivers (1422?–83) (tr.)
The Morale Proverbes of Cristyne V
Translated from *Proverbes Moraux* (*c.*1402) by Christine de Pisan (1364–1430)

1479

- Union of the crowns of Aragon and Castile

Anthony Woodville, Earl Rivers (1422?–83) (tr.)
Cordiale, or Four Last Things V
Translated from J. Miélot's version of the *Cordiale quattuor novissimorum*, attributed to Gerardus de Vliederhoven and to Denis le Chartreux (1402 or 3–1471)

1480

- Turks capture Otranto, on the Italian mainland

Anonymous
Chronicles of England NF
An edition of the *Brut*, the most popular historical chronicle in English in the 15th century. Based on the French *Brut d'Engleterre*, which ended at 1333.

Anonymous
The Court of Sapience NF
Formerly attributed to John Lydgate. Composed *c.*1475 to compliment Edward IV.

Anonymous
Description of Britain NF
A supplement to Caxton's edition of the *Chronicles of England* 1480 (q.v.), taken directly from the geographical sections of John of Trevisa's translation of Ranulf Higden's *Polycronicon* 1482 (q.v.)

1481

- Beginning of the Spanish war against Granada

Anonymous
On Old Age NF
A translation, attributed to William Worcester (1415–82?) and to Stephen Scrope (*d.* 1472), of Cicero's *De senectute* (from the French of Laurent de Premierfait) and *Laelius de amicitia*. The latter was translated by John Tiptoft, earl of Worcester, executed in 1470 for his persecution of the Lancastrians.

William Caxton (1422?–91) (tr.)
Godfrey of Boulogne F
Translated from a French version (*Le Livre d'Eracles*) of the Latin history of the First Crusade written by William, archbishop of Tyre (*c.*1170), with prologue and epilogue by Caxton. Also called *The Siege and Conquest of Jerusalem*, and *Eracles*, this book was part of Caxton's plan to produce works on all the Nine Worthies.

William Caxton (1422?–91) (tr.)
The Mirror of the World NF
A prose translation of a paraphrase by Gautier de Metz of the 13th-century French poem *Image du monde*, attributed to Vincent of Beauvais. An encyclopaedia dealing with God, the seven liberal arts, the four elements, geography, meteorology, and astronomy.

William Caxton (1422?–91) (tr.)
Reynard the Fox F
Derived from a Dutch prose translation of the 14th-century Flemish poem *Reinaerts Historie*, with epilogue by Caxton. A universally popular medieval beast fable with versions in many European languages.

1482

- Death of Mary of Burgundy
  Treaty of Arras

Ranulf Higden (*d.* 1364)
Polycronicon NF
Composed in the 1320s. A 'universal history', edited by Caxton, with prologues and epilogues by him, from the English translation (1387) by John of Trevisa. See also Caxton's *Description of Britain* 1480.

1483

- Death of Edward IV (9 Apr.)
  EDWARD V succeeds: deposed (25 June) by his uncle, Richard, duke of Gloucester
  RICHARD III (–1485)
  Edward V and his brother murdered in the Tower of London
  Death of Louis XI of France: succeeded by Charles VIII
  Spanish Inquisition formally established
- Benet Burgh dies
  Anthony Woodville (*b.* 1422?) dies

- Stephen Gardiner, bishop of Winchester, born?
- Martin Luther born

Anonymous
The Golden Legend NF
A translation and compilation from various sources, the principal Latin source being by Jacobus de Voragine (1230–98). An immensely popular and influential compendium of ecclesiastical lore.

Anonymous
The Pilgrimage of the Soul NF
An English prose version (with some verse) of *Le Pèlerinage de l'âme* (*c.*1355–8) by Guillaume de Deguileville (*b.* 1295). Erroneously attributed to John Lydgate.

William Caxton (1422?–91) (tr.)
The Curial NF/V
A translation of a French version of *De vita curiali* by Alain Chartier (*c.*1385–*c.*1429), with a Ballade, probably by Caxton

Geoffrey Chaucer (1340?–1400)
The House of Fame V
Edited by William Caxton. An unfinished dream-poem, for which Caxton supplied a 12-line conclusion.

Geoffrey Chaucer (1340?–1400)
Troilus and Criseyde V
Anonymous. Publication date conjectural. See also *Troilus and Criseyde* 1526.

John Gower (1325?–1408)
Confessio Amantis V
Written *c.*1390

John Lydgate (1370?–1449)
The Book of the Lyf of Our Lady V
Composed at the request of Henry V. Very popular, with many manuscript copies still extant.

John Mirk (*fl.* 1403)
Festial NF
Anonymous. A collection of sermons for parish priests.

1484

- Peace of Bagnolo ending conflict in Italy

William Caxton (1422?–91) (tr.)
Aesop's Fables F
Includes a life of Aesop and fables by Avianus, Poggio Bracciolini, and others. Translated from Jules de Machault's French version (1483), of a German-Latin collection (*c.*1476).

William Caxton (1422?–91) (tr.)
Caton NF
A version of the *Disticha Catonis*, translated from a Latin-French edition, with commentary in French. See also Benet Burgh, *Parvus Cato* 1476.

William Caxton (1422?–91) (tr.)
The Knight of the Tower NF
Translated from Geffroy de la Tour Landry's *Le Livre du chevalier de la Tour Landry*, written in 1371–2

William Caxton (1422?–91) (tr.)
The Order of Chivalry NF
Translated from a French version of the *Libre del orde de cavayleria* by Ramón Lull (1235–1315)

Nicholas Love (*d.* 1424) (tr.)
The Mirror of the Life of Christ NF
A very popular life of Christ, once attributed to St Bonaventura (1221–74) but now ascribed to Johannes de Caulibus of San Gimignano. Translated into English *c.*1410.

1485

- Battle of Bosworth (22 Aug.): death of Richard III
  HENRY VII (–1509)
- Hugh Latimer born?

William Caxton (1422?–91) (tr.)
Charles the Great King of France NF
A life of Charlemagne, translated from the French compilation of Jean Baignon (*fl.* 1463–94). The third volume in Caxton's 'Nine Worthies' project.

William Caxton (1422?–91) (tr.)
Paris and Vienne F
Translated from an abridgement of a French version (1432) by Pierre de la Cypède of a Provençal (?) original

Sir Thomas Malory (*fl.* 1470)
Le Morte DArthur F
Completed by Malory 1469–70. The second volume in Caxton's 'Nine Worthies' project.

1486

- Henry VII marries Elizabeth of York, uniting rival royal houses

Juliana Berners (*d.* 1388?)
The Book of St Albans MISC

1487

- Battle of Stoke (16 June): final battle of the Wars of the Roses
  Rebellion of Lambert Simnel
  Bartolomeu Diaz circumnavigates the Cape

William Caxton (1422?–91) (tr.)
The Book of Good Manners NF
Translated from Jacques Legrand's *Livre de bonnes moeurs* (1410?). A 'courtesy book', aimed at the young.

1488

- James IV of Scotland succeeds
  Duke Humphrey's Library opened at Oxford
- Miles Coverdale born

William Caxton (1422?–91) (tr.)
Royal Book NF
Publication date conjectural. A translation of Friar Laurent's *La Somme le Roy*, on the Vices and Virtues.

1489

- Rebellion in Yorkshire and north-east England over taxation
  Murder of the duke of Northumberland
  Prince Arthur proclaimed Prince of Wales
- Thomas Cranmer born

William Caxton (1422?–91) (tr.)
The Book of Feats of Arms NF
Translated from Christine de Pisan (1364–1430), *Le livre des fays d'armes et de chevalerie* (1408–9)

1490

- Aldus Manutius founds the Aldine Press at Venice
- Andrew Borde born?
  Sir Thomas Elyot born?
  Sir David Lindsay born

William Caxton (1422?–91) (tr.)
The Art and Craft to Know Well to Die NF
Translated from a French abridgement of the *Ars Moriendi*, adapted for the use of the laity. See also *Ars Moriendi* 1491.

William Caxton (1422?–91) (tr.)
Blanchardine and Eglantine F
A chivalric romance translated from a 13th-century French work, *Blancandin*, in a 15th-century prose version. See also Thomas Pope Goodwin's translation, 1595.

William Caxton (1422?–91) (tr.)
Eneydos F
A translation of a late 14th-century French chivalric romance by Guillaume le Roy, adapted from an Italian paraphrase of Virgil's *Aeneid* and Boccaccio (1313–75), *De casibus virorum illustrium*. Gavin Douglas undertook his own translation of Virgil (1553, q.v.) as a corrective to this version.

William Caxton (1422?–91) (tr.)
The Four Sons of Aymon F
Translated from a 15th-century French prose version of the *chanson de geste, Renaud de Montauban* (*c.*1200). Part of the Charlemagne cycle.

1491

- William Caxton (*b.* 1422?) dies

William Caxton (1422–91?) (tr.)
Ars Moriendi NF
Translated and abbreviated from the French. A miscellany, containing, as well as the *Ars Moriendi*, a devotion on the Eucharist, the twelve degrees of humility, the fifteen degrees of charity, etc. See also *The Art and Craft to Know Well to Die* 1490.

1492

- Ferdinand of Castile conquers of Moorish Granada
  Expulsion of the Jews from Spanish kingdoms
  Siege of Boulogne
  Death of Pope Innocent VIII
  Columbus discovers the West Indies
- Pietro Aretino born
- Lorenzo de' Medici dies

1493

- Christopher Columbus returns to Lisbon from the West Indies (Mar.); leaves on second voyage (Sept.)

Anonymous
Dives and Pauper NF
A prose dialogue, written *c.*1405–10, on the themes of poverty and the Ten Commandments. Formerly

attributed to the Carmelite Henry Parker (*d.* 1470), but probably not by him.

1494

- Charles VIII of France invades Italy
- William Tyndale born?
- François Rabelais born
  Coreggio born

John Lydgate (1370?–1449) (tr.)
The Fall of Princes V
Translated *c.*1431–8 from the *De casibus illustrium virorum* of Boccaccio (1313–75). See also Lydgate, *Proverbs* 1510.

1495

- Jews expelled from Portugal
  Aldine Press begins publishing editions of the Greek classics
- John Bale born
  Thomas Lupset born
  John Taverner born

John of Trevisa (*c.*1330–1402) (tr.)
Bartholomeus de proprietatibus rerum NF
An important encyclopaedic work, written by Bartholomaeus Anglicus (*fl.* 1230–50) and translated by John of Trevisa in the late 14th century. It remained popular throughout the 16th century.

1496

- Henru VII joins the Holy League
  John Colet lectures in Oxford
- William Roper born

Anonymous
The Three Kings of Cologne NF
Publication date conjectural. Translated from Johannes de Hildesheim (*d.* 1375), *Liber de gestit et translatione trium regum* (*c.*1400).

Juliana Berners (*d.* 1388?)
The Manere of Hawkynge and Huntynge MISC
See also *The Book of St Albans* 1486

Sir John Mandeville (*d.* 1342?)
Mandeville's Travels NF
Written in the 1340s. Ostensibly a guide for pilgrims to Jerusalem, but also contains a description of the marvels of the Great Cham's empire in the East.

1497

- Rebellion in Cornwall over taxation
  John Cabot sails from Bristol (May); reaches Newfoundland (June)
  Vasco da Gama reaches India
- John Heywood born?
- Hans Holbein, the younger, born

John Lydgate (1370?–1449)
The Siege of Thebes V
Anonymous. Publication date conjectural. Adapted *c.*1421–2 from an unknown French prose romance. Reflects the influence of Boccaccio, Chaucer, Martianus Capella, the Bible, and Seneca.

1498

- Perkin Warbeck imprisoned
  Girolamo Savonarola executed
  Vasco da Gama reaches India
  Christopher Columbus's third voyage: he arrives off the coast of South America in August
- Edward Halle (chronicler) born *c.*1498
- John Cabot dies

Anonymous
The Assembly of the Gods V
Written after 1422. A dream-vision, misattributed to John Lydgate.

1499

- Perkin Warbeck tried for treason and executed

Anonymous
Promptorium Parvulorum DICT
An English–Latin dictionary, first compiled in the 15th century by Galfridus

John Skelton (1460?–1529)
The Bouge of Court V
Anonymous. Publication date conjectural. Written in 1488. A satirical dream-allegory of court life.

1500

1500

- John Bellenden born *c.*1500
  Nicholas Ridley born?
  John Rogers (editor of the Bible and martyr) born?
- Benvenuto Cellini born

Anonymous
A Gest of Robin Hood V
Publication date conjectural. Possibly compiled from earlier Robin Hood ballads, *c.*1400 or before.

Anonymous
Guy of Warwick V
Publication date conjectural. Derived from the Anglo-Norman *Gui de Warewic* (*c.*1232–42).

Anonymous
Robert the Devil F
Publication date conjectural. An anonymous translation of the prose *La vie du terrible Robert le Diable* (1496).

Anonymous
Sir Bevis of Hampton V
Translated *c.*1300 from the Anglo-Norman *Boeve de Haumtone* (*c.*1200). A printed version was in existence before 1498.

Anonymous
Sir Eglamour of Artois V
Composed in the mid-14th century

Geoffrey Chaucer (1340?–1400)
Mars and Venus V
Anonymous. Publication date conjectural. An amalgamation of Chaucer's *The Complaint of Mars* and *The Complaint of Venus*.

John Lydgate (1370?–1449)
The Virtue of the Mass V
Anonymous. Publication date conjectural. Also called the *Interpretacio Misse*.

1501

- Ferdinand II of Spain proclaims the Kingdom of Granada to be Christian
  Amerigo Vespucci sails from Lisbon (May)
  Arthur, Prince of Wales, marries Catherine of Aragon (Nov.)
  Michelangelo begins his statue of David

Margery Kempe (*c.*1373–*c.*1439)
The Book of Margery Kempe NF

1502

- Arthur, Prince of Wales, dies (Apr.) at the age of 16
  Wittenberg University founded
  Chairs of divinity founded at Oxford and Cambridge by Lady Margaret Beaufort, countess of Richmond, Henry VII's mother
  Christopher Columbus's final voyage

Anonymous
Gesta Romanorum F
Publication date conjectural. An immensely popular and influential collection of 43 fictitious stories in Latin, probably compiled in England in the late 13th century from an Anglo-Norman version.

1503

- Queen Elizabeth, Henry VII's consort, dies
  Henry Tudor created Prince of Wales
  James IV of Scotland marries Margaret Tudor
  Pope Alexander VI dies; succeeded by Pius III and then by Julius II
- Sir Thomas Wyatt born?
- Nostradamus (Michel de Notredame) born

Anonymous
Sir Tryamour V
Publication date conjectural. Composed in the late 14th century.

Richard Arnold (*d.* 1521?)
Arnold's Chronicle NF
Publication date conjectural. Contains the earliest known version of *The Nutbrown Maid*.

William Atkinson (*d.* 1509) (tr.)
Imitation of Christ NF
A translation of Thomas à Kempis (1380–1471), *De Imitatione Christi*. Book iv translated by

Margaret, countess of Richmond and Derby. See also Thomas Rogers, *Imitation of Christ* 1580.

1504

- Isabella of Castile dies
- Matthew Parker, archbishop of Canterbury, born

Anonymous
Generides V
Publication date conjectural. Composed in the late 14th century.

Stephen Hawes (*d.* 1523?)
The Example of Virtue V
Publication date conjectural

1505

- John Knox born
  Margaret Roper (daughter of Sir Thomas More) born
  Richard Taverner born?
  Nicholas Udall born?
  Thomas Tallis born
- Robert Henryson dies (*c.*1505)

Anonymous
Adam Bell, Clim of the Clough, and William of Cloudesly V
An outlaw ballad, reprinted many times up to the mid-17th century. A continuation, *Young Cloudeslie*, was issued in 1608.

Anonymous
Octavian V
Publication date conjectural (1504–6). Composed in the mid-14th century from a French version. The work draws on many romance themes, among which are the 'Calumniated Wife' and the St Eustace Legend.

Anonymous
Sir Torrent of Portingale V
Publication date conjectural. Composed late 14th–early 15th century.

Alexander Barclay (1475?–1552) (tr.)?
The Castle of Labour V
Anonymous. Publication date conjectural. Translated from Pierre Gringoire (*c.*1475–1538).

Andrew Chertsey (*fl.* 1508–32) (tr.)
The Crafte to Lyve Well and to Dye Well NF
Translated from the French. See also *The Art and Craft to Know Well to Die* 1490, and *Ars Moriendi* 1491.

John Stanbridge (1463–1510)
Accidence NF
Publication date conjectural. Stanbridge was one of the most popular grammarians of the period, whose five textbooks were frequently reprinted.

1506

- George Buchanan born
  John Leland born?
- Christopher Columbus dies
  Andrea Mantegna dies

Anonymous
The Kalender of Shepherdes NF
English translation of a Scots version of a French work, *Le Compost et Kalendrier des Bergiers*

Anonymous
The Seven Sages of Rome F
Publication date conjectural. Composed in the early 14th century. One of the earliest examples of a collection of short tales, of Eastern origin, set within a frame-tale.

Margaret Beaufort, countess of Richmond and Derby (1443–1509) (tr.)
The Mirroure of Golde for the Synfull Soule NF
Publication date conjectural. A translation of the *Speculum aureum*, attributed to Jacobus de Gruitroede.

1507

- Cesare Borgia dies

William Dunbar (1460?–1513?)
The Tua Mariit Wemen and the Wedo V
Publication date conjectural. Also contains Dunbar's 'Lament for the Makaris', 'Kynd Kittok', and 'The Testament of Mr Andro. Kennedy'.

1508

- Michelangelo begins painting the Sistine Chapel ceiling (–1512)
- WIlliam Rastell born?
  Andrea Palladio born
- Lodovico Sforza dies

Anonymous
Golagros and Gawain V
A Middle Scots romance, composed not long before 1500 in the alliterative metre. Based on two episodes from the *First Continuation* (*c.*1200) of Chrétien de Troyes's *Perceval, ou le Conte du Graal* (*c.*1190).

Anonymous
The Remedy Against the Troubles of Temptations NF
Misattributed to Richard Rolle of Hampole (*d.* 1349?), though it contains some quotations from him

Andrew Cadiou (*fl.* 1472?) (tr.)
The Porteous of Nobleness V
A Scots version of *Le Bréviaire des Nobles* by Alain Chartier (*c.*1385–*c.*1429)

William Dunbar (1460?–1513?)
The Ballade of Lord Barnard Stewart V
Lord Bernard Stewart, third seigneur of Aubigny (1447?–1508), arrived in Scotland in May 1508 as French envoy to James IV. He died soon afterwards, whilst still in Scotland.

William Dunbar (1460?–1513?)
The Flyting of Dunbar and Kennedy, and Other Poems V
A fragmentary text of *The Flyting*, together with two short poems, 'Wythin a garth', ascribed to Henryson, and the anonymous 'Devise, prowes and eke humilitee'

William Dunbar (1460?–1513?)
The Golden Targe V

John Fisher (1459?–1535)
The Fruitful Sayings of David NF

'Henry, the Minstrel' ('Blind Harry')
Acts and Deeds of Wallace V
Publication date conjectural. Written *c.*1478 in Scots verse, supposedly derived from a Latin original. One of the most popular works of Scottish poetry of the period.

Robert Henryson (*c.*1430–*c.*1505)
Orpheus and Eurydice V
Anonymous. Publication date conjectural.

Richard Holland (*fl.* 1450)
Buke of the Howlat V
Publication date conjectural. Written *c.*1450. The poem pictures an assembly of birds, with the Owl lodging a bitter complaint against Dame Nature for making him so ugly.

John Lydgate (1370?–1449)
The Complaint of the Black Knight V
Anonymous

'Walter, of Henley' (*fl.* 1250)
Boke of Husbandry NF
Anonymous. Publication date conjectural.

1509

- Death of Henry VII (21 Apr.)
  HENRY VIII (–1547)
  Henry VIII marries Catherine of Aragon (June)
  Earthquake destroys Constantinople
  Building of the *Mary Rose* begins (–1510): first use of gunports
- William Atkinson (translator of Thomas à Kempis) dies
  Margaret Beaufort, countess of Richmond and Derby, dies
- John Calvin born

Anonymous
King Ponthus F
Publication date conjectural. Attributed to Henry Watson (*fl.* 1500–18). A French prose romance, *Ponthus et la belle Sidoine*, adapted *c.*1390 from the Anglo-Norman *Horn et Rimnild* (*c.*1170–80) by Geoffrey IV de la Tour Landry, was translated into English prose *c.*1400–50.

Anonymous
Richard Coeur de Lion V
Composed *c.*1300. A combination of historical and romance elements.

Alexander Barclay (1475?–1552) (tr.)
The Ship of Fools V
Translated mainly from Latin and French versions of the celebrated *Narrenschiff* (1494) by Sebastian Brandt (1458–1521). See also Henry Watson, *The Shyppe of Fooles* 1509.

John Fisher (1459?–1535)
A Mourning Remembrance NF

Stephen Hawes (*d.* 1523?)
The Convercyon of Swerers V

Stephen Hawes (*d.* 1523?)
A Joyfull Medytacyon to all Englonde V
On the coronation of Henry VIII

Stephen Hawes (*d.* 1523?)
The Pastyme of Pleasure V

Henry Watson (*fl.* 1500–18) (tr.)
The Shyppe of Fooles F
Translated from J. Drouyn's French prose version of Sebastian Brandt's *Narrenschiff* (1494). See also Alexander Barclay 1509.

1510

- John Colet founds St Paul's School
- John Caius born
  Sir Richard Morison born?
  Thomas Phaer born?
  Robert Record born?
  Robert Wedderburn born *c.*1510
- Sandro Botticelli dies
  Giorgione dies

Anonymous
The Destruction of Jerusalem F
Publication date conjectural. Translated from a French prose version.

Anonymous
Melusine F
First translated into English *c.*1500 from the French prose *Melusine* (*c.*1387), by Jean d'Arras, printed at Geneva in 1478 as *L'Histoire de la Belle Melusine*

Anonymous
Merlin V
Based on the second of two versions of the Middle English romance *Arthur and Merlin*, which derives ultimately from the Old French Prose-*Merlin*, part of the Arthurian Vulgate Cycle (*c.*1215–35)

Robert Copland (*fl.* 1508–47) (tr.)
Apollonius of Tyre F
A translation of Louis Garbin's *Le Romant de Appollin roy de Thir* (Geneva: *c.*1482), itself a close translation of the late classical *Historia Apollonii Regis Tyri*. A very widespread tale of trial and separation. See also Laurence Twyne, *The Patterne of Painefull Adventures* 1594.

John Lydgate (1370?–1449)
Proverbs V
Publication date conjectural. Written *c.*1431–8. Consists largely of extracts from *The Fall of Princes* 1494 (q.v.).

Sir Thomas More (1478–1535) (tr.)
The Lyfe of Johan Picus Erle of Myrandula V
Publication date conjectural. A life of Giovanni Pico della Mirandola (1463–94), Italian humanist and philosopher, member of the Platonic Academy in Florence.

Henry Watson (*fl.* 1500–18) (tr.)
Valentine and Orson F
Publication date conjectural. Translated from an early French romance, *Lystoire des deux vaillans chevaliers Valentin et Orson*. Many editions and adaptations through to the 19th century.

1511

- Erasmus appointed Greek Reader at Cambridge (1511–14)
- Giorgio Vasari born

Anonymous
The Demaundes Joyous NF
The first book of riddles published in England

Anonymous
The Friar and the Boy V
Publication date conjectural (1510–13). A popular fabliau.

Anonymous
Joseph of Arimathea F
Publication date conjectural. Known as *The Prose Life of Joseph of Arimathea*. Based on the *Nova legenda Angliæ* by John Capgrave (*d.* 1464). A fictitious account of the evangelization of Britain by Joseph.

John Lydgate (1370?–1449) (tr.)
The Governance of Kings V
Translated (*c.*1370?) from Aristotle's *Secreta secretorum*. Lydgate's last work. Also referred to as *Secrets of the Old Philisoffres*. See also Robert Copland, *Secreta secretorum* 1528.

1512

- The Spanish invade Navarre
  James V of Scotland born
- Thomas Becon born
- Amerigo Vespucci dies

Anonymous
Syr Degore V
Publication date conjectural. Composed before 1325, in couplets.

Robert Copland (*fl.* 1508–47) (tr.)
The Knight of the Swan F
A free prose translation by Copland of *La genealogie aveques les gestes . . . du . . . Godeffroy de Boulin* by Pierre d'Esrey of Troyes, printed before 1500

1513

- English defeat the French at the 'Battle of the Spurs' (Aug.)
  Battle of Flodden (9 Sept.): death of James IV of Scotland

James V of Scotland succeeds at the age of 17 months

- William Dunbar (*b.* 1460?) dies?
  Robert Fabyan (chronicler) dies
- Sir Edward Howard, Lord Admiral, dies in action

Anonymous
Ars amatoria V
Translated from Ovid

John Lydgate (1370?–1449) (tr.)
Troy Book V
Anonymous. A verse paraphrase (1412–21) of Guido delle Colonne's *Historia destructionis Troiae* (1287), a Latin prose translation of the *Roman de Troie* (*c.*1165) of Benôit de Sainte-Maure. See also *The Life and Death of Hector* 1614.

John Skelton (1460?–1529)
A Ballade of the Scottysshe Kynge V
Anonymous. A celebration of the defeat of the Scots at Flodden.

1514

- The Complutensian Bible (first polyglot Bible) begun (completed 1517; published 1522)
- Sir John Cheke born
  John Ponet born?
  Christophe Plantin born

Simon [Appleby]
The Fruyte of Redempcyon NF
Sometimes attributed to R. Whitford

1515

- Thomas Wolsey made cardinal (Sept.) and appointed Lord Chancellor (Dec.)
- Roger Ascham born
  William Baldwin born c.1515
- Anne of Cleves born

Anonymous
Euryalus and Lucretia NF
Publication date conjectural. Written in Latin by Aeneas Sylvius Piccolomini (Pope Pius II) (1404–65).

Anonymous
Everyman D
Publication date conjectural. Translated from the Dutch *Elkerlijc*. Death summons Everyman from a life of pleasure and riches. All his companions (Fellowship, Kindred, Goods) desert him, except Good Deeds.

Anonymous
Hickscorner D
Publication date conjectural. An interlude. Characters include Pity, Contemplation, Perseverance, Freewill, and Hickscorner himself, a brothel-keeper.

Anonymous
The Informacyon for Pylgrymes unto the Holy Londe NF

Anonymous
William of Palermo F
Publication date conjectural. A prose translation of the Middle English alliterative romance *William of Palerne*, or *William and the Werewolf*, itself translated *c.*1350–61 from the Old French romance *Guillaume de Palerne* (*c.*1194–7). The hero, William, is rescued from danger by a werewolf, a prince who has been magically transformed into this shape by his wicked stepmother.

Alexander Barclay (1475?–1552) (tr.)
Saint George V
Translated from Baptista Spagnuoli Mantuanus (1448–1516)

John Bourchier, Lord Berners (1467–1533) (tr.)
Huon of Bordeaux F
Publication date conjectural. A close translation of a French prose version (*c.*1455) first printed in Paris in 1513.

Stephen Hawes (*d.* 1523?)
The Comforte of Lovers V
Publication date conjectural

Henry Medwall (*b. c.*1462)
Fulgens and Lucrece D
Publication date uncertain (between 1512 and 1516). Medwall took the plot from *De Vera Nobilitate* (*c.*1428) by Buonaccorso da Montemagno (*c.*1392–1429), translated into English *c.*1460 by John Tiptoft, earl of Worcester, and printed by Caxton in his collection *Tulle of Old Age* (1481) as *The Declamacion of Noblesse*, the version used by Medwall.

1516

- Henry VIII's daughter Mary, later Mary I, born (18 Feb.)
- John Foxe born

- Giovanni Bellini dies
  Hieronymus Bosch dies

Robert Fabyan (*d.* 1513)
The New Cronycles of Englande and of Fraunce NF
The 4th edition (continued to the reign of Mary I) was published in 1559

Sir Thomas More (1478–1535)
Utopia NF
The original Latin text of *Utopia*, translated into English in 1551 (q.v.)

1517

- Luther nails his 95 theses to the door of the Schlosskirche in Wittenburg: the Protestant Reformation begins
- Henry Howard, earl of Surrey, born?

Anonymous
Frederick of Jennen F
Publication date conjectural

1518

- Royal College of Physicians founded
- Ninian Winzet born

Anonymous
Cock Laurel's Boat V
Publication date conjectural. Cock Lorell was the head of a gang of thieves in the early 16th century.

Anonymous
The Life and Death of Virgil F
Publication date conjectural. Depicts Virgil as a necromancer.

Anonymous
Mary of Nemmegen F
Publication date conjectural. A translation into English prose of a late medieval Dutch miracle play, *Mariken van Nieumeghen*.

Alexander Barclay (1475?–1552)
Fifth Eclogue V
See also *Eclogues* 1530, *The Boke of Codrus and Mynalcas* 1521

Sir Thomas More (1478–1535)
Epigrammata V

Henry Watson (*fl.* 1500–18) (tr.)
Oliver of Castille F
Translated from the French

1519

- Charles I of Spain elected Holy Roman Emperor as Charles V
  Cortes received by Montezuma
  Magellan sails from Europe: the expedition eventually circumnavigates the earth
  St George's Chapel, Windsor, completed (begun 1473)
- Nicholas Grimald born?
- John Colet (*b.* 1467) dies
- Catherine and Cosimo de' Medici born
- Leonardo da Vinci dies
  Lucretia Borgia dies

1520

- Henry VIII and Francis I meet at the Field of the Cloth of Gold (7–24 June)
  Magellan reaches the Pacific
  Luther declared a heretic
  Cortes conquers Mexico
- William Cecil, Lord Burghley, born
  Thomas Churchyard born?

Anonymous
Alexander the Great V
Publication date conjectural

Anonymous
Andria D
Publication date conjectural. In Latin and English.

Anonymous
Life of St Thomas NF
A life of St Thomas à Becket (1118?–70), sometimes attributed to Alexander Barclay

Anonymous
The Squire of Low Degree V
Publication date conjectural. Also known as *Undo Your Dore*. Composed *c.*1500.

Anonymous
Ypotis NF
Publication date highly conjectural (1520?–30?). Composed *c.*1300–25. A dialogue between the Emperor Hadrian and the child Ypotis (Epictetus), concerning matters of Christian dogma. The child is later identified with Christ. Its most famous appearance is in the list of doggerel romances in Chaucer's *Tale of Sir Thopas*.

John Constable (*fl.* 1520)
Epigrammata V

William Hendred (tr.)
The Pilgrimage of Mankind V
Publication date conjectural

John Lydgate (1370?–1449)
Testament V
Publication date conjectural

John Rastell (1475?–1536)
The Nature of the Four Elements D
Publication date conjectural

1521

- Papal ban on Luther at Diet of Worms
  Title of 'Defender of the Faith' bestowed on Henry VIII by Pope Leo X
  Execution of the 3rd duke of Buckingham
- Anne Askew (Protestant martyr) born *c.*1521
  Sir Thomas Chaloner born
  Richard Eden born?
- Richard Arnold (chronicler) dies

Anonymous
Book of a Ghostly Father V
Publication date conjectural

Anonymous
Christmas Carols V
Includes 'A caroll of huntynge' and 'A carol bringyng in the bores heed'

Brian Anslay (*fl.* 1521) (tr.)
The City of Ladies F
A translation of Christine de Pisan (1364–1430), *Le livre de la cité des dames* (1404–5). A collection of stories about women of exemplary virtue, taken mostly from Boccaccio (1313–75).

Alexander Barclay (1475?–1552)
The Boke of Codrus and Mynalcas V
Barclay's Fourth Eclogue. See also *Eclogues* 1530, *Fifth Eclogue* 1518.

Alexander Barclay (1475?–1552)
The Introductory to Wryte and to Pronounce Frenche NF

Henry Bradshaw (*d.* 1513)
The Life of St Werburgh V

Andrew Chertsey (*fl.* 1508–32) (tr.)
The Passyon of Our Lorde NF/V
Translated from French, with added interspersed verses

John Fisher (1459?–1535)
The Sermon of John the Bysshop of Rochester NF
Publication date conjectural. Sermon preached 12 May 1521.

John Skelton (1460?–1529)
The Tunnyng of Elynour Rummyng V
Publication date conjectural

1522

- War with France
- John Jewel, bishop of Salisbury, born
- Gavin Douglas dies
  William Lily (*b.*1468?) dies

Anonymous
Mundus & Infans D

Alexander Barclay (1475?–1552) (tr.)
Cronycle of the Warre agaynst Jugurth NF
Publication date conjectural. A translation of Sallust's *Bellum Jugurthinum*. In Latin and English.

Robert Copland (*fl.* 1508–47) (tr.)
Ipomadon V
Publication date conjectural. Derived from Hue de Rotelande's Anglo-Norman *Ipomedon* (*c.*1190).

1523

- Richard Edwards born?
- Stephen Hawes dies?

Alexander Barclay (1475?–1552) (tr.)
The Mirror of Good Manners V
Publication date conjectural. Translated from Dominic Mancini (*fl.* 1478–91), *De quatuor virtutibus*. English and Latin.

John Bourchier, Lord Berners (1467–1533) (tr.)
Froissart's Chronicles NF
Volume i. Translated from Jean Froissart (*c.*1337–*c.*1410). Volume ii published 1525 (q.v.).

John Skelton (1460?–1529)
The Garland of Laurel V

1524

- Thomas Tusser born?
  William Whittingham (translator of the Bible) born?
- Ronsard born

- Luis de Camoëns born
- Hans Holbein, the elder, dies

1525

- Peace with France
  Thomas Wolsey endows Cardinal College Oxford (refounded as Christ Church by Henry VIII in 1546)
- John Stow born
- Pieter Breughel born

Anonymous
King Alexander V
Publication date conjectural. Composed in the early 14th century. Freely adapted from Thomas of Kent's 12th-century *Roman de toute chevalerie.*

John Bourchier, Lord Berners (1467–1533) (tr.)
Froissart's Chronicles NF
Volume ii. See also *Froissart's Chronicles* 1523.

John Rastell (1475?–1536) (tr.)?
Celestina D
Publication date conjectural. Adapted from acts 1–4 of *Celestina* by Fernando de Rojas (*d.* 1541), with a new conclusion. Also known as *Calisto and Melebea.*

John Rastell (1475?–1536)
Of Gentleness and Nobility D
Publication date conjectural. Erroneously attributed to John Heywood.

Walter Smith (*fl.* 1523)
The Merry Jests of the Widow Edith F

William Tyndale (1494?–1536) (tr.)
The New Testament BIB
Only partly printed

William Walter (*fl.* 1520) (tr.)
Titus and Gesippus V
Publication date conjectural. Translated from a Latin version of Boccaccio (1313–75), *Decameron*, Day 10, Tale 8.

John Walton (*fl.* 1410) (tr.)
The Consolation of Philosophy V
Translated from Boethius (*d.* 524). See also Chaucer, *Consolation of Philosophy* 1478.

Richard Whitford (*fl.* 1495–1555?) (tr.)
The Rule of St Augustine NF
In two parts: i, the Latin text of Augustine's *Regula*, with Hugh of Saint-Victor's and Richard Whitford's commentaries in English; ii, Whitford's English translation of the *Regula.*

1526

- Mogul dynasty established after the battle of Panipat (27 Apr.)
  Suleiman I defeats the Hungarians at the Battle of Mohács (29–30 Aug.)
- Palestrina born

Anonymous
The Grete Herball NF
Largely based on *Le grand herbier* (Paris, n.d.)

Anonymous
A Hundred Merry Tales F
Publication date conjectural. A jest-book.

Paul Bushe (1490–1558)
The Extirpation of Ignorance V
Publication date conjectural

Geoffrey Chaucer (1340?–1400)
The Canterbury Tales V
The Pynson edition. See *Canterbury Tales* 1477.

Geoffrey Chaucer (1340?–1400)
The House of Fame V
Pynson edition. Publication date conjectural. See also *The House of Fame* 1483.

Geoffrey Chaucer (1340?–1400)
Troilus and Criseyde V
Pynson edition, published anonymously. Publication date conjectural. See also *Troilus and Criseyde* 1483.

Margaret More Roper (1505–44) (tr.)
A Devout Treatise upon the Pater Noster NF
Anonymous. Publication date conjectural. Translated from Erasmus, *Precatio Dominica.*

William Tyndale (1494?–1536) (tr.)
The New Testament BIB
The first complete edition of Tyndale's translation. See also *New Testament* 1525.

1527

- Henry VIII begins negotiations with Rome for a divorce
- Niccolò Machiavelli dies
- Castiglione, *Il Cortegiano*

John Colet (1467?–1519) and **William Lily** (1468?–1522)
The Æditio NF
Colet's *Æditio* and Lily's *Rudimenta* published together in one volume, the latter serving as the basis for part i of 'Lily's Grammar' 1542 (q.v.)

John Skelton (1460?–1529)
Skelton Laureate Agaynste a Comely Coystrowne V
Publication date conjectural. Also contains 'Upon a Dead Man's Head', and 'Womanhood, Wanton, ye want'.

1528

- War with Spain
- Lady Anne Bacon born
- Albrecht Dürer dies

Anonymous
The Jeaste of Syr Gawayne V
Publication date conjectural. An Arthurian romance, adapted from two episodes in the *First Continuation* (*c.*1200) of Chrétien de Troyes's *Perceval, ou le Conte del Graal* (*c.*1190).

William Barlowe (*d.* 1568)
Read Me and Be Not Wroth/The Burial of the Mass V
Written with William Roy

Robert Copland (*fl.* 1508–47) (tr.)
The Rutter of the See NF
Anonymous. Translated from Pierre Garcie's *Le routier de la mer.*

Robert Copland (*fl.* 1508–47) (tr.)
Secreta secretorum NF
Also translated by John Lydgate: see *The Governance of Kings* 1511

Thomas Paynell (*fl.* 1528–67) (tr.)
This Boke Techyng al People to Governe them in Helthe NF
Latin and English. The first English translation of the popular medical treatise *The School of Salern* (*Regimen sanitatis Salerni*).

John Skelton (1460?–1529)
Diverse Ballads V
Publication date conjectural

John Skelton (1460–1529)
A Replication V

William Tyndale (1494?–1536)
The Obedience of a Christen Man NF
Anonymous

Sir Thomas Wyatt (1503?–42) (tr.)
The Quyete of Mynde NF
The only work of Wyatt's to be published in his lifetime. Translated from Plutarch's *De tranquillitate animi* for Katherine of Aragon.

1529

- Thomas Wolsey dismissed: Sir Thomas More appointed Lord Chancellor
  The 'Reformation Parliament' summoned
  Treaty of Cambrai
- John Hall born?
- John Skelton (*b.* 1460?) dies

Anonymous
Solomon and Marcolphus V
Publication date conjectural

Simon Fish (*d.* 1531)
A Supplicacyon for the Beggers NF

Sir Thomas More (1478–1535)
A Dialogue Concernynge Heresyes & Matters of Religion NF
See Tyndale's *An Answere unto Sir Thomas Mores Dialogue* 1531

Sir Thomas More (1478–1535)
The Supplycacyon of Soulys NF

1530

- Tyndale's Bible burned
- Sir Thomas Hoby born
  Richard Mulcaster born?
  George Puttenham born?
  Robert Sempill born?
  John Whitgift born?
- Thomas Lupset dies
  Cardinal Wolsey dies (29 Nov.)
- Ivan IV ('The Terrible') born

Anonymous
Boccus and Sydracke V
Edited by J. Twyne. Publication date conjectural (1530–7). A medieval encyclopaedia, deriving from the Old French *Sidrac*, in dialogue form, with Boccus asking the 847 questions and Sidrac (*b.* 847 years after the Flood) answering them.

Anonymous
Caesar: Commentaries NF
English and Latin in parallel columns. Translated from French, not from Latin, and often misattributed to John Tiptoft, earl of Worcester.

Anonymous
The Dialoges of Creatures Moralysed F
Publication date conjectural. A translation of *Dialogus creaturarum optimé moralizatus*, variously attributed to Nicolaus Pergaminus and to Mayno de' Mayneri (*d.* 1368).

Anonymous
Sir Isumbras V
Publication date uncertain (*c.*1530). A family romance of separation and reunion, based, like *Sir Eglamour* 1500 (q.v.) and *Sir Torrent* 1505? (q.v.), on the St Eustace legend. Composed in the early 14th century in tail-rhyme.

Anonymous
Sir Lamwell V
Publication date conjectural (1530–2?). One of several English versions of this Arthurian tale, derived from Marie de France's *Lai de Lanval* (second half of the 12th century). A 'fairy mistress' tale.

Anonymous
Youth D
Publication date uncertain (*c.*1530)

Alexander Barclay (1475?–1529) (tr.)
Eclogues V
Publication date conjectural. Translated from Enea Silvio de Piccolomini (Pope Pius II, 1405–64), *De miseria curialium*. See also *The Boke of Codrus and Mynalcas* 1521, *Fifth Eclogue* 1518.

John Colet (1467?–1519)
The Sermon of Doctor Colete NF
First published in Latin *c.*1512

Sir Thomas Elyot (1490?–1546) (tr.)
The Educacion or Bringinge up of Children NF
Translated from Plutarch

George Joye (*d.* 1553) (tr.)
The Psalter of David in Englishe BIB

Henry Medwall (*b. c.*1462)
Nature D

Christopher Saint-German (1460?–1540)
Doctor and Student NF
Publication date conjectural. A major work of 16th-century constitutional theory. Latin original published in1528.

John Skelton (1460?–1529)
Magnyfycence D
Publication date conjectural

William Tyndale (1494?–1536) (tr.)
The Pentateuch BIB
Tyndale's translation of the first five books of the Old Testament

William Tyndale (1494?–1536)
The Practyse of Prelates NF

Richard Ullerston (*d.* 1423)
A Compendious Olde Treatyse NF
A mid-15th century revision, with 16th-century modernization, of an English Lollard redaction of a Latin text. Previously attributed to John Purvey.

1531

- Henry VIII becomes Supreme Head of the Church in England
- Simon Fish dies
- Ulrich Zwingli dies

Sir Thomas Elyot (1490?–1546)
The Governor NF

John Skelton (1460?–1529)
Colin Clout V
Publication date conjectural

William Tyndale (1494?–1536)
An Answere unto Sir Thomas Mores Dialogue NF
See Sir Thomas More, *A Dialogue Concernynge Heresyes* 1529

1532

- Sir Thomas More resigns as Lord Chancellor
  Submission of the clergy, recognizing the king's superiority over ecclesiastical matters, passed by convocation
  Anne Boleyn becomes pregnant
- Sir John Hawkins born
  Thomas Norton born

Geoffrey Chaucer (1340?–1400)
The Workes of Geffray Chaucer WKS
Edited by William Thynne. See also *Woorkes* 1561 (ed. Stow), *Workes* 1598 (ed. Speght).

Leonard Cox (*fl.* 1572)
The Arte or Crafte of Rhetoryke NF
Based on Philip Melanchthon's *Institutiones rhetoricae* (1521)

Sir Thomas Elyot (1490?–1546)
Pasquil the Playne NF

Sir Thomas More (1478–1535)
The Confutacyon of Tyndales Answere NF
See also *The Second Parte of the Confutacyon* 1533 and Tyndale's *Answere* 1531

Thomas Paynell (*fl.* 1528–67) (tr.)
De contemptu mundi NF
Publication date conjectural. The original by Erasmus was published in 1521.

William Walter (*fl.* 1520) (tr.)
Guistarde and Sigismonde V

From Boccaccio (1313–75), *Decameron*, Day 4, Tale 1, translated from a Latin version by Leonardo Bruni (1369–1444) and edited by Robert Copland.

1533

- Henry VIII secretly marries Anne Boleyn (Jan.)
  Thomas Cranmer becomes archbishop of Canterbury (Mar.): pronounces Henry VIII's marriage to Catherine of Aragon void (May)
  Anne Boleyn gives birth to Princess Elizabeth, the future Elizabeth I (7 Sept.)
- John Bourchier, 2nd Baron Berners (*b*.1467) dies
- Michel de Montaigne born
- Lodovico Ariosto dies

Anonymous
Old Christmas D
An interlude with the characters Old Christmas, Good Order, Riot, Gluttony, and Prayer

Giles Duwes (*d*. 1535)
An Introductorie for to Lerne Frenche NF
Publication date conjectural. A practical French grammar.

Sir Thomas Elyot (1490?–1546) (tr.)
The Doctrinall of Princis NF
Publication date conjectural. Translated from Isocrates.

Sir Thomas Elyot (1490?–1546)
Of the Knowledge whiche Maketh a Wise Man NF

John Heywood (1497?–1580?)
Johan Johan D
Anonymous

John Heywood (1497?–1580?)
The Pardoner and the Friar D
Anonymous

John Heywood (1497?–1580?)
The Play of the Wether D

Thomas Lupset (1495–1530)
A Treatise of Charitie NF
Anonymous

Sir Thomas More (1478–1535)
The Apologye of Syr Thomas More Knyght NF
Answers Christopher Saint-German's *Treatise Concernynge the Division Betweene the Spirytualtie and Temporaltie* (1532) and answered by Saint-German's *Salem and Bizance* (1533)

Sir Thomas More (1478–1535)
The Debellacyon of Salem and Bizance NF
Answers Christopher Saint-German's *Salem and Bizance* (1533)

Sir Thomas More (1478–1535)
A Letter of Syr Tho. More Knyght NF
Answered by *A Boke Made by John Frith . . . Answeringe unto M. Mores Lettur* (1533) and by Tyndale's *Souper of the Lorde* (1533)

Sir Thomas More (1478–1535)
The Second Parte of the Confutacyon of Tyndales Answere NF
See More, *The Confutacyon* 1532

William Tyndale (1494?–1536)? (tr.)
The Manuell of the Christen Knyght NF
Anonymous. Possibly by Tyndale. Translated from Erasmus, *Enchiridion militis Christiani*.

Nicholas Udall (1505?–56) (tr.)
Floures for Latine Spekynge NF
From Terence

1534

- Act of Supremacy passed setting aside papal authority over the English Church
- George Gascoigne born?
- Wynkyn de Worde dies

John Colet (1467?–1519)
The Ordre of a Good Chrysten Mannes Lyfe NF

Sir Thomas Elyot (1490?–1546) (tr.)
The Mortalitie of Man NF
By St Cyprian. Also includes *The Rules of a Christian Lyfe*, from Giovanni Pico della Mirandola (1463–94).

John Heywood (1497?–1580?)
A Play of Love D

Thomas Lupset (1495–1530) (tr.)
The Counsailes of Saint Isidore NF
Translated from St Isidore of Seville (*c*.AD 602FFL36)

Thomas Lupset (1495–1530)
The Waye of Dyenge Well NF

John Lydgate (1370?–1449) (tr.)
Life of St Alban and St Amphibalus V
Anonymous. Translated from French.

Sir Thomas More (1478–1535)
The Answere to the Poysened Booke Named The Souper of the Lorde NF
The 'poysened booke' was by William Tyndale, printed (in Antwerp?) in April 1533

William Tyndale (1494?–1536) (tr.)
The Newe Testament Corrected BIB
Published 1534, dated 1535. The last edition of Tyndale's translation of the New Testament to be revised by him.

Robert Whittington (*fl.* 1520) (tr.)
The Thre Bookes of Tullyes Offyces NF
A translation of Cicero's *De officiis*

1535

- Thomas Cartwright born
- Jasper Heywood born
  Sir Thomas North born
- John Fisher executed (22 June)
  Sir Thomas More executed (6 July)

Anonymous
The Ploughman's Tale V
Publication date conjectural. Probably 15th century in origin. Misattributed to Chaucer in Thynne's edition of his works 1532 (q.v.).

John Bourchier, Lord Berners (1467–1533) (tr.)
The Golden Boke of Marcus Aurelius NF
Anonymous. Translated from a French version of Antonio de Guevara's *Reloj de principes o libro aureo del emperador Marco Aurelio* (1529). The 'Aurelian' content is spurious. Reprinted many times. See also Sir Thomas North's *Diall of Princes* 1557.

Miles Coverdale (1488–1568) (tr.)
The Bible BIB
Published 4 October 1535. Dedicated to Henry VIII.

Miles Coverdale (1488–1568)
Goostly Psalmes and Spirituall Songes BIB
Publication date conjectural. With music.

Gavin Douglas (1474?–1522)
The Palice of Honour V
Publication date conjectural. Written *c.*1501. An allegory in the form of a vision.

George Joye (*d.* 1553)
An Apologye Made to Satisfye W. Tindale NF
See Tyndale's *Newe Testament Corrected* 1534

George Joye (*d.* 1553) (tr.)
A Compendyouse Somme of the Very Christen Relygyon NF
Anonymous. Translated from the *Summa totius sacrae scripturae.*

John Lydgate (1370?–1449)
The Serpent of Division NF
Anonymous. Publication date conjectural.

1536

- Catherine of Aragon dies (Jan.)
  Dissolution of the monasteries begins
  Anne Boleyn executed (19 May): Henry VIII marries Jane Seymour (30 May)
  The Pilgrimage of Grace (Oct. 1536–Feb. 1537)
- Arthur Golding born?
- John Rastell dies
  William Tyndale executed (Oct.)
- Erasmus dies

Anonymous
Jack Upland V
Publication date conjectural. Misattributed to Chaucer.

Robert Copland (*fl.* 1508–47) (tr.)
The Hye Way to the Spyttell Hous V
Translated from Robert de Balsac (*c.*1440–1503), *Le chemin de l'ospital.* A contribution to the 'vagabond' literature of the period. The hospital in question is St Bartholomew's in London.

Sir Richard Morison (1510?–56)
A Remedy for Sedition NF
Anonymous. Morison was hired as apologist for Henry VIII's policies. This tract was a response to the Pilgrimage of Grace.

1537

- Prince Edward, the future Edward VI, born (12 Oct.)
  Jane Seymour dies after giving birth to Edward (29 Oct.)
- Bartholomew Clerke born?
  Thomas Preston born

Sir Thomas Elyot (1490?–1546)
The Castell of Helthe NF
Publication date conjectural. Medical advice for the ordinary man. Corrected and augmented, 1541.

'Thomas Matthew' [John Rogers (1500?–55)] (tr.)
The Byble BIB
First edition of the 'Matthew Bible'—actually a conflation of Tyndale's and Coverdale's translations

1538

- William Fulke born
  Reginald Scot born?

Anonymous
The Court of Venus V
See also *The Courte of Venus* 1563

Sir Thomas Elyot (1490?–1546)
The Dictionary of Syr Thomas Eliot DICT
In Latin and English. 2nd edition published in 1542 as *Bibliotheca Elyotae.*

Sir David Lindsay (1490–1555)
The Complaynte and Testament of a Popinjay V

William Tyndale (1494?–1536) (tr.)
The Newe Testament in Englyshe and Latyn BIB
The first diglot Bible, using Tyndale's English New Testament and the Latin of Erasmus. Coverdale's diglot also published in 1538.

1539

- Dissolution of the Greater Monasteries
- Sir Geoffrey Fenton born?
  Sir Humphrey Gilbert born?

Miles Coverdale (1488–1568) (ed.)
The Byble in Englyshe BIB
Published in April 1539. First edition of the 'Great Bible' (also known as 'Cromwell's Bible')—a revision by Coverdale of Matthew's Bible 1537 (q.v.)—injuncted to be placed in all churches.

Sir Thomas Elyot (1490?–1546)
The Bankette of Sapience NF

Sir Richard Morison (1510?–56)
An Exhortation to Styrre all Englysshe Men to the Defence of theyr Countreye NF

Sir Richard Morison (1510?–56) (tr.)
An Introduction to Wisdom NF
Anonymous. Translated from *Introductio ad sapientiam* (1524) by Juan Luis Vives (1492–1540). A highly influential and frequently reprinted compendium of learning.

Sir Richard Morison (1510?–56)
An Invective Ayenste the Greate and Detestable Vice, Treason NF

Richard Taverner (1505?–75) (ed.)
The Most Sacred Bible BIB
The first edition of Taverner's Bible, a revision of Matthew's Bible of 1537 (q.v.)

Richard Taverner (1505?–75) (tr.)
Proverbes or Adagies NF
The first English translation of Erasmus's *Adagia*

1540

- Henry VIII marries Anne of Cleves (6 Jan.); the marriage is annulled (9 July)
  Henry VIII marries Catherine Howard (28 July)
  Thomas Cromwell executed (28 July)
  War with France
- William Gilbert born
  Barnabe Googe born
  William Painter born?
  Barnabe Rich born?

John Bellenden (*c.*1500–48?) (tr.)
The Chronicles of Scotland NF
Publication date conjectural. A translation of Boece's *Historia Scotorum* (Paris, 1527). Contains two poems by Bellenden, 'The Proheme to the Cosmographe' and 'The Proheme of the History'.

Miles Coverdale (1488–1568) (ed.)
The Byble in Englyshe BIB
Published in April 1540. The second edition of the 'Great Bible', further revised by Coverdale, and the earliest containing Cranmer's prologue. See *The Byble in Englyshe* 1539.

Sir Thomas Elyot (1490?–1546)
The Defence of Good Women NF

Sir Thomas Elyot (1490?–1546)
The Image of Governance NF

Sir Thomas More (1478–1535)
Lady Fortune V
Publication date conjectural

1541

- Catherine Howard sent to the Tower (Nov.)
- El Greco born
- Paracelsus dies

Anonymous
The Schole House of Women V

Sometimes attributed to Edward Gosynhyll, but in fact replied to by him in *The Prayse of all Women* 1542 (q.v.). Also answered by Robert Burdet in *A Dyalogue Defensyve for Women against Malycyous Detractours* (1542) and by Edward More in *The Defence of Women* (1560).

Thomas Paynell (*fl.* 1528–67) (tr.)
The Conspiracie of Lucius Catiline NF
A translation of Costanzo Felice, *De conjuratione L. Catalinæ*

1542

- Mary Queen of Scots born (8 Dec.)
  Catherine Howard executed (13 Feb.)
  Scottish army defeated at the Battle of Solway Moss (24 Nov.)
- Thomas Newton born?
- Sir Thomas Wyatt dies
- Hans Holbein, the younger, dies

Andrew Borde (1490?–1549)
Dyetary of Helth NF
See also Borde's *Breviary of Helthe* 1547

'Roderigo Mors' [Henry Brinkelow (*d.* 1546)]
The Lamentacion of a Christian, Against the Citie of London NF

Edward Gosynhyll (*fl.* 1560)
The Prayse of all Women V
Publication date conjectural

John Leland (1506?–52)
Naeniae in mortem Thomae Viati V
Neo-Latin poems on the death of Sir Thomas Wyatt the elder (1503?–1542)

William Lily (1468?–1522)
An Introduction of the Eyght Partes of Speche NF
'Lily's Grammar'—the most important school textbook of the period, authorized for use from 1540. See also Colet and Lily 1527.

Nicholas Udall (1505?–56) (tr.)
Apophthegmes NF
A translation of Erasmus's *Apophthegmata*

1543

- Henry VIII marries Catherine Parr (12 July)
  Alliance between Henry and the Holy Roman Emperor, Charles V, against Scotland and France
- William Byrd born
  Thomas Deloney born?
  Thomas Twyne born
- Copernicus, *De Revolutionibus Orbium Coelestium*
- Copernicus dies

Nicholas Grimald (1519?–62)
Christus Redivivus D
A Latin play performed at Brasenose College, Oxford

John Hardyng (1378–*c.*1464)
Chronicle V
A minor source for Malory's *Le Morte DArthur* 1485 (q.v.), the work also contains a version of the Grail quest

George Joye (*d.* 1553)
The Unitie and Scisme of the Olde Chirche NF

Robert Record (1510?–58)
The Worke and Practise of Arithmetike NF
See also *The Whetstone of Witte* 1557

1544

- Henry VIII and Charles V invade France
- Richard Bancroft, archbishop of Canterbury, born
  Alexander Neville born
  George Turberville born c.1544
- Margaret Roper dies
- Torquato Tasso born

John Bale (1495–1563)
The Examinacyon and Death of the Martyr Syr John Oldecastell NF
Anonymous. Publication date conjectural.

John Fisher (1459?–1535)
Psalmes or Prayers Taken Out of Holie Scripture BIB
Anonymous. Translated by Sir Richard Proby from Fisher's Latin original (also published 1544).

John Heywood (1497?–1580?)
The Foure PP D
Publication date conjectural. An interlude of a palmer, a pardoner, a 'potcary', and a pedlar.

George Joye (*d.* 1553)
A Present Consolacion for the Sufferers of Persecution NF

John Leland (1506?–52)
Assertio inclytissimi Arturii regis Britanniæ NF

A passionate defence of the historicity of King Arthur against Polydore Vergil's assertion that he never existed. See also Leland 1582.

1545

- Sinking of Henry VIII's warship, the *Mary Rose*
  The Council of Trent
- Nicholas Breton born?
  John Gerard born

Anonymous
The Four Cardinal Virtues D
Publication date conjectural

Roger Ascham (1515–68)
Toxophilus NF

Robert Burrant (*fl.* 1553) (tr.)
Preceptes of Cato with Annotacions of D. Erasmus V
Main text in verse, with Burrant's prose translation of Erasmus's commentary, together with his own

Sir Thomas Elyot (1490?–1546)
A Preservative Agaynste Deth NF

Henry Howard, earl of Surrey (1517?–47)
An Excellent Epitaffe of Syr Thomas Wyat V
Publication date conjectural. Wyatt (the elder) died in 1542.

Catherine Parr, Queen Consort of Henry VIII (1512–48)
Prayers Stirrying the Mynd unto Heavenlye Medytacions NF
See also *The Monument of Matrones* 1582

John Skelton (1460?–1529)
Certain Books V
Includes *Speke Parrot*; *The Death of Kyng Edward the Fourth*; *A Treatise of the Scottes*; and *The Tunnyng of Elynour Rummyng* (see 1521)

John Skelton (1460?–1529)
Phillip Sparrow V
Publication date conjectural

John Skelton (1460?–1529)
Why Come Ye Not to Court? V
Publication date conjectural

1546

- Cardinal Beaton murdered
  Anne Askew burned at Smithfield
- Robert Parsons born
- Sir Thomas Elyot dies
- Luther dies
- Tycho Brahe born

Anne Askew (*c.*1521–46)
The First Examination NF
Askew was a Protestant martyr, burned at Smithfield. See also *The Later Examination* 1547.

John Bale (1495–1563)
The Actes of Englysh Votaryes NF

Stephen Gardiner (1483?–1555)
A Detection of the Devils Sophistre NF

John Heywood (1497?–1580?)
A Dialogue Conteinyng the Nomber in Effect of all the Proverbes in the Englishe Tongue V

Thomas Langley (*d.* 1581) (ed.)
An Abridgement of the Notable Worke of Polidore Vergile NF
An abridgement of the *De Inventoribus Rerum* (Venice, 1499; enlarged 1521) of Polydore Vergil (1470?–1555?)

John Wycliffe (*d.* 1384)
Wycklyffes Wicket NF

1547

- Henry VIII dies (28 Jan.)
  EDWARD VI (–1553): duke of Somerset becomes Protector
  Ivan the Terrible crowned tsar of Russia
- Richard Stanyhurst born
- Edward Halle dies
  Henry Howard, earl of Surrey, executed
- Cervantes born

Anne Askew (*c.*1521–1546)
The Later Examination NF
See *The First Examination* 1546

William Baldwin (*c.*1515–63)
A Treatise of Morall Phylosophie NF/V

John Bale (1495–1563)
God's Promises D
Publication date conjectural

John Bale (1495–1563)
The Temptation of our Lord D
Publication date conjectural. Probably preceded by the now lost *Brefe comedy or enterlude of Johan Baptystes preachynge in the wyldernesse.*

Andrew Borde (1490?–1549)
The Breviary of Helthe NF
An alphabetical list of diseases by their Latin names, with their remedies and treatment. Intended as a companion to Borde's *Dyetary of Helth* 1542 (q.v.).

Catherine Parr, Queen Consort of Henry VIII (1512–48)
The Lamentacion of a Synner NF
Preface by William Cecil. See also *The Monument of Matrones* 1582.

1548

- John Norden born
  George Pettie born
  Geoffrey Whitney born?
- Catherine Parr dies

John Bale (1495–1563)
The Three Laws D
Publication date conjectural

John Bourchier, Lord Berners (1467–1533) (tr.)
The Castell of Love F
Publication date conjectural. A translation of *La cárcel de amor* [Prison of Love] (1492) by Diego de San Pedro (*c.*1437–*c.*1498).

Sir Francis Bryan (*d.* 1550) (tr.)
A Dispraise of the Life of a Courtier, and a Commendacion of the Life of the Labouryng Man NF
Translated from a Castilian original by Antonio de Guevara (*d.* 1545)

Thomas Cranmer (1489–1556) (tr.)
Catechismus NF
Commonly called 'Cranmer's Catechism'. Translated from Justus Jonas (1493–1555).

Robert Crowley (1518–88)
An Informacion and Peticion Agaynst the Oppressours of the Pore Commons of this Realme NF
Also published in Latin (1549?)

Princess Elizabeth, later **Queen Elizabeth I** (1533–1603) (tr.)
A Godly Medytacyon of the Christen Sowle NF
A translation of Marguerite, consort of Henry II of Navarre, *Le Miroir de l'âme pécheresse*. Edited by John Bale. See also *The Monument of Matrones* 1582.

Edward Halle (*c.*1498–1547)
Halle's Chronicle NF

Hugh Latimer (1485?–1555)
A Notable Sermon [on the plough] *of Maister Hughe Latemer* NF

Sir David Lindsay (1490–1555)
The Tragical Death of David Beaton Bishoppe of Sainct Andrews V
Publication date conjectural. Archbishop Beaton (or Bethune) convicted Wishart (Knox's teacher) of heresy in 1546 and was murdered in the same year.

Luke Shepherd (*fl.* 1548)
Antipus V

Luke Shepherd (*fl.* 1548)
Doctour Doubble Ale V
Publication date conjectural. An anti-Catholic poem.

Luke Shepherd (*fl.* 1548)
John Bon and Mast Person V
Publication date conjectural. Shepherd was twice imprisoned on account of this work.

Luke Shepherd (*fl.* 1548)
Pathos V
Publication date conjectural

Luke Shepherd (*fl.* 1548)
The Upcheering of the Mass V

1549

- Act of Uniformity
  The first Book of Common Prayer
  Prayer Book riots
  Robert Kett's Norfolk rebellion
- Giles Fletcher, the elder, born?
  John Rainolds born
  Sir Henry Savile born
- Andrew Borde dies

Anonymous
The Booke of Common Prayer
Published 7 March 1549. Also an issue on 8 March 1549 and one dated 'mense Martii'. Final version 1662 (q.v.).

William Baldwin (*c.*1515–63)
The Canticles or Balades of Salomon V

Sir Thomas Chaloner (1521–65) (tr.)
The Praise of Folly PS
Misdated 1569. A translation of the edition of Erasmus's *Moriæ Encomium* published in Cologne in 1526. Chaloner also consulted the Italian translation by Antonio Pellegrini (Venice, 1539).

Sir John Cheke (1514–57)
The Hurt of Sedicion NF
Anonymous

Thomas Cooper (1517?–94)
An Epitome of Cronicles of England Continued to the Reigne of Edwarde the Sixt NF
Misdated 1569. Continues Thomas Lanquet's Chronicle. See also *Cooper's Chronicle* 1560.

Robert Crowley (1518–88)
The Voyce of the Laste Trumpet Blowen bi the Seventh Angel V

Hugh Latimer (1485?–1555)
The Fyrste Sermon of Mayster Hughe Latimer NF

John Leland (1506?–52)
The New Year's Gift NF
See also *Itinerary,* edited by Thomas Hearne, 1710

Sir Thomas Wyatt (1503?–42) (tr.)
Certayne Psalmes Chosen Out of the Psalter of David BIB
The first of Wyatt's poems to appear in print

1550

- Fall of the duke of Somerset: the duke of Northumberland becomes Protector
- Thomas Blenerhasset born?
  Robert Browne (Separatist) born?
  Gabriel Harvey born
  Richard Knolles born?

Anonymous
John the Evangelist D

Anonymous
Somebody and Others D
Publication date conjectural

Charles Bansley (*fl.* 1550)
The Pride of Women V

Thomas Cranmer (1489–1556)
A Defence of the True and Catholike Doctrine of the Sacrament of the Body and Bloud of Christ NF

Robert Crowley (1518–88)
One and Thyrtye Epigrammes V
Actually contains 33 epigrams

John Heywood (1497?–1580?)
An Hundred Epigrammes V
See also *Two Hundred Epigrammes* 1555, *A Fourth* [i.e. fifth] *Hundred of Epygrams* 1560, *Works* 1562.

John Hooper (*d.* 1555)
A Godly Confession and Protestacion of the Christian Fayth NF

William Langland (1330?–1400?)
Piers Plowman V
Attributed to Langland. The B text (written *c.*1377–9). Title-page misdated 1505.

William Roy (*fl.* 1527–31) (tr.)
The True Beliefe in Christ and his Sacramentes NF
A translation made in 1526 of Wolfgang Capito's *De pueris instutituendis*

William Thomas (*d.* 1554)
Principal Rules of the Italian Grammer DICT
The first work of its kind in English

Richard Weaver (*fl. c.*1549–53)
Lusty Juventus D
Publication date conjectural

Robert Wedderburn (*c.*1510–*c.*1557)?
The Complaynt of Scotland NF
Possibly by Wedderburn. The framework is taken from Alain Chartier's *Le Quadrilogue Invectif* (1422). Contains a list of tales told by shepherds to pass the time.

1551

- Timothy Bright (inventor of shorthand) born
  William Camden born
  George Whetstone born *c.*1551

Thomas Cranmer (1489–1556)
An Answer Unto a Crafty Cavillation by Stephen Gardiner NF
Answers Gardiner's *Explication and Assertion* 1551 (q.v.)

Robert Crowley (1518–88)
Philargyrie of Greate Britayne; or, The Fable of the Great Giant V
Anonymous

Stephen Gardiner (1483?–1555)
An Explication and Assertion of the True Catholique Fayth NF
Confutation of Cranmer's *Defence* 1550 (q.v.)

Sir Thomas More (1478–1535)
Utopia NF
Translated by Ralph Robinson (*b.* 1521). Original Latin text published 1516 (q.v.).

William Turner (*d.* 1568)
A New Herball NF
The first of a 3-volume work—the first systematic survey of the English flora. Volumes ii and iii published in 1562 and 1568 respectively. See also Gerard's *Herball* 1597.

1552

- Cranmer promulgates Forty-Two Articles of Religion (later reduced to Thirty-Nine: see 1562)
- Sir Edward Coke born
  Abraham Fleming born?
  Richard Hakluyt born?
  Philemon Holland born
  Sir Hugh Plat born
  Sir Walter Ralegh born?
  John Speed born?
  Edmund Spenser born
- Alexander Barclay dies
  John Leland dies

William Barker (*fl.* 1572) (tr.)
Cyropædia NF
Publication date conjectural. A partial translation (in 7 books) of Xenophon. A complete translation (in 8 books) appeared in 1567.

Thomas Churchyard (1520?–1604)
A Myrrour for Man V

1553

- Death of Edward VI (6 July)
  Lady Jane Grey proclaimed queen (10 July): deposed (19 July)
  MARY I (–1558)
  Cranmer committed to the Tower for sedition
  Execution of the duke of Northumberland (22 Aug.)
  Stephen Gardiner appointed Lord Chancellor
- Arthur Dent (Puritan) born
  John Florio born
  Henry Lok born?
  Anthony Munday born
- George Joye (Bible translator) dies
- François Rabelais dies

Anonymous
Pierce the Ploughmans Crede V
Publication date conjectural. See also *Piers Plowman* 1550.

Gavin Douglas (1474?–1522) (tr.)
Aeneid V
Translated 1512–13, while Douglas was Provost of St Giles in Edinburgh. Book xiii is by Maffeo Vegio (1406 or 7–1458).

Gavin Douglas (1474?–1522)
The Palis of Honoure V
2nd edition. Publication date conjectural. 1st edition 1535 (q.v.). This edition differs considerably from the first.

Richard Eden (1521?–76) (tr.)
A Treatyse of the Newe India NF
A translation of *Cosmographia* by Sebastian Münster (1489–1552)

Stephen Gardiner (1483?–1555)
De vera obediencia NF
A translation (attributed to John Bale, Michael Wood, or William Turner) of Gardiner's *De vera obedientia oratio* (1535)

Sir Thomas More (1478–1535)
A Dialoge of Comfort Against Tribulacion NF

Thomas Paynell (*fl.* 1528–67) (tr.)
The Faythfull and True Storye of the Destruction of Troye F
A fictional account, though purporting to be history. Translated from M. Heret's French translation of the (spurious) *De excidio Troiae historia* of Darius Phrygius. See also Lydgate's *Troy Book* 1513.

Thomas Wilson (1525?–81)
The Arte of Rhetorique NF

1554

- Sir Thomas Wyatt's rebellion (Jan.–Feb.): Wyatt executed (Apr.)
  Lady Jane Grey executed (12 Feb.)
  Princess Elizabeth sent to the Tower
  Queen Mary marries Philip of Spain
- Stephen Gosson born
  Fulke Greville, 1st Lord Brooke, born
  Richard Hooker born
  John Lyly born
  Sir Philip Sidney born

Miles Hogarde (*fl.* 1557)
The Assault of the Sacrament of the Altar V
Written 1549. Voices non-elite opposition to the Reformation.

Henry Howard, earl of Surrey (1517?–47) (tr.)
The Fourth Boke of Virgill, Intreating of the Love Betwene Aeneas & Dido V
See also *Certain Bokes* 1557

John Knox (1505–72)
An Admonition or Warning NF

John Knox (1505–72)
A Percel of the VI Psalme Expounded NF
See also *A Fort for the Afflicted* 1580

Sir David Lindsay (1490–1555)
The Monarche V
Includes other works by Lindsay

1555

- Peace of Augsburg
- Lancelot Andrewes born
  Richard Carew, of Antony, born
  William Gager born
  Stephen Gosson born
- Stephen Gardiner dies
  Hugh Latimer and Nicholas Ridley burned in Oxford (16 Oct.)
  Sir David Lindsay dies
  John Rogers burned at Smithfield
- François de Malherbe born

Anonymous
The Image of Idleness F
Publication date conjectural

Anonymous
Till Eulenspiegel F
Publication date conjectural

Andrew Borde (1490?–1549)
The Fyrst Boke of the Introduction of Knowledge NF
Partly in verse

Richard Eden (1521?–76) (tr.)
The Decades of the New Worlde or West India NF
A translation of Decades i–iii of *De orbe novo* (1516) by Pietro Martire d'Anghiera (known as Peter Martyr Anglerius, 1467–1526). 2nd edition, with additions (by R. Willes) and omissions, as *The History of Travayle in the West and East Indies* 1577.

John Heywood (1497?–1580?)
Two Hundred Epigrammes V
See also *An Hundred Epigrammes* 1550, *A Fourth Hundred of Epygrams* 1560, *Works* 1562

Henry Parker, 8th Baron Morley (1476–1556) (tr.)
The Tryumphes of Fraunces Petrarcke V
Publication date conjectural. A translation of Petrarch (1304–74), *Trionfi*.

Nicholas Ridley (1500?–55)
A Brief Declaracion of the Lordes Supper NF
Ridley was burnt at the stake on 16 October 1555

1556

- Abdication of Charles V of Spain: succession of Philip II
  Resignation of the Holy Roman Empire by Charles V to his brother, Ferdinand I
- Alexander Montgomerie born?
  George Peele born
- Thomas Cranmer executed (21 Mar.)
  Sir Richard Morison dies
  Henry Parker, 8th Baron Morley, dies
  John Ponet dies
  Nicholas Udall dies
- Pietro Aretino dies
  Ignatius Loyola dies

Anonymous
The Knight of Curtesy and the Fair Lady of Faguell V
Publication date conjectural. Composed in the late 14th century and based on late 13th-century French originals.

Roger Bieston (*fl.* 1554)
The Bayte and Snare of Fortune V
Published anonymously, though Bieston's name is revealed in an acrostic. Probably translated from the French version of an Italian original.

George Colvile (*fl.* 1556) (tr.)
The Consolation of Philosophy NF
Translated from Boethius. Latin and English.

Thomas Cranmer (1489–1556)
The Recantation of Thomas Cranmer NF

Thomas Cranmer (1489–1556)
Submissions and Recantations NF
The first four are in English, the last two in Latin

Nicholas Grimald (1519?–62) (tr.)
Marcus Tullius Ciceroes Thre Bokes of Duties NF
Grimald was former chaplain to Bishop Ridley (burnt at the stake 1555). A translation of Cicero's *De officiis*.

John Heywood (1497?–1580?)
The Spider and the Flie V

John Ponet (1514?–56)
A Shorte Treatise of Politike Power, and of the True Obedience NF
One of the chief expressions of Protestant resistance theory

Robert Record (1510?–58)
The Castle of Knowledge NF
The first scientific account in English of the elements of astronomy, remaining the standard work throughout the rest of the 16th century.

1557

- War with France
  Stationers' Company incorporated
- Thomas Morley born
  Thomas Watson born?
- Anne of Cleves dies
  Sir John Cheke dies
  Robert Wedderburn dies c.1557

Anonymous
The Deceyte of Women F
Publication date conjectural. Partly translated from the anonymous French work *Les cent nouvelles nouvelles.*

Anonymous
Jacob and Esau D
See also *Jacob and Esau* 1568

John Heywood (1497?–1580?)
A Breefe Balet Touching the Traytorous Takynge of Scarborow Castell V
A patriotic ballad, relating the capture of Scarborough Castle in April 1557 by Thomas Stafford, who held it for two days before the earl of Westmorland recaptured it

Henry Howard, earl of Surrey (1517?–47) and others
Tottel's Miscellany ANTH
Contains 271 poems, of which 40 are by Surrey, 96 by Sir Thomas Wyatt, 40 by Nicholas Grimald (sometimes identified as the editor), and 95 by various authors. Many editions.

Henry Howard, earl of Surrey (1517?–47) (tr.)
Certain Bokes of Virgiles Aeneis V
A translation of the *Aeneid,* books ii and iv. Book iv first published 1554 (q.v.).

Sir Thomas More (1478–1535)
The Workes of Sir Thomas More Knyght, Sometime Lorde Chauncellour of England WKS
Edited by W. Rastell. The first edition of More's collected works.

Sir Thomas North (1535–1601) (tr.)
The Diall of Princes NF
Translated from Antonio de Guevara (*d.* 1545?), *Libro llamado Relox de principes,* through a French version. Revised, with a 4th book, 1568. See also John Bourchier's translation of *The Golden Boke of Marcus Aurelius* 1535.

William Rastell (1508?–65) (ed.)
Rastell's Abridged Statutes NF
After 8 reprints, this essential legal work was printed entirely in English for the first time in 1579

Robert Record (1510?–58)
The Whetstone of Witte NF
See also *The Worke and Practise of Arithmetike* 1543

Thomas Tusser (1524?–80)
A Hundreth Good Pointes of Husbandrie V
The work takes the reader through the farmer's year, month by month. Enlarged 1562. See also *Five Hundreth Points* 1573.

William Whittingham (1524?–79) (tr.)
The Newe Testament of Our Lord Jesus Christ BIB
Ascribed to William Whittingham. The text is based on Tyndale's translation of 1526 (q.v.) and the Great Bible of 1539 (q.v.). A forerunner of the Geneva version of 1560 (q.v.).

1558

- Mary Queen of Scots marries the Dauphin of France (the future Francis II)
  France declares Mary Queen of Scots queen of England
  Loss of Calais
  Death of Mary I (17 Nov.)
  ELIZABETH I (–1603)
- Robert Greene born
  Thomas Kyd born
  Thomas Lodge born
  William Perkins born
  William Warner born?
- Robert Record dies

Thomas Becon (1512–67)
The Pomander of Prayer NF
Anonymous. Many editions.

William Bullein (*d.* 1576)
A Newe Booke Entituled the Governement of Healthe NF

John Knox (1505–72)
The First Blast of the Trumpet Against the Monstruous Regiment of Women NF
Anonymous. See also *An Harborowe for Faithfull and Trewe Subjectes* 1559.

Thomas Phaer (1510?–60) (tr.)
The Seven First Bookes of the Eneidos V
The most widely read 16th-century English translation of Virgil's *Aeneid.* Enlarged to 9 books in 1562 (q.v.); 12 books 1573 (q.v.); 13 books (the 13th composed by Maffeo Vegio, 1406 or 7–1458) 1584 (q.v.).

1559

- Act of Uniformity
- George Chapman born?
- Isaac Casaubon born
- Amyot's translation of Plutarch

John Awdely (*fl.* 1559–77)
The Wonders of England V
An anti-Catholic ballad

John Aylmer (1521–94)
An Harborowe for Faithfull and Trewe Subjectes, Agaynst the Late Blowne Blaste, Concerninge the Government of Wemen NF
Anonymous. A response to John Knox's *The First Blast of the Trumpet* 1558 (q.v.).

William Baldwin (*c.*1515–63) and **George Ferrers** (1500?–79)
A Myrroure for Magistrates V
Earlier suppressed edition 1554 (?). Many editions. See also Blenerhasset, *The Seconde Part* (1578). Further contributions by H. Cavell, Thomas Challoner, John Dolman, Thomas Churchyard, Thomas Phaer, Thomas Sackville, Francis Seager. The 1574 'First Part' was written by John Higgins.

Thomas Brice (*d.* 1570)
A Compendious Register in Metre, Conteining the Names, and Pacient Suffryngs of the Membres of Jesus Christ V

Jasper Heywood (1535–98) (tr.)
The Sixt Tragedie of . . . Lucius Anneus Seneca, entituled Troas D
Reprinted by Thomas Newton in *Seneca his Tenne Tragedies* 1581 (q.v.)

Nicholas Ridley (1500?–55)
A Frendly Farewel, which Master Doctor Ridley . . . did write . . . unto all his true lovers and frendes in God, a litle before that he suffred NF
Edited, with final note, by John Foxe

1560

- Reformation in Scotland
  The Treaty of Edinburgh ends the 'Auld Alliance' between Scotland and France
  Death of Francis II: Mary Queen of Scots returns to Scotland
  Westminster School founded
- Henry Chettle born?
  William Fowler born
  Sir John Harrington born
  Alexander Hume born?
  Christopher Middleton born?
  John Udall born?
- Thomas Phaer dies

Anonymous
The Boke of Secretes of Albertus Magnus, of the Vertues of Herbes NF
A translation of the Latin version, first printed by William de Machlinia *c.*1483. Continued to be reprinted well into the 17th century.

Anonymous
Dane Hew V
Publication date conjectural (1560–84). A 15th-century comic tale of a lecherous monk, murdered by an outraged husband, whose corpse is transferred back and forth between the murder scene and his abbey before being finally 'killed'.

Anonymous
Impatient Poverty D

Anonymous
Nice Wanton D

William Baldwin (*c.*1515)
The Funeralles of King Edward the Sixt V

John Bourchier, Lord Berners (1467–1533) (tr.)
Arthur of Little Britain F
Publication date conjectural. A translation of a 14th-century French romance, *Artus de la Petite Bretagne*, probably in the version prtd by Jean de la Fontaine in Lyon (1496). The hero is a descendant of Lancelot du Lac. The translator's purpose was to keep alive 'the chivalrous feats and martial prowesses of the victorious knights of times past'.

Thomas Churchyard (1520?–1604)
The Contention Betwyxte Churchyeard and Camell, upon David Dycers Dreame V

Thomas Cooper (1517?–94)
Cooper's Chronicle NF
To the death of Queen Mary. See also *An Epitome of Cronicles* 1549. Two further editions

were published in 1565, updating the Chronicle to 1564.

Barnabe Googe (1540–94) (tr.)
The Zodiac of Life [books i–iii] V
Translated from the *Zodiacus vitae* (*c.*1528) of Marcello Palingenio Stellato (*c.*1500–*c.*1543). See also *The Zodiac of Life* 1561, 1565.

Jasper Heywood (1535–98) (tr.)
The Seconde Tragedie of Seneca Entituled Thyestes D
Reprinted by Thomas Newton in *Seneca his Tenne Tragedies* 1581 (q.v.)

John Heywood (1497?–1580?)
A Fourth [i.e. fifth] *Hundred of Epygrams* V
See also *An Hundred Epigrammes* 1550, *Two Hundred Epigrammes* 1555, *Works* 1562

Ann Lok (*fl.* 1560) (tr.)
Sermons of John Calvin NF/V
Part ii consists of Lok's verse 'Meditation of a Penitent Sinner: Written in maner of a paraphrase upon the 51. Psalme of David', generally regarded as the first sonnet sequence in English

Matthew Parker (1504–74)
An Admonition . . . NF
Many editions

William Whittingham (1524?–79), and others (tr.)
The Bible and Holy Scriptures Conteyned in the Olde and Newe Testament BIB
The first edition of the Geneva (or 'Breeches') Bible—an extremely popular version, Calvinistic in tone and consequently much used by Puritans

1561

- Francis Bacon born
  Sir Robert Dallington born
  Mary Herbert, countess of Pembroke, born
  Robert Southwell born?
  Sir Henry Spelman born?

Anonymous
Queen Hester D
Probably written 1529

Thomas Becon (1512–67)
The Sycke Mans Salve NF
Many editions into the 17th century

Thomas Blundeville (*fl.* 1558–61) (tr.)
Three Morall Treatises V/NF
First two treatises in verse. Translated from Plutarch.

Geoffrey Chaucer (1340?–1400)
The Woorkes of Geffrey Chaucer WKS
Edited by John Stow, based on Thynne's edition of 1532 (q.v.). See also *Workes* 1598 (ed. Speght).

Richard Eden (1521?–76) (tr.)
The Arte of Navigation NF
Translated from Spanish, Many editions.

Barnabe Googe (1540–95) (tr.)
The Zodiac of Life [books i–vi] V
Translated from Marcello Palingenio Stellato (*c.*1500–*c.*1543), *Zodiacus vitae* (*c.*1528). See also *The Zodiac of Life* 1560, 1565.

Jasper Heywood (1535–98) (tr.)
Hercules Furens D
Translated from Seneca. Latin and English. Reprinted by Thomas Newton in *Seneca his Tenne Tragedies* 1581 (q.v.).

Sir Thomas Hoby (1530–66) (tr.)
The Book of the Courtier NF
Translated from Baldassare Castiglione (1478–1529), *Il Cortegiano* (1528). See also the Latin edition of 1571.

Thomas Norton (1532–84) (tr.)
The Institution of the Christian Religion NF
A translation of Calvin's *Institutes*. Many editions.

1562

- French Wars of Religion begin
  The Thirty-Nine Articles of Religion submitted to Convocation (see 1571)
- George Abbot, archbishop of Canterbury, born
  Henry Constable born
  Samuel Daniel born
  Sir Richard Hawkins born c.1562
  Robert Tofte born
- Nicholas Grimald dies
  Lewis Wager dies
- Lope de Vega born

Anonymous
Jack Juggler D
Publication date conjectural

Anonymous
Thersytes D
Publication date conjectural. An interlude, adapted from Ravisius Textor (Jean Tixier de Ravisi, *c.*1480–1524), possibly by Nicholas Udall?

Humphrey Baker (*fl.* 1562–87)
The Well Sprynge of Sciences NF

A manual of arithmetic which continued to be reprinted until the end of the 17th century

Thomas Brice (*d.* 1570)
Against Filthy Writing, and Such Like Delighting V

Arthur Brooke (*d.* 1563) (tr.)
The Tragicall Historye of Romeus and Juliet F
Anonymous. Translated from a French version by Pierre Boaistuau (Paris, 1559) of Matteo Bandello's story 'La sfortunata morte di dui infelicissimi manti' (from his *Novelle*, 1554), the source of Shakespeare's *Romeo and Juliet* 1597 (q.v.).

William Bullein (*d.* 1576)
Bulleins Bulwarke of Defence Againste all Sicknes, Sornes, and Woundes NF

Richard Grafton (*d.* 1572?)
An Abridgement of the Chronicles of England NF
Several editions. See also *A Chronicle at Large* 1569.

John Heywood (1497?–1580?)
A Ballad Against Slander and Detraction V

John Heywood (1497?–1580?)
Works V

John Jewel (1522–71)
Apologia ecclesiae anglicanae NF
Anonymous. Translated into English by Lady Ann Bacon in 1564 (q.v.). Many editions. Also translated by Matthew Parker 1562. See also *A Defence of the Apologie* 1567.

Hugh Latimer (1485?–1555)
Twenty-seven Sermons Preached by the Ryght Reverende . . . Maister Hugh Latimer NF
Several subsequent editions

Thomas Phaer (1510?–60) (tr.)
The Nyne First Bookes of the Eneidos of Virgil V
Edited by W. Wightman. See also *The Seven First Bookes* 1558; *The Whole Twelve Bookes* 1573, *The Thirteen Bookes* 1584.

Peter Whitehorne (*fl.* 1560) (tr.)
The Arte of Warre NF
A translation of Niccolò Machiavelli (1469–1527), *Libro dell'arte della guerra*

Ninian Winzet (1518–92)
The Last Blast of the Trompet of Godis Worde Aganis the Ursurpit Auctoritie of John Knox NF
Winzet was exiled in the following year

1563

- Conclusion of the Council of Trent
  Plague in London
- John Dowland born
  Michael Drayton born
  Sir Robert Naunton born
  Joshua Sylvester born
- William Baldwin dies
  John Bale dies
  Arthur Brooke dies

Anonymous
The Courte of Venus V
Publication date conjectural. First published 1538 (q.v.). This edition contains several other ballads.

John Fisher (1459?–1535)
A Godlie Treatisse Declaryng the Benefites of Prayer NF
Anonymous. Dated 1560, but actually published in 1563? Translated by Anthony Browne, 1st Viscount Montague (1528–92), from Fisher's *Tractatus de orando Deum.*

John Foxe (1516–87)
A Brief Exhortation, Fruitfull and Meete to be Read, in This Heavy Tyme of Gods Visitation in London NF

John Foxe (1516–87)
Foxe's Book of Martyrs NF
Actual title: *Actes and Monuments of these Latter and Perillous Dayes.* Translated and enlarged from the original Latin edition (Basle, 1559). Many editions. An abridgement by T. Bright published in 1589.

Arthur Golding (1536?–1606) (tr.)
The Historie of Leonard Aretine NF
Translated from the Latin of Leonardo Bruni (1369–1444)

Barnabe Googe (1540–94)
Eglogs, Epytaphes, and Sonettes V

Alexander Nevyle (1544–1614) (tr.)
The Lamentable Tragedie of Œdipus the Sonne of Laius Kyng of Thebes out of Seneca V
Translated from Seneca and reprinted in *Seneca his Tenne Tragedies*, edited by Thomas Newton, 1581 (q.v.)

Richard Rainold (*d.* 1606)
The Foundation of Rhetoric NF
Based on the *Progymnasmata* of Aphthonius (4th century)

Ninian Winzet (1518–92)
The Buke of Fourscoir-thre Questions NF

1564

- Christopher Marlowe born
  William Shakespeare born
  Galileo born
- Jean Calvin dies
  Michelangelo dies

Anne, Lady Bacon (1528–1610) (tr.)
An Apologie or Answere in Defence of the Churche of Englande NF
Anonymous. A translation of John Jewel's *Apologia ecclesiae anglicanae* 1562 (q.v.).

William Bullein (*d.* 1576)
A Dialogue Both Pleasant and Piety-full, Against the Fever Pestilence NF

Miles Coverdale (1488–1568)
Certain Most Godly, Fruitful, and Comfortable Letters of Such True Saintes and Holy Martyrs as in the Late Bloodye Persecution Gave their Lyves NF

Arthur Golding (1536?–1606) (tr.)
The Abridgment of the Histories of Trogus Pompeius NF
Translation of an epitome of Pompeius Trogus, *Historiae Philippicae*

Matthew Parker (1504–74) (tr.)
A Godly and Necessarye Admonition of the Decrees and Canons of the Counsel of Trent NF
Anonymous

1565

- Mary Queen of Scots marries Henry, Lord Darnley
  Royal Exchange founded by Sir Thomas Gresham (opened 1571)
- Robert Armin born?
  John Davies, of Hereford, born
  Francis Meres born
  Sir Anthony Sherley born
- Sir Thomas Chaloner dies
  William Rastell dies

Anonymous
King Darius D

Anonymous
Wealth and Health D

William Allen (1532–94)
A Defense and Declaration of the Catholike Churchies [sic] *Doctrine, Touching Purgatory* NF

John Awdely (*fl.* 1559–77)
The Fraternitie of Vacabondes NF
Anonymous. See also *Cock Laurel's Boat* 1518.

Thomas Cooper (1517?–94)
Thesaurus linguae Romanae Britannicae DICT
Highly influential successor to Elyot's *Dictionary* 1538 (q.v.) and *Bibliotheca* (1542–59). With an extensive English appendix of historical and literary names and places.

Robert Copland (*fl.* 1508–47)
The Seven Sorrows That Women Have When Theyr Husbandes Be Deade V
Publication date conjectural

Arthur Golding (1536?–1606) (tr.)
Gallic Wars NF
Translated from Julius Caesar

Arthur Golding (1536?–1606) (tr.)
Metamorphoses V
Translated from Ovid (books i–iv). See also *Metamorphosis* [books i–xv] 1567.

Barnabe Googe (1540–94) (tr.)
The Zodiac of Life [books i–xii] V
Translated from Marcello Palingenio Stellato (*c.*1500–*c.*1543), *Zodiacus vitæ* (*c.*1528). See also *The Zodiac of Life* 1560, 1561.

Thomas Norton (1532–84) and **Thomas Sackville, 1st earl of Dorset** (1536–1608)
Gorboduc D
The first English tragedy in blank verse, first performed at the Inner Temple in 1561

Thomas Stapleton (1535–98) (tr.)
The History of the Church of Englande NF
Translation of Bede's *Historia ecclesiastica gentis Anglorum*, published in Latin at Strasbourg, *c.*1475

John Stow (1525–1605)
A Summarie of Englyshe Chronicles NF
Written as a challenge to Grafton's *Abridgement* 1562 (q.v.). See also *Chronicles* 1580, *Annales* 1592.

1566

- Murder of David Rizzio, Mary Queen of Scots' secretary
- Thomas Bastard born
  Robert Chester born

James, later James VI of Scotland and James I of England, born
Fynes Moryson born
- Richard Edwards dies
Sir Thomas Hoby dies
- Nostradamus dies

Anonymous
Albion Knight D

William Adlington (tr.)
The Golden Asse F
The earliest (and most influential) English translation of Apuleius' *Metamorphoses* or *De asino aureo*

Thomas Churchyard (1520?–1604)
Churchyard's Round V

Thomas Churchyard (1520?–1604)
Churchyardes Farewell V

Thomas Churchyard (1520?–1604)
Churchyardes Lamentacion of Freyndshyp V

Thomas Drant (*d.* 1578?) (tr.)
A Medicinable Morall V
The first attempt at a metrical version of Horace. See also *Horace his Arte of Poetrie* 1567.

William Painter (1540?–94) (tr.)
The Palace of Pleasure F
Volume i. Stories translated from Latin, Greek, French, and Italian by Boccaccio, Bandello, Cinthio, etc. Contains the story of Giletta of Narbona, translated from Boccaccio's *Decameron*, the main source for Shakespeare's *All's Well That Ends Well* (see 1623). Volume ii published in 1567 (q.v.).

John Phillips (*fl.* 1564–94)
Patient and Meek Griselda D
Publication date conjectural. The best-known version to English readers of this widely popular tale is Chaucer's *Clerk's Tale*, derived from Petrarch's *De obedientia ac fide uxoria mythologia* (1374), itself a translation of Boccaccio (1313–75), *Decameron*, Day 10, Tale 10.

John Studley (*b. c.*1547) (tr.)
Agamemnon D
Translated from Seneca. Reprinted by Thomas Newton in *Seneca his Tenne Tragedies* 1581 (q.v.).

John Studley (*b. c.*1547) (tr.)
Medea D
Translated from Seneca. Reprinted by Thomas Newton in *Seneca his Tenne Tragedies* 1581 (q.v.).

Nicholas Udall (1505?–56)
Ralph Roister Doister D
Publication date conjectural. Traditionally regarded as the earliest known comedy in English and probably first performed before 1541.

Lewis Wager (*d.* 1562)
The Life and Repentance of Mary Magdalene D

William Wager (*fl.* 1565–9)
The Cruel Debtor D

1567

- Start of revolt of the Netherlands: the duke of Alva's reign of terror
Murder of Lord Darnley
Mary Queen of Scots marries the earl of Bothwell
Assassination of Shane O'Neill, earl of Tyrone
Mary Queen of Scots abdicates
Rugby School founded
Revolt of the Netherlands
- Sir William Alexander born?
Thomas Campion born
Anthony Copley born
Thomas Nashe born

Anonymous
The Merry Tales of Skelton F
Not by Skelton

Anonymous
The Trial of Treasure D

Thomas Drant (*d.* 1578?) (tr.)
Horace his Arte of Poetrie, Pistles, and Satyrs Englished V
See also *A Medicinable Morall* 1566

Sir Geoffrey Fenton (1539?–1608) (tr.)
Certaine Tragicall Discourses F
Translated from Matteo Bandello (1485–1561), *Novelle* (1554). Known as *Fenton's Bandello.*

Arthur Golding (1536?–1606) (tr.)
Metamorphosis [books i–xv] V
See *The fyrst fower bookes* 1565. Many editions into the 17th century.

Henry Grantham (*fl.* 1571–87) (tr.)
Filocolo F
Translated from *Il Filocolo by* Boccaccio (1313–75); also a source for Chaucer's *Franklin's Tale*

John Jewel (1522–71)
A Defence of the Apologie of the Churche of Englande NF
See also Jewel's *Apologia* 1562 and Anne, Lady Bacon's translation 1564. Written in response to a

work by Thomas Harding (1516–72), *A Confutation of a Booke intituled An Apologie of the Church of England* (Antwerp: 1565).

William Painter (1540?–94) (tr.)
The Second Tome of the Palace of Pleasure F
Translated from Matteo Bandello (1485–1561), 'Ariabarzane senescalo del re di Persia' (from *Novelle*, 1554). Contains the story of Romeo and Julietta, which Shakespeare made use of. See also Arthur Brooke, *Romeus and Juliet* 1562 and Thomas Heywood, *The Royall King* 1637.

Matthew Parker (1504–74) (tr.)
The Whole Psalter Translated into English Metre BIB
Publication date conjectural. With four-part settings by Thomas Tallis.

John Pickering (1544–96)
Horestes; or, The New Interlude of Vice D

George Turberville (*c.*1544–*c.*1597) (tr.)
The Eglogs of the Poet B. Mantuan Carmelitan, Turned into English Verse V
Adapted from the *Adolescentia seu Bucolica* of Baptista Spagnuoli Mantuanus (1448–1516)

George Turberville (*c.*1544–*c.*1597) (tr.)
Epitaphes, Epigrams, Songs and Sonets V

George Turberville (*c.*1544–*c.*1597) (tr.)
The Heroycall Epistles of . . . Publius Ovidius Naso, in Englishe Verse V
Translated from Ovid's *Heroides*. Many editions.

Isabella Whitney (*fl.* 1567–73)
The Copy of a Letter V
Publication date conjectural

1568

- Revolt of the Moors in Spain
- Gervase Markham born?
  Sir Henry Wotton born
- Roger Ascham dies
  Miles Coverdale dies

Anonymous
Jacob and Esau D
See also *Jacob and Esau* 1557

Thomas Drant (*d.* 1578?) (tr.)
Epigrams and Sentences Spirituall in Vers V
Translated from St Gregory Nazianzus (329/30–389/90)

Ulpian Fulwell (*d.* 1586)
Like Will to Like D

Thomas Howell (*fl.* 1568)
The Arbor of Amitie V

Sir David Lindsay (1490–1555)
Works WKS

Matthew Parker (1504–74) (ed.) and others
The Holie Bible BIB
First edition of the 'Bishops' Bible', a revision of the Great Bible of 1539 (q.v.) by Matthew Parker, Archbishop of Canterbury, and other bishops and scholars. Copies were ordered to be placed in every cathedral and church by the Convocation of Canterbury in 1571. See also *The Holi Bible* 1569.

John Skelton (1460?–1529)
Pithy Pleasaunt and Profitable Workes of Maister Skelton V
Edited by J. Stow

Edmund Tilney (*d.* 1610)
The Flower of Friendship F

George Turberville (*c.*1544–*c.*1597) (tr.)
A Plaine Path to Perfect Vertue V
Translated from *De quatuor virtutibus* by Dominic Mancini (*fl.* 1478–91)

1569

- Rising of northern earls
- Sir John Davies born
  Aemelia Lanyer born
- Pieter Breughel dies

Stephen Bateman (*d.* 1584)
A Christall Glasse of Christian Reformation NF

Stephen Bateman (*d.* 1584) (tr.)
The Travayled Pylgrime V
An allegorical-theological romance translated from *Le chevalier délibéré* by Olivier de La Marche (*c.*1425–1502)

Barnabe Googe (1540–94)
The Ship of Safeguard V

Richard Grafton (*d.* 1572?)
A Chronicle at Large NF
See also *An Abridgement* 1562

Sir John Hawkins (1532–95)
A True Declaration of the Troublesome Voyadge of J. Haukins to the Parties of Guynea and the West Indies NF

Matthew Parker (1504–74) (ed.) and others
The Holi Bible BIB

The 2nd edition, in quarto, of the Bishops' Bible of 1568 (q.v.). Includes the Book of Common Prayer.

James Sanford (*fl.* 1569) (tr.)
Of the Vanitie and Uncertaintie of Artes and Sciences NF
Translated from Henricus Cornelius Agrippa (1486?–1535)

Thomas Underdowne (*fl.* 1566–87) (tr.)
An Æthiopian Historie written in Greeke by Heliodorus F
Publication date conjectural. Translated from Heliodorus, *Aethiopica*.

Thomas Underdowne (*fl.* 1566–87) (tr.)
Ovid his Invective against Ibis V
Anonymous

William Wager (*fl.* 1565–9)
The Longer Thou Livest D
Publication date conjectural

1570

- English plantation of East Ulster
  Papal Bull declares Elizabeth excommunicated and deposed
  The potato introduced to Europe
- Samuel Rowlands born?
- Guy Fawkes born

Anonymous
The Marriage of Wit and Science D

Roger Ascham (1515–68)
The Scholemaster; or, Plaine and Perfite Way of Teachying Children, to Understand, Write, and Speake, the Latin Tong NF
Many editions

William Baldwin (*c.*1515–63)
Beware the Cat F
Anonymous. Includes some verse.

Thomas Churchyard (1520?–1604)
A Discourse of Rebellion V

Sir Geoffrey Fenton (1539?–1608) (tr.)
A Discourse of the Civile Warres and Late Troubles in Fraunce NF
Translated from Jean de Serres (1540?–98). On the Huguenot Wars.

John Foxe (1516–87)
A Sermon of Christ Crucified NF
Written against Pius V's excommunication of Elizabeth I

Robert Henryson (*c.*1430–*c.*1505) (tr.)
The Morall Fabillis of Esope the Phrygian V
Translated from Aesop. English version, by Richard Smith, published as *The Fabulous Tales of Esope* in 1577.

Thomas Ingelend (*fl.* 1560)
The Disobedient Child D
Publication date conjectural

Sir Thomas North (1535–1601) (tr.)
The Morall Philosophie of Doni NF
Translated from Antonio Francesco Doni (1513–74), itself taken at some removes from the oriental collection commonly known as 'The Fables of Bidpai' (i.e. the *Kalala wa Damna* of Pilpay)

Thomas Norton (1532–84)
A Catechisme, or First Instruction of Christian Religion NF
Anonymous

Thomas Preston (1537–98)
Cambises D
Publication date conjectural. The origin of Shakespeare's phrase 'King Cambyses's vein' (*1 Henry IV*).

'John Scoggin' (*fl.* 1480)
The Jestes of Skogyn F
Publication date conjectural. Supposedly, but probably not, by Skoggin. See also *Scoggins Jestes* 1613, *The First and Best Part of Scoggins Jests* 1626.

William Wager (*fl.* 1565–9)
Enough is as Good as a Feast D
Publication date conjectural

1571

- The Thirty-Nine Articles of Religion authorized by Parliament
  Ridolfi plot to depose Elizabeth
  Battle of Lepanto (Oct.)
  Harrow School founded
- Barnabe Barnes born
  Thomas Mun born
- John Jewel dies
- Johann Kepler born

John Barbour (*c.*1320–95)
The Bruce V
Anonymous. Publication date conjectural. Written 1376.

John Bridges (*d.* 1618)
A Sermon, Preached at Paules Crosse NF

George Buchanan (1506–82)
The Admonitioun NF

George Buchanan (1506–82)
Ane Detectioun of the Duinges of Marie Quene of Scottes NF
Translated by Thomas Wright. Buchanan's Latin version also published 1571.

Bartholomew Clerke (1537?–90) (tr.)
The Courtier NF
A Latin translation of Baldassare Castiglione (1478–1529), *Il Cortegiano*, that was more influential than Hoby's English version of 1561 (q.v.). Many editions into the 18th century.

George Colclough (*fl.* 1571)
The Spectacle to Repentance V

Richard Edwards (1523?–66)
Damon and Pithias D

1572

- St Bartholomew's Day Massacre (24 Aug.)
  Execution of Thomas Howard, 4th duke of Norfolk, for conspiring against Elizabeth
  Society of Antiquaries founded by Matthew Parker
- Thomas Dekker born?
  John Donne born
  John Floyd (Jesuit) born
  Ben Jonson born
  James Mabbe born
- Richard Grafton (chronicler) dies?
  John Knox dies

Anonymous
Rauf Coilyear V
A Scottish alliterative poem written in the late 15th century. Loosely attached to the Charlemagne cycle, it is a 'King and Commoner' story in which the king is taught a lesson in manners by one of his subjects.

Sir Geoffrey Fenton (1539?–1608) (tr.)
Monophylo NF
Translated from Estienne Pasquier (1529–1615)

Thomas Paynell (*fl.* 1528–67) (tr.)
The Treasurie of Amadis de Fraunce F
Translated from *Le trésor de Amadis*, a compilation of extracts from books i–xiii of Nicholas de Herberay's translation of *Amadis de Gaula*

William Tyndale (1494?–1536) and others
The Whole Workes of W. Tyndall, John Frith, and Doct. Barnes WKS

John Whitgift (1530?–1604)
An Answere to a Certen Libel Intituled, An Admonition NF
Written against *An Admonition to the Parliament* (1572) by John Field and Thomas Wilcox. See Cartwright *A Replye* 1573 and Whitgift's *Defense of the Answere* 1574.

1573

- Francis Drake sees the Pacific
- Inigo Jones born
  William Laud, archbishop of Canterbury, born
- John Caius dies

Anonymous
New Custom D
An interlude written as a vindication of the Reformation

John Bridges (*d.* 1618)
The Supremacie of Christian Princes NF

Thomas Cartwright (1535–1603)
A Replye to An Answere Made of M. Doctor Whitgifte NF
Publication date conjectural. Written in response to Whitgift's *Answere* 1572 (q.v.).

George Gascoigne (1534?–77)
A Hundreth Sundrie Flowres Bounde up in One Small Poesie MISC
Includes *Supposes* (first performed at Gray's Inn, 1566), a free translation of Ariosto's *I Suppositi* and the first Italian-style comedy in English; *Jocasta* (translated, with Francis Kinwelmersh, from Euripides and performed at Gray's Inn, 1566), the earliest version of a Greek tragedy in English; and *The Adventures of Master F.J.*, an early example of Elizabethan fiction. See also *The Posies of George Gascoigne* 1575, *The Whole Woorkes* 1587.

Thomas Phaer (1510?–60) (tr.)
The Whole Twelve Bookes of the Æneidos V
The last 3 books translated by Thomas Twyne (1543–1613). See also *The Seven First Bookes* 1558; *The Nyne First Bookes* 1562, *The Thirteen Bookes* 1584.

Thomas Tusser (1524?–80)
Five Hundreth Points of Good Husbandry United to as Many of Good Huswiferie V

See *A Hundreth Good Pointes* 1557. Reprinted many times by the end of the 16th century.

Thomas Twyne (1543–1613) (tr.)
The Breviary of Britayne NF
A translation of Humphrey Llwyd (1527–68), *Commentarioli Descriptionis Britannicæ Fragmentum* (Cologne, 1572)

Isabella Whitney (*fl.* 1567–73)
A Sweet Nosgay, or Pleasant Posye V

1574

- Richard Barnfield born
  John Day born
  Joseph Hall born
  Thomas Heywood born?

John Bale (1495–1563)/**John Studley** (1545?) (tr.)
The Pageant of Popes D
A translation, with additions, by Studley (1545?–90?) of Bale's *Acta Pontificum Romanorum*, written in the 1550s

Arthur Golding (1536?–1606) (tr.)
Sermons . . . upon the Booke of Job NF
Translated from the French of Jean Calvin

Barnabe Rich (1540?–1617)
Dialogue Between Mercury and an English Soldier F

Reginald Scot (1538?–99)
A Perfite Platforme of a Hoppe Garden; and Necessarie Instructions for the Making and Mayntenaunce Thereof NF

Lady Elizabeth Tyrwhit (*fl.* 1574)
Morning and Evening Prayers NF
See also *The Monument of Matrones* 1582

John Whitgift (1530?–1604)
The Defense of the Answere to the Admonition, Against the Replie NF
See Cartwright's *Replye* 1573 and Whitgift's *Answere* 1572

1575

- Augustine Baker born
  Edmund Bolton born?
  William Burton born
  William Haughton born
  William Percy born
  Cyril Tourneur born
  Sir William Vaughan born
- Matthew Parker dies
  Richard Taverner dies
- Guido Reni born
  Jacob Boehme born

Anonymous
Apius and Virginia D

Nicholas Breton (1545?–1626?)
A Smale Handfull of Fragrant Flowers V

Thomas Churchyard (1520?–1604)
The Firste Parte of Churchyardes Chippes MISC
Largely in verse. Part of this work recounts 'the whole order howe oure soveraigne ladye Queene Elizabeth, was receyved into the citie of Bristow'.

Sir Geoffrey Fenton (1539?–1608) (tr.)
Golden Epistles NF
Translated from Antonio de Guevara

Abraham Fleming (1552?–1607) (tr.)
The Bucolikes of Publius Virgilius Maro V
The first printed English translation of Virgil's *Eclogues*. An expanded edition containing the *Georgics* appeared in 1589.

Ulpian Fulwell (*d.* 1586)
The Flower of Fame NF
Partly in verse

George Gascoigne (1534?–77)
The Glasse of Governement D
A prodigal son drama influenced by Dutch sources

George Gascoigne (1534?–77)
The Posies of George Gascoigne Esquire V
The 2nd, much enlarged, edition of *A Hundreth Sundrie Flowres* 1573 (q.v.). Includes 'The Fruits of Warre' (Gascoigne's longest poem) and 'Certayne Notes of Instruction Concerning the Making of Verse or Ryme in English'. See also *The Whole Woorkes* 1587.

Robert Laneham (*fl.* 1575)
A Letter NF
Contains the well-known list of Captain Cox's books and ballads

John Rolland (*fl.* 1560)
The Court of Venus V

William Stevenson (*fl.* 1553)
Gammer Gurton's Needle D
Anonymous

George Turberville (*c.*1544–*c.*1597)
The Booke of Faulconrie or Hauking NF

1576

- Sack of Antwerp
  Martin Frobisher's voyages 1576–7
  James Burbage builds the Theatre in Shoreditch, London
- William Ames born
  John Marston born
  John Weever born

Anonymous
Common Conditions D

Thomas Achelly (*fl.* 1568–95) (tr.)
A Most Lamentable and Tragicall Historie V
Anonymous. Translated from Matteo Bandello (1485–1561), *Novelle* (1554).

Richard Edwards (1523?–66) and others
The Paradyse of Daynty Devises ANTH
Other authors include the Earl of Oxford, Jasper Heywood, William Hunnis, and Lord Vaux. Reprinted many times.

Abraham Fleming (1552?–1607)
A Panoplie of Epistles; or, A Looking-glasse for the Unlearned NF
Collected and translated from Cicero, Ascham, and others

Ulpian Fulwell (*d.* 1586)
The Art of Flattery NF
Eight dialogues, partly in verse

George Gascoigne (1534?–77)
The Droomme of Doomes Day NF
The first part translated from Pope Innocent III (1160?–1216), *De contemptu mundi*

George Gascoigne (1534?–77)
The Spoyle of Antwerpe NF
Anonymous. Publication date conjectural.

George Gascoigne (1534?–77)
The Steele Glas: a Satyre; Togither with The Complainte of Phylomene V
An 'estates' satire: the first non-dramatic poem in blank verse in English

Sir Humphrey Gilbert (1539?–83)
A Discourse of a Discoverie for a New Passage to Cataia NF
Edited by George Gascoigne. A private letter to Gilbert's brother recounting his discovery of a new passage to China, printed without the author's knowledge.

William Lambarde (1536–1601)
A Perambulation of Kent NF
Written 1570 as part of a projected 'Topographicall Dictionarie'. The first topographical survey to be published in Britain.

George Pettie (1548–89)
A Petite Pallace of Pettie his Pleasure F
An influential story collection on the model of Painter's *Palace of Pleasure* 1566 (q.v.)

George Whetstone (*c.*1551–87)
The Rocke of Regard V
Mostly in verse

1577

- Francis Drake departs on his voyage of circumnavigation (1577–80)
  Curtain Theatre opened *c.*1577
- Robert Burton born
  Thomas Coryate born?
  Sir Arthur Gorges born?
  Samuel Purchas born
  Richard Sibbes born
- George Gascoigne dies
- Peter Paul Rubens born

Nicholas Breton (1545?–1626?)
A Floorish upon Fancie V

Nicholas Breton (1545?–1626?)
The Workes of a Young Wyt V

George Buchanan (1506–82)
Baptistes D
In Latin

Arthur Golding (1536?–1606) (tr.)
Abraham's Sacrifice D
Translated from Théodore de Bèze, *Abraham sacrifant*

John Grange (*c.*1577–1611)
The Golden Aphroditis MISC

Gabriel Harvey (1550–1631)
Gabrielis Harveii Ciceronianus NF

Gabriel Harvey (1550–1631)
Rhetor NF
In Latin

Raphael Holinshed (*d.* 1580?)
Chronicles NF
Written in collaboration with William Harrison (1534–93), Richard Stanyhurst (1547–1618), Edmund Campion (1540–81), and Richard Hooker (1554–1600). See also *The First and Second Volumes* 1587.

Henry Peacham, the elder (*fl.* 1577)
The Garden of Eloquence NF

George Whetstone (*c.*1551–87)
A Remembraunce of the Wel Imployed Life, of George Gaskoigne Esquire V

1578

- Robert Daborne born
  George Hakewill born
  William Harvey born
  Henry Peacham, the younger, born?
  George Sandys born
- Thomas Drant dies?
  William Roper dies

Anonymous
Tarleton's Tragical Treatises F
Associated with the actor and clown Richard Tarlton (*d.* 1588)

George Best (*d.* 1584)
A True Discourse of the Late Voyages of Discoverie Under M. Frobisher NF
Included in the 3rd volume (1600) of Hakluyt's *Principall Navigations* (see 1589)

Thomas Blenerhasset (1550?–1624/5)
The Seconde Part of the Mirrour for Magistrates V
See *A Myrroure for Magistrates* 1559

Thomas Churchyard (1520?–1604)
A Lamentable, and Pitifull Description, of the Wofull Warres in Flaunders NF
Includes two poems

Thomas Churchyard (1520?–1604)
A Prayse, and Reporte of Maister Martyne Forboishers Voyage to Meta Incognita NF
Includes one poem

John Fisher (1459?–1535)
A Spirituall Consolation NF
Publication date conjectural. Written in 1535. A sermon on Ezekiel 2: 10.

John Florio (1553–1625?)
Florio His Firste Fruites MISC
See also *Florios Second Frutes* 1591

John Foxe (1516–87)
A Sermon Preached at the Christening of a Certaine Jew NF
Latin original published in Foxe's *De Oliva Evangelica* (1578)

Thomas Garter (*fl.* 1562–89?)
The Commody of the Moste Vertuous and Godlye Susanna D

Thomas Lupton (*fl.* 1583)
All for Money D

John Lyly (1554–1606)
Euphues F
Many editions. See also *Euphues and his England* 1580; both parts published together 1617 (q.v.).

Thomas Proctor (*fl.* 1578–84) (ed.)
A Gorgious Gallery, of Gallant Inventions ANTH
Poems by Owen Raydon, Proctor, Thomas Churchyard, Thomas Howell, Clement Robinson, and Jasper Heywood

Barnabe Rich (1540?–1617)
Allarme to England NF

Margaret Tyler (*fl.* 1578) (tr.)
The Mirrour of Princely Deedes and Knighthood F
Translated from book i, part i, of Diego Ortúnez de Calahorra, *Espejo de principes y cavalleros*. More parts were published over the next 23 years, translated by Robert Parry (books ii–vi, and ix) and 'L.A.' (books vii–viii). Books iv and v written by P. de la Sierra; books vi–ix by M. Martinez.

George Whetstone (*c.*1551–87)
The Right Excellent and Famous Historye, of Promos and Cassandra D
A source for Shakespeare's *Measure for Measure* (see 1623). See also Whetstone, *An Heptameron of Civill Discourses* 1582.

1579

- Sir William Cornwallis born?
  John Fletcher born
  William Lisle born?
  Francis Rous born
- William Whittingham dies

Anonymous
The Forrest of Fancy MISC
By 'H.C.'

George Buchanan (1506–82)
De jure regno apud scotos, dialogus NF
In Latin. An important statement of resistance theory and a possible influence on Shakespeare's *Macbeth*.

Thomas Churchyard (1520?–1604)
The Miserie of Flaunders, Calamitie of Fraunce, Misfortune of Portugall, Unquietnes of Ireland, Troubles of Scotlande: and the Blessed State of Englande V

Sir Geoffrey Fenton (1539?–1608) (tr.)
The Historie of Guicciardin, Conteining the Warres of Italie, and Other Partes NF
Translated fom the Italian of Francesco Guicciardini (1483–1540), *La Historia d'Italia*

John Foxe (1516–87)
Christ Jesus Triumphant NF
Translated by Richard Day. Latin original published in Foxe's *De Oliva Evangelica* (1578).

Stephen Gosson (1554–1624)
The Schoole of Abuse NF

Thomas Lupton (*fl.* 1583)
A Thousand Notable Things, of Sundry Sortes MISC
Many editions

Anthony Munday (1553–1633)
The Mirrour of Mutabilitie, or Principall Part of the Mirrour for Magistrates V

Sir Thomas North (1535–1601) (tr.)
The Lives of the Noble Grecians and Romanes NF
From the French translation of Plutarch's *Vitae paralellae* by Jacques Amyot (1513–93)

'Immerito' [Edmund Spenser (1552?–99)]
The Shepheardes Calender V
Many editions

John Stubbs (1543?–91)
The Discoverie of a Gaping Gulf NF
Anonymous. Stubbs and the publisher paid for this publication with the loss of their right hands.

1580

- Spanish conquest of Portugal
  Drake returns in *The Golden Hind* from his voyage of circumnavigation (begun 1577)
  Jesuit missionaries arrive in England
- William Herbert, 3rd earl of Pembroke, born
  Thomas Middleton born
  Captain John Smith (governor of Virginia) born
  John Taylor ('The Water Poet') born
  John Webster born?
- John Heywood dies?
  Raphael Holinshed (chronicler) dies?
  Thomas Tusser dies
- Franz Hals born
- Luis de Camoëns dies
  Andrea Palladio dies

Anonymous
The Buik of Alexander V
Publication date conjectural. Composed in Middle Scots in 1438. Erroneously attributed to John Barbour (1316?–95?). A close translation of two medieval French originals.

George Buchanan (1506–82)
Paraphrasis psalmorum Davidis V
In Latin

William Bullokar (*fl.* 1586)
Bullokars Booke at Large, For the Amendment of Orthographie for English Speech NF

William Bullokar (*fl.* 1586)
A Short Introduction or Guiding to Print, Write, and Reade Inglish Speech NF

Thomas Churchyard (1520?–1604)
A Pleasaunte Laborinth Called Churchyardes Chance V

Thomas Churchyard (1520?–1604)
A Warning for the Wise, a Feare to the Fond, a Bridle to the Lewde, and a Glasse to the Good MISC

Thomas Cooper (1517?–94)
Certaine Sermons NF

John Foxe (1516–87)
The Pope Confuted NF
Anonymous. A translation of Foxe's *Papa confutatus* (1580).

Humphrey Gifford (*fl.* 1580)
A Posie of Gilloflowers MISC
Part i translated from Italian and French; part ii in verse

John Knox (1505–72)
A Fort for the Afflicted NF
Revised edition of *A Percel of the VI Psalme* 1554 (q.v.)

John Lyly (1554–1606)
Euphues and his England F
Many editions. See *Euphues* 1578; both parts published together in 1617 (q.v.).

Anthony Munday (1553–1633)
The Paine of Pleasure V

Anthony Munday (1553–1633)
Zelauto: The Fountaine of Fame F

Thomas Rogers (*d.* 1616) (tr.)
Of the Imitation of Christ NF
A translation of *De Imitatio Christi* by Thomas à Kempis (1380–1471), purged of 'Romish' doctrine.

Many other editions. See also William Atkinson, *Imitation of Christ* 1503.

Austin Saker (*fl.* 1580)
The Laberynth of Libertie F

Edmund Spenser (1552?–99) and **Gabriel Harvey** (1550–1631)
Three Proper and Wittie, Familiar Letters NF
Signed 'Immerito' (Spenser) and 'G.H.' (Harvey). Another edition published in 1592 (q.v.) under Harvey's name.

John Stow (1525–1605)
The Chronicles of England, from Brute Unto this Present Yeare 1580 NF
See also *Summarie* 1565, *Annales* 1592

1581

- Anti-Catholic legislation passed in Parliament
  Francis Drake knighted at Deptford
- Sir Thomas Overbury born
  James Ussher, archbishop of Armagh, born
- Edmund Campion executed (Dec.)

Anonymous
A Triumph for True Subjects, and a Terrour unto al Traitours V
Ballad on the execution of Edmund Campion (1 December 1561) doubtfully attributed to William Elderton (*d.* 1592?)

Nicholas Breton (1545?–1626?)
A Discourse in Commendation of the Valiant Gentleman, Maister Frauncis Drake NF

Thomas Lupton (*fl.* 1583)
A Persuasion from Papistrie NF

Richard Mulcaster (1530?–1611)
Positions Necessarie for the Training Up of Children NF

Anthony Munday (1553–1633)
A Breefe Discourse of the Taking of Edmund Campion NF
Campion was executed on 1 December 1581

Anthony Munday (1553–1633)
A Courtly Controversie, betweene Loove and Learning NF

Thomas Newton (1542?–1607) (ed.)
Seneca his Tenne Tragedies D
Hercules Furens, *Thyestes*, and *Troas* translated J. Heywood; *Oedipus* translated by A. Nevile; *Hippolytus*, *Medea*, *Agamemnon*, and *Hercules Oetaeus* translated by J. Studley; *Octavia* translated by Newton

George Pettie (1548–89) (tr.)
The Civile Conversation of M. Steeven Guazzo NF
Books i–iii. Translation of a French version of Stefano Guazzo's *La civile conversazione* (1574). 2nd edition, with book iv translated by B. Young, published in 1586.

Barnabe Rich (1540?–1617)
Riche his Farewell to Militarie Profession F
Contains the story of Apolonius and Silla, the main source for Shakespeare's *Twelfth Night* (see 1623)

Barnabe Rich (1540?–1617)
The Straunge and Wonderfull Adventures of Don Simonides, a Gentilman Spaniarde F
See also *The Second Tome* 1584

Thomas Watson (1557?–92) (tr.)
Antigone D
Translated into Latin verse

Nathaniel Woodes (*fl.* 1550–94)
The Conflict of Conscience D

1582

- Gregorian calendar adopted in the Papal States, Spain, and Portugal; later in France and elsewhere in Europe
  Plague in London 1582–3
  Edinburgh University founded
  Shakespeare marries Anne Hathaway
- John Barclay born
  Richard Corbet born
  Joseph Fletcher born?
  Phineas Fletcher born
  William Lithgow born
- George Buchanan dies
  Gregory Martin (Bible translator) dies
- St Teresa of Avila dies

William Allen (1532–94)
A Briefe Historie of the Glorious Martyrdom of XII Priests NF
Anonymous

Thomas Bentley, of Gray's Inn (ed.)
The Monument of Matrones ANTH
A significant anthology containing the work of many women writers, including Frances Abergavenny, Anne Askew, and Lady Jane Dudley. 'Lamp 2' reprints *A Godly Medytacyon of the Christen Sowle*, a translation by Princess Elizabeth (later Elizabeth I) 1548 (q.v.); *The Lamentacion of a Synner* 1547 (q.v.) and *Prayers* 1545 (q.v.) by Catherine Parr; and *Morning and Evening Prayers* 1574 (q.v.) by Elizabeth Tyrwhit.

Thomas Bentley, of Gray's Inn
The Sixt Lampe of Virginitie MISC

Thomas Blenerhasset (1550?–1624/5)
A Revelation of the True Minerva V

George Buchanan (1506–82)
Rerum Scoticarum historia NF
In Latin. Subsequently incorporated into Holinshed's *Chronicles* 1577 (q.v.).

Stephen Gosson (1554–1624)
Playes Confuted in Five Actions NF

Richard Hakluyt (1552?–1615)
Divers Voyages Touching the Discoverie of America, and the Lands Adjacent NF
See also *Principall Navigations* 1589

John Leland (1506?–52)
The Assertion of Arthur NF
Translated by Richard Robinson (*fl.* 1576–1601) from Leland's *Assertio inclytissimi Arturii regis Britanniæ* 1544 (q.v.)

Gregory Martin (*d.* 1582) and others (tr.)
The New Testament of Jesus Christ BIB
First edition of the Roman Catholic version of the New Testament in English, known as the Rheims version; translated from the Latin Vulgate by Gregory Martin and others at the English Roman Catholic College at Rheims. See also *The Holie Bible* (i.e. the New Testament) 1609.

Brian Melbancke (*fl.* 1583)
Philotimus F

Anthony Munday (1553–1633)
A Breefe Aunswer Made Unto Two Seditious Pamphlets NF
Answers the anonymous *A True Reporte of the Death and Martyrdome of Mr Campion* (1582)

Anthony Munday (1553–1633)
The English Romayne Lyfe NF

Robert Parsons, SJ (1546–1610)
The First Booke of the Christian Exercise, Appertayning to Resolution NF

Richard Stanyhurst (1547–1618) (tr.)
The First Foure Bookes of Virgil his Aeneis V

Thomas Watson (1557?–92)
The Hecatompathia; or, Passionate Centurie of Love V

George Whetstone (*c.*1551–87)
An Heptameron of Civill Discourses F
Contains the story of Promos and Cassandra, from which Shakespeare took the plot of *Measure for Measure* (see 1623). Whetstone's source was Cinthio's *Hecatommithi* (1565). Reissued 1593 as *Aurelia* (q.v.). See also Whetstone, *Promos and Cassandra* 1578.

1583

- John Whitgift becomes archbishop of Canterbury
  Somerville Plot against Elizabeth I
  Throckmorton Plot to assassinate Elizabeth
  First royal theatre company established
- Robert Aylet born
  William Basse born
  Sir John Beaumont born
  Orlando Gibbons born
  Edward Herbert, of Cherbury, born
  Philip Massinger born
- Hugo Grotius born

Robert Greene (1558–92)
Mamillia F
Part ii published 1593 as *Mamillia: The triumph of Pallas*

John Knox (1505–72)
A Notable and Comfortable Exposition Upon the Fourth of Mathew NF

Thomas Norton (1532–84)
A Declaration of the Favourable Dealing of Her Majesties Commissioners Appointed for the Examination of Certaine Traitours NF
Anonymous. Sometimes attributed to William Cecil, Lord Burghley (1520–98).

Richard Robinson (*fl.* 1576–1600) (tr.)
The Auncient Order, Societie, and Unitie Laudable, of Prince Arthure, and his Knightly Armory of the Round Table V
Translated from a French treatise on heraldry, *La devise des armes des Chevaliers de la Table Ronde*, in the 1546 edition (Paris), and adapted by Robinson for the purpose of advertising a popular society of archers, Prince Arthur and the London Round Table. The shields of King Arthur and his knights are allotted to the various members of the society, of which Edmund Spenser's schoolmaster, Richard Mulcaster, was one.

Sir Thomas Smith (1513–77)
De Republica Anglorum: The Maner of Government of England NF
Enlarged as *The Common-welth of England* 1589 (q.v.)

Philip Stubbes (*fl.* 1581–93)
The Anatomie of Abuses NF
Second Part, Conteining the Display of Corruptions, also published 1583

1584

- Execution of Francis Throckmorton
  Assassination of William of Orange
  Death of Ivan the Terrible
  Plantation of Munster begins
- Francis Beaumont born
  John Selden born
  John Pym born
  Daniel Tuvil born *c.*1584
- Thomas Norton dies

Anonymous
The Famous Hystory of Herodotus D
Translated by 'B.R.'. Only books i–iii were published.

William Averell (*fl.* 1584)
A Dyall for Dainty Darlings, Rockt in the Cradle of Securitie F

Thomas Churchyard (1520?–1604)
A Scourge for Rebels NF

Robert Greene (1558–92)
Arbasto F
Several editions

Robert Greene (1558–92)
Gwydonius F
Also includes *The Debate betweene Follie and Love* translated from Louise Labé (1526?–66), *Débat de Folie et d'Amour* (Lyon, 1555). Several editions.

Robert Greene (1558–92)
Morando the Tritameron of Love F

Robert Greene (1558–92)
The Myrrour of Modestie F

King James VI of Scotland, afterwards **James I of England** (1566–1625)
The Essayes of a Prentise, in the Divine Art of Poesie V

Thomas Lodge (1558–1625)
An Alarum Against Usurers MISC
A prose satire, followed by a pastoral romance in prose

Thomas Lupton (*fl.* 1583)
A Dream of the Devill, and Dives NF

John Lyly (1554–1606)
Alexander, Campaspe, and Diogenes D
Anonymous. Three editions in 1584 (second and third as *Campaspe*).

John Lyly (1554–1606)
Sapho and Phao D
Anonymous

John Norden (1548–1625?)
A Pensive Mans Practise Very Profitable for all Personnes NF
A prayer book. Part ii 1594 (q.v.); part iii (as *A Progresse of Pietie*) 1598 (q.v.). Many subsequent editions.

George Peele (1556–96)
The Araygnement of Paris D
Anonymous. Based on Anello Paulilli's *Giudito di Paride.*

Thomas Phaer (1510?–60) (tr.)
The Thirteen Books of Æneidos V
Books x–xii translated by Thomas Twyne (1543–1613), book xiii by Maffeo Vegio (1406 or 7–1458). See also *The Seven First Bookes* 1558; *The Nyne First Bookes* 1562, *The Whole Twelve Bookes* 1573.

Barnabe Rich (1540?–1617)
The Second Tome of the Travailes and Adventures of Don Simonides F
See *The Straunge and Wonderfull Adventures of Don Simonides* 1581

Reginald Scot (1538?–99)
The Discoverie of Witchcraft NF

William Warner (1558?–1609)
Pan his Syrinx, or Pipe F
The 2nd edition, 1597, published as *Syrinx; or, A Seavenfold Historie*

Robert Wilson (*fl.* 1572–1600)
The Three Ladies of London D

1585

- Sack of Antwerp by the duke of Parma
  Ralegh's first colony established at Roanoke, Virginia (it fails)
  War with Spain
- Elizabeth Cary born
  William Drummond, of Hawthornden, born
  William Rowley born?
- Thomas Tallis dies
- Pierre de Ronsard dies

Anonymous
The Adventures of Ladie Egeria F
By 'W.C.'

Samuel Daniel (1562–1619) (tr.)
The Worthy Tract of Paulus Jovius NF

Translated from Paolo Giovio (1483–1552), *Dialogo dell' impresse militari et amorose* (1555)

Robert Greene (1558–92)
Planetomachia; or, The First Parte of the Generall Opposition of the Seven Planets F

Anthony Munday (1553–1633) (adap.)
Fedele and Fortunio D
Anonymous. Adapted from Luigi Pasqualigo's *Il Fedele.*

John Norden (1548–1625?)
A Sinfull Mans Solace: Most Sweete and Comfortable, for the Sicke and Sorrowful Soule MISC

1586

- The Babington plot against Elizabeth I: Sir Anthony Babington executed (20 Sept.)
  Sir Philip Sydney fatally wounded at the Battle of Zutphen (22 Sept.); dies 17 Oct.
  Trial of Mary Queen of Scots at Fotheringhay (Oct.)
- Robert Dowland born c.1586
  John Ford born
  Joseph Mede born
  Lady Mary Wroth born?
- Ulpian Fulwell dies

Thomas Bowes (*fl.* 1586) (tr.)
The French Academie NF
Translated from part i of Pierre de la Primaudaye (*b.* c.1545), *Academie françoise.* See also *The Second Part* 1594. Part iii, translated R. Dolman, published in 1601.

William Bullokar (*fl.* 1586)
William Bullokarz Pamphlet for Grammar NF

William Camden (1551–1623)
Britannia Sive Florentissimorum Regnorum Angliae, Scotiae, Hiberniae Chorographica Descriptio NF
Translated into English by Philemon Holland as *Britain* 1610 (q.v.)

Thomas Churchyard (1520?–1604)
The Epitaph of Sir Phillip Sidney V
Sidney was fatally wounded at the Battle of Zutphen and died on 17 October 1586

Angel Day (*fl.* 1575–95)
The English Secretorie NF
An important letter-writing manual in which letters are classified according to types and planned 'for the unlearned'. Many editions.

Thomas Deloney (1543?–1600)
The Lamentation of Beckles V
Ballad

Thomas Deloney (1543?–1600)
A Most Joyfull Songe V
Ballad

William Warner (1558?–1609)
Albions England; or, Historicall Map of the Same Island V
2nd edition (6 books), 1589 (q.v.); 3rd edition (9 books), 1592 (q.v.); 4th edition (12 books), 1596 (q.v.); 5th edition (13 books, with Epitome), 1602 (q.v.); *A Continuance of Albions England* (books xiv–xvi), 1606 (q.v.)

William Webbe (*fl.* 1568–91)
A Discourse of English Poetrie NF
Contains a translation of Virgil's first two Eclogues

George Whetstone (*c.*1551–87)
The English Myrror NF

Geoffrey Whitney (1548?–1601?)
A Choice of Emblemes and Other Devises V
An influential emblem book

1587

- Mary Queen of Scots executed (8 Feb.)
  Drake destroys the Spanish fleet at Cadiz (Apr.): the 'singeing of the King of Spain's beard'
  Sir Christopher Hatton appointed Lord Chancellor
  Rialto Bridge in Venice begun
- Nathaniel Field born
  Sir Francis Kynaston born
- John Foxe dies
  George Whetstone dies

John Bridges (*d.* 1618)
A Defence of the Government Established in the Church of Englande for Ecclesiasticall Matters NF
The immediate cause of the Martin Marprelate controversey. See *The Epitome* 1588. Bridges was Dean of Salisbury.

Thomas Churchyard (1520?–1604)
The Worthines of Wales MISC
Mostly verse

Angel Day (*fl.* 1575–95) (tr.)
Daphnis and Chloe MISC
A translation (from the French of Jacques Amyot (1513–93) of Longus. Partly in verse.

John Foxe (1516–87)?
A Most Breefe Manner of Instruction, to the Principles of Christian Religion NF
A catechism. Probably not by Foxe; possibly by J. Field. Publication date conjectural.

George Gascoigne (1534?–77)
The Whole Woorkes of George Gascoigne Esquyre WKS
See also *A Hundreth Sundrie Flowres* 1573, *The Posies of George Gascoigne* 1575

George Gifford (*d.* 1620)
A Discourse of the Subtill Practises of Devilles by Witches and Sorcerers NF

Arthur Golding (1536?–1606) and **Sir Philip Sidney** (1554–86) (tr.)
The Trueness of the Christian Religion NF
Translated from Philippe de Mornay (1549–1623), *De la verité de la religion Chrestienne*

Robert Greene (1558–92)
Euphues his Censure to Philautus F

Robert Greene (1558–92)
Penelopes Web F

Raphael Holinshed (*d.* 1580?) and others
The First and Second Volumes of Chronicles NF
Authors include Francis Thynne (1545?–1608), Abraham Fleming, and John Stow. It was this edition that Shakespeare probably used as one of his sources for his history plays, *King Lear*, *Cymbeline*, and *Macbeth*. See also *Chronicles* 1577.

John Knox (1505–72)
History of the Reformation of Religion Within the Realm of Scotland NF
Anonymous. Revised by David Buchanan in 1644.

John Phillips (*fl.* 1564–94)
The Life and Death of Sir Philip Sidney V
Sidney died 17 October 1586

Barnabe Rich (1540?–1617)
A Path-way to Military Practise NF

Robert Southwell SJ (1561?–95)
An Epistle of Comfort, to the Reverend Priestes, & to the Laye Sort Restrayned in Durance NF
Anonymous

Thomas Thomas (1553–88)
Dictionarium linguae latinae et anglicanae DICT
Based on Gulielmus Morelius' dictionary of 1583. Many editions.

George Turberville (*c.*1544–*c.*1597) (tr.)
Tragicall Tales V
Translations from Mambrino Roseo (16th century) and Boccaccio (1313–75), *Decameron*

Thomas Watson (1557?–92)
The Lamentations of Amyntas for the Death of Phillis V
A translation by Abraham Fraunce of Watson's *Amyntas*, published in Latin in 1585. See also *The Countesse of Pembroke's Yvychurch* 1591, in which it is reprinted with alterations, and *The Third Part* 1592.

George Whetstone (*c.*1551–87)
The Censure of a Loyall Subject NF
On the Babington conspiracy

George Whetstone (*c.*1551–87)
Sir Philip Sidney, his Honorable Life, his Valiant Death, and his True Vertues V

1588

- Spanish Armada sets sail from Lisbon (May)
  Battle of Gravelines (July/Aug.) and final dispersal of the Armada
  Marprelate Controversy (1588–90)
- Richard Brathwaite born?
  Leonard Digges born
  Sir Robert Filmer born?
  Giles Fletcher, the younger, born?
  Thomas Hobbes born
  Michael Sparke born?
  George Wither born
- Robert Dudley, earl of Leicester, dies (Sept.)
- Paolo Veronese dies

Richard Bancroft (1544–1610)
A Sermon Preached at Paules Crosse NF
On 1 John 4:1; preached 9 February 1588

Timothy Bright (1551?–1615)
Characterie NF
The first manual of shorthand in English. Dedicated to Queen Elizabeth. Bright had a fifteen-year patent to print this.

William Byrd (1543–1623)
Psalmes, Sonets, & Songs of Sadnes and Pietie, Made into Musicke of Five Parts V/MUS

Thomas Deloney (1543?–1600)
A New Ballet of the Straunge and Most Cruell Whippes which the Spanyards Had Prepared

to Whippe and Torment English Men and Women V
Ballad

Thomas Deloney (1543?–1600)
The Queenes Visiting of the Campe at Tilsburie with her Entertainment there V
Ballad

Abraham Fraunce (*fl.* 1587–1633)
The Arcadian Rhetorike; or, The Praecepts of Rhetorike Made Plaine by Examples, Greeke, Latin, English NF

Abraham Fraunce (*fl.* 1587–1633) (tr.)
The Lawiers Logike NF
Derived in part from Pierre de La Ramée's *Dialectica* (1574)

Robert Greene (1558–92)
Pandosto F
Running title: *The Historie of Dorastus and Fawnia.* The main source for Shakespeare's *The Winter's Tale* (see 1623). Shakespeare is thought to have used one of the first three editions of this work. Many editions.

Robert Greene (1558–92)
Perimedes the Blacke-Smith F

Thomas Harriot (1560–1621)
A Briefe and True Report of the New Found Land of Virginia NF

Maurice Kyffin (*d.* 1599) (tr.)
Andria D
An early prose translation of Terence's comedy

'Martin Marprelate'
The Epistle NF
The first part of the first Marprelate tract, answering John Bridges's *A Defence of the Government Established* 1587 (q.v.). See also *The Mineralls, Hay Any Worke for Cooper, Martin Junior, Martin Senior, The Protestatyon* 1589.

'Martin Marprelate'
The Epitome NF
The second part of the first Marprelate tract, answering John Bridges's *A Defence of the Government Established* 1587 (q.v.). See also *The Mineralls, Hay Any Worke for Cooper, Martin Junior, Martin Senior, The Protestatyon* 1589.

Anthony Munday (1553–1633)
A Banquet of Daintie Conceits V

Anthony Munday (1553–1633) (tr.)
Palladine of England F
Translation of part i of *L'histoire Palladienne*, a translation by Claude Colet (16th century) of the first part of the anonymous romance *Florando de Inglaterra.* It has no connection with the Palmerin romances, with which it is sometimes confused.

Anthony Munday (1553–1633) (tr.)
Palmerin D'Oliva: The Mirrour of Nobilitie F
Part ii published in 1597

Robert Parke (*fl.* 1588) (tr.)
The Historie of the Great and Mighty Kingdome of China, and the Situation Thereof NF
Translated from Juan de Mendoza Monteagudo (1575–1660?), *Historia de las cosas mas notables de la China*

John Udall or Uvedale (1560?–92)
A Demonstration of the Trueth of that Discipline which Christe Hath Prescribed for the Government of His Church NF
Anonymous

John Udall or Uvedale (1560?–92)
The State of the Churche of Englande NF
Anonymous

Nicholas Yonge (*d.* 1619)
Musica Transalpina. Cantus V/MUS
See also *Musica Transalpina* 1597

1589

- Nathanael Carpenter born
- William Fulke dies
  George Pettie dies
- Catherine de' Medici dies
  Christophe Plantin dies

Anonymous
The Rare Triumphs of Love and Fortune D

Jane Anger (*fl.* 1589)
Jane Anger Her Protection for Women NF

William Byrd (1543–1623)
Songs of Sundrie Natures V/MUS

Thomas Cooper (1517?–94)
An Admonition to the People of England NF
Answers the first Martin Marprelate tract 1588 (q.v.)

Robert Greene (1558–92)
Ciceronis Amor: Tullies Love F

Robert Greene (1558–92)
Menaphon F
With an introductory epistle by Thomas Nashe

Robert Greene (1558–92)
The Spanish Masquerado F

Richard Hakluyt (1552?–1615)
The Principall Navigations, Voiages and Discoveries of the English Nation Made by Sea or Over Land, to the Most Remote and Farthest Distant Quarters of the Earth NF
Expanded into 3 volumes, 1598–1600, as *The Principal Navigations, Voiages, Traffiques and Discoveries of the English Nation.* See also *Divers Voyages* 1582.

Thomas Lodge (1558–1625)
Scillaes Metamorphosis: Enterlaced with the Unfortunate Love of Glaucus V
2nd edition, 1610, published as *A Most Pleasunt Historie of Glaucus and Scilla*

John Lyly (1554–1606)?
Pappe with an Hatchet NF
An anonymous tract on the Marprelate controversy, attributed to Lyly

John Lyly (1554–1606)?
A Whip for an Ape; or, Martin Displaied NF
An anonymous tract on the Marprelate controversy. Possibly by Lyly.

'Martin Marprelate'
The Mineralls NF
The third Marprelate tract. See also *The Epistle, The Epitome* 1588, *Hay Any Worke for Cooper, Martin Junior, Martin Senior, The Protestatyon* 1589.

'Martin Marprelate'
Hay Any Worke for Cooper NF
The fourth Marprelate tract. See also *The Epistle, The Epitome* 1588, *The Mineralls, Martin Junior, Martin Senior, The Protestatyon* 1589.

'Martin Marprelate'
Martin Junior NF
The fifth Marprelate tract. See also *The Epistle, The Epitome* 1588, *The Mineralls, Hay Any Worke for Cooper, Martin Senior, The Protestatyon* 1589.

'Martin Marprelate'
Martin Senior NF
The sixth Marprelate tract. See also *The Epistle, The Epitome* 1588, *The Mineralls, Hay Any Worke for Cooper, Martin Junior, The Protestatyon* 1589.

'Martin Marprelate'
The Protestatyon of Martin Marprelat NF
The seventh and last Marprelate tract. See also *The Epistle, The Epitome* 1588, *The Mineralls, Hay Any Worke for Cooper, Martin Junior, Martin Senior* 1589.

Anthony Munday (1553–1633) (tr.)
Palmendos F
A translation of chapters 1–20 of part i of a French version by François de Vernassal of the anonymous Spanish romance *Primaleon*, a continuation of *Palmerin de Oliva*, misattributed to Francisco de Moraës (1500?–72). See also *Celestina* 1596.

Thomas Nashe (1567–1601)?
An Almond for a Parrat; or, Cutbert Curry-Knaves Almes NF
An anonymous contribution to the Marprelate controversy often attributed to Nashe

Thomas Nashe (1567–1601)
The Anatomie of Absurditie NF
Attacks romances, singling out *Bevis of Hampton* (published 1500, q.v.) for particular execration

George Peele (1556–96)
An Eglogue Gratulatorie V

George Peele (1556–96)
A Farewell V

George Puttenham (1530?–90)
The Arte of English Poesie NF
The first draft of this work is thought to have been made as early as the mid-1560s, with revisions throughout the intervening period, up to the time of publication

Sir Thomas Smith (1513–77)
The Common-welth of England, and Manner of Government Thereof NF
Enlarged edition of *De Republica Anglorum* 1583 (q.v.)

William Warner (1558?–1609)
The First and Second Parts of Albions England V
2nd edition (6 books). See *Albions England* 1586. 3rd edition, 1592 (q.v.); 4th edition, 1596 (q.v.); 5th edition, 1602 (q.v.); *A Continuance of Albions England* 1606 (q.v.).

1590

- Richard Brome born?
  Lady Eleanor Davies born c.1590
  Richard Zouch born
- Bartholomew Clerke dies
  George Puttenham dies
  Francis Walsingham dies

Anonymous
The Cobler of Caunterburie, or an Invective Against Tarltons Newes Out of Purgatorie F
See *Tarltons Newes Out of Purgatorie* 1590, below

Anonymous
Tarltons Newes Out of Purgatorie F
Associated with the jester and actor Richard Tarlton (*d.* 1588). Sometimes attributed to Robert Armin, a fellow clown. See also *The Cobler of Caunterburie* 1590, above.

Roger Cotton (*fl.* 1590–6)
A Direction to the Waters of Lyfe NF

Robert Greene (1558–92)
Greenes Mourning Garment NF

Robert Greene (1558–92)
Greenes Never Too Late; or, A Powder of Experience NF
In two parts: part ii. entitled *Francescos Fortunes; or, The second part*, published in 1599

Robert Greene (1558–92) (tr.)
The Royal Exchange NF
A translation of *Dottrina delle virtù, et fuga de' vitii* (Padua, 1585) by Orazio Rinaldi (*d. c.*1592), with added commentary

Thomas Lodge (1558–1625)
Rosalynde: Euphues Golden Legacie F
A pastoral romance in prose. Many editions.

Christopher Marlowe (1564–93)
Tamburlane the Great D
Anonymous

Anthony Munday (1553–1633) (tr.)
The First Book of Amadis of Gaule F
Anonymous. Book ii, 1595; books iii, iv, 1618; book v, 1598. Translated from a French translation of a Spanish original.

George Peele (1556–96)
Polyhymnia V

William Perkins (1558–1602)
The Foundation of Christian Religion NF
Many editions

Henry Roberts (*fl.* 1590)
A Defiance to Fortune F

Sir Philip Sidney (1554–86)
The Countesse of Pembrokes Arcadia F
Books i–iii. 2nd edition, 1593 (q.v.). The so-called *New Arcadia*, which breaks off, mid-sentence, in book iii. See augmented editions of 1593, 1598, 1621, etc.

Edmund Spenser (1552?–99)
The Faerie Queene V
Books i–iii. See also *Second Part of the Faerie Queene* 1596, *Faerie Queene* 1609.

Robert Wilson (*fl.* 1572–1600)
The Three Lords and Ladies of London D

1591

- Trinity College, Dublin, founded
- William Browne, of Tavistock, born
  William Cavendish, 2nd earl of Devonshire, born?
  Thomas Goffe born
  Robert Herrick born
  Alexander Ross born
- St John of the Cross dies

Anonymous
Fair Em the Miller's Daughter D
By Robert Wilson? Publication date conjectural.

Anonymous
Philippes Venus F
By 'Jo. M.'

Anonymous
The Troublesome Raigne of John King of England D
A source for Shakespeare's *King John*, written in the late 1590s and first published in the First Folio of 1623 (q.v.). See also *The Second Part* 1591.

Anonymous
The Second Part of the Troublesome Raigne of King John D

Nicholas Breton (1545?–1626?)
Brittons Bowre of Delights ANTH
Anonymous. Only partly by Breton. Includes his elegy on Sir Philip Sidney. Probably compiled and edited by the printer, Richard Jones. See also Breton, *The Arbor of Amourous Devises* 1597.

Michael Drayton (1563–1631)
The Harmonie of the Church V
Republished 1610 as *A Heavenly Harmonie*

Giles Fletcher, the elder (1549?–1611)
Of the Russe Common Wealth; or, Maner of Government by the Russe Emperour NF

John Florio (1553–1625)
Florios Second Frutes MISC
See *Florio His Firste Fruites* 1578

Abraham Fraunce (*fl.* 1587–1633)
The Countesse of Pembrokes Emanuel V

Abraham Fraunce (*fl.* 1587–1633)
The Countesse of Pembrokes Yvychurch V
Part i adapted from Torquato Tasso (1544–95), *Aminta*. Part ii is a revision of Fraunce's translation of *Amyntas* by Thomas Watson 1587 (q.v.). Also includes translations of the second Bucolic of Virgil (first published in Fraunce's *The*

Lawiers Logike), and of the opening of Heliodorus's *Æthiopica*. See also *The Third Part* 1592.

Robert Greene (1558–92)
Greenes Farewell to Folly NF

Robert Greene (1558–92)
A Notable Discovery of Coosenage NF
Running title: *The Art of Cony-catching*

Robert Greene (1558–92)
The Second Part of Conny-Catching NF
See also *A Notable Discovery of Coosenage* 1591, *The Thirde and Last Part* 1592.

Sir John Harington (1560–1612) (tr.)
Orlando Furioso in English Heroical Verse V
Translated from Ludovico Ariosto (1474–1535)

King James VI of Scotland, afterwards **James I of England** (1566–1625)
His Majesties Poeticall Exercises at Vacant Houres V
Also contains *The Lepanto of James the Sixt, King of Scotland*, its French translation by Guillaume de Salluste Du Bartas (1544–90), and *The Furies*

Thomas Lodge (1558–1625)
Catharos: Diogenes in his Singularitie PS

Thomas Lodge (1558–1625)
Robert, Duke of Normandy F
A prose romance with poems. Based on a version of the *Croniques de Normandie* (13th century).

John Lyly (1554–1606)
Endimion, the Man in the Moone D
Published anonymously. See also *The Woman in the Moone* 1597.

George Peele (1556–96)
Descensus Astrææ V
A pageant for the Lord Mayor of London

Richard Perceval (1550–1620)
Bibliotheca Hispanica DICT
A grammar and dictionary in Spanish, English, and Latin

William Perkins (1558–1602)
A Golden Chaine; or, The Description of Theologie NF
Translated by R. Hill from Perkins's *Armilla Aurea* (1590)

Sir Walter Ralegh (1552?–1618)
A Report of the Truth of the Fight about the Iles of the Açores, this Last Somer NF
Published anonymously

Sir Henry Savile (1549–1622) (tr.)
The Ende of Nero and Beginning of Galba NF
The first English translation of Tacitus' *Annals*. The 2nd edition of 1598 was issued with Richard Greneway's translation of the *Annals* (q.v.).

Sir Philip Sidney (1554–86)
Astrophel and Stella V
Published in 1591 first with a corrupt, unauthorized text, containing 107 sonnets and 10 songs by Sidney, with other verse by Daniel, Campion, Greville, and others; then in a corrected edition, also unauthorized, containing only 94 sonnets by Sidney, and none of the additional poems; 3rd edition published 1597?

Henry Smith (1550–91)
The Examination of Usury, in Two Sermons NF

Robert Southwell SJ (1561?–95)
Marie Magdalens Funeral Teares NF
See also *S. Peters Complaint* 1616

Edmund Spenser (1552?–99)
Complaints V
Includes 'The Ruines of Time'; 'The Teares of the Muses'; 'Virgils Gnat'; 'Prosopopoia; or, Mother Hubberds Tale'; 'Muiopotmos'; 'Visions of the Worlds Vanitie'

Edmund Spenser (1552?–99)
Daphnaida V

1592

- Plague in London
  Rose Theatre opened c.1592
  The Greene-Nashe-Harvey quarrel (–1597)
- William Cavendish, 1st duke of Newcastle, born
  Nicholas Ferrar born
  Henry King, bishop of Chichester, born
  Francis Quarles born
- Robert Greene dies
  John Udall dies
  Thomas Watson dies
  Ninian Winzet dies
- Michel de Montaigne dies

Anonymous
Arden of Feversham D
Sometimes attributed to Shakespeare and to Thomas Kyd

Anonymous
Solyman and Perseda D
Sometimes attributed to Thomas Kyd

Lancelot Andrewes (1555–1626)
The Wonderfull Combate (for Gods Glorie and Mans Salvation) Betweene Christ and Satan NF
Published anonymously

Nicholas Breton (1545?–1626?)
The Pilgrimage to Paradise V

Thomas Churchyard (1520?–1604)
A Handful of Gladsome Verses: Given to the Queenes Majesty at Woodstocke V

Henry Constable (1562–1613)
Diana V
Sonnets. See also *Diana* 1594.

Sir Robert Dallington (1561–1637) (tr.)
Hypnerotomachia Poliphili F
Anonymous translation of the first part of the work attributed to Francesco Colonna, reproducing some of the architectural woodcuts of the original Aldine edition of 1499

Samuel Daniel (1562–1619)
Delia V
Sonnets. Dedicated to the countess of Pembroke. See also *Delia and Rosamond Augmented* 1594.

Abraham Fraunce (*fl.* 1587–1633)
The Third Part of the Countesse of Pembrokes Yvychurch: entituled Amintas Dale V
See *The Countesse of Pembrokes Yvychurch* 1591, and Watson's *Lamentations of Amyntas* 1587

Robert Greene (1558–92)
The Third and Last Part of Conny-Catching NF
Sequel to *A Notable Discovery of Coosenage* and *The Second Part of Conny-Catching* 1591 (qq.v.)

Robert Greene (1558–92)
Philomela F

Robert Greene (1558–92)
A Quip for an Upstart Courtier: or, A Quaint Dispute Between Velvet Breeches and Cloth-Breeches NF
Contains an attack on Gabriel Harvey and his brother

Robert Greene (1558–92)
The Blacke Bookes Messenger: Laying open the life and death of Ned Browne one of the most notable cutpurses, crosbiters, and conny-catchers that ever lived in England NF

Robert Greene (1558–92)
A Disputation, Betweene a Hee Conny-Catcher, and a Shee Conny-Catcher NF

Robert Greene (1558–92)
Greenes, Groats-worth of Witte, Bought with a Million of Repentance NF
Published after Greene's death on 3 September 1592. Edited by Henry Chettle.

Robert Greene (1558–92)
The Repentance of Robert Greene Maister of Artes NF

Gabriel Harvey (1550–1631)
Three Letters, and Certaine Sonnets: Especially touching Robert Greene, and other parties, by him abused MISC
Two issues published in this year, one as *Foure Letters and Certain Sonnets.* See also *Three Proper, and Wittie, Familiar Letters* 1580.

Mary Herbert, countess of Pembroke (1561–1621) (tr.)
A Discourse of Life and Death . . . [with] *Antonius: A Tragoedie* NF
Translated from Philippe de Mornay (1549–1623) and Robert Garnier (1544–90)

Richard Johnson (1573–1659?)
The Nine Worthies of London MISC
Verse and prose

Thomas Kyd (1558–94)
The Spanish Tragedie D
Published anonymously. Many editions.

Thomas Lodge (1558–1625)
Euphues Shadow, the Battaile of the Sences F
A prose romance with poems

John Lyly (1554–1606)
Gallathea D
Published anonymously

John Lyly (1554–1606)
Midas D
Published anonymously

Thomas Nashe (1567–1601)
Pierce Penilesse his Supplication to the Divell NF

Thomas Nashe (1567–1601)
Strange Newes, of the Intercepting Certaine Letters NF

William Perkins (1558–1602)
An Exposition of the Lords Prayer, in the Way of Catechising NF

Barnabe Rich (1540?–1617)
The Adventures of Brusanus, Prince of Hungaria F

Henry Smith (1550–91)
Sermons NF

John Stow (1525–1605)
The Annales of England . . . untill this Present Yeere 1592 NF
The final edition, incorporating all additions by Stow and continuations by Edmund Howes (*fl.* 1607–31), was published in 1632. See also *Summarie* 1565 and *Chronicles* 1580.

William Warner (1558?–1609)
Albions England: The Third Time Corrected and Augmented V
3rd edition (9 books). See *Albions England* 1586; 2nd edition, 1589 (q.v.); 4th edition, 1596 (q.v.); 5th edition, 1602 (q.v.); *A Continuance of Albions England* 1606 (q.v.).

1593

- Theatres closed in London because of plague
- George Herbert born
  Izaak Walton born
- Christopher Marlowe murdered at Deptford

Anonymous
The Phoenix Nest ANTH
Contains poems by Thomas Lodge, Nicholas Breton, Sir Walter Ralegh, etc. Opens with three elegies on Sir Philip Sidney (*d.* 1586), the 'Phoenix' of the title.

Richard Bancroft (1544–1610)
Daungerous Positions and Proceedings: Published and practised within this iland of Brytaine, under pretence of Reformation, and for the Presbiteriall discipline NF
Published anonymously

Barnabe Barnes (1571–1609)
Parthenophil and Parthenophe V
Sonnets, madrigals, elegies, and odes

Henry Chettle (1560?–1607)
Kind-Harts Dreame PS

Thomas Churchyard (1520?–1604)
Churchyard's Challenge MISC

Anthony Chute (*d.* 1595?)
Shore's Wife V

Michael Drayton (1563–1631)
Idea: The shepheards garland. Fashioned in nine eglogs V

Giles Fletcher, the elder (1549?–1611)
Licia, or Poemes of Love V
Published anonymously

George Gifford (*d.* 1620)
A Dialogue Concerning Witches and Witchcraftes NF

Gabriel Harvey (1550–1631)
A New Letter of Notable Contents: With a straunge sonet, intituled Gorgon NF

Gabriel Harvey (1550–1631)
Pierces Supererogation; or A New Prayse of the Old Asse NF
A reply to Thomas Nashe, *Strange Newes* 1592 (q.v.) and *Pappe with an Hatchet*, attributed to John Lyly 1589 (q.v.)

Robert Henryson (*c.*1430–*c.*1505)
The Testament of Cresseid V
First printed anonymously in Thynne's edition of Chaucer's works 1532 (q.v.)

Richard Hooker (1554–1600)
Of the Lawes of Ecclesiasticall Politie NF
See also *The Fift Booke* 1597

Thomas Lodge (1558–1625)
The Life and Death of William Long Beard F
Historical romance with poems

Thomas Lodge (1558–1625)
Phillis: Honoured with pastorall sonnets, elegies and amorous delights V

Henry Lok (1553?–1608?)
Sundry Christian Passions Contained in Two Hundred Sonnets V
See also *Ecclesiastes* 1597

Gervase Markham (1568?–1637)
A Discource of Horsmanshippe NF
2nd enlarged edition published in 1595 as *How to Chuse, Traine and Diet Horses*

Thomas Morley (1557–1602?)
Canzonets; or, Little Short Songs to Three Voyces V/MUS
See also *Canzonets* 1597

Thomas Nashe (1567–1601)
Christs Teares Over Jerusalem NF

John Norden (1548–1625)
Speculum Britanniæ the First Parte: An historicall discription of Middlesex NF
See also *The Description of Hertfordshire* 1598

George Peele (1556–96)
The Famous Chronicle of King Edward the First, Sirnamed Edward Longshankes, with his Returne from the Holy Land D

George Peele (1556–96)
The Honour of the Garter V

William Shakespeare (1564–1616)
Venus and Adonis V
Probably Shakespeare's first published work and printed from his own manuscript. Dedicated to Henry Wriothesley, 3rd earl of Southampton. 2nd edition, 1594. Shakespeare's most frequently reprinted work in his lifetime.

Sir Philip Sidney (1554–86)
The Countesse of Pembrokes Arcadia F
The 'composite' or 'hybrid' *Arcadia* in five books (edited by Hugh Sanford) formed by grafting the concluding part of Sidney's original version (the so-called *Old Arcadia*, which circulated in manuscript but which was not printed until 1926) onto the incomplete *New Arcadia* published in 1590 (q.v.). See also *Arcadia* 1598.

George Whetstone (*c.*1551–87)
Aurelia NF
The 2nd edition of *An Heptameron of Civill Discourses* 1582 (q.v.)

1594

- Earl of Tyrone's revolt in Ireland
  Nine Years War in Ireland begins
  Bad harvests
- John Bramhall born
  John Chalkhill born c.1594
  John Goodwin born?
  James Howell born?
  Geffray Minshull born?
  Henry Shirley born c.1594
- Barnabe Googe dies
  Thomas Kyd dies
  William Painter dies
- Nicolas Poussin born
- Palestrina dies

Anonymous
A Knack to Know a Knave D
Sometimes attributed to Robert Greene

Anonymous
The Life and Death of Jacke Straw D
Published 1594, dated 1593

Anonymous
The Taming of a Shrew D
Perhaps a source for, but more likely an imitation of, Shakespeare's *The Taming of the Shrew*, first published in the First Folio of 1623 (q.v.) but written in the early 1590s

Anonymous
The Warres of Cyrus King of Persia, Against Antiochus King of Assyria D

Richard Barnfield (1574–1627)
The Affectionate Shepheard V

Thomas Blundeville (*fl.* 1558–61)
Exercises NF
Treatises for young gentlemen on cosmography, astronomy, geography, and navigation

Thomas Bowes (*fl.* 1586) (tr.)
The Second Part of the French Academie NF
Translated from part ii of Pierre de la Primaudaye (*b. c.*1545), *Academie françoise.* See also *The French Academie* part i 1586. Part iii, translated by R. Dolman, published in 1601.

Richard Carew (1555–1620) (tr.)
Examen de Ingenios. The Examination of Mens Wits NF
Translated from the Spanish of Juan Huarte de San Juan (1529?–88)

Richard Carew (1555–1620) (tr.)
Godfrey of Bulloigne; or, The Recouverie of Hierusalem V
Translated from the first five books of Tasso's *Gerusalemme Liberata* (1580–1). See also Fairfax, *Godfrey of Bulloigne* 1600.

George Chapman (1559?–1634)
Skia Nyktos. The Shadow of Night V
First two words of title in Greek

Henry Constable (1562–1613)
Diana; or, The Excellent Conceitful Sonnets of H.C. V
2nd edition of *Diana* 1592 (q.v.)

Samuel Daniel (1562–1619)
Delia and Rosamond Augmented; [with] *Cleopatra* V
The 3rd edition of *Delia* and of *Rosamond*; 1st edition of *Cleopatra.* See also *Delia* 1592.

John Dickenson (*fl.* 1594)
Arisbas, Euphues Amidst his Slumbers; or, Cupids Journey to Hell F
Also contains verse

Michael Drayton (1563–1631)
Ideas Mirrour V
51 sonnets

Michael Drayton (1563–1631)
Matilda V
Reprinted, corrected and augmented, in *The Tragicall Legend of Robert Duke of Normandy* 1596 (q.v.)

Michael Drayton (1563–1631)
Peirs Gaveston Earle of Cornwall V

Robert Greene (1558–92)
Friar Bacon, and Friar Bungay D

Robert Greene (1558–92)
Orlando Furioso D
Published anonymously

Alexander Hume (1560?–1609)
Ane Treatise of Conscience NF

Thomas Kyd (1558–94) (tr.)
Cornelia D
Translated from Robert Garnier (1544–90). 2nd edition published in 1595 as *Pompey the Great, his Faire Corneliaes Tragedie*

Sir David Lindsay (1490–1555)
Squire Meldrum V
Also contains *The testament of the nobill and vailzeand Squyer Williame Meldrum of the Bynnis*

Thomas Lodge (1558–1625) and **Robert Greene** (1558–92)
A Looking Glasse, for London and Englande V

Thomas Lodge (1558–1625)
The Wounds of Civill War, Lively Set Forth in the True Tragedies of Marius and Scilla D
In verse and prose

John Lyly (1554–1606)
Mother Bombie D
Published anonymously

Christopher Marlowe (1564–93)
Dido Queene of Carthage D
Supposedly co-written with Thomas Nashe, though he had little or nothing to do with this play

Christopher Marlowe (1564–93)
Edward the Second D

Christopher Marlowe (1564–93)
The Massacre at Paris: with the Death of the Duke of Guise D
Publication date conjectural

Thomas Morley (1557–1602?)
Madrigalls to Foure Voyces V/MUS

Thomas Nashe (1567–1601)
The Terrors of the Night; or, A Discourse of Apparitions NF

Thomas Nashe (1567–1601)
The Unfortunate Traveller; or, The Life of Jacke Wilton F

John Norden (1548–1625)
The Pensive Mans Practise. The Second Part; or, The Pensive Mans Complaint and Comfort NF
See *A Pensive Mans Practise* 1584, *A Progresse of Pietie* 1598

George Peele (1556–96)
The Battell of Alcazar D
Published anonymously

William Percy (1575–1648)
Sonnets to the Fairest Cœlia V

William Shakespeare (1564–1616)
Henry VI Part 2 D
Published anonymously. Corrupt text. Reprinted in the First Folio 1623 (q.v.) as *The Second Part of King Henry the Sixth.* Continued in *Henry VI Part 3* 1595 (q.v.). *The First Part of Henry VI* (written after parts 2 and 3) not published until the First Folio.

William Shakespeare (1564–1616)
Lucrece V
Running-title: *The Rape of Lucrece.* Dedicated to Henry Wriothesley, 3rd earl of Southampton. Probably printed from Shakespeare's own manuscript. Seven reprints by 1640.

William Shakespeare (1564–1616)
Titus Andronicus D
Published anonymously. A performance record exists for January 1594, but the play was probably first performed prior to this date. Reprinted 1600, 1611, and in the First Folio of 1623 (q.v.).

Lawrence Twyne (*fl.* 1576) (tr.)
The Patterne of Painefull Adventures F
A version of the story of Apollonius of Tyre, taken from the *Gesta Romanorum.* One of the main sources of Shakespeare's *Pericles* 1609 (q.v.). See also Copland, *Apollonius of Tyre* 1510.

'Henry Willoby'
Willobie his Avisa; or, The True Picture of a Modest Maide, and of a Chast and Constant Wife V
Author unidentified. The work has a possible association with Shakespeare's sonnets.

Robert Wilson (*fl.* 1572–1600)
The Coblers Prophesie D

1595

- Sir Walter Ralegh's voyage to Guyana
- Thomas Carew born
  John Cosin, bishop of Durham, born
  Thomas May born
  Arthur Wilson born
- Sir Francis Drake dies
  Sir John Hawkins dies
  Robert Sempill dies
- Robert Southwell executed
- Torquato Tasso dies

Anonymous
The Fissher-Mans Tale V
A verse paraphrase of Robert Greene's *Pandosto* 1588 (q.v.). A second part, called *Flora's Fortune*, was also published in 1595.

Anonymous
Locrine D
Misattributed to Shakespeare in the second issue of the Third Folio (1664)

Barnabe Barnes (1571–1609)
A Divine Centurie of Spirituall Sonnets V

Richard Barnfield (1574–1627)
Cynthia V

Thomas Bedingfield (*d.* 1613) (tr.)
The Florentine Historie NF
Translated from Niccolò Machiavelli (1469–1527), *Istorie fiorentine*

Nicholas Breton (1545?–1626?)
Marie Magdalens Love; A Solemne Passion of the Soules Love V

George Chapman (1559?–1634)
Ovids Banquet of Sence V
Published anonymously. Ovid's courtship of Corinna, recounted allegorically.

Bartholomew Chappell (*fl.* 1595)
The Garden of Prudence MISC
Partly in verse

Henry Chettle (1560?–1607)
Piers Plainnes Seaven Yeres Prentiship NF

Thomas Churchyard (1520?–1604)
A Musicall Consort of Heavenly Harmonie (Compounded Out of Manie Parts of Musicke) Called Churchyards Charitie V

Anthony Copley (1567–1607)
Wits Fittes and Fancies . . . Also: Loves Owl MISC
An adaptation of Melchor de Santa Cruz de Dueñas (1520–80), *Floresta española* (1574), and Rodrigo de Cota (*d.* after 1504), *Diálogo entre el Amor y un caballerro viejo*

Samuel Daniel (1562–1619)
The First Fowre Bookes of the Civile Warres Betweene the Two Houses of Lancaster and Yorke V
A 5th book later appeared without title-page or date. See also *Poeticall Essayes* 1599 (5 books), *Works* 1601 (6 books), and *Civile Wares* 1609 (first complete edition, in 8 books).

Michael Drayton (1563–1631)
Endimion and Phoebe: Ideas Latmus V

Thomas Pope Goodwin (*fl.* 1595?) (tr.)
Blanchardine and Eglantine F
Reworked from Caxton's version of 1490 (q.v.). Continuation published in 1597.

Thomas Lodge (1558–1625)
A Fig for Momus V
Verse satires

Gervase Markham (1568?–1637)
The Most Honorable Tragedie of Sir Richard Grinvile, Knight D

Robert Parry (*fl.* 1595–7)
Moderatus, the Most Delectable & Famous Historie of the Blacke Knight F
A mixture of popular neo-chivalric and courtly pastoral romance

George Peele (1556–96)
The Old Wives Tale: A pleasant conceited comedie D

William Perkins (1558–1602)
A Salve for a Sicke Man; or, The Right Manner of Dying Well NF

Henry Roberts (*fl.* 1590)
Phaeander, the Mayden Knight F

William Shakespeare (1564–1616)
Henry VI Part 3 D
Published anonymously. Corrupt text. Reprinted in the First Folio 1623 (q.v.) as *The Third Part of Henry the Sixth*. A continuation of *Henry VI Part 2* 1594 (q.v.). *The First Part of Henry VI* (written after parts 2 and 3) not published until the First Folio.

Sir Philip Sidney (1554–86)
The Defence of Poesie NF
The first authorized edition. Another edition published in 1595 as *An Apologie for Poetrie*. Reprinted in editions of the *Arcadia* from 1598–1739.

Robert Southwell SJ (1561?–95)
Moeniae V

Robert Southwell SJ (1561?–95)
Saint Peters Complaint, with Other Poemes V
Published anonymously. Three editions in 1595. Possibly several manuscripts in circulation before the first printed edition appeared. See also *S. Peters Complaint* 1616.

Robert Southwell SJ (1561?–95)
The Triumphs over Death; or, A Consolatorie Epistle NF
Edited by John Trussell. Also circulated in manuscript.

Edmund Spenser (1552?–99)
Amoretti and Epithalamion V

Edmund Spenser (1552?–99)
Colin Clouts Come Home Againe V
Also contains 'Astrophel: A pastorall elegie upon the death of Sidney', and other laments on Sidney's death by Ralegh and others

William Warner (1558?–1609) (tr.)
Menaecmi: A pleasant and fine conceited comœdie D
From Plautus

Thomas Wilcox (1549?–1608) (tr.)
Satire Menippée NF
Translated from the *Satire Menippée* (1594) of Pierre Le Roy

1596

- Sack of Cadiz by Lord Howard of Effingham and the earl of Essex
  Blackfriars Theatre opens
  Robert Cecil becomes Secretary of State
- Henry Lawes born
  James Shirley born
- George Peele dies
- René Descartes born

Anonymous
Celestina F
A translation, with altered names, of part of a French version by François de Vernassal, of the anonymous Spanish romance *Primaleon*, a continuation of *Palmerin de Oliva*, misattributed to Francisco de Morães (1500?–72). Dedication signed by William Barley (*d.* 1614), who may be the translator. See also Anthony Munday, *Palmerin D'Oliva* 1588.

Anonymous
King Edward the Fourth and the Tanner of Tamworth V
Anonymous ballad. Cf. Thomas Heywood, *King Edward the Fourth* 1599.

Anonymous
A Knack to Know an Honest Man: A most pleasant and merie new comedie D
Publication date conjectural

Anonymous
Lazarillo de Tormes. The Second Part F
Original work attributed to Diego Hurtado de Mendoza (1503–75)

Thomas Churchyard (1520?–1604)
A Pleasant Discourse of Court and Wars V

Henoch Clapham (*d.* 1614)
A Briefe of the Bible V

Peter Colse (*fl.* 1596)
Penelopes Complaint; or, A Mirrour for Wanton Minions V

Anthony Copley (1567–1607)
A Fig for Fortune V

Roger Cotton (*fl.* 1590–6)
An Armour of Proofe: Brought from the tower of David, to fight against Spannyardes, and all enimies of the trueth V

Roger Cotton (*fl.* 1590–6)
A Spirituall Song: Conteining an historicall discourse from the infancie of the world, until this present time V

Sir John Davies (1569–1626)
Orchestra; or, A Poeme of Dauncing V
Published anonymously. See also *Nosce Teipsum* 1622.

John Dickenson (*fl.* 1594)
The Shepheardes Complaint V

Michael Drayton (1563–1631)
Mortimeriados V
Revised as *The Barrons Wars* in 1603 (q.v.)

Michael Drayton (1563–1631)
The Tragicall Legend of Robert Duke of Normandy: [with] *The legend of Matilda; The legend of Piers Gaveston* V

'Misacmos' [Sir John Harington (1560–1612)]
The Metamorphosis of Ajax NF
Supplemented by *An Anatomie of the Metamorpho-sed Ajax*, 1596, and *An Apologie* (also 1596). Answered by the anonymous *Ulysses upon Ajax written by Misodiaboles to his Friend Philaretes* (1596).

Richard Johnson (1573–1659?)
The Seven Champions of Christendom F
Part i. Johnson's treatment of the St George legend owes much to *Bevis of Hampton* 1500 (q.v.). Part ii published in 1597 (q.v.); both parts published together in 1608.

Thomas Lodge (1558–1625)
The Divel Conjured NF

Thomas Lodge (1558–1625)
A Margarite of America F

Prose romance with poems. Written 1592 in the Straits of Magellan.

Thomas Lodge (1558–1625)
Wits Miserie, and the Worlds Madnesse PS

Gervase Markham (1568?–1637)
The Poem of Poems; or, Sions Muse V

Christopher Middleton (1560?–1628)
The Historie of Heaven V

Anthony Munday (1553–1633) (tr.)
Palmerin of England F
Published anonymously. *Crónica de Palmeirim de Inglaterra* written in Portuguese 1544, attributed to Francisco de Morães Cabral (1500?–72) and first published in a Spanish version attributed to Luis Hurtado (*c*.1510–*c*.1598), 1547–8. This translation also includes verses by Dekker, Webster, and others.

Thomas Nashe (1567–1601)
Have With You to Saffron-walden NF

William Perkins (1558–1602)
A Declaration of the True Manner of Knowing Christ Crucified NF

Sir Walter Ralegh (1552?–1618)
The Discoverie of the Large, Rich, and Bewtiful Empyre of Guiana NF

William Smith (*fl.* 1596)
Chloris; or, The Complaint of the Passionate Despised Shepheard V

Edmund Spenser (1552?–99)
Fowre Hymnes V
Published with the 2nd edition of *Daphnaida* 1591 (q.v.)

Edmund Spenser (1552?–99)
Prothalamion; or, A Spousall Verse in Honour of the Double Marriage of Ladie Elizabeth and Ladie Katherine Somerset V

Edmund Spenser (1552?–99)
The Second Part of the Faerie Queene: Containing the fourth, fifth, and sixth bookes V
Volume i reprints (with alterations) books i–iii (first published in 1590, q.v.). See also *Faerie Queene* 1609.

William Warner (1558?–1609)
Albions England V
The 4th edition (12 books). See also *Albions England* 1586; 2nd edition, 1589 (q.v.); 3rd edition, 1592 (q.v.); 5th edition, 1602 (q.v.); *A Continuance of Albions England* 1606 (q.v.).

1597

- Christopher Harvey born
  Rachel Speght born
- George Turberville dies c.1597

Francis Bacon (1561–1626)
Essayes NF
Contains 10 essays. See also *Essayes* 1612, *Essayes, Civil and Moral* 1625.

Thomas Beard (*d.* 1632)
The Theatre of Gods Judgements: or, A Collection of Histories out of Sacred, Ecclesiasticall, and Prophane Authours NF
Mainly a translation of Jean de Chassanion (1531–98), *Histoires memorables des grans et merveilleux jugemens et punitions de Dieu*

Nicholas Breton (1545?–1626?)
The Arbor of Amorous Devises ANTH
A verse miscellany, only partly by Breton. Reprints 10 poems from *Brittons Bowre of Delights* 1591 (q.v.). Probably compiled by the printer, Richard Jones.

Nicholas Breton (1545?–1626?)
Auspicante Jehova V

Nicholas Breton (1545?–1626?)
The Wil of Wit, Wits Wil, or Wils Wit, Chuse You Whether NF

Nicholas Breton (1545?–1626?)
Wits Trenchmour NF

William Burton (1575–1645) (tr.)
Clitophon and Leucippe F
Translated from Achilles Tatius

John Dowland (1563–1626)
The First Booke of Songes or Ayres of Fowre Partes V/MUS
See also *Second Booke* 1600; *Third and Last Booke* 1603

Michael Drayton (1563–1631)
Englands Heroicall Epistles V
Enlarged in 1598; reprinted in *The Barrons Wars* 1603 (q.v.)

John Gerard (1545–1612)
The Herball or Generall Historie of Plantes NF
Profusely illustrated with woodcuts. Mostly based on a translation by a Dr Priest of Rembert Dodoens's *Stirpium historiæ pemptades sex, sive libri xxx* (Antwerp, 1583).

Joseph Hall (1574–1656)
Virgidemiarum, Sixe Bookes V

Published anonymously. See also *Virgidemiarum* 1598.

Richard Hooker (1554–1600)
[*Laws of Ecclesiastical Policy*] *The Fift Booke* NF
See *Lawes of Ecclesiasticall Politie* 1593. The last book of the *Polity* to appear in Hooker's lifetime.

King James VI of Scotland, afterwards **James I of England** (1566–1625)
Daemonologie NF

Richard Johnson (1573–1659?)
The Second Part of the Famous History of the Seaven Champions of Christendome F
Part i published in 1596 (q.v.); both parts published together in 1608

Nicholas Ling (*fl.* 1580–1604) (ed.)
Politeuphuia Wits Common Wealth MISC
Published anonymously. Sometimes attributed to John Bodenham. The first in the 'Wits Series'. See also Meres, *Palladis Tamia* 1598; Allot, *Wits Theater* 1599; Wrednot, *Palladis Palatium* 1604.

Henry Lok (1553?–1608?)
Ecclesiastes, Otherwise Called the Preacher V

John Lyly (1554–1606)
The Woman in the Moone D
See also *Endimion* 1591

Gervase Markham (1568?–1637)
Devoreux V
Translated from an untraced original by Geneviève Petau de Maulette. The subjects are Henri III of France (1551–89) and Walter Devereux (1569–91).

Christopher Middleton (1560?–1628)
The Famous Historie of Chinon of England F

Thomas Middleton (1580–1627)
The Wisdome of Solomon Paraphrased V

Alexander Montgomerie (1556?–1610?)
The Cherrie and the Slaye V
An allegory of the Lover's choice between a beautiful cherry tree or an ugly sloe tree, aided by Hope and Courage on the Cherry's side, and hindered by Dread and Danger on the Sloe's

Thomas Morley (1557–1602?)
Canzonets; or, Little Short Songs to Foure Voyces V/MUS
See also *Canzonets* 1593

Thomas Morley (1557–1602?)
A Plaine and Easie Introduction to Practicall Musicke NF
A widely read musical primer

Robert Parry (*fl.* 1595–7)
Sinetes Passion Uppon his Fortunes V

William Shakespeare (1564–1616)
Richard II D
Published anonymously. The first quarto. First performed late 1592 or early 1593. Abdication scene (IV.i.154–318) omitted in this and in the two reprints of 1598, restored in the fourth quarto of 1608.

William Shakespeare (1564–1616)
Richard III D
Published anonymously. The first quarto, written 1592/3 and probably first performed late 1592/early 1593. 2nd edition, attributed to Shakespeare, 1598; revised version reprinted in the First Folio 1623 (q.v.).

William Shakespeare (1564–1616)
Romeo and Juliet D
Published anonymously. The first quarto: an unlicensed edition apparently produced from a reported text assembled from actors' memories. Second quarto, 'newly corrected, augmented, and amended', published in 1599 (q.v.). Written 1594/5. Based on Arthur Brooke's poem *The Tragical History of Romeus and Juliet* 1562 (q.v.).

Robert Tofte (1562–1620)
Laura: The Toyes of a Traveller; or, The Feast of Fancie V
Contains the probably untrue statement that over 30 poems are not by Tofte

Nicholas Yonge (*d.* 1619)
Musica Transalpina. Cantus V/MUS
See *Musica Transalpina* 1588

1598

- Edict of Nantes
  Death of Philip II of Spain
- Jasper Heywood dies
  Thomas Preston dies
- William Cecil, Lord Burghley, dies

Anonymous
Aristotles Politiques, or discourses of government D

Anonymous
The Famous Victories of Henry the Fifth D

An anonymous chronicle play, perhaps written 1588. A possible source for Shakespeare's *1* and *2 Henry IV* and *Henry V*.

Anonymous
Mucedorus and Amadine D
Often attributed to Shakespeare

Richard Barnfield (1574–1627)
The Encomion of Lady Pecunia; or, The Praise of Money V

Thomas Bastard (1566–1618)
Chrestoleros: Seven bookes of epigrammes V

Richard Bernard (1568–1642) (tr.)
Terence in English D
Latin and English

Nicholas Breton (1545?–1626?)
A Solemne Passion of the Soules Love V

Richard Carew (1555–1620)
A Herrings Tale V
Published anonymously

George Chapman (1559?–1634)
The Blinde Begger of Alexandria D

George Chapman (1559?–1634) (tr.)
Seaven Bookes of the Iliades of Homere, Prince of Poets V
Contains books i–ii, vii–xi. See also *Achilles Shield* 1598, *Homer Prince of Poets* 1609; *The Iliads of Homer* 1611; *Homers Odysses* 1614; *Twenty-four Bookes of Homers Odisses* 1615; *The Whole Workes of Homer* 1616.

George Chapman (1559?–1634) (tr.)
Achilles Shield V
See also *Seaven Bookes of the Iliades of Homere* 1598

Geoffrey Chaucer (1340?–1400)
The Workes of Our Antient and Lerned English Poet, Geffrey Chaucer WKS
Edited by Thomas Speght. See also *Workes* 1532 (ed. Thynne), 1561 (ed. Stow). Speght produced a new edition in 1602 in response to Francis Thynne's *Animadversions* on this 1598 edition.

Thomas Churchyard (1520?–1604)
A Wished Reformacion of Wicked Rebellion V

John Dickenson (*fl.* 1594)
Greene in Conceipt F
Robert Greene died in 1592

John Florio (1553–1625)
A Worlde of Wordes, or Most Copious, Dictionarie in Italian and English NF
Enlarged in 1611 as *Queen Anna's New World of Words*

Emanuel Forde (*fl.* 1607)
Parismus, the Renoumed [sic] *Prince of Bohemia* F
Part ii published in 1599 (q.v.)

Robert Greene (1558–92)
The Scottish Historie of James the Fourth, Slaine at Flodden D

Richard Grenewey (*fl.* 1591–8) (tr.)
The Annales of Cornelius Tacitus NF
Issued with the 2nd edition of Sir Henry Savile's *Ende of Nero and Beginning of Galba* (first published in 1591, q.v.)

Everard Guilpin (*fl.* 1598)
Skialetheia. Or, A Shadow of Truth, in Certaine Epigrams or Satyres V
Published anonymously

Joseph Hall (1574–1656)
Virgidemiarum V
Published anonymously. See *Virgidemiarum* 1597.

King James VI of Scotland, afterwards **James I of England** (1566–1625)
The True Lawe of Free Monarchies; or, The Reciprock and Mutuall Dutie Betwixt a Free King, and his Naturall Subjects NF
See also 1603

Christopher Marlowe (1564–93)
Hero and Leander V
Described as 'this unfinished Tragedy', but quite possibly considered complete by Marlowe himself

Christopher Marlowe (1564–93) and **George Chapman** (1559?–1634)
Hero and Leander: Begun by Christopher Marloe; and finished by George Chapman V
Chapman's contribution consisted of dividing Marlowe's poem into two sestiads and adding four more of his own devising

John Marston (1576–1634)
The Metamorphosis of Pigmalions Image V

'William Kinsayder' [**John Marston** (1576–1634)]
The Scourge of Villanie V

Francis Meres (1565–1647)
Palladis Tamia. Wits Treasury V
Important for its inclusion of a list of plays by Shakespeare. The second in the 'Wits Series'. See also Ling, *Politeuphuia* 1597; Allot, *Wits Theater* 1599; Wrednot, *Palladis Palatium* 1604.

John Norden (1548–1625)
The Description of Hertfordshire NF
The second volume in the series. See also *Speculum Britanniæ . . . Middlesex* 1593.

John Norden (1548–1625)
A Progresse of Pietie NF
The third part of *The Pensive Mans Practise*: see 1584, 1594

Henry Roberts (*fl.* 1590)
Honours Conquest F
Draws on themes from Middle English romance, but aimed at the merchant class

Francis Rous (1579–1659)
Thule; or, Vertues Historie V

Samuel Rowlands (1570?–1630?)
The Betraying of Christ; Judas in Despaire; The Seven Words of Our Savior on the Crosse V

William Shakespeare (1564–1616)
Henry IV Part 1 D
Published anonymously. An earlier printing (almost certainly also 1598) survives only in a single, 8-page fragment. Probably written 1596–7. Reprinted, 'newly corrected by W. Shake-speare', in 1599 and in the First Folio 1623 (q.v.). Part 2 published in 1600 (q.v.).

William Shakespeare (1564–1616)
Loves Labors Lost D
The first of Shakespeare's plays to be published under his name, written 1593/4. Reprinted in the First Folio 1623 (q.v.).

Sir Philip Sidney (1554–86)
The Countesse of Pembrokes Arcadia F
The 3rd edition, adding *The Lady of May*, *Certaine Sonets*, the *Defence of Poesie*, and *Astrophel and Stella*. See also *Arcadia* 1590, 1593.

John Stow (1525–1605)
A Survay of London NF

Joshua Sylvester (1563–1618) (tr.)
The Second Weeke or Childhood of the World V
The first instalment of Sylvester's translation of Guillaume de Salluste Du Bartas (1544–90)

Robert Tofte (1562–1620)
Alba: The months minde of a melancholy lover V

Robert Tofte (1562–1620) (tr.)
Orlando Inamorato V
Translated from Matteo Maria Boiardo (1440/41–94), *Orlando Innamorato*

1599

- The earl of Essex appointed Lord Lieutenant of Ireland; arrested (Sept.)
  Globe Theatre opens
- Maurice Kyffin dies
  Henry Porter dies
  Reginald Scot dies
  Edmund Spenser dies
- Oliver Cromwell born
- Anthony Van Dyck born

Anonymous
George a Greene F
Reissued 1632 as a chapbook, *The Pinder of Wakefield*. Sometimes attributed to Robert Greene.

George Abbot (1562–1633)
A Briefe Description of the Whole Worlde NF
Published anonymously

Robert Allott (*fl.* 1600)
Wits Theater of the Little World V
The third in the 'Wits Series'. See also Ling, *Politeuphuia* 1597; Meres, *Palladis Tamia* 1598; Wrednot, *Palladis Palatium* 1604.

Thomas Blundeville (*fl.* 1558–61)
The Art of Logike NF

Nicholas Breton (1545?–1626?)
The Passions of the Spirit V
Published anonymously

George Chapman (1559?–1634)
An Humerous Dayes Myrth D

Thomas Churchyard (1520?–1604)
The Fortunate Farewel to the Most Forward and Noble Earle of Essex V

Samuel Daniel (1562–1619)
The Poeticall Essayes of Sam. Danyel V
The first collected edition. Contains *The Civill Wars* in 5 books. See also *The First Fowre Bookes* 1595, *Works* 1601 (6 books), *Civile Wares* 1609 (8 books).

Sir John Davies (1569–1626)
Hymns of Astraea, in Acrosticke Verse V
Published anonymously

Sir John Davies (1569–1626)
Nosce Teipsum V
See also *Nosce Teipsum* 1619, 1622

Emanuel Forde (*fl.* 1607)
Ornatus and Artesis F
Publication date conjectural

Emanuel Forde (*fl.* 1607)
Parismenos F
Part ii. See *Parismus* 1598.

Robert Greene (1558–92)
The Comicall Historie of Alphonsus, King of Aragon D

Robert Greene (1558–92)
Greenes Orpharion F

Sir John Hayward (1564?–1627)
The First Part of the Life and Raigne of King Henrie the IIII NF

Thomas Heywood (1574?–1641)
The First and Second Partes of King Edward the Fourth D
Published anonymously. See also *King Edward the Fourth and the Tanner of Tamworth* 1596.

Alexander Hume (1560?–1609)
Hymnes, or Sacred Songs NF

King James VI of Scotland, afterwards **James I of England** (1566–1625)
Basilikon Doron NF
Published anonymously. Title in Greek.

Christopher Marlowe (1564–93) (tr.) and **Sir John Davies** (1569–1626)
All Ovids Elegies: 3 Bookes V
Publication date conjectural. Contains epigrams by Davies.

Thomas Middleton (1580–1627)?
Micro-Cynicon V
Spmetimes attributed to Middleton

Thomas Nashe (1567–1601)
Nashes Lenten Stuffe NF

George Peele (1556–96)
The Love of King David and Fair Bethsabe. With the Tragedie of Absalon D

Henry Porter (*d.* 1599)
The Two Angrie Women of Abington D

William Shakespeare (1564–1616)
The Passionate Pilgrime; or, Certaine Amorous Sonnets V
Only two sheets of the 1st edition survive; 2nd edition also 1599. Contains 20 poems, including versions of Sonnets 138 and 144, and three extracts from *Love's Labour's Lost.* Also includes poems by other hands. 1612 edition adds 9 poems by Thomas Heywood.

William Shakespeare (1564–1616)
Romeo and Juliet D
Published anonymously. The second quarto: first quarto published in 1597 (q.v.). This edition was reprinted almost verbatim in the First Folio of 1623 (q.v.).

Thomas Storer (1571–1604)
The Life and Death of Thomas Wolsey Cardinall V

John Weever (1576–1632)
Epigrammes in the Oldest Cut, and Newest Fashion V

1600

1600

- Fortune Theatre opens
  English East India Company receives royal charter (31 Dec.)
- Samuel Hartlib born?
  Peter Heylyn born
  Sir William Lower born
  William Prynne born
  Samuel Rutherford born
- Thomas Deloney dies
  Richard Hooker dies
- Pedro Caldéron born
  Claude Lorraine born
- Giordano Bruno executed

Englands Helicon ANTH
A landmark anthology of lyrical and pastoral poetry. Includes pieces by Sidney, Spenser, Drayton (five previously unpublished poems), Lodge, Marlowe, and poems from Young's *Diana* (1598). Editorship attributed to John Bodenham, to Nicholas Ling, and to 'A.B.'.

Anonymous
The Maydes Metamorphosis D

Anonymous
The Wisdome of Doctor Dodypoll D

Robert Allott (*fl.* 1600) (ed.)
Englands Parnassus; or, The Choysest Flowers of our Moderne Poets, with their Poeticall Comparisons ANTH
Initialled 'R.A.'—usually attributed to Robert Allott

'Clonico de Curtanio Snuffe' [Robert Armin (1565?–1610)]
Foole upon Foole; or, Six Sortes of Sottes PS
Jests and characters. See also *A Nest of Ninnies* 1608.

'Clunnyco [sic] **de Curtanio Snuffe' [Robert Armin** (1565?–1610)]
Quips upon Questions; or, A Clownes Conceite on Occasion Offered V

John Bodenham (*fl.* 1600) (ed.)
Bel-vedére; or, The Garden of the Muses ANTH
Published anonymously, but editorship usually attributed to John Bodenham. Prefatory sonnet to Bodenham initialled 'A.M.' (Anthony Munday?), to whom the editorship is also sometimes attributed.

Nicholas Breton (1545?–1626?)
Melancholike Humours V

Nicholas Breton (1545?–1626?)
Pasquils Mad-cap and his Message V
Published anonymously

'Salochin Treboun' [Nicholas Breton (1545?–1626?)]
Pasquils Mistresse; or, The Worthie and Unworthie Woman V

Nicholas Breton (1545?–1626?)
Pasquils Passe, and Passeth Not V

Nicholas Breton (1545?–1626?)
The Second Part of Pasquils Mad-cap intituled: The Fooles-cap V

Nicholas Breton (1545?–1626?)
The Strange Fortunes of Two Excellent Princes F

Sir William Cornwallis (1579?–1614)
Essayes [pt i] NF
See also *Essayes* part ii 1601. Both parts published together in 1617.

Thomas Dekker (1572?–1632)
Old Fortunatus D
Anonymous

Thomas Dekker (1572?–1632)
The Shoemakers Holiday; or, The Gentle Craft, with the Humorous Life of Simon Eyre, Shoomaker and Lord Mayor of London D
Published anonymously

Thomas Deloney (1543?–1600) (tr.)?
Patient Grissell V
Ballad. Attribution uncertain. Also printed in *The Garland of Good Will* 1628 (q.v.). Based on book 10, novel x, of Boccaccio's *Decameron*. See also John Phillips, *Patient and Meek Griselda* 1566.

John Dowland (1563–1626)
The Second Booke of Songs or Ayres V/MUS
See also *First Booke* 1597; *Third and Last Booke* 1603

Edward Fairfax (*c*.1580–1635) (tr.)
Godfrey of Bulloigne; or, The Recoverie of Jerusalem V
A Spenserian translation of Torquato Tasso (1544–95), *Gerusalemme Liberata* (1580–93). See also *Godfrey of Bulloigne* 1594.

William Gilbert (1540–1603)
De magnete, magneticisque corporibus, et de magno magnete tellure NF
In Latin

Philemon Holland (1552–1637) (tr.)
The Romane Historie NF
Translated from Livy. Also includes a translation of Bartolomeo Marliani's *Topographia antiquae Romae.*

Ben Jonson (1572–1637)
Every Man Out of his Humor D
First performed 1599, by the Chamberlain's Men at the Globe and at court

William Kemp (*fl.* 1600)
Kemps Nine Daies Wonder: Performed in a daunce from London to Norwich NF

Gervase Markham (1568?–1637)
The Teares of the Beloved; or, The Lamentation of Saint John, Concerning the Death and Passion of Christ Jesus our Saviour V

Christopher Marlowe (1564–93) (tr.)
Pharsalia V
Translated from Lucan

Christopher Middleton (1560?–1628)
The Legend of Humphrey Duke of Glocester V

Thomas Middleton (1580–1627)
The Ghost of Lucrece V
A sequel to Shakespeare's *Lucrece* 1594 (q.v.)

Thomas Morley (1557–1602?)
The First Booke of Ayres; or, Little Short Songs, to Sing and Play to the Lute V

Anthony Munday (1553–1633) and others
Sir John Old-castle D
Published anonymously. Written with Michael Drayton, Richard Hathway, and Robert Wilson. Reprinted in 1619 with false ascription to Shakespeare; also misattributed to Shakespeare in the second issue of the Third Folio 1664.

Thomas Nashe (1567–1601)
Summers Last Will and Testament D

John Norden (1548–1625)
Civita Londini
One of the most frequently reproduced maps of the period

John Norden (1548–1625)
Vicissitudo Rerum: An elegaicall poeme, of the interchangeable courses and varietie of things in this world V

Henry Roberts (*fl.* 1590)
Haigh for Devonshire F
An imitation of an early edition of Thomas Deloney's *Thomas of Reading* (no copy now known)

Samuel Rowlands (1570?–1630?)
The Letting of Humors Blood in the Head-vaine V
See also *Humors Antique Faces* 1605, and *Humors Looking Glasse* 1608

William Shakespeare (1564–1616)
A Midsommer Nights Dreame D
Probably printed from Shakespeare's manuscript. Written 1594/5. Reprinted 1619 (q.v.).

William Shakespeare (1564–1616)
The Merchant of Venice D
Probably written 1596 or 1597. Reprinted in 1619 but falsely misdated 1600.

William Shakespeare (1564–1616)
Henry IV Part 2 D
Scene III. i accidentally omitted but included in a second issue, 1600. Probably written 1596/7. Not reprinted, in differing form, until the First Folio 1623 (q.v.). Part 1 published 1598 (q.v.).

William Shakespeare (1564–1616)
Much Adoe About Nothing D
Probably printed from Shakespeare's manuscript. Probably written 1598–9. Reprinted in the First Folio of 1623 (q.v.).

William Shakespeare (1564–1516)
Henry V D
Published anonymously. Probably written 1599. Reissued 1602, 1619 (misdated 1608), and in a superior text in the First Folio of 1623 (q.v.).

Cyril Tourneur (1575?–1626)
The Transformed Metamorphosis V

Sir William Vaughan (1575–1641)
The Golden-grove NF

Sir William Vaughan (1575–1641)
Naturall and Artificial Directions for Health NF
Many editions

John Weever (1576–1632)
Faunus and Melliflora; or, The Original of Our English Satyres V
With a translation of the first satires of Horace, Persius, and Juvenal

1601

- Execution of the earl of Essex (25 Feb.)
  First East India Company voyage
  Spanish force lands at Kinsale, Ireland
- Lodowick Carlell born?
  John Earle born
- Thomas Nashe dies
  Sir Thomas North dies
- Tycho Brahe dies

Sir Francis Bacon (1561–1626)
A Declaration of the Practises & Treasons Attempted and Committed by Robert Late Earle of Essex and his Complices NF
Published anonymously. See also *Apologie* 1604.

Nicholas Breton (1545?–1626?)
A Divine Poeme V
Published anonymously

Robert Chester (1566–1640?)
Loves Martyr; or, Rosalins Complaint V
Supposedly a translation from the Italian, but in fact written by Chester. Appended poems by Shakespeare, John Marston, George Chapman, and Ben Jonson.

Henoch Clapham (*d.* 1614)
Aelohim-triune V

Sir William Cornwallis (1579?–1614)
Discourses Upon Seneca the Tragedian NF

Sir William Cornwallis (1579?–1614)
Essayes [pt ii] NF
See *Essayes* part i 1600. Both parts published together 1617.

Samuel Daniel (1562–1619)
The Works of Samuel Daniel Newly Augmented WKS
The 2nd collected edition. A few copies of this edition are dated 1602. Contains *The Civill Warres* in six books. See also *The First Fowre Bookes* 1595, *Poeticall Essayes* 1599 (5 books), *Civile Wares* 1609 (8 books).

Arthur Dent (1553–1603)
The Plaine Mans Path-way to Heaven NF
Enormously popular. Twenty-five editions by 1640.

Francis Godwin (1562–1633)
A Catalogue of the Bishops of England NF
Revised and enlarged in 1615

Sir John Hayward (1564?–1627)
The Sanctuarie of a Troubled Soule [pt i] NF
Part ii published in 1604. Both parts published together in 1610. Many editions.

Philemon Holland (1552–1637) (tr.)
The Historie of the World NF
Translated from Pliny the elder, *Naturalis historia*

Robert Jones (*fl.* 1616)
The First Booke of Songes or Ayres of Foure Parts V/MUS

Robert Jones (*fl.* 1616)
The Second Booke of Songes and Ayres V/MUS

Ben Jonson (1572–1637)
Every Man in His Humor D
First performed in 1598 by the Lord Chamberlain's Men at the Curtain Theatre, Shoreditch

Ben Jonson (1572–1637)
The Fountaine of Selfe-love. Or Cynthias Revels D
Running-title: *Cynthias Revells*. First performed in 1600.

Thomas Lodge (1558–1625) (tr.)
The Flowers of Lodowicke of Granado NF
Translated from Luis de Granada (1504–88), *Flores*

John Lyly (1554–1606)
Loves Metamorphosis: A wittie and courtly pastorall D

Gervase Markham (1568?–1637)
Marie Magdalens Lamentations for the Losse of Her Master Jesus V

John Marston (1576–1634)
Jacke Drums Entertainment; or, The Comedie of Pasquill and Katherine D
Published anonymously. Mainly by Marston.

Thomas Morley (1557–1602?)
The Triumphes of Oriana V/MUS

Anthony Munday (1553–1633) and **Henry Chettle** (1560?–1607)
The Downfall of Robert, Earle of Huntington, afterward Called Robin Hood of Merrie Sherwodde D
Published anonymously

Anthony Munday (1553–1633) and **Henry Chettle** (1560?–1607)
The Death of Robert, Earle of Huntington. Otherwise Called Robin Hood of Merrie Sherwodde D
Published anonymously. Probably issued with *The Downfall of Robert, Earle of Huntington* (see above).

John Weever (1576–1632)
The Mirror of Martyrs; or, The Life and Death of that Thrice Valiant Captaine, and Most Godly Martyre, Sir John Old-castle Knight Lord Cobham V

Robert Yarington (*fl.* 1601)
Two Lamentable Tragedies D

1602

- Bodleian Library opens
- William Chillingworth born
  Mildmay Fane born
  Owen Felltham born?
  William Lilly born
  William Strode born
- Thomas Morley dies
  William Perkins dies

Anonymous
A Larum for London; or, The Siedge of Antwerpe D

Anonymous
Liberalitie and Prodigalitie D

Anonymous
Thomas Lord Cromwell D
Attributed to Wentworth Smith (*fl.* 1601–23) and misattributed to Shakespeare in second issue (1664) of the Third Folio

William Basse (1583–1653)
Sword and Buckler; or, Serving-Mans Defence V

William Basse (1583–1653)
Three Pastoral Elegies V

Francis Beaumont (1584–1616) (tr.)
Salamacis and Hermaphroditus V
Published anonymously. Translated from Ovid, *Metamorphoses*.

John Beaumont (1583–1627)
The Metamorphosis of Tabacco V
Published anonymously. Includes the first published verses of Francis Beaumont, John Beaumont's younger brother.

Nicholas Breton (1545?–1626?)
The Mother's Blessing V

Nicholas Breton (1545?–1626?)
Olde Mad-Cappes New Gally-Mawfrey V

Nicholas Breton (1545?–1626?)
A Poste with a Madde Packet of Letters [pt i] NF
Part ii published in 1605

Nicholas Breton (1545?–1626?)
The Soules Harmony V

Nicholas Breton (1545?–1626?)
A True Description of Unthankfulnesse; or, An Enemie to Ingratitude V

Nicholas Breton (1545?–1626?)
Wonders Worth the Hearing NF

Thomas Campion (1567–1620)
Observations in the Art of English Poesie NF
See also Samuel Daniel 1603

Thomas Churchyard (1520?–1604)
The Wonders of the Ayre, the Trembling of the Earth, and the Warnings of the World Before the Judgement Day MISC

John Davies (1565–1618)
Mirum in Modum V
See also *Yehovah Summa Totalis* 1607

Thomas Dekker (1572?–1632)
Satiro-Mastix; or, The Untrussing of the Humorous Poet D

Thomas Deloney (1543?–1600)
Strange Histories, of Kings, Princes, Dukes, Earles, Lords, Ladies, Knights, and Gentlemen V/MUS
Published anonymously. With music.

Thomas Heywood (1574?–1641)?
A Good Wife from a Bad D
Published anonymously. Attribution uncertain.

Ben Jonson (1572–1637)
Poetaster or The Arraignment D
First performed in 1601 by the Children of the Chapel at the Blackfriars

Sir David Lindsay (1490–1555)
Ane Satyre of the Thrie Estaits in Commendation of Vertew and Vituperation of Vyce D

Thomas Lodge (1558–1625) (tr.)
The Famous and Memorable Workes of Josephus EDN
Many editions

Sir Robert Mansell (1573–1636)
A True Report of the Service Done Upon Certaine Gallies Passing through the Narrow Seas NF

John Marston (1576–1634)
Antonio and Mellida D

John Marston (1576–1634)
Antonio's Revenge D
Part ii of *Antonio and Mellida* (see above)

Thomas Middleton (1580–1627)
Blurt Master-Constable; or, The Spaniards Night-Walke D
Published anonymously

Anthony Munday (1553–1633) (tr.)
The True Knowledge of a Mans Owne Selfe NF
Translated from Philippe Duplessis-Mornay (1549–1623)

Simon Patrick (*d.* 1613) (tr.)
A Discourse Upon the Means of Wel Governing a Kingdome NF
Translated from Innocent Gentillet (*c.*1535–*c.*1595)

Samuel Rowlands (1570?–1630?)
Greenes Ghost Haunting Conie-Catchers NF
Published anonymously

Samuel Rowlands (1570?–1630?)
'Tis Merrie When Gossips Meete V
Sometimes attributed to Robert Greene (in fact partly plagiarized from him)

William Shakespeare (1564–1616)
The Merrie Wives of Windsor D
Perhaps written *c.*1597. Corrupt text.
Superior text published in the First Folio of 1623 (q.v.).

William Warner (1558?–1609)
Albions England V
The 5th edition (in 13 books), with Epitome. Mostly in verse. See *Albions England* 1586; 2nd edition, 1589 (q.v.); 3rd edition, 1592 (q.v.); 4th edition, 1596 (q.v.); *A Continuance of Albions England* 1606 (q.v.).

1603

- Death of Queen Elizabeth I (24 Mar.)
  JAMES I (VI of Scotland) (–1625)
  Trial of Sir Walter Ralegh
  Plague in London
- Edward Benlowes born?
  Sir Kenelm Digby born
  Marmion Shackerley born
- Thomas Cartwright dies
  Arthur Dent dies
  William Gilbert dies

Sir William Alexander (1567?–1640)
Darius D
Reprinted in *The Monarchick Tragedies* 1604 (q.v.)

Sir Francis Bacon (1561–1626)
A Briefe Discourse, Touching the Happie Union of the Kingdomes of England, and Scotland NF
Published anonymously

Nicholas Breton (1545?–1626?)
A Merrie Dialogue Betwixt the Taker and Mistaker NF

Henry Chettle (1560?–1607)
Englandes Mourning Garment V
On the death of Queen Elizabeth (*d.* 24 March 1603)

Henry Chettle (1560?–1607), **Thomas Dekker** (1572?–1634), and **William Haughton** (1575–1605)
Patient Grissill D
Published anonymously

Henoch Clapham (*d.* 1614)
An Epistle Discoursing Upon the Present Pestilence NF

Elizabeth Melville, later **Lady Colville of Culros** (*fl.* 1603)
Ane Godlie Dreame V
In Scots. English version published in 1604 as *A Godly Dreame.*

Samuel Daniel (1562–1619)
A Panegyrike Congratulatory Delivered to the Kings Most Excellent Majesty . . . With a Defence of Ryme V
The 'Defence of Ryme' was written in answer to Campion's *Observations in the Art of English Poesie* 1602 (q.v.)

John Davies (1565–1618)
Microcosmos V

Thomas Dekker (1572?–1632)
The Wonderfull Yeare: Wherein is shewed the picture of London, lying sicke of the plague F
Published anonymously

John Dowland (1563–1626)
The Third and Last Booke of Songs or Aires V/MUS
See also *First Booke* 1597; *Second Booke* 1600

Michael Drayton (1563–1631)
The Barrons Wars in the Raigne of Edward the Second V
See *Mortimeriados* 1596. *Englands Heroicall Epistles* first published in 1597 (q.v.). Includes the sonnet sequence 'Idea'.

Michael Drayton (1563–1631)
To the Majestie of King James V

Roger Fenton (1565–1616)
A Perfume Against the Noysome Pestilence NF

John Florio (1553–1625) (tr.)
The Essayes or Morall Politicke and Millitaire Discourses of Michaell de Montaigne NF
Translated from Michel de Montaigne (1533–92)

Joseph Hall (1574–1656)
The Kings Prophecie; or, Weeping Joy V

Samuel Harsnett (1561–1631)
A Declaration of Egregious Popish Impostures NF

Philemon Holland (1552–1637) (tr.)
Moralia NF
Translated from Plutarch

King James I of England, formerly **James VI of Scotland** (1566–1625)
His Majesties Lepanto: or, Heroicall Song V
First published in 1591

King James I of England, formerly **James VI of Scotland** (1566–1625)
The True Lawe of Free Monarchies; or, The Reciprock and Mutuall Dutie Betwixt a Free King, and his Naturall Subjects NF
First published in Scots in 1598 (q.v.)

Richard Knolles (1550?–1610)
The Generall Historie of the Turkes NF

Thomas Lodge (1558–1625)
A Treatise of the Plague NF
On the London plague of 1603

Thomas Newton (1542?–1607)
Atropoion Delion; or, The Death of Delia V

John Norden (1548–1625)
A Pensive Soules Delight V

Thomas Robinson (*fl.* 1598–1603)
The Schoole of Musicke NF

Samuel Rowlands (1570?–1630?)
Ave Caesar: God Save the King V

William Shakespeare (1564–1616)
Hamlet D
Probably written 1600–1. Corrupt text, possibly assembled from actors' memories. Superior text published 1604 (q.v.); a shorter version (probably from the prompt copy) published in the First Folio 1623 (q.v.).

Robert Tofte (1562–1620) (tr.)
The Batchelars Banquet; or, A Banquet for Batchelars NF
Published anonymously. Attributed to Tofte by F.P. Wilson in 1929. Formerly attributed to Thomas Dekker. A translation of the anonymous *Les Quinze Joies de Marriage*, attributed to Antoine de La Sale (*b.* 1388?).

1604

- Hampton Court Conference (14–16 Jan.)
  Treaty of London ends war with Spain
  Fall of Ostend (Sept.)
- George Abbot born
  Jasper Mayne born
- Thomas Churchyard dies
  John Whitgift dies

Anonymous
Jacke of Dover F
Part ii published in *The Penniles Parliament of Threed-bare Poets* 1608

Henry Ainsworth (1569?–1623?) and **Francis Johnson** (1562)
An Apologie or Defence of such True Christians as are Commonly (but unjustly) called Brownists NF
Published anonymously

Sir William Alexander (1567?–1640)
Aurora V

Sir William Alexander (1567?–1640)
The Monarchick Tragedies D
Contains *The Tragedie of Croesus* and *Darius* 1603 (q.v.). The 1607 edition adds *Alexandraean Tragedy* and *Julius Caesar.*

Sir William Alexander (1567?–1640)
A Paraenesis to the Prince V
To Henry, Prince of Wales

Sir Francis Bacon (1561–1626)
Apologie NF
See also *A Declaration of the Practises & Treasons* 1601

Sir Francis Bacon (1561–1626)
Certaine Considerations Touching the Better Pacification and Edification of the Church of England NF
Published anonymously

Nicholas Breton (1545?–1626?)
Grimellos Fortunes, with His Entertainment in his Travaile F

'Bonerto' [**Nicholas Breton** (1545?–1626?)]
The Passionate Shepheard; or, The Shepheardes Love V

Robert Cawdry (*fl.* 1604)
A Table Alphabeticall DICT

Thomas Churchyard (1520?–1604)
Churchyards Good Will V
On the death of John Whitgift, archbishop of Canterbury (1530?–1604)

John Cooke (*fl.* 1614)
Epigrames V

Thomas Dekker (1572?–1632) and **Thomas Middleton** (1580?–1627)
The Honest Whore; with The Humours of the Patient Man, and The Longing Wife D
2nd edition, 1604, published as *The Converted Curtezan*. See also *The Second Part of The Honest Whore* 1630.

Thomas Dekker (1572?–1632)?
The Meeting of Gallants at an Ordinarie; or, The Walkes in Powles NF
Published anonymously. Attributed to Dekker, and also to Thomas Middleton.

Thomas Dekker (1572?–1632)
Newes from Graves-end: Sent to Nobody V
Published anonymously

Michael Drayton (1563–1631)
Moyses in a Map of his Miracles V

Michael Drayton (1563–1631)
The Owle V

Michael Drayton (1563–1631)
A Paean Triumphall V

Elizabeth Grimston (*d.* 1603)
Miscelanea. Meditations. Memoratives MISC
Partly in verse

John Hind (*fl.* 1606)
Lysimachus and Varrona F
Published anonymously. Attributed to John Hind. Contains some verse.

King James I of England, formerly **James VI of Scotland** (1566–1625)
A Counter-blaste to Tobacco NF
Published anonymously

Christopher Marlowe (1564–93)
Dr Faustus D
2nd edition, 1609; 3rd edition, 1611; 4th edition, 1616 (revised and enlarged). Many other editions.

John Marston (1576–1634)
The Malcontent D

Thomas Middleton (1580–1627)
The Ant, and the Nightingale; or, Father Hubburds Tales F

Thomas Middleton (1580–1627)
The Black Booke PS

William Perkins (1558–1602)
The First Part of the Cases of Conscience NF
See also *The Whole Treatise* 1606

Barnabe Rich (1540?–1617)
A Souldiers Wishe to Britons Welfare NF

Samuel Rowlands (1570?–1630?)
Looke to it: for, Ile Stabbe Ye V

William Shakespeare (1564–1616)
Hamlet, Prince of Denmarke D
Probably printed from Shakespeare's manuscript. Some copies dated 1605. A shorter version printed in the First Folio 1623 (q.v.). See also *Hamlet* 1603.

William Wrednot (*fl.* 1604)
Palladis Palatium: Wisdomes Pallace; or, The Fourth Part of Wits Commonwealth NF
Published anonymously. The fourth in the 'Wits Series'. See also Ling, *Politeuphuia* 1597; Meres, *Palladis Tamia* 1598; Allot, *Wits Theater* 1599.

1605

- Gunpowder Plot discovered (5 Nov.)
- Sir Thomas Browne born
  Sir William Dugdale born
  William Habington born
  Thomas Nabbes born?
  Thomas Randolph born
  Sir Robert Stapylton born?
- William Haughton dies
  John Stow dies

Anonymous
Euordanus Prince of Denmark F

Anonymous
King Leir, and his Three Daughters D
A source for Shakespeare's *King Lear* 1608 (q.v.)

Anonymous
The Life and Death of Captaine Thomas Stukeley D

Anonymous
The London Prodigall D
Misascribed to Shakespeare on the title-page. Also misattributed to Shakespeare in the second issue of the Third Folio (1664).

Sir Francis Bacon (1561–1626)
The Advancement of Learning, Divine and Humane NF
Traditionally known as *The Advancement of Learning*. A revised and expanded Latin version published as *De Dignitate & Augmentis Scientiarum* in 1623 (q.v.); translated into English as *Of the Advancement and Proficiencie of Learning* in 1640 (q.v.).

Nicholas Breton (1545?–1626?)
The Honour of Valour V

Nicholas Breton (1545?–1626?)
I Pray You Be Not Angrie: A pleasant and merry dialogue, betweene two travellers NF

Nicholas Breton (1545?–1626?)
An Olde Mans Lesson, and a Young Mans Love NF

Nicholas Breton (1545?–1626?)
The Soules Immortall Crowne V

William Camden (1551–1623)
Remaines of a Greater Worke, Concerning Britaine NF

George Chapman (1559?–1634)
All Fooles D
First performance unknown; performed at Court 1 January 1605

George Chapman (1559?–1634), **Ben Jonson** (1573?–1637), and **John Marston** (1576–1634)
Eastward Hoe D

Sir Robert Dallington (1561–1637)
A Method for Travell: Shewed by taking the view of France NF
Publication date conjectural. A pirated edition published in 1604 as *The View of Fraunce*.

Samuel Daniel (1562–1619)
Certaine Small Poems Lately Printed V
The third collected edition. Contains the first publication of *Philotas*. Also contains *Ulisses and the Syren*. *Musophilus* omitted.

John Davies (1565–1618)
Wittes Pilgrimage (by Poeticall Essaies) V

Michael Drayton (1563–1631)
Poems V
Contains *The Barrons Warres, English Heroicall Epistles, Idea, The Legend of Robert Duke of Normandie, The Legend of Matilda, The Legend of Pierce Gaveston.*

Joseph Hall (1574–1656)
Meditations and Vowes Divine and Morall NF

Thomas Heywood (1574?–1641)
If You Know Not Me, You Know No Bodie; or, The Troubles of Queene Elizabeth D
Published anonymously. See also *If You Know Not Me* 1606.

Robert Jones (*fl.* 1616)
Ultimum Vale V/MUS

Ben Jonson (1572–1637)
Sejanus his Fall D
First performed in 1603 by the King's Men

John Marston (1576–1634)
The Dutch Courtezan D

Samuel Rowlands (1570?–1630?)
Hell's Broke Loose V
On the Dutch Anabaptist, John of Leiden

Samuel Rowlands (1570?–1630?)
Humors Antique Faces V
Published anonymously. See also *The Letting of Humors Blood in the Head-vaine* 1600, and *Humors Looking Glasse* 1608.

Samuel Rowley (*d.* 1633?)
When You See Me, You Know Me; or, The famous chronicle historie of King Henry the Eight D

Joshua Sylvester (1563–1618) (tr.)
Bartas: His Devine Weekes and Workes Translated V
Translated from Guillaume de Salluste du Bartas (1544–90). Contains previously published translations. Completed in 1608.

Peter Woodhouse (*fl.* 1605)
The Flea V
A beast fable. Running-title: *Democritus his dreame.*

1606

- Execution of Guy Fawkes (31 Jan.)
- Sir William Davenant born
  Sir William Killigrew born
  Edmund Waller born
- Arthur Golding dies
  John Lyly dies

- Pierre Corneille born
  Rembrandt born

Anonymous
Caesar and Pompey D
Publication date conjectural

Anonymous
Wily Beguilde D

William Burton (*d.* 1616)
Seven Dialogues Both Pithie and Profitable NF
A translation of Erasmus' *Colloquia*

George Chapman (1559?–1634)
The Gentleman Usher D

George Chapman (1559?–1634)
Monsieur D'Olive: A comedie D

George Chapman (1559?–1634)
Sir Gyles Goosecappe Knight: A comedie D
Published anonymously

Samuel Daniel (1562–1619)
The Queenes Arcadia: A pastoral trage-comedie V
Published anonymously

John Davies (1565–1618)
Bien Venu: Greate Britaines welcome to hir greate friendes, and deere breathren the Danes V

John Day (1574–1640)
The Ile of Guls D

Thomas Dekker (1572?–1632)
The Double PP: a Papist in Armes V
Published anonymously

Thomas Dekker (1572?–1632)
Newes from Hell NF
Running-title: 'The devil's answere to Pierce Pennylesse'

Thomas Dekker (1572?–1632)
The Seven Deadly Sinnes of London NF

Michael Drayton (1563–1631)
Poemes Lyrick and Pastorall V

John Ford (1586–1640?)
Fames Memoriall; or, The Earle of Devonshire Deceased V
On the death of Charles Blount (1563–1606)

Joseph Hall (1574–1656)
The Arte of Divine Meditation NF

Joseph Hall (1574–1656)
Heaven Upon Earth; or, Of True Peace and Tranquillitie of Minde NF

Thomas Heywood (1574?–1641)
If You Know Not Me, You Know No Bodie [pt ii] D
Published anonymously. See *If You Know Not Me* 1605.

John Hind (*fl.* 1606)
Eliosto Libidinoso F
Contains some verse

Philemon Holland (1552–1637) (tr.)
The History of Twelve Caesars, Emperours of Rome NF
Translated from Suetonius, *De vita Caesarum*

Philip Howard, earl of Arundel (1557–95)
A Foure-Fould Meditation, of the Foure Last Things V
Ascribed to R[obert] S[outhwell] but actually by Howard

Ben Jonson (1572–1637)
Hymenaei; or, The Solemnities of Masque, and Barriers D
Performed 5 and 6 January 1606

John Marston (1576–1634)
Parasitaster, or The Fawne D

John Marston (1576–1634)
The Wonder of Women or The Tragedie of Sophonisba D

Henry Peacham, the younger (1578?–1642)
The Art of Drawing with the Pen, and Limming in Water Colours NF
Expanded 1612 as *Graphice; or, The Most Auncient and Excellent Art of Drawing and Limming*

William Perkins (1558–1602)
A Christian and Plaine Treatise of the Manner and Order of Pre-Destination NF
Translated by F. Cacot and T. Tuke from Perkins's *De praedestinationis modo et ordine* (Cambridge, 1598)

William Perkins (1558–1602)
The Whole Treatise of the Cases of Conscience NF
See *The First Part* 1604

Barnabe Rich (1540?–1617)
Faultes Faults, and Nothing Else But Faultes NF
See also *Roome for a Gentleman* 1609

Samuel Rowlands (1570?–1630?)
A Terrible Battell Betweene the Two Consumers of the Whole World: Time and Death V

William Warner (1558?–1609)
A Continuance of Albions England V
The 6th edition (books xiv–xvi). See *Albions England* 1586; 2nd edition, 1589; 3rd edition,1592; 4th edition, 1596; 5th edition, 1602.

Richard West (*fl.* 1606–19)
Newes from Bartholomew Fayre V
Published anonymously

1607

- Jamestown, Virginia, founded as an English colony under Captain John Smith
  Flight of the earls of Tyrone and Tyrconnel, preparing way for English and Scottish plantations in Ulster
- Robert Chamberlain born?
- Henry Chettle dies
  Abraham Fleming dies
- Madeleine de Scudéry born

Anonymous
Claudius Tiberius Nero D

Anonymous
The Fayre Mayde of the Exchange D
Sometimes attributed, doubtfully, to Thomas Heywood

Anonymous
The Puritaine; or, The Widdow of Watling-streete D
Misattributed to Shakespeare in the second issue of the Third Folio (1664). Sometimes attributed to Thomas Middleton, and to Wentworth Smith.

Anonymous
The Revengers Tragaedie D
Some copies of the 1st edition dated 1608. Sometimes attributed to Cyril Tourneur and to Thomas Middleton.

Barnabe Barnes (1571–1609)
The Divils Charter: A tragedie D
Includes some echoes of Shakespeare's *Antony and Cleopatra*

Francis Beaumont (1584–1616) and **John Fletcher** (1579–1625)
The Woman Hater D
Published anonymously

Richard Bernard (1568–1642)
The Faithfull Shepherd: The Shepheards Faithfulnesse NF

Nicholas Breton (1545?–1626?)
Wits Private Wealth NF
Many editions

George Chapman (1559?–1634)
Bussy D'Ambois D
Published anonymously. See also *The Revenge of Bussy D'Ambois* 1613.

Samuel Daniel (1562–1619)
Certaine Small Workes V
The fourth collected edition of Daniel's works

John Davies (1565–1618)
Yehovah Summa Totalis; or, All in All, and, the Same for Ever; or, An Addition to Mirum in Modum V
First word of title in Hebrew characters. See *Mirum in Modum* 1602.

John Day (1574–1640), **William Rowley** (1586?–1642?), and **George Wilkins** (*fl.* 1604–8)
The Travailes of the Three English Brothers, Sir Thomas, Sir Anthony, Mr Robert Shirley D

Thomas Dekker (1572?–1632) and **John Webster** (1580?–1635?)
The Famous History of Sir Thomas Wyat D

Thomas Dekker (1572?–1632) and **George Wilkins** (*fl.* 1604–8)
Jests to Make You Merie F

Thomas Dekker (1572?–1632)
A Knights Conjuring F
An enlargement of Dekker's *Newes from Hell* 1606 (q.v.)

Thomas Dekker (1572?–1632) and **John Webster** (1580?–1635?)
North-ward Hoe D

Thomas Dekker (1572?–1632) and **John Webster** (1580?–1635?)
West-ward Hoe D

Thomas Dekker (1572?–1632)
The Whore of Babylon D

Michael Drayton (1563–1631)
The Legend of Great Cromwel V

Edward Grimeston (*fl.* 1607) (tr.)
Admirable and Memorable Histories Containing the Wonders of Our Time NF
A translation of Simon Goulart (1543–1628), *Histoires admirables et memorables de nostre temps*

Joseph Hall (1574–1656)
Holy Observations NF

Sir John Harington (1560–1612) (tr.)
The Englishmans Docter; or, The Schoole of Salerne V
Translated from the Latin of Joannes de Mediolano, *Regimen sanitatis Salernitatum*

Thomas Heywood (1574?–1641)
A Woman Kilde with Kindnesse D

King James I of England, formerly **James VI of Scotland** (1566–1625)
Triplici Nodo, Triplex Cuneus; or, An Apologie for the Oath of Allegiance NF
Published anonymously. 2nd edition, under the king's name, published 1609.

Robert Jones (*fl.* 1616)
The First Set of Madrigals V/MUS

Ben Jonson (1572–1637)
Volpone D

Gervase Markham (1568?–1637)
Cavelarice; or, The English Horseman NF

Gervase Markham (1568?–1637)
The English Arcadia [pt i] F
Part ii published 1613

Gervase Markham (1568?–1637) (tr.)
Rodomonths Infernall; or, The Divell Conquered V
Translated from the French version by Philippe Desportes (1546–1606) of Ariosto's *Orlando Furioso*

John Marston (1576–1634)
What You Will D

Thomas Middleton (1580–1627)
Michaelmas Terme D

Thomas Middleton (1580–1627)
The Phoenix D
Published anonymously

Samuel Rowlands (1570?–1630?)
Democritus; or, Doctor Merry-man his Medicines, Against Melancholy Humors V

Samuel Rowlands (1570?–1630?)
Diogines Lanthorne V

Edward Sharpham (*fl.* 1607)
Cupids Whirligig D
Partly based on day 7, novel 6, of Boccaccio's *Decameron*

Edward Sharpham (*fl.* 1607)
The Fleire D
Adapted from John Marston's *Parasitaster* 1606 (q.v.)

Thomas Tomkis (*fl.* 1604–15)
Lingua; or, the Combat of the Tongue, and the Five Senses for Superiority D
Published anonymously

Edward Topsell (1572–1625)
The Historie of Foure-Footed Beastes NF
Draws on Konrad Gesner (1516–65), *Historia animalium* (1551–8)

George Wilkins (*fl.* 1604–8)
The Miseries of Inforst Marriage D

1608

- Commission of Inquiry into naval affairs
- Sir Aston Cokayne born
  Sir Richard Fanshawe born
  Thomas Fuller born
  John Milton born
- Sir Geoffrey Fenton dies
  Henry Lok dies?

Anonymous
The Merry Devill of Edmonton D

Anonymous
A Yorkshire Tragedy D
Misattributed on title-page to Shakespeare. Also misattributed to Shakespeare in the second issue of the Third Folio 1664 (q.v.).

Robert Armin (1565?–1610)
A Nest of Ninnies PS
An enlarged version of *Foole upon Foole* 1600 (q.v.)

Nicholas Breton (1545?–1626?)
Divine Considerations of the Soule NF

George Chapman (1559?–1634)
The Conspiracie, and Tragedie of Charles Duke of Byron, Marshall of France D

Henoch Clapham (*d.* 1614)
Errour on the Left Hand, through a Frozen Securitie NF

Henoch Clapham (*d.* 1614)
Errour on the Right Hand, through a Preposterous Zeal NF

John Day (1574–1640)
Humour Out of Breath D

John Day (1574–1640)
Law-Trickes; or, Who Woul'd Have Thought It D

Thomas Dekker (1572?–1632)
The Belman of London: Bringing to light the most notorious villanies that are now practised in the kingdome NF
Published anonymously

Thomas Dekker (1572?–1632)
Lanthorne and Candle-light; or, The Bellmans Second Nights Walke NF
A continuation of *The Belman of London* (see above)

Edward Grimeston (*fl.* 1607) (tr.)
A Generall Historie of the Netherlands: Continued unto this present yeare of our Lord 1608 NF
Translated largely from F. Le Petit (1566–*c.*1615), *La grande chronique* (1601)

Joseph Hall (1574–1656)
Characters of Vertues and Vices NF

Joseph Hall (1574–1656)
Epistles the First Volume NF
Second Volume also published 1608; *Third Volume* published 1610

Thomas Heywood (1574?–1641)
The Rape of Lucrece: A true Roman tragedie D

Ben Jonson (1572–1637)
The Characters of Two Royall Masques. The One of Blacknesse, the Other of Beautie D
Known as the *Masques of Blackness and Beauty.* Performed 6 January 1605 and 10 January 1608 respectively.

Gervase Markham (1568?–1637)
The Dumbe Knight: A historicall comedy D
Written with Lewis Machin

Thomas Middleton (1580–1627)
The Famelie of Love D
Published anonymously. Usually attributed to Middleton but also to Lording Barry.

Thomas Middleton (1580–1627)
A Mad World, My Masters D

Thomas Middleton (1580–1627)
A Tricke to Catch the Old-One D
Published anonymously

Thomas Middleton (1580–1627)
Your Five Gallants D
Publication date conjectural

Henry Peacham, the younger (1578?–1642)
The More the Merrier: Containing: threescore and odde head-lesse epigrams V

William Perkins (1558–1602)
A Discourse of the Damned Art of Witchcraft NF

Samuel Rowlands (1570?–1630?)
Humors Looking Glasse V
Largely composed of selections from *Humors Antique Faces* 1605 (q.v.), and the 1607 edition of *Humors Ordinarie* (an expanded edition of *The Letting of Humors Blood in the Head-vaine* 1600, q.v.)

William Shakespeare (1564–1616)
King Lear D
The Pied Bull Quarto (Q1). Reprinted with corrections and additions in 1619 (misdated 1608). The First Folio text of 1623 (q.v.) includes 100 lines not in Q1, which itself includes about 300 lines not in the Folio. Q1 probably represents the first version of the play, written *c.*1605–6; The First Folio text is probably a revision of *c.*1609–10. See also *King Leir, and his Three Daughters* 1605.

Robert Tofte (1562–1620) (tr.)
Ariosto's Satyres V
Despite Gervaise Markham's name on the title-page, this translation was claimed by Tofte in *The Blazon of Jealousie* 1615 (q.v.)

Daniel Tuvill (*c.*1584–1660)
Essaies Politicke, and Morall NF
Sometimes erroneously attributed to John Tovey

George Wilkins (*fl.* 1604–8)
The Painfull Adventures of Pericles Prince of Tyre F
See also Shakespeare, *Pericles, Prince of Tyre* 1609

John Wycliffe (*d.* 1384)
Two Short Treatises, Against the Orders of the Begging Friars NF

1609

- Independence of the seven United Dutch Provinces established
- Sir Matthew Hale born
  Edward Hyde, 1st earl of Clarendon, born
  Sir John Suckling born
  Benjamin Whichcote born
  Gerrard Winstanley born
- Barnabe Barnes dies
  William Warner dies

- Caravaggio dies
  Annibale Carracci dies

Anonymous
Everie Woman in Her Humor D

Anonymous
The Man in the Moone, Telling Strange Stories; or, The English Fortune-Teller NF

Anonymous
Morindos a King of Spaine F

Robert Armin (1565?–1610)
The Italian Taylor, and his Boy V

Robert Armin (1565?–1610)
The Two Maids of More-clacke D

George Chapman (1559?–1634) (tr.)
Homer Prince of Poets V
Publication date conjectural. A translation of Homer's *Iliad* in xii books. Books i, ii, vii, viii, ix, x, and xi from *Seaven Bookes of the Iliades of Homer* 1598 (q.v.); books iii, iv, v, vi, and xii printed for the first time. Dedicatory verses to Queen Anne and to Lady Wroth and the countess of Montgomery. See also *The Iliads of Homer* 1611; *Homers Odysses* 1614; *Twenty-four Bookes of Homers Odisses* 1615; *The Whole Works of Homer* 1616.

Samuel Daniel (1562–1619)
The Civile Wares Betweene the Howses of Lancaster and Yorke Corrected and Continued V
The first complete edition, in eight books. See *First Fowre Bookes* 1595, *Poeticall Essayes* 1599 (five books), *Works* 1601 (six books).

John Davies (1565–1618)
The Holy Roode; or, Christs Crosse V

John Davies (1565–1618)
Humours Heav'n on Earth: With the civile warres of death and fortune V

Thomas Dekker (1572?–1632)
Foure Birds of Noahs Arke NF

Thomas Dekker (1572?–1632)
The Guls Horne-book PS
Based on *Grobianus* by the German author Friedrich Dedekind (1525–98)

Thomas Dekker (1572?–1632)
Worke for Armorours; or, The Peace is Broken NF

Fulke Greville, Lord Brooke (1554–1628)
The Tragedy of Mustapha D
Published anonymously. Unauthorized.

Joseph Hall (1574–1656)
The Discovery of a New World; or, A Description of the South Indies, Hethero Unknowne NF
Pseudonymous translation ('by an English Mercury') by 'J[ohn] H[ealey]' of Hall's *Mundus alter et idem* [1605?]

Joseph Hall (1574–1656)
Salomon's Divine Arts, of 1. Ethickes, 2. Politickes, 3. Oeconomickes NF

Thomas Heywood (1574?–1641)
Troia Britanica; or, Great Britaines Troy V
Partly translated from Ovid

Philemon Holland (1552–1637) (tr.)
The Roman Historie NF
Translated from Ammianus Marcellinus, *Rerum gestarum libri*

Robert Jones (*fl.* 1616)
A Musicall Dreame; or, The Fourth Booke of Ayres V/MUS

Ben Jonson (1572–1637)
The Case is Altered D
Original version written *c.*1597–8; performed 1598?

Ben Jonson (1572–1637)
The Masque of Queenes D
Performed 2 February 1609

Gervase Markham (1568?–1637)
The Famous Whore, or Noble Curtizan V
Based on Joachin Du Bellay, *La vielle courtisane*

Gregory Martin (*d.* 1582) and others (tr.)
The Holie Bible BIB
The first edition of the Roman Catholic version of the Old Testament and Apocrypha: volume i dated 1609, volume ii dated 1610. See also the Rheims New Testament 1582. Both testaments together known as the Douai-Rheims version of the Douai Bible.

Thomas Middleton (1580–1627) (tr.)
Sir Robert Sherley, Sent Ambassadour in the Name of the King of Persia, to Sigismond the Third, King of Poland NF
Published anonymously. A prose translation, with additions, of *Encomia nominis et negocii D.R. Sherlaii* by Andreas Loeaecheus. The subject, Sir Robert Sherley, or Shirley (1581?–1628), was an envoy and traveller.

Barnabe Rich (1540?–1617)
Roome for a Gentleman; or, The Second Part of Faultes Collected and Gathered for the True Meridian of Dublin NF
See *Faultes Faults* 1606

Samuel Rowlands (1570?–1630?)
A Whole Crew of Kind Gossips V
Published anonymously. Includes *'Tis Merrie When Gossips Meete*, published 1602 (q.v.).

William Rowley (1585?–1642?)
A Search for Money D

William Shakespeare (1564–1616)
Troilus and Cressida D
Q1. Written *c.*1602/3. The First Folio text of 1623 (q.v.) includes Prologue and approx. 45 lines not printed in Q1.

William Shakespeare (1564–1616)
Pericles, Prince of Tyre D
A corrupt text, not wholly by Shakespeare and not included in First Folio 1623 (q.v.). Reprinted in the second issue (1664) of the Third Folio 1663 (q.v.). See also Wilkins, *The Painfull Adventures of Pericles Prince of Tyre* 1608.

William Shakespeare (1564–1616)
Shake-speares Sonnets V
Contains 154 sonnets, two of which (138 and 144) were previously published in *The Passionate Pilgrim* 1599 (q.v.) in inferior texts

Edmund Spenser (1552?–99)
The Faerie Queene V
Contains the 'Two Cantos of Mutabilitie', probably part of a projected book vii. See also *Faerie Queene* 1590, *Second Part of the Faerie Queene* 1596.

Daniel Tuvill (*c.*1584–1660)
Essayes, Morall and Theologicall NF

1610

- Scots and English settle in Ulster
  Assassination of Henry IV of France by François Ravaillac
- Lucius Cary born?
  Henry Glapthorne born
- Robert Armin dies
  Richard Bancroft dies
  Richard Knolles dies
  Edmund Tilney dies
- Paul Scarron born

William Camden (1551–1623)
Britain; or, A Chorographicall Description of the Most Flourishing Kingdomes, England, Scotland, and Ireland, and the Ilands Adjoyning NF
Translation by Philemon Holland of *Britannia* 1586 (q.v.)

Thomas Collins (*fl.* 1610–15)
The Penitent Publican V

Samuel Daniel (1562–1619)
Tethys Festival D

John Donne (1572–1631)
Pseudo-Martyr NF
Published anonymously

Robert Dowland (*c.*1586–1641)
A Musicall Banquet V/MUS
Includes songs by John Dowland

Giles Fletcher, the younger (1588?–1623)
Christs Victorie, and Triumph in Heaven, and Earth, Over, and After Death V

John Fletcher (1579–1625)
The Faithfull Shepheardesse D
Publication date uncertain

Thomas Gainsford (1566–1624?)
The Vision and Discourse of Henry the Seventh V

Joseph Hall (1574–1656)
A Common Apologie of the Church of England NF
Reprints, and replies to, *An answer to a censorious epistle* by John Robinson (no copy known)

John Heath (*fl.* 1615)
Two Centuries of Epigrammes V

Robert Jones (*fl.* 1616)
The Muses Gardin for Delights; or, The Fift Book of Ayres V/MUS

Silvester Jourdain (*d.* 1650)
A Discovery of the Barmudas, otherwise called the Ile of Divels NF

Gervase Markham (1568?–1637)
Markhams Maister-peece; or, What Doth a Horse-man Lacke NF
Many editions

John Marston (1576–1634)?
Histrio-Mastix; or, The Player Whipt D
Probably a revision by Marston of an earlier play by an unknown author

Barnabe Rich (1540?–1617)
A New Description of Ireland NF

Richard Rich (*fl.* 1610)
Newes from Virginia V

John Selden (1584–1654)
The Duello or Single Combat NF

Roger Sharpe (*fl.* 1610)
More Fooles Yet V

Robert Tofte (1562–1620) (tr.)
Honours Academie; or, The Famous Pastorall, of the Faire Shepheardess, Julietta MISC
Translated from the French of Nicolas de Montreux (*b. c.*1561), *Les bergeries de Juliette*

1611

- Richard Alleine born
  WIlliam Cartwright born
  James Harrington born
  Sir Thomas Urquhart born
- Giles Fletcher, the elder, dies
  Richard Mulcaster dies
  Sir Hugh Platt dies?

The Holy Bible BIB
The Authorized Version, born out of the Hampton Court Conference of 1604 and based on the Bishops' Bible of 1568 (q.v.). The body of revisers, about fifty strong, sat in six groups, two at Oxford, two at Cambridge, and two at Westminster.

Lancelot Andrewes (1555–1626)
Scala Coeli NF
Published anonymously

Lording Barry (1580–1629)
Ram-Alley; or, Merrie-Trickes D

Richard Brathwaite (1588?–1673)
The Golden Fleece V

William Byrd (1543–1623)
Psalmes, Songs, and Sonnets; Some Solemne, Others Joyfull V/MUS

Thomas Cartwright (1535–1603)
Christian Religion NF
Published anonymously

George Chapman (1559?–1634) (tr.)
The Iliads of Homer, Prince of Poets V
Publication date conjectural. The first complete edition of Chapman's translation of the *Iliad.* Adds books xiii–xxiv and includes new versions of books i–ii. See also *Seaven Bookes of the Iliades of Homer* 1598; *Homer Prince of Poets* 1609; *Homers Odysses* 1614; *Twenty-four Bookes of Homers Odisses* 1615; *The Whole Workes of Homer* 1616.

George Chapman (1559?–1634)
May-Day: A witty comedie D

Thomas Coryate (1577?–1617)
Coryats Crambe; or, His Colwort Twise Sodden NF

Thomas Coryate (1577?–1617)
Coryats Crudities NF

John Davies (1565–1618)
The Scourge of Folly V

John Donne (1572–1631)
An Anatomy of the World: Wherein, by occasion of the untimely death of Mistris Elizabeth Drury the frailty and the decay of this whole world is represented V
Published anonymously. Elizabeth Drury was buried on 17 December 1610. Written in the hope of securing the patronage of Elizabeth's father, Sir Robert Drury. In three parts: 'To the Praise of the Dead and the Anatomy' (probably written by Joseph Hall, afterwards bishop of Exeter and of Norwich), 'The Anatomy of the World', and 'A Funerall Elegie'. See also *The First Anniversarie* 1612.

John Donne (1572–1631)
Ignatius his Conclave: or His Inthronisation in a Late Election in Hell NF
Published anonymously. A Latin version published concurrently as *Conclave Ignati.*

Roger Fenton (1565–1616)
A Treatise of Usurie NF

Thomas Heywood (1574?–1641)
The Golden Age; or, The Lives of Jupiter and Saturne, with the Defining of the Heathen Gods D

Ben Jonson (1572–1637)
Catiline his Conspiracy D
Performed 1611 by the King's Men

Aemilia Lanyer (1569–1645)
Salve Deus Rex Judaeorum V

Thomas Middleton (1580–1627) and **Thomas Dekker** (1572?–1634)
The Roaring Girle; or, Moll Cut-Purse D

John Speed (1552?–1629)
The Genealogies Recorded in the Sacred Scriptures NF
Issued with copies of the Bible. Many editions.

John Speed (1552?–1629)
The History of Great Britaine, Under the Conquests of the Romans, Saxons, Danes and Normans NF
Woodcuts by Christopher Schweitzer. See also *The Theatre of the Empire of Great Britaine* 1612.

Cyril Tourneur (1575?–1626)
The Atheist's Tragedie; or, The Honest Man's Revenge D
Some copies of the first edition dated 1612

1612

- Trial of the Witches of Pendle (July–Aug.)
  Henry, Prince of Wales, dies (5 Nov.)
  The Dutch begin to settle Manhattan Island
- Anne Bradstreet born
  Samuel Butler born
  Richard Crashaw born?
  Thomas Fairfax born
  Thomas Killigrew born
- John Gerard dies
  Sir John Harington dies
- Robert Cecil, earl of Salisbury, dies

Thomas Adams (*c.*1583)
The Gallants Burden NF

Sir William Alexander (1567?–1640)
An Elegie on the Death of Prince Henrie V
On the death of Henry Frederick, Prince of Wales

Francis Bacon (1561–1626)
Essayes NF
38 essays. See also *Essayes* 1597, *Essayes, Civill and Morall* 1625.

Lewis Bayly (1565–1631)
The Practise of Piety NF
The second edition (enlarged). Date of first edition not known (probably also 1612). Many other editions to the 18th century.

John Brinsley, the elder (*fl.* 1633)
Ludus Literarius; or, The Grammar Schoole NF

George Chapman (1559?–1634) (tr.)
Petrarchs Seven Penitentiall Psalms, Paraphrastically Translated V

George Chapman (1559?–1634)
The Widdowes Teares: A comedie D

Robert Daborne (1578?–1628)
A Christian Turn'd Turke; or, The Tragicall Lives and Deaths of the Two Famous Pyrates, Ward and Dansiker D

Samuel Daniel (1562–1619)
The First Part of the Historie of England NF
Published anonymously. Contains books i–iii, to the end of the reign of Stephen. Continued, to the end of the reign of Edward III, 1618.

John Davies (1565–1618)
The Muses Sacrifice V

Sir John Davies (1569–1626)
A Discoverie of the True Causes why Ireland was Never Entirely Subdued NF
Davies was Attorney-General for Ireland 1606–19

Thomas Dekker (1572?–1632)
If It Be Not Good, the Divel is in It D

Thomas Dekker (1572?–1632)
Troia-Nova Triumphans, London Triumphing D

Thomas Deloney (1543?–1600)
Thomas of Reading; or, The Sixe Worthy Yeomen of the West F
The earliest extant edition. First published 1602?

John Donne (1572–1631)
The First Anniversarie. An Anatomie of the World . . . The Second Anniversarie. Of the Progres of the Soule V
Published anonymously. *The Second Anniversarie* has a separate dated title-page. Originally published as *An Anatomy of the World* 1611 (q.v.).

John Dowland (1563–1626)
A Pilgrimes Solace V/MUS

Michael Drayton (1563–1631)
Poly-Olbion [pt i] V
With notes by John Selden. Part ii published 1622 (q.v.).

Nathaniel Field (1587–1633)
A Woman is a Weather-cocke: A new comedy D

Orlando Gibbons (1583–1625)
The First Set of Madrigals and Mottets of 5 Parts V

Joseph Hall (1574–1656)
Contemplations upon the Principall Passages of the Holy Storie: The first volume NF
Second Volume (books v–viii), published 1614; *Third Volume* (books ix–xi), 1615; *Fourth Volume* (books xii, xiii on the Old Testament; book i on the New Testament), 1618; *Fifth Volume* (books xiv, xv on the Old Testament; book ii on the New Testament), 1620; *Sixth Volume* (books xvi, xvii on the Old Testament; book iii on the New Testament), 1622; *Contemplations Upon the Historie of the Old Testament: The Seventh Volume* (books xviii, xix), 1623; *Contemplations Upon the Historicall Part of the Old Testament* (books xx, xxi) 1626 (q.v.)

Thomas Heywood (1574?–1641)
An Apology for Actors NF

Richard Hooker (1554–1600)
The Answere of Mr Richard Hooker to a Supplication Preferred by Mr Walter Travers to the Lords of the Privie Counsell NF
Answers Walter Travers, *A Supplication Made to the Privy Counsel* (1612). The original controversy took place in 1586.

Richard Hooker (1554–1600)
A Learned and Comfortable Sermon of the Certaintie and Perpetuitie of Faith in the Elect NF

Richard Hooker (1554–1600)
A Learned Discourse of Justification, Workes, and How the Foundation of Faith is Overthrowne NF

Richard Hooker (1554–1600)
A Learned Sermon of the Nature of Pride NF

Richard Hooker (1554–1600)
A Remedie Against Sorrow and Feare NF

Richard Johnson (1573–1659?)
A Crowne-Garland of Goulden Roses, Gathered Out of Englands Royal Garden V

Ben Jonson (1572–1637)
The Alchemist D
Performed 1610 by the King's Men at the Globe

Henry Peacham, the younger (1578?–1642)
Minerva Britanna; or, A Garden of Heroical Devises V

Samuel Rowlands (1570?–1630?)
The Knave of Clubbes V
Published anonymously. The first edition (no copy now known), entitled *A Merry Meeting*, was published in 1600 but was ordered to be burned.

Samuel Rowlands (1570?–1630?)
The Knave of Harts V
Published anonymously

Thomas Shelton (*fl.* 1597–1629?) (tr.)
Don Quixote F
The first English translation of Cervantes' *Don Quixote* (1605), using the Roger Valpius edition of 1607. The first part only. Part ii (with revised part i) published in 1620; both parts published together in 1652.

John Speed (1552?–1629)
The Theatre of the Empire of Great Britaine NF
Published 1612, dated 1611. Text mainly taken from Camden's *Britannia* (English translation, 1610, q.v.). Continued in *The History of Great Britaine* 1611 (q.v.), though published after it.
Translated into Latin by Philemon Holland in 1616.

William Strachey (1572–1621) (ed.)
For the Colony in Virginea Britannia NF

Joshua Sylvester (1563–1618)
Lachrimae Lachrimarum; or, The Distillation of Teares Shede for the Untimely Death of the Incomparable Prince Panaretus V
An elegy on the death of Prince Henry Frederick (*d.* 1612). Also includes poems in English, French, Latin, and Italian by Walter Quin.

John Taylor (1580–1653)
The Sculler V

John Webster (1580?–1635?)
The White Divel; or, The Tragedy of Paulo Giordano Ursini, Duke of Brachiano D
Performed early 1612 at the Red Bull in Clerkenwell by Queen Anne's Men

George Wither (1588–1667)
Prince Henries Obsequies; or, Mournefull Elegies Upon his Death V
On the death of Henry Frederick, Prince of Wales (*d.* 1612)

1613

- James I's daughter, Elizabeth, marries the Elector Palatine, Frederick V
  Death of Sir Thomas Overbury by poisoning (14 Sept.)
  Globe Theatre burns down
- John Cleveland born
  Jeremy Taylor born
  Sir Henry Vane born
- Thomas Bedingfield dies
  Henry Constable dies
  Thomas Twyne dies
- François de la Rochfoucauld born

Anonymous
Scoggins Jestes F
Not in fact by John Scogan (Scoggin). See also *The Jestes of Skogyn* 1570, *The First and Best Part of Scoggins Jests* 1626.

Thomas Adams (*c.*1583)
The White Devil; or, The Hypocrite Uncased NF

Francis Beaumont (1584–1616) and **John Fletcher** (1579–1625)
The Knight of the Burning Pestle D

Published anonymously. Probably written and performed in 1607.

Francis Beaumont (1584–1616)
The Masque of the Inner Temple and Grayes Inne D
Performed 20 February 1613

Nicholas Breton (1545?–1626?)
The Uncasing of Machivils Instructions to his Sonne V
Published anonymously

William Browne (1591–1643)
Britannia's Pastorals [bk i] V
Book ii published in 1616 (q.v.); both books published together in 1625

Thomas Campion (1567–1620)
The First Booke of Ayres V/MUS
Publication date conjectural. See also *Two Bookes of Ayres* 1613, *Third and Fourth Booke of Ayres* 1617.

Thomas Campion (1567–1620)
A Relation of the Late Royall Entertainment Given by the Lord Knowles D

Thomas Campion (1567–1620)
Songs of Mourning: Bewailing the Untimely Death of Prince Henry V/MUS
On the death of Henry Frederick, Prince of Wales (*d.* 1612). Music by Giovanni Coperario or Coprario (*c.*1570–1626), said to have been an Englishman by the name of John Cooper.

Thomas Campion (1567–1620)
Two Bookes of Ayres V/MUS
Publication date conjectural. See *Third and Fourth Booke of Ayres* 1617.

Elizabeth Cary, Viscountess Falkland (1585–1639)
The Tragedie of Mariam, the Faire Queene of Jewry D
The first full-length original play to be published by a woman

George Chapman (1559?–1634)
An Epicede or Funerall Song V
Published in 1613, dated 1612. On the death (1612) of Henry Frederick, Prince of Wales.

George Chapman (1559?–1634)
The Memorable Maske of the Two Honorable Houses or Inns of Courte; the Middle Temple and Lyncolns Inne D
Publication date conjectural

George Chapman (1559?–1634)
The Revenge of Bussy D'Ambois: A tragedie D
See *Bussy D'Ambois* 1607

John Davies (1565–1618)
The Muses-Teares for the Losse of their Hope V
On the death of Henry Frederick, Prince of Wales (*d.* 1612)

William Drummond (1585–1649)
Teares on the Death of Meliades V
On the death of Henry Frederick, Prince of Wales (*d.* 1612)

Sir John Hayward (1564?–1627)
The Lives of the III Normans, Kings of England NF

Thomas Heywood (1574?–1641)
The Brazen Age D

Thomas Heywood (1574?–1641)
The Silver Age D

Gervase Markham (1568?–1637)
The English Husbandman: The first part NF
Second part published 1614 (with *The Pleasures of Princes*). Both parts published together in 1635.

John Marston (1576–1634)? and **William Barksted** (*fl.* 1611)
The Insatiate Countesse: A tragedie D
Probably drafted by Marston (whose authorship is not acknowledged) and completed by Barksted (called Bacster on the title-page). Co-authorship spuriously attributed to Lewis Machin.

Henry Parrot (*fl.* 1606–26)
Laquei Ridiculosi; or, Springes for Woodcocks V

Samuel Purchas (1577–1626)
Purchas his Pilgrimage; or, Relations of the World and the Religions Observed in all Ages and Places Discovered, from the Creation unto this Present NF

Barnabe Rich (1540?–1617)
The Excellency of Good Women NF

Barnabe Rich (1540?–1617)
Opinion Diefied [sic] NF

Sir Anthony Sherley (1565–1635?)
Travels into Persia NF

George Wither (1588–1667)
Abuses Stript, and Whipt; or, Satirical Essayes V

George Wither (1588–1667)
Epithalamia; or, Nuptiall Poems V
Published in 1613, dated 1612

Richard Zouch (1590–1661)
The Dove; or, Passages of Cosmography V

1614

- Henry More born
- Sir William Cornwallis dies
  Alexander Neville dies
  Isaac Causaubon dies
- El Greco dies

Anonymous
The Life and Death of Hector V
A free and modernized verse paraphrase of Lydgate's *Troy Book* 1513 (q.v.). Often misattributed to Thomas Heywood.

Anonymous
The Maske of Flowers D
A Relation of all Matters Passed, Especially in France and the Low Countries, Touching the Causes of the Warre now in Cleveland PER
Earliest extant translation, by Robert Booth, of *Mercurius Gallobelgicus*, the first European news serial published annually, and subsequently semi-annually, in Cologne and Frankfurt, between 1594 and 1635

Thomas Adams (*c.*1583)
The Divells Banket [i.e. Banquet] NF

Sir William Alexander (1567?–1640)
Doomes-day; or, The Great Day of the Lords Judgement V

Richard Brathwaite (1588?–1673)
The Poets Willow; or, The Passionate Shepheard V
Published anonymously

Richard Brathwaite (1588?–1673)
The Schollers Medley; or, An Intermixt Discourse Upon Historicall and Poeticall Relations NF

William Browne (1591–1643)
The Shepheard's Pipe V
Includes poems by Christopher Brooke, George Wither, and John Davies and other poems by Wither

Thomas Campion (1567–1620)
The Description of a Maske: Presented at the Mariage of the Earle of Somerset D

George Chapman (1559?–1634)
Andromeda Liberata; or, The Nuptials of Perseus and Andromeda V
On the marriage of Robert Carr, earl of Somerset, and Frances Howard, formerly countess of Essex

George Chapman (1559?–1634) (tr.)
Homers Odysses V
Publication date conjectural. Books i–xii. See also *Seaven Bookes of the Iliades of Homer* 1598; *Homer Prince of Poets* 1609; *The Iliads of Homer* 1611; *Twenty-four Bookes of Homers Odisses* 1615; *The Whole Workes of Homer* 1616.

John Cooke (*fl.* 1614)
Greene's Tu quoque; or, The Cittie Gallant D

William Drummond (1585–1649)
Poems by William Drummond. Of Hawthornden V
Publication date uncertain

Sir Arthur Gorges (1577?–1625) (tr.)
Lucans Pharsalia: Containing the Civill Warres Betweene Caesar and Pompey V

Joseph Hall (1574–1656)
Works NF
Published 1614, dated 1615

Richard Hooker (1554–1600)
Two Sermons Upon Part of S. Judes Epistle NF

William Lithgow (1582–1645?)
A Most Delectable, and True Discourse, of an Admired and Painefull Peregrination in Europe, Asia and Affricke NF
See also *Rare Adventures, and Painefull Peregrinations* 1632

Thomas Lodge (1558–1625) (tr.)
The Workes of Lucius Annaeus Seneca, both Morrall and Natural EDN
With a life of Seneca by Justus Lipsius. 2nd edition, 1620; 3rd edition, 1632.

Gervase Markham (1568?–1637)
Cheape and Good Husbandry NF
Abridged as *Markhams Methode or Epitome* 1616

Richard Niccols (1584–1616)
The Furies. With Vertues Encomium; or, The Image of Honour V

John Norden (1548)
The Labyrinth of Mans Life; or, Vertues Delight and Envies Opposite V

Sir Thomas Overbury (1581–1613)
A Wife, Now a Widdowe V
The enlarged edition of 1614 contain's Overbury's celebrated *Characters*

Sir Walter Ralegh (1552?–1618)
The History of the World NF
Published anonymously. Many editions.

Barnabe Rich (1540?–1617)
The Honestie of this Age PS

John Selden (1584–1654)
Titles of Honor NF

Joshua Sylvester (1563) (tr.)
The Parliament of Vertues Royal V
Translated from Jean Bertaut. Also includes translations of poems by du Bartas. See also *Second Session* 1615.

Robert Tailor (*fl.* 1613–15)
The Hogge Hath Lost His Pearle: A comedy D

George Wither (1588–1667)
A Satyre V

1615

- The Overbury scandal: Lord and Lady Somerset accused of poisoning Sir Thomas Overbury (see 1613)
- Richard Baxter born
  Sir John Denham born
  John Lacy born
  John Lilburne born
  Joshua Poole born (c.1615)
- Richard Hakluyt dies
  Francis Beaumont dies

John Andrewes (*fl.* 1615)
The Anatomie of Basenesse; or, The Foure Quarters of a Knave V

Richard Brathwaite (1588?–1673)
A Strappado for the Divell V
By 'Misosukos' to his friend 'Philokrates'

Nicholas Breton (1545?–1626?)
Characters Upon Essaies Morall, and Divine NF

George Chapman (1559?–1634) (tr.)
Twenty-four Bookes of Homers Odisses V
Publication date conjectural. Books i–xii from *Homers Odysses* 1614 (q.v.). See also *Seaven Bookes of the Iliades of Homer* 1598; *Homer Prince of Poets* 1609; *The Iliads of Homer* 1611; *The Whole Workes of Homer* 1616.

Thomas Collins (*fl.* 1610–15)
The Teares of Love; or, Cupids Progresse V

Samuel Daniel (1562–1619)
Hymens Triumph: A pastorall tragicomaedie V

John Fletcher (1579–1625) and **Francis Beaumont** (1584–1616)
Cupids Revenge D
'By John Fletcher'—in fact in collaboration with Francis Beaumont. Based on Sir Philip Sidney's *Arcadia* 1590 (q.v.). Performed at Court on 5 January 1612.

Sir John Harington (1560–1612)
Epigrams Both Pleasant and Serious V
See also *The Most Elegant and Witty Epigrams* 1618

Thomas Heywood (1574?–1641)
The Foure Prentises of London. With the Conquest of Jerusalem D

Samuel Rowlands (1570?–1630?)
The Melancholie Knight V

George Sandys (1578–1644)
A Relation of a Journey Begun An: Dom: 1610 NF
Many editions

Thomas Scot (*fl.* 1616)
Philomythie or Philomythologie: Wherein outlandish birds, beasts, and fishes, are taught to speake true English plainely V
Published 1615, dated 1616. Second part published in 1616.

Joshua Sylvester (1563–1618) (tr.)
The Second Session of the Parliament of Vertues Reall V
Translations from Pierre Mathieu (1563–1621) and from Guillaume de Salluste du Bartas (1544–90). See *The Parliament of Vertues Royal* 1614.

Robert Tofte (1562–1620) (tr.)
The Blazon of Jealousie V
Translated from Benedetto Varchi (1605–65)

Thomas Tomkis (*fl.* 1604–15)
Albumazar: A comedy D
Published anonymously

George Wither (1588–1667)
Fidelia V
Published anonymously

George Wither (1588–1667)
The Shepherds Hunting V

1616

- Sir Walter Ralegh released from the Tower to undertake a voyage to Guiana (see 1617)
  Trial of Lord and Lady Somerset for their part in the murder of Sir Thomas Overbury (May)

- James I begins to sell peerages
  Sir Edward Coke, Lord Chief Justice, removed from office
- Joseph Beaumont born
  Nicholas Culpeper born
  Sir Roger L'Estrange born
  John Wallis born
- William Shakespeare dies
- Cervantes dies

Anonymous
The Honest Lawyer D

Thomas Adams (*c.*1583)
A Divine Herball NF

Francis Beaumont (1584–1616) and **John Fletcher** (1579)
The Scornful Ladie D

William Browne (1591–1643)
Britannia's Pastorals. The Second Booke V
Book i published in 1613 (q.v.); both books published together in 1625

John Bullokar (*fl.* 1622)
An English Expositor NF

George Chapman (1559?–1634) (tr.)
The Divine Poem of Musœus. First of all Books V
A translation of Musaeus, *De Herone et Leandro* [Hero and Leander]

George Chapman (1559?–1634) (tr.)
The Whole Workes of Homer; Prince of Poetts V
Publication date conjectural. See also *Seaven Bookes of the Iliades of Homer* 1598; *Homer Prince of Poets* 1609; *The Iliads of Homer* 1611; *Homers Odysses* 1614; *Twenty-four Bookes of Homers Odisses* 1615.

Sir William Cornwallis (1579?–1614)
Essayes or Rather, Encomions, Prayses of Sadnesse NF

Sir William Cornwallis (1579?–1614)
Essayes of Certaine Paradoxes NF
Anonymous

Thomas Coryate (1577?)
From the Court of the Great Mogul NF

John Cotta (1575?)
The Triall of Witch-craft NF

John Davies (1565–1618)
A Select Second Husband for Sir Thomas Overburies Wife, Now a Matchlesse Widow V

Thomas Gainsford (1566–1624?)
The Historie of Trebizond F
A collection of romantic stories

Godfrey Goodman (1583–1656)
The Fall of Man; or, The Corruption of Nature NF
See response by George Hakewill, *An Apologie of the Power and Providence of God* 1627

William Haughton (1575–1605)
English-men for my Money; or, A Pleasant Comedy, called, A Woman Will Have Her Will D
Published anonymously

King James I of England, formerly **James VI of Scotland** (1566–1625)
Works WKS

Ben Jonson (1572–1637)
Works WKS
First Folio . See also 1640.

Richard Niccols (1584–1616)
Sir Thomas Overburies Vision V
Published anonymously

Captain John Smith (1580–1631)
A Description of New England; or, The Observations, and Discoveries, of Captain John Smith NF

Robert Southwell SJ (1561?–95)
S. Peters Complaint. And Saint Mary Magdalens Funerall Teares V
'By R.S. of the Society of Jesus'. See also *Marie Magdalens Funeral Teares* 1591 and *Saint Peters Complaint* 1595.

1617

- George Villiers created earl of Buckingham (created duke 1623)
  Sir Walter Ralegh's expedition to Guiana
- Elias Ashmole born
  Ralph Cudworth born
  Sir George Wharton born
- Thomas Coryate dies
  Barnabe Rich dies

Thomas Campion (1567–1620)
The Third and Fourth Booke of Ayres V/MUS
Publication date conjectural. See *First Booke of Ayres, Two Bookes of Ayres* 1613.

William Cecil, Lord Burghley (1520–98)
Certaine Precepts, or Directions, for the Well-Ordering and Carriage of a Mans Life . . . NF
Anonymous

John Davies (1565–1618)
Wits Bedlam V
Published anonymously. Epigrams.

Leonard Digges (1588–1635) (tr.)
The Rape of Proserpine V
A translation of *De raptu Proserpinae* by Claudian (Claudius Claudianus)

William Drummond (1585–1649)
Forth Feasting V
Published anonymously. Written on the occasion of James I's visit to Scotland.

Robert Greene (1558–92)
Alcida Greenes Metamorphosis F

John Lyly (1554–1606)
Euphues the Anatomy of Wit F
Includes *Euphues and his England.* Other editions: 1623, 1630, 1631, 1636. See *Euphues* 1578, 1580.

Thomas Middleton (1580–1727) and **William Rowley** (1585?–1642?)
A Faire Quarrell D

Fynes Moryson (1566–1630)
An Itinerary Written by Fynes Moryson Gent. NF

'Constantia Munda' (*fl.* 1617)
The Worming of a Mad Dogge; or, A Soppe for Cerberus the Jaylor of Hell NF
A reply to Joseph Swetnams' *The Araignment of Lewde, Idle, Froward, and Unconstant Women* 1617. See also Rachel Speght 1617 below.

Barnabe Rich (1540?–1617)
The Irish Hubbub; or, The English Hue and Crie NF

Rachel Speght (*b.* 1597)
A Mouzell for Melastomus, the Cynicall Bayter of, and Foule Mouthed Barker Against Evahs Sex NF
Another reply to Joseph Swetnam, *The Araignment of Lewde, Idle, Froward, and Unconstant Women* 1617. See also 'Constantia Munda', *The Worming of a Mad Dogge* 1617

1618

- Start of the Thirty Years War (1618–48)
  Synod of Dort (Nov.)
  Sir Walter Ralegh executed (29 Oct.)
- Abraham Cowley born
  Richard Lovelace born
  Sir Edward Sherburne born
  Joshua Sprigge born
- John Bridges, bishop of Oxford, dies
  John Davies, of Hereford, dies
  Richard Stanyhurst dies
  Joshua Sylvester dies

Nicholas Breton (1545?–1626)
Conceyted Letters, Newly Layde Open NF
Anonymous. Perhaps edited by Gervase Markham, to whom the work is sometimes attributed.

Nicholas Breton (1545?–1626?)
The Court and Country; or, A Briefe Discourse Betweene the Courtier and Country-Man NF

John Brinsley, the elder (*fl.* 1633) (tr.)
Ovids Metamorphosis Translated Grammatically NF

George Chapman (1559?–1634) (tr.)
The Georgicks of Hesiod V
A translation of Hesiod's *Works and Days*

Thomas Coryate (1577?–1617)
Mr Thomas Coriat to his Friends in England . . . From Agra NF

Nathaniel Field (1587–1633)
Amends for Ladies: A comedie D

Thomas Gainsford (1566–1624?)
The Glory of England; or, A True Description of Blessings Whereby She Triumpheth Over all Nations NF

Sir John Harington (1560–1612)
The Most Elegant and Witty Epigrams of Sir John Harrington V
See also *Epigrams Both Pleasant and Serious* 1615

'Novus Homo' [Geffray Minshul (1594?)**]**
Certaine Characters and Essayes of Prison and Prisoners NF

John Selden (1584–1654)
The Historie of Tithes NF

John Taylor (1580–1653)
The Pennyles Pilgrimage; or, The Money-lesse Perambulation, of John Taylor, Alias the Kings Majesties Water-Poet NF
Partly in verse

1619

- Inigo Jones designs the Banqueting House in Whitehall
- Richard Allestree born
  William Chamberlayne born
  Walter Charleton born
- Samuel Daniel dies

Sir Francis Bacon (1561–1626)
The Wisedome of the Ancients NF
Translated by Sir Arthur Gorges. First published in Latin as *De Sapienta Veterum* in 1609.

Francis Beaumont (1584–1616) and **John Fletcher** (1579–1625)
A King and No King D

Francis Beaumont (1584–1616) and **John Fletcher** (1579–1625)
The Maides Tragedy D
Published anonymously. Performed 1612/13 before Prince Charles, the Lady Elizabeth, and the Elector Palatine.

Edmund Bolton (1575?–post 1634) (tr.)
The Roman Histories of Lucius Julius Florus NF

'Musophilus' [Richard Brathwaite (1588?–1673)]
A New Spring Shadowed in Sundry Pithie Poems V

Sir John Davies (1569–1626)
Nosce Teipsum V
See also *Nosce Teipsum* 1599, 1622

Thomas Deloney (1543?–1600)
The Pleasant History of John Winchcomb: In his younger yeares called Jack of Newberie F
The earliest extant edition

William Drummond (1585–1649)
A Midnights Trance: Wherein is discoursed of death, the nature of soules, and estate of immortalitie NF
Republished as *A Cypresse Grove* in *Flowres of Sion* 1623 (q.v.)

Henry Hutton (*fl.* 1619)
Follie's Anatomie; or, Satyres and Satiricall Epigrams V

Thomas Middleton (1580–1627)
The Inner-Temple Masque: or Masque of Heroes D
Probably performed between 6 January (Twelfth Night) and 2 February (Candlemas) 1619

Thomas Middleton (1580–1627)
The Triumphs of Love and Antiquity D
Performed and published 29 October 1619

Samuel Purchas (1577–1626)
Purchas his Pilgrim NF

William Shakespeare (1564–1616)
A Midsommer Nights Dreame D
Published 1619, dated 1600. See *A Midsommer Nights Dreame* 1600.

George Wither (1588–1667)
A Preparation to the Psalter NF

1620

- The Pilgrim Fathers leave Plymouth in *The Mayflower*, landing at Plymouth Rock on Cape Cod
- Alexander Brome born
  John Evelyn born
  Richard Flecknoe born (c.1620)
  Lucy Hutchinson born
  Marchamont Nedham born
  Henry Neville born
- Thomas Campion dies
  Richard Carew, of Antony, dies
  Robert Tofte dies

Anonymous
The Decameron F
The first English translation (by John Florio?) of Boccaccio

Anonymous
Swetnam, the Woman-hater, Arraigned by Women: A new comedie D
A reply to Joseph Swetnam, *The Araignment of Lewde, Idle, Froward, and Unconstant Women* 1617 and the responses by 'Constantia Munda' and Rachel Speght 1617 (q.v.)

Anonymous
The Two Merry Milke-Maids D
Variously attributed to John Cumber, John Cooke, John Chalkhill, and to John Clapham

Sir Francis Bacon (1561–1626)
Novum Organum NF
In Latin. Part ii of the *Instauratio*.

Francis Beaumont (1584–1616) and **John Fletcher** (1579–1625)
Phylaster; or, Love Lyes a Bleeding D

Richard Brathwaite (1588?–1673)
Essaies Upon the Five Senses, with a Pithie One upon Detraction NF

William Cavendish, 2nd earl of Devonshire (1591?–1628)
Horæ Subseciae: Observations and discourses NF
Published anonymously. Also attributed to Grey Brydges, 5th baron Chandos, to Gilbert Cavendish, and to Thomas Hobbes.

Thomas Dekker (1572?–1632)
Dekker his Dreame V

John Ford (1586–1640?)
A Line of Life: Pointing at the immortalitie of a vertuous name NF

Ben Jonson (1572–1637)
Epicoene; or, The Silent Woman: A comedie D
Performed 1609 or early 1610 by the Children of the Queen's Revels at the Whitefriars. First published in the folio *Workes* of 1616 (q.v.).

Thomas Middleton (1580–1627) and **William Rowley** (1585?–1642?)
The World Tost at Tennis D

Sir Thomas Overbury (1581–1613) (tr.)
The First and Second Part of the Remedy of Love V
Translated from Ovid, *Remedia amoris*

Henry Peacham, the younger (1578?–1642)
Thalias Banquet: Furnished with an hundred and odde dishes of newly devised epigrammes V

Francis Quarles (1592–1644)
A Feast for Wormes: Set forth in a poeme of the history of Jonah V

Samuel Rowlands (1570?–1630?)
The Night-Raven V

Richard Brathwaite (1588?–1673)
Times Curtaine Drawne; or, The Anatomie of Vanitie V

'Democritus Junior' [Robert Burton (1577–1640)]
The Anatomy of Melancholy NF
Eight editions to 1676

Sir Thomas Culpeper, the elder (1578–1662)
A Tract Against Usurie NF
Published anonymously

John Fletcher (1579–1625)
The Tragedy of Thierry King of France, and his Brother Theodoret D
Published anonymously. Written by Fletcher, assisted by Philip Massinger and others.

Peter Heylyn (1600–62)
Microcosmus: or, A Little Description of the Great World NF
Eight editions to 1639. See also *Cosmographie* 1652.

Richard Johnson (1573–1659?)?
The History of Tom Thumbe, the Little F
Published anonymously. Attributed to Johnson.

Thomas Lodge (1558–1625) (tr.)
A Learned Summary upon the Famous Poeme of William of Saluste Lord of Bartas NF
Translated from French

William Mason (*fl.* 1621)
A Handful of Essaies or Imperfect Offers NF

Thomas Middleton (1580–1627)
The Sunne in Aries: A noble solemnity performed through the Citie D
Performed for the confirmation of the Lord Mayor of London in October 1621

Thomas Mun (1571–1641)
A Discourse of Trade, from England unto the East-Indies NF

Francis Quarles (1592–1644)
Hadassa; or, The History of Queene Ester V

George Sandys (1578–1644) (tr.)
The First Five Books of Ovid's Metamorphosis V
Published anonymously. See also *Ovid's Metamorphosis* 1626.

Rachel Speght (*b.* 1597)
Mortalities Memorandum: With a dreame prefixed, imaginarie in manner, reall in matter V

1621

- Trial and condemnation of Francis Bacon
- Roger Boyle, 1st earl of Orrery, born
  Andrew Marvell born
- John Barclay dies
  Mary Herbert, countess of Pembroke, dies
- Jean de la Fontaine born

John Ashmore (*fl.* 1621) (tr.)
Certain Selected Odes of Horace, Englished; and their Arguments Annexed V

Richard Brathwaite (1588?–1673)
Natures Embassie; or, The Wilde-Mans Measures V

John Taylor (1580–1653)
The Praise, Antiquity, and Commodity, of Beggery, Beggers, and Begging V

John Taylor (1580–1653)
Superbiae Flagellum; or, The Whip of Pride V

George Wither (1588–1667) (tr.)
The Songs of the Old Testament V/MUS

Lady Mary Wroth (1586?–post 1640)
The Countesse of Mountgomeries Urania F
Partly in verse. The author was Sir Philip Sidney's niece.

1622

- Sir Richard Hawkins born
  Algernon Sidney born
  Henry and Thomas Vaughan born
- Sir Henry Savile dies
- Molière (Jean-Baptiste Poquelin) born

Henry Ainsworth (1569?–1623)
Annotations upon the Five Bookes of Moses, and the Booke of Psalmes NF
The six parts were first published separately in 1616 (Genesis), 1617 (Exodus, Psalms), 1618 (Leviticus), and 1619 (Numbers, Deuteronomy)

Robert Aylet (1583–1655?)
Peace with Her Foure Garders: Five morall meditations V

Robert Aylet (1583–1655)
Thrifts Equipage: Five divine and morall meditations V

Sir Francis Bacon (1561–1626)
The Historie of the Raigne of King Henry the Seventh NF
Includes a portrait of Henry VII by the engraver John Payne (*d.* 1647?)

Nicholas Breton (1545?–1626?)
Strange Newes Out of Divers Countries NF

Sir John Davies (1569–1626)
Nosce Teipsum V
See also *Nosce Teipsum* 1599, 1619

John Donne (1572–1631)
Sermon on Acts 1:8 NF
Preached to the Honourable Company of the Virginian Plantation, 13 November 1622

John Donne (1572–1631)
Sermon on Judges 20: 15 NF
Preached 15 September 1622

Michael Drayton (1563–1631)
The Second Part, or a Continuance of Poly-Olbion from the Eighteenth Song V
See *Poly-Olbion* part i, 1612

William Gouge (1578–1653)
Of Domesticall Duties Eight Treatises NF

John Hagthorpe (*fl.* 1622–7)
Divine Meditations, and Elegies V

Patrick Hannay (*d.* 1629?)
The Nightingale. Sheretine and Mariana. A Happy Husband. Eligies on the Death of Queene Anne. Songs and Sonnets V
A Happy Husband first published separately in 1619 with Richard Brathwait's *Description of a Good Wife*; *Elegies on Queene Anne* also published separately in 1619

Sir Richard Hawkins (*c.*1562–1622)
The Observations of Sir Richard Hawkins Knight in his Voiage into the South Sea NF

Sir John Hayward (1564?–1627)
Davids Teares NF
Commentary on Psalms vi and xxxii

Ben Jonson (1572–1637)
The Masque of Augures D
Published in 1622, dated 1621, in two states: one anonymous, the other with a final note initialled 'B.J'. Performed 6 January 1622, and, in an expanded version, on 5 or 6 May 1622.

Gervase Markham (1568?–1637) and **William Sampson** (1590?–*c.*1656)
Herod and Antipater D

Philip Massinger (1583–1640) and **Thomas Dekker** (1572?–1634)
The Virgin Martir: A tragedie D

Thomas May (1595–1650)
The Heire: An excellent comedie D

Henry Peacham, the younger (1578?–1642)
The Compleat Gentleman NF

Samuel Rowlands (1570?–1630?)
Good Newes and Bad Newes V

William Shakespeare (1564–1616)
Othello D
Performed before James I on 1 November 1604. A different and longer text published in the First Folio 1623 (q.v.).

John Taylor (1580–1653)
A Memorial of all the English Monarchs V

George Wither (1588–1667)
Faire-Virtue, the Mistresse of Phil'arete V

George Wither (1588–1667)
Juvenilia V

1623

- Prince Charles and the duke of Buckingham travel incognito to Spain in an attempt to arrange marriage between Charles and the Infanta Maria: negotiations broken off (Dec.) leading to war (see 1624)
- Sir William Petty born
- William Byrd dies
  William Camden dies
  Giles Fletcher, the younger, dies
- Blaise Pascal born

John Abbot (1588?–1650)
Jesus Praefigured; or, A Poëm of the Holy Name of Jesus in Five Bookes V
Only two books published

Robert Aylet (1583–1655)
Joseph; or, Pharoah's Favourite V
Published anonymously

Sir Francis Bacon (1561–1626)
De Dignitate & Augmentis Scientiarum NF
A translation, enlarged and edited by William Rawley (1588?–1667), Bacon's chaplain, of *The Advancement of Learning* 1605 (q.v.). See also *Of the Advancement and Proficiencie of Learning* 1640.

John Bingham (*fl.* 1623) (tr.)
Anabasis: The historie of Xenophon NF
A translation of Xenophon's *Anabasis* and Justus Lipsius (1547–1606), *De militia Romana*

Henry Constable (1562–1613) (tr.)
The Catholike Moderator; or, A Moderate Examination of the Doctrine of the Protestants NF
Published anonymously. A translation of a reply to a work by Roberto Francesco Romolo Bellarmino (1542–1621).

Samuel Daniel (1562–1619)
The Whole Workes of Samuel Daniel Esquire in Poetrie WKS

John Donne (1572–1631)
Encaenia NF
A sermon preached at the dedication of the new chapel at Lincoln's Inn, Ascension Day 1623

John Donne (1572–1631)
Three Sermons upon Speciall Occasions NF
See also *Foure Sermons* 1625, *Five Sermons* 1626, *Six Sermons* 1634, *LXXX Sermons* 1640, *Fifty Sermons* 1649

William Drummond (1585–1649)
Flowres of Sion V
See also *A Midnights Trance* 1619

Owen Felltham (1602?–68)
Resolves, Divine, Morall, Politicall MISC
Publication date conjectural. Eight editions to 1661; 12th edition, 1709.

Giles Fletcher, the younger (1588?–1623)
The Reward of the Faithfull. The Labour of the Faithfull. The Grounds of Our Faith NF

William Lisle (1579?–1637) (tr. and ed.)
A Saxon Treatise Concerning the Old and New Testament NF
Translated from Aelfric, Abbot of Eynsham. In Anglo-Saxon and English.

'Don Diego Puede-Ser' [James Mabbe (1572–1642?)] (tr.)
The Rogue; or, The Life of Guzman de Alfarache F
Published in 1623, though one variant dated 1622. Translated from Mateo Alemán (1547–1615), *Guzmán de Alfarache* (published in two parts, 1599, 1602). Alemán's work began the vogue for the picaresque novel.

Philip Massinger (1583–1640)
The Duke of Millaine: A tragaedie D

Edward Misselden (*fl.* 1608–54)
The Circle of Commerce; or, The Balance of Trade NF

William Shakespeare (1564–1616)
Comedies, Histories and Tragedies: Published according to the true originall copies D
The First Folio. The first collected edition of Shakespeare's plays (36 in all), compiled by John Heminges and Henry Condell. Includes eighteen plays not previously printed:
All's Well That Ends Well (probably written 1602–3)
Antony and Cleopatra (written no later than 1606)
As You Like It (no early performances definitely recorded)
The Comedy of Errors (probably performed 1594 and probably printed from Shakespeare's MS)
Coriolanus (written *c.*1608)
Cymbeline (written 1609–10)
Henry VIII (originally called *All is True*; probably a collaboration with John Fletcher)
Henry VI Part 1 (authorship disputed: see *Henry VI Part 2* 1594 and *Henry VI Part 3* 1595)

Julius Caesar (probably written and performed 1599)
King John (written some time before 1598 and probably printed from Shakespeare's MS)
Macbeth (usually dated *c.*1606; probably includes episodes by Thomas Middleton)
Measure for Measure (performed at Court 26 December 1604 and probably written in the same year)
The Taming of the Shrew (see the related, anonymous, play *The Taming of a Shrew* 1594)
The Tempest (written 1610/11 and performed at Court 1 November 1611)
Timon of Athens (possibly written with Thomas Middleton and usually dated 1607–8)
Twelfth Night (probably written *c.*1601)
The Two Gentlemen of Verona (one of Shakespeare's earliest plays, mentioned by Francis Meres in 1598)
The Winter's Tale (probably written 1609–10)
Some previously printed plays also published here in superior texts. Three collaborative plays—*Pericles, Cardenio* (now vanished), and *Two Noble Kinsmen*—omitted. Also contains the Droeshout portrait. Includes commendatory verses by Ben Jonson, Hugh Holland, Leonard Digges, and James Mabbe. Second Folio, 1632; Third Folio, 1663; Fourth Folio, 1685 (qq.v.).

John Webster (1580?–1635?)
The Devils Law-Case; or, When Women Goe to Law, the Devill is Full of Business D
Written *c.*1619 and performed by Queen Anne's Men (probably at the Cockpit)

John Webster (1580?–1635?)
The Duchess of Malfi D
First performed at the Blackfriars and Globe Theatres by the King's Men (in April 1614)

George Wither (1588–1667)
The Hymnes and Songs of the Church V/MUS
Published anonymously. Music by Orlando Gibbons. Several editions in 1623.

1624

- James I declares war on Spain
- Margaret Cavendish, duchess of Newcastle, born?
  George Fox born
  Edward Howard born
- Thomas Blenerhasset dies?
  Stephen Gosson dies
- Jacob Boehme dies

Anonymous
Loves Garland; or, Posies for Rings, Hand-kerchers, and Gloves ANTH
Verse miscellany

Anonymous
The Tragedy of Nero D

George Abbot (1562–1633)
A Treatise of the Perpetuall Visibilitie and Succession of the True Church in All Ages NF
Published anonymously

Sir William Alexander (1567?–1640)
An Encouragement to Colonies NF

'Philonactophil' [Edmund Bolton (1575?–1634)]
Nero Caesar; or, Monarchie Depraved NF

George Chapman (1559?–1634) (tr.)
Batrachomyomachia V
Publication date conjectural. The original work, ascribed to Homer in antiquity, is not by him; nor are the hymns and epigrams also contained in Chapman's translation.

John Donne (1572–1631)
Devotions Upon Emergent Occasions, and Severall Steps in my Sickness NF
Five editions by 1638

Thomas Heywood (1574?–1641)
Gynaikeion; or, Nine Bookes of Various History. Concerninge Women NF/V
Partly in verse

Elizabeth Joceline (1596–1622)
The Mothers Legacie, to her Unborne Childe NF
'The approbation' signed by 'Tho[mas] Goad' (1576–1638)

Ben Jonson (1572–1637)
Neptunes Triumph for the Returne of Albion D
Published anonymously. Intended for performance on 6 January 1624 but abandoned. Revised as *The Fortunate Isles and their Union* (performed and first published in 1625, q.v.).

Philip Massinger (1583–1640)
The Bond-Man D

Francis Quarles (1592–1644)
Job Militant: With meditations divine and morall V

Francis Quarles (1592–1644)
Sions Elegies, Wept by Jeremie the Prophet V
See also *Sions Sonets* 1625

Captain John Smith (1580–1631)
The Generall Historie of Virginia, New-England, and the Summer Isles NF
Largely a collected edition of Smith's previous works on Virginia and New England

George Wither (1588–1667)
The Schollers Purgatory NF
A defence of Wither's patent for *The Hymnes and Songs of the Church* 1623 (q.v.)

Sir Henry Wotton (1568–1639)
The Elements of Architecture NF

1625

- James I dies (27 Mar.)
  CHARLES I (-1649): marries Henrietta Maria of France (June)
- John Caryll born
  Thomas Stanley, the elder, born
- John Fletcher dies
  John Florio dies?
  Orlando Gibbons dies
  Sir Arthur Gorges dies
  Thomas Lodge dies
  John Norden dies?

Sir Francis Bacon (1561–1626)
Apophthegmes New and Old NF

Sir Francis Bacon (1561–1626)
The Essayes or Counsels, Civill and Morall NF
58 essays. See also *Essayes* 1597, *Essayes* 1612.

Sir Francis Bacon (1561–1626) (tr.)
The Translation of Certaine Psalmes into English Verse BIB

John Barclay (1582–1621)
Barclay his Argenis; or, The Loves of Poliarchus and Argenis F
Translated by Kingsmill Long. Partly in verse (translated by Thomas May). First published in Latin (Paris, 1621). Also translated by Sir Robert Le Grys in 1628.

William Camden (1551–1623)
Annales: The true and royall history of the famous Empresse Elizabeth Queene of England France and Ireland NF
Translated by Abraham Darcie from the French translation by Paul de Bellegent of books i–iii of Camden's *Annales rerum Anglicarum, et Hibernicarum, Regnante Elizabetha*, first published in Latin 1615

Nathanel Carpenter (1589–1628?)
Geography Delineated Forth in Two Bookes NF

Lady Eleanor Davies (*c*.1590–1652)
A Warning to the Dragon and all his Angels NF

John Donne (1572–1631)
The First Sermon Preached to King Charles, at Saint James NF
On Ps. xi, 3. Preached 3 April 1625

John Donne (1572–1631)
Foure Sermons Upon Speciall Occasions NF
Reissue of four previously published sermons: *A Sermon Preached at Pauls Crosse* (i.e. *A Sermon on Judges* 1622, q.v.); *To the Honourable, the Virginia Company* (i.e. *Sermon on Acts*, 1622, q.v.); *At the Consecration of Lincolnes Inne Chappell* (i.e. *Encaenia*, 1623, q.v.); and *The First Sermon Preached to King Charles* (1625, q.v.). See also *Three Sermons* 1623, *Five Sermons* 1626, *Six Sermons* 1634, *LXXX Sermons* 1640 *Fifty Sermons* 1649.

Thomas Heywood (1574?–1641) (tr.)
Art of Love V
Publication date conjectural. Published anonymously. Translated from Ovid, *Ars amatoria*.

Thomas Heywood (1574?–1641)
A Funeral Elegie: Upon the much lamented death of . . . King James V

Ben Jonson (1572–1637)
The Fortunate Isles and their Union D
Published anonymously. Performed 9 January 1625. A revised version of *Neptune's Triumph for the Return of Albion*.

Gervase Markham (1568?–1637)
The Souldiers Accidence; or, An Introduction into Military Discipline NF

Thomas Middleton (1580–1627)
A Game at Chess D
Published anonymously. Performed at the Globe Theatre (6 August 1624).

Samuel Purchas (1577–1626)
Purchas his Pilgrimes NF
Purchas inherited many of the MSS of Richard Hakluyt, hence the additional title-page in volume i: *Hakluytus Posthumus or Purchas his Pilgrimes*

Francis Quarles (1592–1644)
Sions Sonets V
See also *Sions Elegies* 1624

1626

- Peace of La Rochelle between the French Crown and the Huguenots
  Impeachment of the duke of Buckingham
  York House Conference upholds Arminian teaching
- John Aubrey born
  Sir Robert Howard born
- Lancelot Andrewes dies
  Sir Francis Bacon dies
  Nicholas Breton dies?
  Sir John Davies dies
  John Dowland dies
  Samuel Purchas dies
  Cyril Tourneur dies
- Richard Cromwell born
- Mme de Sévigné born
  Christina, Queen of Sweden born

Richard Bernard (1568–1642)
The Isle of Man; or, The Legal Proceedings in Man-shire against Sinne F
The 'Isle of Man' is of course an allegorical location. Ten editions to 1635.

Nicholas Breton (1545?–1626?)
Fantasticks: Serving for a Perpetuall Prognostication NF

John Donne (1572–1631)
Five Sermons Upon Speciall Occasions NF
Adds the *Sermon, Preached . . . at Whitehall* 1626 (q.v.) to those collected in *Foure Sermons* 1625 (q.v.). See also *Three Sermons* 1623, *Six Sermons* 1634, *LXXX Sermons* 1640, *Fifty Sermons* 1649.

John Donne (1572–1631)
A Sermon, Preached to the Kings Majestie at Whitehall NF
On Isaiah: 1: i. Preached 24 February 1626.

Joseph Hall (1574–1656)
Contemplations upon the Historicall Part of the Old Testament NF
Completion of the *Contemplations*. See 1612.

John Kennedy (*fl.* 1626)
Calanthrop and Lucilla V
Reissued 1631 as *The Ladies Delight; or, The English Gentlewomans History of Calanthrop and Lucilla*

Thomas May (1595–1650) (tr.)
Pharsalia V
Books i–iii. Published in ten books in 1627 (q.v.). See also *A Continuation* 1630.

William Roper (1496–1578)
The Mirrour of Vertue in Worldly Greatnes; or, The Life of Syr Thomas More NF

George Sandys (1578–1644) (tr.)
Ovid's Metamorphosis Englished V
Complete edition: see *The First Five Books of Ovid's Metamorphosis* 1621; revised 1632 with allegorical commentary and a version of *Aeneid* i.

John Scoggin (*fl.* 1480)
The First and Best Part of Scoggins Jests F
See also *The Jestes of Skogyn* 1570, *Scoggins Jestes* 1613

Captain John Smith (1580–1631)
An Accidence or the Path-way to Experience: Necessary for all young sea-men NF

'Orpheus Junior' [Sir William Vaughan (1575–1641)]
The Golden Fleece NF
Partly in verse

1627

- Henry Bold born
  Robert Boyle born
  John Hall, of Durham, born
  John Harington born
  John Ray born
- Richard Barnfield dies
  Sir John Beaumont dies
  Thomas Middleton dies
  Henry Shirley dies
- Dorothy Osborne born
- Bossuet born

Sir Francis Bacon (1561–1626)
Sylva Sylvarum; or, A Naturall Historie NF
Published in 1627, dated 1626. Contains *The New Atlantis*. Eleven editions to 1685.

George Buchanan (1506–82)
An Assay; or, Buchanan his Paraphrase on the First Twentie Psalmes BIB
In *One and Forty Divine Odes Englished, Set to King Davids Princely Harpe* by 'S.P.L.' (sometimes identified as Sir James Sempill). Buchanan's paraphrase has separate title-page.

Thomas Deloney (1543?–1600)
The Gentle Craft MISC

John Donne (1572–1631)
A Sermon of Commemoration of the Lady Danvers NF

Lady Magdalen Danvers died in 1627. Also includes commemorations of her by her son George Herbert in Latin and Greek verse.

Michael Drayton (1563–1631)
The Battaile of Agincourt V

Phineas Fletcher (1582–1650)
Locustae V
In Latin with an English paraphrase

George Hakewill (1578–1649)
An Apologie of the Power and Providence of God in the Government of the World NF
A reply to Godfrey Goodman (1583–1656), *The Fall of Man* 1616 (q.v.)

Thomas May (1595–1650) (tr.)
Lucan's Pharsalia; or, The Civill Warres of Rome, betweene Pompey the Great, and Julius Caesar V
Complete in ten books. The first three books were published in 1626 (q.v.). See also *A Continuation* 1630.

Thomas Newman (*fl.* 1627) (tr.)
The Two First Comedies of Terence Called Andria, and The Eunuch D
Verse translations of Terence's *Andria* and *Eunuchus*

Richard Niccols (1584–1616)
The Beggers Ape V
Published anonymously

Robert Sanderson (1587–1663)
Ten Sermons Preached NF
Enlarged over several editions

1628

- Charles I accepts the Petition of Rights
  William Laud becomes bishop of London
  Assassination of the duke of Buckingham by John Felton
  William Harvey publishes his *Exercitatio Anatomica de Motu Cordis et Sanguinis*, on the circulation of the blood
- John Bunyan born
  Sir Paul Rycaut born
  Sir William Temple born
  George Villiers, 2nd duke of Buckingham, born
- William Cavendish, 2nd earl of Devonshire, dies
  Fulke Greville, Lord Brooke, dies
  Christopher Middleton dies
- Charles Perrault born
- Malherbe dies

Anonymous
Robin Good-Fellow his Mad Pranks, and Merry Jests F
'The second part'. Earliest extant edition. Partly in verse.

John Clavell (1603–42)
A Recantation of an Ill Led Life; or, A Discoverie of the High-way Law V

Sir Edward Coke (1552–1634)
Coke upon Littleton NF
A commentary on the text of Sir Thomas Littleton (*d.* 1481), *Tenures in Law,* which is reprinted in the original Law French with an English translation.

Thomas Deloney (1543?–1600)
The Garland of Good Will MISC

Sir Francis Drake (*d.* 1637) (ed.)
The World Encompassed by Sir Francis Drake NF
Editor's dedication signed, though this ascription has been disputed

John Earle (1601?–65)
Micro-cosmographie; or, A Peece of the World Discovered; in Essayes and Characters NF
Published anonymously. Seven editions by 1637.

Owen Felltham (1602?–68)
Resolves, a Duple Century MISC
See *Resolves* 1623

Phineas Fletcher (1582–1650)
Brittain's Ida V
Published anonymously. Not by Spenser. Also sometimes attributed to Giles Fletcher the younger.

Robert Gomersall (1602–46?)
The Levites Revenge V

Robert Gomersall (1602–46?)
The Tragedie of Lodovick Sforza Duke of Milan D

Joseph Hall (1574–1656)
The Olde Religion: Wherin is laid downe the difference betwixt the reformed, and Romane church NF

Thomas May (1595–1650) (tr.)
Virgil's Georgicks Englished V

Sir Walter Ralegh (1552?–1618)
The Prerogative of Parlaments in England NF

Henry Reynolds (1563?–1635?) (tr.)
Torquato Tasso's Aminta Englisht V

Michael Sparke (1588?–1653)
Crumms of Comfort, the Valley of Teares, and the Hill of Joy NF
Earliest extant edition (6th); first published 1623? Last edition (44th) published in 1755.

George Wither (1588–1667)
Britain's Remembrancer: Containing a narration of the plague lately past V
See also *Haleluiah* 1641

1629

- The Commons Protestation (Mar.)
  Charter issued for the colony of Salem
  Treaty of Susa ending war with France
  John Selden imprisoned in the Tower
- Lording Barry dies
  Thomas Goffe dies
  John Speed dies

Thomas Adams (*c.*1583–1660)
The Workes of Thomas Adams WKS

Lancelot Andrewes (1555–1626)
XCVI Sermons NF
Edited by William Laud (1573–1645) and John Buckeridge (1562?–1631)

Sir Francis Bacon (1561–1626)
Certaine Miscellany Works NF

Sir John Beaumont (1583–1627)
Bosworth-field: With a taste of the variety of other poems V

Lodowick Carlell (1601/2–75)
The Deserving Favourite D

George Chapman (1559?–1634) (tr.)
A Justification of a Strange Action of Nero V
Part ii is a verse translation of Juvenal's book i, satire 5

William Davenant (1606–68)
The Tragedy of Albovine, King of the Lombards D

John Ford (1586–1640?)
The Lovers Melancholy D
Adapted from Samuel Daniel's *Hymens Triumph* 1615 (q.v.).

Thomas Hobbes (1588–1679) (tr.)
Eight Books of the Peloponnesian Warre NF
Translated from Thucydides

Sir Francis Hubert (*c.*1568–1629)
The Historie of Edward the Second Surnamed Carnarvan V
The authorized edition. A surreptitious edition was published in 1628.

Gervase Markham (1568?–1637)
Markhams Faithful Farrier NF
Derived from *Markhams Maister-peece* 1610 (q.v.)

Philip Massinger (1583–1640)
The Roman Actor: A tragaedie D

Thomas May (1595–1650) (tr.)
Selected Epigrams of Martial V

John Parkinson (1567–1650)
Paradisi in sole Paradisus terrestris: Or a garden of all sorts of pleasant flowers NF

John Preston (1587–1628)
The New Covenant; or, The Saints Portion NF

Francis Quarles (1592–1644)
Argalus and Parthenia V

James Shirley (1596–1666)
The Wedding D

1630

- Sir John Eliot fined and imprisoned in the Tower for his part in the Common Protestation of 1629
  Treaty of Madrid ends Anglo-Spanish war
  The settlement of Boston begins under the governorship of John Winthrop: expansion of the Massachusetts Bay Colony (-1642)
- Robert Baron born
  Isaac Barrow born
  Charles Cotton born
  James Howard born?
  Edward Phillips born
  John Tillotson born
- William Herbert, 3rd earl of Pembroke, dies
  Fynes Moryson dies
  Samuel Rowlands dies?
- Johann Kepler dies

Lancelot Andrewes (1555–1626)
Institutiones Piae; or, Directions to Pray NF
Published anonymously. Reprinted under Andrewes's name as *Holy Devotions*, 1655. Seven editions to 1684.

Lancelot Andrewes (1555–1626)
A Patterne of Catechisticall Doctrine NF
Published anonymously

Sir Francis Bacon (1561–1626)
The Elements of the Common Lawes of England NF

Richard Bernard (1568–1642)
The Common Catechisme NF
Seven editions to 1634

Richard Brathwaite (1588?–1673)
The English Gentleman NF
See also *The English Gentlewoman* 1631, *The English Gentleman; and The English Gentlewoman* 1641

Elizabeth Cary, Viscountess Falkland (1585–1639) (tr.)
The Reply of the Most Illustrious Cardinall of Perron D
Published anonymously. A translation of a reply by Jacques Davy Du Perron (1556–1618) to *The Answere of Master Isaac Casaubon to the Epistle of Cardinall Peron* (1612), written by Casaubon (1559–1614) under the direction of King James and first published in Latin 1612. Cary's book was ordered to be burned.

William Davenant (1606–68)
The Cruell Brother: A tragedy D

William Davenant (1606–68)
The Just Italian D
Includes commendatory poem by Thomas Carew

Thomas Dekker (1572?–1632)
The Second Part of The Honest Whore D
See *The Honest Whore* 1604

Michael Drayton (1563–1631)
The Muses Elizium V

Joseph Hall (1574–1656)
Occasionall Meditations NF

Sir John Hayward (1564?–1627)
The Life, and Raigne of King Edward the Sixt NF

Francis Higginson (1587–1630)
New-Englands Plantation; or, A Short and True Description of the Commodities and Discommodities of that Countrey NF
Published anonymously

Philip Massinger (1583–1640)
The Picture: A tragaecomedie D

Philip Massinger (1583–1640)
The Renegado: A tragaecomedie D

Thomas May (1595–1650)
A Continuation of Lucan's Historicall Poem Till the Death of Julius Caesar V
See also *Lucan's Pharsalia* 1626, 1627

Thomas Middleton (1580–1627)
A Chast Mayd in Cheape-side: A pleasant conceited comedy D
Performed 1613?

John Preston (1587–1628)
The Breast-Plate of Faith and Love NF

Diana Primrose (*fl.* 1630)
A Chaine of Pearle; or a memoriall of the peerless graces, and heroick vertues of Queene Elizabeth V

Francis Quarles (1592–1644)
Divine Poems V

Thomas Randolph (1605–35)
Aristippus; or, The Joviall Philosopher V
Published anonymously

Nathaniel Richards (1612?–54)
The Celestiall Publican V

Alexander Ross (1591–1654)
Three Decads of Divine Meditations V

James Shirley (1596–1666)
The Gratefull Servant: A comedie D

Richard Sibbes (1577–1635)
The Bruised Reede, and Smoaking Flax NF
Six editions by 1638

Captain John Smith (1580–1631)
The True Travels, Adventures, and Observations of Captaine John Smith NF

John Taylor (1580–1653)
All the Workes of John Taylor the Water-Poet V

1631

- Charles I confiscates Sir Robert Cotton's library
- Anne Conway born
  Richard Cumberland born
  John Dryden born
  Katherine Philips born
  John Phillips born
- John Donne dies
  Michael Drayton dies
  Gabriel Harvey dies

Charles Aleyn (*d.* 1640)
The Battailes of Crescey, and Poctiers V

John Barclay (1582–1621)
The Mirrour of Mindes; or, Barclay's Icon Animorum NF
Translated by Thomas May. First published in Latin in 1614.

Richard Brathwaite (1588?–1673)
The English Gentlewoman NF
See *The English Gentleman* 1630, *The English Gentleman; and The English Gentlewoman* 1641

Richard Brathwaite (1588?–1673)
Whimzies; or, A New Cast of Characters NF
Published anonymously

Nicholas Breton (1545?–1626?)
The Figure of Foure; or, A Handful of Sweet Flowers NF

Thomas Brewer (*fl.* 1624)
The Life and Death of the Merry Devill of Edmonton F

George Chapman (1559?–1634)
Caesar and Pompey: A Roman tragedy, declaring their warres D

Henry Chettle (1560?–1607)
The Tragedy of Hoffman; or, A Revenge for a Father D
Published anonymously

Thomas Dekker (1572?–1632)
Match Mee in London D

Thomas Drue (*fl.* 1631)
The Life of the Dutches of Suffolke D
Published anonymously. Performed at the Fortune Theatre, 1623. A Protestant drama drawn from Foxe's *Book of Martyrs* 1563 (q.v.).

Phineas Fletcher (1582–1650)
Sicelides a Piscatory D
Published anonymously. Performed at King's College, Cambridge, 1615.

Thomas Goffe (1591–1629)
The Raging Turke; or, Bajazet the Second: A tragedie D
The subject is Bayezid II, Sultan of the Turks (1447/8–1512)

Thomas Heywood (1574?–1641)
Englands Elizabeth her Life and Troubles, During her Minoritie, from the Cradle to the Crowne NF

Thomas Heywood (1574?–1641)
The Fair Maid of the West; or, A Girle Worth Gold D

King James I of England, formerly **James VI of Scotland** (1566–1625) (tr.)
The Psalmes of King David BIB
In fact largely translated by William Alexander, earl of Stirling (1567?–1640)

Ben Jonson (1572–1637)
Bartholomew Fayre; The Divell is an Asse; The Staple of Newes D
First published as the second volume of the *Workes* 1616 (q.v.). *Bartholomew Fayre* performed by the Lady Elizabeth's Men at the Hope Theatre (31 October 1614). *The Divell is an Asse* performed in 1616. *The Staple of Newes* performed in 1626.

Ben Jonson (1572–1637)
Chloridia: Rites to Chloris and Her Nymphs: Performed in a masque, at Court D
Published anonymously. Performed 22 February 1631.

Ben Jonson (1572–1637) and **Inigo Jones** (1573–1652)
Loves Triumph Through Callipolis: Performed in a masque at Court D
Published 1631, dated 1630. Performed 9 January 1631.

Ben Jonson (1572–1637)
The New Inne; or, The Light Heart D
Performed 1629

Ralph Knevet (1602–72)
Rhodon and Isis: A pastorall D

Francis Lenton (*fl.* 1630–40)
Characterismi; or, Lentons Leasures: Expressed in essayes and characters NF

William Lisle (1579?–1637) (tr.)
The Faire Aethiopian V
Published anonymously. A verse translation of Heliodorus, *Aethiopica*.

David Lloyd (1597–1663) attrib.
The Legend of Captaine Jones [pt i] V
Published anonymously. Attributed to David Lloyd, sometimes to Martin Lluelyn. Part ii published in 1648.

'Don Diego Puede-Ser' [**James Mabbe** (1572–1642?)] (tr.)?
The Spanish Bawd F
Translated from *La tragicomedia de Calisto y Melibea* (first published 1502), popularly known as *La Celestina*, by Fernando de Rojas (*c.*1465–1541)

Thomas May (1595–1650) (tr.)
The Mirrour of Mindes; or, Barclays Icon Animarum NF
Icon Animarum published in Latin in 1614

Thomas May (1595–1650)
The Tragedy of Antigone, the Theban Princesse D

Thomas Powell (1572?–1635?)
Tom of all Trades; or, The Plaine Path-way to Preferment NF

John Preston (1587–1628)
Life Eternall; or, A Treatise of the Divine Essence and Attributes NF

Francis Quarles (1592–1644)
The Historie of Samson V

James Shirley (1596–1666)
The Schoole of Complement D

1632

- Death of Gustavus Adolphus at the Battle of Lützen (Nov.)
  Van Dyck settles in England as Court painter
  Accession of Queen Christina of Sweden
- Anthony à Wood born
  John Locke born
  Thomas Shipman born
  Henry Stubbe born
- Thomas Dekker dies
  Sir John Eliot dies in the Tower
- Christopher Wren born
- Baruch Spinoza born

Richard Brome (1590?–1652?)
The Northern Lasse: A comoedie D

John Donne (1572–1631)
Deaths Duell; or, A Consolation to the Soule, Against the Dying Life, and Living Death of the Body NF
Sermon preached on 25 February 1631, five weeks less a day before Donne's death on 31 March 1631

Phineas Fletcher (1582–1650)
Joy in Tribulation; or, Consolations for Afflicted Spirits NF

Thomas Goffe (1591–1629)
The Couragious Turke; or, Amurath the First: A tragedie D

Nicholas Goodman (*fl.* 1632)
Hollands Leaguer; or, An Historical Discourse of the Life and Actions of Dona Britanica Hollandia the Arch-Mistris of the Wicked Women of Ethiopia F

Thomas Heywood (1574?–1641)
The Iron Age D
Also contains (separate title-page) *The Second Part of the Iron Age*

Philemon Holland (1552–1637) (tr.)
Cyropaedia NF
Translated from Xenophon. Includes a reprint of Abraham Holland's *Naumachia, or Hollands Sea-fight*, first published in 1622.

William Lithgow (1582–1645?)
Rare Adventures, and Painefull Peregrinations NF
A revised and enlarged edition of *A Most Delectable, and True Discourse, of an Admired and Painefull Peregrination* 1614 (q.v.)

Donald Lupton (*d.* 1676)
London and the Countrey Carbonadoed and Quartered into Severall Characters NF

Shackerley Marmion (1603–1639)
Hollands Leaguer: An excellent comedy D

Philip Massinger (1583–1640)
The Emperour of the East: A tragae-comoedie D

Philip Massinger (1583–1640) and **Nathaniel Field** (1587–1633)
The Fatall Dowry: A tragedy D

Philip Massinger (1583–1640)
The Maid of Honour D

Francis Quarles (1592–1644)
Divine Fancies: Digested into epigrammes, meditations, and observations V

Sir Walter Ralegh (1552?–1618)
Sir Walter Raleighs Instructions to his Sonne and to Posterity NF

Thomas Randolph (1605–35)
The Jealous Lovers: A comedie presented to their gracious Majesties D
Performed at Trinity College, Cambridge, 19 March 1632

Henry Reynolds (1563?–1635?)
Mythomystes: Wherein a short survay is taken of the nature and value of true poesy and depth of the Ancients above our moderne poets NF

William Rowley (1585?–1642?)
A New Wonder; a Woman Never Vext: A pleasant conceited comedy D

William Shakespeare (1564–1616)
Comedies, Histories and Tragedies D

The Second Folio. Commendatory poems include a 16-line epigram by Milton, his first printed poem. See also the First Folio 1623, Third Folio 1663, Fourth Folio 1685.

James Shirley (1596–1666)
Changes; or, Love in a Maze: A comedie D

Aurelian Townshend (*fl.* 1601–43)
Albions Triumph: Personated in a maske at court. By the Kings Majestie and his lords D
Published 1632, dated 1631. Performed 8 January 1632.

Aurelian Townshend (*fl.* 1601–43) and **Inigo Jones** (1573–1652)
Tempe Restored: A masque presented by the Queene, and fourteene ladies D
Published 1632, dated 1631. Performed 14 February 1632. Songs by Townshend, the rest by Inigo Jones. Parts of the masque were derived from Baltasar de Beaujoyeulx (*d. c.*1587), *Balet comique de la royne.*

George Wither (1588–1667) (tr.)
The Psalmes of David Translated into Lyrick Verse BIB

1633

- Thomas Wentworth takes up appointment as Lord Deputy in Ireland (July)
  William Laud appointed archbishop of Canterbury (Aug.)
  English trading post established in Bengal
  Trial of the Lancashire Witches
- Nicholas Billingsley born
  Wentworth Dillon born
  Samuel Pepys born
  Samuel Pordage born
  George Savile, marquis of Halifax, born
- George Abbot, archbishop of Canterbury, dies
  Nathaniel Field dies
  George Herbert dies
  Anthony Munday dies
  Samuel Rowley dies?

Anonymous
The Costlie Whore: A comicall historie D

Abraham Cowley (1618–1667)
Poetical Blossomes V

John Donne (1572–1631)
Juvenilia; or, Certaine Paradoxes, and Problemes NF
See also *Paradoxes, Problems, Essayes, Characters,* 1652

John Donne (1572–1631)
Poems, by J.D.: With elegies on the authors death V
Seven editions by 1669

Phineas Fletcher (1582–1650)
The Purple Island; or, The Isle of Man V

John Ford (1586–1640?)
The Broken Heart: A tragedy D

John Ford (1586–1640?)
Loves Sacrifice: A tragedie D

John Ford (1586–1640?)
'Tis Pitty Shee's a Whore D

Emanuel Forde (*fl.* 1607)
Montelyon, Knight of the Oracle F
The earliest extant edition. Presumably posthumous.

Thomas Goffe (1591–1629)
The Tragedy of Orestes D

Robert Gomersall (1602–46?)
Poems by Robert Gomersall D
Contains *The Levites Revenge, The Tragedie of Lodovick Sforza* (both published separately in 1628, q.v.)

Fulke Greville, Lord Brooke (1554–1628)
Certaine Learned and Elegant Workes WKS
Includes *Mustapha* (published surreptitiously in 1609, q.v.), the sonnet sequence *Caelica*, and other works

George Herbert (1593–1633)
The Temple: Sacred poems and private ejaculations V
Edited by Nicholas Ferrar. Eight editions by 1660.

Thomas Heywood (1574?–1641)
The English Traveller D

Christopher Marlowe (1564–93)
The Jew of Malta D
Edited by Thomas Heywood

Shackerley Marmion (1603–39)
A Fine Companion D

John Marston (1576–1634)
The Workes of Mr John Marston WKS

Philip Massinger (1583–1640)
A New Way to Pay Old Debts: A comoedie D

Thomas May (1595–1650)
The Reigne of King Henry the Second V

William Prynne (1600–69)
Histrio-mastix: The players scourge, or actors tragaedie NF
See also Sir Richard Baker, *Theatrum Redivivum* 1662

William Rowley (1585?–1642?)
All's Lost by Lust D

William Rowley (1585?–1642?)
A Match at Mid-night: A pleasant comoedie D

Wye Saltonstall (*fl.* 1630–40) (tr.)
Tristia V
Translated from Ovid

James Shirley (1596–1666)
The Bird in a Cage: A comedie D

James Shirley (1596–1666)
A Contention for Honour and Riches D
Subsequently published, revised and enlarged, as *Honoria and Mammon* 1659

James Shirley (1596–1666)
The Wittie Faire One: A comedie D

1634

- William Prynne sentenced to lose his ears for the publication (1633, q.v.) of *Histrio-mastix*
- Joseph Alleine born
  Robert South born
- William Austin dies
  George Chapman dies
  Sir Edward Coke dies
  John Marston dies
- Marie-Madeleine de La Fayette born

Richard Brathwaite (1588?–1673)
Anniversaries upon his Panarete V
Published anonymously. See also *Anniversaries . . . Continued* 1635.

Richard Brathwaite (1588?–1673)
A Strange Metamorphosis of Man: Deciphered in characters NF
Published anonymously

Thomas Carew (1595–1639?)
Coelum Brittanicum: A masque D
Published anonymously. The masque was designed by Inigo Jones and based in part on Giordano Bruno (1548–1600), *Spaccio de la bestia trionfante.*

John Donne (1572–1631)
Six Sermons Upon Severall Occasions NF
All reprinted in *Fifty Sermons* 1649 (q.v.). See also *Three Sermons* 1623, *Foure Sermons* 1625, *Five Sermons* 1626, *LXXX Sermons* 1640.

John Fletcher (1579–1625) and **William Shakespeare** (1564–1616)
The Two Noble Kinsmen D

John Ford (1586–1640?)
Perkin Warbeck D
Published anonymously

William Habington (1605–54)
Castara V
Published anonymously

George Herbert (1593–1633) (tr.)
Hygiasticon; or, The Right Course of Preserving Life and Health unto Extream Old Age NF
Translated from the Latin version (1613) by Leonardus Lessius of *Della vita sobria* by Luigi Cornaro (1475–1566)

Sir Thomas Herbert (1606–82)
A Relation of Some Yeares Travaile, Begunne Anno 1626 NF

Thomas Heywood (1574?–1641) and **Richard Brome** (1590?–1652?)
The Late Lancashire Witches: A well received comedy D

Thomas Heywood (1574?–1641)
A Mayden-head Well Lost D

Edward Knott (1582–1656)
Mercy & Truth; or, Charity Maintayned by Catholiques NF
Edward Knott was the name assumed by Matthew Wilson in 1602 which he retained for the rest of his life. A reply to Christopher Potter (1591–1646), *Want of charitie justly charged, on all such Romanists, as dare . . . affirme, that Protestancie destroyeth salvation* (Oxford, 1633). See also Chillingworth, *The Religion of Protestants* 1638.

Samuel Rowley (*d.* 1633?)
The Noble Souldier; or, A Contract Broken, Justly Reveng'd D

James Shirley (1596–1666)
The Triumph of Peace: A masque, presented by the foure honourable houses, or Innes of Court D
Dated 1633 for 1634

Alice Sutcliffe (*fl.* 1634)
Meditations of Man's Mortalitie; or, A Way to True Blessednesse MISC
Partly in verse

1635

- Colonization of Connecticut begins
  Académie Française founded
- Thomas Betterton born?
  Thomas Burnet born?
  Sir George Etherege born
  Thomas Sprat born
  Edward Stillingfleet born
- Richard Corbet dies
  Leonard Digges dies
  Edward Fairfax dies
  Sir Robert Naunton dies
  Thomas Randolph dies
  Sir Anthony Sherley dies?
  Richard Sibbes dies
  John Webster dies?
- Madame de Maintenon born
- Lope de Vega dies

Richard Brathwaite (1588?–1673)
Anniversaries upon his Panarete; Continued NF
Published anonymously. Partly in verse. See also *Anniversaries* 1634.

Richard Brathwaite (1588?–1673) (tr.)
The Arcadian Princesse; or, The Triumph of Justice F
A translation of an untraced work by Mariano Silesio, or possibly an original work by Brathwaite

Thomas Heywood (1574?–1641)
The Hierarchie of the Blessed Angells V
Contains the celebrated reference to 'Mellifluous Shakes-peare, whose inchanting Quill/Commanded Mirth or Passion . . . '

Thomas Heywood (1574?–1641)
Philocothonista; or, The Drunkard, Opened, Dissected, and Anatomized V

Thomas May (1595–1650)
The Victorious Reigne of King Edward the Third V

Francis Quarles (1592–1644)
Emblemes V

Joseph Rutter (*fl.* 1633–40)
The Shepheard's Holy-Day: A pastorall tragi-comaedie V

James Shirley (1596–1666)
The Traytor: A tragedie D

John Swan (1605–71)
Speculum Mundi; or, A Glasse Representing the Face of the World NF

George Wither (1588–1667)
A Collection of Emblemes, Ancient and Moderne V
Emblems printed from engravings originally produced by Crispijn van de Passe the Elder for Gabriel Rollenhagen's *Nucleus Emblematorum* (1611–13)

1636

- Roger Williams founds Providence, Rhode Island
  Harvard College (so designated from 1639) founded
- Joseph Glanvill born
- Boileau (Nicolas Boileau-Despréaux) born

Sir Henry Blount (1602–82)
A Voyage into the Levant NF

Richard Brathwaite (1588?–1673)
The Fatall Nuptiall; or, Mournefull Marriage V
Published anonymously

Edward Dacres (*fl.* 1636–40) (tr.)
Machiavels Discourses, upon the First Decade of T. Livius NF
An anonymous translation of Niccolò Machiavelli (1469–1527), *Discorsi sopra la prima deca de Tito Livio*

William Davenant (1606–68)
The Platonick Lovers: A tragaecomedy D

William Davenant (1606–68)
The Triumphs of the Prince d'Amour: A masque D
Published 1636, dated 1635. Performed 24 February 1636. Prince Rupert attended the first performance.

William Davenant (1606–68)
The Witts: A comedie D

Peter Heylyn (1600–62)
The History of the Sabbath NF

Thomas Heywood (1574?–1641)
A Challenge for Beautie D

Thomas Heywood (1574?–1641)
Loves Maistresse; or, The Queens Masque D

Thomas Heywood (1574?–1641)
A True Discourse of the Two Infamous Upstart Prophets, Richard Farnham Weaver of White-Chappell, and John Bull Weaver of Saint Butolphs Algate, now Prisoners NF
Religious fanatics Farnham and Bull (both *d.* 1642) claimed to be prophets inspired 'by the very spirit of God' (*DNB*). They were arrested for heresy in April 1636, their rantings having attracted wide attention.

Philip Massinger (1583–1640)
The Great Duke of Florence: A comicall historie D

Wye Saltonstall (*fl.* 1630–40) (tr.)
Ovids Heroicall Epistles V
A translation of Ovid's *Epistolae heroïdum*

George Sandys (1578–1644) (tr.)
A Paraphrase upon the Psalmes of David BIB
See also *A Paraphrase Upon the Divine Poems* 1638

George Wither (1588–1667) (tr.)
The Nature of Man NF
Translated from two Latin versions of Nemesius of Emesa, *Peri physeos anthropou*

1637

- Ferdinand II becomes Holy Roman Emperor
  English traders establish a factory at Canton
- Thomas Flatman born
  Thomas Ken born
  Thomas Traherne born
- Nicholas Ferrar dies
  Joseph Fletcher dies
  Philemon Holland dies
  Ben Jonson dies
  Gervase Markham dies
- Dietrich Buxtehude born

Sir William Alexander (1567?–1640)
Recreations with the Muses V
Contains *Four Monarchicke Tragedies, Doomes-day, A Paraenesis to Prince Henry* (all previously published), and *Jonathan: An heroicke poem*

William Austin (1587–1634)
Haec Homo: Wherein the excellency of the creation of woman is described NF

John Fletcher (1579–1625)
The Elder Brother: A comedie D
Acts i and v are ascribed to Philip Massinger, who probably completed the play after Fletcher's death

Thomas Heywood (1574?–1641)
Pleasant Dialogues and Dramma's MISC
Pieces from Jacob Cats (1577–1660); Desiderius Erasmus (*d.* 1536); Lucian, of Samosata; Ovid; and Joannes Ravisius Textor (*c.*1480–1524).

Thomas Heywood (1574?–1641)
The Royall King, and the Loyall Subject D
A dramatization of the second volume of William Painter's *Palace of Pleasure* 1567 (q.v.), itself a translation of Matteo Bandello (1485–1561), 'Ariabarzane senescalo del re di Persia', from his *Novelle* (1554).

Thomas Heywood (1574?–1641)
A True Description of His Majesties Royall Ship NF
The ship was the *Sovereign of the Seas*

Thomas Hobbes (1588–1679) (tr.)
A Briefe of the Art of Rhetorique NF
Published anonymously. A translation of Aristotle's *Rhetorica.*

Thomas Jordan (1612?–85)
Poeticall Varieties; or, Varietie of Fancies V

Ralph Knevet (1602–72)
Funerall Elegies V
Elegies on Lady Katherine Paston

Shackerley Marmion (1603–39)
The Legend of Cupid and Psyche V

John Milton (1608–74)
Comus D
Published anonymously. Dated 1637, but probably published early 1638. Performed at Ludlow Castle (29 September 1634). Edited by Henry Lawes.

Thomas Nabbes (1605?–45?)
Hannibal and Scipio: An historicall tragedy D

Thomas Nabbes (1605?–45?)
Microcosmus: A morall maske D

James Shirley (1596–1666)
Hide Parke: A comedie D

James Shirley (1596–1666)
The Lady of Pleasure: A comedie D
Performed 5 November 1635

James Shirley (1596–1666)
The Young Admirall D
Based on Lope de Vega (1562–1635), *Don Lope de Cardona*

James Shirley (1596–1666)
The Example D

James Shirley (1596–1666)
The Gamester D

Richard Sibbes (1577–1635)
A Fountaine Sealed; or, The Duty of the Sealed to the Spirit, and the Worke of the Spirit in Sealing NF

Nathaniel Whiting (1617?–82)
Le hore di recreatione; or, The Pleasant Historie of Albino and Bellama V

1638

- The Scottish National Covenant
- Philip Ayres born
- Joseph Mede dies
- The future Louis XIV born
- Racine born

Charles Aleyn (*d.* 1640)
The History of Henry the Seventh V

Sir Francis Bacon (1561–1626)
The Historie of Life and Death: With observations naturall and experimentall for the prolonging of life NF
First published in Latin as *Historia vitae et mortis* 1623

'Corymboeus' [Richard Brathwaite (1588?–1673)]
Barnabees Journall, under the Names of Mirtilus & Faustulus Shadowed V
Latin and English verse on facing pages

Richard Brathwaite (1588?–1673)
The Psalmes of David the King and Prophet, and of Other Holy Prophets BIB

Richard Brathwaite (1588?–1673)
A Spiritual Spicerie NF
Much of the material translated from Jacobus de Gruytrode (*d.* 1472?)

Robert Chamberlain (1607?–60)
Nocturnall Lucubrations; or, Meditations Divine and Morall V

William Chillingworth (1602–44)
The Religion of Protestants a Safe Way to Salvation NF
A reply to Edward Knott, *Mercy & Truth* 1634, *Christianity Maintained* 1638. See also Floyd *The Church Conquerant* 1638, *The Totall Summe* 1639.

Abraham Cowley (1618–67)
Loves Riddle: A pastorall comaedie D

Robert Crofts (*fl.* 1638)
The Lover; or, Nuptiall Love NF

William Davenant (1606–68)
Madagascar; with Other Poems V

John Donne (1572–1631) and **Thomas Jackson** (1579–1640)
Sapienta Clamitans NF
The first two sermons are by Jackson, President of Corpus Christi College, Oxford, and Dean of Peterborough. The third sermon, on Ecclesiastes 12: 1, is by Donne and was reprinted as sermon 19 in *XXVI Sermons* 1660.

Nicholas Ferrar (1592–1637) (tr.)
The Hundred and Ten Considerations of Signior John Valdesso NF
Published anonymously. The original work, *Ciento y diez consideraciones divinas*, by Juan de Valdés (*c.*1491–1541) and Alfonso de Valdés (1490?–1532), was published in 1539. Notes by George Herbert.

John Floyd [in religion: **Daniel à Jesu**] (1572)
The Church Conquerant Over Humane Wit NF
Published anonymously. Sometimes also attributed to William Lacey. A response to Chillingworth's *Religion of Protestants* 1638. See also Floyd, *The Totall Summe* 1639.

John Ford (1586–1640?)
The Fancies, Chast and Noble D
Published anonymously

Francis Godwin (1562–1633)
The Man in the Moone F
Dedication initialled 'E.M.' (i.e. pseudonymously as 'Edward Mahon'?)

Thomas Heywood (1574?–1641)
The Wise-Woman of Hogsdon: A comedie D

Inigo Jones (1573–1652) and **William Davenant** (1606–68)
Britannia Triumphans: A masque D
Published 1638, dated 1637. Performed 7 January 1638.

Henry Killigrew (1613–1700)
The Conspiracy: A tragedy D

John Kirke (*d.* 1643)
The Seven Champions of Christendome D

John Milton (1608–74) and others
Justa Edouardo King naufrago, ab amicus moerentibus, amoris & mneias charin NF

A Cambridge memorial volume to Edward King (1612–37). *Obsequies to the memorie of Mr Edward King, anno Dom. 1638*, in English, has a separate dated title-page. Includes the first printing of Milton's 'Lycidas'.

Thomas Nabbes (1605?–45?)
Covent Garden: A pleasant comedie D
Performed in 1632

Thomas Nabbes (1605?–45?)
The Springs Glorie D/V

Thomas Nabbes (1605?–45?)
Totenham Court: A pleasant comedie D
Performed in 1633

Francis Quarles (1592–1644)
Hieroglyphikes of the Life of Man V

Thomas Randolph (1605–35)
Poems with the Muses Looking-Glasse: and Amyntas V

William Rowley (1585?–1642?)
A Shoo-Maker a Gentleman D

George Sandys (1578–1644) (tr.)
A Paraphrase upon the Divine Poems V
Enlarged from *A Paraphrase Upon the Psalmes of David* 1636 (q.v.)

Henry Shirley (*c*.1594–1627)
The Martyr'd Souldier D

James Shirley (1596–1666)
The Dukes Mistris D
Performed at the St James's Theatre (22 February 1636)

James Shirley (1596–1666)
The Royall Master D

Richard Sibbes (1577–1635)
Beames of Divine Light, Breaking Forth from Severall Places of Holy Scripture NF
Published 1638, dated 1639

Sir John Suckling (1609–42)
Aglaura D
Published anonymously. Reprinted in *Fragmenta Aurea* 1646 (q.v.).

Jeremy Taylor (1613–67)
A Sermon Preached in Saint Maries Church in Oxford: Upon the anniversary of the Gunpowder-treason NF
Preached 5 November 1638

John Wilkins (1614–72)
The Discovery of a World in the Moone NF
Published anonymously

1639

- The First Bishops' War
  First North American printing-press (Cambridge, Mass.)
- Thomas Ellwood born
  Sir Charles Sedley born
- Thomas Carew dies?
  Elizabeth Cary dies
  Marmion Shackerley dies
  Sir Henry Wotton dies
- Increase Mather born
- Jean Racine born

Lodowick Carell (1601/2–75)
Arviragus and Philicia D
Published anonymously

William Cartwright (1611–43)
The Royall Slave: A tragi-comedy D
Published anonymously. Performed 30 August 1636 at Christ Church, Oxford.

George Chapman (1559?–1634) and **James Shirley** (1596–1666)
The Ball: A comedy D
In fact probably by James Shirley alone

George Chapman (1559?–1634) and **James Shirley** (1596–1666)
Chabot Admirall of France D
The subject was Philippe Chabot (1480–1543)

Robert Davenport (*fl.* 1624–40)
A Crowne for a Conquerour; and Too Late to Call Backe Yesterday V

Robert Davenport (*fl.* 1624–40)
A New Tricke to Cheat the Divill D

John Fletcher (1579–1625)?
The Bloody Brother: A tragedy D
Attribution uncertain. Probably by Fletcher and Ben Jonson, revised by Philip Massinger. Most subsequent editions titled *The Tragoedy of Rollo Duke of Normandy*.

John Fletcher (1579–1625)
Monsieur Thomas: A comedy D

John Floyd [in religion: **Daniel à Jesu**] (1572)
The Totall Summe: Or, No danger of damnation unto Roman Catholiques for any errour in faith NF
Published anonymously. A response to Chillingworth's *Religion of Protestants* 1638 (q.v.). See also *The Church Conquerant* 1638.

John Ford (1586–1640?)
The Ladies Triall D

Thomas Fuller (1608–61)
The Historie of the Holy Warre NF

Henry Glapthorne (1610–43?)
Albertus Wallenstein D

Henry Glapthorne (1610–43?)
Argalus and Parthenia D
The plot is based on Sir Philip Sidney's *Arcadia*

Henry Glapthorne (1610–43?)
Poëms V

William Laud (1573–1645)
A Relation of the Conference betweene William Lawd . . . and Mr Fisher the Jesuite NF
In part a reply to A.C., *True relations of sundry conferences had betweene certaine Protestant doctours, and a Jesuite called M. Fisher* (1626), sometimes attributed to John Sweet, to John Floyd, and to John Fisher, itself a reply to works by Francis White (1564?–1638) and Daniel Featley (1582–1645)

William Lower (1600?–62)
The Phaenix in Her Flames: A tragedy D

Philip Massinger (1583–1640)
The Unnaturall Combat: A tragedie D

Thomas May (1595–1650)
Cleopatra Queen of Aegypt D
Performed in 1626

Thomas May (1595–1650)
Julia Agrippina D

Jasper Mayne (1604–72)
The Citye Match: A comoedye D

George Rivers (*fl.* 1639)
The Heroinae; or, The Lives of Arria, Paulina, Lucrecia, Dido, Theutilla, Cypriana, Aretaphila F
Published anonymously

James Shirley (1596–1666)
The Maides Revenge: A tragedy D

'Mary Make-peace' [John Taylor (1580–1653)]
Divers Crabtree Lectures: Expressing the severall languages that shrews read to their husbands NF

John Taylor (1580–1653)
A Juniper Lecture: With the description of all sorts of women, good and bad NF
Published anonymously

Richard Zouch (1590–1661)
The Sophister: A comedy D
Published anonymously

1640

- Thomas Wentworth created earl of Strafford
  The Short Parliament (15 Apr.–5 May)
  The Long Parliament (Nov. 1640–Apr. 1653)
  Portugal becomes independent under John IV
  Root and Branch petition presented to Parliament (11 Dec.)
  Impeachment of William Laud (18 Dec.)
- Aphra Behn born?
  William Cavendish, 1st duke of Devonshire, born
  Sir James Chamberlaine born
  Benjamin Keach born
  Samuel Parker born
  Robert Plot born
- Sir William Alexander dies
  Robert Burton dies
  Robert Chester dies?
  John Day dies
  John Ford dies?
  Philip Massinger dies
- Rubens dies

Anonymous
Cawwood the Rooke F

George Abbot (1604–49)
The Whole Booke of Job Paraphrased BIB
With the original Bible text in English

Sir Francis Bacon (1561–1626)
Of the Advancement and Proficiencie of Learning or the Partitions of Sciences NF
A translation, by Gilbert Watts (*d.* 1657), of *De Dignitate & Augmentis Scientiarum* 1623 (q.v.). See also *The Advancement of Learning* 1605.

Francis Beaumont (1584–1616)
Poems V
Includes a translation from Ovid's *Metamorphoses* which may not be by Beaumont. Several other pieces definitely not by him.

Francis Beaumont (1584–1616) and **John Fletcher** (1579–1625)
Wit Without Money: A comedie D
Published 1640, dated 1639. Generally regarded as being by Fletcher alone.

'Philogenes Panedonius' [Richard Brathwaite (1588?–1673)]
Ar't Asleepe Husband?: A boulster lecture MISC

'Musæus Palatinus' [Richard Brathwaite (1588?–1673)?]
The Two Lancashire Lovers; or, The Excellent History of Philocles and Doriclea F
Attributed to Brathwaite

Richard Brome (1590?–1652?)
The Sparagus Garden: A comedie D

Thomas Carew (1595–1639?)
Poems V
Includes *Coelum Brittanicum* 1634 (q.v.)

Robert Chamberlain (1607?–60)
The Swaggering Damsell: A comedy D

Edward Dacres (*fl.* 1636–40) (tr.)
The Prince NF
The first printed translation of Machiavelli's *Il Principe* (written 1513) in English and of his *Vita di Castruccio* (written 1520)

William Davenant (1606–68)
Salmacida Spolia: A masque D
Published 1640, dated 1639. Performed at Whitehall on 21 January 1640.

John Donne (1572–1631)
LXXX Sermons NF
Includes Izaak Walton's Life of Donne, published separately in 1658 (q.v.)

Richard Flecknoe (*c.*1620–78)
The Affections of a Pious Soule, unto our Saviour-Christ MISC

John Fletcher (1579–1625)
The Night-Walker; or, The Little Theife: A comedy D

John Fletcher (1579–1625)
Rule a Wife and Have a Wife: A comoedy D

Thomas Fuller (1608–61)
Joseph's Party-colored Coat NF

Henry Glapthorne (1610–43?)
The Hollander: A comedy written 1635 D

Henry Glapthorne (1610–43?)
The Ladies Priviledge D

Henry Glapthorne (1610–43?)
Wit in a Constable: A comedy written 1639 D

John Gough (1610–61)
The Strange Discovery: A tragi-comedy D

William Habington (1605–54)
The Historie of Edward the Fourth, King of England NF

William Habington (1605–54)
The Queene of Arragon: A tragi-comedie D
Published anonymously

Joseph Hall (1574–1656)
Christian Moderation NF

Joseph Hall (1574–1656)
Episcopacie by Divine Right NF

Christopher Harvey (1597–1663)
The Synagogue; or, The Shadow of the Temple V
Published anonymously in imitation of George Herbert's *The Temple* 1633 (q.v.). Six editions by 1667.

George Herbert (1593–1633)
Outlandish Proverbs NF
The *Proverbs* were also printed as part ii of the first edition only of *Witts Recreations . . . With a Thousand Outlandish Proverbs* (1640)

Thomas Heywood (1574?–1641)
The Exemplary Lives and Memorable Acts of Nine the Most Worthy Women of the World NF

James Howell (1594?–1666)
Dendrologia: Dodona's grove; or, The vocall forrest F
A political allegory dealing with events between 1603 and 1640. Second Part published in 1650.

Ben Jonson (1572–1637) (tr.)
Art of Poetry V
Translated from Horace. Also contains the *Execration Against Vulcan*; *The Masque of the Gypsies* (performed 1621, as *The Gypsies Metamorphosed*), and *Epigrams to Severall Noble Personages in this Kingdome.*

Ben Jonson (1572–1637)
The Workes of Benjamin Jonson WKS
The Second Folio. Volume i reprints *Workes* 1616 (q.v.).

'Don Diego Puede-Ser' [James Mabbe (1572–1642?)] (tr.)?
Exemplarie Novells F
A translation of Cervantes' *Novelas ejemplares* (1613)

Thomas Nabbes (1605?–45?)
The Bride: A comedie D

Thomas Nabbes (1605?–45?)
The Unfortunate Mother: A tragedie D

John Parkinson (1567–1650)
Theatrum Botanicum: The Theater of Plants NF

Francis Quarles (1592–1644)
Enchyridion V

Thomas Rawlins (1620?–70)
The Rebellion: A tragedy D

Nathaniel Richards (1612?–54)
The Tragedy of Messallina, the Roman Emperesse V

George Sandys (1578–1644) (tr.)
Christs Passion: A tragedie D
Translated from the Latin of Hugo Grotius (1583–1645), *Christus patiens*

John Selden (1584–1654)
A Briefe Discourse, Concerning the Power of the Peeres and Comons of Parliament, in Point of Judicature NF
Published anonymously. Sometimes also attributed to Sir Robert Cotton (1571–1631) and to Sir Simonds D'Ewes (1602–50).

Lewis Sharpe (*fl.* 1640)
The Noble Stranger D

James Shirley (1596–1666)
Loves Crueltie: A tragedy D

James Shirley (1596–1666)
The Opportunitie: A comedy D
Based on Tirso de Molina (pseudonym of Fray Gabriel Téllez, 1583–1648), *El castigo del penséque*

James Shirley (1596–1666)
The Coronation: A comedy D
Attributed to John Fletcher, but in fact by Shirley

James Shirley (1596–1666)
The Constant Maid: A comedy D

James Shirley (1596–1666)
St Patrick for Ireland D

James Shirley (1596–1666)
The Humorous Courtier: A comedy D

James Shirley (1596–1666)
The Arcadia D
An adaptation of Sir Philip Sidney's *Arcadia*

John Tatham (*fl.* 1632–64)
The Fancies Theater V

1641

- Triennial Act
  Strafford tried (Mar.) and executed (12 May)
  Court of Star Chamber abolished
  Irish Catholic rebellion
  The Grand Remonstrance
- Sir Dudley North born
  Thomas Rymer born
  William Sherlock born?
  William Wycherley born
- Thomas Heywood dies
  Thomas Mun dies
  Sir Henry Spelman dies
- Anthony Van Dyck dies

Sir Francis Bacon (1561–1626)
Three Speeches: Concerning the post-nati, naturalization of the Scotch in England, Union of the lawes of the kingdomes of England and Scotland NF

Thomas Beedome (*d.* 1641?)
Poems Divine, and Humane V

Richard Brathwaite (1588?–1673)
The English Gentleman; and The English Gentlewoman NF
See *The English Gentleman* 1630, *The English Gentlewoman* 1631

Katherine Chidley (*fl.* 1641–5)
The Justification of the Independant Churches of Christ NF
A refutation of the arguments of Thomas Edwards (1599–1647) for centralized Church government. See also *A New-Yeares-Gift* 1645.

William Habington (1605–54)
Observations upon Historie NF
Published anonymously. Six separate essays on: Henry II; Richard I; the battle of Varna; the fall of Constantinople; Louis XI; and Charles V of France

Joseph Hall (1574–1656)
An Humble Remonstrance to the High Court of Parliament NF
Published 1641, dated 1640. See also: 'Smectymnuus', *An Answer to . . . An Humble Remonstrance* 1641; Hall, *Defence* 1641; 'Smectymnuus', *A Vindication* 1641; Hall, *A Short Answer* 1641; Milton, *Of Reformation Touching Church-Discipline* 1641, *Of Prelatical Episcopacy* 1641, *Animadversions* 1641, *Reason of Church-government* 1642, *Apology against a Pamphlet* 1642.

Joseph Hall (1574–1656)
A Defence of the Humble Remonstrance: Against the frivolous and false exceptions of Smectymnuus NF
Published anonymously. With a translation from the Latin of Abraham Scultetus (1566–1624). See Hall, *An Humble Remonstrance* 1641, above.

Joseph Hall (1574–1656)
A Short Answer to the Tedious Vindication of Smectymnuus NF
Published anonymously. A reply to 'Smectymnuus', *A Vindication of the Answer* 1641 (q.v.).

Samuel Hartlib (1600?–62)
A Description of the Famous Kingdome of Macaria NF
Published anonymously. A Utopian work.

Thomas Heywood (1574?–1641)
The Life of Merlin, Sirnamed Ambrosius NF

John Johnson (*fl.* 1641)
The Academy of Love F

Thomas Killigrew (1612–83)
The Prisoners, and Claracilla: Two tragae-comedies D

John Lilburne (1615–57)
The Christian Mans Triall NF

Shackerley Marmion (1603–39)
The Antiquary: A comedy D

John Milton (1608–74)
Of Reformation Touching Church-Discipline in England: and the Causes that Hitherto Have Hindred It NF
Published anonymously. Published between 12 and 31 May 1641. The first of Milton's pamphlets in support of the five Protestant ministers in the 'Smectymnuus' controversy. See also below, and Hall, *An Humble Remonstrance* 1641.

John Milton (1608–74)
Of Prelatical Episcopacy NF
Published anonymously in June or July 1641. See Hall, *An Humble Remonstrance* 1641.

John Milton (1608–74)
Animadversions Upon the Remonstrants Defence, Against Smectymnuus NF
Published anonymously in (?) 1641. See Hall, *An Humble Remonstrance* 1641.

Sir Robert Naunton (1563–1635)
Fragmenta Regalia: Or observations on the late Queen Elizabeth, her times and favorits NF
Written *c.*1630

Martin Parker (*d.* 1656?)
The Poet's Blind Mans Bough; or, Have Among You My Blind Harpers V

Henry Robinson (1605–73?)
Englands Safety, in Trades Encrease NF

'Smectymnuus' [collective pseudonym]
An Answer to a Booke entituled, An Humble Remonstrance NF
Response to Joseph Hall, *An Humble Remonstrance* 1641. Later editions published as *Smectymnuus redivivus*. See also *A Vindication* 1641, below.

'Smectymnuus' [collective pseudonym]
A Vindication of the Answer to the Humble Remonstrance NF
Response to Joseph Hall, *An Humble Remonstrance* 1641 (q.v.). See also *An Answer* 1641, above.

Michael Sparke (1588?–1653)
Scintilla; or, A Light Broken into Dark Warehouses NF
Published anonymously

Sir Thomas Urquhart (1611–60)
Epigrams: Divine and Moral V

George Wither (1588–1667)
Haleluiah; or, Britans [sic] *Second Remembrancer* V
See also *Britains Remembrancer* 1628

1642

- Royal Standard raised at Nottingham (22 Aug.): outbreak of the Civil War
  Parliamentary force defeated by Prince Rupert at Powicke Bridge (23 Sept.)
  Battle of Edgehill (23 Oct.)
  Theatres closed (–1660)
  Discovery of Tasmania
- Isaac Newton born
  Thomas Shadwell born?
- John Chalkhill dies
  Sir Francis Kynaston dies
  James Mabbe dies?
  Henry Peacham, the younger, dies?
  William Rowley dies?
  Sir John Suckling dies

- Galileo dies
  Cardinal Richelieu dies

William Ames (1576–1633)
The Marrow of Sacred Divinity NF
First published in Latin 1623 as *Medula S.S. theologiae*

Lancelot Andrewes (1555–1626)
The Morall Law Expounded NF

Thomas Browne (1605–82)
Religio Medici NF
Published anonymously. The first of two unauthorized anonymous editions in 1642. See also *Religio Medici* 1643.

Ralph Cudworth (1617–88)
The True Notion of the Lords Supper NF

Ralph Cudworth (1617–88)
The Union of Christ and the Church, in a Shadow NF

Sir John Denham (1615–69)
Coopers Hill: A poëme V
Published anonymously. 1st, 2nd, 3rd, and 4th editions unauthorized. First authorized edition 1655 (q.v.).

Sir John Denham (1615–69)
The Sophy D
Published anonymously

Thomas Fuller (1608–61)
The Holy State NF
In five books; book v has special title-page with title *The Profane State*

John Goodwin (1594?–1665)
Anti-Cavalierisme NF

John Hales (1584–1656)
A Tract Concerning Schisme and Schismaticks NF
Published anonymously

Sir Francis Kynaston (1587–1642)
Leoline and Sydanis V

John Milton (1608–74)
The Reason of Church-government Urg'd Against Prelaty NF
Published at the end of January 1642, dated 1641. The first of Milton's tracts published under his own name. See Hall, *An Humble Remonstrance* 1641.

John Milton (1608–74)
An Apology against a Pamphlet call'd A modest confutation of the Animadversions upon the Remonstrant against Smectymnuus NF
Published anonymously in April 1642, Reprinted 1654 as *An Apology for Smectymnuus*. See Hall, *An Humble Remonstrance* 1641.

Henry More (1614–87)
Psychodia Platonica; or, A Platonicall Song of the Soul V

William Prynne (1600–69)
A Soveraigne Antidote to Prevent, Appease and Determine Our Unnaturall and Destructive Civill Wars NF
Published anonymously

Sir Walter Ralegh (1552?–1618)
The Prince; or, Maxims of State NF

Alexander Ross (1591–1654)
Mel Heliconium; or, Poeticall Honey V

John Selden (1584–1654)
The Priviledges of the Baronage of England, when they sit in Parliament NF

Jeremy Taylor (1613–67)
Of the Sacred Order, and Offices of Episcopacy by Divine Institution, Apostolicall Tradition, & Catholike Practice NF

John Taylor (1580–1653)
Mad Fashions, Odd Fashions, All Out of Fashions; or, The Emblems of these Distracted Times V

1643

- Accession of Louis XIV of France
  Confederation of New England
  Siege of Gloucester (Aug.–Sept.)
  First Battle of Newbury (20 Sept.)
  William Dowsing begins destruction of church images in East Anglia
- Gilbert Burnet born
  John Strype born
- William Browne, of Tavistock, dies
  William Cartwright dies
  Lucius Cary dies
  Henry Glapthorne dies?
- John Pym dies
- Claudio Monteverdi dies

William Ames (1576–1633)
The Workes of the Reverend and Faithfull Minister of Christ William Ames WKS
Translated from the Latin originals

Sir Richard Baker (1568?–1645)
A Chronicle of the Kings of England NF

John Bramhall (1594–1663)
The Serpent Salve, or, A Remedie for the Biting of an Aspe NF
Published anonymously

Thomas Browne (1605–82)
Religio Medici NF
The first authorized edition. See *Religio Medici* 1642. Nine other editions in Browne's lifetime. See also Sir Kenelm Digby 1643, below.

Sir William Davenant (1606–68)
The Unfortunate Lovers: A tragedie D
Samuel Pepys refers to this play as *The Ungrateful Lovers*. Davenant was knighted in this year.

Sir Kenelm Digby (1603–65)
Observations on the 22 stanza in the 9th canto of the 2d book of Spencers Faery Queen NF
Written 1628

Sir Kenelm Digby (1603–65)
Observations upon Religio Medici NF
A response to Thomas Browne's *Religio Medici* 1643, above.

Philip Hunton (1604?–82)
A Treatise of Monarchie NF
Published anonymously. Attributed to Hunton. See also Sir Robert Filmer, *The Anarchy of a Limited or Mixed Monarchy* 1648.

John Milton (1608–74)
The Doctrine and Discipline of Divorce NF
Published anonymously

Marchamont Nedham (1620–78) and **Thomas Audley** (*fl.* 1643)
Mercurius Britanicus: Communicating the affaires of Great Britaine PER
Published weekly, on Tuesdays, Thursdays, and later Mondays, from August 1643 to May 1646

Richard Overton (*fl.* 1642–3)
Mans Mortallitie NF

William Prynne (1600–69)
The Opening of the Great Seale of England NF

William Prynne (1600–69)
The Popish Royall Favourite NF

William Prynne (1600–69)
The Treachery and Disloyalty of Papists to their Soveraignes, in Doctrine and Practise NF
Part i of *The Soveraigne Power of Parliaments and Kingdomes* 1643 (see below)

William Prynne (1600–69)
The Soveraigne Power of Parliaments and Kingdomes NF
See *The Treachery and Disloyalty of Papists to their Soveraignes* 1643 (above)

Francis Rous (1579–1659) (tr.)
The Psalmes of David in Meeter BIB

George Wither (1588–1667)
Campo-Musae V

George Wither (1588–1667)
Mercurious Rusticus; or, A Countrey Messenger NF
Published anonymously

1644

- Royalists defeated at the Battle of Marston Moor (2 July)
  End of the Ming dynasty in China
  Matthew Hopkins begins witch-finding in East Anglia
- William Penn born
  Edward Ravenscroft born
- William Chillingworth dies
  Francis Quarles dies
  George Sandys dies

John Bulwer (*fl.* 1648–54)
Chirologia; or, The Naturall Language of the Hand NF

John Cleveland (1613–58)
The Character of a London Diurnall V
Published anonymously

Sir Kenelm Digby (1603–65)
Two Treatises: In the one of which, the nature of bodies; in the other the nature of mans soule, is looked into NF

John Donne (1572–1631)
Biathanatos: A declaration of that paradoxe, or thesis, that selfe-homicide is not so naturally sinne, that it may never be otherwise NF
Written in 1608

John Goodwin (1594?–1665)
Theomaxia; or, the Grand Imprudence of Men Running the Hazard of Fighting against God NF

Joseph Hall (1574–1656)
The Devout Soul; or, Rules of Heavenly Devotion NF

William Lilly (1602–81)
Merlinus Anglicus Junior: The English Merlin Revived; or, A Mathematicall Prediction NF

John Milton (1608–74)
Of Education NF

John Milton (1608–74) (tr.)
The Judgement of Martin Bucer, Concerning Divorce NF
Published anonymously

John Milton (1608–74)
Areopagitica: A speech . . . for the liberty of unlicenc'd printing NF
Published 23 November 1644

William Prynne (1600–69)
A Breviate of the Life of William Laud NF

Francis Quarles (1592–1644)
Barnabas and Boanerges: Or, wine and oyle for afflicted soules V
Part ii also published in 1644 in an unauthorized edition as *Barnabas and Boanerges*. Both parts published together as *Judgement and Mercie for Afflicted Soules* 1646 (q.v.).

Francis Quarles (1592–1644)
The Loyall Convert NF
Published anonymously 1644, dated 1643

Francis Quarles (1592–1644)
The Shepheards Oracle V

Sir Walter Ralegh (1552?–1618)
To day a Man, To morrow None NF
Partly in verse

Samuel Rutherford (1600?–61)
Lex, Rex: The law and the prince. A dispute for the just prerogative of King and people NF
Published anonymously. In part a reply to a work by John Maxwell (1590?–1647), *Sacro-sancta regum majestas*.

George Wither (1588–1667)
Letters of Advice: Touching the Choice of Knights and Burgesses NF

1645

- Execution of William Laud (10 Jan.)
  Self-Denying Ordinance (3 Apr.): beginning of the New Model Army
  Royalists defeated at the Battle of Naseby (14 June)
- Aemelia Lanyer dies
  William Lithgow dies?
  Thomas Nabbes dies?
  William Strode dies
- Hugo Grotius dies

Katherine Chidley (*fl.* 1641–5)
A New-Yeares-Gift NF
Addressed to Thomas Edward (1599–1647). See also *Justification of the Independent Churches* 1641.

Thomas Fuller (1608–61)
Good Thoughts in Bad Times NF
See also *Good Thoughts in Worse Times* 1647, *Good Thoughts in Bad Times* 1649, *Mixt Contemplations in Better Times* 1660

Henry Hammond (1605–60)
A Practicall Catechisme NF
Published anonymously. Many editions.

James Howell (1594?–1666)
Epistolae Ho-Elianae: Familiar letters domestic and forren NF
See also *A Fourth Volume of Familiar Letters* 1655

Edward Hyde, 1st earl of Clarendon (1609–74)
Transcendent and Multiplied Rebellion and Treason Discovered by the Laws of the Land NF
Published anonymously

William Lilly (1602–81)
The Starry Messenger NF

John Milton (1608–74)
Colasterion: A reply to a nameles answer against The Doctrine and Discipline of Divorce NF
See *The Doctrine and Discipline of Divorce* 1643

John Milton (1608–74)
Tetrachordon NF

Francis Quarles (1592–1644)
Solomons Recantation, entituled Ecclesiastes, Paraphrased V

Alexander Ross (1591–1654)
The Philosophicall Touch-stone NF
A response to Sir Kenelm Digby, *Two Treatises* (1644, q.v.). Ross's work is also a reply to Richard Overton, *Mans Mortallitie* 1643 (q.v.).

Sir Robert Stapylton (1605?–69) (tr.)
Erotopaignion V
Translated from Musaeus

James Ussher (1581–1656)
A Body of Divinitie NF

Edmund Waller (1606–87)
Poems V

George Wither (1588–1667)
Vox Pacifica: A Voice Tending to the Pacification of God's Wrath V

1646

- Charles I surrenders to the Scots at Newark (5 May)
  Oxford surrenders to parliamentary forces (June)
  Rise of the Levellers
- Robert Gomersall dies
- Godfrey Kneller born
  John Flamsteed born
- Leibniz born

Thomas Browne (1605–82)
Pseudodoxia Epidemica; or, Enquiries into Very Many Received Tenets, and Commonly Presumed Truths NF
Six editions to 1672

Lucius Cary, Viscount Falkland (1610?–43)
Discourse of Infallibility NF

Richard Crashaw (1612/13–49)
Steps to the Temple: Sacred poems, with other delights of the muses V
Enlarged 1648

Thomas Fuller (1608–61)
Andronicus; or, The Unfortunate Politician NF
Published anonymously

Thomas Fuller (1608–61)
Feare of Losing the Old Light; or, A Sermon Preached in Exeter NF

John Hall, of Durham (1627–56)
Horae Vacivae; or, Essays NF

Joseph Hall (1574–1656)
The Balme of Gilead; or, Comforts for the Distressed, both Morall and Divine NF

Martin Lluelyn (1616–82)
Men-Miracles: With other poemes V

John Milton (1608–74)
Poems of Mr John Milton, Both English and Latin V
Published 1646, dated 1645

Henry More (1614–87)
Democritus Platonissans; or, An Essay Upon the Infinity of Worlds out of Platonick Principles NF
Includes verse

Francis Quarles (1592–1644)
Judgement and Mercie for Afflicted Soules NF
First authorized edition of part ii of *Boanerges and Barnabas*, preceded by unauthorized edition titled *Barnabas and Boanerges*. Part i also published 1646 with title *Judgement & Mercy for Afflicted Soules*. The two parts subsequently published separately and together. The work eventually became known as *Boanerges and Barnabas*. See *Barnabas and Boanerges* 1644.

John Saltmarsh (*c.*1610–47)
Reasons for Unitie, Peace, and Love NF

James Shirley (1596–1666)
Poems V

Sir John Suckling (1609–42)
Fragmenta Aurea WKS
Contains letters, poems, and the four plays (*Aglaura, The Goblins, Francelia, Brennoralt*)

Jeremy Taylor (1613–67)
A Discourse Concerning Prayer ex tempore, or, by Pretence of the Spirit NF
Published anonymously

Henry Vaughan (1622–95)
Poems, with the Tenth Satyre of Juvenal Englished V

George Wither (1588–1667)
Justitiarius Justificatus: The Justice Justified NF
Wither was fined and imprisoned for this tract, which was burned at Guildford by the hangman

George Wither (1588–1667)
Opobalsamum Anglicanum V

1647

- Constitutional debate at Putney
  Cornet Joyce arrests Charles I at Holmby House, Northamptonshire (3 June)
  Charles imprisoned at Carisbrooke Castle (14 Nov.)
- John Wilmot, 2nd earl of Rochester, born
- Francis Meres dies
- Pierre Bayle born

Lancelot Andrewes (1555–1626)
Of Episcopacy NF

A reply to and translation of Pierre Du Moulin (1568–1658), *Epistolae tres*

Lancelot Andrewes (1555–1626)
The Private Devotions [Preces Privatae] NF
Translated by Humphrey Moseley (*d.* 1661). See also *Manual of the Private Devotions* 1648.

Robert Baron (1630–58)
Erotopaignion; or, The Cyprian Academy F
Partly in verse. Plagiarises Milton's minor poems (1645) and includes the play *Gripus and Hegio; or, The Passionate Lovers.*

Francis Beaumont (1584–1616) and **John Fletcher** (1579–1625)
Comedies and Tragedies D
Edited by James Shirley. Includes all the plays not hitherto printed, except *The Wild-Goose Chase* 1652 (q.v.). See also *Fifty Comedies and Tragedies* 1679.

Richard Corbet (1582–1635)
Certain Elegant Poems V
Edited by John Donne the younger (1604–62). See also *Poetica Stromata* 1648.

Abraham Cowley (1618–67)
The Mistresse; or, Severall Copies of Love-Verses V

Ralph Cudworth (1617–88)
A Sermon Preached Before the Honourable House of Commons, March 31 1647 NF

Sir Richard Fanshawe (1608–66) (tr.)
Il Pastor Fido, the Faithfull Shepherd V
Published anonymously. Translated from Battista Guarini (1538–1612). See also *Il Pastor Fido* 1648.

Thomas Fuller (1608–61)
The Cause and Cure of a Wounded Conscience NF

Thomas Fuller (1608–61)
Good Thoughts in Worse Times NF
See also *Good Thoughts in Bad Times* 1645, 1649, *Mixt Contemplations in Better Times* 1660

John Hall, of Durham (1627–56)
Poems V

Christopher Harvey (1597–1663) (tr.)
Schola Cordis . . . in 47 Emblems V
Published anonymously. Adapted from Benedict van Haeften (1588–1648), *Schola Cordis* (1629). Later reprints ascribe this work to Francis Quarles.

William Lilly (1602–81)
Christian Astrology Modestly Treated of in Three Books NF

Henry More (1614–87)
Philosophicall Poems V

Marchamont Nedham (1620–78)
Mercurius Pragmaticus: Communicating intelligence from all parts PER
Anonymous. Published weekly on Tuesdays from September 1647 to May 1649. A much counterfeited newsbook. Some issues probably edited by Samuel Sheppard and John Cleveland.

Henry Neville (1620–94)
The Parliament of Ladies PS
Anonymous. A political satire. See also *The Ladies, a Second Time, Assembled* 1647 (below).

Henry Neville (1620–94)
The Ladies, a Second Time, Assembled in Parliament PS
Anonymous. Continuation of *The Parliament of Ladies* 1647 (above).

Francis Quarles (1592–1644)
Hosanna; or, Divine Poems on the Passion of Christ V

Samuel Rutherford (1600?–61)
Christ Dying and Drawing Sinners to Himselfe NF

John Saltmarsh (*c.*1610–47)
Sparkles of Glory; or, Some Beams of the Morning-Star NF

Joshua Sprigge (1618–84)
Anglia Rediviva: England's Recovery NF

Thomas Stanley, the elder (1625–78) (tr.)
Aurora, & The Prince. Oronta the Cyprian Virgin F
Translated from Juan Pérez de Montalbán (1602–38) and Girolanus Preti (1582–1626)

Sir Robert Stapylton (1605?–69) (tr.)
Juvenal's Sixteen Satyrs; or, A Survey of the Manners and Actions of Mankind V

George Wither (1588–1667)
Amygdala Britannica, Almonds for Parrets V
Anonymous

George Wither (1588–1667)
Carmen Expostulatorium; or, A Timely Expostulation V

1648

- Cromwell defeats the Scots at the Battle of Preston (17–20 Aug.)
  End of the Thirty Years War by the Peace of Westphalia (24 Oct.)
  Colonel Pride's Purge of the House of Commons, leaving the 'Rump' Parliament (6 Dec.)
  Society of Friends founded by George Fox 1648–50
- Robert Barclay born
  Humphrey Prideaux born
  Elkanah Settle born
  John Sheffield, duke of Buckingham, born
  George Jeffreys (Judge Jeffreys) born
- Edward Herbert, Lord Herbert of Cherbury, dies
- Grinling Gibbons born

Lancelot Andrewes (1555–1626)
A Manual of the Private Devotions of the Right Reverend Father in God, Lancelot Andrews NF
Translated by Richard Drake (*d.* 1681). Intended as a correction of Moseley's translation 1647 (q.v.).

Sir Francis Bacon (1561–1626)
The Remaines of the Right Honorable Francis Lord Verulam Viscount of St Albanes NF
Reissued 1656 under the title *The Mirrour of State and Eloquence*

Joseph Beaumont (1616–99)
Psyche; or, Loves Mysterie. In XX Canto's V

Richard Corbet (1582–1635)
Poetica Stromata; or, A Collection of Sundry Peices [sic] *in Poetry* V
The second edition of *Certain Elegant Poems* 1647 (q.v.). See also *Poems* 1672.

Mildmay Fane, 2nd earl of Westmorland (1602–66)
Otia Sacra Optima Fides V
Anonymous. English and Latin verse.

Sir Richard Fanshawe (1608–66)
Il Pastor Fido the Faithfull Shepherd V
Entirely by Fanshawe: intended as an addition to his translation of Guarini's *Il Pastor Fido* 1647 (q.v.)

Sir Robert Filmer (1588?–1653)
The Anarchy of a Limited or Mixed Monarchy NF
Anonymous. A reply to Philip Hunton, *A Treatise of Monarchie* 1643 (q.v.).

Sir Robert Filmer (1588?–1653)
The Necessity of the Absolute Power of Kings NF
Anonymous

Thomas Gage (1603?–56)
The English-American his Travail by Sea and Land; or, A New Survey of the West India's NF

Joseph Hall (1574–1656)
Select Thoughts, One Century NF

Robert Herrick (1591–1674)
Hesperides; or, The Works both Humane and Divine of Robert Herrick Esq. V
In two sections, secular and religious, the latter having a separate title-page, dated 1647: *His Noble Numbers; or, His Pious Pieces*

Jasper Mayne (1604–72)
The Amorous Warre: A tragi-comoedy D

John Wallis (1616–1703)
A Briefe and Easie Explanation of the Shorter Catechism NF
Eight editions by 1662

John Wilkins (1614–72)
Mathematicall Magick: Or, the wonders that may be performed by mechanicall geometry NF

Gerrard Winstanley (1609–76?)
The Breaking of the Day of God NF

Gerrard Winstanley (1609–76?)
The Mysterie of God, Concerning the Whole Creation, Mankinde NF

Gerrard Winstanley (1609–76?)
The Saints Paradise; or, The Fathers Teaching the only Satisfaction to Waiting Souls NF

'Terrae-Filius' [George Wither (1588–1667)]
Prosopopoeia Britannica V

1649

- Charles I tried (beginning 19 Jan.) and executed (30 Jan.)
  England declared a Commonwealth (19 May)
  Sacking of Drogheda by Oliver Cromwell (11 Sept.)
- Sir Thomas Pope Blount born
  Nathaniel Lee born?
  Titus Oates born

- RIchard Crashaw dies
  William Drummond, of Hawthornden, dies

Anonymous
Eikon Basilike: The poutraicture of His Sacred Majestie, in his solitudes and sufferings NF
Published on 9 February 1649, dated 1648. Originally attributed to Charles I himself (executed 30 January 1649), but authorship later claimed by Dr John Gauden (1605–62), bishop of Worcester. Responded to by Milton in *Eikonoklastes* 1649 (q.v.).

Robert Baron (1630–58)
An Apologie for Paris: For rejecting of Juno, and Pallas, and presenting of Ate's golden ball to Venus F

Richard Brome (1590?–1652?) (ed.)
Lachrymae Musarum: The Tears of the Muses V
Anonymous collection of elegies on the death of Henry, Lord Hastings. Generally assumed to have been assembled by Richard Brome.

Sir William Cavendish, later **1st duke of Newcastle** (1592–1676)
The Country Captaine, and The Varietie D
Anonymous

Sir William Davenant (1606–68)
Love and Honour D

William Dell (*c*.1607–70)
The Way of True Peace and Unity among the Faithful and Churches of Christ NF

John Donne (1572–1631)
Fifty Sermons NF
See also *LXXX Sermons* 1640

John Evelyn (1620–1706) (tr.)
Of Liberty and Servitude NF
Anonymous. Translated from the French of François de la Mothe le Vayer (1583–1672), *De la liberté et de la servitude*.

Thomas Fuller (1608–61)
Good Thoughts in Bad Times, Together with Good Thoughts in Worse Times NF
See also *Good Thoughts in Bad Times* 1645, *Good Thoughts in Worse Times* 1647, *Mixt Contemplations in Better Times* 1660

John Hall, of Durham (1627–56)
An Humble Motion to the Parliament of England Concerning the Advancement of Learning: and Reformation of the Universities NF

Joseph Hall (1574–1656)
Resolutions and Decisions of Divers Practicall Cases of Conscienc NF

Edward Herbert, Lord Herbert of Cherbury (1583–1648)
The Life and Raigne of King Henry the Eighth NF

Henry King (1592–1669)
A Groane at the Funerall of that Incomparable and Glorious Monarch, Charles the First V
Charles was executed on 30 January 1649

Richard Lovelace (1618–58)
Lucasta: Epodes, Odes, Sonnets, Songs, &c V
See also *Lucasta: Posthume Poems* 1659

John Milton (1608–74)
The Tenure of Kings and Magistrates NF
Written 15–29 January 1649 and relating to the trial of Charles I, which opened on 19 January 1649 (the king was executed on 30 January)

John Milton (1608–74)
Eikonoklastes: In answer to a book intitl'd Eikon Basilike NF
The anonymous *Eikon Basilike* was published on 9 February 1649: see above

Marchamont Nedham (1620–78)?
Mercurius Pragmaticus, (for King Charles II) PER
Anonymous. Possibly by Nedham. Published weekly on Tuesdays from April 1649 to May 1650. Inspired a hostile counterfeit, possibly edited by Samuel Sheppard.

John Ogilby (1600–76) (tr.)
The Works of Publius Virgilius Maro EDN

William Prynne (1600–69)
A Breife Memento to the Present Unparliamentary Junto NF
Published 1649, dated 1648

Thomas Stanley, the elder (1625–78)
Europa. Cupid Crucified. Venus Vigils V

Jeremy Taylor (1613–67)
The Great Exemplar of Sanctity and Holy Life According to the Christian Institution NF

George Wither (1588–1667)
Carmen Eucharisticon V

1650

- Execution of the marquess of Montrose
  Charles Stuart lands in Scotland (24 June) and is proclaimed king

Cromwell defeats the Scots at Dunbar (Sept.)

- John Banks born (c.1650)
  Jeremy Collier born
- Sir Simonds D'Ewes dies
  Phineas Fletcher dies
  Thomas May dies
- The future William III born
- Descartes dies

Anonymous
Beware the Beare: The strange but pleasing history of Balbulo and Rosina F

Robert Baron (1630–58)
Pocula Castalia V

Jacob Bauthumley (1629–60)
The Light and Dark Sides of God NF
An important Ranter tract

Richard Baxter (1615–91)
The Saints Everlasting Rest; or, A Treatise of the Blessed State of the Saints in their Enjoyment of God in Glory NF
Parts ii–iv have separate title-pages dated 1649. Eleven editions by 1677.

Thomas Bayly (*d.* 1657?)
Herba Parietis; or, The Wall-Flower F

Anne Bradstreet (1612–72)
The Tenth Muse Lately Sprung Up in America V

John Bulwer (*fl.* 1648–54)
Anthropometamorphosis, Man Transform'd, or, The Artificial Changeling NF

Abraham Cowley (1618–67)
The Guardian: A comedie D
Performed at Trinity College, Cambridge, on 12 March 1642. Altered and published as *Cutter of Coleman-Street* 1663 (q.v.).

Thomas Fuller (1608–61)
A Pisgah-Sight of Palestine and the Confines Thereof NF

John Hall, of Durham (1627–56)
Paradoxes NF

Robert Heath (*fl.* 1650)
Clarastella: Together with poems occasional, elegies, epigrams, satyrs V

Thomas Hobbes (1588–1679)
Humane Nature; or, The Fundamental Elements of Policie NF
Elements of Law, part i

Thomas Hobbes (1588–1679)
De Corpore Politico; or, The Elements of Law, Moral & Politick NF
Elements of Law, part ii

Marchamont Nedham (1620–78)
The Case of the Common-Wealth of England, Stated NF

Marchamont Nedham (1620–78)
Mercurius Politicus: Comprising the summ of all intelligence PER
Anonymous. Published weekly on Thursdays from June 1650 to April 1660. Some later issues edited by John Canne (*d.* 1667?).

Henry Neville (1620–94)
Newes From the New Exchange; or, The Commonwealth of Ladies F
See *The Parliament of Ladies, The Ladies, a Second Time* 1647

Sir Walter Ralegh (1552?–1618)
Judicious and Select Essayes and Observations NF

Samuel Sheppard (*fl.* 1646)
The Loves of Amandus and Sophronia F

John Tatham (*fl.* 1632–64)
Ostella; or, The Faction of Love and Beauty Reconcil'd V

Jeremy Taylor (1613–67)
The Rule and Exercises of Holy Living NF
Many editions. See also *The Rule and Exercises of Holy Dying* 1651.

Henry Vaughan (1622–95)
Silex Scintillans; or, Sacred Poems and Private Ejaculations V
See also *Silex Scintillans* 1655

'Eugenius Philalethes' [Thomas Vaughan (1622–66)]
Anima Magica Abscondita: Or a discourse of the universall spirit of nature NF
Probably not issued separately, but issued only with Vaughan's *Anthroposophia Theomagica* 1650 (q.v.)

'Eugenius Philalethes' [Thomas Vaughan (1622–66)]
Anthroposophia Theomagica; or, A Discourse of the Nature of Man and his State After Death V

'Eugenius Philalethes' [Thomas Vaughan (1622–66)]
Magia Adamica; or, The Antiquitie of Magic, and the Descent Thereof from Adam Downwards, Proved NF

'Eugenius Philalethes' [Thomas Vaughan (1622–66)]
The Man-Mouse Taken in a Trap NF
A reply to Henry More's *Observations* 1650 (q.v.)

Sir Anthony Weldon (*d.* 1649?)
The Court and Character of King James NF

1651

- Scots crown Charles II at Scone (1 Jan.)
  Cromwell defeats Charles II at the Battle of Worcester (3 Sept.): Charles flees to France
  First Navigation Act
- Mary Mollineux born
- François de la Mothe Fénelon born

Anonymous
A Hermeticall Banquet V
Published 1651, dated 1652. Sometimes attributed to James Howell or to Thomas Vaughan.

Anonymous
The Tragedy of that Famous Roman Orator Marcus Tullius Cicero D

Sir Francis Bacon (1561–1626)
The Felicity of Queen Elizabeth: and Her Times NF

William Bosworth (1607–50?)
The Chast and Lost Lovers V

Roger Boyle, earl of Orrery (1621–79)
Parthenissa That Most Fam'd Romance F
First issue of the first edition. Contains Part i, books 1–8, and Part ii, books 1–8. Parts iii and iv published 1655; Part v, 1656. Final part (vi) published 1669; complete edition (6 parts) published 1676 (q.v.). The first imitation of French heroico-historical romances.

William Cartwright (1611–43)
Comedies, Tragi-Comedies, with Other Poems WKS

Mary Cary (*fl.* 1636–53)
The Little Horns Doom and Downfall NF
An important millenarian tract

John Cleveland (1613–58)
Poems V
The '6th edition', containing 28 poems, 23 from the 5th edition of *The Character of a London Diurnall* 1647 and adds a prose work, 'The Character of a Country Committee-Man, with the Ear-Mark of a Sequestrator'. Many subsequent editions.

Sir William Davenant (1606–68)
Gondibert: An heroick poem V
Commendatory verses by Edmund Waller and Abraham Cowley. See also *The Seventh and Last Canto . . . of Gondibert* 1685.

Sir John Denham (1615–69)
The Anatomy of Play NF
Anonymous

John Donne (1572–1631)
Essayes in Divinity NF
Edited John Donne the younger (1604–62)

John Donne (1572–1631)
Letters to Severall Persons of Honour NF
Edited by John Donne the younger (1604–62)

Thomas Fuller (1608–61) and others
Abel Redevivus; or, The Dead Yet Speaking: The lives and deaths of the moderne divines NF
Preface and some lives by Fuller. Other biographical sketches by Daniel Featley (1582–1645), Thomas Gataker (1574–1654), and others. Occasional verse by Francis and John Quarles.

Joseph Hall (1574–1656)
The Great Mysterie of Godliness NF
Published 1651, dated 1652

Joseph Hall (1574–1656)
Susurrium Cum Deo: Soliloquies NF

Thomas Hobbes (1588–1679)
Leviathan; or, The Matter, Forme, & Power of a Common-Wealth Ecclesiasticall and Civill NF

Thomas Hobbes (1588–1679)
Philosophicall Rudiments Concerning Government and Society NF
First published in Latin as *Elementorum Philosophiae Sectio Tertia: de Cive*, Paris: 1642

Henry King (1592–1669) (tr.)
The Psalmes of David BIB

William Laud (1573–1645)
Seven Sermons Preached upon Severall Occasions NF

William Lilly (1602–81)
Monarchy or No Monarchy in England NF
Includes 'Several Observations upon the Life and Death of Charles late King of England'

John Milton (1608–74)
Pro Populo Anglicano Defensio, Contra Claudii Anonymi, alias Salmasii, Defensionem Regiam NF

Translated into English by J. Washington, 1692, as *A Defence of the People of England . . . In Answer to Salmasius's Defence of the King*. See also *Pro Populo Anglicano Defensio Secunda* 1654.

Edmund Prestwich (*fl.* 1651) (tr.)
Hippolitus Translated out of Seneca D
A translation of Seneca's *Phaedra*

Sir Walter Ralegh (1552?–1618)
Sir Walter Raleigh's Sceptick, or Speculations NF

Sir Edward Sherburne (1618–1702)
Salmacis. Lyrian & Sylvia. Forsaken Lydia. The Rape of Helen V
Also issued 1651 as *Poems and Translations, Amorous, Lusory, Morall, Divine*

Michael Sparke (1588?–1653)
The Narrative History of King James, for the First Fourteen Years NF

Thomas Stanley, the elder (1625–78)
Poems V
Includes original poems and translations. First privately printed 1647 as *Poems and Translations*.

John Tatham (*fl.* 1632–64)
The Distracted State: A tragedy D

Jeremy Taylor (1613–67)
The Rule and Exercises of Holy Dying NF
Seven editions to 1668. See also *The Rule and Exercises of Holy Living* 1650.

Jeremy Taylor (1613–67)
XXVIII Sermons Preached at Golden Grove NF
See also *XXV Sermons* 1653

Henry Vaughan (1622–95)
Olor Iscanus: A collection of some select poems, and translations V/NF
Includes four prose translations: 'Of the benefit wee may get by our enemies' (from Plutarch); 'Of the diseases of the mind and the body' (Plutarch); 'Of the diseases of the mind, and the body' (from Maximus of Tyre); 'The praise and happinesse of the countrie-life' (from Fray Antonio de Guevara, 1480?–1545)

'Eugenius Philalethes' [Thomas Vaughan (1622–66)]
Lumen de Lumine; or, A New Magicall Light Discovered, and Communicated to the World NF

Izaak Walton (1593–1683)
'The Life of Sir Henry Wotton' NF
Published in *Reliquiae Wottonianae* 1651 (see below)

Leonard Willan (*fl.* 1649–70)
Astraea; or, True Love's Myrrour: A pastoral D

Sir Henry Wotton (1568–1639)
Reliquiae Wottonianae: Or, a collection of lives, letters, poems MISC
Includes 'The Life of Sir Henry Wotton' by Izaak Walton

1652

- First Anglo-Dutch War (1652–4)
- Jane Barker born
  Thomas Otway born
  Nahum Tate born
- Richard Brome dies?
  Lady Eleanor Davies dies
- Inigo Jones dies

Elias Ashmole (1617–92)
Theatrum Chemicum Britannicum NF
In Latin

Francis Beaumont (1584–1616) and **John Fletcher** (1579–1625)
The Wild-Goose Chase: A comedie D
Performed at Court in 1621 but omitted from the 1647 (q.v.) folio edition of Beaumont and Fletcher's works

Edward Benlowes (1603?–76)
Theophila; or, Loves Sacrifice V
Includes some Latin verse and translations

Richard Brome (1590?–1652?)
A Joviall Crew; or, The Merry Beggars D
See also Concanen, *The Jovial Crew* 1731

Samuel Clarke (1599–1683)
A Martyrologie NF

Henry Cogan (*fl.* 1652) (tr.)
Ibrahim; or, The Illustrious Bassa: An excellent new romance F
Translated from Madeleine de Scudéry (1607–1701), *Ibrahim, ou l'Illustre Bassa* (1641–4)

Richard Crashaw (1612/13–49)
Carmen Deo Nostro, Te Decet Hymnus: Sacred poems V
Contains poems from *Steps to the Temple* 1646 (q.v.), with additions

John Donne (1572–1631)
Paradoxes, Problemes, Essayes, Characters NF
The 3rd edition of *Juvenilia* 1633 (q.v.). Prepared by John Donne the younger. Epigrams translated

by Jasper Mayne (1604–72). Also contains *Ignatius his Conclave*, first published in 1611 (q.v.).

John Evelyn (1620–1706)
The State of France NF

Sir Richard Fanshawe (1608–66) (tr.)
Selected Parts of Horace, Prince of Lyricks V
Anonymous. Latin and English verse on facing pages.

Sir Robert Filmer (1588?–1653)
Observations Concerning the Originall of Government NF
Anonymous. With reference to Thomas Hobbes, *Leviathan* 1651 (q.v.); Milton's *Pro Populo Anglicano Defensio*; and Hugo Grotius (1583–1645), *De jure belli et pacis*.

Sir Robert Filmer (1588?–1653)
Observations Upon Aristotles Politiques Touching Forms of Government NF
Anonymous

Fulke Greville, Lord Brooke (1554–1628)
The Life of the Renowned Sr Philip Sidney NF
Written *c.*1611

Joseph Hall (1574–1656)
Holy Raptures; or, Patheticall Meditations of the Love of Christ NF

George Herbert (1593–1633)
Herbert's Remains NF
Contains *A Priest to the Temple; or, The Country Parson his Character, and Rule of Holy Life* (printed separately 1671, q.v.); *Jacula Prudentum; or, Outlandish Proverbs, Sentences, &c* (first published 1640, 1651). Includes a life of Herbert by Barnabas Oley (1602–86), who may have edited the whole volume.

Peter Heylyn (1600–62)
Cosmographie in Four Bookes NF
An expanded version of *Microcosmus* 1621 (q.v.)

William Lilly (1602–81)
Annus Tenebrosus; or, The Dark Year NF

Cosmo Manuche (*fl.* 1642–64)
The Bastard: A tragedy D
Anonymous. Attributed to Manuche. Based on *Geraldo the Unfortunate Spaniard*, a translation by Leonard Digges of Gonzalo de Céspedes y Meneses (1585?–1638), *Poema tragico del pañol Gerado*.

Cosmo Manuche (*fl.* 1642–64)
The Just General: A tragi-comedy D

Cosmo Manuche (*fl.* 1642–64)
The Loyal Lovers: A tragi-comedy D

Thomas Middleton (1580–1627)
The Widdow: A comedie D
Attributed to 'Ben Johnson [sic], John Fletcher, Tho. Middleton gent.'. Now ascribed wholly to Middleton.

Edward Sparke (*d.* 1692)
Scintillula Altaris NF
Later editions published as *Thysiast-erion*

Michael Sparke (1588?–1653)
A Second Beacon Fired by Scintilla NF
'Scintilla' = Michael Sparke

John Tatham (*fl.* 1632–64)
The Scots Figgaries; or, A Knot of Knaves: A comedy D
Anonymous

Sir Thomas Urquhart (1611–60)
Pantochronochanon; or, A Peculiar Promptuary of Time NF

Henry Vaughan (1622–95)
The Mount of Olives; or, Solitary Devotions NF

Thomas Vaughan (1622–66)
Aula Lucis; or, The House of Light NF
'By S.N. a modern speculator'

1653

- Rump Parliament dissolved
  Oliver Cromwell becomes Lord Protector (16 Dec.)
- Thomas D'Urfey born
  John Oldham born
- William Basse dies
  Sir Robert Filmer dies
  William Heminges dies
  John Taylor ('The Water Poet') dies

Richard Baxter (1615–91)
The Right Method for a Settled Peace of Conscience, and Spiritual Comfort NF
An influential work of pastoral counselling

Richard Brome (1590?–1652?)
Five New Playes D
Contains: *A Madd Couple Well Matcht*; *The Novella*; *The Court Begger*; *The City Wit*; *The Damoiselle*. See also *Five New Plays* 1659.

Margaret Cavendish, Lady Newcastle (1624?–74)
Philosophicall Fancies MISC

Margaret Cavendish, Lady Newcastle (1624?–74)
Poems, and Fancies NF/V

Anne Collins (*fl.* 1653)
Divine Songs and Meditacions V

Nicholas Culpeper (1616–54)
The English Physitian Enlarged NF

Sir Robert Filmer (1588?–1653)
An Advertisement to the Jury-Men of England, Touching Witches NF
Anonymous. Partly a reply to William Perkins, *A Discourse of the Damned Art of Witchcraft* 1608 (q.v.).

Richard Flecknoe (*c.*1620–78)
Miscellania; or, Poems of all Sorts MISC
Prose and verse

Henry Hammond (1605–60)
A Paraphrase, and Annotations upon all the Books of the New Testament BIB

William Heminges (1602–53)
The Fatal Contract: A French tragedy D

Edward Johnson (1599?–1672)
A History of New-England NF
Published 1653, dated 1654

Henry Lawes (1596–1662)
Ayres and Dialogues, for One, Two, and Three Voyces V/MUS
See also *Second Book of Ayres* 1655, *Ayres, and Dialogues* 1658

Thomas Middleton (1580–1627) and **William Rowley** (1585?–1642?)
The Changeling D

Thomas Middleton (1580–1627) and **William Rowley** (1585?–1642?)
The Spanish Gipsie D

Henry More (1614–87)
Conjectura Cabbalistica NF

Alexander Ross (1591–1654)
Leviathan Drawn Out With a Hook: Or, animadversions on Mr Hobbes his Leviathan NF

James Shirley (1596–1666)
Six New Playes D
Contains *The Brothers*; *The Doubtful Heir*; *The Imposture*; *The Cardinal*; *The Sisters*; *The Court Secret*

James Shirley (1596–1666)
Cupid and Death: A masque D

Jeremy Taylor (1613–67)
XXV Sermons Preached at Golden-Grove NF
See also *XXVIII Sermons* 1651

Sir Thomas Urquhart (1611–60) (tr.)
The First Book of the Works of Mr Francis Rabelais, Doctor in Physick V
Anonymous translation of *Gargantua and Pantagruel* by François Rabelais (*c.*1494–*c.*1553). *Second Book* also published in 1653; *Third Book*, dated 1693, published in *The Works of F. Rabelais MD by Sir Tho. Urchard Kt and Others* (1694).

Izaak Walton (1593–1683)
The Compleat Angler; or, The Contemplative Man's Recreation NF
5th edition 1676 as *The Universal Angler* (with alterations by Charles Cotton)

George Wither (1588–1667)
The Dark Lantern V

1654

- Treaty of Westminster ends the first Anglo-Dutch War (Apr.)
  Abdication of Queen Christina of Sweden
- Joshua Barnes born
  Sir Richard Blackmore born
  Charles Blount born
- Nicholas Culpeper dies
  William Habington dies
  Nathaniel Richards dies
- John Selden dies

Robert Aylet (1583–1655)
Divine, and Moral Speculations in Metrical Numbers, Upon Various Subjects V
Includes previously published pieces plus 'The Song of Songs' and 'The Brides Ornaments' apparently published here for the first time

Alexander Brome (1620–66)
The Cunning Lovers: A comedy D

George Chapman (1559?–1634)
The Tragedy of Alphonsus Emperour of Germany D
Sometimes also attributed to George Peele

John Cleveland (1613–58)
The Idol of the Clownes; or, Insurrection of Wat the Tyler NF
Anonymous

John Cotton (1584–1652)
A Briefe Exposition with Practicall Observations upon the Whole Book of Ecclesiastes NF

Richard Flecknoe (*c.*1620–78)
Love's Dominion D
Published anonymously and unacted. See *Love's Kingdom* 1664.

George Fox (1624–91)
The Vialls of the Wrath of God NF

Thomas Hobbes (1588–1679)
Of Libertie and Necessitie NF
A reply to John Bramhall (1594–1663), bishop of Londonderry, later archbishop of Armagh

Robert Mead (1616–53)
The Combat of Love and Friendship: A comedy D

John Milton (1608–74)
Pro Populo Anglicano Defensio Secunda NF
See *Pro Populo Anglicano Defensio* 1651. First translated into English in 1806.

John Playford (1623–86)
A Breefe Introduction to the Skills of Musick for Song & Violl V/MUS
Many editions

Anna Trapnel (*fl.* 1642–60)
A Legacy for Saints: Being several experiences of the dealings of God with Anna Trapnel NF

Henry Vaughan (1622–95) (compiler)
Flores Solitudinis: Certaine rare and elegant pieces ANTH

John Webster (1580?–1635?)
Appius and Virginia: A tragedy D

Richard Whitlock (*c.*1616–*c.*1672)
Zootomia; or, Observations of the Present Manners of the English NF

1655

- Penruddock's Rising (Mar.)
  The English occupy Jamaica
  The First Northern War
- John Evelyn, the younger, born
- Robert Aylet dies?

Anonymous
The Comical History of Francion F
Translated 'by a person of honour' from *La Vraie histoire comique de Francion* (1623) by Charles Sorel (*c.*1599–1674), an early example of the picaresque novel.

Robert Baron (1630–58)
Mirza: A tragedie D
Publication date uncertain

Richard Baxter (1615–91)
The Unreasonableness of Infidelity NF
A pioneering work of Christian apologetic on rational grounds

Lodowick Carlell (1601/2–75)
The Passionate Lovers: A tragi-comedy. The first and second parts D
Part i performed at Somerset House (10 July 1638); part ii performed at the Cockpit-in-Court (20 December 1638)

Margaret Cavendish, Lady Newcastle (1624?–74)
The Philosophical and Physical Opinions NF

Margaret Cavendish, Lady Newcastle (1624?–74)
The Worlds Olio NF
Includes two poems

John Cotgrave (*fl.* 1655) (ed.)
The English Treasury of Wit and Language ANTH

John Cotgrave (*fl.* 1655)
Wits Interpreter NF

Robert Davenport (*fl.* 1624–40)
King John and Matilda: A tragedy D

Sir John Denham (1615–69)
Coopers Hill V
The first authorized edition. See also *Coopers Hill* 1642.

William Drummond (1585–1649)
The History of Scotland: From the year 1423 until the year 1542 NF

Sir Richard Fanshawe (1608–66) (tr.)
The Lusiad; or, Portugals Historicall Poem V
Translated from Luis de Camoëns (1524?–80)

Thomas Heywood (1574?–1641) and **William Rowley** (1585?–1642?)
Fortune by Land and Sea: A tragi-comedy D

James Howell (1594?–1666)
A Fourth Volume of Familiar Letters NF
Completes Howell's *Familiar Letters*. See also *Epistolae Ho-Elianae* 1645.

Henry Lawes (1596–1662)
The Second Book of Ayres, and Dialogues, for One, Two, and Three Voyces V/MUS
See *Ayres and Dialogues* 1653, 1658

Sir William Lower (1600?–62) (tr.)
Polyeuctes; or, The Martyr: A tragedy D
Translated from *Polyeucte* (1641/2) by Pierre Corneille (1606–84)

Andrew Marvell (1621–78)
The First Anniversary of the Government Under His Highness the Lord Protector V
Anonymous

Philip Massinger (1583–1640)
Three New Playes D
Contains *The Bashful Lover*; *The Guardian*; *A Very Woman* (written with John Fletcher)

Marchamont Nedham (1620–78)
The Publick Intelligencer: Communicating the chief occurrences and proceedings PER
Anonymous. Published weekly on Mondays from October 1655 to April 1660. Sister journal to *Mercurius Politicus* (1650–60, q.v), with some overlap.

John Phillips (1631–1706)
A Satyr Against Hypocrites V
Anonymous. An attack on Oliver Cromwell and puritanism.

Laurence Price (*fl.* 1625–80?)
The Witch of the Woodlands; or, The Coblers New Translation F

William Prynne (1600–69)
The Quakers Unmasked, and Clearly Detected to be But the Spawn of Romish Frogs NF

William Rider (*fl.* 1655)
The Twins: A tragi-comedy D

James Shirley (1596–1666)
The Gentleman of Venice: A tragi-comedie D

James Shirley (1596–1666)
The Politician: A tragedy D

Jonathan Sidnam (*fl.* 1630) (tr.)
Filli di Sciro; or, Phillis of Scyros: An excellent pastorall D
Translated from Guido Ubaldo de' Bonarelli della Rovere (1563–1608)

John Spottiswood (1565–1639)
The History of the Church of Scotland NF

Thomas Stanley, the elder (1625–78)
The History of Philosophy NF

William Strode (1602–45)
The Floating Island: A tragi-comedy D

Jeremy Taylor (1613–67)
The Golden Grove; or, A Manuall of Daily Prayers and Letanies, Fitted to the Dayes of the Weeke NF
bao *The Great Exemplar*. Twenty-one editions by 1703.

Sir Henry Vane (1613–62)
The Retired Mans Meditations NF

Henry Vaughan (1622–95) (tr.)
Hermetical Physick; or, The Right Way to Preserve and to Restore Health NF
Translated from Heinrich Nolle (*fl.* 1612–19), *Systema Medicinae Hermeticae Generale* (1613)

Henry Vaughan (1622–95)
Silex Scintillans: Sacred poems and private ejaculations V
The 2nd edition. See also *Silex Scintillans* 1650.

'Eugenius Philalethes' [Thomas Vaughan (1622–66)]
Euphrates; or, The Waters of the East NF

Edmund Waller (1606–87)
A Panegyrick to my Lord Protector V

George Wither (1588–1667)
The Protector V

1656

- Anglo-Spanish War (-1659)
  Persecution of the Quakers
- Patrick Abercromby born
  Mary Chudleigh born
  Gerard Langbaine born
- John Hall, of Durham, dies
  Joseph Hall dies
  James Ussher dies
- Edmund Halley born
  Jacob Tonson born

Richard Baxter (1615–91)
Gildas Salvianus: The Reformed Pastor NF

John Bunyan (1628–88)
Some Gospel-Truths Opened According to the Scriptures NF
Bunyan's first publication, written against the Quakers. See also *A Vindication* 1657.

Margaret Cavendish, Lady Newcastle (1624?–74)
Natures Pictures Drawn by Fancies Pencil to the Life MISC
Fiction, verse, and prose

Walter Charleton (1619–1707) (tr.)
Epicurus's Morals NF
Anonymous

Abraham Cowley (1618–67)
Poems V

Sir William Davenant (1606–68)
The Siege of Rhodes D
Anonymous

Sir John Denham (1615–69) (tr.)
The Destruction of Troy V
Anonymous. A partial version of Virgil, *Aeneid* ii.

William Drummond (1585–1649)
Poems V

Sir William Dugdale (1605–86)
The Antiquities of Warwickshire Illustrated NF

John Evelyn (1620–1706) (tr.)
An Essay on the First Book of T. Lucretius Carus V
A translation of Lucretius, *De rerum natura*. English and Latin. Includes commendatory poems by Sir Richard Brown, Edmund Waller, and Christopher Wase (in Latin).

Richard Flecknoe (*c*.1620–78)
The Diarium, or Journall V
Published anonymously

Thomas Fuller (1608–61)
A Collection of Sermons NF

Thomas Goffe (1591–1629)
The Careless Shepherdess: A tragi-comedy D

James Harrington (1611–77)
The Common-wealth of Oceana NF
Anonymous

Thomas Hobbes (1588–1679)
Elements of Philosophy NF
An English translation of Hobbes's *Elementorum Philosophiae: De Corpore* (1655)

Thomas Hobbes (1588–1679)
The Questions Concerning Liberty, Necessity and Chance NF

John Lilburne (1615–57)
The Resurrection of John Lilburne NF

Sir William Lower (1600?–62) (tr.)
Horatius: A Roman tragedie D
Translated from *Horace* (1640) by Pierre Corneille (1606–84)

Philip Massinger (1583–1640), **Thomas Middleton** (1580–1627), and **William Rowley** (1586?–1642?)
The Old Law D

Marchamont Nedham (1620–78)
The Excellencie of a Free-State; or, The Right Constitution of a Common-wealth NF
Anonymous. Reprinted from *Mercurius Politicus* 1650 (q.v.).

Jeremy Taylor (1613–67)
Deus Justificatus: Two discourses of original sin NF

Sir Henry Vane (1613–62)
A Healing Question Propounded and Resolved NF
Anonymous. Calls for the adoption of a new constitution.

1657

- The Humble Petition and Advice offering Cromwell the title of king (he refuses)
- John Dennis born
  Francis Moore ('Old Moore') born
  John Norris born
  Matthew Tindal born
- William Harvey dies
  John Lilburne dies

Anonymous
Lusts Dominion; or, The Lascivious Queen: A tragedie D
Misattributed to Christopher Marlowe on title-page. Probably written collaboratively *c*.1600 by John Marston, Thomas Dekker, John Day, and William Haughton.

Sir Francis Bacon (1561–1626)
Resuscitatio NF
Part i; part ii published 1670 (q.v.). Compiled by William Rawley (1588?–1667), Bacon's chaplain.

Augustine Baker (1575–1641)
Sancta Sophia; or, Directions for the Prayer of Contemplation &c NF

Nicholas Billingsley (1633–1709)
Brachy-Martyrologia V

Henry Bold (1627–83)
Wit a Sporting in a Pleasant Grove of New Fancies V

John Bramhall (1594–1663)
Castigations of Mr Hobbes and his Last Animadversions in the Case Concerning Liberty and Universal Necessity NF
See Hobbes, *Of Liberty and Necessitie* 1654

Richard Brome (1590?–1652?)
The Queenes Exchange: A comedy D

John Bunyan (1628–88)
A Vindication of the Book Called Some Gospel-Truths Opened NF
Written in answer to Edward Burrough, *The True Faith of the Gosepl of Peace Contended For* (1656), itself a reply to Bunyan's *Some Gospel-Truths Opened* 1656 (q.v.).

Lodowick Carlell (1601/2–75)
The Fool Would Be a Favourit; or, The Discreet Lover: A trage-comedy D
Also issued as part of Carlell's *Two New Playes* 1657

Lodowick Carlell (1601/2–75)
Osmond the Great Turk D
Also issued as part of Carlell's *Two New Playes* 1657

Samuel Clarke (1599–1683)
England's Remembrancer NF

John Cosin (1595–1672)
A Scholastical History of the Canon of the Holy Scriptures NF
Repudiates the canon promulgated by the Council of Trent

James Harrington (1611–77)
The Prerogative of Popular Government NF
Published 1657, dated 1658. A partial defence of Harrington's *Common-wealth of Oceana* 1656 (q.v.).

Peter Heylyn (1600–62)
Ecclesia Vindicata; or, The Church of England Justified NF

James Howell (1594?–1666)
Londinopolis: An historicall discourse or perlustration of the City of London NF
Largely derived from John Stow's *Survay of London* 1598 (q.v.)

Henry King (1592–1669)
Poems, Elegies, Paradoxes, and Sonnets V
Anonymous and unauthorized

Thomas Middleton (1580–1627)
No Wit, Help Like a Womans: A comedy D
Edited by James Shirley

Thomas Middleton (1580–1627)
Two New Playes D
Contains *More Dissemblers Beside Women* and *Women Beware Women*

Marchamont Nedham (1620–78)
The Publick Adviser PER
Anonymous. Published weekly from May to September 1657. The first advertising weekly.

Joshua Poole (*c*.1615–*c*.1656)
The English Parnassus; or, A Helpe to English Poesie DICT

'William Allen' [Edward Sexby (*d*. 1658)**]**
Killing Noe Murder NF
An apology for tyrannicide, ironically dedicated to Oliver Cromwell. Possibly co-written with Silius Titus (1623?–1704).

Jeremy Taylor (1613–67)
A Discourse of the Nature, Offices and Measures of Friendship NF
Anonymous

'Eugenius Philalethes' [Henry Vaughan (1622–95)**]** (tr.)?
The Chymists Key to Shut and to Open NF
Translated from Heinrich Nolle (*fl*. 1612–19), *De Generatione Rerum Naturalium* (1613)

1658

- Oliver Cromwell dies (3 Sept.)
  Richard Cromwell becomes Protector (–May 1659)
- John Cleveland dies
  Richard Lovelace dies
- Henry Purcell born
- Alessandro Scarlatti born

Richard Allestree (1619–81)
The Practice of Christian Graces; or, The Whole Duty of Man NF
Anonymous. Many editions.

Richard Baxter (1615–91)
A Call to the Unconverted to Turn and Live and Accept of Mercy While Mercy May Be Had NF
Twenty-eight editions to 1696

Richard Baxter (1615–91)
The Crucifying of the World, by the Cross of Christ NF

Richard Baxter (1615–91)
The Grotian Religion Discovered NF

With reference to Hugo Grotius (1583–1645) and the Synod of Dort (1618–19), and a reply to Thomas Pierce (1622–91)

Nicholas Billingsley (1633–1709)
Kosmobrephia; or, The Infancy of the World V
Mostly in verse

Richard Brathwaite (1588?–1673)
The Honest Ghost; or, A Voice from the Vault V
Anonymous. Mostly in verse.

Thomas Browne (1605–82)
Hydriotaphia, Urne-Buriall; or, A Discourse of the Sepulchrall Urnes Lately Found in Norfolk NF
Also contains *The Garden of Cyrus*

John Bunyan (1628–88)
A Few Sighs from Hell; or, The Groans of a Damned Soul NF
Bunyan's first published sermon treatise, which continued to be reprinted through the 18th century

William Chamberlayne (1619–89)
Loves Victory: A tragi-comedy D

Sir Aston Cokayne (1608–84)
Small Poems of Divers Sorts V
See also *Poems* 1662

Sir William Davenant (1606–68)
The Cruelty of the Spaniards in Peru D
Anonymous

'Philocepos' [John Evelyn (1620–1706)**]** (tr.)
The French Gardiner NF
Translated from the French of Nicolas de Bonnefons, *Le jardinier françois*

Richard Flecknoe (*c.*1620–78)
Enigmaticall Characters NF

Henry Lawes (1596–1662)
Ayres, and Dialogues, for One, Two, and Three Voyces V/MUS
See *Ayres and Dialogues* 1653, *The Second Book of Ayres and Dialogues* 1655

Philip Massinger (1583–1640)
The City-Madam: A comedie D
Some copies dated 1659. Performed in 1632.

Thomas May (1595–1650)
The Old Couple: A comedy D

Thomas Meriton (*b.* 1638)
Love and War D

Edward Phillips (1630–96?)
The New World of English Words; or, A General Dictionary DICT

William Rowley (1585?–1642?), **Thomas Dekker** (1572?–1632), and **John Ford** (1596–1640)
The Witch of Edmonton: A known true story D
Performed *c.*1621

George Starkey (1627–65)
Natures Explication and Helmont's Vindication; or, A Short and Sure Way to a Long and Sound Life NF
Published 1658, dated 1657. With reference to Franciscus Mercurius van Helmont (1614–99).

James Ussher (1581–1656)
The Annals of the World NF

Edmund Waller (1606–87) and **Sidney Godolphin** (1645–1712) (tr.)
The Passion of Dido for Aeneas V
Translated from Virgil

Izaak Walton (1593–1683)
The Life of John Donne NF
The first separate edition. Enlarged from the version published in Donne's *LXXX Sermons* 1640 (q.v.).

Leonard Willan (*fl.* 1649–70)
Orgula; or, The Fatal Error: A known true story D

1659

- Restoration of the Rump Parliament (7 May)
  Richard Cromwell resigns as Protector (25 May)
  Aurangzeb becomes Mogul Emperor
- Thomas Creech born
  John Dunton born
  Thomas Southerne born
  Anne Wharton born
- Francis Rous dies

Richard Baxter (1615–91)
Five Disputations of Church-Government and Worship NF
Each disputation has a separate title-page dated 1658

Richard Baxter (1615–91)
A Holy Commonwealth, or Political Aphorisms NF

Robert Boyle (1627–91)
Some Motives and Incentives to the Love of God NF
6th edition, 1678

Richard Brathwaite (1588?–1673)
Capitall Hereticks; or, The Evill Angels Embattel'd against S. Michael NF

Richard Brome (1590?–1652?)
Five New Plays D
Contains *The English Moor*; *The Love-Sick Court*; *The Weeding of the Covent-Garden*; *The New Academy*; *The Queen and Concubine*. See also *Five New Playes* 1653.

John Bunyan (1628–88)
The Doctrine of the Law and Grace Unfolded NF
Bunyan's most sustained work of systematic theology, expounding a covenantal version of Calvinism. See also *Christian Behaviour* 1663.

William Chamberlayne (1619–89)
Pharonnida: A heroick poem V

John Cleveland (1613–58)
J. Cleaveland Revived: Poems, orations, epistles . . . MISC
See also *Clievelandi Vindiciæ* 1677

John Day (1574–1640) and **Henry Chettle** (1560?–1607)
The Blind-Beggar of Bednal-Green D

John Dryden (1631–1700), and others
Three Poems Upon the Death of His Late Highnesse Oliver Lord Protector of England, Scotland, and Ireland V
By Dryden, Edmund Waller, and Thomas Sprat

John Evelyn (1620–1706)
An Apologie for the Royal Party NF
Anonymous

John Evelyn (1620–1706)
A Character of England NF
Anonymous

John Evelyn (1620–1706) (tr.)
The Golden Book of St John Chrysostom NF
A translation of St John Chrysostom, *De educandis liberis*

Richard Flecknoe (*c.*1620–78)
The Idea of His Highness Oliver, Late Lord Protector NF
Cromwell died on 3 September 1658

George Fox (1624–91)
The Great Mistery of the Great Whore Unfolded NF

John Hales (1584–1656)
Golden Remaines of the Ever Memorable Mr John Hales WKS

James Harrington (1611–77)
Aphorisms Political NF

James Harrington (1611–77) (tr.)
Virgil's Aeneis: The Third, Fourth, Fifth and Sixth Books V

Peter Heylyn (1600–62)
Examen Historicum: Or, a discovery and examination of the mistakes, falsities, and defects in some modern histories NF

Henry King (1592–1669)
An Elegy Upon the Most Incomparable K. Charls the I V
Completed by 11 March 1649 but not printed until this year

Richard Lovelace (1618–58)
Lucasta: Posthume poems V
See *Lucasta* 1649

John Milton (1608–74)
Considerations Touching the Likeliest Means to Remove Hirelings Out of the Church NF

John Milton (1608–74)
A Treatise of Civil Power in Ecclestiastical Causes NF

Henry More (1614–87)
The Immortality of the Soul NF

Marchamont Nedham (1620–78)
Interest Will Not Lie NF
A reply to John Fell (1625–86), *The Interest of England Stated* (1659)

John Pearson (1613–86)
Exposition of the Apostles Creed NF

Thomas Sprat (1635–1713)
The Plague of Athens, which Hapned in the Second Year of the Peloponnesian Warra V

Sir John Suckling (1609–42)
The Last Remains of Sr John Suckling MISC

James Ussher (1581–1656)
Eighteen Sermons Preached in Oxford, 1640 NF

1660

- Declaration of Breda (Apr.)
  Convention Parliament invites Charles II to return to England: he enters London on 29 May
  The Restoration: CHARLES II (-1685)
  Royal Society founded
  Samuel Pepys begins his diary on 1 Jan. (-1669)
  Bunyan imprisoned
- Daniel Defoe born
  White Kennett born
  Anne Killigrew born
- Robert Chamberlain dies
  Sir Thomas Urquhart dies
- Hans Sloan born
  The future George I born
- Paul Scarron dies
  Velazquez dies

Richard Allestree (1619–81)
The Gentlemans Calling NF
Anonymous. Sometimes attributed to Lady Dorothy Pakington (*d.* 1679) and to Richard Sterne (1596?–1683). Many editions. See also *The Ladies Calling* 1673.

Elias Ashmole (1617–92)
Sol in Ascendente; or, The Glorious Appearance of Charles the Second, upon the Horizon of London, in her Horoscopicall Sign, Gemini V
Anonymous. Charles II entered London on 29 May 1660.

Richard Baxter (1615–91)
Catholick Unity: or the Only Way to Bring Us All To Be of One Religion NF

Richard Baxter (1615–91)
The Life of Faith, as it is the Evidence of Things Unseen NF
See also *The Life of Faith* 1670

Robert Boyle (1627–91)
New Experiments Physico-Mechanicall, Touching the Spring of the Air, and its Effects NF
Boyle's first scientific work

Charles Cotton (1630–87)
A Panegyrick to the King's Most Excellent Majesty V

Abraham Cowley (1618–67)
Ode, Upon the Blessed Restoration and Returne of His Sacred Majestie, Charls [sic] *the Second* V
Charles II entered London on 29 May 1660

'Ezekiel Grebner' [**Abraham Cowley** (1618–67)]
The Visions and Prophecies Concerning England, Scotland, and Ireland of Ezekiel Grebner PS/V
Published 1660, dated 1661. A Royalist political satire, partly in verse.

John Dancer (*fl.* 1675) (tr.)
Aminta: The Famous Pastoral V
Translated from Torquato Tasso (1544–95)

Sir William Davenant (1606–68)
Poem, Upon His Sacred Majesties Most Happy Return to His Dominions V

John Dryden (1631–1700)
Astraea Redux: A poem on the happy restoration & return of Charles the Second V

Thomas Fuller (1608–61)
Mixt Contemplations in Better Times NF
See also *Good Thoughts in Bad Times* 1645, *Good Thoughts in Worse Times* 1647, *Good Thoughts in Bad Times* 1649

James Harrington (1611–77)
Political Discourses NF
Abridged 1659 as *The Art of Law-giving*

William Herbert, 3rd earl of Pembroke (1580–1630), and others
Poems V
With Sir Benjamin Rudyerd (1572–1658). Edited by John Donne the younger. Also includes poems by Sir Walter Ralegh, Sir Edward Dyer, Carew, William Strode, and others, and a celebrated epitaph on the countess of Pembroke, attributed partly to Ben Jonson but probably by William Browne of Tavistock.

Sir Robert Howard (1626–98)
Poems V

James Howell (1594?–1666)
Lexicon Tetraglotton: An English-French-Italian-Spanish dictionary DICT

Sir George Mackenzie (1636–91)
Aretina; or, The Serious Romance F
Anonymous

John Milton (1608–74)
The Readie & Easie Way to Establish a Free Commonwealth NF

Published in the last week of February 1660. Parliament invited Charles II to return to England on 25 April 1660. The king entered London on 29 May. See also George Starkey, *The Dignity of Kingship* 1660.

John Milton (1608–74)
Brief Notes Upon a Late Sermon, Titl'd, The Fear of God and the King NF
In answer to a sermon preached by Matthew Giffith (25 March 1660)

John Phillips (1631–1706)
Montelion, 1660; or, The Propheticall Almanack V
By 'Montelion, knight of the oracle, a well-wisher to the mathematicks'. A satire on the almanacs of William Lilly.

Samuel Pordage (1633–91?)
Poems Upon Several Occasions V

Samuel Pordage (1633–91) (tr.)
Troades Englished D
Translated from Seneca

John Sadler (1615–74)
Olbia: The New Iland Lately Discovered F

Robert Sanderson (1587–1663)
Several Cases of Conscience NF
A translation by Robert Codrington (1601–65) of Sanderson's *De obligatione conscientiæ prælectiones decem* (1660)

John Smith (1616?–52)
Select Discourses NF

Robert South (1634–1716)
Interest Deposed, and Truth Restored NF

George Starkey (1627–65)?
The Dignity of Kingship Asserted NF
By 'G.S.'. Also attributed to George Searle and Gilbert Sheldon (1598–1677). A reply to Milton's *Readie & Easie Way* 1660 (see above).

Edward Stillingfleet (1635–99)
Irenicum: A Weapon-salve for the Churches Wounds NF
Published 1660, dated 1661

John Tatham (*fl.* 1632–64)
The Rump; or, The Mirrour of the Late Times: D
A virulent key-play. Rewritten by Aphra Behn as *The Roundheads* 1682 (q.v.).

Jeremy Taylor (1613–67)
Ductor Dubitantium NF

Jeremy Taylor (1613–67)
The Worthy Communicant NF
Many editions

Edmund Waller (1606–87)
To the King, upon His Majesties Happy Return V
Anonymous. Charles II was restored to the throne in May 1660.

Robert Wild (1609–79)
Iter Boreale V

William Winstanley (1628?–98)
England's Worthies NF

George Wither (1588–1667)
Fides-Anglicana NF
Includes a bibliography of Wither's works

George Wither (1588–1667)
Speculum Speculativum; or, A Considering-Glass V

1661

- Death of Cardinal Mazarin
  Beginning of Louis XIV's personal rule in France
  Edward Hyde created earl of Clarendon
  Savoy Conference between Anglicans and Presbyterians
  England acquires Tangier from Portugal
- Anne Finch, countess of Winchilsea, born
  Sir Samuel Garth born
  Charles Montagu, earl of Halifax, born
  John Tutchin born?
- Thomas Fuller dies
  John Gough dies
  Richard Zouch dies
- Robert Harley born
  Nicholas Hawksmoor born

Anonymous
An Antidote Against Melancholy V
One of the earliest and most important collections of 'Drolleries'

Anonymous
The Princess Cloria; or, The Royal Romance F
Attributed to Sir Percy Herbert. In five parts. First published in two parts, 1653–4.

Francis Beaumont (1584–1616) and **John Fletcher** (1579–1625)
The Beggars Bush D
Sometimes attributed to Fletcher and Philip Massinger

Robert Boyle (1627–91)
The Sceptical Chymist; or, Chymico-Physical Doubts & Paradoxes NF

Alexander Brome (1620–66)
Songs and Other Poems V

John Bunyan (1628–88)
Profitable Meditations Fitted to Mans Different Condition V
Bunyan's first prison work, and his first published work in verse

Robert Davenport (*fl.* 1624–40)
The City-Night-Cap; or, Crede Quod Habes, & Habes: A tragi-comedy D
Belated publication of a pre-Civil War work of *c.*1624

Sir Kenelm Digby (1603–65)
A Discourse Concerning the Vegetation of Plants NF

John Dryden (1631–1700)
To His Sacred Majesty, a Panegyrick on his Coronation V
Charles II was crowned on 23 April 1661

John Evelyn (1620–1706)
Fumifugium; or, The Inconvenience of the Aer and Smoak of London Dissipated NF

John Evelyn (1620–1706)
A Panegyric to Charles the Second V

Richard Flecknoe (*c.*1620–78)
Erminia; or, The Fair and Vertuous Lady: A trage-comedy D
Unacted

George Fox (1624–91)
An Answer to the Arguments of the Jewes NF

George Fox (1624–91)
Some Principles of the Elect People of God, who in Scorn Are Called Quakers NF

Joseph Glanvill (1636–80)
The Vanity of Dogmatizing: or Confidence in Opinions NF
Anonymous. Republished 1665 as *Scepsis Scientifica; or, Confest Ignorance, the Way to Science.*

Peter Heylyn (1600–62)
Ecclesia Restaurata; or, History of the Reformation of the Church of England NF

Thomas Middleton (1580–1627)
The Mayor of Quinborough: A comedy D
Performed *c.*1596

Robert Sanderson (1587–1663)
Episcopacy Not Prejudicial to Regal Power: A treatise written in the time of the Long Parliament NF

Edmund Waller (1606–87)
A Poem on St James's Park V

John Webster (1580?–1635?) and **William Rowley** (1585?–1642?)
A Cure for a Cuckold: A pleasant comedy D
Attribution questionable

George Wither (1588–1667)
The Prisoners Plea V

1662

- Act of Uniformity restores Anglican church order and worship (May)
  Revised Anglican Prayer Book
  Charles II marries Catherine of Braganza (21 May)
  Royal Society receives royal charter
  Dunkirk sold to France
- Francis Atterbury born
  Richard Bentley born
  Samuel Wesley, the elder, born
  Thomas Brown born
  William King born
- Samuel Hartlib dies
  Peter Heylyn dies
  Henry Lawes dies
  Sir William Lower dies
  Sir Henry Vane dies
- Richard Bentley born
- Blaise Pascal dies

The Book of Common Prayer BIB
Final version. See *Booke of Common Prayer* 1549.

Anonymous
The Noble Birth and Gallant Atchievements of that Remarkable Out-Law Robin Hood F

Sir Richard Baker (1568?–1645)
Theatrum Redivivum; or, The Theatre Vindicated NF
A reply to Prynne's *Histrio-mastix* 1633 (q.v.)

Richard Baxter (1615–91)
Now or Never NF

Margaret Cavendish, Lady Newcastle (1624?–74)
Playes D
Contains 21 plays and includes verses by William Cavendish, duke of Newcastle. See also *Plays, Never Before Printed* 1668.

Sir Aston Cokayne (1608–84)
Poems V
2nd edition of *Small Poems of Divers Sorts* 1658 (q.v.)

John Dryden (1631–1700)
To My Lord Chancellor, Presented on New-Years-Day V

Sir William Dugdale (1605–86)
The History of Imbanking and Drayning of Divers Fenns and Marshes NF

John Evelyn (1620–1706)
Sculptura; or, The History, and Art of Chalcography and Engraving in Copper NF
Anonymous. The first work in English to treat of mezzotint engraving.

Thomas Fuller (1608–61)
The History of the Worthies of England NF

Joseph Glanvill (1636–80)
Lux Orientalis: Or an enquiry into the opinion of the Eastern sages, concerning the praexistence of souls NF
Anonymous

John Graunt (1620–74)
Natural and Political Observations NF

William Heminges (1602–53)
The Jewes Tragedy; or, Their Fatal and Final Overthrow by Vespatian and Titus his Son D
A pre-Civil War play

Thomas Middleton (1580–1627)
Any Thing for a Quiet Life: A comedy D

Simon Patrick (1626–1707)
A Brief Account of the New Sect of Latitude-Men NF

Sir William Petty (1623–87)
A Treatise of Taxes and Contributions NF
Anonymous

Edward Stillingfleet (1635–99)
Origines Sacrae: Or, a rational account of the grounds of the Christian faith NF
7th edition, 1702

John Wallis (1616–1703)
Hobbius Heauton-timorumenos: Or, a consideration of Mr Hobbes his dialogues NF
A sustained attack on Thomas Hobbes

1663

- Charles II grants charter to Rhode Island
- Delarivière Manley born
  Peter Anthony Motteux born
  Joseph Stennett born
  William Walsh born
- Christopher Harvey dies
- Cotton Mather born

Robert Boyle (1627–91)
Some Considerations Touching the Usefulnesse of Experimentall Naturall Philosophy NF
Anonymous

John Bunyan (1628–88)
Christian Behaviour; or, The Fruits of True Christianity NF
A companion piece to *The Doctrine of the Law and Grace* 1659 (q.v.)

Samuel Butler (1612–80)
Hudibras. The First Part: Written in the time of the late wars V
Anonymous. See also *Hudibras. The Second Part* 1664; *Hudibras. The First and Second Parts* 1674; *Hudibras. The Third and Last Part* 1678; *Hudibras. In Three Parts* 1684.

Abraham Cowley (1618–67)
Cutter of Coleman-Street: A comedy D
Revised version of *The Guardian* 1650 (q.v.)

Abraham Cowley (1618–67)
Verses, Lately Written Upon Several Occasions V

Sir William Davenant (1606–68)
Poem, to the King's Most Sacred Majesty V

Thomas Howard (*fl.* 1663)
The History of the Seven Wise Mistrisses of Rome F

Thomas Jordan (1612?–85)
A Royal Arbor of Loyal Poesie V

Roger L'Estrange (1616–1704)
The Intelligencer PER
Anonymous. Published weekly then bi-weekly August 1663–January 1666.

Sir George Mackenzie (1636–91)
Religio Stoici NF
Anonymous. Attributed to Mackenzie.

Katherine Philips (1631–64) (tr.)
Pompey: A tragoedy D
A translation of *La Mort de Pompée* (1642/3) by Pierre Corneille (1606–84). Performed 1663.

Thomas Porter (1636–80)
The Carnival: A comedy D
Performed *c.*1663

Thomas Porter (1636–80)
The Villain: A tragedy D
Performed October 1662

William Shakespeare (1564–1616)
Comedies, Histories, and Tragedies D
The Third Folio. The second issue, dated 1664, contains *Pericles* (first published in 1609, q.v.) and six apocryphal plays: *The London Prodigall* 1605 (q.v.), *Thomas Lord Cromwell* 1602 (q.v.), *Sir John Old-castle* 1600 (q.v.), *The Puritaine* 1607 (q.v.), *A Yorkshire Tragedy* 1608 (q.v.), and *Locrine* 1595 (q.v.).

Sir Robert Stapylton (1605?–69)
The Slighted Maid: A comedy D
Performed February 1663

Sir Samuel Tuke (*c.*1620–74) (adap.)
The Adventures of Five Hours: A tragi-comedy D
Adaptation of Antonio Coello (1611–52), *Los Empeños de seis horas* (formerly attributed to Calderón). Performed 8 January 1663.

1664

- Conventicles Act, forbidding religious gatherings of more than five people, other than for Anglican ceremonies
  English annex New Netherlands, including New Amsterdam (renamed New York)
- Charles Hopkins born?
  Matthew Prior born
  Sir John Vanbrugh born
- Katherine Philips ('Orinda') dies

Richard Baxter (1615–91)
The Divine Life, in Three Treatises NF

Henry Bold (1627–83)
Poems Lyrique Macaronique Heroique V

Robert Boyle (1627–91)
Experiments and Considerations Touching Colours NF

John Bulteel, the younger (*fl.* 1683)
Birinthea: A romance F

Samuel Butler (1612–80)
Hudibras. The Second Part: By the authour of the First V
A spurious poem entitled *Hudibras. The Second Part,* preceding the genuine second part, was issued in 1663. See *Hudibras, the First Part* 1663; *Hudibras. The First and Second Parts* 1674; *Hudibras. The Third and Last Part* 1678; *Hudibras. In Three Parts* 1684.

Margaret Cavendish, Lady Newcastle (1624?–74)
Philosophicall Letters NF
Commendatory poem by William Cavendish, duke of Newcastle

Margaret Cavendish, Lady Newcastle (1624?–1674)
CCXI Sociable Letters F
Commendatory verse by William Cavendish, duke of Newcastle

Charles Cotton (1630–87) (tr.)
The Morall Philosophy of the Stoicks NF
Translated from Guillaume du Vair (1556–1621)

Charles Cotton (1630–87)
Scarronides; or, Virgile Travestie V
Anonymous. See also *Scarronides* 1665, 1667.

Ralph Cudworth (1617–88)
A Sermon Preached to the Honourable Society of Lincolnes-Inne NF

John Dryden (1631–1700)
The Rival Ladies: A tragi-comedy D
Performed June 1664. The first of Dryden's plays to be printed. Preface inaugurated controversy with Sir Robert Howard on the use of rhyme; answered by Howard in the preface to *Four New Plays* 1665 (q.v.); Dryden's principal response in *Of Dramatick Poesie* 1668 (q.v.). See also *The Indian Emperour* 1667.

Sir George Etherege (1635–91)
The Comical Revenge; or, Love in a Tub D
Performed March 1664

John Evelyn (1620–1706)
Sylva; or, A Discourse of Forest-Trees, and the Propagation of Timber in His Majesties Dominions NF
Also contains *Kalendarium Hortense; or, gard'ners almanac,* published separately in 1666

Richard Flecknoe (*c.*1620–78)
Love's Kingdom: A pastoral trage-comedy D
Performed 1664? Altered from *Love's Dominion* 1654 (q.v.).

George Fox (1624–91)
Three General Epistles to be Read in all the Congregations of the Righteous NF

Thomas Killigrew (1612–83)
Comedies, and Tragedies D
Includes Killigrew's best-known comedy, *The Parson's Wedding* and *Thomaso,* the source of Aphra Behn's *The Rover* 1677 (q.v.)

Sir William Killigrew (1606–95)
Pandora: A comedy D
Anonymous. Performed *c.*1662. Commendatory verses by Edmund Waller, Sir Robert Stapylton, and others. See also *Three Playes* 1665.

Henry More (1614–87)
A Modest Enquiry into the Mystery of Iniquity NF

Thomas Mun (1571–1641)
England's Treasure by Forraign Trade NF
Written *c.*1630

Katherine Philips (1631–64)
Poems by the Incomparable, Mrs K.P. V
See also *Poems* 1667

Sir Charles Sedley (1639–1701) and others (tr.)
Pompey the Great: A tragedy D
Translated from Pierre Corneille's *La mort de Pompée* (1644) by Sedley, Sidney Godolphin, the earl of Dorset, and perhaps others

Sir Robert Stapylton (1605?–69)
The Step-Mother: A tragi-comedy D
Anonymous. Performed *c.*November 1663.

Jeremy Taylor (1613–67)
A Choice Manual, Containing What is To Be Believed, Practised, and Desired or Praied For NF

Jeremy Taylor (1613–67)
A Dissuasive from Popery to the People of Ireland [pt i] NF
Part ii published in 1667

Sir William Temple (1628–99)
Upon the Death of Mrs Catherine Philips V
Anonymous

John Tillotson (1630–94)
The Wisdom of Being Religious NF

John Wilson (1627?–96)
The Cheats: A comedy D
Anonymous

George Wither (1588–1667)
Tuba-Pacifica V

1665

- Second Anglo-Dutch War (1665–7)
  Plague breaks out in London (Apr. 1665–autumn 1666)
- Charles Gildon born
- Sir Kenelm Digby dies
  John Earle dies
- The future Queen Anne born
- Nicholas Poussin dies

Richard Brathwaite (1588?–1673)
A Comment Upon the Two Tales of Our Ancient, Renowned, and Ever-Living Poet Sr Jeffray Chaucer, Knight NF

John Bulteel, the younger (*fl.* 1683) (tr.)
Amorous Orontus; or, The Love in Fashion: A comedy D
Anonymous translation of *Amour à la mode* by Pierre Corneille (1606–84)

John Bulteel, the younger (*fl.* 1683) (tr.)
The Comical Romance; or, A Facetious History of a Company of Stage-players F
Translated from *Le Roman comique* (1651–7) by Paul Scarron (1610–60)

John Bunyan (1628–88)
The Holy City; or, The New Jerusalem NF

John Bunyan (1628–88)
The Resurrection of the Dead, and Eternall Judgement NF

Charles Cotton (1630–87)
Scarronides; or, Virgile Travestie V
Anonymous. See also *Scarronides* 1664, 1667.

John Crowne (*d.* 1703)
Pandion and Amphigenia; or, The History of the Coy Lady of Thessalia F

Richard Head (1637?–86?)
The English Rogue Described: In the life of Meriton Latroon, a witty extravagant F
Anonymous. Reissued 1666 by the bookseller Francis Kirkman (*b.* 1632), who wrote a second part (earliest edition 1671). Parts iii and iv published 1671; all 4 parts published together 1680. Head disclaimed responsibility for any part except the first.

Edward Herbert, Lord Herbert of Cherbury (1583–1648)
Occasional Verses of Edward Lord Herbert, Baron of Cherbury and Castle-Island V

Sir Robert Howard (1626–98)
Four New Plays D
Preface responds to that of Dryden's to *The Rival Ladies* 1664 (q.v.): see also Dryden's *Of Dramatick Poesie* 1668. Contains *The Surprisal*; *The Committee*; *The Indian-Queen*; *The Vestal Virgin.* Reissued as *Five Plays* 1692, adding *The Duke of Lerma* 1668 (q.v.).

Sir William Killigrew (1606–95)
Three Playes D
Contains *Selindra*, *Pandora* (published separately in 1664, q.v.), and *Ormasdes*. *Four Plays* 1666 adds *The Siege of Urbin.*

Henry King (1592–69)
A Sermon Preached the 30th of January at White-Hall 1664 [i.e. 1665] NF
Commemorates the execution of Charles I

David Lloyd (1635–92)
The States-men and Favourites of England since the Reformation NF
Enlarged in 1670 as *State Worthies*

Andrew Marvell (1621–78)
The Character of Holland V
Anonymous

Simon Patrick (1626–1707)
The Parable of the Pilgrim F
Frequently reprinted. A possible source for Bunyan's *Pilgrim's Progress* 1678 (q.v.).

John Phillips (1631–1706) (tr.)
Typhon; or, The Gyants War with the Gods: A mock poem V
Translated from Paul Scarron (1610–60)

Thomas Sprat (1635–1713)
Observations on Monsieur de Sorbier's Voyage into England NF
Addressed to Sir Christopher Wren. *Relation d'un voyage en Angleterre* by Samuel Sorbière (*c*.1615–70) published in 1664.

Izaak Walton (1593–1683)
Life of Richard Hooker NF

George Wither (1588–1667)
Meditations Upon the Lords Prayer V

George Wither (1588–1667)
Three Private Meditations MISC

1666

- Great Plague continues in London to the autumn
  Great Fire of London (2–6 Sept.)
- Mary Astell born
  Mary Pix born
  William Wotton born
- Alexander Brome dies
  Mildmay Fane dies
  Sir Richard Fanshawe dies
  James Howell dies
  James Shirley dies
  Thomas Vaughan dies
- Franz Hals dies
  Claude Lorraine dies

Anonymous
The Princess of Monpensier F
Translation of *La Princesse de Montpensier* (1662) by Marie-Madeleine, comtesse de La Fayette (1634–93)

Robert Boyle (1627–91)
Hydrostatical Paradoxes NF

Robert Boyle (1627–91)
The Origine of Forms and Qualities NF

John Bunyan (1628–88)
Grace Abounding to the Chief of Sinners NF
Bunyan's spiritual autobiography

Margaret Cavendish, duchess of Newcastle (1624?–74)
The Description of a New World, called the Blazing World F

Samuel Parker (1640–88)
A Free and Impartial Censure of the Platonick Philosophie NF

Elkanah Settle (1648–1724)
Mare Clausum; or, A Ransack for the Dutch V

John Tillotson (1630–94)
The Rule of Faith NF
A reply to John Sergeant, *Sure-footing in Christianity* (1665)

Edmund Waller (1606–87)
Instructions to a Painter V
The first 64 lines were published anonymously on a single sheet in 1665

George Wither (1588–1667)
Sigh for the Pitchers V

1667

- The Dutch fleet raids the Medway (June)
  Treaty of Breda (31 July) ends Second Anglo-Dutch War
  The French invade the Spanish Netherlands and begin the War of Devolution (–May 1668)
  Banishment of the Earl of Clarendon
- John Arbuthnot born
  Abel Boyer born
  George Granville, Lord Lansdowne, born
  John Pomfret born
  Jonathan Swift born
  Edward Ward born
- Abraham Cowley dies
  Charles Hoole dies
  Jeremy Taylor dies
  George Wither dies

Richard Allestree (1619–81)
The Causes of the Decay of Christian Piety NF
Anonymous. Frequently reprinted.

Nicholas Billingsley (1633–1709)
Thesauro-Phulakion; or, A Treasury of Divine Raptures V

Margaret Cavendish, duchess of Newcastle (1624?–74)
Life of William Cavendish NF

Charles Cotton (1630–87)
Scarronides; or, Virgile Travestie V
Anonymous. See also *Scarronides* 1664, 1665.

Sir John Denham (1615–69)
On Mr Abraham Cowley His Death, and Burial Amongst the Ancient Poets V

John Dryden (1631–1700)
Annus Mirabilis: The Year of Wonders, 1666 V

John Dryden (1631–1700)
The Indian Emperour; or, The Conquest of Mexico by the Spaniards D
Performed April 1665. Sequel to *The Indian Queen*, first published in Sir Robert Howard's *Four New Plays* 1665 (q.v.). The 2nd edition (1668) contains 'A Defence of an Essay of Dramatique Poesie, Being an Answer to the Preface of The Great Favourite, or the Duke of Lerma [by Howard]'.

Richard Flecknoe (*c.*1620–78)
The Damoiselles a la Mode: A comedy D
Performed September 1668. Based on several plays by Molière.

George Fox (1624–91)
The Arraignment of Popery NF

William Laud (1573–1645)
A Summarie of Devotions NF

Roger L'Estrange (1616–1704) (tr.)
The Visions of Dom Francisco de Quevedo Villagas F
A translation of Francisco Gómez de Quevedo y Villegas (1580–1645), *Los Sueños* (1627), a series of five satirical prose sketches. Frequently reprinted.

John Milton (1608–74)
Paradise Lost: A poem written in ten books V
Published in October 1667. 2nd edition, in twelve books, published in 1674 (q.v.).

Katherine Philips (1631–64)
Poems: By the most deservedly admired Mrs Katherine Philips the Matchless Orinda V
See also *Poems by the Incomparable, Mrs K.P.* 1664

Sir Paul Rycaut (1628–1700)
The Present State of the Ottoman Empire NF

Thomas Sprat (1635–1713)
The History of the Royal-Society of London NF

1668

- The Triple Alliance between England, the Netherlands, and Sweden against France
  Dryden made Poet Laureate
- Sir William Davenant dies
  Owen Felltham dies
- Alain René Lesage born

Roger Boyle, earl of Orrery (1621–79)
The History of Henry the Fifth; The Tragedy of Mustapha, Son of Solyman the Magnificent D
Henry the Fifth performed August 1664; *Mustapha* performed April 1665

Margaret Cavendish, duchess of Newcastle (1624?–74)
Plays, Never Before Printed D
See also *Playes* 1662

Abraham Cowley (1618–67)
The Works of Mr Abraham Cowley WKS

Sir William Davenant (1606–68)
The Rivals: A comedy D

Sir John Denham (1615–69)
Poems and Translations: With The Sophy V
The first collected edition of Denham's poems

John Dryden (1631–1700)
Of Dramatick Poesie NF
Dryden's main contribution to the controversy with Sir Robert Howard on the use of rhyme. See *The Rival Ladies* 1664, Howard's *Four New Plays* 1665.

John Dryden (1631–1700)
Secret-Love; or, The Maiden-Queen D
Performed February 1667

John Dryden (1631–1700) (adap.)
Sir Martin Mar-all; or, The Feign'd Innocence: A comedy D
Performed 15 August 1667. Adapted from Molière's first comedy, *L'Etourdi* (first performed 1655). Partly written by William Cavendish, 1st duke of Newcastle.

Sir George Etherege (1635–91)
She Wou'd if She Cou'd: A comedy D
Performed 6 February 1668

John Evelyn (1620–1706) (tr.)
An Idea of the Perfection of Painting NF
Translated from the French of Roland Freart (1606–76), *L'idée de la perfection de la peinture*

Richard Flecknoe (*c*.1620–78)
Sir William D'Avenant's Voyage to the Other World: with his Adventures in the Poets Elizium: A poetical fiction V
Published anonymously

Joseph Glanvill (1636–80)
Plus Ultra; or, The Progress and Advancement of Knowledge Since the Days of Aristotle NF

Peter Heylyn (1600–62)
Cyprianus Anglicanus NF
A life and defence of William Laud (1573–1645)

Edward Howard (1624–*c*.1700)
The Usurper: A tragedy D
Performed January 1664

Sir Robert Howard (1626–98)
The Duell of the Staggs V

Sir Robert Howard (1626–98)
The Great Favourite; or, The Duke of Lerma D
Performed 20 February 1668. Preface continues Howard-Dryden controversy (see Howard, *Four New Plays* 1665).

Thomas Jordan (1612?–85)
Money is an Asse: A comedy D

David Lloyd (1635–92)
Memoires of the Lives of Those Personages that Suffered for the Protestant Religion NF

Henry Neville (1620–94)
The Isle of Pines; or, A Late Discovery of a Fourth Island in Terra Australis, Incognita F
Anonymous. 2nd edition, 1668 (with part ii, see below).

Henry Neville (1620–94)
A New and Further Discovery of the Islle of Pines F
Anonymous. See *The Isle of Pines* 1668, above.

William Penn (1644–1718)
The Sandy Foundations Shaken NF

William Penn (1644–1718)
Truth Exalted NF

Sir Thomas St Serfe (*fl.* 1668)
Tarugo's Wiles: or, The Coffee-House: A comedy D
Performed (5 October 1667). Based on Agustín Moreto (1618–69), *No puede ser el guardar a una mujer.*

Sir Charles Sedley (1639–1701)
The Mulberry-Garden: A comedy D
Performed 1668

Thomas Shadwell (1642?–92)
The Sullen Lovers; or, The Impertinents: A comedy D
Performed 2 May 1668. Based on Molière's *Les Fâcheux* (1661).

John Wilkins (1614–72)
An Essay Towards a Real Character, and a Philosophical Language NF
Also contains *An Alphabetical Dictionary* with separate title-page

1669

- Pepys' Diary ends on 31 May (see 1660)
- Susanna Centlivre born?
- Sir John Denham dies
  Henry King, bishop of Chichester, dies
  William Prynne dies
  Sir Robert Stapylton dies
- Rembrandt dies

Richard Allestree (1619–81)
Eighteen Sermons NF

Roger Boyle, earl of Orrery (1621–79)
Two New Tragedies: The Black Prince, and Tryphon D
The Black Prince performed 19 October 1667; *Tryphon* performed 8 December 1668

Edward Chamberlayne (1616–1703)
Angliae Notitiae; or, The Present State of England NF

Sir John Denham (1615–69)
Cato Major of Old Age V
A verse paraphrase of Cicero's *De senectute*

John Dryden (1631–1700)
The Wild Gallant: A comedy D
Performed 5 February 1663 (the first of Dryden's plays to be acted)

John Flavel (1630?–91)
Husbandry Spiritualized: Or, the heavenly use of earthly things NF

Richard Flecknoe (*c.*1620–78)
Epigrams of All Sorts V

Sir William Killigrew (1606–95)?
The Imperial Tragedy D
Anonymous (attributed to Killigrew). Unacted.

John Milton (1608–74)
Accedence Commenc't Grammar NF

Simon Patrick (1626–1707)
A Friendly Debate Between a Conformist and a Non-Conformist NF
Anonymous. *A Continuation* also published in 1669; *A Further Continuation* published 1670.

William Penn (1644–1718)
Innocency with her Open Face NF
Anonymous

William Penn (1644–1718)
No Cross, No Crown NF

Thomas Shadwell (1642?–92)
The Royal Shepherdess: A tragi-comedy D
Performed 25 February 1669

Sir Robert Stapylton (1605?–69)
The Tragedie of Hero and Leander D
Unacted

1670

- The Secret Treaty of Dover between Charles II and Louis XIV
- William Congreve born
  Laurence Echard born (c.1670)
  Sarah Egerton born
  Bevil Higgons born
  Bernard Mandeville born?
  John Toland born

Sir Francis Bacon (1561–1626)
The Second Part of the Resuscitatio NF
Edited by William Rawley (1588?–1667), Bacon's chaplain. See *Resuscitatio* 1657.

Richard Baxter (1615–91)
The Cure of Church-Divisions NF

Richard Baxter (1615–91)
The Life of Faith. In Three Parts NF
Greatly expanded edition of *The Life of Faith* 1660 (q.v.), containing Baxter's repudiation of *A Holy Commonwealth* 1659 (q.v.)

John Dryden (1631–1700) and **Sir William Davenant** (1606–68)
The Tempest; or, The Enchanted Island: A comedy D
Performed 7 November 1667. Adapted from Shakespeare.

John Dryden (1631–1700)
Tyrannick Love; or, The Royal Martyr: A tragedy D
Performed 24 June 1669

John Eachard (1636?–97)
The Grounds and Occasions of the Contempt of the Clergy and Religion Enquired into NF
Anonymous

Sir Richard Fanshawe (1608–66) (tr.)
Querer por soló querer: To love only for love sake V
Translated from Antonio Hurtado de Mendoza y Larrea (1586–1644)

Joseph Glanvill (1636–80)
Logou Threskeia NF
Anonymous

Fulke Greville, Lord Brooke (1554–1628)
The Remains of Sir Fulk Grevill Lord Brooke V

Peter Heylyn (1600–62)
Aerius Redivivus; or, The History of the Presbyterians NF

John Milton (1608–74)
The History of Britain, That Part Especially Now Call'd England NF
See also *Character of the Long Parliament* 1681

Samuel Parker (1640–88)
A Discourse of Ecclesiastical Politie NF
See also *A Defence and Continuation* 1671. Replied to by Marvell in *The Rehearsal Transpros'd* 1672 (q.v.); answered by Parker in *A Reproof to the Rehearsal Transprosed* (1673).

John Ray (1627–1705)
A Collection of English Proverbs NF

Henry Stubbe (1632–76)
Campanella Revived; or, An Inquiry into the History of the Royal Society NF
Anonymous

Henry Stubbe (1632–76)
The Plus Ultra reduced to a Non Plus NF
An attack on Joseph Glanvill, Thomas Sprat, and the Royal Society

Izaak Walton (1593–1683)
The Lives of Dr John Donne, Sir Henry Wooton, Mr Richard Hooker, Mr George Herbert NF
First collected edition

Hannah Wolley (*fl.* 1661–84)
The Queen-like Closet; or, Rich Cabinet NF
A highly successful cookery and household management book which passed through many editions

1671

- Edmund Calamy born
  Colley Cibber born
  Anthony Ashley Cooper, 3rd earl of Shaftesbury, born

Anonymous
Westminster-Drollery; or, A Choice Collection of the Newest Songs & Poems Both at Court & Theaters V
Second part published in 1672 (q.v.)

Theodosia Alleine (*fl.* 1671) and others
The Life and Death of Joseph Alleine NF

Isaac Barrow (1630–77)
The Duty and Reward of Bounty to the Poor NF

Aphra Behn (1640?–89)
The Forc'd Marriage; or, The Jealous Bridegroom: A tragi-comedy D
Performed September 1670

Aphra Behn (1640?–89)
The Amorous Prince; or, The Curious Husband: A comedy D
Performed *c.*February 1671. Partly based on Robert Davenport's *The City-Night-Cap* 1661 (q.v.).

Samuel Collins (1619–70)
The Present State of Russia NF
Anonymous

Charles Cotton (1630–87) (tr.)
Horace D
Translated from *Horace* (1640) by Pierre Corneille (1606–84)

John Crowne (*d.* 1703)
Juliana; or, The Princess of Poland: A tragicomedy D
Performed *c.*June 1671

John Dancer (*fl.* 1675) (tr.)
Nicomede: A tragi-comedy D
Translated from *Nicomède* (1651) by Pierre Corneille (1606–84)

John Dryden (1631–1700)
An Evening's Love; or, The Mock-Astrologer D
Performed 12 June 1668

Joseph Glanvill (1636–80)
Philosophia Pia: Or, a discourse of the religious temper of the experimental philosophy which is profest by the Royal Society NF

George Herbert (1593–1633)
A Priest to the Temple; or, The Country Parson his Character, and Rule of Holy Life NF
Preface by Barnabas Oley (1602–86). First published in Herbert's *Remains* 1652 (q.v.).

Thomas Hobbes (1588–1679)
Three Papers Presented to the Royal Society Against Dr Wallis NF
Concerning the distinguished mathematician John Wallis (1616–1703)

Edward Howard (1624–*c.*1700)
The Womens Conquest: A tragi-comedy D
Anonymous. Performed *c.*November 1670.

John Milton (1608–74)
Paradise Regain'd: A poem . . . To which is added Samson Agonistes V
Published in May 1671. *Samson Agonistes* published separately in 1681.

Samuel Parker (1640–88)
A Defence and Continuation of the Ecclesiastical Politie NF
See *A Discourse of Ecclesiastical Politie* 1670

Elkanah Settle (1648–1724)
Cambyses King of Persia: A tragedy D
Performed *c.*February 1667

Thomas Shadwell (1642?–92)
The Humorists: A comedy D
Performed December 1670

John Tillotson (1630–94)
Sermons Preach'd Upon Several Occasions [vol. i] NF
Volume ii, 1678; volume iii, 1686 (as *Sermons and Discourses*)

George Whitehead (1636?–1723) and **William Penn** (1644–1718)
A Serious Apology for the Principles and Practices of the People Call'd Quakers NF
Written in response to confutations of Quakerism written by Thomas Jenner (*fl.* 1631–56) and Timothy Taylor (1611 or 12–1681)

1672

- Third Dutch War (1672–4)
  Charles II's Declaration of Indulgence towards Roman Catholics and Non-Conformists (retracted 1673)
- Joseph Addison born
  Sir Richard Steele born
- Anne Bradstreet dies
  John Cosin dies
  Ralph Knevet dies
  Peter Sterry dies
- Peter the Great born

Anonymous
Westminster Drollery. The Second Part V
First part published in 1671 (q.v.)

Joseph Alleine (1634–68)
An Alarme to Unconverted Sinners NF
Frequently reprinted. See also Theodosia Alleine 1671.

Elias Ashmole (1617–92)
The Institution, Laws and Ceremonies of the Most Noble Order of the Garter NF

John Bramhall (1594–1663)
Bishop Bramhall's Vindication of Himself and the Episcopal Clergy NF
'A Preface shewing what grounds there are of fears and jealousies of popery' by Samuel Parker, responded to by Marvell in *The Rehearsal Transpros'd* 1672 (q.v.). See also Richard Baxter, *The Grotian Religion Discovered* 1658.

John Bunyan (1628–88)
A Confession of My Faith, and a Reason of My Practice NF
Anonymous. Answered by John Denne in *Truth Outweighing Error* (1673) and Thomas Paul, *Some Serious Reflections* (1673). See also Bunyan, *Differences in Judgment* 1673.

John Bunyan (1628–88)
A Defence of the Doctrine of Justification, by Faith in Jesus Christ NF
Written in reply to *The Design of Christianity* (1671) by Edward Fowler (1632–1714)

John Crowne (*d.* 1703)
The History of Charles the Eighth of France; or, The Invasion of Naples by the French D
Performed *c.*December 1671

John Dryden (1631–1700)
The Conquest of Granada by the Spaniards D
Part i performed December? 1670; part ii performed January 1671. Part i contains 'Of Heroique Plays: An Essay'; part ii contains 'Defence of the Epilogue; or, An Essay on the Dramatique Poetry of the Last Age'. See also Richard Leigh, *The Censure of the Rota* 1673, and Charles Blount, *Mr Dreyden Vindicated* 1673.

John Eachard (1636?–97)
Mr Hobbs's State of Nature Considered NF
Anonymous. See also *Some Opinions of Mr Hobbs* 1673.

John Evelyn, the younger (1655–99) (tr.)
Of Gardens V
Translated from the Jesuit scholar and critic Père René Rapin (1621–87), *Hortorum*

James Howard (*b.* 1630?)
All Mistaken; or, The Mad Couple: A comedy D
Performed September 1667

James Janeway (1636?–74)
A Token for Children NF

John Josselyn (*fl.* 1630–75)
New-Englands Rarities NF

John Lacy (1615–81)
The Dumb Lady; or, The Farrier Made Physician D
Performed 1669. Partly based on Molière's *Le médecin malgré lui* (1666) and *L'amour médecin* (1665).

John Lacy (1615–81)
The Old Troop; or, Monsieur Raggou D
Performed *c.*1665

Andrew Marvell (1621–78)
The Rehearsal Transpros'd NF
Anonymous. A reply to Samuel Parker's Preface to John Bramhall's *Vindication of Himself* 1672 (q.v.). The title refers to *The Rehearsal* 1672 (q.v.) by George Villiers. See also Richard Leigh, *The Transposer Rehears'd* 1673. Part ii published in 1673 (q.v.).

William Penn (1644–1718)
The Spirit of Truth Vindicated NF

John Phillips (1631–1706) (tr.)
Maronides or, Virgil Travestie V

Edward Ravenscroft (1644–1704) (adap.)
The Citizen Turn'd Gentleman: A comedy D
Performed July 1672. Adapted from Molière (1622–73), *Le Bourgeois Gentilhomme* (1671) and *Monsieur de Pourceaugnac* (1669).

Thomas Shadwell (1642?–92) (adap.)
The Miser: A comedy D
Performed January 1672. Adapted from Molière (1622–73), *L'Avare* (1668).

Henry Stubbe (1632–76)
Rosemary & Bayes NF
Anonymous. An attack on Marvell's *The Rehearsal Transpros'd* 1672 (q.v.).

George Villiers, duke of Buckingham (1628–87)
The Rehearsal D
Anonymous. Performed 7 December 1671. An attack on Dryden and other contemporary dramatists.

William Wycherley (1641–1716)
Love in a Wood; or, St James's Park: A comedy D
Performed *c.*March 1671

1673

- The Test Act excluding Roman Catholics from public office (Mar.)
- John Oldmixon born
  Richard Brathwaite dies
- Molière (Jean-Baptiste Poquelin) dies

Richard Allestree (1619–81)
The Ladies Calling NF
bao *The Whole Duty of Man* . . . and *The Gentlemans Calling*

Robert Barclay (1648–90)
A Catechism and Confession of Faith NF
Anonymous

Richard Baxter (1615–91)
A Christian Directory: or, A Summ of Practical Theologie, and Cases of Conscience NF
A massive and central work of casuistry: completed by *Catholick Theologie* 1675 (q.v.)

Aphra Behn (1640?–89)
The Dutch Lover: A comedy D
Performed February 1673. Based on Francisco de Quintana (*d.* 1658).

Charles Blount (1654–93)
Mr Dreyden Vindicated NF
Anonymous. A response to Richard Leigh's *The Censure of the Rota* 1673.

John Bunyan (1628–88)
The Barren Fig-Tree; or, The Doom and Downfall of the Fruitless Professor NF

John Bunyan (1628–88)
Differences in Judgment About Water-Baptism, No Bar to Communion NF
See *A Confession of My Faith* 1672

Gilbert Burnet (1643–1715)
The Mystery of Iniquity Unvailed NF

William Cave (1637–1713)
Primitive Christianity; or, The Religion of the Ancient Christians NF

Sir William Davenant (1606–68)
The Works of Sr William D'avenant WKS

John Dryden (1631–1700)
Amboyna: A tragedy D
Performed May 1673

John Dryden (1631–1700)
The Assignation; or, Love in a Nunnery D
Performed October/November 1672

John Dryden (1631–1700)
Marriage-a-la-Mode: A comedy D
Performed April 1672

John Eachard (1636?–97)
Some Opinions of Mr Hobbs Considered in a Second Dialogue between Philautus and Timothy NF
Anonymous. See *Mr Hobbs's State of Nature Considered* 1672.

Joseph Glanvill (1636–80)
An Earnest Invitation to the Sacrament of the Lords Supper NF

Richard Head (1637?–86?)
The Floating Island; or, A New Discovery F
Anonymous. A mimic imaginary journey through London low life.

Edward Hyde, 1st earl of Clarendon (1609–74)
Animadversions upon a Book intituled, Fanaticism Fanatically Imputed to the Catholick Church NF
'By a person of honour'. A response to Serenus Cressy (1605–74) replying to Edward Stillingfleet's *Discourse Concerning the Idolatry Practised in the Church of Rome* (1671).

Benjamin Keach (1640–1704)
War with the Devil; or, The Young Mans Conflict with the Powers of Darkness V
Many editions

Richard Leigh (1649 or 50–1728)
The Censure of the Rota: On Mr Driden's Conquest of Granada NF
Anonymous. See Dryden, *The Conquest of Granada* 1672, and Charles Blount, *Mr Dreyden Vindicated* 1673.

Richard Leigh (1649 or 50–1728)
The Transproser Rehears'd NF

Anonymous. A satirical reply to Marvell's *Rehearsal Transpros'd* 1672 (q.v.). See also John Bramhall's *Vindication of Himself and the Episcopal Clergy* 1672.

Andrew Marvell (1621–78)
The Rehearsall Transpros'd. The Second Part NF
See *The Rehearsal Transpros'd* 1672

John Milton (1608–74)
Of True Religion, Haeresie, Schism, Toleration NF

John Milton (1608–74)
Poems, &c. Upon Several Occasions V
2nd edition (revised and enlarged) of *Poems* 1646 (q.v.)

Henry Nevil Payne (*d. c.*1710)
The Fatal Jealousie: A tragedy D
Anonymous. Performed August 1672.

Henry Nevil Payne (*d. c.*1710)
The Morning Ramble: A comedy D
Anonymous. Performed November 1672.

Samuel Pordage (1633–91)
Herod and Mariamne: A tragedy D
Performed September 1671?

Edward Ravenscroft (1644–1704)
The Careless Lovers: A comedy D
Performed March 1673. Partly taken from Molière (1622–73), *Monsieur de Pourceaugnac* (1669).

John Ray (1627–1705)
Observations Topographical, Moral, & Physiological NF

Elkanah Settle (1648–1724)
The Empress of Morocco: A tragedy D
Performed July 1673 (also probably at Court in 1671). Verse prologue by John Wilmot, earl of Rochester. See also *Notes and Observations* 1674.

Thomas Shadwell (1642?–92)
Epsom-Wells: A comedy D
Performed December 1672

Sir William Temple (1628–99)
An Essay upon the Advancement of Trade in Ireland NF
Anonymous

Sir William Temple (1628–99)
Observations upon the United Provinces of the Netherlands NF

Thomas Traherne (1637–74)
Roman Forgeries NF
'By a faithful son of the Church of England'

William Wycherley (1641–1716)
The Gentleman Dancing-Master: A comedy D
Performed *c.*February 1672. Based on an incident in Calderón (1600–81), *El maestro de danzar.*

1674

- Second Treaty of Westminster between England and the Netherlands
- Mary Davys born
  Ambrose Philips born
  Elizabeth Rowe born
  Nicholas Rowe born
  Catharine Trotter born
  Jethro Tull born
  Isaac Watts born
- Margaret Cavendish, duchess of Newcastle, dies
  Robert Herrick dies
  Edward Hyde, 1st earl of Clarendon, dies
  John Milton dies
  Thomas Traherne dies

Richard Allestree (1619–81)
The Government of the Tongue NF
bao *The Whole Duty of Man*

Richard Baxter (1615–91)
The Poor Man's Family Book NF
In dialogue form, with some fictional tendencies and affinities with Bunyan

Robert Boyle (1627–91)
The Excellency of Theology, compar'd with Natural Philosophy NF
By 'T.H.R.B.E., Fellow of the Royal Society' (i.e. The Honourable Robert Boyle Esq.). Written 1665. Also published in Latin in 1674.

Samuel Butler (1612–80)
Hudibras. The First and Second Parts V
Anonymous. See *Hudibras, the First Part* 1663; *Hudibras. The Second Part* 1664; *Hudibras. The Third and Last Part* 1678; *Hudibras. In Three Parts* 1684.

Charles Cotton (1630–87)
The Compleat Gamester; or, Instructions How to Play at Billiards, Trucks, Bowls, and Chess NF
Anonymous

Sir William Davenant (1606–68) (adap.)
Macbeth: A tragedy D
Altered from Shakespeare

John Dryden (1631–1700) and **Sir William Davenant** (1606–68) (adap.)
The Tempest; or, The Enchanted Island: A comedy D
Adaptation and alteration of Shakespeare's *The Tempest*, with further additions and alterations by Thomas Shadwell. Performed April 1674.

Thomas Duffett (*fl.* 1674–8)
The Spanish Rogue D
Performed *c.*March 1673

Thomas Flatman (1637–88)
Poems and Songs V

Henry Hammond (1605–60)
The Workes of the Reverend and Learned Henry Hammond WKS

Richard Head (1637?–86?)
The Western Wonder; or, O Brazeel F
Anonymous

James Howard (*b.* 1630?)
The English Monsieur: A comedy D
Performed 30 June 1663

Thomas Ken (1637–1711)
A Manual of Prayers for the Use of Scholars of Winchester College NF
25th edition, 1736

John Milton (1608–74)
Paradise Lost: A poem in twelve books V
The 2nd edition, revised and enlarged to twelve books. Published July 1674. Commendatory poems by 'S.B.' in Latin and Andrew Marvell in English. See also *Paradise Lost* 1667.

John Ray (1627–1705)
A Collection of English Words Not Generally Used DICT

Thomas Rymer (1641–1713) (tr.)
Reflections on Aristotles Treatise of Poesie NF
Anonymous. Translated from René Rapin (1621–87), *Réflexions sur la Poétique d'Aristote* (1674).

Elkanah Settle (1648–1724)
Notes and Observations on the Empress of Morocco Revised NF
See *The Empress of Morocco* 1673

Anthony à Wood (1632–95)
Historia et Antiquitates Universitatis Oxoniensis NF
Compiled in English and translated into Latin by Richard Peers and Richard Reeve. Contains much material borrowed from John Aubrey. English text published in parts by J. Gutch 1786–96. See *The History and Antiquities of the University of Oxford* 1786.

1675

- William Somerville born
- Lodowick Carlell dies
  Bulstrode Whitlocke, the elder, dies
- Bernard Lintot born

Richard Allestree (1619–81)
The Art of Contentment NF
Anonymous

Joshua Barnes (1654–1712)
Gerania: A new discovery of a little sort of people anciently discoursed of, called pygmies NF

Richard Baxter (1615–91)
Richard Baxter's Catholick Theologie NF

John Bunyan (1628–88)
Instruction for the Ignorant NF

John Bunyan (1628–88)
Light for Them That Sit in Darkness; or, A Discourse of Jesus Christ NF

Richard Burthogge (1638?–94?)
Causa Dei; or, An Apology for God NF

Charles Cotton (1630–87) (tr.)
Burlesque upon Burlesque; or, The Scoffer Scoft V
Anonymous. A second part published in 1675 as *The Scoffer Scoft.*

John Crowne (*d.* 1703) (adap.)
Andromache: A tragedy D
Performed *c.*August 1674. An anonymous translation of *Andromaque* (1667) by Jean Racine (1639–99), revised and altered (also anonymously) by Crowne.

John Crowne (*d.* 1703)
Calisto; or, The Chaste Nimph: The late masque at court D
Performed February 1675

John Crowne (*d.* 1703)
The Countrey Wit: A comedy D
Performed January 1676. Based on Molière (1622–73), *Le Sicilien* (1666–7).

Sir Francis Fane (*d.* 1689?)
Love in the Dark; or, The Man of Bus'ness: A comedy D

Nathaniel Lee (1649?–92)
The Tragedy of Nero, Emperour of Rome D
Performed May 1674

Richard Leigh (1649 or 50–1728)
Poems, upon Several Occasions, and, to Several Persons V
bao *The Censure of the Rota*

Thomas Otway (1652–85)
Alcibiades: A tragedy D
Performed September 1675

Henry Nevil Payne (*d. c.*1710)
The Siege of Constantinople: A tragedy D
Anonymous. Performed November 1674.

Edward Phillips (1630–96?) (ed.)
Theatrum Poetarum; or, A Compleat Collection of the Poets of all Ages V

Elkanah Settle (1648–1724)
Love and Revenge: A tragedy D
Performed November 1675

Thomas Shadwell (1642?–92) (adap.)
Psyche: A tragedy D
Performed 27 February 1675. Adapted from Molière (1622–73), *Psyché* (1671).

Peter Sterry (1613–72)
A Discourse of the Freedom of the Will NF

Jeremy Taylor (1613–67)
Antiquitates Christianae NF
Includes *Lives of the Apostles* by William Cave (1637–1713)

Thomas Traherne (1637–74)
Christian Ethicks; or, Divine Morality NF
Contains eight poems

William Wycherley (1641–1716)
The Country-Wife: A comedy D
Performed January 1675. Draws on Molière (1622–73), *L'École des femmes* (1662) and *L'École des maris* (1661).

1676

- Anthony Collins born
  Benjamin Hoadly born
  John Phillips born
- Edward Benlowes dies
  William Cavendish, 1st duke of Newcastle, dies
  Sir Matthew Hale dies
  Lucy Hutchinson dies?
  Gerrard Winstanley dies?

Robert Barclay (1648–90)
The Anarchy of the Ranters and Other Libertines NF

Robert Barclay (1648–90)
Quakerism Confirmed NF
Written with George Keith (1639?–1716). Written in refutation of Alexander Shirreff, John Leslie, and Paul Gellie. *Quakerism Canvassed* (1675).

Roger Boyle, earl of Orrery (1621–79)
English Adventures F
'By a person of honour'

Roger Boyle, earl of Orrery (1621–79)
Parthenissa, that Most Fam'd Romance: The six volumes compleat F
Comprising the 3rd edition of part i, books i–vi, and the 2nd edition of part i, books vii–viii; part ii, and part iii

John Bunyan (1628–88)
The Strait Gate; or, Great Difficulty of Going to Heaven NF

John Dryden (1631–1700)
Aureng-Zebe: A tragedy D
Performed 17 November 1675

Thomas D'Urfey (1653–1723)
The Siege of Memphis; or, The Ambitious Queen: A tragedy D
Performed *c.*September 1676

Sir George Etherege (1635–91)
The Man of Mode; or, Sir Fopling Flutter: A comedy D
Performed March 1676

George Fox (1624–91)
Concerning Revelation, Prophecy, Measure and Rule, and the Inspiration and Sufficiency of the Spirit NF

Joseph Glanvill (1636–80)
Essays on Several Important Subjects in Philosophy and Religion NF

Sir Matthew Hale (1609–76)
Contemplations, Moral and Divine NF
'By a person of great learning and judgment'. Many editions.

Thomas Hobbes (1588–1679) (tr.)
Homer's Iliads in English: To which may be added Homer's Odysses V
Hobbes's translation of the *Odyssey* was published in 1675

Thomas Hobbes (1588–1679)
A Letter About Liberty and Necessity NF
Extracted from *Of Libertie and Necessitie* 1654 (q.v.). Includes observations by Benjamin Laney (1591–1675), late bishop of Ely.

Edward Hyde, 1st earl of Clarendon (1609–74)
A Brief View and Survey of the Dangerous and Pernicious Errors to Church and State, in Mr Hobbes's book, entitled Leviathan NF
See Hobbes, *Leviathan* 1651

Nathaniel Lee (1649?–92)
Gloriana; or, The Court of Augustus Cæsar D
Performed January 1676

Nathaniel Lee (1649?–92)
Sophonisba; or, Hannibal's Overthrow: A tragedy D
Performed April 1675

Thomas Otway (1652–85) (adap.)
Don Carlos, Prince of Spain: A tragedy D
Performed June 1676. Adapted from César Vichard, l'abbé de Saint-Réal (1639–92), *Don Carlos* (1672).

Elkanah Settle (1648–1724)
The Conquest of China, by the Tartars: A tragedy D
Performed May 1675

Thomas Shadwell (1642?–92) (adap.)
The Libertine: A tragedy D
Performed June 1675. Adapted from Sieur Rosimond (1645–86), *Nouveau festin de Pierre.*

Thomas Shadwell (1642?–92)
The Virtuoso: A comedy D
Performed 25 May 1676

John Wilmot, earl of Rochester (1647–80)
Corydon and Cloris; or, The Wanton Sheepherdess V
Anonymous. Broadsheet. Publication date conjectural.

1677

- William of Orange marries Princess Mary, daughter of James, duke of York (Nov.)
- Sir Thomas Hanmer born
- Isaac Barrow dies
  James Harrington dies
- Benedict Spinoza dies

Anonymous
The Happy Slave: A novel F
Translated from Gabriel de Brémond, *L'hereux Esclave*

Anonymous
Tunbridge-Wells: or A Days Courtship: A comedy D
Formerly attributed (now questioned) to Thomas Rawlins (1620?–1670). Performed *c.*March 1678.

John Banks (*c.*1650–*c.*1700)
The Rival Kings; or, The Loves of Oroondates and Statira: A tragædy D

Aphra Behn (1640?–89)
Abdelazer; or, The Moor's Revenge: A tragedy D
Performed July 1676. An alteration of *Lust's Dominion* 1657 (q.v.), erroneously attributed to Christopher Marlowe.

Aphra Behn (1640?–89)
The Rover. Or, The Banish't Cavaliers: A comedy D
Anonymous, but reissued under Behn's name 1677. Based on Thomas Killigrew's *Thomaso* (see *Comedies, and Tragedies* 1664). Performed 24 March 1677. See also *The Second Part of The Rover* 1681.

Aphra Behn (1640?–89)
The Town-Fopp; or, Sir Timothy Tawdrey: A comedy D
Performed *c.*September 1676. Based on George Wilkins, *The Miseries of Inforst Mariage* 1607 (q.v.).

William Cavendish, 1st duke of Newcastle (1592–1676)
The Humorous Lovers: A comedy D

William Cavendish, 1st duke of Newcastle (1592–1676)
The Triumphant Widow; or, The Medley of Humours: A comedy D

John Cleveland (1613–58)
Clievelandi Vindiciae; or, Clieveland's Genuine Poems, Orations, Epistles MISC
See also *J. Cleaveland Revived* 1659

John Crowne (*d.* 1703)
The Destruction of Jerusalem by Titus Vespasian D
Performed January 1677

Charles Davenant (1656–1714)
Circe: A tragedy D

John Dryden (1631–1700)
The State of Innocence, and the Fall of Man: An opera D/OP
A dramatization of Milton's *Paradise Lost.* Unacted.

Thomas D'Urfey (1653–1723)
A Fond Husband; or, The Plotting Sisters: A comedy D
Performed May 1677

Thomas D'Urfey (1653–1723)
Madam Fickle; or, The Witty False One: A comedy D
Performed November 1676

John Flavel (1630?–91)
Navigation Spiritualized; or, A New Compass for Seamen NF
Includes verse

Richard Head (1637?–86?)
The Life and Death of Mother Shipton F
Anonymous. Pseudo-biography of the celebrated prophetess.

Nathaniel Lee (1649?–92)
The Rival Queens; or, The Death of Alexander the Great D
Performed 17 March 1677. Commendatory verses by John Dryden. Prologue by Sir Carr Scroope (1649–80).

John Oldham (1653–83)
Upon the Marriage of the Prince of Orange with the Lady Mary V
Anonymous. On the marriage of the future William III and Mary II in November 1677.

Thomas Otway (1652–85) (adap.)
Titus and Berenice: A tragedy D
Performed *c.*December 1676. Adapted from Jean Racine (1639–99), *Bérénice* (1671) Also includes *The Cheats of Scapin* translated and adapted from Molière (1622–73), *Les Fourberies de Scapin* (1671).

John Phillips (1631–1706)
Almahide; or, The Captive Queen: An excellent new romance F
Translated from Madeleine de Scudéry (1607–1701), *Almahide ou l'esclave reine* (1660–3)

Robert Plot (1640–96)
The Natural History of Oxford-Shire NF

Edward Ravenscroft (1644–1704)
King Edgar and Alfreda: A tragi-comedy D
Performed *c.*October 1677

Edward Ravenscroft (1644–1704)
Scaramouch a Philosopher, Harlequin a School-boy, Bravo, Merchant, and Magician: A comedy after the Italian manner D
Performed May 1677. Partly based on Molière (1622–73), *Le Bourgeois gentilhomme* (1671) and *Le mariage forcé*.

Edward Ravenscroft (1644–1704)
The Wrangling Lovers; or, The Invisible Mistress: A comedy D
Anonymous. Performed July 1676.

Sir Charles Sedley (1639–1701)
Antony and Cleopatra: A tragedy D
Performed 1677. Altered and published 1702 as *Beauty the Conqueror*.

Elkanah Settle (1648–1724) (adap.)
Ibrahim the Illustrious Bassa: A tragedy D
Performed *c.*March 1676. Adapted from Madeleine de Scudéry (1607–1701), *Ibrahim, ou l'Illustre Bassa* (1641–4).

Elkanah Settle (1648–1724)
Pastor Fido; or, The Faithful Shepherd: A pastoral D
Performed *c.*December 1676. Altered by Settle from Fanshawe's translation 1647 (q.v.) of the poem by Battista Guarini (1538–1612).

Edward Stillingfleet (1635–99)
A Letter to a Deist NF
Anonymous

Nahum Tate (1652–1715)
Poems V
Enlarged 1684 as *Poems Written on Several Occasions*

John Webster (1610–82)
The Displaying of Supposed Witchcraft NF

William Wycherley (1641–1716)
The Plain-Dealer: A comedy D
Performed December 1676

1678

- The fabricated Popish Plot unveiled by Titus Oates (Sept.)
- George Farquhar born
  Thomas Hearne born
  Mary Monck born (*c.*1678)
  Henry St-John, Viscount Bolingbroke, born
- Richard Flecknoe dies
  Andrew Marvell dies
  Marchamont Nedham dies
  Thomas Stanley, the elder, dies

Anonymous
Tom Essence: or, The Modish Wife: A comedy D
Formerly attributed (now questioned) to Thomas Rawlins (1620?–1670). Performed *c.*September 1676.

Richard Allestree (1619–81)
The Lively Oracle Given to Us NF
bao *The Whole Duty of Man*

Robert Barclay (1648–90)
An Apology for the True Christian Divinity NF
First published in Latin as *Theologiae vere Christianae apologia* (1676), also in French and Dutch. See also *Apology . . . Vindicated* 1679.

Isaac Barrow (1630–77)
Sermons Preached Upon Several Occasions NF

Aphra Behn (1640?–89) attrib.
The Lives of Sundry Notorious Villains F
Anonymous

Aphra Behn (1640?–89)
Sir Patient Fancy: A comedy D
Performed January 1678. Based on several plays by Molière (1622–73), especially *Le Malade imaginaire* (1673).

John Bunyan (1628–88)
Come, & Welcome, to Jesus Christ NF
Nine editions by 1700

John Bunyan (1628–88)
The Pilgrim's Progress From This World, To That Which is To Come F
The 17th century's bestseller, remaining in print, in multiple editions and translations in the majority of languages, ever since. *Pilgrim's Progress . . . The Second Part* published in 1684.

Samuel Butler (1612–80)
Hudibras. The Third and Last Part V
'By the author of the first and second parts'. See *Hudibras, the First Part* 1663; *Hudibras. The Second Part* 1664; *Hudibras. The First and Second Parts* 1674; *Hudibras. In Three Parts* 1684.

Ralph Cudworth (1617–88)
The True Intellectual System of the Universe NF

John Dryden (1631–1700)
All for Love; or, The World Well Lost: A tragedy D
Performed 12 December 1677. Based on Shakespeare's *Antony and Cleopatra*. Dryden's last play for the King's Company.

Thomas Duffett (*fl.* 1674–8)
Psyche Debauch'd: A comedy D
Performed *c.*August 1675. A satire on Shadwell's *Psyche* 1675 (q.v.).

Thomas D'Urfey (1653–1723)
The Fool Turn'd Critick: A comedy D
Performed November 1676

Thomas D'Urfey (1653–1723)
Trick for Trick; or, The Debauch'd Hypocrite: A comedy D
Performed *c.*March 1678. An alteraton of John Fletcher's *Monsieur Thomas* 1639 (q.v.).

'Ephelia' (possibly **Joan Philips**, *fl.* 1678–82)
A Poem to His Sacred Majesty, on the Plot V
On the Popish Plot

Joseph Glanvill (1636–80)
An Essay Concerning Preaching NF
Anonymous

Thomas Hobbes (1588–1679)
Decameron Physiologicum; or, Ten Dialogues of Natural Philosophy NF

Nathaniel Lee (1649?–92)
Mithridates King of Pontus: A tragedy D
Performed *c.*March 1678. Epilogue by Dryden.

Roger L'Estrange (1616–1704) (tr.)
Five Love-letters from a Nun to a Cavalier F
Anonymous. An influential epistolary novel. Translated from *Lettres portuguises*, formerly attributed to Marianna d'Alcoforado (1640–1723), now attributed to Gabriel Joseph de Lavergne, vicomte de Guilleragues (1628–85).

Roger L'Estrange (1616–1704) (tr.)
Seneca's Morals by Way of Abstract NF
Translated from Seneca, *Epistolae morales*. Many editions.

Thomas Otway (1652–85)
Friendship in Fashion: A comedy D
Performed April 1678

Samuel Pordage (1633–91)
The Siege of Babylon D
Performed *c.*September 1677

Thomas Porter (1636–80)
The French Conjurer: A comedy D
Performed *c.*July 1677. Partly based on Mateo Alemán (1547–1614?), *Aventuras y vida de Guzmán de Alfarache*.

Edward Ravenscroft (1644–1704)
The English Lawyer: A comedy D
Anonymous. Performed *c.*December 1677. Adapted from G. Ruggle's Latin play *Ignoramus* (1630), translated by Robert Codrington 1662, which was itself based on *La Trappolaria* by Giambattista della Porta (1535?–1615).

Thomas Rymer (1641–1713)
Edgar; or, The English Monarch: An heroick tragedy D

Thomas Rymer (1641–1713)
The Tragedies of the Last Age Consider'd and Examin'd NF

Thomas Shadwell (1642?–92) (adap.)
The History of Timon of Athens, the Man-hater D
Performed *c.*January 1678. Altered from Shakespeare.

Thomas Shipman (1632–80)
Henry the Third of France, Stabb'd by a Fryer. With the fall of the Guise D

Nahum Tate (1652–1715)
Brutus of Alba; or, The Enchanted Lovers: A tragedy D
Performed *c.*July 1678. Based on Virgil's *Aeneid*, book iv.

Henry Vaughan (1622–95)
Thalia Rediviva V
Includes previously published pieces and Latin poems by Thomas Vaughan ('Eugenius Philalethes')

John Wallis (1616–1703)
A Defence of the Royal Society, and the Philosophical Transactions, particularly those of July, 1670 NF
In answer to William Holder's *Supplement* to the July 1670 *Transactions* of the Royal Society

Izaak Walton (1593–1683)
The Life of Dr Sanderson, Late Bishop of Lincoln NF

1679

- Habeas Corpus Amendment Act (May) forbidding imprisonment without trial
  Exclusion crisis (1679–81): beginning of the 'Tory' and 'Whig' parties
- Charles Johnson born
  Thomas Parnell born
  Joseph Trapp born
- Roger Boyle, 1st earl of Orrery, dies
  Anne Conway dies
  Thomas Hobbes dies

Anonymous
The Princess of Cleves F
Translation of Marie-Madeleine, comtesse de La Fayette (1634–93), *La Princesse de Clèves* (1678). Many editions.

Anonymous
The Protestant Tutor NF

Sir Francis Bacon (1561–1626)
Baconiana NF

John Bancroft (*d.* 1696)
The Tragedy of Sertorius D
Performed *c.*March 1679

John Banks (*c.*1650–1700)
The Destruction of Troy: A tragedy D
Performed *c.*November 1678

Robert Barclay (1648–90)
Robert Barclay's Apology for the True Christian Divinity Vindicated NF
Written in response to John Brown (1610?–79), *Quakerisme the Path-way to Paganisme* (1678). See also Barclay, *An Apology* 1678.

Francis Beaumont (1584–1616) and **John Fletcher** (1579–1625)
Fifty Comedies and Tragedies D
See *Comedies and Tragedies* 1647

Aphra Behn (1640?–89)
The Feign'd Curtizans; or, A Night's Intrigue: A comedy D
Performed *c.*March 1679. Dedicatory epistle to Nell Gwyn.

John Bunyan (1628–88)
A Treatise of the Fear of God NF

Gilbert Burnet (1643–1715)
The History of the Reformation of the Church of England. The First Part NF
Part ii, 1681; part iii, 1715

Abraham Cowley (1618–67)
A Poem on the Late Civil War V

John Crowne (*d.* 1703)
The Ambitious Statesman; or, The Loyal Favourite D
Performed *c.*March 1679

John Dryden (1631–1700) and **Nathaniel Lee** (1649?–92)
Oedipus: A tragedy D
Performed September 1678? Acts i and iii by Dryden.

John Dryden (1631–1700) (adap.)
Troilus and Cressida; or, Truth Found Too Late: A tragedy D
Performed *c.*April 1679. Adapted from Shakespeare.

Thomas D'Urfey (1653–1723)
Squire Oldsapp; or, The Night-Adventurers: A comedy D
Performed *c.*June 1678

'Ephelia' (possibly **Joan Philips,** *fl.* 1678–82)
Female Poems on Several Occasions V
Reissued in 1682 with new material—mostly (possibly all) by other hands, including John Wilmot, earl of Rochester

Thomas Hobbes (1588–1679)
Behemoth; or, An Epitome of the Civil Wars of England NF
Written in 1668 but suppressed

Benjamin Keach (1640–1704)
The Glorious Lover: A divine poem V

John Oldham (1653–83)
Garnets Ghost V
bao *The Satyr Against Virtue*

John Oldham (1653–83)
A Satyr Against Vertue V
Anonymous. Reprinted in *Satyrs Upon the Jesuits* 1681 (q.v.).

John Phillips (1631–1706)
Jockey's Downfall: A poem on the late total defeat given to the Scottish Covenanters V
bao *The Satyr Against Hypocrites*. Broadsheet.

Thomas Shadwell (1642?–92)
A True Widow: A comedy D
Performed 21 March 1678. Prologue by Dryden.

Robert South (1634–1716)
Sermons Preached upon Several Occasions NF

John Wilmot, earl of Rochester (1647–80)
A Letter From Artemiza in the Town to Chloë in the Country V
'By a person of honour'

John Wilmot, earl of Rochester (1647–80)
A Satyr Against Mankind V
'By a person of honour'

John Wilmot, earl of Rochester (1647–80)
Upon Nothing V
'By a person of honour'. Broadsheet.

John Wilmot, earl of Rochester (1647–80)
A Very Heroical Epistle From My Lord All-Pride to Dol-Common V
Anonymous. Broadsheet.

1680

- Execution of Lord Stafford (29 Dec.)
- John Durant Breval born?
  Benjamin Griffin born
- Samuel Butler dies
  Joseph Glanvill dies
  Thomas Shipman dies
  John Wilmot, 2nd earl of Rochester, dies
- François de la Rochfoucauld dies

Anonymous
The Secret History of the Most Renowned Queen Elizabeth, and the Earl of Essex F
The source of John Banks's play *The Unhappy Favourite* 1682 (q.v.)

Philip Ayres (1638–1712) (tr.)
The Count of Gabalis; or, The Extravagant Mysteries of the Cabalists F
Anonymous. Translated from Nicolas-Pierre-Henri de Montfaucon, abbé de Villars (*c.*1635–73), *Le Comte de Gabalis* (1670). Used by Pope in *The Rape of the Lock* 1714 (q.v.).

Isaac Barrow (1630–77)
A Treatise of the Pope's Supremacy NF

Richard Baxter (1615–91)
Church-History of the Government of Bishops and their Councils Abbreviated NF

Aphra Behn (1640?–89) attrib.
The Revenge; or, A Match in Newgate: A comedy D
Anonymous. Performed *c.*June 1680.
Also attributed to Thomas Betterton (1635?–1710).

Charles Blount (1654–93)
Great is Diana of the Ephesians; or, The Original of Idolatry NF
Anonymous

Charles Blount (1654–93) (tr.)
The Two First Books of Philostratus Concerning the Life of Apollonius Tyaneus NF
Anonymous

John Bunyan (1628–88)
The Life and Death of Mr Badman NF

Gilbert Burnet (1643–1715)
Some Passages of the Life and Death of the Earl of Rochester NF
Rochester died in July 1680. Abridged *c.*1690 as *The Libertine Overthrown; or, A Mirror for Atheists* and 1693 as *A Mirror for Atheists*.

Wentworth Dillon, 4th earl of Roscommon (1633–85) (tr.)
Horace's Art of Poetry V

A translation of Horace, *Ars poetica*. Includes an essay by Edmund Waller.

John Dryden (1631–1700)
The Kind Keeper; or, Mr Limberham: A comedy D
Performed 11 March 1678

John Dryden (1631–1700) and others (tr.)
Ovid's Epistles V

Thomas D'Urfey (1653–1723)
The Virtuous Wife; or, Good Luck at Last: A comedy D
Performed *c.*September 1679

Sir Robert Filmer (1588?–1653)
Patriarcha; or, The Natural Power of Kings NF
Written 1635–42

George Fox (1624–91)
Concerning the Living God of Truth and the World's God NF

Thomas Hobbes (1588–1679)
An Historical Narration Concerning Heresie, and the Punishment Thereof NF

Edward Hyde, 1st earl of Clarendon (1609–74)
Two Letters Written by the Right Honourable Edward Earl of Clarendon NF
Publication date conjectural

Francis Kirkman (1632–*c.*1680)
An Exact Catalogue of all the Comedies, Tragedies, Tragi-Comedies, Opera's, Masks, Pastorals and Interludes Printed or Published, Till 1680 NF
Compiled 1671; additions to 1680 by Nicholas Cox

Nathaniel Lee (1649?–92)
Cæsar Borgia; Son of Pope Alexander the Sixth: A tragedy D
Performed *c.*May 1679. Prologue by Dryden.

Nathaniel Lee (1649?–92)
Theodosius; or, The Force of Love: A tragedy D
Performed *c.*September 1680

Roger L'Estrange (1616–1704)
The Casuist Uncas'd PS

Roger L'Estrange (1616–1704)
Citt and Bumpkin: In a dialogue over a pot of ale NF
Anonymous. *Citt and Bumpkin, the Second Part* also published 1680.

Roger L'Estrange (1616–1704)
A Compendious History of the Most Remarkable Passages of the Last Fourteen Years NF
Anonymous

Roger L'Estrange (1616–1704) (tr.)
Twenty Select Colloquies Out of Erasmus Roterodamus NF
Translated from Erasmus (*c.*1467–1536), *Colloquia*

Thomas Otway (1652–85)
The History and Fall of Caius Marius: A tragedy D
Performed September/October 1679. Taken in part from Shakespeare's *Romeo and Juliet.*

Thomas Otway (1652–85)
The Orphan; or, The Unhappy Marriage: A tragedy D
Performed February/March 1680

Thomas Otway (1652–85)
The Poet's Complaint of his Muse; or, A Satyr Against Libells V

John Phillips (1631–1706)
Dr Oates's Narrative of the Popish Plot Vindicated NF

Sir Paul Rycaut (1628–1700)
The History of the Turkish Empire from the Year 1623 to the Year 1677 NF
Continuation of *The General History of the Turks* by Richard Knolles

Elkanah Settle (1648–1724)
Fatal Love; or, The Forc'd Inconstancy: A tragedy D
Performed *c.*September 1680. Based on a Greek romance, *Clitiphon and Leucippe*, by Achilles Tatius.

Elkanah Settle (1648–1724)
The Female Prelate: Being the history of the life and death of Pope Joan. A tragedy. D
Performed 31 May 1680

Thomas Shadwell (1642?–92)
The Woman-Captain: A comedy D
Performed *c.*September 1679

Edward Stillingfleet (1635–99)
The Mischief of Separation NF

Nahum Tate (1652–1715)
The Loyal General: A tragedy D
Performed *c.*December 1679. Prologue by Dryden.

Sir William Temple (1628–99)
Miscellanea NF

See also *Miscellanea: The Second Part* 1690; *Third Part* 1701.

John Wilmot, earl of Rochester (1647–80)
Poems on Several Occasions V
Rochester died in July 1680

1681

- Barton Booth born
- Richard Alleine dies
  Richard Allestree dies
  William Lilly dies
- Georg Telemann born
- Calderón dies

Richard Baxter (1615–91)
A Breviate of the Life of Margaret Baxter NF
A memorial of Baxter's wife

Richard Baxter (1615–91)
Compassionate Counsel to all Young-Men NF

Richard Baxter (1615–91)
Poetical Fragments V

Aphra Behn (1640?–89)
The Second Part of The Rover D
Performed *c.*January 1681. See *The Rover*, part i, 1677.

Charles Cotton (1630–87)
The Wonders of the Peake V

John Crowne (*d.* 1703) (adap.)
Thyestes: A tragedy D
Performed *c.*March 1680. Adapted from Seneca.

John Dryden (1631–1799)
Absalom and Achitophel [pt i] V
Anonymous. A satire on Anthony Ashley Cooper, earl of Shaftesbury (1621–83), and James Scott, duke of Monmouth (1649–85). See also *The Second Part of Absalom and Achitophel* 1682.

John Dryden (1631–1700)
The Spanish Fryar; or, The Double Discovery D
Performed 8 March 1680

Sir William Dugdale (1605–86)
A Short View of the Late Troubles in England NF
Anonymous

Thomas D'Urfey (1653–1723)
The Progress of Honesty; or, A View of a Court and City V
See also *The Malcontent* 1684

Thomas D'Urfey (1653–1723)
Sir Barnaby Whigg; or, No Wit Like a Womans: A comedy D
Performed *c.*September 1681. Based on Shackerley Marmion's *A Fine Companion* 1633 (q.v.) and Gabriel de Brémond, *Le Double Cocu.*

Joseph Glanvill (1636–80)
Saducismus Triumphatus; or, Full and Plain Evidence Concerning Witches and Apparitions NF
The 5th edition of *Some Philosophical Considerations Touching the Being of Witches*, 1666, most copies of which were destroyed in the Fire of London

Thomas Hobbes (1588–1679)
A Dialogue Between a Philosopher and a Student of the Common Laws of England NF

Thomas Hobbes (1588–1679)
Tracts of Thomas Hobb's NF
See also *Tracts* 1682

Sir William Killigrew (1606–95)
Mid-night Thoughts NF
'By a person of quality'. See also *Mid-night and Daily Thoughts* 1694.

Jane Lead (1623–1704)
The Heavenly Cloud Now Breaking NF

Nathaniel Lee (1649?–92)
Lucius Junius Brutus, Father of his Country: A tragedy D
Performed December 1680. Partly based on Madeleine de Scudéry (1608–1701), *Clélie, histoire romaine* (1654–60).

Roger L'Estrange (1616–1704)
The Observator. In Question and Answer PER
Anonymous. Subsequently *The Observator, in dialogue.* Published between two and four times a week from April 1681 to March 1687.

Andrew Marvell (1621–78)
Miscellaneous Poems V

John Milton (1608–74)
Mr John Miltons Character of the Long Parliament and Assembly of Divines NF
Originally written for Milton's *History of Britain* 1670 (q.v.) but omitted from early editions

John Oldham (1653–83)
Satyrs upon the Jesuits V
Anonymous. The first 'Satyr Upon the Jesuits' originally published in 1679 as a broadside under the title *Garnets Ghost* (q.v.).

Thomas Otway (1652–85) (adap.)
The Souldiers Fortune: A comedy D

Performed *c.*June 1680. Based on Molière (1622–73), *L'École des maris* (1661). See also *The Atheist* 1684.

William Penn (1644–1718)
A Brief Account of the Province of Pennsylvania in America NF
Anonymous

George Savile, marquis of Halifax (1633–95)
Observations Upon a Late Libel, called A letter from a person of quality to his friend, concerning the Kings declaration, &c NF
Anonymous. A satirical commentary on the Whigs' reaction to the dissolution of the Oxford parliament.

Nahum Tate (1652–1715) (adap.)
The History of King Lear D
Performed *c.*March 1681. Altered from Shakespeare's *King Lear*.

Nahum Tate (1652–1715) (adap.)
The History of King Richard the Second D
Performed *c.*January 1681. Altered from Shakespeare's *Richard II*.

1682

- Tsaritza Sophia becomes Regent for her infant brothers, Ivan and Peter
- Thomas Newcomb born?
- James Gibbs born
- Sir Thomas Browne dies
  Philip Hunton dies
- Claude Lorraine dies

John Banks (*c.*1650–1700)
The Unhappy Favourite; or, The Earl of Essex: A tragedy D
Performed *c.*May 1681

John Banks (*c.*1650)
Vertue Betray'd; or, Anna Bullen: A tragedy D

Aphra Behn (1640?–89)
The City-Heiress; or, Sir Timothy Treat-All: A comedy D
Performed *c.*March 1682

Aphra Behn (1640?–89)
The False Count; or, A New Way to Play an Old Game D
Performed *c.*December 1681

Aphra Behn (1640?–89)
The Roundheads or, The Good Old Cause: A comedy D
Performed *c.*December 1681. Based on John Tatham's *The Rump* 1660 (q.v.).

John Bunyan (1628–88)
The Holy War, Made by Shaddai Upon Diabolus, for the Regaining of the Metropolis of the World NF

Gilbert Burnet (1643–1715)
The Life and Death of Sir Matthew Hale NF

Samuel Butler (1612–80)
Mercurius Menippeus. The Loyal Satirist; or, Hudibras in Prose NF
Anonymous. Also attributed to Sir John Birkenhead (1616–79).

Matthew Coppinger (*fl.* 1682)
Poems, Songs and Lover-Verses, upon Several Subjects V

Thomas Creech (1659–1700) (tr.)
De Natura Rerum V
Anonymous. Translated into verse from Lucretius.

Sir Simonds D'Ewes (1602–50)
The Journals of all the Parliaments During the Reign of Queen Elizabeth NF

John Dryden (1631–1700)
Mac Flecknoe; or, A Satyr upon the True-Blew-Protestant Poet, T.S. V
bao *Absalom and Achitophel.* Directed against Thomas Shadwell.

John Dryden (1631–1700)
The Medall: A satyre against sedition V
bao *Absalom and Achitophel.* A satire on Anthony Ashley Cooper, earl of Shaftesbury (1621–83). Commendatory poem by Nahum Tate.

John Dryden (1631–1700)
Religio Laici; or, A Laymans Faith V

Thomas D'Urfey (1653–1723)
Butler's Ghost; or, Hudibras. The Fourth Part V
A continuation of Samuel Butler's *Hudibras* (part i, 1663, q.v.)

Thomas D'Urfey (1653–1723)
The Royalist: A comedy D
Performed January 1682

Robert Gould (*d.* 1709)
Love Given O're; or, A Satyr Against the Pride, Lust and Inconstancy of Woman V
Anonymous. See also Sarah Egerton, *The Female Advocate* 1686, and Richard Ames, *Sylvia's Revenge* 1688.

Thomas Hobbes (1588–1679)
Tracts of Mr Thomas Hobbs of Malmsbury NF
Second collection: see also *Tracts* 1681

Samuel Johnson (1649–1702)
Julian the Apostate NF
Written against the succession of the duke of York (later James II)

John Milton (1608–74)
A Brief History of Moscovia NF

Thomas Otway (1652–85) (adap.)
Venice Preserv'd; or, A Plot Discover'd: A tragedy D
Performed 9 February 1682. A translation and adaptation of César Vichard, M. l'abbé de Saint-Réal (1639–92), *Les Conjurations des Espagnols contre la République de Venise.*

Samuel Pordage (1633–91)
The Medal Revers'd: A satyre against persecution V
bao *Azaria and Hushai.* See Dryden, above.

Edward Ravenscroft (1644–1704)
The London Cuckolds: A comedy D
Performed November 1681

Elkanah Settle (1648–1724)
Absalom Senior; or, Achitophel Transpros'd V
Anonymous. A reply to the first part of Dryden's *Absalom and Achitophel* 1681 (q.v.).

Elkanah Settle (1648–1724)
The Heir of Morocco, with the Death of Gayland D
Performed 11 March 1682

Thomas Shadwell (1642?–92)
The Lancashire-Witches, and Tegue o Divelly the Irish Priest: A comedy D
Performed *c.*September 1681. See also *The Amorous Bigotte* 1690.

Thomas Shadwell (1642?–92)
The Medal of John Bayes: A satyr against folly and knavery V
Anonymous. An answer to Dryden's *The Medall* 1682. See also *Mac Flecknoe* 1682.

John Sheffield, duke of Buckingham and **marquess of Normanby** (1648–1721)
An Essay upon Poetry V
Anonymous. An attack on John Wilmot, earl of Rochester (*d.* 1680).

Thomas Southerne (1659–1746)
The Loyal Brother; or, The Persian Prince: A tragedy D
Performed February 1682). Prologue and Epilogue by Dryden. Based on a French novel translated as *Tachmas, Prince of Persia* by P. Porter in 1676.

Nahum Tate (1652–1715) (adap.)
The Ingratitude of a Common-wealth; or, The Fall of Caius Martius Coriolanus D
Performed *c.*December 1681. Adapted from Shakespeare's *Coriolanus.*

Nahum Tate (1652–1715) and **John Dryden** (1631–1700)
The Second Part of Absalom and Achitophel V
A sequel to *Absalom and Achitophel* 1681 (q.v.) and similarly directed against the earl of Shaftesbury and James, duke of Monmouth. Mostly written by Tate.

George Villiers, duke of Buckingham (1628–87)
The Chances: A comedy D
Performed December 1682. Adapted from John Fletcher (1579–1625). Plot taken from Cervantes (1547–1616), 'La Señora Cornelia' (from his *Novelas ejemplares*, 1613).

Bulstrode Whitlocke (1605–75)
Memorials of the English Affairs NF
Anonymous

1683

- The Rye House Plot discovered (June)
  Siege of Vienna by the Turks
  William Dampier begins his voyage round the world
  Evacuation of Tangier
- Conyers Middleton born
  Edward Young born
- Thomas Killigrew dies
  John Oldham dies
  Algernon Sidney executed
  Izaak Walton dies
  Benjamin Whichcote dies

Philip Ayres (1638–1712)
Emblems of Love V
Subsequently reissued as *Cupids Addresse to the Ladies*

Isaac Barrow (1630–77)
The Works of the Learned Isaac Barrow WKS

Richard Baxter (1615–91)
Richard Baxter's Dying Thoughts upon Phil. I.23 NF

Aphra Behn (1640?–89)
The Young King; or, The Mistake D

Performed *c.*1679. Based on part viii of *Cléopatre* by Gaultier de Coste, Seigneur de la Calprenède (*d.* 1663), and on Calderón (1600–81), *La Vida es sueño* (1636).

Sir Thomas Browne (1605–82)
Certain Miscellany Tracts NF

John Bunyan (1628–88)
A Case of Conscience Resolved NF

John Bunyan (1628–88)
The Greatness of the Soul, and Unspeakableness of the Loss Thereof NF

John Chalkhill (*c.*1594–1642)
Thealma and Clearchus: A pastoral history V
Edited by Izaak Walton

John Crowne (*d.* 1703)
City Politiques: A comedy D
Performed 19 January 1683

John Dryden (1631–1700) and **Nathaniel Lee** (1649?–92)
The Duke of Guise: A tragedy D
Performed 30 November 1682

John Dryden (1631–1700)
The Vindication: Or, the parallel of the French Holy-League, and the English League and Covenant NF
A reply to Thomas Hunt (1627?–88), *Defence of the Charter, and Municipal Rights of the City of London* (1683), and to Shadwell, *Some Reflections upon the Pretended Parallel in the Play called The Duke of Guise* (1683)

Thomas D'Urfey (1653–1723)
A New Collection of Songs and Poems V

Thomas Flatman (1637–88)
On the Death of the Illustrious Prince Rupert V
Prince Rupert died on 29 November 1682

Robert Gould (*d.* 1709)
Presbytery Rough-Drawn V
Anonymous

Benjamin Keach (1640–1704)
The Travels of True Godliness F
Anonymous. Bunyanesque allegorical fiction. Many editions.

Jane Lead (1623–1704)
The Revelation of Revelations NF

John Mason (1645?–94)
Spiritual Songs; or, Songs of Praise to Almighty God upon Several Occasions V
Anonymous

John Oldham (1653–83)
Poems, and Translations V
bao *Satyrs Upon the Jesuits*

Sir William Petty (1623–87)
Another Essay in Political Arithmetick: Concerning the growth of the city of London NF

Thomas Shipman (1632–80)
Carolina; or, Loyal Poems V

1684

- John Kelly born (*c.*1684)
  William Pulteney, earl of Bath, born
- Sir Aston Cokayne dies
- Antoine Watteau born
- Pierre Corneille dies

Richard Allestree (1619–81)
Forty Sermons NF
2 parts. Biographical sketch by John Fell (1625–86).

John Banks (*c.*1650)
The Island Queens; or, The Death of Mary, Queen of Scotland D
Prohibited. Later altered as *The Albion Queens* (1704).

Aphra Behn (1640?–89)
Love-Letters Between a Noble-man and his Sister F
Published anonymously. Imaginary letters between Forde Grey, earl of Tankerville (1655–1701) and his sister-in-law, Lady Henrietta Berkeley (1664 or 5–1710). Part ii 1685 (q.v.), Part iii, as *The Amours of Philander and Silvia*, 1687 (q.v.).

Aphra Behn (1640?)
Poems Upon Several Occasions V

John Bunyan (1628–88)
A Holy Life, the Beauty of Christianity; or, An Exhortation to Christians to be Holy NF

John Bunyan (1628–88)
The Pilgrim's Progress From This World to That Which is To Come: The Second Part F
See *Pilgrim's Progress* 1678

John Bunyan (1628–88)
Seasonable Counsel; or, Advice to Sufferers NF
On the persecution endured by nonconformists

Gilbert Burnet (1643–1715) (tr.)
Utopia NF
Translated anonymously

Thomas Burnet (1635?–1715)
The Theory of the Earth NF
With additional title-page: *Sacred Theory of the Earth*. A translation of part i of *Telluris theoria sacra*, first published in Latin 1681–9. See also *The Theory of the Earth* 1690.

Samuel Butler (1612–80)
Hudibras. In Three Parts V
Published anonymously. See *Hudibras, the First Part* 1663; *Hudibras. The Second Part* 1664; *Hudibras. The First and Second Parts* 1674; *Hudibras. The Third and Last Part* 1678.

Thomas Creech (1659–1700) (tr.)
The Idylliums of Theocritus, with Rapin's Discourse of Pastorals Done into English V
Translator's dedication signed. The 'Discourse' translated from Père René Rapin (1621–87), *Treatise de carmine pastorali*.

Thomas Creech (1659–1700) (tr.)
The Odes, Satyrs, and Epistles of Horace V
The only complete translation of Horace's poems until Philip Francis's (see 1743 and 1747)

Wentworth Dillon, 4th earl of Roscommon (1633–85)
An Essay on Translated Verse V
2nd edition, 1684

John Dryden (1631–1700) (tr.)
The History of the League NF
Translated from Louis Maimbourg (1610–86)

John Dryden (1631–1700) and **Jacob Tonson** (1656?–1736) (eds)
Miscellany Poems ANTH
The first in the series of miscellanies published by Tonson 1684–1709. See also *Sylvae* 1685, *Examen Poeticum* 1693, *Annual Miscellany* 1694. *Poetical Miscellanies: Fifth Part* 1704; *Sixth Part* 1709.

Thomas D'Urfey (1653–1723)
Choice New Songs V

Thomas D'Urfey (1653–1723)
The Malecontent: a Satyr V
Published anonymously. Sequel to *The Progress of Honesty* 1681 (q.v.).

John Harington (1627–1700)
The Grecian Story V

Benjamin Keach (1640–1704)
The Progress of Sin F
Published anonymously. Bunyanesque allegorical fiction.

John Lacy (1615–81)
Sir Hercules Buffoon; or, The Poetical Squire D
Performed *c.*June 1684

Nathaniel Lee (1649?–92)
Constantine the Great: A tragedy D
Performed November 1683. Prologue by Thomas Otway, epilogue by John Dryden.

John Norris (1657–1711)
Poems and Discourses. Occasionally Written V

John Oldham (1653–83)
The Works of Mr John Oldham WKS

Thomas Otway (1652–85)
The Atheist; or, The Second Part of the Souldiers Fortune D
Performed *c.*July 1683. See *The Souldiers Fortune* 1681.

Samuel Parker (1640–88)
Religion and Loyalty; or, A Demonstration of the Power of the Christian Church Within It Self NF
See also *Religion and Loyalty* 1685

Edward Ravenscroft (1644–1704)
Dame Dobson: or, The Cunning Woman D
Performed *c.*May 1683. Adapted from *La Devineresse* by Thomas Corneille (1625–1709) and Jean Donneau de Vizé.

Thomas Southerne (1659–1746)
The Disappointment; or, The Mother in Fashion D
Performed *c.*April 1684

1685

- Death of Charles II (6 Feb.)
  JAMES II (–1688)
  Flogging of Titus Oates (May)
  Monmouth's Rebellion (June–July)
  Monmouth defeated at the Battle of Sedgemoor (6 July)
  Monmouth executed (15 July)
  The 'Bloody Assizes' conducted by George Jeffreys (Sept.)
  Revocation of the Edict of Nantes by Louis XIV
- Penelope Aubin born (*c.*1685)
  George Berkeley born
  Jane Brereton born
  William Diaper born

John Gay born
Aaron Hill born
William King (*d.* 1763) born

- Wentworth Dillon, 4th earl of Roscommon, dies
  Anne Killigrew dies
  Thomas Otway dies
  Anne Wharton dies

- Johann Sebastian Bach born
  George Frederick Handel born
  Domenico Scarlatti born

Edmund Arwaker (*c.*1655–1730)
The Vision V

Edmund Arwaker (*c.*1655–1730)
The Second Part of The Vision, a Pindarick Ode V
The coronation of James II, the third son of Charles II and the former duke of York, took place on 23 April 1685

Isaac Barrow (1630–77)
Of Contentment, Patience and Resignation to the Will of God NF

Richard Baxter (1615–91)
A Paraphrase on the New Testament NF
The work for which Baxter was imprisoned on charges of sedition

Aphra Behn (1640?–89)
Love-Letters From a Noble Man and His Sister F
Part i 1684 (q.v.); part iii, as *The Amours of Philander and Silvia*, 1687 (q.v.)

Aphra Behn (1640?–89)
A Pindarick on the Death of Our Late Sovereign V
Charles II died on 6 February 1685

Aphra Behn (1640?–89)
A Pindarick Poem on the Happy Coronation of His Most Sacred Majesty James II V
The coronation of James II took place on 23 April 1685

Henry Bold (1627–83) (tr.)
Latine Songs, with their English: and Poems V
Includes the ballad 'Chevy Chase' and Sir John Suckling's poem 'Why so pale and wan fond lover?'

John Bunyan (1628–88)
A Discourse upon the Pharisee and the Publicane NF

John Bunyan (1628–88)
Questions About the Nature and Perpetuity of the Seventh-Day-Sabbath NF

Gilbert Burnet (1643–1715)
A Collection of Several Tracts and Discourses Written in the Years 1677–85 NF
See also *A Second Collection* 1689, *A Third Collection* 1703

Charles Cotton (1630–87) (tr.)
Essays of Montaigne NF
Published in 3 volumes (1685–6)

John Crowne (*d.* 1703) (adap.)
Sir Courtly Nice; or, It Cannot Be: A comedy D
Performed 9 May 1685. An adaptation of Agustíin Moreto y Cabaña (1618–69), *No puede ser*, itself derived from Lope de Vega.

John Cutts, Baron Cutts (1661?–1707)
La Muse de Cavalier V
Anonymous

Sir William Davenant (1606–68)
The Seventh and Last Canto of the Third Book of Gondibert V
See *Gondibert* 1651

John Dryden (1631–1700)
Albion and Albanius: An opera D/OP
Performed 3 June 1685. Music (not included) by Louis Grabu (*d.* 1694). See also *King Arthur* 1691.

John Dryden (1631–1700) and **Jacob Tonson** (1656?–1736) (eds)
Sylvae; or, The Second Part of Poetical Miscellanies V
The second in a series of miscellanies published by Tonson 1684–1709. Contains translations from Virgil, Lucretius, Theocritus, and Horace, mainly by Dryden. See also *Miscellany Poems* 1684, *Examen Poeticum* 1693, *Annual Miscellany* 1694. *Poetical Miscellanies: Fifth Part* published 1704; *Sixth Part* 1709.

John Dryden (1631–1700)
Threnodia Augustalis V
On the death of Charles II (6 February 1685)

Thomas Ken (1637–1711)
An Exposition on the Church-Catechism NF

Thomas Otway (1652–85)
Windsor Castle V
On the death of Charles II (6 February 1685). Otway died in April of this year.

Samuel Parker (1640–88)
Religion and Loyalty. The Second Part NF
See also *Religion and Loyalty* 1684

William Shakespeare (1564–1616)
Comedies, Histories, and Tragedies D
The Fourth Folio

Thomas Sprat (1635–1713)
A True Account and Declaration of the Horrid Conspiracy Against the Late King NF
Anonymous. An account, written at the behest of Charles II, of the Rye House Plot (1683).

Edward Stillingfleet (1635–99)
Origines Britannicae; or, The Antiquities of the British Church NF

Nahum Tate (1652–1715)
Cuckolds-Haven: or, An Alderman no Conjurer: A farce D
Performed *c.*July 1685

Nahum Tate (1652–1715)
A Duke and No Duke: A farce D
Performed *c.*August 1684

Nahum Tate (1652–1715) (ed.)
Poems by Several Hands, and on Several Occasions V
Poems by Cowley, Rochester, Sir Francis Fane, Philip Ayes, John Evelyn, Waller, Tate, and others

John Tutchin (1661?–1707)
Poems on Several Occasions V

Edmund Waller (1606–87)
Divine Poems V

Samuel Wesley (1662–1735)
Maggots; or, Poems on Several Subjects, Never Before Handled V
Anonymous

John Wilmot, earl of Rochester (1647–80)
Valentinian: A tragedy D
Adaptation of a play by John Fletcher. First prologue by Aphra Behn. See also *Poems* 1691.

1686

- The League of Augsberg formed against Louis XIV
- Thomas Carte born
  William Law born
  Samuel Madden born
  Allan Ramsay born
  Thomas Tickell born
- Sir William Dugdale dies

Edmund Arwaker (*c.*1655) (tr.)
Pia Desideria; or, Divine Addresses V
Translated from Herman Hugo (1588–1629), *Pia Desideria Emblematis* (1624)

Sir Thomas Browne (1605–82)
The Works of the Learned Sir Thomas Brown WKS
The first collected edition

John Bunyan (1628–88)
A Book for Boys and Girls; or, Country Rhimes for Children NF

Gilbert Burnet (1643–1715)
Some Letters: Containing an account of . . . Switzerland, Italy, etc. NF
Written to Robert Boyle

Thomas D'Urfey (1653–1723)
The Banditti; or, A Ladies Distress D
Performed *c.*February 1686

Thomas D'Urfey (1653–1723)
A Common-wealth of Women D
Performed *c.*August 1685

Sarah Fyge Egerton, later **Field** (1670–1723)
The Female Advocate V
Anonymous. A reply to Robert Gould's *Love Given O're* 1682 (q.v.).

Sir Francis Fane (*d.* 1689?)
The Sacrifice: A tragedy D
Unacted

Thomas Flatman (1637–88)
A Song for St Caecilia's Day V

Anne Killigrew (1660–85)
Poems by Mrs Anne Killigrew V

Thomas Otway (1652–85) (tr.)
The History of the Triumvirates NF
Lives of Julius Caesar, Pompey, Crassus, Augustus, Anthony, and Lepidus. Translated from Samuel de Broë, Seigneur de Citri.

Richard Parr (1617–91)
The Life of James Usher NF

Robert Plot (1640–96)
The Natural History of Stafford-Shire NF

Edward Stillingfleet (1635–99)
The Doctrines and Practices of the Church of Rome Truly Represented NF
Anonymous

1687

- Declaration of Indulgence issued by James II
- Daniel Bellamy, the elder, born
  Henry Carey born?

Mary Chandler born
Thomas Sheridan born
William Stukeley born
Nicholas Tindal born

- Charles Cotton dies
Henry More dies
Sir William Petty dies
George Villiers, 2nd duke of Buckingham, dies
Edmund Waller dies

Anonymous
Letters Writ by a Turkish Spy F
Translated from Giovanni Paolo Marana (1642–93), *L'Esploratore Turco*. Many editions.

Philip Ayres (1638–1712)
Lyric Poems: Made in imitation of the Italians V
Includes translations

Aphra Behn (1640?–89)
The Amours of Philander and Silvia F
The third part of *Love-Letters Between a Nobleman and his Sister*. Part i 1684 (q.v.), part ii 1685 (q.v.).

Aphra Behn (1640?–89)
The Emperor of the Moon: A farce D
Performed March/April 1687. Based on Anne Mauduit de Fatouville, *Arlequin Empereur dans la Lune*.

Aphra Behn (1640?–89)
The Luckey Chance; or, An Alderman's Bargain: A comedy D
Performed by April 1686

Martin Clifford (*d.* 1677)
Notes Upon Mr Dryden's Poems in Four Letters NF
Includes 'Reflections upon the Hind and the Panther' by 'another hand'—i.e. Thomas Brown (1663–1704)

John Dryden (1631–1700)
The Hind and the Panther V
Anonymous

John Dryden (1631–1700)
A Song for St Cecilia's Day V

Thomas D'Urfey (1653–1723)
A Compleat Collection of Mr D'Urfey's Songs and Odes V

Gerard Langbaine, the younger (1656–92)
A New Catalogue of English Plays NF
Published 1687, dated 1688. Two unauthorized issues published in 1687 as *Momus Triumphans*.

Sir Roger L'Estrange (1616–1704) (tr.)
The Spanish Decameron; or, Ten Novels F
Five novels from Cervantes (1547–1616), *Novelas ejemplares* (1613); five from Alonso de Castillo Solórzano (1584–1648), *La Garduña de Sevilla* (1642)

Isaac Newton (1642–1727)
Philosophiae Naturalis Principia Mathematica NF
In Latin. English translation published in 1729 (q.v.).

John Norris (1657–1711)
A Collection of Miscellanies MISC

Sir William Petty (1623–87)
Two Essays in Political Arithmetick NF

Matthew Prior (1664–1721) and **Charles Montagu** (1661–1715)
The Hind and the Panther Transvers'd to the Story of the Country-Mouse and the City-Mouse V
Anonymous. A burlesque of Dryden's *The Hind and the Panther* 1687 (q.v.). Montagu later became earl of Halifax.

Edward Ravenscroft (1644–1704)
Titus Andronicus; or, The Rape of Lavinia D
Performed *c.*December 1677

Sir Charles Sedley (1639–1701)
Bellamira; or, The Mistress: A comedy D
Performed 1687. Based on Terence, *Eunuchus*.

Thomas Shadwell (1642?–92) (tr.)
The Tenth Satyr of Juvenal V
English and Latin on facing pages

Nahum Tate (1652–1715) (adap.)
The Island-Princess D
Performed April 1687. An adaptation of John Fletcher's *The Island Princess* (published posthumously in 1669). See also Motteux, *The Island Princess* 1699.

1688

- Trial of the Seven Bishops (June)
The 'Glorious Revolution': William of Orange lands at Torbay (5 Nov); enters London (19 Dec.)
James II, wife, and son flee to France
Convention Parliament

- Laurence Eusden born
Zachary Grey born
William Meston born?
Alexander Pope born

Lewis Theobald born
Thomas Warton, the elder, born?
Leonard Welsted born
- John Bunyan dies
Ralph Cudworth dies
Thomas Flatman dies
- James Edward Stuart ('The Old Pretender') born
- Emanuel Swedenborg born

Richard Ames (*d.* 1693)
Sylvia's Revenge; or, A Satyr Against Man V
Anonymous response to Robert Gould, *Love Given O're* 1682 (q.v.). See also *Sylvia's Complaint* 1692.

Jane Barker (1652–1732) and others
Poetical Recreations V

Joshua Barnes (1654–1712)
The History of that Most Victorious Monarch, Edward III NF

Aphra Behn (1640?–89)
A Congratulatory Poem to Her Most Sacred Majesty V
Addressed to Queen Mary, who gave birth to James Francis Edward Stuart, Prince of Wales, known later as the Old Pretender, on 10 June 1688

Aphra Behn (1640?–89)
The Fair Jilt; or, The History of Prince Tarquin and Miranda F

Aphra Behn (1640?–89)
Oroonoko; or, The Royal Slave: A true history F
See also Thomas Southerne's dramatization 1696

Aphra Behn (1640?–89)
Three Histories F
Includes *Oroonoko, The Fair Jilt,* and *Agnes de Castro; or, The force of generous love,* translated from Jean-Baptiste de Brilhac

Robert Boyle (1627–91)
A Disquisition About the Final Causes of Natural Things NF

Thomas Brown (1663–1704)
The Reasons of Mr Bays Changing his Religion V
Anonymous. 'Mr Bays' = Dryden. See also *The Late Converts Exposed* 1690.

John Bunyan (1628–88)
A Discourse of the Building, Nature, Excellency, and Government of the House of God V

John Bunyan (1628–88)
Good News for the Vilest of Men NF

John Bunyan (1628–88)
Solomon's Temple Spiritualized NF

John Bunyan (1628–88)
The Water of Life NF

John Crowne (*d.* 1703)
Darius, King of Persia: A tragedy D
Performed May 1688

John Dryden (1631–1700)
Britannia Rediviva V
On the birth of James Edward Francis, Prince of Wales, on 10 June 1685

Thomas D'Urfey (1653–1723)
A Fool's Preferment; or, The Three Dukes of Dunstable D
Performed *c.*April 1688

William Mountfort (1664–92)
The Injur'd Lovers; or, The Ambitious Father: A tragedy D
Performed *c.*February 1688

John Norris (1657–1711)
The Theory and Regulation of Love NF
Includes letters between Norris and Henry More

George Savile, marquis of Halifax (1633–95)
The Anatomy of an Equivalent NF
Anonymous

George Savile, marquis of Halifax (1633–95)
The Lady's New-Years Gift; or, Advice to a Daughter NF
Anonymous

Thomas Shadwell (1642?–92)
The Squire of Alsatia: A comedy D
Performed May 1688

George Wither (1588–1667)
Divine Poems on the Ten Commandments V

1689

- Parliament declares abdication of James II
WILLIAM III (–1702) and MARY II (–1694) proclaimed King and Queen (Feb.)
Toleration Act (May)
Bill of Rights (July)
Battle of Killecrankie (27 July)
Nine Years War (1689–97)
Peter the Great becomes Tsar of Russia

Kensington Palace remodelled by Christopher Wren (-1696)
Thomas Shadwell succeeds Dryden as Poet Laureate

- William Broome born
  Lady Mary Wortley Montagu born
  Samuel Richardson born
- Aphra Behn dies
  William Chamberlayne dies
  Judge George Jeffreys dies
- Montesquieu born

Anonymous *The Amours of Messalina late Queen of Albion* PS
A satire on Mary of Modena (1658–1718), consort of James II

Philip Ayres (1638–1712)
Mythologia Ethica; or, Three Centuries of Aesopian Fables, in English Prose F

Aphra Behn (1640?–89)
The History of the Nun; or, The Fair Vow-Breaker F

Aphra Behn (1640?–89)
A Pindaric Poem to the Reverend Doctor Burnet V
Addressed to Gilbert Burnet (1643–1715)

John Bunyan (1628–88)
The Acceptable Sacrifice; or, The Excellency of a Broken Heart NF
The manuscript of this work was delivered to the press by Bunyan shortly before his death

John Bunyan (1628–88)
Mr John Bunyan's Last Sermon NF

Gilbert Burnet (1643–1715)
A Second Collection of Several Tracts and Discourses NF
See also *A Collection of Several Tracts and Discourses* 1685, *A Third Collection* 1703

Charles Cotton (1630–87)
Poems on Several Occasions V

Robert Gould (*d.* 1709)
Poems V

White Kennett (1660–1728)
A Dialogue Between Two Friends: Occasioned by the late revolution NF

Nathaniel Lee (1649?–92)
On the Death of Mrs Behn V
Aphra Behn died on 16 April 1689

Nathaniel Lee (1649?–92)
The Princess of Cleve D
Performed 1680/1. Based on the novel by Madeleine de la Fayette (published 1678).

John Locke (1632–1704)
A Letter Concerning Toleration NF
Anonymous. A translation by William Popple (*d.* 1708) of Locke's *Epistola de tolerantia* (1689). See also *A Second Letter* 1690, *A Third Letter* 1692.

John Selden (1584–1654)
Table-Talk NF

Thomas Shadwell (1642?–92)
Bury-Fair: A comedy D
Performed *c.*April 1689

William Sherlock (1641?–1707)
A Practical Discourse Concerning Death NF

John Tutchin (1661?–1707) and others
The Bloody Assizes: Or, a compleat history of the life of George Lord Jefferies NF
Anonymous. Written by John Tutchin and John Shirley (*fl.* 1680–1702), with contributions by Titus Oates (1649–1705) and John Dunton (1659–1733).

1690

- English and Dutch fleets defeated by the French at Beachy Head (29 June)
  James II defeated by William III at the Battle of the Boyne (1 July)
- Mary Barber born?
  Samuel Croxall born?
  William Duncombe born
  Martha Sansom born
  George Sewell born?
- Robert Barclay dies

Aphra Behn (1640?–89)
The Widdow Ranter; or, The History of Bacon in Virginia: A tragi-comedy D
Performed November 1689. Prologue by Dryden.

Thomas Betterton (1635?–1710) (adap.)
The Prophetess; or, The History of Dioclesian D/OP
Anonymous. Performed June 1690. Supposedly adapted from Francis Beaumont and John Fletcher; more probably the original was written by John Fletcher and Philip Massinger. Without the music by Purcell.

Roger Boyle, earl of Orrery (1621–79)
Mr Anthony: A comedy D
Performed *c.*1671

Thomas Brown (1663–1704)
The Late Converts Exposed V
Anonymous. See *The Reasons of Mr Bays Changing his Religion* 1688.

Sir Thomas Browne (1605–82)
A Letter to a Friend NF

Thomas Burnet (1635?–1715)
The Theory of the Earth NF
A translation of part ii of Burnet's *Telluris theoria sacra* (1681–9). See also *The Theory of the Earth* 1684.

John Crowne (*d.* 1703)
The English Frier; or, The Town Sparks: A comedy D
Performed *c.*March 1690

John Dryden (1631–1700)
Amphitryon; or, The Two Socia's: A comedy D
Performed October 1690. Based on Plautus and Molière. Music by Purcell.

John Dryden (1631–1700)
Don Sebastian, King of Portugal: A tragedy D
Performed 4 December 1689

Thomas D'Urfey (1653–1723)
Collin's Walk Through London and Westminster V

Thomas D'Urfey (1653–1723)
New Poems V

John Glanvill (1664?–1735)
Some Odes of Horace Imitated with Relation to His Majesty and the Times V

Nathaniel Lee (1649?–92)
The Massacre of Paris: A tragedy D
Performed November 1689. On the St Bartholomew's Day Massacre (1572). Partly published in *The Duke of Guise* 1683 (q.v.).

John Locke (1632–1704)
An Essay Concerning Humane Understanding NF
2nd edition, much enlarged, published in 1694; 3rd edition, 1695; 4th edition, 1700; 5th edition, 1706 (posthumous)

John Locke (1632–1704)
A Second Letter Concerning Toleration NF
Signed 'Philanthropus'. A reply to Jonas Proast, *The Argument of the Letter Concerning Toleration* (1690). See *A Letter Concerning Toleration* 1689, *A Third Letter* 1692.

John Locke (1632–1704)
Two Treatises of Government NF
Anonymous. Part i is a response to Sir Robert Filmer's *Patriarcha* 1680 (q.v.).

Sir George Mackenzie (1636–91)
Reason NF

Charles Montagu, earl of Halifax (1661–1715)
An Epistle to the Right Honourable Charles Earl of Dorset and Middlesex V
Anonymous. On William III's victories in Ireland.

William Mountfort (1664–92)
The Successfull Straingers: A tragi-comedy D
Performed *c.*December 1689

John Norris (1657–1711)
Christian Blessedness NF
See John Locke, *Essay Concerning Humane Understanding* 1690

Sir William Petty (1623–87)
Political Arithmetick NF

George Powell (1658?–1714)
The Treacherous Brothers: A tragedy D
Performed *c.*December 1689

Thomas Shadwell (1642?–92)
The Amorous Bigotte: With the second part of Tegue o Divelly D
Performed *c.*March 1690. See also *The Lancashire-Witches* 1682.

Sir William Temple (1628–99)
Miscellanea: the Second Part NF
See also *Miscellanea* 1680, *Third Part* 1701

Edmund Waller (1606–87)
The Maid's Tragedy Altered V
A fragment, probably intended by Waller to turn Beaumont and Fletcher's *The Maides Tragedy* 1619 (q.v.) into a comedy. With other pieces.

Edward Ward (1667–1731)
The School of Politicks; or, The Humours of a Coffee-House V
Anonymous

1691

- Jacobites defeated at the Battle of Aughrim (12 July)
  Treaty of Limerick ends war in Ireland
- Thomas Amory born?
  George Bubb Dodington born
- Richard Baxter dies
  Robert Boyle dies: Boyle Lectures founded
  Sir George Etherege dies
  George Fox dies

Sir Dudley North dies
Samuel Pordage dies?

- Purcell, *King Arthur*

Anonymous
The Ingenious and Diverting Letters of the Lady ---------'s Travels into Spain F
Translation of Marie-Catherine, comtesse d'Aulnoy (*c.*1650–1705), *Relation du voyage en Espagne* (1690). Parts i and ii, 1691; part iii, 1692.

Richard Ames (*d.* 1693)
The Female Fire-Ships: A satyr against whoring V
Anonymous

Richard Ames (*d.* 1693)
Islington-Wells; or, The Threepenny-academy V
Anonymous

John Bancroft (*d.* 1696)
King Edward the Third, with the Fall of the Earl of March D
Performed *c.*December 1690

Richard Baxter (1615–91)
Richard Baxter's Penitent Confession, and his Necessary Vindication NF
A reply to Thomas Long (1621–1707), *The Unreasonableness of Separation: The second part* (1682)

Sir Thomas Pope Blount (1649–97)
Essays on Several Subjects NF

John Dryden (1631–1700)
King Arthur; or, The British Worthy: A dramatick opera D/OP
Performed *c.*May 1691. Music by Purcell (partially extant). Sequel to *Albion and Albanius* 1685 (q.v.), written for Charles II, who died before its performance.

John Dunton (1659–1733) and others
The Athenian Gazette PER
Anonymous. Alternatively *The Athenian Mercury*. Published bi-weekly from March 1691 to June 1697.

Thomas D'Urfey (1653–1723)
Love for Money; or, The Boarding School: A comedy D
Performed *c.*January 1691

Laurence Echard (*c.*1670–1730)
An Exact Description of Ireland NF

Joseph Harris (*c.*1650–*c.*1715)
The Mistakes; or, The False Report: A tragi-comedy D
Performed *c.*December 1690

Benjamin Keach (1640–1704)
Spiritual Melody V

Gerard Langbaine, the younger (1656–92)
An Account of the English Dramatick Poets NF

Sir Dudley North (1641–91)
Discourses Upon Trade NF
Anonymous

George Powell (1658?–1714)
Alphonso: King of Naples: A tragedy D
Performed *c.*December 1690

John Ray (1627–1705)
The Wisdom of God Manifested in the Works of the Creation NF

Elkanah Settle (1648–1724)
Distress'd Innocence; or, The Princess of Persia: A tragedy D
Performed *c.*October 1690

Thomas Shadwell (1642?–92)
The Scowrers D
Performed *c.*December 1690

William Sherlock (1641?–1707)
The Case of the Allegiance Due to Soveraign Powers NF

Thomas Southerne (1659–1746)
Sir Anthony Love; or, The Rambling Lady: A comedy D
Performed *c.*December 1690

Nahum Tate (1652–1715)
Characters of Vertue and Vice V
A verse paraphrase of Joseph Hall's *Characters of Vertues and Vices* 1608 (q.v.)

William Walsh (1663–1708)
A Dialogue Concerning Women NF
Anonymous

Edward Ward (1667–1731)
The Poet's Ramble After Riches V
Anonymous

John Wilmot, earl of Rochester (1647–80)
Poems on Several Occasions: with Valentinian, a Tragedy V
See also *Valentinian* 1685

Anthony à Wood (1632–95)
Athenae Oxonienses [vol. i] NF
Anonymous. Volume ii published 1692 (q.v.).

1692

- Massacre of the Macdonalds by the Campbells at Glencoe (13 Feb.)
  French navy defeated by the English at La Hogue (May)
  Salem witch hunts begin
  Chelsea Hospital opened
  Thomas Rymer becomes Historiographer Royal
- Joseph Butler born
  John Byrom born
- Elias Ashmole dies
  Gerard Langbaine, the younger, dies
  Nathaniel Lee dies
  Thomas Shadwell dies: Nahum Tate becomes Poet Laureate
- Purcell, *The Fairy Queen*

Richard Ames (*d.* 1693)
The Double Descent V
Anonymous

Richard Ames (*d.* 1693)
The Jacobite Coventicle V
Anonymous

Richard Ames (*d.* 1693)
Sylvia's Complaint, of Her Sexes Unhappiness V
Anonymous reply to Robert Gould, *Love Given O're* 1682 (q.v.). See *Sylvia's Revenge* 1688.

Robert Barclay (1648–90)
Truth Triumphant through the Spiritual Warfare, Christian Labours, and Writings of Robert Barclay WKS

Richard Baxter (1615–91) (tr.)
Paraphrase on the Psalms of David V

Richard Bentley (1662–1742)
The Folly of Atheism, and (what is now called) Deism NF
Boyle Lecture 1, delivered 7 March 1692

Richard Bentley (1662–1742)
Matter and Motion Cannot Think; or, A Confutation of Atheism from the Faculties of the Soul NF
Boyle Lecture 2

Richard Bentley (1662–1742)
A Confutation of Atheism from the Structure and Origin of Humane Bodies NF
In three separately published parts (Boyle Lectures 3, 4, and 5)

Richard Bentley (1662–1742)
A Confutation of Atheism from the Origin and Frame of the World NF
In three separately published parts (Boyle Lectures 6, 7, and 8)

Nicholas Brady (1659–1726)
The Rape; or, The Innocent Impostors: A tragedy D
Anonymous. Performed February 1692.

John Bunyan (1628–88)
The Works of That Eminent Servant of Christ, Mr John Bunyan WKS
Edited by Charles Doe. Contains ten previously unpublished and ten previous published works. Announced as the first volume of an intended complete edition, but no second volume published until the 2nd edition, edited by Ebenezer Chandler and Samuel Wilson in 1736–7.

Gilbert Burnet (1643–1715)
A Discourse of the Pastoral Care NF

William Congreve (1670–1729)
Incognita; or, Love and Duty Reconcil'd: A novel F
Signed 'Cleophil' (= Congreve)

Anne Conway, Viscountess Conway (1631–79)
The Principles of the Most Ancient and Modern Philosophy NF
Anonymous. Attributed to Lady Anne Conway.

John Dennis (1657–1734)
Poems in Burlesque V
Anonymous

John Dryden (1631–1700)
Cleomenes, the Spartan Hero: A tragedy D
Performed April 1692. Act v completed by Thomas Southerne. Includes 'The Life of Cleomenes' translated from Plutarch by Thomas Creech.

John Dryden (1631–1700)
Eleonora V
A memorial to the countess of Abingdon

Thomas D'Urfey (1653–1723)
The Marriage-Hater Match'd: A comedy D
Performed January 1692

Thomas Fletcher (1666–1713)
Poems on Several Occasions, and Translations V

Charles Gildon (1665–1724) (ed.)
Miscellany Poems upon Several Occasions ANTH

Sir Roger L'Estrange (1616–1704) (tr.)
Fables, of Aesop and other Eminent Mythologists F
Fables by Aesop, Barlandus, Avianus, Abstemius, and Poggius. See also *Fables and Storyes Moralized* 1699.

John Locke (1632–1704)
Some Considerations of the Consequences of the Lowering of Interest and Raising the Value of Money NF
Anonymous. See also *Further Considerations* 1695.

John Locke (1632–1704)
A Third Letter for Toleration NF
Anonymous. See *A Letter Concerning Toleration* 1689, *A Second Letter* 1690.

Matthew Prior (1664–1721)
An Ode in Imitation of the Second Ode of the Third Book of Horace V

John Ray (1627–1705)
Miscellaneous Discourses Concerning the Dissolution and Changes of the World NF

Elkanah Settle (1648–1724)?
The Fairy Queen: An opera D/OP
Anonymous. Performed 2 May 1692. Libretto possibly by Settle. Music by Purcell. Based on Shakespeare's *Midsummer Night's Dream*.

Robert South (1634–1716)
Twelve Sermons Preached upon Several Occasions NF

Thomas Southerne (1659–1746)
The Wives Excuse; or, Cuckolds Make Themselves: A comedy D
Performed December 1691

Sir William Temple (1628–99)
Memoirs of What Past in Christendom: From the war begun in 1672 to the peace concluded 1679 NF
Anonymous. See also *Memoirs* 1709.

William Walsh (1663–1708)
Letters and Poems, Amorous and Gallant V
Anonymous

Anthony à Wood (1632–95)
Athenae Oxonienses [vol. ii] NF
Anonymous. Volume i published 1691 (q.v.).

1693

- The French capture Charleroi
  The English bombard St Malo
  Long-term national debt begins
- Eliza Haywood born (c.1693)
  Jacob Hildebrand born
  George Lillo born
- Richard Ames dies
  Charles Blount dies
- Marie-Madeleine de La Fayette dies

Richard Ames (*d.* 1693)
Fatal Friendship; or, The Drunkards Misery V
bao *The Search After Claret*

John Bancroft (*d.* 1696)
Henry the Second, King of England: With the death of Rosamond, a tragedy D
Performed November 1692

Roger Boyle, earl of Orrery (1621–79)
Guzman: A comedy D
Performed April 1669

William Congreve (1670–1729)
The Old Batchelour: A comedy D
Performed 9 March 1693. Commendatory poems by Thomas Southerne and others.

John Dennis (1657–1734)
The Impartial Critick NF
A response to Thomas Rymer, *A Short View of Tragedy* 1693 (q.v.)

John Dryden (1631–1700) and **Jacob Tonson** (1656?–1736) (eds)
Examen Poeticum: Being the Third Part of Miscellany Poems ANTH
The third of the series of miscellanies published by Tonson 1684–1709. See also *Miscellany Poems* 1684, *Sylvae* 1685, *Annual Miscellany* 1694. *Poetical Miscellanies: Fifth Part* 1704, *Sixth Part* 1709.

John Dryden (1631–1700) and others (tr.)
The Satires of Decimus Junius Juvenalis ANTH
Other translators include Nahum Tate and William Congreve

John Dunton (1659?–1733)?
The Ladies Mercury PER
Possibly by Dunton. Irregular, appearing in 4 issues in February and March 1693. The first periodical specifically addressed to women.

Thomas D'Urfey (1653–1723)
The Richmond Heiress; or, A Woman Once in the Right: A comedy D
Performed c.April 1693

John Evelyn (1620–1706) (tr.)
The Compleat Gard'ner NF

Translated from the French of Jean de la Quintinie (1626–88)

Robert Gould (*d.* 1709)
The Corruption of the Times by Money V

John Locke (1632–1704)
Some Thoughts Concerning Education NF
Anonymous

William Penn (1644–1718)
Some Fruits of Solitude NF
Anonymous

Thomas Rymer (1641–1713)
A Short View of Tragedy NF
See also John Dennis, *The Impartial Critick* 1693

Thomas Shadwell (1642?–92)
The Volunteers; or, The Stock-Jobbers: A comedy D
Performed November 1692. Shadwell's last play. Prologue by Thomas D'Urfey.

Thomas Southerne (1659–1746)
The Maids Last Prayer; or Any, Rather Than Fail: A comedy D
Performed January 1693

John Tillotson (1630–94)
Sermons Concerning the Divinity and Incarnation of Our Blessed Saviour NF

Catharine Trotter, later **Cockburn** (1674–1749)
Olinda's Adventures; or, The Amours of a Young Lady F
Anonymous. Published in the miscellany *Letters of Love and Gallantry. And Several Other Subjects. All written by ladies.*

Samuel Wesley (1662–1735)
The Life of Our Blessed Lord V

'Anthony Harmer' [Henry Wharton (1664–95)]
A Specimen of Some Errors and Defects in the History of the Reformation by Gilbert Burnet NF
An attack on Bishop Burnet (see 1679)

1694

- Bank of England founded (July)
  Construction of Greenwich Hospital begins
  Triennial Act
  Death of Queen Mary (28 Dec.): William III reigns alone
- James Bramston born?
  Francis Hutcheson born
  Mary Masters born?
  Philip Dormer Stanhope, 4th earl of Chesterfield, born
  Elizabeth Tollet born
- John Tillotson dies
- Voltaire (Francois-Marie Arouet) born

Edmund Arwaker (*c.*1655–1730)
An Epistle to Monsieur Boileau V
Addressed to Nicholas Boileau-Despréaux (1636–1711)

Mary Astell (1666–1731)
A Serious Proposal to the Ladies NF
'By a lover of her sex'. See also *A Serious Proposal Part II* 1697.

John Banks (*c.*1650)
The Innocent Usurper; or, The Death of the Lady Jane Grey: A tragedy D

Sir Thomas Pope Blount (1649–97)
De Re Poetica; or, Remarks upon Poetry NF

Roger Boyle, earl of Orrery (1621–79)
Herod the Great: A tragedy D
Unacted

Gilbert Burnet (1643–1715)
Four Discourses NF

Richard Burthogge (1638?–94?)
An Essay Upon Reason and the Nature of Spirits NF

Jeremy Collier (1650–1726)
Miscellanies NF
See also *Miscellanies upon Moral Subjects* 1695

William Congreve (1670–1729)
The Double-Dealer: A comedy D
Performed October 1693

John Crowne (*d.* 1703)
The Married Beau; or, The Curious Impertinent: A comedy D
Performed *c.*April 1694. Based on the *Curioso Impertinente* in Cervantes (1547–1616), *Don Quixote*, part i.

John Dryden (1631–1700) and **Jacob Tonson** (1656?–1736) (eds)
The Annual Miscellany: for the Year 1694 V
The fourth in the series of miscellanies published by Tonson 1684–1709. See also *Miscellany Poems* 1684, *Sylvae* 1685, *Examen Poeticum* 1693. *Poetical Miscellanies: Fifth Part*, 1704, *Sixth Part* 1709.

John Dryden (1631–1700)
Love Triumphant; or, Nature Will Prevail: A tragi-comedy D
Performed January 1694

Thomas D'Urfey (1653–1723)
The Comical History of Don Quixote D
Performed *c.*May 1694. Based on *Don Quixote* by Cervantes (1547–1616). *Part the Second* 1694 (see below); *The Third Part* 1696 (q.v.). Some songs in parts i and ii by Purcell.

Thomas D'Urfey (1653–1723)
The Comical History of Don Quixote D
Performed *c.*June 1694. Part i 1694 (see above). *The Third Part* 1696 (q.v.).

Laurence Echard (*c.*1670–1730) (tr.)
Plautus's Comedies: Amphytrion, Epidicus, and Rudens D

Laurence Echard (*c.*1670–1730) and others (tr.)
Terence's Comedies D

George Fox (1624–91)
Journal NF
Preface by William Penn

Charles Gildon (1665–1724) (ed.)
Chorus Poetarum; or, Poems on Several Occasions V
Contains poems by Aphra Behn, the duke of Buckingham, Sir John Denham, Sir George Etherege, Marvell, and others

Charles Hopkins (1664?–1700)
Epistolary Poems V

Sir William Killigrew (1606–95)
Mid-night and Daily Thoughts MISC
See also *Mid-night Thoughts* 1681

Jane Lead (1623–1704)
The Enochian Walks with God NF

John Milton (1608–74)
Letters of State MISC
A translation by Edward Phillips of *Literae pseudo-senatûs Anglicani*, published surreptitiously in 1676. The account of Milton's life is also by Phillips. Includes the first printing of Milton's sonnets to Cromwell, Fairfax, Vane, and Skinner.

George Savile, marquis of Halifax (1633–95)
A Rough Draft of a New Model at Sea NF
Anonymous

Elkanah Settle (1648–1724)
The Ambitious Slave; or, A Generous Revenge: A tragedy D
Performed 21 March 1694

Thomas Southerne (1659–1746)
The Fatal Marriage; or, The Innocent Adultery D
Performed February 1694

John Strype (1643–1737)
Memorials of Thomas Cranmer NF

Matthew Tindal (1657–1733)
An Essay Concerning the Laws of Nations, and the Rights of Soveraigns NF

William Wotton (1666–1727)
Reflections upon Ancient and Modern Learning NF
Part i. 2nd edition, with Bentley's 'Dissertation upon the Epistles of Phalaris', published in 1697 (q.v.). The 3rd edition of 1705 adds 'A Defense' of the Reflections and 'Observations upon The Tale of a Tub'. Part ii published in 1698.

James Wright (1643–1713)
Country Conversations NF
Anonymous

1695

- William III takes Namur
  Establishment of dockyard at Plymouth
- Thomas Fitzgerald born?
  Francis Hutcheson born
  Thomas Purney born
- Sir William Killigrew dies
  Mary Mollineux dies
  Dorothy Osborne, Lady Temple, dies
  George Savile, marquis of Halifax, dies
  Henry Vaughan dies
  Anthony à Wood dies
- Henry Purcell dies
- Jean de la Fontaine dies

Joseph Addison (1672–1719)
A Poem to His Majesty V

Sir Richard Blackmore (1654–1729)
Prince Arthur V
See also *King Arthur* 1697

Charles Blount (1654–93)
Miscellaneous Works WKS
Edited anonymously by Charles Gildon

Gilbert Burnet (1643–1715)
An Essay on the Memory of the Late Queen NF
On the death of Mary II (28 December 1694)

Colley Cibber (1671–1757)
A Poem on the Death of Our Late Sovereign Lady, Queen Mary V
On the death of Mary II (28 December 1694)

Jeremy Collier (1650–1726)
Miscellanies upon Moral Subjects: The second part NF
See *Miscellanies* 1694. Both parts published together as *Essays upon Several Moral Subjects* in 1697.

William Congreve (1670–1729)
Love for Love: A comedy D
Performed 30 April 1695

William Congreve (1670–1729)
The Mourning Muse of Alexas: A pastoral V
On the death of Mary II (28 December 1694)

John Dennis (1657–1734)
The Court of Death V
On the death of Mary II (28 December 1694)

John Dryden (1631–1700) (tr.)
De Arte Graphica NF
Translated from Charles-Alphonse du Fresnoy (1611–68)

Laurence Echard (*c.*1670–1730)
The Roman History NF
Volume ii published in 1698; both volumes published together in 1699

Charles Hopkins (1664?–1700)
Pyrrhus King of Epirus: A tragedy D
Performed *c.*August 1695

William Laud (1573–1645)
The History of the Troubles and Tryal of William Laud NF

John Locke (1632–1704)
Further Considerations Concerning Raising the Value of Money NF
See *Some Considerations* 1692

John Locke (1632–1704)
The Reasonableness of Christianity as Delivered in the Scriptures NF
See also below

John Locke (1632–1704)
A Vindication of the Reasonableness of Christianity NF
Anonymous. A reply to John Edwards (1637–1715), whose reflections on Locke's *Reasonableness of Christianity* were published 1695. See also *A Second Vindication* 1697.

John Milton (1608–74)
The Poetical Works of Mr John Milton V
Edited by Patrick Hume

John Norris (1657–1711)
Letters Concerning the Love of God NF
Letters between Norris and Mary Astell. See her *Serious Proposal to the Ladies* 1694.

John Phillips (1631–1706)
A Reflection on Our Modern Poetry NF
Anonymous

Matthew Prior (1664–1721)
An English Ballad: In answer to Mr Despreaux's Pindarique ode on the taking of Namure V
'Mr Despreaux' = Nicholas Boileau-Despréaux (1636–1711). The text of Boileau's 'Ode sur la prise de Namur' is given in French with Prior's ballad on opposite pages.

Edward Ravenscroft (1644–1704)
The Canterbury Guests; or, A Bargain Broken: A comedy D
Performed September 1694

Elkanah Settle (1648–1724)
Philaster; or, Love Lies A-Bleeding: A tragi-comedy D
Performed *c.*December 1695

Robert South (1634–1716)
Tritheism NF
Anonymous. A refutation of William Sherlock's *Vindication of the Doctrine of the Holy and Ever Blessed Trinity* (1690).

Richard Steele (1672–1729)
The Procession: A poem on Her Majesties funeral V
'By a gentleman of the army'

Sir William Temple (1628–99)
An Introduction to the History of England NF

Edward Ward (1667–1731)
Female Policy Detected; or, The Arts of a Designing Woman Laid Open V

1696

- Trial of Treasons Act
  Board of Trade established
  Kit Kat Club founded
- Matthew Green born
  John Hervey born
  Henry Home, Lord Kame, born
  Batty Langley born
  William Oldys born
- John Bancroft dies
  Robert Plot dies

- Giovanni Tiepolo born
- Madame de Sévigné dies

Anonymous
An Essay in Defence of the Female Sex NF
'By a lady'. Usually now attributed to Judith Drake; formerly attributed to Mary Astell.

Anonymous
Bonduca; or, The British Heroine: A tragedy D
Performed *c.*September 1695. Altered from John Fletcher. Dedication signed by George Powell (1658–1714), but probably not by him. Without the music by Purcell.

John Aubrey (1626–97)
Miscellanies NF
Aubrey's only work to be published in his lifetime

Philip Ayres (1638–1712)
The Revengeful Mistress F

John Banks (*c.*1650–1700)
Cyrus the Great; or, The Tragedy of Love D

Richard Baxter (1615–91)
Reliquiae Baxterianae NF
Edited by Matthew Sylvester (1636?–1708)

Aphra Behn (1640?–89)
The Histories and Novels of the Late Ingenious Mrs Behn F

Aphra Behn (1640?–89)
The Younger Brother; or, The Amorous Jilt: A comedy D
Performed *c.*February 1696

Colley Cibber (1671–1757)
Love's Last Shift; or, The Fool in Fashion: A comedy D
Performed January 1696

Gerard Croese (1642–1710)
The General History of the Quakers NF
A translation of Croese's *Historia Quakeriana*

John Dryden (1631–1700)
An Ode on the Death of Mr Henry Purcell V

Thomas D'Urfey (1653–1723)
The Comical History of Don Quixote. The Third Part D
Performed c.November 1695. From Cervantes (1547–1616). Parts i and ii published 1694 (q.v.).

Robert Gould (*d.* 1709)
The Rival Sisters; or, The Violence of Love: A tragedy D
Performed 1696

George Granville, Lord Lansdowne (1667–1735)
The She-Gallants: A comedy D
Anonymous. Performed *c.*December 1695.

Joseph Harris (*c.*1650–1715)
The City Bride; or, The Merry Cuckold: A comedy D
Performed *c.*March 1696. Taken mostly from *A Cure for a Cuckold* 1661 (q.v.), attributed to John Webster and William Rowley.

Charles Hopkins (1664?–1700)
Neglected Virtue; or, The Unhappy Conquerour D
Performed 1696

Charles Leslie (1650–1722)
The Snake in the Grass NF
Anonymous. Written against the Quakers.

Delarivière Manley (1663–1724)
Letters Writen [sic] *by Mrs Manley* NF

Delarivière Manley (1663–1724)
The Lost Lover; or, The Jealous Husband: A comedy D
Performed *c.*April 1696

Delarivière Manley (1663–1724)
The Royal Mischief: A tragedy D
Performed *c.*April 1696

Peter Anthony Motteux (1663–1718)
Love's a Jest: A comedy D
Performed *c.*June 1696

John Oldmixon (1673–1742)
Poems on Several Occasions V

William Penn (1644–1718)
Primitive Christianity Revived in the Faith and Practice of the People called Quakers NF

Mary Pix (1666–1720)
Ibrahim, the Thirteenth Emperour of the Turks: A tragedy D
Performed *c.*May 1696

Mary Pix (1666–1720)
The Inhumane Cardinal; or, Innocence Betray'd: F
'Written by a gentlewoman, for the entertainment of the sex'

Mary Pix (1666–1720)
The Spanish Wives: A farce F
Based on *The Pilgrim* by Gabriel de Brémond, translated into English in 1680

'Philomela' [**Elizabeth Rowe** (1674–1737)]
Poems on Several Occasions V

John Sheffield, duke of Buckingham (1648–1721)
The Character of Charles II, King of England V

Thomas Southerne (1659–1746)
Oroonoko: A tragedy D
Performed *c.*November 1695. Based on Aphra Behn's novel of the same name 1688 (q.v.). Epilogue by Congreve. An altered version by John Hawkesworth (1715?–73) was published in 1759.

Sir John Suckling (1609–42)
The Works of Sir John Suckling WKS
First collected edition

Nahum Tate (1652–1715) (ed.)
Miscellanea Sacra; or, Poems on Divine & Moral Subjects ANTH

Nahum Tate (1652–1715) and **Nicholas Brady** (1659–1726)
A New Version of the Psalms of David BIB
A metrical version accepted for use in churches

John Tillotson (1630–94)
The Works of John Tillotson WKS

John Toland (1670–1722)
Christianity Not Mysterious NF
Anonymous

Catharine Trotter, later **Cockburn** (1674–1749)
Agnes de Castro: A tragedy D
'Written by a young lady'. Performed *c.*December 1695. Based on Aphra Behn's novel of the same name.

1697

- Treaty of Ryswick between England, France, Holland, and Spain ends Nine Years War
  Standing army controversy begins
- Nicholas Amhurst born
  Sir George Anson born
  WIlliam Hogarth born
  Charles Macklin born?
  Robert Paltock born
- John Aubrey dies
  Sir Thomas Pope Blount dies

Mary Astell (1666–1731)
A Serious Proposal to the Ladies, Part II NF
Anonymous. See *A Serious Proposal* 1694.

Sir Richard Blackmore (1654–1729)
King Arthur V
First edition published in ten books 1695 (q.v.) as *Prince Arthur*

Thomas Burnet (1635?–1715)
Remarks upon An Essay Concerning Humane Understanding NF
Anonymous. See Locke 1690. *Second Remarks* published 1697; *Third Remarks*, 1699.

Colley Cibber (1671–1757)
Womans Wit; or, The Lady in Fashion: A comedy D
Performed December? 1696

William Cleland (1661?–89)
A Collection of Several Poems and Verses V

William Congreve (1670–1729)
The Birth of the Muse V
Dated 1698, but advertised November 1697

William Congreve (1670–1729)
The Mourning Bride: A tragedy D
Performed February 1697

William Dampier (1652–1715)
A New Voyage Round the World NF

Daniel Defoe (1660–1731)
An Essay Upon Projects NF
Anonymous. Reissued as *Several Essays . . . Now Communicated to the World for Publick Good* in 1700.

John Dennis (1657–1734)
A Plot and No Plot: A comedy D
Performed 8 May 1697

John Dryden (1631–1700)
Alexander's Feast; or, The Power of Musique V

John Dryden (1631–1700) (tr.)
The Works of Virgil V

Thomas D'Urfey (1653–1723)
Cinthia and Endimion D/OP

Thomas D'Urfey (1653–1723)
The Intrigues at Versailles; or, A Jilt in all Humours: A comedy D
Performed *c.*May 1697

John Evelyn (1620–1706)
Numismata: A discourse of medals NF

Charles Gildon (1665–1724)
The Roman Brides Revenge: A tragedy D
Anonymous. Performed 1697.

Charles Hopkins (1664?–1700)
Boadicea Queen of Britain: A tragedy D
Performed *c.*November 1697

Jane Lead (1623–1704)
A Fountain of Gardens NF

John Locke (1632–1704)
A Letter to the Right Reverend Edward Ld Bishop of Worcester NF
See Locke 1690. See also *Mr Locke's Reply* 1697 (below), and 1699.

John Locke (1632–1704)
Mr Locke's Reply to the Right Reverend the Lord Bishop of Worcester's Answer to his Letter NF
See also Locke *A Letter* 1697, *Mr Locke's Reply* 1699

John Locke (1632–1704)
A Second Vindication of the Reasonableness of Christianity NF
Anonymous. See *A Vindication* 1695.

John Phillips (1631–1706)
Augustus Britannicus V
On the Treaty of Ryswick (September 1697)

Humphrey Prideaux (1648–1724)
The True Nature of Imposture Fully Display'd in the Life of Mahomet NF

Sir John Vanbrugh (1664–1726)
The Relapse; or, Virtue in Danger D
Anonymous. Performed 21 November 1696. A sequel to Colley Cibber's *Love's Last Shift; or, The Fool in Fashion* 1696 (q.v.).

Sir John Vanbrugh (1664–1726)
Aesop: A comedy D
Anonymous. Part i performed *c.*December 1696; part ii performed *c.*March 1697, and published 1697. Translated from Edme Boursault (1638–1701).

Sir John Vanbrugh (1664–1726)
The Provok'd Wife: A comedy D
bao *The Relapse.* Performed May 1697.

John Wilmot, earl of Rochester (1647–80)
Familiar Letters NF

William Wotton (1666–1727)
Reflections upon Ancient and Modern Learning NF
Includes Richard Bentley's *Dissertation on Phalaris,* published separately in 1699 (q.v.)

1698

- Peter the Great of Russia arrives in England (Jan.)
  New East India Company chartered by William III
  Society for Promoting Christian Knowledge (SPCK) founded
- Edward Chicken born
  John Jortin born
  William Warburton born
- Sir Robert Howard dies

Anonymous
The Maxims of the Saints Explained, Concerning the Interiour Life NF
Translation of *Explication des maximes des saints* (1697) by the French theologian François Fénelon (1651–1715)

Francis Atterbury (1662–1732)
A Discourse Occasion'd by the Death of the Right Honourable the Lady Cutts NF
Concerning Elizabeth Pickering Cutts (1678 or 9–1697)

Aphra Behn (1640?–89)
All the Histories and Novels Written by the late ingenious Mrs Behn F
The 3rd edition of *The Histories and Novels* 1696 (q.v.)

Charles Boyle, 4th earl of Orrery (1676–1731)
Dr Bentley's Dissertations on the Epistles of Phalaris, and the Fables of Aesop NF

John Bunyan (1628–88)
The Heavenly Foot-Man; or, A Description of the Man that Gets to Heaven NF
Almost certainly the work on 'the Way/And Race of Saints' mentioned in the prefatory verses to *The Pilgrim's Progress* which Bunyan put aside when, in the course of its composition, he 'Fell suddenly into an Allegory' which became *The Pilgrim's Progress*

Jeremy Collier (1650–1726)
A Short View of the Immorality, and Profaneness of the English Stage NF
See also *A Defence of the Short View* 1699, *A Second Defence* 1700, *Mr Collier's Dissuasive* 1703, *A Further Vindication* 1708, and Gildon, *Phaeton* 1698.

William Congreve (1670–1729)
Amendments of Mr Collier's False and Imperfect Citations, &c. NF
Anonymous. A reply to Collier's *Short View* 1698 (q.v.).

John Crowne (*d.* 1703)
Caligula: A tragedy D
Performed *c.*March 1698

Daniel Defoe (1660–1731)
An Enquiry into the Occasional Conformity of Dissenters, in Cases of Preferment NF
Anonymous. Published 1698, dated 1697.

Daniel Defoe (1660–1731)
The Poor Man's Plea NF
Anonymous

John Dennis (1657–1734)
The Usefulness of the Stage, to the Happiness of Mankind, to Government and to Religion NF
A reply to Collier's *Short View* 1698 (q.v.)

Thomas D'Urfey (1653–1723)
The Campaigners; or, The Pleasant Adventures at Brussels D
Performed June? 1698. The Preface replies to Collier's *Short View* 1698 (q.v.).

George Farquhar (1678–1707)
Love and a Bottle: A comedy D
Published 1698, dated 1699. Performed December 1698.

Andrew Fletcher (1655–1716)
A Discourse of Government with Relation to Militia's NF
Published anonymously

George Fox (1624–91)
A Collection of Many Select and Christian Epistles, Letters and Testimonials NF
The 'second volume': see *Journal* 1694. Preface by George Whitehead.

Charles Gildon (1665–1724)
Phaeton; or, The Fatal Divorce D
Anonymous. Performed 1698. With reflections on Collier, *A Short View* 1698 (q.v.).

Robert Gould (*d.* 1709)
A Satyr Against Wooing V
bao the *Satyr Against Women*

George Granville, Lord Lansdowne (1667–1735)
Heroick Love: A tragedy D
Performed *c.*December 1697

Charles Hopkins (1664?–1700)
White-hall; or, The Court of England V

John Hughes (1677–1720)
The Triumph of Peace V

John Lacy (1615–81) (adap.)
Sauny the Scot; or, The Taming of the Shrew: A comedy D
Performed April 1667. Adapted from Shakespeare, *The Taming of the Shrew.*

Charles Leslie (1650–1722)
A Short and Easie Method with the Deists NF
Anonymous

Edmund Ludlow (1617?–92)
Memoirs of Edmund Ludlow Esq. NF

Peter Anthony Motteux (1663–1718)
Beauty in Distress: A tragedy D
Performed *c.*April 1698

John Oldmixon (1673–1742) (tr.)
Amintas: A pastoral D
Translated from Torquato Tasso (1544–95)

William Philips (*d.* 1734)
The Revengeful Queen: A tragedy D
Anonymous. Performed *c.*June 1698.

Mary Pix (1666–1720)
Queen Catharine; or, The Ruines of Love: A tragedy D
Performed *c.*June 1698

Walter Pope (1630?–1714)
Moral and Political Fables, Ancient and Modern V

Edward Ravenscroft (1644–1704)
The Italian Husband: A tragedy D
Performed *c.*December 1677

Elkanah Settle (1648–1724)
A Defence of Dramatick Poetry NF
A response to Collier 1698 (q.v.)

Algernon Sidney (1622–83)
Discourses Concerning Government NF
In answer to Sir Robert Filmer, *Patriarcha* 1680 (q.v.)

Catharine Trotter, later **Cockburn** (1674–1749)
Fatal Friendship: A tragedy D
Performed *c.*May 1698

Sir John Vanbrugh (1664–1726)
A Short Vindication of The Relapse and The Provok'd Wife, from Immorality and Prophaneness by the Author NF
Anonymous. A reply to Collier 1698 (q.v.). See also *The Relapse, The Provok'd Wife* 1697.

Edward Ward (1667–1731)
The London Spy PER
Anonymous. Published monthly from November 1698 to April 1700. Collected as *The London-Spy Compleat in Eighteen-Parts* (1703).

Edward Ward (1667–1731)
A Trip to Jamaica NF
Anonymous

Benjamin Whichcote (1609–83)
Select Sermons of Dr Whichcot NF
Edited by Anthony Ashley Cooper, earl of Shaftesbury (1671–1713)

1699

- Size of the British army reduced
  Castle Howard, designed by John Vanbrugh, begun
- Charles Beckingham born
  Robert Blair born
  John Dyer born
  Thomas Edwards born
  Christopher Pitt born
  Alexander Ross born
  Joseph Spence born
- Joseph Beaumont dies
  John Evelyn, the younger, dies
  Sir William Temple dies
- Jean Racine dies

Richard Bentley (1662–1742)
A Dissertation upon the Epistles of Phalaris NF
First published in William Wotton's *Reflections upon Ancient and Modern Learning* 1697 (q.v.). See also Charles Boyle 1698.

Thomas Brown (1663–1704)
A Collection of Miscellany Poems, Letters, etc. MISC
Brown was the (undergraduate) author of the celebrated quatrain beginning 'I do not love thee, Dr Fell'

Colley Cibber (1671–1757)
Xerxes: A tragedy D
Performed February? 1699

Jeremy Collier (1650–1726)
A Defence of the Short View of the Profaneness and Immorality of the English Stage NF
See *A Short View* 1698, *A Second Defence* 1700, *Mr Collier's Dissuasive* 1703, *A Further Vindication* 1708

William Dampier (1652–1715)
Voyages and Descriptions NF
Volums ii of Dampier's *New Voyage Round the World* 1697 (q.v.)

John Dennis (1657–1734)
Rinaldo and Armida: A tragedy D
Performed November 1698? Based on Torquato Tasso's *Gerusalemme Liberata*.

John Dunton (1659–1733)
The Dublin Scuffle NF
A discursive account of Dunton's trip to Ireland in 1698

Thomas D'Urfey (1653–1723)
A Choice Collection of New Songs and Ballads V

George Farquhar (1678–1707)
The Adventures of Covent-Garden F
Anonymous

George Farquhar (1678–1707)
The Constant Couple; or, A Trip to the Jubilee: A comedy D
Published 1699, dated 1700. Performed November 1699. See also *Sir Harry Wildair* 1701.

Sir Samuel Garth (1661–1719)
The Dispensary V
Anonymous. A satire on the opponents of the dispensary set up by the Royal College of Physicians. See also *A Compleat Key to the . . . Dispensary* 1714.

John Hughes (1677–1720)
The Court of Neptune V

George Keith (1639?–1716)
The Deism of William Penn, and his Brethren NF
A reply to Penn's *Discourse of the General Rule of Faith* (1699)

William King (1663–1712)
Dialogues of the Dead NF
bao *The Journey to London*. Responds to Bentley, *Dissertation upon the Epistles of Phalaris* 1699 (q.v.)

William King (1663–1712)
The Furmetary V
Anonymous

Gerard Langbaine, the younger (1656–92)
The Lives and Characters of the English Dramatick Poets NF
Includes a contemporary continuation by Charles Gildon

Sir Roger L'Estrange (1616–1704) (tr.)
Fables and Storyes Moralized V
Second part of *Fables, of Aesop* 1692. Both volumes were frequently reprinted in the 18th century.

John Locke (1632–1704)
Mr Locke's Reply to the Right Reverend the Lord Bishop of Worcester's Answer to his Second Letter NF
See *A Letter*, and *Mr Locke's Reply* 1697

Peter Anthony Motteux (1663–1718) (adap.)
The Island Princess; or, The Generous Portuguese D/OP
Performed *c.*November 1698. Adapted from John Fletcher, *The Island Princess.*

John Oldmixon (1673–1742)
Reflections on the Stage, and Mr Collier's Defence of the Short View NF
Anonymous. See Collier 1699.

Mary Pix (1666–1720)
The False Friend; or, The Fate of Disobedience: A tragedy D
Performed *c.*May 1699

John Pomfret (1667–1702)
The Choice V
Published 1699, dated 1700

Nahum Tate (1652–1715)
Elegies V
Subjects: Mary II (1662–94); John Tillotson (1630–94); James, duke of Ormond (1610–88); Thomas, earl of Ossory (1634–80); Anne Herbert, countess of Pembroke (1590–1676)

Sir William Temple (1628–99)
Letters Written by Sir William Temple During his Being Ambassador at The Hague NF

John Toland (1670–1722)
The Life of John Milton NF
Anonymous. See also *Amyntor* 1699.

John Toland (1670–1722)
Amyntor; or, A Defence of Milton's Life NF
Anonymous. See also *Life of John Milton* 1699.

Thomas Traherne (1637–74)
A Serious and Pathetical Contemplation of the Mercies of God NF
Anonymous. Edited by George Hickes (1642–1715). Attributed to Traherne by Bertram Dobell.

William Wake (1657–1737)
The Principles of the Christian Religion Explained NF

Edward Ward (1667–1731)
A Trip to New-England NF
Anonymous. Contains some verse.

James Wright (1643–1713)
Historia Histrionica: An historical account of the English-stage NF
Anonymous

1700

1700

- Great Northern War (–1721)
- James Arbuckle born
  Phanuel Bacon born
  Charles Jennens born
  Matthew Pilkington born (*c.*1700)
  James Thomson born
- John Banks dies (*c.*1700)
  Thomas Creech dies
  John Dryden dies
  Edward Howard dies
  Sir Paul Rycaut dies

Mary Astell (1666–1731)
Some Reflections upon Marriage NF
Anonymous

Aphra Behn (1640?–89)
Histories, Novels, and Translations F/NF

Sir Richard Blackmore (1654–1729)
A Satyr Against Wit V
Anonymous. An attack on the 'wits' of the time, including Dryden.

Abel Boyer (1667–1729)
Achilles; or, Iphigenia in Aulis: A tragedy D
Performed December? 1699. Based on Racine's *Iphigénie*.

Thomas Brown (1663–1704)
Amusements Serious and Comical F

Thomas Brown (1663–1704)
A Description of Mr Dryden's Funeral V
Anonymous. Dryden died on 1 May 1700.

Susanna Centlivre (1669?–1723)
The Perjur'd Husband; or, The Adventures of Venice: A tragedy D
Published under the name of S[usanna] Carroll. Performed October? 1700.

Colley Cibber (1671–1757)
The Tragical History of King Richard III D
Performed *c.*February 1700

Samuel Cobb (1675–1713)
Poetae Britannici V
Anonymous

Jeremy Collier (1650–1726)
A Second Defence of the Short View of the Profaneness and Immorality of the English Stage, &c NF
See *A Short View* 1698, *A Defence of the Short View* 1699, *Mr Collier's Dissuasive* 1703, *A Further Vindication* 1708

William Congreve (1670–1729)
The Way of the World: A comedy D
Performed March 1700

Daniel Defoe (1660–1731)
The Pacificator V
Anonymous verse satire contributing to the literary war between the 'Men of Sense' and the 'Men of Wit'

John Dennis (1657–1734)
Iphigenia: A tragedy D
Performed December 1699

John Dryden (1631–1700)
Fables Ancient and Modern V

Charles Gildon (1665–1724) (adap.)
Measure for Measure; or, Beauty the Best Advocate D
Anonymous. Performed 1699.

Charles Hopkins (1664?–1700)
Friendship Improv'd; or, The Female Warriour: A tragedy D
Performed 7 November 1699

William King (1663–1712)
The Transactioneer With Some of his Philosophical Fancies V
Anonymous. A satire on Sir Hans Sloane, who edited the *Transactions* of the Royal Society.

Francis Moore (1657–1714)
Vox Stellarum: An almanac for 1701 NF
The first 'Old Moore's Almanac'

Peter Anthony Motteux (1663–1718) (ed.)
The History of the Renown'd Don-Quixote de la Mancha F
Translated by several hands from Cervantes (1547–1616). Volume i only. Volumes ii–iv printed in 1712 as part of the 3rd edition.

Mary Pix (1666–1720)
The Beau Defeated: or, The Lucky Younger Brother: A comedy D
Anonymous. Performed *c.*March 1700.

John Pomfret (1667–1702)
Reason V
bao *The Choice*

Thomas Southerne (1659–1746)
The Fate of Capua: A tragedy D
Performed *c.*April 1700

Nahum Tate (1652–1715)
Panacea: A poem upon tea V

Sir William Temple (1628–99)
Letters Written by Sir W. Temple, and Other Ministers of State, Both at Home and Abroad NF
Edited by Jonathan Swift

John Tutchin (1661?–1707)
The Foreigners V
Anonymous. Provoked a reply from Defoe in *The True-Born Englishman* 1701 (q.v.).

Sir John Vanbrugh (1664–1726)
The Pilgrim: A comedy D
Anonymous. Performed April 1700.

Edward Ward (1667–1731)
The Reformer V
Anonymous

Edward Ward (1667–1731)
A Step to the Bath: With a character of the place NF
Anonymous

Thomas Yalden (1670–1736)
The Temple of Fame V

1701

- The War of the Spanish Succession (–1713)
  Act of Settlement
  Death of the former James II (6 Sept.)
- Matthew Concanen born
  Alexander Cruden born
  Matthew Pilkington born
- Sir Charles Sedley dies
- Madeleine de Scudéry dies

Mary, Lady Chudleigh (1656–1710)
The Ladies Defence; or, The Bride-woman's Counsellor Answer'd V
Written 'by a lady' in reply to a wedding sermon by John Sprint, preached May 1699 (published in 1709 as *The Bride-Womans Counseller*)

Colley Cibber (1671–1757)
Love Makes a Man; or, The Fop's Fortune: A comedy D
Performed 13 December 1700. An amalgamation of two plays by Beaumont and Fletcher, *The Custom of the Country* and *The Elder Brother.*

Jeremy Collier (1650–1726) (tr.)
The Great Historical, Geographical, Genealogical and Poetical Dictionary DICT
Translated from Louis Moréri (1643–80), *Le grand dictionnaire historique*. A continuation ('by another hand') published in 1705.

William Congreve (1670–1729)
The Judgment of Paris: A masque D
Performed March 1701

Daniel Defoe (1660–1731)
The Original Power of the Collective Body of the People of England NF
Anonymous. Published 1701, dated 1702. An attack on Sir Humphrey Mackworth's *A Vindication of the Rights of the Commons of England* (1701).

Daniel Defoe (1660–1731)
The True-Born Englishman: A satyr V
Anonymous. Published 1701, dated 1700. Inspired by John Tutchin's *The Foreigners* 1700 (q.v.). Tutchin's *The Apostates* (1701) is his anonymous reply. Inspired many other responses, adaptations, and attacks.

John Dennis (1657–1734)
The Advancement and Reformation of Modern Poetry NF

John Dryden (1631–1700)
Poems on Various Occasions; and Translations from Several Authors V

Thomas D'Urfey (1653–1723)
The Bath; or, The Western Lass: A comedy D

George Farquhar (1678–1707)
Sir Harry Wildair D
Performed *c.*April 1701. Sequel to *The Constant Couple* 1699 (q.v.).

Charles Gildon (1665–1724)
Love's Victim; or, the Queen of Wales: A tragedy D
Anonymous. Performed 1701.

Charles Gildon (1665–1724) (ed.)
A New Miscellany of Original Poems ANTH

Includes 'The Spleen' and other poems by Anne Finch, countess of Winchilsea

George Granville, Lord Lansdowne (1667–1735)
The Jew of Venice: A comedy D
Anonymous. Performed *c.*May 1701.

Peter Anthony Motteux (1663–1718)
The Masque of Acis and Galatea D
Performed c.March 1701

John Norris (1657–1711)
An Essay Towards the Theory of the Ideal or Intelligible World NF
Volume i; volume ii published in 1704

John Philips (1676–1709)?
The Sylvan Dream; or, The Mourning Muses V
Anonymous. Commonly attributed to Philips but perhaps not by him.

Mary Pix (1666–1720)
The Double Distress: A tragedy D
Performed *c.*March 1701

Nicholas Rowe (1674–1718)
The Ambitious Step-Mother D
Performed December? 1700

Sir Edward Sherburne (1618–1702) (tr. and ed.)
The Tragedies of L. Annaeus Seneca EDN

Richard Steele (1672–1729)
The Christian Hero NF

Richard Steele (1672–1729)
The Funeral; or, Grief a-la-mode: A comedy D
Published 1701, dated 1702. Performed some time between 9 October and 11 December 1701.

Jonathan Swift (1667–1745)
A Discourse of the Contests and Dissensions Between the Nobles and the Commons in Athens and Rome NF
Anonymous

Sir William Temple (1628–99)
Miscellanea: the Third Part NF
See also *Miscellanea: The First Part* 1680; *Second Part* 1690

John Toland (1670–1722)
The Art of Governing by Partys NF

Catharine Trotter, later **Cockburn** (1674–1749)
Love at a Loss; or, Most Votes Carry It: A comedy D
Performed 23 November 1700

Catharine Trotter, later **Cockburn** (1674–1749)
The Unhappy Penitent: A tragedy D
Performed 4 February 1701

Benjamin Whichcote (1609–83)
Several Discourses NF
4 volumes, 1701–7

1702

- Death of William III (8 Mar.)
  QUEEN ANNE (–1714)
  War declared against France
- Judith Cowper born
  Philip Doddridge born
- John Pomfret dies

Thomas Brown (1663–1704) and others
Letters From the Dead to the Living F
Partly original, partly translated from the French. *A Continuation or Second Part of the Letters From the Dead to the Living* published in 1703.

Edmund Calamy (1671–1732)
An Abridgement of Mr [Richard] *Baxter's History of His Life and Times* NF

Susanna Centlivre (1669?–1723)
The Beau's Duel; or, A Soldier for the Ladies: A comedy D

Colley Cibber (1671–1757)
She Wou'd and She Wou'd Not; or, The Kind Impostor D
Performed 26 November 1702

Daniel Defoe (1660–1731)
An Enquiry into Occasional Conformity NF
bao *The Preface to Mr Howe*

Daniel Defoe (1660–1731)
The Mock-Mourners: A satyr, by way of an elegy on King William V
bao *The True-Born Englishman*

Daniel Defoe (1660–1731)
A New Test of the Church of England's Loyalty NF
Anonymous

Daniel Defoe (1660–1731)
Reformation of Manners: A satyr V
Anonymous

Daniel Defoe (1660–1731)
The Shortest Way with the Dissenters NF
Anonymous. See also *A Brief Explanation* 1703, *A Dialogue* 1703, *More Short-Ways* 1704. Many

responses. See also John Dunton, *The Shortest Way with Whores and Rogues* 1703, and Mary Astell, *A Fair Way with Dissenters* 1704.

Daniel Defoe (1660–1731)
The Spanish Descent V
bao *The True-Born Englishman*

John Dennis (1657–1734)
The Monument V
Memorial poem on the death of William III (8 March 1702)

Laurence Echard (*c.*1670–1730)
A General Ecclesiastical History NF

George Farquhar (1678–1707)
The Inconstant; or, The Way to Win Him: A comedy D
Performed *c.*February 1702. An adaptation of John Fletcher's *The Wild Goose Chase.*

George Farquhar (1678–1707)
Love and Business MISC
Verse and prose

George Farquhar (1678–1707)
The Twin-Rivals: A comedy D
Published 1702, dated 1703. Performed 14 December 1702.

Edmund Gibson (1669–1748)
Synodus Anglicana; or, The Constitution and Proceedings of an English Convocation NF

Charles Gildon (1665–1724)?
A Comparison Between the Two Stages NF
Anonymous. Attribution doubtful. A comparison between Drury Lane and Lincoln's Inn Fields theatres.

Charles Gildon (1665–1724) (ed.)
Examen Miscellaneum MISC
Anonymous

Bevil Higgons (1670–1735)
The Generous Conqueror; or, The Timely Discovery: A tragedy D
Performed *c.*December 1701

Edward Hyde, 1st earl of Clarendon (1609–74)
The History of the Rebellion and Civil Wars in England NF
3 volumes, 1702–4. See also *History of the Rebellion . . . in Ireland* 1720.

George Keith (1639?–1716)
The Standard of the Quakers Examined; or, An Answer to the Apology of Robert Barclay NF

William King (1650–1729)
De Origine Mali NF
English translation published in 1731 (q.v.)

Mary Mollineux (1651–95)
Fruits of Retirement; or, Miscellaneous Poems, Moral and Divine V

John Pomfret (1667–1702)
Miscellany Poems on Several Occasions V
bao *The Choice*

Matthew Prior (1664–1721)
To a Young Gentleman in Love V
Anonymous

Nicholas Rowe (1674–1718)
Tamerlane: A tragedy D
Performed December? 1701. The hero was intended as a portrait of William III and the play was subsequently produced annually at Drury Lane on the anniversary of William's landing (5 November) until 1815.

Joseph Stennett (1663–1713)
A Poem to the Memory of His Late Majesty William the Third V
King William died on 8 March 1702

John Toland (1670–1722)
Paradoxes of State NF
Anonymous

Catharine Trotter, later **Cockburn** (1674–1749)
A Defence of the Essay of Human Understanding NF
Anonymous. See John Locke, *An Essay Concerning Humane Understanding* 1690.

Sir John Vanbrugh (1664–1726)
The False Friend: A comedy D
Anonymous. Performed February? 1702.

1703

- Henry Brooke born
  Thomas ('Hesiod') Cooke born
  Robert Dodsley born
  John Wesley born
  Gilbert West born
- John Crowne dies
  Samuel Pepys dies
  John Wallis dies
- Charles Perrault dies

Joseph Addison (1672–1719)
A Letter from Italy, to the Right Honourable Charles Lord Halifax NF

Abel Boyer (1667–1729) (ed.)
The History of the Reign of Queen Anne NF
Anonymous.

Gilbert Burnet (1643–1715)
A Third Collection of Several Tracts and Discourses NF
See also *A Collection of Several Tracts* 1685, *A Second Collection* 1689

Edmund Calamy (1671–1732)
A Defence of Moderate Non-Conformity NF

Susanna Centlivre (1669?–1723)
Love's Contrivance; or, Le Médecin malgré lui: A comedy D
Performed 4 June 1703. Some scenes taken from Molière's play of the same name (performed 1666).

Susanna Centlivre (1669?–1723)
The Stolen Heiress; or, The Salamanca Doctor Outplotted: A comedy D
Anonymous. Performed 31 December 1702. Taken from Thomas May's *The Heir* 1622 (q.v.).

Mary, Lady Chudleigh (1656–1710)
Poems on Several Occasions V

Jeremy Collier (1650–1726)
Mr Collier's Dissuasive from the Play-House NF
See *A Short View* 1698, *A Defence of the Short View* 1699, *A Second Defence* 1700, *A Further Vindication* 1708

William Congreve (1670–1729)
A Hymn to Harmony V

William Congreve (1670–1729)
The Tears of Amaryllis for Amyntas V

William Dampier (1652–1715)
A Voyage to New Holland, &c in the Year 1699 NF

Daniel Defoe (1660–1731)
A Brief Explanation of a Late Pamphlet, entituled, The Shortest Way with the Dissenters NF
Anonymous. See *The Shortest Way with the Dissenters* 1702, *A Dialogue* 1703, *More Short-Ways* 1704.

Daniel Defoe (1660–1731)
A Collection of the Writings of the Author of the True-Born English-Man NF
An unauthorized collection

Daniel Defoe (1660–1731)
A Dialogue Between a Dissenter and the Observator, Concerning The Shortest Way with the Dissenters NF
Anonymous. The 'Observator' = John Tutchin. See also *The Shortest Way with the Dissenters* 1702, *A Brief Explanation* 1703, *More Short-Ways* 1704.

Daniel Defoe (1660–1731)
A Hymn to the Funeral Sermon V
Anonymous. Most probably by Defoe.

Daniel Defoe (1660–1731)
A Hymn to the Pillory V
Anonymous

Daniel Defoe (1660–1731)
More Reformation: A satyr upon himself V
bao *The True-Born Englishman*

Daniel Defoe (1660–1731)
The Shortest Way to Peace and Union NF
bao *The Shortest Way with the Dissenters*

Daniel Defoe (1660–1731)
A True Collection of the Writings of the Author of the True-Born English-man MISC
Anonymous. A collection of poems and prose tracts. See *A Second Volume of the Writings* 1705.

John Dunton (1659–1733)
The Shortest Way with Whores and Rogues NF
Anonymous. A reply to Defoe's *Shortest Way with the Dissenters* 1702 (q.v.).

Sarah Fyge Egerton, later **Field** (1670–1723)
Poems on Several Occasions V
Prefatory verses by Susanna Centlivre

Charles Gildon (1665–1724)
The Patriot; or, The Italian Conspiracy: A tragedy D
Anonymous. Performed 1703. An adaptation of Nathaniel Lee's *Lucius Junius Brutus* 1681 (q.v.).

Thomas Hearne (1678–1735) (ed.)
Reliquiae Bodleianae; or, Some Genuine Remains of Sir Thomas Bodley NF

Benjamin Hoadly (1676–1761)
The Reasonableness of Conformity to the Church of England NF

Bernard Mandeville (1670?–1733)
Some Fables After the Easie and Familiar Method of Monsieur de la Fontaine V
Anonymous

John Oldmixon (1673–1742)
The Governour of Cyprus: A tragedy D
Performed 1703

Nicholas Rowe (1674–1718)
The Fair Penitent: A tragedy D
Performed May? 1703. Adapted from Massinger's *Fatal Dowry* 1632 (q.v.). The villain, 'the gallant, the gay Lothario', gained a proverbial reputation.

Edward Ward (1667–1731)?
The Secret History of the Calves-head Clubb; or, The Republican Unmasqu'd NF
Anonymous. Sometimes also attributed to John Dunton.

Benjamin Whichcote (1609–83)
Moral and Religious Aphorisms NF
Anonymous

1704

- Battle of Blenheim (13 Aug.)
  Capture of Gibraltar by Sir George Rooke
- Moses Brown born
  Soame Jenyns born
- Thomas Brown dies
  Benjamin Keach dies
  Jane Lead dies
  Sir Roger L'Estrange dies
  John Locke dies
  Edward Ravenscroft dies

Joseph Addison (1672–1719)
The Campaign V
Published 1704, dated 1705

Edmund Arwaker (*c.*1655–1730)
An Embassy from Heav'n; or, The Ghost of Queen Mary V

Mary Astell (1666–1731)
A Fair Way with Dissenters and their Patrons NF
Anonymous response to Defoe's *Shortest Way with the Dissenters* 1702 (q.v.). See also Charles Leslie 1704.

Mary Astell (1666–1731)
An Impartial Enquiry into the Causes of Rebellion and Civil War in this Kingdom NF
Anonymous

William Chillingworth (1602–43)
The Works of William Chillingworth WKS

Mary Davys (1674–1732)
The Amours of Alcippus and Leucippe F
'Written by a lady'

Daniel Defoe (1660–1731)
The Address V
Anonymous. A satirical ballad attacking the House of Commons for the persecution of Dissenters.

Daniel Defoe (1660–1731)
The Dissenters Answer to the High-Church Challenge NF
Anonymous. Defoe's response to Charles Leslie's *The Wolf Stript of his Shepherd's Cloathing* 1704 (q.v.).

Daniel Defoe (1660–1731)
An Elegy on the Author of the True-Born English-man V
bao *The Hymn to the Pillory*

Daniel Defoe (1660–1731)?
An Essay on the Regulation of the Press NF
Anonymous. Probably by Defoe.

Daniel Defoe (1660–1731)
Giving Alms No Charity, and Employing the Poor a Grievance to the Nation NF
Anonymous

Daniel Defoe (1660–1731)
A Hymn to Victory V

Daniel Defoe (1660–1731)?
The Lay-Man's Sermon upon the Late Storm NF
Anonymous. Probably by Defoe.

Daniel Defoe (1660–1731)
More Short-Ways with the Dissenters NF
Anonymous. See *The Shortest Way with the Dissenters* 1702, *A Brief Explanation* 1703, *A Dialogue* 1703.

Daniel Defoe (1660–1731) (ed.)
A Review of the Affairs of France: and of All Europe PER
Published from February 1704–June 1713. Edited by Defoe and published under the guidance of Robert Harley (1661–1724), first earl of Oxford.

John Dennis (1657–1734)
The Grounds of Criticism in Poetry NF

John Dennis (1657–1734)
Liberty Asserted: A tragedy D
Performed 24 February 1704

John Dennis (1657–1734)
The Person of Quality's Answer to Mr Collier's Letter NF
Anonymous

George Farquhar (1678–1707)
The Stage-Coach: A farce D
Anonymous. An adaptation of Jean de la Chapelle's *Les carosses d'Orléans*.

Andrew Fletcher (1655–1716)
An Account of a Conversation Concerning a Right Regulation of Governments for the Good of Mankind NF
Published anonymously

White Kennett (1660–1728)
The Christian Scholar NF
Anonymous. Sometimes attributed to Samuel Brewster the elder.

Charles Leslie (1650–1722)
The Wolf Stript of his Shepherd's Cloathing NF
'By one call'd an High Church Man'. An answer to *Moderation a Virtue* (1703) by James Owen (1654–1706). Replied to by Defoe in *The Dissenters Answer to the High-Church Challenge* 1704 (q.v.). See also Mary Astell 1704.

Bernard Mandeville (1670–1733)
Typhon; or, The Wars Between the Gods and Giants V

Isaac Newton (1642–1727)
Opticks; or, A Treatise of the Reflexions, Refractions, Inflexions and Colours of Light NF

Mary Pix (1666–1720) (tr.)
Violenta; or, The Rewards of Virtue V
Anonymous. Based on the 8th tale of the 2nd day of Boccaccio's *Decameron*.

Matthew Prior (1664–1721)
A Letter to Monsieur Boileau Depreaux V
Anonymous. On the Battle of Blenheim (13 August 1704).

Richard Steele (1672–1729)
The Lying Lover; or, The Ladies Friendship: A comedy D
Performed 2 December 1703

Jonathan Swift (1667–1745)
A Tale of a Tub PS
Anonymous

William Taverner (*d.* 1731)
The Faithful Bride of Granada D
Anonymous. Performed *c.*May 1704.

Joseph Trapp (1679–1747)
Abra-Mule; or, Love and Empire: A tragedy D

William Wycherley (1641–1716)
Miscellany Poems V

1705

- Thomas Birch born
  Isaac Hawkins Brown, the elder, born
  Stephen Duck born
  David Hartley born
  David Mallet born?
  Abraham Tucker born
- Titus Oates dies
  John Ray dies

Joseph Addison (1672–1719)
Remarks on Several Parts of Italy NF

Mary Astell (1666–1731)
The Christian Religion as Profess'd by a Daughter of the Church NF
Anonymous

Susanna Centlivre (1669?–1723)
The Gamester D
Anonymous. Performed January 1705. Adapted from *Le Joueur* (performed 1696) by Jean-François Regnard (1655–1709).

Susanna Centlivre (1669?–1723)
The Basset-Table: A comedy D
bao *The Gamester*. Published 1705, dated 1706. Performed 20 November 1705.

George Cheyne (1671–1743)
Philosophical Principles of Natural Religion NF

Colley Cibber (1671–1757)
The Careless Husband: A comedy D
Performed 7 December 1704

Samuel Clarke (1675–1729)
A Demonstration of the Being and Attributes of God NF

Mary Davys (1674–1732)
The Fugitive F
Humorous, loosely organized tale, based on her own life. Rewritten as *The Merry Wanderer* (1725).

Daniel Defoe (1660–1731)
The Consolidator; or, Memoirs of Sundry Transactions from the World in the Moon F
bao *The True-born Englishman*

Daniel Defoe (1660–1731)
The Double Welcome: A poem to the Duke of Marlbro' V
Anonymous

Daniel Defoe (1660–1731)
The Dyet of Poland V
Anonymous. A verse history of 'Poland' during the three sessions of Queen Anne's first parliament.

'Sobieski' is King William; 'Grave Casmir' is Godolphin; 'The Dyet's Marshall' is Harley.

Daniel Defoe (1660–1731)
A Second Volume of the Writings of the Author of the True-Born Englishman MISC
Anonymous. A collection of 18 poems and prose tracts.

John Dennis (1657–1734)
Gibraltar; or, The Spanish Adventure: A comedy D
Performed 16 February 1705

John Dunton (1659–1733)
The Life and Errors of John Dunton Late Citizen of London NF

Edmund Gibson (1669–1748)
Family-Devotion; or, A Plain Exhortation to Morning and Evening Prayer in Families NF

Charles Gildon (1665–1724)
The Deist's Manual; or, A Rational Enquiry into the Christian Religion NF

Bernard Mandeville (1670–1733)
The Grumbling Hive; or, Knaves Turn'd Honest V
A piracy. Incorporated into *The Fable of the Bees* 1714 (q.v.).

Delarivière Manley (1663–1724)
The Secret History, of Queen Zarah, and the Zarazians F
Part ii published in 1705; both parts published together 1711

Peter Anthony Motteux (1663–1718)
Arsinoe, Queen of Cyprus: An opera D/OP
Performed 16 January 1705

William Mountfort (1664–92)
Zelmane; or, The Corinthian Queen D
Performed 1705

John Philips (1676–1709)
Blenheim V
Anonymous

John Philips (1676–1709)
The Splendid Shilling: An imitation of Milton V
Anonymous. See also Bramston, *The Crooked Sixpence* 1743.

Katherine Philips (1631–64)
Letters from Orinda to Poliarchus NF

Mary Pix (1666–1720)
The Conquest of Spain: A tragedy D
Anonymous. Performed May 1705. Adapted from William Rowley's *All's Lost by Lust* 1633 (q.v.).

Matthew Prior (1664–1721)
An English Padlock V
Anonymous

Richard Steele (1672–1729)
The Tender Husband; or, The Accomplish'd Fools: A comedy D
Performed 23 April 1705

Sir John Vanbrugh (1664–1726)
The Confederacy: A comedy D
bao *The Relapse*. Performed 30 October 1705.

Edward Ward (1667–1731)
Hudibras Redivivus; or, A Burlesque Poem on the Times V
Anonymous. In two volumes of twelve parts each (published August 1705–July 1706; August 1706–June 1707).

Isaac Watts (1674–1748)
Horae Lyricae V
Published in 1705, dated 1706. Many editions.

1706

- Battle of Ramillies (23 May)
- Benjamin Hoadly, the younger, born
  James Miller born
- William Burnaby dies
  John Evelyn dies
  John Phillips dies
- Benjamin Franklin born
- Pierre Bayle dies

Anonymous
Arabian Nights Entertainments F
Lengthy serialization from this date. Translated from *Les Mille et une nuits, contes arabes* (first parts published in 1704) by Antoine Galland (1646–1715).

Daniel Baker (1654?–1723)
The History of Job V

Arthur Bedford (1668–1745)
The Evil and Dangers of Stage-Plays NF

Thomas Betterton (1635?–1710) (adap.)
The Amorous Widow; or, The Wanton Wife D
Anonymous. Performed *c.*November 1670. Adapted from Molière's *Georges Dandin* (1668).

Sir Richard Blackmore (1654–1729)
Advice to the Poets V
Anonymous. See also *Instructions to Vander Bank* 1709.

Susanna Centlivre (1669?–1723)
Love at a Venture: A comedy D
bao *The Gamester*

Colley Cibber (1671–1757)
Perolla and Izadora: A tragedy D

Samuel Clarke (1675–1729)
A Discourse Concerning the Unchangeable Obligations of Natural Religion NF

Stephen Clay (*b.* 1672)
An Epistle from the Elector of Bavaria to the French King: After the Battel of Ramilles V
Anonymous. Sometimes misattributed to Matthew Prior.

William Congreve (1670–1729)
A Pindarique Ode . . . on the Victorious Progress of Her Majesties Arms, Under the Conduct of the Duke of Marlborough V

Daniel Defoe (1660–1731)
Caledonia V

Daniel Defoe (1660–1731)
An Essay at Removing National Prejudices Against a Union with Scotland NF
Anonymous

Daniel Defoe (1660–1731)
A Hymn to Peace V
bao *The True-born Englishman*

Daniel Defoe (1660–1731)
Jure Divino V
bao *The True-born Englishman.* A meditation on the 'divine right' theory of monarchy.

Daniel Defoe (1660–1731)?
A True Relation of the Apparition of one Mrs Veal, the Next Day after her Death NF
Anonymous. Probably by Defoe. Most subsequent reprints contained in *The Christian's Defence Against the Fears of Death* by Charles Drelincourt.

Daniel Defoe (1660–1731)
The Vision V
Anonymous. Written in favour of the Union of Scotland and England and an attack on John Hamilton, Lord Belhaven.

John Dennis (1657–1734)
The Battle of Ramillia; or, the Power of Union V

John Dennis (1657–1734)
An Essay on the Opera's after the Italian Manner NF

Thomas D'Urfey (1653–1723)
Wonders in the Sun; or, The Kingdom of the Birds: A comick opera D/OP
Libretto only. Performed April 1706.

George Farquhar (1678–1707)
The Recruiting Officer: A comedy D
Performed 8 April 1706

George Granville, Lord Lansdowne (1667–1735)
The British Enchanters; or, No Magick Like Love: A tragedy D
Anonymous. Performed 21 February 1706.

William Harison (1685–1713)
Woodstock Park V

White Kennett (1660–1728)
The History of England from the Commencement of the Reign of Charles I to the End of William III NF
Volume iii of *A Complete History of England* (volumes i and ii edited by John Hughes)

John Locke (1632–1704)
Posthumous Works of Mr John Locke NF

Delarivière Manley (1663–1724)
Almyna; or, The Arabian Vow: A tragedy D
Anonymous. Published 1706, dated 1707. Performed 16 December 1706.

John Philips (1676–1709)?
Cerealia: An imitation of Milton V
Anonymous. Also attributed to Elijah Fenton.

Matthew Prior (1664–1721)
The Squirrel V
Anonymous

Nicholas Rowe (1674–1718)
Ulysses: A tragedy D
Performed 23 November 1705

Thomas Tickell (1686–1740)
Oxford V
Anonymous. Published 1706, dated 1707.

Matthew Tindal (1657–1733)
The Rights of the Christian Church Asserted NF
Anonymous. See also *A Defence* 1707.

Catharine Trotter, later **Cockburn** (1674–1749)
The Revolution of Sweden: A tragedy D
Performed 11 February 1706

Sir John Vanbrugh (1664–1726)
The Mistake: A comedy D

bao *The Provok'd Wife*. Performed 27 December 1705.

1707

- Union of England and Scotland (12 May) and abolition of the Scottish Parliament
- Henry Fielding born
  Charles Wesley born
- George Farquhar dies
  John Tutchin dies
- Dietrich Buxtehude dies

Anonymous
The Diverting Works of the Countess D'Anois [i.e. d'Aulnoy] F/NF
Translation of novels, letters, memoirs, and tales by Marie-Catherine, comtesse d'Aulnoy (*c*.1650–1705)

Anonymous
Memoirs of the Court of England F
Translation of *Mémoires de la Cour d'Angleterre* (1695) by Marie-Catherine, comtesse d'Aulnoy (*c*.1650–1705). Includes part i of Delarivière Manley's *The Lady's Pacquet of Letters* 1707 (q.v.).

Anonymous
The History of the Earl of Warwick, Sirnam'd the King-maker F
Translation of *Le Comte de Warwick* (1703) by Marie-Catherine, comtesse d'Aulnoy (*c*.1650–1705). The 2nd edition of 1708 includes part ii of Delarivière Manley's *The Lady's Pacquet of Letters* 1707 (q.v.).

Joseph Addison (1672–1719)
Rosamund: An opera D/OP
Performed March 1707. Music by Thomas Clayton.

Richard Baxter (1615–91)
The Practical Works of the Late Richard Baxter NF

Thomas Brown (1663–1704)
The Works of Mr Thomas Brown, in Prose and Verse WKS

Susanna Centlivre (1669?–1723)
The Platonick Lady: A comedy D
bao *The Gamester* and *Love's Contrivance*. Performed 25 November 1706.

Colley Cibber (1671–1757)
The Double Gallant; or, The Sick Lady's Cure: A comedy D
Performed 1 November 1707. Compiled by Cibber from Susanna Centlivre's *Love at a Venture* 1706 (q.v.).

Colley Cibber (1671–1757)
The Lady's Last Stake; or, The Wife's Resentment: A comedy D
Performed 4 February 1707

Samuel Cobb (1675–1713)
Poems on Several Occasions V

Anthony Collins (1676–1729)
An Essay Concerning the Use of Reason NF
Anonymous

Thomas D'Urfey (1653–1723)
Stories, Moral and Comical V/F
Publication date conjectural

Laurence Echard (*c*.1670–1730)
The History of England [vol. i] NF
Volumes ii and iii published in 1718, with a reissued volume i

George Farquhar (1678–1707)
The Beaux' Stratagem: A comedy D
Performed 8 March 1707

Delarivière Manley (1663–1724)
The Lady's Pacquet of Letters F
Part i published in *Memoirs of the Court of England* by the comtesse d'Aulnoy 1707 (q.v.); part ii in d'Aulnoy's *The History of the Earl of Warwick* 1707 (q.v.). Both parts published as *Court Intrigues, in a Collection of Original Letters, From the Island of the New Atalantis*, 1711.

Peter Anthony Motteux (1663–1718)
Thomyris, Queen of Scythia: An opera D/OP
Performed 1 April 1707

John Oldmixon (1673–1742) (ed.)
The Muses Mercury; or, The Monthly Miscellany PER
Published monthly (January 1707–January 1708)

John Pomfret (1667–1702)
Quae Rara, Chara: A poem on Panthea's confinement V
bao *The Choice*

Nahum Tate (1652–1715)
Injur'd Love; or, The Cruel Husband: A tragedy D

Nahum Tate (1652–1715)
The Triumph of Union V

Matthew Tindal (1657–1733)
A Defence of the Rights of the Christian Church NF
Anonymous. See *The Rights of the Christian Church* 1706. *A Second Defence* published in 1709.

Catharine Trotter, later **Cockburn** (1674–1749)
A Discourse Concerning a Guide in Controversies NF
Anonymous. The 'Guide in Controversies' (1677?) was written by Abraham Woodhead (1609–78).

Isaac Watts (1674–1748)
Hymns and Spiritual Songs V
Many editions throughout the 18th century and beyond

John Wilmot, earl of Rochester (1647–80) and others
The Miscellaneous Works of the Late Earls of Rochester and Roscommon WKS

1708

- Battle of Oudenarde (11 July)
- Richard Bentley, the younger, born
  Samuel Boyse born
  John Collier ('Tim Bobbin') born
  Philip Francis born
  Laetitia Pilkington born?

Joseph Addison (1672–1719)
The Present State of the War NF

Edmund Arwaker (*c*.1655–1730) (tr.)
Truth in Fiction; or, Morality in Masquerade V
Fables by Aesop and others

Francis Atterbury (1662–1732)
Fourteen Sermons Preach'd on Several Occasions NF

Joseph Bingham (1668–1723)
Origines Ecclesiae; or, The Antiquities of the Christian Church [vols i, ii] NF
Volumes iii–x published 1711–22

Sir Richard Blackmore (1654–1729)
The Kit-Cats V

Jeremy Collier (1650–1726)
An Ecclesiastical History of Great Britain, Chiefly of England [vol. i] NF
Volume ii published in 1714

Jeremy Collier (1650–1726)
A Farther Vindication of the Short View of the Profaneness and Immorality of the English Stage NF
Reply to Filmer's *A Defence of Dramatick Poetry* 1698. See *A Short View* 1698, *A Defence of the Short View* 1699, *A Second Defence* 1700, *Mr Collier's Dissuasive* 1703.

Anthony Ashley Cooper, 3rd earl of Shaftesbury (1671–1713)
A Letter Concerning Enthusiasm NF
Anonymous

Elijah Fenton (1683–1730) (ed.)
Oxford and Cambridge Miscellany Poems V

John Gay (1685–1732)
Wine V
Anonymous

Charles Gildon (1665–1724)
Libertas Triumphans V
On the Battle of Oudenarde (11 July 1708)

Charles Gildon (1665–1724)
The New Metamorphosis NF
An original work by Gildon, though purporting to be a translation from the Italian

Aaron Hill (1685–1750) (tr.)
The Celebrated Speeches of Ajax and Ulysses, for the Armour of Achilles V
Anonymous. Translated from Ovid's *Metamorphosis*.

Benjamin Hoadly (1676–1761)
The Happiness of the Present Establishment, and the Unhappiness of Absolute Monarchy NF

William King (1663–1712)
The Art of Cookery V

John Locke (1632–1704)
Some Familiar Letters NF

Peter Anthony Motteux (1663–1718)
Love's Triumph: An opera D/OP
Performed 26 February 1708

Simon Ockley (1678–1720)
The Conquest of Syria, Persia, and Aegypt by the Saracens NF
Volume i; volume ii (*The History of the Saracens*) published in 1718

Matthew Prior (1664–1721)
Poems on Several Occasions V
Published 1708, dated 1709. See also *Poems on Several Occasion* 1719.

Nicholas Rowe (1674–1718)
The Royal Convert: A tragedy D
Performed 25 November 1707

Jonathan Swift (1667–1745)
Predictions for the Year 1708 PS
Anonymous

Jonathan Swift (1667–1745)
The Accomplishment of the First of Mr Bickerstaff's Predictions PS
Anonymous

1709

- Peter the Great defeats Charles XII at the Battle of Poltava (8 July)
  Battle of Malplaquet (11 Sept.)
  First Copyright Act
- John Armstrong ('Launcelot Temple') born
  John Banks born
  John Cleland born
  Samuel Johnson born
  George Lyttelton, 1st Baron Lyttelton, born
  Robert Craggs Nugent born
  John Shebbeare born

The Female Tatler PER
'By Mrs Crackenthorpe'. Published between 8 July 1709 and 31 March 1710. The original Mrs Crackenthorpe is generally identified as Delarivière Manley.

Anonymous
Memoirs of the Life and Adventures of Signor Rozelli, at the Hague F
Translated from *L'Infortuné Napolitain, ou les avantures du seigneur Rozelli* (1704) by the Abbé Olivier. Sometimes misattributed to Defoe.

Mary Astell (1666–1731)
Bart'lemy Fair; or, An Inquiry After Wit NF
'By Mr Wotton' (i.e. Astell). A response to Shaftesbury's *Letter Concerning Enthusiasm* 1708 (q.v.).

George Berkeley (1685–1753)
An Essay Towards a New Theory of Vision NF

Sir Richard Blackmore (1654–1729)
Instructions to Vander Bank V
Anonymous. Sequel to *Advice to the Poets* 1706 (q.v.).

Susanna Centlivre (1669?–1723)
The Busie Body: A comedy D
Performed 12 May 1709. Introduces the celebrated character of Marplot. Part of the play's plot is based on Ben Jonson's *The Devil is an Ass* 1631 (q.v.). See also *Mar-Plot* 1711.

Susanna Centlivre (1669?–1723)
The Man's Bewitch'd; or, The Devil to Do About Her: A comedy D
Performed 12 December 1709

Samuel Cobb (1675–1713)
The Female Reign V

Anthony Ashley Cooper, 3rd earl of Shaftesbury (1671–1713)
Sensus Communis NF
Anonymous

Daniel Defoe (1660–1731)
The History of the Union of Great Britain NF
Anonymous

John Dennis (1657–1734)
Appius and Virginia: A tragedy D
Performed 5 February 1709

Charles Gildon (1665–1724)
The Golden Spy; or, A Political Journal of the British Nights Entertainments of War and Peace, and Love and Politics PS
Anonymous. A prose satire, published 1709–10.

Charles Johnson (1679–1748)
Love and Liberty: A tragedy D
Unacted

White Kennett (1660–1728)
A Vindication of the Church and Clergy of England NF
Anonymous

William King (1663–1712)
Miscellanies in Prose and Verse MISC

Delarivière Manley (1663–1724)
Secret Memoirs and Manners of Several Persons of Quality, of Both Sexes F
Anonymous. See also *Memoirs of Europe* 1710; and Oldmixon (ed.), *The Court of Atalantis* 1714.

Mary Pix (1666–1720)
The Adventures in Madrid: A comedy D
Anonymous. Possibly by Pix. Performed *c.*June 1706.

John Reynolds (1667–1727)
Death's Vision Represented in a Philosophical Sacred Poem V

William Shakespeare (1564–1616)
The Works of Mr William Shakespear EDN
Edited by Nicholas Rowe. The first edition of Shakespeare after the four Folios. Text based on the Fourth Folio of 1685 (q.v.). See also *Works of Mr William Shakespear* 1714.

Richard Steele (1672–1729), **Joseph Addison** (1672–1719), and others
The Tatler PER
'By Isaac Bickerstaff'. Published in 271 numbers from 12 April 1709–19 May 1711 and in 4 volumes 1710–11. About 188 numbers by Steele alone, about

42 numbers by Addison alone, and 36 numbers by Steele and Addison together, who were no longer associated with the periodical after number 271.

John Strype (1643–1737)
Annals of the Reformation and Establishment of Religion NF

Jonathan Swift (1667–1745)
Baucis and Philemon V
Anonymous

Jonathan Swift (1667–1745)
A Famous Prediction of Merlin, the British Wizard V

Jonathan Swift (1667–1745)
A Project for the Advancement of Religion, and the Reformation of Manners NF
'By a person of quality'

Jonathan Swift (1667–1745)
A Vindication of Isaac Bickerstaff Esq. NF
Anonymous

Sir William Temple (1628–99)
Memoirs: Part III NF
Edited by Jonathan Swift. See also *Memoirs* 1692.

Various
Poetical Miscellanies: The Sixth Part ANTH
Edited by John Dryden and usually known as Dryden's, or Tonson's, Miscellanies. The sixth in the series of miscellanies published by Tonson 1684–1709. Contains three pieces by Pope. See also *Miscellany Poems* 1684, *Sylvae* 1685, *Examen Poeticum* 1693, *Annual Miscellany* 1694, *Poetical Miscellanies: Fifth Part* 1704.

1710

- Sarah Fielding born
  James Hammond born
  Thomas Reid born
  William Melmoth, the younger, born
- Thomas Betterton dies
  Mary Chudleigh dies
- Thomas Arne born

Joseph Addison (1672–1719)
The Whig Examiner PER
Published in 5 numbers (September–October 1710)

George Berkeley (1685–1753)
A Treatise Concerning the Principles of Human Knowledge NF

Susanna Centlivre (1669?–1723)
A Bickerstaff's Burying; or, Work for the Upholders: A farce D

Mary, Lady Chudleigh (1656–1710)
Essays upon Several Subjects in Verse and Prose MISC

Colley Cibber (1671–1757)
The Secret History of Arlus and Odolphus F
Anonymous. A satirical fable on Harley, Marlborough, and Godolphin.

Anthony Collins (1676–1729)
A Vindication of the Divine Attributes NF
Anonymous

Anthony Ashley Cooper, 3rd earl of Shaftesbury (1671–1713)
Soliloquy; or, Advice to an Author NF
Anonymous

Daniel Defoe (1660–1731)
Atalantis Major F
Anonymous. Published 1710, dated 1711. A political allegory.

Daniel Defoe (1660–1731)
An Essay Upon Publick Credit NF
Anonymous. Sometimes erroneously attributed to Robert Harley (1661–1724), first earl of Oxford

George Farquhar (1678–1707)
Barcellona V

Aaron Hill (1685–1750)
Elfrid; or, The Fair Inconstant: A tragedy D
Performed 3 January 1710

Charles Johnson (1679–1748)
The Force of Friendship: A tragedy D
Performed 20 April 1710

John Leland (1506?–52)
The Itinerary of John Leland the Antiquary NF
Edited by Thomas Hearne. Published in 9 volumes (1710–12).

Delarivière Manley (1663–1724)
Memoirs of Europe, Towards the Close of the Eighth Century F
Anonymous. A contemporary satire. See also *Secret Memoirs* 1709.

Ambrose Philips (1674–1749)
Pastorals V

Jonathan Swift (1667–1745)
A Meditation Upon a Broom-Stick PS

Various
The Examiner; or, Remarks upon Papers and Occurrences PER
Published weekly 1710–14. Begun as an 'ultra-Tory' journal by Henry St John, Francis Atterbury, Matthew Prior, and John Freind. Originally edited by William King. Under the editorship of Swift (also a major contributor) from November 1710–June 1711.

Various
The Medley PER
Originated by Arthur Maynwaring (1668–1712). Contributors include Richard Steele and John Oldmixon. Published weekly, October 1710–August 1711.

1711

- Robert Harley created earl of Oxford
- Cornelius Arnold born
  Alban Butler born
  Catherine ('Kitty') Clive born
  David Hume born
- John Caryll dies
  Thomas Ken dies
- Boileau dies

Francis Atterbury (1662–1732)
The Mitre and the Crown; or, A Real Distinction Between Them NF
Anonymous

Sir Richard Blackmore (1654–1729)
The Nature of Man V
Anonymous

Abel Boyer (1667–1729)
The Political State of Great Britain NF
Continued to 40 volumes after Boyer's death

Susanna Centlivre (1669?–1723)
Mar-Plot; or, The Second Part of the Busie-Body D
Performed 30 December 1710. See *The Busie Body* 1709.

Anthony Ashley Cooper, 3rd earl of Shaftesbury (1671–1713)
Characteristicks of Men, Manners, Opinions, Times NF
Contains *A Letter Concerning Enthusiasm* 1708 (q.v.), *Sensus Communis* 1709 (q.v.), *Soliloquy* 1710 (q.v.) and other pieces

Daniel Defoe (1660–1731)?
The British Visions; or, Isaac Bickerstaff, Sen. NF
Anonymous. Probably by Defoe. A hoax, in which Bickerstaff appears to foretell events which have already occurred, inspired in part by Swift's *Predictions for the Year 1708* (q.v.).

Daniel Defoe (1660–1731)
An Essay on the History of Parties, and Persecution in Britain NF
Anonymous. An attack on the bill against Occasional Conformity, then pending in Parliament.

Daniel Defoe (1660–1731)
An Essay on the South-Sea Trade NF
bao *The Review*. Published 1711, dated 1712.

Daniel Defoe (1660–1731)
The Present State of the Parties in Great Britain NF
Anonymous. Almost certainly by Defoe.

Daniel Defoe (1660–1731)?
The Secret History of the October Club NF
Anonymous. Probably by Defoe.

John Dennis (1657–1734)
An Essay Upon Publick Spirit NF

John Dennis (1657–1734)
Reflections Critical and Satyrical, Upon a Late Rhapsody call'd, An Essay upon Criticism NF
A response to Pope's *Essay on Criticism* 1711 (see below)

John Gay (1685–1732)
The Present State of Wit NF

William King (1663–1712)
An Historical Account of the Heathen Gods and Heroes V

George Mackenzie, earl of Cromarty (1630–1714)
Several Proposals Conducting to a Further Union of Britain NF
Anonymous

Alexander Pope (1688–1744)
An Essay on Criticism V

Richard Steele (1672–1729), **Joseph Addison** (1672–1719), **Eustace Budgell** (1686–1737), and others
The Spectator PER
Published in 555 numbers (March 1711–1712)

John Strype (1643–1737)
The Life and Acts of Matthew Parker NF

Jonathan Swift (1667–1745)
Miscellanies in Prose and Verse ANTH
Contains 25 pieces by Swift

Jonathan Swift (1667–1745)
The Conduct of the Allies, and of the Late Ministry NF
Published 1711, dated 1712. See also Defoe 1712.

Edward Ward (1667–1731)
The Life and Notable Adventures of that Renown'd Knight Don Quixote de la Mancha V
Originally published in six monthly parts, 1710–11

1712

- Henry St-John created Viscount Bolingbroke
- Richard Glover born
  Edward Moore born
- Philip Ayres dies
  William King dies
- Jean-Jacques Rousseau born
- Richard Cromwell dies
  Sidney, Earl Godolphin, dies

John Arbuthnot (1667–1735)
'The History of John Bull' NF
Anonymous. A collection of five pamphlets advocating an end to the war with France, published 4 March–31 July 1712. See also 1714.

George Berkeley (1685–1753)
Passive Obedience; or, The Christian Doctrine of Not Resisting the Supreme Power NF

Sir Richard Blackmore (1654–1729)
Creation V

Sir Thomas Browne (1605–82)
Posthumous Works of the Learned Sir Thomas Browne, NF

Susanna Centlivre (1669?–1723)
The Perplex'd Lovers: A comedy D
Performed 19 January 1712

Samuel Clarke (1675–1729)
The Scripture-Doctrine of the Trinity NF

Daniel Defoe (1660–1731)?
A Further Search into the Conduct of the Allies NF
Anonymous. Probably by Defoe. Presented as a sequel to Swift's *Conduct of the Allies* 1711 (q.v.).

John Dennis (1657–1734)
An Essay upon the Genius and Writings of Shakespear NF

William Diaper (1685–1717)
Dryaides; or, The Nymphs Prophecy V
Published 1712, dated 1713

William Diaper (1685–1717)
Nereides; or, Sea-Eclogues V

Thomas Ellwood (1639–1713)
Davideis: The Life of King David of Israel V

John Gay (1685–1732)
The Mohocks: A tragi-comical farce D
Unacted

George Granville, Lord Lansdowne (1667–1735)
Poems Upon Several Occasions V

John Hughes (1677–1720)
Calypso and Telemachus: An opera D/OP
Performed 17 May 1712

Bernard Mandeville (1670–1733)
Typhon; or, The Wars Between the Gods and Giants V
Anonymous

Peter Anthony Motteux (1663–1718)
A Poem Upon Tea V

John Oldmixon (1673–1742)
The Dutch Barrier Our's; or, The Interest of England and Holland Inseparable NF
Anonymous. A reply to Swift's *Conduct of the Allies* 1711 (q.v.).

John Oldmixon (1673–1742)
Reflections on Dr Swift's Letter to the Earl of Oxford, About the English Tongue NF
Anonymous

John Oldmixon (1673–1742)
The Secret History of Europe NF
Anonymous. Parts i, ii. Part iii published in 1713; part iv, 1715.

Thomas Otway (1652–85)
The Works of Mr Thomas Otway WKS

Ambrose Philips (1674–1749) (tr.)
The Distrest Mother: A tragedy D
Performed 17 March 1712. Translated from Jean Racine (1639–99), *Andromaque* (1667).

John Philips (1676–1709)
Poems V

Alexander Pope (1688–1744) (ed.)
Miscellaneous Poems and Translations ANTH
Contains the two-canto version of Pope's 'The Rape of the Lock', without the letter to Miss Fermor. See *The Rape of the Lock* 1714.

Matthew Prior (1664–1721)
Erle Robert's Mice: A tale, in imitation of Chaucer V
Anonymous

Nicholas Rowe (1674–1718) (tr.)
Callipaedia V
Translated from Claude Quillet (1602–61)

George Sewell (1690?–1726)
The Patriot V

'Scoto-Brittanus' [Richard Steele (1672–1729)] (ed.)
The Englishman's Thanks to the Duke of Marlborough NF

Jonathan Swift (1667–1745)
Some Advice Humbly Offer'd to the Members of the October Club PS
Anonymous

Jonathan Swift (1667–1745)
A Proposal for Correcting, Improving and Ascertaining the English Tongue NF
One of Swift's few signed publications

Thomas Tickell (1686–1740)
A Poem, to his Excellency the Lord Privy-Seal, on the Prospect of Peace V

Leonard Welsted (1688–1747) (tr.)
The Works of Dionysius Longinus, on the Sublime NF

John Wright (*fl.* 1708–27)
The Best Mirth; or, The Melody of Sion V
A collection of hymns

1713

- Peace of Utrecht: Britain gains French territory in North America, and Gibraltar and Minorca from Spain
  Scriblerus Club founded by Pope, Swift, Congreve, and others
- Edward Capell born
  Laurence Sterne born
- Anthony Ashley Cooper dies
  Thomas Rymer dies
  Thomas Sprat dies
- Denis Diderot born
- Arcangelo Corelli dies

Joseph Addison (1672–1719)
Cato: A tragedy D
Performed April 1713

Jane Barker (1652–1732)
Love Intrigues; or, The History of the Amours of Bosvil and Galesia F
'Written by a young lady'

'Phileleutherus Lipsiensis' [Richard Bentley (1662–1742)]
Remarks upon a Late Discourse of Free-thinking NF
Written in response to Anthony Collins' *Discourse of Free-thinking* 1713 (q.v.). Part ii published in 1714.

George Berkeley (1685–1753)
Three Dialogues Between Hylas and Philonous NF

Henry Carey (1687?–1743)
Poems on Several Occasions V
Contains the celebrated lyric 'Sally in Our Alley' and 'Namby-Pamby', written in ridicule of Ambrose Philips

Anthony Collins (1676–1729)
A Discourse of Free-thinking NF
Anonymous

Daniel Defoe (1660–1731)
And What if the Pretender Should Come? NF
Anonymous. An ironic pamphlet advancing pro-Jacobite arguments for the succession of the Pretender. See also *Reasons Against the Succession of the House of Hanover* 1713.

Daniel Defoe (1660–1731)
A General History of Trade NF
Anonymous

Daniel Defoe (1660–1731)
Reasons Against the Succession of the House of Hanover NF
Anonymous. A highly ironic pamphlet arguing that it would be best for the country if the Pretender, rather than the Elector George, were to succeed Queen Anne. See also *And What if the Pretender Should Come?* 1713.

John Dennis (1657–1734)
Remarks upon Cato, a Tragedy NF
See Addison, *Cato* (above)

Abel Evans (1679–1737)
Vertumnus V
bao *The Apparition*

Anne Finch, countess of Winchilsea (1661–1720)
Miscellany Poems on Several Occasions V
'Written by a lady'

John Gay (1685–1732)
Rural Sports V

John Gay (1685–1732)
The Wife of Bath: A comedy D
Performed 12 May 1713

John Gay (1685–1732)
The Fan V
Published 1713, dated 1714

Edmund Gibson (1669–1748)
Codex Juris Ecclesiastici Anglicani NF
On the statutes, canons, etc., of the Church of England

John Hughes (1677–1720) (tr.)
Letters of Abelard and Heloise NF
Anonymous. Partly translated from Pierre Bayle (1647–1706), *Dictionnaire historique et critique*. Many editions.

Charles Johnson (1679–1748)
The Successful Pyrate D
Performed 7 November 1712

Thomas Parnell (1679–1718)
An Essay on the Different Stiles of Poetry V
Anonymous

Alexander Pope (1688–1744)
Windsor-Forest V

Alexander Pope (1688–1744)
Ode for Musick V

Richard Steele (1672–1729) and **Joseph Addison** (1672–1719)
The Guardian PER
Published in 175 number (March–October 1713). 53 numbers by Addison.

Richard Steele (1672–1729)
The Englishman PER
Published in 56 numbers (October 1713–February 1714). See also *The Englishman* 1714, *The Englishman: Second Series* 1715.

Jonathan Swift (1667–1745)
Mr C[olli]n's Discourse of Free-thinking, Put into Plain English NF
Anonymous. Written in response to Anthony Collins's *Discourse of Free-thinking* 1713 (q.v.).

Jonathan Swift (1667–1745)
Part of the Seventh Epistle of the First Book of Horace Imitated V
Anonymous

John Toland (1670–1722)
Reasons for Naturalizing the Jews in Great Britain and Ireland NF
Anonymous

Edward Ward (1667–1731)
The History of the Grand Rebellion V

Edward Young (1683–1765)
An Epistle to the Right Honourable the Lord Lansdown V

Edward Young (1683–1765)
A Poem on the Last Day V

1714

- Death of Queen Anne (1 Aug.)
  GEORGE I (-1727)
- James Burnett, Lord Monboddo, born
  Richard Griffith born?
  James Hervey born
  Catherine Jemmat born
  William Shenstone born
  James Townley born
  George Whitefield born

Anonymous
A Compleat Key to the Seventh Edition of the Dispensary NF
See Samuel Garth, *The Dispensary* 1699

Anonymous
The Court of Atalantis F
Variously attributed to John Oldmixon, Jodocus Crull, and Delarivière Manley. See also Delarivière Manley, *Secret Memoirs* 1709.

Anonymous
The Ladies Tale F
Short stories in a frame narrative

Anonymous
The Ladies Library ANTH
'Written by a lady'. Edited by Richard Steele. Variously attributed to Mary Wray, to Steele himself, and to George Berkeley.

John Arbuthnot (1667–1735)
A Continuation of the History of the Crown-Inn NF
Anonymous. See *'The History of John Bull'* 1712.

John Arbuthnot (1667–1735)
A Postscript to John Bull NF
Anonymous. See *'The History of John Bull'* 1712.

Susanna Centlivre (1669?–1723)
The Wonder! A Woman Keeps a Secret: A comedy D
bao *The Gamester*. Performed 27 April 1714.

Daniel Defoe (1660–1731)
The Secret History of the White-Staff NF

Anonymous. Defoe's defence of his patron Robert Harley, 1st earl of Oxford (1661–1724), who had resigned the Lord Treasurer's white staff of office and was facing calls for his impeachment. Part ii published in 1714, part iii, 1715.

William Diaper (1685–1717)
An Imitation of the Seventeenth Epistle of the First Book of Horace V

Thomas Ellwood (1639–1713)
The History of the Life of Thomas Ellwood NF

Laurence Eusden (1688–1739)
A Letter to Mr Addison, on the King's Accession to the Throne V

Abel Evans (1679–1737)
Prae-existence: A poem, in imitation of Milton V

John Gay (1685–1732)
The Shepherd's Week V

Charles Gildon (1665–1724)
A New Rehearsal; or, Bays the Younger NF
Anonymous

Anthony Hamilton (1646?–1720)
Memoirs of the Life of the Count de Grammont F
Translated by Abel Boyer. First published anonymously in French in 1713.

Charles Johnson (1679–1748)
The Victim: A tragedy D
Performed 5 January 1714

Samuel Jones (*d.* 1732)
Poetical Miscellanies on Several Occasions V

William King (1663–1712) and others (tr.)
The Persian and the Turkish Tales, Compleat F
Translated from François Pétis de la Croix *fils* (1653–1713), *Les Milles et un jours, contes persans* (1710–12) and *Histoire de la sultane de Perse et des vizirs, contes turcs* (1707)

John Locke (1632–1704)
The Works of John Locke WKS

Bernard Mandeville (1670–1733)
The Fable of the Bees; or, Private Vices Publick Benefits NF
Anonymous

Delarivière Manley (1663–1724)
The Adventures of Rivella; or, The History of the Author of the Atalantis F
Anonymous

Alexander Pope (1688–1744)
The Rape of the Lock: An heroi-comical poem V
First edition in enlarged, 5-canto form. See also *Miscellaneous Poems and Translations* 1712.

Nicholas Rowe (1674–1718)
Poems on Several Occasions V

Nicholas Rowe (1674–1718)
The Tragedy of Jane Shore D
Performed 2 February 1714

William Shakespeare (1564–1616)
The Works of Mr William Shakespear EDN
Edited by Nicholas Rowe. Ostensibly the second (actually the third) edition of Rowe's *Works of Mr William Shakespear* 1709 (q.v.).

Alexander Smith (*fl.* 1714–26)
The History of the Lives of the Most Noted Highway-men, Foot-pads, House-breakers, Shop-lifts and Cheats of Both Sexes . . . F
Volume ii published 1714; volume iii, 1720

Richard Steele (1672–1729) (ed.)
The Crisis; or, A Discourse Representing the Just Causes of the Late Happy Revolution NF

Richard Steele (1672–1729)
The Englishman: Being the Close of the Paper So Called PER
Reprints Number 57. See also *The Englishman* 1713, *The Englishman: Second Series* 1715.

Richard Steele (1672–1729)
The Lover PER
'By Marmaduke Myrtle, Gent.'. Published in 40 numbers (February–May 1714). Numbers 10 and 39 are by Joseph Addison. See *The Reader* 1714.

Richard Steele (1672–1729)
Mr Steele's Apology for Himself and his Writings NF

Richard Steele (1672–1729) (ed.)
Poetical Miscellanies V
Includes works by Pope, Thomas Parnell, Thomas Tickell, John Gay, Thomas Warton, Edward Young, and Steele himself

Richard Steele (1672–1729)
The Publick Spirit of the Tories NF
Anonymous. Attributed to Steele. A response to Swift's *Publick Spirit of the Whigs* 1714 (q.v.).

Richard Steele (1672–1729)
The Reader PER
Anonymous. Published in nine numbers (April–May 1714).

Jonathan Swift (1667–1745) (tr.)
The First Ode of the Second Book of Horace Paraphras'd V
Published 1714, dated 1713

Jonathan Swift (1667–1745)
The Publick Spirit of the Whigs PS
Anonymous. Some subsequent editions censored, losing five paragraphs attacking Scots peers. See also Steele, *Publick Spirit of the Tories* 1714.

Edward Ward (1667–1731)
The Field-Spy; or, The Walking Observator V
bao *The London Spy*

Edward Young (1683–1765)
The Force of Religion; or, Vanquish'd Love V

1715

- Death of Louis XIV: accession of the infant Louis XV under the regentship of Philippe II, Duc d'Orléans
  Jacobite rising in Scotland ('The Fifteen')
  Jacobites defeated at Sheriffmuir and Preston (13–14 Nov.)
- Jane Collier born
  Richard Graves born
  John Hawkesworth born
  Richard Jago born
  William Whitehead born
- Gilbert Burnet dies
  Mary Monck dies
  Charles Montagu, earl of Halifax, dies
  Nahum Tate dies: Nicholas Rowe appointed Poet Laureate
- William Dampier dies

Joseph Addison (1672–1719)
The Free-Holder; or, Political Essays PER
Published in 55 numbers (December 1715–June 1716)

Jane Barker (1652–1732)
Exilius; or, The Banish'd Roman F

Richard Bentley (1662–1742)
A Sermon upon Popery NF

Christopher Bullock (1690?–1724)
A Woman's Revenge; or, A Match in Newgate: A comedy D
Performed 24 October 1715. An alteration of *The Revenge* 1680 (q.v.), attributed to Aphra Behn.

Henry Carey (1687?–1743)
The Contrivances; or, More Ways Than One D
Anonymous. Performed 9 August 1715.

Susanna Centlivre (1669?–1723)
The Gotham Election: A farce D
Unacted

Charles Cotton (1630–87)
The Genuine Works of Charles Cotton V

Samuel Croxall (1690?–1752)
The Vision V

Daniel Defoe (1660–1731)
An Appeal to Honour and Justice NF

Daniel Defoe (1660–1731)
The Family Instructor NF
Anonymous. See also *A New Family Instructor* 1727.

Daniel Defoe (1660–1731)?
A Hymn to the Mob V
Anonymous. Probably by Defoe.

Elizabeth Elstob (1683–1758)
The Rudiments of Grammar for the English-Saxon Tongue NF

John Gay (1685–1732)
The What D'Ye Call It: A tragi-comi-pastoral farce D
Performed 23 February 1715

Benjamin Griffin (1680–1740)
Injured Virtue; or, The Virgin Martyr: A tragedy D
Performed 1 November 1714

Charles Johnson (1679–1748)
The Country Lasses; or, The Custom of the Manor D
Performed 4 February 1715

Charles Montagu, earl of Halifax (1661–1715)
The Works and Life of the Late Earl of Halifax WKS

Alexander Pope (1688–1744)
The Temple of Fame V

Alexander Pope (1688–1744) (tr.)
The Iliad of Homer [vol. i] V
Books i–iv. Volume ii (books v–viii) 1716; volume iii (books ix–xii) 1717; volume iv (books xiii–xvi) 1718; volumes v (books xvii–xxi) and vi (books xxii–xxiv) 1720 (qq.v.).

Jonathan Richardson (1665–1745)
An Essay on the Theory of Painting NF

Nicholas Rowe (1674–1718)
The Tragedy of the Lady Jane Grey D
Performed 20 April 1715

Alexander Smith (*fl.* 1714–26)
The Secret History of the Lives of the Most Celebrated Beauties, Ladies of Quality, and Jilts F

Sir Richard Steele (1672–1729)
The Englishman: Second Series PER
Anonymous. Published in 28 numbers (July–November 1715) and in 1 volume, 1716. A resurrected version of *The Englishman* 1713–14 (q.v.). Steele was knighted in this year.

Sir Richard Steele (1672–1729)
Town-Talk PER
Published in 9 numbers (December 1715–February 1716)

'William Symson' [pseud.] (*fl.* 1715)
A New Voyage to the East Indies F
A possible source for Swift's *Gulliver's Travels* 1726 (q.v.)

Lewis Theobald (1688–1744)
The Perfidious Brother: A tragedy D
In fact by Henry Mestayer, revised by Theobald. Performed 21 February 1716.

Thomas Tickell (1686–1740) (tr.)
The First Book of Homer's Iliad V

Sir John Vanbrugh (1664–1726) (tr.)
The Country House: A farce D
Anonymous. Performed 18 January 1698. A translation of *La maison de campagne* by Florent Carton Dancourt (1661–1725).

Isaac Watts (1674–1748)
Divine Songs V
Many editions

Isaac Watts (1674–1748)
A Guide to Prayer NF
Ten editions by 1753

1716

- Septennial Act, prolonging the life of Parliament to seven years
- Thomas Gray born
- George Keith dies
  Robert South dies
  William Wycherley dies
- Lancelot ('Capability') Brown born
- Leibniz dies

Anonymous
The History and Adventures of Gil Blas of Santillane F
Anonymous translation of *Histoire de Gil Blas de Santillane* (volumes i and ii, 1715) by Alain René Lesage (1668–1747).

Joseph Addison (1672–1719)
The Drummer; or, The Haunted House: A comedy D
Anonymous. Performed 1715. Preface by Sir Richard Steele.

Sir Richard Blackmore (1654–1729)
Essays upon Several Subjects [vol. i] NF
Volume ii (1717) was issued with the second edition of volume i

Barton Booth (1681–1733)
The Death of Dido: A masque D
Performed 17 April 1716

Jane Brereton (1685–1740)
The Fifth Ode of the Fourth Book of Horace, Imitated V

Sir Thomas Browne (1605–82)
Christian Morals NF

'Mr [Joseph] Gay' [Francis Chute (*d.* 1745)]
The Petticoat: An heroi-comical poem V
Often misattributed to John Durant Breval

Anthony Ashley Cooper, 3rd earl of Shaftesbury (1671–1713)
Several Letters Written by a Noble Lord to a Young Man at the University NF
Anonymous

Mary Davys (1674–1732)
The Northern Heiress; or, The Humors of York: A comedy D

John Dennis (1657–1734)
A True Character of Mr Pope, and his Writings NF
Anonymous

John Gay (1685–1732)
Trivia; or, The Art of Walking the Street V

Aaron Hill (1685–1750)
The Fatal Vision; or, The Fall of Siam: A tragedy D
Anonymous. Performed 7 February 1716.

John Hughes (1677–1720)
Apollo and Daphne: A masque D
Performed 12 January 1716

Charles Johnson (1679–1748)
The Cobler of Preston D
Performed 3 February 1716

Lady Mary Wortley Montagu (1689–1762)
Court Poems: i. The basset-table. ii. The drawing-room. iii. The toilet. V
Anonymous. Published 1716, misdated 1706. Authorship problematic, though it is generally agreed that the greatest share in the authorship of these verses is that of Lady Mary Wortley Montagu.

John Oldmixon (1673–1742)
Memoirs of Ireland from the Restoration, to the Present Times NF
bao *The Secret History of Europe*. Sometimes erroneously attributed to Thomas Salmon.

Alexander Pope (1688–1744) (tr.)
The Iliad of Homer [vol. ii] V
Books v–viii. Volume i (books i–iv) 1715; volume iii (books ix–xii) 1717; volume iv (books xiii–xvi) 1718; volumes v (books xvii–xxi) and vi (books xxii–xxiv) 1720 (qq.v.).

Humphrey Prideaux (1648–1724)
The Old and New Testament Connected in the History of the Jews and Neighbouring Nations NF

Thomas Purney (1695–1730)
Pastorals V
Published 1716, dated 1717

George Sewell (1690?–1726)
A Vindication of the English Stage NF

Lewis Theobald (1688–1744) (tr.)
The Odyssey of Homer V
Published 1716, dated 1717

1717

- First performance of Handel's *Water Music*
- Richard Owen Cambridge born
  Elizabeth Carter born
  David Garrick born
  Horace Walpole born
- William Diaper dies

Elias Ashmole (1617–92)
Memoirs of the Life of Elias Ashmole, Drawn up by Himself by Way of a Diary NF

John Durant Breval (1680?–1738)
The Art of Dress V
Anonymous

John Durant Breval (1680?–1738)
The Confederates: A farce D
'By Mr Gay'. A satire on Pope, Gay, and Arbuthnot's *Three Hours After Marriage* 1717 (q.v.).

Susanna Centlivre (1669?–1723)
The Cruel Gift: A tragedy D
Performed 17 December 1716

Susanna Centlivre (1669?–1723)
An Epistle to the King of Sweden V
Anonymous

Anthony Collins (1676–1729)
A Philosophical Inquiry Concerning Human Liberty NF
Anonymous

John Dennis (1657–1734)
Remarks upon Mr Pope's Translation of Homer NF

Wentworth Dillon, 4th earl of Roscommon (1633–85) and others
Poems by the Earl of Roscomon [sic] V

Elijah Fenton (1683–1730)
Poems on Several Occasions V

John Gay (1685–1732) [with **Alexander Pope** (1688–1744) and **John Arbuthnot** (1667–1735)]
Three Hours After Marriage: A comedy D
Performed 16 January 1717. See also Breval, *The Confederates* 1717.

Benjamin Hoadly (1676–1761)
The Nature of the Kingdom, or Church of Christ NF
See also William Law *The Bishop of Bangor's Late Sermon* 1717.

Jane Holt (*fl.* 1701–17)
A Fairy Tale V

Charles Johnson (1679–1748)
The Sultaness: A tragedy D
Performed 25 February 1717

William Law (1686–1761)
The Bishop of Bangor's Late Sermon NF
A response to Benjamin Hoadly's *Nature of the Kingdom or Church of Christ* 1717 (q.v.)

Delarivière Manley (1663–1724)
Lucius, the First Christian King of Britain: A tragedy D
Performed 11 May 1717

Thomas Parnell (1679–1718) (tr.)
Homer's Battle of the Frogs and Mice V

Anonymous. The original was erroneously attributed in antiquity to Homer.

Alexander Pope (1688–1744) (tr.)
The Iliad of Homer [vol. iii] V
Books ix–xii. Volume i (books i–iv) 1715; volume ii (books v–viii) 1716; volume iv (books xiii–xvi) 1718; volumes v (books xvii–xxi) and vi (books xxii–xxiv) 1720 (qq.v.).

Alexander Pope (1688–1744)
The Works of Mr Alexander Pope WKS
The first collected edition of Pope's works. Contains new pieces, including 'Verses to the Memory of an Unfortunate Lady' and 'Eloisa to Abelard'. See also *Works* 1735, 1736, 1737.

Matthew Prior (1664–1721)
The Dove V
Anonymous

Thomas Purney (1695–1730)
A Full Enquiry into the True Nature of Pastoral NF

Richard Savage (1697?–1743)
The Convocation; or, A Battle of Pamphlets V

Thomas Tickell (1686–1740)
An Epistle from a Lady in England; to a Gentleman at Avignon V
Anonymous

John Toland (1670–1722)
The State-Anatomy of Great Britain [pt i] NF
Signed 'Patricola'. Part ii also published in 1717.

Thomas Traherne (1637–74)
Hexameron; or, Meditations on the Six Days of Creation NF
Anonymous, in *A Collection of Meditations and Devotions* by Susanna Hopton. Shown to be by Traherne by G.I. Wade in 1944. Includes poems.

Joseph Trapp (1679–1747)
The Real Nature of the Church or Kingdom of Christ NF

Various
Ovid's Metamorphoses V
Contributing translators include Dryden, Addison, Eusden, Gay, Pope, and Rowe. Many editions.

Edward Ward (1667–1731)
British Wonders; or, A Poetical Description of the Several Prodigies . . . That Have Happen'd in Britain Since the Death of Queen Anne V
Anonymous

Edward Ward (1667–1731)
A Collection of Historical and State Poems, Satyrs, Songs, and Epigrams V
bao *The London Spy*

Leonard Welsted (1688–1747)
Palaemon to Caelia, at Bath; or, The Triumvirate V
Anonymous

1718

- Hugh Blair born
  Thomas Chippendale born
- Peter Anthony Motteux dies
  Thomas Parnell dies
  William Penn dies
  Nicholas Rowe dies: Laurence Eusden appointed Poet Laureate

Anonymous
A Vindication of the Press NF
Sometimes misattributed to Defoe

Joseph Addison (1672–1719) and others
Poems on Several Occasions V
Published 1718, dated 1719

Joseph Addison (1672–1719)
The Resurrection V
Latin text by Addison followed by an English translation attributed to Nicholas Amhurst

Nicholas Amhurst (1697–1742)
Protestant Popery; or, The Convocation V

Charles Beckingham (1699–1731)
Scipio Africanus: A tragedy D

Susanna Centlivre (1669?–1723)
A Bold Stroke for a Wife: A comedy D
bao *The Busie-body* and *The Gamester*. Performed 3 February 1718.

Colley Cibber (1671–1757)
The Non-Juror: A comedy D
Performed 6 December 1717. An adaptation of Molière's *Le Tartuffe* (1664).

Charles Gildon (1665–1724)
The Complete Art of Poetry NF

Mary Hearne
The Lover's Week; or, The Six Days Adventures of Philander and Amaryllis F
'By a young lady'. An epistolary novel.

Richardson Pack (1682–1728)
Miscellanies in Verse and Prose MISC
Published 1718, dated 1719

Ambrose Philips (1674–1749) (ed.)
The Free-Thinker PER
Published in 350 numbers, March 1718–July 1721. Collected edition published in 1722.

Alexander Pope (1688–1744) (tr.)
The Iliad of Homer [vol. iv] V
Books xiii–xvi. Volume i (books i–iv) 1715; volume ii (books v–viii) 1716; volume iii (books ix–xii) 1717; volumes v (books xvii–xxi) and vi (books xxii–xxiv) 1720 (qq.v.).

Thomas Purney (1695–1730)
The Chevalier de St George: An heroi-comick poem V

Allan Ramsay (1686–1758)
Christ's Kirk on the Green V
Canto i supposedly by James I. Three cantos (ii and iii ascribed to Ramsay) also published in 1718.

John Ray (1627–1705)
Philosophical Letters NF

John Strype (1643–1737)
The Life and Acts of John Whitgift NF

Lewis Theobald (1688–1744)
Orestes: A dramatic opera D/OP
Performed 3 April 1731

Lewis Theobald (1688–1744)
Pan and Syrinx: An opera D/OP
Performed 14 January 1718

John Wilmot, earl of Rochester (1647–80)
Remains of the Earl of Rochester V

1719

- James Cawthorn born
  Charles Johnstone born?
  Edward Kimber born
  Esther Lewis born
- Joseph Addison dies
  Sir Samuel Garth dies
  John Flamsteed dies
- Madame de Maintenon dies

Anonymous
Heroick Friendship: A tragedy D
Falsely ascribed to Thomas Otway

Anonymous
Zulima: or, Pure Love F
Translated from *Zulima, ou l'Amour pur* (1694) by Eustache Le Noble de Tennelière (1643–1711)

Joseph Addison (1672–1719)
Maxims, Observations, and Reflections, Moral, Political, and Divine NF
Part ii published in 1720

Joseph Addison (1672–1719)
Notes upon the Twelve Books of Paradise Lost NF

Joseph Addison (1672–1719)
The Old Whig. Numb. I V
Anonymous. Published on 19 March 1719.

Joseph Addison (1672–1719)
The Old Whig. Numb. II V
Anonymous. Published on 2 April 1719.

Thomas Betterton (1635?–1710)
The Bond-Man; or, Love and Liberty: A tragi-comedy D
Anonymous. Performed 1719.

John Durant Breval (1680?–1738)
Mac-Dermot; or, The Irish Fortune-Hunter V
bao *The Art of Dress*

John Durant Breval (1680?–1738)
Ovid in Masquerade V
'By Mr Joseph Gay' (i.e. Breval), but this pseudonym also used by Francis Chute (*d.* 1745)

Colley Cibber (1671–1757)
Ximena; or, The Heroick Daughter: A tragedy D
Performed 28 November 1712

Daniel Defoe (1660–1731)
The Manufacturer; or, The British Trade Truly Stated PER
Published in 86 issues (October 1719–March 1721). Commissioned by the London Company of Weavers to illustrate the damaging effects of the importation of Indian printed calicoes.

Daniel Defoe (1660–1731)
Robinson Crusoe F
Anonymous. Full title: *The Life and Strange Surprizing Adventures of Robinson Crusoe, of York, Mariner*. See also *Serious Reflections* 1720.

Daniel Defoe (1660–1731)
The Farther Adventures of Robinson Crusoe F
Anonymous. See also previous entry and *Serious Reflections* 1720.

Charles Gildon (1665–1724)
The Life and Strange Surprizing Adventures of Mr D[aniel] DeF[oe], of London, Hosier NF
Anonymous

Eliza Haywood (*c.*1693–1756)
Love in Excess; or, The Fatal Enquiry F
Part i. Part ii published 1719?; part iii, 1720.

Benjamin Hoadly (1676–1761)
The Common Rights of Subjects, Defended NF

Giles Jacob (1686–1744)
The Poetical Register; or, The Lives and Characters of the English Dramatick Poets NF

Matthew Prior (1664–1721)
Poems on Several Occasions V
Dated 1718, but not ready for subscribers until March 1719. See also *Poems on Several Occasions* 1709.

Allan Ramsay (1686–1758)
Content V

Nicholas Rowe (1674–1718) (tr.)
Lucan's Pharsalia, Translated into English Verse V
Published 1719, dated 1718. With a life of Rowe by James Welwood.

Richard Savage (1697?–1743) (tr.)
Love in a Veil: A comedy D
Performed 17 June 1718. Translated from Pedro Calderón de la Barca (1600–81).

George Sewell (1690?–1726)
The Tragedy of Sir Walter Raleigh D
Performed 16 January 1719

George Sewell (1690?–1726)
Poems on Several Occasions V

Thomas Southerne (1659–1746)
The Spartan Dame: A tragedy D
Performed 11 December 1719

Sir Richard Steele (1672–1729)
The Plebian PER
'By a Member of the House of Commons'. Published in 4 numbers (March–April 1719).

Isaac Watts (1674–1748) (tr.)
The Psalms of David BIB
Many editions

Edward Young (1683–1765)
Busiris, King of Egypt: A tragedy D
Performed 7 March 1719

Edward Young (1683–1765)
A Letter to Mr Tickell V
On the death of Joseph Addison (17 June 1719)

1720

- The 'South Sea Bubble' begins to burst (Oct.)
- Samuel Foote born
  Elizabeth Griffith born
  Richard Hurd born
  James Merrick born
  Elizabeth Montagu born
  Gilbert White born
- Anne Finch, countess of Winchilsea, dies
  Mary Pix dies
- Charles Edward Stuart ('The Young Pretender') born

Charles Beckingham (1699–1731)
The Tragedy of King Henry IV of France D

Arthur Blackamore (*b.* 1679)
The Perfidious Brethren; or, The Religious Triumvirate F

Thomas Boston, the elder (1677–1732)
Human Nature in its Four-fold State NF
Anonymous

Jane Brereton (1685–1740)
An Expostulatory Epistle to Sir Richard Steele upon the Death of Mr Addison V
Anonymous

Thomas Brown (1663–1704)
The Remains of Mr Thomas Brown, Serious and Comical MISC
See also *Works* 1707

William Rufus Chetwood (*d.* 1766)
The Voyages, Dangerous Adventures, and Miraculous Escapes of Capt. Richard Falconer F
Anonymous. Written in the manner of Defoe's *Robinson Crusoe* 1719 (q.v.).

Samuel Croxall (1690?–1752)
The Fair Circassian V
Poetical adaptation of the Song of Solomon

Daniel Defoe (1660–1731)
The Life, Adventures, and Pyracies, of the Famous Captain Singleton F
Anonymous

Daniel Defoe (1660–1731)?
Memoirs of a Cavalier; or, A Military Journal of the Wars in Germany, and the Wars in England; from the Year 1632 to the Year 1648 F
Anonymous. Probably by Defoe.

Daniel Defoe (1660–1731)
Serious Reflections During the Life and Surprising Adventures of Robinson Crusoe F
Anonymous. Sometimes attributed to Thomas Gent. See *Robinson Crusoe* 1719.

John Dennis (1657–1734)
The Invader of His Country; or, The Fatal Resentment: A tragedy D
Performed 11 November 1719

John Gay (1685–1732)
Poems on Several Occasions V

Charles Gildon (1665–1724)
All for the Better; or, The World Turn'd Upside Down F
Dedication signed 'Philopatris'

Thomas Hearne (1678–1735)
A Collection of Curious Discourses NF

Aaron Hill (1685–1750)
The Creation V

John Hughes (1677–1720)
The Siege of Damascus: A tragedy D
Performed 17 February 1720

Edward Hyde, 1st earl of Clarendon (1609–74)
The History of the Rebellion and Civil Wars in Ireland NF
See also *History of the Rebellion . . . in England* 1702

Hildebrand Jacob (1693–1739)
The Curious Maid V
Anonymous

Delarivière Manley (1663–1724)
The Power of Love F
Contains seven novels, five of which are adapted from Painter's *Palace of Pleasure* (1566)

John Mottley (1692–1750)
The Imperial Captives: A tragedy D
Performed 29 February 1720

Alexander Pennecuik (*d.* 1730)
Streams From Helicon; or, Poems on Various Subjects V

Alexander Pope (1688–1744) (tr.)
The Iliad of Homer [vols v, vi] V
Books xvii–xxi, xxii–xxiv. Volume i (books i–iv) 1715; volume ii (books v–viii) 1716; volume iii (books ix–xii) 1717; volume iv (books xii–xvi) 1718 (qq.v.).

Matthew Prior (1664–1721)
The Conversation V
Anonymous

Allan Ramsay (1686–1758)
A Poem on the South-Sea V

Allan Ramsay (1686–1758)
Poems V

Richard Rawlinson (1690–1755)
The English Topographer NF

Martha Sansom (1690–1736)
The Epistles of Clio and Strephon MISC
Anonymous. Letters in prose and verse written with William Bond (*d.* 1735).

George Sewell (1690?–1726)
A New Collection of Original Poems V
bao *Sir Walter Raleigh*

Sir Richard Steele (1672–1729) (ed.)
The Crisis of Property NF
See also *A Nation a Family* 1720

Sir Richard Steele (1672–1729) (ed.)
A Nation a Family NF
See also *The Crisis of Property* 1720

Jonathan Swift (1667–1745)
A Proposal for the Universal Use of Irish Manufacture NF
Anonymous

Sir William Temple (1628–99)
The Works of Sir William Temple WKS

Various
A New Miscellany of Original Poems, Translations and Imitations V
Known as 'Hammonds Miscellany'. Pieces by Pope, Lady Mary Wortley Montagu, Bevil Higgons, and Nicholas Amhurst, and letters by the earl of Rochester.

Edward Ward (1667–1731)
The Delights of the Bottle; or, The Compleat Vintner V
bao *The Cavalcade*

1721

- Inoculation for smallpox introduced by Lady Mary Wortley Montagu
- Mark Akenside born
  William Collins born
  Thomas Francklin born
  Tobias George Smollett born
  Catherine Talbot born
- Matthew Prior dies
  John Sheffield, duke of Buckingham, dies
- Grinling Gibbons dies
- Antoine Watteau dies

Joseph Addison (1672–1719)
The Works of Joseph Addison WKS
Edited by Thomas Tickell

Penelope Aubin (*c.*1685–1731)
The Life of Madam de Beaumont F

Penelope Aubin (*c.*1685–1731)
The Strange Adventures of the Count de Vinevil and his Family F

Nathan Bailey (*d. c.*1742)
An Universal Etymological Dictionary DICT

George Berkeley (1685–1753)
An Essay Towards Preventing the Ruine of Great Britain NF
Anonymous

Sir Richard Blackmore (1654–1729)
A New Version of the Psalms of David BIB

Colley Cibber (1671–1757)
The Refusal; or, The Ladies Philosophy: A comedy D
Performed 14 February 1721. Adapted from Molière's *Les Femmes Savantes* (1672).

Anthony Ashley Cooper, 3rd earl of Shaftesbury (1671–1713)
Letters from the Late Earl of Shaftesbury, to Robert Molesworth NF

Charles Gildon (1665–1724)
The Laws of Poetry NF

Eliza Haywood (*c*.1693–1756)
The Fair Captive: A tragedy D
Performed 4 March 1721

Eliza Haywood (*c*.1693–1756) (tr.)
Letters From a Lady of Quality to a Chevalier F
Translated from Edmé Bursault

John Mottley (1692–1750)
Antiochus: A tragedy D
Performed 13 April 1721

Alexander Pennecuik (*d*. 1730)
An Ancient Prophecy Concerning Stock-Jobbing, and the Conduct of the Directors of the South-Sea-Company V

Matthew Prior (1664–1721)
Colin's Mistakes V
Anonymous

John Strype (1643–1737)
Ecclesiastical Memorials NF

Jonathan Swift (1667–1745)
The Bubble V

Jonathan Swift (1667–1745)
A Letter to a Young Gentleman, Lately Enter'd into Holy Orders NF

Thomas Tickell (1686–1740)
Kensington Garden V
Anonymous. Published 1721, dated 1722.

Robert Wodrow (1679–1734)
The History of the Sufferings of the Church of Scotland NF

Edward Young (1683–1765)
The Revenge: A tragedy D
Performed 18 April 1721

1722

- William Wood obtains concession to issue new copper coinage in Ireland
  The Atterbury Plot to proclaim 'James III' king
- Mary Leapor born
  Christopher Smart born
  Joseph Warton born
- John Toland dies
- John Burgoyne born
- John Churchill, duke of Marlborough, dies (16 June)

Penelope Aubin (*c*.1685–1731)
The Life and Amorous Adventures of Lucinda, an English Lady F
Anonymous

Penelope Aubin (*c*.1685–1731)
The Noble Slaves; or, The Lives and Adventures of Two Lords and Two Ladies F

Phanuel Bacon (1700–83)
The Kite: An heroi-comical poem V

Daniel Bellamy, the elder (*b*. 1687)
The Cambro-Britannic Engineer; or, The Original Mouse-Trapp Maker V
Anonymous

Thomas Cooke (1703–56)
Marlborough V
The Duke of Marlborough died on 16 June 1722

Samuel Croxall (1690?–1752) (tr.)
Fables of Aesop and Others F

Daniel Defoe (1660–1731)
Colonel Jack F
Anonymous. Published 1722, dated 1723.

Daniel Defoe (1660–1731)
Due Preparations for the Plague NF
Anonymous

Daniel Defoe (1660–1731)
A Journal of the Plague Year F
Anonymous

Daniel Defoe (1660–1731)
Moll Flanders F
Anonymous. Published 1722, dated 1721.

Daniel Defoe (1660–1731)
Religious Courtship F
Anonymous. Many further editions and abridgements.

John Dennis (1657–1734)
A Defence of Sir Fopling Flutter NF
See Etherege, *The Man of Mode* 1676

William Hamilton [of Gilbertfield] (1665?–1751) (ed.)
The Life and Heroick Actions of the Renoun'd Sir William Wallace EDN

Eliza Haywood (*c*.1693–1756)
The British Recluse; or, The Secret History of Cleomira, Suppos'd Dead F
Written in imitation of Penelope Aubin

Hildebrand Jacob (1693–1739)
Bedlam V
Published 1722, dated 1723

Thomas Parnell (1679–1718)
Poems on Several Occasions V

Ambrose Philips (1674–1749)
The Briton: A tragedy D
Performed 19 February 1722

Allan Ramsay (1686–1758)
Fables and Tales V

William Sewel (1654–1720)
The History of the Rise, Increase, and Progress of the Christian People Called Quakers NF

Sir Richard Steele (1672–1729)
The Conscious Lovers: A comedy D
Published 1722, dated 1723. Performed 7 November 1722.

Elizabeth Thomas (1675–1731)
Miscellany Poems on Several Subjects V
Anonymous

Matthew Tindal (1657–1733)
A Defence of Our Present Happy Establishment NF
Anonymous. A reply to 'Cato's Letters' by John Trenchard (1662–1723) and Thomas Gordon (*d.* 1750), published November 1720–July 1723 (first in the *London Journal* and later in the *British Journal)*, and to Mathias Earbery the younger.

Isaac Watts (1674–1748)
Death and Heaven NF

William Wollaston (1660–1724)
The Religion of Nature Delineated NF

1723

- Louis XV of France obtains his majority
- Sir William Blackstone born
  John Gilbert Cooper born
  Adam Ferguson born
  Richard Price born
  Sir Joshua Reynolds born
  Sara Scott born
  Adam Smith born
- Susanna Centlivre dies
  Thomas D'Urfey dies
  Sarah Egerton dies
  George Whitehead dies
- Sir Godfrey Kneller dies
  Sir Christopher Wren dies
- Increase Mather dies
- J.S. Bach, *Magnificat*

Penelope Aubin (*c*.1685–1731)
The Life of Charlotta du Pont, an English Lady F

Henry Baker (1698–1774)
An Invocation of Health V

Jane Barker (1652–1732)
A Patch-Work Screen for the Ladies; or, Love and Virtue Recommended F
See also *The Lining of the Patch-Work Screen* 1726

Arthur Blackamore (*b.* 1679)
Luck at Last; or, The Happy Unfortunate F

Sir Richard Blackmore (1654–1729)
Alfred: An epick poem V

Susanna Centlivre (1669?–1723)
The Artifice: A comedy D
Performed 2 October 1722

Elijah Fenton (1683–1730)
Mariamne: A tragedy D
Performed 22 February 1723

Eliza Haywood (*c*.1693–1756)
Idalia; or, The Unfortunate Mistress F

Charles Johnson (1679–1748)
Love in a Forest: A comedy D
Performed 9 January 1723

Ambrose Philips (1674–1749)
Humfrey, Duke of Gloucester: A tragedy D
Performed 15 February 1723

Ambrose Philips (1674–1749)
Ode on the Death of William, Earl Cowper V

Matthew Prior (1664–1721)
Down-Hall V

Matthew Prior (1664–1721)
The Turtle and the Sparrow V

Allan Ramsay (1686–1758)
The Fair Assembly V

Allan Ramsay (1686–1758)
The Tea-Table Miscellany [vol. i] ANTH
Anonymous. This collection of Scots songs grew in size and reputation, becoming one of the most popular miscellanies of the century. Volume ii published in 1726; volume iii, 1727; volume iv, 1737.

Edward Ward (1667–1731)
Nuptial Dialogues and Debates V
bao *The London Spy*

1724

- Christopher Anstey born
  Frances Brooke born
  William Gilpin born
  Frances Sheridan born
- Delarivière Manley dies
  Humphrey Prideaux dies
  Elkanah Settle dies
- George Stubbs born
- Robert Harley, earl of Oxford, dies
- Immanuel Kant born
  G.F. Klopstock born
- J.S. Bach, *St John Passion*

Anonymous
A Narrative of All the Robberies, Escapes, &c of John Sheppard F
Feigned autobiography. Sometimes misattributed to Defoe.

Gilbert Burnet (1643–1715)
Bishop Burnet's History of His Own Time [vol. i] NF
Volume ii published in 1734

Anthony Collins (1676–1729)
A Discourse of the Grounds and Reasons of the Christian Religion NF
Anonymous

Matthew Concanen (1701–49) (ed.)
Miscellaneous Poems, Original and Translated ANTH

Mary Davys (1674–1732)
The Reform'd Coquet F

Daniel Defoe (1660–1731)
A New Voyage Round the World F
Anonymous. Published 1724, dated 1725.

Daniel Defoe (1660–1731)
Roxana F
Anonymous. Full title: *The Fortunate Mistress; or, a History of the Life . . . of Mademoiselle de Beleau . . . Being the person known by the name of the Lady Roxana.*

Daniel Defoe (1660–1731)
A Tour Thro' the Whole Island of Great Britain, Divided into Circuits or Journies NF
'By a gentleman'. 3 volumes (1724–6).

John Dennis (1657–1734)
Vice and Luxury Publick Mischiefs; or, Remarks on a Book intitul'd, the Fable of the Bees NF
See Mandeville, *The Fable of the Bees* 1714

Richard Fiddes (1671–1725)
A General Treatise of Morality NF
A response to Mandeville's *Fable of the Bees* 1714 (q.v.)

Richard Fiddes (1671–1725)
The Life of Cardinal Wolsey NF

John Gay (1685–1732)
The Captives: A tragedy D
Performed 15 January 1724

Eliza Haywood (*c*.1693–1756) (tr.)
La Belle Assemblé; or, The Adventures of Six Days F
Anonymous. Translated from *Les journées amusantes* by Madeleine, Madame de Gomez (1684–1770).

Eliza Haywood (*c*.1693–1756)
The Fatal Secret; or, Constancy in Distress F

Eliza Haywood (*c*.1693–1756)
Lasselia; or, The Self-abandon'd F

Eliza Haywood (*c*.1693–1756)
The Masqueraders; or, Fatal Curiosity F
Part ii published in 1725

Eliza Haywood (*c*.1693–1756)
Poems on Several Occasions V
Anonymous. Issued in volume iv of a collection, *Works;* probably not published separately.

Eliza Haywood (*c*.1693–1756)
A Wife to be Lett: A comedy D
Performed 12 August 1723

Thomas Hearne (1678–1735) (ed.)
Robert of Gloucester's Chronicle EDN

Edward Hyde, 1st earl of Clarendon (1609–74)
An Appendix to the History of the Grand Rebellion NF

William Law (1686–1761)
Remarks Upon a Late Book, entituled, The Fable of the Bees NF
Response to Mandeville's *Fable of the Bees* 1714 (q.v.)

John Oldmixon (1673–1742)
The Critical History of England, Ecclesiastical and Civil NF
Anonymous. 2 volumes (1724–6). See also Zachary Grey, *Defence of Our Antient and Modern Historians* 1725; Oldmixon, *Review of Dr Zachary Grey's Defence* 1725; and *Clarendon and Whitlock Compar'd* 1727.

William Philips (*d.* 1734)
Belisarius: A tragedy D
Performed 14 April 1724

Allan Ramsay (1686–1758) (ed.)
The Ever Green: Being a collection of Scots poems ANTH

Allan Ramsay (1686–1758)
Health V

Richard Savage (1697?–1743)
The Tragedy of Sir Thomas Overbury D
Performed 12 June 1723

William Stukeley (1687–1765)
Itinerarium Curiosum; or, An Account of the Antiquitys and Remarkable Curiositys in Nature or Art NF

'M.B. Drapier' [Jonathan Swift (1667–1745)]
A Letter to the Shop-keepers, Tradesmen, Farmers and Common-people of Ireland NF
See also *A Letter to Mr Harding, Some Observations, A Letter to the Whole People of Ireland, Seasonable Advice, A Letter to Viscount Molesworth* (all 1724), and *Fraud Detected* 1725

'M.B. Drapier' [Jonathan Swift (1667–1745)]
A Letter to Mr Harding the Printer NF

'M.B. Drapier' [Jonathan Swift (1667–1745)]
Some Observations Upon a Paper Relating to Woods's Half-pence NF

'M.B. Drapier' [Jonathan Swift (1667–1745)]
A Letter to the Whole People of Ireland NF
On William Wood's coinage. Harding, the printer, was arrested.

Jonathan Swift (1667–1745)
Seasonable Advice NF
Anonymous

'M.B. Drapier' [Jonathan Swift (1667–1745)]
A Letter to the Right Honourable the Lord Viscount Molesworth NF
On William Wood's coinage

Elizabeth Tollet (1694–1754)
Poems on Several Occasions V
Anonymous

William Warburton (1698–1779)
Miscellaneous Translations, in Prose and Verse MISC

Leonard Welsted (1688–1747)
Epistles, Odes, &c., Written on Several Subjects V

1725

- Death of Peter the Great of Russia
- John Delap born
  William Kenrick born
  Mary Latter born
  William Mason born
  John Newton born
- Robert Clive born

Joseph Addison (1672–1719)
Miscellanies, in Verse and Prose MISC

Henry Baker (1698–1774)
Original Poems: Serious and Humorous V
See *The Second Part of Original Poems* 1726

Colley Cibber (1671–1757)
Caesar in Aegypt: A tragedy D

Thomas Cooke (1703–56)
The Battle of the Poets V
Anonymous

Mary Davys (1674–1732)
The Works of Mrs Davys MISC

Daniel Defoe (1660–1731)
The Complete English Tradesman, in Familiar Letters NF
Anonymous. Published in 1725, dated 1726. Volume ii published in 1727.

George Bubb Dodington (1691–1762)
An Epistle to Sir Robert Walpole V
Anonymous. Published 1725, dated 1726.

John Dyer (1699–1757) and others
A New Miscellany MISC
Prints the first version of Dyer's 'Grongar Hill'. Second (pindaric) version in R. Savage's *Miscellaneous Poems and Translations* (1726). Final version published in *Miscellaneous Poems by Several Hands* (1726),

Laurence Echard (*c.*1670–1730)
The History of the Revolution, and the Establishment of England in 1688 NF

John Glanvill (1664?–1735)
Poems V

Zachary Grey (1688–1766)
A Defence of Our Antient and Modern Historians NF
A response to Oldmixon's *Critical History of England* 1724 (q.v.). See also Oldmixon, *A Review of Dr Zachary Grey's Defence* 1725, and *Clarendon and Whitlock Compar'd* 1727.

Eliza Haywood (*c.*1693–1756)
Bath-Intrigues F
Anonymous. Also attributed to Delarivière Manley.

Eliza Haywood (*c.*1693–1756)
Fantomina; or, Love in a Maze F

Eliza Haywood (*c.*1693–1756)
Memoirs of a Certain Island Adjacent to the Kingdom of Utopia F

Eliza Haywood (*c.*1693–1756)
Secret Histories, Novels and Poems F

Francis Hutcheson (1695–1747)
An Inquiry into the Original of Our Ideas of Beauty and Virtue NF
Anonymous

John Oldmixon (1673–1742)
A Review of Dr Zachary Grey's Defence of Our Ancient and Modern Historians NF
bao *The Critical History of England.* See Zachary Grey, *A Defence of Our Antient and Modern Historians* 1725, and also Oldmixon's *Critical History of England* 1724, *Clarendon and Whitlock Compar'd* 1727.

Richardson Pack (1682–1728)
A New Collection of Miscellanies in Verse and Prose MISC

Christopher Pitt (1699–1748) (tr.)
Vida's Art of Poetry V
Translated from Marco Girolamo Vida (*c.*1485–1566)

Alexander Pope (1688–1744) (tr.)
The Odyssey of Homer [vols i, ii, iii] V
Volume i, books i–iv; volume ii, books v–ix; volume iii, books x–xiv. Volume iv (books xv–xix) 1726; volume v (books xx–xxiv) 1726 (qq.v.). Pope was assisted by Elijah Fenton and William Broome.

Allan Ramsay (1686–1758)
The Gentle Shepherd: A Scots pastoral comedy V

Richard Savage (1697?–1743)
The Authors of the Town V
Anonymous

William Shakespeare (1564–1616)
The Works of Shakespear EDN
Edited by Alexander Pope

Thomas Sheridan (1687–1738) (tr.)
The Philoctetes of Sophocles D

Jonathan Swift (1667–1745)
Fraud Detected; or, The Hibernian Patriot NF
Anonymous

Isaac Watts (1674–1748)
Logick NF
See also *The Improvement of the Mind* 1741

George Whitehead (1636?–1723)
The Christian Progress of George Whitehead NF

Edward Young (1683–1765)
The Universal Passion: Satire i V
Anonymous. Satire ii published April 1725; Satire iii, *To Mr Dodington*, April 1725; Satire iv, *To Sir Spencer Compton*, June 1725; Satire v, *On Women*, February 1727; Satire vi, *On Women*, February 1728; *Satire the Last. To Sir Robert Walpole*, published 1726. Collected as *Love of Fame: The Universal Passion, in Seven Characteristical Satires. The second edition* (1728).

1726

- Voltaire banished from France: begins three-year stay in England
- Charles Burney born
  Maria Frances Cowper born
  John Howard born
  Maurice Morgann born
  Thomas Pennant born
- Jeremy Collier dies
  Sir John Vanbrugh dies

Anonymous
Gulliver Decyphered NF
See Swift, *Gulliver's Travels* 1726

Penelope Aubin (*c.*1685–1731)
The Life and Adventures of the Lady Lucy F
See also *The Life and Adventures of the Young Count Albertus* 1728

Henry Baker (1698–1774)
The Second Part of Original Poems: Serious and Humorous V
See *Original Poems* 1725

Jane Barker (1652–1732)
The Lining of the Patch-Work Screen F
See also *A Patch-Work Screen for the Ladies* 1723

Joseph Butler (1692–1752)
Fifteen Sermons Preached at the Rolls Chapel NF

William Rufus Chetwood (*d.* 1766)
The Voyages and Adventures of Captain Robert Boyle F
Anonymous. Extremely popular. Sometimes erroneously attributed to Defoe, or to Benjamin Victor.

Anthony Collins (1676–1729)
The Scheme of Literal Prophecy Considered NF
Anonymous. A Reply to Edward Chandler (1668?–1750), Bishop of Lichfield, who had written against Collins's *Discourse of the Grounds and Reason of the Christian Religion* 1724 (q.v.).

Daniel Defoe (1660–1731)
An Essay Upon Literature; or, An Enquiry into the Antiquity and Original of Letters NF
Anonymous

Daniel Defoe (1660–1731)
The Political History of the Devil, as well Ancient as Modern NF
Anonymous

Daniel Defoe (1660–1731)
A System of Magick; or, A History of the Black Art NF
Anonymous. Published 1726, dated 1727.

John Dennis (1657–1734)
The Stage Defended NF
A reply to William Law's *The Absolute Unlawfulness of the Stage-Entertainment* 1726 (q.v.)

Eliza Haywood (*c.*1693–1756)
The City Jilt; or, The Alderman Turn'd Beau F
Anonymous

Eliza Haywood (*c.*1693–1756)
The Mercenary Lover; or, The Unfortunate Heiress F

Aaron Hill (1685–1750)
The Fatal Extravagance: A tragedy . . . By Joseph Mitchell D
In fact written by Hill for the benefit of Joseph Mitchell (1684–1738). Performed 21 April 1721.

William Law (1686–1761)
The Absolute Unlawfulness of the Stage-Entertainment Fully Demonstrated NF
See also John Dennis, *The Stage Defended* 1726

William Law (1686–1761)
A Practical Treatise upon Christian Perfection NF

William Penn (1644–1718)
A Collection of the Works of William Penn WKS

William Penn (1644–1718)
Fruits of a Father's Love NF

Alexander Pope (1688–1744) (tr.)
The Odyssey of Homer [vols iv, v] V
Volume iv (books xv–xix), volume v (books xx–xxiv). Volume i (books i–iv), volume ii (books v–ix), volume iii (books x–xiv), 1725 (q.v.).

William Pulteney (1684–1764) and **Alexander Pope** (1688–1744)
The Discovery; or, The Squire Turn'd Ferret V
Anonymous. Published 1726, dated 1727. A satirical ballad on the claim of Mary Toft to have given birth to rabbits.

Richard Savage (1697?–1743) (ed.)
Miscellaneous Poems and Translations V
Includes Savage's account of his early life. Poems by Savage, Aaron Hill, John Dyer, and others.

William Somervile (1675–1742)
Occasional Poems, Translations, Fables, Tales, &c V
Published 1726, dated 1727

Thomas Southerne (1659–1746)
Money the Mistress D
Performed 19 February 1726. Based on Madame d'Aulnoy (*c.*1650–1705), *Relation du voyage d'Espagne*.

Joseph Spence (1699–1768)
An Essay on Pope's Odyssey NF
Anonymous

Jonathan Swift (1667–1745)
Cadenus and Vanessa V
Anonymous. Written in 1713 for Esther Vanhomrigh ('Vanessa').

Jonathan Swift (1667–1745)
Gulliver's Travels F

Anonymous. Published October 1726. Full title: *Travels into Several Remote Nations of the World. In four parts, by Lemuel Gulliver*. Part i: 'A Voyage to Lilliput'; part ii: 'A Voyage to Brobdingnag'; part iii: 'A Voyage to Laputa, Balnibarbi, Glubbdubdrib, Luggnagg and Japan'; part iv: 'A Voyage to the Houyhnhnms'.

Lewis Theobald (1688–1744)
Shakespeare Restored NF
A criticism of Pope's edition 1725 (q.v.)

James Thomson (1700–48)
Winter V
Published in April 1726. Five editions by March 1728. The poem was increased to 787 lines in 1730. See also *Summer* 1727; *Spring* 1728; *The Seasons* 1730.

Various
The Craftsman PER
Begun December 1726 by 'Caleb D'Anvers' (Nicholas Amhurst and others). The final number published in May 1727. Other contributors included Henry Pulteney and Henry St-John, Lord Bolingbroke.

1727

- Siege of Gibraltar (Feb.) begins the Anglo-Spanish War (–1728)
  Death of George I (11 June)
  GEORGE II (–1760)
- Hester Chapone born
  John Hoole born
- Thomas Gainsborough born
  John Wilkes born
- Sir Isaac Newton dies
  William Wotton dies

Anonymous
Memoirs of the Court of Lilliput F
Sometimes attributed to Eliza Haywood

Anonymous
Several Copies of Verses on Occasion of Mr Gulliver's Travels V
Usually attributed to Pope, but possibly a joint production of Pope, John Gay, and John Arbuthnot

'Louisa' [Elizabeth Boyd (*fl.* 1727–45)]
Variety V

Mary Davys (1674–1732)
The Accomplish'd Rake; or, Modern Fine Gentleman F
Anonymous

Daniel Defoe (1660–1731)?
Conjugal Lewdness; or, Matrimonial Whoredom NF
Anonymous. Probably by Defoe.

Daniel Defoe (1660–1731)
An Essay on the History and Reality of Apparitions NF
Anonymous. Republished in 1728 as *The Secrets of the Invisible World Disclos'd; or, An Universal History of Apparitions, by Andrew Moreton, Esq.*

Daniel Defoe (1660–1731)
A New Family Instructor NF
Anonymous. See also *The Family Instructor* 1715.

Philip Frowde (*d.* 1738)
The Fall of Saguntum: A tragedy D
Performed 16 January 1727

John Gay (1685–1732)
Fables V
A second volume published in 1738 (q.v.); both volumes published together in 1750. See also Cotton, *Visions in Verse* 1751.

Eliza Haywood (*c.*1693–1756)
Cleomelia; or, The Generous Mistress F

Eliza Haywood (*c.*1693–1756)
The Fruitless Enquiry F

Eliza Haywood (*c.*1693–1756)
The Perplex'd Dutchess; or, Treachery Rewarded F
Anonymous. A political satire on George I.

Eliza Haywood (*c.*1693–1756)
Philidore and Placentia; or, L'amour trop delicat F
Anonymous

Eliza Haywood (*c.*1693–1756)
The Secret History of the Present Intrigues of the Court of Caramania F
Anonymous. A key-novel based on the English court.

Edward Hyde, 1st earl of Clarendon (1609–74)
A Collection of Several Tracts NF

John Oldmixon (1673–1742)
Clarendon and Whitlock Compar'd NF
bao *The Critical History of England*

Christopher Pitt (1699–1748)
Poems and Translations V

James Ralph (1705?–62)
The Tempest; or, The Terror of Death V

Henry St-John, Viscount Bolingbroke (1678–1751)
The Occasional Writer PER
Anonymous. Published in 4 numbers.

Jonathan Swift (1667–1745), **Alexander Pope** (1688–1744), and others
Miscellanies in Prose and Verse ANTH
The three volumes called 'First', 'Second', and 'Last'. Contains prose and verse by Swift, Pope, John Arbuthnot, and John Gay. 'Last Volume' published in 1728, dated 1727. 'The Third Volume' (actually the fourth) published in 1732 (q.v.). 'Volume the Fifth' published in 1735 (q.v.), contains nothing by Pope.

Lewis Theobald (1688–1744)
The Rape of Proserpine D
Anonymous. Performed 13 February 1727.

James Thomson (1700–48)
A Poem Sacred to the Memory of Sir Isaac Newton V
Newton died on 20 March 1727

James Thomson (1700–48)
Summer V
See also *Winter* 1726, *Spring* 1728, *The Seasons* 1730

William Warburton (1698–1779)
A Critical and Philosophical Enquiry into the Causes of Prodigies and Miracles NF
Anonymous

John Wright (*fl.* 1708–27)
Spiritual Songs for Children V

1728

- Robert Bage born
  James Cook born
  Francis Gentleman born
  Oliver Goldsmith born
  Thomas Warton, the younger, born
- White Kennett dies
- Robert Adam born
- Cotton Mather dies

Joseph Addison (1672–1719)
The Christian Poet: A miscellany of divine poems V

Penelope Aubin (*c*.1685–1731)
The Life and Adventures of the Young Count Albertus F
Sequel to *The Life and Adventures of the Lady Lucy* 1726 (q.v.)

Peter Browne (*c*.1665–1735)
The Procedure, Extent, and Limits of Human Understanding NF
Anonymous

'Captain George Carleton'
The Memoirs of an English Officer F
Sometimes misattributed to Defoe. Possibly partly factual. Widely reprinted.

Thomas Cooke (1703–56) (tr.)
The Works of Hesiod V

John Dennis (1657–1734)
Remarks on Mr Pope's Rape of the Lock NF

Henry Fielding (1707–54)
Love in Several Masques: A comedy D
Performed 16 February 1728

Henry Fielding (1707–54)
The Masquerade V
'By Lemuel Gulliver, Poet Laureat to the King of Lilliput'

John Gay (1685–1732)
The Beggar's Opera D/OP
Performed 29 January 1728. See also *Polly* 1729.

James Gibbs (1682–1754)
A Book of Architecture NF

Eliza Haywood (*c*.1693–1756)
The Agreeable Caledonian; or, Memoirs of Signiora di Morella F
Part ii published in 1729. Revised in 1768 as *Clementina*.

Francis Hutcheson (1695–1747)
An Essay on the Nature and Conduct of the Passions and Affections NF
bao *The Inquiry into the Original of Our Ideas of Beauty and Virtue*

David Mallet (1705?–65)
The Excursion V

John Mottley (1692–1750)
Penelope: A dramatic opera D/OP
Anonymous. Performed 8 May 1728. A comic opera satirizing Pope's *Odyssey*. Mottley was assisted by Thomas Cooke.

John Oldmixon (1673–1742) (tr. and ed.)
The Arts of Logick and Rhetorick NF
Anonymous. Translated from Dominique Bouhours (1628–1702), *Manière de bien penser.*

John Oldmixon (1673–1742)
An Essay on Criticism NF
bao *The Critical History of England*. Issued with the 1728 edition of *The Critical History of England* (first published in 1724, q.v.).

Christopher Pitt (1699–1748) (tr.)
An Essay on Virgil's Aeneid V
See also *The Aeneid of Virgil* 1740, *Works of Virgil* 1753

Alexander Pope (1688–1744)
The Dunciad: An heroic poem V
Published 18 May 1728. Enlarged in 1729 (q.v.).

James Ralph (1705?–62)
Night V

James Ralph (1705?–62)
Sawney: An heroic poem. Occasion'd by the Dunciad V
Anonymous. Addressed to John Toland, James Moore Smith, and Lawrence Eusden.

James Ralph (1705?–62)
Zeuma; or, The Love of Liberty V
Published 1728, dated 1729

Allan Ramsay (1686–1758)
Poems by Allan Ramsay V

Elizabeth Rowe (1674–1737) (tr.)
Friendship in Death NF
Anonymous. Dedicated to Edward Young.

Richard Savage (1697?–1743)
The Bastard V

Richard Savage (1697?–1743)?
Nature in Perfection; or, The Mother Unveil'd V
Anonymous. Authorship uncertain.

George Sewell (1690?–1726)
Posthumous Works of Dr George Sewell WKS

Thomas Sheridan (1687–1738) (tr.)
The Satyrs of Persius V
In Latin and English

Jonathan Swift (1667–1745)
A Short View of the State of Ireland NF

Jonathan Swift (1667–1745) and **Thomas Sheridan** (1687–1738)
The Intelligencer PER
Published in 20 numbers. Numbers 1, 3, 5, 7–10, 15, 19, and 20 are by Swift.

Lewis Theobald (1688–1744)
Double Falsehood; or, The Distrest Lovers . . . Written originally by W. Shakespeare D
Performed 13 December 1727. Based on *Cardenio*, apparently a lost play by Shakespeare and Fletcher, acted in 1613. Theobald claimed to have used a prompt copy but failed to produce or publish it.

James Thomson (1700–48)
Spring V
See also *Winter* 1726, *Summer* 1727, *The Seasons* 1730

Sir John Vanbrugh (1664–1726)
The Provok'd Husband D
Performed, completed by Colley Cibber, 10 January 1728

Edward Ward (1667–1731)
Durgen; or, A Plain Satyr upon a Pompous Satyrist . . . V
Anonymous. Published 1728, dated 1729.

William Wycherley (1641–1716)
The Posthumous Works of William Wycherley WKS
Edited by Lewis Theobald. See also *Posthumous Works* 1729.

Edward Young (1683–1765)
Ocean V
bao *The Universal Passion*

Edward Young (1683–1765)
A Vindication of Providence; or, A True Estimate of Human Life NF

1729

- Edmund Burke born
  John Cunningham born
  John Duncombe born
  Charlotte Lennox born?
  John Moore born
  Thomas Percy born
  Clara Reeve born
- Sir Richard Blackmore dies
  Abel Boyer dies
  Anthony Collins dies
  William Congreve dies
  William King, archbishop of Dublin, dies
  Sir Richard Steele dies
- Catherine the Great born
  G.E. Lessing born
- J.S. Bach, *St Matthew Passion*

Anonymous
The Adventures of Abdalla, Son of Hanif F
Translated by W. Hatchett from Jean Paul Bignon (1662–1743), *Les avantures d'Abdalla*

Anonymous
The Fair Hebrew; or, A True but Secret History of Two Jewish Ladies F
Sometimes attributed to Eliza Haywood

James Bramston (1694?–1744)
The Art of Politicks V
Anonymous

Moses Browne (1704–87)
Piscatory Eclogues V

Henry Carey (1687?–1743)
Poems on Several Occasions V
The third edition, 'much enlarged'. First published in 1713 (q.v.).

Colley Cibber (1671–1757)
Love in a Riddle: A pastoral D
Published 1729, misdated 1719. Performed 7 January 1729) Written in imitation of Gay's *Beggar's Opera* 1728 (q.v.). Converted to *Damon and Phillida* (also 1729), a ballad opera.

Thomas Cooke (1703–56)
Tales, Epistles, Odes, Fables, &c. V
Anonymous

John Gay (1685–1732)
Polly: An opera D/OP
Unacted sequel to *The Beggar's Opera* 1728 (q.v.). First performed, in a cut version by George Colman, 19 June 1777.

Eliza Haywood (*c.*1693–1756)
Frederick, Duke of Brunswick-Lunenburgh: A tragedy D
Performed 4 March 1729

Soame Jenyns (1704–87)
The Art of Dancing V
Anonymous

Charles Johnson (1679–1748)
The Village Opera D/OP
Performed 6 February 1729

William Law (1686–1761)
A Serious Call to a Devout and Holy Life NF
Ten editions by 1772

Daniel Mace (*d.* 1753) (tr.)
The New Testament in Greek and English BIB
A diglot New Testament, containing the Greek text with an English translation, and a precursor of modern critical texts.

Sir Isaac Newton (1642–1727)
The Mathematical Principles of Natural Philosophy NF
A translation of Newton's *Philosophiae Naturalis Principia Mathematica* 1687 (q.v.)

John Oldmixon (1673–1742)
The History of England, During the Reigns of the Royal House of Stuart NF
bao *The Critical History of England*. Published 1729, dated 1730. See also *History of England* 1735, 1739.

Alexander Pope (1688–1744)
The Dunciad, Variorum V

William Pulteney (1684–1764)
The Honest Jury; or, Caleb Triumphant V
Anonymous

James Ralph (1705?–62)
Clarinda; or, The Fair Libertine V
Anonymous

Elizabeth Rowe (1674–1737)
Letters on Various Occasions, in Prose and Verse MISC
bao *Friendship in Death*. See also *Letters Moral and Entertaining* 1731, 1733.

Richard Savage (1697?–1743)
The Wanderer V

Thomas Sherlock (1678–1761)
The Tryal of the Witnesses of the Resurrection of Jesus NF

Jonathan Swift (1667–1745)
The Journal of a Dublin Lady V
Anonymous

Jonathan Swift (1667–1745)
A Modest Proposal PS

Jonathan Swift (1667–1745)
An Epistle Upon an Epistle From a Certain Doctor to a Certain Great Lord V
Anonymous. Published 1729, dated 1730. A satire on Patrick Delany (1685?–1768), *Epistle to His Exellency John Lord Carteret* (1729, dated 1730). See also *A Libel on D--- D------* 1730.

James Thomson (1700–48)
Britannia V
Anonymous

William Wycherley (1641–1716)
The Posthumous Works of William Wycherley [vol. ii] WKS
Volume i published in 1728 (q.v.)

1730

- Colley Cibber appointed Poet Laureate
- David Erskine Baker born
  John Scott born
  Thomas Tyrwhitt born
- Laurence Echard dies
  Elijah Fenton dies
- Josiah Wedgwood born

The Grub-Street Journal PER
Edited by John Martyn and R. Russel. Published in 418 weekly numbers (January 1730–December 1737).

Joseph Addison (1672–1719)
The Evidences of the Christian Religion NF
First published in *Works* 1721 (q.v.). Many editions through the 18th century.

John Banks (1709–51)
The Weaver's Miscellany V

Theophilus Cibber (1703–58)
Patie and Peggy; or, The Fair Foundling: A Scottish ballad opera D/OP
Performed 25 November 1730

'Scriblerus Tertius' [Thomas Cooke (1703–56)?]
The Candidates for the Bays V
Possibly by Cooke

Philip Doddridge (1702–51)
Free Thoughts on the Most Probable Means of Reviving the Dissenting Interest NF
A reply to Strickland Gough (*d.* 1752), *An Enquiry into the Causes of the Decay of the Dissenting Interest* (1730)

Stephen Duck (1705–56)
Poems on Several Subjects V

Henry Fielding (1707–54)
The Author's Farce; and The Pleasures of the Town D
Performed 30 March 1730

Henry Fielding (1707–54)
Rape upon Rape; or, The Justice Caught in his own Trap: A comedy D
Anonymous. Performed 23 June 1730. Republished 1730 as *The Coffee-House Politician.*

Henry Fielding (1707–54)
The Temple Beau: A comedy D
Performed 26 January 1730

Henry Fielding (1707–54)
Tom Thumb: A tragedy D
Anonymous. Performed 24 April 1730. Revised 1731 as *The Tragedy of Tragedies; or, The life and death of Tom Thumb the great.*

John Hervey, 2nd Baron Hervey (1696–1743)
Observations on the Writings of the Craftsman NF
Anonymous. With reference to *The Craftsman* 1726 (q.v.). *Farther Observations* 1730; *A Supplement to the Observations* 1731.

George Lillo (1693–1739)
Silvia; or, The Country Burial: An opera D/OP
Published 1730, dated 1731. Performed 10 November 1730.

George Lyttelton, 1st Baron Lyttelton (1709–73)
An Epistle to Mr Pope V
Anonymous

James Miller (1706–44)
The Humours of Oxford: A comedy D
'By a gentleman of Wadham College'. Performed 9 January 1730.

John Mottley (1692–1750)
The Widow Bewitch'd: A comedy D
Anonymous. Performed 8 June 1730.

Matthew Pilkington (*c.*1700–74)
Poems on Several Occasions V

Jonathan Swift (1667–1745)
A Libel on D---- D--------, and a Certain Great Lord V
Anonymous. A satire on Patrick Delany (1685?–1768), *Epistle to His Exellency John Lord Carteret* (1729, dated 1730). See also *An Epistle Upon an Epistle* 1729.

Lewis Theobald (1688–1744)
Perseus and Andromeda D
Anonymous. Performed 2 January 1730.

Elizabeth Thomas (1675–1731)
The Metamorphosis of the Town; or, A View of the Present Fashions V
Anonymous.

James Thomson (1700–48)
The Seasons, A Hymn, A Poem to the Memory of Sir Isaac Newton, and Britannia, a Poem V
Includes *Autumn.* See also *Winter* 1726; *Summer* 1727; *Spring* 1728.

James Thomson (1700–48)
The Tragedy of Sophonisba D
Performed 28 February 1729

Matthew Tindal (1657–1733)
Christianity as Old as the Creation; or, The Gospel, a Republication of the Religion of Nature NF
Anonymous

William Wotton (1666–1727)
A Discourse Concerning the Confusion of Languages at Babel NF

Edward Young (1683–1765)
Two Epistles to Mr Pope V
Anonymous

1731

- Charles Churchill born
  William Cowper born
  Erasmus Darwin born
  Catherine Macaulay born
- Mary Astell dies
  Penelope Aubin dies
  Charles Boyle, 4th earl of Orrery, dies
  Daniel Defoe dies
  Edward Ward dies

The Gentleman's Magazine PER
'By Sylvanus Urban of Aldermanbury'. Published monthly (January 1731–September 1731). Continued well into the 19th century with various changes of subtitle. Begun and edited by Edward Cave ('Sylvanus Urban', 1691–1754).

Anonymous
The Jovial Crew: A comic-opera D/OP
Performed 2 February 1731. Based on Richard Brome's *A Jovial Crew* (1652, q.v., performed 1641), with new songs by Matthew Concanen and others.

Anonymous
The Life of Mr Cleveland, Natural Son of Oliver Cromwell F
Extremely popular translation of *Le Philosophe anglais ou Histoire de monsieur Cleveland* (1731–9) by Antoine-François, abbé Prévost d'Exiles (1697–1763).

'Caleb D'Anvers' [Nicholas Amhurst (1697–1742)]
A Collection of Poems on Several Occasions V

Samuel Boyse (1708–49)
Translations and Poems Written on Several Subjects V

Thomas Cooke (1703–56)
The Triumphs of Love and Honour D
Performed 18 August 1731

Ralph Cudworth (1617–88)
A Treatise Concerning Eternal and Immutable Morality NF

Robert Dodsley (1703–64)
An Epistle from a Footman in London to the Celebrated Stephen Duck V
Anonymous

Robert Dodsley (1703–64)
A Sketch of the Miseries of Poverty V
Anonymous

Henry Fielding (1707–54)
The Letter-Writers; or, A New Way to Keep a Wife at Home: A farce D
Performed 24 March 1731

Philip Frowde (*d.* 1738)
Philotas: A tragedy D
Performed 3 February 1731

Aaron Hill (1685–1750)
Advice to the Poets V

Aaron Hill (1685–1750)
Athelwold: A tragedy D
Performed 10 December 1731

Charles Johnson (1679–1748)
The Tragedy of Medea D
Performed 11 December 1730

William King (1650–1729)
An Essay on the Origin of Evil NF
A translation of King's *De Origine Mali* 1702 (q.v.). Includes an 'Account of the origin of the passions and affections' by John Gay.

William Law (1686–1761)
The Case of Reason; or, Natural Religion, Fairly Stated NF
A response to Matthew Tindal, *Christianity as Old as the Creation* 1730 (q.v.)

George Lillo (1693–1739)
The London Merchant; or, The History of George Barnwell D
Performed 22 June 1731

David Mallet (1705?–65)
Eurydice: A tragedy D
Performed 22 February 1731

William Oldys (1696–1761)
A Dissertation Upon Pamphlets NF

Alexander Pope (1688–1744)
An Epistle to the Right Honourable Richard Earl of Burlington V
The Epistle 'Of Taste', known subsequently as 'Of False Taste'. See also Bramston, *The Man of Taste* 1733.

James Ralph (1705?–62)
The Fall of the Earl of Essex D
Performed 1 February 1731. Altered from John Banks, *The Unhappy Favourite* (1682, q.v., performed 1681).

Elizabeth Rowe (1674–1737)
Letters Moral and Entertaining NF
bao *Friendship in Death*. See also *Letters on Various Occasions* 1729, *Letters Moral and Entertaining* 1733.

Joseph Trapp (1679–1747) (tr.)
The Works of Virgil V
Trapp's translation of the *Aeneid* was first published in two volumes, 1718–20

1732

- Covent Garden Theatre opened
- George Colman, the elder, born
  Richard Cumberland born
  William Falconer born
  John Ogilvie born
- Francis Atterbury dies
  Jane Barker dies
  Mary Davys dies
  John Gay dies
- Warren Hastings born
- Franz Joseph Haydn born
  Jacques Necker born
  George Washington born

Anonymous
Castle-Howard V
Sometimes attributed to Anne Ingram, Viscountess Irwin (*c*.1696–1764)

Anonymous
The Gentleman's Study in Answer to the Lady's Dressing-Room V
'By Miss W----'. A reply to Swift's *The Lady's Dressing-Room* 1732 (q.v.).

The London Magazine; or, Gentleman's Monthly Intelligencer PER
Launched in April 1732 as a rival to the *Gentleman's Magazine* 1731 (q.v.). Edited by Isaac Kimber from 1732–55.

George Berkeley (1685–1753)
Alciphron; or, The Minute Philosopher, in Seven Dialogues NF
Anonymous. Contains a revised version of *An Essay Towards a New Theory of Vision* 1709 (q.v.).

Elizabeth Boyd (*fl.* 1727–45)
The Happy-Unfortunate; or, The Female-Page F

Henry Carey (1687?–1743)
Amelia: A new English opera D/OP

Henry Carey (1687?–1743)
Teraminta: An opera D/OP

Mary Davys (1674–1732)
The False Friend; or, The Treacherous Portugueze F
A version of *The Cousins*, included in Davys' *Works* (1725)

Philip Doddridge (1702–51)
Sermons on the Religious Education of Children NF

Robert Dodsley (1703–64)
A Muse in Livery; or, The Footman's Miscellany V

Henry Fielding (1707–54)
The Lottery: A farce D
Anonymous. Performed 1 January 1732.

Henry Fielding (1707–54)
The Modern Husband: A comedy D
Performed 14 February 1732

Henry Fielding (1707–54)
The Covent-Garden Tragedy D
Anonymous. Performed 1 June 1732.

Henry Fielding (1707–54)
The Old Debauchees: A comedy D
bao *The Modern Husband*. Performed 1 June 1732.

Henry Fielding (1707–54) (tr.)
The Mock Doctor; or, The Dumb Lady Cur'd: A comedy D
Anonymous. Performed 23 June 1732. Translated from Molière (1622–73), *Le Médecin malgré lui* (1666).

John Gay (1685–1732)
Acis and Galatea: An English pastoral opera D/OP

George Granville, Lord Lansdowne (1667–1735)
The Genuine Works in Verse and Prose WKS

William King (1685–1763)
The Toast: An epic poem V
Supposedly a translation from the Latin of 'Frederick Scheffer'—in fact an original work by King

George Lyttelton, 1st Baron Lyttelton (1709–73)
The Progress of Love V
Anonymous

John Milton (1608–74)
Milton's Paradise Lost EDN
Edited by Richard Bentley

Daniel Neal (1678–1743)
The History of the Puritans or Protestant Non-Conformists NF
4 volumes (1732–8)

Richard Savage (1697?–1743)
An Epistle to the Right Honourable Sir Robert Walpole V

Jonathan Swift (1667–1745)
The Grand Question Debated V
Anonymous

Jonathan Swift (1667–1745)
The Lady's Dressing-Room V
See also the anonymous (by 'Miss W----') *The Gentleman's Study* 1732, and Wortley Montagu, *The Dean's Provocation* 1734

Jonathan Swift (1667–1745), **Alexander Pope** (1688–1744), and others
Miscellanies: The Third Volume MISC
Actually the fourth volume. See *Miscellanies* 1727. Prose and verse by Swift, Pope, John Arbuthnot, and John Gay. See also *Miscellanies* 1735.

Anonymous
A Collection of Pieces in Verse and Prose . . . Publish'd on Occasion of the Dunciad ANTH
Edited by Richard Savage. Contains pieces by Edward Young, W. Harte, and James Miller, and four previously published pamphlets.

Isaac Watts (1674–1748)
A Short View of the Whole Scripture History NF

Leonard Welsted (1688–1747)
Of Dulness and Scandal V

Gilbert West (1703–56)
Stowe V
Anonymous

1733

- Robert Lloyd born
  Joseph Priestley born
  James Scott born
- John Dunton dies
  Bernard Mandeville dies
  Matthew Tindal dies
- Franz Anton Mesmer born
  Christoph Martin Wieland born
- François Couperin dies
- J.S. Bach, *Mass in B Minor* (first version)

Anonymous
Verses Address'd to the Imitator of the First Satire of the Second Book of Horace V
'By a lady' (probably Lady Mary Wortley Montagu)

John Banks (1709–51)
Poems on Several Occasions V

George Berkeley (1685–1753)
The Theory of Vision: or Visual Language NF
bao *Alciphron*. See also *An Essay Towards a New Theory of Vision* 1709.

Samuel Bowden (*fl.* 1726–71)
Poetical Essays on Several Occasions [vol. i] V
Volume ii published in 1735

James Bramston (1694?–1744)
The Man of Taste V
bao *The Art of Politicks*. A response to Pope's *Epistle to Burlington* 1731 (q.v.). See also Newcomb, *The Woman of Taste* 1733.

'Joseph Gay' [John Durant Breval (1680?–1738)**]**
Morality in Vice: An heroi-comical poem V
Reissued as *The Lure of Venus* in 1733

Peter Browne (*c.*1665–1735)
Things Supernatural and Divine Conceived by Analogy with things Natural and Human NF
bao *The Procedure, Extent, and Limits of Human Understanding*

Mary Chandler (1687–1745)
A Description of Bath V

Henry Fielding (1707–54) (adap.)
The Miser: A comedy D
Performed 17 February 1733. From Molière's *L'avare* (performed 1668), itself an adaptation of the *Aulularia* of Plautus.

Thomas Fitzgerald (1695?–1752)
Poems on Several Occasions V

John Gay (1685–1732)
Achilles: An opera D/OP
Performed 10 February 1733. Gay died in December 1732.

'Peter Drake' [Matthew Green (1696–1737)**]**
The Grotto V

James Hammond (1710–42)
An Elegy to a Young Lady, in the Manner of Ovid V
Anonymous

Eliza Haywood (*c.*1693–1756)
The Opera of Operas; or, Tom Thumb the Great D/OP
Anonymous. Written with William Hatchett. Performed 31 May 1733. Altered from Fielding's *Tragedy of Tragedies* (1731), itself a revision of his *Tom Thumb* 1730 (q.v.).

John Hervey, 2nd Baron Hervey (1696–1743)
An Epistle from a Nobleman to a Doctor of Divinity V
Anonymous

George Lyttelton, 1st Baron Lyttelton (1709–73)
Advice to a Lady V
Anonymous

Samuel Madden (1686–1765)
Memoirs of the Twentieth Century F
A satire on George II and his court

David Mallet (1705?–65)
Of Verbal Criticism: An epistle to Mr Pope V

Mary Masters (1694?–1771)
Poems on Several Occasions V

Thomas Newcomb (1682?–1765)
The Woman of Taste V
Anonymous. Attribution to Newcomb is probable. Occasioned by James Bramston's *The Man of Taste* 1733 (above).

Alexander Pope (1688–1744)
Of the Use of Riches: An Epistle to Lord Bathurst V
Published 1733, dated 1732

Alexander Pope (1688–1744)
The First Satire of the Second Book of Horace V
Parallel English and Latin texts. See also *First Satire* 1734.

Alexander Pope (1688–1744)
An Essay on Man [Epistles i–iii] V
Anonymous. See also *An Essay on Man* 1734.

Alexander Pope (1688–1744)
The Impertinent; or, A Visit to the Court V
Anonymous

Elizabeth Rowe (1674–1737)
Letters Moral and Entertaining, in Prose and Verse MISC
bao *Friendship in Death*. See also *Letters on Various Occasions* 1729, *Letters Moral and Entertaining* 1731.

William Shakespeare (1564–1616)
The Works of Shakespeare EDN
Edited by Lewis Theobald

Jonathan Swift (1667–1745)
The Life and Genuine Character of Doctor Swift V
See also *Verses on the Death of Dr Swift* 1739

Jonathan Swift (1667–1745)
On Poetry V
Anonymous. See also *A Rap at the Rhapsody* 1734.

Isaac Watts (1674–1748)
Philosophical Essays on Various Subjects NF

1734

- James Arbuckle dies
  John Dennis dies
- George Romney born

Anonymous
A Rap at the Rhapsody V
A response to Swift's *On Poetry* 1733 (q.v.)

Jane Adams (1710–65)
Miscellany Poems V

Joseph Addison (1672–1719)
A Discourse on Antient and Modern Learning NF

John Arbuthnot (1667–1735)
Gnothi Seauton: Know Yourself V
Anonymous

Francis Atterbury (1662–1732)
Sermons on Several Occasions NF
Two further volumes published in 1734

Mary Barber (1690?–1757)
Poems on Several Occasions V

Isaac Hawkins Browne, the elder (1705–60)
On Design and Beauty V
Anonymous

'Benjamin Bounce' [Henry Carey (1687?–1743)]
The Tragedy of Chrononhotonthologos D
Performed 22 February 1734

Robert Dodsley (1703–64)
An Epistle to Mr Pope V

Stephen Duck (1705–56)
Truth and Falsehood V

William Dunkin (1709?–65)
The Lover's Web V

William Dunkin (1709?–65)
The Poet's Prayer V

Henry Fielding (1707–54)
Don Quixote in England: A comedy D
Performed 5 April 1734

Henry Fielding (1707–54)
The Intriguing Chambermaid: A comedy D
Performed 15 January 1734. Taken from Jean-François Regnard (1655–1709), *Le Retour imprévu.*

John Jortin (1698–1770)
Remarks on Spenser's Poems NF

Lady Mary Wortley Montagu (1689–1762)
The Dean's Provocation for Writing the Lady's Dressing-Room V
Anonymous. See Swift, *The Lady's Dressing-Room* 1732.

Alexander Pope (1688–1744)
An Epistle to Lord Cobham V
Published 1734; dated 1733. The first moral epistle, 'Of the Knowledge and Characters of Men'.

Alexander Pope (1688–1744)
An Essay on Man [Epistle iv] V
Anonymous. Epistles i–iii published in 1733 (q.v.); all four Epistles published together 1734.

Alexander Pope (1688–1744)
The First Satire of the Second Book of Horace V
See the *First Satire of Horace* 1733. Also includes the *Second Satire of the Second Book of Horace* (also published separately 1734).

Alexander Pope (1688–1744)
Sober Advice From Horace V
Anonymous. Parallel English and Latin texts.

Jonathan Richardson (1665–1745)
Explanatory Notes on Milton's Paradise Lost NF
Written with his son Jonathan (1694–1771)

George Sale (1697?–1736) (tr.)
The Koran NF

Jonathan Swift (1667–1745)
A Beautiful Young Nymph Going to Bed V
Anonymous

Robert Tatersal (*fl.* 1734)
The Bricklayer's Miscellany; or, Poems on Several Subjects V

Joseph Trapp (1679–1747)
Thoughts Upon the Four Last Things V
Anonymous. Published in four parts (*Death, Judgment, Heaven, Hell*), 1734–5.

1735

- James Beattie born
  Isaac Bickerstaffe born?
  John Langhorne born
- John Arbuthnot dies
  Thomas Hearne dies
  Samuel Wesley, the elder, dies
- Rameau, *Les Indes Galantes*

Anonymous
The Dramatic Historiographer; or, The British Theatre Delineated NF
Sometimes attributed to Eliza Haywood

George Berkeley (1685–1753)
The Querist [pt i] NF
Anonymous. Misdated 1725. Part ii published in 1736; part iii, 1737.

Jane Brereton (1685–1740)
Merlin V
'By a lady'

Henry Brooke (1703–83)
Universal Beauty V
Anonymous. Published in six parts, 1735–6.

Henry Carey (1687?–1743)
The Honest Yorkshireman: A ballad farce D
Published 1735, dated 1736. Performed 11 July 1735.

Robert Dodsley (1703–64)
Beauty; or, The Art of Charming V
Anonymous

Robert Dodsley (1703–64)
The Toy-Shop: A dramatick satire D
Performed 3 February 1735

William Duncombe (1690–1769)
Junius Brutus: A tragedy D
Performed November 1734

Henry Fielding (1707–54)
An Old Man Taught Wisdom; or, The Virgin Unmask'd: A farce D
Anonymous. Performed 6 January 1735.

Henry Fielding (1707–54)
The Universal Gallant; or, The Different Husbands: A comedy D
Performed 10 February 1735

Benjamin Hoadly (1676–1761)
A Plain Account of the Nature and End of the Sacrament of the Lord's-Supper NF
Anonymous. See also William Law 1737.

John Hughes (1677–1720)
Poems on Several Occasions V

Hildebrand Jacob (1693–1739)
Brutus the Trojan, Founder of the British Empire V

Hildebrand Jacob (1693–1739)
The Works of Hildebrand Jacob WKS

Samuel Johnson (1709–84) (tr.)
A Voyage to Abyssinia V
Translated from Jerónymo Lobo (1596?–1678)

George Lillo (1693–1739)
The Christian Hero: A tragedy D
Performed 13 January 1735

George Lyttelton, 1st Baron Lyttelton (1709–73)
Letters from a Persian in England, to his Friend at Isphahan F
Popular and influential

William Melmoth, the younger (1710–99)
Of Active and Retired Life V
Anonymous

James Miller (1706–44) (adap.)
The Man of Taste: A comedy D
Anonymous. Performed 6 March 1735. Adapted from Molière.

John Oldmixon (1673–1742)
The History of England, During the Reigns of William and Mary, Anne, George I NF
See also *History of England* 1730, 1739

Alexander Pope (1688–1744)
An Epistle from Mr Pope to Dr Arbuthnot V
Published 1735, dated 1734

Alexander Pope (1688–1744)
Of the Characters of Women V
The second moral essay

Alexander Pope (1688–1744)
The Works of Mr Alexander Pope [vol. ii] WKS
Works printed for first time include 'The Author to the Reader', 'The Second Satire of Dr John Donne', 'On Charles Earl of Dorset', 'On Mr Elijah Fenton'. See also *Works* 1717, 1736, 1737.

Alexander Pope (1688–1744)
Letters of Mr Pope, and Several Eminent Persons NF
Curll's unauthorized edition. See also *Letters of Mr Alexander Pope* 1737.

Alexander Pope (1688–1744)
Mr Pope's Literary Correspondence for Thirty Years, 1704 to 1734 NF
Volume the Second and *Volume the Third* published 1735; *Volume the Fourth*, 1736; *Volume the Fifth*, 1737. See also *Letters of Mr Pope* 1735, *Letters of Mr Alexander Pope* 1737.

Samuel Richardson (1689–1761)
A Seasonable Examination of the Pleas and Pretensions of the Proprietors of, and Subscribers to, Play-Houses NF
Anonymous

Henry St-John, Viscount Bolingbroke (1678–1751)
A Dissertation upon Parties NF
First published in *The Craftsman* 1733. 'Caleb D'Anvers' was a pseudonym adopted by Bolingbroke, Nicholas Amhurst, and others.

Richard Savage (1697?–1743)
The Progress of a Divine V

William Somervile (1675–1742)
The Chace V

Jonathan Swift (1667–1745) and others
Miscellanies in Prose and Verse: Volume the Fifth ANTH
Anonymous. 'Completes' the previous four volumes of *Miscellanies* (see 1727, 1732).

Jonathan Swift (1667–1745)
The Works of Jonathan Swift WKS
The first authoritative edition of Swift's works

Lewis Theobald (1688–1744)
The Fatal Secret: A tragedy D
Performed 4 April 1733

James Thomson (1700–48)
Antient and Modern Italy Compared V
The first part of *Liberty*. See also *Greece* 1735; *Rome* 1735; *Britain, The Prospect* 1736.

James Thomson (1700–48)
Greece V
Part ii of *Liberty*. See also *Antient and Modern Italy* 1735, *Rome* 1735; *Britain, The Prospect* 1736.

James Thomson (1700–48)
Rome V
Part iii of *Liberty*. See also *Antient and Modern Italy* 1735, *Greece* 1735; *Britain, The Prospect* 1736.

1736

- Charles Jenner born
  Robert Jephson born
  James Macpherson born
  James Ridley born
  John Horne Tooke born
- George Sale dies
- James Watt born
- Nicholas Hawksmoor dies
  Bernard Lintot dies

Anonymous
*The Life of Marianne; or, The Adventures of the Countess of **** F
Translation (in 3 volumes, 1736–42?) of *La Vie de Marianne* (1731–41, unfinished) by Pierre Carlet de Chamblain de Marivaux (1688–1763). Also adapted by Mary Collyer in *The Virtuous Orphan* (1742).

John Armstrong (1709–79)
The Oeconomy of Love V
Anonymous

Isaac Hawkins Browne, the elder (1705–60)
A Pipe of Tobacco V
Anonymous. Imitates Colley Cibber, Ambrose Philips, James Thomson, Edward Young, Pope, and Swift.

Joseph Butler (1692–1752)
The Analogy of Religion, Natural and Revealed, to the Constitution and Course of Nature NF

Thomas Carte (1686–1754)
A History of the Life of James, Duke of Ormond NF

William Rufus Chetwood (*d.* 1766)
The Voyages, Travels and Adventures of William Owen Gwin Vaughan F
Anonymous

Stephen Duck (1705–56)
Poems on Several Occasions V

Henry Fielding (1707–54)
Pasquin: A dramatick satire on the times D
Performed 5 March 1736

Eliza Haywood (*c.*1693–1756)
Adventures of Eovaai, Princess of Ijaveo F
Reissued 1741 as *The Unfortunate Princess*

Aaron Hill (1685–1750) (tr.)
The Tragedy of Zara D
Performed 12 January 1736. From Voltaire (1694–1778), *Zaïre* (1732).

Aaron Hill (1685–1750) (tr.)
Alzira: A tragedy D
Performed 18 June 1736. From Voltaire (1694–1778), *Alzire* (1736).

William Melmoth, the younger (1710–99)
Two Epistles of Horace Imitated V

Sir Isaac Newton (1642–1727)
The Method of Fluxions and Infinite Series NF
A translation of Newton's *Analysis per quantitatum series*

Alexander Pope (1688–1744)
The Works of Alexander Pope
[vols iii–iv] WKS
Volume iii: fables, translations, and imitations; volume iv: *Dunciad*, etc. See also *Works* 1717, 1735, 1737.

Elizabeth Rowe (1674–1737)
The History of Joseph V
bao *Friendship in Death*

William Stukeley (1687–1765)
Palaeographia Sacra NF

James Thomson (1700–48)
Britain V
Part iv of *Liberty*. See also *Antient and Modern Italy, Greece, Rome* 1735; *The Prospect* 1736.

James Thomson (1700–48)
The Prospect V
Fifth and last part of *Liberty*. See also *Antient and Modern Italy, Greece, Rome* 1735; *Britain* 1736. Revised text of complete poem published in Thomson's *Works* 1738 (q.v.).

William Warburton (1698–1779)
The Alliance Between Church and State NF
Anonymous

1737

- Death of Queen Caroline (20 Nov.)
  Licensing Act reduces number of London theatres and increases censorship
- Edward Gibbon born
  Edward Jerningham born
  Thomas Paine born
  Richard Watson born
- Elizabeth Rowe dies

Anonymous
A Letter from Mrs Jane Jones, alias Jenny Diver, in Drury Lane F
On being a mistress. Possibly by Jane Webb.

Henry Carey (1687?–1743)
The Dragon of Wantley: A burlesque opera D/OP
Performed 26 October 1737

Henry Carey (1687?–1743)
The Musical Century, in One Hundred English Ballads V/MUS
With Carey's own musical settings

Philip Doddridge (1702–51)
Submission to Divine Providence in the Death of Children NF

Robert Dodsley (1703–64)
The King and the Miller of Mansfield D
Performed 29 January 1737. See also *Sir John Cockle at Court* 1738.

Stephen Duck (1705–56)
The Vision V
On the death of Queen Caroline (20 November 1737)

Henry Fielding (1707–54)
The Historical Register for the Year 1736 D
bao *Pasquin*. Performed 21 March 1737. Also includes *Eurydice Hiss'd* (performed 13 April 1737). Fielding's *Eurydice; or, The devil hen-peck'd* had been performed in February 1737 and was published in his *Miscellanies* 1743 (q.v.).

Richard Glover (1712–85)
Leonidas V
Enlarged from 9 to 12 books in 1770

Robert Gould (*d.* 1709)
Innocence Distress'd; or, The Royal Penitents: A tragedy D

Matthew Green (1696–1737)
The Spleen V

William Law (1686–1761)
A Demonstration of the Gross and Fundamental Errors of a Late Book NF
A critical response to Benjamin Hoadly, *A Plain Account* 1735 (q.v.)

George Lillo (1693–1739)
Fatal Curiosity: A true tragedy D
Performed 27 May 1736. Prologue by Henry Fielding.

William Oldys (1696–1761)
The British Librarian NF
Anonymous. First published in six parts 1737.

Alexander Pope (1688–1744)
Horace His Ode to Venus V

Alexander Pope (1688–1744)
The Second Epistle of the Second Book of Horace, Imitated V

Alexander Pope (1688–1744)
Letters of Mr Alexander Pope, and Several of his Friends NF
The first 'authorized' edition. See *Letters of Mr Pope* 1735, *Mr Pope's Literary Correspondence* 1735.

Alexander Pope (1688–1744)
The First Epistle of the Second Book of Horace, Imitated V

Alexander Pope (1688–1744)
The Works of Alexander Pope [vols v–vi] WKS
Letters. See also *Works* 1717, 1735, 1736.

Elizabeth Rowe (1674–1737)
Devout Exercises of the Heart NF
Edited by Isaac Watts

William Shenstone (1714–63)
Poems Upon Various Occasions V
Anonymous. Contains the earliest version (in 12 stanzas) of 'The School-mistress'. Extended version (28 stanzas) published separately in 1742 (q.v.). The final text (35 stanzas) published in volume i of Dodsley's *Collection of Poems* (1748).

Jonathan Swift (1667–1745)
A Proposal for Giving Badges to the Beggars in all the Parishes of Dublin NF

1738

- Parliamentary debate on 'Jenkins' Ear'
- Mary Darwall born
  John Wolcot ('Peter Pindar') born
- John Durant Breval dies

Anonymous
Memoirs of a Man of Quality F
Translation of Antoine-François, abbé Prévost d'Exiles (1697–1763), *Mémoires et aventures d'un homme de qualité* (1728–31, the 7th and final volume of which contained the story of Manon Lescaut, later published separately).

Mark Akenside (1721–70)
A British Philippic V
Anonymous

John Banks (1709–51)
Miscellaneous Works in Verse and Prose MISC

Elizabeth Carter (1717–1806)
Poems Upon Particular Occasions V
Anonymous

Alexander Cruden (1701–70)
A Complete Concordance to the Holy Scriptures of the Old and New Testament DICT

Robert Dodsley (1703–64)
The Art of Preaching V
Anonymous

Robert Dodsley (1703–64)
Sir John Cockle at Court D
Performed 23 February 1738. See *The King and the Miller of Mansfield* 1737.

John Gay (1685–1732)
Fables: Volume the Second V
See *Fables* 1727

Samuel Johnson (1709–84)
London V

George Lillo (1693–1739)
Marina D
Performed 1 August 1738

Alexander Pope (1688–1744)
The Sixth Epistle of the First Book of Horace Imitated V

Alexander Pope (1688–1744)
The First Epistle of the First Book of Horace Imitated V

Alexander Pope (1688–1744) and **Jonathan Swift** (1667–1745)
An Imitation of the Sixth Satire of the Second Book of Horace V
Pope's portion was anonymous. Swift's contribution (part i) was first published in *Miscellanies*, 'The Last Volume' (i.e. the third) 1727 (q.v.).

Alexander Pope (1688–1744)
One Thousand Seven Hundred and Thirty Eight V

Alexander Pope (1688–1744)
The Universal Prayer V
bao *The Essay on Man*

Alexander Pope (1688–1744)
One Thousand Seven Hundred and Thirty Eight: Dialogue II V

Frances Seymour, countess of Hertford, later **duchess of Somerset** (1699–1754)
The Story of Inkle and Yarrico V
Anonymous. Includes 'An Epistle From Yarrico to Inkle, after he had left her in slavery', an imitation of Pope's 'Eloisa to Abelard' (in *Works* 1717, q.v.).

Jonathan Swift (1667–1745)
The Beasts Confession to the Priest V

Jonathan Swift (1667–1745)
A Complete Collection of Genteel and Ingenious Conversation PS
Anonymous. See also *Tittle Tattle* 1749.

James Thomson (1700–48)
Agamemnon: A tragedy D
Performed 6 April 1738

James Thomson (1700–48)
The Works of Mr Thomson WKS

William Warburton (1698–1779)
The Divine Legation of Moses Demonstrated NF
Published in 2 volumes 1738–41. See also *A Vindication* 1738.

William Warburton (1698–1779)
A Vindication of the author of the Divine Legation of Moses NF
See above

John Wesley (1703–91)
A Collection of Psalms and Hymns V
First published at Charlestown, 1737. See also *A Collection of Psalms and Hymns* 1741.

George Whitefield (1714–70)
A Journal of a Voyage from London to Savannah in Georgia NF
See also *A Continuation* 1739

1739

- War declared on Spain
  Dick Turpin hanged (7 Apr.)
- Hugh Kelly born
- Laurence Eusden dies
  Hildebrand Jacob dies
  George Lillo dies
- Handel, *Saul*; *Israel in Egypt*

The Works of Molière, French and English EDN
Edited and translated by Henry Baker (1698–1774) and James Miller (1706–44)

The Scots Magazine PER
Published monthly (February 1739–December 1803)

Penelope Aubin (*c*.1685–1731)
A Collection of Entertaining Histories and Novels F

Samuel Boyse (1708–49)
Deity V

Moses Browne (1704–87)
Poems on Various Subjects V

Henry Carey (1687?–1743)
Nancy; or, The Parting Lovers D
Performed 1 December 1739. Music by Carey.

Elizabeth Carter (1717–1806) (tr.)
Examination of Mr Pope's Essay on Man NF
Anonymous. Translated from Jean-Pierre Crousaz (1663–1750).

Elizabeth Carter (1717–1806) (tr.)
Sir Isaac Newton's Philosophy Explain'd for the Use of Ladies NF
Anonymous. Translated from Francesco Algarotti (1712–64).

Mary Collier (1688?–1762)
The Woman's Labour: An epistle to Mr Stephen Duck V

Thomas Cooke (1703–56)
The Mournful Nuptials; or, Love the Cure of all Woes: A tragedy D

Philip Doddridge (1702–51) (ed.)
The Family Expositor; or, A Paraphrase and Version of the New Testament NF
Published in 6 volumes 1739–56

'Capt. Hercules Vinegar' [Henry Fielding (1707–54) (ed.)]
The Champion; or, British Mercury PER
Edited with James Ralph. Published between November 1739 and June 1741.

Richard Glover (1712–85)
London; or, The Progress of Commerce V

David Hume (1711–76)
A Treatise of Human Nature NF
Anonymous. A third book ('Of Morals') published in 1740. See also *An Abstract* 1740.

William Law (1686–1761)
The Grounds and Reasons of Christian Regeneration NF

David Mallet (1705?–65)
Mustapha: A tragedy D
Performed 13 February 1739

'Elijah Jenkins' [John Mottley (1692–1750)]
Joe Miller's Jests; or, The Wits Vade-Mecum NF

Robert Craggs Nugent (1709–88)
An Epistle to the Right Honourable, Sir Robert Walpole V
Attributed to Nugent

Robert Craggs Nugent (1709–88)
An Ode on Mr Pulteney V
Anonymous

Robert Craggs Nugent (1709–88)
An Ode, to His Royal Highness on His Birthday V
Anonymous. 'His Royal Highness' = Frederick Louis.

Robert Craggs Nugent (1709–88)
Odes and Epistles V
Anonymous

John Oldmixon (1673–1742)
The History of England During the Reigns of Henry VIII. Edward VI. Queen Mary. Queen Elizabeth NF
See also *History of England* 1730, 1735

Laetitia Pilkington (1708?–50)
The Statues; or, The Trial of Constancy V
Anonymous

Samuel Richardson (1689–1761) (ed.)
Aesop's Fables F
Published 1739, dated 1740. Based on L'Estrange's version 1692 (q.v.).

Elizabeth Rowe (1674–1737)
Miscellaneous Works in Prose and Verse WKS

Thomas Sheridan (1687–1738) (ed.)
The Satires of Juvenal Translated V
Anonymous. Latin and English on facing pages.

William Shirley (*fl.* 1739–80)
The Parricide; or, Innocence in Distress: A tragedy D
Performed 17 January 1639

Jonathan Swift (1667–1745)
Verses on the Death of Dr Swift, Written by Himself V
Revised and enlarged version of *The Life and Genuine Character of Doctor Swift* 1731 (q.v.)

James Thomson (1700–48)
Edward and Eleonora: A tragedy D

Joseph Trapp (1679–1747)
The Nature, Folly, Sin, and Danger, of Being Righteous Over-much NF
With reference to George Whitefield

Isaac Watts (1674–1748)
The World To Come NF

John Wesley (1703–91)
Hymns and Sacred Poems V
See also *A Collection of Psalms and Hymns* 1741

George Whitefield (1714–70)
A Continuation of the Reverend Mr Whitefield's Journal NF
See *A Journal of a Voyage* 1738

Paul Whitehead (1710–74)
Manners: A satire V

1740

- Death of Charles VI, the last Hapsburg Emperor: accession of Maria Theresa
  Death of Frederick William I of Prussia: accession of Frederick II ('the Great')
  War of the Austrian Succession (-1748)
  George Anson begins his voyage round the world (Sept. 1740-June 1744)
- James Boswell born
  Charlotte Brooke born?
  Sir Philip Francis born
  Susannah Gunning born?
  Augustus Toplady born
- Jane Brereton dies
  Thomas Tickell dies

Colley Cibber (1671–1757)
An Apology for the Life of Mr Colley Cibber NF

John Dyer (1699–1757)
The Ruins of Rome V

Richard Glover (1712–85)
Admiral Hosier's Ghost V
Anonymous. Publication date uncertain. Single sheet slip-song.

David Hume (1711–76)
An Abstract of a Book Lately Published; Entituled, A Treatise of Human Nature NF
Anonymous. See *A Treatise of Human Nature* 1739.

William Law (1686–1761)
An Earnest and Serious Answer to Dr Trapp's Discourse NF
See Joseph Trapp 1739

William Law (1686–1761)
An Appeal to all that Doubt, or Disbelieve the Truths of the Gospel NF

George Lillo (1693–1739)
Britannia and Batavia: A masque D
Unacted

George Lillo (1693–1739)
Elmerick; or, Justice Triumphant: A tragedy D
Performed 23 February 1740

William Oldys (1696–1761)
The Life of Sir Walter Ralegh NF
First published in Raleigh's *History of the World* (1736)

Christopher Pitt (1699–1748) (tr.)
The Aeneid of Virgil V
Books i–iv first published in 1736. See also *An Essay on Virgil's Aeneid* 1728, *Works of Virgil* 1753.

William Pulteney (1684–1764)
An Epistle from L---- to Lord C----------d V
Anonymous. Written as from Thomas Coke, Baron Lovel and subsequently earl of Leicester, to Lord Chesterfield.

Samuel Richardson (1689–1761)
Pamela; or, Virtue Rewarded [vols i, ii] F
Anonymous. Published 1740, dated 1741. Volumes iii and iv published in 1741 (q.v.). Published complete in 4 volumes in 1742.

Henry St-John, Viscount Bolingbroke (1678–1751)
The Idea of a Patriot King NF

William Stukeley (1687–1765)
Stonehenge: A temple restor'd to the British Druids NF

James Thomson (1700–48) and **David Mallet** (1705?–65)
Alfred: A masque D
Anonymous. Performed 1 August 1740. See also *Alfred* 1751.

William Warburton (1698–1779)
A Vindication of Mr Pope's Essay on Man NF
bao *The Divine Legation of Moses*. Revised and enlarged as *A Critical and Philosophical Commentary on Mr Pope's Essay on Man* 1742 (q.v.).

George Whitefield (1714–70)
A Short Account of God's Dealings with the Reverend George Whitefield NF
A Full Account also published in 1740; *A Further Account* published at London in 1747 (first published Boston, 1746)

1741

- Henry Fuseli born
  Edmond Malone born
  Hester Lynch Piozzi (Mrs Thrale) born
  Sarah Trimmer born
  Arthur Young born
- Angelica Kauffmann born
- Jethro Tull dies
- Pierre Choderlos de Laclos born

Anonymous
The Life of Pamela F
An unattributed piratical adaptation of Richardson's *Pamela* 1740 (q.v.).

Anonymous
Pamela Censured NF
See Samuel Richardson, *Pamela* 1740. Answered by John Kelly, *Pamela's Conduct in High Life* 1741.

Anonymous
Pamela; or, Virtue Triumphant: A comedy D
See Richardson, *Pamela* 1740. No acting history. Possibly written by James Dance.

Thomas Betterton (1635?–1710)
The History of the English Stage, From the Restauration to the Present Time NF
Anonymous. Compiled by John Oldys and Curll from Betterton's papers.

Geoffrey Chaucer (1340?–1400)
The Canterbury Tales of Chaucer EDN
Edited by George Ogle

Robert Dodsley (1703–64)
The Blind Beggar of Bethnal Green D
Performed 3 April 1741

Stephen Duck (1705–56)
Every Man in his Own Way V

'Mr Conny Keyber' [Henry Fielding (1707–54)]
An Apology for the Life of Mrs Shamela Andrews F
See Richardson, *Pamela* 1740

Thomas Francklin (1721–84) (ed.)
Of the Nature of the Gods V
An anonymous edition of Cicero's *De natura deorum*

David Garrick (1717–79)
The Lying Valet D
Published 1741, dated 1742. Performed 30 November 1741.

Eliza Haywood (*c.*1693–1756)
Anti-Pamela; or, Feign'd Innocence Detected; in a Series of Syrena's Adventures F
Anonymous. See Richardson, *Pamela* 1740.

David Hume (1711–76)
Essays Moral and Political [vol. i] NF
Anonymous. Volume ii published in 1742 (q.v.); both volumes published together 1743. See also *Three Essays* 1748.

John Kelly (*c.*1684)
Pamela's Conduct in High Life F
Anonymous. An unauthorized continuation of the first two volumes of Richardson's *Pamela* 1740 (q.v.), this work was largely responsible for Richardson's writing the third and fourth volumes of *Pamela* 1741 (q.v.). See also *Pamela Censured* 1741.

Robert Craggs Nugent (1709–88)
An Ode to Mankind V
Anonymous

Alexander Pope (1688–1744)
Memoirs of the Extraordinary Life, Works, and Discoveries of Martinus Scriblerus F
In *The Works of Mr Alexander Pope, in Prose, Vol. ii.* Written with John Arbuthnot.

Charles Povey (1652?–1743)
The Virgin in Eden; or, The State of Innocency F
Anonymous

Samuel Richardson (1689–1761)
Letters Written to and for Particular Friends NF
Anonymous. Known as *Familiar Letters.*

Samuel Richardson (1689–1761)
Pamela; or, Virtue Rewarded [vols iii, iv] F
Anonymous. Published 1741, dated 1742. Sometimes known as *Pamela in her Exalted Condition.* See *Pamela* volumes i, ii 1740.

William Shenstone (1714–63)
The Judgment of Hercules V
Anonymous

Jonathan Swift (1667–1745)
Dean Swift's Literary Correspondence NF
Pope filed a bill against the publisher, Curll, for piratically publishing these letters

Jonathan Swift (1667–1745)
Some Free Thoughts on the Present State of Affairs NF
Anonymous

Isaac Watts (1674–1748)
The Improvement of the Mind NF
Supplement to *Logick* 1725 (q.v.)

Leonard Welsted (1688–1747)
The Summum Bonum; or, Wisest Philosophy V

John Wesley (1703–91) and **Charles Wesley** (1707–88)
A Collection of Psalms and Hymns V
See also *Hymns and Sacred Poems* 1739

George Whitefield (1714–70)
A Letter to the Reverend John Wesley NF
First published Boston, 1740

Edward Young (1683–1765)
Poetical Works of the Reverend Edward Young V

1742

- Resignation of Robert Walpole
- Mary Alcock born (c.1742)
  William Combe born
  Joseph Cradock born
  Thomas Penrose born
  Isaac Reed born
  Anna Seward born
- Nicholas Amhurst dies
  Richard Bentley dies
  John Oldmixon dies
- Handel's *Messiah* first performed in Dublin (8 Apr.)

Colley Cibber (1671–1757)
A Letter from Mr Cibber, to Mr Pope NF
See also *A Second Letter* 1743, *Another Occasional Letter* 1744

William Collins (1721–59)
Persian Eclogues V
Anonymous. Supposedly a translation. The second edition of 1757 was called *Oriental Eclogues.*

Thomas Cooke (1703–56)
Mr Cooke's Original Poems V

Philip Doddridge (1702–51)
Evidences of Christianity NF

Henry Fielding (1707–54)
Joseph Andrews F
Full title: *The History of the Adventures of Joseph Andrews . . . Written in imitation of the manner of Cervantes*

James Hammond (1710–42)
Love Elegies V
Anonymous. Published 1742, dated 1743. Preface by the earl of Chesterfield.

Eliza Haywood (*c.*1693–1756) (tr.)
The Virtuous Villager, or Virgin's Victory F
A translation of *La paysanne parvenue* by Charles de Fieux, chevalier de Mouhy (1701–84)

David Hume (1711–76)
Essays Moral and Political [vol. ii] NF
Anonymous. Volume i published in1741 (q.v.); both volumes published together, 1743. See also *Three Essays* 1748.

Charles Jennens (1700–73)
Messiah V/MUS
Libretto, from biblical text, with music by Handel. Performed 23 March 1742.

James Merrick (1720–69) (tr.)
The Destruction of Troy V
A translation from the Greek of Triphiodorus

John Oldmixon (1673–1742)
Memoirs of the Press, Historical and Political NF

William Shenstone (1714–63)
The School-Mistress V
bao *The Judgment of Hercules*. The second version (28 stanzas). First version (12 stanzas) in *Poems* 1737 (q.v.); final version (35 stanzas) in Dodsley's *Collection* volume i, 1748 (q.v.).

William Somervile (1675–1742)
Field Sports V

Horace Walpole (1717–97) and **Sir Charles Hanbury Williams** (1708–59)?
The Lessons for the Day PS
Anonymous. Published 1742, dated 1741. A mock-biblical satire on William Pulteney and his friends. The 'second lesson' is by Walpole. Co-authorship attributed to Sir C.H. Williams. The work created a fashion for the mock-biblical 'lesson' and 'chronicle' as a form of political satire.

William Warburton (1698–1779)
A Critical and Philosophical Commentary on Mr Pope's Essay on Man NF
See *A Vindication of Mr Pope's Essay on Man* 1740

John Wesley (1703–91)
The Character of a Methodist NF

John Wesley (1703–91)
The Principles of a Methodist NF
See *The Principles of a Methodist Farther Explain'd* 1746

George Whitefield (1714–70)
Nine Sermons NF

Sir Charles Hanbury Williams (1708–59)
The Country Girl: An ode V
Anonymous

Edward Young (1683–1765)
The Complaint; or, Night-Thoughts on Life, Death and Immortality: Night the First V
Anonymous. *Night the Second* ('On Time, Death, Friendship') and *Night the Third* ('Narcissa') also published in 1742; *Night the Fourth* ('The Christian Triumph') and *Night the Fifth* ('The Relapse'), 1743; *Night the Sixth* ('The Infidel Reclaim'd', Part the First) and *Night the Seventh*, ('Being the Second Part of the Infidel Reclaim'd'), 1744; *Night the Eighth* ('Virtue's

Apology; or, The Man of the World Answer'd'), 1745; *Night the Ninth* ('The Consolation'), 1746 (dated 1745).

1743

- Battle of Dettingen (27 June)
- Anna Laetitia Barbauld born
  Jane Bowdler born
  Hannah Cowley born
  Lady Eleanor Fenn ('Mrs Teachwell') born
  William Paley born
- Henry Carey dies
  John Hervey, 2nd Baron Hervey, dies
  Richard Savage dies
- Thomas Jefferson born

Robert Blair (1699–1746)
The Grave V

Samuel Boyse (1708–49)
Albion's Triumph V

James Bramston (1694?–1744)
The Crooked Six-pence V
Anonymous. Attributed to Bramston in Isaac Reed's *Repository* 1777 (q.v.). A parody of John Philips' *The Splendid Shilling* 1705 (q.v.), the text of which is included.

John Brown (1715–66)
Honour V
Anonymous

William Rufus Chetwood (*d.* 1766)
The Twins; or, The Female Traveller F

Colley Cibber (1671–1757)
The Egotist; or, Colley Upon Cibber NF
Includes several references to the Pope–Cibber quarrel

Colley Cibber (1671–1757)
A Second Letter from Mr Cibber to Mr Pope NF
See *A Letter from Mr Cibber* 1742, *Another Occasional Letter* 1744

William Collins (1721–59)
Verses Humbly Address'd to Sir Thomas Hanmer on his Edition of Shakespear's Works V
'By a Gentleman of Oxford'

Thomas Cooke (1703–56)
An Epistle to the Countess of Shaftesbury V

Philip Doddridge (1702–51)
The Principles of the Christian Religion V

Robert Dodsley (1703–64)
Pain and Patience V

Henry Fielding (1707–54)
Miscellanies MISC
Volume ii contains *A Journey from this World to the Next*; volume iii contains *The Life of Mr Jonathan Wild the Great* (see also *Jonathan Wild* 1754)

Henry Fielding (1707–54)
The Wedding-Day: A comedy D
Performed 17 February 1743. Also included in volume ii of Fielding's *Miscellanies* 1743 (q.v.).

Philip Francis (1708?–73) (tr.)
The Odes, Epodes, and Carmen Seculare of Horace V
Two further volumes published in 1746 as *The Satires of Horace* and *The Epistles and Art of Poetry of Horace* respectively. An immensely popular and much reprinted translation of Horace's poems. See also *A Poetical Translation of the Works of Horace* 1747.

John Gay (1685–1732)
The Distress'd Wife: A comedy D
Performed 5 March 1734

Eliza Haywood (*c.*1693–1756)
A Present for a Servant-Maid; or, The Sure Means of Gaining Love and Esteem NF
Anonymous. A conduct book.

Aaron Hill (1685–1750)
The Fanciad: An heroic poem V
Anonymous

David Mallet (1705?–65)
Poems on Several Occasions V

Henry St-John, Viscount Bolingbroke (1678–1751)
Remarks on the History of England NF
First published in *The Craftsman* (December 1730–May 1731). Dedication signed 'Caleb D'Anvers' (i.e. Bolingbroke).

William Shakespeare (1564–1616)
The Works of Shakespear EDN
Edited by Sir Thomas Hanmer. The dramatic works only.

William Stukeley (1687–1765)
Abury: A temple of the British Druids NF
Intended as a companion volume to Stukeley's *Stonehenge* 1740 (q.v.)

William Whitehead (1715–85)
An Essay on Ridicule V

1744

- Elizabeth Bonhote born
  Richard Lovell Edgeworth born
  Rowland Hill born
- James Bramston dies
  James Miller dies
  Alexander Pope dies
  Lewis Theobald dies

Mark Akenside (1721–70)
The Pleasures of Imagination V
Anonymous. Published in January 1744. The poem remained in print throughout most of the 18th century.

Mark Akenside (1721–70)
An Epistle to Curio V
Anonymous. Published in November 1744. 'Curio' = William Pulteney, earl of Bath.

John Armstrong (1709–79)
The Art of Preserving Health V

George Berkeley (1685–1753)
Siris NF
Published in March 1744

Jane Brereton (1685–1740)
Poems on Several Occasions V
Dated 1744 but possibly published in January 1745

Colley Cibber (1671–1757)
Another Occasional Letter from Mr Cibber to Mr Pope NF
See *A Letter from Mr Cibber* 1742, *A Second Letter* 1743

Mary Collyer (*d.* 1763)
Felicia to Charlotte F
Anonymous

Thomas Cooke (1703–56)
Love the Cause and Cure of Grief; or, The Innocent Murderer D
Performed 19 December 1743

Robert Dodsley (1703–64) (ed.)
A Select Collection of Old Plays EDN

Sarah Fielding (1710–68)
The Adventures of David Simple F
'By a Lady'. Published in May? 1744. The second edition was revised by Henry Fielding, with preface, in 1744. See also *Familiar Letters* 1747, *Adventures of David Simple: Volume the Last* 1753.

David Garrick (1717–79)
An Essay on Acting NF
Anonymous. Attributed to Garrick.

William Havard (1710?–78)
Regulus: A tragedy D
Performed 21 February 1744

Eliza Haywood (*c.*1693–1756) (ed.)
The Female Spectator PER
Published in 24 number (April 1744–March 1746). Issues of this women's periodical included essays on conduct and philosophy, poetry, and letters (genuine and fictitious) from readers. Frequently reprinted during the 18th century.

Eliza Haywood (*c.*1693–1756)
The Fortunate Foundlings F
Anonymous

Samuel Johnson (1709–84) (ed.)
An Account of the Life of John Philip Barretier NF
Anonymous. Compiled by Johnson from the letters of François Baratier (1682–1751).

Samuel Johnson (1709–84)
An Account of the Life of Mr Richard Savage NF
Anonymous. Published in February 1744. See also *The Works of Richard Savage* 1775.

James Miller (1706–44)
Joseph and his Brethren: A sacred drama D
Performed March 1744. Music by Handel.

James Miller (1706–44)
Mahomet the Imposter: A tragedy D
Anonymous. Performed 25 April 1744.

Edward Moore (1712–57)
Fables for the Female Sex V
Anonymous. The last three fables were written by Henry Brooke.

William Oldys (1696–1761) (ed.)
The Harleian Miscellany EDN
Anonymous. Published in 8 volumes (1744–6). Introduction by Samuel Johnson.

Jonathan Swift (1667–1745)
Three Sermons NF
Published in October/November 1744

Joseph Warton (1722–1800)
The Enthusiast; or, The Lover of Nature V
Anonymous. Published on 8 March 1744.

Paul Whitehead (1710–74)
The Gymnasiad; or, Boxing Match V

1745

- Charles Edward Stuart ('The Young Pretender') lands in Scotland (23 July): second Jacobite uprising (see 1715)

English army defeated by the Jacobites at Prestonpans (21 Sept.)
Mme de Pompadour installed as Louis XV's mistress at Versailles

- Charles Dibdin born
  William Hayley born
  Thomas Holcroft born
  Henry Mackenzie born
  Hannah More born
  Henry James Pye born
- Mary Chandler dies
  William Meston dies
  Jonathan Swift dies
  Thomas Warton, the elder, dies
- Robert Walpole, earl of Orford, dies

Mark Akenside (1721–70)
Odes on Several Subjects V
Anonymous

Thomas Broughton (1704–74)
Hercules: A musical drama D
Anonymous. Libretto only. The music was written by Handel.

John Brown (1715–66)
An Essay on Satire: Occasion'd by the death of Mr Pope V
Anonymous. Pope had died on 30 May 1744.

John Gilbert Cooper (1723–69)
The Power of Harmony V
Anonymous

Philip Doddridge (1702–51)
The Rise and Progress of Religion in the Soul NF

Robert Dodsley (1703–64)
Rex et Pontifex D
Unacted

Henry Fielding (1707–54)
A Serious Address to the People of Great Britain NF
Anonymous. On the events following the landing of Charles Edward Stuart, the Young Pretender, on Eriskay Island in Scotland on 23 July 1745.

Henry Fielding (1707–54)
The True Patriot; and The History of Our Own Times PER
Published between November 1745 and June 1746

Charles Jennens (1700–73)
Belshazzar: An oratorio V/MUS
Performed March 1745. Music by Handel.

Samuel Johnson (1709–84)
Miscellaneous Observations on the Tragedy of Macbeth NF
Anonymous

Samuel Johnson (1709–84)
Proposals for Printing a New Edition of the Plays of William Shakespear NF
Anonymous. The proposed work was never published.

Samuel Madden (1686–1765)
Boulter's Monument V
Assisted by Samuel Johnson

Moses Mendes (*d.* 1758) (tr.)
Henry and Blanche; or, The Revengeful Marriage V
Translated from Alain-René Lesage (1668–1747)

Glocester Ridley (1702–74)
Jovi Eleutherio; or, An Offering to Liberty V
Anonymous

Thomas Scott (1705–75)
England's Danger and Duty V
Anonymous

Jonathan Swift (1667–1745)
Directions to Servants PS

William Thompson (1712?–66)
Sickness V
The first two books. Book iii published in 1746.

James Thomson (1700–48)
Tancred and Sigismunda: A tragedy D
Performed 18 March 1745

1746

- Battle of Falkirk (17 Jan.)
  Final defeat of the Jacobites at Culloden by the duke of Cumberland (16 Apr.)
  Charles Edward Stuart escapes to France with the help of Flora MacDonald
- Robert Blair dies
  Sir Thomas Hanmer dies
  Mary Leapor dies
  Thomas Southerne dies
- Madame de Genlis born
  James Wyatt born
- Handel, *Judas Maccabaeus*

John Arbuthnot (1667–1735)
Miscellanies MISC

Thomas Blacklock (1721–91)
Poems on Several Occasions V

'Tim Bobbin' [John Collier (1708–86)]
A View of the Lancashire Dialect F

William Collins (1721–59)
Odes on Several Descriptive and Allegoric Subjects V
Published 1746, dated 1747

Thomas Cooke (1703–56)
A Hymn to Liberty V

Zachary Grey (1688–1766)
A Word or Two of Advice to William Warburton NF
See also *A Free and Familiar Letter* 1750

James Hervey (1714–58)
Meditations Among the Tombs NF

Soame Jenyns (1704–87)
The Modern Fine Gentleman V
Anonymous. See also *The Modern Fine Lady* 1751.

Tobias George Smollett (1721–71)
Advice V
Anonymous

John Upton (1707–60)
Critical Observations on Shakespeare NF

Horace Walpole (1717–97)
The Beauties V
Anonymous

Joseph Warton (1722–1800)
Odes on Various Subjects V

John Wesley (1703–91)
The Principles of a Methodist Farther Explain'd NF
See *The Principles of a Methodist* 1742

John Wesley (1703–91)
Sermons on Several Occasions NF
Published in three volumes, 1746–50

1747

- British defeated by the French at Lauffeldt
  David Garrick becomes joint manager of Drury Lane Theatre
- John Aikin born
  Susanna Blamire born
  John O'Keeffe born
  Samuel Parr born
  Sir Uvedale Price born
- Joseph Trapp dies
  Leonard Welsted dies
- Alain-René Le Sage dies
- Voltaire, *Zadig*

Sir William Blackstone (1723–80)?
The Pantheon V
Anonymous. Attribution uncertain.

Thomas Carte (1686–1754)
A General History of England NF
Published in four volumes, 1747–55

John Cunningham (1729–73)
Love in a Mist: A farce D
Performed April 1747

William Dunkin (1709?–65)
Boeotia V

Thomas Edwards (1699–1757)
A Supplement to Mr Warburton's Edition of Shakespear NF
Second edition, 1748, entitled *The Canons of Criticism*

'John Trott Plaid' [Henry Fielding (1707–54)]
The Jacobite's Journal PER
Published between December 1747 and November 1748

Sarah Fielding (1710–68)
Familiar Letters Between the Principal Characters in David Simple, and Some Others F
bao *David Simple*. See *Adventures of David Simple* 1744, 1753. The preface and letters xl–xliv are by Henry Fielding.

Samuel Foote (1720–77)
The Roman and English Comedy Consider'd and Compar'd NF

Philip Francis (1708?–73) (tr.)
A Poetical Translation of the Works of Horace V
The first editions of the constituent parts were published as *The Odes, Epodes and Carmen Seculare of Horace* 1743 (q.v.). This is the first collected edition, with parallel Latin and English texts.

Hannah Glasse (1708–70)
The Art of Cookery, Made Plain and Easy NF
'By a lady'

Thomas Gray (1716–71)
Ode on a Distant Prospect of Eton College V
Anonymous

Benjamin Hoadly 'the younger' (1706–57)
The Suspicious Husband: A comedy D
Performed 12 February 1747. Prologue by David Garrick (who also acted in it).

Henry Home, Lord Kames (1696–1782)
Essays Upon Several Subjects Concerning British Antiquities NF
Anonymous

Samuel Johnson (1709–84)
The Plan of a Dictionary of the English Language NF
Anonymous. See *A Dictionary of the English Language* 1755.

Charlotte Lennox (1729?–1804)
Poems on Several Occasions V

David Mallet (1705?–65)
Amyntor and Theodora; or, The Hermit V

William Mason (1725–97)
Musaeus: A monody to the memory of Pope V
Anonymous. In imitation of Milton's 'Lycidas'.

William Melmoth, the younger (1710–99) (tr.)
The Letters of Pliny the Consul NF

Lady Mary Wortley Montagu (1689–1762)
Six Town Eclogues V

Josiah Relph (1712–43)
A Miscellany of Poems V

Samuel Richardson (1689–1761)
Clarissa; or, The History of a Young Lady [vols i, ii] F
'By the editor of *Pamela*'. Published 1747, dated 1748. Volumes iii–vii published 1748 (q.v.).

William Shakespeare (1564–1616)
The Works of Shakespear EDN
Edited by WIlliam Warburton

Tobias George Smollett (1721–71)
Reproof: A satire V
Anonymous. Sequel to *Advice* 1746 (q.v.).

Joseph Spence (1699–1768)
Polymetis; or, An Enquiry Concerning the Agreement Between the Works of the Roman Poets, and the Remains of the Antient Artists NF

Laurence Sterne (1713–68)
The Case of Elijah and the Widow of Zerephath, Consider'd NF

Horace Walpole (1717–97)
A Letter to the Whigs NF
Anonymous. A reply to the anonymous *Letter to the Tories* (attributed to George Lyttelton and Styan Thirlby), 1747. See *A Second and Third Letter* 1748.

Joseph Warton (1722–1800)
Ranelagh House PS
Anonymous

Thomas Warton, the younger (1728–90)
The Pleasures of Melancholy V
Anonymous

1748

- French raise the English siege of Pondicherry
  Treaty of Aix-la-Chapelle ends the War of the Austrian Succession
  Holywell Music Room, Oxford, opened
- Jeremy Bentham born
  Thomas Day born
  Eliza Parsons born
- Charles Johnson dies
  Christopher Pitt dies
  James Thomson dies
  Isaac Watt dies
- William Kent dies
- Gottfried August Bürger born

Mark Akenside (1721–70)
An Ode to the Earl of Huntingdon V

Sir George Anson (1697–1762)
A Voyage Round the World NF

John Cleland (1709–89)
Memoirs of a Woman of Pleasure F
Anonymous. Published in two volumes 1748–9 (both volumes dated 1749). See also *Memoirs of Fanny Hill* 1750.

Robert Dodsley (1703–64) (ed.)
A Collection of Poems ANTH
Volume ii contains Gray's 'Ode [on the Spring]', 'Ode on the Death of a Favourite Cat', and 'Ode on a Distant Prospect of Eton College' (published separately in 1747, q.v.)

Eliza Haywood (*c.*1693–1756)
Life's Progress through the Passions; or, The Adventures of Natura F
bao *The Fortunate Foundlings*

James Hervey (1714–58)
Meditations and Contemplations NF
Styled the 'second edition' because both parts of volume i (*Meditations Among the Tombs* 1746, q.v., and *Reflections on a Flower-garden*) had been published separately in 1746. This second work had its own title-page, dated 1747. This is the first collection gathering Hervey's writings into *Meditations and Contemplations*, which went into more than 25 editions before 1800.

David Hume (1711–76)
Philosophical Essays Concerning Human Understanding NF
bao *Essays Moral and Political*

David Hume (1711–76)
Three Essays, Moral and Political NF
See *Essays Moral and Political* 1741, 1742

William Kenrick (1725?–79)
The Town V

Mary Leapor (1722–46)
Poems upon Several Occasions V
See also *Poems Upon Several Occasions* 1751

'Sir Thomas Fitzosborne, bart.' [William Melmoth, the younger (1710–99)]
Letters on Several Subjects NF
Many editions. A second volume was published in 1749. The work was also reprinted under the title *The Letters of Sir Thomas Fitzosborne, on several subjects.*

Edward Moore (1712–57)
The Foundling: A comedy D
Performed 13 February 1748

Ambrose Philips (1674–1749)
Pastorals, Epistles, Odes and Other Original Poems V

Laetitia Pilkington (1708?–50)
The Memoirs of Mrs Laetitia Pilkington NF
A 'Third and Last Volume', edited by John Carteret Pilkington in 1754, is of questionable authenticity

Samuel Richardson (1689–1761)
Clarissa; or, The History of a Young Lady [vols iii, iv; v–vii] F
'By the editor of *Pamela*'. Volumes iii and iv published in April. 1748; volumes v, vi, and vii published in December. See *Clarissa* volumes i–ii 1747.

Thomas Sheridan (1687–1738)
The Simile; or, Woman: a Cloud V

Tobias George Smollett (1721–71) (tr.)
The Adventures of Gil Blas of Santillane F
Anonymous. Published 1748, dated 1749. Translated from Alain-René Le Sage (1668–1747).

Tobias George Smollett (1721–71)
The Adventures of Roderick Random F
Anonymous

James Thomson (1700–48)
The Castle of Indolence V

Horace Walpole (1717–97)
A Second and Third Letter to the Whigs NF
Anonymous. See *A Letter to the Whigs* 1747.

Thomas Warton, the elder (1688?–1745)
Poems on Several Occasions V
Edited by Joseph Warton (who also contributed two odes)

John Wesley (1703–91)
A Letter to a Person Lately Join'd with the People call'd Quakers NF
Anonymous

Peter Whalley (1722–91)
An Enquiry into the Learning of Shakespeare NF

1749

- Samuel Jackson Pratt born
  Charlotte Smith born
  Joseph Strutt born
- Samuel Boyse dies
  Matthew Concanen dies
  Ambrose Philips dies
  Catharine Trotter dies
- Charles James Fox born
- Vittorio Alfieri born
  Johann Wolfgang von Goethe born
- Handel's *Music for the Royal Fireworks* performed in Green Park, London, to mark the Peace of Aix-la-Chapelle
- Buffon, *Histoire Naturelle*

The Monthly Review PER
Published between May 1749 and December 1800

Anonymous
Tittle Tattle; or, Taste a-la-mode: A new farce D
Dramatized version of Swift's *A Complete Collection of Genteel and Ingenious Conversation* 1738 (q.v.)

Joseph Ames (1689–1759)
Typographical Antiquities NF

George Berkeley (1685–1753)
A Word to the Wise; or, An Exhortation to the Roman Catholic Clergy of Ireland NF
'By a member of the established church'

John Brown (1715–66)
On Liberty V

William Rufus Chetwood (*d.* 1766)
A General History of the Stage NF

John Cleland (1709–89)?
The Case of the Unfortunate Bosavern Penlez NF

Attributed to Cleland. See also Fielding, *A True State of the Case of Bosavern Penlez* 1749 (below).

William Collins (1721–59)
Ode Occasion'd by the Death of Mr Thomson V
James Thomson died in August 1748

Thomas Cooke (1703–56)
An Ode on Beauty V
Anonymous

John Gilbert Cooper (1723–69)
The Life of Socrates NF
See also *Cursory Remarks* 1751

Henry Fielding (1707–54)
The History of Tom Jones, a Foundling F

Henry Fielding (1707–54)
A True State of the Case of Bosavern Penlez NF
See also Cleland, above

Sarah Fielding (1710–68)
The Governess; or, Little Female Academy F
bao *David Simple*. Often considered to be the first novel written for children.

Sarah Fielding (1710–68)?
Remarks on 'Clarissa' NF
Anonymous pamphlet. Attributed to Sarah Fielding.

David Hartley (1705–57)
Observations on Man, his Frame, his Duty, and his Expectations NF
See also Priestley (ed.), *Hartley's Theory of the Human Mind* 1775

William Hawkins (1722–1801)
Henry and Rosamund: A tragedy D

Eliza Haywood (*c.*1693–1756)?
Dalinda; or, The Double Marriage F
Anonymous. Sometimes attributed to Eliza Haywood.

Aaron Hill (1685–1750)
Gideon; or, The Patriot V

Aaron Hill (1685–1750) (tr.)
Meropé: A tragedy D
Performed 15 April 1749. Translated and adapted from the play of the same name by Voltaire.

Samuel Johnson (1709–84)
Irene: A tragedy D
Performed February 1749

Samuel Johnson (1709–84)
The Vanity of Human Wishes: The tenth satire of Juvenal, imitated V

Henry Jones (1721–70)
Poems on Several Occasions V

William Law (1686–1761)
The Spirit of Prayer NF
Part ii published in 1750. See also *The Spirit of Love* 1752.

William Mason (1725–97)
Isis: An elegy V

Moses Mendes (*d.* 1758)
The Chaplet: A musical entertainment D
Performed 2 December 1749. Music by William Boyce.

Henry St-John, Viscount Bolingbroke (1678–1751)
Letters on the Spirit of Patriotism NF
Anonymous

Tobias George Smollett (1721–71)
The Regicide; or, James the First, of Scotland: A tragedy D
bao *Roderick Random*

James Thomson (1700–48)
Coriolanus: A tragedy D
Performed 13 January 1749

John Wesley (1703–91)
A Plain Account of the People Called Methodists NF

Gilbert West (1703–56) (tr.)
Odes of Pindar V

1750

- English Jockey Club founded
  Hambledon Cricket Club founded
- Maria Anna Bennett born
  Catherine Ann Dorset born
  Robert Fergusson born
  Richard Payne Knight born
  Sophia Lee born
- Aaron Hill dies
  Laetitia Pilkington dies
- Joanna Southcott born
- Antonio Salieri born
- J.S. Bach dies

Anonymous
The History of Charlotte Summers, the Fortunate Parish Girl F
The heroine is a female Tom Jones. Introduces the character of Lady Bountiful. Sometimes attributed to Sarah Fielding.

The Rambler PER
Most issues by Samuel Johnson. Published in 208 numbers, March 1750–March 1752.

Sir William Blackstone (1723–89)
An Essay on Collateral Consanguinity NF

Henry Brooke (1703–83)
A New Collection of Fairy Tales F
Anonymous

John Campbell (1708–75)
The Present State of Europe NF

John Cleland (1709–89)
Memoirs of Fanny Hill F
Anonymous. An abridgement of Cleland's *Memoirs of a Woman of Pleasure* 1749 (q.v.).

William Collins (1721–59)
The Passions: An ode V

Thomas Cooke (1703–56)
An Ode on Martial Virtue V
Anonymous

Robert Dodsley (1703–64)
The Oeconomy of Human Life V
Anonymous. Sometimes ascribed to Philip Dormer Stanhope, earl of Chesterfield. Published 1750, dated 1751.

David Garrick (1717–79) (adap.)
Romeo and Juliet D
Anonymous. Performed November 1748. From Shakespeare.

Zachary Grey (1688–1766)
A Free and Familiar Letter to William Warburton NF
See also *A Word or Two of Advice* 1746

Eliza Haywood (*c.*1693–1756)
A Present for Women Addicted to Drinking NF
A conduct book

Francis Hutcheson (1695–1747)
Reflections Upon Laughter NF

Mary Jones (1707–78)
Miscellanies in Prose and Verse MISC

Edward Kimber (1719–69)
The Life and Adventures of Joe Thompson F
Anonymous

Charlotte Lennox (1729?–1804)
The Life of Harriot Stuart, Written by Herself F
Anonymous. Published 1750, dated 1751.

Robert Paltock (1697–1767)
The Life and Adventures of Peter Wilkins, a Cornish Man F
Anonymous. Published 1750, dated 1751.

Sarah Scott (1723–95)
The History of Cornelia F
Anonymous

William Shirley (*fl.* 1739–80)
Edward the Black Prince; or, The Battle of Poictiers: An historical tragedy D
Performed 6 January 1750

Laurence Sterne (1713–68)
The Abuses of Conscience NF

Thomas Warton, the younger (1728–90)
New-market V
Anonymous. Published 1750, dated 1751.

Thomas Warton, the younger (1728–90)
The Triumph of Isis V
Published 1750, dated 1749

William Whitehead (1715–85)
The Roman Father D
Performed 24 February 1750

Edward Young (1683–1765)
The Complaint; or, Night-Thoughts on Life, Death and Immortality V
Anonymous. The collected edition of Nights i–ix: see *The Complaint* 1742.

1751

- Robert Clive takes Arcot (31 Aug.)
- Richard Brinsley Sheridan born
  Richard Tickell born
- Philip Doddridge dies
  Batty Langley dies
  Henry St-John, 1st Viscount Bolingbroke, dies
- Thomas Sheraton born
- Frederick Lewis, Prince of Wales, dies
- *L'Encyclopédie* (–1776), ed. Denis Diderot

John Arbuthnot (1667–1735)
Miscellaneous Works of the Late Dr Arbuthnot WKS

Richard Owen Cambridge (1717–1802)
The Scribleriad V
The six books were first published separately January–March 1751

John Cleland (1709–89)
Memoirs of a Coxcomb; or, The History of Sir William Delamere F
Anonymous

Thomas Cooke (1703–56)
An Ode on the Powers of Poetry V
Anonymous

John Gilbert Cooper (1723–69)
Cursory Remarks on Mr Warburton's New Edition of Mr Pope's Works NF
See *Life of Socrates* 1749

Nathaniel Cotton (1705–88)
Visions in Verse V
Anonymous. Versifies the *Fables* of Gay 1727 (q.v.), adapting their morals for children. Cotton ran the madhouse in which Cowper was confined 1763–5.

Francis Coventry (1725–54)
The History of Pompey the Little; or, The Life and Adventures of a Lap-dog F
Anonymous. Many editions.

Henry Fielding (1707–54)
Amelia F
Published 1751, dated 1752

Henry Fielding (1707–54)
An Enquiry into the Causes of the Late Increase of Robbers NF

Thomas Gray (1716–71)
An Elegy Wrote in a Country Church Yard V
Anonymous. Published on 15 February 1751 in a quarto pamphlet, with preface by Horace Walpole. Reprinted in *Designs by Mr R. Bentley* 1753 (q.v.) and in Gray's *Poems* 1768 (q.v.).

James Harris (1709–80)
Hermes; or, A Philosophical Inquiry Concerning Language and Universal Grammar NF

Eliza Haywood (*c*.1693–1756)
The History of Miss Betsy Thoughtless F
Anonymous

Henry Home, Lord Kames (1696–1782)
Essays on the Principles of Morality and Natural Religion NF
Anonymous

David Hume (1711–76)
An Enquiry Concerning the Principles of Morals NF
Reprinted in *Essays and Treatises* 1753 (q.v.)

Soame Jenyns (1704–87)
The Modern Fine Lady V
See also *The Modern Fine Gentleman* 1746

John Jortin (1698–1770)
Remarks on Ecclesiastical History NF
Published in five volumes, 1751–73

Mary Leapor (1722–46)
Poems Upon Several Occasions V
See also *Poems upon Several Occasions* 1748. Edited by Samuel Richardson and Isaac Hawkins Browne.

David Mallet (1705?–65)
Alfred: A masque D
Performed 23 February 1751. A rewritten version by Mallet of *Alfred* 1740 (q.v.).

Moses Mendes (*d.* 1758)
Robin Hood: A new musical entertainment D
Performed 13 December 1750

Moses Mendes (*d.* 1758)
The Seasons V

Alexander Pope (1688–1744)
The Works of Alexander Pope WKS
Edited by William Warburton

Tobias George Smollett (1721–71)
The Adventures of Peregrine Pickle F
Anonymous

Catharine Cockburn, formerly **Trotter** (1674–1749)
The Works of Mrs Catharine Cockburn WKS

John Wesley (1703–91)
Serious Thoughts upon the Perseverance of Saints NF
Anonymous

Benjamin Whichcote (1609–83)
The Works of the Learned Benjamin Whichcote WKS

1752

- Britain adopts the Gregorian Calendar (14 Sept.)
- Frances Burney born
  Thomas Chatterton born
  Vicesimus Knox born
  Humphry Repton born
- Joseph Butler dies
  Samuel Croxall dies
  William Whiston dies
- John Nash born

George Ballard (1706–55)
Memoirs of Several Ladies of Great Britain NF

George Berkeley (1685–1753)
A Miscellany NF
'By the Bishop of Cloyne'

Thomas Birch (1705–66)
The Life of John Tillotson NF

Francis Blackburne (1705–87)
A Serious Inquiry into the Use and Importance of External Religion NF
Anonymous

Moses Browne (1704–87)
The Works and Rest of the Creation V

John Byrom (1692–1763)
Enthusiasm: A poetical essay V

Richard Owen Cambridge (1717–1802)
A Dialogue Between a Member of Parliament and His Servant V

Thomas Cooke (1703–56)
Pythagoras: An ode V
Anonymous

William Dodd (1729–77) (ed.)
The Beauties of Shakespeare ANTH

'Sir Alexander Drawcansir' [Henry Fielding (1707–54) (ed.)]
The Covent-Garden Journal PER
Published between January and November 1752

Samuel Foote (1720–77)
Taste: A comedy D
Performed 11 January 1752

John Hawkesworth (1715?–73) (ed.)
The Adventurer PER
Published between November 1752 and March 1754. Contributors include Samuel Johnson, Richard Bathurst, and Joseph Warton.

David Hume (1711–76)
Political Discourses NF

William Law (1686–1761)
The Spirit of Love NF
Part ii published in 1754 (q.v.). See also *The Spirit of Prayer* 1749.

William Law (1686–1761)
The Way to Divine Knowledge NF

Charlotte Lennox (1729?–1804)
The Female Quixote; or, The Adventures of Arabella F
Anonymous

William Mason (1725–97)
Elfrida: A dramatic poem V

Henry St-John, Viscount Bolingbroke (1678–1751)
Letters on the Study and Use of History NF
Edited by David Mallet. Written 1736–8 and first privately printed before Bolingbroke's death.

Christopher Smart (1722–71)
Poems on Several Occasions V

1753

- Act for the naturalization of Jews in England
  British Museum Charter
- Elizabeth Inchbald born
  Dugald Stewart born
- George Berkeley dies
- Thomas Bewick born
- Sir Hans Sloane dies
- James Lind, *A Treatise of the Scurvy*

John Armstrong (1709–79)
Taste: An epistle to a young critic V

Richard Bentley, the younger (1708–82) and **Thomas Gray** (1716–71)
Designs by Mr R. Bentley, for Six Poems by Mr T. Gray NF
Contains Gray's 'Ode on the Spring', 'Ode on the Death of a Favourite Cat', 'Ode on a Distant Prospect of Eton College', 'Hymn to Adversity', 'Elegy Wrote in a Country Church Yard', and 'A Long Story' (the only publication of this in Gray's lifetime)

Theophilus Cibber (1703–58)
The Lives and Characters of the Most Eminent Actors and Actresses NF

Theophilus Cibber (1703–58)
The Lives of the Poets of Great Britain and Ireland NF
Mainly compiled by Robert Shiels with revisions and additions by Cibber

Catherine ('Kitty') Clive (1711–85)
The Rehearsal; or, Bays in Petticoats: A comedy D
Performed 15 March 1750

Thomas Cooke (1703–56)
An Ode on Benevolence V
Anonymous

Robert Dodsley (1703–64)
Public Virtue V

Sarah Fielding (1710–68)
The Adventures of David Simple: Volume the Last F

Anonymous. Sequel to *Adventures of David Simple* 1744 (q.v.). See also *Familiar Letters* 1747.

Samuel Foote (1720–77)
The Englishman in Paris: A comedy D
Performed 24 March 1753. See also *The Englishman Return'd from Paris* 1756.

Thomas Francklin (1721–84)
Translation: A poem V

Richard Gifford (1725–1807)
Contemplation: A poem V
Anonymous

Richard Glover (1712–85)
Boadicea: A tragedy D
Performed 1 December 1753

Eliza Haywood (*c*.1693–1756)
The History of Jemmy and Jenny Jessamy F
bao *The History of Betsy Thoughtless*

William Hogarth (1697–1764)
The Analysis of Beauty NF

David Hume (1711–76)
Essays and Treatises on Several Subjects NF

Henry Jones (1721–70)
The Earl of Essex: A tragedy D

Henry Jones (1721–70)
Merit: A poem V

William Kenrick (1725?–79)
The Whole Duty of Woman V
Anonymous

Charlotte Lennox (1729?–1804)
Shakespear Illustrated ANTH
A third volume was published in 1754. Dedication by Samuel Johnson, to whom Malone ascribes many of the notes.

William Melmoth, the younger (1710–99) (tr.)
The Letters of Marcus Tullius Cicero to Several of his Friends NF
A translation of Cicero's *Ad familiares*

Edward Moore (1712–57)
The Gamester: A tragedy D
Performed 7 February 1753

John Ogilvie (1732–1813)
The Day of Judgment V
Anonymous

Christopher Pitt (1699–1748) and others (tr.)
The Works of Virgil, in Latin and English EDN
See also *An Essay on Virgil's Aeneid* 1728, *The Aeneid of Virgil* 1740

Samuel Richardson (1689–1761)
The History of Sir Charles Grandison F
'By the editor of *Pamela* and *Clarissa*'. Published in 7 volumes (1753–4).

Henry St-John, Viscount Bolingbroke (1678–1751)
A Letter to Sir William Windham NF

Christopher Smart (1722–71)
The Hilliad: An epic poem V
Written against John Hill. M.D. (1716?–75), editor of the *British Magazine*, who had abused Smart in the first, and only, number of *The Impertinent* (August 1752).

Tobias George Smollett (1721–71)
The Adventures of Ferdinand Count Fathom F
bao *Roderick Random*

John Toland (1670–1722)
Hypatia NF
Anonymous

William Warburton (1698–1779)
The Principles of Natural and Revealed Religion NF
A third volume published in 1767 as *Sermons and Discourses . . . Volume the third* (q.v.)

Thomas Warton, the younger (1728–90) (ed.)
The Union; or, Select Scots and English Poems ANTH
Anonymous

George Whitefield (1714–70)
Hymns for Social Worship ANTH

Edward Young (1683–1765)
The Brothers: A tragedy D
Performed 3 March 1753. Based on Corneille's *Persée et Démétrius*.

1754

- Duke of Newcastle becomes Prime Minister on the death of his brother, Henry Pelham
  Anglo-French war breaks out in North America
- Thomas and Henrietta Bowdler born
  Jane Cave born (c.1754)
  George Crabbe born
  Robert Charles Dallas born
- Jane Collier dies
  Henry Fielding dies
  James Gibbs dies

- Birth of the future Louis XVI
  Charles Maurice de Talleyrand-Périgord born

Anonymous
Critical Remarks on Sir Charles Grandison, Clarissa and Pamela NF
'By a Lover of Virtue'

Thomas Birch (1705–66)
Memoirs of the Reign of Queen Elizabeth NF

Thomas Cooke (1703–56)
An Ode on Poetry, Painting, and Sculpture V
Anonymous

John Gilbert Cooper (1723–69)
Letters Concerning Taste NF
Anonymous. Published 1754, dated 1755.

Thomas Denton (1724–77)
Immortality; or, The Consolation of Human Life V
Anonymous

John Duncombe (1729–86)
The Feminiad V

Henry Fielding (1707–54)
The Life of Mr Jonathan Wild the Great F
Corrected and enlarged from the first version published in volume iii of *Miscellanies* 1743 (q.v.)

Sarah Fielding (1710–68) and **Jane Collier** (1715–1754/5)
The Cry: A new dramatic fable F
Anonymous

John Gay (1685–1732)
The Rehearsal at Goatham D
Unacted

John Gillies (1712–96)
Historical Collections Relating to Remarkable Periods of the Success of the Gospel NF

Zachary Grey (1688–1766)
Critical, Historical, and Explanatory Notes on Shakespeare NF

Benjamin Hoadly (1676–1761)
Sixteen Sermons NF

David Hume (1711–76)
The History of Great Britain NF
Volume ii published in 1756 (q.v.). See also *History of England* 1759

Henry Jones (1721–70)
The Relief; or, Day Thoughts V
Occasioned by Edward Young, *The Complaint* 1742 (q.v.)

William Law (1686–1761)
The Second Part of the Spirit of Love NF
See *The Spirit of Love* 1752, *The Spirit of Prayer* 1749

Francis Plumer (*d.* 1794)?
A Candid Examination of the History of Sir Charles Grandison NF
Anonymous. Attributed to Francis Plumer.

Henry St-John, Viscount Bolingbroke (1678–1751)
Philosophical Works WKS
Edited by David Mallet

Sarah Scott (1723–95) (tr.)
Agreeable Ugliness; or, The Triumph of the Graces F
Anonymous. Translated from Pierre Antoine de la Place.

Sarah Scott (1723–95)
A Journey Through Every Stage of Life F
'By a person of quality'

John Shebbeare (1709–88)
The Marriage Act F
Anonymous. Written in protest at the act against runaway marriages.

Jonathan Swift (1667–1745)
Brotherly Love NF

Jonathan Swift (1667–1745)
The Works of Jonathan Swift WKS
Edited by John Hawkesworth. A further five volumes were published 1764–75, as well as 6 volumes of letters 1766–8.

William Warburton (1698–1779)
A View of Lord Bolingbroke's Philosophy NF
Anonymous. *Letter the Third* and *Letter the Fourth* were published in 1755.

Thomas Warton, the younger (1728–90)
Observations on the Faerie Queene of Spenser NF

William Whitehead (1715–85)
Poems on Several Occasions V

1755

- General Braddock defeated by the French near Fort Duquesne (9 July)
  Lisbon earthquake (Nov.)
- George Dyer born
  Robert Merry born
- George Ballard dies
  George Jeffreys dies

- Sarah Kemble (Mrs Siddons) born
  John Flaxman born
- Marie Antoinette born
  The future Louis XVIII born
  Charles Louis, Baron de Montesquieu dies

Thomas Amory (1691?–1788)
Memoirs: Containing the Lives of Several Ladies of Great Britain F
Anonymous

John Brown (1715–66)
Barbarossa: A tragedy D
Performed 17 December 1754

John Byrom (1692–1763)
Epistle in Defence of Rhyme V
In Roger Comberbach (*d.* 1757), *A Dispute*, also issued in 1755 as *The Contest*

Theophilus Cibber (1703–58)
An Epistle to David Garrick NF

John Cleland (1709–89)
Titus Vespasian: A tragedy D
Based on Pietro Metastasio's *La Clemenza di Tito*

George Colman, the elder (1732–94) and **Bonnell Thornton** (1724–68) (eds)
Poems by Eminent Ladies ANTH
Contains poems by 18 women poets, including Aphra Behn, Elizabeth Carter, Mrs Leapor, Anne Finch, Katherine Philips, and the duchess of Newcastle

John Gilbert Cooper (1723–69)
The Tomb of Shakespear V
Second edition, 'corrected; with considerable alterations', 1755 (with subtitle 'A vision')

Sir David Dalrymple, Lord Hailes (1726–92) (ed.)
Edom of Gordon: An Ancient Scottish Poem V

Philip Doddridge (1702–51)
Hymns Founded on Various Texts in the Holy Scripture NF

Stephen Duck (1705–56)
Caesar's Camp; or, St George's Hill V

Henry Fielding (1707–54)
The Journal of a Voyage to Lisbon NF

Thomas Francklin (1721–84) (tr.)
The Orphan of China D
Published anonymously in 1755, dated 1756. A translation of Voltaire's *L'Orphelin de la Chine* (1755). See also the play of the same name by Arthur Murphy 1759.

David Garrick (1717–79) (adap.)
The Fairies: An opera D/OP
Anonymous. Performed 3 February 1755. Adapted from Shakespeare's *A Midsummer Night's Dream.*

'Exploralibus' [**Eliza Haywood** (*c.*1693–1756)]
The Invisible Spy F

James Hervey (1714–58)
Theron and Aspasio; or, A Series of Dialogues and Letters NF

Benjamin Hoadly (1676–1761)
Twenty Sermons NF

Francis Hutcheson (1695–1747)
A System of Moral Philosophy NF

Samuel Johnson (1709–84)
A Dictionary of the English Language DICT

David Mallet (1705?–65)
Britannia: A masque D
Performed 9 May 1755

Samuel Richardson (1689–1761)
A Collection of the Moral and Instructive Sentiments . . . Contained in the Histories of Pamela, Clarissa, and Sir Charles Grandison ANTH
Anonymous

John Shebbeare (1709–88)
Letters on the English Nation F
Supposedly translated from Batista Angeloni, a Jesuit—in fact written by Shebbeare. A spy-letter novel.

Tobias George Smollett (1721–71) (tr.)
The History and Adventures of the Renowned Don Quixote F
Translated from Cervantes (1547–1616)

Charles Wesley (1707–88)
An Epistle to John Wesley NF

Edward Young (1683–1765)
The Centaur not Fabulous NF
Anonymous

1756

- Outbreak of the Seven Years War (–1763)
  The Black Hole of Calcutta
- William Gifford born
  William Godwin born
  Harriet Lee born

- Thomas Cooke ('Hesiod Cooke') dies
  Stephen Duck dies
  Eliza Haywood dies
  Gilbert West dies
- Henry Raeburn born
  Thomas Rowlandson born
- Wolfgang Amadeus Mozart born

The Literary Magazine PER
Edited and published by William Faden. Monthly, January 1756–July 1758.

Anonymous
The Life and Memoirs of Mr Ephraim Tristram Bates F
An anticipation of Sterne's *Tristram Shandy* 1759 (q.v.)

Anonymous
The Paths of Virtue Delineated; or, The History in Miniature of the Celebrated Pamela, Clarissa Harlowe, and Sir Charles Grandison F
Adapted 'to the capacities of youth'

Thomas Amory (1691?–1788)
The Life of John Buncle, Esq. F
Anonymous. Part ii published in 1766.

Isaac Bickerstaffe (1735?–1812?)
Leucothoe V
Anonymous

Thomas Birch (1705–66)
The History of the Royal Society of London NF
Published in 4 volumes, 1756–7

Sir William Blackstone (1723–89)
An Analysis of the Laws of England NF
Anonymous

Frances Brooke (1724–89)
Virginia: A tragedy D/V
Also contains poems

John Brown (1715–66)
Athelstan: A tragedy D
Performed 27 February 1756

Edmund Burke (1729–97)
A Vindication of Natural Society NF
Anonymous. In imitation of Henry St-John Bolingbroke.

Alban Butler (1711–73)
The Lives of the Fathers, Martyrs, and Other Principal Saints NF
Anonymous. Published in 4 volumes, 1756–9.

Richard Owen Cambridge (1717–1802)
An Elegy Written in an Empty Assembly Room V
A parody of Pope's *Eloisa to Abelard*

Theophilus Cibber (1703–58)
Dissertations on Theatrical Subjects NF

Thomas Cole (1726?–96)
The Arbour; or, The Rural Philosopher V
Anonymous

Samuel Foote (1720–77)
The Englishman Return'd from Paris D
Performed 3 February 1756. See *The Englishman in Paris* 1753.

David Garrick (1717–79) (adap.)
Catherine and Petruchio: A comedy D
Performed 21 January 1756

David Garrick (1717–79) (adap.)?
The Tempest: An opera D/OP
Anonymous. Adapted from Shakespeare and performed 11 February 1756. Though he once denied it, Garrick probably had a significant role in the adaptation as manager of Drury Lane.

'Mira' [**Eliza Haywood** (*c.*1693–1756)]
The Wife NF
A conduct piece. A companion piece, *The Husband: In answer to the wife*, also published in 1756.

David Hume (1711–76)
The History of Great Britain [vol. ii] NF
Published 1756, dated 1757. Volume i published 1754 (q.v.). See also *History of England* 1759

William Kenrick (1725?–79)
Epistles to Lorenzo V
Anonymous

Charlotte Lennox (1729?–1804) (tr.)
The Memoirs of the Countess of Berci F
Anonymous. Adapted from *L'Histoire tragi-comique de nostre temps* by Vital d'Audiguier (1569–1624).

William Mason (1725–97)
Odes V

Christopher Pitt (1699–1748)
Poems . . . Together with The Jordan V
'By the celebrated translator of Virgil's Aeneid'

Christopher Smart (1722–71)
Hymn to the Supreme Being V

Christopher Smart (1722–71) (tr.)
The Works of Horace EDN
See also *Works of Horace, Translated into Verse* 1767

Tobias George Smollett (1721–71)
A Compendium of Authentic and Entertaining Voyages NF
Anonymous

Tobias George Smollett (1721–71) (ed.) and others
The Critical Review; or, Annals of Literature PER
Semi-annually, 1756–90

Joseph Warton (1722–1800)
An Essay on the Writings and Genius of Pope [vol. i] NF
Volume ii published 1782 (q.v.)

John Wesley (1703–91)
An Address to the Clergy NF

1757

- J.-F. Damiens attempts to assassinate Louis XV
  Admiral Byng executed for the loss of Minorca (in May 1756)
  Robert Clive defeats Nawab Siraj-ud-Daula at the Battle of Plassey (23 June)
  Horace Walpole sets up the Strawberry Hill Press
  John Baskerville's first volume (a Latin Virgil) printed at Birmingham
- William Blake born
  Dr Charles Burney born
  Georgiana, duchess of Devonshire born
  Francis Douce born
  John Philip Kemble born
  William Sotheby born
- Mary Barber dies
  Colley Cibber dies: William Whitehead appointed Poet Laureate
  John Dyer dies
  Thomas Edwards dies
  David Hartley dies
  Benjamin Hoadly, the younger, dies
  Edward Moore dies
- Samuel Romilly born
  Thomas Telford born
- Antonio Canova born

Anonymous
An Account of the European Settlements in America NF
Probably a collaboration between Edmund Burke and William Burke (1730–98)

Anonymous
The Taxes: A dramatick entertainment D
Sometimes attributed to Phanuel Bacon (1700–83)

Robert Andrews (1723–66)
Eidyllia; or, Miscellaneous Poems V
The preface contains a violent attack on rhyme

Cornelius Arnold (1711–57)
Poems on Several Occasions V
Includes a play, *Osman: An historical tragedy*

Samuel Boyce (*d.* 1775)
Poems on Several Occasions V

John Brown (1715–66)
An Estimate of the Manners and Principles of the Times NF
bao *Essays on the Characteristics*. See also *An Explanatory Defence* 1758.

Edmund Burke (1729–97)
A Philosophical Enquiry into the Origin of Our Ideas of the Sublime and Beautiful NF
Anonymous. Half-title: 'On the Sublime and the Beautiful'. Nine editions to 1782.

Robert Colvill (*d.* 1788)
Britain V
Anonymous

'Aristippus' [John Gilbert Cooper (1723–69)]
Epistles to the Great V
See also *The Call of Aristippus* 1758

Sir John Dalrymple (1726–1810)
An Essay Towards a General History of Feudal Property in Great Britain NF

John Duncombe (1729–86)
The Feminead; or, Female Genius V
See *The Feminiad* 1754 and also Mary Scott, *The Female Advocate* 1774

William Duncombe (1690–1769) (ed.)
The Works of Horace in English Verse EDN
By various hands. The epodes and first book of the epistles were translated by John Duncombe; William Duncombe also translated parts of the work.

John Dyer (1699–1757)
The Fleece V

Adam Ferguson (1723–1816)
The Morality of Stage-Plays Seriously Considered NF
Anonymous

Sarah Fielding (1710–68)
The Lives of Cleopatra and Octavia F
bao *David Simple*

Samuel Foote (1720–77)
The Author: A comedy D
Performed 5 February 1757

David Garrick (1717–79)
Lilliput: A dramatic entertainment D
Anonymous. An afterpiece, performed 3 December 1756.

Thomas Gray (1716–71)
Odes by Mr Gray V
Contains 'The Progress of Poesy' and 'The Bard'. The first book to be printed by Horace Walpole's Press at Strawberry Hill.

Richard Griffith (1714?–88) and **Elizabeth Griffith** (1720?–93)
A Series of Genuine Letters Between Henry and Frances [vols i, ii] F
Published anonymously. The partly fictionalized courtship letters of Elizabeth and Richard Griffith. Volumes iii and iv published in 1766; volumes v and vi, 1770.

John Home (1722–1808)
Douglas: A tragedy D
Performed in Edinburgh in 1765 and in London 14 March 1757

David Hume (1711–76)
Four Dissertations NF
i: 'The Natural History of Religion'; ii: 'Of the Passions'; iii: 'Of Tragedy'; iv: 'Of the Standard of Taste'. See also Warburton, *Remarks on Mr David Hume's Essay* 1757.

Soame Jenyns (1704–87)
A Free Inquiry into the Nature and Origin of Evil NF

Tobias George Smollett (1721–71)
A Complete History of England NF
Published in 4 volumes, 1757–8. *Continuation* published 1760–5.

Tobias George Smollett (1721–71)
The Reprisal; or, The Tars of Old England: A comedy D
Anonymous. Performed 22 January 1757.

William Thompson (1712?–66)
Poems on Several Occasions V

William Warburton (1698–1779)
Remarks on Mr David Hume's Essay on the Natural History of Religion NF
Anonymous. By Warburton and Richard Hurd (1720–1808). See Hume, *Four Dissertations* 1757.

John Wesley (1703–91)
The Doctrine of Original Sin NF

William Wilkie (1721–72)
The Epigoniad V
Anonymous

Edward Young (1683–1765)
The Works of the Author of the Night Thoughts WKS

1758

- Elizabeth Hamilton born
  Ellis Cornelia Knight born
  Mary Robinson ('Perdita') born
  Thomas Taylor ('the Platonist') born
  Jane West born
- Theophilus Cibber dies
  James Hervey dies
  Allan Ramsay dies
- Horatio Nelson born
- Jonathan Edwards dies

Mark Akenside (1721–70)
An Ode to the Country Gentlemen of England V

'Launcelot Temple' [John Armstrong (1709–79)]
Sketches; or, Essays on Various Subjects NF

Sir William Blackstone (1723–89)
A Discourse on the Study of Law NF
See also *Analysis of the Laws of England* 1756

John Brown (1715–66)
An Explanatory Defence of the Estimate of the Manners and Principles of the Times NF
See *An Estimate* 1757

Elizabeth Carter (1717–1806) (tr.)
All the Works of Epictetus EDN

John Gilbert Cooper (1723–69)
The Call of Aristippus V
bao *Epistles to the Great* 1757 (q.v.)

Robert Dodsley (1703–64)
Cleone: A tragedy D/V
Performed 2 December 1758. The work also contains Dodsley's poem on the sublime, 'Melpomene'.

David Garrick (1717–79) (adap.)
Florizel and Perdita: A dramatic pastoral D
Performed 21 January 1756

'James Willington' [Oliver Goldsmith (1728–74) (tr.)]
The Memoirs of a Protestant, Condemned to the Galleys of France, For his Religion NF
Translated from Jean Marteilhe (1684–1777)

William Hawkins (1722–1801)
Tracts in Divinity MISC

Henry Home, Lord Kames (1696–1782)
Historical Law-Tracts NF
Anonymous

John Home (1722–1808)
Agis: A tragedy D
bao *Douglas*. Performed 21 February 1758.

Samuel Johnson (1709–84) and others
The Idler PER
bao *The Rambler*. Published in 104 numbers (April 1758–April 1760). Published as part of *The Universal Chronicle, or Weekly Gazette*, numbers 2–105. Though the name of the periodical underwent several changes over time, its lead article remained 'The Idler'.

Charlotte Lennox (1729?–1804)
Henrietta F
bao *The Female Quixote*. Later dramatized as *The Sister* 1769 (q.v.).

Charlotte Lennox (1729?–1804)
Philander: A dramatic pastoral D
bao *The Female Quixote*

Robert Lowth (1710–87)
The Life of William of Wykeham, Bishop of Winchester NF

James Macpherson (1736–96)
The Highlander V

Arthur Murphy (1727–1805)
The Upholsterer; or, What News? D
Performed 30 March 1758

Thomas Parnell (1679–1718)
Posthumous Works V

Richard Price (1723–91)
A Review of the Principal Questions and Difficulties in Morals NF

George Alexander Stevens (1710–84)
Albion Restored; or, Time Turned Oculist D
Anonymous

Jonathan Swift (1667–1745)
The History of the Last Four Years of the Queen NF

Horace Walpole (1717–97)
A Catalogue of the Royal and Noble Authors of England NF
See also *Postscript to the Royal and Noble Authors* 1786

Horace Walpole (1717–97)
A Dialogue Between Two Great Ladies PS
Anonymous. A prose satire in the form of a dialogue between Maria Theresa of Austria-Hungary and the Empress of Russia on the German war.

Horace Walpole (1717–97)
Fugitive Pieces in Verse and Prose MISC

Arthur Young (1741–1820)
The Theatre of the Present War in North America NF

1759

- British Museum opens (Jan.)
  British troops under General Wolfe scale the Heights of Abraham and defeat the French (13 Sept.); surrender of Quebec (18 Sept.)
  French navy defeated at Quiberon Bay
- Robert Burns born
  Mary Wollstonecraft (later Godwin) born
- William Collins dies
- Richard Porson born
  Charles Simeon born
  William Wilberforce born
- George Frederick Handel dies
  James Wolfe dies
- J.C.F. von Schiller born

Edmund Burke (1729–97) (ed.)
The Annual Register PER
First published on 15 May 1759. Edited by Edmund Burke until 1788.

Samuel Butler (1612–80)
The Genuine Remains in Verse and Prose WKS

Edward Capell (1713–81) (ed.)
Prolusions; or, Select Pieces of Antient Poetry ANTH
Anonymous. Published 1759, dated 1760.

John Gilbert Cooper (1723–69) (tr.)
Ver-Vert; or, The Nunnery Parrot V
Anonymous. Translated from the mock-epic *Ver-Vert* (1733) by the poet and dramatist Jean-Baptiste-Louis Gresset (1709–77).

Sarah Fielding (1710–68)
The History of the Countess of Dellwyn F
bao *David Simple*

Alexander Gerard (1728–95)
An Essay on Taste NF

Oliver Goldsmith (1728–74)
The Bee NF
First issued in eight weekly numbers. Reprinted in *Essays* 1765 (q.v.).

Oliver Goldsmith (1728–74)
An Enquiry into the Present State of Polite Learning in Europe NF
Anonymous

William Hawkins (1722–1801) (adap.)
Cymbeline: A tragedy D
Performed 15 February 1759. Adapted from Shakespeare.

David Hume (1711–76)
The History of England, Under the House of Tudor NF
See also *History of Great Britain* 1754, 1756

Richard Hurd (1720–1808)
Moral and Political Dialogues NF

Edward Hyde, 1st earl of Clarendon (1609–74)
The Life of Edward Earl of Clarendon Written by Himself NF

Samuel Johnson (1709–84)
The Prince of Abissinia F
Anonymous. Known to modern readers as *Rasselas*.

Mary Latter (1725–77)
The Miscellaneous Works WKS

William Mason (1725–97)
Caractacus V
bao *Elfrida*

Arthur Murphy (1727–1805)
The Orphan of China: A tragedy D
Anonymous. Performed 21 April 1759. Based on Voltaire's *L'Orphelin de la Chine* (performed 1755). See also Thomas Francklin's translation 1755.

William Rider (1723–85) (tr.)
Candidus; or, The Optimist F
A translation of Voltaire's *Candide* (1759)

William Robertson (1721–93)
The History of Scotland During the Reigns of Queen Mary and of King James VI NF

Adam Smith (1723–90)
The Theory of Moral Sentiments NF

Laurence Sterne (1713–68)
The Life and Opinions of Tristram Shandy, Gentleman [vols i, ii] F
Anonymous. On sale in December 1759, dated 1760. Volumes iii and iv published in 1761 (q.v.); volumes v and vi, 1762 (q.v.); volumes vii and viii, 1765 (q.v.); volume ix, 1767 (q.v.).

Augustus Montague Toplady (1740–78)
Poems on Sacred Subjects V
Anonymous

James Townley (1714–78)
High Life Below Stairs: A farce D
Anonymous

Arthur Young (1741–1820)
Reflections on the Present State of Affairs at Home and Abroad NF

Edward Young (1683–1765)
Conjectures on Original Composition NF
Anonymous

1760

- Death of George II (25 Oct.)
  GEORGE III (–1820)
- William Beckford born
  William Gilbert born
  Mary Hays born
- Isaac Hawkins Browne, the elder, dies
- Thomas Clarkson born
- Marie Tussaud born

Anonymous
Yorick's Meditations upon Various Interesting and Important Subjects F
Digressive and essayistic fiction in the manner of Sterne's *Tristram Shandy* 1759 (q.v.)

James Beattie (1735–1803)
Original Poems and Translations V

Frances Brooke (1724–89) (tr.)
Letters from Juliet, Lady Catesby F
Published 1760, dated 1759. Translated from the French of Marie-Jeanne Riccoboni (1713–92).

John Cleland (1709–89)?
The Romance of a Day; or, An Adventure in Greenwich-Park F
Attributed to Cleland

George Colman, the elder (1732–94)
Polly Honeycombe: A dramatick novel of one act D
Anonymous. Performed 5 December 1760.

George Colman, the elder (1732–94) and **Robert Lloyd** (1733–64)
Two Odes V
i: 'To Obscurity'; ii: 'To Oblivion'. Written in parody of Thomas Gray.

John Delap (1725–1812)
Elegies V

Sarah Fielding (1710–68)
The History of Ophelia F
bao *David Simple*

Samuel Foote (1720–77)
The Minor: A comedy D
Performed 28 January 1760

John Home (1722–1808)
The Siege of Aquileia: A tragedy D
Performed 21 February 1760

Charles Johnstone (1719?–1800?)
Chrysal; or, The Adventures of a Guinea [vols i, ii] F
Anonymous. Volumes iii and iv published in 1765. First complete edition published in 1767.

William Law (1686–1761)
Of Justification by Faith and Works NF

Robert Lloyd (1733–64)
The Actor V
Anonymous

Robert Lloyd (1733–64)
The Tears and Triumphs of Parnassus V

George Lyttelton, 1st Baron Lyttelton (1709–73)
Dialogues of the Dead V
Anonymous. Numbers 26, 27, and 28 are by Elizabeth Montagu.

James Macpherson (1736–96)
Fragments of Ancient Poetry V

Arthur Murphy (1727–1805)
The Desert Island D
Performed 24 January 1760

Arthur Murphy (1727–1805)
The Way to Keep Him D
Performed 24 January 1760

James Scott (1733–1814)
Heaven: A vision V
Seatonian Prize poem

John Scott (1730–83)
Four Elegies: Descriptive and Moral V
Anonymous

John Shebbeare (1709–88)
The History of the Sumatrans PS
A political satire on the Whig opponents of George III

Tobias George Smollett (1721–71) (ed.)
The British Magazine PER
Published in 8 volumes, 1760–7. Volumes i and ii contain the first publication of *Launcelot Greaves* 1762 (q.v.).

Laurence Sterne (1713–68)
The Sermons of Mr Yorick [vols i, ii] NF
Anonymous. Volumes iii and iv, 1766 (q.v.); volumes v, vi, and vii, 1769.

William Tytler (1711–92)
An Historical and Critical Inquiry into the Evidence Against Mary Queen of Scots NF
Anonymous

1761

- Eyre Coote takes Pondicherry (16 Jan.)
- John Williams ('Anthony Pasquin') born
- Benjamin Hoadly, the elder, bishop of Winchester, dies
  William Law dies
  William Oldys dies
  Samuel Richardson dies
- August von Kotzebue born
- Rousseau, *Julie ou la Nouvelle Héloïse*

John Armstrong (1709–79)
A Day: An epistle to John Wilkes V
Anonymous. Misdated 1661.

Isaac Bickerstaffe (1735?–1812)
Thomas and Sally; or, The Sailor's Return D
Performed 28 November 1760. Libretto only, without the music by Thomas Arne.

Henry Brooke (1703–83)
The Earl of Essex: A tragedy D
Performed May 1750

Charles Churchill (1731–64)
The Apology V

Charles Churchill (1731–64)
Night: An epistle to Robert Lloyd V
Anonymous

Charles Churchill (1731–64)
The Rosciad V

Thomas Cole (1726?–96)
Discourses on Luxury, Infidelity, and Enthusiasm NF

George Colman, the elder (1732–94)
Critical Reflections on the Old English Dramatick Writers NF
Anonymous

George Colman, the elder (1732–94)
The Jealous Wife: A comedy D
Performed 12 February 1761. Partly derived from Fielding's *Tom Jones* 1749 (q.v.).

Robert Dodsley (1703–64)
Select Fables of Esop and Other Fabulists F
Collected, partly translated, and partly written by Dodsley, who also added 'An essay on fable'. Other contributors included William Melmoth, William Shenstone, and Richard Graves.

Francis Fawkes (1720–77)
Original Poems and Translations V

Richard Glover (1712–85)
Medea: A tragedy D
Not intended for the stage but acted in 1767, 1768, and 1776 for the benefit of Mary Ann Yates (1728–87)

John Hawkesworth (1715?–73)
Almoran and Hamet: An oriental tale F
Anonymous

Henry Home, Lord Kames (1696–1782)
Introduction to the Art of Thinking NF
Anonymous

David Hume (1711–76)
The History of England, from the Invasion of Julius Caesar to the Accession of Henry VII NF
Published in 2 volumes (1761–2). See also *History of Great Britain* 1754, [1756]; *History of England* 1759.

Edward Jerningham (1737–1812)
Andromache to Pyrrhus: An heroick epistle V

William Kenrick (1725?–79) (tr.)
Eloisa; or, A Series of Original Letters F
Anonymous. The earliest translation of *Julie ou la Nouvelle Héloïse* (1761) by Jean-Jacques Rousseau (1712–78).

Robert Lloyd (1733–64)
An Epistle to Charles Churchill V

Arthur Murphy (1727–1805)
All in the Wrong D
Performed 15 June 1761

Arthur Murphy (1727–1805)
The Old Maid D
Performed 2 July 1761

Thomas Percy (1729–1811) (ed. and tr.)
Hau Kiou Choaan; or, The Pleasing History F
Anonymous. Volumes i–iii translated by James Wilkinson; volume iv translated by Percy.

Joseph Priestley (1733–1804)
The Rudiments of English Grammar NF

'Sir Charles Morell' [James Ridley (1736–65)]
The History of James Lovegrove, Esquire F

James Scott (1733–1814)
Odes on Several Subjects V

Frances Sheridan (1724–66)
Memoirs of Miss Sidney Bidulph F
Anonymous. See also *Conclusion of the Memoirs of Miss Sidney Bidulph* 1767.

Laurence Sterne (1713–68)
The Life and Opinions of Tristram Shandy, Gentleman [vols iii, iv] F
Anonymous. Published January 1761. Volumes i, ii published in 1759 (q.v.); volumes v, vi 1762 (q.v.); volumes vii, viii 1765 (q.v.); volume ix 1767 (q.v.).

Edward Thompson (1739?–86)
The Meretriciad V
A satire on Kitty Fisher, a London courtesan

1762

- Assassination of Peter III of Russia (17 July); accession of Catherine the Great
  Library of the Sorbonne founded
  The 'Cock Lane Ghost' hoax
- Joanna Baillie born
  James Boaden born
  William Lisle Bowles born
  Sir Samuel Egerton Brydges born
  George Colman, the younger, born
  Susanna Rowson born
  Helen Maria Williams born
- George Bubb Dodington dies
  Lady Mary Wortley Montagu dies
- George Anson dies
  Richard ('Beau') Nash dies
- Johann Gottlieb Fichte born
- Rousseau, *Contrat Social*; Émile

The North Briton PER
Principally written by John Wilkes (1727–97), with contributions from Charles Churchill. First

number published on 5 June 1762. Publication ceased in November 1763.

James Boswell (1740–95)
The Cub at Newmarket V
Anonymous

George Campbell (1719–96)
A Dissertation on Miracles NF

Elizabeth Carter (1717–1806)
Poems on Several Occasions V

Charles Churchill (1731–64)
The Ghost [bks i, ii] V
Book iii published in 1762; book iv, 1763

John Cleland (1709–89)?
The Romance of a Night; or, The Covent-Garden Adventure F
Attributed to Cleland

Mary Collier (1690?–1762)
Poems, on Several Occasions V

John Cunningham (1729–73)
The Contemplatist V

John Delap (1725–1812)
Hecuba: A tragedy D
Anonymous. Performed 11 December 1761.

Thomas Denton (1724–77)
The House of Superstition V
Prefixed to Gilpin's *Lives of the Reformers*. Written in imitation of Spenser.

Henry Fielding (1707–54)
The Works of Henry Fielding WKS

Samuel Foote (1720–77)
The Orators D
Performed 30 August 1762

David Garrick (1717–79) (adap.)
Cymbeline: A tragedy D
Anonymous. Performed 28 November 1761. From Shakespeare.

Oliver Goldsmith (1728–74)
The Citizen of the World; or, Letters From a Chinese Philosopher Residing in London to his Friends in the East F
Anonymous. Published 1 May 1762. Serialized in *The Public Ledger* (January 1760–August 1761) as *Chinese Letters*.

Oliver Goldsmith (1728–74)
The Life of Richard Nash, of Bath NF
Anonymous

Oliver Goldsmith (1728–74)
The Mystery Revealed NF
Anonymous. Attributed to Goldsmith. On the celebrated Cock Lane ghost.

Henry Home, Lord Kames (1696–1782)
Elements of Criticism NF

Richard Hurd (1720–1808)
Letters on Chivalry and Romance NF
Anonymous

Edward Jerningham (1737–1812)
The Nunnery: An elegy in imitation of the Elegy in a Churchyard V
In imitation of Thomas Gray

Charles Johnstone (1719?–1800?)
The Reverie; or, A Flight to the Paradise of Fools F

William Kenrick (1725?–79) (tr.)
Emilius and Sophia; or A New System of Education F
Anonymous. The earliest translation of Rousseau's *Émile, ou De l'education* (1762). A sequel, *Emilius and Sophia; or, The Solitaries*, published in 1783.

John Langhorne (1735–79)
Letters on Religious Retirement, Melancholy and Enthusiasm NF

John Langhorne (1735–79)
Solyman and Almena: An oriental tale F
Anonymous

Charlotte Lennox (1729?–1804)
Sophia F

Robert Lloyd (1733–64)
Poems by Robert Lloyd V

Robert Lowth (1710–87)
A Short Introduction to English Grammar NF

'Ossian' [James Macpherson (1736–96)**]**
Fingal: An ancient epic poem . . . Together with several other poems translated from the Galic language V
Macpherson posed as the translator of this supposed ancient Gaelic epic by one Ossian, son of Fingal, but in fact he had liberally edited and loosely translated parts of many Gaelic poems, inserting extended passages of his own composition. See also *Fragment of Ancient Poetry* 1760, and *Temora* 1763.

John Ogilvie (1732–1813)
Poems on Various Subjects V

Joseph Priestley (1733–1804)
A Course of Lectures on the Theory of Language, and Universal Grammar NF

Sarah Scott (1723–95)
A Description of Millenium Hall, and the Country Adjacent F
Anonymous. Sometimes thought to have been written with Lady Barbara Montagu. Also attributed to Oliver Goldsmith and Christopher Smart.

Tobias George Smollett (1721–71)
The Life and Adventures of Sir Launcelot Greaves F
bao *Roderick Random*. Serialized in *The British Magazine* (January 1760-December 1761).

Laurence Sterne (1713–68)
The Life and Opinions of Tristram Shandy, Gentleman [vols v, vi] F
Anonymous, but dedication to volume v signed. Volumes i, ii 1759 (q.v.); volumes iii, iv 1761 (q.v.); volumes vii, viii 1765 (q.v.); volume ix 1767 (q.v.).

Horace Walpole (1717–97) (ed.)
Anecdotes of Painting in England NF
Published in 4 volumes (1762–71). Volume iv contained Walpole's 'Essay on Modern Gardening', published separately in 1785

William Whitehead (1715–85)
A Charge to the Poets V

Edward Young (1683–1765)
Resignation V
Anonymous. First privately printed in 1761.

1763

- Peace of Paris (10 Feb.) ends Seven Years War
  Arrest of John Wilkes for attacking the government in *The North Briton* No. 45 (Apr.)
  James Boswell meets Samuel Johnson (16 May)
  Almack's gaming club opens in London
- William Cobbett born
  Samuel Rogers born
  Elizabeth Sophia Tomlins born
- John Byrom dies
  Mary Collyer dies
  William Shenstone dies
- Johann Paul Friedrich Richter ('Jean Paul') born
  Almanack de Gotha first issued

Anonymous
The Peregrinations of Jeremiah Grant, Esq; the West-Indian F

John Ash (1724?–79)
Grammatical Institutes NF

Richard Bentley, the younger (1708–82)
Patriotism V
Anonymous

Isaac Bickerstaffe (1735?–1812)
Love in a Village: A comic opera D/OP
Anonymous. Performed 8 December 1762.

Hugh Blair (1718–1800)
A Critical Dissertation on the Poems of Ossian, the Son of Fingal NF
Anonymous

Frances Brooke (1724–89)
The History of Lady Julia Mandeville F
'By the translator of *Lady Catesby's Letters*'. Ten editions by 1792.

John Brown (1715–66)
A Dissertation on Poetry and Music NF

Charles Churchill (1731–64)
The Author V

Charles Churchill (1731–64)
The Conference V

Charles Churchill (1731–64)
An Epistle to William Hogarth V

Charles Churchill (1731–64)
Poems V

Charles Churchill (1731–64)
The Prophecy of Famine V

John Collier (1708–86)
Tim Bobbin's Toy-shop; or, His Whimsical Amusements V

George Colman, the elder (1732–94)
The Deuce is in Him: A farce D
Performed 4 November 1763

Philip Doddridge (1702–51)
A Course of Lectures on the Principal Subjects in Pneumatology, Ethics, and Divinity NF

Susannah Minifie, later **Gunning** (1740?–1800) and **Margaret Minifie** (*fl.* 1768–83)
The Histories of Lady Frances S----- and Lady Caroline S----- F

George Keate (1729–97)
The Alps V

John Langhorne (1735–79)
The Letters that Passed Between Theodosius and Constantia F
Anonymous

Mary Latter (1725–77)
The Siege of Jerusalem, by Titus Vespasian: A tragedy D
Anonymous

Robert Lloyd (1733–64) (tr.)
The Death of Adam: A tragedy V
Translated from Friedrich Gottlieb Klopstock (1724–1803), *Der Tod Adams*

Catherine Macaulay (1731–91)
The History of England from the Accession of James I to that of the Brunswick Line NF
Published in 8 volumes (1763–83)

'Ossian' [James Macpherson (1736–96)**]**
Temora: An ancient epic poem V
In this work, as in *Fingal* 1762 (q.v.), Macpherson posed as the translator of a supposed ancient Gaelic epic by one Ossian, son of Fingal. See also *Fingal* 1762 and *Works of Ossian* 1765.

David Mallet (1705?–65)
Elvira: A tragedy D
Performed 19 January 1763

William Mason (1725–97)
Elegies V

James Merrick (1720–69)
Poems on Sacred Subjects V

Lady Mary Wortley Montagu (1689–1762)
Letters Written, During her Travels in Europe, Asia and Africa, to Persons of Distinction NF

Arthur Murphy (1727–1805)
The Citizen D
Performed 2 July 1761

Robert Orme (1728–1801)
A History of the Military Transactions of the British Nation in Indostan from the Year 1745 NF
Anonymous

Frances Sheridan (1724–66)
The Discovery: A comedy D
Performed 3 February 1763

Christopher Smart (1722–71)
A Song to David V
See also *A Translation of the Psalms of David* 1765

Henry Venn (1725–97)
The Complete Duty of Man NF

William Warburton (1698–1779)
The Doctrine of Grace NF

John Wesley (1703–91)
A Survey of the Wisdom of God in the Creation NF

1764

- John Wilkes expelled from the House of Commons (Jan.)
  Samuel Johnson founds The Literary Club
- Sir John Barrow born
  James Beresford born
  Thomas Morton born?
  Ann Radcliffe born
  Frederic Reynolds born
  John Thelwall born
- Charles Churchill dies
  Robert Dodsley dies
  Robert Lloyd dies
- William Hogarth dies
- Jean Philippe Rameau dies
- Voltaire, *Dictionnaire philosophique*

David Erskine Baker (1730–67)
The Companion to the Play-house; or, An Historical Account of all the Dramatic Writers (and their Works) that have Appeared in Great Britain and Ireland DICT
Anonymous. Expanded by Isaac Reed as *Biographia Dramatica* 1782 (q.v.).

Charles Churchill (1731–64)
The Candidate V

Charles Churchill (1731–64)
The Duellist V
Anonymous

Charles Churchill (1731–64)
The Farewell V

Charles Churchill (1731–64)
Gotham [bk i] V
Book ii, 1764; book iii, 1764

Charles Churchill (1731–64)
Independence V
Anonymous

Charles Churchill (1731–64)
The Times V

John Gilbert Cooper (1723–69)
Poems on Several Subjects V
bao *The Life of Socrates*. Edited by Robert Dodsley.

Samuel Foote (1720–77)
The Patron: A comedy D
Performed 26 June 1764

Phebe Gibbes (*fl.* 1777–89)
The History of Lady Louisa Stroud, and the Honourable Miss Caroline Stretton F
Anonymous

Oliver Goldsmith (1728–74)
An History of England NF
Anonymous. Published on 26 June 1764.

Oliver Goldsmith (1728–74)
The Traveller; or, A Prospect of Society V
Published on 19 December 1764, dated 1765

James Grainger (1721–66)
The Sugar-Cane V

Susannah Minifie, later **Gunning** (1740?–1800)
Family Pictures F
Anonymous

Edward Herbert, Lord Herbert of Cherbury (1583–1648)
The Life of Edward Lord Herbert of Cherbury NF
Edited by Horace Walpole

Edward Jerningham (1737–1812)
The Nun V
bao *The Magdalens*

George Keate (1729–97)
The Ruins of Netley Abbey V

Mary Latter (1725–77)
Liberty and Interest V

William Mason (1725–97)
Poems V

Arthur Murphy (1727–1805)
No One's Enemy But His Own: A comedy D
Anonymous. Performed 9 January 1764. Based on Voltaire's *L'indiscret.*

Arthur Murphy (1727–1805)
What We Must All Come To: A comedy D
Anonymous. Performed 9 January 1764.

John Newton (1725–1807)
An Authentic Narrative of Some Remarkable and Interesting Particulars in the Life of [Newton] NF
Anonymous

Kane O'Hara (1714?–82)
Midas: An English burletta D
Anonymous Performed in Dublin 22 January 1762.

'George Psalmanazar' (1679?–1763)
*Memoirs of ****. Commonly Known by the Name of George Psalmanazar; a Reputed Native of Formosa* F
'George Psalmanazar' is a pseudonym

Anthony Purver (1702–77) (tr.)
A New and Literal Translation of all the Books of the Old and New Testament BIB
Anonymous. Known as the 'Quaker Bible'. Begun in 1733, published in parts *c.*1742.

Thomas Reid (1710–96)
An Inquiry into the Human Mind NF

'Sir Charles Morell' [**James Ridley** (1736–65)]
The Tales of the Genii F
Based on the Arabian Nights. Originally issued in shilling parts.

William Shenstone (1714–63)
Works, in Verse and Prose WKS
Edited by Robert Dodsley. A third volume published in 1769.

Frances Sheridan (1724–66)
The Dupe: A comedy D
bao *The Discovery.* Performed 10 December 1763.

Christopher Smart (1722–71)
Hannah: An oratorio D

Christopher Smart (1722–71) (tr.)
A Poetical Translation of the Fables of Phaedrus V

Horace Walpole (1717–97)
The Castle of Otranto F
Anonymous. Published on 24 December 1764, dated 1765. Many editions.

Thomas Warton, the younger (1728–90) (ed.)
The Oxford Sausage; or, Select Poetical Pieces ANTH

1765

- Stamp Act passed (Mar.) for taxing the American colonies
- James Grahame born
  Henry Luttrell born
  William Taylor born
  Robert Plumer Ward born
- Samuel Madden dies
  David Mallet dies
  James Ridley dies
  Edward Young dies

Anonymous
The History of Little Goody Twoshoes F
Often attributed to Oliver Goldsmith and sometimes to Giles Jones. Many subsequent editions.

James Beattie (1735–1803)
The Judgment of Paris V

James Beattie (1735–1803)
Verses Occasioned by the Death of Charles Churchill V
Churchill died in November 1764

Isaac Bickerstaffe (1735?–1812)
Daphne and Amintor: A comic opera D/OP
Adapted from *L'Oracle* by G.F. Poullain de Saint-Foix (1698–1776). Performed 8 October 1765.

Isaac Bickerstaffe (1735?–1812)
The Maid of the Mill: A comic opera D/OP
Performed 31 January 1765. Based on Richardson's *Pamela* 1741 (q.v.).

Sir William Blackstone (1723–89)
Commentaries on the Laws of England NF
Published in 4 volumes (1765–9)

John Bunyan (1628–88)
A Relation of [*the*] *Imprisonment of Mr John Bunyan* NF

William Collins (1721–59)
The Poetical Works of William Collins V
The first collected edition

George Colman, the elder (1732–94) (tr.)
The Comedies of Terence D

Charles Dibdin (1745–1814)
The Shepherd's Artifice: A dramatic pastoral D
Performed 21 May 1764

Henry Fuseli (1741–1825) (tr.)
Reflections on the Painting and Sculpture of the Greeks NF
A translation of *Gedanken uber die Nachahmung der griechischen Werke* by Johann Joachim Winckelman (1717–68)

Oliver Goldsmith (1728–74)
Essays by Mr Goldsmith NF

Elizabeth Griffith (1720?–93) (adap.)
The Platonic Wife: A comedy D
Published anonymously. Performed January 1765. Adapted from the story 'L'heureuse divorce' in the *Contes moraux* of Jean-François Marmontel (1723–99).

Thomas Hull (1728–1808)
Pharnaces: An opera D/OP
Performed 15 February 1765

Edward Jerningham (1737–1812)
An Elegy Written Among the Ruins of an Abbey V
bao *The Nun*

William Kenrick (1725?–79)
A Review of Doctor Johnson's New Edition of Shakespeare NF
See Johnson, *The Plays of William Shakespeare* 1765

James Macpherson (1736–96)
The Works of Ossian V
Contains both *Fingal* 1762 (q.v.) and *Temora* 1763 (q.v.), as well as Hugh Blair's *Critical Dissertation on the Poems of Ossian*, first published 1763 (q.v.). Macpherson posed as the translator of ancient Gaelic poetry by 'Ossian, son of Fingal', but in fact he had liberally edited and loosely translated parts of many Gaelic poems and supplemented these by passages of his own composition.

Thomas Percy (1729–1811) (ed.)
Reliques of Ancient English Poetry ANTH

Joseph Priestley (1733–1804)
An Essay on a Course of Liberal Education for Civil and Active Life NF

William Shakespeare (1564–1616)
The Plays of William Shakespeare, with the Corrections and Illustrations of Various Commentators EDN
Edited by Samuel Johnson. Revised by George Steevens in 1773 (q.v.)

William Shirley (*fl.* 1739–80)
Electra: A tragedy D

Christopher Smart (1722–71) (tr.)
A Translation of the Psalms of David V
Includes *A Song to David* 1763 (q.v.) and Smart's 'Hymns and Spiritual Songs for the Fasts and Festivals of the Church of England'

Laurence Sterne (1713–68)
The Life and Opinions of Tristram Shandy, Gentleman [vols vii, viii] F
Anonymous. Published January 1765. Volumes i, ii, 1759 (q.v.); volumes iii, iv, 1761 (q.v.); volumes v, vi, 1762 (q.v.); volume ix, 1767 (q.v.).

George Alexander Stevens (1710–84)
The Celebrated Lecture on Heads NF
Anonymous. Lecture first delivered in 1764.

Percival Stockdale (1736–1811)
Churchill Defended V

1766

- Stamp Act repealed (Mar.) but Declaratory Act passed asserting sovereignty over the American assemblies
- Robert Bloomfield born
  Isaac D'Israeli born
  Thomas Malthus born
  Mary Pilkington born
- Thomas Birch dies
  William Rufus Chetwood dies
  Zachary Grey dies
  Frances Sheridan dies
  William Thompson dies
- James Edward Stuart ('The Old Pretender') dies
- Anne-Louise-Germaine Necker, Madame de Staël, born
- G.E. Lessing, *Laocoön*
  C.M. Wieland, *Agathon*

Anonymous
Genuine Memoirs of the Celebrated Miss Maria Brown F
Although the title-page associates the novel with 'the author of *A Woman of Pleasure*' (i.e. John Cleland), this was almost certainly a commercial ploy

Mark Akenside (1721–70)
An Ode to the Late Thomas Edwards V

Christopher Anstey (1724–1805)
The New Bath Guide; or, Memoirs of the B[lunde]R[hea]D Family in a Series of Poetical Epistles V
Twelve editions by 1784

James Beattie (1735–1803)
Poems on Several Subjects V
Beattie styled this collection 'A new edition, corrected' because it used some poems from his 1760 (q.v.) *Original Poems and Translations*, which he had tried to suppress. This collection reprints none of the translations from his earlier volume.

Francis Blackburne (1705–87)
The Confessional; or, A Full and Free Inquiry into Establishing Systematical Confessions of Faith and Doctrine in Protestant Churches NF
Anonymous. The book inspired a considerable controversy.

Henry Brooke (1703–83)
The Fool of Quality; or, The History of Henry Earl of Moreland F
Published in 5 volumes (1766–70)

Edmund Burke (1729–97)
A Short Account of a Late Short Administration NF
Anonymous. Possibly a collaboration with John Christopher Roberts and William Mellish.

George Colman, the elder (1732–94) and **David Garrick** (1717–79)
The Clandestine Marriage: A comedy D
Performed 20 February 1766

John Cunningham (1729–73)
Poems, Chiefly Pastoral V

Thomas Francklin (1721–84)
The Earl of Warwick: A tragedy D
Anonymous. Performed 13 December 1766. Altered from *Le comte de Warwick* by Jean-François de La Harpe (1739–1803).

John Freeth (1731?–1808)
The Political Songster V

Oliver Goldsmith (1728–74) (ed.)
Poems for Young Ladies ANTH
Published 1766, dated 1767

Oliver Goldsmith (1728–74)
The Vicar of Wakefield: A tale, supposed to be written by himself F
Anonymous. Published 27 March 1766. Seven editions in 1766; 66 editions to 1800.

Elizabeth Griffith (1720?–93)
The Double Mistake: A comedy D
Published anonymously. Performed 9 January 1766.

Susannah Minifie, later **Gunning** (1740?–1800) and **Margaret Minifie** (*fl.* 1768–83)
The Picture F

Thomas Hull (1728–1808)
The Fairy Favour: A masque D
Anonymous. Performed 31 January 1767.

Catherine Jemmat (1714–66)
Miscellanies in Prose and Verse MISC

Charles Jenner (1736–74)
Poems V

Hugh Kelly (1739–77)
Memoirs of a Magdalen; or, The History of Louisa Mildmay F
Anonymous. Published 1766, dated 1767.

Charlotte Lennox (1729?–1804)?
The History of Eliza F
Anonymous. Published 1766, dated 1767. Sometimes attributed to Lennox.

Thomas Pennant (1726–98)
The British Zoology NF
Anonymous

Henry James Pye (1745–1813)
Beauty V

Sarah Scott (1723–95)
The History of Sir George Ellison F
Anonymous. Subsequently published as *The Man of Real Sensibility*.

William Shakespeare (1564–1616)
Twenty of the Plays of Shakespeare EDN
Edited by George Steevens

Samuel Sharp (1700?–78)
Letters from Italy NF

Tobias George Smollett (1721–71)
Travels Through France and Italy NF

Laurence Sterne (1713–68)
The Sermons of Mr Yorick [vols iii, iv] NF
Volumes i, ii 1760 (q.v.); volumes v, vi, and vii published posthumously in 1769 as *Sermons by the Late Rev. Mr Sterne* (q.v.).

Thomas Tyrwhitt (1730–86)
Observations and Conjectures Upon Some Passages of Shakespeare NF
Anonymous

John Wesley (1703–91)
A Plain Account of Christian Perfection NF

Anna Williams (1706–83) (ed.)
Miscellanies in Prose and Verse MISC

1767

- Taxes imposed on the American colonies on imports of tea, paper, and other goods
- Alexander Balfour born
  Maria Edgeworth born
- David Erskine Baker dies
  Robert Paltock dies
- John Quincy Adams born
  Benjamin Constant born
  Andrew Jackson born

Anonymous
Belisarius F
Translation of *Bélisaire* (1767) by Jean-François Marmontel (1723–99). A great popular success.

Richard Bentley, the younger (1708–82)
Philodamus D
Anonymous. Performed 14 December 1782.

Isaac Bickerstaffe (1735?–1812)
Love in the City: A comic opera D/OP
Performed 21 February 1767

James Boswell (1740–95)
Dorando: A Spanish tale F
Anonymous

John Byrom (1692–1763)
The Universal English Short-hand NF

George Colman, the elder (1732–94)
The English Merchant: A comedy D
Performed 21 February 1767. From Voltaire.

William Duff (1732–1815)
An Essay on Original Genius NF
Anonymous. See also *Critical Observations* 1770.

Richard Farmer (1735–97)
An Essay on the Learning of Shakespeare NF

Francis Fawkes (1720–77)
Partridge-Shooting: An eclogue V

Adam Ferguson (1723–1816)
An Essay on the History of Civil Society NF

David Garrick (1717–79)
Cymon: A dramatic romance D
Anonymous. Performed 2 January 1767.

Phebe Gibbes (*fl.* 1777–89)
The Woman of Fashion; or, The History of Lady Diana Dormer F
Anonymous

Oliver Goldsmith (1728–74) (ed.)
The Beauties of English Poesy ANTH

Susannah Minifie, later **Gunning** (1740?–1800)
Barford Abbey F
Anonymous. Published 1767, dated 1768. An epistolary novel.

Hall Hartson (*d.* 1773)
The Countess of Salisbury: A tragedy D
Performed 2 May 1765

Richard Jago (1715–81)
Edge-Hill; or, The Rural Prospect Delineated and Moralised V

Henry Jones (1721–70)
Kew Garden V

Catherine Macaulay (1731–91)
Loose Remarks on Mr Hobbes's Philosophical Rudiments of Government and Society NF
Anonymous. See Thomas Hobbes, *Philosophicall Rudiments* 1651.

Moses Mendes (*d.* 1758) and others
A Collection of the Most Esteemed Pieces of Poetry ANTH

William Mickle (1735–88)
The Concubine V
Reissued as *Sir Martin* 1778

Arthur Murphy (1727–1805)
The School for Guardians D
Performed 10 January 1767

Joseph Priestley (1733–1804)
The History and Present State of Electricity NF

Frances Sheridan (1724–66)
Conclusion of the Memoirs of Miss Sidney Bidulph F
Anonymous. See *Memoirs of Miss Sidney Bidulph* 1761.

Frances Sheridan (1724–66)
The History of Nourjahad F
'By the editor of *Sidney Bidulph*'

Christopher Smart (1722–71) (tr.)
The Works of Horace, Translated into Verse EDN
See also *Works of Horace* 1756

Laurence Sterne (1713–68)
The Life and Opinions of Tristram Shandy, Gentleman [vol. ix] F
Anonymous. Published January 1767. Volumes i, ii, 1759 (q.v.); volumes iii, iv, 1761 (q.v.); volumes v, vi, 1762 (q.v.); volumes vii, viii, 1765 (q.v.).

William Warburton (1698–1779)
Sermons and Discourses on Various Subjects and Occasions NF
Volume iii of *The Principles of Natural and Revealed Religion* 1753 (q.v.)

Arthur Young (1741–1820)
The Adventures of Emmera; or, The Fair American F
Anonymous

Arthur Young (1741–1820)
The Farmer's Letters to the People of England NF
Anonymous

1768

- John Wilkes elected MP for Middlesex
  Royal Academy founded, with Joshua Reynolds as its first president
- Charles Dibdin born
- Sarah Fielding dies
  Joseph Spence dies
  Laurence Sterne dies
- François-René de Chateaubriand born

Anonymous
L'ingénu; or, The Sincere Huron F
Translation of Voltaire's *L'Ingénu* (1767)

Isaac Bickerstaffe (1735?–1812)
Lionel and Clarissa: A comic opera D/OP
Anonymous. Performed 25 February 1768. Revised as *The School for Fathers* in 1770.

Isaac Bickerstaffe (1735?–1812)
The Padlock: A comic opera D/OP
Anonymous. Performed 3 October 1768. Based on Cervantes's *El celoso extremono.*

James Boswell (1740–95)
An Account of Corsica NF

Isaac Hawkins Browne, the elder (1705–60)
Poems Upon Various Subjects, Latin and English V
Edited by Isaac Hawkins Browne, the younger

John Cleland (1709–89)?
The Woman of Honor F
Sometimes attributed to Cleland

Alexander Dow (*d.* 1779) (tr.)
Tales Translated from the Persian of Inatulla of Delhi F
The author of the original was In-ayat All-ah (*d. c.*1671)

Oliver Goldsmith (1728–74)
The Good Natur'd Man: A comedy D
Performed 29 January 1768. Prologue by Samuel Johnson.

Oliver Goldsmith (1728–74)
The Present State of the British Empire in Europe, America, Africa, and Asia NF
Anonymous

Richard Gough (1735–1809)
Anecdotes of British Topography NF
Anonymous

Thomas Gray (1716–71)
Poems, by Mr Gray V
The first collected edition. Includes 'The Fatal Sisters', 'The Descent of Odin', 'The Triumphs of Owen', but omits 'A Long Story'.

John Hoole (1727–1803)
Cyrus: A tragedy D
Performed 3 December 1768

Thomas Hull (1728–1808) (adap.)
The Royal Merchant: An opera D/OP
Anonymous. Performed 14 December 1767. Adapted from *The Beggar's Bush*, attributed to Beaumont and Fletcher.

Richard Jago (1715–81)
Labour and Genius; or, The Mill-Stream, and the Cascade V

Edward Jerningham (1737–1812)
Amabella V

Hugh Kelly (1739–77)
False Delicacy: A comedy D
Performed 23 January 1768. Prologue and epilogue by David Garrick.

Lady Mary Wortley Montagu (1689–1762)
Poetical Works V

Arthur Murphy (1727–1805)
Zenobia: A tragedy D
bao *The Orphan of China*. Performed 27 February 1768.

Joseph Priestley (1733–1804)
An Essay on the First Principles of Government NF

Henry James Pye (1745–1813)
Elegies on Different Occasions V
Anonymous

Alexander Ross (1699–1784)
The Fortunate Shepherdess V

William Shakespeare (1564–1616)
Mr William Shakespeare His Comedies, Histories and Tragedies EDN
Edited by Edward Capell

Christopher Smart (1722–71)
The Parables of Our Lord and Saviour Jesus Christ V

Tobias George Smollett (1721–71)
The Present State of all Nations NF
Published in 8 volumes (1766–9)

Laurence Sterne (1713–68)
A Sentimental Journey Through France and Italy NF
Published in February 1768

Gilbert Stuart (1742–86)
An Historical Dissertation Concerning the Antiquity of the English Constitution NF
Anonymous

'Edward Search' [Abraham Tucker (1705–74)]
The Light of Nature Pursued NF
A third volume was published posthumously in 1777. See also William Hazlitt, *An Abridgement* . . . 1807.

Horace Walpole (1717–97)
Historic Doubts on the Life and Reign of King Richard III NF

Horace Walpole (1717–97)
The Mysterious Mother: A tragedy D
Limited edition. First public edition published in 1781.

William Wilkie (1721–72)
Fables V

Arthur Young (1741–1820)
A Six Weeks' Tour Through the Southern Counties of England and Wales NF
bao *The Farmer's Letters*

1769

- John Wilkes expelled from Parliament
  Tea duty in the American colonies retained
  Josiah Wedgwood opens the Etruria pottery works
  Shakespeare Jubilee at Stratford-upon-Avon
- John Hookham Frere born
  Elizabeth Gunning born
  Amelia Opie born
- WIlliam Duncombe dies
  Edward Kimber dies
  James Merrick dies
- Thomas Lawrence born
  Arthur Wellesley, duke of Wellington, born
- Napoleon born
  Alexander von Humboldt born

Sir William Blackstone (1723–1789)
A Reply to Dr Priestley's Remarks on the Fourth Volume of the Commentaries on the Laws of England NF

Elizabeth Bonhote (1744–1818)
Hortensia F
Anonymous

Frances Brooke (1724–89)
The History of Emily Montague F
bao *Lady Julia Mandeville*

William Buchan (1729–1805)
Domestic Medicine; or, The Family Physician NF

Edmund Burke (1729–97)
Observations on a Late State of the Nation NF
Anonymous. Answers William Knox, *The Present State of the Nation* 1768

Charles Burney (1726–1814)
An Essay Towards a History of the Principal Comets that have Appeared Since 1742 NF
Anonymous

George Colman, the elder (1732–94)
The Oxonian in Town: A comedy D
Published 1769, dated 1770. Performed 7 November 1767.

Alexander Dow (*d.* 1779)
Zingis: A tragedy D
Performed 17 December 1768

Adam Ferguson (1723–1816)
Institutes of Moral Philosophy NF

'Junius' [probably Sir Philip Francis (1740–1818)]
The Political Contest [pt i] NF
Fourteen letters, January–July 1769, the last dated 8 July

'Junius' [probably Sir Philip Francis (1740–1818)]
The Political Contest [pt ii] NF
Seven letters, the last dated 25 September 1769

'Junius' [probably Sir Philip Francis (1740–1818)]
*Two Letters from Junius to the D*** of G******* NF
'D*** of G***' = the duke of Grafton

Oliver Goldsmith (1728–74)
The Roman History NF
Many editions. Abridged for the use of schools in 1772.

James Granger (1723–76)
Biographical History of England from Egbert the Great to the Revolution NF

Thomas Gray (1716–71)
Ode Performed in the Senate-House at Cambridge, July 1, 1769 V

Elizabeth Griffith (1720?–93) (adap.)
The School for Rakes: A comedy D
Published anonymously. Performed February 1769. Adapted from Beaumarchais's *Eugénie* (1767).

Richard Griffith (1714?–88) and **Elizabeth Griffith** (1720?–93)
Two Novels: in Letters F
bao *Henry and Frances*. Contains *The Delicate Distress* by Elizabeth Griffith and *The Gordian Knot* by Richard Griffith.

Susannah Gunning, formerly **Minifie** (1740?–1800)
The Cottage F

John Home (1722–1808)
The Fatal Discovery D
Performed 23 February 1769

Charles Jenner (1736–74)
The Placid Man; or, Memoirs of Sir Charles Beville F
Anonymous. Published 1769, dated 1770.

Charlotte Lennox (1729?–1804)
The Sister: A comedy D
Performed 18 February 1769, with prologue by George Colman and epilogue by Oliver Goldsmith. Adapted from Lennox's novel *Henrietta* 1758 (q.v.).

Margaret Minifie (*fl.* 1768–83) [and **Susannah Gunning,** formerly **Minifie** (1740?–1800)]
The Hermit F

Elizabeth Montagu (1720–1800)
An Essay on the Writings and Genius of Shakespear NF
Anonymous

John Ogilvie (1732–1813)
Paradise V
Anonymous

Clara Reeve (1729–1807)
Original Poems on Several Occasions V

Sir Joshua Reynolds (1723–92)
A Discourse NF
The first of Reynolds Discourses, delivered at the opening of the Royal Academy on 2 January 1769. Fourteen more discourses published between 1769 and 1791. Collected edition published posthumously in 1820.

William Robertson (1721–93)
The History of the Reign of the Emperor Charles V NF

Tobias George Smollett (1721–71)
The History and Adventures of an Atom F
Anonymous

Laurence Sterne (1713–68)
A Political Romance NF
Anonymous. A satire on ecclesiastical disputes at York. The first edition of 1759 was suppressed.

Laurence Sterne (1713–68)
Sermons by the Late Rev. Mr Sterne [*Sermons of Mr Yorick*, v, vi, vii] NF
Volumes i and ii published in 1760 (q.v.); volumes iii, iv 1766 (q.v.)

William Tooke (1744–1820)
The Loves of Othniel and Achsah F
Anonymous. Supposedly 'translated from the Chaldee', but actually an original work by Tooke.

1770

- Lord North becomes Prime Minister
  James Cook discovers Botany Bay (Apr.)
- Joseph Cottle born
  Barbara Hofland born
  James Hogg born
  James Plumptre born
  William Wordsworth born
- Mark Akenside dies
  Thomas Chatterton dies
  Alexander Cruden dies
  Catherine Talbot dies
  George Whitefield dies
- George Canning born
  William Huskisson born
- Friedrich Hölderlin born
  Ludwig van Beethoven born
- Giovanni Tiepolo dies
- Paul Holbach, *Système de la Nature*

John Armstrong (1709–79)
Miscellanies MISC

James Beattie (1735–1803)
An Essay on the Nature and Immutability of Truth NF

Isaac Bickerstaffe (1735?–1812)
The Recruiting Serjeant D
Anonymous

Frances Brooke (1724–89) (tr.)
Memoirs of the Marquis de St Forlaix D
A translation of *Mémoires de M. le Marquis de S. Forlaix* (1770) by Nicolas-Étienne Framéry

Michael Bruce (1746–67)
Poems on Several Occasions V

Edmund Burke (1729–97)
Thoughts on the Cause of the Present Discontents NF
See also Catherine Macaulay, *Observations on a Pamphlet* 1770

George Colman, the elder (1732–94)
Man and Wife; or, The Shakespeare Jubilee: A comedy D
Performed 9 October 1769

Richard Cumberland (1732–1811)
The Brothers: A comedy D
Anonymous. Performed 2 December 1769

Sir David Dalrymple, Lord Hailes (1726–92) (ed.)
Ancient Scottish Poems ANTH

William Duff (1732–1815)
Critical Observations on the Writings of the Most Celebrated Geniuses in Poetry NF
See *Essay on Original Genius* 1767

Samuel Foote (1720–77)
The Lame Lover: A comedy D
Performed 22 June 1770

Francis Gentleman (1728–84)
The Sultan; or, Love and Fame D
Published anonymously. Performed *c*.1754.

Edward Gibbon (1737–94)
Critical Observations on the Sixth Book of the Aeneid NF
Anonymous pamphlet—Gibbon's first publication in English. On *A Dissertation on the Sixth Book of Virgil's Aeneis* and *The Divine Legation of Moses* 1738 (q.v.) by William Warburton.

Oliver Goldsmith (1728–74)
The Deserted Village V
Published in May 1770

Oliver Goldsmith (1728–74)
The Life of Thomas Parnell NF

Oliver Goldsmith (1728–74)
Life of Henry St John, Lord Viscount Bolingbroke NF
Anonymous

Ukawsaw Gronniosaw
A Narrative of the Most Remarkable Particulars in the Life of Ukawsaw Gronniosaw, an African Prince NF

John Hoole (1727–1803)
Timanthes: A tragedy D
Performed 24 February 1770

Samuel Johnson (1709–84)
The False Alarm NF
Anonymous

Hugh Kelly (1739–77)
A Word to the Wise: A comedy D
Performed 3 March 1770

Catherine Macaulay (1731–91)
Observations on a Pamphlet Entitled, Thoughts on the Present Discontents NF
A response to Burke's *Thoughts on the Cause of the Present Discontents* 1770 (q.v.)

William Mickle (1735–88)
Voltaire in the Shades; or, Dialogues on the Deistical Controversy V
Anonymous

Thomas Percy (1729–1811) (tr.)
Northern Antiquities; or, A Description of the Manners, Customs, Religion and Laws of the Ancient Danes, and Other Northern Nations . . . NF
Anonymous. From the French of Paul Henri Mallet (1730–1807).

George Alexander Stevens (1710–84)
The Court of Alexander: An opera D/OP
Performed 5 January 1770

Catherine Talbot (1721–70)
Reflections on the Seven Days of the Week NF
Anonymous. Many editions.

Augustus Montague Toplady (1740–78)
A Letter to the Rev. Mr John Wesley NF

William Woty (1731?–91)
Poetical Works V

Arthur Young (1741–1820)
A Six Months Tour Through the North of England NF

1771

- Thomas John Dibdin born
  John Lingard born
  James Montgomery born
  Sir Walter Scott born
  Sydney Smith born
- Thomas Gray dies
  Christopher Smart dies
  Tobias George Smollett dies
- Robert Owen born
  Mungo Park born
- Klopstock, *Oden*

Anonymous
The History of Sir William Harrington F
Variously attributed to Anna Meades and to Thomas Hull

James Beattie (1735–1803)
The Minstrel; or, The Progress of Genius V
Anonymous. Book ii published in 1774 (q.v.).

Isaac Bickerstaffe (1735?–1812)
He Wou'd If He Cou'd; or, An Old Fool Worse Than Any D
Anonymous. Performed 12 April 1771. Loosely based on *La serva padrona* by G.A. Frederico.

John Brown (1715–66)
Description of the Lake of Keswick NF
Written in 1753

Charles Burney (1726–1814)
The Present State of Music in France and Italy NF
See also *The Present State of Music in Germany* 1773

James Cawthorn (1719–61)
Poems V

Joseph Cradock (1742–1826)
Zobeide: A tragedy D
Performed 11 December 1771. Prologue by Oliver Goldsmith. Based on Voltaire's *Les Scythes* (1767).

Richard Cumberland (1732–1811)
The West Indian: A comedy D
bao *The Brothers*. Performed 19 January 1771.

Sir John Dalrymple (1726–1810)
Memoirs of Great Britain and Ireland NF

Oliver Goldsmith (1728–74)
The History of England NF
To the death of George II

Elizabeth Griffith (1720?–93)
The History of Lady Barton F

Samuel Johnson (1709–84)
Thoughts on the Late Transactions Respecting Falkland's Islands NF
Anonymous

Hugh Kelly (1739–77)
Clementina: A tragedy D
Anonymous. Performed 23 February 1771.

John Langhorne (1735–79)
The Fables of Flora V

John Langhorne (1735–79)
Letters to Eleonora F
Anonymous

Henry Mackenzie (1745–1831)
The Man of Feeling F
Anonymous

Thomas Pennant (1726–98)
A Tour in Scotland NF
Enlarged as *A Tour in Scotland and Voyage to the Hebrides* (1778–81)

Thomas Percy (1729–1811)
The Hermit of Warkworth V
Anonymous

Henry James Pye (1745–1813)
The Triumph of Fashion V

William Smellie (1740–95) (ed.)
Encyclopaedia Britannica; or, A Dictionary of Arts and Sciences DICT
Issued in 100 parts 1768–73

Tobias Smollett (1721–71)
The Expedition of Humphry Clinker F
bao *Roderick Random*. Published in June 1771.

John Wesley (1703–91)
The Works of the Rev. John Wesley WKS
Published in 32 volumes (1771–4)

Arthur Young (1741–1820)
The Farmer's Tour Through the East of England NF

1772

- First Partition of Poland
  Warren Hastings appointed governor of Bengal
- Henry Cary born
  Samuel Taylor Coleridge born
  Pierce Egan, the elder, born
  James Hook born
  William Barnes Rhodes born
  David Ricardo born
- James Graeme dies
  William Wilkie dies
- Emanuel Swedenborg dies

Mark Akenside (1721–71)
The Poems of Mark Akenside V

Elizabeth Bonhote (1744–1818)
The Rambles of Mr Frankly F
Anonymous. Two further volumes published in 1776.

Sophia Briscoe (*fl.* 1771–2)
The Fine Lady F
bao *Miss Melmoth*

Moses Browne (1704–87) (tr.)
The Excellency of the Knowledge of Jesus Christ NF
Translated from John Liborius Zimmerman (1702–34)

Sir William Chambers (1726–96)
A Dissertation on Oriental Gardening NF

Thomas Chatterton (1752–70)
The Execution of Sir Charles Bawdin V
Anonymous. Attributed to 'Thomas Rowlie', the spurious author invented by Chatterton, in another 1772 edition.

Richard Cumberland (1732–1811)
The Fashionable Lover: A comedy D
Performed 20 January 1772

'Junius' [probably Sir Philip Francis (1740–1818)]
Junius: Stat Nominis Umbra NF
Publication date assumed. Many editions. Variously attributed. See also *The Political Contest, Two Letters from Junius* 1769.

David Garrick (1717–79)
The Irish Widow D
Anonymous. Performed 23 October 1772.

Francis Grose (1731–91)
The Antiquities of England and Wales NF
Published in 4 volumes (1772–6), with later supplementary volumes

Richard Hurd (1720–1808)
An Introduction to the Study of Prophecies Concerning the Christian Church NF

Charles Jenner (1736–74)
Town Eclogues V

Sir William Jones (1746–94)
Poems V
Anonymous

William Kenrick (1725?–79)
Love in the Suds: A Town Eclogue V

William Mason (1725–97)
The English Garden V
An early draft of this first book was privately printed *c.*1771 for Mason, who subsequently attempted to destroy all the copies. *Book the Second* privately printed in 1776 (trade edition, 1777).

Arthur Murphy (1727–1805)
The Grecian Daughter: A tragedy D
Anonymous. Performed 26 February 1772.

Joseph Priestley (1733–1804)
The History and Present State of Discoveries Relating to Vision, Light, and Colours NF

Sarah Scott (1723–95)
The Test of Filial Duty F
Anonymous

Christopher Smart (1722–71)
Hymns, for the Amusement of Children V
Anonymous

George Alexander Stevens (1710–84)
Songs, Comic and Satyrical V

Catherine Talbot (1721–70)
Essays on Various Subjects NF
bao *Reflections on the Seven Days of the Week*

1773

- The Boston Tea Party (16 Dec.)
- Francis Jeffrey born
  James Mill born
  Regina Maria Roche born
- Alban Butler dies
  John Hawkesworth dies
  George Lyttelton, 1st Baron Lyttelton, dies
  Philip Dormer Stanhope, 4th earl of Chesterfield, dies
- Robert Clive dies
- Ludwig Johann Tieck born
- Gottfried August Bürger, *Leonore*
  Goethe, *Goetz von Berlichingen*

Anonymous
The History of Agathon F
Translation of *Geschichte des Agathon* (1776/7) by Christoph Martin Wieland (1733–1813)

Anonymous
Reason Triumphant Over Fancy F
Translation of *Der Sieg der Natur über die Schäwrmerey* (1764) by Christoph Martin Wieland (1733–1813)

Anna Laetitia Barbauld (1743–1825) and **John Aikin** (1747–1822)
Miscellaneous Pieces in Prose MISC

Anna Laetitia Barbauld (1743–1825)
Poems V

Elizabeth Bonhote (1744–1818)
The Fashionable Friend F
Anonymous

Patrick Brydone (1736–1818)
A Tour Through Sicily and Malta NF

James Burnett, Lord Monboddo (1714–99)
Of the Origin and Progress of Language NF
Anonymous. Published in 6 volumes (1773–92).

Charles Burney (1726–1814)
The Present State of Music in Germany, the Netherlands, and United Provinces NF
See also *The Present State of Music in France* 1771

Hester Chapone (1727–18-1)
Letters on the Improvement of the Mind NF
Anonymous

Sir David Dalrymple, Lord Hailes (1726–92)
Remarks on the History of Scotland NF

Thomas Day (1748–89)
The Dying Negro V

Charles Dibdin (1745–1814)
The Deserter: A new musical drama D
Performed 2 November 1773. An adaptation of *Le déserteur* by Michael Jean Sedaine (1719–97).

Robert Fergusson (1750–74)
Auld Reikie V

Robert Fergusson (1750–74)
Poems V
See also *Poems on Various Subjects* 1779

Oliver Goldsmith (1728–74)
She Stoops to Conquer; or, The Mistakes of a Night: A comedy D
Performed 15 March 1773. Published on 25 March 1773.

Richard Graves (1715–1804)
The Love of Order V
Published anonymously

Richard Graves (1715–1804)
The Spiritual Quixote; or, The Summer's Ramble of Mr Geoffrey Wildgoose F
Published anonymously

John Hawkesworth (1715?–73)
An Account of the Voyages for Making Discoveries in the Southern Hemisphere NF
Includes an account of Captain James Cook's circumnavigation

John Home (1722–1808)
Alonzo: A tragedy D
Performed 27 February 1773

Edward Jerningham (1737–1812)
Faldoni and Teresa V

George Keate (1729–97)
The Monument in Arcadia V

William Kenrick (1725?–79)
The Duellist: A comedy D
Performed 20 November 1773

Thomas Leland (1722–85)
The History of Ireland NF

Henry Mackenzie (1745–1831)
The Man of the World F
Anonymous

Henry Mackenzie (1745–1831)
The Prince of Tunis D
Anonymous. Performed 8 March 1773.

James Macpherson (1736–96) (tr.)
The Iliad V

William Melmoth, the younger (1710–99) (tr.)
Cato; or, An Essay on Old-Age NF
Anonymous. Translated from Cicero.

Hannah More (1745–1833)
A Search After Happiness V
'By a young lady'

Arthur Murphy (1727–1805)
Alzuma: A tragedy D
Anonymous. Performed 23 February 1773.

John Scott (1730–83)
Observations on the Present State of the Parochial and Vagrant Poor NF
Anonymous

Thomas Scott (1705–75)
Lyric Poems, Devotional and Moral V
Contain most of Scott's hymns

William Shakespeare (1564–1616)
The Plays of William Shakespeare EDN
Edited by George Steevens and based on Samuel Johnson's edition of 1765 (q.v.). Revised in 1778 (by Steevens), in 1785 (by Isaac Reed), and in 1793 (again by Steevens) 1793. See also *The Plays of William Shakespeare* 1803.

Laurence Sterne (1713–68)
Letters from Yorick to Eliza NF
'Yorick' = Sterne

John Wolcot (1738–1819)
Persian Love Elegies V

1774

- Accession of Louis XVI
  Philadelphia Congress of American Colonies
  John Wilkes becomes Lord Mayor of London
  Joseph Priestley discovers oxygen
- Robert Southey born
  Robert Tannahill born
- Henry Baker dies
  Robert Fergusson dies
  Oliver Goldsmith dies
  Abraham Tucker dies

Miles Peter Andrews (*d.* 1814)
The Election D
Anonymous. Performed 21 October 1774.

James Beattie (1735–1803)
The Minstrel; or, The Progress of Genius V
Book ii. Book i published in 1771 (q.v.). Both books published together, with other poems, in 1775.

Jeremy Bentham (1748–1832) (tr.)
The White Bull: An oriental history F
Anonymous translation by Bentham of Voltaire's *Le Taureau blanc* (1774)

Henry Brooke (1703–83)
Juliet Grenville; or, The History of the Human Heart F

John Burgoyne (1722–92)
The Maid of the Oaks D
Anonymous. Performed 5 November 1744.
Epilogue by David Garrick.

George Colman, the elder (1732–94)
The Man of Business: A comedy D
Performed 29 January 1774

Joseph Cradock (1742–1826)
Village Memoirs NF
Anonymous. Misdated 1765.

Charles Dibdin (1745–1814)
The Waterman; or, The First of August D/OP
Anonymous. Performed 8 August 1774.

William Dunkin (1709?–65)
The Poetical Works of the Late William Dunkin V
Volume i includes Latin and Greek verse with English translations

Oliver Goldsmith (1728–74)
Retaliation V
Published on 19 April 1774, soon after Goldsmith's death

Oliver Goldsmith (1728–74)
The Grecian History NF

Oliver Goldsmith (1728–74)
An History of the Earth and Animated Nature NF

Richard Graves (1715–1804)
The Progress of Gallantry V
Published anonymously

Henry Home, Lord Kames (1696–1782)
Sketches of the History of Man NF
Anonymous

Thomas Hull (1728–1808)
Henry the Second; or, The Fall of Rosamond: A tragedy D
Performed 1 May 1773. Epilogue by George Colman.

Samuel Johnson (1709–84)
The Patriot NF
Anonymous

Charles Johnstone (1719?–1800?)
The History of Arsaces, Prince of Betlis F
'By the editor of *Chrysal*'

Hugh Kelly (1739–77)
The School for Wives: A comedy D
Anonymous. Performed 11 December 1773.

William Mason (1725–97)
An Heroic Postscript to the Public V
Anonymous

Hannah More (1745–1833)
The Inflexible Captive: A tragedy V

Joseph Priestley (1733–1804)
Experiments and Observations on Different Kinds of Air NF
Published in 3 volumes (1774–7). Later abridged as part of *Experiments and Observations on Different Kinds of Air, and Other Branches of Natural Philosophy* (1790).

Henry James Pye (1745–1813)
Farringdon Hill V

William Richardson (1743–1814)
A Philosophical Analysis and Illustration of Some of Shakespeare's Remarkable Characters NF

Mary Scott (1752?–93)
The Female Advocate V
A response to John Duncombe, *The Feminead* 1754 (q.v.)

Philip Dormer Stanhope, 4th earl of Chesterfield (1694–1773)
Letters to his Son NF
Many editions

Horace Walpole (1717–97)
A Description of Strawberry-Hill NF

Thomas Warton, the younger (1728–90)
The History of English Poetry NF
Published in 3 volumes (1774–81)

John Wesley (1703–91)
Thoughts upon Slavery NF

William Whitehead (1715–85)
Plays and Poems, by William Whitehead, Esq. Poet Laureat D/V
See also *Poems* 1788

1775

- War of American Independence begins (Apr.): defeat of the British at Lexington and Concord
  George Washington appointed Commander-in-Chief of American forces
  British defeat American forces at Bunker Hill (17 June)
- Jane Austen born
  Sir Alexander Boswell born
  Lady Charlotte Bury born
  Charles Lamb born
  Walter Savage Landor born
  Matthew Gregory Lewis born
  Charles Lloyd born
  Henry Crabb Robinson born
  Mary Martha Sherwood born
  James Smith born
  Joseph Blanco White born
- Daniel O'Connell born
- Beaumarchais, *Le Barbier de Séville*

Anonymous
Moral Tales F
Translation of *Contes moraux* (1774) by Marie Leprince de Beaumont (1711–80)

Edmund Burke (1729–97)
Speech on American Taxation, April 19, 1774 NF

Edmund Burke (1729–97)
Speech on Conciliation with the Colonies, March 22, 1775 NF

Hester Chapone (1727–1801)
Miscellanies in Prose and Verse MISC

Geoffrey Chaucer (1340?–1400)
The Canterbury Tales of Chaucer EDN
Edited by Thomas Tyrwhitt

William Combe (1742–1823) attrib.
Letters from Eliza to Yorick NF
Anonymous. Spurious letters supposedly written by Eliza Draper to Laurence Sterne. See *Letters from Yorick to Eliza* 1773.

George Crabbe (1754–1832)
Inebriety V
Anonymous

Richard Cumberland (1732–1811)
The Choleric Man: A comedy D
Performed 19 December 1774

Hugh Downman (1740–1809)
The Drama V

Thomas Francklin (1721–84)
Matilda: A tragedy D
bao *The Earl of Warwick*. Performed 21 January 1775.

David Garrick (1717–79)
Bon Ton; or, High Life Above Stairs: A comedy D
Anonymous. Performed 18 March 1775.

Thomas Gray (1716–71)
Poems of Mr Gray V
Edited by William Mason

John Howie (1735–93)
Biographia Scoticana NF

Thomas Hull (1728–1808)
Edward and Eleonora: A tragedy D
Performed 18 March 1775

Robert Jephson (1736–1803)
Braganza: A tragedy D
Performed 17 February 1775

Edward Jerningham (1737–1812)
The Fall of Mexico V

Samuel Johnson (1709–84)
A Journey to the Western Islands of Scotland NF
Anonymous

Samuel Johnson (1709–84)
Taxation No Tyranny NF
Anonymous

Charles Johnstone (1719?–1800?)
The Pilgrim; or, A Picture of Life F
'By the editor of *Chrysal*'

Henrietta Knight, Lady Luxborough (1699–1756)
Letters Written to William Shenstone NF

Charlotte Lennox (1729?–1804)
Old City Manners: A comedy D
Performed 9 November 1775. Prologue by George Colman.

James Macpherson (1736–96)
The History of Great Britain NF

'Courtney Melmoth' [Samuel Jackson Pratt (1749–1814)]
Liberal Opinions, upon Animals, Man, and Providence F
Published in 6 volumes (1775–7)

Joseph Priestley (1733–1804)
Hartley's Theory of the Human Mind NF
Contains selections from Hartley's *Observations on Man* 1749 (q.v.), edited by Priestley

Mary Robinson (1758–1800)
Poems V

Richard Savage (1697?–1743)
The Works of Richard Savage WKS
Edited, with a life of Savage, by Samuel Johnson. The life was reprinted in Johnson's *Prefaces . . . to the Works of the English Poets* 1779 (q.v.). See also *An Account of the Life of Mr Richard Savage* 1744.

Richard Brinsley Sheridan (1751–1816)
The Rivals: A comedy D
Anonymous. Performed 17 January 1775. The printed text derived from a revised version performed 28 January 1775.

Laurence Sterne (1713–68)
Letters of the Late Rev Mr L. Sterne NF

Laurence Sterne (1713–68)
Sterne's Letters to his Friends on Various Occasions NF

John Wesley (1703–91)
A Calm Address to Our American Colonies NF

1776

- The British evacuate Boston (Mar.)
  American Declaration of Independence (4 July)
- Mary Matilda Betham born
  Thomas Frognall Dibdin born
  Jane Porter born
- David Hume dies
- John Constable born
- E.T.A. Hoffmann born

James Beattie (1735–1803)
Essays NF

James Beattie (1735–1803)
Poems on Several Occasions V

Jeremy Bentham (1748–1832)
A Fragment on Government NF

An examination of the introduction to William Blackstone's *Commentaries on the Laws of England* 1765 (q.v.)

Charles Burney (1726–1814)
A General History of Music NF
Published in 4 volumes (1776–89)

George Campbell (1719–96)
The Philosophy of Rhetoric NF

Hannah Cowley (1743–1809)
The Runaway: A comedy D
Anonymous. Performed 15 February 1776. Produced by David Garrick, who also wrote the epilogue.

Sir David Dalrymple, Lord Hailes (1726–92)
Annals of Scotland [vol. i] NF
To the reign of Robert I. Volume ii (to the House of Stuart) published in 1779.

Samuel Foote (1720–77)
The Bankrupt: A comedy D
Performed 21 July 1773

Edward Gibbon (1737–94)
The History of the Decline and Fall of the Roman Empire: Volume the First NF
Published 17 February 1776. Volumes ii and iii published in 1781 (q.v.); volumes iv, v, and vi, 1788 (q.v.).

Oliver Goldsmith (1728–74)
A Survey of Experimental Philosophy NF

Richard Graves (1715–1804)
Euphrosyne; or, Amusements on the Road of Life V
bao *The Spiritual Quixote*

Elizabeth Griffith (1720?–93)
The Story of Lady Juliana Harley F

Sir John Hawkins (1719–89)
A General History of the Science and Practice of Music NF

David Herd (1732–1810) (ed.)
Ancient and Modern Scottish Songs ANTH

Soame Jenyns (1704–87)
A View of the Internal Evidence of the Christian Religion NF
Anonymous

William Mickle (1735–88) (tr.)
The Lusiad; or, The Discovery of India V
Translated from Luis de Camoëns (1524–80)

Hannah More (1745–1833)
Sir Eldred of the Bower, and The Bleeding Rock V

Thomas Paine (1737–1809)
The American Crisis NF
bao *Common Sense*. Sixteen separate publications, 1776–83.

Thomas Paine (1737–1809)
Common Sense NF

'Courtney Melmoth' [Samuel Jackson Pratt (1749–1814)]
The Pupil of Pleasure; or, The New System Illustrated F

Richard Price (1723–91)
Observations on the Nature of Civil Liberty NF

Jonathan Richardson (1665–1745)
Morning Thoughts; or, Poetical Meditations, Moral, Divine and Miscellaneous V

John Scott (1730–83)
Amwell V

Adam Smith (1723–90)
An Inquiry into the Nature and Causes of the Wealth of Nations NF
Published 9 March 1776

Augustus Montague Toplady (1740–78)
Psalms and Hymns for Public and Private Worship V

William Whitehead (1715–85)
Variety V
Anonymous

1777

- Washington defeats the British at Princeton (3 Jan.)
  Burgoyne capitulates to the Americans at Saratoga (17 Oct.)
  Suspension of Habeas Corpus Act
- Thomas Campbell born
  William Henry Ireland born
  Francis Lathom born
- Samuel Foote dies
  Hugh Kelly dies
  Mary Latter dies
- Henry Hallam born

Hugh Blair (1718–1800)
Sermons [vol. i] NF
Many subsequent editions. Volume ii, 1780; volume iii, 1790; volume iv, 1794, volume v (with life by J. Finlayson), 1801.

Frances Brooke (1724–89)
The Excursion F

Edmund Burke (1729–97)
Letter to the Sheriffs of Bristol, on the Affairs of America NF

Thomas Chatterton (1752–70)
Poems, Supposed to Have Been Written at Bristol, by Thomas Rowley, and Others, in the Fifteenth Century V
Anonymous. Edited by Thomas Tyrwhitt. Published 8 February 1777. See also Tyrwhitt, *A Vindication* 1782.

William Combe (1742–1823)
The Diaboliad V
Anonymous. Misdated 1677. Directed at Simon, Lord Irnham.

William Combe (1742–1823)
The First of April; or, The Triumphs of Folly V
bao *The Diaboliad*

James Cook (1728–79)
A Voyage Towards the South Pole, and Round the World NF

Thomas Day (1748–89)
The Desolation of America V
Anonymous

Charles Dibdin (1745–1814)
The Quaker: A comic opera D/OP
Anonymous. Performed 7 October 1777.

William Dodd (1729–77)
Thoughts in Prison V

Phebe Gibbes (*fl.* 1777–89)
Modern Seduction; or, Innocence Betrayed F
bao *Lady Louisa Stroud*

John Howard (1726–90)
The State of the Prisons in England and Wales NF

David Hume (1711–76)
The Life of David Hume NF

Henry Mackenzie (1745–1831)
Julia de Roubigné F
bao *The Man of Feeling*, and *The Man of the World*

Hannah More (1745–1833)
Essays on Various Subjects NF

Maurice Morgann (1726–1802)
An Essay on the Dramatic Character of Sir John Falstaff NF

Samuel Jackson Pratt (1749–1814)
Charles and Charlotte F
Anonymous

'Courtney Melmoth' [Samuel Jackson Pratt (1749–1814)]
Travels for the Heart F

Joseph Priestley (1733–1804)
Disquisitions Relating to Matter and Spirit NF
See also *Doctrine of Philosophical Necessity Illustrated* 1777, below

Joseph Priestley (1733–1804)
The Doctrine of Philosophical Necessity Illustrated NF
Appendix to the *Disquisitions* 1777, above

Isaac Reed (1742–1807) (ed.)
The Repository ANTH

Clara Reeve (1729–1807)
The Champion of Virtue: A gothic story F
'By the editor of the Phoenix'. Reissued as *The Old English Baron* 1778 (q.v.).

William Robertson (1721–93)
The History of America NF
Many editions

William Roscoe (1753–1831)
Mount Pleasant V
Anonymous

Philip Dormer Stanhope, 4th earl of Chesterfield (1694–1773)
Characters of Eminent Personages of His Own Time NF

Thomas Warton, the younger (1728–90)
Poems: A new edition V

Paul Whitehead (1710–74)
Poems and Miscellaneous Compositions V

1778

- France supports the American Colonists
  Washington defeats the British at Monmouth (28 June)
- Henry Brougham born
  Thomas Brown born
  Mary Brunton born
  Sir Humphrey Davy born
  William Hazlitt born
- James Townley dies

- Humphry Davy born
- Thomas Arne dies
  William Pitt, earl of Chatham, dies
- Carl Linnaeus dies
  Jean-Jacques Rousseau dies
  Voltaire dies
- J.G. Herder, *Volkslieder*

John Codrington Bampfylde (1754–96)
Sixteen Sonnets V

Anna Laetitia Barbauld (1743–1825)
Lessons for Children of Two to Three Years Old NF
Lessons for Children of Three Years Old also 1778; *Lessons for Children from Three to Four Years Old* 1779 (q.v.)

Edmund Burke (1729–97)
Two Letters on the Trade of Ireland NF

Frances Burney (1752–1840)
Evelina; or, a Young Lady's Entrance into the World F
Anonymous. Published January 1778. At least eighteen editions in Frances Burney's lifetime.

Thomas Chatterton (1752–70)
Miscellanies in Prose and Verse MISC
See also *A Supplement to the Miscellanies* 1784

William Combe (1742–1823)
The Auction V

Charles Dibdin (1745–1814)
Poor Vulcan: A burletta D
Anonymous. Performed 4 February 1778. Based on P.A. Motteux's *The Loves of Mars and Venus*.

'Sir Gregory Gander' [George Ellis (1753–1815)]
Poetical Tales V

Samuel Foote (1720–77)
The Devil upon Two Sticks: A comedy D
Performed 30 May 1768

Samuel Foote (1720–77)
The Nabob: A comedy D
Performed 26 June 1772

Samuel Foote (1720–77)
The Taylors: A tragedy for warm weather D
Anonymous. Performed 2 July 1767.

William Hayley (1745–1820)
A Poetical Epistle to an Eminent Painter V
Anonymous. Addressed to George Romney.

John Home (1722–1808)
Alfred: A tragedy D
Performed 21 January 1778

Hannah More (1745–1833)
Percy: A tragedy D
Prologue and Epilogue by David Garrick

Ann Murry (*c*.1755–post 1812)
Mentoria; or, The Young Lady's Instructor in Familiar Conversations NF

Thomas Pennant (1726–98)
A Tour in Wales NF

Clara Reeve (1729–1807)
The Old English Baron: A Gothic story F
The second, substantially revised, edition of *The Champion of Virtue* 1777 (q.v.)

John Scott (1730–83)
Moral Eclogues V
Anonymous

Gilbert Stuart (1742–86)
A View of Society in Europe, in its Progress from Rudeness to Refinement NF

'Peter Pindar' [John Wolcot (1738–1819)]
A Poetical, Supplicating, Modest and Affecting Epistle to those Literary Colossuses the Reviewers V

1779

- Spain declares war on Britain
  John Paul Jones in *Serapis* defeats HMS *Countess of Scarborough*
  The Derby horse race established at Epsom
- John Galt born
  Thomas Moore born
  Horatio Smith born
  Frances Trollope born
- John Armstrong dies
  David Garrick dies
  William Warburton dies
- William Lamb, 2nd Viscount Melbourne, born
- Thomas Chippendale dies
  Captain James Cook dies

Anonymous
The Sorrows of Werter: A German story F
A translation by Daniel Malthus (or Richard Graves?) of Goethe's *Die Leiden des jungen Werthers* (1774), apparently using the French translation of 1776

Anna Laetitia Barbauld (1743–1825)
Lessons for Children from Three to Four Years Old NF
See *Lessons for Children of Two to Three Years Old* 1778

James Burnett, Lord Monboddo (1714–99)
Antient Metaphysics; or, The Science of Universals NF
Anonymous. Published in 6 volumes (1779–99).

Edward Capell (1713–81)
Notes and Various Readings to Shakespeare NF
Published in 3 volumes (1779–80). Part i first published in 1774.

George Chalmers (1742–1825)
Political Annals of the Present United Colonies NF

Hannah Cowley (1743–1809)
Albina, Countess Raimond: A tragedy D
Performed 31 July 1779

Hannah Cowley (1743–1809)
Who's the Dupe? D
Performed 10 April 1779

William Cowper (1731–1800) and **John Newton** (1725–1807)
Olney Hymns V
Sixty-six hymns by Cowper, the remainder (282) by Newton. Cowper's hymns marked 'C' to distinguish them from Newton's. Many editions.

Richard Cumberland (1732–1811)
Calypso: A masque D
Performed 20 March 1779

Hugh Downman (1740–1809)
Lucius Junius Brutus; or, The Expulsion of the Tarquins D

Robert Fergusson (1750–1774)
Poems on Various Subjects V
Part ii of *Poems* 1773 (q.v.)

Edward Gibbon (1737–94)
A Vindication of Some Passages in the History of the Decline and Fall of the Roman Empire NF
Anonymous

Richard Graves (1715–1804)
Columella; or, The Distressed Anchoret F
'By the editor of *The Spiritual Quixote*'

William Hayley (1745–1820)
Epistle to Admiral Keppel V
Anonymous

David Hume (1711–76)
Dialogues Concerning Natural Religion NF

Robert Jephson (1736–1803)
The Law of Lombardy: A tragedy D
Performed 8 February 1779

Samuel Johnson (1709–84)
Prefaces, Biographical and Critical, to the Works of the English Poets NF
Published in 10 volumes (1779–81). Later editions entitled *Lives of the English Poets.*

Vicesimus Knox (1752–1821)
Essays, Moral and Literary NF

John Moore (1729–1802)
A View of Society and Manners in France, Switzerland, and Germany NF
Anonymous. See also *A View of Society and Manners in Italy* 1781.

Hannah More (1745–1833)
The Fatal Falsehood: A tragedy D
bao *Percy*

Ann Murry (*c.*1755–post 1812)
Poems on Various Subjects V

'Courtney Melmoth' [Samuel Jackson Pratt (1749–1814)]
Shenstone-Green; or, The New Paradise Lost F

Samuel Jackson Pratt (1749–1814)
The Tutor of Truth F
bao *The Pupil of Pleasure*

Horace Walpole (1717–97)
A Letter to the Editor of the Miscellanies of Thomas Chatterton NF
Anonymous

1780

- The Gordon Riots in London (June)
  Death of Maria Theresa of Austria; succession of Joseph II
  The first Sunday School established at Gloucester
- John Wilson Croker born
  George Croly born
  William Hone born
  James Justinian Morier born
  Anna Maria Porter born
- Sir William Blackstone dies
- C.M. Wieland, *Oberon*

William Beckford (1760–1844)
Biographical Memoirs of Extraordinary Painters F
Anonymous. Satirical fictitious memoirs.

Elizabeth Blower (*b.* 1763)
The Parsonage House F

'By a young lady'. An imitation of Frances Burney's *Evelina* 1778 (q.v.).

Jacob Bryant (1715–1804)
An Address to Dr Priestley NF
Anonymous. See Priestley, *The Doctrine of Philosophic Necessity Illustrated* 1777. Rejoinder by Priestley published in 1780.

Edmund Burke (1729–97)
Speech on Oeconomical Reformation NF

William Combe (1742–1823)
Letters of the Late Lord Lyttelton NF
Anonymous. Spurious letters.

Hannah Cowley (1743–1809)
The Maid of Arragon V
Part i only. Completed in *The Works of Mrs Cowley* (1813).

George Crabbe (1754–1832)
The Candidate V
Anonymous. Published July 1780.

Sir Herbert Croft (1751–1816)
The Abbey of Kilkhampton; or, Monumental Records for the Year 1980 V
Anonymous. Satirical epitaphs on contemporary figures.

Sir Herbert Croft (1751–1816)
Love and Madness F
Anonymous

Susanna Harrison (1752–84)
Songs in the Night V
'By a Young Woman Under Deep Afflictions'. Fifteen editions by 1823.

William Hayley (1745–1820)
An Essay on History V

Thomas Holcroft (1745–1809)
Alwyn; or, The Gentleman Comedian F
Anonymous. Written with some assistance from William Nicholson (1753–1815).

Sophia Lee (1750–1824)
The Chapter of Accidents: A comedy F

Martin Madan (1726–90)
Thelyphthora; or, A Treatise on Female Ruin NF
Anonymous. A controversial argument in favour of polygamy. See also Cowper, *Anti-Thelyphthora* 1781.

Margaret Minifie (*fl.* 1768–83)
The Count de Poland F
Sometimes incorrectly attributed to the author's sister, Susannah Minifie (later Gunning).

John Nichols (1745–1826) (ed.)
A Select Collection of Poems ANTH
Edited with Isaac Reed, with assistance from Thomas Percy, Robert Lowth, and Joseph Warton. Published in 8 volumes (1780–2).

John O'Keeffe (1747–1833)
Tony Lumpkin in Town D
Performed 14 August 1778. Based on Oliver Goldsmith's *She Stoops to Conquer* 1773 (q.v.).

Samuel Jackson Pratt (1749–1814)
Emma Corbett; or, The Miseries of Civil War F
bao *Liberal Opinions, Pupil of Pleasure, Shenstone Green*

Richard Price (1723–91)
An Essay on the Population of England NF

Isaac Reed (1742–1807) (ed.)
[R. Dodsley] *A Select Collection of Old Plays* ANTH
Anonymous. The second edition. See Dodsley, *A Select Collection of Old Plays* 1744.

Anna Seward (1742–1809)
Elegy on Captain Cook V
James Cook died on 13 February 1779

William Shakespeare (1564–1616)
Supplement to the Edition of Shakespeare's Plays Published in 1778 by Samuel Johnson and George Steevens EDN
Edited by Edmond Malone

Sarah Trimmer (1741–1810)
An Easy Introduction to the Knowledge of Nature, and Reading the Holy Scriptures NF
Adapted for children

John Wesley (1703–91)
Reflections on the Rise and Progress of the American Rebellion NF
Anonymous

Arthur Young (1741–1820)
A Tour in Ireland NF

1781

- Cornwallis capitulates at Yorktown (19 Oct.)
- Lucy Aikin born
  Sir David Brewster born
  Ebenezer Elliott born
  Robert Eyres Landor born
- Edward Capell dies
  Richard Jago dies

- George Stephenson born
- G.E. Lessing dies
- Rousseau, *Confessions*

Miles Peter Andrews (*d.* 1814)
Dissipation: A comedy D
Performed 10 March 1781

Robert Bage (1728–1801)
Mount Henneth F
Anonymous. Published 1781, dated 1782.

Anna Laetitia Barbauld (1743–1825)
Hymns in Prose for Children NF

Frances Brooke (1724–89)
The Siege of Sinope: A tragedy D
Performed 31 January 1781. Based on the libretto of the opera *Mitridate a Sinope* by Giuseppe Sarti (1729–1802).

William Combe (1742–1823)
Letters of an Italian Nun and an English Gentleman F
Anonymous. Spuriously described as being translated from Rousseau.

William Cowper (1731–1800)
Anti-Thelyphthora V
Anonymous. See Martin Madan, *Thelyphthora* 1780.

George Crabbe (1754–1832)
The Library V
Anonymous

John Delap (1725–1812)
The Royal Suppliants: A tragedy D
Performed 17 February 1781

Anne Francis (1738–1800) (tr.)
A Poetical Translation of the Song of Solomon V

Edward Gibbon (1737–94)
The History of the Decline and Fall of the Roman Empire: Volume the Second/Volume the Third NF
Published 1 March 1781. Volume i published 1776 (q.v.); volumes iv, v, and vi, 1788 (q.v.).

William Hayley (1745–1820)
The Triumphs of Temper V

Thomas Holcroft (1745–1809)
Duplicity: A comedy D
Performed 13 October 1781

Henry Home, Lord Kames (1696–1782)
Loose Hints Upon Education NF

Robert Jephson (1736–1803)
The Count of Narbonne: A tragedy D
Performed 17 November 1781

Samuel Johnson (1709–84)
The Beauties of Johnson [pt i] NF
Part ii published in 1782

Charles Johnstone (1719?–1800?)
The History of John Juniper, Esq, alias Juniper Jack F
'By the Editor of *The Adventures of a Guinea*'

George Keate (1729–97)
An Epistle to Angelica Kauffmann V

George Keate (1729–97)
Poetical Works V

John Moore (1729–1802)
A View of Society and Manners in Italy NF
See also *A View of Society and Manners in France* 1779

John Newton (1725–1807)
Cardiphonia; or, The Utterance of the Heart NF
bao *Omicron's Letters.*

John Nichols (1745–1826)
Biographical Anecdotes of William Hogarth NF
Anonymous. The Anecdotes were first privately printed in 1780, with additions by Isaac Reed and George Steevens.

Samuel Jackson Pratt (1749–1814)
Sympathy; or, A Sketch of the Social Passion V
Anonymous

Samuel Jackson Pratt (1749–1814)
The Fair Circassian: A tragedy D
bao *Sympathy: A Poem.* Based on Hawkesworth's *Almoran and Hamet* 1761 (q.v.).

Glocester Ridley (1702–74)
Melampus V

Anna Seward (1742–1809)
Monody on Major André V/NF

Richard Brinsley Sheridan (1751–1816)
A Trip to Scarborough: A comedy D
Performed 24 February 1777

Richard Brinsley Sheridan (1751–1816)
The School for Scandal: A comedy D
Anonymous. Performed 8 May 1777.

Richard Brinsley Sheridan (1751–1816)
The Critic; or, A Tragedy Rehearsed D
Performed 30 October 1779

1782

- Spanish capture Minorca
  George Rodney defeats the French Fleet at the Battle of the Saints in the West Indies (12 Apr.)—the last major naval engagement in the American War of Independence
- Charlotte Dacre born?
  Susan Ferrier born
  William Jerdan born
  Charles Robert Maturin born
  Ann Taylor born
- Richard Bentley, the younger, dies
  Henry Home, Lord Kames, dies
- J.C. Bach dies
- Laclos, *Les Liaisons dangereuses*

Elizabeth Blower (*b.* 1763)
George Bateman F
Anonymous

Frances Burney (1752–1840)
Cecilia; or, Memoirs of an Heiress F
bao *Evelina*

Hannah Cowley (1743–1809)
The Belle's Stratagem: A comedy D
Performed 22 February 1780

William Cowper (1731–1800)
'The Diverting History of John Gilpin' V
Anonymous. Published in the *Public Advertiser* (14 November 1782). Published separately with *The Task* 1785 (q.v.).

William Cowper (1731–1800)
Poems V
See also *Poems* 1815

Thomas Day (1748–89)
Reflections upon the Present State of England, and the Independence of America NF

John Freeth (1731?–1808)
Modern Songs, on Various Subjects V

William Gilpin (1724–1804)
Observations on the River Wye, and Several Parts of South Wales NF

William Hayley (1745–1820)
An Essay on Epic Poetry in Five Epistles to Mason V

Edmond Malone (1741–1812)
Cursory Observations on the Poems Attributed to Thomas Rowley NF
Anonymous. See Thomas Chatterton, *Poems, Supposed to Have Been Written . . . by Thomas Rowley* 1777.

William Mason (1725–97)?
An Archaeological Epistle to Jeremiah Milles . . . Editor of a Superb Edition of the Poems of Thomas Rowley V
Attributed to Mason. Written in the Rowleian dialect. See Thomas Chatterton, *Poems, Supposed to Have Been Written . . . by Thomas Rowley* 1777.

William Mason (1725–97)
King Stephen's Watch V
bao *The Heroic Epistle to Sir William Chambers*

Hannah More (1745–1833)
Sacred Dramas, Chiefly Intended for Young Persons V
Anonymous. Twenty-four editions by 1829.

John Nichols (1745–1826)
Biographical and Literary Anecdotes of William Bowyer NF
An enlarged version of *Anecdotes, Biographical and Literary, of the Late Mr William Bowyer, Printer* (privately printed, 1778)

Thomas Pennant (1726–98)
The Journey from Chester to London NF

Isaac Reed (1742–1807) (ed.)
Biographia Dramatica; or, A Companion to the Playhouse NF
Expansion of David Erskine Baker's *Companion to the Play-house* 1764 (q.v.)

Joseph Ritson (1752–1803)
Observations on the First Three Volumes of the History of English Poetry NF
See Thomas Warton 1774

Edward Rushton (1756–1814)?
The Dismember'd Empire V
Anonymous. Attribution conjectural.

Ignatius Sancho (1729?–80)
Letters of the Late Ignatius Sancho, an African NF
Includes a life of the author by Joseph Jekyll, M.P.

John Scott (1730–83)
The Poetical Works of John Scott V

Laurence Sterne (1713–68)
The Beauties of Sterne NF

Thomas Tyrwhitt (1730–86)
A Vindication of the Appendix to the Poems, called Rowley's NF
See Thomas Chatterton, *Poems, Supposed to Have Been Written . . . by Thomas Rowley* 1777

Joseph Warton (1722–1800)
An Essay on the Writings and Genius of Pope NF
Anonymous. Volume ii. See 1756.

Thomas Warton, the younger (1728–90)
An Enquiry into the Authenticity of the Poems Attributed to Thomas Rowley NF
See Thomas Chatterton, *Poems, Supposed to Have Been Written . . . by Thomas Rowley* 1777

Helen Maria Williams (1762–1827)
Edwin and Eltruda V

'Peter Pindar' [**John Wolcot** (1738–1819)]
Lyric Odes, to the Royal Academicians V
See also *More Lyric Odes* 1783

1783

- The Peace of Versailles between Britain, France, Spain, and the USA: Britain recognizes American independence
  Fox's India Bill defeated
  Pitt's first ministry
  The first steamboat
- Reginald Heber born
  Lady Sydney Morgan (*née* Owenson) born
  Jane Taylor born
- Henry Brooke dies
  John Scott dies
- Marie Henri Beyle ('Stendhal') born
  Simón Bolívar born
  Washington Irving born

James Beattie (1735–1803)
Dissertations Moral and Critical NF

William Beckford (1760–1844)
Dreams, Waking Thoughts and Incidents NF
Anonymous. Suppressed by Beckford. Reissued in revised form in *Italy* 1834 (q.v.).

Hugh Blair (1718–1800)
Lectures on Rhetoric and Belles Lettres NF

William Blake (1757–1827)
Poetical Sketches V

Frances Brooke (1724–89)
Rosina: A comic opera D/OP
Performed 31 December 1782

Edmund Burke (1729–97)
Letter on the Penal Laws Against Irish Catholics NF
Anonymous. A piracy. Addressed to Lord Kenmare.

Jane Cave, later **Winscom** (*c.*1754–1813)
Poems on Various Subjects, Entertaining, Elegiac, and Religious V

Hannah Cowley (1743–1809)
Which is the Man? D
Performed 9 February 1782

Judith Cowper, later **Madan** (1702–81)
The Progress of Poetry V

George Crabbe (1754–1832)
The Village V
Published 23 May 1783

Thomas Day (1748–89)
The History of Sandford and Merton F
Anonymous. For children. Volume ii published in 1786; volume iii, 1789 (qq.v). Based on the philosophy of Rousseau.

'Mrs Teachwell' [**Lady Eleanor Fenn** (1743–1813)]
Fables by Mrs Teachwell F

Adam Ferguson (1723–1816)
The History of the Progress and Termination of the Roman Republic NF

Thomas Holcroft (1745–1809)
The Family Picture; or, Domestic Dialogues on Amiable and Interesting Subjects F

Vicesimus Knox (1752–1821) (ed.)
Elegant Extracts; or, Useful and Entertaining Passages in Prose ANTH

Sophia Lee (1750–1824)
The Recess; or, A Tale of Other Times [vol. i] F
bao *The Chapter of Accidents*. Republished with two further volumes in 1785.

Anna Maria Mackenzie (*fl.* 1783–98)
Burton-Wood F
'By a lady'

Clara Reeve (1729–1807)
The Two Mentors F
bao *The Old English Baron*

Joseph Ritson (1752–1803) (ed.)
A Select Collection of English Songs ANTH

'Peter Pindar' [**John Wolcot** (1738–1819)]
More Lyric Odes, to the Royal Academicians V
See *Lyric Odes* 1782

1784

- Pitt's India Act
  John Wesley establishes Methodism

- Bernard Barton born
  Allan Cunningham born
  Leigh Hunt born
  James Sheridan Knowles born
  David Richard Morier born
- Samuel Johnson dies
  Matthew Pilkington dies
  Alexander Ross dies
  George Alexander Stevens dies
- Henry Temple, Viscount Palmerston, born
- Denis Diderot dies
- Beaumarchais, *Le Mariage de Figaro*

Anonymous
*Dangerous Connections; or, Letters Collected in a Society and Published for the Instruction of Other Societies. By M. C*** de L**** F
Translation of *Les liaisons dangereuses* (1782) by Choderlos de Laclos (1741–1803)

Mary Alcock (*c.*1742–98)
The Air Balloon V

Thomas Astle (1735–1803)
The Origin and Progress of Writing NF

Robert Bage (1728–1801)
Barham Downs F
bao *Mount Henneth*

George Berkeley (1685–1753)
The Works of George Berkeley WKS

Edmund Burke (1729–97)
Speech on the East India Bill NF
Published 22 January 1784

Thomas Chatterton (1752–70)
A Supplement to the Miscellanies of Thomas Chatterton MISC
See *Miscellanies* 1778

William Combe (1742–1823)
Original Love-letters, Between a Lady of Quality and a Person of Inferior Station F
Anonymous

James Cook (1728–79)
A Voyage to the Pacific Ocean NF
Volumes i and ii written by Cook; volume iii by Captain James King (1750–84)

Hannah Cowley (1743–1809)
A Bold Stroke for a Husband: A comedy D
Performed 25 February 1783

Hannah Cowley (1743–1809)
More Ways Than One: A comedy D
Performed 6 December 1783

Richard Cumberland (1732–1811)
The Carmelite: A tragedy D
Performed 2 December 1784

George Bubb Dodington (1691–1762)
The Diary of the Late George Bubb Dodington NF

William Godwin (1756–1836)
Damon and Delia F
Anonymous

William Godwin (1756–1836)
Italian Letters; or, The History of the Count de St Julian F
Anonymous

Thomas Holcroft (1745–1809) (tr.)
Tales of the Castle; or, Stories of Instruction and Delight F
Published 1784, dated 1785. Translated from *Les Veillées du château* (1782) by Madame de Genlis (1746–1830).

Samuel Horsley (1733–1806)
Letters from the Archdeacon of St Albans, in Reply to Dr Priestley NF
Archdeacon of St Albans = Horsley

Richard Jago (1715–81)
Poems, Moral and Descriptive V

William Mitford (1744–1827)
The History of Greece [vol. i] NF
Volume ii, 1790; volume iii, 1798

Anna Seward (1742–1809)
Louisa: A poetical novel V

Charlotte Smith (1749–1806)
Elegaic Sonnets, and Other Essays V
See also *Elegaic Sonnets* 1797

Helen Maria Williams (1762–1827)
An Ode on the Peace V
bao *Edwin and Eltruda*

Helen Maria Williams (1762–1827)
Peru V

Arthur Young (1741–1820)
Annals of Agriculture, and Other Useful Arts NF

1785

- Steam-powered engine for spinning cotton set up by Matthew Bolton and James Watt in Nottinghamshire

- Thomas De QuIncey born
  Lady Caroline Lamb born
  Sir William Napier born
  Thomas Love Peacock born
  Henry Kirke White born
  John Wilson ('Christopher North') born
- Catherine ('Kitty') Clive dies
  Richard Glover dies
  William Whitehead dies: Thomas Warton, the younger, appointed Poet Laureate
- David Wilkie born
- Jacob Grimm born
  Alessandro Manzoni born

Anna Maria Bennett (*c.*1750–1808)
Anna; or, Memoirs of a Welch Heiress F
Anonymous

Elizabeth Blower (*b.* 1763)
Maria F
bao *George Bateman*. An imitation of Frances Burney's *Evelina* 1778 (q.v.).

James Boswell (1740–95)
The Journal of a Tour to the Hebrides with Samuel Johnson NF

Samuel Egerton Brydges (1762–1837)
Sonnets and Other Poems V
Anonymous

Edmund Burke (1729–97)
Speech on the Nabob of Arcot's Debts NF
Published 23 August 1785

George Colman, the younger (1762–1836)
Two to One: A comic opera D/OP
Performed 19 June 1784

William Combe (1742–1823)
The Royal Dream; or, The P[rince] *in a Panic* V
Anonymous

William Cowper (1731–1800)
The Task V
Volume ii of *Poems* 1782 (q.v.). See also *Poems* 1815. Also includes 'An Epistle to Joseph Hill, Esq.', 'Tirocinium; or, A Review of Schools', and 'The History of John Gilpin' (first published in 1782, q.v.). Many editions.

George Crabbe (1754–1832)
The News-Paper V

Richard Cumberland (1732–1811)
The Natural Son: A comedy D
Performed 22 December 1784

Richard Graves (1715–1804)
Eugenius; or, Anecdotes of the Golden Vale F
Published anonymously

Francis Grose (1731–91)
A Classical Dictionary of the Vulgar Tongue DICT
Anonymous

William Hayley (1745–1820)
A Philosophical, Historical and Moral Essay on Old Maids V

Elizabeth Inchbald (1753–1821)
Appearance is Against Them: A farce D
Anonymous. Performed 22 October 1785.

Samuel Johnson (1709–84)
The Poetical Works of Samuel Johnson V

Samuel Johnson (1709–84)
Prayers and Meditations NF

Samuel Johnson (1709–84)
The Works of Samuel Johnson WKS
Published in 11 volumes. A further 2 volumes issued in 1787; another volume issued in 1788.

Edward Lovibond (1724–75)
Poems on Several Occasions V

John O'Keeffe (1747–1833)
The Poor Soldier: A comic opera D/OP
Anonymous

William Paley (1743–1805)
The Principles of Moral and Political Philosophy NF
Many editions

Clara Reeve (1729–1807)
The Progress of Romance NF
'By C.R., author of *The English Baron*, etc.'

Thomas Reid (1710–96)
Essays on the Intellectual Powers of Man NF

John Scott (1730–83)
Critical Essays on Some of the Poems, of Several English Poets NF

'Peter Pindar' [John Wolcot (1738–1819)**]**
The Lousiad: Canto i V
Canto ii published in 1787; canto iii, 1791; canto iv, 1792; canto v, 1795

'Peter Pindar' [John Wolcot (1738–1819)**]**
Lyric Odes, for the Year 1785 V

Ann Yearsley (1752–1806)
Poems, on Several Occasions V

1786

- Pitt establishes sinking fund for reducing the National Debt
- Eaton Stannard Barrett born
  Caroline Anne Bowles (later Southey) born
  Sir John Franklin born
  Benjamin Robert Haydon born
  John Cam Hobhouse born
  Peter George Patmore born
- John Duncombe dies
  Thomas Tyrwhitt dies
- Wilhelm Grimm born
  Carl Maria von Weber born
- Frederick the Great dies
- Mozart, *The Marriage of Figaro*

Baron Munchausen's Narrative of his Marvellous Travels and Campaigns in Russia F
A selective translation from Rudolphe Erich Raspe (1737–94)

James Beattie (1735–1803)
Evidences of the Christian Religion Briefly Stated NF

William Beckford (1760–1844)
Vathek F
Published 7 June 1786. The first (supposedly unauthorized) translation of Beckford's *Vathek* (titled *An Arabian Tale*) by the Revd Samuel Henley. First published in French (1786, dated 1787).

Anna Maria Bennett (*c.*1750–1808)
Juvenile Indiscretions F
bao *Anna; or, The Welch Heiress*

Jane Bowdler (1743–84)
Poems and Essays MISC
'By a Lady Lately Deceased'. Seventeen editions by 1830.

John Burgoyne (1722–92)
The Heiress: A comedy D
Performed 14 January 1786

John Burgoyne (1722–92) (tr.)
Richard Coeur de Lion D
Anonymous. Performed 24 October 1786. Translated from Michel-Jean Sedaine (1719–97), *Richard Coeur de Lion* (1784).

Robert Burns (1759–96)
Poems Chiefly in the Scottish Dialect V
See also *Poems* 1787, 1793

Thomas Clarkson (1760–1846)
An Essay on the Slavery and Commerce of the Human Species, Particularly the African NF

Hannah Cowley (1743–1809)
A School for Greybeards; or, The Mourning Bride: A comedy D
Performed 25 November 1786

Hannah Cowley (1743–1809)
The Scottish Village; or, Pitcairn Green V

Thomas Day (1748–89)
The History of Sandford and Merton F
Anonymous. Volume i published in 1783; volume iii, 1789 (qq.v).

William Gilpin (1724–1804)
Observations, Relative Chiefly to Picturesque Beauty . . . Particularly the Mountains, and Lakes of Cumberland, and Westmoreland NF
See also *Observations* 1789

Richard Graves (1715–1804)
Lucubrations MISC
'By the late Peter of Pontefract'

Thomas Holcroft (1745–1809) (tr.)
Caroline of Lichtfield F
Translated from *Caroline* (1786) by Jeanne-Isabelle-Pauline de Bottens, baronne de Montolieu (1751–1832)

Elizabeth Inchbald (1753–1821)
I'll Tell You What: A comedy D
Performed 4 August 1785

Charles Johnstone (1719?–1800?)
The Adventures of Anthony Varnish; or, A Peep at the Manners of Society F
Anonymous

Harriet Lee (1756–1851)
The Errors of Innocence F
Anonymous

Anna Maria Mackenzie (*fl.* 1783–98)
The Gamesters F
bao *Burton-Wood, Joseph*

John Newton (1725–1807)
Messiah NF

John O'Keeffe (1747–1833)
Patrick in Prussia; or, Love in a Camp: A comic opera D/OP
Performed 17 February 1786. Sequel to *The Poor Soldier* 1785 (q.v.).

Hester Lynch Piozzi (1741–1821)
Anecdotes of the Late Samuel Johnson NF

Frederic Reynolds (1764–1841)
Werter: A tragedy D
Anonymous. Performed 25 November 1785. Based on the novel by Goethe.

Samuel Rogers (1763–1855)
An Ode to Superstition, with Some Other Poems V
Anonymous

Susanna Rowson (1762–1824)
Victoria F
Published under the author's maiden name, Susanna Haswell

Charlotte Smith (1749–1806) (tr.)
Manon Lescaut; or, The Fatal Attachment F
Translated from *L'Histoire du chevalier des Grieux et de Manon Lescaut* (1731) by Antoine-François, abbé Prévost d'Exiles (1697–1763)

John Horne Tooke (1736–1812)
Epea Pteroenta; or, The Diversions of Purley NF

Sarah Trimmer (1741–1810)
Fabulous Histories F
Later called *History of the Robins*

Horace Walpole (1717–97)
Postscript to the Royal and Noble Authors NF
See *A Catalogue of the Royal and Noble Authors of England* 1758, of which this is a continuation

Helen Maria Williams (1762–1827)
Poems V

'Peter Pindar' [John Wolcot (1738–1819)**]**
Bozzy and Piozzi; or, The British Biographers V
Ten editions by 1788

'Peter Pindar' [John Wolcot (1738–1819)**]**
Farewel [sic] *Odes. For the Year 1786* V

'Peter Pindar' [John Wolcot (1738–1819)**]**
A Poetical and Congratulatory Epistle to James Boswell V
On Boswell's *Journal of a Tour to the Hebrides* 1785 (q.v.)

Anthony à Wood (1632–95)
The History and Antiquities of the Colleges and Halls in the University of Oxford NF
A translation of the second division of Part 2 of *Historia et Antiquitates Universitatis Oxoniensis* 1674 (q.v.). An 'Appendix' published in 1790.

1787

- Impeachment of Warren Hastings (May)
  Signing of the American Constitution (17 Sept.)
- Charles Cowden Clarke born
  'Barry Cornwall' (Bryan Waller Procter) born
  Caroline Fry born
  Mary Russell Mitford born
  Catharine Ward born
- Moses Brown dies
  Soame Jenyns dies
- Edmund Kean born
- Mozart, *Don Giovanni*

Robert Bage (1728–1801)
The Fair Syrian F
bao *Mount Henneth* and *Barham Downs*

James Beattie (1735–1803)
Scoticisms NF
Anonymous

Jeremy Bentham (1748–1832)
Defence of Usury NF

Elizabeth Bonhote (1744–1818)
Olivia; or, Deserted Bride F
bao *Hortensia*

Robert Burns (1759–96)
Poems Chiefly in the Scottish Dialect V
See also *Poems* 1786, 1793

George Colman, the elder (1732–94)
Prose on Several Occasions NF

George Colman, the younger (1762–1836)
Inkle and Yarico: An opera D/OP
Performed 4 August 1787

Ottobah Cugoano
Thoughts and Sentiments on the Evil and Wicked Traffic of the Slavery and Commerce of the Human Species NF

Anne Francis (1738–1800)
Charlotte to Werter V

Richard Glover (1712–85)
The Athenaid V
bao *Leonidas*

Sir John Hawkins (1719–89)
The Life of Samuel Johnson NF

Elizabeth Helme (*d.* 1816)
Louisa; or, The Cottage on the Moor F
Anonymous. A bestseller.

Thomas Holcroft (1745–1809)
Seduction: A comedy D
Performed 12 March 1787

Ann Howell (*fl.* 1787–97)
Rosa de Montmorien F
Published under the author's maiden name, Ann Hilditch

Anne Hughes (*fl.* 1787–95)
Caroline; or, The Diversities of Fortune F
Anonymous

Robert Jephson (1736–1803)
Julia; or, The Italian Lover: A tragedy D
Performed 17 April 1787

James Johnson (*c.*1750–1811) (ed.)/**Robert Burns** (1759–96)
The Scots Musical Museum ANTH
Published in 6 volumes (1787–1803). Volumes ii–v edited by Burns, who contributed 177 of the 600 songs and collected many others.

George Keate (1729–97)
The Distressed Poet V

Sophia Lee (1750–1824)
A Hermit's Tale V
Anonymous

Robert Merry (1755–98)
Paulina; or, The Russian Daughter V

John Nichols (1745–1826) (ed.)
The Epistolary Correspondence of Sir Richard Steele NF

John Ogilvie (1732–1813)
The Fane of the Druids V
Anonymous

William Roscoe (1753–1831)
The Wrongs of Africa V
Anonymous

Edward Rushton (1756–1814)
West-Indian Eclogues V
Anonymous

Charlotte Smith (1749–1806)
The Romance of Real Life F
A collection of tales based on F. Gayot de Pitaval's *Cause célèbres et interéssantes*

Thomas Taylor (1758–1835) (tr.)
Concerning the Beautiful; NF
Translated from Plotinus

John Thelwall (1764–1834)
Poems on Various Subjects V

'Peter Pindar' [John Wolcot (1738–1819)**]**
Ode Upon Ode; or, A Peep at St James V

Mary Wollstonecraft (1759–97)
Thoughts on the Education of Daughters NF

Ann Yearsley (1752–1806)
Poems, on Various Subjects V

1788

- Parliamentary motion for the abolition of the slave trade
  Linnaean Society founded
  Trial of Warren Hastings begins (Feb.)
- Edwin Atherstone born
  Richard Harris Barham born
  George Gordon, Lord Byron, born
  George Combe born
  Sir Aubrey De Vere born
  Theodore Hook born
  Thomas Medwin born
- Thomas Amory dies
  William Julius Mickle dies
  Robert Craggs Nugent dies
  John Shebbeare dies
  Charles Wesley dies
- Charles Edward Stuart ('The Young Pretender') dies
  Thomas Gainsborough dies
- C.P.E. Bach dies
- Goethe, *Egmont*
  Jean Lemprière, *Classical Dictionary*

The Times
Begun as *The Daily Universal Register*, January 1785

Anonymous
Paul and Virginie F
Translation of *Paul et Viriginie* (1788) by Jacques-Henri-Bernadin de Saint Pierre (1737–1814). Also translated by Helen Maria Williams 1795 (q.v.).

Robert Bage (1728–1801)
James Wallace F
bao *Mount Henneth, Barham Downs*, and *The Fair Syrian*

William Blake (1757–1827)
All Religions Are One NF
An illustrated philosophical tractate with ten relief-etched plates. Date uncertain. Two series.

William Blake (1757–1827)
There is No Natural Religion NF
Illustrated philosophical tractate. Date uncertain. Two series.

Elizabeth Blower (*b*.1763)
Features from Life; or, A Summer Visit F
bao *George Bateman, Maria*

Edmund Burke (1729–97)
A Letter to Philip Francis NF
On the pending trial of Warren Hastings

Henry Cary (1772–1844)
Sonnets and Odes V

William Collins (1721–59)
Ode on the Popular Superstitions of the Highlands of Scotland V

George Colman, the younger (1762–1836)
Ways and Means; or, A Trip to Dover: A comedy D
Performed 10 July 1788

Hannah Cowley (1743–1809)
The Fate of Sparta; or, The Rival Kings: A tragedy D
Performed 31 January 1788

William Crowe (1745–1829)
Lewesdon Hill V
Anonymous

Thomas Day (1748–89)
The History of Little Jack F
Anonymous. See also *The History of Sandford and Merton* [1783, etc], similarly based on the philosophy of Rousseau.

Maria Falconar (1771?) and **Harriet Falconar** (1774?)
Poems V

Maria Falconar (1771?) and **Harriet Falconar** (1774?)
Poems on Slavery V

Edward Gibbon (1737–94)
The History of the Decline and Fall of the Roman Empire [vols iv, v, vi] NF
Published 8 May 1788. Volume i published in 1776 (q.v.); volumes ii and iii, 1781 (q.v.). Abridgement of whole work published in 1789.

James Hurdis (1763–1801)
The Village Curate V

Elizabeth Inchbald (1753–1821)
A Mogul Tale; or, The Descent of the Balloon D
Anonymous. Performed 6 July 1784.

Elizabeth Inchbald (1753–1821)
Such Things Are D
Performed 10 February 1787

Samuel Johnson (1709–84)
Letters To and From the Late Samuel Johnson NF

Vicesimus Knox (1752–1821)
Winter Evenings; or, Lucubrations on Life and Letters NF

Anna Maria Mackenzie (*fl.* 1783–98)
Retribution F
bao *The Gamesters*

'Della Crusca' [**Robert Merry** (1755–98)]
Diversity V

Hannah More (1745–1833)
Slavery V

Hannah More (1745–1833)
Thoughts on the Importance of the Manners of the Great to General Society NF

John Newton (1725–1807)
Thoughts Upon the African Slave Trade NF

Clara Reeve (1729–1807)
The Exiles; or, Memoirs of the Count de Cronstadt F

Charlotte Smith (1749–1806)
Emmeline, the Orphan of the Castle F

William Whitehead (1715–85)
Poems by William Whitehead V
Edited by William Mason. Whitehead had been Poet Laureate. See also *Plays and Poems* 1774.

'Peter Pindar' [**John Wolcot** (1738–1819)]
Tales and Fables V

Mary Wollstonecraft (1759–97)
Mary: A fiction F
Anonymous

Mary Wollstonecraft (1759–97) (tr.)
Of the Importance of Religious Opinions NF
Anonymous. A translation of *De l'importance des opinions religieuses* by Jacques Necker (1732–1804)

Mary Wollstonecraft (1759–97)
Original Stories, from Real Life F
Anonymous

Ann Yearsley (1752–1806)
A Poem on the Inhumanity of the Slave-Trade V

1789

- Regency Bill introduced by Pitt but not enacted

George Washington inaugurated as the first President of the USA (30 Apr.)
Estates-General meet at Versailles (5 May)
Third Estate takes the Tennis Court Oath (20 June)
Storming of the Bastille (14 July)
The 'October Days'—Louis XVI and the Estates-General are removed to Paris

- Marguerite Gardiner, countess of Blessington, born
John Payne Collier born
Charlotte Elliott born
Sir James Stephen born
- Frances Brooke dies
John Cleland dies
Thomas Day dies
John Wilson dies
- James Fenimore Cooper born
J.L.M. Daguerre born

Anna Maria Bennett (*c.*1750–1808)
Agnes De-Courci F

Jeremy Bentham (1748–1832)
An Introduction to the Principles of Morals and Legislation NF

William Blake (1757–1827)
Songs of Innocence V
Blake's first major illuminated book, with 31 relief-etched plates. See also *Songs of Innocence and of Experience* 1794.

William Blake (1757–1827)
The Book of Thel V
With eight relief-etched plates

Elizabeth Bonhote (1744–1818)
Darnley Vale; or, Emelia Fitzroy F

William Lisle Bowles (1762–1850)
Fourteen Sonnets, Elegaic and Descriptive V
Anonymous. Revised in 1789 as *Sonnets Written Chiefly on Picturesque Spots.*

William Lisle Bowles (1762–1850)
Verses to John Howard V

Charlotte Brooke (1740?–93) (tr.)
Reliques of Irish Poetry ANTH

George Colman, the elder (1732–94)
Ut Pictura Poesis!; or, The Enraged Musician: A musical entertainment D
Performed 18 May 1789

Richard Cumberland (1732–1811)
Arundel F
bao *The Observer*

Erasmus Darwin (1731–1802)
The Botanic Garden V

Erasmus Darwin (1731–1802)
The Loves of the Plants V
Republished as part ii of *The Botanic Garden* in 1789

Thomas Day (1748–89)
The History of Sandford and Merton F
Anonymous. Volume i published in 1783; volume ii 1786 (qq.v).

'Mrs Teachwell' [Lady Eleanor Fenn (1743–1813)]
Fairy Spectator F

'Mrs Teachwell' [Lady Eleanor Fenn (1743–1813)]
Juvenile Tatler F

William Gilpin (1724–1804)
Observations, Relative Chiefly to Picturesque Beauty . . . Particularly the High-lands of Scotland NF
See also *Observations* 1786

John Philip Kemble (1757–1823) (adap.)
King Henry V; or, The Conquest of France: A tragedy D
Performed 1 October 1789. Adapted from Shakespeare.

John Moore (1729–1802)
Zeluco F
Anonymous

John Ogilvie (1732–1813)
The Fane of the Druids V
Anonymous. See also 1787.

Ann Radcliffe (1764–1823)
The Castles of Athlin and Dunbayne F
Anonymous. Ann Radcliffe's first romance.

Thomas Russell (1762–88)
Sonnets and Miscellaneous Poems V

Charlotte Smith (1749–1806)
Ethelinde; or, The Recluse of the Lake F

William Warburton (1698–1779)
Tracts, by Warburton and a Warburtonian NF
Edited by Samuel Parr. 'A Warburtonian' = Richard Hurd. Includes translations of several classical texts.

Gilbert White (1720–93)
The Natural History and Antiquities of Selborne NF

James White (1759?–99)
Earl Strongbow; or, The History of Richard de Clare and the Beautiful Geralda F
Anonymous

'Anthony Pasquin' [John Williams (1761–1818)]
Poems: by Anthony Pasquin V

'Mrs Cresswick' [Mary Wollstonecraft (1759–97) (ed.)]
The Female Reader; or, Miscellaneous Pieces in Prose and Verse ANTH

1790

- Festival of the Champ de Mars (14 July)
  Resignation of Jacques Necker (Sept.)
  Wolf Tone founds Society of United Irishmen
- Anna Eliza Bray born
  Richard Carlile born
  Catherine Crowe born
  Nassau William Senior born
  George Soane born
  Charlotte Elizabeth Tonna born
- Adam Smith dies
  Thomas Warton, the younger, dies: Henry James Pye appointed Poet Laureate
- Alphonse de Lamartine born
- Benjamin Franklin dies

Archibald Alison (1757–1839)
Essays on the Nature and Principles of Taste NF

Joanna Baillie (1762–1851)
Poems V
Anonymous

James Beattie (1735–1803)
Elements of Moral Science NF

William Blake (1757–1827)
The Marriage of Heaven and Hell V
Anonymous. Undated illuminated book with 27 relief-etched plates.

William Bligh (1754–1817)
A Narrative of the Mutiny, on Board His Britannic Majesty's Ship Bounty NF
See also *A Voyage to the South Sea* 1792

Elizabeth Bonhote (1744–1818)
Ellen Woodley F

Frances Brooke (1724–89)
The History of Charles Mandeville F
Sequel to *The History of Lady Julia Mandeville* 1763 (q.v.)

James Bruce (1730–94)
Travels to Discover the Source of the Nile NF

Edmund Burke (1729–97)
Reflections on the Revolution in France NF
Seven editions in 1790

Edmund Burke (1729–97)
Speech on the Army Estimates NF

George Colman, the younger (1762–1836)
The Battle of Hexham: A comedy D
Anonymous. Performed 11 August 1789.

George Colman, the younger (1762–1836)
The Surrender of Calais D
Anonymous. Performed 30 July 1791.

William Combe (1742–1823)
The Devil upon Two Sticks in England F
Anonymous. Published in four volumes, with two further volumes appearing in 1791. A continuation of *Le Diable boiteux* (1707) by Alain-René Le Sage (1668–1747), itself an imitation of *El Diablo cojuelo* (1641) by Luis Vélez de Guevara (1570–1644).

Anne Francis (1738–1800)
Miscellaneous Poems V
'By a lady'. Reissued in the same year under the author's name.

Richard Graves (1715–1804)
Plexippus; or, The Aspiring Plebeian F
Published anonymously

Samuel Johnson (1709–84)
The Celebrated Letter from Samuel Johnson to Philip Dormer Stanhope NF
Edited by James Boswell

Ellis Cornelia Knight (1758–1837)
Dinarbas F
Anonymous. A continuation of Samuel Johnson's *The Prince of Abissinia* [*Rasselas*] 1759 (q.v.).

Charlotte Lennox (1729?–1804)
Euphemia F

Catherine Macaulay (1731–91)
Letters on Education NF

Robert Merry (1755–98)
The Laurel of Liberty V

Amelia Opie (1769–1853)
Dangers of Coquetry F
Anonymous

William Paley (1743–1805)
Horae Paulinae; or, The Truth of the Scripture History of St Paul Evinced NF

Thomas Pennant (1726–98)
Of London NF

Ann Radcliffe (1764–1823)
A Sicilian Romance F
bao *The Castles of Athlin and Dunbayne*

Frederic Reynolds (1764–1841)
Better Late Than Never: A comedy D
Performed 17 November 1790. Co-written with Miles Peter Andrews.

Frederic Reynolds (1764–1841)
The Dramatist; or, Stop Him Who Can! A comedy D
Performed 15 May 1789

William Shakespeare (1564–1616)
The Plays and Poems of William Shakespeare EDN
Edited by Edmond Malone

William Sotheby (1757–1833)
Poems V

Helen Maria Williams (1762–1827)
Julia F

Helen Maria Williams (1762–1827)
Letters Written in France, in the Summer of 1790 NF

Mary Wollstonecraft (1759–97) (tr.)
Elements of Morality for the Use of Children NF
Translated from C.G. Salzmann (1744–1811)

Mary Wollstonecraft (1759–97)
A Vindication of the Rights of Men NF
Anonymous

Ann Yearsley (1752–1806)
Stanzas of Woe V

1791

- Mirabeau elected President of the French Assembly (Jan.) but dies in Apr.
  Louis XVI attempts to flee France: turned back at Varennes (20 June)
- Michael Faraday born
  Anne Marsh-Caldwell born
  Henry Hart Milman born
  Edward Quillinan born
  Richard Lalor Sheil born
- Catherine Macaulay dies
  John Wesley dies
- Wolfgang Amadeus Mozart dies
- Marquis de Sade, *Justine*
  Mozart, *The Magic Flute*

John Aikin (1747–1822)
Poems V

Anna Laetitia Barbauld (1743–1825)
Epistle to William Wilberforce V

Jeremy Bentham (1748–1832)
Panopticon; or, The Inspection-House NF
Written in 1787

William Blake (1757–1827)
The French Revolution V
Anonymous

James Boswell (1740–95)
The Life of Samuel Johnson NF

Edmund Burke (1729–97)
An Appeal from the New to the Old Whigs NF

Edmund Burke (1729–97)
Letter to a Member of the National Assembly NF
Addressed to François-Louis-Thibault Menonville. First published in French by 27 April 1791.

Edmund Burke (1729–97)
Two Letters on the Revolution in France NF
Unauthorized. Letter to Pierre-Gaëton Dupont dated 2 January 1791; letter to Captain W[oodford] dated 11 February 1791.

Robert Burns (1759–96)
'Tam O'Shanter' V
Published in the *Edinburgh Herald* (18 March 1791). Also published in volume ii of F. Grose, *The Antiquities of Scotland* 1791 (q.v.).

William Cowper (1731–1800) (tr.)
The Iliad and the Odyssey V

Isaac D'Israeli (1766–1848)
Curiosities of Literature [1st ser., vol. i] NF
Anonymous. See also *Curiosities of Literature* 1793, 1817, 1823, 1834.

William Gifford (1756–1826)
The Baviad V
Anonymous

William Gilpin (1724–1804)
Remarks on Forest Scenery NF

Francis Grose (1731–91)
The Antiquities of Scotland [vol. ii] NF

Contains Burns's 'Tam O'Shanter' (see above). Volume i published in 1789.

George Huddesford (1749–1809) (ed.)
Salmagundi: A miscellaneous combination of original poetry V
Anonymous. Edited and largely written by Huddesford.

Elizabeth Inchbald (1753–1821)
A Simple Story F
Many editions

Charlotte Lennox (1729?–1804)
Hermione; or, The Orphan Sisters F
Anonymous

James Mackintosh (1765–1832)
Vindiciae Gallicae NF
A defence of the French Revolution

Robert Merry (1755–98)
Lorenzo: A tragedy D

Hannah More (1745–1833)
An Estimate of the Religion of the Fashionable World NF
'By one of the laity'

Thomas Paine (1737–1809)
Rights of Man NF
Part i. Published on 13 March 1791 and dedicated to George Washington. Part ii published in 1792. Many editions.

Eliza Parsons (1748–1811)
The Errors of Education F

Richard Polwhele (1760–1838)
Poems V

Ann Radcliffe (1764–1823)
The Romance of the Forest F
bao *A Sicilian Romance*. Many editions into the 19th century.

Clara Reeve (1729–1807)
The School for Widows F

Joseph Ritson (1752–1803) (ed.)
Pieces of Ancient Popular Poetry ANTH

Susanna Rowson (1762–1824)
Charlotte F
Anonymous

Christopher Smart (1722–71)
Poems of the Late Christopher Smart V
Edited by Francis Newbey, assisted by Smart's nephew, Christopher Hunter

Charlotte Smith (1749–1806)
Celestina F

Mariana Starke (1762?–1838)
The Widow of Malabar: A tragedy D
Performed 5 May 1790. Adapted from Antoine Marin Lemierre (1723–93), *La veuve du Malabar*.

Alexander Fraser Tytler, Lord Woodhouselee (1747–1813)
Essay on the Principles of Translation NF
Anonymous

Ann Yearsley (1752–1806)
Earl Goodwin: An historical play D
'By Ann Yearsley, milk-woman'

1792

- Girondin ministry in France
  Assassination of Gustavus III of Sweden
  France declares war on Austria and Prussia
  Guillotine used for the first time (25 Apr.)
  Paris mob invades the Tuileries (10 Aug.)
  French royal family imprisoned (13 Aug.)
  September massacres in Paris (2–6 Sept.)
  Trial of Louis XVI opens (5 Dec.)
- Charles Babbage born
  George Cruikshank born
  Thomas Colley Grattan born
  Augustus Hare born
  Thomas Jefferson Hogg born
  William Howitt born
  John Keble born
  Frederick Marrayat born
  Percy Bysshe Shelley born
  Edward John Trelawny born
- Sir John Herschel born
  Lord John Russell born
- Robert Adam dies
  Sir Joshua Reynolds dies
- Gioacchino Rossini born

Robert Anderson (1750–1830) (ed.)
A Complete Edition of the Poets of Great Britain EDN
Published in 13 volumes (1792–5), with a 14th volume appearing in 1807

Robert Bage (1728–1801)
Man as He Is F
Anonymous

Anna Laetitia Barbauld (1743–1825) and **John Aikin** (1747–1822)
Evenings at Home; or, The Juvenile Budget Opened MISC
Anonymous. Published in 6 volumes (1792–6).

William Bligh (1754–1817)
A Voyage to the South Sea NF
Anonymous. Chapters xiii–xx are adapted from *A Narrative of the Mutiny, on Board His Majesty's Ship Bounty* 1790 (q.v.).

Samuel Egerton Brydges (1762–1837)
Mary de-Clifford F
Anonymous

Edmund Burke (1729–97)
The Works of the Right Honourable Edmund Burke WKS
Concluded in 1827

Maria Cowper (1726–97)
Original Poems on Various Occasions V
Revised before publication with the help of William Cowper, the author's cousin

George Dyer (1755–1841)
Poems V

Adam Ferguson (1723–1816)
Principles of Moral and Political Science NF

William Gilpin (1724–1804)
Three Essays on Picturesque Beauty NF

Susannah Gunning, formerly **Minifie** (1740?–1800)
Anecdotes of the Delborough Family F

Thomas Holcroft (1745–1809)
Anna St Ives F

Thomas Holcroft (1745–1809)
The Road to Ruin: A comedy D
Performed 18 February 1792

James Hurdis (1763–1801)
Sir Thomas More: A tragedy D
bao *The Village Curate*

Edward Jerningham (1737–1812)
Stone Henge V

Ellis Cornelia Knight (1758–1837)
Marcus Flaminius; or, A View of the Military, Political and Social Life of the Romans F

Janet Little (1759–1813)
The Poetical Works of Janet Little, the Scotch Milkmaid V

Anna Maria Mackenzie (*fl.* 1783–98)
Slavery; or, The Times F
bao *Monmouth, The Danish Massacre, &c*

Edmond Malone (1741–1812)
A Letter to Richard Farmer NF
See Malone (ed.), *The Plays and Poems of William Shakespeare* 1790. A reply to criticisms by Joseph Ritson 1792, below.

John Moore (1729–1802)
A Journal During a Residence in France NF
Volume ii published in 1794

Charlotte Palmer (*fl.* 1790–1800)
Integrity and Content F

Charlotte Palmer (*fl.* 1790–1800)
It is, and it is not a Novel F

Joseph Ritson (1752–1803)
Cursory Criticisms on the Edition of Shakespeare Published by Edmond Malone NF
Anonymous. See Malone (ed.), *The Plays and Poems of William Shakespeare* 1790, and *A Letter to the Rev. Richard Farmer* 1792, above.

Mary Robinson (1758–1800)
Vancenza; or, The Dangers of Credulity F

Samuel Rogers (1763–1855)
The Pleasures of Memory V
bao *An Ode to Superstition.* Fifteen editions by 1806.

Susanna Rowson (1762–1824)
The Fille de Chambre F
bao *The Inquisitor*

Charlotte Smith (1749–1806)
Desmond F

Dugald Stewart (1753–1828)
Elements of the Philosophy of the Human Mind [vol. i] NF
Published in 3 volumes (1792–1827)

Thomas Taylor (1758–1835)
A Vindication of the Rights of Brutes NF
Anonymous

Sarah Trimmer (1741–1810)
Reflections upon the Education of Children in Charity Schools NF

Mary Wollstonecraft (1759–97)
A Vindication of the Rights of Woman NF

Arthur Young (1741–1820)
Travels, During the Years 1787, 1788, and 1790 NF

1793

- Execution of Louis XVI (21 Jan.)
  France declares war on Britain and Holland (1 Feb.)
  First Coalition against France formed by Britain, Austria, Prussia, Holland, and Spain

Committee of Public Safety established (Apr.)
Overthrow of the Girondins; Reign of Terror begins in France (June)
Jean Marat murdered by Charlotte Corday (13 July)
Christianity abolished in France (5 Oct.)
Execution of Marie Antoinette (16 Oct.)
Second partition of Poland

- John Clare born
  Felicia Dorothea Hemans born
  Edward Howard born
  William Maginn born
- Charlotte Brooke dies
  Richard Tickell dies
  Gilbert White dies

William Blake (1757–1827)
America: A prophecy V
Illuminated book with 18 relief-etched plates

William Blake (1757–1827)
For Children V
Illuminated book with 18 intaglio plates

William Blake (1757–1827)
Visions of the Daughters of Albion V
Illuminated book with 11 relief-etched plates

Lady Sophia Burell (1750?–1802)
Poems V

Frances Burney (1752–1840)
Brief Reflections Relative to the Emigrant French Clergy NF
bao *Evelina* and *Cecilia*

Robert Burns (1759–96)
Poems Chiefly in the Scottish Dialect V
Enlarged from *Poems* 1787 (q.v.)

Charles Dibdin (1745–1814)
The Younger Brother F

Isaac D'Israeli (1766–1848)
Curiosities of Literature [1st ser., vol. ii] NF
See also *Curiosities of Literature* 1791, 1817, 1823, 1834

William Godwin (1756–1836)
An Enquiry Concerning Political Justice NF
Published in February 1793

Susannah Gunning, formerly **Minifie** (1740?–1800)
Memoirs of Mary F

Mary Hays (1760–1843)
Letters and Essays NF

Gilbert Imlay (*fl.* 1793)
The Emigrants; or, The History of an Expatriated Family F
Formerly misattributed largely to Mary Wollstonecraft

Elizabeth Inchbald (1753–1821)
Every One Has His Fault: A comedy D
Performed 29 January 1793

Charles Macklin (1697?–1797)
Love à la Mode: A farce D
First authorized edition. Performed 12 December 1759.

Charles Macklin (1697?–1797)
The Man of the World: A comedy D
First authorized edition. Performed 10 May 1781.

John Newton (1725–1807)
Letters to a Wife NF
bao *Cardiphonia*

John Ogilvie (1732–1813)
The Theology of Plato NF

Eliza Parsons (1748–1811)
Castle of Wolfenbach: A German story F
One of the seven 'horrid novels' mentioned in Jane Austen's *Northanger Abbey*, chapter vi (see 1817)

Eliza Parsons (1748–1811)
Ellen and Julia F

Eliza Parsons (1748–1811)
Woman as She Should Be; or, Memoirs of Mrs Menville F

Thomas Pennant (1726–98)
Literary Life of the Late Thomas Pennant NF

Anna Maria Porter (1780–1832)
Artless Tales F
A second volume was published in 1795

Clara Reeve (1729–1807)
Memoirs of Sir Roger de Clarendon F

Frederic Reynolds (1764–1841)
How to Grow Rich: A comedy D
Performed 18 April 1793

Joseph Ritson (1752–1803) (ed.)
The English Anthology ANTH

Charlotte Smith (1749–1806)
The Emigrants V
Dedicated to William Cowper

Charlotte Smith (1749–1806)
The Old Manor House F
See also *The Wanderings of Warwick* 1794

William Taylor (1765–1836) (tr.)
Iphigenia in Tauris D
Translated from J.W. von Goethe

George Thomson (1757–1851) (ed.)
A Select Collection of Original Scottish Airs for the Voice V
Published in 4 volumes (1793–9). Volume i contains 59 songs by Robert Burns.

'Prudentia Homespun' [Jane West (1758–1852)]
The Advantages of Education; or, The History of Maria Williams F

John Whitehead (1740?–1804)
The Life of John Wesley NF

William Wordsworth (1770–1850)
Descriptive Sketches V

William Wordsworth (1770–1850)
An Evening Walk V
Addressed to Dorothy Wordsworth

Ann Yearsley (1752–1806)
Reflections on the Death of Louis XVI V

1794

- Execution of Danton and Camille Desmoulins (Apr.)
  Lord Howe defeats French fleet in the English Channel (1 June)
  French forces invade Spain (June)
  Fall of Robespierre
- William Carleton born
  George Grote born
  Anna Jameson born
  John Gibson Lockhart born
  John Hamilton Reynolds born
  William Whewell born
- George Colman, the elder, dies
  Edward Gibbon dies
- André Chenier dies
  Marie Jean Antoine Condorcet dies
  Antoine Laurent Lavoisier dies

Anna Maria Bennett (*c*.1750–1808)
Ellen, Countess of Castle Howel F

William Blake (1757–1827)
Europe: A prophecy V
Illuminated book. Twelve copies known, usually with 17 relief-etched plates.

William Blake (1757–1827)
The First Book of Urizen V
Illuminated book. No further books.

William Blake (1757–1827)
Songs of Innocence and of Experience: Shewing the two contrary states of the human soul V
Illuminated book. See also *Songs of Innocence* 1789.

James Boaden (1762–1839)
Fontainville Forest D
Performed 25 March 1794. Adapted from Ann Radcliffe's *The Romance of the Forest* 1791 (q.v.).

S.T. Coleridge (1772–1834) and **Robert Southey** (1774–1843)
The Fall of Robespierre D
Act i by Coleridge, acts ii and iii by Southey

George Colman, the younger (1762–1836)
The Mountaineers D
Anonymous. Performed 3 August 1793.

Richard Cumberland (1732–1811)
The Jew: A comedy D
Performed 8 May 1794

Erasmus Darwin (1731–1802)
The Golden Age V
Addressed to Thomas Beddoes

Erasmus Darwin (1731–1802)
Zoonomia; or, The Laws of Organic Life NF

Thomas Gisborne (1758–1846)
Walks in a Forest V
Anonymous

William Godwin (1756–1836)
Things as They Are; or, The Adventures of Caleb Williams F
Published in May 1794. See also George Colman, *The Iron Chest* (1796).

James Grahame (1765–1811)
Poems in English, Scotch and Latin V

Elizabeth Gunning, later **Plunkett** (1769–1823)
Lord Fitzhenry F

Elizabeth Gunning, later **Plunkett** (1769–1823)
The Packet F

Thomas Holcroft (1745–1809)
The Adventures of Hugh Trevor [vols i–iii] F
Volumes iv, v, and vi published in 1797 (q.v.)

Edward Jerningham (1737–1812)
The Siege of Berwick: A tragedy D
Performed 13 November 1793

Isabella Kelly (*c*.1759–1857)
Madeleine; or, The Castle of Montgomery F
Anonymous

Richard Payne Knight (1750–1824)
The Landscape V
Addressed to Uvedale Price

Thomas James Mathias (1754?–1835)
The Pursuits of Literature V
Anonymous. Concluded in 1797.

Joseph Moser (1748–1819)
Turkish Tales F

Thomas Paine (1737–1809)
The Age of Reason NF
Part i. Part ii published in 1795.

William Paley (1743–1805)
A View of the Evidences of Christianity NF

Eliza Parsons (1748–1811)
Lucy F

Sir Uvedale Price (1747–1829)
An Essay on the Picturesque NF

Ann Radcliffe (1764–1823)
The Mysteries of Udolpho: A romance F
Many editions into the 19th century

Joseph Ritson (1752–1803) (ed.)
Scottish Song ANTH

Mary Robinson (1758–1800)
The Widow; or, A Picture of Modern Times F

Charlotte Smith (1749–1806)
The Banished Man F

Charlotte Smith (1749–1806)
The Wanderings of Warwick F
Sequel to *The Old Manor House* 1793 (q.v.)

Mary Wollstonecraft (1759–97)
An Historical and Moral View of the Origin and Progress of the French Revolution NF

1795

- Third partition of Poland
  Warren Hastings acquitted of treason (Apr.)
  Belgium annexed to France
  Rule of the Directory in France (Nov.)
- Dr Thomas Arnold born
  Thomas Carlyle born
  George Darley born
  John Keats born
  John William Polidori born
  Thomas Noon Talfourd born
- James Boswell dies
- Josiah Wedgwood dies

William Blake (1757–1827)
The Book of Ahania V
Illuminated book continuing with the layout, imagery, and themes of *The First Book of Urizen* 1794 (q.v.). One known copy, with 5 intaglio plates.

William Blake (1757–1827)
The Book of Los V
Illuminated book with 5 intaglio plates

William Blake (1757–1827)
The Song of Los V
Illuminated book. Five copies known, with 8 plates.

Thomas Chatterton (1752–70)
The Revenge: A burletta D
No record of performance

S.T. Coleridge (1772–1834)
Conciones ad Populum; or, Addresses to the People NF
Published in November 1795

S.T. Coleridge (1772–1834)
A Moral and Political Lecture NF
Lecture delivered in February 1795

S.T. Coleridge (1772–1834)
The Plot Discovered; or, An Address to the People, Against Ministerial Treason NF

George Colman, the elder (1732–94)
Some Particulars of the Life of the Late George Colman NF

Joseph Cottle (1770–1853)
Poems V
Anonymous

Hannah Cowley (1743–1809)
The Town Before You: A comedy D
Performed 6 December 1794

Anne Batten Cristall (*b*. 1769)
Poetical Sketches V

Richard Cumberland (1732–1811)
Henry F
bao *Arundel*

Richard Cumberland (1732–1811)
The Wheel of Fortune: A comedy D
Performed 28 February 1795

Isaac D'Israeli (1766–1848)
An Essay on the Manners and Genius of the Literary Character NF

Maria Edgeworth (1767–1849)
Letters for Literary Ladies NF
Anonymous

William Gifford (1756–1826)
The Maeviad V
bao *The Baviad*, with which it was republished (see 1791)

William Hayley (1745–1820)
The National Advocates V
Anonymous

Robert Huish (1777–1850) (tr.)
The Sorcerer F
Anonymous translation of *Die Teufelsbeschwörung* by 'Veit Weber' (G.P.L.L. Wächter, 1762–1835)

Samuel Ireland (*d.* 1800) (ed.)
Miscellaneous Papers and Legal Instruments Under the Hand and Seal of William Shakespeare NF
Published 1795, dated 1796. Forgeries created by his son, William Henry Ireland. Demolished by Malone in his *Inquiry* 1796 (q.v.).

Walter Savage Landor (1775–1864)
Moral Epistle to Earl Stanhope V
Anonymous

Walter Savage Landor (1775–1864)
The Poems of Walter Savage Landor V
Suppressed by Landor

Francis Lathom (1777–1832)
The Castle of Ollada F
Anonymous

Charles Lloyd (1775–1839)
Poems on Various Subjects V

Mary Meeke (*d.* 1818)
Count St Blanchard; or, The Prejudiced Judge F

John Moore (1729–1802)
A View of the Causes and Progress of the French Revolution NF

Thomas Paine (1737–1809)
Dissertation on First Principles of Government NF

Henry James Pye (1745–1813)
The Democrat F
Anonymous. Pye was Poet Laureate 1790–1813.

Ann Radcliffe (1764–1823)
A Journey Made in the Summer of 1794, Through Holland and the Western Frontier of Germany NF

Adam Smith (1723–90)
Essays on Philosophical Subjects NF

Charlotte Smith (1749–1806)
Montalbert F

Robert Southey (1774–1843)
Poems V
Written by Southey and Robert Lovell, a fellow student of Southey's at Balliol College, Oxford

William Taylor (1765–1836) (tr.)
Dialogues of the Gods F
Translated from Christoph Martin Wieland (1733–1813)

William Taylor (1765–1836) (tr.)
Select Fairy Tales F
Anonymous translation from Christoph Martin Wieland (1733–1813)

John Thelwall (1764–1834)
The Natural and Constitutional Right of Britons to Annual Parliaments NF
Anonymous. Thelwall was arrested in 1794, and sent to the Tower of London. See also below.

John Thelwall (1764–1834)
Poems Written in Close Confinement in the Tower and Newgate V
See above

John Horne Tooke (1736–1812)
The Proceedings at Large, on the Trial of John Horne Tooke, for High Treason NF
Tooke was tried for High Treason, but acquitted. See also Thelwall, above.

Gilbert White (1720–93)
A Naturalist's Calendar NF

Helen Maria Williams (1762–1827)
Letters Containing a Sketch of the Politics of France NF

Helen Maria Williams (1762–1827) (tr.)
Paul and Virginia F
A popular translation from Jacques-Henri Bernadin de Saint Pierre (1737–1814). See also *Paul and Viriginie* 1788.

'Peter Pindar' [John Wolcot (1738–1819)**]**
The Cap: A satiric poem V

1796

- Napoleon Bonaparte marries Josephine Beauharnais (9 Mar.)
  Bonaparte invades Italy
  Bonaparte defeats the Austrians at Lodi and enters Milan (May)

William Beckford begins construction of Fonthill Abbey
Edward Jenner vaccinates against smallpox

- Michael Banim born
  Frederick Chamier born
  Hartley Coleridge born
  Richard Ford born
  Agnes Strickland born
- Robert Burns dies
  James Macpherson dies
  Thomas Reid dies

Robert Bage (1728–1801)
Hermsprong; or, Man as He is Not F
bao *Man as He Is*

'Lady Harriet Marlow' [William Beckford (1760–1844)]
Modern Novel Writing F

Mary Matilda Betham (1776–1852)
Elegies, and Other Small Poems V

William Lisle Bowles (1762–1850)
Hope V

Sir James Burges (1752–1824)
The Birth and Triumph of Love V

Edmund Burke (1729–97)
A Letter to a Noble Lord NF
Fourteen editions in 1796

Edmund Burke (1729–97)
Two Letters Addressed on the Proposals for Peace with the Regicide Directory of France NF
A third letter published in 1797

Charles Burney (1726–1814)
Memoirs of the Life and Writings of the Abate Metastasio NF

Frances Burney (1752–1840)
Camilla; or, A Picture of Youth F
bao *Evelina* and *Cecilia*

S.T. Coleridge (1772–1834)
Ode on the Departing Year V

S.T. Coleridge (1772–1834)
Poems on Various Subjects V
See also *Poems* 1797

S.T. Coleridge (1772–1834)
The Watchman NF
Published in 10 numbers (1 March–13 May 1796)

George Colman, the younger (1762–1836)
The Iron Chest D
Performed 12 March 1796. Adapted from Godwin's *Caleb Williams* 1794 (q.v.).

Isaac D'Israeli (1766–1848)
Miscellanies; or, Literary Recreations NF
Revised and enlarged in 1801 as *Literary Miscellanies*

Maria Edgeworth (1767–1849)
The Parent's Assistant; or, Stories for Children F
Some stories reprinted in *Early Lessons* 1801 (q.v.)

Edward Gibbon (1737–94)
Miscellaneous Works WKS

Elizabeth Hamilton (1758–1816)
Translation of the Letters of a Hindoo Rajah F

William Hayley (1745–1820)
The Life of Milton NF

Mary Hays (1760–1843)
Memoirs of Emma Courtney F

Elizabeth Helme (*d.* 1816)
The Farmer of Inglewood Forest F
Frequently reprinted throughout the 19th century

Thomas Holcroft (1745–1809)
The Man of Ten Thousand: A comedy D
Performed 23 January 1796

Elizabeth Inchbald (1753–1821)
Nature and Art F

Samuel Ireland (*d.* 1800) (ed.)
Mr Ireland's Vindication . . . of the Supposed Shakspeare MSS NF
See Malone, *Inquiry* 1796, and Ireland, *Miscellaneous Papers* 1795

W.H. Ireland (1777–1835)
An Authentic Account of the Shaksperian Manuscripts NF
See also *Confessions* 1805

Robert Jephson (1736–1803)
Conspiracy: A tragedy D
Performed 15 November 1796

Isabella Kelly (*c.*1759–1857)
The Ruins of Avondale Priory F

Sophia Lee (1750–1824)
Almeyda, Queen of Granada: A tragedy D

M.G. Lewis (1775–1818)
The Monk: A romance F
Published on 12 March 1796

M.G. Lewis (1775–1818)
Village Virtues V
Anonymous

'Ellen of Exeter' [Anna Maria Mackenzie (*fl.* 1783–98)]
The Neapolitan; or, The Test of Integrity F

Edmond Malone (1741–1812)
An Inquiry into the Authenticity of Certain Miscellaneous Papers Attributed to Shakspeare NF
Written to expose the forgeries of William Henry Ireland. See *Miscellaneous Papers* 1795 and S. Ireland, *Vindication* 1796.

Thomas Morton (1764?–1838)
The Way to Get Married: A comedy D
Performed 23 January 1796

Joseph Moser (1748–1819)
The Hermit of Caucasus: An oriental romance F

Eliza Parsons (1748–1811)
The Mysterious Warning F
One of the seven 'horrid novels' mentioned in Jane Austen's *Northanger Abbey*, chapter vi (see 1817)

Eliza Parsons (1748–1811)
Women as They Are F

Ann Radcliffe (1764–1823)
The Italian; or, The Confessional of the Black Penitents F
Published 1796, dated 1797

Mary Robinson (1758–1800)
Angelina F

Mary Robinson (1758–1800)
Hubert de Sevrac F

Regina Maria Roche (1773–1845)
The Children of the Abbey F
Many editions and cheap reissues

Walter Scott (1771–1832) (tr.)
The Chase, and William and Helen V
Anonymous. Translated from Gottfried August Bürger (1747–94), *Der Wilde Jäger* and *Lenore*.

Anna Seward (1742–1809)
Llangollen Vale, with Other Poems V

Charlotte Smith (1749–1806)
Marchmont F

Robert Southey (1774–1843)
Joan of Arc V

Robert Southey (1774–1843)
Poems V
Published 1796, dated 1797. See also *Poems* 1799, *Minor Poems* 1815.

William Taylor (1765–1836) (tr.)
Ellenore V
Anonymous translation of *Lenore* (1774) by Gotfried August Bürger (1747–94), itself based on a Scottish ballad

John Thelwall (1764–1834)
The Rights of Nature, Against the Usurpations of Establishments NF

Jane West (1758–1852)
A Gossip's Story, and A Legendary Tale F
bao *The Advantages of Education*

Mary Wollstonecraft (1759–97)
Letters Written During a Short Residence in Sweden, Norway and Denmark NF

Ann Yearsley (1752–1806)
The Rural Lyre V

1797

- Spanish fleet defeated by Nelson and Jervis off Cape St Vincent (14 Feb.)
  John Adams inaugurated President of the USA (Mar.)
- Emily Eden born
  Samuel Lover born
  Sir Charles Lyell born
  Mary Shelley (*née* Godwin) born
  Alaric Alexander Watts born
- Edmund Burke dies
  Maria Cowper dies
  Charles Macklin dies
  William Mason dies
  Horace Walpole dies
  Mary Godwin (*née* Wollstonecraft) dies
- Connop Thirlwall born
- John Wilkes dies
- Alfred de Vigny born
  Heinrich Heine born
  Franz Schubert born

'Jaquetta Agneta Mariana Jenks' [William Beckford (1760–1844)]
Azemia F
Dedicated to 'The Right Honourable Lady Harriet Marlow' (i.e. another of Beckford's pseudonyms: see *Modern Novel Writing* 1796)

Anna Maria Bennett (*c*.1750–1808)
The Beggar Girl and Her Benefactors F

James Boaden (1762–1839)
The Italian Monk D
Performed 15 August 1797

Elizabeth Bonhote (1744–1818)
Bungay Castle F

Edmund Burke (1729–97)
Letter on the Conduct of the Minority in Parliament NF
Pirated

Edmund Burke (1729–97)
A Third Letter on the Proposals for Peace with the Regicide Directory of France NF
See *Two Letters . . . on the Proposals for Peace* 1796

Edmund Burke (1729–97)
Three Memorials on French Affairs NF

Edmund Burke (1729–97)
Two Letters on the Conduct of Our Domestick Parties NF

'Peter Porcupine' [William Cobbett (1763–1835)]
The Life and Adventures of Peter Porcupine F
First published Philadelphia, 1796

S.T. Coleridge (1772–1834)
Poems . . . Second Edition V
See also *Poems* 1796, 1803

Charles Dibdin (1745–1814)
A Complete History of the English Stage NF

Isaac D'Israeli (1766–1848)
Vaurien; or, Sketches of the Times F
Anonymous

George Dyer (1755–1841)
The Poet's Fate V

Thomas Erskine (1750–1823)
A View of the Causes and Consequences of the Present War with France NF
Thirty-five editions in 1797

William Gifford (1756–1826) (ed.)
The Anti-Jacobin; or, Weekly Examiner PER
Published in 36 numbers (November 1797–July 1798)

William Godwin (1756–1836)
The Enquirer NF

Elizabeth Gunning, later **Plunkett** (1769–1823)
The Orphans of Snowdon F

Susannah Gunning, formerly **Minifie** (1740?–1800)
Love at First Sight F

Thomas Holcroft (1745–1809)
The Adventures of Hugh Trevor [vols iv–vi] F
Volumes i–iii published in 1794 (q.v.)

Elizabeth Inchbald (1753–1821)
Wives as They Were, and Maids as They Are: A comedy D
Performed 4 March 1797

Harriet Lee (1756–1851)
Canterbury Tales for the Year 1797 F
Volume ii (*Canterbury Tales*, by Sophia Lee), published in 1798; volume iii (by Sophia and Harriet Lee), 1799; volume iv (by Harriet Lee), 1801; volume v (by Harriet Lee), 1805

M.G. Lewis (1775–1818) (tr.)
The Minister: A tragedy D
Unacted. Translated from *Kabale und Liebe* by J.C.F. Schiller (1759–1805)

'Gabrielli' [Mary Meeke (*d.* 1818)]
The Mysterious Wife F

Alexander Pope (1688–1744)
The Works of Alexander Pope WKS
Edited by Joseph Warton

Anna Maria Porter (1780–1832)
Walsh Colville; or, A Young Man's First Entrance into Life F
Anonymous

Samuel Jackson Pratt (1749–1814)
Family Secrets, Literary and Domestic F

Frederic Reynolds (1764–1841)
The Will: A comedy D
Performed 19 April 1797

Mary Robinson (1758–1800)
Walsingham; or, The Pupil of Nature F

Edward Rushton (1756–1814)
Expostulatory Letter to George Washington V
On Washington's ownership of slaves

Charlotte Smith (1749–1806)
Elegaic Sonnets, and Other Poems [vol. ii] V
Sequel to *Elegaic Sonnets* 1784 (q.v.)

Robert Southey (1774–1843)
Letters Written During a Short Residence in Spain and Portugal NF

William Wilberforce (1759–1833)
A Practical View of the Prevailing Religious System of Professed Christians NF

1798

- Napoleon leads an expedition to conquer Italy
  Battle of the Nile: Nelson destroys the French fleet off Aboukir (1 Aug.)
  Income tax introduced in Britain
- John Banim born
  Henry Nelson Coleridge born
  George Lillie Craik born
  Thomas Crofton Croker born
  Alexander Dyce born
  Catherine Godwin born
  Elizabeth Caroline Grey born
- Robert Merry dies
  Thomas Pennant dies
- Auguste Comte born
  Giacomo Leopardi born

Robert Anderson (1770–1833)
Poems on Various Subjects V

Joanna Baillie (1762–1851)
A Series of Plays [vol. i] D
Known as *Plays on the Passions*. Includes *Count Basil, The Tryal, De Montfort* (published separately in 1807, q.v.). See also 1802, 1812, 1821.

William Lisle Bowles (1762–1850)
St Michael's Mount V

Thomas Brown (1778–1820)
Observations on the Zoonomia of Erasmus Darwin NF
See Darwin, *Zoonomia* 1794

Samuel Egerton Brydges (1762–1837)
Arthur Fitz-Albini F
Anonymous

S.T. Coleridge (1772–1834)
Fears in Solitude V
Also includes 'France: An Ode' and 'Frost at Midnight'

Joseph Cottle (1770–1853)
Malvern Hills V

Thomas John Dibdin (1771–1841)
The Mouth of the Nile; or, The Glorious First of August D
Performed 25 October 1798. On the destruction of the French fleet by Nelson at the Battle of Aboukir (1 August 1798).

Nathan Drake (1766–1836)
Literary Hours; or, Sketches Critical and Narrative NF

Maria Edgeworth (1767–1849) and **Richard Lovell Edgeworth** (1744–1817)
Practical Education NF

William Gilpin (1724–1804)
Picturesque Remarks on Western Parts of England and the Isle of Wight NF

Thomas Gisborne (1758–1846)
Poems, Sacred and Moral V

William Godwin (1756–1836)
Memoirs of the Author of A Vindication of the Rights of Women NF
Memoirs of Mary Wollstonecraft Godwin

Mary Hays (1760–1843)
An Appeal to the Men of Great Britain in Behalf of Women NF
Anonymous. Attributed to Mary Hays.

Thomas Holcroft (1745–1809)
He's Much to Blame: A comedy D
Anonymous. Performed 13 February 1798. Also attributed to John Fenwick.

Elizabeth Inchbald (1753–1821) (tr.)
Lovers' Vows D
Performed 11 October 1798. Translated from *Das Kind der Liebe* (1790) by August von Kotzebue (1761–1819).

Charles Lamb (1775–1834) and **Charles Lloyd** (1775–1839)
Blank Verse V
Includes Lamb's 'The Old Familiar Faces'

Charles Lamb (1775–1834)
A Tale of Rosamund Gray and Old Blind Margaret F

Walter Savage Landor (1775–1864)
Gebir V
Anonymous. See also *Gebir* 1831.

M.G. Lewis (1775–1818)
The Castle Spectre D
Performed 14 December 1797

Charles Lloyd (1775–1839)
Edmund Oliver F

Anna Maria Mackenzie (*fl.* 1783–98)
Dusseldorf; or, The Fratricide F

T.R. Malthus (1766–1834)
An Essay on the Principle of Population NF
Anonymous

Mary Meeke (*d.* 1818)
The Sicilian F
bao *The Mysterious Wife*

Mary Pilkington (1766–1839)
Tales of the Cottage; or, Stories, Moral and Amusing for Young Persons F
Anonymous

James Plumptre (1770–1832)
The Lakers: A comic opera D/OP
Anonymous. Unacted.

Anna Maria Porter (1780–1832)
Octavia F

Regina Maria Roche (1773–1845)
Clermont F
One of the 'horrid' novels mentioned in Jane Austen's *Northanger Abbey* (see 1817)

Samuel Rogers (1763–1855)
An Epistle to a Friend, with Other Poems V
bao *The Pleasures of Memory*

Eleanor Sleath (*fl.* 1798–1811)
The Orphan of the Rhine F
Another of the 'horrid' novels mentioned in Jane Austen's *Northanger Abbey* (see 1817)

Charlotte Smith (1749–1806)
The Young Philosopher F
Charlottle Smith's last novel

William Sotheby (1757–1833) (tr.)
Oberon V
A translation of *Oberon* (1780) by Christoph Martin Wieland (1733–1813). See also *Oberon; or, Huon of Bordeaux* 1802.

George Vancouver (1757–98)
A Voyage of Discovery to the North Pacific Ocean, and Round the World NF

Horace Walpole (1717–97)
The Works of Horatio Walpole WKS
Edited by Robert Walpole, assisted by Mary Berry. Further volumes added in 1818, 1822, and 1825.

Helen Maria Williams (1762–1827)
A Tour in Switzerland NF

Mary Wollstonecraft (1759–97)
The Wrongs of Woman F
Unfinished. Published as volumes i and ii of *Posthumous Works of the Author of a Vindication of the Rights of Woman* (edited by William Godwin).

William Wordsworth (1770–1850) and **S.T. Coleridge** (1772–1834)
Lyrical Ballads with a Few Other Poems V
Anonymous. Published in September 1798. Contains Coleridge's 'The Rime of the Ancyent Marinere'. See also *Lyrical Ballads* 1801, 1802, 1805, 1815.

1799

- Second Coalition against France
  Napoleon Bonaparte overthrows the Directory and becomes First Consul
  Talleyrand appointed French Foreign Minister
  Religious Tract Society founded
- Eliza Acton born
  Louisa Costello born
  Eyre Evans Crowe born
  Catherine Gore born
  John Abraham Heraud born
  Thomas Hood born
  Mary Howitt born
  George Payne Rainsford James born
- James Burnett, Lord Monboddo, dies
  William Melmoth, the younger, dies
- Honoré de Balzac born
  Alexander Pushkin born
- Beaumarchais dies
  George Washington dies
- F. Schiller, *Wallenstein*

Mary Alcock (*c.*1742–98)
Poems V

James Boaden (1762–1839)
Aurelio and Miranda D
Performed 29 December 1798. Adapted from M.G. Lewis's *The Monk* 1796 (q.v.).

William Lisle Bowles (1762–1850)
Song of the Battle of the Nile V
Nelson destroyed the French fleet off Aboukir (Battle of the Nile) on 1 August 1798

Thomas Campbell (1777–1844)
The Pleasures of Hope, with Other Poems V
See also 1855

Isaac D'Israeli (1766–1848)
Romances F

Maria Edgeworth (1767–1849) and **Richard Lovell Edgeworth** (1744–1817)
A Rational Primer NF
bao *Practical Education*

William Godwin (1756–1836)
St Leon: A tale of the sixteenth century F
Published in November 1799

Elizabeth Gunning, later **Plunkett** (1769–1823)
The Gipsy Countess F

Mary Hays (1760–1843)
The Victim of Prejudice F

George Huddesford (1749–1809)
Bubble and Squeak V
Anonymous. A second part also published in 1799 as *Crambe Repetita.*

Elizabeth Inchbald (1753–1821) (tr.)
The Wise Man of the East D
Performed 30 November 1799. Translation of *Das Schreibepult* by August von Kotzebue (1761–1819).

W.H. Ireland (1777–1835)
Vortigern: An historical tragedy D
Performed 2 April 1796. The play was supposedly written by Shakespeare but was in fact by Ireland, See *An Authentic Account* 1796, *Confessions* 1805.

M.G. Lewis (1775–1818) (tr.)
Rolla; or, The Peruvian Hero: A tragedy D
Translation of *Die Spanier in Peru* (1797) by August von Kotzebue (1761–1819)

M.G. Lewis (1775–1818) [and others]
Tales of Terror V
Imitations, translations, etc., including contributions by Sir Walter Scott, Robert Southey, and John Leyden. See also Walter Scott, *An Apology for Tales of Terror* 1799, below.

Hannah More (1745–1833)
Strictures on the Modern System of Female Education NF

Mungo Park (1771–1806)
Travels in the Interior Districts of Africa NF

Eliza Parsons (1748–1811)
The Valley of St Gothard F
Dedicated to M.G. Lewis

Mary Anne Radcliffe (*c.*1746–post 1810)
The Female Advocate; or, An Attempt to Recover the Rights of Women from Male Usurpation NF

Clara Reeve (1729–1807)
Destination; or, Memoirs of a Private Family F

Frederic Reynolds (1764–1841)
Management: A comedy D
Performed 31 October 1799

Mary Robinson (1758–1800)
The False Friend F

'Anne Frances Randall' [Mary Robinson (1758–1800)]
A Letter to the Women of England, on the Injustice of Mental Subordination NF

Mary Robinson (1758–1800)
The Natural Daughter F

Susanna Rowson (1762–1824)
Reuben and Rachel; or, Tales of Old Times F

Walter Scott (1771–1832) (tr.)
Goetz of Berlichingen; with The Iron Hand V
Translated from J.W. von Goethe (1749–1832)

Walter Scott (1771–1832)
An Apology for Tales of Terror V
Anonymous. Also attributed to M.G. Lewis. See *Tales of Terror* 1799, above.

Anna Seward (1742–1809)
Original Sonnets on Various Subjects V

Richard Brinsley Sheridan (1751–1816) (tr.)
Pizarro D
Performed 24 May 1799). Translated from *Die Spanier in Peru* (1797) by August von Kotzebue (1761–1819).

Horatio Smith (1779–1849)
A Family Story F
Published 1799, dated 1800

William Sotheby (1757–1833)
The Battle of the Nile V
Nelson defeated the French at Aboukir on 1 August 1798

Robert Southey (1774–1843)
Poems . . . The Second Volume V
Contains the original book ix of *Joan of Arc* ('The Vision of the Maid of Orleans') and new material. See also *Poems* 1796.

1800

1800

- Napoleon Bonaparte defeats the Austrians at the Battle of Marengo (14 June)
  British capture Malta (Sept.)
  Library of Congress established in Washington
- Anna Maria Hall (Mrs S.C. Hall, *née* Fielding) born
  Thomas Babington Macaulay born
  Edward Bouverie Pusey born
  Sir Henry Taylor born
  Charles Jeremiah Wells born
- Hugh Blair dies
  William Cowper dies
  Susannah Gunning (*née* Minifie) dies
  Charles Johnstone dies
  Elizabeth Montagu dies
  Mary Robinson ('Perdita', *née* Darby) dies
  Joseph Warton dies
- William Henry Fox Talbot born
- Schiller, *Maria Stuart*

The Armenian; or, The Ghost-Seer F
Translation by Wilhelm Render of *Der Geisterseher* (1789) by J.C.F. Schiller (1759–1805)

Anonymous
The Rival Mothers; or, Calumny F
Anonymous translation of *Les Mères rivales, ou la calomnie* (1800) by Madame de Genlis (1746–1830)

Christopher Anstey (1724–1805)
Contentment; or, Hints to Servants on the Present Scarcity V

Robert Bloomfield (1766–1823)
The Farmer's Boy V
Published on 1 March 1800, with engravings by Thomas Bewick. Fifteen editions by 1827.

Frances Brooke (1724–89)
Marian: A comic opera D/OP

Robert Burns (1759–96)
The Works of Robert Burns WKS

William Cobbett (1763–1835) (ed.)
The Porcupine PER
A staunchly anti-republican daily periodical (365 numbers, October 1800–December 1801)

S.T. Coleridge (1772–1834) (tr.)
Wallenstein D
Translated from J.C.F. Schiller (1759–1805). Part i *The Piccolomini*; part ii *The Death of Wallenstein.*

Joseph Cottle (1770–1853)
Alfred V

Erasmus Darwin (1731–1802)
Phytologia; or, The Philosophy of Agriculture and Gardening NF

Sir Humphry Davy (1778–1829)
Researches, Chemical and Philosophical NF

Maria Edgeworth (1767–1849)
Castle Rackrent: An Hibernian tale F
Anonymous. Published in January 1800.

William Gifford (1756–1826)
Epistle to Peter Pindar V
bao *The Baviad*. Satire addressed at John Wolcot.

William Godwin (1756–1836)
Antonio: A tragedy D
Performed 13 December 1800

Susannah Gunning, formerly **Minifie** (1740?–1800)
Fashionable Involvements F

William Hayley (1745–1820)
An Essay on Sculpture V

Walter Savage Landor (1775–1864) (tr.)
Poems from the Arabic and Persian V
bao *Gebir*

M.G. Lewis (1775–1818)
The East Indian: A comedy D
bao *The Monk*. Performed 22 April 1799. Based partly on *Die Indianer in England* by August von Kotzebue (1761–1819).

M.G. Lewis (1775–1818) and others
Tales of Wonder F/V
Published 1800, dated 1801. Includes poems by Walter Scott.

T.R. Malthus (1766–1834)
An Investigation of the Cause of the Present High Price of Provisions NF
bao *The Essay on the Principle of Population*

Mary Meeke (*d.* 1818)
Anecdotes of the Altamont Family F
Anonymous

John Moore (1729–1802)
Mordaunt F
bao *Zeluco* & *Edward*

Thomas Moore (1779–1852) (tr.)
Odes of Anacreon V

Thomas Morton (1764?–1838)
Speed the Plough: A comedy D
Performed 8 February 1800. The play introduced the character of Mrs Grundy.

Eliza Parsons (1748–1811)
The Miser and his Family F

Henry James Pye (1745–1813)
Adelaide: A tragedy D
Pye was Poet Laureate 1790–1813

Mary Robinson (1758–1800)
Lyrical Tales V

Walter Scott (1771–1832)
The Eve of Saint John V

Charlotte Smith (1749–1806)
The Letters of a Solitary Wanderer F
Published in 5 volumes (1800–2)

William Sotheby (1757–1833) (tr.)
The Georgics of Virgil V

William Sotheby (1757–1833)
The Siege of Cuzco: A tragedy V

Thomas Warton, the younger (1728–90) and others
Essays on Gothic Architecture NF

1801

- Union of Great Britain and Ireland (1 Jan.)
  Thomas Jefferson inaugurated as President of the USA (Mar.)
  Suspension of Habeas Corpus Act
  Peace preliminaries between Britain and France
- William Barnes born
  Caroline Clive born
  John Henry Newman born
- Robert Bage dies
  Hester Chapone dies
- Friedrich von Hardenberg ('Novalis') dies
- Chateaubriand, *Atala*

Lucy Aikin (1781–1864) (ed.)
Poetry for Children V
Poems by various authors, including Dryden, Pope, and Mrs Barbauld. Some poems signed 'original'.

Sir John Barrow (1764–1848)
An Account of Travels into the Interior of Southern Africa NF

William Lisle Bowles (1762–1850)
The Sorrows of Switzerland V

Sir James Burges (1752–1824)
Richard the First V

Robert Burns (1759–96)
Poems Ascribed to Robert Burns V

Hannah Cowley (1743–1809)
The Siege of Acre V

R. C. Dallas (1754–1824)
Percival; or, Nature Vindicated F

George Dyer (1755–1841)
Poems V

Maria Edgeworth (1767–1849)
Belinda F

Maria Edgeworth (1767–1849)
Early Lessons F
bao *The Parent's Assistant*. Contains: *Harry and Lucy* (parts i and ii); *Rosamond* (parts i, ii, and iii); *Frank* (parts i, ii, iii, and iv); and *The Little Dog Trusty* (with other stories). See also *Continuation* 1814; *Rosamond* 1821; *Frank* 1822, and *Harry and Lucy* 1825.

Maria Edgeworth (1767–1849)
Moral Tales for Young People F

William Godwin (1756–1836)
Thoughts Occasioned by Dr Parr's Spital Sermon NF
See Samuel Parr 1801, below

Rowland Hill (1744–1833)
Village Dialogues F

James Hogg (1770–1835)
Scottish Pastorals, Poems, Songs V

Thomas Hull (1728–1808)
Elisha; or, The Woman of Shunem D

Leigh Hunt (1784–1859)
Juvenilia NF

M.G. Lewis (1775–1818)
Adelmorn the Outlaw D

M.G. Lewis (1775–1818)
Alfonso, King of Castile: A tragedy D

Charles Lucas (1769–1854)
The Infernal Quixote F

Thomas Moore (1779–1852)
Corruption, and Intolerance V
Anonymous

Thomas Moore (1779–1852)
The Poetical Works of the Late Thomas Little V

Arthur Murphy (1727–1805)
The Life of David Garrick NF

Amelia Opie (1769–1853)
The Father and Daughter F/V
Later dramatized by W.T. Moncrieff as *The Lear of Private Life* 1820 (q.v.)

Samuel Parr (1747–1825)
A Spital Sermon NF
Sermon preached on Gal. vi: 10 on 15 April 1800. See also William Godwin 1801, above.

Eliza Parsons (1748–1811)
The Peasant of Ardenne Forest F

Henry James Pye (1745–1813)
Alfred V
Pye was Poet Laureate 1790–1813

Frederic Reynolds (1764–1841)
Life: A comedy D
Performed 1 November 1800

William Barnes Rhodes (1772–1826) (tr.)
The Satires of Juvenal V

Horatio Smith (1779–1849)
Trevanion; or, Matrimonial Errors F

William Sotheby (1757–1833)
Julian and Agnes; or, The Monks of the Great St Bernard: A tragedy D
Performed 25 April 1800, with Mrs Siddons in the part of Agnes

Robert Southey (1774–1843)
Thalaba the Destroyer V
bao *Joan of Arc*

'John Beaufort' [John Thelwall (1764–1834)]
The Daughter of Adoption F

Helen Maria Williams (1762–1827)
Sketches of the State of Manners and Opinions in the French Republic NF

William Wordsworth (1770–1850) and **S.T. Coleridge** (1772–1834)
Lyrical Ballads, with Other Poems V
Published in two volumes in January 1801, dated 1800, under Wordsworth's name but containing poems by Coleridge. Includes new preface containing 'a systematic defence of the theory upon which the poems were written'. Volume ii contains new poems. See also *Lyrical Ballads* 1798, 1802, 1805.

1802

- Peace of Amiens (27 Mar.) between Britain and France
- Thomas Aird born
  Selina Bunbury born
  Lady Bulwer-Lytton (*née* Rosina Wheeler) born
  Robert Chambers born
  Sara Coleridge born
  Letitia Elizabeth Landon born
  Harriet Martineau born
  Winthrop Mackworth Praed born
  Isaac Williams born
- Richard Owen Cambridge dies
  Erasmus Darwin dies
- John Moore dies
- Alexandre Dumas born
  Victor Hugo born
- Chateaubriand, *Le Génie du Christianisme*
  Madame de Staël, *Delphine*

Atala F
A translation of *Atala, ou les amours de deux sauvages dans le désert* (1801) by François-René de Chateaubriand (1768–1848)

The Edinburgh Review, or Critical Journal PER
Begun by Sydney Smith, Francis Jeffrey, and Henry Brougham. Published quarterly (October 1802–October 1829).

Joanna Baillie (1762–1851)
A Series of Plays [vol. ii] D
Known as *Plays on the Passions*. See also 1798 1812, 1821. Includes *The Election, Ethwald, The Second Marriage.*

Robert Bloomfield (1766–1823)
Rural Tales, Ballads and Songs V
Illustrated by Thomas Bewick

Sir Alexander Boswell (1775–1822)
Songs, Chiefly in the Scottish Dialect V
Anonymous

Samuel Egerton Brydges (1762–1837)
Le Forester F
bao *Arthur Fitz-Albini*

William Cobbett (1763–1835) (ed.)
Cobbett's Political Register PER
Published weekly (January 1802–February 1836) under various titles. Mostly written by Cobbett himself until his death

George Colman, the younger (1762–1836)
The Poor Gentleman: A comedy D
Performed 11 February 1801

Thomas John Dibdin (1771–1841)
The Cabinet: A comic opera D/OP
Performed 9 February 1802

George Dyer (1755–1841)
Poems V

Richard Lovell Edgeworth (1744–1817) and **Maria Edgeworth** (1767–1849)
Essay on Irish Bulls NF

William Gifford (1756–1826) (tr.)
The Satires of Decimus Junius Juvenalis V

Thomas Holcroft (1745–1809)
A Tale of Mystery: A melodrama D
Performed 13 November 1802

Charles Lamb (1775–1834)
John Woodvil: A tragedy D
Also contains Mary Lamb's poem 'Helen' (her first appearance in print)

Walter Savage Landor (1775–1864)
Poetry by the author of Gebir V

Amelia Opie (1769–1853)
Poems V

William Paley (1743–1805)
Natural Theology NF
Twenty editions by 1820

Joseph Ritson (1752–1803)
Bibliographia Poetica NF

Walter Scott (1771–1832) (ed.)
Minstrelsy of the Scottish Border ANTH
Anonymous. Volume iii published in 1803.

William Sotheby (1757–1833)
Oberon; or, Huon de Bourdeaux D
See also *Oberon* 1798

William Wordsworth (1770–1850) and **S.T. Coleridge** (1772–1834)
Lyrical Ballads, with Pastoral and Other Poems V
Published under Wordsworth's name but containing poems by Coleridge. The Preface of 1801 expanded and texts of poems amended in many cases. See also *Lyrical Ballads* 1798, 1801, 1805.

1803

- The Louisiana Purchase (Apr.)
  Renewal of hostilities between Britain and France (May)
- Thomas Lovell Beddoes born
  George Borrow born
  Edward George Bulwer-Lytton, 1st Baron Lytton, born
  Richard Hurrell Froude born
  R.H. Horne born
  Douglas Jerrold born
- James Beattie dies
  Joseph Ritson dies
- Hector Berlioz born
  Ralph Waldo Emerson born
  Prosper Mérimée born
- Vittorio Alfieri dies
  Friedrich Gottlieb Klopstock dies

Delphine F
Translation of *Delphine* (1802) by Madame de Staël (1766–1817)

Sir Alexander Boswell (1775–1822)
The Spirit of Tintoc; or, Johnny Bell and the Kelpie V
Anonymous

William Lisle Bowles (1762–1850)
The Picture V

Henry Brougham (1778–1868)
An Inquiry into the Colonial Policy of the European Powers NF

Thomas Campbell (1777–1844)
Poems V
Contains the 7th edition of *The Pleasures of Hope* 1799 (q.v.) and new pieces, including 'Lochiel's Warning', 'Hohenlinden', and 'The Soldier's Dream'

Thomas Chatterton (1752–70)
The Works of Thomas Chatterton EDN
Edited by Robert Southey and Joseph Cottle

S.T. Coleridge (1772–1834)
Poems: Third Edition V
Substantially a reprint of *Poems . . . Second Edition* 1797 (q.v.), omitting the poems of Lamb and Lloyd. See also *Poems* 1796.

Erasmus Darwin (1731–1802)
The Temple of Nature; or, The Origin of Society V

Charles Dibdin (1745–1814)
The Professional Life of Mr Dibdin NF/V

Isaac D'Israeli (1766–1848)
Narrative Poems V

William Godwin (1756–1836)
Life of Geoffrey Chaucer, the Early English Poet NF

William Hayley (1745–1820)
The Life and Posthumous Writings of William Cowper MISC
Published in 3 volumes (1803–4). Contains previously unpublished poems. Plates engraved by William Blake.

Mary Hays (1760–1843)
Female Biography NF

Elizabeth Helme (*d.* 1816)
St Clair of the Isles; or, The Outlaws of Barra F

Thomas Holcroft (1745–1809)
Hear Both Sides: A comedy D
Performed 12 February 1803

Lady Mary Wortley Montagu (1689–1762)
The Works of the Right Honorable Lady Mary Wortley Montagu WKS
Edited by James Dallaway. See also *Letters and Works* 1837.

Sydney Owenson, later **Lady Morgan** (1783?–1859)
St Clair; or, The Heiress of Desmond F

William Mudford (1782–1848)
Augustus and Mary; or, The Maid of Buttermere F

Jane Porter (1776–1850)
Thaddeus of Warsaw F

Humphry Repton (1752–1818)
Observations on the Theory and Practice of Landscape Gardening NF

William Shakespeare (1564–1616)
The Plays of William Shakespeare EDN
Edited by Isaac Reed. The First Variorum Edition (i.e. the 5th reprint of George Steevens's edition, 1773, q.v., revised by Reed in 1785).

Robert Southey (1774–1843) (tr.)
Amadis of Gaul F
Translated from Vasco Lobeira using the Spanish version (1508) of Garci Rodríguez de Montalvo (*fl.* 1500)

Henry Kirke White (1785–1806)
Clifton Grove V

1804

- Napoleon Bonaparte assumes imperial title as Napoleon I (18 May)
- Laman Blanchard born
  Richard Cobden born
  Benjamin Disraeli born
  Sir Richard Owen born
- William Gilpin dies
  Richard Graves dies
  Charlotte Lennox dies
  Joseph Priestley dies
  John Wilkes dies
- Nathaniel Hawthorne born
  Charles-Augustin Sainte-Beuve born
  George Sand (Aurore Dupin) born
- Immanuel Kant dies
  Jacques Necker dies
- Schiller, *Wilhelm Tell*

Joanna Baillie (1762–1851)
Miscellaneous Plays D
Includes *Rayner, The Country Inn, Constantine Paleologus; or, The Last of the Caesars*

Sir John Barrow (1764–1848)
Travels in China NF

Mary Matilda Betham (1776–1852)
A Biographical Dictionary of the Celebrated Women of Every Age and Country DICT

Robert Bloomfield (1766–1823)
Good Tidings; or, News from the Farm V

William Lisle Bowles (1762–1850)
The Spirit of Discovery; or, The Conquest of Ocean V

Thomas Brown (1778–1820)
Poems V

Andrew Cherry (1762–1812)
The Soldier's Daughter: A comedy D
Twelve editions by 1805

William Cobbett (1763–1835) (ed.)
Cobbett's Parliamentary Debates NF
Edited jointly with John Wright until 1811, thereafter by Wright alone. The first attempt to provide a complete report of parliamentary

proceedings; known as *Hansard's Parliamentary Debates* from 1818 after T.C. Hansard (1776–1833), the printer of the work from 1808.

William Cobbett (1763–1835)
The Political Proteus NF
Taken largely from the *Political Register* of 1803

John Collins (1742?–1808)
Scripscrapologia; or Collins's Doggerel Dish of all Sorts V

John Wilson Croker (1780–1857)
An Intercepted Letter from J- T-, Esq. V
'J- T-' = Croker. A satire on the city of Dublin.

Richard Cumberland (1732–1811)
The Sailor's Daughter: A comedy D
Performed 7 April 1804

R.C. Dallas (1754–1824)
Aubrey F

Maria Edgeworth (1767–1849)
Popular Tales F

Pierce Egan, the elder (1772–1849)
Sporting Anecdotes, Original and Select NF
'By an amateur sportsman'

John Galt (1779–1839)
The Battle of Largs V
Anonymous. Galt's first published work.

James Grahame (1765–1811)
The Sabbath V
Anonymous

William Hayley (1745–1820)
The Triumph of Music V

Sophia Lee (1750–1824)
The Life of a Lover F

John Nichols (1745–1826)
Brief Memoirs of John Nichols NF

Thomas Love Peacock (1785–1866)
The Monks of St Mark V
Anonymous

Anna Maria Porter (1780–1832)
The Lake of Killarney F

Anna Seward (1742–1809)
Memoirs of the Life of Erasmus Darwin NF

Ann Taylor (1782–1866), **Jane Taylor** (1783–1824), and others
Original Poems for Infant Minds V
Many editions

Thomas Taylor (1758–1835) and **Floyer Sydenham** (1710–87) (tr.)
The Works of Plato NF

1805

- Thomas Jefferson begins second term as US President (Mar.)
  Napoleon crowned King of Italy (May)
  Third coalition (Britain, Austria, Russia, and Sweden) formed against France; war resumes (Aug.)
  Austrian army capitulates at Ulm (20 Oct.)
  Battle of Trafalgar (21 Oct.): Lord Nelson dies in action
  Battle of Austerlitz (2 Dec.)
- Sarah Fuller Adams born
  William Harrison Ainsworth born
  James Martineau born
  Frederick Denison Maurice born
  Robert Surtees born
- Christopher Anstey dies
  William Paley dies
- Hans Christian Andersen born
  Giuseppe Mazzini born
  Charles Alexis de Tocqueville born
- Schiller dies

Robert Anderson (1770–1833)
Ballads in the Cumberland Dialect V

Thomas Brown (1778–1820)
Observations on the Nature and Tendency of the Doctrine of Mr Hume NF

Samuel Egerton Brydges (1762–1837)
Censura Literaria NF

Henry Cary (1772–1844) (tr.)
The Inferno of Dante Alighieri V
See also *The Vision* 1814

George Colman, the younger (1762–1836)
John Bull; or, The Englishman's Fireside: A comedy D
Performed 5 March 1803

Richard Cumberland (1732–1811)
The Victory and Death of Lord Viscount Nelson D
Performed 11 November 1805

'Rosa Matilda' [Charlotte Dacre (1782?–1841?)]
The Confessions of the Nun of St Omer F
Dedicated to M.G. Lewis

Charlotte Dacre (1782?–1841?)
Hours of Solitude V

R.C. Dallas (1754–1824)
The Morlands F

Isaac D'Israeli (1766–1848)
Flim-flams!; or, The Life and Errors of My Uncle, and the Amours of My Aunt! F
Anonymous

Maria Edgeworth (1767–1849)
The Modern Griselda F

George Ellis (1753–1815) (ed.)
Specimens of Early English Metrical Romances ANTH

'Edward Baldwin' [William Godwin (1756–1836)]
Fables Ancient and Modern F
For children

William Godwin (1756–1836)
Fleetwood; or, The New Man of Feeling F

William Hayley (1745–1820)
Ballads V

William Hazlitt (1778–1830)
An Essay on the Principles of Human Action NF
Anonymous. Hazlitt's first book. See also *Essays on the Principles of Human Action* 1836.

Thomas Holcroft (1745–1809)
The Lady of the Rock: A melo-drama D
Performed 12 February 1805

Thomas Holcroft (1745–1809)
Memoirs of Bryan Perdue F

Elizabeth Inchbald (1753–1821)
To Marry or not to Marry: A comedy D
Performed 16 February 1805

W.H. Ireland (1777–1835)
The Confessions of William Henry Ireland NF
Expansion of *An Authentic Account* 1796 (q.v.)

Samuel Johnson (1709–84)
An Account of the Life of Dr Samuel Johnson, Written by Himself NF
A fragment of autobiography taken by Francis Barber, Johnson's black servant, from the personal papers Johnson ordered to be burnt a few days before his death

Richard Payne Knight (1750–1824)
An Analytical Enquiry into the Principles of Taste NF

Charles Lamb (1775–1834)
The King and Queen of Hearts V
Anonymous. For children.

M.G. Lewis (1775–1818) (tr.)
The Bravo of Venice F
A free translation of *Aboellino, der grosse Bandit* (1803) by Heinrich Daniel Zschokke (1771–1848)

Thomas Morton (1764?–1838)
The School of Reform; or, How to Rule a Husband: A comedy D
Performed 15 January 1805

Amelia Opie (1769–1853)
Adeline Mowbray; or, The Mother and Daughter F

Henry James Pye (1745–1813)
A Prior Claim: A comedy D
Performed 29 October 1805. Written with Samuel James Arnold (1774–1852).

Walter Scott (1771–1832)
The Lay of the Last Minstrel V
Published 12 January 1805 in Edinburgh. Sixteen editions by 1823.

Robert Southey (1774–1843)
Madoc V

Robert Southey (1774–1843)
Metrical Tales, and Other Poems V
See also *Minor Poems* 1815

William Taylor (1765–1836) (tr.)
Nathan the Wise V
Translated from the German of G.E. Lessing (1729–81). First privately printed in 1791.

John Thelwall (1764–1834)
The Trident of Albion V
On the Battle of Trafalgar, in which Lord Nelson was mortally wounded (21 October 1805)

William Wordsworth (1770–1850) and **S.T. Coleridge** (1772–1834)
Lyrical Ballads, with Pastoral and Other Poems V
The last separate edition. Includes Coleridge's work. Some textual variants. See also *Lyrical Ballads* 1798, 1801, 1802.

1806

- 'Ministry of All the Talents' formed (Feb.)
  Napoleon makes his brother Joseph king of Naples (Mar.)
  End of the Holy Roman Empire (Aug.)
  Prussian armies defeated at the dual battle of Jena and Auerstedt (14 Oct.)

- Elizabeth Barrett (Browning) born
  Charles Lever born
  John Stuart Mill born
- Elizabeth Carter dies
  Mungo Park dies
  Charlotte Smith dies
  Henry Kirke White dies
- Isambard Kingdom Brunel born
- Georgiana Cavendish, duchess of Devonshire, dies
  Charles James Fox dies
  William Pitt dies (23 Jan.)

Sir John Barrow (1764–1848)
A Voyage to Cochin-China NF

Anna Maria Bennett (*c*.1750–1808)
Vicissitudes Abroad; or, The Ghost of my Father F

James Beresford (1764–1840)
The Miseries of Human Life; or, The Groans of Timothy Testy, and Samuel Sensitive V
Anonymous

Robert Bloomfield (1766–1823)
Wild Flowers; or, Pastoral and Local Poetry V

George Gordon, Lord Byron (1788–1824)
Fugitive Pieces V
Anonymous. Privately printed. Byron's first publication.

John Wilson Croker (1780–1857)
The Amazoniad; or, Figure and Fashion V
Anonymous

Richard Cumberland (1732–1811)
A Hint to Husbands: A comedy D
Performed 8 March 1806

Charlotte Dacre (1782?–1841?)
Zofloya; or, The Moor F

Maria Edgeworth (1767–1849)
Leonora F

William Hazlitt (1778–1830)
Free Thoughts on Public Affairs; or, Advice to a Patriot NF
Anonymous

Thomas Holcroft (1745–1809)
Tales in Verse V

Lucy Hutchinson (1620–76?)
Memoirs of the Life of Colonel Hutchinson NF

Walter Savage Landor (1775–1864)
Simonidea V
Anonymous. In English and Latin.

M.G. Lewis (1775–1818)
Adelgitha; or, The Fruits of a Single Error: A tragedy D

M.G. Lewis (1775–1818) (tr.)
Feudal Tyrants; or, The Counts of Carlshein and Sargans F
A free translation of *Elisabeth Erbin von Toggenburg* (1789) by Christiane Benedicte Eugenie Naubert

John Lingard (1771–1851)
The Antiquities of the Anglo-Saxon Church NF

James Montgomery (1771–1854)
The Wanderer of Switzerland, and Other Poems V

Thomas Moore (1779–1852)
Epistles, Odes and Other Poems V

Sydney Owenson, later **Lady Morgan** (1783?–1859)
The Novice of St Dominick F

Sydney Owenson, later **Lady Morgan** (1783?–1859)
The Wild Irish Girl F

Amelia Opie (1769–1853)
Simple Tales F

Thomas Love Peacock (1785–1866)
Palmyra, and Other Poems V

Alexander Pope (1688–1744)
The Works of Alexander Pope, in Verse and Prose WKS
Edited in 10 volumes by William Lisle Bowles

Mary Robinson (1758–1800)
The Poetical Works of the Late Mrs Mary Robinson V

Walter Scott (1771–1832)
Ballads and Lyrical Pieces V

Ann Taylor (1782–1866), **Jane Taylor** (1783–1824), and others
Rhymes for the Nursery V
bao *Original Poems*

1807

- Slave trade abolished in all British possessions (Mar.)
  Treaties of Tilsit (July) ends the continental war
  The British bombard Copenhagen (Sept.)
- Robert Montgomery born

Richard Chenevix Trench born

- John Newton dies
  Clara Reeve dies
- Henry Wadsworth Longfellow born
  Giuseppe Garibaldi born
  John Greenleaf Whittier born
- Madame de Staël, *Corinne*

Corinna; or, Italy F
Translation of *Corinne, ou l'Italie* (1807) by Madame de Staël (1766–1817)

Joanna Baillie (1762–1851)
De Montfort: A tragedy D
Performed 29 April 1800. See also *A Series of Plays* [i] 1798.

'Polypus' [Eaton Stannard Barrett (1786–1820)]
All the Talents: A satirical poem V
Nineteen editions in 1807. See also *The Talents Run Mad* 1816.

Henrietta Bowdler (1754–1830) (ed.)
The Family Shakespeare EDN
Anonymous. Contains twenty expurgated plays. See also *The Family Shakespeare* 1818.

Samuel Egerton Brydges (1762–1837)
Poems V
The fourth, enlarged, edition of *Sonnets and Other Poems* 1785 (q.v.)

George Gordon, Lord Byron (1788–1824)
Poems on Various Occasions V
Anonymous. Privately printed.

George Gordon, Lord Byron (1788–1824)
Hours of Idleness V
See also *Poems* 1808

Elizabeth Carter (1717–1806)
Memoirs of the Life of Mrs Elizabeth Carter MISC

George Chalmers (1742–1825)
Caledonia; or, An Account, Historical and Topographic, of North Britain NF

George Crabbe (1754–1832)
Poems V
Includes 'The Parish Register'. Nine editions by 1817.

Richard Cumberland (1732–1811) and **Sir James Burges** (1752–1824)
The Exodiad V

Richard Cumberland (1732–1811)
Memoirs of Richard Cumberland NF

Charlotte Dacre (1782?–1841?)
The Libertine F

Catharine Ann Dorset (1750?–1817?)
The Peacock 'At Home' V
'Written by a lady'. For children. Enormously popular. A sequel to William Roscoe's *The Butterfly's Ball* 1807 (q.v.).

William Godwin (1756–1836)
Faulkener: A tragedy D
Performed in December 1807. Based on an incident in Defoe's *Roxana* 1724 (q.v.). Prologue, in verse, by Charles Lamb.

James Grahame (1765–1811)
Poems V

Lady Anne Hamilton (1766–1846)
The Epics of the Ton; or, The Glories of the Great World V
A probable influence on Byron's *English Bards, and Scotch Reviewers* 1809 (q.v.)

William Hazlitt (1778–1830)
An Abridgement of the Light of Nature Pursued NF
Anonymous. See Abraham Tucker, *The Light of Nature Pursued* 1768.

William Hazlitt (1778–1830)
The Eloquence of the British Senate ANTH
Anonymous

William Hazlitt (1778–1830)
A Reply to the Essay on Population NF
Anonymous. See Malthus 1798.

James Hogg (1770–1835) and others
The Forest Minstrel V
By Hogg, Thomas Mouncey Cunningham, and several anonymous writers

James Hogg (1770–1835)
The Mountain Bard V

Leigh Hunt (1784–1859) (ed.)
Classic Tales, Serious and Lively ANTH
Tales by Goldsmith, Johnson, Henry Mackenzie, John Hawkesworth, Sterne, Voltaire, and others

Leigh Hunt (1784–1859)
Critical Essays on the Performers of the London Theatres NF
Anonymous. Published 1807, dated 1808.

Charles Lamb (1775–1834) and **Mary Lamb** (1764–1847)
Tales from Shakespear F
Published under Charles Lamb's name but fourteen of the twenty pieces are by Mary Lamb

'Dennis Jasper Murphy' [**C.R. Maturin** (1782–1824)]
Fatal Revenge; or, The Family of Montorio F

Sydney Owenson, later **Lady Morgan** (1783?–1859)
The Lay of an Irish Harp; or, Metrical Fragments V

Thomas Morton (1764?–1838)
Town and Country D
Performed 10 March 1807

Anna Maria Porter (1780–1832)
The Hungarian Brothers F

William Roscoe (1753–1831)
The Butterfly's Ball and the Grasshopper's Feast V
First published in the *Gentleman's Magazine* in November 1806

Charlotte Smith (1749–1806)
Beachy Head, with Other Poems V

'Peter Plymley' [**Sydney Smith** (1771–1845)]
Two Letters on the Subject of the Catholics NF
Written in support of Catholic emancipation. *Three More Letters* also published in 1807.

William Sotheby (1757–1833)
Saul V

Robert Southey (1774–1843)
Letters from England F
Anonymous

Robert Southey (1774–1843) (ed. and tr.)
Palmerin of England F
First translated by A. Munday 1588 (q.v.) and extensively corrected by Southey. The original was written in 1544 and is attributed to the Portuguese writer Francisco de Morães Cabal (1500?–72).

Robert Southey (1774–1843) (ed.)
Specimens of the Later English Poets ANTH
Intended to complement George Ellis's *Specimens of the Early English Poems* 1790

Henry Kirke White (1785–1806)
The Remains of Henry Kirke White V
Edited, with an account of the author's life, by Robert Southey

William Wordsworth (1770–1850)
Poems, in Two Volumes V
Includes 'Ode to Duty', 'Ode: Intimations of Immortality', 'Miscellaneous Sonnets'

1808

- Rising against the French in Madrid (May)
  Napoleon makes his brother Joseph king of Spain
  Britain sends an expeditionary force to Spain (Aug.)
  Convention of Cintra (30 Aug.): French troops withdraw from Portugal
- Clara Balfour (Mrs C.L. Balfour, *née* Liddell) born
  James Ballantine born
  Horatius Bonar born
  Henry Edward Manning (later Cardinal) born
  Caroline Norton born
  Philip Meadows Taylor born
- Anna Maria Bennett dies
  John Home dies
- Gérard de Nerval born
- Ackermann's *Microcosm of London* begins publication (–1811)
  Beethoven, 5th Symphony and 'Pastoral' Symphony
  Goethe, *Faust*, pt i

Christina; or, Memoirs of a German Princess F
Translation of *La Princesse de Wolfenbuttel* (1807) by Isabelle de Montolieu (1751–1832)

The Examiner PER
Published weekly (January 1808–February 1881). Edited by Leigh Hunt until 1821.

Christopher Anstey (1724–1805)
The Poetical Works of the Late Christopher Anstey V

Mary Matilda Betham (1776–1852)
Poems V

William Blake (1757–1827)
Milton V
Illuminated book. Dated 1804 on the title-page, but this was probably when the plates were begun. Probably printed *c.*1808.

Robert Burns (1759–96)
Reliques of Robert Burns V

George Gordon, Lord Byron (1788–1824)
Poems Original and Translated V
The second edition of *Hours of Idleness* 1807 (q.v.)

Thomas Clarkson (1760–1846)
The History of the Rise, Progress and Accomplishment of the Abolition of the African Slave-Trade NF

George Colman, the younger (1762–1836)
The Heir at Law: A comedy D
Performed 15 July 1797

William Cowper (1731–1800) (tr.)
Latin and Italian Poems of Milton Translated into English Verse V

William Cowper (1731–1800) (tr.)
Poems Translated from the French of Mme de la Mothe Guion V

John Dalton (1766–1844)
A New System of Chemical Philosophy NF

James Grahame (1765–1811)
The Siege of Copenhagen V

Elizabeth Hamilton (1758–1816)
The Cottagers of Glenburnie F

Felicia Dorothea Browne, later **Hemans** (1793–1835)
Poems V

Felicia Dorothea Browne, later **Hemans** (1793–1835)
England and Spain; or, Valour and Patriotism V

'Alfred Allendale, Esq.' [Theodore Hook (1788–1841)]
The Man of Sorrow F

Elizabeth Inchbald (1753–1821) (ed.)
The British Theatre EDN
Published in 25 volumes

Charles Lamb (1775–1834)
The Adventures of Ulysses F

Charles Lamb (1775–1834)
Specimens of English Dramatic Poets, who Lived about the Time of Shakespeare ANTH

Charles Lamb (1775–1834) and **Mary Lamb** (1764–1847)
Mrs Leicester's School F
Anonymous. Published 1808, dated 1809.

M.G. Lewis (1775–1818)
Romantic Tales F

Charles Lucas (1769–1854)
The Abissinian Reformer; or, The Bible and Sabre F

C.R. Maturin (1782–1824)
The Wild Irish Boy F
bao *Montorio*

James Mill (1773–1836)
Commerce Defended NF

Thomas Moore (1779–1852)
A Selection of Irish Melodies [pts i, ii] V/MUS
Published in 10 parts (1808–34). See also *Irish Melodies* 1821.

Amelia Opie (1769–1853)
The Warrior's Return, and Other Poems V

Walter Scott (1771–1832)
Marmion V
Published on 22 February 1808 in Edinburgh. Ten editions by 1821.

Robert Southey (1774–1843) (tr.)
Chronicles of the Cid NF

'Peter Pindar' [John Wolcot (1738–1819)]
The Fall of Portugal; or, The Royal Exiles D

1809

- Battle of Corunna (16 Jan.): Sir John Moore fatally wounded
  James Madison becomes US President (Mar.)
  British forces under Arthur Wellesley land in Portugal (Apr.): French defeated at Oporto (12 May)
  Napoleon defeats Austrians at the Battle of Wagram (6 July)
  Wellesley defeats the French at Talavera (28 July) and is created duke of Wellington
  Lord Castlereagh and George Canning fight a duel
  Napoleon divorces Josephine
  Drury Lane Theatre burns
- Mary Cowden Clarke (*née* Novello) born
  Charles Darwin born
  Edward Fitzgerald born
  Margaret Gatty born
  Frances Kemble born
  Mark Lemon born
  Alexander William Kinglake born
  Richard Monckton Milnes, 1st Baron Houghton, born
  Alfred Tennyson, 1st Baron Tennyson, born
- Hannah Cowley dies
  Thomas Holcroft dies
  Thomas Paine dies
  Anna Seward dies
- William Ewart Gladstone born
- Felix Mendelssohn-Bartholdy born
  Edgar Allan Poe born
  Oliver Wendell Holmes born
  Abraham Lincoln born
- Haydn dies

- Beethoven, 5th Piano Concerto ('Emperor')
  Chateaubriand, *Les Martyrs*

The Quarterly Review PER
First number published in February 1809. Edited by William Gifford 1809–24.

William Blake (1757–1827)
A Descriptive Catalogue of Pictures, Poetical and Historical Inventions NF

George Gordon, Lord Byron (1788–1824)
English Bards, and Scotch Reviewers V
Anonymous. Published in March 1809.

Thomas Campbell (1777–1844)
Gertrude of Wyoming: A Pennsylvanian Tale, and Other Poems V
See also *Gertrude* 1857

William Cobbett (1763–1835)
The Life of William Cobbett NF
An abridged version of *The Life and Adventures of Peter Porcupine* (Philadelphia, 1796)

S.T. Coleridge (1772–1834)
The Friend PER
Published in 27 weekly numbers (irregularly, June 1809–March 1810). Complete edition published in 1812. See also *Essays on His Own Times* 1850.

Richard Cumberland (1732–1811)
John de Lancaster F

Thomas Frognall Dibdin (1776–1847)
The Bibliomania, or Book Madness NF

Maria Edgeworth (1767–1849)
Tales of Fashionable Life [vols i–iii] F
See also *Tales of Fashionable Life* 1812

Richard Lovell Edgeworth (1744–1817) [and **Maria Edgeworth** (1767–1849)]
Essays on Professional Education NF

William Godwin (1756–1836)
Essay on Sepulchres NF

John Cam Hobhouse (1786–1869) and others
Imitations and Translations from the Ancient and Modern Classics V
Contains twenty-nine pieces by Hobhouse, nine by Lord Byron, and twenty-seven by other hands

Margaret Holford, later **Hodson** (1778–1852)
Wallace; or, The Fight of Falkirk V

Charles Lamb (1775–1834) and **Mary Lamb** (1764–1847)
Poetry for Children, Entirely Original V
bao *Mrs Leicester's School.* See also *The First Book of Poetry* 1810.

M.G. Lewis (1775–1818)
Monody on the Death of Sir John Moore V

Elizabeth Montagu (1720–1800)
Letters of Mrs Elizabeth Montagu NF
Published in 4 volumes (1809–13)

Thomas Moore (1779–1852)
The Sceptic V
bao *Corruption and Intolerance*

Hannah More (1745–1833)
Coelebs in Search of a Wife F
Anonymous. Published in 1809, dated 1808.

Sydney Owenson, later **Lady Morgan** (1783?–1859)
Woman; or, Ida of Athens F

Anna Maria Porter (1780–1832)
Don Sebastian; or, The House of Braganza F

Mary Anne Radcliffe (*c.*1746–post 1810)?
Manfroné; or, The One-Handed Monk F
Ascribed to Radcliffe, but authorship later claimed by Louisa Theresa Bellenden Ker

Jane West (1758–1852)
The Mother V

William Wordsworth (1770–1850)
Concerning the Relations of Great Britain, Spain, and Portugal . . . as Affected by the Convention of Cintra NF
Appendix by Thomas De Quincey

1810

- Napoleon marries Marie-Louise of Austria (Feb.)
  Napoleon annexes the Netherlands to France
  The duke of Wellington holds the Lines of Torres Vedras (Oct.)
  Coleridge lectures on Shakespeare
- Robert Curzon born
  Elizabeth Gaskell born
  Philip Henry Gosse born
  Thomas Adolphus Trollope born
  Martin Tupper born
- Sarah Trimmer dies
- Frédéric Chopin born
  Alfred de Musset born
  Robert Schumann born
- Madame de Staël, *De l'Allemagne*

Lucy Aikin (1781–1864)
Epistles on Women V

Joanna Baillie (1762–1851)
The Family Legend: A tragedy D
Performed 29 January 1810. Prologue by Walter Scott; epilogue by Henry Mackenzie.

Anna Laetitia Barbauld (1743–1825) (ed.)
The British Novelists EDN

'Simon Gray' [Sir Alexander Boswell (1775–1822)]
Edinburgh; or, The Ancient Royalty V

Samuel Egerton Brydges (1762–1837)
The British Bibliographer NF
With J. Haslewood

George Crabbe (1754–1832)
The Borough V
Published in April 1810. Six editions by 1816.

Richard Lovell Edgeworth (1744–1817) and **Maria Edgeworth** (1767–1849)
Readings on Poetry NF

Ebenezer Elliott (1781–1849)
Night V
Anonymous

Mary Elliott (1794?–1870)
The Mice, and the Pic Nic V
'By a Looking-glass Maker'. For children.

William Hazlitt (1778–1830)
A New and Improved Grammar of the English Tongue NF

James Hogg (1770–1835)
The Spy PER
Edited and largely written by Hogg. Published in 52 numbers (September 1810–August 1811).

'W.F. Mylius' [Charles Lamb (1775–1834) and **Mary Lamb** (1764–1847)]
The First Book of Poetry V
Published 1810, dated 1811. Contains 22 items from *Poetry for Children* 1809 (q.v.), plus selections from various authors and a new poem, 'A Birth-Day Thought', apparently by Lamb. Ten editions by 1828.

Mary Russell Mitford (1787–1855)
Poems V

James Montgomery (1771–1854)
The West Indies, and Other Poems V

Thomas Love Peacock (1785–1866)
The Genius of the Thames V

Anne Plumptre (1760–1818)
Narrative of a Three Years' Residence in France NF

Isaac Pocock (1782–1835)
Hit or Miss! D
Performed 26 February 1810

Jane Porter (1776–1850)
The Scottish Chiefs F

Samuel Rogers (1763–1855)
The Voyage of Columbus V
Anonymous

Walter Scott (1771–1832) (ed.)
English Minstrelsy ANTH
Anonymous

Walter Scott (1771–1832)
The Lady of the Lake V
Published on 8 May 1810. Five editions in 1810.

Anna Seward (1742–1809)
Poetical Works V
Edited by Walter Scott

P.B. Shelley (1792–1822)
Original Poetry by Victor and Cazire V
Anonymous. Written by Shelley and his sister Elizabeth.

P.B. Shelley (1792–1822)
Posthumous Fragments of Margaret Nicholson V
Anonymous. Written with Thomas Jefferson Hogg.

P.B. Shelley (1792–1822)
Zastrozzi F
'By P.B.S.'

William Sotheby (1757–1833)
Constance of Castille V
An imitation of Scott's *The Lady of the Lake* 1810 (see above)

Robert Southey (1774–1843)
The Curse of Kehama V

Robert Southey (1774–1843)
History of Brazil . . . Part the First NF
Volume ii published in 1817 (q.v.); volume iii, 1819 (q.v.)

Dugald Stewart (1753–1828)
Philosophical Essays NF

Ann Taylor (1782–1866), **Jane Taylor** (1783–1824), and others
Hymns for Infant Minds V
bao *Original Poems*. Many editions.

1811

- The Prince of Wales becomes Regent due to the insanity of George III
  Luddites begin destroying factory machinery (Mar.)
  Shelley expelled from Oxford
- Gilbert Abbott à Beckett born
  Arthur Henry Hallam born
  William Makepeace Thackeray born
- Richard Cumberland dies
  Charles Kean dies
  Eliza Parsons dies
  Thomas Percy dies
- John Bright born
- Harriet Beecher Stowe born
  Théophile Gautier born
  Franz Liszt born
- Heinrich von Kleist dies
- Friedrich Fouqué, *Undine*

Jane Austen (1775–1817)
Sense and Sensibility F
'By a lady'. First version written *c.*1795.

'Cervantes Hogg' [Eaton Stannard Barrett (1786–1820)]
The Metropolis; or, A Cure for Gaming F

Robert Bloomfield (1766–1823)
The Banks of Wye V

Mary Brunton (1778–1818)
Self-Control F
Anonymous

Richard Cumberland (1732–1811)
Retrospection V

'Rosa Matilda' [Charlotte Dacre (1782?–1841?)]
The Passions F

Thomas John Dibdin (1771–1841)
The Lady of the Lake; or, Roderick vich Alpine D
Performed 24 September 1810. Based on Scott's poem of 1810 (q.v.). See also Dibdin, *Ivanhoe* 1820, *The Pirate* 1822.

Elizabeth Inchbald (1753–1821) (ed.)
The Modern Theatre ANTH

Robert Kerr (1755–1813)
A General History and Collection of Voyages and Travels NF

Charles Lamb (1775–1834)
Prince Dorus; or, Flattery Put Out of Countenance V
Anonymous. For children.

Mary Russell Mitford (1787–1855)
Christina, the Maid of the South Seas V

Hannah More (1745–1833)
Practical Piety; or, The Influence of the Religion of the Heart on the Conduct of Life NF

Sydney Owenson, later **Lady Morgan** (1783?–1859)
The Missionary: An Indian tale F

Thomas Morton (1764?–1838)
The Knight of Snowdoun D
Performed 5 February 1811. Based on Scott's *The Lady of the Lake* 1810 (q.v.).

Anna Maria Porter (1780–1832)
Ballad Romances, and Other Poems V

Henry Crabb Robinson (1775–1867) (tr.)
Amatonda F
Anonymous. A translation of *Persiche Märchen: Amathonte* (1799) by 'Anton Wall' (Christian Lebrecht Heyne, 1751–1821).

Jonathan Scott (1754–1829) (tr.)
The Arabian Nights Entertainments F

Walter Scott (1771–1832)
The Vision of Don Roderick V

P.B. Shelley (1792–1822)
The Necessity of Atheism NF
Anonymous. The cause of Shelley's expulsion from Oxford, 25 March 1811.

P.B. Shelley (1792–1822)
St Irvyne; or, The Rosicrucian F
'By a Gentleman of the University of Oxford'

Dugald Stewart (1753–1828)
Biographical Memoirs, of Adam Smith, W. Robertson, and Thomas Reid NF

Mary Tighe (1772–1810)
Psyche, with Other Poems V

John Wolcot (1738–1819)
Carlton House Fete; or, The Disappointed Bard V

1812

- Wellington takes Ciudad Rodrigo (19 Jan.)
  Frame-breaking becomes a capital offence

- The British capture Badajoz (6 Apr.)
- Prime Minister Spencer Perceval assassinated (11 May)
- The USA declares war on Britain (June)
- Napoleon begins the invasion of Russia (24 June)
- Wellington defeats the French at Salamanca (22 July): enters Madrid (12 Aug.)
- Battle of Borodino (7 Sept.)
- Napoleon enters Moscow (14 Sept.): French retreat begins a month later
- Roxburghe Club founded by Thomas Dibdin and others

- Robert Browning born
- Charles Dickens born
- Sarah Ellis (*née* Stickney) born
- John Forster born
- Lady Georgiana Fullerton born
- Geraldine Jewsbury born
- Edward Lear born
- Henry Mayhew born
- William Johnson Neale born
- Augustic Welby Pugin born
- Samuel Smiles born

- Edmond Malone dies
- John Horne Tooke dies

- Jacob and Wilhelm Grimm, *Kinder- und Hausmärchen*

Joanna Baillie (1762–1851)
A Series of Plays [vol. iii] D
Known as *Plays on the Passions*. See also 1798 1802, 1821. Includes *Orra, The Dream, The Siege, The Beacon*.

Anna Laetitia Barbauld (1743–1825)
Eighteen Hundred and Eleven V

Bernard Barton (1784–1849)
Metrical Effusions; or, Verses on Various Occasions V
Anonymous

Lady Charlotte Bury (1775–1861)
Self-Indulgence F
Anonymous

George Gordon, Lord Byron (1788–1824)
Childe Harold's Pilgrimage [cantos i–ii] V
Published on 10 March 1812. Also contains fourteen shorter poems. Seven editions by February 1814. See also *Childe Harold* 1816, 1818.

George Gordon, Lord Byron (1788–1824)
The Curse of Minerva V

Maria, Lady Callcott (1785–1842)
Journal of a Residence in India NF

S.T. Coleridge (1772–1834) and **Robert Southey** (1774–1843)
Omniana; or, Horae Otiosiores MISC
Contains 45 contributions by Coleridge, 201 by Southey

William Combe (1742–1823)
The Tour of Dr Syntax, in Search of the Picturesque V
Anonymous. Illustrated by Thomas Rowlandson. First published in monthly parts in 1809. See *The Second Tour of Doctor Syntax* 1820, *The Third Tour* 1821. The work inspired several imitations (e.g. *The Tour of Doctor Syntax Through London* and *Doctor Syntax in Paris*, both 1820).

George Crabbe (1754–1832)
Tales V
Seven editions by 1815

Thomas Frognall Dibdin (1776–1847)
Bibliography V

Isaac D'Israeli (1766–1848)
Calamities of Authors NF

Maria Edgeworth (1767–1849)
Tales of Fashionable Life [vols iv, v, vi] F
Contains 'The Absentee' (volumes v–vi). See also *Tales of Fashionable Life* 1809.

Pierce Egan, the elder (1772–1849)
Boxiana; or, Sketches of Ancient and Modern Pugilism NF

Mary Elliott (1794?–1870)
Simple Truths in Verse V
Under the author's maiden name, Mary Belson. For children.

Reginald Heber (1783–1826)
Poems and Translations V

Felicia Dorothea Browne, later Hemans (1793–1835)
The Domestic Affections, and Other Poems V

Leigh Hunt (1784–1859)
The Prince of Wales v The Examiner NF
Anonymous. Written with his brother, John Hunt (1775–1848).

Walter Savage Landor (1775–1864)
Count Julian: A tragedy V

M.G. Lewis (1775–1818)
Poems V

Elizabeth Macauley (1785?–1837)
Effusions of Fancy V

C.R. Maturin (1782–1824)
The Milesian Chief F
bao *Montorio* and *The Wild Irish Boy*

Mary Russell Mitford (1787–1855)
Watlington Hill V

James Morier (1780–1849)
A Journey Through Persia, Armenia, and Asia Minor, to Constantinople, in the Years 1808 and 1809 NF
See also *Second Journey* 1818

John Nichols (1745–1826)
Literary Anecdotes of the Eighteenth Century NF

Amelia Opie (1769–1853)
Temper; or, Domestic Scenes F

Robert Owen (1771–1858)
A Statement Regarding the New Lanark Establishment NF

Thomas Love Peacock (1785–1866)
The Genius of the Thames, Palmyra, and Other Poems V
See also *Palmyra* 1806, *The Genius of the Thames* 1810

Thomas Love Peacock (1785–1866)
The Philosophy of Melancholy V

Samuel Rogers (1763–1855)
Poems by Samuel Rogers V

P.B. Shelley (1792–1822)
An Address to the Irish People NF

P.B. Shelley (1792–1822)
Declaration of Rights NF
Published in February 1812

P.B. Shelley (1792–1822)
The Devil's Walk V
Published in February 1812. A broadside ballad on a single sheet.

P.B. Shelley (1792–1822)
A Letter to Lord Ellenborough NF
Pamphlet published in February 1812

P.B. Shelley (1792–1822)
Proposals for an Association of Philanthropists NF
Published in February 1812

Horatio Smith (1779–1849) and **James Smith** (1775–1839)
Rejected Addresses; or, The New Theatrum Poetarum V
Anonymous. Many editions (the 18th, 1833, with new preface by Horatio Smith; 21st edition, 1847).

John Wilson (1785–1854)
The Isle of Palms, and Other Poems V

1813

- Wellington defeats the French at Vitoria (21 June)
  Battle of Dresden (26–7 Aug.)
  Wellington enters France (Oct.)
  Napoleon defeated at the Battle of Leipzig (16–19 Oct.)
  Prussian army under Blücher begins the invasion of France
  James Madison starts second term as US President
- Leigh Hunt imprisoned (–1815)
- William Edmonstoune Aytoun born
  Isaac Butt born
  Sir Arthur Helps born
  Mark Pattison born
- David Livingstone born
- Henry James Pye dies: Robert Southey appointed Poet Laureate
- Søren Kierkegaard born
  Giuseppe Verdi born
  Richard Wagner born
- C.M. Wieland dies

John Aubrey (1626–97)
Lives of Eminent Men NF
Now known as *Brief Lives*. Published in *Letters Written by Eminent Persons in the Seventeenth and Eighteenth Centuries*, edited by John Walker (1770–1831).

Jane Austen (1775–1817)
Pride and Prejudice F
bao *Sense and Sensibility*

Eaton Stannard Barrett (1786–1820)
The Heroine; or, Adventures of a Fair Romance Reader F

William Lisle Bowles (1762–1850)
The Missionary V
Anonymous

David Brewster (1781–1868)
A Treatise on New Philosophical Instruments NF

'Horace Hornem Esq.' [George Gordon, Lord Byron (1788–1824)]
Waltz V

George Gordon, Lord Byron (1788–1824)
The Giaour: A fragment of a Turkish tale V

George Gordon, Lord Byron (1788–1824)
The Bride of Abydos: A Turkish tale V

S.T. Coleridge (1772–1834)
Remorse: A tragedy D
Performed 23 January 1813. A revision of *Osorio*, written in 1797.

Richard Cumberland (1732–1811)
Posthumous Dramatick Works WKS

Allan Cunningham (1784–1842)
Songs V

Selina Davenport
The Sons of the Viscount, and the Daughters of the Earl F
'By a lady'

Thomas John Dibdin (1771–1841)
A Metrical History of England V

John Galt (1779–1839)
Letters from the Levant NF

John Cam Hobhouse (1786–1869)
A Journey Through Albania NF

James Hogg (1770–1835)
The Queen's Wake V

Thomas Jefferson Hogg (1792–1862)
Memoirs of Prince Alexy Haimatoff F

Mary Russell Mitford (1787–1855)
Narrative Poems on the Female Character V

James Montgomery (1771–1854)
The World Before the Flood V

'Thomas Brown, the younger' [Thomas Moore (1779–1852)]
Intercepted Letters; or, The Twopenny Post-Bag V
Several editions in 1813

Hannah More (1745–1833)
Christian Morals NF

James Northcote (1746–1831)
Memoirs of Sir Joshua Reynolds NF

Amelia Opie (1769–1853)
Tales of Real Life F

Robert Owen (1771–1858)
A New View of Society NF

Isaac Pocock (1782–1835)
The Miller and his Men: A melo-drama D
Anonymous. Performed 21 October 1813.

Walter Scott (1771–1832)
Rokeby V
Published in January 1813 in Edinburgh. Five editions in 1813. An anonymous parody, *Jokeby*, written by John Roby (1793–1850) also published 1813.

Walter Scott (1771–1832)
The Bridal of Triermain; or, The Vale of St John V

P.B. Shelley (1792–1822)
Queen Mab V

P.B. Shelley (1792–1822)
A Vindication of Natural Diet NF
Anonymous

Horatio Smith (1779–1849) and **James Smith** (1775–1839)
Horace in London V
bao *Rejected Addresses.* Mostly by James Smith.

Robert Southey (1774–1843)
The Life of Nelson NF
Southey was appointed Poet Laureate in this year

1814

- The Allies enter Paris (30–31 Mar.)
  Napoleon abdicates and is exiled to Elba (6 Apr.)
  Louis XVIII enters Paris (May)
  The British burn Washington (Aug.)
  Congress of Vienna opens (Nov.)
  Treaty of Ghent ends war between Britain and the USA (Dec.)
- Caroline Bray born
  John William Colenso born
  Aubrey Thomas de Vere born
  Pierce Egan, the younger, born
  Frederick William Faber born
  Joseph Sheridan Le Fanu born
  Charles Reade born
  G.W.M. Reynolds born
  Emma Robinson born
  Ellen Wood (Mrs Henry Wood, *née* Price) born
- Charles Burney dies
  Charles Dibdin dies
  Samuel Jackson Pratt dies
- Johann Gottlieb Fichte dies

Anonymous
The Family Robinson Crusoe F
Ostensibly translated (possibly by William Godwin) from the German *Schweizerische Robinson* (1812–13) by Johan David Wyss (1743–1818), though utilizing material from the French translation by Madame de Montolieu. Retitled *The Swiss Family Robinson* from 1818.

The New Monthly Magazine PER
Published under various titles from January 1814-December 1871. Later editors included Thomas Campbell 1820–30; S.C. Hall 1830–1; Theodore Hook 1836–41; Thomas Hood 1841–3; and W.H. Ainsworth 1845–71.

Lucy Aikin (1781–1864)
Lorimer F
Anonymous

Jane Austen (1775–1817)
Mansfield Park F
bao *Sense and Sensibility,* and *Pride and Prejudice*

Thomas Brown (1778–1820)
The Paradise of Coquettes V
Anonymous

Mary Brunton (1778–1818)
Discipline F
bao *Self-Control*

Frances Burney (1752–1840)
The Wanderer; or, Female Difficulties F
bao *Evelina, Cecilia,* and *Camilla*

George Gordon, Lord Byron (1788–1824)
The Corsair V

George Gordon, Lord Byron (1788–1824)
Ode to Napoleon Buonaparte V
Anonymous

George Gordon, Lord Byron (1788–1824) and **Samuel Rogers** (1763–1855)
Lara, a Tale; Jacqueline, a Tale V
Anonymous. *Lara* by Byron; *Jacqueline* by Rogers.

Henry Cary (1772–1844) (tr.)
The Vision; or, Hell, Purgatory and Paradise of Dante Alighieri V
See also *Inferno* 1805

R.C. Dallas (1754–1824)
Recollections of the Life of Lord Byron NF

George Daniel (1789–1864)
The Modern Dunciad V
Anonymous

Selina Davenport
The Hypocrite; or, The Modern Janus F

Isaac D'Israeli (1766–1848)
Quarrels of Authors; or, Some Memoirs for Our Literary History NF

Maria Edgeworth (1767–1849)
Continuation of Early Lessons F
Anonymous. See also *Early Lessons* 1801; *Rosamond* 1821; *Frank* 1822, and *Harry and Lucy* 1825.

Maria Edgeworth (1767–1849)
Patronage F

Pierce Egan, the elder (1772–1849)
The Mistress of Royalty; or, The Loves of Florizel and Perdita V
Anonymous. Concerning the relationship between the Prince of Wales ('Florizel') and Mrs Mary Robinson ('Perdita').

'J.H. Craig, of Douglas' [James Hogg (1770–1835)]
The Hunting of Badlewe V

Leigh Hunt (1784–1859)
The Feast of the Poets V
Revised and enlarged in 1815. First published in *The Reflector* in 1810.

John Jea (*b.* 1773)
The Life, History and Unparalleled Sufferings of John Jea, the African Preacher NF

'Calvus' [Walter Savage Landor (1775–1864)]
Letters Addressed to Lord Liverpool, and the Parliament NF

Isabella Lickbarrow (1784–1847)
Poetical Effusions V

T.R. Malthus (1766–1834)
Observations on the Effects of the Corn Laws NF

Sydney, Lady Morgan, formerly **Owenson** (1783?–1859)
O'Donnel F

Thomas Love Peacock (1785–1866)
Sir Hornbrook; or, Childe Launcelot's Expedition V

'P.M. O'Donovan' [Thomas Love Peacock (1785–1866)]
Sir Proteus: A satirical ballad V
Dedicated to Lord Byron

Anna Maria Porter (1780–1832)
The Recluse of Norway F

J.H. Reynolds (1794–1852)
The Eden of the Imagination V

J.H. Reynolds (1794–1852)
Safie: An eastern tale V

Legh Richmond (1772–1827)
Annals of the Poor F

Originally published, under the pseudonym 'Simplex', in the *Christian Guardian* 1809–14. Enormously popular.

Walter Scott (1771–1832)
Waverley; or, 'tis Sixty Years Since F
Anonymous. Published on 7 July 1814. Four editions in 1814; 8th edition, 1821.

Richard Lalor Sheil (1791–1851)
Adelaide; or, The Emigrants: A tragedy D
Performed 19 February 1814

P.B. Shelley (1792–1822)
A Refutation of Deism: in a Dialogue NF
Anonymous

William Sotheby (1757–1833)
Tragedies D
Contains *The Death of Darnley; Ivan; Zamorin and Zama; The Confession; Orestes*

Robert Southey (1774–1843)
Odes to the Prince Regent, the Emperor of Russia, and the King of Prussia V
Southey's first productions as Poet Laureate (appointed 1813). The second edition, 1821, given the title *Carmen Triumphale, for the Commencement of the Year 1814.*

Robert Southey (1774–1843)
Roderick, the Last of the Goths V

William Wordsworth (1770–1850)
The Excursion: Being a portion of The Recluse, a poem V
See also *The Prelude* 1850, *The Recluse* 1888

1815

- Napoleon returns to France from Elba (1 Mar.) and enters Paris (20 Mar.): beginning of the 'Hundred Days'
  First Corn Law passed (23 Mar.)
  Congress of Vienna concludes (June)
  Napoleon finally defeated by Wellington and Blücher at the Battle of Waterloo (18 June)
  Napoleon banished to St Helena (Aug.)
  Byron marries Annabella Milbanke
  John Nash begins the Brighton Pavilion (completed 1823)
- George Boole born
  Richard William Church born
  Sir Thomas Erskine May born
  Elizabeth Missing Sewell born
  Arthur Penrhyn Stanley born
  Anthony Trollope born
- Benjamin Constant, *Adolphe*

Jane Austen (1775–1817)
Emma F
bao *Pride and Prejudice*. Published in December 1815, dated 1816. Dedicated to the Prince Regent.

Jeremy Bentham (1748–1832)
Chrestomathia NF

Barbarina Brand, Lady Dacre (1768–1854)
Ina: A tragedy D
Performed 22 April 1815

George Gordon, Lord Byron (1788–1824)
Hebrew Melodies V

John Campbell (1766–1840)
Travels in South Africa NF

Louisa Costello (1799–1879)
The Maid of the Cyprus Isle, and Other Poems V

William Cowper (1731–1800)
Poems, by William Cowper V
Edited by John Johnson

John Galt (1779–1839)
The Majolo F
Anonymous

'Verax' [William Godwin (1756–1836)**]**
Letters of Verax, to the Editor of the Morning Chronicle NF

James Hogg (1770–1835)
The Pilgrims of the Sun V
See also *The Three Perils of Woman* 1823

Leigh Hunt (1784–1859)
The Descent of Liberty: A masque V

Charles Lloyd (1775–1839) (tr.)
The Tragedies of Vittorio Alfieri D
Translated from the Italian dramatist Vittorio Alfieri (1749–1803)

T.R. Malthus (1766–1834)
An Inquiry into the Nature and Progress of Rent NF

Henry Hart Milman (1791–1868)
Fazio: A tragedy D

Robert Owen (1771–1858)
Observations on the Effect of the Manufacturing System NF

Ann Radcliffe (1764–1823)
Poems V

Walter Scott (1771–1832)
The Lord of the Isles V

Published on 5 January 1815 in Edinburgh. Five editions in 1815.

Walter Scott (1771–1832)
Guy Mannering; or, The Astrologer F
bao *Waverley*

Walter Scott (1771–1832)
The Field of Waterloo V
The Battle of Waterloo took place on 18 June 1815

Robert Southey (1774–1843)
The Minor Poems of Robert Southey V
Reissue of *Poems* 1797 (q.v.) and *Metrical Tales* 1805 (q.v.)

Robert Tannahill (1774–1810)
Poems and Songs V

Jane Taylor (1783–1824)
Display F
For children. Many editions.

Helen Maria Williams (1762–1827)
A Narrative of the Events which have Taken Place in France NF

William Wordsworth (1770–1850)
Poems V
A third volume was published in 1820. Includes *Lyrical Ballads*, published separately in 1798, 1800, 1802, 1805 (q.v.).

William Wordsworth (1770–1850)
The White Doe of Rylstone; or, The Fate of the Nortons V
Dedicatory sonnet to Mary Wordsworth

Sir Nathaniel Wraxall (1751–1831)
Historical Memoirs of My Own Time NF

1816

- Spa Fields Riot (2 Dec.)
  Shelley marries Mary Godwin after the suicide of Harriet Westbrook
  Byron's final departure from England
  Coleridge settles at Highgate
- Grace Aguilar born
  Philip James Bailey born
  Charlotte Brontë born
  [Charles WIlliam] Shirley Brooks born
  Frances Browne born
  Sir Theodore Martin born
- Adam Ferguson dies
  Richard Brinsley Sheridan dies

Eaton Stannard Barrett (1786–1820)
The Talents Run Mad; or, Eighteen Hundred and Sixteen V
bao *All the Talents*

Mary Matilda Betham (1776–1852)
The Lay of Marie V

Thomas Brown (1778–1820)
The Wanderer in Norway V

Sir Samuel Egerton Brydges (1762–1837)
Bertram V
First privately printed in 1814

George Gordon, Lord Byron (1788–1824)
The Siege of Corinth: a Poem; Parisina: a Poem V
The Siege of Corinth published separately in 1824

George Gordon, Lord Byron (1788–1824)
A Sketch From Private Life V
A poem on the separation from his wife Augusta, printed for private circulation. Unauthorized publication in *The Champion* (14 April 1816). See also *Fare Thee Well* 1816.

George Gordon, Lord Byron (1788–1824)
Fare Thee Well V
Like *A Sketch From Private Life* (see above), a poem on the separation from his wife Augusta and printed for private circulation. Unauthorized publication in *The Champion* (Sunday 14 April 1816).

George Gordon, Lord Byron (1788–1824)
Monody on the Death of the Right Honourable R.B. Sheridan V
Written at the request of Douglas Kinnaird and spoken at Drury Lane Theatre by Mrs Maria Davison on 16 September 1816

George Gordon, Lord Byron (1788–1824)
Childe Harold's Pilgrimage: Canto the Third V
Published on 18 November 1816. See also *Childe Harold* 1812, 1818.

George Gordon, Lord Byron (1788–1824)
The Prisoner of Chillon, and Other Poems V
Published on 5 December 1816

George Gordon, Lord Byron (1788–1824)
Poems V

S.T. Coleridge (1772–1834)
Christabel; Kubla Khan: A Vision; The Pains of Sleep V
Published in February 1816

S.T. Coleridge (1772–1834)
The Statesman's Manual NF

William Cowper (1731–1800)
Memoir of the Early Life of William Cowper NF

George Crabbe (1754–1832)
The Works of the Reverend George Crabbe WKS
Includes *Poems* 1807, *The Borough* 1810, *Tales* 1812 (qq.v.). See also 1834.

James Hogg (1770–1835)
Mador of the Moor V

James Hogg (1770–1835)
The Poetic Mirror; or, The Living Bards of Britain V
Anonymous. Contains parodies of Wordsworth, Coleridge, and Southey.

Thomas Holcroft (1745–1809)
Memoirs of the Late Thomas Holcroft NF
Includes a continuation to the time of Holcroft's death by William Hazlitt

Leigh Hunt (1784–1859)
The Story of Rimini V

Lady Caroline Lamb (1785–1828)
Glenarvon F
Anonymous. See also *Verses from Glenarvon* 1819.

C.R. Maturin (1782–1824)
Bertram; or, The Castle of St Aldobrand D
Performed 9 May 1816

Thomas Moore (1779–1852)
Lines on the Death of [*R.B. Sheridan*] V
Published in the *Morning Chronicle* (5 August 1816) and also published separately

Hannah More (1745–1833)
Poems V

Amelia Opie (1769–1853)
Valentine's Eve F

Thomas Love Peacock (1785–1866)
Headlong Hall F
Anonymous. See also *Headlong Hall* etc 1849.

Edward Quillinan (1791–1851)
The Sacrifice of Isabel V

J.H. Reynolds (1794–1852)
The Naiad, with Other Poems V
Anonymous

David Ricardo (1772–1823)
Proposals for an Economical and Secure Currency NF

Walter Scott (1771–1832)
The Antiquary F
bao *Waverley* and *Guy Mannering*

Walter Scott (1771–1832)
Tales of My Landlord [1st ser.] F
Anonymous. Contains 'The Black Dwarf' and 'Old Mortality'. Second series, 1818 (q.v.), third series, 1819 (q.v.), fourth series, 1832 (q.v.).

P.B. Shelley (1792–1822)
Alastor; or, The Spirit of Solitude: and Other Poems V
Published in March 1816

Robert Southey (1774–1843)
The Lay of the Laureate: Carmen nuptiale V
A privately printed edition was published in 1816 with title *Carmen Nuptiale*. Written on the marriage of Princess Charlotte.

Robert Southey (1774–1843)
The Poet's Pilgrimage to Waterloo V

Jane Taylor (1783–1824)
Essays in Rhyme, on Morals and Manners V

John Wilson (1785–1854)
The City of the Plague, and Other Poems V

William Wordsworth (1770–1850)
Thanksgiving Ode, January 18, 1816 V

1817

- James Monroe becomes President of the USA
  Habeas Corpus Act suspended
  Act to prevent seditious meetings passed
  William Hone imprisoned
- Branwell Brontë born
  Benjamin Jowett born
  Sir Austine Henry Layard born
  George Henry Lewes born
  Denis MacCarthy born
  Tom Taylor born
- John Leech born
- Jane Austen dies
  Dr Charles Burney dies
  Richard Lovell Edgeworth dies
- Henry David Thoreau born
- Madame de Staël dies

Blackwood's Edinburgh Magazine PER
Begun as *Blackwood's Edinburgh Monthly Magazine* (April–September 1817); continued as *Blackwood's Edinburgh Magazine* (October 1817–December 1905), then as *Blackwood's Magazine* from January 1906

Jane Austen (1775–1817)
Northanger Abbey; and Persuasion F
bao *Pride and Prejudice, Mansfield Park*, &c.

Published in December 1817, dated 1818. Biographical notice (naming the author) by Henry Austen.

Eaton Stannard Barrett (1786–1820)
Six Weeks at Long's F
Anonymous. Three editions in 1817.

Jeremy Bentham (1748–1832)
Papers Relative to Codification and Public Instruction NF
Written in 1809

Sir James Burges (1752–1824)
Dramas D

George Gordon, Lord Byron (1788–1824)
Manfred D
Published on 16 June 1817

George Gordon, Lord Byron (1788–1824)
The Lament of Tasso V

Richard Carlile (1790–1843)
The Political Litany, Diligently Revised NF

Thomas Chalmers (1780–1847)
Astronomical Discourses NF
See also *Commercial Discourses* 1820

S.T. Coleridge (1772–1834)
Biographia Literaria; or, Biographical Sketches of my Literary Life and Opinions NF
Published in July 1817

S.T. Coleridge (1772–1834)
Sybilline Leaves V

S.T. Coleridge (1772–1834)
Zapolya: A Christmas tale V

William Combe (1742–1823)
The Dance of Life V
bao *Doctor Syntax*. Illustrated by Thomas Rowlandson.

George Croly (1780–1860)
Paris in 1815 V

Thomas Frognall Dibdin (1776–1847)
The Bibliographical Decameron NF

Isaac D'Israeli (1766–1848)
Curiosities of Literature [1st ser., vol. iii] NF
See also *Curiosities of Literature* 1791, 1793, 1823, 1834

Nathan Drake (1766–1836)
Shakespeare and his Times NF

Maria Edgeworth (1767–1849)
Comic Dramas D

Maria Edgeworth (1767–1849)
Harrington, a Tale; and Ormond, a Tale F

Thomas Erskine (1750–1823)
Armata NF
Anonymous. Four editions in 1817. Part ii also published in 1817.

John Hookham Frere (1769–1846)
Prospectus and Specimen of an Intended National Work by William and Robert Whistlecraft Relating to King Arthur and his Round Table [cantos i, ii] V
Cantos iii and iv published in 1818

William Godwin (1756–1836)
Mandeville F

William Hazlitt (1778–1830) and **Leigh Hunt** (1784–1859)
The Round Table NF
Contains 52 essays (12 by Leigh Hunt) mostly written for *The Examiner* between May 1814 and January 1817

William Hazlitt (1778–1830)
Characters of Shakespear's Plays NF

Felicia Dorothea Hemans (1793–1835)
Modern Greece V

James Hogg (1770–1835)
Dramatic Tales MISC
bao *The Poetic Mirror*

John Keats (1795–1821)
Poems V

C.R. Maturin (1782–1824)
Manuel: A tragedy D
bao *Bertram*. Performed 8 March 1817.

Thomas Moore (1779–1852)
Lalla Rookh: An oriental romance V
Six editions in 1817

John Nichols (1745–1826)
Illustrations of the Literary History of the Eighteenth Century NF
Continued by J.B. Nichols after his father's death

Thomas Love Peacock (1785–1866)
Melincourt F
bao *Headlong Hall*

Anna Maria Porter (1780–1832)
The Knight of St John F

Jane Porter (1776–1850)
The Pastor's Fire-side F

David Ricardo (1772–1823)
On the Principles of Political Economy and Taxation NF

Walter Scott (1771–1832)
Harold the Dauntless V
Anonymous

Walter Scott (1771–1832)
The Border Antiquities of England and Scotland NF
First issued in seventeen separate parts (June 1812–September 1817)

Richard Lalor Sheil (1791–1851)
The Apostate: A tragedy D
Performed 3 May 1817

Mary Shelley (1797–1851)
History of a Six Weeks' Tour Through a Part of France, Switzerland, Germany, and Holland NF
Anonymous. Written with P.B. Shelley.

P.B. Shelley (1792–1822)
Laon and Cythna; or, The Revolution of the Golden City V
Published late 1817, dated 1818, but suppressed. Passages were removed at the insistence of the publisher, Ollier, and the poem reissued as *The Revolt of Islam* in late 1817 (see below).

P.B. Shelley (1792–1822)
A Proposal for Putting Reform to the Vote Throughout the Kingdom NF
'By the Hermit of Marlow'

P.B. Shelley (1792–1822)
The Revolt of Islam V
Published late 1817, dated 1818. A revised version of *Laon and Cythna* 1817 (see above). Some copies dated 1817.

Robert Southey (1774–1843)
History of Brazil . . . Part the Second NF
Volume i published in 1810 (q.v.); volume iii, 1819 (q.v.)

Robert Southey (1774–1843)
Wat Tyler V

1818

- Shelley's final departure from England
  Anonymous attack on Keats in *Blackwood's*
- Cecil Frances Alexander (Mrs C.F. Alexander, *née* Humphreys) born
  Emily Brontë born
  James Anthony Froude born
  John Mason Neale born
  Thomas Mayne Reid born
- Mary Brunton dies
  Sir Philip Francis ('Junius'?) dies
  Matthew Gregory Lewis dies
  Mary Meeke dies
- Humphry Repton dies
- Karl Marx born
  Ivan Turgenev born

Sir John Barrow (1764–1848)
A Chronological History of Voyages into the Arctic Regions NF

Bernard Barton (1784–1849)
The Convict's Appeal V

Bernard Barton (1784–1849)
Poems V
'By an amateur'

'Q. in the Corner' [Thomas Haynes Bayly (1797–1839)]
Parliamentary Letters, and Other Poems V

Mary Matilda Betham (1776–1852)
Vignettes V

William Blake (1757–1827)
Jerusalem: The emanation of the giant Albion V
Illuminated book (100 plates). Dated 1804, but this probably indicates the date when Blake began the work. The first copies were probably printed in 1818.

Thomas Bowdler (1754–1825) (ed.)
The Family Shakespeare EDN
Continues *The Family Shakespeare* 1807 (q.v.) prepared by his sister Henrietta

Sir James Burges (1752–1824)
The Dragon Knight V

George Gordon, Lord Byron (1788–1824)
Beppo: A Venetian story V
Anonymous. Published on 24 February 1818.

George Gordon, Lord Byron (1788–1824)
Childe Harold's Pilgrimage: Canto the Fourth V
Published on 28 April 1818. See also *Childe Harold* 1812, 1816.

George Chalmers (1742–1825)
The Life of Mary, Queen of Scots NF

William Cobbett (1763–1835)
A Grammar of the English Language, in a Series of Letters NF
Published 1818, dated 1819

Thomas Doubleday (1790–1870)
Sixty-Five Sonnets V
Anonymous

John Evelyn (1620–1706)
Memoirs of John Evelyn NF
The first, though defective, edition of Evelyn's diary

Susan Edmonstone Ferrier (1782–1854)
Marriage F
Anonymous

William Godwin (1756–1836)
Letters of Advice to a Young American NF

Henry Hallam (1777–1859)
View of the State of Europe During the Middle Ages NF

William Hazlitt (1778–1830)
Lectures on the English Poets NF
Lectures delivered in January 1818

William Hazlitt (1778–1830)
A View of the English Stage; or, A Series of Dramatic Criticisms NF

Felicia Dorothea Hemans (1793–1835) (tr.)
Translations from Camoens and Other Poets, with Original Poetry V
bao *Modern Greece*

James Hogg (1770–1835)
The Brownie of Bodsbeck, and Other Tales F

Leigh Hunt (1784–1859)
Foliage; or, Poems Original and Translated V

Leigh Hunt (1784–1859)
Literary Pocket-Book MISC
Concluded in 1822

John Keats (1795–1821)
Endymion: A poetic romance V

Charles Lamb (1775–1834)
The Works of Charles Lamb WKS

Henry Hart Milman (1791–1868)
Samor: Lord of the bright city V

'Thomas Brown the Younger' [Thomas Moore (1779–1852)]
The Fudge Family in Paris V
At least nine editions in 1818. See also *The Fudges in England* 1835.

Hannah More (1745–1833)
Tragedies V

Sydney, Lady Morgan, formerly **Owenson** (1783?–1859)
Florence Macarthy F

James Morier (1780–1849)
A Second Journey Through Persia, Armenia and Asia Minor NF
See *Journey* 1812

Amelia Opie (1769–1853)
New Tales F

Thomas Love Peacock (1785–1866)
Nightmare Abbey F
bao *Headlong Hall*. See also *Headlong Hall* etc 1849.

Thomas Love Peacock (1785–1866)
Rhododaphne; or, The Thessalian Spell V

Isaac Pocock (1782–1835)
Rob Roy Macgregor; or, Auld Lang Syne: A musical drama D
Performed 12 March 1818. The libretto was based on Scott's novel 1818 (see below).

Anna Maria Porter (1780–1832)
The Feast of St Magdalen F

Walter Scott (1771–1832)
Rob Roy F
bao *Waverley*, *Guy Mannering*, and *The Antiquary*. Published on 1 January 1818. Four editions in 1818.

Walter Scott (1771–1832)
Tales of My Landlord, Second Series F
Comprises 'The Heart of Midlothian'. First series published in 1816 (q.v.); third series, 1819 (q.v.); fourth series, 1832 (q.v.).

Richard Lalor Sheil (1791–1851)
Bellamira; or, The Fall of Tunis: A tragedy D
Performed 22 April 1818

Mary Shelley (1797–1851)
Frankenstein; or, The Modern Prometheus F
Dedicated to William Godwin

Mary Martha Sherwood (1775–1851)
The History of the Fairchild Family; or, The Child's Manual F
Part ii published in 1842; part iii, 1847

William Sotheby (1757–1833)
Farewell to Italy, and Occasional Poems V

Horace Walpole (1717–97)
Letters to George Montagu NF

Horace Walpole (1717–97)
Letters to William Cole, and Others NF

1819

- The 'Peterloo Massacre' (16 Aug.)
  Simón Bolívar becomes President of the newly formed Republic of Colombia
- Maria Charlesworth born
  Arthur Hugh Clough born
  George Eliot (Mary Ann Evans) born
  Charles Kingsley born
  John Ruskin born
- Princess (later Queen) Victoria born
  Albert, later Prince Consort, born
- James Watt dies
  John Wolcot ('Peter Pindar') dies
- James Russell Lowell born
  Herman Melville born
  Walt Whitman born
- August von Kotzebue assassinated

Alexander Balfour (1767–1829)
Campbell; or, The Scottish Probationer F
Anonymous

William Lisle Bowles (1762–1850)
The Invariable Principles of Poetry NF
See also *Two Letters* 1821, *A Final Appeal* 1825, and *Lessons in Criticism* 1826

Mary Brunton (1778–1818)
Emmeline F
Unfinished at the author's death

Charles Bucke (1781–1846)
The Fall of the Leaf, and Other Poems V

George Gordon, Lord Byron (1788–1824)
Mazeppa V

George Gordon, Lord Byron (1788–1824)
Don Juan [cantos i–ii] V
Anonymous. Published on 15 July 1819. See also *Don Juan* 1821, 1823, 1824.

Thomas Campbell (1777–1844) (ed.)
Specimens of the British Poets ANTH

William Cobbett (1763–1835)
A Year's Residence in the United States of America NF
First issued in 3 parts, 1818–19

George Combe (1788–1858)
Elements of Phrenology NF
See also *Essays on Phrenology* below

George Combe (1788–1858)
Essays on Phrenology NF
See also *Elements of Phrenology* above

'Barry Cornwall' [Bryan Waller Procter (1787–1874)]
Dramatic Scenes, and Other Poems V

Louisa Costello (1799–1879)
Redwald: A Tale of Mona; and Other Poems V

George Crabbe (1754–1832)
Tales of the Hall V
Crabbe's last work

Charles Dibdin (1768–1833)
Young Arthur; or, The Child of Mystery V

William Hazlitt (1778–1830)
Lectures on the English Comic Writers NF
Lectures delivered November 1818–January 1819

William Hazlitt (1778–1830)
Political Essays, with Sketches of Public Characters NF

Felicia Dorothea Hemans (1793–1835)
Tales and Historic Scenes, in Verse V

Felicia Dorothea Hemans (1793–1835)
Wallace's Invocation to Bruce V

William Hone (1780–1842)
The Political House that Jack Built V
Anonymous. Illustrated by George Cruikshank.

Thomas Hope (1770?–1831)
Anastasius; or, Memoirs of a Greek F
Anonymous. The first 3-decker novel to be published at a guinea and a half (31s 6d). Widely attributed to Lord Byron on its publication.

Leigh Hunt (1784–1859)
Hero and Leander, and Bacchus and Ariadne V

Lady Caroline Lamb (1785–1828)
Verses from Glenarvon V
Anonymous. See *Glenarvon* 1816.

John Lingard (1771–1851)
The History of England [vols i, ii, iii] NF
Published in 8 volumes (1819–30)

Charles Lloyd (1775–1839)
Nugae Canorae V

'Peter Morris' [J.G. Lockhart (1794–1854)]
Peter's Letters to His Kinfolk NF
'By Peter Morris the Odontist'. Written with John Wilson ('Christopher North').

Thomas Babington Macaulay (1800–59)
Pompeii V

C.R. Maturin (1782–1824)
Fredolfo: A tragedy D
Performed 12 May 1819

James Montgomery (1771–1854)
Greenland, and Other Poems V

Thomas Moore (1779–1852)
Tom Crib's Memorial to Congress V

Hannah More (1745–1833)
Moral Sketches of Prevailing Opinions and Manners NF

John William Polidori (1795–1821)
Ernestus Berchtold; or, The Modern Oedipus F

John William Polidori (1795–1821)
The Vampyre F
Anonymous

J.H. Reynolds (1794–1852)
Benjamin the Waggoner V
Anonymous. A parody on Wordsworth.

J.H. Reynolds (1794–1852)
Peter Bell: A lyrical ballad V
'By W.W.' (i.e. satirically purporting to be William Wordsworth)

Samuel Rogers (1763–1855)
Human Life V

John Ross (1777–1856)
A Voyage of Discovery NF

Walter Scott (1771–1832)
The Provincial Antiquities and Picturesque Scenery of Scotland NF
Issued in 10 parts (May 1819–December 1826). Many of the plates are from drawings by J.M.W. Turner. All 10 parts published together in 1826.

Walter Scott (1771–1832)
Tales of My Landlord, Third Series F
Comprises 'The Bride of Lammermoor', and 'A Legend of Montrose'. First series published in 1816 (q.v.); second series, 1818 (q.v.), fourth series, 1832 (q.v.).

Walter Scott (1771–1832)
Novels and Tales of the Author of Waverley F
Contains *Waverley, Guy Mannering, The Antiquary, Rob Roy, Tales of my Landlord*

Walter Scott (1771–1832)
Ivanhoe F
bao *Waverley*, &c. Published on 20 December 1819 in Edinburgh, dated 1820. See also George Soane, *The Hebrew* 1820.

Richard Lalor Sheil (1791–1851)
Evadne; or, The Statue: A tragedy D
Performed 10 February 1819

P.B. Shelley (1792–1822)
The Cenci: A tragedy V
Not performed until 7 May 1886, under the auspices of the Shelley Society

P.B. Shelley (1792–1822)
Rosalind and Helen: a Modern Eclogue; with Other Poems V

Charles Simeon (1759–1836)
Horae Homilecticae; or, Discourses upon the Whole Scriptures NF
The first collected edition (11 volumes, 1819–20). First volume published in 1796.

Robert Southey (1774–1843)
History of Brazil . . . Part the Third NF
Volume i published in 1810 (q.v.); volume ii, 1817 (q.v.)

William Wordsworth (1770–1850)
Peter Bell: A tale in verse V
Dedicated to Robert Southey. Parodied in advance of publication by J.H. Reynolds in *Peter Bell* 1819 (above), and later by Shelley in 'Peter Bell the Third'.

William Wordsworth (1770–1850)
The Waggoner V

1820

- Death of George III (29 Jan.)
  GEORGE IV (-1830)
  The Cato Street Conspiracy to murder members of the Cabinet discovered (23 Feb.)
  Trial of Queen Caroline
- Edward Litt Laman Blanchard born
  Dion Boucicault born?
  Anne Brontë born
  Sir George Grove born
  Jean Ingelow born
  Anna Sewell born
  Herbert Spencer born
- Florence Nightingale born
  John Tenniel born
- William Hayley dies
  Arthur Young dies
- Friedrich Engels born

Alexander Balfour (1767–1829)
Contemplation V

R.H. Barham (1788–1845)
Baldwin; or, A Miser's Heir F
'By an Old Bachelor'

William Barnes (1801–86)
Poetical Pieces v

Bernard Barton (1784–1849)
A Day in Autumn v

Bernard Barton (1784–1849)
Poems v

Caroline Bowles, later **Southey** (1786–1854)
Ellen Fitzarthur v
Anonymous

Thomas Brown (1778–1820)
Lectures on the Philosophy of the Human Mind NF

Elizabeth Barrett Barrett, later **Browning** (1806–61)
The Battle of Marathon v
Privately printed by Elizabeth Barrett's father, Edward Barrett

Edward Lytton Bulwer, later **Bulwer-Lytton** (1803–73)
Ismael: An Oriental Tale, with Other Poems v

Thomas Chalmers (1780–1847)
Commercial Discourses NF
See also *Astronomical Discourses* 1817

John Clare (1793–1864)
Poems Descriptive of Rural Life and Scenery v

John Payne Collier (1789–1883)
The Poetical Decameron NF

William Combe (1742–1823)
The Second Tour of Doctor Syntax, in Search of Consolation v
Anonymous. Illustrated by Thomas Rowlandson and first published in monthly parts. See *The Tour of Doctor Syntax* 1812, *The Third Tour* 1821.

'Barry Cornwall' [Bryan Waller Procter (1787–1874)]
Marcian Colonna v/D

'Barry Cornwall' [Bryan Waller Procter (1787–1874)]
A Sicilian Story, with Diego de Montilla, and Other Poems v

George Croly (1780–1860)
The Angel of the World; Sebastion; with Other Poems v

Thomas John Dibdin (1771–1841)
Ivanhoe; or, The Jew's Daughter: A melo dramatic romance D
Performed 20 January 1820. Based on Scott's novel of 1819 (q.v.). See also Dibdin, *The Lady of the Lake* 1811, *The Pirate* 1822.

Maria Edgeworth (1767–1849)
Memoirs of Richard Lovell Edgeworth NF
Volume i by Richard Lovell Edgeworth (died 1817), volume ii by Maria

Ebenezer Elliott (1781–1849)
Peter Faultless to his Brother Simon, and Other Poems v
bao *Night*

Thomas Erskine (1788–1870)
Remarks on the Internal Evidence for the Truth of Revealed Religion NF

John Galt (1779–1839)
The Earthquake F
bao *The Ayrshire Legatees*

John Galt (1779–1839)
Glenfell; or, Macdonalds and Campbells F
Anonymous

'Revd T. Clarke' [John Galt (1779–1839)]
The Wandering Jew; or, The Travels and Observations of Hareach the Prolonged F

William Godwin (1756–1836)
Of Population NF
See Malthus, *Essay on the Principle of Population* 1798, and Francis Place, *Illustrations and Proofs of the Principle of Population* 1822

William Hazlitt (1778–1830)
Lectures Chiefly on the Dramatic Literature of the Age of Elizabeth NF
Lectures delivered in January 1820

Felicia Dorothea Hemans (1793–1835)
The Sceptic v

John Abraham Heraud (1799–1887)
The Legend of St Loy, with Other Poems v

John Abraham Heraud (1799–1887)
Tottenham v

James Hogg (1770–1835)
Winter Evening Tales F

William Hone (1780–1842)
The Man in the Moon v
Anonymous. Illustrated by George Cruikshank. Ironically dedicated to George Canning.

William Hone (1780–1842)
The Queen's Matrimonial Ladder v
bao *The Political House that Jack Built*. Published in August 1820. On the Bill of Pains and Penalities

against Queen Caroline. Illustrated by George Cruikshank.

Leigh Hunt (1784–1859) (tr.)
Amyntas V
Translated from TorquatoTasso (1544–95) and dedicated to John Keats

John Keats (1795–1821)
Lamia, Isabella, The Eve of St Agnes, and Other Poems V
Also includes 'Ode to a Nightingale', 'Ode on a Grecian Urn', 'Ode to Psyche', 'To Autumn', and 'Hyperion'

James Sheridan Knowles (1784–1862)
Virginius; or, The Liberation of Rome D
Performed in London 17 May 1820

T.R. Malthus (1766–1834)
Principles of Political Economy NF

C.R. Maturin (1782–1824)
Melmoth the Wanderer F
bao *Bertram*

Henry Hart Milman (1791–1868)
The Fall of Jerusalem V

'William Thomas Moncrieff' [William Thomas Thomas (1794–1857)]
The Lear of Private Life; or, Father and Daughter D
Performed 27 April 1820. A dramatization of *Father and Daughter* by Amelia Opie.

Amelia Opie (1769–1853)
Tales of the Heart F

Thomas Love Peacock (1785–1866)
'The Four Ages of Poetry' NF
Published in *Ollier's Literary Miscellany*. Responded to by Shelley's 'Defence of Poetry', written in 1821 and published in 1840 in *Essays, Letters from Abroad, Translations and Fragments* (q.v.).

Sir Walter Scott (1771–1832)
The Poetical Works of Sir Walter Scott V
The first collected edition (in 12 volumes). Scott was created baronet in 1820.

Sir Walter Scott (1771–1832)
The Monastery F
bao *Waverley*

Sir Walter Scott (1771–1832)
The Abbot F
bao *Waverley*

P.B. Shelley (1792–1822)
Oedipus Tyrannus; or, Swellfoot the Tyrant V
Anonymous. A burlesque on the trial of Queen Caroline.

P.B. Shelley (1792–1822)
Prometheus Unbound: A lyrical drama V
Poems include: 'The Sensitive Plant', 'A Vision of the Sea', 'Ode to Heaven', 'Ode to the West Wind'. 'To a Cloud', 'To a Skylark', 'Ode to Liberty'

George Soane (1790–1860)
The Hebrew: A drama D
Performed 2 March 1820. Based on Scott's *Ivanhoe* 1819 (q.v.).

Robert Southey (1774–1843)
The Life of Wesley, and the Rise and Progress of Methodism NF

Horace Walpole (1717–97)
Private Correspondence of Horace Walpole NF
The first collected edition

William Wordsworth (1770–1850)
The Miscellaneous Poems of William Wordsworth V
See also *Poetical Works* 1827 and *Poetical Works* 1836, *Poetical Works* 1840, *Poems* 1845, *Poetical Works* 1857, *Poetical Works* (Centenary Edition) 1870

William Wordsworth (1770–1850)
The River Duddon V
See also *A Description of the Scenery of the Lakes* 1822 and *A Guide Through the District of the Lakes* 1835

1821

- James Monroe begins second term as US President
  Greek War of Independence begins
  Revolution in the Piedmont; abdication of Victor Emmanuel
  John Scott (editor of the *London Magazine*) killed in a duel
  Manchester Guardian started
- Henry Thomas Buckle born
  Sir Richard Burton born
  Elizabeth Charles born
  Dora Greenwell born
  George John Whyte-Melville born
- Elizabeth Inchbald dies
  John Keats dies
  Vicesimus Knox dies
  Hester Lynch Piozzi (Mrs Thrale) dies
  John William Polidori dies
- Queen Caroline dies (7 Aug.)
- Charles Baudelaire born
  Fyodor Dostoevsky born

Gustave Flaubert born

- Death of Napoleon (5 May)
- Constable, *The Hay Wain*
  James Fenimore Cooper, *The Spy*

John Leycester Adolphus (1795–1862)
Letters to Richard Heber NF
Anonymous

Edwin Atherstone (1788–1872)
The Last Days of Herculaneum V

Joanna Baillie (1762–1851)
Metrical Legends of Exalted Characters V

Joanna Baillie (1762–1851)
A Series of Plays [vols i–iii] D
Known as *Plays on the Passions*. See also 1798, 1802, 1812.

John Banim (1798–1842)
The Celt's Paradise V
Anonymous

John Banim (1798–1842)
Damon and Pythias: A tragedy D
Performed May 1821

Thomas Lovell Beddoes (1803–49)
The Improvisatore, in Three Fyttes, with Other Poems V

William Lisle Bowles (1762–1850)
Two Letters to the Right Honourable Lord Byron NF
See also *Invariable Principles* 1819, *A Final Appeal* 1825, and *Lessons in Criticism* 1826

George Gordon, Lord Byron (1788–1824)
Marino Faliero, Doge of Venice; The Prophecy of Dante V
Marino Faliero performed 25 April 1821

George Gordon, Lord Byron (1788–1824)
Don Juan [cantos iii–v] V
Anonymous. Published on 8 August 1821. See also *Don Juan* 1819, 1823, 1824.

George Gordon, Lord Byron (1788–1824)
Sardanapalus; The Two Foscari; Cain V/D
Sardanapalus and *The Two Foscari* not performed until 10 April 1834 and 7 April 1837 respectively. *Cain* published separately in 1822.

John Clare (1793–1864)
The Village Minstrel, and Other Poems V

William Cobbett (1763–1835)
The American Gardener NF
Written by Cobbett (a former gardener's boy) during his second stay in America; later revised as *The English Gardener* 1828 (q.v.)

William Cobbett (1763–1835)
Cottage Economy NF
Issued in seven monthly parts, August 1821–March 1822

William Combe (1742–1823)
The Third Tour of Doctor Syntax, in Search of a Wife V
Anonymous. Illustrated by Thomas Rowlandson. See *The Tour of Doctor Syntax* 1812, *The Second Tour* 1820.

'Barry Cornwall' [Bryan Waller Procter (1787–1874)]
Mirandola: A tragedy V/D

Maria Edgeworth (1767–1849)
Rosamond F
A sequel to *Early Lessons* 1801 (q.v.). See also *Continuation* 1814; *Frank* 1822, and *Harry and Lucy* 1825.

Pierce Egan, the elder (1772–1849)
Life in London; Or, the day and night scenes of Jerry Hawthorn, and his elegant friend Corinthian Tom F
Illustrated by I.R. and George Cruikshank and issued in monthly numbers from 1820

Pierce Egan, the elder (1772–1849)
Real Life in London; Or, the rambles and adventures of Bob Tallyho, and his cousin, the Hon. Tom Dashall F
'By an amateur'. Published in 2 volumes (1821–2).

John Galt (1779–1839)
Annals of the Parish; or, The Chronicle of Dalmailing F
'Arranged and edited by the author of *The Ayrshire Legatees*'

John Galt (1779–1839)
The Ayrshire Legatees; or, The Pringle Family F
bao *Annals of the Parish*

William Gifford (1756–1826) (tr.)
The Satires of Aulus Persius Flaccus V
In Latin and English

James Haynes (1788–1851)
Conscience; or, The Bridal Night: A tragedy D
Performed 21 February 1821

William Hazlitt (1778–1830)
Table-Talk; or, Original Essays NF
See also *Table-Talk* 1822

Felicia Dorothea Hemans (1793–1835)
Dartmoor V

William Hone (1780–1842)
The Political Showman—At Home! V
bao *The Political House that Jack Built*. Illustrated by George Cruikshank. Establishment figures lampooned include Wellington, Lord Liverpool (the prime minister), George IV, Castlereagh, and John Stoddart (editor of *The Times*).

Leigh Hunt (1784–1859)
The Months V

'L.E.L.' [Letitia Elizabeth Landon (1802–38)]
The Fate of Adelaide, and Other Poems V

Charles Lloyd (1775–1839)
Desultory Thoughts in London; Titus and Gisippus, with Other Poems V

J.G. Lockhart (1794–1854)
Valerius: A Roman story F
Anonymous

Thomas Medwin (1788–1869)
Sketches in Hindoostan, with Other Poems V

James Mill (1773–1836)
Elements of Political Economy NF

Thomas Moore (1779–1852)
Irish Melodies V
The first authorized edition of Moore's lyrics. Ten editions by 1832. See also *A Selection of Irish Melodies* 1808.

Hannah More (1745–1833)
Bible Rhymes V

John Henry Newman, later **Cardinal** (1801–90)
St Bartholomew's Eve V
Anonymous. Written with J.W. Bowden (1798–1844).

Anna Maria Porter (1780–1832)
The Village of Mariendorpt F
See also *Roche-Blanche* 1822. James Sheridan Knowles's play *The Maid of Mariendorpt* (performed 9 October 1838) was based on this novel.

J.H. Reynolds (1794–1852)
The Garden of Florence, and Other Poems V
Includes two verse tales translated from Boccaccio, intended as part of a Boccaccio volume to have been written with John Keats

Sir Walter Scott (1771–1832)
Kenilworth F
bao *Waverley, Ivanhoe*

Sir Walter Scott (1771–1832)
The Pirate F
bao *Waverley, Kenilworth*. Published in December 1821, dated 1822.

Sir Walter Scott (1771–1832)
Lives of the Novelists NF
Prefatory memoirs by Scott included in *Ballantyne's Novelist's Library*, published in 10 volumes (1821–5)

Richard Lalor Sheil (1791–1851)
Damon and Pythias: A tragedy D
Performed 28 May 1821

P.B. Shelley (1792–1822)
Adonais: An elegy on the death of John Keats V
Keats died in Rome on 23 February 1821

P.B. Shelley (1792–1822)
Epipsychidion V
Anonymous. Addressed to Emilia Viviani.

Horatio Smith (1779–1849)
Amarynthus, the Nympholept V
Anonymous

Robert Southey (1774–1843)
A Vision of Judgement V
See also Byron's *The Vision of Judgment* 1822

1822

- Lord Castlereagh commits suicide; succeeded as Foreign Secretary by George Canning
  Brazil becomes independent
  Liberia founded
  The Sunday Times started
- Matthew Arnold born
- James Grant born
  Thomas Hughes born
  Eliza Linton (*née* Lynn) born
  Sir Henry Maine born
  David Masson born
- Percy Bysshe Shelley dies
- Sir Francis Galton born
- César Franck born
  Edmond de Goncourt born
- E.T.A. Hoffmann dies
- Washington Irving, *Bracebridge Hall*

William Barnes (1801–86)
Orra: A Lapland tale V

Bernard Barton (1784–1849)
Napoleon, and Other Poems V

Bernard Barton (1784–1849)
Verses on the Death of Percy Bysshe Shelley V

Shelley was drowned off the Italian coast in July 1822

Thomas Haynes Bayly (1797–1839)
Erin, and Other Poems V

Thomas Lovell Beddoes (1803–49)
The Bride's Tragedy V

Jeremy Bentham (1748–1832)
The Analysis of the Influence of Natural Religion upon the Temporal Happiness of Mankind NF
Edited by 'Philip Beaumont' (i.e. George Grote, 1794–1871) from Bentham's MSS

Marguerite Gardiner, countess of Blessington (1789–1849)
The Magic Lantern; or, Sketches and Scenes in the Metropolis NF
Anonymous

Robert Bloomfield (1766–1823)
May Day with the Muses V

Caroline Bowles, later **Southey** (1786–1854)
The Widow's Tale, and Other Poems V
bao *Ellen Fitzarthur*

William Lisle Bowles (1762–1850)
The Grave of the Last Saxon; or, The Legend of the Curfew V

'Quevedo Redivivus' [George Gordon, Lord Byron (1788–1824)]
The Vision of Judgment V
First published in *The Liberal* on 15 October 1822; published separately on 19 December. Written in response to Southey's *A Vision of Judgement* 1821 (q.v.).

William Cobbett (1763–1835)
Cobbett's Sermons NF
First issued in twelve monthly parts, 1821–2

George Croly (1780–1860)
Catiline: A tragedy V
Also includes poems

Allan Cunningham (1784–1842)
Sir Marmaduke Maxwell; The Mermaid of Galloway; The Legend of Richard Faulder; and Twenty Scottish Songs V

Allan Cunningham (1784–1842)
Traditional Tales of the English and Scottish Peasantry F

George Darley (1795–1846)
The Errors of Ecstasie: A dramatic poem V

Thomas De Quincey (1785–1859)
Confessions of an English Opium Eater NF
Published in August 1822. Serialized in the *London Magazine* (September–October 1821, with an appendix in September 1822). See also *Confessions of an English Opium Eater* 1856.

Sir Aubrey de Vere (1788–1846)
Julian the Apostate V

Charles Dibdin (1768–1833)
Life in London; or, The Larks of Logic, Tom, & Jerry: An extravaganza D
Based on Pierce Egan's *Life in London* 1821 (q.v.)

Thomas John Dibdin (1771–1841)
The Pirate; or, The Wild Woman of Zetland: A melo dramatic romance D
Performed 7 January 1822 and based on Scott's novel of 1821 (q.v.). See also Dibdin, *The Lady of the Lake* 1811, *Ivanhoe* 1820.

Maria Edgeworth (1767–1849)
Frank F
See also *Early Lessons* 1801; *Continuation* 1814; *Rosamond* 1821; and *Harry and Lucy* 1825

Thomas Erskine (1788–1870)
An Essay on Faith NF

Caroline Fry (1787–1846)
Serious Poetry V

John Galt (1779–1839)
Sir Andrew Wylie of that Ilk F
bao *Annals of the Parish*

John Galt (1779–1839)
The Provost F
bao *Annals of the Parish, Ayrshire Legatees,* and *Sir Andrew Wylie*

John Galt (1779–1839)
The Steam-Boat F
bao *Annals of the Parish*

William Hazlitt (1778–1830)
Table-Talk; or, Original Essays [vol. ii] NF
See also *Table-Talk* 1821

James Hogg (1770–1835)
The Poetical Works of James Hogg V

James Hogg (1770–1835)
The Royal Jubilee: A Scottish mask V/D
'By the Ettrick Shepherd'

James Hogg (1770–1835)
The Three Perils of Man; or, War, Women and Witchcraft F
See also *The Three Perils of Woman* 1823

Lady Caroline Lamb (1785–1828)
Graham Hamilton F
Anonymous

Charles Lloyd (1775–1839)
The Duke d'Ormond; and Beritola V

J.G. Lockhart (1794–1854)
Some Passages in the Life of Mr Adam Blair F
Anonymous

Henry Hart Milman (1791–1868)
Belshazzar V

Henry Hart Milman (1791–1868)
The Martyr of Antioch V

Amelia Opie (1769–1853)
Madeline F

Thomas Love Peacock (1785–1866)
Maid Marian F
bao *Headlong Hall.* Written in 1818 (except last three chapters). See also *Headlong Hall* etc 1849.

Francis Place (1771–1854)
Illustrations and Proofs of the Principle of Population NF
See Malthus, *Essay on the Principle of Population* 1798, and William Godwin, *Of Population* 1820

Francis Place (1771–1854)
Improvement of the Working People NF

Anna Maria Porter (1780–1832)
Roche-Blanche; or, The Hunters of the Pyrenees F
Sequel to *The Village of Mariendorpt* 1821 (q.v.)

Samuel Rogers (1763–1855)
Italy: Part the first V
Anonymous. *Part the Second* published in 1828 (q.v.). Both parts published together in 1830 (illustrated by J.M.W. Turner and Thomas Stothard).

Sir Walter Scott (1771–1832)
The Fortunes of Nigel F
bao *Waverley, Kenilworth,* &c. Published in May 1822.

Sir Walter Scott (1771–1832)
Halidon Hill V

Sir Walter Scott (1771–1832)
Historical Romances of the Author of Waverley F
Published in June 1822 in Edinburgh. Contains *Ivanhoe, The Monastery, The Abbot, Kenilworth.*

P.B. Shelley (1792–1822)
Hellas V
Shelley's last work published in his lifetime

Horace Walpole (1717–97)
Memoirs of the Last Ten Years of the Reign of George II NF
Edited by Lord Holland

Joseph Blanco White (1775–1841)
Vargas F
Anonymous

William Wordsworth (1770–1850)
Memorials of a Tour on the Continent, 1820 NF

William Wordsworth (1770–1850)
A Description of the Scenery of the Lakes in the North of England NF
First published in abbreviated form as an introduction to Joseph Wilkinson's *Select Views in Cumberland, Westmoreland, and Lancashire* (1810); reprinted in *The River Duddon* 1820 (q.v.). See also *A Guide Through the District of the Lakes* 1835.

William Wordsworth (1770–1850)
Ecclesiastical Sonnets V

1823

- Daniel O'Connell forms Catholic Association of Ireland (May)
  The Monroe Doctrine closing America to colonial settlement by European powers
  The Lancet started
  Oxford Union Society founded
- Coventry Patmore born
  Friedrich Max Müller born
  Alfred Russel Wallace born
  Charlotte Mary Yonge born
- Robert Bloomfield dies
  William Combe dies
  Elizabeth Gunning dies
  Ann Radcliffe dies
  David Ricardo dies
- Edward Augustus Freeman born
- Ernest Renan born
- John Cumberland's *British Theatre*

Robert Bloomfield (1766–1823)
Hazelwood Hall V/D

William Lisle Bowles (1762–1850)
Ellen Gray; or, The Dead Maiden's Curse V
'By the late Dr Archibald Macleod' (i.e. Bowles)

Edward Lytton Bulwer, later **Bulwer-Lytton** (1803–73)
Delmour; or, A Tale of a Sylphid, and Other Poems V
Anonymous

George Gordon, Lord Byron (1788–1824)
The Age of Bronze; or, Carmen Seculare et Annus Haud Mirabilis V
Anonymous

George Gordon, Lord Byron (1788–1824)
Don Juan [cantos vi–viii; ix–xi; xii–xiv] V
Anonymous. Cantos vi–viii published on 15 July 1823; cantos ix–xi, 29 August; cantos xii–xiv, 17 December. See also *Don Juan* 1819 1821, 1824.

George Gordon, Lord Byron (1788–1824)
The Island; or, Christian and His Comrades V

George Gordon, Lord Byron (1788–1824)
Werner: A tragedy D
Not performed until 1830

'Barry Cornwall' [Bryan Waller Procter (1787–1874)**]**
The Flood of Thessaly, The Girl of Provence, and Other Poems V

Sir Aubrey de Vere (1788–1846)
The Duke of Mercia; The Lamentation of Ireland; and Other Poems V

Isaac D'Israeli (1766–1848)
A Second Series of Curiosities of Literature NF
See also *Curiosities of Literature* 1791, 1793, 1817, 1834

Ebenezer Elliott (1781–1849)
Love V

Sir John Franklin (1786–1847)
Narrative of a Journey to the Shores of the Polar Sea NF

John Galt (1779–1839)
The Entail; or, The Lairds of Grippy F
bao *Annals of the Parish*

John Galt (1779–1839)
The Gathering of the West F
bao *The Ayrshire Legatees*

John Galt (1779–1839)
Ringan Gilhaize; or, The Covenanters F
bao *Annals of the Parish*

John Galt (1779–1839)
The Spaewife F
bao *Annals of the Parish*

Basil Hall (1788–1844)
Fragments of Voyages and Travels [1st ser.] NF
Second series published in 1832; third series, 1833

William Hayley (1745–1820)
Memoirs NF

James Haynes (1788–1851)
Durazzo: A tragedy D
Performed November 1838

William Hazlitt (1778–1830)
Characteristics NF

William Hazlitt (1778–1830)
Liber Amoris; or, The New Pygmalion NF
Anonymous

Felicia Dorothea Hemans (1793–1835)
The Siege of Valencia; The Last Constantine; with Other Poems V

Felicia Dorothea Hemans (1793–1835)
The Vespers of Palermo: A tragedy V/D

James Hogg (1770–1835)
The Three Perils of Woman; or, Love, Leasing and Jealousy F
See also *The Three Perils of Man* 1822

Mary Howitt (1799–1888) and **William Howitt** (1792–1879)
The Forest Minstrel, and Other Poems V

Leigh Hunt (1784–1859)
Ultra-Crepidarius V
A satire on William Gifford

James Sheridan Knowles (1784–1862)
Caius Gracchus: A tragedy D
Performed in London on 18 November 1823

Lady Caroline Lamb (1785–1828)
Ada Reis F
Anonymous

Charles Lamb (1775–1834)
Elia [1st ser.] NF
Anonymous. Essays mostly published in the *London Magazine* (August 1820–October 1822). See also *Elia: Second Series* 1828, *Last Essays* 1833.

Charles Lloyd (1775–1839)
Poems V

J.G. Lockhart (1794–1854) (tr.)
Ancient Spanish Ballads, Historical and Romantic ANTH

J.G. Lockhart (1794–1854)
Reginald Dalton F
bao *Valerius,* and *Adam Blair*

T.R. Malthus (1766–1834)
The Measure of Value Stated and Illustrated NF

Mary Russell Mitford (1787–1855)
Julian: A tragedy D

'Thomas Brown the Younger' [Thomas Moore (1779–1852)]
Fables for the Holy Alliance; Rhymes on the Road V

Thomas Moore (1779–1852)
The Loves of the Angels V

Robert Owen (1771–1858)
An Exploration of the Cause of the Distress which Pervades the Civilized Parts of the World NF

Isaac Pocock (1782–1835)
Nigel; or, The Crown Jewels D
Performed 28 January 1823. Based on Scott's *The Fortunes of Nigel* 1822 (q.v.).

Winthrop Mackworth Praed (1802–39)
Lillian V

Sir Walter Scott (1771–1832)
Peveril of the Peak F
bao *Waverley, Kenilworth*, &c. Published in January 1823, dated 1822.

Sir Walter Scott (1771–1832)
Quentin Durward F
bao *Waverley, Peveril of the Peak*, &c. Published in May 1823.

Sir Walter Scott (1771–1832)
Novels and Romances of the Author of Waverley F
Published in December 1823, dated 1824. Contains *The Pirate, The Fortunes of Nigel, Peveril of the Peak, Quentin Durward.*

Sir Walter Scott (1771–1832)
St Ronan's Well F
bao *Waverley, Quentin Durward*, &c. Published in December 1823, dated 1824.

Mary Shelley (1797–1851)
Valperga; or, The Life and Adventures of Castruccio, Prince of Lucca F
bao *Frankenstein*

P.B. Shelley (1792–1822)
Poetical Pieces by the Late Percy Bysshe Shelley V
Contains *Prometheus Unbound* 1820 (q.v.), *Hellas* 1822 (q.v.), *The Cenci* 1819 (q.v.), *Rosalind and Helen* 1819 (q.v.)

Robert Southey (1774–1843)
History of the Peninsular War [vol. i] NF
Volume ii published in 1827 (q.v.), volume iii, 1832 (q.v.)

Catharine G. Ward (*b.* 1787)
The Cottage on the Cliff F

William Wilberforce (1759–1833)
An Appeal to the Inhabitants of the British Empire, in Behalf of the Negro Slaves of the West Indies NF

Helen Maria Williams (1762–1827)
Poems on Various Subjects V

1824

- Death of Louis XVIII; succeeded by Charles X
- William Allingham born
  [William] Wilkie Collins born
  Sydney Thompson Dobell born
  George MacDonald born
  Francis Turner Palgrave born
  Louisa Shore born
- Lord Byron dies at Missolonghi (19 Apr.)
  Robert Charles Dallas dies
  Richard Payne Knight dies
  Sophia Lee dies
  Charles Robert Maturin dies
  Susanna Rowson dies
  Jane Taylor dies
- Anton Bruckner born

The Westminster Review PER
Published quarterly from January 1824. Founded by Jeremy Bentham. Editors included J.S. Mill.

Edwin Atherstone (1788–1872)
A Midsummer Day's Dream V

John Banim (1798–1842)
Revelations of the Dead-Alive F
Anonymous

Bernard Barton (1784–1849)
Poetic Vigils V

Jeremy Bentham (1748–1832)
The Book of Fallacies NF

Robert Bloomfield (1766–1823)
The Remains of Robert Bloomfield V

Sir Samuel Egerton Brydges (1762–1837)
Letters on the Character and Poetical Genius of Lord Byron NF

See also *An Impartial Portrait of Lord Byron* 1825

George Gordon, Lord Byron (1788–1824)
The Deformed Transformed: A drama D
Published in February 1824

George Gordon, Lord Byron (1788–1824)
Don Juan [cantos xv–xvi] V
Anonymous. Published on 26 March 1824. See also *Don Juan* 1819 1821, 1823.

Thomas Campbell (1777–1844)
Miscellaneous Poems V

Thomas Campbell (1777–1844)
Theodric, and Other Poems V

Thomas Carlyle (1795–1881) (tr.)
Wilhelm Meister's Apprenticeship F
Anonymous. Published in May 1824. Translated from J.W. von Goethe's *Wilhelm Meisters Lehrjahre* (1795–6).

William Cowper (1731–1800)
Private Correspondence of William Cowper NF
Includes some poems

Joseph Cradock (1742–1826)
The Czar: An historical tragedy D

John Davison (1777–1832)
Discourses on Prophecy NF

Susan Edmonstone Ferrier (1782–1854)
The Inheritance F
bao *Marriage*

John Galt (1779–1839)
The Bachelor's Wife F

John Galt (1779–1839)
Rothelan F
bao *Annals of the Parish*. Includes three additional tales in volume iii.

Robert Pearse Gillies (1788–1858) (tr.)
The Devil's Elixir F
Anonymous translation of *Die Elixiere des Teufels* (1815–16) by E.T.A. Hoffmann (1776–1822)

Catherine Grace Godwin (1798–1845)
The Night Before the Bridal; Sappho; and Other Poems V
Under the author's maiden name, Catherine Grace Garnett

William Godwin (1756–1836)
History of the Commonwealth of England NF

Catherine Frances Gore (1799–1861)
Theresa Marchmont; or, The Maid of Honour F

William Hazlitt (1778–1830) (ed.)
Select British Poets ANTH

William Hazlitt (1778–1830) (ed.)
Sketches of the Principal Picture-Galleries in England NF

James Hogg (1770–1835)
The Private Memoirs and Confessions of a Justified Sinner F
Anonymous

Theodore Hook (1788–1841)
Sayings and Doings F
Second series published in 1825; third series, 1828 (qq.v)

'L.E.L.' [Letitia Elizabeth Landon (1802–1838)]
The Improvisatrice, and Other Poems V

Walter Savage Landor (1775–1864)
Imaginary Conversations of Literary Men and Statesmen [vols i, ii] NF
Published in March 1824. Essentially personal essays in the form of dialogues between historical characters and having a contemporary, rather than historical, relevance. See also *Imaginary Conversations* 1828, 1829, 1848, 1853, and *Last Fruit* 1853.

J.G. Lockhart (1794–1854)
The History of Matthew Wald F
Anonymous

C.R. Maturin (1782–1824)
The Albigenses F
bao *Bertram, Woman,* &c

Thomas Medwin (1788–1869)
Journal of the Conversations of Lord Byron NF
Fifteen editions between 1824 and 1842

Mary Russell Mitford (1787–1855)
Our Village [vol. i] F
First published in *The Lady's Magazine* from 1819. Volume ii published in 1826; volume iii, 1828; volume iv, 1830; volume v, 1832.

Thomas Moore (1779–1852)
Memoirs of Captain Rock, the Celebrated Irish Chieftain F
Anonymous

James Morier (1780–1849)
The Adventures of Hajji Baba, of Ispahan F
Anonymous. See also *Adventures of Hajji Baba, in England* 1828.

Amelia Opie (1769–1853)
The Negro Boy's Tale V

Sir William Edward Parry (1790–1855)
Journal of a Second Voyage for the Discovery of a North-West Passage NF

Jane Porter (1776–1850)
Duke Christian of Luneburg; or, Tradition From the Harz F

Sir Walter Scott (1771–1832)
Redgauntlet F
bao *Waverley*. Published on 14 June 1824 in Edinburgh.

P.B. Shelley (1792–1822)
Posthumous Poems of Percy Bysshe Shelley V
Contains 'Julian and Maddalo', 'The Witch of Atlas', 'Prince Athanese', 'Ode to Naples', 'Mont Blanc', *Alastor* 1816 (q.v.), 'The Triumph of Life', 'Marianne's Dream', 'Letter to [Maria Gisborne]', and other pieces, including translations

Robert Southey (1774–1843)
The Book of the Church NF
See also Joseph Blanco White, *Practical Internal Evidence* 1825 and Southey, *Vindiciae Ecclesiae Anglicanae* 1826

William Thompson (1775–1833)
An Inquiry into the Principles of the Distribution of Wealth NF

1825

- John Quincy Adams becomes President of the USA
  Bolivia and Uruguay gain independence
  Tsar Alexander I dies; 'Decembrist revolt' following the succession of Nicholas I
  Stockton and Darlington Railway opened
- R.M. Ballantyne born
  Richard Doddridge Blackmore born
  Annie Hector ('Mrs Alexander', *née* French) born
  Thomas Henry Huxley born
  Adelaide Anne Procter born
  William Stubbs born
  Brooke Foss Westcott born
- Anna Laetitia Barbauld dies
  Thomas Bowdler dies
  Henry Fuseli dies
  Samuel Parr dies
- Johann Strauss born
- J.P.F. Richter ('Jean Paul') dies
- Alessandro Manzoni, *I Promessi Sposi* (1825–7)
  Pushkin, *Boris Godunov*

John Banim (1798–1842) and **Michael Banim** (1796–1874)
Tales, by the O'Hara Family F
Published in September 1825. See also *Tales by the O'Hara Family* 1826.

Anna Laetitia Barbauld (1743–1825)
The Works of Anna Laetitia Barbauld WKS
Edited by Lucy Aikin

George Borrow (1803–81) (tr.)
Faustus: His Life, Death and Descent into Hell D
A translation of *Fausts Leben, Thaten und Höllenfahrt* (1791) by Friedrich Maximilian von Klinger (1752–1831)

William Lisle Bowles (1762–1850)
A Final Appeal to the Literary Public, Relative to Pope NF
See also *Invariable Principles* 1819, *Two Letters* 1821, and *Lessons in Criticism* 1826

Henry Brougham (1778–1868)
Practical Observations upon the Education of the People NF
A bestseller. Twenty editions by 1825.

Sir Samuel Egerton Brydges (1762–1837)
An Impartial Portrait of Lord Byron as a Poet and a Man NF
See also *Letters on the Character and Poetical Genius of Lord Byron* 1824

Thomas Carlyle (1795–1881)
The Life of Friedrich Schiller NF
Published in March 1825. A shortened version appeared in the *London Magazine*, 1823–4.

S.T. Coleridge (1772–1834)
Aids to Reflection NF
Published in July 1825

Sara Coleridge (1802–52) (tr.)
The History of the Chevalier Bayard V
Anonymous. Translated from the French of Jacques de Mailles (*fl.* 1527).

Louisa Costello (1799–1879)
Songs of a Stranger V

Allan Cunningham (1784–1842) (ed.)
The Songs of Scotland, Ancient and Modern ANTH

Thomas De Quincey (1785–1859) (tr.)
Walladmor F
Anonymous. A translation of *Walladmor* by G.W.H. Häring, an imitation of Scott's Waverley novels.

Charles Dibdin (1768–1833)
Comic Tales and Lyrical Fancies V

Thomas Doubleday (1790–1870)
Babington: A tragedy D

Alexander Dyce (1798–1869) (ed.)
Specimens of British Poetesses ANTH

Maria Edgeworth (1767–1849)
Harry and Lucy Concluded F
See also *Early Lessons* 1801, *Continuation* 1814, *Rosamond* 1821, *Frank* 1822

Maria Edgeworth (1767–1849)
Tales and Miscellaneous Pieces F
The first collected edition

John Galt (1779–1839)
The Omen F
Anonymous

George Robert Gleig (1796–1888)
The Subaltern F

William Hazlitt (1778–1830)
The Spirit of the Age; or, Contemporary Portraits NF

Felicia Dorothea Hemans (1793–1835)
The Forest Sanctuary, and Other Poems V

Thomas Hood (1799–1845) and **J.H. Reynolds** (1794–1852)
Odes and Addresses to Great People V
Anonymous

Theodore Hook (1788–1841)
Sayings and Doings; or, Sketches from Life F
Anonymous. First series published in 1824; third series, 1828 (qq.v.).

Leigh Hunt (1784–1859) (tr.)
Bacchus in Tuscany V
Translated from the Italian of Francesco Redi (1626–98)

James Sheridan Knowles (1784–1862)
William Tell D
Performed 11 May 1825

'L.E.L.' [Letitia Elizabeth Landon (1802–38)]
The Troubador, Catalogue of Pictures, and Historical Sketches V

James Mill (1773–1836)
Essays on Government, Jurisprudence, Liberty of the Press, Prisons and Prison Discipline, Law of Nations, Education NF
Written for the Supplement to the *Encyclopaedia Britannica*

Thomas Moore (1779–1852)
Memoirs of the Life of Richard Brinsley Sheridan NF

Amelia Opie (1769–1853)
Tales of the Pemberton Family F
For children

Sir Walter Scott (1771–1832)
Tales of the Crusaders F
bao *Waverley, Quentin Durward*. Published in June 1825 in Edinburgh. Comprises 'The Betrothed' and 'The Talisman'.

George Soane (1790–1860)
Faustus: A romantic drama D

Robert Southey (1774–1843)
A Tale of Paraguay V

Connop Thirlwall (1797–1875) (tr.)
The Pictures; The Betrothing F
Anonymous translations of *Die Gemälde* (1823) and *Die Verlobung* (1823) by Ludwig Tieck (1773–1853)

Thomas Wade (1805–75)
Tasso and the Sisters: Tasso's Spirit: The Nuptials of Juno: The Skeletons: The Spirits of the Ocean D

Robert Plumer Ward (1765–1846)
Tremaine; or, The Man of Refinement F
Anonymous

Joseph Blanco White (1775–1841)
Practical Internal Evidence Against Catholicism NF
A reply in part to Charles Butler's *Book of the Roman Church* 1825 itself a response to Southey's *Book of the Church* 1824 (q.v.)

John Wilson (1785–1854)
The Foresters F
bao *Lights and Shadows of Scottish Life, The Trials of Margaret Lyndsay*

1826

- Zoological Society founded by Stamford Raffles
  University College, London, founded
- Charles Hamilton Aïdé born
  Walter Bagehot born
  Rolf Boldrewood (Thomas Alexander Brown) born
  Dina Maria Craik (*née* Mulock) born
  R.H. Hutton born
  Augustus Mayhew born

- William Gifford dies
  Reginald Heber dies
- Gustave Moreau born
- Thomas Jefferson dies
  Carl Maria von Weber dies
- James Fenimore Cooper, *The Last of the Mohicans*

Anonymous
Aben-Hamet, the Last of the Abencerages F
Translation of *Les Aventures du dernier Abencérage* (1826) by François-René de Chateaubriand (1768–1848)

Thomas Aird (1802–76)
Murtzoufle: A tragedy V

Joanna Baillie (1762–1851)
The Martyr D
Unacted

John Banim (1798–1842)
The Boyne Water F
'By the O'Hara Family' (or rather John Banim solely)

John Banim (1798–1842) and **Michael Banim** (1796–1874)
Tales by the O'Hara Family: Second series F
Anonymous. Published in September 1826. See also *Tales, by the O'Hara Family* 1825.

Anna Laetitia Barbauld (1743–1825)
A Legacy for Young Ladies MISC
Edited by Lucy Aikin

George Borrow (1803–81) (tr.)
Romantic Ballads V
Translated from Danish and German

Caroline Bowles, later **Southey** (1786–1854)
Solitary Hours MISC
bao *Ellen Fitzarthur* and *The Widow's Tale*

William Lisle Bowles (1762–1850)
Lessons in Criticism to William Roscoe NF
See also *Invariable Principles* 1819, *Two Letters* 1821, *A Final Appeal* 1825

Anna Eliza Bray (1790–1883)
De Foix; or, Sketches of the Manners and Customs of the Fourteenth Century F

Henry Brougham (1778–1868)
Thoughts on Negro Slavery NF

Elizabeth Barrett Barrett, later **Browning** (1806–61)
An Essay on Mind, with Other Poems V
Anonymous. Published in March 1826.

Selina Bunbury (1802–82)
The Pastor's Tales F
bao *Early Recollections*

John Burke (1787–1848)
A General and Heraldic Dictionary of the Peerage and Baronetage of the United Kingdom DICT

Richard Carlile (1790–1843)
Every Man's Book; or, What is God? NF

'Dr Waters' [**Richard Carlile** (1790–1843)]
The Philosophy of the Sexes; or, Every Woman's Book NF
An early sex manual

William Cobbett (1763–1835)
Cobbett's Poor Man's Friend NF
Issued in five numbers, 1826–7

Henry Nelson Coleridge (1798–1843)
Six Months in the West Indies in 1825 NF
Anonymous

T. Crofton Croker (1798–1854)
Fairy Legends and Traditions of the South of Ireland [vol. i] F
Anonymous. Four of the tales are by William Maginn. Volumes ii and iii published in 1828 (q.v.).

Allan Cunningham (1784–1842)
Paul Jones F

'Guy Penseval' [**George Darley** (1795–1846)]
The Labours of Idleness; or, Seven Nights Entertainments F
See also *The New Sketch Book* 1829

Benjamin Disraeli (1804–81)
Vivian Grey [vols i, ii] F
Anonymous. Volumes iii–v published in 1827 (q.v.).

John Galt (1779–1839)
The Last of the Lairds; or, The Life and Opinions and Malachi Mailings F
bao *Annals of the Parish, The Entail*

William Hazlitt (1778–1830)
Notes of a Journey Through France and Italy NF
Anonymous

William Hazlitt (1778–1830)
The Plain Speaker NF
Anonymous

W.B. Hockley (1792–1860)
Pandurang Hari; or, Memoirs of a Hindoo F

Anonymous. Apparently written by Cyrus Redding, from notes sent from India by Hockley.

James Hogg (1770–1835)
Queen Hynde V

Thomas Hood (1799–1845)
Whims and Oddities MISC
See also *Whims and Oddities* 1827

J.G. Lockhart (1794–1854) and **John Wilson** (1785–1854)
Janus; or, The Edinburgh Literary Almanack NF
Anonymous. Intended as an annual series but no more published.

Henry Hart Milman (1791–1868)
Anne Boleyn V

Mary Russell Mitford (1787–1855)
Foscari: A tragedy D

Amelia Opie (1769–1853)
The Black Man's Lament; or, How to Make Sugar V

Sir William Edward Parry (1790–1855)
Journal of a Third Voyage for the Discovery of a North-West Passage NF

Peter George Patmore (1786–1855)
Rejected Articles NF
Anonymous parodies

Jane Porter (1776–1850) and **Anna Maria Porter** (1780–1832)
Tales Round a Winter Hearth F

Ann Radcliffe (1764–1823)
Gaston de Blondeville; Keeping Festival in Ardenne; St Alban's Abbey MISC
With a memoir by Thomas Noon Talfourd

Sir Walter Scott (1771–1832)
Woodstock; or, The Cavalier F
bao *Waverley, Tales of the Crusaders*. Published in April 1826.

Mary Shelley (1797–1851)
The Last Man F

P.B. Shelley (1792–1822)
Miscellaneous and Posthumous Poems of Percy Bysshe Shelley V
Unauthorized. Selections reissued in 1826 as *Miscellaneous Poems.*

Horatio Smith (1779–1849)
Brambletye House; or, Cavaliers and Roundheads F
'By one of the authors of the *Rejected Addresses*'

Robert Southey (1774–1843)
Vindiciae Ecclesiae Anglicanae NF
See also *The Book of the Church* 1824

Richard Whately (1787–1863)
Elements of Logic NF

1827

- Lord Liverpool resigns as Prime Minister after a stroke
  The Evening Standard started
- Edward Bradley ('Cuthbert Bede') born
  Barbara Bodichon born
  [Edward James] Mortimer Collins born
  George Alfred Lawrence born
  Emily Pfeiffer born
  John Hanning Speke born
- William Blake dies
  George Canning dies
  Helen Maria Williams dies
- William Holman Hunt born
- Ludwig van Beethoven dies

Anonymous
The Military Sketch-Book F
'By an officer of the line'. See also *Tales of Military Life* 1829.

Anonymous
The Natchez: An Indian tale F
Translation of *Les Natchez* (1826) by François-René de Chateaubriand (1768–1848)

Bernard Barton (1784–1849)
A Widow's Tale, and Other Poems V

Jeremy Bentham (1748–1832)
The Rationale of Judicial Evidence NF
Edited by J.S. Mill

Robert Bloomfield (1766–1823)
The Poems of Robert Bloomfield V

Edward Lytton Bulwer, later **Bulwer-Lytton** (1803–73)
Falkland F
Anonymous

Edward Lytton Bulwer, later **Bulwer-Lytton** (1803–73)
O'Neill; or, The Rebel V
Anonymous

Selina Bunbury (1802–82)
Cabin Conversations and Castle Scenes F
bao *Early Recollections, A Visit to my Birth-place*

Lady Charlotte Bury (1775–1861)
Flirtation F
Anonymous

Richard Carlile (1790–1843)
The Gospel According to Richard Carlile NF

Thomas Carlyle (1795–1881)
German Romance ANTH
'By the translator of *Wilhelm Meister*'

John Clare (1793–1864)
The Shepherd's Calendar; with Village Stories and Other Poems V

George Darley (1795–1846)
Sylvia; or, The May Queen V

Thomas John Dibdin (1771–1841)
The Reminiscences of Thomas Dibdin NF

Benjamin Disraeli (1804–81)
Vivian Grey [vols iii, iv, v] F
Anonymous. Volumes i and ii published in 1826 (q.v.).

Maria Edgeworth (1767–1849)
Little Plays for Children D

Catherine Frances Gore (1799–1861)
The Lettre de Cachet; a Tale. The Reign of Terror; a Tale F
Anonymous

Henry Hallam (1777–1859)
The Constitutional History of England NF
To the death of George II

Julius Charles Hare (1795–1855) and **Augustus William Hare** (1792–1834)
Guesses at Truth [1st ser.] NF
Second series published in 1848

Reginald Heber (1783–1826)
Hymns V

Thomas Hood (1799–1845)
National Tales F
Novelettes in the manner of Boccaccio

Thomas Hood (1799–1845)
The Plea of the Midsummer Fairies; Hero and Leander; Lycus the Centaur; and Other Poems V

Thomas Hood (1799–1845)
Whims and Oddities in Prose and Verse [2nd ser.] MISC
See also *Whims and Oddities* 1826

Mary Howitt (1799–1888) and **William Howitt** (1792–1879)
The Desolation of Eyam; The Emigrant: A Tale of the American Woods, and Other Poems V

John Keble (1792–1866)
The Christian Year V
Anonymous. A hundred editions by 1866.

'L.E.L.' [Letitia Elizabeth Landon (1802–38)]
The Golden Violet, and Other Poems V

T.R. Malthus (1766–1834)
Definitions in Political Economy NF

Mary Russell Mitford (1787–1855)
Dramatic Scenes, Sonnets, and Other Poems V

James Montgomery (1771–1854)
The Pelican Island, and Other Poems V

Thomas Moore (1779–1852)
The Epicurean F

Sydney, Lady Morgan, formerly **Owenson** (1783?–1859)
The O'Briens and the O'Flahertys F

Sir Walter Scott (1771–1832)
Tales and Romances of the Author of Waverley F
Published in May 1827 in Edinburgh. Contains *St Ronan's Well, Redgauntlet, Tales of the Crusaders, Woodstock*.

Sir Walter Scott (1771–1832)
The Life of Napoleon Buonaparte NF
bao *Waverley* &c. Published in June 1827 in Edinburgh.

Sir Walter Scott (1771–1832)
Chronicles of the Canongate F
bao *Waverley, &c.* Published in November 1827. Contains 'The Highland Widow', 'The Two Drovers', 'The Surgeon's Daughter'. Second series published in 1828 (q.v.).

Sir Walter Scott (1771–1832)
Tales of a Grandfather NF
Anonymous. Published on 15 December 1827 in Edinburgh, dated 1828. Second series, 1828 (q.v.); third series, 1829 (q.v.); fourth series, 1830 (q.v.).

Robert Southey (1774–1843)
History of the Peninsular War [vol. ii] NF
Volume i published in 1823 (q.v.), volume iii, 1832 (q.v.)

Agnes Strickland (1796–1874)
The Seven Ages of Woman, and Other Poems V

Henry Taylor (1800–86)
Isaac Comnenus D

Alfred Tennyson (1809–92), **Charles Tennyson** (1808–79), and **Frederick Tennyson** (1807–98)
Poems, by Two Brothers V
Anonymous. Published in March 1827. Despite the title, the volume also includes poems by Frederick Tennyson.

Robert Plumer Ward (1765–1846)
De Vere; or, The Man of Independence F
bao *Tremaine*

John Wesley (1703–91)
The Journal of John Wesley NF

William Wordsworth (1770–1850)
The Poetical Works of William Wordsworth V
Text drastically revised from *Miscellaneous Poems* 1820 (q.v.). See also *Poetical Works* 1836, *Poetical Works* 1840, *Poems* 1845, *Poetical Works* 1857, and *Poetical Works* (Centenary Edition) 1870.

1828

- The duke of Wellington forms Tory administration
  Test and Corporation Acts repealed
  Thomas Arnold becomes Head Master of Rugby School
- William Delafield Arnold ('Punjabee') born
  Charles Alston Collins born
  George Meredith born
  Margaret Oliphant (*née* Wilson) born
  Dante Gabriel Rossetti born
  George Augustus Sala born
- Lady Caroline Lamb dies
  Dugald Stewart dies
- Henrik Ibsen born
  Hippolyte-Adolphe Taine born
  Leo Tolstoy born
  Jules Verne born
- Franz Schubert dies

The Athenaeum PER
Published weekly, beginning in January 1828 and continuing until February 1921

The Keepsake PER
Published annually 1828–57. Editors included W.H. Ainsworth (1828); Caroline Norton (1836); and the countess of Blessington (1841–50).

The Spectator PER
Published weekly, beginning 5 July 1828

Anonymous
The English in France F
bao *The English in Italy*. Attributed to Eyre Evans Crowe and also to Constantine Henry Phipps, marquess of Normanby.

Edwin Atherstone (1788–1872)
The Fall of Nineveh V
Books i–xiii. See also *The Fall of Nineveh* 1847.

Joanna Baillie (1762–1851)
The Bride D
Unacted

John Banim (1798–1842)
The Anglo-Irish of the Nineteenth Century F
Anonymous

John Banim (1798–1842) and **Michael Banim** (1796–1874)
The Croppy F
'By the authors of *The O'Hara Tales*, *The Nowlans*, and *The Boyne Water*'

Bernard Barton (1784–1849)
A New Year's Eve, and Other Poems V

Laman Blanchard (1804–45)
Lyric Offerings V

William Lisle Bowles (1762–1850)
Days Departed; or, Banwell Hill V

Anna Eliza Bray (1790–1883)
The White Hoods F

Mary Ann Browne (1812–1844)
Ada, and Other Poems V

Edward Lytton Bulwer, later **Bulwer-Lytton** (1803–73)
Pelham; or, The Adventures of a Gentleman F
Anonymous

Selina Bunbury (1802–82)
The Abbey of Innismoyle F
bao *Early Recollections, A Visit to my Birth-Place*

Thomas Campbell (1777–1844)
The Poetical Works of Thomas Campbell V

William Cobbett (1763–1835)
The English Gardener NF
Published 1828, dated 1829. A revised and enlarged version of *The American Gardener* 1821 (q.v.).

William Cobbett (1763–1835)
A Treatise on Cobbett's Corn NF
The first book printed on paper made from the husks and stalks of corn

S.T. Coleridge (1772–1834)
The Poetical Works of S.T. Coleridge V

George Combe (1788–1858)
The Constitution of Man Considered in Relation to External Objects NF

T. Crofton Croker (1798–1854)
Fairy Legends and Traditions of the South of Ireland [vols ii, iii] F
Anonymous . Volume i published in 1825 (q.v.).

George Croly (1780–1860)
Salathiel F
Anonymous

Nathan Drake (1766–1836) (ed.)
Memorials of Shakespeare ANTH

Thomas Erskine (1788–1870)
The Unconditional Freeness of the Gospel NF

Sir John Franklin (1786–1847)
Narrative of a Second Expedition to the Shores of the Polar Sea NF

James Baillie Fraser (1783–1856)
The Kuzzilbash F
Published anonymously. See also *The Persian Adventurer* 1830.

William Hazlitt (1778–1830)
The Life of Napoleon Buonaparte [vols i, ii] NF
See *Life of Napoleon* volumes iii, iv 1830

Reginald Heber (1783–1826)
Narrative of a Journey Through India 1824–5 NF

Felicia Dorothea Hemans (1793–1835)
Records of Woman, with Other Poems V

Theodore Hook (1788–1841)
Sayings and Doings; or, Sketches from Life F
Anonymous. First series, 1824; second series, 1825 (qq.v.).

Leigh Hunt (1784–1859)
Lord Byron and Some of his Contemporaries NF

Charles Lamb (1775–1834)
Elia: Second series NF
Anonymous. Unauthorized. See *Elia* 1823, *Last Essays* 1833.

'L.E.L.' [Letitia Elizabeth Landon (1802–38)]
The Venetian Bracelet; The Lost Pleiad; A History of the Lyre; and Other Poems V

Walter Savage Landor (1775–1864)
Imaginary Conversations of Literary Men and Statesmen [vol. iii] NF
Published in May 1828. See also *Imaginary Conversations* 1824, 1829, 1848, 1853, and *Last Fruit* 1853.

J.G. Lockhart (1794–1854)
Life of Robert Burns NF

Mary Russell Mitford (1787–1855)
Rienzi: A tragedy D
Performed 9 October 1828

Robert Montgomery (1807–55)
The Omnipresence of the Deity V

James Morier (1780–1849)
The Adventures of Hajji Baba, of Ispahan, in England F
Anonymous. See *Adventures of Hajji Baba* 1824.

Sir William Napier (1785–1860)
History of the War in the Peninsula and the South of France NF

Sir William Edward Parry (1790–1855)
Narrative of an Attempt to Reach the North Pole NF

Thomas Jeffery Llewelyn Prichard (1790–1862)
The Adventures and Vagaries of Twm Shon Catti F
Sometimes said to be the first novel in English by a Welsh author

Samuel Rogers (1763–1855)
Italy: a Poem. Part the Second V
Part the First published in 1822 (q.v.)

Sir Walter Scott (1771–1832)
Chronicles of the Canongate: Second series F
bao *Waverley*, &c. Published in May 1828. Comprises 'Saint Valentine's Day; or, The Fair Maid of Perth'.

Sir Walter Scott (1771–1832)
Religious Discourses NF

Sir Walter Scott (1771–1832)
Tales of a Grandfather. Second Series NF
Published on 27 November 1828 in Edinburgh, dated 1829. First series, 1827 (q.v.); third series, 1829 (q.v.); fourth series, 1830 (q.v.).

Dugald Stewart (1753–1828)
The Philosophy of the Active and Moral Powers of Man NF

Richard Whately (1787–1863)
Elements of Rhetoric NF

1829

- Andrew Jackson becomes President of the USA
  Catholic Emancipation in Britain
  First Oxford and Cambridge boat race
  Stephenson's *Rocket* wins the Liverpool–Manchester Railway competition (Oct.)
- William Booth born
  Samuel Rawson Gardiner born
  Laurence Oliphant born
  William Michael Rossetti born
  Sir James Fitzjames Stephen born
- Sir Humphry Davy dies
  Sir Uvedale Price dies
- William Booth born
  John Everett Millais born
- Goethe, *Wilhelm Meisters Wanderjahre*

Anonymous
Tales of Military Life F
bao *The Military Sketch-Book* 1827 (q.v.). Attributed, probably erroneously, to William Maginn.

Dr Thomas Arnold (1795–1842)
Sermons NF
Published in 3 volumes (1823–34)

Caroline Bowles, later **Southey** (1786–1854)
Chapters on Churchyards F
bao *Ellen Fitzarthur, Widow's Tale, Solitary Hours, &c*

Edward Lytton Bulwer, later **Bulwer-Lytton** (1803–73)
Devereux F
bao *Pelham*

Edward Lytton Bulwer, later **Bulwer-Lytton** (1803–73)
The Disowned F
bao *Pelham*

Selina Bunbury (1802–82)
Retrospections F
bao *A Visit to my Birth-Place, Abbey of Innismoyle*

William Carleton (1794–1869)
Father Butler; The Lough Dearg Pilgrim F
Anonymous

William Cobbett (1763–1835)
The Emigrant's Guide NF

George Crabbe (1754–1832)
The Poetical Works of George Crabbe V
The first one-volume collected works

Allan Cunningham (1784–1842)
Lives of the Most Eminent British Painters, Sculptors and Architects NF

'Geoffrey Crayon jun.' [George Darley (1795–1846)]
The New Sketch Book NF

Thomas Doubleday (1790–1870)
Dioclesian V

Ebenezer Elliott (1781–1849)
The Village Patriarch V

Catherine Frances Gore (1799–1861)
Romances of Real Life F
bao *Hungarian Tales*

Anna Maria Hall [Mrs S.C. Hall] (1800–81)
Sketches of Irish Character F

Basil Hall (1788–1844)
Travels in North America in the Years 1827 and 1828 NF

Reginald Heber (1783–1826)
Sermons Preached in England NF

James Hogg (1770–1835)
The Shepherd's Calendar NF

Thomas Hood (1799–1845)
The Epping Hunt V
Illustrated by George Cruikshank

Thomas Hood (1799–1845) (ed.)
The Gem PER
A literary annual published 1829–32

G.P.R. James (1799–1860)
Richelieu F
Anonymous

Douglas Jerrold (1803–57)
Black-Eyed Susan; or, All in the Downs D
Performed 8 June 1829

Walter Savage Landor (1775–1864)
Imaginary Conversations of Literary Men and Statesmen: Second Series [vols iv, v] NF
Published in May 1829. See also *Imaginary Conversations* 1824 1828, 1848, 1853, and *Last Fruit* 1853.

J.G. Lockhart (1794–1854)
The History of Napoleon Buonaparte NF
Anonymous

Frederick Marryat (1792–1848)
The Naval Officer; or, Scenes and Adventures in the Life of Frank Mildmay F
Anonymous

James Mill (1773–1836)
Analysis of the Phenomena of the Human Mind NF

Henry Hart Milman (1791–1868)
The History of the Jews NF
Anonymous

Caroline Norton (1808–77)
The Sorrows of Rosalie: A Tale; with Other Poems V
Anonymous

Thomas Love Peacock (1785–1866)
The Misfortunes of Elphin F
bao *Headlong Hall*

Sir Walter Scott (1771–1832)
Anne of Geierstein; or, The Maiden of the Mist F
bao *Waverley, &c.* Published in May 1829.

Sir Walter Scott (1771–1832)
Tales of a Grandfather [3rd ser.] NF
Anonymous. Published on 21 December 1829, dated 1830. First series, 1827 (q.v.); second series, 1828 (q.v.); fourth series, 1830 (q.v.).

Sir Walter Scott (1771–1832)
Waverley Novels F
The 'Magnum Opus' Edition (48 volumes, 1829–33, with Scott's last revisions and notes. The first two volumes, comprising *Waverley*, were published on 1 June 1829. Successive volumes were published at monthly intervals, beginning on 1 August 1829 and concluding in May 1833. Later collected editions include the Centenary Edition (1870–1) with revised text, and the Dryburgh Edition (1892–4), with further revisions.

Robert Southey (1774–1843)
Sir Thomas More; or, Colloquies on the Progress and Prospects of Society NF

Isaac Taylor (1787–1865)
The Natural History of Enthusiasm NF
Anonymous. See also *Fanaticism* 1833 and *Spiritual Despotism* 1835.

Alfred Tennyson (1809–92)
Timbuctoo V
In *Prolusiones Academicae*, which also contains poems by C.R. Kennedy and C. Merivale. First printed in the *Cambridge Chronicle* (10 July 1829).

Thomas Wade (1805–75)
Woman's Love; or, The Triumph of Patience D
Performed 17 December 1828

1830

- Death of George IV (26 June)
  WILLIAM IV (–1837)
  Revolution in France (July): abdication of Charles X of France; succeeded by Louis Philippe, duke of Orleans
  William Huskisson killed by a train at the opening of the Liverpool–Manchester Railway
  Resignation of the duke of Wellington as Prime Minister
  Belgian independence
  King's College, London, founded
- Thomas Edward Brown born
  Frederick Greenwood born
  Henry Kingsley born
  Justin McCarthy born
  James Payn born
  Christina Rossetti born
  Alexander Smith born
- Henrietta Bowdler dies
  William Hazlitt dies
- Jules de Goncourt born
- Benjamin Constant dies
  Simón Bolívar dies
- Victor Hugo, *Hernani*
  Stendhal, *Le Rouge et le Noir*

Fraser's Magazine PER
Published monthly from February 1830

Thomas Aird (1802–76)
The Captive of Fez V

Edwin Atherstone (1788–1872)
The Sea-Kings in England F
bao *The Fall of Nineveh*

Edward Lytton Bulwer, later **Bulwer-Lytton** (1803–73)
Paul Clifford F
bao *Pelham, Devereux*. Published in May 1830.

George Gordon, Lord Byron (1788–1824)
Letters and Journals of Lord Byron NF
Edited by Thomas Moore

William Carleton (1794–1869)
Traits and Stories of the Irish Peasantry [1st ser.] F
Anonymous. See also *Traits and Stories* 1833

William Cobbett (1763–1835)
Advice to Young Men NF
Published 1830, dated 1829. First issued in parts, 1829–30.

William Cobbett (1763–1835)
Eleven Lectures on the French and Belgian Revolutions NF
First issued in parts (September–October 1830)

William Cobbett (1763–1835)
History of the Regency and Reign of King George the Fourth NF

William Cobbett (1763–1835)
Rural Rides NF
First published intermittently in the *Political Register*, 1821–6

S.T. Coleridge (1772–1834) and **Robert Southey** (1774–1843)
The Devil's Walk V
Anonymous. Published in July 1830. Original version published in the *Morning Post* (6 September 1799) as 'The Devil's Thoughts'.

S.T. Coleridge (1772–1834)
On the Constitution of the Church and State NF

George Lillie Craik (1798–1866)
The Pursuit of Knowledge Under Difficulties NF
Anonymous. See also *The Pursuit of Knowledge* 1847.

George Croly (1780–1860)
Poetical Works V

Ebenezer Elliott (1781–1849)
Corn Law Rhymes: The Ranter V

James Baillie Fraser (1783–1856)
The Persian Adventurer F
bao *A Tour to the Himala Mountains*, *Travels in Persia*, etc. A sequel to *The Kuzzilbash* 1828 (q.v.).

Caroline Fry (1787–1846)
The Listener MISC
Anonymous. Many editions.

John Galt (1779–1839)
Lawrie Todd; or, The Settlers in the Woods F
Anonymous

John Galt (1779–1839)
The Life of Lord Byron NF

William Godwin (1756–1836)
Cloudesley F
bao *Caleb Williams*

Catherine Frances Gore (1799–1861)
Women As They Are; or, The Manners of the Day F
Anonymous

William Hazlitt (1778–1830)
Conversations of James Northcote NF

William Hazlitt (1778–1830)
The Life of Napoleon Buonaparte [vols iii, iv] NF
See *Life of Napoleon* volumes i, ii 1828

Felicia Dorothea Hemans (1793–1835)
Songs of the Affections, with Other Poems V

John Abraham Heraud (1799–1887)
The Descent into Hell V
Anonymous

Sir John Herschel (1792–1871)
A Preliminary Discourse on the Study of Natural Philosophy NF

Thomas Hood (1799–1845) (ed.)
The Comic Annual PER
Published 1830–9, 1842

Theodore Hook (1788–1841)
Maxwell F
bao *Sayings and Doings*

G.P.R. James (1799–1860)
Darnley; or, The Field of the Cloth of Gold F
bao *Richelieu*

G.P.R. James (1799–1860)
De l'Orme F
bao *Richelieu*, and *Darnley*

Sir Charles Lyell (1797–1875)
Principles of Geology NF

Frederick Marryat (1792–1848)
The King's Own F
bao *The Naval Officer*

Harriet Martineau (1802–76)
Traditions of Palestine NF

Robert Montgomery (1807–55)
Satan V

Anna Maria Porter (1780–1832)
The Barony F

Sir Walter Scott (1771–1832)
The Doom of Devorgoil; Auchindrane; or, The Ayrshire Tragedy D
Published in April 1830

Sir Walter Scott (1771–1832)
Letters on Demonology and Witchcraft NF
Published in September 1830

Sir Walter Scott (1771–1832)
Tales of a Grandfather [4th ser.] NF

Published on 21 December 1830, dated 1831. First series, 1827 (q.v.); second series, 1828 (q.v.); third series, 1829 (q.v.).

Mary Shelley (1797–1851)
The Fortunes of Perkin Warbeck F
bao *Frankenstein*

Alfred Tennyson (1809–92)
Poems, Chiefly Lyrical V
Published in September 1830. Includes 'Mariana', 'The Kraken'. See also *Poems* 1842.

Charles Tennyson, later **Turner** (1808–79)
Sonnets and Fugitive Pieces V

1831

- Bristol riots following defeat of first and second Reform Bills
  Charles Darwin leaves on HMS *Beagle*
  Third Reform Bill introduced in the House of Commons
- Amelia Barr born
  Isabella Bird born
  Isabel Burton, Lady Burton (*née* Arundell), born
  Edward Robert Bulwer, Earl Lytton ('Owen Meredith') born
  Charles Calverley born
  Amelia Edwards born
  Frederic William Farrar born
  George Manville Fenn born
  William Hale White ('Mark Rutherford') born
  Edmund Yates born
- Henry Mackenzie dies
  William Roscoe dies
  Sarah Siddons dies
- Hegel dies
- Balzac, *La Peau de chagrin*
  John Cumberland's *Minor Theatre*
  Victor Hugo, *Notre-Dame de Paris*

Figaro in London PER
Published December 1831–August 1839. Edited by Gilbert Abbott à Beckett 1831–4.

John Banim (1798–1842)
The Smuggler F
bao *Tales by the O'Hara Family*

John Banim (1798–1842) and **Michael Banim** (1796–1874)
The Chaunt of the Cholera V
'By the authors of *The O'Hara Tales, The Smuggler*'

Sir John Barrow (1764–1848)
The Eventful History of the Mutiny and Piratical Seizure of HMS Bounty NF

Henry Glassford Bell (1803–74)
Summer and Winter Hours V

David Brewster (1781–1868)
The Life of Sir Isaac Newton NF

David Brewster (1781–1868)
A Treatise on Optics NF

Thomas Campbell (1777–1844)
Poland: A Poem. Lines on the View from St Leonard's V

William Cobbett (1763–1835)
Cobbett's Two-Penny Trash; or, Politics for the Poor NF
First issued in parts (July 1830–July 1832)

William Cobbett (1763–1835)
A Spelling Book NF

Benjamin Disraeli (1804–81)
The Young Duke F
Anonymous

Susan Edmonstone Ferrier (1782–1854)
Destiny; or, The Chief's Daughter F
bao *Marriage*, and *The Inheritance*

John Galt (1779–1839)
Bogle Corbet; or The Emigrants F
bao *Lawrie Todd, The Life of Lord Byron*

John Galt (1779–1839)
The Lives of the Players NF

William Godwin (1756–1836)
Thoughts on Man, his Nature, Productions and Discoveries NF

Catherine Frances Gore (1799–1861)
Mothers and Daughters: A tale of the year 1830 F
Anonymous

James Hogg (1770–1835)
Songs, by the Ettrick Shepherd V

Thomas Hood (1799–1845)
The Dream of Eugene Aram: the Murderer V
First published in *The Gem* for 1829

G.P.R. James (1799–1860)
Philip Augustus; or, The Brothers in Arms F
bao *Darnley, De l'Orme*

Charles Lamb (1775–1834)
Satan in Search of a Wife V
Anonymous. Cf. the title of Hannah More's *Coelebs in Search of a Wife* 1809 (q.v.).

'L.E.L.' [Letitia Elizabeth Landon (1802–38)]
Romance and Reality F

Walter Savage Landor (1775–1864)
Gebir, Count Julian and Other Poems V
Gebir first published in 1798 (q.v.); *Count Julian* published 1812 (q.v.)

Frederick Marryat (1792–1848)
Newton Forster; or, The Merchant Service F
bao *The King's Own*. Published 1831, dated 1832.

Harriet Martineau (1802–76)
Five Years of Youth; or, Sense and Sentiment F

W. Johnson Neale (1812–93)
Cavendish; or, The Patrician at Sea F

Thomas Love Peacock (1785–1866)
Crotchet Castle F
bao *Headlong Hall*

Anna Maria Porter (1780–1832)
The Tuileries F

Winthrop Mackworth Praed (1802–39)
The Ascent of Elijah V

Mary Prince
The History of Mary Prince, a West Indian Slave NF
Edited by the anti-slavery campaigner Thomas Pringle (1789–1834)

Sir Walter Scott (1771–1832)
Tales of My Landlord: Fourth and Last Series F
Published in December 1831, dated 1832. Comprises 'Count Robert of Paris' and 'Castle Dangerous'. First series, 1816; (q.v.); second series, 1818 (q.v.); third series, 1819 (q.v.).

E.J. Trelawny (1792–1881)
Adventures of a Younger Son F
Anonymous

1832

- Reform Bill passes the House of Lords (4 June)
  Greek independence recognized
  Mazzini founds 'Young Italy'
  Andrew Jackson elected for second term as US President
- Sir Edwin Arnold born
  Stopford Augustus Brooke born
  Lewis Carroll (Charles Lutwidge Dodgson) born
  G.A. Henty born
  Charlotte Elizabeth Riddell (Mrs J.H. Riddell, *née* Cowan) born
  Sir Leslie Stephen born
  Theodore Watts-Dunton born
- Jeremy Bentham dies
  George Crabbe dies
  Francis Lathom dies
  Anna Maria Porter dies
  Sir Walter Scott dies
- Goethe dies; *Faust ii*

Chambers's Edinburgh Journal PER
Published weekly, beginning in February 1832

W.E. Aytoun (1813–65)
Poland, Homer, and Other Poems V

Charles Babbage (1792–1871)
On the Economy of Machinery and Manufactures NF

Henry Glassford Bell (1803–74)
My Old Portfolio; or, Tales and Sketches V

William Lisle Bowles (1762–1850)
St John in Patmos V
Anonymous

Sir David Brewster (1781–1868)
Letters on Natural Magic NF
Addressed to Sir Walter Scott

Edward Lytton Bulwer, later **Bulwer-Lytton** (1803–73)
Eugene Aram F
bao *Pelham, Devereux*. Published on 1 January 1832.

Frances Burney (1752–1840)
Memoirs of Dr Burney NF
'By Madame d'Arblay'

Frederick Chamier (1796–1870)
The Life of a Sailor F
'By a Captain in the Navy'

William Cobbett (1763–1835)
Cobbett's Manchester Lectures NF

William Cobbett (1763–1835)
A Geographical Dictionary of England and Wales NF

'Barry Cornwall' [Bryan Waller Procter (1787–1874)]
English Songs V

Thomas De Quincey (1785–1859)
Klosterheim; or, The Masque D
'By the English Opium-Eater'

Thomas Frognall Dibdin (1776–1847)
Bibliophobia NF
Anonymous

Benjamin Disraeli (1804–81)
Contarini Fleming F
Anonymous

Maria Edgeworth (1767–1849)
Garry Owen; or, The Snow-Woman; and Poor Bob, the Chimney-Sweeper F

John Galt (1779–1839)
The Member F
bao *The Ayrshire Legatees*

'The Ettrick Shepherd' [James Hogg (1770–1835)]
Altrive Tales V

Leigh Hunt (1784–1859)
Christianism; or, Belief and Unbelief Reconciled NF
Limited edition, not for sale. Enlarged in 1853 as *The Religion of the Heart.*

Leigh Hunt (1784–1859)
The Poetical Works of Leigh Hunt V

G.P.R. James (1799–1860)
Henry Masterton; or, The Adventures of a Young Cavalier F
bao *Richelieu, Darnley*

Anna Jameson (1794–1860)
Characteristics of Women, Moral, Poetical and Historical NF

Frances Kemble (1809–93)
Francis the First: An historical drama D
Performed 15 March 1832

James Sheridan Knowles (1784–1862)
The Hunchback D
Performed 5 April 1832

Harriet Martineau (1802–76)
Illustrations of Political Economy F

Thomas Miller (1807–74)
Songs of the Sea Nymphs V

James Morier (1780–1849)
Zohrab the Hostage F
bao *Hajji Baba*

P.B. Shelley (1792–1822)
The Masque of Anarchy V
Preface by Leigh Hunt

Robert Southey (1774–1843)
Essays, Moral and Political NF

Robert Southey (1774–1843)
History of the Peninsular War [vol. iii] NF
Volume i published in 1823 (q.v.); volume ii, 1827 (q.v.)

Alfred Tennyson (1809–92)
Poems V
Published in December 1832, dated 1833. Includes 'The Lady of Shalott', 'Mariana in the South', 'Oenone', 'The Palace of Art', 'The Lotos-Eaters', 'A Dream of Fair Women'. See also *Poems* 1842.

Frances Trollope (1779–1863)
Domestic Manners of the Americans NF

Frances Trollope (1779–1863)
The Refugee in America F

1833

- Lord Ashley (later earl of Shaftesbury) introduces the Factory Act, providing restrictions on the employment of women and children
  John Keble's sermon on National Apostasy (14 July): start of the Oxford Movement
  Dramatic Copyright Act and foundation of Dramatic Authors' Society
- Richard Watson Dixon born
- Charles Isaac Munro Dibdin dies
  Arthur Henry Hallam dies
  Hannah More dies
  William Sotheby dies
  William Wilberforce dies
- Johannes Brahms born
  Edward Burne-Jones born
- Balzac, *Eugénie Grandet*
  Charles Knight's *Penny Cyclopaedia* (–1844)
  Pushkin, *The Queen of Spades*

The Dublin University Magazine PER
Published monthly, beginning in January 1833, concluding in December 1877. Edited by J.S. Le Fanu, 1861–70.

Michael Banim (1796–1874)
The Ghost-Hunter and His Family F
'By John [or rather Michael solely] Banim author of *Tales by the O'Hara Family*'

Edward Bickersteth (1786–1850)
Christian Psalmody V

Marguerite Gardiner, countess of Blessington (1789–1849)
The Repealers F
A *roman à clef.* The second edition of 1834 was published as *Grace Cassidy; or, The Repealers.*

Caroline Bowles, later **Southey** (1786–1854)
Tales of the Factories V
bao *Ellen Fitzarthur, The Widow's Tale, Solitary Hours*

Elizabeth Barrett Barrett, later **Browning** (1806–61) (tr.)
Prometheus Bound V
Anonymous. Published in May 1833. Translated from Aeschylus.

Robert Browning (1812–89)
Pauline: A fragment of a confession V
Anonymous. Browning's first published poem. Not reprinted until *Poetical Works* 1868 (q.v.), with apologetic preface and minor revisions.

Edward Lytton Bulwer, later **Bulwer-Lytton** (1803–73)
England and the English NF
Published in July 1833

Edward Lytton Bulwer, later **Bulwer-Lytton** (1803–73)
Godolphin F
Anonymous

Selina Bunbury (1802–82)
Tales of My Country F
bao *Early Recollections*

William Carleton (1794–1869)
Traits and Stories of the Irish Peasantry [2nd ser.] F
See also *Traits and Stories* 1830

Charles Cowden Clarke (1787–1877)
Tales From Chaucer, in Prose F
For young people

William Cobbett (1763–1835)
Cobbett's Tour in Scotland NF

Hartley Coleridge (1796–1849)
Biographia Borealis; or, Lives of Distinguished Northerns NF

Hartley Coleridge (1796–1849)
Poems V

Allan Cunningham (1784–1842)
The Maid of Elvar V

Benjamin Disraeli (1804–81)
Ixion in Heaven F
Serialized in the *New Monthly Magazine* (December 1832–February 1833)

Benjamin Disraeli (1804–81)
The Wondrous Tale of Alroy. The Rise of Iskander F
bao *Vivian Grey, Contarini Fleming*. Published on 5 March 1833.

Ebenezer Elliott (1781–1849)
The Splendid Village; Corn Law Rhymes; and Other Poems V

John Galt (1779–1839)
The Autobiography of John Galt NF

John Galt (1779–1839)
Eben Erskine; or, The Traveller F
bao *The Ayrshire Legatees, Lawrie Todd, Stanley Buxton*

William Godwin (1756–1836)
Deloraine F

Felicia Dorothea Hemans (1793–1835)
Hymns on the Works of Nature V

R.H. Horne (1803–84)
Exposition of the False Medium and Barriers Excluding Men of Genius From the Public NF
Anonymous

John Keble (1792–1866)
National Apostasy NF
A sermon preached in Oxford on 14 July 1833

Charles Lamb (1775–1834)
The Last Essays of Elia NF
Mostly first published in the *London Magazine*. Preface by 'A Friend of the Late Elia' (i.e. Lamb himself).

Frederick Marryat (1792–1848)
Peter Simple F
bao *Newton Forster*. First serialized in the *Metropolitan Magazine* (June 1832–December 1833).

Thomas Medwin (1788–1869)
The Shelley Papers NF
First published in *The Athenaeum*, 1832–3

Robert Montgomery (1807–55)
Woman: The Angel of Life V

Thomas Moore (1779–1852)
Travels of an Irish Gentleman in Search of a Religion NF
'By the editor of Captain Rock's Memoirs'. See also Joseph Blanco White, *Second Travels of an Irish Gentleman* 1833.

W. Johnson Neale (1812–93)
The Port Admiral F
Anonymous

John Henry Newman, later **Cardinal** (1801–90)
The Arians of the Fourth Century NF

Leman Rede (1802–47)
The Rake's Progress D
Performed 28 January 1833

Sir Walter Scott (1771–1832)
Tales and Romances of the Author of Waverley F
Published in May 1833. Contains *Chronicles of the Canongate, Tales of my Landlord* [fourth series].

Sir Walter Scott (1771–1832)
The Poetical Works of Sir Walter Scott, Bart. V
The final revised edition (12 volumes, 1833–4), edited by J.G. Lockhart and illustrated by J.M.W. Turner. Volume i published on 1 May 1833; volume xii, 1 April 1834.

Robert Southey (1774–1843)
Lives of the British Admirals [vols i, ii] NF
Volume iii published in 1834, volume iv, 1837, volume v, 1840 (continued by R. Bell)

Isaac Taylor (1787–1865)
Fanaticism NF
bao *Natural History of Enthusiasm*. See also *The Natural History of Enthusiasm* 1830 and *Spiritual Despotism* 1835.

Horace Walpole (1717–97)
Letters to Sir Horace Mann NF

Joseph Blanco White (1775–1841)
Second Travels of an Irish Gentleman in Search of a Religion NF
Written in answer to Thomas Moore's *Travels of an Irish Gentleman* 1833 (q.v.)

1834

- The 'Tolpuddle Martyrs' sentenced to transportation
  Civil War in Spain breaks out
  Houses of Parliament destroyed by fire
  Resignation of Lord Melbourne: Tory administration formed by Robert Peel
  Chimney Sweeps Act
  Abolition of slavery in all British possessions
- John Emerich Acton, Lord Acton, born
  Sabine Baring-Gould born
  George du Maurier born
  William Morris born
  Sir John Seeley born
  J.H. Shorthouse born
  Charles Spurgeon born
  James Thomson born
- Samuel Taylor Coleridge dies
  Augustus Hare dies
  Charles Lamb dies
  Thomas Malthus dies
  John Thelwall dies
- Edgar Degas born
  James MacNeil Whistler born
- Balzac, *Le Père Goriot* (1834–5)

Gilbert Abbott à Beckett (1811–56)
The Revolt of the Workhouse D/OP
Performed 24 February 1834. Acknowledged by Dickens as an influence on *Oliver Twist* 1838 (q.v.).

W.H. Ainsworth (1805–82)
Rookwood F
Anonymous. Published in May 1834.

William Beckford (1760–1844)
Italy; with Sketches of Spain and Portugal NF
bao *Vathek*

Jeremy Bentham (1748–1832)
Deontology; or, Science of Morality NF

John Stuart Blackie (1809–95) (tr.)
Faust: a Tragedy D
Translated from J.W. von Goethe (1749–1832)

Marguerite Gardiner, countess of Blessington (1789–1849)
Conversations of Lord Byron with the Countess of Blessington NF
Serialized in the *New Monthly Magazine*, 1832–3

Anna Eliza Bray (1790–1883)
Trials of Domestic Life F

Sir Samuel Egerton Brydges (1762–1837)
Autobiography NF

Edward Lytton Bulwer, later **Bulwer-Lytton** (1803–73)
The Last Days of Pompeii F
bao *Pelham, Eugene Aram*. Published in September 1834.

Edward Lytton Bulwer, later **Bulwer-Lytton** (1803–73)
The Pilgrims of the Rhine F
bao *Pelham*

Thomas Carlyle (1795–81)
Sartor Resartus NF
Privately printed. First serialized in *Fraser's Magazine* (November 1833–August 1834). See also *Sartor Resartus* 1838.

Sara Coleridge (1802–52)
Pretty Lessons in Verse for Good Children V

George Crabbe (1754–1832)
The Poetical Works of George Crabbe V

Published in 8 volumes (February–September 1834). With letters, journals, and life by Crabbe's son.

Isaac D'Israeli (1766–1848)
Curiosities of Literature NF
The first two series combined. See also *Curiosities of Literature* 1791, 1793, 1817, 1823.

Maria Edgeworth (1767–1849)
Helen F

Charlotte Elliott (1789–1871) (ed.)
The Invalid's Hymn Book ANTH

Catherine Frances Gore (1799–1861)
The Hamiltons; or, The New Era F
bao *Mothers and Daughters*

A.H. Hallam (1811–33)
Remains in Verse and Prose MISC
Includes a memoir by Henry Hallam

R.S. Hawker (1803–75)
Records of the Western Shore V

Felicia Dorothea Hemans (1793–1835)
National Lyrics, and Songs for Music V

Felicia Dorothea Hemans (1793–1835)
Scenes and Hymns of Life V

James Hogg (1770–1835)
The Domestic Manners and Private Life of Sir Walter Scott NF

Thomas Hood (1799–1845)
Tylney Hall F

Mary Howitt (1799–1888)
The Seven Temptations V

John Keble (1792–1866)
Tracts for the Times [Nos 4, 13, 40, 52, 54, 57, 60] NF
The ninety Tracts for the Times were published between 9 September 1833 and 27 February 1841. See also Keble, Tract 89, 1841.

Walter Savage Landor (1775–1864)
Citation and Examination of Wil. Shakespeare, NF
Anonymous. A piece in the syle of Landor's imaginary conversations. Also contains 'A Conference of Master Edmund Spenser, with the Earl of Essex'.

Frederick Marryat (1792–1848)
Jacob Faithful F

F.D. Maurice (1805–72)
Eustace Conway; or, The Brother and Sister F
Anonymous

Richard Monckton Milnes (1809–85)
Memorials of a Tour in Some Parts of Greece, Chiefly Poetical V

Mary Russell Mitford (1787–1855)
Charles the First: An historical tragedy D
Performed 9 July 1834

James Morier (1780–1849)
Ayesha, the Maid of Kars F
bao *Zohrab*

Amelia Opie (1769–1853)
Lays for the Dead V

Sir Walter Scott (1771–1832)
The Miscellaneous Prose Works of Sir Walter Scott NF
The final revised edition (28 volumes, 1834–6), edited by J.G. Lockhart. Volume i published on 1 May 1834; the remaining volumes appearing monthly thereafter, concluding 1 August 1836.

P.B. Shelley (1792–1822)
The Works of Percy Bysshe Shelley, with his Life V
Unauthorized. Selections reissued 1834 as *Posthumous Poems.*

Robert Southey (1774–1843)
The Doctor [vols i, ii] NF
Volume iii published in 1835 (q.v.); volume iv, 1837 (q.v.); volume v, 1838 (q.v.); volumes vi and vii published poshtumously in 1847 (q.v.)

Robert Southey (1774–1843)
Lives of the British Admirals [vol. iii] NF
Volumes i and ii published in 1833 (q.v.); volume iv, 1837 (q.v.); volume v, 1840 (continued by R. Bell)

Henry Taylor (1800–86)
Philip van Artevelde V

1835

- Robert Peel resigns: Lord Melbourne forms Whig ministry
  New York Herald first published
- Alfred Austin born
  Mary Elizabeth Braddon born
  Samuel Butler born
  Edward Caird born
  Emily Faithfull born
  Richard Garnett born
  Thomas (Tom) Hood born
  Mark Twain (Samuel Clemens) born
- William Cobbett dies
  Felicia Dorothea Hemans dies

James Hogg dies
William Henry Ireland dies
Thomas Taylor ('The Platonist') dies

- Gogol, *Dead Souls*

'Nimrod' [Charles James Apperley (1779–1843)]
Memoirs of the Life of John Mytton NF
Reprinted from the *New Sporting Magazine*

'Nimrod' [Charles James Apperley (1779–1843)]
Nimrod's Hunting Tours NF

Michael Banim (1796–1874)
The Mayor of Windgap F

William Beckford (1760–1844)
Recollections of an Excursion to the Monasteries of Alcobaça and Batalha NF
bao *Vathek*

'Isaac Tomkins, Gent.' [Henry Brougham, Baron Brougham and **Vaux** (1778–1868)]
Thoughts upon the Aristocracy of England NF
See also *'We Can't Afford It'* 1835, below

'Isaac Tomkins, Gent.' [Henry Brougham, Baron Brougham and **Vaux** (1778–1868)]
'We Can't Afford It!' NF
Part ii of *Thoughts upon the Aristocracy of England* 1835 (see above)

Robert Browning (1812–89)
Paracelsus V
Reprinted in *Poems* 1849 (q.v.)

Edward Lytton Bulwer, later **Bulwer-Lytton** (1803–73)
Rienzi, the Last of the Tribunes F
bao *Eugene Aram, Last Days of Pompeii*

Maria, Lady Callcott (1785–1842)
Little Arthur's History of England NF

Richard Carlile (1790–1843)
Church Reform NF

John Clare (1793–1864)
The Rural Muse V

William Cobbett (1763–1835)
Cobbett's Legacy to Labourers NF
Published 1835, dated 1834

William Cobbett (1763–1835)
Cobbett's Legacy to Parsons NF

Richard Cobden (1804–65)
England, Ireland, and America NF
'By a Manchester Manufacturer'

S.T. Coleridge (1772–1834)
Specimens of the Table Talk of the Late Samuel Taylor Coleridge NF
Edited by H.N. Coleridge. Coleridge died in July 1834.

Eliza Cook (1818–89)
Lays of a Wild Harp V

William Cowper (1731–1800)
The Works of William Cowper WKS
Edited (in 15 volumes, 1835–7) by Robert Southey

George Darley (1795–1846)
Nepenthe V

Felicia Dorothea Hemans (1793–1835)
Poetical Remains V

James Hogg (1770–1835)
Tales of the Wars of Montrose F

Leigh Hunt (1784–1859)
Captain Sword and Captain Pen V

Frances Kemble (1809–93)
Journal NF

Charles Lamb (1775–1834)
Recollections of Christ's Hospital NF
The *Recollections* were first published in 1813. The volume also reprints *Rosamund Gray* 1798 (q.v.) and other pieces.

'L.E.L.' [Letitia Elizabeth Landon (1802–38)]
The Vow of the Peacock, and Other Poems V

Frederick Marryat (1792–1848)
The Pacha of Many Tales F
bao *Peter Simple, Jacob Faithful.* Collects stories first published in the *Metropolitan Magazine,* 1831–5.

Frederick Marryat (1792–1848)
The Pirate and the Three Cutters F
Published 1835, dated 1836

Mary Russell Mitford (1787–1855)
Belford Regis; or, Sketches of a Country Town F

Thomas Moore (1779–1852)
The Fudges in England V
See *The Fudge Family in Paris* 1818

Sydney, Lady Morgan, formerly **Owenson** (1783?–1859)
The Princess; or, The Beguine F

Caroline Norton (1808–77)
The Wife, and Woman's Reward F
Anonymous

John Oxenford (1812–77)
My Fellow Clerk: A farce D
Performed 20 April 1835

A.W.N. Pugin (1812–52)
Gothic Furniture in the Style of the 15th Century NF
Published in two parts, 1835–6

Mary Shelley (1797–1851)
Lodore F
bao *Frankenstein*

Robert Southey (1774–1843)
The Doctor [vol. iii] NF
Volumes i, ii published in 1834 (q.v.); volume iv, 1837 (q.v.); volume v, 1838 (q.v.); volumes vi and vii published posthumously in 1847 (q.v.)

Isaac Taylor (1787–1865)
Spiritual Despotism NF
bao *Natural History of Enthusiasm*. See also *The Natural History of Enthusiasm* 1830 and *Fanaticism* 1833.

Connop Thirlwall (1797–1875)
A History of Greece NF
Published in 8 volumes (1835–44)

Joseph Blanco White (1775–1841)
Observations on Heresy and Orthodoxy NF

William Wordsworth (1770–1850)
A Guide Through the District of the Lakes in the North of England NF
Enlarged version of *A Description of the Scenery of the Lakes* 1822 (q.v.). See also *The River Duddon* 1820.

William Wordsworth (1770–1850)
Yarrow Revisited, and Other Poems V

1836

- Texas declares independence from Mexico
  Beginning of the Chartist movement (-1848)
  Irish Constabulary formed (Royal Irish Constabulary from 1867)
- Isabella Beeton (*née* Mayson) born
  Sir Walter Besant born
  Matilda Betham-Edwards born
  Francis Cowley Burnand born
  William Schwenck Gilbert born
  Francis Bret Harte born
- George Colman, the younger, dies
  Richard Hurrell Froude dies
  William Godwin dies
  James Mill dies
  Charles Simeon dies
  William Taylor dies

Bernard Barton (1784–1849)
The Reliquary V
Written with Lucy Barton

Thomas Haynes Bayly (1797–1839)
Perfection; or, The Lady of Munster D
Performed 25 March 1830

Marguerite Gardiner, countess of Blessington (1789–1849)
The Confessions of an Elderly Gentleman F
See also *Confessions of an Elderly Lady* 1838

Edward Lytton Bulwer, later **Bulwer-Lytton** (1803–73)
The Duchess de la Vallière D
bao *Eugene Aram, The Last Days of Pompeii, Rienzi*. Performed 4 January 1837.

Frederick Chamier (1796–1870)
Ben Brace F

S.T. Coleridge (1772–1834)
Letters, Conversations and Recollections of S.T. Coleridge NF

S.T. Coleridge (1772–1834)
The Literary Remains of Samuel Taylor Coleridge [vols i, ii] NF
Edited by H.N. Coleridge. See also *Literary Remains* 1838 and 1839.

'Boz' [Charles Dickens (1812–70)]
Sketches by 'Boz' [1st ser.] F
Published on 8 February 1836. Dickens's first book, illustrated by George Cruikshank. Contains previous published sketches and stories and three new pieces written for the volume. See also below.

'Boz' [Charles Dickens (1812–70)]
Sketches by 'Boz' [2nd ser.] F
Published on 17 December 1836, dated 1837. Illustrated by George Cruikshank. See above.

Benjamin Disraeli (1804–81)
Henrietta Temple F
bao *Vivian Grey*. Published in December 1836, dated 1837.

Benjamin Disraeli (1804–81)
The Letters of Runnymede NF
Anonymous. First published in *The Times*.

Catherine Frances Gore (1799–1861)
Mrs Armytage; or, Female Domination F
bao *Mothers and Daughters*

William Hazlitt (1778–1830)
Essays on the Principles of Human Action NF

Edited by Hazlitt's son William (1811–93). See also *Essay on the Principles of Human Action* 1805.

William Hazlitt (1778–1830)
Literary Remains of the Late William Hazlitt NF

Theodore Hook (1788–1841)
Gilbert Gurney F
bao *Sayings and Doings*. See also *Gurney Married* 1838.

Edward Howard (1793?–1841)
Rattlin the Reefer F
'Edited by the author of Peter Simple'—i.e. fallaciously ascribing the book to Captain Marryat, Howard's friend and colleague. Partly serialized in the *Metropolitan Magazine*, 1834–6.

Mary Howitt (1799–1888)
Wood Leighton; or, A Year in the Country F

'L.E.L.' [Letitia Elizabeth Landon (1802–38)]
Traits and Trials of Early Life F/V

Walter Savage Landor (1775–1864)
The Letters of a Conservative NF

Walter Savage Landor (1775–1864)
Pericles and Aspasia F
Imaginary letters

Walter Savage Landor (1775–1864)
A Satire on Satirists, and Admonition to Detractors V

Frederick Marryat (1792–1848)
Japhet in Search of a Father F
bao *Peter Simple, Jacob Faithful*. Serialized in the *Metropolitan Magazine*, 1834–6.

Frederick Marryat (1792–1848)
Mr Midshipman Easy F
bao *Peter Simple, Jacob Faithful*. One instalment published in the *Metropolitan Magazine* (July 1836).

James Martineau (1805–1900)
The Rationale of Religious Enquiry NF

John Henry Newman (1801–90) and others
Lyra Apostolica V
Contains 109 poems by Newman, including the untitled hymn now known as 'Lead, Kindly Light' (first published anonymously as 'Faith' in the *British Magazine* in February 1834). Most of Newman's poems were republished in *Verses on Various Occasions* 1868.

Caroline Norton (1808–77)
A Voice From the Factories V

A.W.N. Pugin (1812–52)
Contrasts. Or, a parallel between the noble edifices of the fourteenth and fifteenth centuries and similar buildings of the present day NF

Nassau W. Senior (1790–1864)
An Outline of the Science of Political Economy NF
Offprint of an article published in the *Encyclopaedia Metropolitana*

Catherine Sinclair (1800–64)
Modern Accomplishments; or, The March of Intellect F
See also *Modern Society* 1837

Thomas Noon Talfourd (1795–1854)
Ion: A tragedy D
Performed 26 May 1836. First printed for private circulation in 1835.

Frances Trollope (1779–1863)
The Life and Adventures of Jonathan Jefferson Whitlaw; or, Scenes on the Mississippi F

William Wordsworth (1770–1850)
The Poetical Works of William Wordsworth V
Published in 6 volumes (1836–7). Text further revised from *Poetical Works* 1827. Reissued with corrections in 1839. See also *Miscellaneous Poems* 1820, *Poetical Works* 1840, *Poems* 1845, *Poetical Works* 1857, and *Poetical Works* (Centenary Edition) 1870.

1837

- Martin Van Buren becomes President of the USA
  Death of William IV (20 June)
  VICTORIA (–1901)
- Gilbert Arthur à Beckett born
  Anne Isabella Ritchie, Lady Ritchie (*née* Thackeray) born
  Algernon Charles Swinburne born
  Augusta Webster ('Cecil Home', *née* Davies) born
- Sir Samuel Egerton Brydges dies
  Ellis Cornelia Knight dies
  William Dean Howells born
- John Constable dies
  Alexander Pushkin dies

Bentley's Miscellany PER
Published monthly, beginning in January 1837. Edited by Charles Dickens, 1837–January 1839, and by W.H. Ainsworth, 1839–41.

W.H. Ainsworth (1805–82)
Crichton F
Published on 27 February 1837

Robert Browning (1812–89)
Strafford: An historical tragedy V
Performed 1 May 1837

Edward Lytton Bulwer, later **Bulwer-Lytton** (1803–73)
Ernest Maltravers F
bao *Pelham, Eugne Aram, Rienzi.* See also *Alice* 1838.

George Gordon, Lord Byron (1788–1824)
Dramas V

Thomas Campbell (1777–1844)
Letters From the South NF

Thomas Carlyle (1795–1881)
The French Revolution NF
Published in May 1837

Frederick Chamier (1796–1870)
The Arethusa F

Georgiana, Lady Chatterton (1806–76)
Aunt Dorothy's Tale; or, Geraldine Morton F

Sara Coleridge (1802–52)
Phantasmion F
Anonymous

Joseph Cottle (1770–1853)
Early Recollections: Chiefly relating to the late Samuel Taylor Coleridge NF
Reprinted in 1847 as *Reminiscences of Samuel Taylor Coleridge and Robert Southey*

'Boz' [**Charles Dickens** (1812–70)]
The Posthumous Papers of the Pickwick Club F
Published on 17 November 1837, illustrated by Robert Seymour and Hablot K. Browne ('Phiz'). First published in parts (31 March 1836–30 October 1837).

Benjamin Disraeli (1804–81)
Venetia; or, The Poet's Daughter F
bao *Vivian Grey* and *Henrietta Temple*

Catherine Frances Gore (1799–1861)
Stokeshill Place; or, The Man of Business F
bao *Mrs Armytage, Mothers and Daughters*

Theodore Hook (1788–1841)
Jack Brag F
bao *Sayings and Doings*

Edward Howard (1793?–1841)
The Old Commodore F
bao *Rattlin the Reefer*

James Sheridan Knowles (1784–1862)
The Love-Chase: A comedy D
Performed 9 October 1837

Charles Lamb (1775–1834)
The Letters of Charles Lamb NF
With a life by Thomas Noon Talfourd

Letitia Elizabeth Landon (1802–38)
Ethel Churchill; or, The Two Brides F
bao *The Improvisatrice, Francesca Carrara*

Walter Savage Landor (1775–1864)
The Pentameron and Pentalogia NF/F
Anonymous. The 'Pentameron' consists of imaginary conversations between Boccaccio and Petrach; the 'Pentalogia' contains five dramatic scenes between Essex and Bacon, Walter Tyrrel and William Rufus, the parents of Luther, and Orestes and Electra.

J.G. Lockhart (1794–1854)
Memoirs of the Life of Sir Walter Scott NF

Samuel Lover (1797–1868)
Rory O'More F
Based on one of Lover's own ballads and subsequently dramatized (performed 29 September 1837)

Frederick Marryat (1792–1848)
Snarleyyow; or, The Dog Fiend F
bao *Peter Simple, Frank Mildmay.* First serialized in the *Metropolitan Magazine* (February 1836–July 1837).

Harriet Martineau (1802–76)
Society in America NF

Mary Russell Mitford (1787–1855)
Country Stories F

Lady Mary Wortley Montagu (1689–1762)
Letters and Works WKS
Includes introductory anecdotes by Lady Louisa Stuart. See also *Works* 1803.

W. Johnson Neale (1812–93)
Gentleman Jack F
bao *Cavendish*

Mary Shelley (1797–1851)
Falkner F
bao *Frankenstein*

Catherine Sinclair (1800–64)
Modern Society; or, The March of Intellect F
Sequel to *Modern Accomplishments* 1836 (q.v.)

Robert Southey (1774–1843)
The Doctor [vol. iv] NF
Volumes i, ii published in 1834 (q.v.); volume iii, 1835 (q.v.); volume v, 1838 (q.v.); volumes vi and vii published posthumously in 1847 (q.v.)

Robert Southey (1774–1843)
Lives of the British Admirals [vol. iv] NF
Volumes i and ii published in 1833 (q.v.); volume iii, 1834 (q.v.); volume v, 1840 (continued by R. Bell)

Robert Southey (1774–1843)
The Poetical Works of Robert Southey [vols i, ii] V
Volumes iii–x published in 1838 (q.v.)

William Whewell (1794–1866)
The History of the Inductive Sciences NF
See also *Philosophy of the Inductive Sciences* 1840

1838

- First Afghan War
  Public Record Office established
  English HIstorical Society founded
  Camden Society publications begin
- Benjamin Leopold Farjeon born
  William Edward Lecky born
  Florence Marryat born
  John Morley, 1st Viscount Morley, born
  [William] Winwood Reade born
  Henry Sidgwick born
  Sir George Otto Trevelyan born
- Letitia Elizabeth Landon dies
  Thomas Morton dies
- Georges Bizet born
  Henry Irving born

'Nimrod' [Charles James Apperley (1779–1843)]
Nimrod's Northern Tour NF

John Banim (1798–1842)
The Bit o' Writin', and Other Tales F
'By the O'Hara Family' (or rather John Banim solely)

Alexander Bethune (1804–43)
Tales and Sketches of the Scottish Peasantry V
Written with John Bethune

Marguerite Gardiner, countess of Blessington (1789–1849)
The Confessions of an Elderly Lady F
See also *Confessions of an Elderly Gentleman* 1836

Elizabeth Barrett Barrett, later **Browning** (1806–61)
The Seraphim, and Other Poems V
Published in June 1838

Edward Lytton Bulwer, later **Bulwer-Lytton** (1803–73)
Alice; or, The Mysteries F
bao *Pelham, Rienzi, The Student.* See also *Ernest Maltravers* 1837.

Edward Lytton Bulwer, later **Bulwer-Lytton** (1803–73)
The Lady of Lyons; or, Love and Pride D
bao *Eugene Aram.* Performed 15 February 1838.

Edward Lytton Bulwer, later **Bulwer-Lytton** (1803–73)
Leila; Calderon the Courtier F
bao *Eugene Aram, Rienzi*

Thomas Carlyle (1795–1881)
Sartor Resartus NF
First English trade edition (privately printed in 1834, q.v.). First published in the USA, 1836.

S.T. Coleridge (1772–1834)
The Literary Remains of Samuel Taylor Coleridge [vol. iii] NF
Edited by H.N. Coleridge. See also *Literary Remains* 1836 and 1839.

Charles Darwin (1809–82) (ed.)
The Zoology of the Voyage of HMS Beagle NF
Consists of i: *Fossil Mammalia* by Richard Owen (1840), with geological introduction by Darwin; ii: *Mammalia* by George R. Waterhouse, with notice by Darwin (1839); iii: *Birds* by John Gould, with notice by Darwin (1841); iv: *Fish* by Leonard Jenyns (1842); v: *Reptiles* by Thomas Bell (1843)

'Boz' [Charles Dickens (1812–70)]
Oliver Twist; or, The Parish Boy's Progress F
Published on 9 November 1838. Illustrated by George Cruikshank. First serialized in *Bentley's Miscellany* (31 January 1837–April 1839 [except June and October 1837, and September 1838]); later published in ten monthly parts (January–October 1846).

R.H. Froude (1803–36)
Remains of the late Richard Hurrell Froude MISC
Edited by John Keble and John Henry Newman

W.E. Gladstone (1809–98)
The State in its Relations with the Church NF

Catherine Frances Gore (1799–1861)
The Woman of the World F
bao *Diary of a Désennuyé*

Lady Charlotte Guest (1812–95) (tr.)
The Mabinogion F
See also *Mabinogion* 1877

Charles Hennell (1809–50)
An Inquiry Concerning the Origin of Christianity NF

Theodore Hook (1788–1841)
Gurney Married F
bao *Sayings and Doings*. See *Gilbert Gurney* 1836.

Edward Howard (1793?–1841)
Outward Bound; or, A Merchant's Adventures F
bao *Rattlin the Reefer, The Old Commodore*. Partly serialized in the *Metropolitan Magazine* as *Ardent Troughton*.

G.P.R. James (1799–1860)
The Robber F
bao *Richelieu, The Gipsy, Attila*

Letitia Elizabeth Landon (1802–38)
Duty and Inclination F

Sir Charles Lyell (1797–1875)
Elements of Geology NF

Robert Southey (1774–1843)
The Doctor [vol. v] NF
Volumes i, ii published in 1834 (q.v.); volume iii, 1835 (q.v.); volume iv, 1837 (q.v.); volumes vi and vii published posthumously in 1847 (q.v.)

Robert Southey (1774–1843)
The Poetical Works of Robert Southey, [vols iii–x] V
Volumes i and ii published in 1837 (q.v.)

R.S. Surtees (1805–64)
Jorrocks' Jaunts and Jollities F
Illustrated by Hablot K. Browne ('Phiz'). First serialized in the *New Sporting Magazine* (July 1831–September 1834).

'Arthur Pendennis, Esq.' [W.M. Thackeray (1811–63)]
The Yellowplush Correspondence F
Papers first published in *Fraser's Magazine* (November 1837, January–July 1838). The first appearance in book form of any of Thackeray's work, published in Philadelphia. First published in book form in England in *Comic Tales and Sketches* 1841 (q.v.).

Martin Farquhar Tupper (1810–89)
Proverbial Philosophy MISC
Three series, 1838–67; complete, 1876. Many editions.

Isaac Williams (1802–65)
The Cathedral; or, The Catholic and Apostolic Church in England V

William Wordsworth (1770–1850)
The Sonnets of William Wordsworth V

1839

- William Fox Talbot announces a system of making photographic prints on silver chloride paper (Jan.)
  National Convention of Chartists (Feb.)
  Chartist riots
  Anglo-Chinese Opium War breaks out
  National Anti-Corn Law League, led by Richard Cobden, established
- William de Morgan born
  Mary Louisa Molesworth (*née* Stewart) born
  'Ouida' (Marie Louise de la Ramée) born
  Walter Pater born
- John Galt dies
  Charles Lloyd dies
  Mary Pilkington dies
  James Smith dies
  Winthrop Mackworth Praed dies
- Paul Cézanne born
- Stendhal, *La Chartreuse de Parme*

W.H. Ainsworth (1805–82)
Jack Sheppard F
Published in October 1839 illustrated by George Cruikshank. First serialized in *Bentley's Miscellany* (January 1839–February 1840).

Philip James Bailey (1816–1902)
Festus V
Numerous editions to 1889 (the 50th anniversary edition)

Marguerite Gardiner, countess of Blessington (1789–1849)
The Governess F

Marguerite Gardiner, countess of Blessington (1789–1849)
The Idler in Italy NF

Anna Eliza Bray (1790–1883)
Trials of the Heart F
Anonymous

Edward Lytton Bulwer, later **Bulwer-Lytton** (1803–73)
Richelieu; or, The Conspiracy D
bao *The Lady of Lyons, Eugene Aram*. Performed 7 March 1839.

Lady [Rosina] Bulwer-Lytton (1802–82)
Cheveley; or, The Man of Honour F

Robert Burns (1759–96)
The Prose Works of Robert Burns NF

Edited by Robert Chambers. See also *Life and Works* 1851.

William Carleton (1794–1869)
Fardorougha the Miser; or, The Convicts of Lisnamona F
Serialized in the *Dublin University Magazine* (February–May 1837, December 1837-February 1838)

Thomas Carlyle (1795–1881)
Critical and Miscellaneous Essays NF
Published September 1839. First published in the USA, 1838.

Thomas Carlyle (1795–1881)
Chartism NF
Published in December 1839, dated 1840

S.T. Coleridge (1772–1834)
The Literary Remains of Samuel Taylor Coleridge [vol. iv] NF
Edited by H.N. Coleridge. See also *Literary Remains* 1836 and 1838.

'Boz' [Charles Dickens (1812–70)**]**
Nicholas Nickleby F
Published on 23 October 1839. Illustrated by Hablot K. Browne ('Phiz'). First published in separate parts (31 March 1838–1 October 1839). Wrapper title: *The Life and Adventures of Nicholas Nickleby.*

Sarah Ellis, formerly **Stickney** (1812–72)
The Women of England NF
See also *The Daughters of England* 1842

Michael Faraday (1791–1867)
Experimental Researches in Electricity NF

Catherine Frances Gore (1799–1861)
The Cabinet Minister F
bao *Mothers and Daughters*

William Hazlitt (1778–1830)
Sketches and Essays NF

Walter Savage Landor (1775–1864)
Andrea of Hungary, and Giovanna of Naples D
The first two parts of a trilogy. See also *Fra Rupert* 1840.

Charles Lever (1806–72)
The Confessions of Harry Lorrequer F
'Edited by Harry Lorrequer'. Serialized in the *Dublin University Magazine* (irregularly February 1837–June 1842) and published in monthly parts (March 1839–January 1840), illustrated by Hablot K. Browne ('Phiz').

Frederick Marryat (1792–1848)
A Diary in America, with Remarks on its Institutions NF

Frederick Marryat (1792–1848)
The Phantom Ship F
First serialized in the *New Monthly Magazine* (March 1837–August 1839)

Harriet Martineau (1802–76)
Deerbrook F

Henry Hart Milman (1791–1868)
Poetical Works V

Thomas Moore (1779–1852)
Alciphron V
Illustrated by J.M.W. Turner. Also includes *The Epicurean* (first published in 1827, q.v.).

W. Johnson Neale (1812–83)
The Flying Dutchman F
bao *Cavendish*

John Henry Newman (1801–90) and others
Plain Sermons by Contributors to the 'Tracts for the Times' NF
Sermons by John Keble, Isaac Williams, E.B. Pusey, Newman, Thomas Keble, Sir George Prevost, and Robert Francis Wilson (indicated by the letters A, B, C, D, E, F, G respectively)

G.W.M. Reynolds (1814–79)
Alfred de Rosann; or, The Adventures of a French Gentleman F

G.W.M. Reynolds (1814–79)
Grace Darling; or, The Heroine of the Fern Islands F

G.W.M. Reynolds (1814–79)
Pickwick Abroad; or, The Tour in France F
First published in monthly numbers, 1838–9

P.B. Shelley (1792–1822)
The Poetical Works of Percy Bysshe Shelley V
Edited by Mary Shelley, with preface and notes. Reprinted in 1847 (q.v.) with *Essays, Letters from Abroad, Translations and Fragments* 1840 (q.v.).

Sydney Smith (1771–1845)
The Works of the Rev. Sydney Smith NF

Philip Meadows Taylor (1808–76)
Confessions of a Thug F
Published in September 1839

'Ikey Solomons, Esq., Jr' [W.M. Thackeray (1811–63)**]**
Catherine F
Serialization in *Fraser's Magazine* (May 1839–February 1840). Reprinted, 1869.

Frances Trollope (1779–1863)
The Widow Barnaby F
See also *The Widow Married* 1840, *The Barnabys in America* 1843

1840

- Queen Victoria marries Prince Albert of Saxe-Coburg-Gotha (10 Feb.)
  End of Carlist wars in Spain
  Attempted rising by Louis Napoleon fails
  The Tablet begins publication
- Wilfrid Scawen Blunt born
  Rhoda Broughton born
  Rosa Nouchette Cary born
  Austin Dobson born
  Thomas Hardy born
  John Addington Symonds born
- Frances Burney (Madame D'Arblay) dies
- Henry Morton Stanley born
- Claude Monet born
  Auguste Rodin born
  Piotr Ilyich Tchaikovsky born
  Émile Zola born
- Edgar Allan Poe, *Tales of the Grotesque and Arabesque*

W.H. Ainsworth (1805–82)
The Tower of London F
Published in December 1840. Illustrated by George Cruikshank. First published in monthly parts (January–December 1840).

Thomas Aird (1802–76)
Orthuriel, and Other Poems V

Matthew Arnold (1822–88)
Alaric at Rome V

'Thomas Ingoldsby' [R.H. Barham (1788–1845)]
The Ingoldsby Legends; or, Mirth and Marvels [1st ser.] MISC
First published in *Bentley's Miscellany*. See also *Ingoldsby Legends* 1842, 1847.

Robert Browning (1812–89)
Sordello V

Edward Lytton Bulwer, later **Bulwer-Lytton** (1803–73)
Money D
bao *The Lady of Lyons*. Performed 8 December 1840.

Lady [Rosina] Bulwer-Lytton (1802–82)
The Budget of the Bubble Family F

Lady Charlotte Bury (1775–1861)
The History of a Flirt, Related by Herself F
Anonymous

Frederick Chamier (1796–1870)
The Spitfire F

'V' [Caroline Clive (1801–73)**]**
IX Poems by 'V' V

S.T. Coleridge (1772–1834)
Confessions of an Inquiring Spirit NF
Edited by H.N. Coleridge

Charles Dickens (1812–70)
Master Humphrey's Clock [vol. i] F
Published in October 1840. Illustrated by Hablot K. Browne ('Phiz') and George Cattermole. First published in weekly numbers (from 4 April 1840), then in twenty monthly parts (April 1840–November 1841). Volume ii published in 1841 (q.v.).

Frederick William Faber (1814–63)
The Cherwell Water-Lily, and Other Poems V

Theodore Hook (1788–1841)
Precepts and Practice F
Illustrated by Hablot K. Browne ('Phiz')

Walter Savage Landor (1775–1864)
Fra Rupert D
The final part of a trilogy: see also *Andrea of Hungary* 1839

Frederick Marryat (1792–1848)
Olla Podrida MISC

Henry Hart Milman (1791–1868)
The History of Christianity NF

Thomas Moore (1779–1852)
The Poetical Works of Thomas Moore V
Published in 10 volumes (1840–1)

Robert Owen (1771–1858)
Manifesto of Robert Owen NF

Robert Owen (1771–1858)
The Social Bible V

P.B. Shelley (1792–1822)
Essays, Letters from Abroad, Translations and Fragments MISC
Edited by Mary Shelley. Includes 'The Defence of Poetry' (written 1821 in reply to Peacock's 'Four Ages of Poetry' 1820, q.v.).

James Smith (1775–1839)
Comic Miscellanies MISC
Edited by Horatio [Horace] Smith

W.M. Thackeray (1811–63)
An Essay on the Genius of George Cruikshank NF
Anonymous. First published in the *Westminster Review* (June 1840).

'Mr Titmarsh' [W.M. Thackeray (1811–63)**]**
The Paris Sketch Book NF
Illustrated by Thackeray

Frances Trollope (1779–1863)
The Life and Adventures of Michael Armstrong: the Factory Boy F
First published in monthly parts (March 1839–February 1840)

Frances Trollope (1779–1863)
The Widow Married F
Sequel to *The Widow Barnaby* 1839 (q.v.). See also *The Barnabys in America* 1843.

William Whewell (1794–1866)
The Philosophy of the Inductive Sciences NF
See also *History of the Inductive Sciences* 1837

William Wordsworth (1770–1850)
The Poetical Works of William Wordsworth V
In six volumes. Includes supplement to volume v containing twelve sonnets from *The Sonnets of William Wordsworth* 1838 (q.v.). Reprinted in 1841 and 1842 (with additional volume consisting of *Poems, Chiefly of Early and Late Years* [1842]). See also *Miscellaneous Poems* 1820, *Poetical Works* 1827, *Poetical Works* 1836, *Poems* 1845, *Poetical Works* 1857, *Poetical Works* (Centenary Edition) 1870.

1841

- Britain claims sovereignty over Hong Kong
  John Tyler becomes President of the USA after the death of W.H. Harrison
  Second Afghan war begins (-1842)
  Jewish Chronicle begins publication
  New York Tribune started
- William Black born
  Mathilde Blind born
  Robert Buchanan born
  Julia Horatia Ewing born
  William Henry Hudson born
  Rosa Mulholland, Lady Gilbert, born
- Charlotte Dacre dies
  Thomas John Dibdin dies
  Theodore Hook dies
  Joseph Blanco White dies
- Sir Henry Morton Stanley born
- Bradshaw's first *Railway Guide*

Punch: or the London Charivari PER
Published from 17 July 1841 onwards. Edited by Mark Lemon 1841–70, C.W. Shirley Brooks 1870–4, Tom Taylor 1874–80, and F.C. Burnand 1880–1906. Ceased publication in 1992; relaunched 1996.

Sarah Flower Adams (1805–48)
Vivia Perpetua: A dramatic poem V

W.H. Ainsworth (1805–82)
Guy Fawkes; or, The Gunpowder Treason F
Published on 29 July 1841. Illustrated by George Cruikshank. Serialized in *Bentley's Miscellany* (January 1840–November 1841).

W.H. Ainsworth (1805–82)
Old Saint Paul's F
First serialized in the *Sunday Times* (January–December 1841) and published in monthly parts over same period.

'Thomas Ingoldsby' [R.H. Barham (1788–1845)**]**
Some Account of My Cousin Nicholas F
Serialized in *Blackwood's Magazine*

E.L.L. Blanchard (1820–89)
The Life of George Barnwell; or, The London Apprentice of the Last Century F

George Borrow (1803–81)
The Zincali; or, An Account of the Gypsies of Spain NF
Published in April 1841

Dion Boucicault (1820?–90)
London Assurance: A comedy D
Performed 4 March 1841

Robert Browning (1812–89)
Pippa Passes [*Bells and Pomegranates* i] D
Reprinted, with considerable revisions, in *Poems* 1849 (q.v.). See also *Bells and Pomegranates* 1842, 1843, 1844, 1845, 1846.

Thomas Carlyle (1795–1881)
On Heroes, Hero-Worship, and the Heroic in History NF
Collection of lectures delivered in May 1840

Frederick Chamier (1796–1870)
Tom Bowling F

Catherine Crowe (1790–1876)
Adventures of Susan Hopley; or, Circumstantial Evidence F
Anonymous

Charles Dickens (1812–70)
Master Humphrey's Clock [vols ii, iii] F
Volume ii published in April 1841; volume iii, December 1841. Volume i published 1840 (q.v.).

Charles Dickens (1812–70)
Barnaby Rudge: A tale of the riots of 'eighty F
Published on 15 December 1841. Illustrated by Hablot K. Browne ('Phiz') and George Cattermole. First published in weekly numbers in *Master Humphrey's Clock* (13 February–27 November 1841) and in monthly parts. Also published in volumes ii and iii of the book edition of *Master Humphrey's Clock* 1841.

Charles Dickens (1812–70)
The Old Curiosity Shop F
Published on 15 December 1841. Illustrated by Hablot K. Browne ('Phiz') and George Cattermole. First published in weekly numbers in *Master Humphrey's Clock* (25 April 1840–6 February 1841) and in monthly parts. Also published in volumes i and ii of the book edition of *Master Humphrey's Clock* 1841.

Isaac D'Israeli (1766–1848)
Amenities of Literature NF

Elizabeth, Lady Eastlake (1809–93)
A Residence on the Shores of the Baltic NF

W.J. Fox (1786–1864) (comp.)
Hymns and Anthems ANTH
Contains 150 numbered hymns without music, thirteen of which are by Sarah Flower Adams, including 'Nearer, my God, to thee'

Catherine Frances Gore (1799–1861)
Cecil; or, The Adventures of a Coxcomb F
Anonymous. See also *Cecil a Peer*, below.

Catherine Frances Gore (1799–1861)
Cecil a Peer F
See also *Cecil*, above

Catherine Frances Gore (1799–1861)
Greville; or, A Season in Paris F

J.O. Halliwell-Phillipps (1820–89)
Shakesperiana NF

John Keble (1792–1866)
Tracts for the Times [No. 89] NF
The ninety *Tracts for the Times were* published between 9 September 1833 and 27 February 1841. See also Keble 1834.

James Sheridan Knowles (1784–1862)
Dramatic Works WKS

Charles Lever (1806–72)
Charles O'Malley, the Irish Dragoon F
'Edited by Harry Lorrequer'. Illustrated by Hablot K. Browne ('Phiz'). Serialized in the *Dublin University Magazine* (March 1840–December 1841) and published in monthly parts over same period.

Frederick Marryat (1792–1848)
Masterman Ready; or, The Wreck of the Pacific F
Published in three separate volumes (May 1841, April 1842, and December 1842)

Harriet Martineau (1802–76)
The Hour and the Man F
Based on the life of Toussaint L'Ouverture (1743?–1803)

James Morier (1780–1849)
The Mirza F

W. Johnson Neale (1812–93)
The Naval Surgeon F
Anonymous

W. Johnson Neale (1812–93)
Paul Periwinkle; or, The Press Gang F
bao *Cavendish*. Illustrated by Hablot K. Browne ('Phiz').

John Henry Newman, later **Cardinal** (1801–90)
Remarks on Certain Passages in the Thirty-Nine Articles NF
Tracts for the Times 90 (27 February 1841)

Arthur Philip Perceval (1799–1853)
A Vindication of the Principles of the Authors of the Tracts for the Times NF

A.W.N. Pugin (1812–52)
The True Principles of Pointed or Christian Architecture NF

Horatio Smith (1779–1849)
The Moneyed Man; or, The Lesson of a Life F

Philip Meadows Taylor (1808–76)
Tippoo Sultaun F
Published 1841, dated 1840

'Michael Angelo Titmarsh' [**W.M. Thackeray** (1811–63)]
Comic Tales and Sketches F
Illustrated by Thackeray. Papers previously published in magazines.

W.M. Thackeray (1811–63)
The History of Samuel Titmarsh and the Great Hoggarty Diamond F
Serialization in *Fraser's Magazine* (September–December 1841). Published in book form in the USA (1848) as *The Great Hoggarty Diamond*, and in Britain (1849) under the original title.

'Mr M.A. Titmarsh' [**W.M. Thackeray** (1811–63)]
The Second Funeral of Napoleon MISC

W.M. Thackeray (1811–63)
Some Passages in the Life of Major Gahagan F
Serialized in the *New Monthly Magazine* (February 1838–February 1839)

'Charlotte Elizabeth' [**Charlotte Elizabeth Tonna** (1790–1846)]
Helen Fleetwood: A tale of the factories F

Robert Plumer Ward (1765–1846)
De Clifford; or, The Constant Man F
bao *Tremaine*

Samuel Warren (1807–77)
Ten Thousand a-Year F
Anonymous. Serialized in *Blackwood's Magazine* (October 1839–August 1841). One of the most popular comic novels of the 19th century.

1842

- Copyright Act (extending protection to 42 years from publication or 7 years after author's death)
  Mines Act introduced by Lord Ashley (later the earl of Shaftesbury), forbidding the employment of women underground, and of boys under the age of 10
  Treaty of Nanking ends Anglo-Chinese War
- Harry Buxton Forman born
- Dr Thomas Arnold dies
  Allan Cunningham dies
  John Banim dies
  Charles Armitage Brown dies
  Allan Cunningham dies
  William Hone dies
  William Maginn dies
- William James born
  Stéphane Mallarmé born
- Stendhal dies

The Illustrated London News PER
Published weekly from 14 May 1842

Robert Armitage (1805–52)
Doctor Hookwell; or, The Anglo-Catholic Family F
Anonymous

Michael Banim (1796–1874)
Father Connell F
'By the O'Hara Family' (or rather Michael Banim solely)

'Thomas Ingoldsby' [**R.H. Barham** (1788–1845)]
The Ingoldsby Legends; or, Mirth and Marvels: Second series MISC
Illustrated by George Cruikshank and John Leech. See also *Ingoldsby Legends* 1840, 1847.

Henry Brougham, Baron Brougham and **Vaux** (1778–1868)
Political Philosophy NF

Robert Browning (1812–89)
King Victor and King Charles [*Bells and Pomegranates* ii] D
See also *Bells and Pomegranates* 1841, 1843, 1844, 1845, 1846

Robert Browning (1812–89)
Dramatic Lyrics [*Bells and Pomegranates* iii] V
Browning's first collection of shorter poems, including 'My Last Duchess' and 'The Pied Piper of Hamelin'. Reprinted, with some revisions and omissions, in *Poems* 1849 (q.v.). See also *Bells and Pomegranates* 1841, 1843, 1844, 1845, 1846.

Sir Edward Bulwer-Lytton (1803–73)
Eva; The Ill-Omened Marriage; and Other Tales and Poems F

Sir Edward Bulwer-Lytton (1803–73)
Zanoni F
bao *Night and Morning, Rienzi*

Frances Burney, Madame d'Arblay (1752–1840)
Diary and Letters of Madame D'Arblay NF
See also *Early Diary of Frances Burney* 1889

Thomas Campbell (1777–1844)
The Pilgrim of Glencoe, with Other Poems V

Charles Darwin (1809–82)
The Structure and Distribution of Coral Reefs NF
See also *Geological Observations* 1844, 1846

Charles Dickens (1812–70)
American Notes for General Circulation NF
Published on 19 October 1842

Sarah Ellis, formerly **Stickney** (1812–72)
The Daughters of England NF
See also *The Women of England* 1839

Frederick William Faber (1814–63)
The Styrian Lake, and Other Poems V

J.O. Halliwell-Phillipps (1820–89) (ed.)
The Nursery Rhymes of England ANTH

Theodore Hook (1788–1841)
Peregrine Bunce; or, Settled at Last F

Leigh Hunt (1784–1859)
The Palfrey V

Douglas Jerrold (1803–57)
Cakes and Ale F

'L.E.L.' [Letitia Elizabeth Landon (1802–38)]
Lady Anne Granard; or, Keeping Up Appearances F

Samuel Lover (1797–1868)
Handy Andy F
Illustrated by Lover. Serialized in *Bentley's Miscellany* (January 1837–May 1839) and published in monthly parts in 1842.

Thomas Babington Macaulay (1800–59)
Lays of Ancient Rome V

Henry Edward Manning, later **Cardinal** (1808–92)
Sermons NF

Henry Edward Manning, later **Cardinal** (1808–92)
The Unity of the Church NF

Frederick Marryat (1792–1848)
Percival Keene F

Thomas Miller (1807–74)
Godfrey Malvern; or, The Life of an Author F

Robert Montgomery (1807–55)
Luther V

William Shakespeare (1564–1616)
The Works of William Shakespeare EDN
Edited in 8 volumes (1842–4) by John Payne Collier

Elizabeth Stone (*b.* 1803)
William Langshawe, the Cotton Lord F

Alfred Tennyson (1809–92)
Poems V
Published in September 1842. Volume i contains reprinted poems; volume ii contains new poems, including 'Morte d'Arthur', 'Locksley Hall', 'The Vision of Sin', and 'Godiva'.

John Wilson (1785–1854)
The Recreations of Christopher North NF

William Wordsworth (1770–1850)
Poems, Chiefly of Early and Late Years V
Includes *The Borderers*

Thomas Wright (1810–77)
Biographia Britannica Literaria; or, Biography of Literary Characters of Great Britain and Ireland [vol. i] DICT
Covers the Anglo-Saxon period. Volume ii (Anglo-Norman period) published in 1846.

1843

- Britain annexes Natal and Sind
  Pusey suspended by Oxford University for his sermon on the Holy Eucharist
  Theatre Regulation Act: abolition of Drury Lane and Covent Garden monopoly and extension of Lord Chamberlain's censorship powers
  The Economist started
- Christabel Rose Coleridge born
  Mandell Creighton born
  Sir Charles Wentworth Dilke born
  Edward Dowden born
  Charles Montagu Doughty born
  Henry James born
  Frederic Myers born
- Richard Carlile dies
  Henry Nelson Coleridge dies
  Mary Hays dies
  Robert Southey dies: William Wordsworth appointed Poet Laureate
- Edvard Grieg born
- Liddell and Scott's *Greek Lexicon*

W.H. Ainsworth (1805–82)
Windsor Castle F
Illustrated by George Cruikshank. First serialized in *Ainsworth's Magazine* (July 1842–June 1843).

James Ballantine (1808–77)
The Gaberlunzie's Wallet F
Continued in *The Miller of Deanhaugh* 1844 (q.v.)

George Borrow (1803–81)
The Bible in Spain NF

Robert Browning (1812–89)
The Return of the Druses [*Bells and Pomegranates* iv] D
See also *Bells and Pomegranates* 1841, 1842, 1844, 1845, 1846

Robert Browning (1812–89)
A Blot in the 'Scutcheon [*Bells and Pomegranates* v] D
Performed February 1843 but closed after three nights. See aso *Bells and Pomegranates* 1841, 1842, 1844, 1845, 1846.

Sir Edward Bulwer-Lytton (1803–73)
The Last of the Barons F
bao *Rienzi.* Published in September 1843.

Thomas Carlyle (1795–1881)
Past and Present NF
Published in April 1843

Aubrey Thomas de Vere (1814–1902)
The Search after Proserpine; Recollections of Greece, and Other Poems V

Charles Dickens (1812–70)
A Christmas Carol in Prose F
Published on 19 December 1843. Illustrated by John Leech. The first of Dickens's Christmas Books. See also *The Chimes* 1844; *The Cricket on the Hearth* 1845; *The Battle of Life* 1846; *The Haunted Man* 1848.

Elizabeth, Lady Eastlake (1809–93)
The Jewess F
Reprinted in *Livonian Tales* 1846 (q.v.)

Catherine Frances Gore (1799–1861)
The Banker's Wife; or, Court and City F

R.S. Hawker (1803–75)
Reeds Shaken with the Wind V

Thomas Hood (1799–1845)
'The Song of the Shirt' V
Publication in *Punch* (Christmas 1843)

R.H. Horne (1803–84)
Orion: An epic poem V

Douglas Jerrold (1803–57)
Punch's Letters to His Son NF
Illustrated by Kenny Meadows. Published in *Punch* (July–December 1842).

James Sheridan Knowles (1784–1862)
The Secretary D
Performed 24 April 1843

Charles Lever (1806–72)
Jack Hinton, the Guardsman F
The first volume of *Our Mess.* Illustrated by Hablot K. Browne ('Phiz'). First published in monthly parts (January–December 1842), See also *Tom Burke of 'Ours'* 1844.

Thomas Babington Macaulay (1800–59)
Critical and Historical Essays NF
Contributions to the *Edinburgh Review*

Frederick Marryat (1792–1848)
Narrative of the Travels and Adventures of Monsieur Violet F

James Martineau (1805–1900)
Endeavours After the Christian Life [1st ser.] NF

John Stuart Mill (1806–73)
A System of Logic, Ratiocinative and Inductive NF

A.W.N. Pugin (1812–52)
An Apology for the Revival of Christian Architecture in England NF

John Ruskin (1819–1900)
Modern Painters [vol. i] NF
'By a Graduate of Oxford'. Published on 5 April 1843. Seven editions by 1867. Volume ii published in 1846 (q.v.).

Herbert Spencer (1820–1903)
The Proper Sphere of Government NF

Elizabeth Stone (*b.* 1803)
The Young Milliner F

R.S. Surtees (1805–64)
Handley Cross; or, The Spa Hunt F
bao *Jorrocks' Jaunts and Jollities.* Serialized in the *New Sporting Magazine* (1840–1). Reissued and enlarged in irregular monthly parts (March 1853–October 1854), illustrated by John Leech.

'Mr M.A. Titmarsh' [W.M. Thackeray (1811–63)]
The Irish Sketch-Book NF
Illustrated by Thackeray

W.M. Thackeray (1811–63)
Men's Wives F
Serialization of a trio of short stories published in *Fraser's Magazine* (March–November 1843). First published in book form in the USA, 1852.

Frances Trollope (1779–1863)
The Barnabys in America; or, Adventures of the Widow Wedded F
Illustrated by John Leech. See also *The Widow Barnaby* 1839, *The Widow Married* 1840.

Frances Trollope (1779–1863)
Hargrave; or, The Adventures of a Man of Fashion F

1844

- YMCA founded
  Musical Times begins publication
- Arthur William à Beckett born
  Robert Bridges born
  Ada Cambridge born
  Caroline Emily Cameron (Mrs Lovett Cameron, *née* Sharp) born
  Edward Carpenter born
  Charlotte Despard born

- Gerard Manley Hopkins born
  Andrew Lang born
  Arthur O'Shaughnessy born
- William Beckford dies
  Thomas Campbell dies
  Henry Francis Cary dies
  John Dalton dies
- Anatole France born
  Paul Verlaine born
  Friedrich Wilhelm Nietzsche born
- Robert Chambers's *Cyclopaedia of English Literature*
  Dumas, *Les Trois Mousquetaires; Le Comte de Monte-Cristo* (1844–5)

Grace Aguilar (1816–47)
Records of Israel F

W.H. Ainsworth (1805–82)
Saint James's; or, The Court of Queen Anne F
Illustrated by George Cruikshank. Serialized in *Ainsworth's Magazine* (January–December 1844).

James Ballantine (1808–77)
The Miller of Deanhaugh F
Continuation of *The Gaberlunzie's Wallet* 1843 (q.v.)

William Barnes (1801–86)
Poems of Rural Life in the Dorset Dialect V
See also 1859, 1862, 1868

Henry Brougham, Baron Brougham and **Vaux** (1778–1868)
Albert Lunel; or, The Chateau of Languedoc F
Written as a memorial to Brougham's daughter

Henry Brougham, Baron Brougham and **Vaux** (1778–1868)
The British Constitution NF

Frances Browne (1816–79)
The Star of Attéghéi; The Vision of Schwartz, and Other Poems V

Elizabeth Barrett Barrett, later **Browning** (1806–61)
Poems V
Published in August 1844. Dedicated to the author's father, Edward Barrett. Includes 'A Drama of Exile' (published separately with other poems in the USA, 1844) and ballads.

Robert Browning (1812–89)
Colombe's Birthday [*Bells and Pomegranates* vi] D
Browning's last play written for the stage. See also *Bells and Pomegrantes* 1841, 1842, 1843, 1845, 1846.

Robert Chambers (1802–71)
Vestiges of the Natural History of Creation NF
Anonymous. See also *Explanations* 1845.

Charles Darwin (1809–82)
Geological Observations on the Volcanic Islands, Visited During the Voyage of HMS Beagle NF
See also *Structure and Distribution* 1842, *Geological Observations* 1846

Thomas De Quincey (1785–1859)
The Logic of Political Economy NF

'Boz' [Charles Dickens (1812–70)]
Martin Chuzzlewit F
Published on 16 July 1844. Illustrated by Hablot K. Browne ('Phiz'). First published in monthly parts (31 December 1842–30 June 1844). Wrapper title: *The Life and Adventures of Martin Chuzzlewit.*

Charles Dickens (1812–70)
The Chimes F
Published on 16 December 1844. Illustrated by John Leech, Richard Doyle, Daniel Maclise, and Clarkson Stanfield. Dickens's second Christmas Book. See also *A Christmas Carol* 1843; *The Cricket on the Hearth* 1845; *The Battle of Life* 1846; *The Haunted Man* 1848.

Benjamin Disraeli (1804–81)
Coningsby; or, The New Generation F

Sir Francis Hastings Doyle (1810–88)
The Two Destinies V

Frederick William Faber (1814–63)
Sir Lancelot V

Lady Georgiana Fullerton (1812–85)
Ellen Middleton F

Benjamin Robert Haydon (1786–1846)
Lectures on Painting and Design NF
Concluded in 1846

Thomas Hood (1799–1845)
Whimsicalities MISC

R.H. Horne (1803–84) (ed.)
A New Spirit of the Age NF
Edited and largely written by Horne

Leigh Hunt (1784–1859)
Imagination and Fancy NF

Francis, Lord Jeffrey (1773–1850)
Contributions to the Edinburgh Review NF

A.W. Kinglake (1809–91)
Eothen; or, Traces of Travel Brought Home from the East NF
Anonymous

Charles Lever (1806–72)
Arthur O'Leary F
'Edited by his friend Harry Lorrequer'. Illustrated by George Cruikshank. First serialized in the *Dublin University Magazine* (January–December 1843).

Charles Lever (1806–72)
Tom Burke, of 'Ours' F
Volumes ii–iii of *Our Mess*. Illustrated by Hablot K. Browne ('Phiz'). First published in monthly parts (February 1843–September 1844). See also *Jack Hinton* 1843.

Samuel Lover (1797–1868)
Treasure Trove F

Harriet Martineau (1802–76)
Life in the Sick-Room; or, Essays by an Invalid NF

Thomas Erskine May (1815–86)
A Treatise upon the Law, Privileges, Proceedings and Usage of Parliament NF

John Stuart Mill (1806–73)
Essays on Some Unsettled Questions of Political Economy NF

John Henry Newman (1801–90) and others
Lives of the English Saints NF
A series (published in 16 volumes, 1844–5) projected by Newman and at first edited by him; he withdrew after the publication of volumes i and ii

Coventry Patmore (1823–96)
Poems V

Hannah Mary Rathbone (1798–1878)
So Much of the Diary of Lady Willoughby as Relates to Her Domestic History, and to the Eventful Period of the Reign of Charles I F
A fictitious diary, widely interpreted as an authentic historical document. Its fictional nature was acknowledged in the preface to the third edition (1845). A sequel was published in 1847.

Emma Robinson (1814–90)
Whitefriars; or, The Days of Charles the Second F
Anonymous. Dramatic version by W. Thompson Townsend performed 4 April 1844.

Elizabeth M. Sewell (1815–1906)
Amy Herbert F
'By a lady'

Mary Shelley (1797–1851)
Rambles in Germany and Italy, in 1840, 1842, and 1843 NF

Arthur Penrhyn Stanley (1815–81)
The Life and Correspondence of Thomas Arnold NF

W.M. Thackeray (1811–63)
The Luck of Barry Lyndon F
Serialization in *Fraser's Magazine* (January–September, November–December 1844). First published in book form in Britain in 1856 (q.v.).

Frances Trollope (1779–1863)
The Laurringtons; or, Superior People F

W. G. Ward (1812–82)
The Ideal of a Christian Church NF
Responds to William Palmer, *A Narrative of Events* 1843

Charlotte M. Yonge (1823–1901)
Abbeychurch; or, Self-control and Self-conceit F
Anonymous

1845

- The USA annexes Texas
  James K. Polk becomes President of the USA
  Outbreak of Anglo-Sikh War
  John Franklin's expedition to find the North-West Passage
  A.H. Layard begins excavations at Nineveh
  Much of the Irish potato crop destroyed by fungus: start of the Irish famine (-1851)
  Oxford University condemns William Ward's *Ideal of a Christian Church* (1844, q.v.)
  John Newman joins the Church of Rome (Oct.)
  Robert Browning and Elizabeth Barrett begin their correspondence
- Sidney Colvin born
  Emily Lawless born
  George Saintsbury born
  Henry Sweet born
- Richard Harris Barham dies
  Laman Blanchard dies
  Catherine Godwin dies
  Thomas Hood dies
  Regina Maria Roche dies
  Sydney Smith dies
- *Encyclopaedia Metropolitana*

Eliza Acton (1799–1859)
Modern Cookery, in all its Branches NF

Grace Aguilar (1816–47)
The Women of Israel; or, Characters and Sketches from the Holy Scripture NF

'Bon Gaultier' [W.E. Aytoun (1813–65)]
The Book of Ballads V
Parodies written with Theodore Martin

Bernard Barton (1784–1849)
Household Verses V

Marguerite Gardiner, countess of Blessington (1789–1849)
Strathern; or, Life at Home and Abroad F

Horatius Bonar (1808–89)
The Bible Hymn-Book V

Robert Browning (1812–89)
Dramatic Romances and Lyrics [*Bells and Pomegranates* vii] V
Includes 'How They Brought the Good News from Ghent to Aix', 'The Lost Leader', and 'The Flight of the Duchess'. Reprinted in *Poems* 1849 (q.v.). See also *Bells and Pomegranates* 1841, 1842, 1843, 1844, 1846.

William Carleton (1794–1869)
Parra Sashta; or, The History of Paddy Go-Easy and His Wife, Nancy F

William Carleton (1794–1869)
Tales and Sketches F
Previously published stories

Robert Chambers (1802–71)
Explanations NF
Anonymous. A sequel to *Vestiges of the Natural History of Creation* 1844 (q.v.).

Mary Cowden Clarke (1809–98)
The Complete Concordance to Shakespeare NF
First published in monthly parts

Richard Cobbold (1797–1877)
The History of Margaret Catchpole, a Suffolk Girl F
Anonymous

Thomas Cooper (1805–92)
The Purgatory of Suicides V
Written in Stafford Gaol

Louisa Costello (1799–1879) (ed.)
The Rose Garden of Persia ANTH
Translations from Persian poetry

Catherine Crowe (1790–1876) (tr.)
The Seeress of Prevorst NF
Translated from the German original (1829) of J.A.C. Kerner (1786–1862)

Charles Dickens (1812–70)
The Cricket on the Hearth F
Published on 20 December 1845, dated 1846. Illustrated by John Leech, Richard Doyle, Edwin Landseer, and Clarkson Stanfield. Dickens's third Christmas Book. See also *A Christmas Carol* 1843; *The Chimes* 1844; *The Battle of Life* 1846; *The Haunted Man* 1848.

Benjamin Disraeli (1804–81)
Sybil; or, The Two Nations F
Published in May 1845

Frederick William Faber (1814–63)
The Rosary, and Other Poems V

Richard Ford (1796–1858)
A Hand-Book for Travellers in Spain, and Readers at Home NF

George Gilfillan (1813–78)
A Gallery of Literary Portraits [1st ser.] NF
Includes portraits of Hazlitt, Shelley, Carlyle, De Quincey, Landor, Coleridge, Wordsworth, Charles Lamb, and Southey. Second series published in 1850; third series, 1854.

Anna Maria Hall [Mrs S.C. Hall] (1800–81)
The Whiteboy F

G.P.R. James (1799–1860)
The Smuggler F
bao *Darnley, De l'Orme, Richelieu*

Geraldine Jewsbury (1812–80)
Zoe: The history of two lives F

J.S. Le Fanu (1814–73)
The Cock and Anchor F
Anonymous. Reprinted as *Morley Court* in 1873.

Charles Lever (1806–72)
The O'Donoghue F
Illustrated by Hablot K. Browne ('Phiz')

G.H. Lewes (1817–78)
A Biographical History of Philosophy NF

Frederick Marryat (1792–1848)
The Mission; or, Scenes in Africa F

Harriet Martineau (1802–76)
Dawn Island F
Written for the National Anti-Corn Law Bazaar

Harriet Martineau (1802–76)
Forest and Game-Law Tales F
A third volume published in 1846

Harriet Martineau (1802–76)
Letters on Mesmerism NF

G.W.M. Reynolds (1814–79)
The Mysteries of London [1st ser.] F

Published October 1845. A second volume published in September 1846. Also published in weekly penny numbers and monthly parts. Second series published in 1847. A third series, written by Thomas Miller, 1848; fourth series, written by E.L. Blanchard, 1849.

Robert Southey (1774–1843)
Oliver Newman: A New-England tale V
Unfinished. Also includes other poems.

R.S. Surtees (1805–64)
Hillingdon Hall; or, The Cockney Squire F
bao *Handley Cross*. First serialized in the *New Sporting Magazine* (February–June 1844).

W.M. Thackeray (1811–63)
Jeames's Diary F
Serialization in *Punch* (2 August 1845–7 February 1846). Published in book form in the USA, 1846.

Joseph Blanco White (1775–1841)
The Life of Joseph Blanco White NF

William Wordsworth (1770–1850)
The Poems of William Wordsworth, Poet Laureate V
Includes further revisions to texts and a number of poems published for the first time. Wordsworth had been made Poet Laureate in 1843 following the death of Robert Southey. See also *Miscellaneous Poems* 1820, *Poetical Works* 1827, *Poetical Works* 1836, *Poetical Works* 1840, *Poetical Works* 1857, and *Poetical Works* (Centenary Edition) 1870.

1846

- American-Mexican War: the US annexes New Mexico
  Repeal of the Corn Laws (23 May)
  The Guardian started
  Dickens starts *The Daily News*
  Robert Browning marries and elopes with Elizabeth Barrett (Sept.)
- Francis Herbert Bradley born
  Ernest Hartley Coleridge born
  Kate Greenaway born
- Thomas Clarkson dies
  George Darley dies
  John Hookham Frere dies
  Caroline Fry dies
  Benjamin Robert Haydon dies
  Robert Plumer Ward dies
- Felix Mendelssohn-Bartholdy dies
- Balzac, *La Cousine Bette*
  Bohn's *Standard Library*
  Melville, *Typee*

Reynolds's Miscellany of Romance, General Literature, Science, and Art PER
Published weekly, 7 November 1846–19 June 1869. Edited by G.W.M. Reynolds.

Danish Fairy Legends and Tales F
Translation by Caroline Peachey from Hans Christian Andersen (1805–75). See also *A Danish Story-Book, The Nightingale* 1846, *The Dream of Little Tuk* 1848.

Gilbert Abbott à Beckett (1811–56)
The Comic Blackstone F
Illustrated by George Cruikshank

William Barnes (1801–86)
Poems, Partly of Rural Life V
Not in dialect

Charles Boner (1815–70) (tr.)
A Danish Story-Book F
Translated from Hans Christian Andersen (1805–75). See also *The Nightingale* 1846, *The Dream of Little Tuk* 1848; *Danish Fairy Legends and Tales* 1846

Charles Boner (1815–70) (tr.)
The Nightingale, and Other Tales F
Translated from Hans Christian Andersen: see above

'Currer, Ellis, and Acton Bell' [Charlotte Brontë (1816–55), **Emily Brontë** (1818–48), and **Anne Brontë** (1820–49)]
Poems by Currer, Ellis and Acton Bell V
Published on 26 May 1846. See also *The Professor* 1857.

Robert Browning (1812–89)
Luria: a Tragedy; A Soul's Tragedy [*Bells and Pomegranates* viii] D
See also *Bells and Pomegranates* 1841, 1842, 1843, 1844, 1845

Henry Cary (1772–1844)
Lives of English Poets, from Johnson to Kirke White V
First published in the *London Magazine*, 1821–4

Charles Darwin (1809–82)
Geological Observations on South America NF
See also *Structure and Distribution* 1842, *Geological Observations* 1844

Charles Dickens (1812–70)
Pictures from Italy F

Published on 18 May 1846. Illustrated by Samuel Palmer. Partly serialized in the *Daily News* (21 January–11 March 1846).

Charles Dickens (1812–70)
The Battle of Life F
Published on 19 December 1846. Illustrated by John Leech, Richard Doyle, Daniel Maclise, and Clarkson Stanfield. Dickens's fourth Christmas Book. See also *A Christmas Carol* 1843; *The Chimes* 1844; *The Cricket on the Hearth* 1845; *The Haunted Man* 1848.

Elizabeth, Lady Eastlake (1809–93)
Livonian Tales F
bao *Letters from the Baltic*. Includes *The Jewess* 1843 (q.v.), *The Disponent*, and *The Wolves*.

'George Eliot' [Mary Ann Evans (1819–80)] (tr.)
The Life of Jesus NF
Anonymous. Published on 15 June 1846. Translated from David Friedrich Strauss (1808–74), *Das Leben Jesu*.

Catherine Frances Gore (1799–1861)
Sketches of English Character F

George Grote (1794–1871)
A History of Greece NF
Published in 12 volumes (1846–56)

Thomas Hood (1799–1845)
Poems V

Douglas Jerrold (1803–57)
Mrs Caudle's Curtain Lectures F
Serialized in *Punch* (January–December 1845), illustrated by John Leech

John Keble (1792–1866)
Lyra Innocentium: Thoughts in verse on Christian children V

'Derry Down Derry' [Edward Lear (1812–88)]
A Book of Nonsense V
Illustrated by Lear. Enlarged in 1861 and 1863. See also *Nonsense Songs* 1870, *More Nonsense* 1871, *Laughable Lyrics* 1877.

Frederick Marryat (1792–1848)
The Privateer's-Man F
Serialized in the *New Monthly Magazine* (August 1845–June 1846)

Thomas Peckett Prest (1810?–79)
A String of Pearls; or, The Sailor's Gift F
Published in Edward Lloyd's penny journal *The People's Periodical* (92 instalments beginning 21 November 1846), this was the source of the popular melodrama, *Sweeney Todd, the Demon Barber of Fleet Street*. According to Montague Summers, the opening chapters were written by George Macfarren (1788–1843).

John Ruskin (1819–1900)
Modern Painters: Volume II NF
'By a Graduate of Oxford'. Published on 24 April 1846. See also *Modern Painters* 1843.

'Mr M.A. Titmarsh' [W.M. Thackeray (1811–63)]
Notes of a Journey from Cornhill to Grand Cairo NF
Illustrated by Thackeray

1847

- Communist League founded
  The Mormons found Salt Lake City
- George Barlow born
  Annie Besant born
  Alice Meynell (*née* Thompson) born
  Flora Annie Steel born
  Bram Stoker born
- Grace Aguilar dies
  Thomas Frognall Dibdin dies
- Sir John Franklin dies
  Sharon Turner dies
- Alexander Graham Bell born
  Thomas Alva Edison born
- Daniel O'Connell dies
- Merimée, *Carmen*

Gilbert Abbott à Beckett (1811–56)
The Comic History of England F
Illustrated by John Leech. First issued in parts (July 1846–February 1848).

Grace Aguilar (1816–47)
Home Influence F
See also *A Mother's Recompense* 1850

Edwin Atherstone (1788–1872)
The Fall of Nineveh V
Enlarged edition in thirty books. See also *The Fall of Nineveh* 1828.

'Thomas Ingoldsby, Esq.' [R.H. Barham (1788–1845)]
The Ingoldsby Legends; or, Mirth and Marvels V/F
Illustrated by George Cruikshank and John Leech. See also *Ingoldsby Legends* 1840, 1842.

George Boole (1815–1864)
The Mathematical Analysis of Logic NF

'Currer Bell' [**Charlotte Brontë** (1816–55)]
Jane Eyre: An autobiography F
Published on 19 October 1847

'Ellis Bell' and 'Acton Bell' [**Emily Brontë** (1818–48) and **Anne Brontë** (1820–49)]
Wuthering Heights; Agnes Grey F
Published on 4 December 1847 in 3 volumes. Volumes i–ii: *Wuthering Heights* (EB); volume iii: *Agnes Grey* (AB).

William Carleton (1794–1869)
The Black Prophet: A tale of Irish famine F
Serialized in the *Dublin University Magazine* (May–December 1846)

'V' [**Caroline Clive** (1801–73)]
The Queen's Ball V

George Lillie Craik (1798–1866)
The Pursuit of Knowledge Under Difficulties, Illustrated by Female Examples NF
Anonymous. Continuation of *The Pursuit of Knowledge* 1830 (q.v.).

Benjamin Disraeli (1804–81)
Tancred; or, The New Crusade F
Published in March 1847

'Malcolm J. Errym' [**James Malcom Rymer** (1804–82)]
Varney the Vampire; or, The Feast of Blood F
Sometimes attributed to T.P. Prest (1810?–79)

'Zeta' [**J.A. Froude** (1818–94)]
Shadows of the Clouds F

Leigh Hunt (1784–1859)
Men, Women, and Books NF

G.P.R. James (1799–1860)
The Castle of Ehrenstein F
bao *Heidelberg, The Step-Mother, The Smuggler*

John Keble (1792–1866)
Sermons, Academical and Occasional NF
See also *Sermons* 1868

Walter Savage Landor (1775–1864)
The Hellenics of Walter Savage Landor V

J.S. Le Fanu (1814–73)
The Fortunes of Colonel Torlogh O'Brien F
Illustrated by Hablot K. Browne ('Phiz'). First published in monthly parts (April 1846–January 1847).

G.H. Lewes (1817–78)
Ranthorpe F

Eliza Lynn, later **Linton** (1822–98)
Azeth the Egyptian F
Anonymous

Frederick Marryat (1792–1848)
The Children of the New Forest F
Published in 2 volumes (July 1847, October 1847)

Augustus Mayhew (1826–75) and **Henry Mayhew** (1812–87)
The Greatest Plague of Life; or, The Adventures of a Lady in Search of a Good Servant F
Illustrated by George Cruikshank. First published in monthly parts.

Thomas Medwin (1788–1869)
The Life of Percy Bysshe Shelley NF

James Morier (1780–1849)
Misselmah: A Persian tale F

John Maddison Morton (1811–91)
Box and Cox: A romance of real life D
Performed 1 November 1847

Christina Rossetti (1830–94)
Verses by Christina G. Rossetti V

P.B. Shelley (1792–1822)
The Works of Percy Bysshe Shelley V
Edited by Mary Shelley

Charles Simeon (1759–1836)
Memoirs of the Life of the Rev. Charles Simeon NF

Robert Southey (1774–1843)
The Doctor [vols. vi, vii] NF
Volumes i, ii published in 1834 (q.v.); volume iii, 1835 (q.v.); volume iv, 1837 (q.v.); volume v, 1838 (q.v.)

Robert Southey (1774–1843) and **Caroline Bowles Southey** (1786–1854)
Robin Hood V

R.S. Surtees (1805–64)
Hawbuck Grange; or, The Sporting Adventures of Thomas Scott, Esq. F
bao *Handley Cross*. Illustrated by Hablot K. Browne ('Phiz'). First serialized in *Bell's Sporting Life*.

Alfred Tennyson (1809–92)
The Princess V
Published in November 1847

'M.A. Titmarsh' [**W.M. Thackeray** (1811–63)]
Mrs Perkins's Ball F
Illustrated by Thackeray. The first of Thackeray's Christmas books. See also *Our Street* 1848, *Doctor Birch and His Young Friends* 1849, *The Kickleburys on the Rhine* 1850, and *The Rose and the Ring* 1855.

Anthony Trollope (1815–82)
The Macdermots of Ballycloran F

Charlotte M. Yonge (1823–1901)
Scenes and Characters; or, Eighteen Months at Beechcroft F
bao *Abbeyfield*. See also *The Two Sides of the Shield* 1885 and *Beechcroft at Rockstone* 1888.

1848

- Marx and Engels, *Communist Manifesto* (Feb.)
  Abdication of Louis Philippe (Feb.): republic proclaimed
  Resignation of Metternich
  Venetian Republic proclaimed
  'June Days' in Paris (22–6 June): radical revolt suppressed
  Abdication of Ferdinand I of Austria: succeeded by Franz Joseph I
  Louis Napoleon elected President of the French Republic (10 Dec.)
  Second Sikh War
  Holman Hunt, Millais, and Rossetti form the Pre-Raphaelite Brotherhood
- Grant Allen born
  Arthur James Balfour born
  Bernard Bosanquet born
  John Churton Collins born
  Lanoe Falconer (Mary Elizabeth Hawker) born
  Richard Jefferies born
- Sarah Fuller Adams dies
  Branwell Brontë dies
  Emily Brontë dies
  Isaac D'Israeli dies
  Frederick Marryat dies
- Paul Gaugin born
  Joel Chandler Harris ('Uncle Remus') born
  J.-K. Huysmans born
- Bohn's *Classical Library*
  Chateaubriand, *Mémoires d'Outre-tombe*
  Dumas (*fils*), *La Dame aux Camélias*
  Thomas Lacy's Acting Editions begun (–1873)

The English Struwwelpeter; or, Pretty Stories and Funny Pictures for Little Children F
Translation of *Lustige Geschichten und drollige Bilder* (1845; 3rd edition retitled *Der Struwwelpeter*) by Heinrich Hoffmann (1809–44)

W.H. Ainsworth (1805–82)
James the Second; or, The Revolution of 1688 F
Serialized in *Ainsworth's Magazine* (January–December 1847)

Cecil Frances Alexander (1818–95)
The Baron's Little Daughter, and Other Tales in Prose and Verse MISC

Cecil Frances Alexander (1818–95)
Hymns for Little Children V
Dedicated to John Keble

R.M. Ballantyne (1825–94)
Hudson's Bay; or, Every-day Life in the Wilds of North America NF
Illustrated by Ballantyne

John Stanyan Bigg (1828–65)
The Sea-King V

E.L.L. Blanchard (1820–89)
Adams's Illustrated Descriptive Guide to the Watering-Places of England NF

Charles Boner (1815–70) (tr.)
The Dream of Little Tuk, and Other Tales F
Translated fron Hans Christian Andersen (1805–75). See also *A Danish Story-Book* and *The Nightingale* 1846.

'Acton Bell' [Anne Brontë (1820–49)]
The Tenant of Wildfell Hall F
Published on 27 June 1848

Sir Edward Bulwer-Lytton (1803–73)
Harold, the Last of the Saxon Kings F
Anonymous. Published in June 1848.

William Carleton (1794–1869)
The Emigrants of Ahadarra F

Maria Charlesworth (1819–80)
A Book for the Cottage; or, The History of Mary and Her Family F
bao *The Female Visitor to the Poor*

A.H. Clough (1819–61)
The Bothie of Toper-na-Fuosich V
Published in December 1848. The title was changed in the posthumous 1862 *Poems* [q.v.] to *The Bothie of Tober-na-Vuolich*.

Wilkie Collins (1824–89)
Memoirs of the Life of William Collins NF
Published in November 1848

Catherine Crowe (1790–1876)
The Night-Side of Nature; or, Ghosts and Ghost-Seers F
Supposedly true supernatural tales and phenomena

Aubrey Thomas de Vere (1814–1902)
English Misrule and Irish Deeds V

Charles Dickens (1812–70)
Dombey and Son F
Published in April 1848. Illustrated by Hablot K. Browne ('Phiz'). First published in monthly parts (30 September 1846–31 March 1848). Wrapper title: *Dealings with the Firm of Dombey and Son. Wholesale, Retail, and for Exportation.*

Charles Dickens (1812–70)
The Haunted Man and the Ghost's Bargain F
Published on 19 December 1848. Illustrated by John Leech, Clarkson Stanfield, John Tenniel, and Frank Stone. Dickens's fifth Christmas Book. See also *A Christmas Carol* 1843; *The Chimes* 1844; *The Cricket on the Hearth* 1845; *The Battle of Life* 1846.

Elizabeth Gaskell (1810–65)
Mary Barton F
Anonymous. Published in October 1848.

James Grant (1822–87)
Adventures of an Aide-de-Camp; or, A Campaign in Calabria F

Dora Greenwell (1821–82)
Poems V

James Hannay (1827–73)
Biscuits and Grog F
'Edited' [i.e. written] by Hannay

Leigh Hunt (1784–1859)
A Jar of Honey from Mount Hybla V

Leigh Hunt (1784–1859)
The Town NF

Geraldine Jewsbury (1812–80)
The Half-Sisters F

Julia Kavanagh (1824–77)
Madeleine F

Charles Kingsley (1819–75)
The Saint's Tragedy V

Walter Savage Landor (1775–1864)
Imaginary Conversation of King Carlo-Alberto and the Duchess Belgioso NF
See also *Imaginary Conversations* 1824, 1828, 1829, 1853, and *Last Fruit* 1853

Walter Savage Landor (1775–1864)
The Italics of Walter Savage Landor V

G.H. Lewes (1817–78)
Rose, Blanche, and Violet F

John Stuart Mill (1806–73)
Principles of Political Economy NF

Richard Monckton Milnes (1809–85)
The Life, Letters and Literary Remains of John Keats NF

John Henry Newman, later **Cardinal** (1801–90)
Loss and Gain F
Anonymous. Later editions add the subtitle 'The story of a convert'.

Angus Bethune Reach (1821–56)
The Natural History of 'Bores' NF

W.M. Thackeray (1811–63)
The Book of Snobs NF
Illustrated by Thackeray. First published in *Punch* (28 February 1846–27 February 1847).

W.M. Thackeray (1811–63)
Vanity Fair F
Illustrated by Thackeray. First published in monthly parts (January 1847–July 1848).

'Mr M.A. Titmarsh' [W.M. Thackeray (1811–63)]
'Our Street' F
Illustrated by Thackeray. The second of Thackeray's Christmas books. See also *Mrs Perkins's Ball* 1847, *Doctor Birch and His Young Friends* 1849, *The Kickleburys on the Rhine* 1850, and *The Rose and the Ring* 1855.

Anthony Trollope (1815–82)
The Kelleys and the O'Kellys; or, Landlords and Tenants F
Published in July 1848

1849

- Britain annexes the Punjab
  Zachary Taylor becomes President of the USA
- Frances Burnett (*née* Hodgson) born
  Lucy Clifford (Mrs W.K. Clifford, *née* Lane) born
  Sir Edmund Gosse born
  William Ernest Henley born
  Selwyn Image born
  Hume Nisbet born
- Thomas Lovell Beddoes dies
  Bernard Barton dies
  Marguerite Gardiner Blessington, countess of Blessington, dies
  Anne Brontë dies
  Hartley Coleridge dies
  Maria Edgeworth dies
  Pierce Egan, the elder, dies
  Ebenezer Elliott dies
  James Morier dies
  Horatio Smith dies

- August Strindberg born
- Frédéric Chopin dies
  Edgar Allan Poe dies

Notes and Queries PER
Commenced 3 November 1849

W.H. Ainsworth (1805–82)
The Lancashire Witches F
Serialized in the *Sunday Times* (1848) and in *Ainsworth's Magazine* (July 1850–September 1853)

Cecil Frances Alexander (1818–95)
Moral Songs V

'A' [Matthew Arnold (1822–88)]
The Strayed Reveller, and Other Poems V

W.E. Aytoun (1813–65)
Lays of the Scottish Cavaliers, and Other Poems V

Dion Boucicault (1820?–90)
Old Heads and Young Hearts: A comedy D
Performed 18 November 1849

'Currer Bell' [Charlotte Brontë (1816–55)]
Shirley F
Published on 26 October 1849

Robert Browning (1812–89)
Poems V
The first collected edition

Sir Edward Bulwer-Lytton (1803–73)
The Caxtons F
First published in *Blackwood's Magazine*, 1848–9

Sir Edward Bulwer-Lytton (1803–73)
King Arthur V
First published in 3 parts, 1848–9

Lady [Rosina] Bulwer-Lytton (1802–82)
The Peer's Daughters F

William Carleton (1794–1869)
The Tithe-Proctor F

Edward Caswall (1814–78)
Lyra Catholica V

A.H. Clough (1819–61)
Ambarvalia V
Published in January 1849

S.T. Coleridge (1772–1834)
Notes and Lectures Upon Shakespeare and Some of the Old Poets and Dramatists NF

Dinah Mulock, later **Craik** (1826–87)
The Ogilvies F

Robert Curzon (1810–73)
Visits to Monasteries in the Levant NF

William Hepworth Dixon (1821–79)
John Howard and the Prison-World of Europe NF

'Zeta' [J.A. Froude (1818–94)]
The Nemesis of Faith F
The book was burned in the quad of Exeter College, Oxford, by William Sewell

Leigh Hunt (1784–1859)
Readings for Railways ANTH

Douglas Jerrold (1803–57)
A Man Made of Money F
Illustrated by John Leech. First published in six parts (October 1848–January 1849).

Charles Lever (1806–72)
Confessions of Con. Cregan, the Irish Gil Blas F
Anonymous. Illustrated by Hablot K. Browne ('Phiz').

Thomas Babington Macaulay (1800–59)
The History of England from the Accession of James II [vols i, ii] NF
Volumes ii and iv published in 1855 (q.v.)

Anne Manning (1807–79)
Cherry and Violet F

Anne Manning (1807–79)
The Maiden and Married Life of Mary Powell, Afterwards Mistress Milton F
Anonymous. First published in *Sharpe's Magazine*, 1849.

Harriet Martineau (1802–76)
Household Education NF

Francis William Newman (1805–97)
The Soul NF

Margaret Oliphant (1828–97)
Passages in the Life of Mrs Margaret Maitland F
Anonymous. See also *Lilliesleaf* 1855.

Thomas Love Peacock (1785–1866)
Headlong Hall, Nightmare Abbey, Maid Marian, Crotchet Castle F
A volume in Bentley's Standard Novels and Romances. Contains minor revisions to texts: see *Headlong Hall* 1816, *Nightmare Abbey* 1818, *Maid Marian* 1822, *Crotchet Castle* 1831.

Angus Bethune Reach (1821–56)
Clement Lorimer; or, The Book with the Iron Clasps F
Illustrated by George Cruikshank. First published in monthly parts, 1848–9.

G.W.M. Reynolds (1814–79)
Mysteries of the Court of London [1st ser.] F
Published in weekly penny numbers and monthly parts, commencing September 1848. Intended as a third series of *The Mysteries of London* 1845 (q.v.). The work ran to four series (1848–56).

John Ruskin (1819–1900)
The Seven Lamps of Architecture NF
Published on 10 May 1849

Catherine Sinclair (1800–64)
Sir Edgar Graham; or, Railway Speculators F

Robert Southey (1774–1843)
Southey's Common-place Book: First Series MISC
Edited by John Wood Warter. Second series, 1849 (below); third and fourth series, 1850 (q.v.).

Robert Southey (1774–1843)
Southey's Common-place Book: Second Series MISC
See above. Third and fourth series, 1850 (q.v.).

Robert Southey (1774–1843)
The Life and Correspondence of the Late Robert Southey NF
Edited by Cuthbert Southey

Philip Henry Stanhope (1805–75)
Historical Essays Contributed to the 'Quarterly Review' NF

Sir James Stephen (1789–1859)
Essays in Ecclesiastical Biography NF

'Mr M.A. Titmarsh' [W.M. Thackeray (1811–63)]
Doctor Birch and his Young Friends F
Illustrated by Thackeray. The third of Thackeray's Christmas books. See also *Mrs Perkins's Ball* 1847, *Our Street* 1848, *The Kickleburys on the Rhine* 1850, and *The Rose and the Ring* 1855.

W.M. Thackeray (1811–63)
The History of Pendennis F
Volume i published in 1849, dated 1850; volume ii, 1850. First published in monthly parts (November 1848–September 1849, January–December 1850). Illustrated by Thackeray.

W.M. Thackeray (1811–63)
The History of Samuel Titmarsh and the Great Hoggarty Diamond F
Serialized in *Fraser's Magazine* in 1841 (q.v.)

'Mr M.A. Titmarsh' [W.M. Thackeray (1811–63)]
Rebecca and Rowena F
Published in December 1849, dated 1850. Illustrated by Richard Doyle. First version published in *Fraser's Magazine* (August–September 1846).

Frances Trollope (1779–1863)
The Old World and the New F

Isaac Williams (1802–65)
The Christian Scholar V
bao *The Cathedral*

1850

- Death of US President Zachary Taylor: succeeded by Millard Fillmore
  Harper's Magazine started
- Robert Barr born
  Augustine Birrell born
  Lafcadio Hearn born
  Frederic William Maitland born
  Robert Louis Stevenson born
- William Lisle Bowles dies
  Francis Jeffrey, Lord Jeffrey, dies
  Jane Porter dies
  William Wordsworth dies: Alfred Tennyson appointed Poet Laureate
- Robert Peel dies
- Guy de Maupassant born
- Honoré de Balzac dies
- Hawthorne, *The Scarlet Letter*

Household Words PER
Published weekly from 30 March 1850–28 May 1859. Edited by Charles Dickens. Succeeded by *All the Year Round* 1859 (q.v.).

Grace Aguilar (1816–47)
A Mother's Recompense F
See *Home Influence* 1847

Grace Aguilar (1816–47)
The Vale of Cedars; or, The Martyr F
Written 1831–5

Grace Aguilar (1816–47)
Woman's Friendship F

W.H. Ainsworth (1805–82)
Auriol F
Serialized in *Ainsworth's Magazine* (October 1844–May 1845) and in the *New Monthly Magazine* (August 1845–January 1846)

William Allingham (1824–89)
Poems V

Philip James Bailey (1816–1902)
The Angel World, and Other Poems V
See also *Festus* 1839

Thomas Spencer Baynes (1823–87)
An Essay on the New Analytic of Logical Forms NF

Thomas Lovell Beddoes (1803–49)
Death's Jest-Book; or, The Fool's Tragedy V
Anonymous

[Charles William] Shirley Brooks (1816–74)
Timour the Tartar! An extravaganza D
Written with John Oxenford

Elizabeth Barrett Browning (1806–61)
Poems V
Published on 1 November 1850. Dedicated to her father, Edward Barrett. Her first book published as Elizabeth Barrett Browning (she was married to Robert Browning in September 1846). Includes *Sonnets from the Portuguese* (first printed separately in Boston, 1866). See also *Poems* 1844, 1853, 1856.

Robert Browning (1812–89)
Christmas-Eve and Easter-Day V

Thomas Carlyle (1795–1881)
Latter-Day Pamphlets NF
Published in August 1850. First published as eight separate pamphlets (February–August 1850.

S.T. Coleridge (1772–1834)
Essays on His Own Times NF
Edited by Sara Coleridge

Wilkie Collins (1824–89)
Antonina; or, The Fall of Rome F
Published in February 1850

Dinah Mulock, later **Craik** (1826–87)
Olive F
bao *The Ogilvies*

Charles Dickens (1812–70)
David Copperfield F
Published on 15 November 1850. Illustrated by Hablot K. Browne ('Phiz'). First published in monthly parts (30 April 1849–30 October 1850). Wrapper title: *The Personal History, Adventures, Experience, and Observation of David Copperfield the Younger.*

'Sydney Yendys' [Sydney Dobell (1824–74)]
The Roman V

Elizabeth Gaskell (1810–65)
Libbie Marsh's Three Eras F
Anonymous. First published in *Howitt's Journal* (1847) under the pseudonym 'Cotton Mather Mills'.

Elizabeth Gaskell (1810–65)
The Moorland Cottage F
bao *Mary Barton.* Published in December 1850. Illustrated by Birket Foster.

James Grant (1822–87)
The Scottish Cavalier F

Dora Greenwell (1821–82)
Stories That Might Be True, with Other Poems V

Leigh Hunt (1784–1859)
The Autobiography of Leigh Hunt NF

Jean Ingelow (1820–97)
A Rhyming Chronicle of Incidents and Feelings V

Charles Kingsley (1819–75)
Alton Locke, Tailor and Poet F
Anonymous

Charles Lever (1806–72)
Roland Cashel F
Illustrated by Hablot K. Browne ('Phiz')

James McCosh (1811–94)
The Method of the Divine Government, Physical and Moral NF

Francis William Newman (1805–97)
Phases of Faith; or, Passages from the History of my Creed NF

Thomas Mayne Reid (1818–83)
The Rifle Rangers; or Adventures of an Officer in Southern Mexico F

John Ruskin (1819–1900)
The King of the Golden River; or, The Black Brothers F
Published on 21 December 1850, dated 1851. Illustrated by Richard Doyle. Written in 1841 for Effie Gray (Ruskin's future wife), then twelve years of age.

John Ruskin (1819–1900)
Poems V

Robert Southey (1774–1843)
Southey's Common-place Book: Third/Fourth Series MISC
Edited by John Wood Warter. First and second series, 1849 (q.v.).

Tom Taylor (1817–80)
The Fool's Revenge D
Performed 18 October 1859

Alfred Tennyson (1809–92)
In Memoriam A.H.H. V
Published in June 1850. In memory of Tennyson's friend, Arthur Hallam. Following Wordsworth's death in April 1850, Tennyson was appointed Poet Laureate (the post having been refused by Samuel Rogers on the ground of age).

'Mr M.A. Titmarsh' [W.M. Thackeray (1811–63)]
The Kickleburys on the Rhine F
Illustrated by Thackeray. The fourth of Thackeray's Christmas books. See also *Mrs Perkins's Ball* 1847, *Our Street* 1848, *Doctor Birch and His Young Friends* 1849, and *The Rose and the Ring* 1855.

Anthony Trollope (1815–82)
La Vendée F
Published in June 1850

Frances Trollope (1779–1863)
Petticoat Government F

Anna Laetitia Waring (1820–1910)
Hymns and Meditations V
Numerous editions

Isaac Williams (1802–65)
The Seven Days; or, The Old and New Creation V
bao *The Cathedral*

William Wordsworth (1770–1850)
The Prelude; or, Growth of a Poet's Mind V
2nd edition, 1851. Intended to form the introduction to *The Recluse*, of which *The Excursion* 1814 (q.v.) was the second part. See also *The Recluse* 1888.

1851

- The Great Exhibition
  Louis Napoleon carries out *coup d'état*; declared Emperor Napoleon III (Dec.)
  New York Times begins publication
- A.C. Bradley born
  Ella D'Arcy born
  Henry Arthur Jones born
  Sir Oliver Lodge born
  Mary Augusta Ward (Mrs Humphrey Ward, *née* Arnold) born
- Joanna Baillie dies
  Harriet Lee dies
  John Lingard dies
  Mary Shelley, *née* Godwin dies
- J.M.W. Turner dies
- Louis Daguerre dies
  James Fenimore Cooper dies
- Hawthorne, *The House of the Seven Gables*
  Melville, *Moby Dick*

Gilbert Abbott à Beckett (1811–56)
A Comic History of Rome F

Charles Babbage (1792–1871)
The Exposition of 1851 NF

Thomas Lovell Beddoes (1803–49)
Poems Posthumous and Collected V

Edward Henry Bickersteth (1825–1906)
Nineveh V

George Borrow (1803–81)
Lavengro: The scholar—the gypsy—the priest F
Published on 7 February 1851. See also *The Romany Rye* 1857.

Elizabeth Barrett Browning (1806–61)
Casa Guidi Windows V
Published on 31 May 1851

Robert Burns (1759–96)
Life and Works of Robert Burns NF
Edited by Robert Chambers. See also *Prose Works* 1839.

Thomas Carlyle (1795–1881)
The Life of John Sterling NF

'Lord B****' [Frederick Richard Chichester, earl of Belfast** (1827–53)]
Masters and Workmen F

'V' [Caroline Clive (1801–73)]
The Valley of the Rea V

Hartley Coleridge (1796–1849)
Essays and Marginilia NF
Edited by Derwent Coleridge

Hartley Coleridge (1796–1849)
Poems by Hartley Coleridge V
Edited by Derwent Coleridge

Wilkie Collins (1824–89)
Rambles Beyond Railways; or, Notes in Cornwall Taken A-Foot NF
Published in January 1851. First serialized in *Household Words*.

Sir Edward Shepherd Creasy (1812–78)
Fifteen Decisive Battles of the World NF
Twenty-one editions by 1874

Edward FitzGerald (1809–83)
Euphranor NF
Anonymous

Margaret Gatty (1809–73)
The Fairy Godmothers, and Other Tales F

R.H. Horne (1803–84)
The Dreamer and the Worker F

Leigh Hunt (1784–1859)
Table Talk NF

Geraldine Jewsbury (1812–80)
Marian Withers F

Charles Kingsley (1819–75)
Yeast: A problem F
Anonymous. Revised from the serialization in *Fraser's Magazine* (July–December 1848).

W.H.G. Kingston (1814–80)
Peter the Whaler F
Juvenile

Edward Lear (1812–88)
Journals of a Landscape Painter in Albania, Illyria etc NF
Illustrated by Lear. See also *Journals* 1852, 1870.

J.S. Le Fanu (1814–73)
Ghost Stories and Tales of Mystery F
Illustrated by Hablot K. Browne ('Phiz')

Henry Mayhew (1812–87)
1851; or, The Adventures of Mr and Mrs Sandboys and Family F
Illustrated by George Cruikshank. Written with John Binny.

Henry Mayhew (1812–87)
London Labour and the London Poor NF
Some material first published in the *Morning Chronicle*, 1849–50. Expanded in 1861–2.

George Meredith (1828–1909)
Poems V
Includes the first version of 'Love in the Valley'

Margaret Oliphant (1828–97)
John Drayton F
Anonymous

John Ruskin (1819–1900)
The Stones of Venice: Volume the First NF
Published on 3 March 1851. Volume ii published in 1853 (q.v.); volume iii, 1853 (q.v.).

John Ruskin (1819–1900)
Pre-Raphaelitism NF
bao *Modern Painters*. Published in August 1851.

Herbert Spencer (1820–1903)
Social Statics NF

1852

- Second Empire proclaimed in France with Napoleon III as Emperor
- R.B. Cunninghame Graham born
  Isabella, Lady Gregory, born
  George Moore born
  Talbot Baines Reed born
- Sara Coleridge dies
  Thomas Moore dies
  Augustus Pugin dies
  John Hamilton Reynolds dies
  Jane West dies
- Arthur Wellesley, duke of Wellington, dies (14 Sept.)
- Nocolai Gogol dies
- Harriet Beecher Stowe, *Uncle Tom's Cabin*
  Gautier, *Émaux et Camées*

'A' [Matthew Arnold (1822–88)]
Empedocles on Etna, and Other Poems V

E.L.L. Blanchard (1820–89)
Adams's Illustrated Guide to the Lake District NF

Dion Boucicault (1820?–90)
The Corsican Brothers: A dramatic romance D
Performed 24 February 1852

Wilkie Collins (1824–89)
Basil: A story of modern life F
Published in November 1852

Wilkie Collins (1824–89)
Mr Wray's Cash Box; or, The Mask and the Mystery F
Published on 17 December 1852

Dinah Mulock, later **Craik** (1826–87)
Bread Upon the Waters: A governess's life F
bao *Olive*

Charles Kingsley (1819–75)
Sermons on National Subjects NF

Edward Lear (1812–88)
Journals of a Landscape Painter in Southern Calabria NF
Illustrated by Lear. See also *Journals* 1851, 1870.

Charles Lever (1806–72)
Maurice Tiernay, The Soldier of Fortune F
First serialized in the *Dublin University Magazine* (April 1850–December 1851)

Henry Edward Manning, later **Cardinal** (1808–92)
The Grounds of Faith NF

Harriet Martineau (1802–76)
Letters from Ireland NF

Mary Russell Mitford (1787–1855)
Recollections of a Literary Life NF

Laurence Oliphant (1829–88)
A Journey to Katmandu with the Camp of Jung Bahadoor NF

'Henry J. Thurstan' [Francis Turner Palgrave (1824–97)]
Preciosa F

Charles Reade (1814–84)
Peg Woffington F
Published in December 1852, dated 1853. Adapted from Reade's play *Masks and Faces* (1852), published in 1854.

Thomas Mayne Reid (1818–83)
The Desert Home; or, The Adventures of a Lost Family in the Wilderness F
Subtitled 'The English Family Robinson'

P.M. Roget (1779–1869)
Thesaurus of English Words and Phrases D

Alfred Tennyson (1809–92)
Ode on the Death of the Duke of Wellington V
Wellington died on 14 September 1852

W.M. Thackeray (1811–63)
The Confessions of Fitz-Boodle; and Some Passages in the Life of Major Gahagan F
The first book publication of the *Confessions* (papers first published in *Fraser's Magazine,* 1842–3). *Some Passages* first published in book form in 1841 (q.v.).

W.M. Thackeray (1811–63)
The History of Henry Esmond, Esq. F

W.M. Thackeray (1811–63)
A Shabby Genteel Story, and Other Tales F

William Whewell (1794–1866)
Lectures on the History of Moral Philosophy in England NF

1853

- Napoleon III marries Eugénie de Montijo
  Franklin Pierce becomes President of the USA
  Russia occupies the Danubian Principalities
  Turkey declares war on Russia (4 Oct.): beginning of the Crimean War (-1856)
  Turkish fleet destroyed by the Russians at Sinope (30 Nov.)
- Clementina Black born
  Kathleen Mannington Caffyn ('Iota') born
  Hall Caine born
  Helen Mathers (Ellen Mathews) born
- Joseph Cottle dies
  Amelia Opie dies
- Cecil Rhodes born
- Vincent Van Gogh born
- Johann Ludwig Tieck dies
- Hawthorne, *Tanglewood Tales*
  Charles Knight's *English Cyclopaedia* (-1861)

Grace Aguilar (1816–47)
Home Scenes and Heart Studies F

Cecil Frances Alexander (1818–95)
Narrative Hymns for Village Schools V

Matthew Arnold (1822–88)
Poems: a New Edition V
The first collected edition of Arnold's poems, known as *Poems: First Series*. See also 1855.

'Punjabee' [William Delafield Arnold (1828–59)]
Oakfield; or, Fellowship in the East F

'Cuthbert Bede B.A.' [Edward Bradley (1827–89)]
The Adventures of Mr Verdant Green, an Oxford Freshman F
Published in October 1853. See also *Further Adventures of Mr Verdant Green* 1854, *Mr Verdant Green, Married and Done For* 1857; *Little Mr Bouncer* 1873.

'Melanter' [R.D. Blackmore (1825–1900)]
Poems by Melanter V

'Currer Bell' [Charlotte Brontë (1816–55)]
Villette F
Published on 28 January 1853

Elizabeth Barrett Browning (1806–61)
Poems V
Published on 12 October 1853. Dedicated to the author's father, Edward Barrett. See also *Poems* 1844, 1850, 1856.

'Pisistratus Caxton' [Sir Edward Bulwer-Lytton (1803–73)]
'My Novel'; or, Varieties in English Life F

George Cayley (1826–78)
Las Alforjas; or, The Bridle Roads of Spain NF
Anonymous

'V' [Caroline Clive (1801–73)]
The Morlas V

S.T. Coleridge (1772–1834)
Hints Towards the Formation of a More Comprehensive Theory of Life NF

S.T. Coleridge (1772–1834)
Notes, Theological, Poetical, and Miscellaneous NF
Edited by Derwent Coleridge

Thomas De Quincey (1785–1859)
Autobiographic Sketches NF
Volume i of *Selections Grave and Gay*. See also *Autobiographic Sketches* 1854.

Charles Dickens (1812–70)
Bleak House F
Published in September 1853. Illustrated by Hablot K. Browne ('Phiz'). First published in monthly parts (28 February 1852–31 August 1853).

Charles Dickens (1812–70)
A Child's History of England NF
Serialized in *Household Words* (25 January 1851–10 December 1853)

Sydney Dobell (1824–74)
Balder V
bao *The Roman*

Francis Galton (1822–1911)
The Narrative of an Explorer in Tropical Southern Africa NF

Elizabeth Gaskell (1810–65)
Cranford F
bao *Mary Barton, Ruth*. First serialized in *Household Words* (13 December 1851–21 May 1853).

Elizabeth Gaskell (1810–65)
Ruth F
bao *Mary Barton*. Published in January 1853.

Benjamin Robert Haydon (1786–1846)
The Life of Benjamin Robert Haydon NF
Edited by Tom Taylor. See also *Correspondence* 1876.

Geraldine Jewsbury (1812–80)
The History of an Adopted Child F

Charles Kingsley (1819–75)
Hypatia; or, New Foes with an Old Face F
First serialized in *Fraser's Magazine* (January 1852–April 1853)

Walter Savage Landor (1775–1864)
Imaginary Conversations of Greeks and Romans NF
See also *Imaginary Conversations* 1824, 1828, 1829, 1848; *Last Fruit* 1853

Walter Savage Landor (1775–1864)
The Last Fruit off an Old Tree NF
Contains eighteen imaginary conversations and ten satiric letters addressed to Cardinal Wiseman

Denis MacCarthy (1817–82) (tr.)
Dramas of Calderón D
See also *The Two Lovers of Heaven* 1870

Harriet Martineau (1802–76) (tr. and ed.)
The Positive Philosophy of August Comte NF

F.D. Maurice (1805–72)
Theological Essays NF

Thomas Moore (1779–1852)
Memoirs, Journal, and Correspondence of Thomas Moore NF
Edited by Lord John Russell

Coventry Patmore (1823–96)
Tamerton Church-Tower, and Other Poems V
See also *Amelia* 1878

Charles Reade (1814–84)
Christie Johnstone F
Published in August 1853. Developed from an earlier play by Reade of the same name.

Thomas Mayne Reid (1818–83)
The Boy Hunters; or, Adventures in Search of a White Buffalo F
Juvenile

John Ruskin (1819–1900)
The Stones of Venice: Volume the Second NF
Published on 28 July 1853. Volume i, 1851 (q.v.); volume iii, 1853 (see below).

John Ruskin (1819–1900)
The Stones of Venice: Volume the Third NF
Published on 2 October 1853. Volume i, 1851 (q.v.); volume ii, 1853 (see above).

R.S. Surtees (1805–64)
Mr Sponge's Sporting Tour F
bao *Handley Cross*. Illustrated by John Leech. First published in monthly parts (January–December 1852). Earlier version serialized in the *New Monthly Magazine*, 1849–51.

W.M. Thackeray (1811–63)
The English Humourists of the Eighteenth Century NF
Published in June 1853. Lectures delivered in London May–July 1853.

Alfred R. Wallace (1823–1913)
A Narrative of Travels on the Amazon and Rio Negro NF

G.J. Whyte-Melville (1821–78)
Digby Grand F

Charlotte M. Yonge (1823–1901)
The Heir of Redclyffe F
bao *The Two Guardians*

1854

- France and Britain declare war on Russia
  Republican Party established in the USA
  Allied forces land in the Crimea (14 Sept.)
  Battle of the Alma (20 Sept.)
  Siege of Sebastopol begins (Oct.)
  Battle of Balaclava; Charge of the Light Brigade (25 Oct.)
  Battle of Inkerman (5 Nov.)
- J.G. Frazer born
  Sarah Grand (Frances McFall, *née* Clarke) born
  Oscar Wilde born
- Caroline Southey (*née* Bowles) dies
  Thomas Crofton Croker dies
  Susan Ferrier dies
  Hannah Jones dies
  John Gibson Lockhart dies
  James Montgomery dies
  Thomas Noon Talfourd dies
  John Wilson ('Christopher North') dies
- Arthur Rimbaud born
- Thoreau, *Walden*

William Allingham (1824–89)
Day and Night Songs V
See also *The Music-Master* 1855

'T. Percy Jones' [W.E. Aytoun (1813–65)**]**
Firmilian; or, The Student of Badajoz V
Subtitled 'A Spasmodic tragedy'

'Cuthbert Bede B.A.' [Edward Bradley (1827–89)]
The Further Adventures of Mr Verdant Green, an Oxford Undergraduate F
See also *Verdant Green* 1853, *Mr Verdant Green, Married and Done For* 1857; *Little Mr Bouncer* 1873

Barbara Leigh Smith, later **Bodichon** (1827–91)
A Brief Summary in Plain Language, of the Most Important Laws Concerning Women NF

Mary Elizabeth Braddon (1835–1915)
Three Times Dead; or, The Secret of the Heath F
The author's first novel. Reissued as *The Trail of the Serpent; or, Three Times Dead* (1861).

Elizabeth Barrett Browning (1806–61) and **Robert Browning** (1812–89)
Two Poems V
Published in April 1854. Contains 'A Plea for the Ragged Schools of London' (EBB) and 'The Twins' (RB). Publication was paid for by the Brownings and proceeds donated to the Ragged Schools.

Wilkie Collins (1824–89)
Hide and Seek F

Thomas De Quincey (1785–1859)
Autobiographic Sketches NF
Published in February 1854. Volume ii of *Selections Grave and Gay.* See also *Autobiographic Sketches* 1853.

Thomas De Quincey (1785–1859)
Miscellanies [i] NF
Published in June 1854. Volume iii of *Selections Grave and Gay.*

Thomas De Quincey (1785–1859)
Miscellanies [ii] NF
Published in December 1854. Volume iv of *Selections Grave and Gay.*

Charles Dickens (1812–70)
Hard Times, For These Times F
Published in August 1854. First serialized in *Household Words* (1 April–12 August 1854).

Marian Evans ['George Eliot' (1819–80)**]** (tr.)
The Essence of Christianity NF
Published in July 1854. Translated from Ludwig Feuerbach (1804–72). The only book to be published under the author's real name.

Elizabeth Gaskell (1810–65)
Lizzie Leigh, and Other Tales F
bao *Mary Barton, Ruth.* Published in September 1854.

Annie French, later **Hector** (1825–1902)
Kate Vernon F
Anonymous

T.H. Huxley (1825–95)
On the Educational Value of the Natural History Sciences NF

John Keats (1795–1821)
The Poetical Works of John Keats V
Edited by Richard Monckton Milnes

Charles Kingsley (1819–75)
Sermons on National Subjects NF
Second series. See *Sermons on National Subjects* 1852.

Thomas Babington Macaulay (1800–59)
Speeches NF

Henry Hart Milman (1791–1868)
History of Latin Christianity, Including that of the Popes to Nicolas V NF
Published in 6 volumes (1854–5)

Mary Russell Mitford (1787–1855)
Atherton, and Other Tales F

Mary Russell Mitford (1787–1855)
Dramatic Works D

Margaret Oliphant (1828–97)
Magdalen Hepburn F
bao *Passages in the Life of Margaret Maitland*

Coventry Patmore (1823–96)
The Betrothal [*The Angel in the House* i] V
See also *The Espousals* 1856, *Faithful for Ever* 1860, *The Victories of Love* 1863

John Ruskin (1819–1900)
Lectures on Architecture and Painting NF
Published in April 1854. Lectures delivered in November 1853.

John Ruskin (1819–1900)
The Opening of the Crystal Palace NF
Published in July 1854

'Arthur Pendennis' [W.M. Thackeray (1811–63)]
The Newcomes F
Illustrated by Richard Doyle. First published in monthly parts (October 1853–August 1855) and also serialized in *Harper's Monthly Magazine* (November 1853–October 1855).

Frances Trollope (1779–1863)
The Life and Adventures of a Clever Woman F

Edmund Yates (1831–94)
My Haunts and their Frequenters F

Charlotte M. Yonge (1823–1901)
The Little Duke; or, Richard the Fearless F
bao *The Heir of Redclyffe*. First serialized in *The Monthly Packet* (January–October 1851).

Charlotte M. Yonge (1823–1901)
Heartsease; or, The Brother's Wife F
bao *The Heir of Redclyffe*

1855

- Death of Tsar Nicholas I; succeeded by Alexander II
  Fall of Sebastopol (11 Sept.)
  Daily Chronicle started
  Daily Telegraph started
- W.P. Ker born
  Oliver Madox Brown born
  Marie Corelli born
  Arthur Wing Pinero born
  William Sharp ('Fiona Macleod') born
  Olive Schreiner born
  Howard Sturgis born
  Stanley Weyman born
- Charlotte Brontë dies
  Julius Hare dies
  Mary Russell Mitford dies
  Robert Montgomery dies
  Samuel Rogers dies
- Søren Kierkegaard dies
  Gérard de Nerval dies
- Whitman, *Leaves of Grass*

The Saturday Review of Politics, Literature, Science and Art PER
Published weekly from 3 November 1856–July 1938

William Allingham (1824–89)
The Music-Master V
Published in June 1855. Illustrated by Arthur Hughes, D.G. Rossetti, and J.E. Millais. See also *Day and Night Songs* 1854.

Matthew Arnold (1822–88)
Poems: Second Series V
See also *Poems* 1853

Philip James Bailey (1816–1902)
The Mystic, and Other Poems V
See also *Festus* 1839

Alexander Bain (1818–1903)
The Senses and the Intellect NF

William Cox Bennett (1820–95)
Anti-Maud V
'By a poet of the people'. A parody of Tennyson's *Maud* 1855 (q.v.).

William Cox Bennett (1820–95)
War Songs V

Robert Browning (1812–89)
Men and Women V
Published in November 1855

Richard F. Burton (1821–90)
Personal Narrative of a Pilgrimage to El-Medinah and Meccah NF
Published in 3 volumes (1855–6)

Thomas Campbell (1777–1844)
The Pleasures of Hope, with Other Poems V
First published in 1799 (q.v.). Illustrated by Birket Foster, George Thomas, and Harrison Weir.

Caroline Clive (1801–73)
Paul Ferroll F
bao *IX Poems by 'V'*. See also *Why Paul Ferroll Killed His Wife* 1860.

'Adam Hornbrook' [Thomas Cooper (1805–92)]
The Family Feud F

'S. Yendys' [Sydney Dobell (1824–74)] and **Alexander Smith** (1830–67)
Sonnets on the War V

Elizabeth Gaskell (1810–65)
North and South F
bao *Mary Barton, Ruth, Cranford*. Published in March 1855. First serialized in *Household Words* (2 September 1854–27 January 1855). This text differs substantially from the serial.

Saba, Lady Holland (1802–66)
A Memoir of the Reverend Sydney Smith NF
Sydney Smith died in February 1845. His daughter Saba married the physician Sir Henry Holland in 1834.

Leigh Hunt (1784–1859)
Stories in Verse V

Geraldine Jewsbury (1812–80)
Constance Herbert F

Charles Kingsley (1819–75)
Glaucus; or, The Wonders of the Shore NF
For children. Based on an article published in the *North British Review* (November 1854).

Charles Kingsley (1819–75)
Westward Ho!; or, The Voyages and Adventures of Sir Amyas Leigh F

'Holme Lee' [Harriet Parr (1828–1900)]
Gilbert Massenger F

'Owen Meredith' [Edward Robert Bulwer Lytton (1831–91)]
Clytemnestra; The Earl's Return; The Artist, and Other Poems V

Thomas Babington Macaulay (1800–59)
The History of England from the Accession of James II [vols iii, iv] NF
Published in December 1855. Volumes i and ii published in 1849 (q.v.).

George MacDonald (1824–1905)
Within and Without V
Published on 18 May 1855. MacDonald's first published book.

Augustus Mayhew (1826–75)
Kitty Lamere; or, A Dark Page in London Life F

George Meredith (1828–1909)
The Shaving of Shagpat: An Arabian entertainment F
Published on 19 December 1855, dated 1856

Margaret Oliphant (1828–97)
Lilliesleaf F
Anonymous. Published in December 1855. Sequel to *Passages in the Life of Mrs Margaret Maitland* 1849 (q.v.).

Margaret Oliphant (1828–97)
Zaidee F
Published in December 1855, dated 1856. Serialized in *Blackwood's Magazine* (December 1854–December 1855).

E.B. Pusey (1800–82)
The Doctrine of the Real Presence NF

Louisa Shore (1824–95)
War Lyrics V
Anonymous. Written with her sister, Arabella Shore.

Tom Taylor (1817–80)
'Still Waters Run Deep': An original comedy D
Performed 14 May 1855. Based on the novel *De Gendre* by 'Charles de Bernard' (i.e. Pierce Marie Charles Bernard du Grail de la Villette).

Alfred Tennyson (1809–92)
Maud, and Other Poems V
Published in August 1855. Includes 'The Charge of the Light Brigade' (first published in the *Examiner*, 9 December 1854) and *Ode on the Death of the Duke of Wellington* 1852 (q.v.).

'Mr M.A. Titmarsh' [W.M. Thackeray (1811–63)]
The Rose and the Ring; or, The History of Prince Giglio and Prince Bulbo F
Illustrated by Thackeray. The fifth, and last, of Thackeray's Christmas books. See also *Mrs Perkins's Ball* 1847, *Our Street* 1848, *Doctor Birch and His Young Friends* 1849, and *The Kickleburys on the Rhine* 1850.

Anthony Trollope (1815–82)
The Warden F

Published in January 1855. The first of the six Barsetshire novels. See also *Barchester Towers* 1857, *Doctor Thorne* 1858, *Framley Parsonage* 1861, *The Small House at Allington* 1864, *The Last Chronicle of Barset* 1867.

Catherine Winkworth (1827–78) (tr.)
Lyra Germanica [1st ser.] v
A popular translation of *Versuch eines allgemeinen evangelischen Gesang- und Gebetbuchs* by Christian Karl Josias, Freiherr von Busen (1791–1860). A second series was published in 1858 (q.v.).

Nicholas Patrick Wiseman, Cardinal Wiseman (1802–65)
Fabiola; or, The Church of the Catacombs F
Anonymous

Charlotte M. Yonge (1823–1901)
The Lances of Lynwood F
bao *The Little Duke.* Published in October 1855. First serialized in *The Monthly Packet* (January 1853–December 1854).

Charlotte M. Yonge (1823–1901)
The Railroad Children F
bao *The Heir of Redclyffe. First* serialized in *Mozley's Magazine for the Young* (1849).

1856

- Victoria Cross instituted by Queen Victoria
  Treaty of Paris ending the Crimean War (30 Mar.)
- F. Anstey (Thomas Anstey Guthrie) born
  William Archer born
  Henry Rider Haggard born
  Frank Harris born
  Vernon Lee (Violet Paget) born
  George Bernard Shaw born
- Gilbert Abbott à Beckett dies
  Hugh Miller dies
- Keir Hardie born
- Sigmund Freud born
- Heinrich Heine dies
  Robert Schumann dies
- Flaubert, *Madame Bovary*
  Hugo, *Les Contemplations*

Isabella L. Bird (1831–1904)
An Englishwoman in America NF

Elizabeth Barrett Browning (1806–61)
Poems v
Published on 1 November 1856. Dedicated to Edward Barrett. See also *Poems* 1844, 1850, 1853.

Elizabeth Barrett Browning (1806–61)
Aurora Leigh v
Published on 15 November 1856, dated 1857

Wilkie Collins (1824–89)
After Dark F
Published in February 1856

Dinah Mulock, later **Craik** (1826–87)
John Halifax, Gentleman F
bao *The Head of the Family*

Thomas De Quincey (1785–1859)
Confessions of an English Opium Eater NF
Volume v of *Selections Grave and Gay.* Enlarged from 1822 (q.v.) and including 'The Daughters of Lebanon'.

Sydney Dobell (1824–74)
England in Time of War v

Edward FitzGerald (1809–83) (tr.)
Salámán and Absál v
Anonymous. See also *Rubáiyát* 1859.

Tom Hood (1835–74)
Pen and Pencil Pictures NF
Published 1856, dated 1857

Geraldine Jewsbury (1812–80)
The Sorrows of Gentility F

Charles Kingsley (1819–75)
The Heroes; or, Greek Fairy Tales for My Children F
Illustrated by Kingsley

Walter Savage Landor (1775–1864)
Antony and Octavius v

Charles Lever (1806–72)
The Martins of Cro' Martin F
Illustrated by Hablot K. Browne ('Phiz')

David Masson (1822–1907)
Essays Biographical and Critical NF

John Henry Newman, later **Cardinal** (1801–90)
Callista F
Anonymous

Coventry Patmore (1823–96)
The Espousals [*The Angel in the House* ii] v
See also *The Betrothal* 1854, *Faithful for Ever* 1860, *The Victories of Love* 1863

Charles Reade (1814–84)
'It Is Never Too Late To Mend': A matter-of-fact novel F
Published on 1 August 1856. Developed from Reade's play *Gold* (1853).

Samuel Rogers (1763–1855)
Recollections of the Table-Talk of Samuel Rogers NF
Memoir by Alexander Dyce

John Ruskin (1819–1900)
Modern Painters: Volume III NF
Published on 15 January 1856. Volume i, 1843 (q.v.); volume ii, 1846 (q.v.); volume iv, 1856 (below)

John Ruskin (1819–1900)
Modern Painters: Volume IV NF
Published on 14 April 1856. Volume i, 1843 (q.v.), volume ii, 1846 (q.v.); volume iii, 1856 (above).

W.M. Thackeray (1811–63)
The Memoirs of Barry Lyndon F
Serialized in *Fraser's Magazine* 1844 (q.v.) as *The Luck of Barry Lyndon*. The first British edition. First book publication in the USA, 1853.

Frances Trollope (1779–1863)
Fashionable Life; or, Paris and London F

Charlotte M. Yonge (1823–1901)
The Daisy Chain; or, Aspirations F
bao *The Heir of Redclyffe*. Part i serialized in *The Monthly Packet* (July 1853–December 1855). See also *The Trial* 1864.

1857

- James Buchanan becomes President of the USA
  Revolt of Sepoys at Meerut (10 May): beginning of the Indian Mutiny
  Massacre of Cawnpore
  Relief of Lucknow (17 Nov.)
  British forces recapture Cawnpore (6 Dec.)
  Matthew Arnold becomes Professor of Poetry at Oxford
  The Christian World started
  The Atlantic Monthly started
- Jane Barlow born
  Joseph Conrad born
  John Davidson born
  George Gissing born
  Edwin Arnold Lester born
- John Wilson Croker dies
  Douglas Jerrold dies
  Isabella Kelly dies
- Robert Baden-Powell born
  Edward Elgar born
- Auguste Comte dies
  Alfred de Musset dies
- Baudelaire, *Les Fleurs du mal*

R.M. Ballantyne (1825–94)
The Coral Island F
Published in November 1857, dated 1858. Illustrated by Ballantyne.

'Cuthbert Bede B.A.' [Edward Bradley (1827–89)]
Mr Verdant Green, Married and Done For F
See also *Verdant Green* 1853, *Further Adventures of Mr Verdant Green* 1854; *Little Mr Bouncer* 1873

Matilda Betham-Edwards (1836–1919)
The White House by the Sea NF

George Borrow (1803–81)
The Romany Rye F
Published on 18 May 1857. Sequel to *Lavengro* 1851 (q.v.).

'Currer Bell' [Charlotte Brontë (1816–55)**]**
The Professor F
Published on 6 June 1857

Frances Browne (1816–79)
Granny's Wonderful Chair, and Its Tales of Fairy Times F

Henry Thomas Buckle (1821–62)
History of Civilization in England NF
Published in 2 volumes (1857–61)

Thomas Campbell (1777–1844)
Gertrude of Wyoming; or, The Pennsylvanian Cottage V
First published in 1809 (q.v.). Illustrated by Birket Foster, William Harvey, Thomas Dalziel, and Harrison Weir.

Wilkie Collins (1824–89)
The Dead Secret F
Published in June 1857. First serialized in *Household Words* (January–June 1857).

Thomas De Quincey (1785–1859)
Sketches, Critical and Biographic NF
Volume vi of *Selections Grave and Gay*

Charles Dickens (1812–70)
Little Dorrit F
Illustrated by Hablot K. Brown ('Phiz'). First published in monthly parts (30 November 1855–30 June 1857).

Elizabeth Gaskell (1810–65)
The Life of Charlotte Brontë NF
Published on 25 March 1857

Anna Maria Hall [Mrs S.C. Hall] (1800–81)
A Woman's Story F

Thomas Hughes (1822–96)
Tom Brown's Schooldays F

Published on 24 April 1857. Six editions by 1858. See also *Tom Brown at Oxford* 1861.

Annie Keary (1825–79)
The Heroes of Asgard F
bao *Mia and Charlie*. Co-written with her sister Eliza Keary.

Charles Kingsley (1819–75)
Two Years Ago F

G.A. Lawrence (1827–76)
Guy Livingstone; or, Thorough F
Anonymous

Charles Lever (1806–72)
The Fortunes of Glencore F
Serialized in the *Dublin University Magazine*, 1855–7

David Livingstone (1813–73)
Missionary Travels and Researches in South Africa NF

'Owen Meredith' [Edward Robert Bulwer Lytton (1831–91)]
The Wanderer V

Denis MacCarthy (1817–82)
Underglimpses, and Other Poems V

George MacDonald (1824–1905)
Poems V

Theodore Martin (1816–1909) (tr.)
Aladdin; or, The Wonderful Lamp V
Translated from Adam Oehlenschläger (1779–1850)

Theodore Martin (1816–1909)
The Life of His Royal Highness the Prince Consort NF
Published in 5 volumes (1875–80)

George Meredith (1828–1909)
Farina F

David Morier (1784–1877)
Photo the Suliote F

Robert Owen (1771–1858)
Life, Written by Himself NF

Emily Pfeiffer (1827–90)
Valisneria; or, A Midsummer Night's Dream F

Charles Reade (1814–84)
The Course of True Love Never Did Run Smooth F

John Ruskin (1819–1900)
The Political Economy of Art NF
Published on 3 December 1857

Mary Seacole (1805–81)
Wonderful Adventures of Mrs Seacole in Many Lands NF
Preface by W.H. Russell, correspondent of *The Times*

Samuel Smiles (1812–1904)
The Life of George Stephenson, Railway Engineer NF

Anthony Trollope (1815–82)
Barchester Towers F
Published in May 1857. The second of the six Barsetshire novels. See also *The Warden* 1855, *Doctor Thorne* 1858, *Framley Parsonage* 1861, *The Small House at Allington* 1864, *The Last Chronicle of Barset* 1867.

Anthony Trollope (1815–82)
The Three Clerks F
Published in December 1857, dated 1858

William Wordsworth (1770–1850)
The Poetical Works of William Wordsworth V
Includes notes dictated by Wordsworth to Miss Fenwick. See also *Miscellaneous Poems* 1820, *Poetical Works* 1827, *Poetical Works* 1836, *Poetical Works* 1840, *Poems* 1845, and *Poetical Works* (Centenary Edition) 1870.

Charlotte M. Yonge (1823–1901)
Dynevor Terrace; or, The Clue of Life F
bao *The Heir of Redclyffe*

1858

- Powers of the East India Company transferred to the British Crown
  Dickens begins his public readings
  Sinn Fein founded in Ireland
- John Meade Falkner born
  Henry Watson Fowler born
  Edith Nesbit born
  Edith Œnone Somerville born
  Sir William Watson born
  Beatrice Webb born
- Richard Ford dies
  Robert Owen dies
- Giacomo Puccini born
- Oliver Wendell Holmes, *The Autocrat of the Breakfast Table*

John Leycester Adolphus (1795–1862)
Letters from Spain in 1856 and 1857 NF

Charles Hamilton Aïdé (1826–1906)
Rita F
Anonymous

W.H. Ainsworth (1805–82)
The Life and Adventures of Mervyn Clitheroe F
Illustrated by Hablot K. Browne ('Phiz'). First published in monthly parts (December 1851–March 1852, December 1857–June 1858)

Cecil Frances Alexander (1818–95)
Hymns Descriptive and Devotional for the Use of Schools V

Matthew Arnold (1822–88)
Merope V

Walter Bagehot (1826–77)
Estimates of Some Englishmen and Scotchmen NF
See also *Literary Studies* 1879

R.M. Ballantyne (1825–94)
Martin Rattler; or, A Boy's Adventures in the Forests of Brazil F
Published in November 1858. Juvenile.

R.M. Ballantyne (1825)
Ungava F
Illustrated by Ballantyne. Juvenile.

John Brown (1810–82)
Horae Subsecivae NF
Published in 3 volumes (1858–82)

Thomas Carlyle (1795–1881)
History of Frederick II of Prussia, called Frederick the Great [vols i–iv] NF
Published in February 1858. See also *History of Frederick II* 1865.

Elizabeth Rundle Charles (1821–89)
The Voice of Christian Life in Song V
bao *Tales and Sketches of Christian Life*

A.H. Clough (1819–61)
'Amours de Voyage' V
Publication in the *Atlantic Monthly* (February–May 1858). Reprinted in the posthumous *Poems* 1862 (q.v.).

William Johnson Cory (1823–92)
Ionica V
Anonymous. See also *Ionica II* 1877.

Charles Davies (1829–85)
Philip Paternoster: A Tractarian love-story F
'By an ex-Puseyite'

Thomas De Quincey (1785–1859)
Studies on Secret Records, Personal and Historic NF
Volume vii of *Selections Grave and Gay*

Thomas De Quincey (1785–1859)
Essays Sceptical and Anti-sceptical, on Problems Neglected or Misconceived NF
Volume viii of *Selections Grave and Gay*

Thomas De Quincey (1785–1859)
Leaders in Literature, with a Notice of Traditional Errors Affecting Them NF
Volume ix of *Selections Grave and Gay*

'George Eliot' [Mary Ann Evans (1819–80)**]**
Scenes of Clerical Life F
Published in January 1858. Contains *Amos Barton; Janet's Repentance* (serialized in *Blackwood's Magazine*, July–November 1857); 'The Sad Fortunes of the Revd Amos Barton' (serialized in *Blackwood's*, January–February 1857); and 'Mr Gilfil's Love Story' (serialized in *Blackwood's*, March–June 1857).

Frederic W. Farrar (1831–1903)
Eric; or, Little by Little F

John Forster (1812–76)
Historical and Biographical Essays NF

W.E. Gladstone (1809–98)
Studies on Homer and the Homeric Age NF

Thomas Jefferson Hogg (1792–1862)
The Life of Percy Bysshe Shelley NF

Charles Kingsley (1819–75)
Andromeda, and Other Poems V

Walter Savage Landor (1775–1864)
Dry Sticks, Fagoted V

George MacDonald (1824–1905)
Phantastes: A faerie romance for men and women F
Published in October 1858

Augustus Mayhew (1826–75)
Paved with Gold; or, The Romance and Reality of London Streets F
Illustrated by Hablot K. Browne ('Phiz')

William Morris (1834–96)
The Defence of Guenevere, and Other Poems V
Morris's first book. Dedicated to D.G. Rossetti.

Thomas Love Peacock (1785–1866)
'Memoirs of Percy Bysshe Shelley' NF
Publication in *Fraser's Magazine* (June 1858). See also 'Memoirs of Shelley' 1860.

Adelaide A. Procter (1825–64)
Legends and Lyrics [1st ser.] V
Procter was author of the well-known lyric 'The Lost Chord', set to music by Sir Arthur Sullivan.

'F.G. Trafford' [Charlotte Elizabeth Riddell (1832–1906)]
The Moors and the Fens F

Herbert Spencer (1820–1903)
Essays: Scientific, Political, and Speculative [1st ser.] NF

R.S. Surtees (1805–64)
'Ask Mamma'; or, The Richest Commoner in England F
bao *Handley Cross*. Illustrated by John Leech.

W.M. Thackeray (1811–63)
The Virginians F
Volume i dated 1858, volume ii dated 1859. Illustrated by Thackeray. First published in monthly parts (November 1857–October 1859) and serialized in *Harper's Monthly Magazine* (December 1857–November 1859).

E.J. Trelawny (1792–1881)
Recollections of the Last Days of Shelley and Byron NF

Anthony Trollope (1815–82)
Doctor Thorne F
Published in June 1858. The third of the six Barsetshire novels. See also *The Warden* 1855, *Barchester Towers* 1857, *Framley Parsonage* 1861, *The Small House at Allington* 1864, *The Last Chronicle of Barset* 1867.

G.J. Whyte-Melville (1821–78)
The Interpreter: A tale of the war F

Catherine Winkworth (1827–78) (tr.)
Lyra Germanica: Second Series V
See *Lyra Germanica* 1855

1859

- US abolitionist John Brown raids Harpers Ferry and is subsequently executed
  War of Italian Liberation begins
  Sporting Life started
- Mary Cholmondeley born
  Sir Arthur Conan Doyle born
  George Egerton (Mary Chavelita Dunne) born
  Havelock Ellis born
  Kenneth Grahame born
  A.E. Housman born
  Jerome K. Jerome born
  Sir Sidney Lee born
  A.W. Pollard born
  Ernest Rhys born
  Francis Thompson born
  Sidney Webb born
- William Delafield Arnold dies
  Thomas de Quincey dies
  Henry Hallam dies
  Leigh Hunt dies
  Lord Macaulay dies
  Sir James Stephen dies
- Isambard Kingdom Brunel dies
- Henri Bergson born
  Theodore Roosevelt born
- Washington Irving dies
  Alexander von Humboldt dies
- *Chambers's Encyclopaedia* (–1868)

All the Year Round PER
Published weekly from 30 April 1859–1893. Owned and edited by Charles Dickens until his death in 1870. Editorship taken over by Dickens's eldest son Charley until 1888.

Macmillan's Magazine PER
Published monthly from November 1859–October 1907

Once a Week PER
Published weekly from 2 July 1859–May 1879. Editors included E.S. Dallas, Mark Lemon, and George Manville Fenn.

Walter Bagehot (1826–77)
Parliamentary Reform NF

William Barnes (1801–86)
Hwomely Rhymes V
See also 1844, 1862, 1868

William Barnes (1801–86)
The Song of Solomon in the Dorset Dialect V

Andrew Kennedy Boyd (1825–99)
Recreations of a Country Parson [1st ser.] NF
Anonymous. Two further series in 1861 and 1878.

John Brown (1810–82)
Rab and His Friends NF

Wilkie Collins (1824–89)
The Queen of Hearts F
Published in October 1859. Short stories.

Catherine Crowe (1790–1876)
Spiritualism, and the Age We Live In NF

Charles Darwin (1809–82)
On the Origin of Species by Natural Selection NF
Sixth edition published in 1872 as *The Origin of Species*

Thomas De Quincey (1785–1859)
Classic Records Reviewed or Deciphered NF
Volume x of *Selections Grave and Gay*

Thomas De Quincey (1785–1859)
Critical Suggestions on Style and Rhetoric NF
Volume xi of *Selections Grave and Gay*

Thomas De Quincey (1785–1859)
Speculations, Literary and Philosophic NF
Volumes xii–xiii of *Selections Grave and Gay*

Charles Dickens (1812–70)
A Tale of Two Cities F
Published in November 1859. Illustrated by Hablot K. Browne ('Phiz')—the last of Dickens's books to be illustrated by Browne. First serialized in *All the Year Round* (30 April–26 November 1859); also published in monthly parts (June–December 1859).

'Lady Theresa Lewis' [Emily Eden (1797–1869)]
The Semi-Detached House F

'George Eliot' [Mary Ann Evans (1819–80)]
Adam Bede F
Published on 1 February 1859. Seven editions in 1859.

'George Eliot' [Mary Ann Evans (1819–80)]
'The Lifted Veil' F
Publication in *Blackwood's Edinburgh Magazine* (July 1859)

Edward FitzGerald (1809–83) (tr.)
The Rubáiyát of Omar Khayyám V
Anonymous. Revised in 1868, 1872, 1879 (with the *Salámán* and *Absál* of Jámí: see 1856).

Elizabeth Gaskell (1810–65)
Round the Sofa F
bao *Mary Barton, The Life of Charlotte Brontë*

Margaret Gatty (1809–73)
Aunt Judy's Tales F
See also *Aunt Judy's Letters* 1862

Geraldine Jewsbury (1812–80)
Right or Wrong F

Henry Kingsley (1830–76)
The Recollections of Geoffrey Hamlyn F

Charles Lever (1806–72)
Davenport Dunn; or, The Man of the Day F
Illustrated by Hablot K. Browne ('Phiz'). First published in monthly parts (July 1857–April 1859).

Harriet Martineau (1802–76)
England and her Soldiers NF

George Meredith (1828–1909)
The Ordeal of Richard Feverel F
Published on 20 June 1859

John Stuart Mill (1806–73)
Dissertations and Discussions NF

John Stuart Mill (1806–73)
On Liberty NF

John Stuart Mill (1806–73)
Thoughts on Parliamentary Reform NF

Charles Reade (1814–84)
'Love Me Little, Love Me Long' F
Published in April 1859

Winwood Reade (1838–75)
Charlotte and Myra F

John Ruskin (1819–1900)
The Two Paths NF
Lectures delivered 1858–9

George Augustus Sala (1828–95)
Twice Round the Clock; or, The Hours of the Day and Night in London F
Published in October 1859. First published in *The Welcome Guest* from May 1858.

Nassau W. Senior (1790–1864)
A Journal Kept in Turkey and Greece NF

P.B. Shelley (1792–1822)
Shelley Memorials NF
Edited by Lady Shelley

Louisa Shore (1824–95)
Gemma of the Isles V
Anonymous. Written with her sister, Arabella Shore.

Samuel Smiles (1812–1904)
Self-Help NF

Alfred Tennyson (1809–92)
Idylls of the King V
Published in June 1859. See also *The Holy Grail* 1869, *Idylls of the King* 1870, 'The Last Tournament' 1871, *Gareth and Lynette* 1872, 'Balin and Balan' in *Tiresias* 1885, *Idylls of the King* 1889.

Anthony Trollope (1815–82)
The Bertrams F
Published in March 1859

1860

- Garibaldi enters Naples (7 Sept.); Victor Emmanuel proclaimed King of Italy (26 Oct.)
  Emancipation of serfs in Russia
  Abraham Lincoln secures majority of popular votes in US presidential election; South Carolina secedes from the Union in protest
  The Wilberforce-Huxley debate in Oxford
- Sir J.M. Barrie born

S.R. Crockett born
W.R. Inge born
L.P. Jacks born
Sir Charles Oman born
Frederick Rolfe ('Baron Corvo') born

- George Croly dies
  G.P.R. James dies
  Anna Jameson dies
  Ebenezer Jones dies
  Sir William Napier dies
- Anton Chekhov born
  Gustave Mahler born
- Arthur Schopenhauer dies

The Cornhill Magazine PER
First series published monthly from January 1860–June 1883. Edited by W.M. Thackeray from January 1860–May 1862.

Temple Bar PER
Published mothly from December 1860–December 1905. Edited by George Sala 1860–3, and by Edmund Yates 1863–7.

Hymns Ancient and Modern V

W.H. Ainsworth (1805–82)
Ovingdean Grange F
Illustrated by Hablot K. Browne ['Phiz']. Serialized in *Bentley's Miscellany* (November 1859–July 1860).

Walter Bagehot (1826–77)
The History of the Unreformed Parliament and its Lessons NF

Clara Lucas Balfour [Mrs C.L. Balfour] (1808–78)
'Scrub'; or, The Workhouse Boy's First Start in Life F

Dion Boucicault (1820?–90)
The Colleen Bawn; or, The Brides of Garryowen D
Performed in London 10 September 1860. Based on Gerald Griffin's novel *The Collegians* 1829

William Bright (1824–1901)
A History of the Church from the Edict of Milan to the Council of Chalcedon NF

Robert Brough (1828–1860)
Marston Lynch F
Completed after the author's death by G.A. Sala

Elizabeth Barrett Browning (1806–61)
Poems Before Congress V
Published on 12 March 1860

Caroline Clive (1801–73)
Why Paul Ferroll Killed His Wife F
bao *Paul Ferroll* [see 1855]

Wilkie Collins (1824–89)
The Woman in White F
Published on 15 August 1860. Six editions in 1860. First serialized in *All the Year Round* (26 November 1859–25 August 1860). Stage version performed October 1871.

Thomas De Quincey (1785–1859)
Letters to a Young Man whose Education has been Neglected NF
The final volume (xiv) of *Selections Grave and Gay* Partly prepared before De Quincey's death in December 1859.

Charles Dickens (1812–70)
The Uncommercial Traveller F
First series, published on 15 December 1860, dated 1861. Sketches first published in *All the Year Round* in 1860.

Emily Eden (1797–1869)
The Semi-Attached Couple F
bao *The Semi-Detached House*

'George Eliot' [Mary Ann Evans (1819–80)]
The Mill on the Floss F
Published on 4 April 1860

Elizabeth Gaskell (1810–65)
Right at Last, and Other Tales F
bao *Mary Barton, The Life of Charlotte Brontë, Round the Sofa*. Published on 10 May 1860.

Philip Henry Gosse (1810–88)
The Romance of Natural History NF

J.O. Halliwell-Phillipps (1820–89)
A Dictionary of Old English Plays DICT

W.H.G. Kingston (1814–80)
The Cruise of the 'Frolic'; or, Yachting Adventures of Barnaby Brine, Esq. F
Juvenile

W.E.H. Lecky (1838–1903)
The Religious Tendencies of the Age NF
Anonymous

Samuel Lover (1797–1868)
Metrical Tales, and Other Poems V
Illustrated by Hablot K. Browne, Kenny Meadows, and others

Coventry Patmore (1823–96)
Faithful for Ever [The Angel in the House iii] V
See also *The Betrothal* 1854, *The Espousals* 1856, *The Victories of Love* 1863

Thomas Love Peacock (1785–1866)
'Memoirs of Percy Bysshe Shelley, Part II' NF
Publication in *Fraser's Magazine* (January 1860). See also 'Memoirs of Shelley' 1858.

John Ruskin (1819–1900)
Modern Painters: Volume V NF
The final volume, published on 14 June 1860. Volume i, 1843 (q.v.); volume ii, 1846 (q.v.); volumes iii and iv, 1856 (q.v.).

Herbert Spencer (1820–1903)
A System of Synthetic Philosophy NF

R.S. Surtees (1805–64)
Plain or Ringlets? F
bao *Handley Cross, Sponge's Sporting Tour.* First published in monthly parts, 1860.

Algernon Charles Swinburne (1837–1909)
The Queen-Mother; Rosamond D

Anthony Trollope (1815–82)
Castle Richmond F
Published in May 1860

T. Adolphus Trollope (1810–92)
Filippo Strozzi F

'George F. Preston' [John Leicester Warren (1835–95)]
Ballads and Metrical Sketches V

G.J. Whyte-Melville (1821–78)
Holmby House F

Ellen Wood [Mrs Henry Wood] (1814–87)
Danesbury House F
Ellen Wood's first novel

1861

- Congress of Montgomery (4 Feb.): Jefferson Davies elected President of the Confederate States
  Abraham Lincoln becomes President of the USA (4 Mar.)
  American Civil War begins (–1865): Battle of Bull Run (21 July)
  Death of the Prince Consort (14 Dec.)
- Mary Elizabeth Coleridge born
  Maurice Hewlett born
  Sir Walter Raleigh born
- Elizabeth Barrett Browning dies
  Arthur Hugh Clough dies
  Catherine Gore dies
- Rabindranath Tagore born

The St James's Magazine PER
First series published monthly from April 1861–March 1868

W.H. Ainsworth (1805–82)
The Constable of the Tower F
Serialized in *Bentley's Miscellany* (February–September 1861)

Matthew Arnold (1822–88)
On Translating Homer NF
See also F.W. Newman, *Homeric Translation* 1861 and *On Translating Homer* 1862

Isabella Beeton (1836–65)
The Book of Household Management NF
First published in monthly parts (September 1859–61)

Sir Henry Stewart Cunningham (1832–1920)
Wheat and Tares F
Anonymous

Charles Dickens (1812–70)
Great Expectations F
Published on 6 July 1861. First serialized in *All the Year Round* (1 December 1860–3 August 1861).

Richard Watson Dixon (1833–1900)
Christ's Company, and Other Poems V

'George Eliot' [Mary Ann Evans (1819–80)]
Silas Marner, the Weaver of Raveloe F
Published on 2 April 1861

Elizabeth Gaskell (1810–65)
Lois the Witch, and Other Tales F

Margaret Gatty (1809–73)
Parables from Nature F
bao *Proverbs Illustrated, Worlds Not Realized,* and *The Fairy Godmothers.* Many editions.

Thomas Hughes (1822–96)
Tom Brown at Oxford F
bao *Tom Brown's Schooldays.* Published in November 1861.

Friedrich Max Müller (1823–1900)
Lectures on the Science of Language NF

Thomas Erskine May (1815–86)
The Constitutional History of England NF
Published in 2 volumes (1861–3)

George Meredith (1828–1909)
Evan Harrington F
The first British edition. First serialized in *Once a Week* (11 February–13 October 1860).

John Stuart Mill (1806–73)
Considerations on Representative Government NF

Francis William Newman (1805–97)
Homeric Translation in Theory and Practice NF
A reply to Matthew Arnold's *On Translating Homer* 1861 (q.v.)

Francis Turner Palgrave (1824–97) (ed.)
The Golden Treasury of Songs and Lyrics ANTH
Many subsequent editions. Revised and enlarged in 1891; second series published in 1897.

Thomas Love Peacock (1785–1866)
Gryll Grange MISC
bao *Headlong Hall.* First serialized in *Fraser's Magazine* (April–December1860).

Adelaide A. Procter (1825–64) (ed.)
The Victoria Regia ANTH
An anthology set up in type by women compositors at Emily Faithfull's Victoria Press

Charles Reade (1814–84)
The Cloister and the Hearth F
Published in October 1861. Original version serialized as 'A Good Fight' in *Once a Week* (2 July–1 October 1859).

'F.G. Trafford' [Charlotte Elizabeth Riddell (1832–1906)]
City and Suburb F

Dante Gabriel Rossetti (1828–82) (tr.)
The Early Italian Poets V
Reissued in 1874 as *Dante and his Circle*

W.M. Thackeray (1811–63)
The Four Georges NF
Published in November 1861. Lectures delivered in the USA 1855–6. Serialized in the *Cornhill Magazine* (June–August, October 1860).

W.M. Thackeray (1811–63)
Lovel the Widower F
Published in November 1861. Illustrated by Thackeray. Serialized in the *Cornhill Magazine* (January–June 1860).

Anthony Trollope (1815–82)
Framley Parsonage F
Published in May 1861. Illustrated by J.E. Millais. Serialized in the *Cornhill Magazine* (January 1860–April 1861). The fourth of the six Barsetshire novels. See also *The Warden* 1855, *Barchester Towers* 1857, *Doctor Thorne* 1858, *The Small House at Allington* 1864, *The Last Chronicle of Barset* 1867.

Anthony Trollope (1815–82)
Tales of All Countries [1st ser.] F
Published in November 1861. Serialized in *Cassell's Illustrated Family Paper* (May–October 1860).

Anthony Trollope (1815–82)
Orley Farm F
Volume i published on 3 December 1861, dated 1862; volume ii published on 25 September 1862. Illustrated by J.E. Millais. First published in monthly parts (March 1861–October 1862).

Ellen Wood [Mrs Henry Wood] (1814–87)
East Lynne F
First serialized in the *New Monthly Magazine* (January 1860–August 1861). Many editions and reprints ('200th thousand', 1888).

1862

- Second Battle of Bull Run (30 Aug.): Union army defeated by 'Stonewall' Jackson
  Battle of Antietam, Maryland (17 Sept.)
  Abraham Lincoln declares all US slaves to be free from 1 Jan. 1863 (22 Sept.)
  Battle of Fredericksburg: Confederates under Robert E. Lee defeat Unionists
  Bismarck becomes Prime Minister of Prussia
- A.C. Benson born
  Goldsworthy Lowes Dickinson born
  M.R. James born
  Sir Henry Newbolt born
  Eden Phillpotts born
- Henry Thomas Buckle dies
  Thomas Jefferson Hogg dies
  James Sheridan Knowles dies
- Claude Debussy born
  Maurice Maeterlinck born
  Edith Wharton born
- Henry David Thoreau dies
- Flaubert, *Salammbô*
  Victor Hugo, *Les Misérables*
  Turgenev, *Fathers and Sons*

Bow Bells PER
First series published weekly from 12 November 1862–27 July 1864. Co-owned and edited by G.M.W. Reynolds.

Matthew Arnold (1822–88)
On Translating Homer: Last Words NF
Reply to F.W. Newman's *Homeric Translation in Theory and Practice* 1861 (q.v.). See also *On Translating Homer* 1861.

Walter Bagehot (1826–77)
Count Your Enemies and Economise Your Expenditure NF

William Barnes (1801–86)
Poems of Rural Life in the Dorset Dialect: Third Collection V
See also 1844, 1859, 1868

Isabella Beeton (1836–65)
The Englishwoman's Cooking-Book NF

George Borrow (1803–81)
Wild Wales NF
Published in December 1862

Mary Elizabeth Braddon (1835–1915)
Lady Audley's Secret F
Published in October 1862. Serialized in *Robin Goodfellow* (6 July–28 September 1861) amd elsewhere.

Elizabeth Barrett Browning (1806–61)
Last Poems V
Published posthumously on 20 March 1862. The edition was prepared by Robert Browning.

Sir Edward Bulwer-Lytton (1803–73)
A Strange Story F
Anonymous. Serialized in *All the Year Round* (10 August 1861–5 March 1862).

C.S. Calverley (1831–84)
Verses and Translations V
Anonymous

William Carleton (1794–1869)
Redmond Count O'Hanlon, the Irish Rapparee F

A.H. Clough (1819–61)
Poems V
Memoir by F.T. Palgrave

Wilkie Collins (1824–89)
No Name F
Published on 31 December 1862. Serialized in *All the Year Round* (15 March 1862–17 January 1863).

Juliana Horatia Gatty, later **Ewing** (1841–85)
Melchior's Dream, and Other Tales F
Illustrated by Margaret Gatty. First published in *The Monthly Packet*, 1861.

Richard Garnett (1835–1906) (ed.)
Relics of Shelley NF
Poems include the 'Prologue to Hellas' and 'The Magic Plant'

Margaret Gatty (1809–73)
Aunt Judy's Letters NF
See also *Aunt Judy's Tales* 1859

Henry Kingsley (1830–76)
Ravenshoe F

James McCosh (1811–94)
The Supernatural in Relation to the Natural NF

George Meredith (1828–1909)
Modern Love and Poems of the English Roadside V
Published on 28 April 1862. See also *Modern Love* 1892.

Adelaide A. Procter (1825–64)
A Chaplet of Verses V
Illustrated by Richard Doyle

Christina Rossetti (1830–94)
Goblin Market, and Other Poems V
See also *Poems* 1890

John Ruskin (1819–1900)
'Unto This Last': Four essays on the first principles of political economy NF
Published on 13 June 1862

W.M. Thackeray (1811–63)
The Adventures of Philip on His Way Through the World F
Published on 21 July 1862. Serialized in the *Cornhill Magazine* (January 1861–August 1862).

Anthony Trollope (1815–82)
North America NF
Published in May 1862

Ellen Wood [Mrs Henry Wood] (1814–87)
The Channings F
See also *Roland Yorke* 1869

Ellen Wood [Mrs Henry Wood] (1814–87)
Mrs Halliburton's Troubles F

Charlotte M. Yonge (1823–1901)
Countess Kate F
bao *The Heir of Redclyffe*. Serialized in *Mozley's Magazine for the Young* (October 1861–December 1862).

Charlotte M. Yonge (1823–1901)
The Sea Spleenwort, and Other Stories F
bao *The Heir of Redclyffe*

1863

- Confederate victory at Chancellorsville, Virginia (May): 'Stonewall' Jackson fatally wounded

Confederate forces under Robert E. Lee defeated at Gettysburg, Pennsylvania (1–3 July)
Confederates defeated at Vicksburg, Mississippi (4 July)
The Church Times started
Football Association established

- Anthony Hope (Sir Anthony Hope Hawkins) born
W.W. Jacobs born
Arthur Machen born
Sir Arthur Quiller-Couch born
May Sinclair born
Henry de Vere Stacpoole born
- William Makepeace Thackeray dies
Frances Trollope dies
- David Lloyd George born
- Gabriele D'Annunzio born
Edvard Munch born
- Eugène Delacroix dies
Alfred de Vigny dies
Jacob Grimm dies
- *The Cambridge Shakespeare* commences (-1866)

Henry Walter Bates (1825–92)
The Naturalist on the River Amazon NF

Mary Elizabeth Braddon (1835–1915)
Aurora Floyd F
Serialized in *Temple Bar* (January 1862–January 1863)

Mary Elizabeth Braddon (1835–1915)
John Marchmont's Legacy F
bao *Lady Audley's Secret*. Serialized in *Temple Bar* (December 1862–January 1864).

Elizabeth Barrett Browning (1806–61)
The Greek Christian Poets and the English Poets NF
Published on 9 March 1863. Essays first published in the *Athenaeum* (1842) but revised before the author's death.

Robert Browning (1812–89)
Poetical Works V
In this edition Browning redistributed the poems of *Dramatic Lyrics* 1842, *Dramatic Romances and Lyrics* 1845, and *Men and Women* 1855 (qq.v.). Further amendments made for the *Poetical Works* of 1868 (q.v.).

Sir Edward Bulwer-Lytton (1803–73)
Caxtoniana: A series of essays on life, literature and manners NF

Samuel Butler (1835–1901)
A First Year in Canterbury Settlement NF

Elizabeth Rundle Charles (1821–89)
The Chronicles of the Schönberg-Cotta Family F
bao *The Voice of Christian Life in Song*. Published in 1863, dated 1864.

Edward Dowden (1843–1913)
Mr Tennyson and Mr Browning NF

'George Eliot' [Mary Ann Evans (1819–80)**]**
Romola F
Published on 6 July 1863. Serialized in the *Cornhill Magazine* (July 1862–August 1863).

S. R. Gardiner (1829–1902)
History of England 1603–16 NF
See also *Prince Charles* 1869, *History of England* 1875, *Personal Government* 1877, *Fall of the Monarchy* 1882, *History of England* 1883

Elizabeth Gaskell (1810–65)
Sylvia's Lovers F
Published in February 1863

Elizabeth Gaskell (1810–65)
A Dark Night's Work F
Published in May 1863. Short stories, illustrated by George du Maurier.

William Gilbert (1804–90)
Shirley Hall Asylum; or, The Memoirs of a Monomaniac F
bao *Dives and Lazarus*

Alexander Gilchrist (1828–61)
Life of William Blake NF
Completed by Gilchrist's widow

T.H. Huxley (1825–95)
Evidence as to Man's Place in Nature NF

T.H. Huxley (1825–95)
On Our Knowledge of the Causes of the Phenomena of Organic Nature NF

Jean Ingelow (1820–97)
Poems V
Twenty-three editions by 1880. See also *Poems* 1880, *Poems: Third Series* 1885.

Frances Kemble (1809–93)
Plays D

A.W. Kinglake (1809–91)
The Invasion of the Crimea NF
Published in 8 volumes (1863–77)

Charles Kingsley (1819–75)
The Water-Babies F
Illustrated by J. Noel Paton. Serialized in *Macmillan's Magazine* (August 1862–March 1863).

Walter Savage Landor (1775–1864)
Heroic Idyls with Additional Poems V
Landor's last published book

J.S. Le Fanu (1814–73)
The House by the Churchyard F
Serialized in the *Dublin University Magazine* (October 1861–February 1863)

Charles Lever (1806–72)
Barrington F
Illustrated by Hablot K. Browne ('Phiz'). First published in monthly parts (February 1862–January 1863).

George MacDonald (1824–1905)
David Elginbrod F

F.D. Maurice (1805–72)
The Claims of the Bible and of Science NF

John Stuart Mill (1806–73)
Utilitarianism NF
Revised in 1864, 1867, and 1871

Caroline Norton (1808–77)
Lost and Saved F
Four editions in 1863

Margaret Oliphant (1828–97)
The Rector; and The Doctor's Family F
Anonymous. The first of the 'Chronicles of Carlingford' series. *The Rector* first published in *Blackwood's Magazine* (September 1861); *The Doctor's Family* serialized in *Blackwood's* (October 1861–January 1862). See also *Salem Chapel* 1863 (below), *The Perpetual Curate* 1864, *Miss Marjoribanks* 1866, *Phoebe Junior* 1876.

Margaret Oliphant (1828–97)
Salem Chapel F
Anonymous. The second of the 'Chronicles of Carlingford' series. Serialized in *Blackwood's Magazine* (February 1862–January 1863). See also *The Rector and The Doctor's Family* 1863 (above), *The Perpetual Curate* 1864, *Miss Marjoribanks* 1866, *Phoebe Junior* 1876.

'Ouida' [Marie Louise de la Ramée (1839–1908)]
Held in Bondage F
Serialized under a different title in the *New Monthly Magazine* (January 1861–June 1863)

Coventry Patmore (1823–96)
The Victories of Love [The Angel in the House iv] V
First British edition. First published in *Macmillan's Magazine* (September–November 1861). See also *The Betrothal* 1854, *The Espousals* 1856, *Faithful for Ever* 1860.

Charles Reade (1814–84)
Hard Cash: A matter-of-fact romance F
Published on 15 December 1863. First serialized in *All the Year Round* (28 March–26 December 1863) as *Very Hard Cash.*

Anne Thackeray, later **Lady Ritchie** (1837–1919)
The Story of Elizabeth F
Serialized in the *Cornhill Magazine* (September 1862–January 1863)

George Augustus Sala (1828–95)
The Strange Adventures of Captain Dangerous F
Serialized in *Temple Bar* (January 1862–February 1863)

Menella Smedley (1820–77)
The Story of Queen Isabel, and Other Verses V
Anonymous

John Hanning Speke (1827–64)
Journal of the Discovery of the Source of the Nile NF

W.M. Thackeray (1811–63)
Roundabout Papers NF
Serialized in the *Cornhill Magazine* (January 1860–February 1863)

Anthony Trollope (1815–82)
Tales of All Countries [2nd ser.] F
Published in February 1863. See *Tales of All Countries* 1861.

Anthony Trollope (1815–82)
Rachel Ray F
Published in October 1863

T. Adolphus Trollope (1810–92)
Giulio Malatesta F

Ellen Wood [Mrs Henry Wood] (1814–87)
The Shadow of Ashlydyat F

1864

- Union army under William Sherman march into Georgia (May)
  Confederates abandon Atlanta (Sept.)
  Abraham Lincoln re-elected as US President (Nov.)
  The Kingsley–Newman controversy begins
  Early English Text Society founded
- Arthur St John Adcock born
  Elinor Glyn born
  Robert Hichens born
  Stephen Phillips born

Israel Zangwill born

- Lucy Aikin dies
George Boole dies
John Clare dies
Walter Savage Landor dies
Adelaide Procter dies
Nassau Senior dies
Robert Surtees dies
Alaric Alexander Watts dies
- Henri Toulouse-Lautrec born
Frank Wedekind born
- Nathaniel Hawthorn dies
- Tolstoy, *War and Peace* (-1869)

William Allingham (1824–89)
Laurence Bloomfield in Ireland V

William Allingham (1824–89) (ed.)
The Ballad Book ANTH

Michael Banim (1796–1874)
The Town of the Cascades F

Matilda Betham-Edwards (1836–1919)
Doctor Jacob F
bao *John and I*

R.D. Blackmore (1825–1900)
Clara Vaughan F
Anonymous

Mary Elizabeth Braddon (1835–1915)
Henry Dunbar F
bao *Lady Audley's Secret.* Serialized under a different title in the *London Journal* (12 September 1863–26 March 1864).

Robert Browning (1812–89)
Dramatis Personae V

Elizabeth Rundle Charles (1821–89)
Diary of Mrs Kitty Trevylyan F
bao *Chronicles of the Schönberg-Cotta Family.* Published in 1864, dated 1865.

Amelia B. Edwards (1831–92)
Barbara's History F

'George Eliot' [Mary Ann Evans (1819–80)]
'Brother Jacob' F
Anonymous publication in the *Cornhill Magazine* (June 1864)

Charles Kingsley (1819–75)
'What, Then, Does Dr Newman Mean?' NF
See J.H. Newman, *Apologia Pro Vita Sua* and *Mr Kingsley and Dr Newman* 1864

Charles Lamb (1775–1834)
Eliana NF
Uncollected writings

J.S. Le Fanu (1814–73)
Uncle Silas F
Published in December 1864. Serialized in the *Dublin University Magazine* (July–December 1864).

J.S. Le Fanu (1814–73)
Wylder's Hand F

George MacDonald (1824–1905)
Adela Cathcart F/V
Published in April 1864. Fairy tales, parables and poems.

George Meredith (1828–1909)
Emilia in England F
Published in April 1864. See also *Sandra Belloni* 1886.

John Henry Newman, later **Cardinal** (1801–90)
Apologia Pro Vita Sua V
A reply to Charles Kingsley (1864, q.v.). First published as eight pamphlets (21 April–2 June 1864, and 16 June 1864). The second edition of 1865 was retitled *History of My Religious Opinions.* Many editions and reprints.

John Henry Newman (1801–90)
Mr Kingsley and Dr Newman NF

Margaret Oliphant (1828–97)
The Perpetual Curate F
bao *Salem Chapel.* Serialized in *Blackwood's Magazine* (June 1863–March 1864, May–September 1864). The third of the 'Chronicles of Carlingford' volumes. See also *The Rector and The Doctor's Family* 1863, *Salem Chapel* 1863, *Miss Marjoribanks* 1866, *Phoebe Junior* 1876.

James Payn (1830–98)
Lost Sir Massingberd F
Anonymous

Winthrop Mackworth Praed (1802–39)
Poems V
Memoir by Derwent Coleridge

William Brighty Rands (1823–82)
Lilliput Levee V
Anonymous. For children.

'F.G. Trafford' [Charlotte Elizabeth Riddell (1832–1906)]
George Geith of Fen Court F

Alfred Tennyson (1809–92)
Enoch Arden V

Anthony Trollope (1815–82)
The Small House at Allington F
Published in March 1864. Illustrated by J.E. Millais. Serialized in the *Cornhill Magazine*

(September 1862–April 1864). The fifth of the six Barsetshire novels. See also *The Warden* 1855, *Barchester Towers* 1857, *Doctor Thorne* 1858, *Framley Parsonage* 1861, *The Last Chronicle of Barset* 1867.

Anthony Trollope (1815–82)
Can You Forgive Her? F
Volume i published in October 1864; volume ii published in August 1865. First published in monthly parts (January 1864–August 1865).

Charlotte M. Yonge (1823–1901)
The Trial F
bao *The Heir of Redclyffe*. Serialized in *The Monthly Packet* (January 1862–April 1864).

1865

- Robert E. Lee surrenders to Ulysses S. Grant at Appomattox (9 Apr.)
  Abraham Lincoln assassinated by J.W. Booth (14 Apr.): succeeded as President by Andrew Johnson
  Last Confederate army surrenders at Shreveport (26 May): end of the American Civil War
  Salvation Army founded by William Booth
  Sporting Times started
- Laurence Housman born
  Rudyard Kipling born
  A.E.W. Mason born
  Baroness Orczy born
  Logan Pearsall Smith born
  Arthur Symons born
  W.B. Yeats born
- William Edmonstoune Aytoun dies
  Isabella Beeton dies
  Richard Cobden dies
  Elizabeth Gaskell dies
  Isaac Williams dies
  Nicholas Wiseman (Cardinal Wiseman) dies
- Wagner, *Tristan*

The Argosy PER
Published monthly from December 1865–December 1901. Edited by Ellen (Mrs Henry) Wood, 1865–87, who positioned it as a rival to Mary Elizabeth Braddon's *Belgravia*.

Matthew Arnold (1822–88)
Essays in Criticism [1st ser.] NF
See also *Essays in Criticism* 1888, 1910

Isabella Beeton (1836–65)
Mrs Beeton's Dictionary of Every-day Cookery DICT

Robert Browning (1812–89)
Poetical Works: Fourth edition V

Ada Cambridge (1844–1926)
The Two Surplices F

Thomas Carlyle (1795–1881)
History of Frederick II of Prussia [vols v–vi] NF
Published in March 1865. See also *History of Frederick II* 1858.

'Lewis Carroll' [C.L. Dodgson (1832–98)]
Alice's Adventures in Wonderland F
Illustrated by John Tenniel. See also *Through the Looking-Glass* 1871.

A.H. Clough (1819–61)
Letters and Remains of Arthur Hugh Clough MISC
Includes *Dipsychus*. See also *Poems and Prose* 1869.

Mortimer Collins (1827–76)
Who is the Heir? F

Charles Dickens (1812–70)
Our Mutual Friend F
Volume i published in February 1865; volume ii, published November 1865. Illustrated by Marcus Stone. First published in monthly parts (May 1864–November 1865).

Elizabeth Gaskell (1810–65)
The Grey Woman, and Other Tales F
Published in October 1865. Illustrated by George du Maurier.

Elizabeth Gaskell (1810–65)
Cousin Phillis, and Other Tales F
Published in December 1865. Illustrated by George du Maurier.

Annie French Hector ['Mrs Alexander' (1825–1902)]
Look Before You Leap F
Anonymous

John Cam Hobhouse (1786–1869)
Some Account of a Long Life NF
Published in 5 volumes (1865–7)

W.E.H. Lecky (1838–1903)
History of the Rise and Influence of the Spirit of Rationalism in Europe NF

J.S. Le Fanu (1814–73)
Guy Deverell F
Serialized in the *Dublin University Magazine* (January–July 1865)

David Livingstone (1813–73)
Narrative of an Expedition to the Zambesi and its Tributaries NF

George MacDonald (1824–1905)
Alec Forbes of Howglen F

Henry Edward Manning, later **Cardinal** (1808–92)
The Temporal Mission of the Holy Ghost; or, Reason and Revelation NF
Manning had been enthroned as Archbishop of Westminster in June 1865, following the death of Cardinal Wiseman

George Meredith (1828–1909)
Rhoda Fleming F
Published in October 1865

John Stuart Mill (1806–73)
Auguste Comte and Positivism NF

'Ouida' [Marie Louise de la Ramée (1839–1908)]
Stratmore F

E.B. Pusey (1800–82)
An Eirenicon NF
See also *Eirenicon* 1869, 1870

'F.G. Trafford' [Charlotte Elizabeth Riddell (1832–1906)]
Maxwell Drewitt F

T.W. Robertson (1829–71)
Society: A comedy D
Performed in London 11 November 1865

John Ruskin (1819–1900)
The Ethics of the Dust NF
Published in December 1865, dated 1866

John Ruskin (1819–1900)
Sesame and Lilies NF

R.S. Surtees (1805–64)
Mr Facey Romford's Hounds F
bao *Handley Cross, Mr Sponge's Sporting Tour.* First published in monthly parts, illustrated by John Leech, who died during serial issue; illustrations completed by Hablot K. Browne ('Phiz').

Algernon Charles Swinburne (1837–1909)
Atalanta in Calydon V

Algernon Charles Swinburne (1837–1909)
Chastelard V

Anthony Trollope (1815–82)
Miss Mackenzie F
Published in March 1865

Charlotte M. Yonge (1823–1901)
The Clever Woman of the Family F
bao *The Heir of Redclyffe.* Serialized in *The Churchman's Family Magazine* (1864–5).

1866

- Benjamin Disraeli becomes Leader of the House of Commons
  Alfred Nobel invents dynamite
- E.W. Hornung born
  Violet Hunt born
  Richard Le Gallienne born
  Gilbert Murray born
  Beatrix Potter born
  Dora Sigerson born
  H.G. Wells born
- Saba Holland, Lady Holland, dies
  John Keble dies
  Jane Welsh Carlyle dies
  John Mason Neale dies
  Thomas Love Peacock dies
  Ann Taylor dies
  William Whewell dies
- Dostoevsky, *Crime and Punishment*

Aunt Judy's Magazine PER
First series published monthly (May 1866–October 1881). Edited by Margaret (Mrs Alfred) Gatty (1866–73), and by Horatia K.F. Gatty (1874–85).

Belgravia PER
Published monthly (November 1866–June 1899). Edited by Mary Elizabeth Braddon (1866–76).

Sir Samuel White Baker (1821–93)
The Albert N'yanza, Great Basin of the Nile, and Explorations of the Nile Sources NF

R.D. Blackmore (1825–1900)
Cradock Nowell F
Serialized in *Macmillan's Magazine* (May 1865–August 1866)

Barbara Leigh Smith Bodichon (1827–91)
Objections to the Enfranchisement of Women Considered NF

Jane Octavia Brookfield (1821–96)
Only George F
Anonymous

F.C. Burnand (1836–1917)
Happy Thoughts NF

Wilkie Collins (1824–89)
Armadale F

Published in May 1866. Serialized in the *Cornhill Magazine* (November 1864–June 1866).

E.S. Dallas (1828–79)
The Gay Science NF

Sir Francis Hastings Doyle (1810–88)
The Return of the Guards, and Other Poems V

'George Eliot' [Mary Ann Evans (1819–80)**]**
Felix Holt, the Radical F
Published on 15 June 1866

Elizabeth Gaskell (1810–65)
Wives and Daughters F
Unfinished at Elizabeth Gaskell's death on 12 November 1865. Published in February 1866. Illustrated by George du Maurier. Serialized in the *Cornhill Magazine* (August 1864–January 1866).

Charles Kingsley (1819–75)
Hereward the Wake F
Serialized in *Good Words* (January–December 1865)

J.S. Le Fanu (1814–73)
All in the Dark F
Serialized in the *Dublin University Magazine* (February–June 1866)

Mark Lemon (1809–70)
Falkner Lyle; or, The Story of Two Wives F

Charles Lever (1806–72)
Sir Brooke Fossbrooke F

Eliza Lynn Linton (1822–98)
Lizzie Lorton of Greyrigg F

James McCosh (1811–94)
An Examination of Mill's Philosophy NF

John Henry Newman, later **Cardinal** (1801–90)
The Dream of Gerontius V
First published in *The Month* (May–June 1865)

Margaret Oliphant (1828–97)
Miss Marjoribanks F
bao *Salem Chapel*. Serialized in *Blackwood's Magazine* (February–December 1865, February–May 1866). The fourth of the 'Chronicles of Carlingford' volumes. See also *The Rector and The Doctor's Family* 1863, *Salem Chapel* 1863, *The Perpetual Curate* 1864, *Phoebe Junior* 1876.

'Ouida' [Marie Louise de la Ramée (1839–1908)**]**
Chandos F

Charles Reade (1814–84)
Griffith Gaunt; or, Jealousy F
Serialized in *The Argosy* (December 1865–November 1866)

Christina Rossetti (1830–94)
The Prince's Progress, and Other Poems V

W.M. Rossetti (1829–1919)
Swinburne's Poems and Ballads NF

John Ruskin (1819–1900)
The Crown of Wild Olive NF
Published on 14 May 1866

Algernon Charles Swinburne (1837–1909)
Notes on Poems and Reviews NF

Algernon Charles Swinburne (1837–1909)
Poems and Ballads [1st ser.] V
Second series, 1878 (q.v.); third series, 1889 (q.v.)

Tom Taylor (1817–80)
The Overland Route: A comedy D
Performed 23 February 1860

Anthony Trollope (1815–82)
The Belton Estate F
Published in January 1866. Serialized in the *Fortnightly Review* (May 1865–January 1866).

Charlotte M. Yonge (1823–1901)
The Dove in the Eagle's Nest F
bao *The Heir of Redclyffe*. Serialized in *Macmillan's Magazine* (May–December 1865).

1867

- Second Reform Act
  Fenian risings in Ireland
  British North America Act establishes the Dominion of Canada (Mar.)
  Garibaldi marches on Rome
  T.J. Barnardo founds the East End Juvenile Mission
  Bicycles begin to be manufactured in France
- Arnold Bennett born
  Ernest Dowson born
  Pearl Mary Craigie ('John Oliver Hobbes') born
  John Galsworthy born
  Lionel Johnson born
  C.E. Montague born
  George William Russell ('Æ') born
- Sir Archibald Alison dies
  Henry Crabb Robinson dies
  Alexander Smith dies
- Michael Faraday dies
- Arturo Toscanini born
- Charles Baudelaire dies
  Jean Dominique Ingres dies
- Marx, *Das Kapital* (vol. i)
  Zola, *Thérèse Raquin*

Tinsleys' Magazine PER
First series published monthly from August 1867–May 1887. Edited by Edmund Yates 1867–9.

Matthew Arnold (1822–88)
New Poems V

Matthew Arnold (1822–88)
On the Study of Celtic Literature NF

Walter Bagehot (1826–77)
The English Constitution NF

Philip James Bailey (1816–1902)
Universal Hymn V
See also *Festus* 1839

Sir Samuel White Baker (1821–93)
The Nile Tributaries of Abyssinia NF

'Claude Lake' [Mathilde Blind (1841–96)]
Poems V

Rhoda Broughton (1840–1920)
Cometh Up as a Flower F
Anonymous. Published in March 1867. Serialized in the *Dublin University Magazine* (July 1866–January 1867).

Rhoda Broughton (1840–1920)
Not Wisely But Too Well F
Anonymous. Serialized in the *Dublin University Magazine*.

Richard Cobden (1804–65)
The Political Writings of Richard Cobden NF

E.A. Freeman (1823–92)
The History of the Norman Conquest of England NF
Published in 6 volumes (1867–79)

Jean Ingelow (1820–97)
A Story of Doom, and Other Poems V

J.S. Le Fanu (1814–73)
The Tenants of Malory F
Serialized in the *Dublin University Magazine* (February–October 1867)

George MacDonald (1824–1905)
Dealings with the Faeries F
Five stories for children

George Meredith (1828–1909)
Vittoria F
Published in December 1867. Serialized in the *Fortnightly Review* (15 January–1 December 1866).

William Morris (1834–96)
The Life and Death of Jason V

'Ouida' [Marie Louise de la Ramée (1839–1908)]
Under Two Flags F
Partly serialized in the *British Army and Navy Review* from August 1865

Anne Thackeray, later **Lady Ritchie** (1837–1919)
The Village on the Cliff F
bao *The Story of Elizabeth*

T.W. Robertson (1829–71)
Caste: An original comedy D
Performed 6 April 1867

Samuel Smiles (1812–1904)
Lives of the Engineers NF

'Hesba Stretton' [Sarah Smith (1832–1911)]
Jessica's First Prayer F
See also *Jessica's Mother* 1868

Algernon Charles Swinburne (1837–1909)
A Song of Italy V

W.M. Thackeray (1811–63)
Denis Duval F
Thackeray's last work, unfinished at his death. Serialized in the *Cornhill Magazine* (March–June 1864).

Anthony Trollope (1815–82)
Nina Balatka F
Published on 1 February 1867. Serialized in *Blackwood's Magazine* (July 1866–January 1867).

Anthony Trollope (1815–82)
The Last Chronicle of Barset F
Volume i published on 16 March 1867; volume ii published on 6 July 1867. Illustrated by George H. Thomas. First published in monthly parts (December 1866–July 1867). The sixth and last of the Barsetshire novels. See also *The Warden* 1855, *Barchester Towers* 1857, *Doctor Thorne* 1858, *Framley Parsonage* 1861, *The Small House at Allington* 1864.

Anthony Trollope (1815–82)
The Claverings F
Published on 20 April 1867. Serialized in the *Cornhill Magazine* (February 1866–January 1867).

Anthony Trollope (1815–82)
Lotta Schmidt, and Other Stories F
Published in August 1867

Augusta Webster (1837–94)
A Woman Sold, and Other Poems V

Edmund Yates (1831–94)
Black Sheep F

Serialized in *All the Year Round* (August 1866–March 1867)

1868

- Disraeli becomes Prime Minister (Feb.) for the first time; resigns (Dec.); Liberal ministry formed by W.E. Gladstone (–1874)
  Royal Historical Society founded
- Gertrude Bell born
  Norman Douglas born
  Marie Belloc Lowndes born
  E.V. Lucas born
- Samuel Lover dies
  Henry Hart Milman dies
- Sir David Brewster dies
  Henry Brougham dies
- Robert Falcon Scott born
- Paul Claudel born
  Maxim Gorky born
  Edmond Rostand born
- Louisa M. Alcott, *Little Women*
  Dostoevsky, *The Idiot*
  A.B. Grosart, *Fuller Worthies Library* (–1876)
- Wagner, *Die Meistersinger*

W.H. Ainsworth (1805–82)
Myddleton Pomfret F
Serialized in *Bentley's Miscellany* (July 1867–March 1868)

William Barnes (1801–86)
Poems of Rural Life in Common English V
See also 1844, 1859, 1862

Walter Besant (1836–1901)
Studies in Early French Poetry NF

Robert Browning (1812–89)
Poetical Works V
In 6 volumes

Robert Browning (1812–89)
The Ring and the Book [vols i, ii] V
Volume i published in November 1868; volume ii, December 1868. See also *The Ring and the Book* 1869.

Rosa Nouchette Carey (1840–1909)
Nellie's Memories F

Wilkie Collins (1824–89)
The Moonstone: A romance F
Published in July 1868. Serialized in *All the Year Round* (4 January–8 August 1868). Stage version performed 17 September 1877.

'George Eliot' [**Mary Ann Evans** (1819–80)]
The Spanish Gypsy V
Published on 29 April 1868

Emily Faithfull (1835–95)
Change Upon Change F

John Keble (1792–1866)
Sermons, Occasional and Parochial NF
See also *Sermons* 1847

J.S. Le Fanu (1814–73)
Haunted Lives F
Serialized in the *Dublin University Magazine* (May–December 1868)

J.S. Le Fanu (1814–73)
A Lost Name F
Serialized in *Temple Bar* (May 1867–May 1868)

Eliza Lynn Linton (1822–98)
The Girl of the Period NF
Anonymous. Reprinted from the *Saturday Review* (14 March 1868). See also *The Girl of the Period, and Other Social Essays* 1883.

George MacDonald (1824–1905)
Robert Falconer F
Serialized in *Argosy* (December 1866–November 1867)

John Stuart Mill (1806–73)
England and Ireland NF

William Morris (1834–96)
The Earthly Paradise [pts i & ii] V
Part iii published in 1869 (dated 1870, q.v.); part iv published in 1870 (q.v.). Complete work published in 10 volumes in 1872.

Menella Smedley (1820–77)
Poems Written for a Child V
'By two friends'. Written with Fanny Hart.

'Hesba Stretton' [**Sarah Smith** (1832–1911)]
Jessica's Mother F
Sequel to *Jessica's First Prayer* 1867 (q.v.)

Algernon Charles Swinburne (1837–1909)
Siena V

Anthony Trollope (1815–82)
Linda Tressel F
Published in May 1868. Serialized in *Blackwood's Magazine* (October 1867–May 1868).

Charlotte M. Yonge (1823–1901)
The Chaplet of Pearls; or, The White and Black Ribaumont F
bao *The Heir of Redclyffe*. See also *Stray Pearls* 1883, and *The Release* 1896.

1869

- General Ulysses S. Grant becomes President of the USA
  Suez Canal opened (17 Nov.)
  Girton College, Cambridge, founded
- Harleian Society founded
  Nature started
  The Academy started
  The Graphic started
- Laurence Binyon born
  Algernon Blackwood born
  Angela Brazil born
  Charlotte Mew born
- William Carleton dies
  Alexander Dyce dies
  Emily Eden dies
  Elizabeth Caroline Grey dies
  John Cam Hobhouse dies
  Thomas Medwin dies
- Neville Chamberlain born
- Gandhi born
  André Gide born
  Henri Matisse born
- Alphonse de Lamartine dies
  Hector Berlioz dies
  Charles Augustin Sainte-Beuve dies
- Flaubert, *L'Éducation sentimentale*
  Bret Harte, *The Outcasts of Poker Flat*
  Jules Verne, *Vingt mille lieues sous les mers*
- Wagner, *Das Rheingold*

Matthew Arnold (1822–88)
Culture and Anarchy NF

J.E. Austen-Leigh (1798–1874)
A Memoir of Jane Austen NF
Published in December 1869. See also 1871.

R.D. Blackmore (1825–1900)
Lorna Doone F

Robert Browning (1812–89)
The Ring and the Book [vols iii, iv] V
Volume iii published in January 1869; volume iv, February 1869. See also *The Ring and the Book* 1868.

C.S. Calverley (1831–84) (tr.)
Theocritus Translated into English Verse V

'Lewis Carroll' [**C.L. Dodgson** (1832–98)]
Phantasmagoria, and Other Poems V

A.H. Clough (1819–61)
Poems and Prose Remains MISC
See also *Letters* 1865

Juliana Horatia Ewing [**Mrs J.H. Ewing**] (1841–85)
Mrs Overtheway's Remembrances F
bao *Melchior's Dream and Other Tales*

Francis Galton (1822–1911)
Hereditary Genius NF

S. R. Gardiner (1829–1902)
Prince Charles and the Spanish Marriage 1617–23 NF
See also *History of England* 1863, *History of England* 1875, *Personal Government* 1877, *Fall of the Monarchy* 1882, *History of England* 1883

W.S. Gilbert (1836–1911)
The 'Bab' Ballads V
First published in the comic journal *Fun*. See also *More 'Bab' Ballads* 1872.

Jean Ingelow (1820–97)
Mopsa the Fairy F

John Keble (1792–1866)
Miscellaneous Poems V

J.S. Le Fanu (1814–73)
The Wyvern Mystery F
Serialized in the *Dublin University Magazine* (February–November 1869)

Eliza Lynn Linton (1822–98)
Ourselves: A series of essays on women NF

F.D. Maurice (1805–72)
Social Morality NF

John Stuart Mill (1806–73)
The Subjection of Women NF
Many editions

'Ennis Graham' [**Mary Louisa Molesworth** (1839–1921)]
Lover and Husband F

William Morris (1834–96)
The Earthly Paradise [pt iii] V
Published in November 1869, dated 1870. Parts i and ii published in 1868; part iv, 1870 (qq.v.).

William Morris (1834–96) and **Eiríkr Magnússon** (1833–1913) (tr.)
Grettis Saga: the Story of Grettir the Strong F
Translated from Icelandic. See also *Völsunga Saga* 1870, *Three Northern Love Stories* 1875, *The Story of Gunnlaug the Worm-Tongue* 1891.

Rosa Mulholland (1841–1921)
Hester's History F

E.B. Pusey (1800–82)
An Eirenicon: Part 2 NF
See also *An Eirenicon* 1865, 1870

Henry Crabb Robinson (1775–1867)
Diary, Reminiscences, and Correspondence NF

C.H. Spurgeon (1834–92)
John Ploughman's Talk; or, Plain Advice for Plain People NF
See also *John Ploughman's Pictures* 1880

Alfred Tennyson (1809–92)
The Holy Grail, and Other Poems V
Published in December 1869, dated 1870. The volume begins with the first publication of four Idylls of the King. See also *Idylls of the King* 1859, *Idylls of the King* 1870, 'The Last Tournament' 1871, *Gareth and Lynette* 1872, 'Balin and Balan' in *Tiresias* 1885, *Idylls of the King* 1889.

Anthony Trollope (1815–82)
Phineas Finn; the Irish Member F
Published in March 1869. Illustrated by J.E. Millais. Serialized in *St Paul's Magazine* (October 1867–May 1869).

Anthony Trollope (1815–82)
He Knew He Was Right F
Published in May 1869. Illustrated by Marcus Stone. First published in weekly numbers (17 October 1868–22 May 1869) and monthly from November 1868.

Ellen Wood [Mrs Henry Wood] (1814–87)
Roland Yorke F
Sequel to *The Channings* 1862 (q.v.)

1870

- Franco-Prussian War begins (–1871)
  French defeated at the Battle of Sedan (1 Sept.): Napoleon III taken prisoner
  Republic proclaimed in France
  Siege of Paris begins (19 Sept.)
  Married Women's Property Act
  Education Act, establishing a system of elementary schools
  Italians enter Rome
- Hilaire Belloc born
  [Robert] Erskine Childers born
  Hubert Crackanthorpe born
  Lord Alfred Douglas born
  Thomas Sturge Moore born
  'Saki' (Hector Hugh Monro) born
- Frederick Chamier dies
  Charles Dickens dies
  Mark Lemon dies
  Nikolai Lenin born
- Alexandre Dumas (*père*) dies
  Jules de Goncourt dies
  Prosper Mérimée dies
- Wagner, *Die Walküre*

Arthur William à Beckett (1844–1909)
Fallen Among Thieves F

Deborah Alcock (1835–1913)
The Spanish Brothers F
bao *The Dark Year of Dundee*. Published 870, dated 1871. Juvenile.

Matthew Arnold (1822–88)
St Paul and Protestantism NF

Alfred Austin (1835–1913)
The Poetry of the Period NF

E. Cobham Brewer (1810–97)
A Dictionary of Phrase and Fable DICT

Rhoda Broughton (1840–1920)
Red as a Rose is She F
bao *Cometh Up as a Flower*. Serialized in *Temple Bar* (May 1869–March 1870).

Christabel Rose Coleridge (1843–1921)
Lady Betty F

Wilkie Collins (1824–89)
Man and Wife F
Published in June 1870. Serialized in *Harper's Weekly* (11 December 1869–6 August 1870) and in *Cassell's Magazine* (January–September 1870).

Charles Dickens (1812–70)
The Mystery of Edwin Drood F
Published in September 1870. Illustrated by Luke Fildes. Unfinished at Dickens's death on 9 June 1870. First published in six (of a projected twelve) monthly parts (April–September 1870).

Benjamin Disraeli (1804–81)
Lothair F
Published in May 1870

Amelia B. Edwards (1831–92)
Debenham's Vow F
Serialized in *Good Words* (January–December 1869)

Juliana Horatia Ewing [Mrs J.H. Ewing] (1841–85)
The Brownies and Other Tales F
bao *Melchior's Dream* and *Mrs Overtheway's Remembrances*. Illustrated by George Cruikshank.

B.L. Farjeon (1838–1903)
Grif F

G.A. Henty (1832–1902)
Out on the Pampas; or, The Young Settlers F
Juvenile

Edward Lear (1812–88)
Journal of a Landscape Painter in Corsica NF
See also *Journals* 1851, 1852

Edward Lear (1812–88)
Nonsense Songs, Stories, Botany, and Alphabets V
Published in December 1870, dated 1871. See also *Book of Nonsense* 1846, *More Nonsense* 1871, *Laughable Lyrics* 1877.

Denis MacCarthy (1817–82) (tr.)
The Two Lovers of Heaven: Chrysanthus and Daria D
See also *Dramas of Calderón* 1853

George MacDonald (1824–1905)
At the Back of the North Wind F
Published in December 1870, dated 1871. Illustrated by Arthur Hughes. Serialized in *Good Words for the Young* (November 1868–October 1869).

William Morris (1834–96)
The Earthly Paradise [pt iv] V
Parts i and ii published in 1868; part iii, 1869 (qq.v.)

William Morris (1834–96) and **Eiríkr Magnússon** (1833–1913) (tr.)
Völsunga Saga: the Story of the Volsungs and Niblungs F
See also *Grettis Saga* 1869, *Three Northern Love Stories* 1875, *The Story of Gunnlaug the Worm-Tongue* 1891

Laurence Oliphant (1829–88)
Piccadilly F
Illustrated by Richard Doyle

Arthur O'Shaughnessy (1844–81)
An Epic of Women, and Other Poems V

E.B. Pusey (1800–82)
An Eirenicon: Part 3 NF
See also *An Eirenicon* 1865, 1869

Charles Reade (1814–84)
Put Yourself in His Place F
Published in May 1870. Serialized in the *Cornhill Magazine* (March 1869–July 1870).

Charlotte Elizabeth Riddell [**Mrs J.H. Riddell**] (1832–1906)
Austin Friars F

Christina Rossetti (1830–94)
Commonplace, and Other Short Stories F

Dante Gabriel Rossetti (1828–82)
Poems V
Published on 26 April 1870

John Ruskin (1819–1900)
Lectures on Art NF

Arthur Penrhyn Stanley (1815–81)
Essays, Chiefly on Questions of Church and State NF

Alfred Tennyson (1809–92)
Idylls of the King V
Published in January 1870, dated 1869. Contains eight Idylls in the arrangement Tennyson wanted at this point in their development. See also *Idylls of the King* 1859, *The Holy Grail* 1869, 'The Last Tournament' 1871, *Gareth and Lynette* 1872, 'Balin and Balan' in *Tiresias* 1885, *Idylls of the King* 1889.

Anthony Trollope (1815–82)
The Vicar of Bullhampton F
Published in April 1870. First published in monthly parts (July 1869–May 1870).

Anthony Trollope (1815–82)
The Struggles of Brown, Jones, and Robinson F
Published in November 1870. Serialized in the *Cornhill Magazine* (August 1861–March 1862).

Anthony Trollope (1815–82)
Sir Harry Hotspur of Humblethwaite F
Published in November 1870, dated 1871. Serialized in *Macmillan's Magazine* (May–December 1870).

Alfred Russel Wallace (1823–1913)
Contributions to the Theory of Natural Selection NF

Augusta Webster (1837–94)
Portraits V

Ellen Wood [**Mrs Henry Wood**] (1814–87)
George Canterbury's Will F

William Wordsworth (1770–1850)
The Poetical Works of William Wordsworth: The Centenary Edition V
See also *Miscellaneous Poems* 1820, *Poetical Works* 1827, *Poetical Works* 1836, *Poetical Works* 1840, *Poems* 1845, *Poetical Works* 1857

1871

- German Empire established: William I of Prussia becomes Emperor
  France and Germany sign armistice (28 Jan.)
  Commune Rising in Paris (Mar.–May)
  Abolition of religious tests at the universities of Oxford, Cambridge, and Durham

Robert Buchanan attacks Rossetti in the *Contemporary Review*

- Robert Hugh Benson born
  W.H. Davies born
  John Millington Synge born
- Charles Babbage dies
  Robert Chambers dies
  George Grote dies
  Sir John Herschel dies
- Stephen Crane born
  Marcel Proust born
  Paul Valéry born
- Whitman, *Democratic Vistas*
  Zola, *Les Rougon-Macquart* (1871–93)

Sir John Acton, Baron Acton (1834–1902)
The War of 1870 NF

William Alexander (1826–94)
Johnny Gibb of Gushetneuk in the Parish of Pyketillim F

J.E. Austen-Leigh (1798–1874)
A Memoir of Jane Austen NF
Published on 16 December 1871. Contains the first printed texts of Jane Austen's *Lady Susan*, *The Watsons*, the cancelled chapter of *Persuasion*, and extracts from *Sanditon* (completed by Anne Lefroy in the 1830s and first published in 1983). See also Catherine Hubback, *Memoir of Jane Austen* 1869 and *Sanditon* 1925.

William Black (1841–98)
A Daughter of Heth F

William Black (1841–98)
The Monarch of Mincing Lane F

Robert Browning (1812–89)
Balaustion's Adventure V

Robert Browning (1812–89)
Prince Hohenstiel-Schwangau, Saviour of Society V

Sir Edward Bulwer-Lytton (1803–73)
The Coming Race F
Anonymous

'Lewis Carroll' [C.L. Dodgson (1832–98)]
Through the Looking-Glass, and What Alice Found There F
Published in 1871, dated 1872. Illustrated by John Tenniel. See also *Alice's Adventures* 1865.

George Chesney (1830–95)
The Battle of Dorking F
Anonymous. First published in *Blackwood's Magazine* (May 1871).

George Manville Fenn (1831–1909)
The Sapphire Cross F

E.A. Freeman (1823–92)
Historical Essays [1st ser.] NF
See also *Historical Essays* 1873, 1879, 1892

Thomas Hardy (1840–1928)
Desperate Remedies F
Anonymous. Published on 25 March 1871. Hardy's first published novel.

R.H. Hutton (1826–97)
Essays Theological and Literary NF

Edward Lear (1812–88)
More Nonsense, Pictures, Rhymes, Botany, etc. V
Published in 1871, dated 1872. See also *Book of Nonsense* 1846, *Nonsense Songs* 1870, *Laughable Lyrics* 1877.

J.S. Le Fanu (1814–73)
Checkmate F
Serialized in *Cassell's Magazine* (September 1870–March 1871)

J.S. Le Fanu (1814–73)
Chronicles of Golden Friars F
Short stories

J.S. Le Fanu (1814–73)
The Rose and the Key F

George MacDonald (1824–1905)
The Princess and the Goblin F
Published in December 1871, dated 1872. Illustrated by Arthur Hughes. See also *The Princess and Curdie* 1882.

George Meredith (1828–1909)
The Adventures of Harry Richmond F
Published on 26 October 1871. Serialized in the *Cornhill Magazine* (September 1870–November 1871).

John Morley (1838–1923)
Critical Miscellanies [1st ser.] NF

'Ouida' [Marie Louise de la Ramée (1839–1908)]
Folle-Farine F

John Ruskin (1819–1900)
Fors Clavigera [vol. i] NF
Letters originally isssued as separate publications and collected into eight volumes of twelve lettters each (published 1871–84).

Samuel Smiles (1812–1904)
Character NF

Leslie Stephen (1832–1904)
The Playground of Europe NF

Algernon Charles Swinburne (1837–1909)
Songs Before Sunrise V

Alfred Tennyson (1809–92)
'The Last Tournament' V
Publication in the *Contemporary Review* (December 1871). One of the Arthurian Idylls, subsequently published in *Gareth and Lynette* 1872 (q.v.). See also *Idylls of the King* 1859, *The Holy Grail* 1869, *Idylls of the King* 1870, 'Balin and Balan' in *Tiresias* 1885, *Idylls of the King* 1889.

Anthony Trollope (1815–82)
Ralph the Heir F
Serialized in *St Paul's Magazine* (January 1870–July 1871)

1872

- Royal Albert Hall in London opened
- Aubrey Beardsley born
  Sir Max Beerbohm born
  John Cowper Powys born
  Bertrand Russell born
- Edwin Atherstone dies
  Sarah Ellis (*née* Stickney) dies
  Charles Lever dies
  Frederick Denison Maurice dies
- Serge Diaghilev born
- Théophile Gautier dies
  Giuseppe Mazzini dies
- Nietzsche, *Die Geburt der Tragödie*
  Turgenev, *A Month in the Country*

Alfred Austin (1835–1913)
Interludes V

Walter Bagehot (1826–77)
Physics and Politics NF

Walter Besant (1836–1901) and **James Rice** (1843–82)
Ready-Money Mortiboy F
Dramatic version by Rice and W. Maurice performed 12 March 1874)

William Black (1841–98)
The Strange Adventures of a Phaeton F
Serialized in *Macmillan's Magazine* (January–November 1872)

R.D. Blackmore (1825–1900)
The Maid of Sker F
Serialized in *Blackwood's Magazine* (August 1871–July 1872)

Robert Browning (1812–89)
Fifine at the Fair V

Robert Buchanan (1841–1901)
The Fleshly School of Poetry, and Other Phenomena of the Day NF
The celebrated title essay first published in the *Contemporary Review* (October 1871). See also Swinburne, *Under the Microscope*, below.

F.C. Burnand (1836–1917)
The New History of Sandford and Merton F
Anonymous. See Thomas Day, *The History of Sandford and Merton* 1783.

Samuel Butler (1835–1902)
Erewhon; or, Over the Range F
Anonymous. See also *Erewhon Revisited* 1901.

C.S. Calverley (1831–84)
Fly Leaves V
Anonymous

Frances Power Cobbe (1822–1904)
Darwinism in Morals and Other Essays NF

Wilkie Collins (1824–89)
Poor Miss Finch F
Published on 26 January 1872. Serialized in *Cassell's Magazine* (October 1871–March 1872).

Thomas Cooper (1805–92)
The Life of Thomas Cooper NF

'George Eliot' [Mary Ann Evans (1819–80)**]**
Middlemarch F
Published on 1 December 1872 in 4 volumes. The eight separate parts published from December 1871–December 1872.

John Forster (1812–76)
The Life of Charles Dickens NF

W.S. Gilbert (1836–1911)
More 'Bab' Ballads V
See also *'Bab' Ballads* 1869

Thomas Hardy (1840–1928)
Under the Greenwood Tree: A rural painting of the Dutch School F
bao *Desperate Remedies*. Published in June 1872.

Jean Ingelow (1820–97)
Off the Skelligs F
See also *Fated to be Free* 1875

Andrew Lang (1844–1912) (tr.)
Ballads and Lyrics of Old France, with Other Poems V

J.S. Le Fanu (1814–73)
In a Glass Darkly F
Stories

Charles Lever (1806–72)
Lord Kilgobbin F

Lever's last novel. Serialized in the *Cornhill Magazine* (October 1870–March 1872).

John Henry Newman, later Cardinal (1801–90)
Essays Critical and Historical NF

Winwood Reade (1838–75)
The Martyrdom of Man V
Eighteen editions by 1910

Christina Rossetti (1830–94)
Sing-Song V
Illustrated by Arthur Hughes

Henry Morton Stanley (1841–1904)
How I Found Livingstone NF

Algernon Charles Swinburne (1837–1909)
Under the Microscope NF
Swinburne's reply to Robert Buchanan's attack in 'The Fleshly School of Poetry' (*Contemporary Review*, October 1871). See also Buchanan, above.

Alfred Tennyson (1809–92)
Gareth and Lynette V
Published in December 1872. See also *Idylls of the King* 1859, *The Holy Grail* 1869, *Idylls of the King* 1870, 'The Last Tournament' 1871, 'Balin and Balan' in *Tiresias* 1885, *Idylls of the King* 1889.

Anthony Trollope (1815–82)
The Golden Lion of Granpere F
Published in May 1872. Serialized in *Good Words* (January–August 1872).

Anthony Trollope (1815–82)
The Eustace Diamonds F
Published in December 1872, dated 1873. Serialized in the *Fortnightly Review* (July 1871–February 1873).

1873

- Death of Napoleon III at Chiselhurst
  Ashanti War breaks out
- The New Shakespeare Society founded by F.J. Furnivall
- Walter de la Mare born
  Ford Madox Ford (Ford Hermann Hueffer) born
  G.E. Moore born
  C.T. Onions born
  Oliver Onions born
  A.R. Orage born
  H.M. Tomlinson born
- Edward Bulwer-Lytton, 1st Baron Lytton, dies
  Caroline Clive dies
  Charles Allston Collins dies
  Margaret Gatty dies
  J.S. Le Fanu dies
  John Stuart Mill dies
- David Livingstone dies
  Samuel Wilberforce dies
- Sergei Rachmaninov born
- Rimbaud, *Une Saison en Enfer*
  Tolstoy, *Anna Karenina* (–1875)
  Jules Verne, *Le Tour du monde en quatre-vingt jours*

Gilbert Arthur à Beckett (1837–91)
The Happy Land D
Written with W.S. Gilbert (under the pseudonym 'F. Tomline')

Alexander Anderson (1845–1909)
A Song of Labour, and Other Poems V

Matthew Arnold (1822–88)
Literature and Dogma NF

'Cuthbert Bede' [Edward Bradley (1827–89)]
Little Mr Bouncer and His Friend, Verdant Green F
See also *Verdant Green* 1853, *Further Adventures of Verdant Green* 1854, *Mr Verdant Green, Married and Done For* 1857

Robert Bridges (1844–1930)
Poems by Robert Bridges V
See also *Poems* 1879, 1880

Oliver Madox Brown (1855–74)
Gabriel Denver F

Robert Browning (1812–89)
Red Cotton Night-Cap Country; or, Turf and Towers V

Edward Carpenter (1844–1929)
Narcissus, and Other Poems V

Wilkie Collins (1824–89)
Miss or Mrs? and Other Stories in Outline F
Anonymous. Published on 17 January 1873.

Charles Davies (1829–85)
Unorthodox London NF
See also *Orthodox London* 1874

Austin Dobson (1840–1921)
Vignettes in Rhyme V

E.A. Freeman (1823–92)
Historical Essays: Second Series NF
See also *Historical Essays* 1871, 1879, 1892

Dora Greenwell (1821–82)
Songs of Salvation V

Thomas Hardy (1840–1928)
A Pair of Blue Eyes F
Published in May 1873. Serialized (anonymously) in *Tinsleys' Magazine* (September 1872–July 1873),

'Mrs Alexander' [Annie French Hector (1825–1902)]
The Wooing O't F
Serialized in *Temple Bar* (June 1872–Nov. 1873)

J.S. Le Fanu (1814–73)
Willing to Die F

John Stuart Mill (1806–73)
Autobiography NF

William Morris (1834–96)
Love is Enough; or, The Freeing of Pharamond V

John Henry Newman, later **Cardinal** (1801–90)
The Idea of a University NF

Walter Pater (1839–94)
Studies in the History of the Renaissance NF
Revised in 1877 as *The Renaissance: Studies in Art and Poetry*

Emily Pfeiffer (1827–90)
Gerard's Monument, and Other Poems V

Charles Reade (1814–84)
A Simpleton F
Serialized in *London Society* (August 1872–August 1873)

William Stubbs (1825–1901)
The Constitutional History of England: in its Origin and Development [vol. i] NF
Published in 3 volumes (1873–8)

Anthony Trollope (1815–82)
Phineas Redux F
Published in December 1873, dated 1874. Serialized in *The Graphic* (19 July 1873–10 January 1874).

Charlotte M. Yonge (1823–1901)
The Pillars of the House; or, Under Wode, Under Rode F
Serialized in *The Monthly Packet* (January 1870–December 1873)

1874

- Conservatives win British general election: resignation of Gladstone; Disraeli becomes Prime Minister (–1880)

First Impressionist exhibition in Paris

- Maurice Baring born
Gordon Bottomley born
G.K. Chesterton born
Sir Winston Churchill born
Somerset Maugham born
Gertrude Stein born
- Michael Banim dies
[Charles William] Shirley Brooks dies
Oliver Madox Brown dies
Sydney Dobell dies
Thomas (Tom) Hood dies
Agnes Strickland dies
Bryan Waller Procter ('Barry Cornwall') dies
- Ernest Shackleton born
- Gustav Holst born

Cassell's Family Magazine PER
First series published monthly, December 1874–November 1897

The World PER
Published weekly from 8 July 1874–25 March 1922. Co-owned by Edmund Yates and edited by him 1874–94.

Alfred Austin (1835–1913)
The Tower of Babel V

William Black (1841–98)
A Princess of Thule F
Serialized in *Macmillan's Magazine* (March–December 1873)

Walter Richard Cassels (1826–1907)
Supernatural Religion [vols i–ii] NF
Anonymous. Volume iii published in 1877.

Wilkie Collins (1824–89)
The Frozen Deep, and Other Stories F
Published on 2 November 1874. The title story (serialized in *Temple Bar,* August–October 1874) was based on a play written and acted by Dickens, Collins, and others on 6 January 1857.

Robert William Dale (1829–95)
The English Hymn Book V

Charles Davies (1829–85)
Orthodox London NF
See also *Unorthodox London* 1873

Charlotte Despard (1844–1939)
Chaste as Ice, Pure as Snow F

'George Eliot' [Mary Ann Evans (1819–80)]
The Legend of Jubal, and Other Poems V
Published in May 1874

Frederic W. Farrar (1831–1903)
The Life of Christ NF

Francis Galton (1822–1911)
English Men of Science NF

J.R. Green (1837–83)
A Short History of the English People NF

Thomas Hardy (1840–1928)
Far From the Madding Crowd F
Published in November 1874. Illustrated by Helen Allingham. Serialized (anonymously) in the *Cornhill Magazine* (January–December 1874).

Richard Jefferies (1848–87)
The Scarlet Shawl F

Edward Robert Bulwer Lytton (1831–91)
Fables in Song V

'Ennis Graham' [Mary Louisa Molesworth (1839–1921)]
Cicely F

John Henry Newman, later **Cardinal** (1801–90)
Tracts Theological and Ecclesiastical NF

Arthur O'Shaughnessy (1844–81)
Music and Moonlight V

Charlotte Elizabeth Riddell [Mrs J.H. Riddell] (1832–1906)
Frank Sinclair's Wife, and Other Stories F

Henry Sidgwick (1838–1900)
The Methods of Ethics NF

Leslie Stephen (1832–1904)
Hours in a Library [1st ser.] NF
Second series, 1876; third series, 1879

Algernon Charles Swinburne (1837–1909)
Bothwell: A tragedy D

Anthony Trollope (1815–82)
Lady Anna F
Published in May 1874. Serialized in the *Fortnightly Review* (April 1873–April 1874).

Anthony Trollope (1815–82)
Harry Heathcote of Gangoil F
Published in October 1874. First published in *The Graphic* (Christmas Number, 1873).

Ellen Wood [Mrs Henry Wood] (1814–87)
Johnny Ludlow [1st ser.] F
Anonymous. Six series, 1874–89.

1875

- Matthew Webb becomes the first man to swim the English Channel (24–5 Aug.)
- E.C. Bentley born
  John Buchan born
  J.W. Dunne born
  Sir Walter Wilson Greg born
  Theodore Francis Powys born
  Forrest Reid born
  Rafael Sabatini born
  Evelyn Underhill born
  Edgar Wallace born
- Sir Arthur Helps dies
  Charles Kingsley dies
  Sir Charles Lyell dies
  Augustus Mayhew dies
  [William] Winwood Reade dies
  Connop Thirlwall dies
- Maurice Ravel born
  Rainer Maria Rilke born
  Albert Schweitzer born
- Hans Christian Andersen dies
  Georges Bizet dies
- Twain, *The Adventures of Tom Sawyer*

Matthew Arnold (1822–88)
God and the Bible NF
See *Literature and Dogma* 1873

George Barlow (1847–1913)
Under the Dawn V

'Proteus' [Wilfrid Scawen Blunt (1840–1922)]
Sonnets and Songs V
See also *Love Sonnets* 1881, *Love Lyrics* 1892

Robert Browning (1812–89)
Aristophanes' Apology V

Lady [Isabel] Burton (1831–96)
The Inner Life of Syria, Palestine, and the Holy Land NF

Marcus Clarke (1846–81)
His Natural Life F
First published Melbourne, 1874. The first one-volume edition of 1878 was titled *For the Term of His Natural Life.*

Wilkie Collins (1824–89)
The Law and the Lady F
Published in February 1875. Serialized in *The Graphic* (26 September 1874–13 March 1875).

S. R. Gardiner (1829–1902)
A History of England Under the Duke of Buckingham and Charles I NF
See also *History of England* 1863, *Prince Charles* 1869, *Personal Government* 1877, *Fall of the Monarchy* 1882, *History of England* 1883

W.S. Gilbert (1836–1911)
Trial by Jury: A novel original dramatic cantata D
Performed 25 March 1875. Music by Arthur Sullivan. The first Gilbert and Sullivan opera.

Frederic Harrison (1831–1923)
Order and Progress NF

Jean Ingelow (1820–97)
Fated to be Free F
Sequel to *Off the Skelligs* 1872 (q.v.)

Henry James (1843–1916)
A Passionate Pilgrim, and Other Tales F
Published in the USA on 31 January 1875. No separate British edition.

John Keble (1792–1866)
Sermons for the Christian Year NF

'Helen Mathers' [Ellen Buckingham Mathers (1853–1920)]
Comin' Thro' the Rye F

George Meredith (1828–1909)
Beauchamp's Career F
Published in November 1875, dated 1876. A condensed version was serialized in the *Fortnightly Review* (August 1874–December 1875).

Alice Meynell (1847–1922)
Preludes V

William Morris (1834–96) and **Eiríkr Magnússon** (1833–1913) (tr.)
Three Northern Love Stories, and Other Tales F
See also *Grettis Saga* 1869, *Völsunga Saga* 1870, *The Story of Gunnlaug the Worm-Tongue* 1891

Francis Turner Palgrave (1824–97) (ed.)
The Children's Treasury of English Song ANTH

Algernon Charles Swinburne (1837–1909)
Essays and Studies NF

Sir Henry Taylor (1800–86)
A Sicilian Summer; St Clement's Eve; The Eve of the Conquest V

Alfred Tennyson (1809–92)
Queen Mary D
Published in May 1875. Performed 18 April 1876.

Anthony Trollope (1815–82)
The Way We Live Now F
Published in July 1875. First published in monthly parts (February 1874–September 1875).

1876

- Alexander Graham Bell patents the telephone
  First complete performance of Wagner's *Ring* cycle at the newly opened Bayreuth Theatre
- Frank Richards (Charles Hamilton, creator of Billy Bunter) born
  G.M. Trevelyan born
- Mortimer Collins dies
  Catherine Crowe dies
  John Forster dies
  Henry Kingsley dies
  G.A. Lawrence dies
  Harriet Martineau dies
  Philip Meadows Taylor dies
- George Sand (Aurore Dupin) dies
- Mallarmé, *L'Après-midi d'un faune*
  Henry Sweet, *Anglo-Saxon Reader*

Isabella Banks [Mrs G. Linnaeus Banks] (1821–97)
The Manchester Man F
Serialized in *Cassell's Family Magazine* (January–November 1874)

Walter Besant (1836–1901) and **James Rice** (1843–82)
The Case of Mr Lucraft, and Other Tales F

Walter Besant (1836–1901) and **James Rice** (1843–82)
The Golden Butterfly F
'By the authors of *Ready-Money Mortiboy*'

William Black (1841–98)
Madcap Violet F
Serialized in *Macmillan's Magazine* (January–December 1876)

F.H. Bradley (1846–1924)
Ethical Studies NF

Robert Bridges (1844–193-)
The Growth of Love V
Revised and enlarged in 1889

Oliver Madox Brown (1855–74)
The Dwale Bluth, Hebditch's Legacy, and Other Literary Remains F
Edited by W.M. Rossetti and F. M. Hueffer

Robert Browning (1812–89)
Pacchiarotto and How He Worked in Distemper; with Other Poems V

Frederick Burnaby (1842–85)
On Horseback Through Asia Minor NF

'Lewis Carroll' [C.L. Dodgson (1832–98)]
The Hunting of the Snark V
Illustrated by Henry Holiday

Wilkie Collins (1824–89)
The Two Destinies F
Serialized in *Temple Bar* (January–September 1876)

Edward Dowden (1843–1913)
Poems V

'George Eliot' [Mary Ann Evans (1819–80)]
Daniel Deronda F
Published on 26 August 1876 in 4 volumes. The eight parts published separately between January and September 1876.

W.S. Gilbert (1836–1911)
Original Plays V
Second series, 1881; third series, 1895; fourth series, 1911

Dora Greenwell (1821–82)
Camera Obscura V

Thomas Hardy (1840–1928)
The Hand of Ethelberta F
Published in April 1876. Illustrated by George du Maurier. Serialized in the *Cornhill Magazine* (July 1875–May 1876).

Benjamin Robert Haydon (1786–1846)
Correspondence and Table-Talk NF

'Mrs Alexander' [Annie French Hector (1825–1902)]
Her Dearest Foe F
Serialized in *Temple Bar* (June 1875–Aug. 1876)

Emma Marshall (1828–99)
Life's Aftermath F

'Ennis Graham' [Mary Louisa Molesworth (1839–1921)]
'Carrots': Just a little boy F

Margaret Oliphant (1828–97)
The Curate in Charge F
Serialized in *Macmillan's Magazine* (August 1875–January 1876)

Margaret Oliphant (1828–97)
Phoebe Junior F
The fifth and last of the 'Chronicles of Carlingford' volumes. See also *The Rector and The Doctor's Family* 1863, *Salem Chapel* 1863, *The Perpetual Curate* 1864, *Miss Marjoribanks* 1866.

Emily Pfeiffer (1827–90)
Poems V

P.B. Shelley (1792–1822)
The Works of Percy Bysshe Shelley WKS
Edited by Harry Buxton Forman (8 volumes, 1876–80)

Leslie Stephen (1832–1904)
History of English Thought in the Eighteenth Century NF
See also *The English Utilitarians* 1900

Algernon Charles Swinburne (1837–1909)
Erechtheus: A tragedy D

Anthony Trollope (1815–82)
The Prime Minister F
Published in May 1876. First published in monthly parts (November 1875–June 1876).

William Wordsworth (1770–1850)
The Prose Works of William Wordsworth EDN
Edited by A.B. Grosart

1877

- Queen Victoria proclaimed Empress of India (1 Jan.)
  R.B. Hayes becomes President of the USA
  Russo-Turkish War (–1878)
  First All-England Lawn tennis championship at Wimbledon
  Thomas Edison invents the phonograph
- James Agate born
  [George] Warwick Deeping born
  Harley Granville-Barker born
  Sir Desmond MacCarthy born
  Flora Thompson born
- Walter Bagehot dies
  James Ballantine dies
  Charles Cowden Clarke dies
  Caroline Norton dies
- Leon Trotsky born
- Gustave Courbet dies
- Flaubert, *Trois Contes*
  Ibsen, *Pillars of Society*
  Zola, *L'Assommoir*

The Nineteenth Century PER
Published monthly, March 1877–December 1900

William Allingham (1824–89)
Songs, Ballads, and Stories V

Matthew Arnold (1822–88)
Last Essays on Church and Religion NF

Thomas Carlyle (1795–1881)
Characteristics NF

William Johnson Cory (1823–92)
Ionica II V
Anonymous. See also *Ionica* 1858.

Austin Dobson (1840–1921)
Proverbs in Porcelain V

S. R. Gardiner (1829–1902)
The Personal Government of Charles I NF
See also *History of England* 1863, *Prince Charles* 1869, *History of England* 1875, *Fall of the Monarchy* 1882, *History of England* 1883

Lady Charlotte Guest (1812–95) (tr.)
The Mabinogion F
The first complete, popular translation of the medieval Welsh tales found in *The Red Book of Hergest*. See also *The Mabinogion* 1838.

John Abraham Heraud (1799–1887)
Uxmal; Macée de Léodepart V

Richard Jefferies (1848–87)
The World's End F

Edward Lear (1812–88)
Laughable Lyrics V
See also *Book of Nonsense* 1846, *Nonsense Songs* 1870, *More Nonsense* 1871

George MacDonald (1824–1905)
The Marquis of Lossie F
A sequel to *Malcolm* 1874. Serialized in *Lippincott's Magazine* (November 1876–September 1877).

W.H. Mallock (1849–1923)
The New Republic; or, Culture, Faith, and Philosophy in an English Country House F
Serialized in *Belgravia* (June–December 1876)

Harriet Martineau (1802–76)
Harriet Martineau's Autobiography NF

George Moore (1852–1933)
Flowers of Passion V
Published in 1877, dated 1878

William Morris (1834–96)
The Story of Sigurd the Volsung, and the Fall of the Niblungs V

John Henry Newman, later **Cardinal** (1801–90)
The Via Media of the Anglican Church NF

Coventry Patmore (1823–96)
The Unknown Eros, and Other Odes V
Anonymous. Odes i–xxxi. The second, enlarged, edition was published under Patmore's name in 1878 (Odes i–xlvi).

Anna Sewell (1820–78)
Black Beauty: The autobiography of a horse, translated from the original Equine F

Alfred Tennyson (1809–92)
Harold D
Published in November 1877

Anthony Trollope (1815–82)
The American Senator F
Published in July 1877. Serialized in *Temple Bar* (May 1876–July 1877) as *The Senator*.

1878

- Congress of Berlin (July) on the Eastern Question
  English Men of Letters series begins
- H.C. Bailey born
  A.E. Coppard born
  Lord Dunsany born
  Jeffery Farnol born
  Wilfrid Gibson born
  John Masefield born
  Edward Thomas born
- Clara Balfour dies
  George Cruikshank dies
  George Henry Lewes dies
  Anna Sewell dies
  G.J. Whyte-Melville dies
- Lord John Russell, 1st Earl Russell, dies
- Tchaikovsky, *Swan Lake*

Wilfrid Scawen Blunt (1840–1922)
Proteus and Amadeus V

Robert Browning (1812–89)
La Saisiaz; The Two Poets of Croisic V

Robert Buchanan (1841–1901)
Poetical Works V

Samuel Butler (1835–1902)
Life and Habit NF

Wilkie Collins (1824–89)
The Haunted Hotel F
Published in November 1878, dated 1879. Serialized in *Belgravia* (June–November 1878).

W.S. Gilbert (1836–1911)
HMS Pinafore; or, The Lass That Loved a Sailor D/OP

Performed 25 May 1878. Music by Arthur Sullivan.

Thomas Hardy (1840–1928)
The Return of the Native F
Published in November 1878. Serialized in *Belgravia* (January–December 1878).

Henry James (1843–1916)
The Europeans F
Published on 18 September 1878. Serialized in the *Atlantic Monthly* (July–October 1878).

Richard Jefferies (1848–87)
The Gamekeeper at Home NF
Anonymous

W.E.H. Lecky (1838–1903)
A History of England in the Eighteenth Century NF
Published in 8 volumes (1878–90). Expanded to 12 volumes, 1892.

W.H. Mallock (1849–1923)
The New Paul and Virginia; or, Positivism on an Island F

'Helen Mathers' [Ellen Buckingham Mathers (1853–1920)]
Cherry Ripe! F
bao *Comin' Thro' the Rye*. Serialized in *Temple Bar* (January 1877–January 1878).

William Morris (1834–96)
The Decorative Arts NF

Coventry Patmore (1823–96)
Amelia; Tamerton Church-Tower V
Tamerton Church-Tower first published in 1853 (q.v.)

Sir Henry Morton Stanley (1841–1904)
Through the Dark Continent NF

Leslie Stephen (1832–1904)
Samuel Johnson NF
The inaugural volume of the English Men of Letters series

R.L. Stevenson (1850–94)
Edinburgh: Picturesque Notes NF

R.L. Stevenson (1850–94)
An Inland Voyage NF

Algernon Charles Swinburne (1837–1909)
Poems and Ballads: Second Series V
See also *Poems and Ballads* 1866, 1889

John Addington Symonds (1840–93)
Many Moods V

John Addington Symonds (1840–93)
Shelley NF

Anthony Trollope (1815–82)
Is He Popenjoy? F
Published in April 1878. Serialized in *All the Year Round* (October 1877–July 1878).

Oscar Wilde (1854–1900)
Ravenna V

1879

- Zulu War
  The Cambridge Review starts
- Joseph Campbell born
  E.M. Forster born
  Percy Lubbock born
  Harold Monro born
- Frances Browne dies
  E.S. Dallas dies
  G.W.M. Reynolds dies
  Charles Jeremiah Wells dies
- Albert Einstein born
  Joseph Stalin born
- Ibsen, *A Doll's House*
  Strindberg, *The Red Room*
- Tchaikovsky, *Eugene Onegin*

The Boy's Own Paper PER
Published weekly, 18 January 1879–February 1967. See also *The Girls' Own Paper* 1880.

Edwin Arnold (1832–1904)
The Light of Asia; or, The Great Renunciation V
See also *The Light of the World* 1891

Matthew Arnold (1822–88)
Mixed Essays NF

Walter Bagehot (1826–77)
Literary Studies NF
Edited by R.H. Hutton

A.J. Balfour (1848–1930)
A Defence of Philosophic Doubt NF

Louisa Sarah Bevington (1845–95)
Key-Notes V

Robert Bridges (1844–1930)
Poems V
bao *The Growth of Love*. See also *Poems* 1873, 1880.

Robert Browning (1812–89)
Dramatic Idyls [1st ser.] V
See also *Dramatic Idyls* 1880

Lady [Isabel] Burton (1831–96)
Arabia, Egypt, India NF

Samuel Butler (1835–1902)
Evolution, Old and New NF

Wilkie Collins (1824–89)
The Fallen Leaves F
Published in July 1879. Serialized in *The World* (1 January–23 July 1879).

Charlotte Despard (1844–1939)
A Modern Iago F

'George Eliot' [**Mary Ann Evans** (1819–80)]
Impresssions of Theophrastus Such NF
Published on 19 May 1879

E.A. Freeman (1823–92)
Historical Essays: Third Series NF
See also *Historical Essays* 1871, 1873, 1892

Edmund Gosse (1849–1928)
New Poems V

Kate Greenaway (1846–1901)
Under the Window: Pictures & rhymes for children V

George Grove (1820–1900) (ed.)
A Dictionary of Music and Musicians DICT

Henry James (1843–1916)
Daisy Miller; An International Episode; Four Meetings F
First British edition, published on 15 February 1879. Title story serialized in the *Cornhill Magazine* (June–July 1878).

Henry James (1843–1916)
The American F
First authorized edition, published in March 1879

Henry James (1843–1916)
Roderick Hudson F
First British edition, published on 11 June 1879

Henry James (1843–1916)
The Madonna of the Future, and Other Tales F
Published in October 1879

Henry James (1843–1916)
Confidence F
Published on 10 December 1879, dated 1880. Serialized in *Scribner's Monthly* (August 1879–January 1880).

Richard Jefferies (1848–87)
The Amateur Poacher NF
Anonymous

Richard Jefferies (1848–87)
Wild Life in a Southern County NF
Anonymous

Justin McCarthy (1830–1912)
A History of Our Own Times [vols i, ii] NF
Volumes iii and iv, 1880. Expanded to 5 volumes (1889–97) and to 7 volumes (1897–1905).

George Meredith (1828–1909)
The Egoist F
Published in October 1879. Serialized in the *Glasgow Weekly Herald* (21 June 1879–10 January 1880).

Margaret Oliphant (1828–97)
A Beleaguered City F
Published 1879, dated 1880. First published in the *New Quarterly Magazine* (January1879).

Emily Pfeiffer (1827–90)
Quarterman's Grace, and Other Poems V

R.L. Stevenson (1850–94)
Travels with a Donkey in the Cévennes NF

John Addington Symonds (1840–93)
Sketches and Studies in Italy NF

Alfred Tennyson (1809–92)
The Lover's Tale V
Published in May 1879

Anthony Trollope (1815–82)
An Eye for an Eye F
Published in January 1879. Serialized in the *Whitehall Review* (August 1878–February 1879). Written in 1871.

Anthony Trollope (1815–82)
John Caldigate F
Published in June 1879. Serialized in *Blackwood's Magazine* (April 1878–June 1879).

Anthony Trollope (1815–82)
Cousin Henry F
Published in November 1879. Serialized in the *Manchester Weekly Times* (May–December 1879).

1880

- Liberals win British general election: Gladstone becomes Prime Minister for the second time (–1885)
  Charles Bradlaugh elected to Parliament but as an atheist refuses to take the oath and is excluded from the House of Commons
  Transvaal Boers proclaim a republic
  The Stage started
- Sir Ernest Gowers born
  Radclyffe Hall born
  Alfred Noyes born
  Sean O'Casey born

Marie Stopes born
Lytton Strachey born
R.H. Tawney born
Leonard Woolf born

- Maria Charlesworth dies
  Pierce Egan, the younger, dies
  George Eliot (Mary Ann Cross, *née* Evans) dies
  Geraldine Jewsbury dies
  Tom Taylor dies
- Guillaume Apollinaire (Wilhelm de Kostrowitsky) born
  Jacob Epstein born
- Gustave Flaubert dies
  Jacques Offenbach dies
- Maupassant, *Boule de Suif*
  Dostoevsky, *The Brothers Karamazov*
  Lew Wallace, *Ben Hur*
  Zola, *Nana*

The Girl's Own Paper PER
Published weekly, 3 January 1880–26 September 1908. See also *The Boy's Own Paper* 1879.

Walter Bagehot (1826–77)
Economic Studies NF
Edited by R.H. Hutton

William Black (1841–98)
White Wings F
Serialized in the *Cornhill Magazine* (July 1879–Oct. 1880)

Robert Bridges (1844–1930)
Poems V
bao *The Growth of Love*. See also *Poems* 1873, 1879.

Robert Browning (1812–89)
Dramatic Idyls [2nd ser.] V
See also *Dramatic Idyls* 1879

Wilkie Collins (1824–89)
Jezebel's Daughter F
Book version of Collins's unpublished play *The Red Vial* (performed in 1858)

Charles Dickens (1812–70)
The Mudfog Papers F
Illustrated by George Cruikshank. Three pieces first published in *Bentley's Miscellany* (January and October 1837, September 1838).

Benjamin Disraeli (1804–81)
Endymion F
bao *Lothair*

W.S. Gilbert (1836–1911)
The Pirates of Penzance; or, The Slave of Duty D/OP
Performed 30 December 1879. Music by Arthur Sullivan.

George Gissing (1857–1903)
Workers in the Dawn F
Published in March 1880. Gissing's first novel, published at his own expense.

Thomas Hardy (1840–1928)
The Trumpet-Major F
Published in October 1880. Serialized in *Good Words* (January–December 1880).

Frederic Harrison (1831–1923)
The Present and the Future NF

Jean Ingelow (1820–97)
Poems V
Volume i reprints the twenty-third edition of *Poems* 1863 (q.v.); volume ii reprinted from the sixth edition of *A Story of Doom* (1867, q.v.). See also *Poems: Third Series* 1885.

Richard Jefferies (1848–87)
Hodge and his Masters F

Andrew Lang (1844–1912)
XXII Ballades in Blue China V

'Vernon Lee' [Violet Paget (1856–1935)]
Studies of the Eighteenth Century in Italy NF

J.S. Le Fanu (1814–73)
The Purcell Papers F
Stories, with memoir by A.P. Graves

George Meredith (1828–1909)
The Tragic Comedians F
Published on 15 December 1880. Serialized in the *Fortnightly Review* (October 1880–February 1881).

Mary Louisa Molesworth (1839–1921)
A Christmas Child F
Illustrated by Walter Crane

Mary Louisa Molesworth (1839–1921)
Miss Bouverie F

Emily Pfeiffer (1827–90)
Sonnets and Songs V

Charlotte Elizabeth Riddell [Mrs J.H. Riddell] (1832–1906)
The Mystery in Palace Gardens F

C.H. Spurgeon (1834–92)
John Ploughman's Pictures; or, More of his Plain Talk for Plain People NF
See also *John Ploughman's Talks* 1869

Algernon Charles Swinburne (1837–1909)
The Heptalogia; or, The Seven Against Sense V
Parodies of seven contemporaries (Tennyson, Robert Browning, Elizabeth Browning, Coventry

Patmore, Robert, Lord Lytton, D.G. Rossetti, and Swinburne himself)

Algernon Charles Swinburne (1837–1909)
Songs of the Springtides V

Algernon Charles Swinburne (1837–1909)
Studies in Song V

John Addington Symonds (1840–93)
New and Old V

Alfred Tennyson (1809–92)
Ballads, and Other Poems V
Published in November 1880

James Thomson (1834–82)
The City of Dreadful Night, and Other Poems V
Title poem first published in the *National Reformer* (22 March–17 May 1874)

Anthony Trollope (1815–82)
The Duke's Children F
Published in May 1880. Serialized in *All the Year Round* (4 October 1879–24 July 1880).

William Watson (1858–1935)
The Prince's Quest, and Other Poems V

Oscar Wilde (1854–1900)
Vera; or, The Nihilists D
Performed in New York in August 1883

1881

- Hostilities with the Transvaal Boers; Britain recognizes independence of the Transvaal (Apr.)
  James A. Garfield becomes President of the USA (Mar.) but is subsequently assassinated; succeeded by Chester Arthur (Sept.)
  Assassination of Tsar Alexander II
- Lascelles Abercrombie born
  Daisy Ashford born
  Clive Bell born
  Padraic Colum born
  Eleanor Farjeon born
  Constance Holme born
  E.V. Knox born
  Rose Macaulay born
  Mary Webb born
  P.G. Wodehouse born
- George Borrow dies
  Thomas Carlyle dies
  Benjamin Disraeli dies
  Anna Maria Hall (Mrs S.C. Hall) dies
  Arthur O'Shaughnessy dies
  Arthur Penrhyn Stanley dies
- Alexander Fleming born
- Pablo Picasso born
- Feodor Dostoevsky dies
- Ibsen, *Ghosts*
  Flaubert, *Bouvard et Pécuchet*
  Verlaine, *Sagesse*

The New Testament BIB
The Revised Version of the Bible, published on 17 May 1881. See also *Holy Bible* 1885, *Apocrypha* 1895.

Tit-Bits PER
Published weekly from 22 October 1881. Owned and edited by George Newnes.

W.H. Ainsworth (1805–82)
Stanley Brereton F

Walter Bagehot (1826–77)
Biographical Studies NF
Edited by R.H. Hutton

Walter Besant (1836–1901) and **James Rice** (1843–82)
The Chaplain of the Fleet F

Wilfrid Scawen Blunt (1840–1922)
The Love Sonnets of Proteus V
See also *Sonnets and Songs* 1875, *Love Lyrics* 1892

'Arran and Isla Leigh' [Katherine Harris Bradley (1846–1914) and **Edith Emma Cooper** (1862–1913)]
Bellerophon, and Other Poems V

Thomas Carlyle (1795–1881)
Reminiscences NF
Published in February 1881, the month Carlyle died. Edited by J.A. Froude.

Wilkie Collins (1824–89)
The Black Robe F
First published in the *Canadian Monthly* (November 1880–June 1881)

E.A. Freeman (1823–92)
The Historical Geography of Europe NF

S.R. Gardiner (1829–1902)
Introduction to the Study of English History NF

W.S. Gilbert (1836–1911)
Patience; or, Bunthorne's Bride D
First performed 23 April 1881. Music by Arthur Sullivan.

Thomas Hardy (1840–1928)
A Laodicean; or, The Castle of the De Stancys F

Published in December 1881. Serialized in *Harper's New Monthly Magazine* (December 1880–December 1881).

T.H. Huxley (1825–95)
Science and Culture, and Other Essays NF

Henry James (1843–1916)
Washington Square; The Pension Beaurepas; A Bundle of Letters F
First British edition, published in January 1881. *Washington Square* serialized in the *Cornhill Magazine* (June–November 1880).

Henry James (1843–1916)
The Portrait of a Lady F
Published in November 1881. Serialized in *Macmillan's Magazine* (October 1880–November 1881).

Amy Levy (1861–89)
Xantippe, and Other Verse V

W.H. Mallock (1849–1923)
A Romance of the Nineteenth Century F

George Moore (1852–1933)
Pagan Poems V
Published in March 1881

David Christie Murray (1847–1907)
Joseph's Coat F
Serialized in *Belgravia* (November 1880–December 1881)

Rosa Caroline Praed [Mrs Campbell Praed] (1851–1935)
Policy and Passion F

Charlotte Elizabeth Riddell [Mrs J.H. Riddell] (1832–1906)
The Senior Partner F

Christina Rossetti (1830–94)
A Pageant, and Other Poems V

Dante Gabriel Rossetti (1828–82)
Ballads and Sonnets V

'Mark Rutherford' [William Hale White (1831–1913)]
The Autobiography of Mark Rutherford, Dissenting Minister F
See also *Mark Rutherford's Deliverance* 1885

J.H. Shorthouse (1834–1903)
John Inglesant F
Anonymous. First privately printed in 1880.

R.L. Stevenson (1850–94)
Virginibus Puerisque, and Other Papers NF
Title piece first published in the *Cornhill Magazine* (August 1876)

Bram Stoker (1847–1912)
Under the Sunset F
Published in November 1881, dated 1882. Stories.

Algernon Charles Swinburne (1837–1909)
Mary Stuart: A tragedy D

Anthony Trollope (1815–82)
Dr Wortle's School F
Published in February 1881. Serialized in *Blackwood's Magazine* (May–December 1880).

Anthony Trollope (1815–82)
Ayala's Angel F
Published in June 1881

Mary Ward [Mrs Humphry Ward] (1851–1920)
Milly and Olly; or, A Holiday Among the Mountains F
Published December 1881

Oscar Wilde (1854–1900)
Poems V
Published in June 1881. Three editions in 1881.

1882

- Murder of Lord Frederick Cavendish and T.H. Burke by the 'Irish Invincibles' in Phoenix Park, Dublin (6 May)
  Society for Psychical Research founded
  Dictionary of National Biography (ed. Sir Leslie Stephen) begins publication
- John Drinkwater born
  James Joyce born
  [Percy] Wyndham Lewis born
  A.A. Milne born
  James Stephens born
  Virginia Woolf (*née* Stephen) born
  G.M. Young born
- William Harrison Ainsworth dies
  Rosina Bulwer-Lytton dies
  Charles Darwin dies
  Dora Greenwell dies
  Dennis MacCarthy dies
  E.B. Pusey dies
  Dante Gabriel Rossetti dies
  James Thomson dies
  Anthony Trollope dies
- Jean Giraudoux born
  Igor Stravinsky born
- Franklin D. Roosevelt born
- Ralph Waldo Emerson dies
  Giuseppe Garibaldi dies

Henry Wadsworth Longfellow dies
- Wagner, *Parsifal*

Longman's Magazine PER
Published mothly, November 1882–October 1905

William Allingham (1824–89)
Evil May-Day V

'F. Anstey' [Thomas Anstey Guthrie (1856–1934)]
Vice Versa; or, A Lesson to Fathers F

William Archer (1856–1924)
English Dramatists of Today NF

Walter Besant (1836–1901)
All Sorts and Conditions of Men F
Dedicated to Besant's writing partner, James Rice (1843–82). Serialized in *Belgravia* (January–December 1882).

Walter Besant (1836–1901)
The Revolt of Man F
Anonymous. Besant's first independent novel following the death of his writing partner, James Rice.

R.D. Blackmore (1825–1900)
Christowell F
Serialized in *Good Words* (January–December 1881)

Hall Caine (1853–1931)
Recollections of Dante Gabriel Rossetti NF

Lucy Clifford [Mrs W.K. Clifford] (1849–1929)
Anyhow Stories F
For children

Mandell Creighton (1843–1901)
History of the Papacy [vols i, ii] NF
Volumes iii and iv, 1887 (q.v.); volume v, 1894 (q.v.)

Juliana Horatia Ewing [Mrs J.H. Ewing] (1841)
Old Fashioned Fairy Tales F

E.A. Freeman (1823–92)
The Reign of William Rufus and the Accession of Henry the First NF

J.A. Froude (1818–94)
Thomas Carlyle NF
See also *Letters and Memorials* 1883, *Thomas Carlyle* 1884

S. R. Gardiner (1829–1902)
The Fall of the Monarchy of Charles I, 1637–1649 NF
See also *History of England* 1863, *Prince Charles* 1869, *History of England* 1875, *Personal Government* 1877, *History of England* 1883

H. Rider Haggard (1856–1925)
Cetawayo and His White Neighbours NF
Published in June 1882

Thomas Hardy (1840–1928)
Two on a Tower F
Published in October 1882

'Lucas Malet' [Mary St Leger Harrison (1852–1931)]
Mrs Lorimer F

Richard Jefferies (1848–87)
Bevis: The story of a boy F
bao *The Gamekeeper at Home, Wild Life in a Southern County*

Henry Arthur Jones (1851–1929)
The Silver King D
Performed 16 November 1882. Not published until 1907. Co-written with Henry Herman (1832–94).

Frances Kemble (1809–93)
Records of Later Life NF
See also *Further Records* 1890

Emily Lawless (1845–1913)
A Chelsea Householder F

George MacDonald (1824–1905)
The Princess and Curdie F
Published in 1882, dated 1883. Sequel to *The Princess and the Goblin* 1871 (q.v.). Serialized in *Good Things* (January–June 1877).

Margaret Oliphant (1828–97)
A Little Pilgrim in the Unseen F
Published in October 1882. Title story first published in *Macmillan's Magazine* (May 1882). See also *The Land of Darkness* 1888.

Charlotte Elizabeth Riddell [Mrs J.H. Riddell] (1832–1906)
The Prince of Wales's Garden Party, and Other Stories F

R.L. Stevenson (1850–94)
Familiar Studies of Men and Books NF

R.L. Stevenson (1850–94)
New Arabian Nights F
See also *More New Arabian Nights* 1885

Algernon Charles Swinburne (1837–1909)
Tristram of Lyonesse, and Other Poems V

Anthony Trollope (1815–82)
The Fixed Period F

Serialized in *Blackwood's Magazine* (October 1881–March 1882)

Anthony Trollope (1815–82)
Kept in the Dark F
Published in October 1882. Serialized in *Good Words* (May–December 1882).

Anthony Trollope (1815–82)
Marion Fay F
Serialized in *The Graphic* (December 1881–June 1882)

Anthony Trollope (1815–82)
Why Frau Frohmann Raised Her Prices, and Other Stories F
Stories mainly published in magazines December 1876–December 1878

1883

- Paul Kruger elected President of the Transvaal (South African Republic)
  Britain evacuates the Sudan
- T.E. Hulme born
  Edward Fitzgerald born
  John Maynard Keynes born
  Compton Mackenzie born
- J.W. Colenso dies
  Edward Fitzgerald dies
  Thomas Mayne Reid dies
- Franz Kafka born
  Benito Mussolini born
- Karl Marx dies
  Ivan Turgenev dies
  Richard Wagner dies
- H.B. Forman's edition of Keats
  Nietzsche, *Also sprach Zarathustra*
  Maupassant, *Une Vie*

William Allingham (1824–89)
The Fairies V
Includes 'Up the airy mountain . . .', reprinted from *Poems* 1850 (q.v.)

Wilfrid Scawen Blunt (1840–1922)
The Wind and the Whirlwind V

Robert Bridges (1844–1930)
Prometheus the Firegiver V
Published in July 1883

Robert Browning (1812–89)
Jocoseria V

Jane Welsh Carlyle (1801–66)
Letters and Memorials of Jane Welsh Carlyle NF
Edited by J.A. Froude. See also Froude, *Thomas Carlyle* 1882, 1884.

Thomas Carlyle (1795–1881)
The Correspondence of Thomas Carlyle and Ralph Waldo Emerson NF
Published in Britain in February 1883

S R. Gardiner (1829–1902)
History of England 1603–42 NF
Collected edition (10 volumes, 1883–4) of previously published works. See *History of England* 1863, *Prince Charles* 1869, *History of England* 1875, *Personal Government* 1877, *Fall of the Monarchy* 1882.

G.A. Henty (1832–1902)
Under Drake's Flag F
Juvenile

Richard Jefferies (1848–87)
The Story of My Heart NF
bao *The Gamekeeper at Home, Wild Life in a Southern County*

Eliza Lynn Linton (1822–98)
The Girl of the Period, and Other Social Essays NF
Published in November 1883. Title essay first published in 1868 (q.v.).

George Meredith (1828–1909)
Poems and Lyrics of the Joy of Earth V
Published on 7 June 1883

George Moore (1852–1933)
A Modern Lover F
Rewritten as *Lewis Seymour and Some Women* (1917)

'Ralph Iron' [Olive Schreiner (1855–1920)]
The Story of an African Farm F

R.L. Stevenson (1850–94)
The Silverado Squatters F
Published in December 1883. Serialized in *The Century Illustrated Magazine* (November–December 1883).

R.L. Stevenson (1850–94)
Treasure Island F
Serialized in *Young Folks* (1 October 1881–28 January 1882)

Algernon Charles Swinburne (1837–1909)
A Century of Roundels V
Dedicatory verse to Christina Rossetti

Anthony Trollope (1815–82)
Mr Scarborough's Family F
Published in May 1883. Serialized in *All the Year Round* (May 1882–June 1883).

Anthony Trollope (1815–82)
The Landleaguers F
Published in October 1883. Unfinished at Trollope's death in December 1882. Serialized in *Life* (November 1882–October 1883).

Anthony Trollope (1815–82)
An Autobiography NF
Published in November 1883

Charlotte M. Yonge (1823–1901)
Stray Pearls F
See *A Chaplet of Pearls* 1868. Serialized in *The Monthly Packet* (January 1881–May 1883).

1884

- German occupation of South-West Africa
  Third Reform Bill extending suffrage
  Oxford English Dictionary (ed. Sir James Murray) commences (-1928)
  Fabian Society founded
  Buffalo Bill's first open-air Wild West show, in Nebraska
- Gilbert Cannan born
  Ivy Compton-Burnett born
  James Elroy Flecker born
  Naomi Jacob born
  Sean O'Casey born
  Llewellyn Powys born
  Arthur Ransome born
  Sir John Collings Squire born
  Frank Swinnerton born
  Alison Uttley born
  Sir Hugh Walpole born
  Francis Brett Young born
- Charles Stuart Calverley dies
  R.H. Horne dies
  Mark Pattison dies
  Charles Reade dies
- Huysmans, *A rebours*

'Cecil Power' [**Grant Allen** (1848–99)]
Philistia F

Augustine Birrell (1850–1933)
Obiter Dicta [1st ser.] NF
See also *Obiter Dicta* 1887, 1924

Robert Browning (1812–89)
Ferishtah's Fancies V
Published in November 1884

Richard F. Burton (1821–90)
Book of the Sword NF

John Wilson Croker (1780–1857)
The Croker Papers NF

J.A. Froude (1818–94) (ed.)
Thomas Carlyle NF
See also *Thomas Carlyle* 1882, *Letters and Memorials* 1883

W.S. Gilbert (1836–1911)
Princess Ida; or, Castle Adamant D
Performed 5 January 1884. Music by Arthur Sullivan.

George Gissing (1857–1903)
The Unclassed F
Published in May 1884

W.E. Henley (1849–1903) and **R.L. Stevenson** (1850–94)
Admiral Guinea D
Performed 29 November 1897

W.E. Henley (1849–1903) and **R.L. Stevenson** (1850–94)
Beau Austin D
Performed 3 November 1890

Richard Jefferies (1848–87)
Red Deer NF
bao *The Gamekeeper at Home, Wild Life in a Southern County, The Story of My Heart*, etc

Richard Jefferies (1848–87)
The Life of the Fields NF
bao *The Gamekeeper at Home, Nature Near London, Red Deer*, etc

Andrew Lang (1844–1912)
Custom and Myth NF

Andrew Lang (1844–1912)
Rhymes à la Mode V
Published 1884, dated 1885

Amy Levy (1861–89)
A Minor Poet, and Other Verse V

'Leolinus Siluriensis' [**Arthur Machen** (1863–1947)]
The Anatomy of Tobacco; or, Smoking Methodised NF

George Moore (1852–1933)
A Mummer's Wife F
Published 1884, dated 1885

William Morris (1834–96)
A Summary of the Principles of Socialism NF
Written with H.M. Hydnman

Charlotte Elizabeth Riddell [**Mrs J.H. Riddell**] (1832–1906)
Weird Stories F
A celebrated ghost-story collection

John Ruskin (1819–1900)
The Art of England NF
Originally published in seven parts (May 1883–July 1884)

John Ruskin (1819–1900)
The Pleasures of England NF

Herbert Spencer (1820–1903)
The Man Versus the State NF

Algernon Charles Swinburne (1837–1909)
A Midsummer Holiday, and Other Poems V

Alfred, Lord Tennyson (1809–92)
Becket D
Published in November 1884. Performed (produced by Henry Irving) 6 February 1893. Tennyson accepted a peerage from Queen Victoria in January 1884.

Alfred, Lord Tennyson (1809–92)
The Cup; and The Falcon D
The Cup performed 3 January 1881

Anthony Trollope (1815–82)
An Old Man's Love F

Mary Ward [Mrs Humphry Ward] (1851–1920)
Miss Bretherton F
Published in November 1884

1885

- Fall of Khartoum (26 Jan.): death of General Charles Gordon
  Leopold II of Belgium establishes the Congo State
  Grover Cleveland becomes President of the USA
- D.H. Lawrence born
  Ezra Pound born
  Gwen Raverat born
  Humbert Wolfe born
  P.C. Wren born
  Dornford Yates (Cecil William Mercer) born
- Juliana Horatia Ewing (Mrs J.H. Ewing) dies
  Richard Monckton Milnes, Lord Houghton, dies
- Alban Berg born
  François Mauriac born
  Ezra Pound born
- Victor Hugo dies
- Maupassant, *Bel-Ami*
  Marx, *Das Kapital* (vol. ii)
  Zola, *Germinal*

The Holy Bible BIB
Published on 19 May 1885. Contains the first publication of the Revised Version of the Old Testament (volumes i–iv) and the New Testament published in 1881 (q.v.). The Apocrypha published in 1895 (q.v.).

Matthew Arnold (1822–88)
Discourses in America NF

Alfred Austin (1835–1913)
At the Gate of the Convent, and Other Poems V

Amelia Barr (1831–1919)
Jan Vedder's Wife F

Robert Bridges (1844–1930)
Eros and Psyche V
Published in December 1885

Robert Bridges (1844–1930)
Nero: Part 1 D
Part 2 published in 1894 (q.v.)

Sir Richard F. Burton (1821–90) (tr.)
A Plain and Literal Translation of the Arabian Nights' Entertainments NF
Lady Burton's edition, prepared 'for household reading' by J.H. McCarthy, was published in 1886

C.S. Calverley (1831–84)
Literary Remains V

Lucy Clifford [Mrs W.K. Clifford] (1849–1929)
Mrs Keith's Crime F
Anonymous

'George Eliot' [Mary Ann Evans (1819–80)**]**
George Eliot's Life, as Related in Her Letters and Journals NF
Edited by her husband, J.W. Cross

W.S. Gilbert (1836–1911)
Iolanthe; or, The Peer and the Peri D/OP
Performed 25 November 1882. Music by Arthur Sullivan.

W.S. Gilbert (1836–1911)
The Mikado; or, The Town of Titipu D/OP
Performed 14 March 1885. Music by Arthur Sullivan.

H. Rider Haggard (1856–1925)
King Solomon's Mines F
Published on 30 September 1885 and reprinted in October, November, and December

W.H. Hudson (1841–1922)
The Purple Land that England Lost F

Jean Ingelow (1820–97)
Poems: Third Series V
See also *Poems* 1863, *Poems* 1880

Richard Jefferies (1848–87)
After London; or, Wild England F
bao *The Gamekeeper at Home, Wood Magic, Red Deer, The Dewy Morn.* Set in a vague, post-catastrophic future.

George Meredith (1828–1909)
Diana of the Crossways F
Published on 16 February 1885. Twenty-six chapters were serialized in the *Fortnightly Review* (June–July, September–December 1884).

William Morris (1834–96)
Chants for Socialists V

William Morris (1834–96)
The Manifesto of the Socialist League NF

Walter Pater (1839–94)
Marius the Epicurean: His sensations and ideas F

Mark Pattison (1813–84)
Memoirs NF

Charles Reade (1814–84)
A Perilous Secret F
Published in March 1885, dated 1884. Serialized in *Temple Bar* (September 1884–May 1885).

Charlotte Elizabeth Riddell [Mrs J.H. Riddell] (1832–1906)
Mitre Court F
Serialized in *Temple Bar* (January 1885-January 1886)

Christina Rossetti (1830–94)
Time Flies: A reading diary NF
Contains 130 poems

John Ruskin (1819–1900)
On the Old Road NF

'Mark Rutherford' [William Hale White (1831–1913)]
Mark Rutherford's Deliverance F

'John Strange Winter' [Henrietta Eliza Stannard (1856–1911)]
Bootles' Baby F
See also *Bootles' Children* 1888

R.L. Stevenson (1850–94)
A Child's Garden of Verses V

R.L. Stevenson (1850–94)
More New Arabian Nights: The Dynamiter F
Published in April 1885. Written with Fanny Van de Grift Stevenson. See *New Arabian Nights* 1882.

R.L. Stevenson (1850–94)
Prince Otto F
Serialized in *Longman's Magazine* (April–October 1885)

Algernon Charles Swinburne (1837–1909)
Marino Faliero: A tragedy D

Alfred, Lord Tennyson (1809–92)
Tiresias, and Other Poems V
Published in November 1885. Includes 'Balin and Balan'—one of the *Idylls of the King*. See also *Idylls of the King* 1859, *The Holy Grail* 1869, *Idylls of the King* 1870, 'The Last Tournament' 1871, *Gareth and Lynette* 1872, *Idylls of the King* 1889.

Katharine Tynan (1861–1931)
Louise de la Vallière, and Other Poems V

Charlotte M. Yonge (1823–1901)
The Two Sides of the Shield F
A sequel to *Scenes and Characters* 1847 (q.v.). See also *Beechcroft at Rockstone* 1888.

1886

- Gladstone's Liberal administration defeated on Irish Home Rule Bill: Lord Salisbury forms Conservative ministry
  Scribner's Magazine started
  English Historical Review (ed. Mandell Creighton) started
- Clifford Bax born
  Marjorie Bowen born
  Ronald Firbank born
  Sir Harold Nicolson born
  Lennox Robinson born
  Siegfried Sassoon born
  Charles Williams born
- William Barnes dies
  Sir Henry Taylor dies
  Richard Chevenix Trench dies
- Alain-Fournier (Henri Alban Fournier) born
- Franz Liszt dies
- Ibsen, *Rosmersholm*
  Nietzsche, *Jenseits von Gut und Böse* (Beyond Good and Evil)
  Rimbaud, *Les Illuminations*

William Alexander (1824–1911)
St Augustine's Holiday, and Other Poems V

Grant Allen (1848–99)
For Mamie's Sake: A tale of love and dynamite F

Amelia Barr (1831–1919)
The Bow of Orange Ribbon F

Frances Hodgson Burnett (1849–1924)
Little Lord Fauntleroy F

Serialized in *St Nicholas* (November 1885–October 1886)

Marie Corelli (1855–1924)
A Romance of Two Worlds F
Published in February 1886. See also *Ardath* 1889.

Emilia Frances, Lady Dilke (1840–1904)
The Shrine of Death, and Other Stories F
See also *The Shrine of Love* 1891

Edward Dowden (1843–1913)
The Life of Percy Bysshe Shelley NF

E.A. Freeman (1823–92)
The Methods of Historical Study NF

George Gissing (1857–1903)
Demos: A story of English Socialism F
Anonymous. Published in March 1886.

George Gissing (1857–1903)
Isabel Clarendon F
Published in June 1886

'Maxwell Gray' [Mary Gleed Tuttiett (1847–1923)]
The Silence of Dean Maitland F

Thomas Hardy (1840–1928)
The Mayor of Casterbridge: The life and death of a man of character F
Published on 10 May 1886. Serialized in *The Graphic* (2 January–15 May 1886).

Fergus Hume (1859–1932)
The Mystery of a Hansom Cab F

Henry James (1843–1916)
The Bostonians F
Published on 16 February 1886. Serialized in the *Century Magazine* (February 1885–February 1886).

Henry James (1843–1916)
The Princess Casamassima F
Published on 22 October 1886. Serialized in the *Atlantic Monthly* (September 1885–October 1886).

Jerome K. Jerome (1859–1927)
The Idle Thoughts of an Idle Fellow NF
See also *Second Thoughts of an Idle Fellow* 1898

Rudyard Kipling (1865–1936)
Departmental Ditties, and Other Verses V

Emily Lawless (1845–1913)
Hurrish F

W.H. Mallock (1849–1923)
The Old Order Changes F

George Meredith (1828–1909)
Sandra Belloni F
Published in February 1886. The second edition of *Emilia in England* 1864 (q.v.).

George Moore (1852–1933)
A Drama in Muslin F
Published in June 1886. Serialized in the *Court and Society Review* (14 January–1 July 1886). Extensively rewritten as *Muslin* (1915).

William Morris (1834–96)
Useful Work Versus Useless Toil NF

E[dith] Nesbit (1858–1924)
Lays and Legends [1st ser.] V
Second series, 1892

Dante Gabriel Rossetti (1828–82)
Collected Works V
Edited by W.M. Rossetti

W.M. Rossetti (1829–1919)
A Memoir of Shelley NF
Reprinted from Rossetti's edition of Shelley (1870)

John Ruskin (1819–1900)
Dilecta NF
Correspondence, diary notes, etc; published in three parts, 1886–1900. See also *Praeterita* 1886, 1887, 1888.

John Ruskin (1819–1900)
Praeterita: Outlines of scenes and thoughts perhaps worthy of memory in my past life NF
Volume i. Volume ii, 1887 (q.v.); volume iii, 1888–9 (q.v.). See also *Dilecta* 1886.

Bernard Shaw (1856–1950)
Cashel Byron's Profession F
Serialized in *To-Day* (April 1885–March 1886)

R.L. Stevenson (1850–94)
Strange Case of Dr Jekyll and Mr Hyde F
Published in January 1886

R.L. Stevenson (1850–94)
Kidnapped F
Serialized in *Young Folks* (1 May–13 July 1886). See also *Catriona* 1893.

Arthur Symons (1865–1945)
An Introduction to the Study of Browning NF

Alfred, Lord Tennyson (1809–92)
Locksley Hall Sixty Years After V
Published in December 1886

W.B. Yeats (1865–1939)
Mosada V
Probably published in October 1886

1887

- Queen Victoria's Diamond Jubilee (21 June)
  British annexation of Zululand
- C.D. Broad born
  Rupert Brooke born
  Elizabeth Daryush born
  Sir Julian Huxley born
  Sir Geoffrey Keynes born
  Edwin Muir born
  Edith Sitwell born
- Dinah Maria Craik dies
  James Grant dies
  Richard Jefferies dies
  Henry Mayhew dies
  Ellen Wood (Mrs Henry Wood) dies
- Marc Chagall born
- Zola, *La Terre*

William Allingham (1824–89)
Rhymes for Young Folk V

J.M. Barrie (1860–1937)
Better Dead F
Published in November 1887, dated 1888

Augustine Birrell (1850–1933)
Obiter Dicta [2nd ser.] NF
See also *Obiter Dicta* 1884, 1924

R.D. Blackmore (1825–1900)
Springhaven F
Serialized in *Harper's Magazine* (April 1886–April 1887)

'Michael Field' [Katherine Harris Bradley (1846–1914) and **Edith Emma Cooper** (1862–1913)]
Canute the Great; The Cup of Water D

Thomas Edward Brown (1830–97)
The Doctor, and Other Poems V

Robert Browning (1812–89)
Parleyings with Certain People of Importance in their Day V

Hall Caine (1853–1931)
The Deemster F

Hall Caine (1853–1931)
A Son of Hagar F

'Pax' [Mary Cholmondeley (1859–1925)]
The Danvers Jewels F
Published on 9 August 1887. Serialized in *Temple Bar* (January–March 1887). See also *Sir Charles Danvers* 1889.

Wilkie Collins (1824–89)
Little Novels F

Mandell Creighton (1843–1901)
History of the Papacy [vols iii, iv] NF
Volumes i and ii published in 1882 (q.v.); volume v, 1894, (q.v.)

W.S. Gilbert (1836–1911)
Ruddygore; or, The Witch's Curse D/OP
Performed 22 January 1887. Music by Arthur Sullivan. Title spelling subsequently changed to *Ruddigore*.

George Gissing (1857–1903)
Thyrza F
Serialized in the *Cornhill Magazine* (January–December 1888)

H. Rider Haggard (1856–1925)
She: A history of adventure F
Published on 1 January 1887. Serialized in *The Graphic* (2 October 1886–8 January 1887). See also *Ayesha* 1905, *She and Allan* 1921, *Wisdom's Daughter* 1923.

H. Rider Haggard (1856–1925)
Allan Quatermain F
Published on 1 July 1887. Serialized in *Longman's Magazine* (January–August 1887).

Thomas Hardy (1840–1928)
The Woodlanders F
Published on 15 March 1887. Serialized in *Macmillan's Magazine* (May 1886–April 1887).

Richard Jefferies (1848–87)
Amaryllis at the Fair F
bao *The Gamekeeper at Home, Greene Ferne Farm, After London*. Jefferies died on 14 August 1887.

Andrew Lang (1844–1912)
Myth, Ritual and Religion NF

Richard Le Gallienne (1866–1947)
My Lady's Sonnets V

'Edna Lyall' [Ada Ellen Bayly (1857–1903)]
The Autobiography of a Slander F
See also *The Autobiography of a Truth* 1896

George Meredith (1828–1909)
Ballads and Poems of Tragic Life V
Published on 10 May 1887

George Moore (1852–1933)
A Mere Accident F

William Morris (1834–96)
The Aims of Art NF

Walter Pater (1839–94)
Imaginary Portraits NF

'Q' [A.T. Quiller-Couch (1863–1944)]
Dead Man's Rock F

John Ruskin (1819–1900)
Praeterita [vol. ii] NF
Volume i published in 1886 (q.v.); volume iii, 1888–9 (q.v.). See also *Dilecta* 1886.

'Mark Rutherford' [William Hale White (1831–1913)]
The Revolution in Tanner's Lane F

Bernard Shaw (1856–1950)
An Unsocial Socialist F
First published in *To-Day* (March–December 1884)

R.L. Stevenson (1850–94)
Memories and Portraits NF

R.L. Stevenson (1850–94)
The Merry Men, and Other Tales and Fables F
Includes 'Markheim' (published in *Unwin's Christmas Annual* for 1885) and 'Thrawn Janet' (*Cornhill Magazine*, October 1881)

R.L. Stevenson (1850–94)
Underwoods V

Algernon Charles Swinburne (1837–1909)
The Jubilee V
Published in June 1887

Algernon Charles Swinburne (1837–1909)
Locrine: A tragedy D
Performed 20 March 1899

Alfred, Lord Tennyson (1809–92)
Carmen Saeculare: An ode in honour of the Jubilee of Queen Victoria V
Published in April 1887

Katharine Tynan (1861–1931)
Shamrocks V

1888

- Accession of Kaiser Wilhelm II
  Cecil Rhodes is granted mining rights in Matabeleland by King Lobengula
  Pasteur Institute founded in Paris
  Nansen crosses Greenland
  Football League founded
- Joyce Cary born
  Clemence Dane (Winifred Ashton) born
  T.S. Eliot born
  F. Tennyson Jesse born
  Ronald Knox born
  T.E. Lawrence born
  Herman Cyril McNeile ('Sapper') born
  Katherine Mansfield born
  Sir Lewis Namier born
  Michael Sadleir born
  Eugene O'Neill born
- Matthew Arnold dies
  Philip Henry Gosse dies
  Edward Lear dies
  Sir Henry Maine dies
  Laurence Oliphant dies
- Irving Berlin born
- Maupassant, *Pierre et Jean*

William Allingham (1824–89)
Flower Pieces, and Other Poems V
Illustrated by D.G. Rossetti.

William Archer (1856–1924)
Masks or Faces? A study in the psychology of acting NF

Sir Edwin Arnold (1832–1904)
With Sa'di in the Garden; or, The Book of Love V
Translated from the Persian

Matthew Arnold (1822–88)
Essays in Criticism [2nd ser.] NF
See also *Essays in Criticism* 1865, 1910

J.M. Barrie (1860–1937)
Auld Licht Idylls F
Published in April 1888

'Gavin Ogilvy' [J.M. Barrie (1860–1937)]
When a Man's Single F
Published in October 1888. Serialized in *The British Weekly* (7 October 1887–23 March 1888).

'Rolf Boldrewood' [Thomas Alexander Browne (1826–1915)]
Robbery Under Arms F
First serialized in the *Sydney Mail* (1 July–11 August 1883)

Rosa Nouchette Carey (1840–1909)
Only the Governess F

Thomas Carlyle (1795–1881)
Letters of Thomas Carlyle 1826–1836 NF

Charles Doughty (1843–1926)
Travels in Arabia Deserta NF

A. Conan Doyle (1859–1930)
A Study in Scarlet F
Published in July 1888. The first Sherlock Holmes adventure. First published in *Beeton's Christmas*

Annual for 1887. See also *The Sign of Four* 1890, *Adventures of Sherlock Holmes* 1892, *Memoirs of Sherlock Holmes* 1893, *The Hound of the Baskervilles* 1902, *Return of Sherlock Holmes* 1905, *The Valley of Fear* 1915, *His Last Bow* 1917, *Case-Book of Sherlock Holmes* 1927.

Richard Garnett (1835–1906)
The Twilight of the Gods, and Other Tales F

George Gissing (1857–1903)
A Life's Morning F
Published on 15 November 1888. Serialized in the *Cornhill Magazine* (January–December 1888).

'Sarah Grand' [Frances Elizabeth McFall (1854–1943)]
Ideala F
Anonymous

H. Rider Haggard (1856–1925)
Maiwa's Revenge; or, The War of the Little Hand F
Published on 3 August 1888

H. Rider Haggard (1856–1925)
Colonel Quaritch, V.C. F
Published on 3 December 1888

Thomas Hardy (1840–1928)
Wessex Tales F
Published on 4 May 1888

W.E. Henley (1849–1903)
A Book of Verses V

W.E. Henley (1849–1903) and **R.L. Stevenson** (1850–94)
Deacon Brodie; or, The Double Life D
First version private printed in 1880. Performed in Bradford, 28 December 1882.

Henry James (1843–1916)
The Reverberator F
Published in June 1888. Serialized in *Macmillan's Magazine* (February–July 1888).

Henry James (1843–1916)
The Aspern Papers F
Stories. Published in September 1888. Title story serialized in the *Atlantic Monthly* (March–May 1888).

Rudyard Kipling (1865–1936)
Soldiers Three F
Stories. Published in Allahabad. First British edition, 1890. See also *Soldiers Three*, etc., 1895.

Rudyard Kipling (1865–1936)
The Story of the Gadsbys F
Stories. Published in Allahabad. First British edition, 1890. See also *Soldiers Three*, etc., 1895.

Rudyard Kipling (1865–1936)
In Black and White F
Stories. Published in Allahabad. First British edition, 1890. See also *Soldiers Three*, etc., 1895.

Rudyard Kipling (1865–1936)
Under the Deodars F
Stories. Published in Allahabad. First British edition, 1890. See also *Wee Willie Winkie*, etc., 1895.

Rudyard Kipling (1865–1936)
The Phantom 'Rickshaw, and Other Tales F
Stories, including 'The Man Who Would Be King' and 'The Strange Ride of Morrowbie Jukes'. Published in Allahabad. First British edition, 1890. See also *Wee Willie Winkie*, etc., 1895.

Rudyard Kipling (1865–1936)
Wee Willie Winkie, and Other Child Stories F
Stories. Published in Allahabad. First British edition, 1890. See also *Wee Willie Winkie*, etc., 1895.

Rudyard Kipling (1865–1936)
Plain Tales From the Hills F
Stories. Published in Calcutta. First British edition, 1890.

Andrew Lang (1844–1912)
Grass of Parnassus V

Amy Levy (1861–89)
The Romance of a Shop F

George Meredith (1828–1909)
A Reading of Earth V
Published on 20 December 1888

'Henry Seton Merriman' [Hugh Stowell Scott (1862–1903)]
The Phantom Future F

George Moore (1852–1933)
Confessions of a Young Man NF
Published in February 1888

George Moore (1852–1933)
Spring Days F
Published in August or September 1888. Serialized in the *Evening News* (3 April–31 May 1888).

William Morris (1834–96)
A Dream of John Ball; and A King's Lesson F
John Ball serialized in *The Commonweal* (November 1886–January 1887); *A King's Lesson* first published in *The Commonweal* (September 1886) as *An Old Story Re-Told.*

William Morris (1834–96)
Signs of Change NF

Margaret Oliphant (1828–97)
The Land of Darkness F
Stories. See also *A Little Pilgrim in the Unseen* 1882.

'Q' [A.T. Quiller-Couch (1863–1944)]
The Astonishing History of Troy Town F

John Ruskin (1819–1900)
Praeterita [vol. iii] NF
Published in four parts, 1888–9. Volume i, 1886 (q.v.); volume ii, 1887 (q.v.). See also *Dilecta* 1886.

'John Strange Winter' [Henrietta Eliza Stannard (1856–1911)]
Bootles' Children F
See also *Bootles' Baby* 1885

R.L. Stevenson (1850–94)
The Black Arrow: A tale of two roses F
Serialized in *Young Folks* (30 June–20 October 1888)

Mary Ward [Mrs Humphry Ward] (1851–1920)
Robert Elsmere F
Published on 24 February 1888. Nine editions in 1888. See also *The Case of Richard Meynell* 1911.

Oscar Wilde (1854–1900)
The Happy Prince, and Other Tales F
Published in May 1888

William Wordsworth (1770–1850)
The Recluse V
Printed from the original MS. The plan of *The Recluse*, never completed, was for a long autobiographical poem consisting of three parts and a prelude. See *The Excursion* 1814 and *The Prelude* 1850.

Charlotte M. Yonge (1823–1901)
Beechcroft at Rockstone F
Sequel to *Scenes and Characters* 1847 and *The Two Sides of the Shield* 1885 (qq.v.). Serialized in *The Monthly Packet* (January 1887–December 1888).

1889

- Benjamin Harrison becomes President of the USA
  Cecil Rhodes's British South Africa Company granted royal charter
  Parnell Commission
  Eiffel Tower in Paris completed
  The Granta started
- Enid Bagnold born
  G.D.H. Cole born
  R.G. Collingwood born
  Philip Guedalla born
  Hugh Kingsmill born
  John Middleton Murry born
  C.K. Ogden born
  Arnold Toynbee born
  Arthur Waley born
- William Allingham dies
  Edward Bradley ('Cuthbert Bede') dies
  Robert Browning dies
  Wilkie Collins dies
  Gerard Manley Hopkins dies
  Martin Tupper dies
- Charles Chaplin born
  Adolf Hitler born
  Paul Nash born
- Tolstoy, *The Kreutzer Sonata*

J.M. Barrie (1860)
A Window in Thrums F
Published in July 1889

Wilfrid Scawen Blunt (1840–1922)
A New Pilgrimage, and Other Poems V

Robert Bridges (1844–1930)
The Feast of Bacchus V
Published in November 1889

Thomas Edward Brown (1830–97)
The Manx Witch, and Other Poems V

Robert Browning (1812–89)
Asolando: Fancies and facts V
Published on 12 December 1889 (the day of Browning's death), dated 1890

Frances Burney, Madame d'Arblay (1752–1840)
The Early Diary of Frances Burney 1768–78 NF
See also *Diary and Letters of Madame d'Arblay* 1842

Lady Colin Campbell (1861–1911)
Darell Blake F

'Lewis Carroll' [C.L. Dodgson (1832–98)]
Sylvie and Bruno F
Illustrated by Harry Furniss. See also *Sylvie and Bruno Concluded* 1893.

Mary Cholmondeley (1859–1925)
Sir Charles Danvers F
bao *The Danvers Jewels*. Serialized in *Temple Bar* (May–December 1889). Sequel to *The Danvers Jewels* 1887 (q.v.).

Marie Corelli (1855–1924)
Ardath F
Sequel to *A Romance of Two Worlds* 1886 (q.v.)

George Nathaniel Curzon (1859–1925)
Russia in Central Asia in 1889 NF

A. Conan Doyle (1859–1930)
Micah Clarke F
Published on 25 February 1889

W.S. Gilbert (1836–1911)
The Gondoliers; or, The King of Barataria D/OP
Performed 7 December 1889. Music by Arthur Sullivan.

George Gissing (1857–1903)
The Nether World F
Published on 3 April 1889

H. Rider Haggard (1856–1925)
Cleopatra F
Published on 24 June 1889. Serialized in *The Illustrated London News* (5 January–29 June 1889).

H. Rider Haggard (1856–1925)
Allan's Wife, and Other Tales F
Published in December 1889

'Rita' [Eliza Humphreys (1856–1938)]
Sheba F

Henry James (1843–1916)
A London Life F
Stories. Published in April 1889.

Richard Jefferies (1848–87)
Field and Hedgerow NF

Jerome K. Jerome (1859–1927)
Three Men in a Boat (To Say Nothing of the Dog) F
See also *Three Men on the Bummel* 1900

Andrew Lang (1844–1912) (ed.)
The Blue Fairy Book ANTH
Illustrated by H.J. Ford and G.P. Jacomb-Hood. The first of the Fairy Book series. Followed by *The Red Fairy Book* 1890, *Green Fairy Book* 1892, *Yellow Fairy Book* 1894, *Pink Fairy Book* 1897, *Grey Fairy Book* 1900, *Violet Fairy Book* 1901, *Brown Fairy Book* 1904, *Orange Fairy Book* 1906, *Lilac Fairy Book* 1910.

Andrew Lang (1844–1912)
Letters on Literature NF

Amy Levy (1861–89)
A London Plane-Tree, and Other Verse V

Amy Levy (1861–89)
Miss Meredith F

George Moore (1852–1933)
Mike Fletcher F
Published in December 1889

William Morris (1834–96)
A Tale of the House of the Wolfings and All the Kindreds of the Mark F/V
In prose and verse

Walter Pater (1839–94)
Appreciations NF

Mark Pattison (1813–84)
Essays by the Late Mark Pattison NF

Emily Pfeiffer (1827–90)
Flowers of the Night V

'Geilles Herring' [Edith Somerville (1858–1949)] and **'Martin Ross' [Violet Martin** (1862–1915)]
An Irish Cousin F

R.L. Stevenson (1850–94) and **Lloyd Osbourne** (1868–1947)
The Wrong Box F
Published in June 1889

R.L. Stevenson (1850–94)
The Master of Ballantrae: A winter's tale F
Published in August 1889. Serialized in *Scribner's Magazine* (November 1888–October 1889).

Algernon Charles Swinburne (1837–1909)
Poems and Ballads: Third Series V
See also *Poems and Ballads* 1866, 1878

Arthur Symons (1865–1945)
Days and Nights V

Alfred, Lord Tennyson (1809–92)
Demeter, and Other Poems V
Published in December 1889

Alfred, Lord Tennyson (1809–92)
Idylls of the King V
Complete edition of the Idylls, with final titles and running order. See also *Idylls of the King* 1859, *The Holy Grail* 1869, *Idylls of the King* 1870, 'The Last Tournament' 1871, *Gareth and Lynette* 1872, 'Balin and Balan' in *Tiresias* 1885.

Alfred Russel Wallace (1823–1913)
Darwinism NF

W.B. Yeats (1865–1939)
The Wanderings of Oisin, and Other Poems V
Published in January 1889

1890

- Resignation of Bismarck (Mar.)
  Cecil Rhodes becomes Prime Minister of Cape Colony
  William Morris founds the Kelmscott Press

Charles Parnell resigns as leader of the Irish Nationalists: succeeded by Justin McCarthy

- Agatha Christie born
  Richmal Crompton born
  E.M. Delafield (Edmée Monica de la Pasture) born
  Ivor Gurney born
  Sir A.P. Herbert born
  Jean Rhys (Ella Rees Williams) born
  Isaac Rosenberg born
  Gladys Stern born
  Angela Thirkell born
- Dion Boucicault dies
  Sir Richard Burton dies
  Richard William Church dies
  John Henry Newman dies
  Emily Pfeiffer dies
  William Bell Scott dies
- Michael Collins born
  Charles de Gaulle born
  Dwight D. Eisenhower born
  Man Ray born
- César Franck dies
  Vincent van Gogh dies
- Ibsen, *Hedda Gabler*
- William James, *Principles of Psychology*

'F. Anstey' [Thomas Anstey Guthrie (1856–1934)]
Voces Populi [1st ser.] F

William Archer (1856–1924) (ed.)
Ibsen's Prose Dramas EDN
Published in 6 volumes (1890–1905), mostly translated by Archer

Edwin Lester Arnold (1857–1935)
The Wonderful Adventures of Phra the Phonecian F
Published in 1890, dated 1891

J.M. Barrie (1860–1937)
My Lady Nicotine F
Published in April 1890

William Booth (1829–1912)
In Darkest England, and the Way Out NF

Robert Bridges (1844–1930)
Palicio: A romantic drama in the Elizabethan manner D

Robert Bridges (1844–1930)
The Return of Ulysses: A drama in a mixed manner D

Robert Bridges (1844–1930)
The Christian Captives: A tragedy in a mixed manner D

Robert Bridges (1844–1930)
Achilles in Scyros: A drama in a mixed manner D

Hall Caine (1853–1931)
The Bondman F

Wilkie Collins (1824–89)
Blind Love F
Published in January 1890. Wilkie Collins died in September 1889. Completed, with preface, by Walter Besant. Serialized in the *Illustrated London News* (July–December 1889).

Wilkie Collins (1824–89) and **Charles Dickens** (1812–72)
The Lazy Tour of Two Idle Apprentices; No Thoroughfare; The Perils of Certain English Prisoners F
The Lazy Tour of Two Idle Apprentices first published in *Household Words* (3–31 October 1857)

John Davidson (1857–1909)
Perfervid F

A. Conan Doyle (1859–1930)
The Sign of Four F
Published on 15 October 1890. First published in *Lippincott's Monthly Magazine* (February 1890). See also *A Study in Scarlet* 1888, *Adventures of Sherlock Holmes* 1892, *Memoirs of Sherlock Holmes* 1893, *The Hound of the Baskervilles* 1902, *Return of Sherlock Holmes* 1905, *The Valley of Fear* 1915, *His Last Bow* 1917, *Case-Book of Sherlock Holmes* 1927.

Sara Jeannette Duncan [Mrs Everard Cotes] (1861–1922)
A Social Departure NF

Havelock Ellis (1859–1939)
The New Spirit NF

J.G. Frazer (1854–1941)
The Golden Bough NF
Completed in 1915

Richard Garnett (1835–1906)
Iphigenia in Delphi V

W.S. Gilbert (1836–1911)
Songs of a Savoyard V

George Gissing (1857–1903)
The Emancipated F
Published on 22 March 1890

Edmund Gosse (1849–1928)
The Life of Philip Henry Gosse NF

H. Rider Haggard (1856–1925) and **Andrew Lang** (1844–1912)
The World's Desire F
Published on 5 November 1890. Serialized in the *New Review* (April–December 1890).

'Anthony Hope' [Anthony Hope Hawkins (1863–1933)]
A Man of Mark F

E.W. Hornung (1866–1921)
A Bride from the Bush F
Seialized in the *Cornhill Magazine* (July–November 1890)

Douglas Hyde (1860–1949) (ed.)
Beside the Fire: A collection of Irish and Gaelic folk stories F

Henry James (1843–1916)
The Tragic Muse F
Published in June 1890. First published in the USA. Serialized in the *Atlantic Monthly* (January 1889–May 1890).

Frances Kemble (1809–93)
Further Records NF
See also *Records of Later Life* 1882

'Vernon Lee' [Violet Paget (1856–1935)]
Hauntings F

Catherine Martin (1848?–1937)
An Australian Girl F

William Morris (1834–96)
The Roots of the Mountains F

Christina Rossetti (1830–94)
Poems V
New and enlarged edition

'Mark Rutherford' [William Hale White (1831–1913)]
Miriam's Schooling, and Other Papers F

Sir Henry Morton Stanley (1841–1904)
In Darkest Africa NF

R.L. Stevenson (1850–94)
Ballads V

John Addington Symonds (1840–93)
Essays Speculative and Suggestive NF

William Watson (1858–1935)
Wordsworth's Grave, and Other Poems V

Sidney Webb (1859–1947)
Socialism in England NF

Stanley J. Weyman (1855–1928)
The House of the Wolf F

1891

- Chace Act (partial US copyright protection for non-US authors)
  Germany, Austria, and Italy renew their Triple Alliance
  Construction of the Trans-Siberian Railway begins
  Carnegie Hall, New York, opened
- C.E.M. Joad born
- Gilbert Arthur à Beckett dies
  Barbara Bodichon dies
  Alexander William Kinglake dies
  Edward Robert Bulwer Lytton, Earl Lytton ('Owen Meredith') dies
- Max Ernst born
  Henry Miller born
- James Russell Lowell dies
  Herman Melville dies
  Arthur Rimbaud dies
- Huysmans, *Là-bas*

The Bookman PER
Published monthly, October 1891–December 1934. Edited by William Robertson Nicoll 1899–1903.

The Strand Magazine PER
Published monthly, January 1891–March 1950

Sir Edwin Arnold (1832–1904)
The Light of the World; or, The Great Consummation V
See also *The Light of Asia* 1879

Alfred Austin (1835–1913)
Lyrical Poems V

'Brandon Roy' [Florence Barclay (1862–1921)]
Guy Mervyn F

J.M. Barrie (1860–1937)
The Little Minister F
Published in October 1891. Serialized in *Good Words* (January–December 1891).

Isabella L. Bird (1831–1904)
Journeys in Persia and Kurdistan NF

Hall Caine (1853–1931)
The Scapegoat F

John Churton Collins (1848–1908)
The Study of English Literature NF

John Davidson (1857–1909)
In a Music-Hall, and Other Poems V

Emilia Frances, Lady Dilke (1840–1904)
The Shrine of Love, and Other Stories F
See also *The Shrine of Death* 1886.

A. Conan Doyle (1859–1930)
The White Company F
Published on 26 October 1891. Serialized in the *Cornhill Magazine* (January–December 1891).

Sara Jeannette Duncan [Mrs Everard Cotes] (1861–1922)
An American Girl in London F

'Lanoe Falconer' [Mary Elizabeth Hawker (1848–1908)]
Cecilia de Noël F

'Lanoe Falconer' [Mary Elizabeth Hawker (1848–1908)]
Mademoiselle Ixe F

'Lanoe Falconer' [Mary Elizabeth Hawker (1848–1908)]
The Hôtel d'Angleterre, and Other Stories F

George Gissing (1857–1903)
New Grub Street F
Published on 7 April 1891

Clotilde Graves (1863–1932)
Dragon's Teeth F

H. Rider Haggard (1856–1925)
Eric Brighteyes F
Published on 13 May 1891

Thomas Hardy (1840–1928)
A Group of Noble Dames F
Stories. Published on 30 May 1891.

Thomas Hardy (1840–1928)
Tess of the d'Urbervilles: A pure woman faithfully presented F
Published in November 1891. Serialized in *The Graphic* (4 July–26 December 1891).

Jerome K. Jerome (1859–1927)
Diary of a Pilgrimage (and Six Essays) NF

Jerome K. Jerome (1859–1927)
Told After Supper F
Stories

Rudyard Kipling (1865–1936)
Life's Handicap F
Stories

Rudyard Kipling (1865–1936)
The Light That Failed F
First published in the USA, 1890

George MacDonald (1824–1905)
There and Back F
Published in March or April 1891. Serialized in *The Sun* (7 September 1889–30 August 1890).

George Meredith (1828–1909)
One of Our Conquerors F
Published on 15 April 1891. Thirty-two chapters were serialized in the *Fortnightly Review* (October 1890–May 1891).

George Moore (1852–1933)
Impressions and Opinions NF
Published in March 1891

George Moore (1852–1933)
Vain Fortune F
Published in October 1891. Serialized in the *Lady's Pictorial* (4 July–17 October 1891).

William Morris (1834–96)
News from Nowhere; or, An Epoch of Rest F
First British edition. First (unauthorized) publication in the USA, 1890. Serialized in *The Commonweal* (January–October1890).

William Morris (1834–96)
The Story of the Glittering Plain F
The first book published at Morris's Kelmscott Press. First published in the *English Illustrated Magazine* (1890).

William Morris (1834–96)
Poems By the Way V

William Morris (1834–96) and **Eiríkr Magnússon** (1833–1913) (tr.)
The Story of Gunnlaug the Worm-Tongue and Raven the Scald F
See also *Grettis Saga* 1869, *Völsunga Saga* 1870, *Three Northern Love Stories* 1875

Eden Phillpotts (1862–1960)
The End of a Life F

Arthur Wing Pinero (1855–1934)
The Times: A comedy D
Performed 24 October 1891

Bernard Shaw (1856–1950)
The Quintessence of Ibsenism NF
Published in September 1891

May Sinclair (1863–1946)
Essays in Verse V

E[dith] Œ[none] Somerville (1858–1949) and **'Martin Ross' [Violet Martin** (1862–1915)]
Naboth's Vineyard F

J.K. Stephen (1859–92)
Lapsus Calami V

H.O. Sturgis (1855–1920)
Tim F
Anonymous

Katharine Tynan (1861–1931)
Ballads and Lyrics V

Beatrice Webb (1858–1943)
The Co-operative Movement in Great Britain NF

Oscar Wilde (1854–1900)
The Picture of Dorian Gray F
Published in April 1891. First version published in *Lippincott's Monthly Magazine* (July 1890).

Oscar Wilde (1854–1900)
Intentions NF
Published on 2 May 1891

Oscar Wilde (1854–1900)
Lord Arthur Savile's Crime, and Other Stories F
Published in July 1891. Title story first published in the *Court and Society Review* (11, 18, 25 May 1887). Also includes 'The Canterville Ghost'.

Oscar Wilde (1854–1900)
A House of Pomegranates F
Stories. Published in November 1891.

1892

- Resignation of Lord Salisbury: Gladstone forms Liberal government
  Famine in Russia
  Sewanee Review started
- Richard Aldington born
  Stella Benson born
  Lucy Boston born
  E.H. Carr born
  David Garnett born
  J.B.S. Haldane born
  Hugh MacDiarmid (Christopher Murray Grieve) born
  Vita Sackville-West born
  Sir Osbert Sitwell born
  J.R.R. Tolkien born
  Rebecca West (Cicily Andrews, *née* Fairfield) born
- Amelia Edwards dies
  Edward Augustus Freeman dies
  Henry Manning dies
  Sir Richard Owen dies
  Charles Spurgeon dies
  Alfred, Lord Tennyson dies
  Thomas Adolphus Trollope dies
- Ernest Renan dies
  Walt Whitman dies
- Maeterlinck, *Pelléas et Mélisande*
  Zola, *La Débâcle*

The Idler Magazine PER
Published monthly, February 1892–March 1911. Edited by J.K. Jerome and Robert Barr 1892–5, and by Jerome alone 1895–7.

The Book of the Rhymers' Club ANTH
Contributors to the anthology included Ernest Dowson, Lionel Johnson, Richard Le Gallienne, Ernest Radford, Ernest Rhys, T.W. Rolleston, Arthur Symons, and W.B. Yeats. See also *Second Book of the Rhymers' Club* 1894.

Jane Barlow (1857–1917)
Bog-Land Studies V

Jane Barlow (1857–1917)
Irish Idylls F
See also *Strangers at Lisconnel* 1895

'Luke Sharp' [Robert Barr (1850–1912)]
In a Steamer Chair, and Other Shipboard Stories F

A.C. Benson (1862–1925)
Le Cahier Jaune V

Wilfrid Scawen Blunt (1840–1922)
Esther, Love Lyrics, and Natalia's Resurrection V

Charles Booth (1840–1916)
Life and Labour of the People in London NF

Edward Caird (1835–1908)
Essays on Literature and Philosophy NF

Thomas Carlyle (1795–1881)
Last Words of Thomas Carlyle NF
Published on 28 May 1892. Includes the unfinished novel, *Wotten Reinfred.*

Austin Dobson (1840–1921)
The Ballad of Beau Brocade, and Other Poems of the XVIIIth Century V

Austin Dobson (1840–1921)
Eighteenth Century Vignettes [1st ser.] NF
See also *Eighteenth Century Vignettes* 1894, 1896

A. Conan Doyle (1859–1930)
The Adventures of Sherlock Holmes F
Published on 14 October 1892. Illustrated by Sidney Paget. Stories first published in the *Strand Magazine* (July 1891–June 1892). See also *A Study in Scarlet* 1888, *The Sign of Four* 1890, *Memoirs of Sherlock Holmes* 1893, *The Hound of the*

Baskervilles 1902, *Return of Sherlock Holmes* 1905, *The Valley of Fear* 1915, *His Last Bow* 1917, *Case-Book of Sherlock Holmes* 1927.

George du Maurier (1834–96)
Peter Ibbetson F
Serialized in *Harper's Monthly Magazine* (June–December 1891)

Ford Madox Ford (1873–1939)
The Shifting of the Fire F

E.A. Freeman (1823–92)
Historical Essays: Fourth Series NF
See also *Historical Essays* 1871, 1873, 1879

George Gissing (1857–1903)
Denzil Quarrier F
Published on 5 February 1892

George Gissing (1857–1903)
Born in Exile F
Published on 29 April 1892

George Grossmith (1847–1912) and **Weedon Grossmith** (1854–1919)
The Diary of a Nobody F
Illustrated by Weedon Grossmith. Originally published in *Punch* (26 May 1888–11 May 1889).

H. Rider Haggard (1856–1925)
Nada the Lily F
Published on 9 May 1892. Serialized in the *Illustrated London News* (2 January–7 May 1892).

W.E. Henley (1849–1903)
The Song of the Sword, and Other Verses V

G.A. Henty (1832–1902)
The Dash for Khartoum F
Juvenile

'John Oliver Hobbes' [Pearl Craigie (1867–1906)**]**
The Sinner's Comedy F

W.H. Hudson (1841–1922)
The Naturalist in La Plata NF

Henry James (1843–1916)
The Lesson of the Master F
Stories. Published in February 1892.

Rudyard Kipling (1865–1936)
Barrack-Room Ballads, and Other Verses V

Richard Le Gallienne (1866–1947)
English Poems V

'Mrs Alick Macleod' [Catherine Martin (1848?–1937)**]**
The Silent Sea F

George Meredith (1828–1909)
Modern Love: a Reprint V
Published on 26 January 1892. See *Modern Love* 1862.

George Meredith (1828–1909)
Poems V
Published in October 1892

Arthur Wing Pinero (1855–1934)
The Cabinet Minister: A farce D
Performed 23 April 1890

Anne Thackeray Ritchie, Lady Ritchie (1837–1919)
Records of Tennyson, Ruskin, Robert and Elizabeth Browning NF

Christina Rossetti (1830–94)
The Face of the Deep: A devotional commentary on the Apocalypse NF
Contains poems and verse fragments

James Fitzjames Stephen (1829–94)
Horae Sabbaticae NF
Articles first published in the *Saturday Review*

R.L. Stevenson (1850–94)
Across the Plains, with Other Memories and Essays NF

R.L. Stevenson (1850–94) and **Lloyd Osbourne** (1868–1947)
The Wrecker F
Published in July 1892. Serialized in *Scribner's Magazine* (August 1891–July 1892).

Algernon Charles Swinburne (1837–1909)
The Sisters D

Arthur Symons (1865–1945)
Silhouettes V

Alfred, Lord Tennyson (1809–92)
The Foresters D
Published on 29 March 1892. Performed in New York (17 March 1892).

Alfred, Lord Tennyson (1809–92)
The Silent Voices V
Published on 11 October 1892, on the day before Tennyson's funeral

Alfred, Lord Tennyson (1809–92)
The Death of Oenone, Akbar's Dream, and Other Poems V
Published on 28 October 1892

Mary Ward [Mrs Humphry Ward] (1851–1920)
The History of David Grieve F
Published in January 1892

William Watson (1858–1935)
Lachrymae Musarum, and Other Poems V
On the death of Tennyson (6 October 1892)

W.B. Yeats (1865–1939)
The Countess Kathleen, and Various Legends and Lyrics D/V
Published in September 1892. Contains 'The Lake Isle of Innisfree' (first published in the *National Observer*, 13 December 1890).

Israel Zangwill (1864–1926)
The Big Bow Mystery F

1893

- Keir Hardie establishes the Independent Labour Party
  Grover Cleveland becomes President of the USA for the second time
  Nansen begins expedition to the North Pole
  Completion of the Manchester Ship Canal
- Vera Brittain born
  Richard Church born
  Anthony Berkeley Cox born
  W.E. Johns born
  Harold Laski born
  Robert Nichols born
  Wilfred Owen born
  Sir Herbert Read born
  Ivor Richards born
  Dorothy L. Sayers born
  Freya Stark born
  Sylvia Townsend Warner born
- Sir Samuel White Baker dies
  Benjamin Jowett dies
  Frances Kemble dies
  Talbot Baines Reed dies
  John Addington Symonds dies
- Mao Tse-tung born
  Joan Miró born
  Cole Porter born
- Guy de Maupassant dies
  Hippolyte Taine dies
  Tchaikovsky dies

The Pall Mall Magazine PER
Published monthly, May 1893–September 1914

James Adderley (1861–1942)
Stephen Remarx F

'F. Anstey' [Thomas Anstey Guthrie (1856–1934)]
Mr Punch's Pocket Ibsen MISC

R.M. Ballantyne (1825–94)
The Walrus Hunters F
Ballantyne's last book for boys published in his lifetime

Jane Barlow (1857–1917)
Kerrigan's Quality F

E.F. Benson (1867–1940)
Dodo: A detail of the day F
See also *Dodo the Second* 1914, *Dodo Wonders* 1921

Annie Besant (1847)
An Autobiography NF

Wilfrid Scawen Blunt (1840–1922)
Griselda V
Anonymous

F.H. Bradley (1846–1924)
Appearance and Reality NF

'Michael Field' [Katherine Harris Bradley (1846–1914) and **Edith Emma Cooper** (1862–1913)]
Underneath the Bough V

Robert Bridges (1844–1930)
The Humours of the Court: a Comedy; and Other Poems V
Published in November 1893

Lady [Isabel] Burton (1831–96)
The Life of Captain Sir Richard F. Burton NF

'Lewis Carroll' [C.L. Dodgson (1832–98)]
Sylvie and Bruno Concluded F
Illustrated by Harry Furniss. See also *Sylvie and Bruno* 1889.

Mary Elizabeth Coleridge (1861–1907)
The Seven Sleepers of Ephesus F

Marie Corelli (1855–1924)
Barabbas F

Hubert Crackanthorpe (1870–96)
Wreckage F
Stories

S.R. Crockett (1860–1914)
The Stickit Minister and Some Common Men F
Stories

John Davidson (1857–1909)
Fleet Street Eclogues [1st ser.] V
See also *Fleet Street Eclogues* 1896

Ernest Dowson (1867–1900)
A Comedy of Masks F
Written with Arthur Moore

A. Conan Doyle (1859–1930)
The Memoirs of Sherlock Holmes F
Published on 13 December 1893. Illustrated by Sidney Paget. Stories first published in the *Strand Magazine* (December 1892–December 1893). See also *A Study in Scarlet* 1888, *The Sign of Four* 1890, *Adventures of Sherlock Holmes* 1892, *The Hound of the Baskervilles* 1902, *Return of Sherlock Holmes* 1905, *The Valley of Fear* 1915, *His Last Bow* 1917, *Case-Book of Sherlock Holmes* 1927.

'George Egerton' [Mary Chavelita Dunne (1859–1945)]
Keynotes F
Stories

George Gissing (1857–1903)
The Odd Women F
Published on 10 April 1893

Kenneth Grahame (1859–1932)
Pagan Papers MISC
Published in 1893, dated 1894. Essays and stories.

'Sarah Grand' [Frances Elizabeth McFall (1854–1943)]
The Heavenly Twins F

W.E. Henley (1849–1903)
London Voluntaries; The Song of the Sword; and Other Verses V

W.H. Hudson (1841–1922)
Idle Days in Patagonia NF

T.H. Huxley (1825–95)
Evolution and Ethics NF

Henry James (1843–1916)
The Real Thing, and Other Tales F
Published in March 1893

Henry James (1843–1916)
The Private Life F
Stories. Published on 3 June 1893.

Rudyard Kipling (1865–1936)
Many Inventions F
Stories

Richard Le Gallienne (1866–1947)
The Religion of a Literary Man NF

George MacDonald (1824–1905)
Poetical Works V

Alice Meynell (1847–1922)
Poems V

George Moore (1852–1933)
Modern Painting NF
Published in May 1893

William Morris (1834–96)
Gothic Architecture NF

William Morris (1834–96)
Socialism NF
Written with E.B. Bax

E[dith] Nesbit (1858–1924)
Grim Tales F
Ghost stories

Coventry Patmore (1823–96)
Religio Poetae NF

'Mark Rutherford' [William Hale White (1831–1913)]
Catharine Furze F

Bernard Shaw (1856–1950)
Widowers' Houses: A comedy D
Published in May 1893. Performed 9 December 1892.

Flora Annie Steel (1847–1929)
Miss Stuart's Legacy F

Leslie Stephen (1832–1904)
An Agnostic's Apology, and Other Essays NF

R.L. Stevenson (1850–94)
Catriona F
Sequel to *Kidnapped* 1886 (q.v.). Serialized in *Atalanta* (December 1892, January–September 1893).

R.L. Stevenson (1850–94)
Island Nights' Entertainments F
Stories. Published on 7 April 1893.

John Addington Symonds (1840–93)
In the Key of Blue, and Other Prose Essays NF

Francis Thompson (1859–1907)
Poems V

Stanley J. Weyman (1855–1928)
A Gentleman of France F

Oscar Wilde (1854–1900)
Lady Windermere's Fan: A play about a good woman D
Published on 9 November 1893. Performed 20 February 1892.

W.B. Yeats (1865–1939)
The Celtic Twilight V/NF
Published in December 1893

Israel Zangwill (1864–1926)
Ghetto Tragedies F
See also *Ghetto Comedies* 1907

1894

- Gladstone resigns: Lord Rosebery becomes Prime Minister
  Uganda becomes a British protectorate
  Japan declares war on China over Korea
  Arrest and trial of Alfred Dreyfus
- Aldous Huxley born
  Charles Morgan born
  Eric Partridge born
  J.B. Priestley born
- R.M. Ballantyne dies
  James Anthony Froude dies
  Walter Pater dies
  Christina Rossetti dies
  Robert Louis Stevenson dies
  Edmund Yates dies
- Harold Macmillan born
  James Thurber born
- Oliver Wendell Holmes dies

The Yellow Book PER
Published quarterly, April 1894–April 1897. Edited by Aubrey Beardsley and Henry Harland.

Second Book of the Rhymers' Club ANTH
Contributors included Ernest Dowson, Lionel Johnson, Richard Le Gallienne, Ernest Radford, Ernest Rhys, T.W. Rolleston, Arthur Symons, and W.B. Yeats. See also *Book of the Rhymers' Club* 1892.

A. St John Adcock (1864–1930)
An Unfinished Martyrdom, and Other Stories F

Alfred Austin (1835–1913)
The Garden That I Love NF

Laurence Binyon (1869–1943)
Lyric Poems V

Robert Bridges (1844–1930)
Nero: Part 2 D
Published on 18 June 1894. See *Nero: Part 1* 1885.

'Iota' [Kathleen Mannington Caffyn (1853–1926)]
A Yellow Aster F

Hall Caine (1853–1931)
The Manxman F

Mona Caird (1858–1932)
The Daughters of Danaus F

Edward Carpenter (1844–1929)
Homogenic Love and its Place in a Free Society NF
Printed for private circulation

Edward Carpenter (1844–1929) (ed.)
Woman, and Her Place in a Free Society NF

Mandell Creighton (1843–1901)
History of the Papacy [vol. v] NF
Volumes i and ii, 1882 (q.v.); volumes iii and iv, 1887 (q.v.)

S.R. Crockett (1860–1914)
The Raiders F

John Davidson (1857–1909)
Ballads and Songs V

Ella Hepworth Dixon (1855–1932)
The Story of a Modern Woman F

Austin Dobson (1840–1921)
Eighteenth Century Vignettes [2nd ser.] NF
See also *Eighteenth Century Vignettes* 1892, 1896

George du Maurier (1834–96)
Trilby F
bao *Peter Ibbetson.* Illustrated by du Maurier. Serialized in *Harper's Monthly Magazine* (January–July 1894).

Sara Jeannette Duncan [Mrs Everard Cotes] (1861–1922)
A Daughter of To-day F

'George Egerton' [Mary Chavelita Dunne (1859–1945)]
Discords F
Stories

Havelock Ellis (1859–1939)
Man and Woman NF

George Gissing (1857–1903)
In the Year of the Jubilee F

Edmund Gosse (1849–1928)
In Russet and Silver V

H. Rider Haggard (1856–1925)
The People of the Mist F
Published on 15 October 1894. Serialized in *Tit-Bits Weekly* (23 December 1893–18 August 1894).

Thomas Hardy (1840–1928)
Life's Little Ironies F
Stories. Published on 22 February 1894.

Beatrice Harraden (1864–1936)
In Varying Moods F
Stories

Robert Hichens (1864–1950)
The Green Carnation F
Anonymous

'Anthony Hope' [Anthony Hope Hawkins (1863–1933)]
The Dolly Dialogues F

'Anthony Hope' [Anthony Hope Hawkins (1863–1933)]
The Prisoner of Zenda F
See also *Rupert of Hentzau* 1898

'Rita' [Eliza Humphreys (1856–1938)]
A Husband of No Importance F
Oscar Wilde's play *A Woman of No Importance* opened in 1893

Violet Hunt (1866–1942)
The Maiden's Progress F

Selwyn Image (1849–1930)
Poems and Carols V

Lionel Johnson (1867–1902)
The Art of Thomas Hardy NF

Rudyard Kipling (1865–1936)
The Jungle Book F
See also *The Second Jungle Book* 1895

Andrew Lang (1844–1912)
Cock Lane and Common Sense NF
On spiritualism and psychic phenomena, etc.

William Le Queux (1864–1927)
The Great War in England in 1897 F

Arthur Machen (1863–1947)
The Great God Pan, and The Inmost Light F

George Meredith (1828–1909)
Lord Ormont and His Aminta F
Published on 18 June 1894. Serialized in the *Pall Mall Magazine* (December 1893–July 1894).

George Moore (1852–1933)
Esther Waters F
Published in March 1894

William Morris (1834–96)
The Wood Beyond the World F

Arthur Morrison (1863–1945)
Martin Hewitt, Investigator F
Illustrated by Sidney Paget. Stories first published in the *Strand Magazine*.

'George Paston' [Emily Morse Symonds (1860–1936)]
A Modern Amazon F

'Warwick Simpson' [W. Pett Ridge (1860–1930)]
Eighteen of Them F
Stories

'C.E. Raimond' [Elizabeth Robins (1862–1952)]
George Mandeville's Husband F

'Æ' [George William Russell (1867–1935)]
Homeward V

Henry de Vere Stacpoole (1863–1951)
The Intended F

Algernon Charles Swinburne (1837–1909)
Astrophel, and Other Poems V

Algernon Charles Swinburne (1837–1909)
Studies in Prose and Poetry NF

Katharine Tynan (1861–1931)
Cuckoo Songs V

William Watson (1858–1935)
Odes and Other Poems V

Sidney Webb (1859–1947) and **Beatrice Webb** (1858–1943)
The History of Trade Unionism NF

Stanley J. Weyman (1855–1928)
Under the Red Robe F

Oscar Wilde (1854–1900)
Salomé: A tragedy D
Published on 9 February 1894. Illustrated by Aubrey Beardsley. Translated by Lord Alfred Douglas. First published in French, 1893. Performed in Paris, 11 February 1896.

Oscar Wilde (1854–1900)
The Sphinx V
Published on 11 June 1894

Oscar Wilde (1854–1900)
A Woman of No Importance D
Published on 9 October 1894. Performed 19 April 1893.

W.B. Yeats (1865–1939)
The Land of Heart's Desire D
Published in April 1894. Yeats's first acted play, performed 29 March 1894.

Israel Zangwill (1864–1926)
The King of Schnorrers F

1895

- Massacre of Armenians in Constantinople
  The Jameson Raid into the Transvaal (29 Dec.)
- Michael Arlen (Dikran Kouyoumdjian) born
  William Gerhardie born
  Robert Graves born

- Sir Basil Liddell Hart born
  L.P. Hartley born
  F.R. Leavis born
  Henry Williamson born
- Cecil Frances Alexander (Mrs C.F. Alexander) dies
  Emily Faithfull dies
  T.H. Huxley dies
  George Augustus Sala dies
  Sir John Seeley dies
- J. Edgar Hoover born
- Friedrich Engels dies
  Louis Pasteur dies

The Apocrypha BIB
Last portion of the Revised Version of the King James Bible. See also *The New Testament* 1881, *The Holy Bible* 1885.

Sir John Acton, Baron Acton (1834–1902)
A Lecture on the Study of History NF

Grant Allen (1848–99)
The British Barbarians: A hill-top novel F

Grant Allen (1848–99)
The Woman Who Did F

Jane Barlow (1857–1917)
Strangers at Lisconnel F
Second series of *Irish Idylls* 1892 (q.v.)

Guy Boothby (1867–1905)
A Bid for Fortune; or, Dr Nikola's Vendetta F
See also *Doctor Nikola* 1896, *'Farewell, Nikola'* 1901

Mary Elizabeth Braddon (1835–1915)
Sons of Fire F
bao *Lady Audley's Secret*. The last of Braddon's three-decker novels.

Robert Bridges (1844–1930)
Invocation to Music V

John Buchan (1875–1940)
Sir Quixote of the Moors F

Caroline Emily Cameron [Mrs H. Lovett Cameron] (1844–1921)
The Man Who Didn't; or, The Triumph of a Snipe Pie F
See Grant Allen, *The Woman Who Did* 1895

'Lucas Cleeve' [Adelina Georgina Kingscote (1860–1908)]
The Woman Who Wouldn't F
See Grant Allen, *The Woman Who Did* 1895

Joseph Conrad (1857–1924)
Almayer's Folly: A story of an eastern river F
Published on 29 April 1895

Marie Corelli (1855–1924)
The Sorrows of Satan; or, The Strange Experience of One Geoffrey Tempest, Millionaire F

Hubert Crackanthorpe (1870–96)
Sentimental Studies F

S.R. Crockett (1860–1914)
The Men of the Moss-Hags F

'Victoria Cross' [Annie Sophie Cory (1868–1952)]
The Woman Who Didn't F
See Grant Allen, *The Woman Who Did* 1895

Ella D'Arcy (1851–1937?)
Monochromes F
Stories

John Davidson (1857–1909)
Fleet Street Eclogues [2nd ser.] V
Published 1895, dated 1896. See also *Fleet Street Eclogues* 1893.

Austin Dobson (1840–1921)
The Story of Rosina, and Other Verses V

Ernest Dowson (1867–1900)
Dilemmas F
Stories

J. Meade Falkner (1858–1932)
The Lost Stradivarius F

George Gissing (1857–1903)
Eve's Ransom F
Serialized in the *Illustrated London News* (5 January–30 March 1895)

George Gissing (1857–1903)
The Paying Guest F

George Gissing (1857–1903)
Sleeping Fires F
Published in December 1895

Kenneth Grahame (1859–1932)
The Golden Age F
Stories

H. Rider Haggard (1856–1925)
Joan Haste F
Published on 12 August 1895. Serialized in the *Pall Mall Magazine* (September 1894–July 1895).

Thomas Hardy (1840–1928)
Jude the Obscure F

Published on 1 November 1895, dated 1896. Serialized in *Harper's New Monthly Magazine* (December 1894–November 1895).

Thomas Hardy (1840–1928)
The Wessex Novels WKS
The first uniform and complete edition (16 volumes, 1895–6)

Maurice Hewlett (1861–1923)
A Masque of Dead Florentines V

Violet Hunt (1866–1942)
A Hard Woman F

Henry James (1843–1916)
Terminations F
Stories. Published on 15 May 1895.

Lionel Johnson (1867–1902)
Poems V

Rudyard Kipling (1865–1936)
The Second Jungle Book F
See *The Jungle Book* 1894

Rudyard Kipling (1865–1936)
Soldiers Three; The Story of the Gadsbys; In Black and White F
All first published in 1888 (q.v.)

Rudyard Kipling (1865–1936)
Wee Willie Winkie; Under the Deodars; The Phantom 'Rickshaw F
All first published in 1888 (q.v.)

Richard Le Gallienne (1866–1947)
Robert Louis Stevenson, and Other Poems V

Arthur Machen (1863–1947)
The Three Impostors; or, The Transmutations F

A.E.W. Mason (1865–1948)
A Romance of Wastdale F

George Meredith (1828–1909)
The Tale of Chloe, and Other Stories F
Published in January 1895. Title story first published in the *New Quarterly Magazine* (July 1879).

George Meredith (1828–1909)
The Amazing Marriage F
Published on 15 November 1895. Serialized in *Scribner's Magazine* (January–December 1895).

George Moore (1852–1933)
Celibates F
Stories

William Morris (1834–96)
Child Christopher and Goldilind the Fair F

William Morris (1834–96) (tr.)
The Tale of Beowulf V

Arthur Morrison (1863–1945)
Chronicles of Martin Hewitt F
Stories first published in the *Windsor Magazine* (January–June 1895). See also *Martin Hewitt, Investigator* 1894

Walter Pater (1839–94)
Greek Studies NF

Walter Pater (1839–94)
Miscellaneous Studies NF

Coventry Patmore (1823–96)
The Rod, the Root, and the Flower V

Arthur Wing Pinero (1855–1934)
The Notorious Mrs Ebbsmith D
Performed 13 March 1895

Arthur Wing Pinero (1855–1934)
The Second Mrs Tanqueray D
Privately printed 1892. Performed 27 May 1893.

'Q' [**A.T. Quiller-Couch** (1863–1944)]
Wandering Heath F
Stories and sketches

M.P. Shiel (1865–1947)
Prince Zaleski F
Stories

Logan Pearsall Smith (1865–1946)
The Youth of Parnassus, and Other Stories F

R.L. Stevenson (1850–94)
Vailima Letters NF
Published on 2 November 1895

Arthur Symons (1865–1945)
London Nights V

James Thomson (1834–82)
Poetical Works V
Edited, with memoir, by Bertram Dobell

William Watson (1858–1935)
The Father of the Forest, and Other Poems V

H.G. Wells (1866–1946)
The Stolen Bacillus, and Other Incidents F

H.G. Wells (1866–1946)
The Time Machine: An invention F

H.G. Wells (1866–1946)
The Wonderful Visit F

Oscar Wilde (1854–1900)
The Soul of Man NF

First published as 'The Soul of Man Under Socialism' in the *Fortnightly Review* (February 1891)

W.B. Yeats (1865–1939) (ed.)
A Book of Irish Verse ANTH
Published in March 1895

W.B. Yeats (1865–1939)
Poems V/D
Published in October 1895. The first edition of Yeats's collected poems.

1896

- Alfred Austin appointed Poet Laureate
  The 'Kruger Telegram', sent from Kaiser Wilhelm II to Paul Kruger, leader of the Transvaal
  Cecil Rhodes resigns as Prime Minister of Cape Colony
  The Daily Mail started
- J.R. Ackerley born
  Edmund Blunden born
  A.J. Cronin born
  Margaret Kennedy born
  R.C. Sheriff born
  Dodie Smith born
- Matilda Blind dies
  Isabel Burton, Lady Burton, dies
  Huber Crackanthorpe dies
  George du Maurier dies
  Thomas Hughes dies
  William Morris dies
  Coventry Patmore dies
- Sir John Everett Millais dies
- André Breton born
  John Dos Passos born
- Anton Bruckner dies
  Harriet Beecher Stowe dies
  Edmond de Goncourt dies
  Paul Verlaine dies
- Puccini, *La Bohème*
  Richard Strauss, *Also sprach Zarathustra*

Pearson's Magazine PER
Published monthly, January 1896–November 1939

The Savoy PER
Numbers 1–2 published in January and April 1896. Continued monthly, July–December 1896. Edited by Arthur Symons.

J.M. Barrie (1860–1937)
Margaret Ogilvy F
Published in December 1896

J.M. Barrie (1860–1937)
Sentimental Tommy F
Published October 1896. See also *Tommy and Grizel* 1900.

Max Beerbohm (1872–1956)
Caricatures of Twenty-Five Gentlemen NF

Hilaire Belloc (1870–1953)
The Bad Child's Book of Beasts V
See *More Beasts (for Worse Children)* 1897

Hilaire Belloc (1870–1953)
Verses and Sonnets V

Laurence Binyon (1869–1943)
First Book of London Visions V
See also *Second Book of London Visions* 1899

R.D. Blackmore (1825–1900)
Tales from the Telling House F

Guy Boothby (1867–1905)
Doctor Nikola F
See also *A Bid for Fortune* 1895, *'Farewell, Nikola'* 1901

'Anodos' [Mary Elizabeth Coleridge (1861–1907)]
Fancy's Following V
See also *Fancy's Guerdon* 1897

Joseph Conrad (1857–1924)
An Outcast of the Islands F
Published on 4 March 1896

Hubert Crackanthorpe (1870–96)
Vignettes F
Stories

Goldsworthy Lowes Dickinson (1862–1932)
The Greek View of Life NF

Austin Dobson (1840–1921)
Eighteenth Century Vignettes [3rd ser.] NF
See also *Eighteenth Century Vignettes* 1892, 1894

Ménie Muriel Dowie (1867–1945)
Some Whims of Fate F
Stories collected from *The Yellow Book*

Ernest Dowson (1867–1900)
Verses V

A. Conan Doyle (1859–1930)
The Exploits of Brigadier Gerard F
Published on 15 February 1896. Stories first published in the *Strand Magazine* (December 1894–December 1895). See also *Adventures of Gerard* 1903.

A. Conan Doyle (1859–1930)
Rodney Stone F

Published on 13 November 1896. Illustrated by Sidney Paget. Serialized in the *Strand Magazine* (February–December 1896).

A.E. Housman (1859–1936)
A Shropshire Lad V

Laurence Housman (1865–1959)
Green Arras V

W.W. Jacobs (1863–1943)
Many Cargoes F
Stories

Henry James (1843–1916)
Embarrassments F
Stories. Published on 12 June 1896.

Henry James (1843–1916)
The Other House F
Published on 1 October 1896. Serialized in the *Illustrated London News* (4 July–26 September 1896).

Rudyard Kipling (1865–1936)
The Seven Seas V

Richard Le Gallienne (1866–1947)
The Quest of the Golden Girl F.

'Edna Lyall' [Ada Ellen Bayly (1857–1903)]
The Autobiography of a Truth F
See also *The Autobiography of a Slander* 1887

'Henry Seton Merriman' [Hugh Stowell Scott (1862–1903)]
The Sowers F
Serialized in the *Cornhill Magazine* (January 1895–January 1896)

Alice Meynell (1847–1922)
Other Poems V

William Morris (1834–96)
The Well at the World's End F

Arthur Morrison (1863–1945)
A Child of the Jago F

John Cowper Powys (1872–1963)
Odes, and Other Poems V

A.T. Quiller-Couch (1863–1944)
Adventures in Criticism NF
Published in March 1896

Christina Rossetti (1830–94)
New Poems V
Edited by W.M. Rossetti

George Saintsbury (1845–1933)
A History of Nineteenth-Century Literature NF

Flora Annie Steel (1847–1929)
On the Face of the Waters F
Published in 1896, dated 1897

R.L. Stevenson (1850–94)
Weir of Hermiston: An unfinished romance F
Published on 20 May 1896

R.L. Stevenson (1850–94)
Songs of Travel, and Other Verses V
Published on 1 September 1896

Algernon Charles Swinburne (1837–1909)
The Tale of Balen V

William Watson (1858–1935)
The Purple East V

H.G. Wells (1866–1946)
The Island of Dr Moreau F

H.G. Wells (1866–1946)
The Wheels of Chance F

Charlotte M. Yonge (1823–1901)
The Release; or Caroline's French Kindred F
See also *The Chaplet of Pearls* 1868, and *Stray Pearls* 1883

1897

- William McKinley becomes President of the USA
  Turkey declares war on Greece
  Germany begins to build a major battle fleet
  Tate Gallery, London, opened
  Country Life started
- Storm Jameson born
  G. Wilson Knight born
  Naomi Mitchison born
  Ruth Pitter born
  Sir Sacheverell Sitwell born
  Dennis Wheatley born
- Thomas Edward Brown dies
  R.H. Hutton dies
  Jean Ingelow dies
  Margaret Oliphant dies
  Francis Turner Palgrave dies
- Enid Blyton born
- Alphonse Daudet dies
- Edmond Rostand, *Cyrano de Bergerac*

A. St John Adcock (1864–1930)
East End Idylls F

'Olive Pratt Rayner' [Grant Allen (1848–99)]
The Type-Writer Girl F

Alfred Austin (1835–1913)
The Conversion of Winckelmann, and Other Poems V
Austin was appointed Poet Laureate in 1896

Hilaire Belloc (1870–1953)
More Beasts (for Worse Children) V
See *The Bad Child's Book of Beasts* 1896

E.F. Benson (1867–1940)
The Babe, B.A. F

Lady [Isabel] Burton (1831–96)
The Romance of Isabel, Lady Burton NF

Hall Caine (1853–1931)
The Christian F

'Anodos' [Mary Elizabeth Coleridge (1861–1907)]
Fancy's Guerdon V
See also *Fancy's Following* 1896

Joseph Conrad (1857–1924)
The Nigger of the 'Narcissus' F
Seven copies published for copyright purposes on 29 July 1897, followed by US edition (November 1897) and British edition (2 December 1897). Serialized in the *New Review* (August–December 1897).

Hubert Crackanthorpe (1870–96)
Last Studies F
Stories. Includes an appreciation by Henry James.

John Davidson (1857–1909)
New Ballads V

Ernest Dowson (1867–1900)
The Pierrot of the Minute: A dramatic phantasy V

A. Conan Doyle (1859–1930)
Uncle Bernac F
Published on 14 May 1897

George du Maurier (1834–96)
The Martian F
Illustrated by du Maurier. Serialized in *Harper's Monthly Magazine* (October 1896–July 1897).

'George Egerton' [Mary Chavelita Dunne (1859–1945)]
Symphonies F
Stories

Havelock Ellis (1859–1939)
Sexual Inversion NF

'John Sinjohn' [John Galsworthy (1867–1933)]
From the Four Winds F
Stories

George Gissing (1857–1903)
The Whirlpool F
Published on 6 April 1897

'Sarah Grand' [Frances Elizabeth McFall (1854–1943)]
The Beth Book F
Published in 1897, dated 1898

Thomas Hardy (1840–1928)
The Well-Beloved: A sketch of a temperament F
Published on 16 March 1897. Serialized in the *Illustrated London News* (1 October–17 December 1892).

'John Oliver Hobbes' [Pearl Craigie (1867–1906)]
The School for Saints F
See also *Robert Orange* 1900

Henry James (1843–1916)
The Spoils of Poynton F
Published on 6 February 1897. Serialized in the *Atlantic Monthly* (April–October 1896).

Henry James (1843–1916)
What Maisie Knew F
Published on 17 September 1897

Jerome K. Jerome (1859–1927)
Sketches in Lavender, Blue, and Green F
Stories

Lionel Johnson (1867–1902)
Ireland, with Other Poems V

W.P. Ker (1855–1923)
Epic and Romance NF

Mary Kingsley (1862–1900)
Travels in West Africa NF

Rudyard Kipling (1865–1936)
'Captains Courageous': A story of the Grand Banks F
Serialized in *Pearson's Magazine* (December 1896–April 1897)

Somerset Maugham (1874–1965)
Liza of Lambeth F
Published in September 1897

George Meredith (1828–1909)
An Essay on Comedy and the Uses of the Comic Spirit NF
Published in March 1897. Lectures delivered at the London Institution in February 1877. First published in the *New Quarterly Magazine* (April 1877).

Henry Newbolt (1862–1938)
Admirals All, and Other Verses V
Includes 'Drake's Drum' (first published in the *St James's Gazette*, 1896)

Arthur Wing Pinero (1855–1934)
The Princess and the Butterfly; or, The Fantastics D
Performed 29 March 1897

'Æ' [George William Russell (1867–1935)]
The Earth Breath, and Other Poems V

Dora Sigerson (1866–1918)
The Fairy Changeling, and Other Poems V

E[dith] Œ[none] Somerville (1858–1949) and **'Martin Ross' [Violet Martin** (1862–1915)]
The Silver Fox F

Bram Stoker (1847–1912)
Dracula F

Arthur Symons (1865–1945)
Amoris Victima V

Edward Thomas (1878–1917)
The Woodland Life NF

Francis Thompson (1859–1907)
New Poems V

Sidney Webb (1859–1947) and **Beatrice Webb** (1858–1943)
Industrial Democracy NF

H.G. Wells (1866–1946)
Certain Personal Matters NF
Published 1897, dated 1898

H.G. Wells (1866–1946)
The Invisible Man: A grotesque romance F
Serialized in *Pearson's Weekly* (June–July 1897)

H.G. Wells (1866–1946)
The Plattner Story, and Others F

Charles Whibley (1859–1930)
A Book of Scoundrels NF

W.B. Yeats (1865–1939)
The Secret Rose F
Published in April 1897. See also *Stories of Red Hanrahan* 1905.

W.B. Yeats (1865–1939)
The Tables of the Law. The Adoration of the Magi F
Privately printed. *The Tables of the Law* first published in *The Savoy* (November 1896). See also 1904.

1898

- The USA declares war on Spain
  Hawaii transferred to the USA
  Kitchener defeats the Dervishes at Omdurman (2 Sept.)
  The Fashoda Crisis
- Maurice Bowra born
  Winifred Holtby born
  C.S. Lewis born
  Alec Waugh born
- Aubrey Beardsley dies
  William Black dies
  Lewis Carroll (Charles Lutwidge Dodgson) dies
  Mary Cowden Clarke dies
  Eliza Lynn Linton dies
  James Payn dies
- William Ewart Gladstone dies
- Bertolt Brecht born
  Ernest Hemingway born
- Stéphane Mallarmé dies
  Gustave Moreau dies

A. St John Adcock (1864–1930)
In the Image of God F
Sequel to *East End Idylls* 1897 (q.v.)

'Elizabeth' [Mary Annette Gräfin von Arnim-Schlagenthin (1866–1941)]
Elizabeth and her German Garden F
Anonymous

Alfred Austin (1835–1913)
Lamia's Winter-Quarters V

Alfred Austin (1835–1913)
Songs of England V

Arnold Bennett (1867–1931)
A Man From the North F

Laurence Binyon (1869–1943)
Porphyrion, and Other Poems V

Robert Bridges (1844–1930)
Poetical Works [vol. i] V
Published in 6 volumes (1898–1905)

'Lewis Carroll' [C.L. Dodgson (1832–98)]
Life and Letters NF
Edited by S.G. Collingwood

Winston Spencer Churchill (1874–1965)
The Story of the Malakand Field Force NF

Joseph Conrad (1857–1924)
Tales of Unrest F
Published on 4 April 1898

S.R. Crockett (1860–1914)
The Red Axe F
See also *Joan of the Sword Hand* 1900

Ella D'Arcy (1851–1937?)
The Bishop's Dilemma F

Ella D'Arcy (1851–1937?)
Modern Instances F
Stories

A. Conan Doyle (1859–1930)
The Tragedy of the Korosko F
Published on 1 February 1898. Illustrated by Sidney Paget. Serialized in the *Strand Magazine* (May–December 1897).

'George Egerton' [Mary Chavelita Dunne (1859–1945)]
Fantasies F
Stories

'George Egerton' [Mary Chavelita Dunne (1859–1945)]
The Wheel of God F

J. Meade Falkner (1858–1932)
Moonfleet F
bao *The Lost Stradivarius*

Ellen Thorneycroft Fowler (1860–1929)
Concerning Isabel Carnaby F

'John Sinjohn' [John Galsworthy (1867–1933)]
Jocelyn F

George Gissing (1857–1903)
The Town Traveller F
Published on 29 August 1898

Kenneth Grahame (1859–1932)
Dream Days F
Stories. Published in 1898, dated 1899.

Thomas Hardy (1840–1928)
Wessex Poems, and Other Verses V
Published in December 1898

James Hastings (1862–1922) (ed.)
A Dictionary of the Bible DICT

W.E. Henley (1849–1903)
Poems V

Maurice Hewlett (1861–1923)
The Forest Lovers F

'Anthony Hope' [Anthony Hope Hawkins (1863–1933)]
Rupert of Hentzau F
Sequel to *The Prisoner of Zenda* 1894 (q.v.)

Henry James (1843–1916)
The Two Magics ['The Turn of the Screw', 'Covering End'] F
Published on 5 October 1898. 'The Turn of the Screw' serialized in *Collier's Weekly* (27 January–16 April 1898).

Jerome K. Jerome (1859–1927)
The Second Thoughts of an Idle Fellow NF
See also *Idle Thoughts* 1886

Rudyard Kipling (1865–1936)
The Day's Work F
Stories

Marie Connor Leighton (1869–1941)
Convict 99 F
Written with the author's husband, Robert Leighton

E.V. Lucas (1868–1938) and **C.L. Graves** (1856–1944)
The War of the Wenuses F
A parody of H.G. Wells's *The War of the Worlds* 1898 (q.v.)

Somerset Maugham (1874–1965)
The Making of a Saint F
Published on 25 June 1898

George Moore (1852–1933)
Evelyn Innes F
Published in May 1898. See also *Sister Teresa* 1901.

William Morris (1834–96)
Art and the Beauty of the Earth NF

Henry Newbolt (1862–1938)
The Island Race V

E. Phillips Oppenheim (1866–1946)
The Mysterious Mr Sabin F

Stephen Phillips (1864–1915)
Poems V

Eden Phillpotts (1862–1960)
Children of the Mist F
First of the 'Dartmoor Cycle'. See also *Sons of the Morning* 1900, *The River* 1902, *The Secret Woman* 1905, *The Mother* 1908, *The Thief of Virtue* 1910, *Widecombe Fair* 1913.

Arthur Wing Pinero (1855–1934)
Trelawny of the 'Wells': A comedietta D
Performed 20 January 1898

'Baron Corvo' [Frederick William Rolfe (1860–1913)]
Stories Toto Told Me F

George Saintsbury (1845–1933)
A Short History of English Literature NF

Bernard Shaw (1856–1950)
Plays Pleasant and Unpleasant D
Published on 19 April 1898

Bernard Shaw (1856–1950)
The Perfect Wagnerite NF
Published on 1 December 1898

R.L. Stevenson (1850–94)
St Ives F
Unfinished at Stevenson's death; completed by A. Quiller-Couch. Serialized in the *Pall Mall Magazine* (November 1896–November 1897).

William Watson (1858–1935)
The Hope of the World, and Other Poems V

Theodore Watts-Dunton (1832–1914)
The Coming of Love, and Other Poems V

H.G. Wells (1866–1946)
The War of the Worlds F
Serialized in *Pearson's Magazine* (April–December 1897)

Oscar Wilde (1854–1900)
The Ballad of Reading Gaol V
'By C.3.3.'. Published on 13 February 1898. The seventh edition (June 1898) carried Wilde's name.

Israel Zangwill (1864–1926)
Dreamers of the Ghetto NF

1899

- First Hague Conference
  Dreyfus pardoned
  Kruger's ultimatum precipitates the Second Anglo-Boer War (Oct.)
- Elizabeth Bowen born
  Noël Coward born
  C.S. Forester (Cecil Troughton Smith) born
  Eric Linklater born
  Antonia White (Eirene Botting) born
- Grant Allen dies
  Florence Marryat dies
- Alfred Hitchcock born
  Jorge Luis Borges born
  Vladimir Nabokov born
- Johann Strauss dies
- Elgar, *Enigma Variations*
  Tolstoy, *Resurrection*

Helen Bannerman (1863–1946)
The Story of Little Black Sambo F
For children

Robert Barr (1850–1912)
Jennie Baxter, Journalist F
Anonymous

Hilaire Belloc (1870–1953)
A Moral Alphabet V

Arnold Bennett (1867–1931)
Polite Farces for the Drawing-Room D
Published 1899, dated 1900

Laurence Binyon (1869–1943)
Second Book of London Visions V
See also *First Book of London Visions* 1896

Wilfrid Scawen Blunt (1840–1922)
Satan Absolved V

Gordon Bottomley (1874–1948)
Poems at White-Nights V

'Kennedy King' [George Douglas Brown (1869–1902)]
Love and a Sword F

Robert Buchanan (1841–1901)
The New Rome: Poems and ballads of our empire V

Kathleen Mannington Caffyn (1853–1926)
Anne Mauleverer F

Mary Cholmondeley (1859–1925)
Red Pottage F

John Davidson (1857–1909)
The Last Ballad, and Other Poems V

Lord Alfred Douglas (1870–1945)
The City of the Soul V

Ernest Dowson (1867–1900)
Decorations: In Verse and Prose MISC

John Fortescue (1859–1933)
The History of the British Army NF
Published in 13 volumes (1899–1930)

George Gissing (1857–1903)
The Crown of Life F
Published on 23 October 1899

Maurice Hewlett (1861–1923)
Little Novels of Italy F

E.W. Hornung (1866–1921)
The Amateur Cracksman F
Stories. See also *The Black Mask* 1901, *A Thief in the Night* 1905, *Mr Justice Raffles* 1909.

Douglas Hyde (1860–1949)
A Literary History of Ireland NF

W.R. Inge (1860–1954)
Christian Mysticism NF

Henry James (1843–1916)
The Awkward Age F
Published on 25 April 1899. Serialized in *Harper's Weekly* (1 October 1898–7 January 1899).

Rudyard Kipling (1865–1936)
Stalky & Co. F
Stories

Richard Le Gallienne (1866–1947)
Young Lives F

William Le Queux (1864–1927)
England's Peril F

Somerset Maugham (1874–1965)
Orientations F
Stories. Published in June 1899.

E[dith] Nesbit (1858–1924)
The Story of the Treasure Seekers F
See also *The Would-Be-Goods* 1901, *New Treasure Seekers* 1904

Arthur Wing Pinero (1855–1934)
The Gay Lord Quex: An original comedy D
Performed 8 April 1899

John Cowper Powys (1872–1963)
Poems V

W. Pett Ridge (1860–1930)
Outside the Radius F

Dora Sigerson (1866–1918)
Ballads and Poems V

E[dith] Œ[none] Somerville (1858–1949) and **'Martin Ross' [Violet Martin** (1862–1915)]
Some Experiences of an Irish R.M. F
First published in in the *Badminton Magazine*. See also *Some Further Experiences* 1908 and *Mr Knox's Country* 1915.

Algernon Charles Swinburne (1837–1909)
Rosamund, Queen of the Lombards D

Arthur Symons (1865–1945)
Images of Good and Evil V

Arthur Symons (1865–1945)
The Symbolist Movement in Literature NF

Theodore Watts-Dunton (1832–1914)
Aylwin F

H.G. Wells (1866–1946)
Tales of Space and Time F
Published in 1899, dated 1900

H.G. Wells (1866–1946)
When the Sleeper Wakes F
Serialized in *The Graphic* (1898–9)

Oscar Wilde (1854–1900)
The Importance of Being Earnest: A trivial comedy for serious people D
bao *Lady Windermere's Fan.* Published in February 1899 and dedicated to Robert Ross. Performed 14 February 1895.

Oscar Wilde (1854–1900)
An Ideal Husband D
bao *Lady Windermere's Fan.* Published in July 1899. Performed 3 January 1895.

W.B. Yeats (1865–1939)
The Wind Among the Reeds V
Published in April 1899

1900

1900

- British Labour Party founded (27 Feb.)
  Ladysmith relieved by Redvers Buller (28 Feb.)
  Boxer Rising in China
  The Daily Express started
- Basil Bunting born
  Geoffrey Household born
  Richard Hughes born
  Stephen Potter born
  V.S. Pritchett born
  A.J.A. Symons born
- Richard Doddridge Blackmore dies
  Ernest Dowson dies
  James Martineau dies
  Friedrich Max Müller dies
  John Ruskin dies
  Henry Sidgwick dies
  Oscar Wilde dies
- Antoine de Saint-Exupéry born
- Stephen Crane dies
  Friedrich Nietzsche dies
- Chekhov, *Uncle Vanya*
- Elgar, *The Dream of Gerontius*
  Puccini, *Tosca*
  Sibelius, *Finlandia*

'F. Anstey' [Thomas Anstey Guthrie (1856–1934)]
The Brass Bottle F

J.M. Barrie (1860–1937)
Tommy and Grizel F
Published in October 1900. See also *Sentimental Tommy* 1896.

'Ernest Bramah' [Ernest Bramah Smith (1868–1942)]
The Wallet of Kai Lung F
Stories

G.K. Chesterton (1874–1936)
Greybeards at Play V
Published in October 1900

G.K. Chesterton (1874–1939)
The Wild Knight, and Other Poems V
Published in November 1900

Winston Spencer Churchill (1874–1965)
London to Ladysmith via Pretoria NF

Joseph Conrad (1857–1924)
Lord Jim F
Published on 9 October 1900. Serialized in *Blackwood's Magazine* (October 1899–November 1900).

Marie Corelli (1855–1924)
The Master-Christian F

S.R. Crockett (1860–1914)
Joan of the Sword Hand F
Sequel to *The Red Axe* 1898 (q.v.)

S.R. Crockett (1860–1914)
The Stickit Minister's Wooing, and Other Galloway Stories F
See also *The Stickit Minister* 1893

Ford Madox Ford (1873–1939)
Poems for Pictures and for Notes of Music V
See also *The Face of the Night* 1904

Elinor Glyn (1864–1943)
The Visits of Elizabeth F
See also *Elizabeth Visits America* 1909

Henry Harland (1861–1905)
The Cardinal's Snuff-Box F

W.E. Henley (1849–1903)
For England's Sake V

G.A. Henty (1832–1902)
With Buller to Natal F
Juvenile. Published in 1900, dated 1901.

'John Oliver Hobbes' [Pearl Craigie (1867–1906)]
Robert Orange F
Sequel to *The School for Saints* 1897 (q.v.)

W.H. Hudson (1841–1922)
Nature in Downland NF

Henry James (1843–1916)
The Soft Side F
Stories. Published on 30 August 1900.

Jerome K. Jerome (1859–1927)
Three Men on the Bummel F
See also *Three Men in a Boat* 1889

Rudyard Kipling (1865–1936)
From Sea to Sea, and Other Sketches NF
Published in March 1900

Richard Le Gallienne (1866–1947)
Sleeping Beauty, and Other Prose Fancies NF

George Moore (1852–1933)
The Bending of the Bough: A comedy D
Published on 21 February 1900. Performed in Dublin, 19 February 1900.

E[dith] Nesbit (1858–1924)
The Book of Dragons F
Published in November 1900, dated 1901

'Barry Pain' [Eric Odell (1864–1928)**]**
Eliza F
See also *Eliza Getting On* 1911, *Exit Eliza* 1912, *Eliza's Son* 1913

Eden Phillpotts (1862–1960)
Sons of the Morning F
Second novel in the 'Dartmoor Cycle'. See also *Children of the Mist* 1898, *The River* 1902, *The Secret Woman* 1905, *The Mother* 1908, *The Thief of Virtue* 1910, *Widecombe Fair* 1913.

A.T. Quiller-Couch (1863–1944)
Old Fires and Profitable Ghosts F
Stories

A.T. Quiller-Couch (1863–1944) (ed.)
The Oxford Book of English Verse 1250–1900 ANTH
See also *The New Oxford Book of English Verse* 1972

Bernard Shaw (1856–1950)
Fabianism and the Empire NF
Published on 2 October 1900

Leslie Stephen (1832–1904)
The English Utilitarians NF
Sequel to *History of English Thought in the Eighteenth Century* 1876 (q.v.)

H.G. Wells (1866–1946)
Love and Mr Lewisham F

W.B. Yeats (1865–1939)
The Shadowy Waters V
Published in December 1900

1901

- Australia becomes a dominion
  Death of Queen Victoria (22 Jan.)
  EDWARD VII (–1910)
  US President McKinley assassinated (Sept.); succeeded by Theodore Roosevelt
  British Academy established
- Roy Campbell born
  James Hanley born
  Rosamond Lehmann born
  Gladys Mitchell born
  Laura Riding born
- Sir Walter Besant dies
  Robert Buchanan dies
  Mandell Creighton dies
  Kate Greenaway dies
  William Stubbs dies
  Brooke Foss Westcott dies
  Charlotte Mary Yonge dies
- Marlene Dietrich born
  Walt Disney born
  André Malraux born
- Henri Toulouse-Lautrec dies
- Giuseppe Verdi dies
- Chekhov, *Three Sisters*
  Thomas Mann, *Buddenbrooks*
  Strindberg, *Dance of Death*
  Oxford World's Classics series launched

H.C. Bailey (1878–1961)
My Lady of Orange F

'Michael Fairless' [Margaret Fairless Barber (1869–1901)**]**
The Gathering of Brother Hilarius F

Jane Barlow (1857–1917)
Ghost-Bereft, with Other Stories and Studies in Verse V

Annie Besant (1847–1933)
Esoteric Christianity NF

Guy Boothby (1867–1905)
'Farewell, Nikola' F
See also *A Bid for Fortune* 1895, *Doctor Nikola* 1896

'George Douglas' [George Douglas Brown (1869–1902)**]**
The House With the Green Shutters F

'Shan F. Bullock' [John William Bullock (1865–1935)**]**
Irish Pastorals F

Samuel Butler (1835–1902)
Erewhon Revisited Twenty Years Later F
See also *Erewhon* 1872

Hall Caine (1853–1931)
The Eternal City F

C.S. Calverley (1831–84)
Complete Works WKS
See also 1885

G.K. Chesterton (1874–1936)
The Defendant NF
Published in December 1901

Joseph Conrad (1857–1924) and **F.M. Hueffer [Ford Madox Ford** (1873–1939)**]**
The Inheritors F
Published on 26 June 1901

John Davidson (1857–1909)
Self's the Man: A tragi-comedy D

John Davidson (1857–1909)
The Testament of a Man Forbid V

John Davidson (1857–1909)
The Testament of a Vivisector V

'George Egerton' [Mary Chavelita Dunne (1859–1945)**]**
Rosa Amorosa F

'John Sinjohn' [John Galsworthy (1867–1933)**]**
A Man of Devon F
Includes the first appearance of the Forsyte family

George Gissing (1857–1903)
Our Friend the Charlatan F
Published in May 1901

Thomas Hardy (1840–1928)
Poems of the Past and the Present V
Published in November 1901, dated 1902

G.A. Henty (1832–1902)
With Roberts to Pretoria F
Juvenile. Published in 1901, dated 1902.

E.W. Hornung (1866–1921)
The Black Mask F
Eight Raffles episodes. See *The Amateur Cracksman* 1899, *A Thief in the Night* 1905, *Mr Justice Raffles* 1909.

Rudyard Kipling (1865–1936)
Kim F
Serialized in *Cassell's Magazine* (December 1900–October 1901)

Richard Le Gallienne (1866–1947)
The Life Romantic NF

Somerset Maugham (1874–1965)
The Hero F
Published on 3 July 1901

George Meredith (1828–1909)
A Reading of Life, with Other Poems V
Published in May 1901

James Moffatt (1870–1944) (ed. and tr.)
The Historical New Testament BIB

George Moore (1852–1933)
Sister Teresa F
Sequel to *Evelyn Innes* 1898 (q.v.). Rewritten in 1928.

E[dith] Nesbit (1858–1924)
The Wouldbegoods F
See also *Treasure Seekers* 1899, *New Treasure Seekers* 1904

Stephen Phillips (1864–1915)
Herod: A tragedy D

'Frederick, Baron Corvo' [Frederick William Rolfe (1860–1913)**]**
In His Own Image F
Stories

Bernard Shaw (1856–1950)
Three Plays for Puritans D
Published on 15 January 1901

H.G. Wells (1866–1946)
The First Men in the Moon F

1902

- Boer War ended by the Treaty of Vereeniging (31 May)
  Further renewal of Triple Alliance between Germany, Austria, and Italy
  Arthur Balfour becomes British Prime Minister
  TImes Literary Supplement begins publication
- Lord David Cecil born
  Stella Gibbons born
  Georgette Heyer born
  Nikolaus Pevsner born
  Stevie Smith born
- Lord Acton dies
  Philip James Bailey dies
  Samuel Butler dies
  S.R. Gardiner dies
  Francis Bret Harte dies
  Annie French Hector ('Mrs Alexander') dies
  G.A. Henty dies
  Lionel Johnson dies
- Cecil Rhodes dies
- John Steinbeck born
- Émile Zola dies
- Gide, *L'Immoraliste*
- Debussy, *Pelléas et Mélisande*

Alfred Austin (1835–1913)
A Tale of True Love, and Other Poems V

Margaret Fairless Barber (1869–1901)
The Roadmender, and Other Papers NF

Maurice Baring (1874–1945)
The Black Prince, and Other Poems V
Published 1902, dated 1903

J.M. Barrie (1860–1937)
The Little White Bird F
Published in November 1902. Serialized in *Scribner's Magazine* (August–November 1902).

Arnold Bennett (1867–1931)
Anna of the Five Towns F

Arnold Bennett (1867–1931)
The Grand Babylon Hotel F

Sir Walter Besant (1836–1901)
Autobiography NF

John Buchan (1875–1940)
The Watcher by the Threshold, and Other Tales F

Mary Cholmondeley (1859–1925)
Moth and Rust F

Joseph Conrad (1857–1924)
Youth F
Published on 13 November 1902. Contains 'Youth' (first published in *Blackwood's Magazine*, September 1898); 'The Heart of Darkness' (first published in *Blackwood's Magazine*, February–April 1899); and 'The End of the Tether' (serialized in *Blackwood's Magazine*, July–December 1902).

John Davidson (1857–1909)
The Testament of an Empire-Builder V

'Walter Ramal' [Walter de la Mare (1873–1956)]
Songs of Childhood V
Published in January 1902

A. Conan Doyle (1859–1930)
The Hound of the Baskervilles F
Published on 25 March 1902. Illustrated by Sidney Paget. Serialized in the *Strand Magazine* (August 1901–April 1902). See also *A Study in Scarlet* 1888, *The Sign of Four* 1890, *Adventures of Sherlock Holmes* 1892, *Memoirs of Sherlock Holmes* 1893, *Return of Sherlock Holmes* 1905, *The Valley of Fear* 1915, *His Last Bow* 1917, *Case-Book of Sherlock Holmes* 1927.

W.H. Hudson (1841–1922)
El Ombú, and Other Tales F

W.W. Jacobs (1863–1943)
The Lady of the Barge, and Other Stories F
Stories, including Jacobs's celebrated ghost story, 'The Monkey's Paw' (first published in *Harper's Monthly Magazine*, September 1902)

Henry James (1843–1916)
The Wings of the Dove F
Published on 30 August 1902

Rudyard Kipling (1865–1936)
Just So Stories for Little Children F

Sidney Lee (1859–1926)
Queen Victoria NF

John Masefield (1878–1967)
Salt-Water Ballads V

A.E.W. Mason (1865–1948)
The Four Feathers F

Somerset Maugham (1874–1965)
Mrs Craddock F
Published in November 1902

Alice Meynell (1847–1922)
Later Poems V

E[dith] Nesbit (1858–1924)
Five Children and It F

Henry Newbolt (1862–1938)
The Sailing of the Long Ships, and Other Poems V

Alfred Noyes (1880–1958)
The Loom of Years V

Stephen Phillips (1864–1915)
Ulysses D

Eden Phillpotts (1862–1960)
The River F
Part of the 'Dartmoor Cycle'. See also *Children of the Mist* 1898, *Sons of Morning* 1900, *The Secret Woman* 1905, *The Mother* 1908, *The Thief of Virtue* 1910, *Widecombe Fair* 1913.

Arthur Wing Pinero (1855–1934)
Iris D
Performed 21 September 1901

Beatrix Potter (1866–1943)
The Tale of Peter Rabbit F
The first Beatrix Potter book; first privately printed in 1901 and 1902

'Saki' [Hector Hugh Munro (1870–1916)]
The Westminster Alice NF
Political satires reprinted from the *Westminster Gazette*

Bernard Shaw (1856–1950)
Mrs Warren's Profession D

Published on 12 March 1902. First commercially performed 5 January 1902 and first published in *Plays Pleasant and Unpleasant* 1898 (q.v.).

Dora Sigerson (1866–1918)
The Woman Who Went to Hell, and Other Ballads and Lyrics V

H.G. Wells (1866–1946)
The Sea Lady: A tissue of moonshine F

P.G. Wodehouse (1881–1975)
The Pothunters F
Wodehouse's first published novel

W.B. Yeats (1865–1939)
Cathleen ni Hoolihan D
Published in October 1902. See also *The Hour-Glass* 1904.

1903

- *Burlington Magazine* started
  Daily Mirror started
- Kenneth Clark born
  Cyril Connolly born
  George Orwell (Eric Blair) born
  William Plomer born
  A.L. Rowse born
  Evelyn Waugh born
  John Wyndham born
- Frederick William Farrar dies
  George Gissing dies
  W.E. Henley dies
  William Henry Lecky dies
  Herbert Spencer dies
- Paul Gaugin dies
  Camille Pissarro dies
  James MacNeil Whistler dies

Laurence Binyon (1869–1943)
The Death of Adam, and Other Poems V

Robert Bridges (1844–1930)
Now in Wintry Delights V
Published on 6 March 1903

Samuel Butler (1835–1902)
The Way of All Flesh F
Written 1873–84

E.K. Chambers (1866–1954)
The Mediaeval Stage NF

Erskine Childers (1870–1922)
The Riddle of the Sands: A record of secret service recently achieved F

Joseph Conrad (1857–1924)
Typhoon, and Other Stories F
Published on 22 April 1903. 'Typhoon' serialized in the *Pall Mall Magazine* (January–March 1902).

John Davidson (1857–1909)
A Rosary V

Warwick Deeping (1877–1950)
Uther & Igraine F

A. Conan Doyle (1859–1930)
Adventures of Gerard F
Published on 22 September 1903. Stories first published in the *Strand Magazine* (betwen January 1900 and May 1903). See also *The Exploits of Brigadier Gerard* 1896.

J. Meade Falkner (1858–1932)
The Nebuly Coat F
bao *The Lost Stradivarius, Moonfleet*

George Gissing (1857–1903)
The Private Papers of Henry Ryecroft F
Published in January 1903. Serialized in the *Fortnightly Review* (May, August, November 1902, and February 1903).

Isabella Augusta, Lady Gregory (1852–1932)
Poets and Dreamers MISC

W.E. Henley (1849–1903)
A Song of Speed V

'Rita' [Eliza Humphreys (1856–1938)]
Souls F

Henry James (1843–1916)
The Better Sort F
Stories. Published on 26 February 1903.

Henry James (1843–1916)
The Ambassadors F
Published on 24 September 1903. Serialized in the *North American Review* (January–December 1903).

Rudyard Kipling (1865–1936)
The Five Nations V

John Masefield (1878–1967)
Ballads V

Somerset Maugham (1874–1965)
A Man of Honour D
Performed 23 February 1903

George Moore (1852–1933)
The Untilled Field F
Stories. Published on 20 April 1903.

G.E. Moore (1873–1958)
Principia Ethica NF

Alfred Noyes (1880–1958)
The Flower of Old Japan V

Rosa Caroline Praed [Mrs Campbell Praed] (1851–1935)
The Other Mrs Jacobs F

Bertrand Russell (1872–1970)
The Principles of Mathematics NF

'Æ' [George William Russell (1867–1935)]
The Nuts of Knowledge V

Bernard Shaw (1856–1950)
Man and Superman D
Published in August 1903. First commercial performance, 21 May 1905.

Arthur Symons (1865–1945)
Cities NF

Thomas Traherne (1637–74)
The Poetical Works of Thomas Traherne V
Edited by Bertram Dobell

H.G. Wells (1866–1946)
Mankind in the Making NF

H.G. Wells (1866–1946)
Twelve Stories and a Dream F

W.B. Yeats (1865–1939)
Ideas of Good and Evil NF
Published in May 1903

W.B. Yeats (1865–1939)
Where There is Nothing D
Published in May 1903. See also *The Hour-Glass*, and *The King's Threshold* 1904, *Deirdre* 1907.

W.B. Yeats (1865–1939)
In the Seven Woods V
Published in August 1903

W.B. Yeats (1865–1939)
The Hour-Glass D
Copyright edition. See also *The Hour-Glass* 1904.

1904

- *Entente Cordiale* between Britain and France formally established (8 Apr.)
  War between Russia and Japan begins
  Abbey Theatre, Dublin, opened
  Admiral Fisher becomes First Sea Lord
- Sir Harold Acton born
  Margery Allingham born
  C. Day Lewis born
  Graham Greene born
  Patrick Hamilton born
  Christopher Isherwood born
  Patrick Kavanagh born
  Nancy Mitford born
- Sir Edwin Arnold dies
  Lafcadio Hearn dies
  Samuel Smiles dies
  Sir Henry Morton Stanley dies
  Sir Leslie Stephen dies
- Anton Chekhov dies

Aubrey Beardsley (1872–98)
Last Letters of Aubrey Beardsley NF

Aubrey Beardsley (1872–98)
Under the Hill, and Other Essays in Prose and Verse MISC
See also *The Story of Venus and Tannhäuser* 1907

Arnold Bennett (1867–1931)
Teresa of Watling Street F

A.C. Benson (1862–1925)
The House of Quiet F

Phyllis Bottome (1884–1963)
The Master Hope F

A.C. Bradley (1851–1935)
Shakespearean Tragedy NF

Henry Bradley (1845–1923)
The Making of English NF

Angela Brazil (1869–1947)
A Terrible Tomboy F
Angela Brazil's first novel

G.K. Chesterton (1874–1936)
The Napoleon of Notting Hill F
Published on 22 March 1904. Chesterton's first novel.

Joseph Conrad (1857–1924)
Nostromo: A tale of the seaboard F
Published on 14 October 1904. Serialized in *T.P.'s Weekly* (29 January–7 October 1904).

John Davidson (1857–1909)
The Testament of a Prime Minister V

Warwick Deeping (1877–1950)
Love Among the Ruins F

Walter de la Mare (1873–1956)
Henry Brocken F

Edith Durham (1863–1944)
Through the Lands of the Serbs NF

Ford Madox Ford (1873–1939)
The Face of the Night V
A second series of *Poems for Pictures* 1900 (q.v.)

John Galsworthy (1867–1933)
The Island Pharisees F
Galsworthy's first work under his own name

George Gissing (1857–1903)
Veranilda F
Published in October 1904. Incomplete at Gissing's death on 28 December 1903.

Thomas Hardy (1840–1928)
The Dynasts: A drama of the Napoleonic Wars V
Published on 13 January 1904. See also *The Dynasts, Part second* 1906; *Part third* 1908.

Robert Hichens (1864–1950)
The Garden of Allah F

W.H. Hudson (1841–1922)
Green Mansions F

M.R. James (1862–1936)
Ghost Stories of an Antiquary F
Illustrated by James McBryde. See also *More Ghost Stories* 1911, *A Thin Ghost* 1919, *A Warning to the Curious* 1925.

Rudyard Kipling (1865–1936)
Traffics and Discoveries F
Stories

'Vernon Lee' [Violet Paget (1856–1935)]
Pope Jacynth, and Other Fantastic Tales F

Marie Belloc Lowndes (1868–1947)
The Heart of Penelope F

Somerset Maugham (1874–1965)
The Merry-Go-Round F
Published on 19 September 1904

E[dith] Nesbit (1858–1924)
The New Treasure Seekers F
See also *Treasure Seekers* 1899, *The Would-Be-Goods* 1901, *Complete History* 1928

E[dith] Nesbit (1858–1924)
The Phoenix and the Carpet F

Henry Newbolt (1862–1938)
Songs of the Sea V

Alfred Noyes (1880–1958)
Poems V

Forrest Reid (1875–1947)
The Kingdom of Twilight F

Frederick William Rolfe (1860–1913)
Hadrian the Seventh F

'Æ' [George William Russell (1867–1935)]
The Divine Vision, and Other Poems V

'Æ' [George William Russell (1867–1935)]
The Mask of Apollo, and Other Stories F

Rafael Sabatini (1875–1950)
The Tavern Knight F

'Saki' [Hector Hugh Munro (1870–1916)]
Reginald F
Stories

May Sinclair (1863–1946)
The Divine Fire F

H.O. Sturgis (1855–1920)
Belchamber F

Algernon Charles Swinburne (1837–1909)
A Channel Passage, and Other Poems V

G.M. Trevelyan (1876–1962)
England Under the Stuarts NF
Revised in 1925 and 1946

William Watson (1858–1935)
For England V

H.G. Wells (1866–1946)
The Food of the Gods, and How It Came to Earth F

W.B. Yeats (1865–1939)
The Hour-Glass; Cathleen ni Houlihan; The Pot of Broth D
Published in March 1904. See also *Where There is Nothing* 1903, *The King's Threshold* 1904, *Deirdre* 1907.

W.B. Yeats (1865–1939)
The King's Threshold: and On Baile's Strand D
Published in March 1904. See also *Where There is Nothing* 1903, *The Hour-Glass* 1904, *Deirdre* 1907.

W.B. Yeats (1865–1939)
The Tables of the Law; The Adoration of the Magi F
First privately printed 1897 (q.v.)

1905

- Workers fired on in St Petersburg on 'Bloody Sunday' (22 Jan.)
  General strike in Russia
  Sinn Féin party founded by Arthur Griffith and Bulmer Hobson
  Sir Henry Campbell Bannerman becomes British Prime Minister
  Royal Naval College at Dartmouth founded
  Automobile Association founded
- H.E. Bates born
  Norman Cameron born

Henry Green (Henry Vincent Yorke) born
Geoffrey Grigson born
Arthur Koestler born
Anthony Powell born
C.P. Snow born

- Guy Boothby dies
George MacDonald dies
William Sharp dies
- Sir Henry Irving dies
- Greta Garbo born
Jean-Paul Sartre born
- Jules Verne dies

Arnold Bennett (1867–1931)
The Loot of Cities F
Stories

Arnold Bennett (1867–1931)
Tales of the Five Towns F

A.C. Benson (1862–1925)
The Upton Letters F
Anonymous

R.H. Benson (1871–1914)
The King's Achievement F

E.C. Bentley (1875–1956)
Biography for Beginners V

Robert Bridges (1844–1930)
Demeter V
Published in May 1905

Frances Hodgson Burnett (1849–1924)
A Little Princess F
Extended version of *Sara Crewe* 1888

Joseph Campbell (1879–1944)
The Garden of Bees V

G.K. Chesterton (1874–1936)
The Club of Queer Trades F
Published in March 1905. Serialized in *The Idler* (1904).

G.K. Chesterton (1874–1936)
Heretics NF
Published on 6 June 1905

Padraic Colum (1881–1972)
The Land D
The first popular success for the Abbey Theatre

John Davidson (1857–1909)
The Theatrocrat: A tragic play of Church and stage D

W.H. Davies (1871–1940)
The Soul's Destroyer NF

Goldsworthy Lowes Dickinson (1862–1932)
A Modern Symposium NF

Richard Watson Dixon (1833–1900)
Last Poems V

Ernest Dowson (1867–1900)
The Poems of Ernest Dowson V
Illustrated by Aubrey Beardsley; with memoir by Arthur Symons

A. Conan Doyle (1859–1930)
The Return of Sherlock Holmes F
Published on 7 March 1905. Illustrated by Sidney Paget. Stories first published in the *Strand Magazine* (between October 1903 and December 1904). See also *A Study in Scarlet* 1888, *The Sign of Four* 1890, *Adventures of Sherlock Holmes* 1892, *Memoirs of Sherlock Holmes* 1893, *The Hound of the Baskervilles* 1902, *The Valley of Fear* 1915, *His Last Bow* 1917, *Case-Book of Sherlock Holmes* 1927.

'George Egerton' [Mary Chavelita Dunne (1859–1945)]
Flies in Amber F
Stories

Ronald Firbank (1886–1926)
Odette d'Antrevernes; and A Study in Temperament F

Ford Madox Ford (1873–1939)
The Benefactor F

E.M. Forster (1879–1970)
Where Angels Fear to Tread F

Francis Galton (1822–1911)
Eugenics NF

George Gissing (1857–1903)
Will Warburton F
Published in June 1905. Serialized in *New Age* (5 January–8 June 1904).

H. Rider Haggard (1856–1925)
Ayesha F
Published on 6 October 1905. Serialized in the *Windsor Magazine* (December 1904–October 1905).

E.W. Hornung (1866–1921)
A Thief in the Night F
Stories. See also *The Amateur Cracksman* 1899, *The Black Mask* 1901, *Mr Justice Raffles* 1909.

Henry James (1843–1916)
The Golden Bowl F
Published on 10 February 1905

E.V. Lucas (1868–1938)
A Wanderer in Holland NF
First of the Wanderer series

John Masefield (1878–1967)
A Mainsail Haul F
Stories

A.A. Milne (1882–1956)
Lovers in London F

George Moore (1852–1933)
The Lake F
Published on 10 November 1905

E[dith] Nesbit (1858–1924)
Oswald Bastable and Others F
See also *Treasure Seekers* 1899, *Complete History* 1928

Baroness Orczy (1865–1947)
The Scarlet Pimpernel F
First of the Scarlet Pimpernel series. Based on a play of the same name, written with Montagu Barstow and performed in 1903.

Eden Phillpotts (1862–1960)
The Secret Woman F
Part of the 'Dartmoor Cycle'. See also *Children of the Mist* 1898, *Sons of the Morning 1900*, *The River* 1902, *The Mother* 1908, *The Thief of Virtue* 1910, *Widecombe Fair* 1913. Dramatic version published 1912.

Frederick William Rolfe (1860–1913)
Don Tarquinio: A kataleptic phantasmatic romance F

Bernard Shaw (1856–1950)
The Irrational Knot F
Published on 13 October 1905

Dora Sigerson (1866–1918)
The Country-House Party F

Algernon Charles Swinburne (1837–1909)
Love's Cross-Currents F
First published in *The Tatler* (25 August–29 December 1877) as *A Year's Letters, By Mrs Horace Manners.*

Algernon Charles Swinburne (1837–1909)
The Poems of Algernon Charles Swinburne V

Arthur Symons (1865–1945)
A Book of Twenty Songs V

Arthur Symons (1865–1945)
Spiritual Adventures NF

J.M. Synge (1871–1909)
The Shadow of the Glen and Riders to the Sea D
Shadow of the Glen performed 8 October 1903; *Riders to the Sea* performed 25 February 1904

J.M. Synge (1871–1909)
The Well of the Saints D
Performed 4 February 1905

Katharine Tynan (1861–1931)
Innocencies V

Edgar Wallace (1875–1932)
The Four Just Men F

H.G. Wells (1866–1946)
Kipps: The story of a simple soul F

H.G. Wells (1866–1946)
A Modern Utopia F

Oscar Wilde (1854–1900)
De Profundis NF
Published on 23 February 1905. Six editions in 1905.

W.B. Yeats (1865–1939)
Stories of Red Hanrahan F
Published on 16 May 1905, dated 1904. Stories from *The Secret Rose* 1897 (q.v.), rewritten with Lady Gregory. See also *Stories of Red Hanrahan* 1927.

1906

- Liberal landslide in British general election
- Samuel Beckett born
  Sir John Betjeman born
  Catherine Cookson born
  Sir William Empson born
  Richard Llewellyn born
  R.K. Narayan born
  J.I.M. Stewart ('Michael Innes') born
  A.J.P. Taylor born
  Vernon Watkins born
  T.H. White born
- Charles Hamilton Aïdé dies
  Pearl Mary Craigie ('John Oliver Hobbes') dies
  Richard Garnett dies
  F.W. Maitland dies
  Charlotte Elizabeth Riddell dies
- Paul Cézanne dies
  Henrik Ibsen dies
- Everyman's Library started
  The English Hymnal published

Robert Barr (1850–1912)
The Triumphs of Eugène Valmont F
Stories

J.M. Barrie (1860–1937)
Peter Pan in Kensington Gardens F
Published in December 1906. Illustrated by Arthur Rackham. The original play, *Peter Pan; or, The Boy Who Would Not Grow Up*, performed 27 December 1904. See also *Peter and Wendy* 1911.

A.C. Benson (1862–1925)
From a College Window NF

Algernon Blackwood (1869–1951)
The Empty House, and Other Ghost Stories F

'Marjorie Bowen' [Gabrielle Margaret Vere Campbell (1886–1952)**]**
The Viper of Milan F

Joseph Campbell (1879–1944)
The Rushlight V

Mary Cholmondeley (1859–1925)
Prisoners (Fast Bound in Misery and Iron) F
Serialized in the *Lady's Realm* (November 1905–October 1906)

Joseph Conrad (1857–1924)
The Mirror of the Sea NF
Published on 4 October 1906

John Davidson (1857–1909)
Holiday, and Other Poems V

Walter de la Mare (1873–1956)
Poems V
Published in September 1906

William De Morgan (1839–1917)
Joseph Vance F

A. Conan Doyle (1859–1930)
Sir Nigel F
Published on 15 November 1906. Serialized in the *Strand Magazine* (December 1905–December 1906).

John Drinkwater (1882–1937)
The Death of Leander, and Other Poems V

Lord Dunsany (1878–1957)
Time and the Gods F

Ford Madox Ford (1873–1939)
The Fifth Queen and How She Came to Court F
The Fifth Queen Trilogy i. See also *Privy Seal* 1907, *The Fifth Queen Crowned* 1908.

H.W. Fowler (1858–1933) and **F.G. Fowler** (1870–1918)
The King's English NF

John Galsworthy (1867–1933)
The Man of Property F
The first novel in The Forsyte Saga. See also *In Chancery* 1920, *To Let* 1921, *The Forsyte Saga* 1922. See also *Two Forsyte Interludes* 1927, *Four Forsyte Stories* 1929, *On Forsyte 'Change* 1930, *Soames and the Flag* 1930.

George Gissing (1857–1903)
The House of Cobwebs, and Other Stories F

'Radclyffe Hall' [Marguerite Antonia Radclyffe-Hall (1880–1943)**]**
'Twixt Earth and Stars V

Thomas Hardy (1840–1928)
The Dynasts V
Published on 9 February 1906. See also *The Dynasts* 1904, 1908.

Rudyard Kipling (1865–1936)
Puck of Pook's Hill F
Stories first published in the *Strand Magazine*

William Le Queux (1864–1927)
The Invasion of 1910 F

Rose Macaulay (1881–1958)
Abbots Verney F

Arthur Machen (1863–1947)
The House of Souls F

Somerset Maugham (1874–1965)
The Bishop's Apron F
Published in February 1906. The basis of Maugham's play *Loaves and Fishes* 1924 (q.v.).

George Moore (1852–1933)
Memoirs of My Dead Life NF
Published in June 1906

George Moore (1852–1933)
Reminiscences of the Impressionist Painters NF

E[dith] Nesbit (1858–1924)
The Railway Children F
Illustrated by C.E. Brock

Alfred Noyes (1880–1958)
Drake [vol. i] V
Volume ii published in 1908

A.R. Orage (1873–1934)
Friedrich Nietzsche: The Dionysian spirit of the age NF

'Q' [A.T. Quiller-Couch (1863–1944)**]**
The Mayor of Troy F

'Æ' [George William Russell (1867–1935)**]**
By Still Waters V

Arthur Symons (1865–1945)
The Fool of the World, and Other Poems V

Katharine Tynan (1861–1931)
The Adventures of Alicia F

Katharine Tynan (1861–1931)
The Yellow Domino, and Other Stories F

H.G. Wells (1866–1946)
In the Days of the Comet F

W.B. Yeats (1865–1939)
Poems, 1899–1905 V/D
Published in October 1906

1907

- Second Hague Peace Conference
  Lenin leaves Russia
  Boy Scouts founded by R. Baden-Powell
- W.H. Auden born
  Daphne du Maurier born
  Peter Fleming born
  Christopher Fry born
  Rumer Godden born
  John Lehmann born
  Louis MacNeice born
- Mary Coleridge dies
  David Masson dies
  Francis Thompson dies
- John Wayne born
- Edvard Grieg dies
  J.-K. Huysmans dies

Sir John Acton, Baron Acton (1834–1902)
Historical Essays and Studies NF

Sir John Acton, Baron Acton (1834–1902)
The History of Freedom, and Other Essays NF

J.M. Barrie (1860–1937)
Walker London: A farcical comedy D
Published in March 1907. Performed 25 February 1892 as *The Houseboat*.

Aubrey Beardsley (1872–98)
The Story of Venus and Tannhäuser NF
Original, unexpurgated version of *Under the Hill* 1904 (q.v.)

Max Beerbohm (1872–1956)
A Book of Caricatures NF

Gertrude Bell (1868–1926)
The Desert and the Sown NF

Arnold Bennett (1867–1931)
The Grim Smile of the Five Towns F
Stories

A.C. Benson (1862–1925)
Beside Still Waters F

Algernon Blackwood (1869–1951)
The Listener, and Other Stories F

Gordon Bottomley (1874–1948)
Chambers of Imagery [1st ser.] V
Second series, 1912

Joseph Campbell (1879–1944)
The Gilly of Christ V

Padraic Colum (1881–1972)
The Fiddler's House D

Padraic Colum (1881–1972)
Wild Earth V

Joseph Conrad (1857–1924)
The Secret Agent F
Published on 12 September 1907

John Davidson (1857–1909)
God and Mammon V
Published in two parts, 1907–8

W.H. Davies (1871–1940)
New Poems V

William De Morgan (1839–1917)
Alice-For-Short F

A. Conan Doyle (1859–1930)
Through the Magic Door NF
Autobiography. Published on 20 November 1907. Serialized in *Cassell's Magazine* (December 1906–November 1907).

Jeffery Farnol (1878–1952)
My Lady Caprice F
Farnol's first novel

James Elroy Flecker (1884–1915)
The Bridge of Fire V

Ford Madox Ford (1873–1939)
An English Girl F

Ford Madox Ford (1873–1939)
From Inland, and Other Poems V

Ford Madox Ford (1873–1939)
Privy Seal F
The Fifth Queen Trilogy ii. See also *The Fifth Queen* 1906, *The Fifth Queen Crowned* 1908.

E.M. Forster (1879–1970)
The Longest Journey F
Published in April 1907

R. Austin Freeman (1862–1943)
The Red Thumb Mark F

First appearance of Freeman's detective Dr John Thorndyke

John Galsworthy (1867–1933)
The Country House F

Edward Garnett (1868–1936)
The Breaking Point D

Wilfrid Gibson (1878–1962)
The Stonefolds D

Elinor Glyn (1864–1943)
Three Weeks F

Edmund Gosse (1849–1928)
Father and Son NF
Anonymous

Frederic Harrison (1831–1923)
The Philosophy of Common Sense NF

Holbrook Jackson (1874–1948)
Bernard Shaw NF

Jerome K. Jerome (1859–1927)
The Passing of the Third Floor Back, and Other Stories F

James Joyce (1882–1941)
Chamber Music V

Ada Leverson (1862–1933)
The Twelfth Hour F

Arthur Machen (1863–1947)
The Hill of Dreams F

Alfred Noyes (1880–1958)
Forty Singing Seamen, and Other Poems V

Arthur Ransome (1884–1967)
Bohemia in London NF

'Æ' [George William Russell (1867–1935)]
Deirdre D

Bernard Shaw (1856–1950)
John Bull's Other Island, and Major Barbara D
Published on 19 June 1907. *John Bull's Other Island* performed 1 November 1904; *Major Barbara* performed 28 November 1905.

Dora Sigerson (1866–1918)
Collected Poems V
Introduction by George Meredith

May Sinclair (1863–1946)
The Helpmate F

J.M. Synge (1871–1909)
The Aran Islands NF

J.M. Synge (1871–1909)
The Playboy of the Western World D
Performed in Dublin, 26 January 1907

J.M. Synge (1871–1909)
The Tinker's Wedding D
Performed 11 November 1909

W.B. Yeats (1865–1939)
Deirdre D
Published in August 1907. See also *Where There is Nothing* 1903, *The Hour-Glass*, and *The King's Threshold* 1904.

W.B. Yeats (1865–1939)
Discoveries NF
Published on 15 December 1907

Israel Zangwill (1864–1926)
Ghetto Comedies F
See also *Ghetto Tragedies* 1893

1908

- Austria-Hungary annexes Bosnia-Herzegovina
  Herbert Asquith becomes British Prime Minister
  English Review founded by Ford Madox Ford
- Ian Fleming born
  Pamela Frankau born
  Sir Osbert Lancaster born
  Norman Lewis born
  Kathleen Raine born
- Edward Caird dies
  John Churton Collins dies
  Lanoe Falconer (Mary Elizabeth Hawker) dies
  Frances Hoey (Mrs Cashel Hoey) dies
  'Ouida' (Marie Louise de la Ramée) dies
- Simone de Beauvoir born
- Joel Chandler Harris dies
  Nicolai Rimsky-Korsakov dies

Lascelles Abercrombie (1881–1938)
Interludes and Poems V

Hilaire Belloc (1870–1953)
Cautionary Tales for Children V
See also *New Cautionary Tales* 1930

Arnold Bennett (1867–1931)
Buried Alive F
See also *The Great Adventure* 1913

Arnold Bennett (1867–1931)
The Old Wives' Tale F

Algernon Blackwood (1869–1951)
John Silence: Physician Extraordinary F
Stories

G.K. Chesterton (1874–1936)
The Man Who Was Thursday: A nightmare F
Published in February 1908

Joseph Conrad (1857–1924)
A Set of Six F
Stories. Published on 6 August 1908.

John Davidson (1857–1909)
The Testament of John Davidson V

W.H. Davies (1871–1940)
The Autobiography of a Super-Tramp NF
Preface by George Bernard Shaw

W.H. Davies (1871–1940)
Nature Poems and Others V

Ford Madox Ford (1873–1939)
The Fifth Queen Crowned F
The Fifth Queen Trilogy iii. See also *The Fifth Queen* 1906, *Privy Seal* 1907.

Ford Madox Ford (1873–1939)
Mr Apollo F

E.M. Forster (1879–1970)
A Room With a View F
Published on 14 October 1908

Edmund Gosse (1849–1928)
The Autumn Garden V
Published 1908, dated 1909

Kenneth Grahame (1859–1932)
The Wind in the Willows F

Thomas Hardy (1840–1928)
The Dynasts V
Published on 11 February 1908. See also *The Dynasts* 1904, 1906.

Maurice Hewlett (1861–1923)
Halfway House F
First of trilogy. See also *Open Country* 1909 and *Rest Harrow* 1910.

Sheila Kaye-Smith (1887–1956)
The Tramping Methodist F

Ada Leverson (1862–1933)
Love's Shadow F
First volume of trilogy with *Tenterhooks* 1912 and *Love at Second Sight* 1916 (qq.v.)

Marie Belloc Lowndes (1868–1947)
The Uttermost Farthing F

Somerset Maugham (1874–1965)
The Magician F
Published in November 1908

E[dith] Nesbit (1858–1924)
Ballads and Lyrics of Socialism V

Stephen Phillips (1864–1915)
New Poems V
Includes the verse drama *Iole*

Eden Phillpotts (1862–1960)
The Mother F
Part of the 'Dartmoor Cycle'. See also *Children of the Mist* 1898, *Sons of the Morning* 1900, *The River* 1902, *The Secret Woman* 1905, *The Thief of Virtue* 1910, *Widecombe Fair* 1913.

E[dith] Œ[none] Somerville (1858–1949) and **'Martin Ross' [Violet Martin** (1862–1915)]
Further Experiences of an Irish R.M. F
See also *Some Experiences of an Irish R.M.* 1899 and *Mr Knox's Country* 1915

Henry de Vere Stacpoole (1863–1951)
The Blue Lagoon F

Algernon Charles Swinburne (1837–1909)
The Duke of Gandia D
Performed 25, 27 May 1919

Thomas Traherne (1637–74)
Centuries of Meditations NF
Edited by Bertram Dobell

Katharine Tynan (1861–1931)
Experiences V

H.G. Wells (1866–1946)
First and Last Things NF

H.G. Wells (1866–1946)
New Worlds for Old: A plain account of modern socialism NF

H.G. Wells (1866–1946)
The War in the Air F

W.B. Yeats (1865–1939)
The Collected Works in Verse and Prose WKS

W.B. Yeats (1865–1939) and **Isabella Augusta, Lady Gregory** (1852–1932)
The Unicorn From the Stars, and Other Plays D
Published on 13 May 1908

1909

- W.H. Taft becomes President of the USA
  US Copyright Act
  Girl Guides founded
  Louis Blériot crosses the English Channel by monoplane
  Henry Ford's 'Model T' car produced

- Eric Ambler born
  Isaiah Berlin born
  Ernst Gombrich born
  Malcolm Lowry born
  James Reeves born
  Stephen Spender born
- Arthur William à Beckett dies
  Rosa Nouchette Carey dies
  John Davidson dies
  George Manville Fenn dies
  Frederick Greenwood dies
  Sir Theodore Martin dies
  George Meredith dies
  Algernon Charles Swinburne dies
  John Millington Synge dies

Florence Barclay (1862–1921)
The Rosary F

Maurice Baring (1874–1945)
Orpheus in Mayfair, and Other Stories and Sketches F

Gertrude Bell (1868–1926)
The Thousand and One Churches NF
With W.M. Ramsay

Arnold Bennett (1867–1931)
What the Public Wants D
Performed 2 May 1909

Laurence Binyon (1869–1943)
England, and Other Poems V

A.C. Bradley (1851–1935)
Oxford Lectures on Poetry NF

Joseph Campbell (1879–1944)
The Mountainy Singer V

Gilbert Cannan (1884–1955)
Peter Homunculus F

G.K. Chesterton (1874–1936)
Orthodoxy NF
Published on 25 September 1908, dated 1909

John Davidson (1857–1909)
Fleet Street, and Other Poems V

William De Morgan (1839–1917)
It Never Can Happen Again F

Lord Alfred Douglas (1870–1945)
Sonnets V

Edith Durham (1863–1944)
High Albania NF

F.S. Flint (1885–1960)
In the Net of the Stars V

Ford Madox Ford (1873–1939)
The 'Half Moon' F

John Galsworthy (1867–1933)
Fraternity F

Elinor Glyn (1864–1943)
Elizabeth Visits America F
Sequel to *The Visits of Elizabeth* 1900 (q.v.)

Harley Granville-Barker (1877–1946)
The Marrying of Ann Leete: A comedy D
Performed 26 January 1902

Harley Granville-Barker (1877–1946)
The Voysey Inheritance D
Performed 7 November 1905

Harley Granville-Barker (1877–1946)
Waste: A tragedy D
Performed 24 November 1907

Isabella Augusta, Lady Gregory (1852–1932)
Seven Short Plays D

Thomas Hardy (1840–1928)
Time's Laughingstocks, and Other Verses V
Published on 3 December 1909. Hardy's first new collection since 1901.

Maurice Hewlett (1861–1923)
Open Country F
Second of trilogy. See also *Halfway House* 1908 and *Rest Harrow* 1910.

E.W. Hornung (1866–1921)
Mr Justice Raffles F
See also *The Amateur Cracksman* 1899, *The Black Mask* 1901, *A Thief in the Night* 1905

Rudyard Kipling (1865–1936)
Actions and Reactions F
Stories

William Le Queux (1864–1927)
Spies of the Kaiser F

C.F.G. Masterman (1874–1927)
The Condition of England NF

Alfred Noyes (1880–1958)
The Enchanted Island, and Other Poems V

Baroness Orczy (1865–1947)
The Old Man in the Corner F
Detective stories

Arthur Wing Pinero (1855–1934)
The Thunderbolt D
Performed 9 May 1908

'Q' [**A.T. Quiller-Couch** (1863–1944)]
True Tilda F

James Stephens (1882–1950)
Insurrections V

Arthur Symons (1865–1945)
The Romantic Movement in English Poetry NF

J.M. Synge (1871–1909)
Poems and Translations V
Preface by W.B. Yeats

Francis Thompson (1859–1907)
Shelley NF

Hugh Walpole (1884–1941)
The Wooden Horse F

H.G. Wells (1866–1946)
Ann Veronica F

H.G. Wells (1866–1946)
Tono-Bungay F

1910

- Death of Edward VII (6 May)
  GEORGE V (-1936)
  Union of South Africa becomes a dominion (July)
  Japan annexes Korea (Aug.)
  Arthur Evans excavates Knossos
- A.J. Ayer born
  William Cooper (Harry Summerfield Hoff) born
  Norman MacCaig born
  Wilfred Thesiger born
  C.V. Wedgwood born
- F.J. Furnivall dies
  A.J. Munby dies
  William Michael Rossetti dies
  Anna Laetitia Waring dies
- William Holman Hunt dies
  Florence Nightingale dies
- Jean Anouilh born
- William James dies
  Leo Tolstoy dies
- Elgar, Violin Concerto
  Stravinsky, *The Firebird*

Sir Norman Angell (1872–1967)
The Great Illusion NF
One of the most influential books of the early 20th century—over a million copies sold

Matthew Arnold (1822–88)
Essays in Criticism: Third Series NF
See also *Essays in Criticism* 1865, 1888

Hilaire Belloc (1870–1953)
Verses V

Arnold Bennett (1867–1931)
Clayhanger F
Volume i of the Clayhanger Trilogy. See also *Hilda Lessways* 1911, *These Twain* 1916.

John Buchan (1875–1940)
Prester John F

Gilbert Cannan (1884–1955)
Devious Ways F

G.K. Chesterton (1874–1936)
The Ball and the Cross F
Published on 24 February 1910. Serialized in *The Commonwealth* (1905–6).

G.K. Chesterton (1874–1936)
Alarms and Discursions NF
Published on 3 November 1910

Padraic Colum (1881–1972)
Thomas Muskerry D

Frances Cornford (1886–1960)
Poems V

W.H. Davies (1871–1940)
Farewell to Poesy, and Other Pieces V

Walter de la Mare (1873–1956)
The Return F

Walter de la Mare (1873–1956)
The Three Mulla-Mulgars F
Published in November 1910. The second edition, 1935, was retitled *The Three Royal Monkeys*.

William De Morgan (1839–1917)
An Affair of Dishonour F

Jeffery Farnol (1878–1952)
The Broad Highway F

James Elroy Flecker (1884–1915)
Thirty-Six Poems V

Ford Madox Ford (1873–1939)
A Call F

Ford Madox Ford (1873–1939)
The Portrait F

Ford Madox Ford (1873–1939)
Songs from London V

E.M. Forster (1879–1970)
Howards End F
Published on 18 October 1910

John Galsworthy (1867–1933)
Justice: A tragedy D
Performed 21 February 1910

John Galsworthy (1867–1933)
Strife D
Performed 9 March 1909

Wilfrid Gibson (1878–1962)
Daily Bread V

Maurice Hewlett (1861–1923)
Rest Harrow F
Third of trilogy. See also *Halfway House* 1908 and *Open Country* 1909.

W.H. Hudson (1841–1922)
A Shepherd's Life NF

Henry James (1843–1916)
The Finer Grain F
Stories. Published on 13 October 1910. First published in the USA.

Rudyard Kipling (1865–1936)
Rewards and Fairies F

Richard Le Gallienne (1866–1947)
New Poems V

John Masefield (1878–1967)
Ballads and Poems V

John Masefield (1878–1967)
Martin Hyde, the Duke's Messenger F
For children

A.E.W. Mason (1865–1948)
At the Villa Rose F

Eden Phillpotts (1862–1960)
The Thief of Virtue F
Part of the 'Dartmoor Cycle'. See also *Children of the Mist* 1898, *Sons of the Morning* 1900, *The River* 1902, *The Secret Woman* 1905, *The Mother* 1908, *Widecombe Fair* 1913.

Arthur Wing Pinero (1855–1934)
Mid-Channel D
Performed 2 September 1909

Lennox Robinson (1886–1958)
The Cross-Roads D

Bertrand Russell (1872–1970)
Philosophical Essays NF

Bertrand Russell (1872–1970) and **A.N. Whitehead** (1861–1947)
Principia Mathematica NF
Published in 3 volumes (1910–13). Revised by Russell 1925–7.

'Saki' [Hector Hugh Munro (1870–1916)]
Reginald in Russia, and Other Sketches F

J.M. Synge (1871–1909)
Deirdre of the Sorrows D
Unfinished. Performed in Dublin, 13 January 1909.

Edward Thomas (1878–1917)
Rest and Unrest F

Hugh Walpole (1884–1941)
Maradick at Forty F

William Watson (1858–1935)
Sable and Purple, with Other Poems V

H.G. Wells (1866–1946)
The History of Mr Polly F

W.B. Yeats (1865–1939)
The Green Helmet, and Other Poems V/D
Published in December 1910. *The Green Helmet* performed at the Abbey Theatre, Dublin, 10 February 1910.

W.B. Yeats (1865–1939)
Poems: Second Series V
Published in March 1910, dated 1909

1911

- Agadir crisis (July)
  Chinese Republic proclaimed (Oct.)
  Suffragette riots in Whitehall (Nov.)
  Roald Amundsen reaches the South Pole (15 Dec.)
  Copyright Act (extending protection to 50 years from author's death)
- Walter Allen born
  Sybille Bedford born
  William Golding born
  Flann O'Brien (Brian O'Nolan) born
  Mervyn Peake born
  Terence Rattigan born
- Sir Charles Wentworth Dilke dies
  Sir Francis Galton dies
  Sir William Schwenck Gilbert dies
- Gustav Mahler dies
- Theodore Dreiser, *Jennie Gerhardt*
  Hofmannsthal, *Der Rosenkavalier*

J.M. Barrie (1860–1937)
Peter and Wendy F
Published in October 1911. Original play, *Peter Pan; or, The Boy Who Would Not Grow Up*, performed 27 December 1904. See also *Peter Pan in Kensington Gardens* 1906.

Max Beerbohm (1872–1956)
Zuleika Dobson: An Oxford love story F

Gertrude Bell (1868–1926)
Amurath to Amurath NF

Arnold Bennett (1867–1931)
The Card F

Arnold Bennett (1867–1931)
Hilda Lessways F
Volume ii of the Clayhanger Trilogy. See also *Clayhanger* 1910, *These Twain* 1916.

Rupert Brooke (1887–1915)
Poems V

Frances Hodgson Burnett (1849–1924)
The Secret Garden F

G.K. Chesterton (1874–1936)
The Innocence of Father Brown F
Published in July 1911. See also *The Wisdom of Father Brown* 1914, *The Incredulity of Father Brown* 1926, *The Secret of Father Brown* 1927, *The Scandal of Father Brown* 1935.

G.K. Chesterton (1874–1936)
The Ballad of the White Horse V
Published on 31 August 1911

I. Compton-Burnett (1884–1969)
Dolores F

Joseph Conrad (1857–1924)
Under Western Eyes F
Published on 5 October 1911. Serialized in the *English Review* (December 1910–October 1911).

Elizabeth Daryush (1887–1977)
Charitesse V

W.H. Davies (1871–1940)
Songs of Joy and Others V

William De Morgan (1839–1917)
A Likely Story F

Norman Douglas (1868–1952)
Siren Land NF

John Drinkwater (1882–1937)
Cophetua D
Performed 18 November 1911

John Drinkwater (1882–1937)
Poems of Men and Hours V

St John Ervine (1883–1971)
Mixed Marriage D
Performed at the Abbey Theatre, Dublin, 30 March 1911

Ford Madox Ford (1873–1939)
Ladies Whose Bright Eyes F

E.M. Forster (1879–1970)
The Celestial Omnibus, and Other Stories F
Published on 11 May 1911

H.W. Fowler (1858–1933) and **F.G. Fowler** (1870–1918)
The Concise Oxford Dictionary of Current English DICT

John Galsworthy (1867–1933)
The Patrician F

Harley Granville-Barker (1877–1946)
The Madras House: A comedy D
Performed 9 March 1910

Henry James (1843–1916)
The Outcry F
Published on 5 October 1911

M.R. James (1862–1936)
More Ghost Stories of an Antiquary F
See also *Ghost Stories of an Antiquary* 1904, *A Thin Ghost* 1919, *A Warning to the Curious* 1925

Lionel Johnson (1867–1902)
Post Liminium NF

E.V. Knox (1881–1971)
The Brazen Lyre V

D.H. Lawrence (1885–1930)
The White Peacock F
Published on 20 January 1911. Lawrence's first novel.

Patrick MacGill (1889–1963)
Songs of a Navvy V

Compton Mackenzie (1883–1972)
The Passionate Elopement F

'Katherine Mansfield' [Kathleen Mansfield Beauchamp (1888–1923)]
In a German Pension F
Stories

John Masefield (1878–1967)
The Everlasting Mercy V

John Masefield (1878–1967)
Jim Davis; or, The Captive of Smugglers F
For children

Somerset Maugham (1874–1965)
Lady Frederick D
Published in December 1911, dated 1912. Performed 26 October 1907.

George Moore (1852–1933)
The Apostle D
Published on 30 May 1911. Rewritten as *The Passing of the Essenes* 1930 (q.v.).

George Moore (1852–1933)
Ave NF
Published on 19 October 1911. First of the Hail and Farewell Trilogy. See also *Salve* 1912 and *Vale* 1914.

Oliver Onions (1873–1961)
Widdershins F
Ghost stories

'Barry Pain' [Eric Odell (1864–1928)**]**
Eliza Getting On F
See also *Eliza* 1900, *Exit Eliza* 1912, *Eliza's Son* 1913

Stephen Phillips (1864–1915)
The New Inferno V

Forrest Reid (1875–1947)
The Bracknels: A family chronicle F

'Æ' [George William Russell (1867–1935)**]**
The Renewal of Youth NF

Bernard Shaw (1856–1950)
The Doctor's Dilemma; Getting Married; and The Shewing-Up of Blanco Posnet D
Published on 21 February 1911. *The Doctor's Dilemma* performed 20 November 1906; *Getting Married* performed 12 May 1908; *The Shewing-Up of Blanco Posnet* performed at the Abbey Theatre, Dublin, 25 August 1909.

E[dith] Œ[none] Somerville (1858–1949) and **'Martin Ross' [Violet Martin** (1862–1915)**]**
Dan Russel the Fox F

Bram Stoker (1847–1912)
The Lair of the White Worm F

Katharine Tynan (1861–1931)
New Poems V

Evelyn Underhill (1875–1941)
Mysticism NF

Edgar Wallace (1875–1932)
Sanders of the River F
Stories

Hugh Walpole (1884–1941)
Mr Perrin and Mr Traill F

Mary Ward [Mrs Humphry Ward] (1851–1920)
The Case of Richard Meynell F
Published in October 1911. Serialized in the *Cornhill Magazine* (January–December 1911). Sequel to *Robert Elsmere* 1888 (q.v.).

H.G. Wells (1866–1946)
The Country of the Blind, and Other Stories F

H.G. Wells (1866–1946)
The New Machiavelli F

W.B. Yeats (1865–1939)
Synge and the Ireland of his Time NF
Published on 26 July 1911

1912

- Scott reaches the South Pole (18 Jan.)
  Sinking (15 Apr.) of the *Titanic* on her maiden voyage
  London dock strike (May)
  First Balkan War
  The faked 'Piltdown Man' remains produced
- Kenneth Allott born
  R.L. Delderfield born
  Nigel Dennis born
  Lawrence Durrell born
  Roy Fuller born
  William Douglas Home born
  Pamela Hansford Johnson born
  Mary Lavin born
  Anne Ridler born
  William Sansom born
  R.W. Southern born
  Julian Symons born
  Elizabeth Taylor born
- Robert Barr dies
  George Grossmith dies
  Andrew Lang dies
  Justin McCarthy dies
  W.W. Skeat dies
  Bram Stoker dies
  Henry Sweet dies
  William Booth dies
- John Cage born
  Tennessee Williams born
- Robert Falcon Scott dies
- Anatole France, *Les Dieux ont soif*
  Stravinsky, *Petruschka*

William Archer (1856–1924)
Play-Making NF

Max Beerbohm (1872–1956)
A Christmas Garland NF

Arnold Bennett (1867–1931)
The Matador of the Five Towns, and Other Stories F

Arnold Bennett (1867–1931)
Milestones D
Written with Edward Knoblock. Performed 5 March 1912.

E.F. Benson (1867–1940)
The Room in the Tower, and Other Stories F
Ghost stories

Robert Bridges (1844–1930)
Poetical Works Excluding the Eight Dramas V

John Buchan (1875–1940)
The Moon Endureth F
Stories

Gilbert Cannan (1884–1955)
Little Brother F
Lawrie Saga i: see also *Round the Corner* 1913, *Three Pretty Men* 1916, *The Stucco House* 1917, *Time and Eternity* 1919, *Annette and Bennett* 1922

Joseph Conrad (1857–1924)
'Twixt Land and Sea: Three tales F
Published on 14 October 1912

S.R. Crockett (1860–1914)
The Moss Troopers F

Walter de la Mare (1873–1956)
The Listeners, and Other Poems V

Ethel M. Dell (1881–1939)
The Way of an Eagle F
First published in the USA, 1911. The first of Ethel M. Dell's many romantic novels and a huge bestseller. See also *The Keeper of the Door* 1915 and *By Request* 1927.

A. Conan Doyle (1859–1930)
The Lost World F
Published on 15 October 1912. Serialized in the *Strand Magazine* (April–November 1912). See also *The Poison Belt* 1913, *The Land of Mist* 1926.

John Drinkwater (1882–1937)
Poems of Love and Earth V

Oliver Elton (1861–1945)
A Survey of English Literature 1780–1830 NF
See also *A Survey of English Literature* 1920

Ford Madox Ford (1873–1939)
The Panel F

Wilfrid Gibson (1878–1962)
Fires V

Thomas Hardy (1840–1928)
Wessex Edition WKS
The definitive edition of Hardy's work, published in 24 volumes (1912–31), commencing 30 April 1912

Stanley Houghton (1881–1913)
Hindle Wakes D

T.E. Hulme (1883–1917)
The Complete Poetical Works V
Five poems

'Mark Time' [Henry Crossly Irwin (1848–1924)]
A Derelict Empire F
A celebrated imperialist scare story

Rudyard Kipling (1865–1936)
Collected Verse V

D.H. Lawrence (1885–1930)
The Trespasser F
Published on 23 May 1912

Ada Leverson (1862–1933)
Tenterhooks F
Second volume of trilogy with *Love's Shadow* 1908 and *Love at Second Sight* 1916 (qq.v.)

Compton Mackenzie (1883–1972)
Carnival F
See also *Coral* 1925

George Moore (1852–1933)
Salve NF
Published on 10 October 1912. Second of the Hail and Farewell Trilogy. See also *Ave* 1911 and *Vale* 1914.

'Barry Pain' [Eric Odell (1864–1928)]
Exit Eliza F
See also *Eliza* 1900, *Eliza Getting On* 1911, *Eliza's Son* 1913

Sir A.T. Quiller-Couch (1863–1944) (ed.)
The Oxford Book of Victorian Verse ANTH

Morley Roberts (1857–1942)
The Private Life of Henry Maitland F
A fictionalized account of the life of George Gissing

Isaac Rosenberg (1890–1918)
Night and Day V

'Saki' [Hector Hugh Munro (1870–1916)]
The Chronicles of Clovis F
Stories

'Saki' [Hector Hugh Munro (1870–1916)]
The Unbearable Bassington F

Dora Sigerson (1866–1918)
New Poems V

May Sinclair (1863–1946)
Feminism NF

J.C. Squire (1884–1958)
Imaginary Speeches, and Other Parodies in Prose and Verse MISC

James Stephens (1882–1950)
The Crock of Gold F

James Stephens (1882–1950)
The Hill of Vision V

Lytton Strachey (1880–1932)
Landmarks in French Literature NF

B.H. Streeter (1874–1937) (ed.)
Foundations NF
Contributors include William Temple. See also Ronald Knox, *Absolute and Abitofhell* 1915.

R.H. Tawney (1880–1962)
The Agrarian Problem in the Sixteenth Century NF

Ernest Weekley (1865–1954)
The Romance of Words NF

H.G. Wells (1866–1946)
Marriage F

Charles Williams (1886–1945)
The Silver Stair V

1913

- Second and Third Balkan Wars
  Woodrow Wilson becomes President of the USA
  Society for Pure English founded by Robert Bridges
  New Statesman started
- Barbara Pym born
  R.S. Thomas born
  Angus Wilson born
- Alfred Austin dies: Robert Bridges appointed Poet Laureate
  Edward Dowden dies
  Emily Lawless dies
  Frederick Rolfe dies
  Alfred Russel Wallace dies
  William Hale White ('Mark Rutherford') dies
- Benjamin Britten born
- Albert Camus born
- Alain-Fournier, *Le Grand Meaulnes*
  Thomas Mann, *Der Tod in Venedig* (Death in Venice)
  Marcel Proust, *A la recherche du temps perdu* (1913–28)
  Edith Wharton, *The Custom of the Country*
- Stravinsky, *The Rite of Spring*

The New Statesman PER
Edited by Clifford Sharp, with J.C. Squire as Literary Editor. Relaunched in 1931.

Lascelles Abercrombie (1881–1938)
Speculative Dialogues NF

Sir J.M. Barrie (1860–1937)
Quality Street D
Published in November 1913. Illustrated by Hugh Thomson. Performed 17 September 1902. Barrie was created baronet this year.

Max Beerbohm (1872–1956)
Fifty Caricatures NF

Arnold Bennett (1867–1931)
The Great Adventure D
Performed 25 March 1913. Based on Bennett's novel *Buried Alive* 1908 (q.v.).

Arnold Bennett (1867–1931)
The Regent: A five towns story of adventure in London F

E.C. Bentley (1875–1956)
Trent's Last Case F

Laurence Binyon (1869–1943)
Auguries V

Joseph Campbell (1879–1944)
Irishry V

Gilbert Cannan (1884–1955)
Round the Corner F
Lawrie Saga ii: see also *Little Brother* 1912, *Three Pretty Men* 1916, *The Stucco House* 1917, *Time and Eternity* 1919, *Annette and Bennett* 1922

G.D.H. Cole (1889–1959)
The World of Labour NF

W.H. Davies (1871–1940)
Foliage V

Walter de la Mare (1873–1956)
Peacock Pie V
Published in June 1913. For children.

A. Conan Doyle (1859–1930)
The Poison Belt F
Published on 13 August 1913. The second Professor Challenger adventure. Serialized in the *Strand Magazine* (March–July 1913). See also *The Lost World* 1912, *The Land of Mist* 1926.

John Drinkwater (1882–1937)
Cromwell, and Other Poems V

Jeffery Farnol (1878–1952)
The Amateur Gentleman F

James Elroy Flecker (1884–1915)
The Golden Journey to Samarkand V
See also *Hassan* 1922

Ford Madox Ford (1873–1939)
Collected Poems EDN
Published 1913, dated 1914

Ford Madox Ford (1873–1939)
Mr Fleight F

Ford Madox Ford (1873–1939)
The Young Lovell F

John Galsworthy (1867–1933)
The Dark Flower F

John Galsworthy (1867–1933)
The Fugitive D
Performed 16 September 1913

Isabella Augusta, Lady Gregory (1852–1932)
Our Irish Theatre NF

'Radclyffe Hall' [Marguerite Antonia Radclyffe-Hall (1880–1943)]
Songs of Three Counties, and Other Poems V
Intro. by R.B. Cunninghame-Graham

Thomas Hardy (1840–1928)
A Changed Man; The Waiting Supper; and Other Tales F
Published on 24 October 1913

Constance Holme (1881–1955)
Crump Folk Going Home F

T.E. Hulme (1883–1917) (tr.)
An Introduction to Metaphysics NF
Translated from Henri Bergson (1858–1941)

L.P. Jacks (1860–1955)
All Men are Ghosts NF

Holbrook Jackson (1874–1948)
The Eighteen Nineties NF

Ronald Knox (1888–1957)
Naboth's Vineyard in Pawn NF

D.H. Lawrence (1885–1930)
Love Poems and Others V
Published in February 1913

D.H. Lawrence (1885–1930)
Sons and Lovers F
Published in May 1913

Richard Le Gallienne (1866–1947)
The Lonely Dancer, and Other Poems V
Published in 1913, dated 1914

Marie Belloc Lowndes (1868–1947)
The Lodger F
Based on the Jack the Ripper murders

Compton Mackenzie (1883–1972)
Sinister Street [vol. i] F
Volume ii, 1914 (q.v.)

John Masefield (1878–1967)
Dauber V

Somerset Maugham (1874–1965)
The Tenth Man: A tragic comedy D
Performed 24 February 1910

Somerset Maugham (1874–1965)
Landed Gentry: A comedy D
Performed 15 October 1910 as *Grace*

Somerset Maugham (1874–1965)
The Land of Promise: A comedy D
Performed in New York 25 December 1913, in London 26 February 1914

F.M. Mayor (1872–1932)
The Third Miss Symons F

James Moffatt (1870–1944) (tr.)
The New Testament BIB
Revised in 1914. See also *The Old Testament* 1924, *The Bible* 1926.

George Moore (1852–1933)
Elizabeth Cooper: A comedy D
Published in July 1913. Performed 22 June 1913. Rewritten as *The Coming of Gabrielle* (1920).

Alfred Noyes (1880–1958)
Tales of the Mermaid Tavern V

'Barry Pain' [Eric Odell (1864–1928)]
Eliza's Son F
See also *Eliza* 1900, *Eliza Getting On* 1911, *Exit Eliza* 1912

Eden Phillpotts (1862–1960)
Widecombe Fair F
Part of the 'Dartmoor Cycle'. See also *Children of the Mist* 1898, *Sons of the Morning* 1900, *The River* 1902, *The Secret Woman* 1905, *The Mother* 1908, *The Thief of Virtue* 1910.

'Sax Rohmer' [Arthur Henry Sarsfield Ward (1883–1959)]
The Mystery of Dr Fu-Manchu F
First of the Fu-Manchu series

'Æ' [George William Russell (1867–1935)]
Collected Poems V
Enlarged in 1919, 1926, and 1935

Dora Sigerson (1866–1918)
Madge Linsey, and Other Poems V

J.C. Squire (1884–1958)
The Three Hills, and Other Poems V

Francis Thompson (1859–1907)
The Works of Francis Thompson WKS
Published in May 1909

Katharine Tynan (1861–1931)
Irish Poems V

H.G. Wells (1866–1946)
The Passionate Friends F

Leonard Woolf (1880–1969)
The Village in the Jungle F

1914

- Suffragettes damage the 'Rokeby Venus' by Velasquez in the National Gallery
  Assassination of the Archduke Franz Ferdinand at Sarajevo (28 June)
  Germany declares war on Russia (1 Aug.)
  Germany declares war on France and invades Belgium (3 Aug.)
  Britain declares war on Germany (4 Aug.)
  Opening of the Panama Canal (15 Aug.)
  Battles of Namur and Mons (Aug.)
  German invasion of France halted at the Battle of the Marne (5–14 Sept.)
  First Battle of Ypres (Oct.–Nov.)
- Patric Dickinson born
  Ronald Duncan born
  Laurie Lee born
  Gavin Maxwell born
  Patrick O'Brian born
  Henry Reed born
  C.H. Sisson born
  Dylan Thomas born
- Robert Hugh Benson dies
  S.R. Crockett dies
  Theodore Watts-Dunton dies
  Sir Arthur Eddington dies
- Alain-Fournier dies
- Vaughan Williams, *The Lark Ascending*

Sir J.M. Barrie (1860)
The Admirable Crichton D
Published in December 1914. Illustrated by Hugh Thomson. Performed 4 November 1902.

E.F. Benson (1867–1940)
Dodo the Second F
See also *Dodo* 1893, *Dodo Wonders* 1921

Laurence Binyon (1869–1943)
The Winnowing-Fan V
Includes Binyon's celebrated poem 'For the Fallen'

Wilfrid Scawen Blunt (1840–1922)
Poetical Works V

'Ernest Bramah' [Ernest Bramah Smith (1868–1942)]
Max Carrados F
Stories

C.D. Broad (1887–1971)
Perception, Physics and Reality NF

G.K. Chesterton (1874–1936)
The Flying Inn F
Published on 22 January 1914

G.K. Chesterton (1874–1936)
The Wisdom of Father Brown F
Published in October 1914. See also *The Innocence of Father Brown* 1911, *The Incredulity of Father Brown* 1926, *The Secret of Father Brown* 1927, *The Scandal of Father Brown* 1935.

Joseph Conrad (1857–1924)
Chance F
Conrad's first popular success. English published in January Serialized in the *New York Herald* (21 January–30 June 1912).

W.H. Davies (1871–1940)
The Bird of Paradise, and Other Poems V

William De Morgan (1839–1917)
When Ghost Meets Ghost F

Lord Alfred Douglas (1870–1945)
Oscar Wilde and Myself NF

John Galsworthy (1867–1933)
The Mob D
Performed 20 April 1914

Wilfrid Gibson (1878–1962)
Borderlands V

Thomas Hardy (1840–1928)
Satires of Circumstance V
Published on 17 November 1914

Constance Holme (1881–1955)
The Lonely Plough F

James Joyce (1882–1941)
Dubliners F
Stories

D.H. Lawrence (1885–1930)
The Prussian Officer, and Other Stories F
Published on 26 November 1914

Ada Leverson (1862–1933)
Bird of Paradise F

Wyndham Lewis (1882–1957) (ed.)
Blast: Review of the great English vortex PER
Two numbers, 20 June 1914 and July 1915

Patrick MacGill (1889–1963)
Children of the Dead End F

Compton Mackenzie (1883–1972)
Sinister Street [vol. ii] F
Volume i, 1913 (q.v.)

John Masefield (1878–1967)
Philip the King, and Other Poems V

George Moore (1852–1933)
Vale NF
Published on 4 March 1914. Third of the Hail and Farewell Trilogy. See also *Ave* 1911 and *Salve* 1912.

'Robert Tressall' [Robert P. Noonan (1870–1911)]
The Ragged Trousered Philanthropists F
Abridged version, published in April 1914. Full version published in 1955.

Berta Ruck (1878–1978)
His Official Fiancée F

'Saki' [Hector Hugh Munro (1870–1916)]
Beasts and Super-Beasts F
Stories

'Saki' [Hector Hugh Munro (1870–1916)]
When William Came F

Bernard Shaw (1856–1950)
Misalliance; The Dark Lady of the Sonnets; and Fanny's First Play D
Published on 18 May 1914. *Misalliance* performed 23 February 1910; *The Dark Lady of the Sonnets* performed 24 November 1910; *Fanny's First Play* performed 19 April 1911.

Bernard Shaw (1856–1950)
Love Among the Artists F
Published in September 1914

Bernard Shaw (1856–1950)
Common Sense About the War NF
Published on 14 November 1914

H.G. Wells (1866–1946)
The War That Will End War NF
Published in October 1914

H.G. Wells (1866–1946)
The Wife of Sir Isaac Harman F

H.G. Wells (1866–1946)
The World Set Free F

Leonard Woolf (1880–1969)
The Wise Virgins F

'Dornford Yates' [Cecil William Mercer (1885–1960)]
The Brother of Daphne F
Stories

W.B. Yeats (1865–1939)
Responsibilities V
See also *Responsibilities* 1916

Francis Brett Young (1884–1954)
Deep Sea F

1915

- Second Battle of Ypres (Apr.–May)
  Germans use poison gas on the western front
  Anglo-French forces land at Gallipoli (22 Apr.)
  Italy declares war on Germany and Austria-Hungary (23 May)
  First Zeppelin attack on London (June)
  Edith Cavell executed in Brussels (11 Oct.)
- Monica Dickens born
  Patrick Leigh Fermor born
  Marghanita Laski born
  Alun Lewis born
  Olivia Manning born
- Rolf Boldrewood (Thomas Alexander Brown) dies
  Mary Elizabeth Braddon dies
  Rupert Brooke dies
  James Elroy Flecker dies
  Stephen Phillips dies
- W.G. Grace dies
- Saul Bellow born
  Arthur Miller born
- Ezra Pound, *Cathay*
- Holst, *The Planets*
  D.W. Griffith, *Birth of a Nation*

Richard Aldington (1892–1962)
Images 1910–15 V

'F. Anstey' [Thomas Anstey Guthrie (1856–1934)]
In Brief Authority F

Stella Benson (1892–1933)
I Pose F

Rupert Brooke (1887–1915)
1914, and Other Poems V

John Buchan (1875–1940)
The Thirty-Nine Steps F

G.K. Chesterton (1874–1936)
Poems V
Published in April 1915

Joseph Conrad (1857–1924)
Within the Tides F
Published on 24 February 1915. Contains four stories written 1910–14.

Joseph Conrad (1857–1924)
Victory F
Published in Britain on 24 September 1915. First published in *Munsey's Magazine* (February 1915) and serialized in the London *Star* (24 August–9 November 1915).

Ethel M. Dell (1881–1939)
The Keeper of the Door F
Sequel to *The Way of an Eagle* 1912 (q.v.). See also *By Request* 1927.

A. Conan Doyle (1859–1930)
The Valley of Fear F
Published on 3 June 1915. Serialized in the *Strand Magazine* (September 1914–May 1915). See also *A Study in Scarlet* 1888, *The Sign of Four* 1890, *Adventures of Sherlock Holmes* 1892, *Memoirs of Sherlock Holmes* 1893, *The Hound of the Baskervilles* 1902, *Return of Sherlock Holmes* 1905, *His Last Bow* 1917, *Case-Book of Sherlock Holmes* 1927.

John Drinkwater (1882–1937)
Swords and Ploughshares V

Ronald Firbank (1886–1926)
Vainglory F

F.S. Flint (1885–1960)
Cadences V

Ford Madox Ford (1873–1939)
The Good Soldier F

Wilfrid Gibson (1878–1962)
Battle V

Ronald Knox (1888–1957)
Absolute and Abitofhell V
First published in the *Oxford Magazine* (28 November 1912, 27 February 1913). A verse satire on *Foundations* 1912 (q.v.).

D.H. Lawrence (1885–1930)
The Rainbow F
Published on 30 September 1915

Richard Le Gallienne (1866–1947)
The Silk-Hat Soldier, and Other Poems V

Richard Le Gallienne (1866–1947)
Vanishing Roads, and Other Essays NF

Arthur Machen (1863–1947)
The Angels of Mons; The Bowmen; and Other Legends of the War F
'The Bowmen' first published in the *Evening News* on 29 September 1914

Arthur Machen (1863–1947)
The Great Return F

Somerset Maugham (1874–1965)
Of Human Bondage F
Published on 13 August 1915

Alice Meynell (1847–1922)
Poems on the War V

Robert Nichols (1893–1944)
Invocation V

Stephen Phillips (1864–1915)
Armageddon D

Herbert Read (1893–1968)
Songs of Chaos V

Dorothy M. Richardson (1873–1957)
Pointed Roofs F
Pilgrimage sequence i. See *Pilgrimage* 1938.

Isaac Rosenberg (1890–1918)
Youth V

'Æ' [George William Russell (1867–1935)**]**
Gods of War, with Other Poems V

'Æ' [George William Russell (1867–1935)**]**
Imaginations and Reveries V

Rafael Sabatini (1875–1950)
The Sea-Hawk F

E[dith] Œ[none] Somerville (1858–1949) and **'Martin Ross' [Violet Martin** (1862–1915)**]**
In Mr Knox's Country F
See also *Some Experiences of an Irish R.M.* 1899 and *Some Further Experiences* 1908

James Stephens (1882–1950)
The Adventures of Seumas Beg; The Rocky Road to Dublin V

James Stephens (1882–1950)
Songs from the Clay V

Arnold Toynbee (1889–1975)
Nationality and the War NF

H.G. Wells (1866–1946)
Bealby F

P.G. Wodehouse (1881–1975)
Psmith, Journalist F

Virginia Woolf (1882–1941)
The Voyage Out F
Published on 26 March 1915

1916

- Battle of Verdun begins (Feb.)
  Easter Rising in Dublin (23 Apr.)
  Battle of Jutland (31 May)
  Battle of the Somme begins (July)
  Execution of Roger Casement (3 Aug.)
  Strikes and mutinies in Russia (Sept.)
  David Lloyd George becomes British Prime Minister
  Tanks used for the first time
- Jack Clemo born
  Roald Dahl born
  Gavln Ewart born
  Penelope Fitzgerald born
- Stopford Brooke dies
  Julia Frankau dies
  Henry James dies
  'Saki' (Hector Hugh Munro) dies
- Jung, *Psychology of the Unconscious*

Arnold Bennett (1867–1931)
These Twain F
First published in the USA, 1915. Serialized in *Munsey's Magazine* (September–October 1915). Volume iii of the Clayhanger Trilogy. See also *Clayhanger* 1910, *Hilda Lessways* 1911.

E.F. Benson (1867–1940)
David Blaize F
See also *David Blaize and the Blue Door* 1918, *David of King's* 1924

Laurence Binyon (1869–1943)
The Anvil, and Other Poems V

Edmund Blunden (1896–1974)
Pastorals V
Published on 16 June 1916

Harold Brighouse (1882–1958)
Hobson's Choice D

Rupert Brooke (1887–1915)
Letters From America NF
Preface by Henry James

John Buchan (1875–1940)
Greenmantle F

John Buchan (1875–1940)
The Power-House F

Gilbert Cannan (1884–1955)
Mendel F

Gilbert Cannan (1884–1955)
Three Pretty Men F
Lawrie Saga iii. See also *Little Brother* 1912, *Round the Corner* 1913, *The Stucco House* 1917, *Time and Eternity* 1919, *Annette and Bennett* 1922.

R.G. Collingwood (1889–1943)
Religion and Philosophy NF

Daniel Corkery (1878–1964)
A Munster Twilight F
Stories

Elizabeth Daryush (1887–1977)
Verses V

W.H. Davies (1871–1940)
Child Lovers, and Other Poems V
Reissued 1921

W.H. Davies (1871–1940)
Collected Poems V
Second series, 1923 (q.v.). See also *Collected Poems* 1928, *Poems* 1934.

Eleanor Farjeon (1881–1965)
Nursery Rhymes of London Town V

Ronald Firbank (1886–1926)
Inclinations F

Robert Graves (1895–1985)
Over the Brazier V

Thomas Hardy (1840–1928)
Selected Poems V
Published on 3 October 1916

Constance Holme (1881–1955)
The Old Road From Spain F

Violet Hunt (1866–1942) and **F.M. Hueffer [Ford Madox Ford** (1873–1939)**]**
Zeppelin Nights F

Aldous Huxley (1894–1963)
The Burning Wheel V

James Joyce (1882–1941)
Portrait of the Artist as a Young Man F
First British edition. First published in the USA. Serialized in *The Egoist* 1–2 (1914–15). See also *Stephen Hero* 1944.

D.H. Lawrence (1885–1930)
Amores V
Published in July 1916

Ada Leverson (1862–1933)
Love at Second Sight F

Third volume of trilogy with *Love's Shadow* 1908 and *Tenterhooks* 1912 (qq.v.)

John Masefield (1878–1967)
Good Friday D
Performed 25 February 1917

Charlotte Mew (1869–1928)
The Farmer's Bride V

George Moore (1852–1933)
The Brook Kerith F
Based on *The Apostle* 1911 (q.v.)

John Middleton Murry (1889–1957)
Fyodor Dostoevsky NF

Sir A.T. Quiller-Couch (1863–1944)
On the Art of Writing NF

Dorothy M. Richardson (1873–1957)
Backwater F
Pilgrimage sequence ii. See *Pilgrimage* 1938.

Isaac Rosenberg (1890–1918)
Moses D
Includes poems

'Sapper' [Herman Cyril McNeile (1888–1937)]
Men, Women, and Guns F
Stories

Bernard Shaw (1856–1950)
Androcles and the Lion; Overruled; Pygmalion D
Published on 25 May 1916. *Androcles and the Lion* performed 1 September 1913 and first published in English in *Everybody's Magazine* (September 1914). *Overruled* performed 14 October 1912 and first published in English in the *English Review* (May 1913). *Pygmalion* performed in Vienna 16 October 1913 and first published in English in *Everybody's Magazine* (November 1914) and *Nash's Magazine* (November–December 1914). See also *Pygmalion* 1941.

Edith Sitwell (1887–1964) and **Osbert Sitwell** (1892–1969)
Twentieth Century Harlequinade, and Other Poems V
Published on 7 June 1916

Charles Sorley (1895–1915)
Marlborough, and Other Poems V

Katharine Tynan (1861–1931)
The Holy War V

Mary Webb (1881–1927)
The Golden Arrow F

H.G. Wells (1866–1946)
Mr Britling Sees It Through F

H.G. Wells (1866–1946)
What is Coming? NF

W.B. Yeats (1865–1939)
Easter, 1916 V

W.B. Yeats (1865–1939)
Responsibilities, and Other Poems V
See also *Responsibilities* 1914

W.B. Yeats (1865–1939)
Reveries Over Childhood and Youth NF
Published on 10 October 1916

Francis Brett Young (1884–1954)
The Iron Age F

1917

- Revolution in Russia: Nicholas II abdicates (Feb.)
  USA enters the war against Germany (6 Apr.)
  Lenin arrives in Petrograd
  US forces land in France (26 June)
  Bolshevik *coup d'état* in Russia (Oct.)
  Balfour Declaration on Palestine (Nov.)
  Germany and Russia sign armistice at Brest-Litovsk (Dec.)
  Pulitzer Prizes established (see 1918)
- Anthony Burgess (John Anthony Burgess Wilson) born
  Charles Causley born
  Arthur C. Clarke born
  Richard Cobb born
  Robert Conquest born
  Eric Hobsbawm born
  Jessica Mitford born
  Conor Cruise O'Brien born
- Jane Barlow dies
  Sir F.C. Burnand dies
  Harry Buxton Forman dies
  T.E. Hulme dies
  William de Morgan dies
  Edward Thomas dies
- John F. Kennedy born
  Robert Lowell born
- Edgar Degas dies
  François Auguste Rodin dies
- Paul Valéry, *La jeune parque*

Rupert Brooke (1887–1915)
Selected Poems V

Gilbert Cannan (1884–1955)
The Stucco House F
Lawrie Saga iv. See also *Little Brother* 1912, *Round the Corner* 1913, *Three Pretty Men* 1916, *Time and Eternity* 1919, *Annette and Bennett* 1922.

Richard Church (1893–1972)
The Flood of Life V

Joseph Conrad (1857–1924)
The Shadow-Line F
Published in March 1917. Serialized in the *English Review* (September 1916–March 1917).

Daniel Corkery (1878–1964)
The Threshold of Quiet F

'Clemence Dane' [Winifred Ashton (1888–1965)]
Regiment of Women F

'E.M. Delafield' [Edmée Monica de la Pasture (1890–1943)]
Zella Sees Herself F

Walter de la Mare (1873–1956)
The Sunken Garden, and Other Poems V

Norman Douglas (1868–1952)
South Wind F

A. Conan Doyle (1859–1930)
His Last Bow: Some reminiscences of Sherlock Holmes F
Published on 22 October 1917. Stories first published in the *Strand Magazine* between 1893 and 1917. See also *A Study in Scarlet* 1888, *The Sign of Four* 1890, *Adventures of Sherlock Holmes* 1892, *Memoirs of Sherlock Holmes* 1893, *The Hound of the Baskervilles* 1902, *Return of Sherlock Holmes* 1905, *The Valley of Fear* 1915, *Case-Book of Sherlock Holmes* 1927.

John Drinkwater (1882–1937)
Tides V

T.S. Eliot (1888–1965)
Prufrock and Other Observations V
Published in June 1917

Ronald Firbank (1886–1926)
Caprice F
Frontispiece by Augustus John

Gilbert Frankau (1884–1952)
The Woman of the Horizon F

Robert Graves (1895–1985)
Fairies and Fusiliers V

Ivor Gurney (1890–1937)
Severn and Somme V

Thomas Hardy (1840–1928)
Collected Poems V
Published on 10 October 1919

Thomas Hardy (1840–1928)
Moments of Vision and Miscellanous Verses V
Published on 30 November 1917

Henry James (1843–1916)
The Sense of the Past F
Published on 5 September 1917. Unfinished at James's death on 28 February 1916. Preface by Percy Lubbock.

Henry James (1843–1916)
The Ivory Tower F
Published on 6 September 1917. Unfinished. See also *The Sense of the Past* 1917.

Rudyard Kipling (1865–1936)
A Diversity of Creatures F
Stories

John Masefield (1878–1967)
Lollingdon Downs, and Other Poems V

Alice Meynell (1847–1922)
A Father of Women, and Other Poems V

George Moore (1852–1933)
Lewis Seymour and Some Women F
Published in March 1917. First published in the USA.

A.R. Orage (1873–1934)
An Alphabet of Economics NF

John Cowper Powys (1872–1963)
Wood and Stone F
First published in the USA, 1915

Dorothy M. Richardson (1873–1957)
Honeycomb F
Pilgrimage sequence iii. See *Pilgrimage* 1938.

'Æ' [George William Russell (1867–1935)]
Salutation V

Vita Sackville-West (1892–1962)
Poems of East and West V

Siegfried Sassoon (1886–1967)
The Old Huntsman, and Other Poems V

Bernard Shaw (1856–1950)
How to Settle the Irish Question NF
Published in December 1917

Arthur Symons (1865–1945)
Tristan and Iseult D

William Temple (1881–1944)
Mens Creatrix NF
See also *Christus Veritas* 1924

Edward Thomas (1878–1917)
A Literary Pilgrim in England NF

Sir William Watson (1858–1935)
The Man Who Saw, and Other Poems Arising Out of the War V
Watson was knighted in this year

Sir William Watson (1858–1935)
Retrogression, and Other Poems V

Alec Waugh (1898–1981)
The Loom of Youth F

H.G. Wells (1866–1946)
The Soul of a Bishop F

Charles Williams (1886–1945)
Poems of Conformity V

W.B. Yeats (1865–1939)
The Wild Swans at Coole, Other Verses and a Play in Verse V
Published on 17 November 1917. See also *The Wild Swans at Coole* 1919.

1918

- Germans begin spring offensive on the western front (21 Mar.)
  British Royal Air Force (RAF) formed (Apr.), amalgamating the Royal Flying Corps and the Royal Naval Air Service
  Women over 30 granted the vote in Britain
  German offensive halted on the Marne (July)
  Russian imperial family murdered by Bolsheviks (16 July)
  Germany signs armistice at Compiègne (11 Nov): end of the First World War
  First Pulitzer Prize for Fiction awarded (to Ernest Poole for *His Family*)
- A.L. Barker born
  Richard Ellmann born
  John Heath-Stubbs born
  Richard Hoggart born
  James Kirkup born
  Penelope Mortimer (*née* Fletcher) born
  P.H. Newby born
  Muriel Spark born
- Wilfred Owen dies
  Isaac Rosenberg dies
  Dora Sigerson dies
- Nelson Mandela born
  Alexander Solzhenitsyn born
- Guillaume Apollinaire dies
  Claude Debussy dies
  Frank Wedekind dies

Enid Bagnold (1889–1981)
A Diary Without Dates NF
Frank account of the author's experiences as a nurse in France

Sir J.M. Barrie (1860–1937)
What Every Woman Knows: A comedy D
Performed 3 September 1908

E.F. Benson (1867–1940)
David Blaize and the Blue Door F
See also *David Blaize* 1916, *David of King's* 1924

J.D. Beresford (1873–1947)
Nineteen Impressions F
Stories

Laurence Binyon (1869–1943)
The New World V

Rupert Brooke (1887–1915)
The Collected Poems of Rupert Brooke V
With an anonymous memoir by Edward Marsh

Walter de la Mare (1873–1956)
Motley, and Other Poems V

John Galsworthy (1867–1933)
Five Tales F
Contains 'Indian Summer of a Forsyte', reprinted in *The Forsyte Saga* 1922 (q.v.)

Wilfrid Gibson (1878–1962)
Whin V

Oliver St John Gogarty (1878–1957)
The Ship, and Other Poems V

'Frank' Harris (1856–1931)
Oscar Wilde NF
First published in the USA, 1916. Includes 'Memories of Oscar Wilde' by Bernard Shaw.

A.P. Herbert (1890–1971)
The Bomber Gipsy, and Other Poems V

Gerard Manley Hopkins (1844–89)
Poems of Gerard Manley Hopkins V
Edited, with notes, by Robert Bridges, Hopkins's friend. Hopkins began writing poetry as a schoolboy in the 1860s but sortly before joining the Jesuits in 1868 he burned everything he had written as a sacrifice to his vocation. He resumed writing poetry in 1875 and continued writing, unpublished, until his death in 1889. See also *Poems* 1930.

Aldous Huxley (1894–1963)
The Defeat of Youth, and Other Poems V

James Joyce (1882–1941)
Exiles D

D.H. Lawrence (1885–1930)
New Poems V
Published in October 1918

Wyndham Lewis (1882–1957)
Tarr F

Desmond MacCarthy (1877–1952)
Remnants NF

'Katherine Mansfield' [Kathleen Mansfield Beauchamp (1888–1923)]
Prelude F

'Edward Moore' [Edwin Muir (1887–1959)]
We Moderns NF

Sir Henry Newbolt (1862–1938)
St George's Day, and Other Poems V

Morley Roberts (1857–1942)
War Lyrics V

Lennox Robinson (1886–1958)
The Lost Leader D

'Æ' [George William Russell (1867–1935)]
The Candle of Vision NF

Siegfried Sassoon (1886–1967)
Counter-Attack, and Other Poems V

Dora Sigerson (1866–1918)
The Sad Years, and Other Poems V
Introduction by Katharine Tynan

Sacheverell Sitwell (1897–1988)
The People's Palace V
Published on 15 June 1918

Logan Pearsall Smith (1865–1946)
Trivia NF
See also *More Trivia* 1922, *Afterthoughts* 1931

'Solomon Eagle' [J.C. Squire (1884–1958)]
Books in General F
Second series, 1920; third series, 1921

J.C. Squire (1884–1958)
Poems, First Series V

Marie Stopes (1880–1958)
Married Love NF
See also *Wise Parenthood*, below

Marie Stopes (1880–1958)
Wise Parenthood NF
Sequel to *Married Love* (see above). Introduction by Arnold Bennett.

Lytton Strachey (1880–1932)
Eminent Victorians NF
Essays on Cardinal Manning, Florence Nightingale, Thomas Arnold, and General Gordon

Edward Thomas (1878–1917)
Last Poems V

'Douglas Valentine' [George Valentine Williams (1883–1946)]
The Man With the Club Foot F

Arthur Waley (1889–1966) (tr.)
One Hundred & Seventy Chinese Poems V

'Rebecca West' [Cicily Isabel Andrews (1892–1983)]
The Return of the Soldier F

W.B. Yeats (1865–1939)
Per Amica Silentia Lunae MISC
Published on 18 January 1918. Poems and essays.

W.B. Yeats (1865–1939)
Nine Poems V

1919

- Irish Free State proclaimed (21 Jan.)
  Alcock and Brown fly across the Atlantic (14 June)
  Treaty of Versailles signed (29 June)
- Doris Lessing born
  Iris Murdoch born
  Amelia Barr dies
- Matilda Betham-Edwards dies
  Weedon Grossmith dies
  Anne Isabella Ritchie, Lady Ritchie (*née* Thackeray), dies
  William Michael Rossetti dies
- Primo Levi born
- Pierre Auguste Renoir dies
  Theodore Roosevelt dies

Richard Aldington (1892–1962)
Images of Desire V

Richard Aldington (1892–1962)
Images of War V

Daisy Ashford (1881–1972)
The Young Visiters F

Max Beerbohm (1872–1956)
Seven Men F
Stories

John Buchan (1875–1940)
Mr Standfast F

Gilbert Cannan (1884–1955)
Time and Eternity F
Lawrie Saga v. See also *Little Brother* 1912, *Round the Corner* 1913, *Three Pretty Men* 1916,

The Stucco House 1917, *Annette and Bennett* 1922.

Joseph Conrad (1857–1924)
The Arrow of Gold F
Published on 6 August 1919. Serialized in *Lloyd's Magazine* (December 1918–February 1920).

John Drinkwater (1882–1937)
Loyalties V

T.S. Eliot (1888–1965)
Poems V
Published in May 1919

Ronald Firbank (1886–1926)
Valmouth F

Ivor Gurney (1890–1937)
War's Embers V

W.R. Inge (1860–1954)
Outspoken Essays [1st ser.] NF
See also *Outspoken Essays* 1922

M.R. James (1862–1936)
A Thin Ghost, and Others F
See also *Ghost Stories of an Antiquary* 1904, *More Ghost Stories* 1911, *A Warning to the Curious* 1925

Storm Jameson (1897–1986)
The Pot Boils F

C.E.M. Joad (1891–1953)
Essays in Common Sense Philosophy NF

J.M. Keynes (1883–1946)
The Economic Consequences of the Peace NF
See also *A Revision of the Treaty* 1922

'Hugh Kingsmill' [Hugh Kingsmill Lunn (1889–1949)]
The Will to Love F

Rudyard Kipling (1865–1936)
The Years Between V

Somerset Maugham (1874–1965)
The Moon and Sixpence F
Published in April 1919

Charles Morgan (1894–1958)
The Gunroom F

Dorothy M. Richardson (1873–1957)
Interim F
Pilgrimage sequence iv. See *Pilgrimage* 1938.

Dorothy M. Richardson (1873–1957)
The Tunnel F
Pilgrimage sequence v. See *Pilgrimage* 1938.

Siegfried Sassoon (1886–1967)
The War Poems of Siegfried Sassoon V

Bernard Shaw (1856–1950)
Heartbreak House; Great Catherine; and Playlets of the War D
Published on 23 September 1919. *Heartbreak House* first performed in London 18 October 1921. *Great Catherine* performed 18 November 1913. Also contains *O'Flaherty V.C.*, *The Inca of Jerusalem*, *Augustus Does His Bit*, and *Annajanska, the Bolshevik Empress.*

Dora Sigerson (1866–1918)
Sixteen Dead Men, and Other Ballads of Easter Week V

Osbert Sitwell (1892–1969)
Argonaut and Juggernaut V
Published on 30 October 1919

E[dith] Œ[none] Somerville (1858–1949) and **'Martin Ross' [Violet Martin** (1862–1915)]
Mount Music F

J.C. Squire (1884–1958)
The Birds, and Other Poems V

H.G. Wells (1866–1946) and others
The Outline of History NF
Published in 24 parts, 1919–20

H.G. Wells (1866–1946)
The Undying Fire F

A.N. Whitehead (1861–1947)
An Enquiry Concerning the Principles of Natural Knowledge NF

P.G. Wodehouse (1881–1975)
My Man Jeeves F
Stories. The first Jeeves title.

Virginia Woolf (1882–1941)
Kew Gardens F
Stories. Published on 12 May 1919. See also *Monday or Tuesday* 1921, *A Haunted House, and Other Short Stories* 1944.

Virginia Woolf (1882–1941)
Night and Day F
Published on 20 October 1919

W.B. Yeats (1865–1939)
Two Plays for Dancers V
Published in January 1919. See also *Four Plays for Dancers* 1921.

W.B. Yeats (1865–1939)
The Wild Swans at Coole V
Published on 11 March 1919. Contains the poems from 1917 edition (q.v.) and others, including 'An Irish Airman Foresees his Death' and 'The Phases of the Moon'.

1920

- The League of Nations established (10 Jan.)
  Prohibition in the USA (Jan.)
  First public broadcasting stations opened in Britain (by Marconi, Feb.) and the US (Nov.)
- Richard Adams born
  Keith Douglas born
  D.J. Enright born
  P.D. James born
  Paul Scott born
- A.H. Bullen dies
  Rhoda Broughton dies
  Ernest Hartley Coleridge dies
  Olive Schreiner dies
  Howard Sturgis dies
  Mary Augusta Ward (Mrs Humphry Ward) dies
- William Dean Howells dies
- Sinclair Lewis, *Main Street*
  Spengler, *Decline of the West*
- *The Cabinet of Dr Caligari*

'Michael Arlen' [Dikran Kouyoumdjian (1895–1956)]
The London Venture F

H.C. Bailey (1878–1961)
Call Mr Fortune F
Detective stories

Maurice Baring (1874–1945)
Poems 1914–1919 V

E.F. Benson (1867–1940)
Queen Lucia F
See also *Miss Mapp* 1922, *Lucia in London* 1927, *Mapp and Lucia* 1931, *Lucia's Progress* 1935

Edmund Blunden (1896–1974)
The Waggoner, and Other Poems V
Published on 15 August 1920

Robert Bridges (1844–1930)
October, and Other Poems V
Published on 18 March 1920

Joseph Conrad (1857–1924)
The Rescue F
Published in August 1920. Serialized in *Land and Water* (30 January–31 July 1919).

Freeman Wills Crofts (1879–1957)
The Cask F

W.H. Davies (1871–1940)
The Song of Life, and Other Poems V

Walter de la Mare (1873–1956)
Poems 1901 to 1918 V

Norman Douglas (1868–1952)
They Went F

T.S. Eliot (1888–1965)
The Sacred Wood NF
Published in November 1920

Oliver Elton (1861–1945)
A Survey of English Literature 1830–80 NF
See also *A Survey of English Literature* 1912

Roger Fry (1866–1934)
Vision and Design NF

John Galsworthy (1867–1933)
Awakening F
A Forsyte interlude, reprinted in *The Forsyte Saga* 1922 (q.v.). See also *Two Forsyte Interludes* 1927.

John Galsworthy (1867–1933)
In Chancery F
The second novel in The Forsyte Saga. See also *The Man of Property* 1906, *To Let* 1921, *The Forsyte Saga* 1922. See also *Two Forsyte Interludes* 1927, *Four Forsyte Stories* 1929, *On Forsyte 'Change* 1930, *Soames and the Flag* 1930.

Robert Graves (1895–1985)
Country Sentiment V

Frederic Harrison (1831–1923)
Novissima Verba NF
See also *De Senectute* 1923

James Hilton (1900–54)
Catherine Herself F

Aldous Huxley (1894–1963)
Leda V

Aldous Huxley (1894–1963)
Limbo F

D.H. Lawrence (1885–1930)
The Lost Girl F
Published in November 1920

David Lindsay (1876–1945)
A Voyage to Arcturus F

Hugh Lofting (1886–1947)
The Story of Dr Dolittle F
First of the Dr Dolittle series

Percy Lubbock (1879–1965) (ed.)
The Letters of Henry James NF

Rose Macaulay (1881–1958)
Potterism F

'Katherine Mansfield' [Kathleen Mansfield Beauchamp (1888–1923)]
Bliss, and Other Stories F

John Masefield (1878–1967)
Enslaved, and Other Poems V

John Middleton Murry (1889–1957)
The Evolution of an Intellectual NF
Mostly reprinted from the *Times Literary Supplement*

Wilfred Owen (1893–1918)
Poems V
Introduction by Siegfried Sassoon

Ruth Pitter (1897–1992)
First Poems V

Lennox Robinson (1886–1958)
The Whiteheaded Boy: A comedy D

'Sapper' [Herman Cyril McNeile (1888–1937)]
Bull-Dog Drummond F
Published as H.C. McNeile

Edward Thomas (1878–1917)
Collected Poems V
Foreword by Walter de la Mare

Charles Williams (1886–1945)
Divorce V

Humbert Wolfe (1885–1940)
London Sonnets V

Humbert Wolfe (1885–1940)
Shylock Reasons with Mr Chesterton, and Other Poems V

1921

- Warren G. Harding becomes President of the USA
  Lenin introduces the New Economic Policy
  British Legion founded
  Anglo-Irish treaty established the Irish Free State (6 Dec.)
- George Mackay Brown born
  Edmund Crispin (Robert Bruce Montgomery) born
  Geoffrey Elton born
  Leon Garfield born
  Brian Moore born
  Raymond Williams born
- Florence Barclay ('Brandon Roy') dies
  Christabel Rose Coleridge dies
  Austin Dobson dies
  E.W. Hornung dies
  Mary Louisa Molesworth dies
  Rosa Mulholland (Lady Gilbert) dies
  Hume Nisbet dies
- *New Cambridge Shakespeare* (ed. A. Quiller-Couch to 1931, then J. Dover Wilson)
  John Dos Passos, *Three Soldiers*
  Prokofiev, *Love of Three Oranges*

Clifford Bax (1886–1962)
Antique Pageantry D
Verse plays

E.F. Benson (1867–1940)
Dodo Wonders F
See also *Dodo* 1893, *Dodo the Second* 1914

Agatha Christie (1890–1976)
The Mysterious Affair at Styles F
First published in the USA, 1920

A.E. Coppard (1878–1957)
Adam and Eve and Pinch Me F
Stories

'Clemence Dane' [Winifred Ashton (1888–1965)]
A Bill of Divorcement D
Performed 14 March 1921

Walter de la Mare (1873–1956)
Memoirs of a Midget F
Published in May 1921

Walter de la Mare (1873–1956)
The Veil, and Other Poems V
Published in December 1921

John Galsworthy (1867–1933)
To Let F
The third novel in the Forsyte Saga. See also *The Man of Property* 1906, *In Chancery* 1920, *The Forsyte Saga* 1922. See also *Two Forsyte Interludes* 1927, *Four Forsyte Stories* 1929, *On Forsyte 'Change* 1930, *Soames and the Flag* 1930.

Robert Graves (1895–1985)
The Pier-Glass V

H. Rider Haggard (1856–1925)
She and Allan F
Published on 17 February 1921. Serialized (as *She Meets Allan*) in *Hutchinson's Story Magazine* (July 1919–March 1920). See also *She* 1887, *Wisdom's Daughter* 1923.

Georgette Heyer (1902–74)
The Black Moth F

Aldous Huxley (1894–1963)
Crome Yellow F

Sheila Kaye-Smith (1887–1956)
Joanna Godden F

D.H. Lawrence (1885–1930)
Women in Love F
Published in June 1921. First privately printed in the USA, 1920.

Percy Lubbock (1879–1965)
The Craft of Fiction NF

Somerset Maugham (1874–1965)
The Trembling of a Leaf F
Stories. Published on 6 October 1921.

Harold Nicolson (1886–1968)
Sweet Waters F

Dorothy M. Richardson (1873–1957)
Deadlock F
Pilgrimage sequence vi. See *Pilgrimage* 1938.

Bertrand Russell (1872–1970)
The Analysis of Mind NF

'Æ' [George William Russell (1867–1935)]
The Inner and the Outer Ireland NF

Rafael Sabatini (1875–1950)
Scaramouche: A romance of the French Revolution F

Vita Sackville-West (1892–1962)
Orchard and Vineyard V

George Sampson (1873–1950)
English for the English NF

Bernard Shaw (1856–1950)
Back to Methuselah D
Published on 23 June 1921. Performed in New York, 10 November 1920. First performed in London, 18 February 1924.

Lytton Strachey (1880–1932)
Queen Victoria NF

R.H. Tawney (1880–1962)
The Acquisitive Society NF

Flora Thompson (1877–1947)
Bog-Myrtle and Peat V

Mary Tourtel (1874–1948)
The Adventures of Rupert the Little Bear F

H.G. Wells (1866–1946)
The Salvaging of Civilization NF

Henry Williamson (1895–1977)
The Beautiful Years F
The Flax of Dream sequence i. See *Dandelion Days* 1922, *The Dream of Fair Women* 1924, *The Pathway* 1928. Revised and published together as *The Flax of Dream* 1936.

Virginia Woolf (1882–1941)
Monday or Tuesday F
Stories. Published in April 1921. Contains 'A Haunted House', 'A Society', 'Monday or Tuesday', 'An Unwritten Novel', 'The String Quartet', 'Blue & Green', 'Kew Gardens' (see 1919), 'The Mark on the Wall' (first published in 1917). See also *A Haunted House, and Other Stories* 1944.

'Dornford Yates' [Cecil William Mercer (1885–1960)]
Berry and Co. F
Stories

W.B. Yeats (1865–1939)
Michael Robartes and the Dancer V
Published in February 1921, dated 1920

W.B. Yeats (1865–1939)
Four Plays for Dancers D
Published on 28 October 1921. Adds 'At the Hawk's Well' and 'Calvary' to *Two Plays for Dancers* 1919 (q.v.).

1922

- Stalin becomes general secretary of the Communist Party (Mar.)
  Andrew Bonar Law becomes British Prime Minister
  British Broadcasting Company (later Corporation) founded: first broadcast 14 Nov.
  Lord Carnarvon and Howard Carter discover the tomb of Tutankhamun at Luxor (Nov.)
  Reader's Digest started
- Kingsley Amis born
  Ronald Blythe born
  John Braine born
  Donald Davie born
  Philip Larkin born
  Alan Ross born
  Vernon Scannell born
- Wilfrid Scawen Blunt dies
  Erskine Childers executed
  W.H. Hudson dies
  Alice Meynell dies
  Sir Walter Raleigh dies
- Michael Collins dies
  Ernest Shackleton dies
- Marcel Proust dies
- Sinclair Lewis, *Babbitt*

Jane Austen (1775–1817)
Love & Freindship [sic] *and Other Early Works* F

First printed from the original MS. Preface by G.K. Chesterton.

Sir J.M. Barrie (1860–1937)
Dear Brutus: A comedy D
Published in November 1922. Performed 17 October 1917.

Arnold Bennett (1867–1931)
Mr Prohack F
Serialized in *The Delineator* (July 1921–January 1922)

E.F. Benson (1867–1940)
Miss Mapp F
See also *Queen Lucia* 1920, *Lucia in London* 1927, *Mapp and Lucia* 1931, *Lucia's Progress* 1935

Phyllis Bentley (1894–1977)
Environment F
See also *Cat-in-the-Manger* 1923

Edmund Blunden (1896–1974)
The Shepherd, and Other Poems of Peace and War V
Published in April 1922

John Buchan (1875–1940)
Huntingtower F

Gilbert Cannan (1884–1955)
Annette and Bennett F
Lawrie Saga vi. See also *Little Brother* 1912, *Round the Corner* 1913, *Three Pretty Men* 1916, *The Stucco House* 1917, *Time and Eternity* 1919.

G.K. Chesterton (1874–1936)
Eugenics, and Other Evils NF
Published in February 1922

G.K. Chesterton (1874–1936)
The Man Who Knew Too Much, and Other Stories F
Published in November 1922

A.E. Coppard (1878–1957)
Clorinda Walks in Heaven F
Stories

'Richmal Crompton' [Richmal Crompton Lamburn (1890–1969)]
Just—William F
Published in May 1922. The first William collection, containing stories published in *Home* magazine (April 1919–July 1921).

W.H. Davies (1871–1940)
The Hour of Magic, and Other Poems V

John Drinkwater (1882–1937)
Preludes 1921–1922 V

James Elroy Flecker (1884–1915)
Hassan D
Performed 20 September 1923. See also *The Golden Journey to Samarkand* 1913.

John Galsworthy (1867–1933)
The Forsyte Saga F
Collects *The Man of Property* 1906, *In Chancery* 1920, *To Let* 1921, together with 'Indian Summer of a Forsyte' (first published in *Five Tales* 1918, q.v.) and *Awakening* 1920 (q.v.). See also *Two Forsyte Interludes* 1927, *Four Forsyte Stories* 1929, *On Forsyte 'Change* 1930, *Soames and the Flag* 1930.

David Garnett (1892–1981)
Lady into Fox F

William Gerhardie (1895–1977)
Futility F

Wilfrid Gibson (1878–1962)
Krindlesdyke V

Elinor Glyn (1864–1943)
Man and Maid F
The novel that introduced the word 'It' as a euphemism for sex

Thomas Hardy (1840–1928)
Late Lyrics and Earlier, with Many Other Verses V
Published on 23 May 1922

'Frank' Harris (1856–1931)
My Life and Loves NF

A.E. Housman (1859–1936)
Last Poems V

Aldous Huxley (1894–1963)
Mortal Coils F
Stories, including 'The Gioconda Smile'. See also 1948.

W.R. Inge (1860–1954)
Outspoken Essays [2nd ser.] NF
See also *Outspoken Essays* 1919

James Joyce (1882–1941)
Ulysses F
Some episodes published in the *Little Review* (March 1918–December 1920), and in *The Egoist 6* (1919). First edition published in Paris. See also *Ulysses* 1936, 1986.

J.M. Keynes (1883–1946)
A Revision of the Treaty NF
See *The Economic Consequences of the Peace* 1919

D.H. Lawrence (1885–1930)
Aaron's Rod F
Published in June 1922

Compton Mackenzie (1883–1972)
The Altar Steps F
See also *The Parson's Progress* 1923

'Katherine Mansfield' [**Kathleen Mansfield Beauchamp** (1888–1923)]
The Garden-Party, and Other Stories F

Somerset Maugham (1874–1965)
On a Chinese Screen F
Stories. Published on 9 November 1922.

A.A. Milne (1882–1956)
The Red House Mystery F

John Middleton Murry (1889–1957)
Countries of the Mind NF

John Middleton Murry (1889–1957)
The Problem of Style NF

Alfred Noyes (1880–1958)
The Watchers of the Sky V
Volume i of the Torch-Bearers Trilogy, followed by *The Book of the Earth* 1925, *The Last Voyage* 1930, *The Torch-Bearers* 1937

C.K. Ogden (1889–1957), **I.A. Richards** (1893–1979), and **James Wood**
The Foundations of Aesthetics NF

J.B. Priestley (1894–1984)
Brief Diversions MISC

Rafael Sabatini (1875–1950)
Captain Blood, his Odyssey F

Michael Sadleir (1888–1957)
Excursions in Victorian Bibliography NF

Edith Sitwell (1887–1964)
Façade V
Concert version, with music by William Walton, performed in January 1922

Sacheverell Sitwell (1897–1988)
The Hundred and One Harlequins, and Other Poems V
Published in July 1922

Logan Pearsall Smith (1865–1946)
More Trivia NF
See also *Trivia* 1918, *Afterthoughts* 1931

J.C. Squire (1884–1958)
Poems: Second Series V
See *Poems, First Series* 1918

Lytton Strachey (1880–1932)
Books and Characters, French and English NF

Ben Travers (1886–1980)
A Cuckoo in the Nest F
Later adapted into a farce (first performed in London 25 July 1925)

Hugh Walpole (1884–1941)
The Cathedral F

H.G. Wells (1866–1946)
A Short History of the World NF

'Rebecca West' [**Cicily Isabel Andrews** (1892–1983)]
The Judge F

Henry Williamson (1895–1977)
Dandelion Days F
The Flax of Dream sequence ii. See *The Beautiful Years* 1921, *The Dream of Fair Women* 1924, *The Pathway* 1928. Revised and published together as *The Flax of Dream* 1936.

Virginia Woolf (1882–1941)
Jacob's Room F
Published on 27 October 1922

W.B. Yeats (1865–1939)
The Trembling of the Veil NF
Published in October 1922

W.B. Yeats (1865–1939)
Later Poems V
Published on 3 November 1922 as the first volume in Macmillan's Collected Edition of Yeats's Works. See also *Plays in Prose and Verse* 1922, *Plays and Controversies* 1923, *Essays* 1924, *Autobiographies* 1926.

W.B. Yeats (1865–1939)
Plays in Prose and Verse D
Published on 3 November 1922. Collected Edition volume ii.

W.B. Yeats (1865–1939)
The Player Queen D
Published on 21 November 1922

1923

- Union of Soviet Socialist Republics (USSR) established (1 Jan.)
  French occupation of the Ruhr (Jan.)
  Stanley Baldwin forms Conservative administration
  Death of US president Harding: succeeded by Calvin Coolidge (Aug.)
  Adolf Hitler's abortive 'beer-hall' putsch in Munich (Nov.)
  Nonesuch Press started
- Dannie Abse born
  Brendan Behan born

Christine Brooke-Rose born
Dorothy Dunnett (*née* Halliday) born
Elizabeth Jane Howard born
Francis King born
Alistair Maclean born
John Mortimer born

- Henry Bradley dies
Maurice Hewlett dies
W.P. Ker dies
W.H. Mallock dies
Katherine Mansfield dies
John Morley, Viscount Morley, dies
- Sarah Bernhardt dies
- F. Scott Fitzgerald, *Tales of the Jazz Age*
Adolf Hitler, *Mein Kampf* (completed 1927; English translation 1933)

Harold Acton (1904–94)
Aquarium V

'Michael Arlen' [Dikran Kouyoumdjian (1895–1956)]
These Charming People F
Stories. See also *May Fair* 1925.

Arnold Bennett (1867–1931)
Riceyman Steps F

Phyllis Bentley (1894–1977)
Cat-in-the-Manger F
Sequel to *Environment* 1922 (q.v.)

Edmund Blunden (1896–1974)
To Nature V
Published in June 1923

Elizabeth Bowen (1899–1973)
Encounters F
Stories

Vera Brittain (1893–1970)
The Dark Tide F

John Buchan (1875–1940)
Midwinter F

Joseph Conrad (1857–1924)
The Rover F
Published on 3 December 1923

W.H. Davies (1871–1940)
Collected Poems [2nd ser.] V
First series, 1916 (q.v.). See also *Collected Poems* 1928, *Poems* 1934.

Walter de la Mare (1873–1956)
The Riddle, and Other Stories F

John Drinkwater (1882–1937)
Collected Poems V
Published in 3 volumes (1923–37)

T.S. Eliot (1888–1965)
The Waste Land V
Published on 12 September 1923. First published in *Criterion i* (October 1922), and *The Dial* (November 1922), without notes. Published in this form in *The Dial*, 73 (1922). See also *The Waste Land* 1940.

Harley Granville-Barker (1877–1946)
Prefaces to the Players' Shakespeare NF
Published in 7 volumes (1923–7). See also *Prefaces to Shakespeare* 1927.

Robert Graves (1895–1985)
Whipperginny V

H. Rider Haggard (1856–1925)
Wisdom's Daughter: The life and love story of She-Who-Must-Be-Obeyed F
Published on 9 March 1923. Serialized in *Hutchinson's Magazine* (March 1922–March 1923). See also *She* 1887, *Ayesha* 1905, *She and Allan* 1921.

Thomas Hardy (1840–1928)
The Famous Tragedy of the Queen of Cornwall at Tintagel in Lyonesse D
Published on 15 November 1923. Performed in Dorchester 28–30 November 1923, and in London on 21 February 1924.

Frederic Harrison (1831–1923)
De Senectute NF
See also *Novissima Verba* 1920

Winifred Holtby (1898–1935)
Anderby Wold F

Laurence Housman (1865–1959)
Followers of St Francis D
Contains *Cure of Souls; Lovers Meeting; The Fool's Errand; The Last Disciple*. See also *Little Plays of St Francis* 1935.

Aldous Huxley (1894–1963)
Antic Hay F

Sheila Kaye-Smith (1887–1956)
The End of the House of Alard F

D.H. Lawrence (1885–1930)
The Ladybird; The Fox; The Captain's Doll F
Published in March 1923. 'The Fox' serialized in *The Dial* (May–August 1922).

D.H. Lawrence (1885–1930)
Psychoanalysis and the Unconscious NF
Published on 10 May 1923. First published in the USA, 1921.

D.H. Lawrence (1885–1930)
Fantasia of the Unconscious NF

Published in September 1923. First published in the USA, 1922.

D.H. Lawrence (1885–1930)
Kangaroo NF
Published in September 1923

D.H. Lawrence (1885–1930)
Birds, Beasts and Flowers V
Published in November 1923. First published in the USA, October 1923.

J.S. Le Fanu (1814–73)
Madam Crowl's Ghost, and Other Tales of Mystery F
Previously uncollected stories, edited by M.R. James

'Hugh MacDiarmid' [Christopher Murray Grieve (1892–1978)]
Annals of the Five Senses V
As Christopher Murray Grieve

Compton Mackenzie (1883–1972)
The Parson's Progress F
Sequel to *The Altar Steps* 1922 (q.v.)

Compton Mackenzie (1883–1972)
The Seven Ages of Woman F

'Katherine Mansfield' [Kathleen Mansfield Beauchamp (1888–1923)]
The Dove's Nest F
Stories. Edited by John Middleton Murry.

John Masefield (1878–1967)
Collected Poems V

John Masefield (1878–1967)
King Cole, and Other Poems V

Alice Meynell (1847–1922)
Last Poems V

Naomi Mitchison (1897–1999)
The Conquered F

C.K. Ogden (1889–1957) and **I.A. Richards** (1893–1979)
The Meaning of Meaning NF

T.F. Powys (1875–1953)
Black Bryony F

Arthur Ransome (1884–1967)
'Racundra's' First Cruise NF

Herbert Read (1893–1968)
Mutations of the Phoenix V

Dorothy M. Richardson (1873–1957)
Revolving Lights F
Pilgrimage sequence vii. See *Pilgrimage* 1938.

Dorothy L. Sayers (1893–1957)
Whose Body? F
The first Lord Peter Wimsey novel

Edith Sitwell (1887–1964)
Bucolic Comedies V
Published on 24 April 1923

Osbert Sitwell (1892–1969)
Out of the Flame V
Published in June 1923

James Stephens (1882–1950)
Deirdre F

Ben Travers (1886–1980)
Rookery Nook F
Later adapted as a farce (performed 30 June 1926)

Alec Waugh (1898–1981)
Myself When Young NF
Autobiography

P.G. Wodehouse (1881–1975)
The Inimitable Jeeves F
Stories

W.B. Yeats (1865–1939)
Plays and Controversies D
Published on 27 November 1923. Collected Edition volume iii.

1924

- Ramsay MacDonald forms first Labour government in Britain (22 Jan.)
  Stanley Baldwin forms Conservative administration (Nov.)
- Patricia Beer born
  James Berry born
  Robert Bolt born
  E.P. Thompson born
- William Archer dies
  F.H. Bradley dies
  Frances Hodgson Burnett dies
  Joseph Conrad dies
  Marie Corelli dies
  Edith Nesbit dies
- C.V. Stanford dies
- James Baldwin born
- Anatole France dies
  Franz Kafka dies
  Lenin dies
  Giacomo Puccini dies
- André Breton, *Manifeste du Surréalisme*
- George Gershwin, *Rhapsody in Blue*
  Puccini, *Turandot*

'Michael Arlen' [Dikran Kouyoumdjian (1895–1956)]
The Green Hat F

Sir J.M. Barrie (1860–1937)
Mary Rose D
Published in December 1924. Performed 22 April 1920.

E.F. Benson (1867–1940)
David of King's F
See also *David Blaize* 1916, *David Blaize and the Blue Door* 1918

Augustine Birrell (1850–1933)
More Obiter Dicta NF
See also *Obiter Dicta* 1884, 1887

Roy Campbell (1901–57)
The Flaming Terrapin V

Agatha Christie (1890–1976)
Poirot Investigates F
Stories

Joseph Conrad (1857–1924) and **Ford Madox Ford** (1873–1939)
The Nature of a Crime F
Published on 26 September 1924, soon after Conrad's death on 3 August. Serialized psedonymously in the *English Review* (April–May 1909).

Noël Coward (1899–1973)
The Young Idea D
First performed in London 1 February 1923

Noël Coward (1899–1973)
The Rat Trap D
Performed 18 October 1926

Lord Dunsany (1878–1957)
The King of Elfland's Daughter F

T.S. Eliot (1888–1965)
Homage to John Dryden NF
Published on 30 October 1924

Ronald Firbank (1886–1926)
Sorrow in Sunlight F
First published in the USA as *Prancing Nigger*

Ford Madox Ford (1873–1939)
Some Do Not F
Parade's End (Tietjens) Tetralogy i. See also *No More Parades* 1925, *A Man Could Stand Up* 1926, *Last Post* 1928.

E.M. Forster (1879–1970)
A Passage to India F
Published on 4 June 1924

L.P. Hartley (1895–1972)
Night Fears, and Other Stories F

Aldous Huxley (1894–1963)
Little Mexican, and Other Stories V

Margaret Irwin (1889–1967)
Still She Wished For Company F

Margaret Kennedy (1896–1967)
The Constant Nymph F
Dramatized, by Kennedy and Basil Dean in 1926. Film 1933. See also *The Fool of the Family* 1930.

D.H. Lawrence (1885–1930)
England, My England F
Published in January 1924. First published in the USA, 1922.

'Katherine Mansfield' [Kathleen Mansfield Beauchamp (1888–1923)]
Something Childish, and Other Stories F

John Masefield (1878–1967)
Sard Harker F

Somerset Maugham (1874–1965)
Loaves and Fishes: A comedy D
Performed 24 February 1911. Based on Maugham's novel *The Bishop's Apron* 1906 (q.v.).

A.A. Milne (1882–1956)
When We Were Very Young V

James Moffatt (1870–1944) (tr.)
The Old Testament BIB
See also *The New Testament* 1913, *The Bible* 1926

George Moore (1852–1933)
Conversations in Ebury Street NF
Published in January 1924

George Moore (1852–19833) (tr.)
The Pastoral Loves of Daphnis and Chloe F
Translated from Longus

George Moore (1852–1933)
Avowals F
Published in November 1924. First privately printed in 1919.

R.H. Mottram (1883–1971)
The Spanish Farm F
Hawthornden Prize. The Spanish Farm Trilogy i. See also *Sixty-Four, Ninety-Four!* 1925, *The Crime at Vanderlynden's* 1926.

I.A. Richards (1893–1979)
Principles of Literary Criticism NF

Lennox Robinson (1886–1958)
Crabbed Youth and Age D
Performed 14 November 1922

Bernard Shaw (1856–1950)
Saint Joan D

Published on 25 June 1924. Performed in New York, 28 December 1923, and in London on 26 March 1924.

Edith Sitwell (1887–1964)
The Sleeping Beauty V
Published in March 1924

J.C. Squire (1884–1958)
The Grub Street Nights Entertainment F

G.B. Stern (1890–1973)
Tents of Israel F
The Rakonitz Chronicles i, followed by *A Deputy Was King* 1926, *Petruchio* 1929, *Shining and Free* 1935, and *The Young Matriarch* 1942.

William Temple (1881–1944)
Christus Veritas NF
Sequel to *Mens Creatrix* 1917 (q.v.)

Mary Webb (1881–1927)
Precious Bane F

Henry Williamson (1895–1977)
The Dream of Fair Women F
The Flax of Dream sequence iii. See *The Beautiful Years* 1921, *Dandelion Days* 1922, *The Pathway* 1928. Revised and published together as *The Flax of Dream* 1936.

Humbert Wolfe (1885–1940)
Kensington Gardens V

P.C. Wren (1885–1941)
Beau Geste F
See also *Beau Sabreur* 1926, *Beau Ideal* 1928

W.B. Yeats (1865–1939)
The Cat and the Moon, and Certain Poems D/V
Published in July 1924

W.B. Yeats (1865–1939)
Essays NF
Published on 6 May 1924. Collected Edition volume iv.

1925

- David Lloyd George becomes Liberal leader (Jan.)
  Hindenburg becomes President of Germany
  Locarno pact
  The New Yorker started
- Brian Aldiss born
  Nina Bawden born
  John Bayley born
  Gerald Durrell born
  John Wain born
- A.C. Benson dies
  Mary Cholmondeley dies
  Sir Henry Rider Haggard dies
- George Curzon, Marquess Curzon of Kedleston, dies
- Pierre Boulez born
  Gore Vidal born
- John Dos Passos, *Manhattan Transfer*
  Gide, *Les Faux-Monnayeurs*
  Kafka, *The Trial* (posthumous)
- Eisenstein, *The Battleship Potemkin*

J.R. Ackerley (1896–1967)
The Prisoners of War D
Performed 5 July 1925

'Michael Arlen' [Dikran Kouyoumdjian (1895–1956)]
May Fair F
Stories

Jane Austen (1775–1817)
Lady Susan F
Written *c.*1805, first published in 1871 in *A Memoir of Jane Austen* (q.v.).

Jane Austen (1775–1817)
Sanditon F
See also *A Memoir of Jane Austen* 1871

Edmund Blunden (1896–1974)
Masks of Time V
Published in June 1925

Gordon Bottomley (1874–1948)
Poems of Thirty Years V

Elinor M. Brent-Dyer (1894–1969)
The School at the Chalet F
The first of the Chalet School series (59 books in all)

Robert Bridges (1844–1930)
New Verse Written in 1921 V
Published in December 1925

John Buchan (1875–1940)
John Macnab F

G.K. Chesterton (1874–1936)
The Everlasting Man NF
Published on 30 September 1925

I. Compton-Burnett (1884–1969)
Pastors and Masters F

Joseph Conrad (1857–1924)
Tales of Hearsay F
Published on 23 January 1925

Joseph Conrad (1857–1924)
Suspense F

Conrad's last, unfinished novel. Published on 16 September 1925. A version serialized in *Hutchinson's Magazine* (February–August 1925).

Noël Coward (1899–1973)
The Vortex D
Performed 25 November 1924

Noël Coward (1899–1973)
Hay Fever: A comedy D
Performed 8 June 1925

Anthony Berkeley Cox (1893–1971)
The Layton Court Mystery F
Anonymous. The first appearance of the detective Roger Sheringham.

Freeman Wills Crofts (1879–1957)
Inspector French's Greatest Case F
The first of the Inspector French novels

W.H. Davies (1871–1940)
A Poet's Alphabet V

C. Day Lewis (1904–72)
Beechen Vigil, and Other Poems V

Warwick Deeping (1877–1950)
Sorrell and Son F

Walter de la Mare (1873–1956)
Broomsticks, and Other Tales F
For children. Published in November 1925.

John Drinkwater (1882–1937)
Collected Plays D

Ford Madox Ford (1873–1939)
No More Parades F
Parade's End (Tietjens) Tetralogy ii. See also *Some Do Not* 1924, *A Man Could Stand Up* 1926, *Last Post* 1928.

William Gerhardie (1895–1977)
The Polyglots F

Robert Graves (1895–1985)
Welchman's Hose V

Graham Greene (1904–91)
Babbling April V
Published in April 1925

Thomas Hardy (1840–1928)
Human Shows, Far Phantasies, Songs and Trifles V
Published on 20 November 1925. The last of Hardy's works published during his lifetime.

Aldous Huxley (1894–1963)
Those Barren Leaves F

M.R. James (1862–1936)
A Warning to the Curious, and Other Ghost Stories F
Published in October 1925. See also *Ghost Stories of an Antiquary* 1904, *More Ghost Stories* 1911, *A Thin Ghost* 1919.

Harold Laski (1893–1950)
A Grammar of Politics NF

'Hugh MacDiarmid' [Christopher Murray Grieve (1892–1978)]
Sangshaw V

Arthur Machen (1863–1947)
The Shining Pyramid F

Compton Mackenzie (1883–1972)
Coral F
Sequel to *Carnival* 1912 (q.v.)

Somerset Maugham (1874–1965)
The Painted Veil F
Published on 23 April 1925

Naomi Mitchison (1897–1999)
Cloud Cuckoo Land F

George Moore (1852–1933)
Héloise and Abelard F
Published in November 1925

R.H. Mottram (1883–1971)
Sixty-Four, Ninety-Four! F
The Spanish Farm Trilogy ii. See also *The Spanish Farm* 1924, *The Crime at Vanderlynden's* 1926.

Edwin Muir (1887–1959)
First Poems V

John Middleton Murry (1889–1957)
Keats and Shakespeare NF

Sean O'Casey (1880–1964)
Two Plays D
Contains *Juno and the Paycock* (performed Abbey Theatre, Dublin, 3 March 1924) and *The Shadow of a Gunman* (performed Abbey Theatre, 12 April 1923)

Llewelyn Powys (1884–1939)
Black Laughter NF

Llewelyn Powys (1884–1939)
Skin for Skin NF

T.F. Powys (1875–1953)
Mr Tasker's Gods F

J.B. Priestley (1894–1984)
The English Comic Characters NF

Dorothy M. Richardson (1873–1957)
The Trap F
Pilgrimage sequence viii. See *Pilgrimage* 1938.

Edith Sitwell (1887–1964)
Troy Park V
Published on 12 March 1925

E[dith] Œ[none] Somerville (1858–1949) and **'Martin Ross' [Violet Martin** (1862–1915)]
The Big House of Inver F

Edgar Wallace (1875–1932)
The Mind of Mr J.G. Reeder F

Sylvia Townsend Warner (1893–1978)
The Espalier V

P.G. Wodehouse (1881–1975)
Carry On, Jeeves! F
Stories

Humbert Wolfe (1885–1940)
The Unknown Goddess V

Virginia Woolf (1882–1941)
The Common Reader [1st ser.] NF
Published on 23 April 1925. Second series published in 1932 (q.v.).

Virginia Woolf (1882–1941)
Mrs Dalloway F
Published on 14 May 1925

W.B. Yeats (1865–1939)
A Vision NF
Published on 15 January 1925. See also *A Vision* 1937.

1926

- General Strike in Britain (May)
  Trotsky expelled from the Politburo
  Book-of-the-Month Club started in the USA
- John Berger born
  J.P. Donleavy born
  John Fowles born
  Elizabeth Jennings born
  Christopher Logue born
  Peter Shaffer born
- Gertrude Bell dies
  Emma Frances Brooke dies
  Ada Cambridge dies
  Charles Montagu Doughty dies
  Ronald Firbank dies
  Sir Sidney Lee dies
  Israel Zangwill dies
- Princess Elizabeth, the future Elizabeth II, born
- Claude Monet dies
  Rudolph Valentino dies
- Theodore Dreiser, *An American Tragedy*
  William Faulkner, *Soldiers' Pay*
  Pollard and Redgrave, *Short-Title Catalogue of English Books 1475–1640*

H.E. Bates (1905–74)
The Two Sisters F
Published on 24 June 1926

Edmund Blunden (1896–1974)
English Poems V
Published in January 1926

Robert Byron (1905–41)
Europe in the Looking-Glass NF

G.K. Chesterton (1874–1936)
The Incredulity of Father Brown F
Published in June 1926. See also *The Innocence of Father Brown* 1911, *The Wisdom of Father Brown* 1914, *The Secret of Father Brown* 1927, *The Scandal of Father Brown* 1935.

Agatha Christie (1890–1976)
The Murder of Roger Ackroyd F

W.H. Davies (1871–1940)
The Birth of Song V

Walter de la Mare (1873–1956)
The Connoisseur, and Other Stories F
Published in May 1926

A. Conan Doyle (1859–1930)
The Land of Mist F
Published on 19 March 1926. Serialized in the *Strand Magazine* (July 1925–March 1926). See also *The Lost World* 1912, *The Poison Belt* 1913.

Ronald Firbank (1886–1926)
Concerning the Eccentricities of Cardinal Pirelli F

Ford Madox Ford (1873–1939)
A Man Could Stand Up F
Parade's End (Tietjens) Tetralogy iii. See also *Some Do Not* 1924, *No More Parades* 1925, *Last Post* 1928.

'C.S. Forester' [Cecil Louis Troughton Smith (1899–1966)]
Payment Deferred F

H.W. Fowler (1858–1933) and **F.G. Fowler** (1870–1918)
A Dictionary of Modern English Usage DICT

'Henry Green' [Henry Vincent Yorke (1905–73)]
Blindness F

Patrick Hamilton (1904–62)
Craven House F

L.P. Jacks (1860–1955)
The Heroes of Smokeover F
See also *Last Legend of Smokeover* 1939

Rudyard Kipling (1865–1936)
Debits and Credits F
Stories

D.H. Lawrence (1885–1930)
The Plumed Serpent (Quetzalcoatl) F
Published in January 1926

T.E. Lawrence (1888–1935)
Seven Pillars of Wisdom NF
First published in an edition of eight copies in 1922. See also *Revolt in the Desert* 1927, *Seven Pillars of Wisdom* 1935.

'Hugh MacDiarmid' [Christopher Murray Grieve (1892–1978)]
A Drunk Man Looks at the Thistle V

'Hugh MacDiarmid' [Christopher Murray Grieve (1892–1978)]
Penny Wheep V

Somerset Maugham (1874–1965)
The Casuarina Tree F
Published on 2 September 1926

A.A. Milne (1882–1956)
Winnie-the-Pooh F

James Moffatt (1870–1944) (tr.)
The Bible BIB
See also *The New Testament* 1913, *The Old Testament* 1924

R.H. Mottram (1883–1971)
The Crime at Vanderlynden's F
The Spanish Farm Trilogy iii. See also *The Spanish Farm* 1924, *Sixty-Four, Ninety-Four!* 1925.

Edwin Muir (1887–1959)
Chorus of the Newly Dead V

Sean O'Casey (1880–1964)
The Plough and the Stars D
Performed at the Abbey Theatre, Dublin, 8 February 1926

William Plomer (1903–73)
Turbott Wolfe F

Herbert Read (1893–1968)
Reason and Romanticism NF

Laura Riding (1901–91)
The Close Chaplet V

Vita Sackville-West (1892–1962)
The Land V
Published in September 1926

Siegfried Sassoon (1886–1967)
Satirical Poems V

Dorothy L. Sayers (1893–1957)
Clouds of Witness F

'Nevil Shute' [Nevil Shute Norway (1899–1960)]
Marazan F

G.M. Trevelyan (1876–1962)
History of England NF

Hugh Walpole (1884–1941)
Harmer John F

Sylvia Townsend Warner (1893–1978)
Lolly Willowes; or, The Loving Huntsman F

Alec Waugh (1898–1981)
Love in These Days F

Beatrice Webb (1858–1943)
My Apprenticeship NF

H.G. Wells (1866–1946)
The World of William Clissold F

Humbert Wolfe (1885–1940)
Humoresque V

Humbert Wolfe (1885–1940)
News of the Devil V

P.C. Wren (1885–1941)
Beau Sabreur F
See also *Beau Geste* 1924, *Beau Ideal* 1928

W.B. Yeats (1865–1939)
Autobiographies NF
Published on 5 November 1926. Collected Edition volume vi. See also *Later Poems* 1922, *Plays in Prose and Verse* 1922, *Plays and Controversies* 1923, *Essays* 1924, *Autobiography* 1938.

1927

- Economic collapse in Germany
  Charles Lindbergh flies from New York to Paris
- Ruth Prawer Jhabvala born
  R.D. Laing born
  Simon Raven born
  Charles Tomlinson born
  Kenneth Tynan born
- Sir Sidney Colvin dies
  Jerome K. Jerome dies
  William Le Queux dies
  Mary Webb dies

- Ernest Hemingway, *Men Without Women*
  Sinclair Lewis, *Elmer Gantry*
  Thornton Wilder, *The Bridge of San Luis Rey*

E.F. Benson (1867–1940)
Lucia in London F
See also *Queen Lucia* 1920, *Miss Mapp* 1922, *Mapp and Lucia* 1931, *Lucia's Progress* 1935

John Buchan (1875–1940)
Witch Wood F

G.K. Chesterton (1874–1936)
Collected Poems V
Published in June 1927

G.K. Chesterton (1874–1936)
The Secret of Father Brown F
Published in September 1927. See also *The Innocence of Father Brown* 1911, *The Wisdom of Father Brown* 1914, *The Incredulity of Father Brown* 1926, *The Scandal of Father Brown* 1935.

W.H. Davies (1871–1940)
A Poet's Calendar V

Ethel M. Dell (1881–1939)
By Request F
Sequel to *The Way of an Eagle* 1912 and *The Keeper of the Door* 1915 (qq.v.)

A. Conan Doyle (1859–1930)
The Case-Book of Sherlock Holmes F
Published on 16 June 1927. Stories first published in the *Strand Magazine* 1921–7. See also *A Study in Scarlet* 1888, *The Sign of Four* 1890, *Adventures of Sherlock Holmes* 1892, *Memoirs of Sherlock Holmes* 1893, The *Hound of the Baskervilles* 1902, *Return of Sherlock Holmes* 1905, *The Valley of Fear* 1915, *His Last Bow* 1917.

J.W. Dunne (1875–1949)
An Experiment with Time NF

T.S. Eliot (1888–1965)
Journey of the Magi V
Published on 25 August 1927

E.M. Forster (1879–1970)
Aspects of the Novel NF
Published on 20 October 1927

Pamela Frankau (1908–1967)
The Marriage of Harlequin F

John Galsworthy (1867–1933)
Two Forsyte Interludes F

William Gerhardie (1895–1977)
Pretty Creatures F
Stories

Harley Granville-Barker (1877–1946)
Prefaces to Shakespeare NF
Based on *Prefaces to the Players' Shakespeare* (see 1923) with additional prefaces

Robert Graves (1895–1985)
Lars Porsena; or, The Future of Swearing and Improper Language NF

Robert Graves (1895–1985)
Poems 1914–26 V

Robert Graves (1895–1985) and **Laura Riding** (1901–91)
A Survey of Modernist Poetry NF

Winifred Holtby (1898–1935)
The Land of Green Ginger F

Storm Jameson (1897–1986)
The Lovely Ship F
The Triumph of Time Trilogy i. Followed by *The Voyage Home* 1930, *A Richer Dust* 1931, *The Triumph of Time* 1932.

James Joyce (1882–1941)
Pomes Penyeach V
Published in Paris

D.H. Lawrence (1885–1930)
Mornings in Mexico NF

T.E. Lawrence (1888–1935)
Revolt in the Desert NF
An abridgement of *Seven Pillars of Wisdom* 1926 (q.v.). See also *Seven Pillars of Wisdom* 1935.

Rosamond Lehmann (1901–90)
Dusty Answer F

Wyndham Lewis (1882–1957)
Time and Western Man NF

'Katherine Mansfield' [Kathleen Mansfield Beauchamp (1888–1923)]
Journal NF
Edited by John Middleton Murry

A.A. Milne (1882–1956)
Now We Are Six V

George Moore (1852–1933)
Celibate Lives F
Stories

H.V. Morton (1892–1979)
In Search of England NF
First of the 'In Search of' series

William Plomer (1903–73)
I Speak of Africa F
Stories

J.B. Priestley (1894–1984)
Adam in Moonshine F

J.B. Priestley (1894–1984)
The English Novel NF

'Jean Rhys' [Ella Gwendolen Rhys Williams (1890–1979)]
The Left Bank, and Other Stories F
Preface by Ford Madox Ford

Dorothy M. Richardson (1873–1957)
Oberland F
Pilgrimage sequence ix. See *Pilgrimage* 1938.

Edith Sitwell (1887–1964)
Rustic Elegies V
Published in March 1927

Osbert Sitwell (1892–1969)
England Reclaimed V
Published on 20 October 1927. See also *Wrack at Tidesend* 1952, *On the Continent* 1958.

Sylvia Townsend Warner (1893–1978)
Mr Fortune's Maggot F

Henry Williamson (1895–1977)
Tarka the Otter F

Humbert Wolfe (1885–1940)
Cursory Rhymes V

Humbert Wolfe (1885–1940)
Requiem V

Virginia Woolf (1882–1941)
To the Lighthouse F
Published on 5 May 1927

W.B. Yeats (1865–1939)
October Blast V
Published in August 1927. Contains 'Sailing to Byzantium'.

W.B. Yeats (1865–1939)
Stories of Red Hanrahan and the Secret Rose V/F
Published on 11 November 1927

1928

- Women's suffrage in Britain reduced to the age of 21
  Alexander Fleming discovers penicillin
- Evelyn Anthony (Evelyn Ward-Thomas) born
  Stan Barstow born
  Anita Brookner born
  Jane Gardam born
  David Mercer born
  Bernice Rubens born
  Tom Sharpe born
  Alan Sillitoe born
  William Trevor (William Trevor Cox) born
- Sir Edmund Gosse dies
  Thomas Hardy dies
  Jane Harrison dies
  Charlotte Mew dies
  C.E. Montague dies
  Barry Pain (Eric Odell) dies
  Sir George Trevelyan dies
  Stanley Weyman dies
- Upton Sinclair, *Boston*
  George Gershwin, *An American in Paris*
  Ravel, *Bolero*
  Kurt Weill and Bertolt Brecht, *The Threepenny Opera*

Sir J.M. Barrie (1860–1937)
The Plays of J.M. Barrie D

Edmund Blunden (1896–1974)
Undertones of War MISC
Published in November 1928

'Ernest Bramah' [Ernest Bramah Smith (1868–1942)]
Kai Lung Unrolls his Mat F
Stories. See also *The Wallet of Kai Lung* 1900.

John Buchan (1875–1940)
The Runagates Club F
Stories

Roy Campbell (1901–57)
The Wayzgoose V

Kenneth Clark (1903–83)
The Gothic Revival NF
Revised and enlarged, 1950

W.H. Davies (1871–1940)
Collected Poems V
See also *Collected Poems*, 1st series, 1916; 2nd series, 1923; *Poems* 1934

T.S. Eliot (1888–1965)
For Lancelot Andrewes NF
Published on 20 November 1928

Ford Madox Ford (1873–1939)
Last Post F
Parade's End (Tietjens) Tetralogy iv. See also *Some Do Not* 1924, *No More Parades* 1925, *A Man Could Stand Up* 1926.

E.M. Forster (1879–1970)
The Eternal Moment, and Other Stories F
Published on 27 March 1928

William Gerhardie (1895–1977)
Jazz and Jasper F

Robert Graves (1895–1985)
Mrs Fisher; or, The Future of Humour NF

'Radclyffe Hall' [Marguerite Antonia Radclyffe-Hall (1880–1943)]
The Well of Loneliness F

Thomas Hardy (1840–1928)
The Short Stories of Thomas Hardy F
Published posthumously on 23 March 1928

Thomas Hardy (1840–1928)
Winter Words in Various Moods and Metres V
Published posthumously on 2 October 1928

Thomas Hardy (1840–1928)
The Early Life of Thomas Hardy 1840–1891 NF
Published posthumously on 2 November 1928. Supposedly compiled by Hardy's wife, Florence Emily Hardy (1879–1937), this is in reality Hardy's autobiography. See also *The Later Years of Thomas Hardy* 1930.

Aldous Huxley (1894–1963)
Point Counter Point F

Christopher Isherwood (1904–86)
All the Conspirators F

D.H. Lawrence (1885–1930)
The Woman Who Rode Away, and Other Stories F
Published on 24 May 1928

D.H. Lawrence (1885–1930)
Lady Chatterley's Lover F
Published in July 1928, privately printed in Florence. See also *Lady Chatterley's Lover* 1929, 1932, 1933, 1960.

D.H. Lawrence (1885–1930)
Collected Poems V
Published in September 1928

Wyndham Lewis (1882–1957)
The Childermass F
Revised in 1956 as book i of The Human Age Trilogy. See *Monstre Gai. Malign Fiesta* 1955.

John Masefield (1878–1967)
Midsummer Night, and Other Tales in Verse V

Somerset Maugham (1874–1965)
Ashenden; or, The British Agent F
Stories. Published on 29 March 1928.

Somerset Maugham (1874–1965)
The Sacred Flame D
Performed in New York, 19 November 1928, and in London on 8 February 1929

A.A. Milne (1882–1956)
The House at Pooh Corner F

Naomi Mitchison (1897–1999)
Black Sparta F
Stories

George Moore (1852–1933)
The Making of an Immortal D
Published on 8 December 1928. Performed 1 April 1928.

Edwin Muir (1887–1959)
The Structure of the Novel NF

E[dith] Nesbit (1858–1924)
The Complete History of the Bastable Family F
See also *Treasure Seekers* 1899, *The Would-Be-Goods* 1901, *New Treasure Seekers* 1904

Sean O'Casey (1880–1964)
The Silver Tassie: A tragi-comedy D
Performed 11 October 1929

T.F. Powys (1875–1953)
The House with the Echo F
Stories

T.F. Powys (1875–1953)
Mr Weston's Good Wine F

J.B. Priestley (1894–1984)
Apes and Angels NF

V.S. Pritchett (1900–97)
Marching Spain NF

'Jean Rhys' [Ella Gwendolen Rhys Williams (1890–1979)]
Postures F

Laura Riding (1901–91)
Love as Love, Death as Death V

Lennox Robinson (1886–1958)
The Big House D

Siegfried Sassoon (1886–1967)
The Heart's Journey V

Siegfried Sassoon (1886–1967)
Memoirs of a Fox-Hunting Man F
Anonymous fictionalized autobiography. See also *Memoirs of an Infantry-Officer* 1930, *Sherston's Progress* 1936, *The Complete Memoirs of George Sherston* 1937.

Dorothy L. Sayers (1893–1957)
The Unpleasantness at the Bellona Club F

Bernard Shaw (1856–1950)
The Intelligent Woman's Guide to Socialism and Capitalism NF
Published on 1 June 1928

A.J.A. Symons (1900–41) (ed.)
An Anthology of 'Nineties' Verse ANTH

Evelyn Waugh (1903–66)
Decline and Fall F

Henry Williamson (1895–1977)
The Pathway F
The Flax of Dream sequence iv. See *The Beautiful Years* 1921, *Dandelion Days* 1922, *The Dream of Fair Women* 1924; revised and published together as *The Flax of Dream* 1936.

Humbert Wolfe (1885–1940)
The Silver Cat, and Other Poems V

Humbert Wolfe (1885–1940)
This Blind Rose V

Virginia Woolf (1882–1941)
Orlando: A biography F
Published on 11 October 1928

P.C. Wren (1885–1941)
Beau Ideal F
See also *Beau Geste* 1924, *Beau Sabreur* 1926

W.B. Yeats (1865–1939)
The Tower V
Published on 14 February 1928

W.B. Yeats (1865–1939)
The Death of Synge, and Other Passages from an Old Diary V
Published in June 1928

1929

- Trotsky exiled (Jan.)
  Herbert Hoover becomes President of the USA
  The Wall Street Crash (29 October): beginning of the Great Depression
  Ramsay MacDonald becomes British Prime Minister
  First Academy Awards (Oscars) ceremony
- Lynne Reid Banks born
  Brigid Brophy born
  Len Deighton born
  U.A. Fanthorpe born
  Thom Gunn born
  John Osborne born
  Peter Porter born
  George Steiner born
  Keith Waterhouse born
  Robert Westall born
- Edward Carpenter dies
  Lucy Clifford dies
  Henry Arthur Jones dies
  Flora Annie Steel dies
- Martin Luther King born
- Cocteau, *Les Enfants terribles*
  William Faulkner, *The Sound and the Fury*
  Ernest Hemingway, *A Farewell to Arms*
  Thomas Wolfe, *Look Homeward Angel*
  Remarque, *Im Westen nichts Neues* (All Quiet on the Western Front)

Richard Aldington (1892–1962)
Death of a Hero F

Margery Allingham (1904–66)
The Crime at Black Dudley F

Edmund Blunden (1896–1974)
Near and Far V
Published on 26 September 1929

Gordon Bottomley (1874–1948)
Scenes and Plays D

Elizabeth Bowen (1899–1973)
Joining Charles, and Other Stories F

Elizabeth Bowen (1899–1973)
The Last September F

Robert Bridges (1844–1930)
The Testament of Beauty V
Published on 24 October 1929

Lord David Cecil (1902–86)
The Stricken Deer; or, The Life of Cowper NF

I. Compton-Burnett (1884–1969)
Brothers and Sisters F

Noël Coward (1899–1973)
Bitter Sweet D
Performed in Manchester, 2 July 1929, and in London on 18 July 1929

'Anthony Berkeley' [Anthony Berkeley Cox (1893–1971)]
The Poisoned Chocolates Case F

W.H. Davies (1871–1940)
Ambition, and Other Poems V

C. Day Lewis (1904–72)
Transitional Poem V

T.S. Eliot (1888–1965)
Animula V
Published on 9 October 1929

John Galsworthy (1867–1933)
Four Forsyte Stories F

John Galsworthy (1867–1933)
A Modern Comedy F

Robert Graves (1895–1985)
Goodbye to All That NF
See also *But It Still Goes On* 1930

'Henry Green' [Henry Vincent Yorke (1905–73)]
Living F

Graham Greene (1904–91)
The Man Within F
Published in June 1929. Greene's first published novel.

Richard Hughes (1900–76)
A High Wind in Jamaica F

Aldous Huxley (1894–1963)
Arabia Infelix, and Other Poems V

Aldous Huxley (1894–1963)
Holy Face, and Other Essays NF

F. Tennyson Jesse (1888–1958)
The Lacquer Lady F

D.H. Lawrence (1885–1930)
Lady Chatterley's Lover F
Published in May 1929 in Paris. Also includes the essay 'My Skirmish with Jolly Roger' on the various piracies of the novel. See also *Lady Chatterley's Lover* 1928, 1932, 1933, 1960; and *A Propos of Lady Chatterley's Lover* 1930.

D.H. Lawrence (1885–1930)
Pansies V
Published in July 1929

D.H. Lawrence (1885–1930)
Pornography and Obscenity NF
Published on 14 November 1929

Wyndham Lewis (1882–1957)
Paleface: The philosophy of the 'melting pot' NF

Eric Linklater (1899–1974)
White-Maa's Saga F

Louis MacNeice (1907–1963)
Blind Fireworks V

Charlotte Mew (1869–1928)
The Rambling Sailor V

A.A. Milne (1882–1956) (adap.)
Toad of Toad Hall D
Performed 17 December 1930. Adapted from *The Wind in the Willows* 1908 (q.v.).

Gladys Mitchell (1901–83)
Speedy Death F
First of the Beatrice Lestrange Bradley novels

Charles Morgan (1894–1958)
Portrait in a Mirror F

C.K. Ogden (1889–1957)
The ABC of Psychology NF

William Plomer (1903–73)
The Family Tree V

William Plomer (1903–73)
Paper Houses F
Stories

John Cowper Powys (1872–1963)
Wolf Solent F

Llewelyn Powys (1884–1939)
The Cradle of God NF

J.B. Priestley (1894–1984)
The Good Companions F
Later dramatized (with Edward Knoblock), performed 14 May 1931

V.S. Pritchett (1900–97)
Clare Drummer F

I.A. Richards (1893–1979)
Practical Criticism NF

R.C. Sherriff (1896–1975)
Journey's End D
Performed 10 December 1928.
Subsequently a novel (1930), written with V. Bartlett.

Alison Uttley (1884–1976)
The Squirrel, the Hare, and the Little Grey Rabbit F
First of the Little Grey Rabbit books. Illustrated by Margaret Tempest.

Sylvia Townsend Warner (1893–1978)
The True Heart F

Alec Waugh (1898–1981)
Three Score and Ten F

H.G. Wells (1866–1946)
The Science of Life NF

T.H. White (1906–64)
Loved Helen, and Other Poems V

P.G. Wodehouse (1881–1975)
Summer Lightning F

Virginia Woolf (1882–1941)
A Room of One's Own NF
Published on 24 October 1929

Sir Leonard Woolley (1880–1960)
Ur of the Chaldees NF

W.B. Yeats (1865–1939)
A Packet for Ezra Pound V
Published in August 1929

1930

- Gandhi begins campaign of civil disobedience in India
  Hitler's National Socialist Workers Party becomes second strongest party in the German parliament
  Prince Ras Tafari becomes Emperor Haile Selassie of Abyssinia
- John Arden born
  J.G. Ballard born
  Elaine Feinstein born
  Roy Fisher born
  Ted Hughes born
  Harold Pinter born
  Ruth Rendell born
  Jon Silkin born
  Anthony Thwaite born
- Arthur St John Adcock dies
  A.J. Balfour dies
  Florence Bell dies
  Robert Bridges dies
  Sir Arthur Conan Doyle dies
  D.H. Lawrence dies
- William Faulkner, *As I Lay Dying*
  John Dos Passos, *42nd Parallel*
- *The Blue Angel* (starring Marlene Dietrich)

Rodney Ackland (1908–91)
Improper People D

W.H. Auden (1907–73)
Poems V
Published on 18 September 1930

Samuel Beckett (1906–89)
Whoroscope V
Beckett's first separately published work

Hilaire Belloc (1870–1953)
New Cautionary Tales V
Illustrated by Nicholas Bentley. See *Cautionary Tales for Children* 1908.

Arnold Bennett (1867–1931)
Imperial Palace F

Arnold Bennett (1867–1931)
Journal, 1929 NF

Edmund Blunden (1896–1974)
The Poems of Edmund Blunden V
Published in December 1930

'James Bridie' [Osborne Henry Mavor (1888–1951)]
The Switchback; The Pardoner's Tale; The Sunlight Sonata D
The Switchback performed 9 March 1929; *The Sunlight Sonata* performed 20 March 1928

Roy Campbell (1901–57)
Adamastor V

Winston Spencer Churchill (1874–1965)
My Early Life NF

John Collier (1901–80)
His Monkey Wife; or, Married to a Chimp F

Noël Coward (1899–1973)
Private Lives: An intimate comedy D
Performed in Edinburgh, 18 August 1930, and in London on 24 September 1930

'E.M. Delafield' [Edmée Monica de la Pasture (1890–1943)]
Diary of a Provincial Lady F

Walter de la Mare (1873–1956)
On the Edge F
Stories. Published in September 1930.

T.S. Eliot (1888–1965)
Ash-Wednesday V
Published on 29 April 1930

T.S. Eliot (1888–1965)
Marina V
Published on 25 September 1930

William Empson (1906–84)
Seven Types of Ambiguity NF

Marjorie Firminger (1899–1976)
Jam To-Day F
Published 1930, dated 1931. A epistolary *roman-à-clef*, banned in England for obscenity. The author was a model for Valerie Ritter in Wyndham Lewis's *Snooty Baronet* 1932 (q.v.).

John Galsworthy (1867–1933)
On Forsyte 'Change F
Stories

John Galsworthy (1867–1933)
Soames and the Flag F
See *The Forsyte Saga* 1922

William Gerhardie (1895–1977)
Pending Heaven F

'Lewis Grassic Gibbon' [James Leslie Mitchell (1901–35)]
Stained Radiance F
As James Leslie Mitchell

Stella Gibbons (1902–89)
The Mountain Beast, and Other Poems V

Robert Graves (1895–1985)
But It Still Goes On NF
Sequel to *Goodbye to All That* 1929 (q.v.)

Graham Greene (1904–91)
The Name of Action F
Published in October 1930

James Hanley (1901–85)
Drift F

Thomas Hardy (1840–1928)
The Later Years of Thomas Hardy 1892–1928 NF
Published on 29 April 1930. Like *The Early Life of Thomas Hardy* 1928 (q.v.), this is in reality an autobiography.

Gerard Manley Hopkins (1844–89)
Poems of Gerard Manley Hopkins V
Edited by Charles Williams. See also *Poems* 1918.

Aldous Huxley (1894–1963)
Brief Candles F
Stories

James Joyce (1882–1941)
Anna Livia Plurabelle F

Margaret Kennedy (1896–1967)
The Fool of the Family F
Sequel to *The Constant Nymph* 1924 (q.v.)

J.M. Keynes (1883–1946)
A Treatise on Money NF

G. Wilson Knight (1897–1985)
The Wheel of Fire NF
See also *The Imperial Theme* 1931, *The Crown of Life* 1947, *The Mutual Flame* 1955

D.H. Lawrence (1885–1930)
Nettles V
Published on 13 March 1930, soon after Lawrence's death on 2 March

D.H. Lawrence (1885–1930)
A Propos of Lady Chatterley's Lover NF
Published on 24 June 1930

D.H. Lawrence (1885–1930)
The Triumph of the Machine V
Published in October 1930

D.H. Lawrence (1885–1930)
The Virgin and the Gypsy F
Published in October 1930

D.H. Lawrence (1885–1930)
Love Among the Haystacks NF
Published on 25 November 1930

Wyndham Lewis (1882–1957)
The Apes of God F

'Hugh MacDiarmid' [Christopher Murray Grieve (1892–1978)]
To Circumjack Cencrastus; or, The Curly Snake V
In English and Scots

Somerset Maugham (1874–1965)
Cakes and Ale; or, The Skeleton in the Cupboard F
Published on 29 September 1930

Somerset Maugham (1874–1965)
The Bread-Winner: A comedy D
Performed 30 September 1930

George Moore (1852–1933)
The Passing of the Essenes D
Published on 20 September 1930. Performed 1 October 1930. A revision of *The Apostle* 1911 (q.v.).

George Moore (1852–1933)
Aphrodite in Aulis F
Published on 1 December 1930

C.K. Ogden (1889–1957)
Basic English NF

J.B. Priestley (1894–1984)
Angel Pavement F

V.S. Pritchett (1900–97)
The Spanish Virgin, and Other Stories F

Arthur Ransome (1884–1967)
Swallows and Amazons F

'Æ' [George William Russell (1867–1935)]
Enchantment, and Other Poems V

Vita Sackville-West (1892–1962)
The Edwardians F

Siegfried Sassoon (1886–1967)
In Sicily V

Siegfried Sassoon (1886–1967)
Memoirs of an Infantry-Officer F
Fictionalized autobiography, bao *Memoirs of a Fox-Hunting Man* 1928 (q.v.). See also *Sherston's Progress* 1936, *The Complete Memoirs of George Sherston* 1937.

Bernard Shaw (1856–1950)
Immaturity F
Published on 26 July 1930. Shaw's first novel, written in 1879 and here silently revised.

Bernard Shaw (1856–1950)
The Apple Cart: A political extravaganza D
Published on 11 December 1930. Performed in Warsaw, 14 June 1929, and at the Malvern Festival on 19 August 1929.

Edith Sitwell (1887–1964)
Collected Poems V
Published on 5 June 1930

Stephen Spender (1909–95)
Twenty Poems V

H.M. Tomlinson (1873–1958)
All Our Yesterdays F

Hugh Walpole (1884–1941)
Rogue Herries F
Herries Chronicle i. See also *Judith Paris* 1931, *The Fortress* 1932, *Vanessa* 1933.

Alec Waugh (1898–1981)
'"Sir", She Said' F
Revised in 1977 as *Love in Conflict*

Evelyn Waugh (1903–66)
Vile Bodies F

Charles Williams (1886–1945)
War in Heaven F

P.G. Wodehouse (1881–1975)
Very Good, Jeeves F
Stories

Humbert Wolfe (1885–1940)
The Uncelestial City V

1931

- Ramsay MacDonald becomes British Prime Minister for the third time
  Spain becomes a republic on the abdication of Alfonso XIII
  Britain abandons the gold standard
- Alan Brownjohn born
  Isabel Colegate born
  P.J. Kavanagh born
  John le Carré (David John Moore Cornwell) born
  Peter Levi born
  Frederic Raphael born
  Fay Weldon born
- Arnold Bennett dies
  Sir Hall Caine dies
  Mary St Leger Harrison ('Lucas Malet') dies
  Katharine Tynan dies
- Eugene O'Neill, *Mourning Becomes Electra*

Samuel Beckett (1906–89)
Proust NF

E.F. Benson (1867–1940)
Mapp and Lucia F
See also *Queen Lucia* 1920, *Miss Mapp* 1922, *Lucia in London* 1927, *Lucia's Progress* 1935

John Betjeman (1906–84)
Mount Zion; or, In Touch with the Infinite V

Laurence Binyon (1869–1943)
Collected Poems V

Edmund Blunden (1896–1974)
Themis V
Published in December 1931

Robert Bridges (1844–1930)
Shorter Poems V

'James Bridie' [Osborne Henry Mavor (1888–1951)]
The Anatomist, and Other Plays D

Roy Campbell (1901–57)
The Georgiad V

I. Compton-Burnett (1884–1969)
Men and Wives F

A.E. Coppard (1878–1957)
Nixey's Harlequin F
Stories

A.J. Cronin (1896–1981)
Hatter's Castle F

C. Day Lewis (1904–72)
From Feathers to Iron V

Daphne du Maurier (1907–89)
The Loving Spirit F

T.S. Eliot (1888–1965)
Triumphal March V
Published on 8 October 1931

William Gerhardie (1895–1977)
Memoirs of a Polyglot NF

Robert Graves (1895–1985)
Poems 1926–1930 V

Graham Greene (1904–91)
Rumour at Nightfall F
Published in November 1931

James Hanley (1901–85)
Boy F
Published in October 1931. Hanley was prosecuted for obscenity in March 1935.

James Hilton (1900–54)
And Now Good-bye F

Aldous Huxley (1894–1963)
The Cicadas, and Other Poems V

Aldous Huxley (1894–1963)
The World of Light: A comedy V
Performed 30 March 1931

G. Wilson Knight (1897–1985)
The Imperial Theme NF
See also *The Wheel of Fire* 1930, *The Crown of Life* 1947, *The Mutual Flame* 1955

D.H. Lawrence (1885–1930)
The Man Who Died F
Novelette. Published in March 1931.

John Lehmann (1907–87)
A Garden Revisited, and Other Poems V

'Hugh MacDiarmid' [Christopher Murray Grieve (1892–1978)]
First Hymn to Lenin, and Other Poems V
Introductory essay by 'Æ' [George William Russell]. See also *Second Hymn to Lenin* 1932.

Somerset Maugham (1874–1965)
Six Stories Written in the First Person Singular F
Published on 28 September 1931

Naomi Mitchison (1897–1999)
The Corn King and the Spring Queen F

Nancy Mitford (1904–73)
Highland Fling F

Kate O'Brien (1897–1974)
Without my Cloak F

'Frank O'Connor' [Michael Francis O'Donovan (1903–66)]
Guests of the Nation F
Stories

Anthony Powell (1905–2000)
Afternoon Men F

Llewelyn Powys (1884–1939)
Impassioned Clay NF

Llewelyn Powys (1884–1939)
A Pagan's Pilgrimage NF

Herbert Read (1893–1968)
The Meaning of Art NF

Forrest Reid (1875–1947)
Uncle Stephen F
Tom Barber Trilogy i, followed by *The Retreat* 1936 and *Young Tom* 1944

Dorothy M. Richardson (1873–1957)
Dawn's Left Hand F
Pilgrimage sequence x. See *Pilgrimage* 1938.

'Æ' [George William Russell (1867–1935)]
Vale, and Other Poems V

Vita Sackville-West (1892–1962)
All Passion Spent F

Bernard Shaw (1856–1950)
Complete Plays D
Published on 14 May 1931

Osbert Sitwell (1892–1969)
The Collected Satires and Poems V
Published on 2 June 1931

'C.L. Anthony' [Dodie Smith (1896–1990)]
Autumn Crocus D
Performed 6 April 1931

Logan Pearsall Smith (1865–1946)
Afterthoughts NF
See also *Trivia* 1918, *More Trivia* 1922

William Soutar (1898–1943)
Conflict V

Arthur Symons (1865–1945)
Jezebel Mort, and Other Poems V

Hugh Walpole (1884–1941)
Judith Paris F
Herries Chronicle ii. See also *Rogue Herries* 1930, *The Fortress* 1932, *Vanessa* 1933.

Sylvia Townsend Warner (1893–1978)
A Moral Ending, and Other Stories F

Evelyn Waugh (1903–66)
Remote People NF

Charles Williams (1886–1945)
Many Dimensions F

Charles Williams (1886–1945)
The Place of the Lion F

Humbert Wolfe (1885–1940)
Snow V

Virginia Woolf (1882–1941)
The Waves F
Published on 8 October 1931

1932

- Nazis become strongest party in the German parliament
  Éamon de Valéra becomes President of Ireland
  F.D. Roosevelt becomes President of the USA
  Charles Lindbergh's son kidnapped
- Malcolm Bradbury born
  Alice Thomas Ellis born
  Eva Figes born
  Penelope Gilliat born
  Adrian Henri born
  Geoffrey Hill born
  George MacBeth born
  Adrian Mitchell born
  V.S. Naipaul born
  Edna O'Brien born
  Sylvia Plath born
  Arnold Wesker born
- Mona Caird dies
  W.G. Collingwood dies
  Goldsworthy Lowes Dickinson dies
  John Meade Falkner dies
  Kenneth Grahame dies
  Isabella, Lady Gregory, dies
  Lytton Strachey dies
  Edgar Wallace dies
- Ernest Hemingway, *Death in the Afternoon*

Scrutiny PER
Published quarterly, 1932–53. Dominated editorially by F.R. and Q.D. Leavis.

W.H. Auden (1907–73)
The Orators: An English study V
Published on 19 May 1932

Arnold Bennett (1867–1931)
The Journals of Arnold Bennett NF

Edmund Blunden (1896–1974)
Halfway House V
Published on 4 November 1932

John Buchan (1875–1940)
The Gap in the Curtain F
Published in July 1932

Roy Campbell (1901–57)
Pomegranates V

Joyce Cary (1888–1957)
Aissa Saved F

A.E. Coppard (1878–1957)
Crotty Shinkwin F
Stories

Noël Coward (1899–1973)
Cavalcade D
Performed 13 October 1931

W.H. Davies (1871–1940)
Poems, 1930–31 V

Lawrence Durrell (1912–90)
Ten Poems V

T.S. Eliot (1888–1965)
Selected Essays 1917–1932 NF
Published on 15 September 1932

T.S. Eliot (1888–1965)
Sweeney Agonistes: Fragments of an Aristophanic melodrama D
Published on 1 December 1932

David Gascoyne (1916)
Roman Balcony, and Other Poems V

'Lewis Grassic Gibbon' [James Leslie Mitchell (1901–35)**]**
Sunset Song F
A Scots Quair Trilogy i, followed by *Cloud Howe* 1933 and *Grey Granite* 1934. Published together as *A Scots Quair* in 1946.

Stella Gibbons (1902–89)
Cold Comfort Farm F
See also *Christmas at Cold Comfort Farm* 1940, *Conference at Cold Comfort Farm* 1949

Graham Greene (1904–91)
Stamboul Train F
Published in December 1932

[Basil] Liddell Hart (1895–1970)
The British Way in Warfare NF

L.P. Hartley (1895–1971)
The Killing Bottle F
Stories

Aldous Huxley (1894–1963)
Brave New World F
See also *Brave New World Revisited* 1959

Christopher Isherwood (1904–86)
The Memorial F

W.E. Johns (1893–1968)
The Camels Are Coming F
The first collection of Biggles stories. See also *Worrals of the WAAF* 1941.

Rudyard Kipling (1865–1936)
Limits and Renewals F
Stories

Ronald Knox (1888–1957)
Broadcast Minds NF

Criticism of science popularizers such as Julian Huxley and H.G. Wells

D.H. Lawrence (1885–1930)
Lady Chatterley's Lover F
Published in February 1932. The first authorized English edition (expurgated). See also *Lady Chatterley's Lover* 1928, 1929, 1933, 1960.

D.H. Lawrence (1885–1930)
Etruscan Places NF
Published in September 1932

D.H. Lawrence (1885–1930)
The Letters of D.H. Lawrence NF
Published on 26 September 1932. Edited by Aldous Huxley.

F.R. Leavis (1895–1978)
New Bearings in English Poetry NF

Rosamond Lehmann (1901–90)
Invitation to the Waltz F

Wyndham Lewis (1882–1957)
Enemy of the Stars D

Wyndham Lewis (1882–1957)
Snooty Baronet F

Rose Macaulay (1881–1958)
They Were Defeated F

'Hugh MacDiarmid' [Christopher Murray Grieve (1892–1978)]
Second Hymn to Lenin, and Other Poems V
See *First Hymn to Lenin* 1931

Somerset Maugham (1874–1965)
The Narrow Corner F
Published on 7 November 1932

Somerset Maugham (1874–1965)
For Services Rendered D
Published on 14 December 1932. Performed 1 November 1932.

Charles Morgan (1894–1958)
The Fountain F

'Frank O'Connor' [Michael Francis O'Donovan (1903–66)]
The Saint and Mary Kate F

Sean O'Faolain (1900–91)
Midsummer Night Madness, and Other Stories F

C.K. Ogden (1889–1957)
The Basic Dictionary DICT
See *Basic English* 1930

William Plomer (1903–73)
The Case is Altered F

William Plomer (1903–73)
The Fivefold Screen V

Anthony Powell (1905–2000)
Venusberg F

J.B. Priestley (1894–1984)
Dangerous Corner D
Performed 17 May 1932

V.S. Pritchett (1900–97)
Shirley Sanz F

Herbert Read (1893–1968)
Form in Modern Poetry NF

'Æ' [George William Russell (1867–1935)]
Song and its Fountains V

'Sapper' [Herman Cyril McNeile (1888–1937)]
The Return of Bull-Dog Drummond F
See *Bull-Dog Drummond* 1920

'C.L. Anthony' [Dodie Smith (1896–1900)]
Service D
Performed 12 October 1932

C.P. Snow (1905–80)
Death Under Sail F

Bertram Thomas (1892–1950)
Arabia Felix NF
Foreword by T.E. Lawrence

Hugh Walpole (1884–1941)
The Fortress F
Herries Chronicle iii. See also *Rogue Herries* 1930, *Judith Paris* 1931, *Vanessa* 1933.

Sylvia Townsend Warner (1893–1978)
The Salutation F
Stories

Evelyn Waugh (1903–66)
Black Mischief F

Charles Williams (1886–1945)
The Greater Trumps F

Virginia Woolf (1882–1941)
The Common Reader: Second Series NF
Published on 13 October 1932. First series, 1925 (q.v.).

W.B. Yeats (1865–1939)
Words for Music Perhaps, and Other Poems V
Published on 14 November 1932

1933

- Hitler becomes German Chancellor (30 Jan.)
  The Reichstag fire (27 Feb.): civil liberties abolished in Germany

- The 'New Deal' in the USA
  Hitler granted dictatorial powers
- Michael Frayn born
  B.S. Johnson born
  Penelope Lively born
  Joe Orton born
  David Storey born
  Claire Tomalin born
- Stella Benson dies
  Annie Besant dies
  Augustine Birrell dies
  Sir John Fortescue dies
  Henry Watson Fowler dies
  John Galsworthy dies
  Anthony Hope (Sir Anthony Hope Hawkins) dies
  George Moore dies
  George Saintsbury dies
- Mario Praz, *The Romantic Agony*
  André Malraux, *La Condition humaine*
  Gertrude Stein, *The Autobiography of Alice B. Toklas*
- *King Kong*

W.H. Auden (1907–73)
Poems: Second Edition V
Published on 2 November 1933

W.H. Auden (1907–73)
The Dance of Death D
Published on 9 November 1933. Performed 1 October 1934.

George Barker (1913–91)
Thirty Preliminary Poems V

John Betjeman (1906–84)
Ghastly Good Taste; or, A Depressing Story of the Rise and Fall of English Architecture NF

'Marjorie Bowen' [Gabrielle Margaret Vere Campbell (1886–1952)]
The Last Bouquet F
Stories

Vera Brittain (1893–1970)
Testament of Youth NF
See also *Testament of Friendship* 1940, *Testament of Experience* 1957

Roy Campbell (1901–57)
Flowering Reeds V

Joyce Cary (1888–1957)
An American Visitor F

I. Compton-Burnett (1884–1969)
More Women Than Men F

A.E. Coppard (1878–1957)
Dunky Fitlow F
Stories

C. Day Lewis (1904–72)
The Magnetic Mountain V

Walter de la Mare (1873–1956)
The Fleeting, and Other Poems V
Published in May 1933

Norman Douglas (1868–1952)
Looking Back NF

John Drinkwater (1882–1937)
Summer Harvest V

T.S. Eliot (1888–1965)
The Use of Poetry and the Use of Criticism NF
Published on 2 November 1933

Havelock Ellis (1859–1939)
Psychology of Sex NF

Eleanor Farjeon (1881–1965)
Over the Garden Wall V
Illustrated by Gwen Raverat

David Gascoyne (1916)
Opening Day F

'John Gawsworth' [Terence Ian Fytton Armstrong (1912–71)]
Poems 1930–32 V

Robert Graves (1895–1985)
Poems 1930–1933 V

Walter Greenwood (1903–74)
Love on the Dole F

James Hilton (1900–54)
Lost Horizon F

A.E. Housman (1859–1936)
The Name and Nature of Poetry NF

Elizabeth Jenkins (1905)
Harriet F
Published in 1933, dated 1934

L.C. Knights (1906–97)
How Many Children Had Lady Macbeth? NF

D.H. Lawrence (1885–1930)
The Lovely Lady F
Stories. Published in January 1933, dated 1932.

D.H. Lawrence (1885–1930)
Last Poems V
Published in April 1933

D.H. Lawrence (1885–1930)
The Plays of D.H. Lawrence D
Published in July 1933

D.H. Lawrence (1885–1930)
Lady Chatterley's Lover F
Unexpurgated edition (published abroad), with prefatory note by Frieda Lawrence. See also *Lady Chatterley's Lover* 1928, 1929, 1932, 1960.

C.S. Lewis (1898–1963)
The Pilgrim's Regress NF

Malcolm Lowry (1909–57)
Ultramarine F

A.G. Macdonell (1895–1941)
England, their England F

Sean O'Casey (1880–1964)
Within the Gates D
Performed 7 February 1934

Sean O'Faolain (1900–91)
A Nest of Simple Folk F

'George Orwell' [Eric Arthur Blair (1903–50)]
Down and Out in Paris and London NF
Published on 9 January 1933

Anthony Powell (1905–2000)
From a View to a Death F

John Cowper Powys (1872–1963)
A Glastonbury Romance F

Herbert Read (1893–1968)
Art Now NF

Herbert Read (1893–1968)
The End of a War V

Laura Riding (1901–91)
Poet: a Lying Word V

'Æ' [George William Russell (1867–1935)]
The Avatars F

Siegfried Sassoon (1886–1967)
The Road to Ruin V

Dorothy L. Sayers (1893–1957)
Murder Must Advertise F

Edith Sitwell (1887–1964)
The English Eccentrics NF
Published in May 1933

Osbert Sitwell (1892–1969)
Miracle on Sinai F
Published in October 1933

Stephen Spender (1909–95)
Poems V

Angela Thirkell (1890–1961)
Ankle Deep F

Hugh Walpole (1884–1941)
Vanessa F
Herries Chronicle iv. See also *Rogue Herries* 1930, *Judith Paris* 1931, *The Fortress* 1932.

Alec Waugh (1898–1981)
Wheels Within Wheels F

H.G. Wells (1866–1946)
The Shape of Things to Come F

'Antonia White' [Eirene Botting (1899–1980)]
Frost in May F
Frost in May Quartet i, followed by *The Lost Traveller* 1950, *The Sugar House* 1952, and *Beyond the Glass* 1954 (qq.v.)

Charles Williams (1886–1945)
Shadows of Ecstasy F

Virginia Woolf (1882–1941)
Flush: A biography NF
Published on 5 October 1933

W.B. Yeats (1865–1939)
The Winding Stair, and Other Poems V
Published on 19 September 1933

W.B. Yeats (1865–1939)
Collected Poems V
Published on 28 November 1933

1934

- Hitler begins to eliminate opponents, including the leader of the SA, Ernst Röhm (June)
  Purges begin in the USSR (Dec.)
  Glyndebourne Festival founded
- Fleur Adcock born
  Beryl Bainbridge born
  Alan Bennett born
  Edward Bond born
  Alan Garner born
  Alasdair Gray born
- F. Anstey (Thomas Anstey Guthrie) dies
  Roger Fry dies
  A.R. Orage dies
  Sir Arthur Wing Pinero dies
- Sir Edward Elgar dies
- Gustav Holst dies

- Carter and Pollard, *An Enquiry into the Nature of Certain XIXth Century Pamphlets* (exposure of forgeries perpetrated by T.J. Wise)
- Jean Cocteau, *La Machine infernale*
  F. Scott Fitzgerald, *Tender is the Night*
  Sholokhov, *Quiet Flows the Don*

Samuel Beckett (1906–89)
More Pricks Than Kicks F
Stories

Edmund Blunden (1896–1974)
The Mind's Eye NF
Published on 30 April 1934

Edmund Blunden (1896–1974)
Choice or Chance V
Published in November 1934

Elizabeth Bowen (1899–1973)
The Cat Jumps, and Other Stories F

Roy Campbell (1901–57)
Broken Record NF

Agatha Christie (1890–1976)
Murder on the Orient Express F

W.H. Davies (1871–1940)
Poems V
See also *Collected Poems*, 1st series, 1916; 2nd series, 1923; *Collected Poems* 1928

J.W. Dunne (1875–1949)
The Serial Universe NF

Lawrence Durrell (1912–90)
Transition V

T.S. Eliot (1888–1965)
After Strange Gods NF
Published on 22 February 1934

T.S. Eliot (1888–1965)
The Rock D
Published on 31 May 1934. Performed 28 May–9 June 1934.

Ronald Firbank (1886–1926)
The Artificial Princess F

William Gerhardie (1895–1977)
Resurrection F

Robert Graves (1895–1985)
Claudius the God and his Wife Messalina F

Robert Graves (1895–1985)
I, Claudius F

Graham Greene (1904–91)
It's a Battlefield F
Published in February 1934

James Hilton (1900–54)
Good-bye Mr Chips F
See also *To You, Mr Chips* 1938

Storm Jameson (1897–1986)
Company Parade F
The Mirror in Darkness Trilogy i, followed by *Love in Winter* 1935 and *None Turn Back* 1936

F. Tennyson Jesse (1888–1958)
A Pin to See the Peepshow F

D.H. Lawrence (1885–1930)
Reflections on the Death of a Porcupine, and Other Essays NF

John Lehmann (1907–87)
The Noise of History V

Wyndham Lewis (1882–1957)
Men Without Art NF

'Hugh MacDiarmid' [Christopher Murray Grieve (1892–1978)]
At the Sign of the Thistle NF

'Hugh MacDiarmid' [Christopher Murray Grieve (1892–1978)]
Stony Limits, and Other Poems V

Kate O'Brien (1897–1974)
The Ante-Room F

Sean O'Casey (1880–1964)
Windfalls: Stories, poems, and plays MISC

Ruth Pitter (1897–1992)
A Mad Lady's Garland V
Preface by Hilaire Belloc

William Plomer (1903–73)
The Invaders F

J.B. Priestley (1894–1984)
English Journey NF

'Æ' [George William Russell (1867–1935)]
The House of the Titans, and Other Poems V

Dorothy L. Sayers (1893–1957)
The Nine Tailors F
Published in January 1934

Bernard Shaw (1856–1950)
Too True to be Good; Village Wooing; and On the Rocks D
Published on 15 February 1934

Bernard Shaw (1856–1950)
Short Stories, Scraps and Shavings MISC
Published on 17 May 1934

Bernard Shaw (1856–1950)
Prefaces NF
Published on 12 June 1934

William Soutar (1898–1943)
The Solitary Way V

Stephen Spender (1909–95)
Vienna V

Howard Spring (1889–1965)
Shabby Tiger F

Freya Stark (1893–1993)
The Valleys of the Assassins, and Other Persian Travels NF

A.J.A. Symons (1900–41)
The Quest for Corvo: An experiment in biography NF

Angela Thirkell (1890–1961)
Wild Strawberries F

Dylan Thomas (1914–53)
18 Poems V

Arnold Toynbee (1889–1975)
A Study of History NF

P.L. Travers (1906–96)
Mary Poppins F
Illustrated by Mary Shepard

Alec Waugh (1898–1981)
The Balliols F

Evelyn Waugh (1903–66)
A Handful of Dust F

H.G. Wells (1866–1946)
Experiment in Autobiography NF

P.G. Wodehouse (1881–1975)
Right Ho, Jeeves F

W.B. Yeats (1865–1939)
The Words Upon the Window Pane D
Published in April 1934

W.B. Yeats (1865–1939)
Wheels and Butterflies D
Published on 13 November 1934

W.B. Yeats (1865–1939)
Collected Plays D
Published on 30 November 1934

W.B. Yeats (1865–1939)
The King of the Great Clock Tower V
Published on 14 December 1934

G.M. Young (1882–1959) (ed.)
Early Victorian England 1830–65 NF
See also *Victorian England* 1936

1935

- Hitler repudiates the disarmament clauses of the Treaty of Versailles (Mar.)
  Stanley Baldwin becomes British Prime Minister
  Italy invades Abyssinia (Oct.)
  Persia changes its name to Iran
- J.G. Farrell born
  Michael Holroyd born
  David Lodge born
  Alan Plater born
  Dennis Potter born
  Jon Stallworthy born
  D.M. Thomas born
- Edwin Lester Arnold dies
  A.C. Bradley dies
  Silas Hocking dies
  Winifred Holtby dies
  T.E. Lawrence dies
  Vernon Lee (Violet Paget) dies
  Rosa Caroline Praed dies
  George William Russell ('Æ') dies
  Sir William Watson dies
- Alban Berg dies
- William Saroyan, *The Daring Young Man on the Flying Trapeze*
- George Gershwin, *Porgy and Bess*
  Rachmaninov, *Rhapsody on a Theme of Paganini*

James Evershed Agate (1877–1947)
Ego: The autobiography of Agate NF
Published in 9 parts, 1935–48

W.H. Auden (1907–73) and **Christopher Isherwood** (1904–86)
The Dog Beneath the Skin; or, Where is Francis? D
Published on 30 May 1935. Performed 12 January 1936.

Enid Bagnold (1889–1981)
'National Velvet' F

H.C. Bailey (1878–1961)
Mr Fortune Objects F
Detective stories. See also *Call Mr Fortune* 1920.

George Barker (1913–91)
Poems V

Samuel Beckett (1906–89)
Echo's Bones and Other Precipitates V

E.F. Benson (1867–1940)
Lucia's Progress F
See also *Queen Lucia* 1920, *Miss Mapp* 1922, *Lucia in London* 1927, *Mapp and Lucia* 1931

Norman Cameron (1905–53)
The Winter House V

G.K. Chesterton (1874–1936)
The Scandal of Father Brown F
Published in March 1935. See also *The Innocence of Father Brown* 1911, *The Wisdom of Father Brown* 1914, *The Incredulity of Father Brown* 1926, *The Secret of Father Brown* 1927.

I. Compton-Burnett (1884–1969)
A House and its Head F

A.E. Coppard (1878–1957)
Polly Oliver F
Stories

A.J. Cronin (1896–1981)
The Stars Look Down F

W.H. Davies (1871–1940)
Love Poems V

C. Day Lewis (1904–72)
Collected Poems 1929–1933 V

C. Day Lewis (1904–72)
A Time to Dance, and Other Poems V

Walter de la Mare (1873–1956)
Poems 1919 to 1934 V
Published in November 1935

T.S. Eliot (1888–1965)
Murder in the Cathedral D
Published on 13 June 1935

William Empson (1906–84)
Poems V

William Empson (1906–84)
Some Versions of Pastoral NF

'C.S. Forester' [Cecil Louis Troughton Smith (1899–1966)]
The African Queen F
Later made into a celebrated film starring Humphrey Bogart and Katherine Hepburn

Graham Greene (1904–91)
England Made Me F
Published in June 1935

Graham Greene (1904–91)
The Basement Room, and Other Stories F
Published in November 1935. See also *Nineteen Stories* 1947 and *Twenty-One Stories* 1954.

Patrick Hamilton (1904–62)
Twenty Thousand Streets Under the Sky F
Introduction by J.B. Priestley. Comprises *The Midnight Bell* 1929, *The Siege of Pleasure* 1932, *The Plains of Cement* 1934.

James Hanley (1901–85)
The Furys F
Furys Chronicle i. Followed by *The Secret Journey* 1936, *Our Time is Gone* 1940, *Winter Song* 1950, and *An End and a Beginning* 1958.

Christopher Hassall (1912–63)
Poems of Two Years V

Georgette Heyer (1902–74)
Regency Buck F

Laurence Housman (1865–1959)
Little Plays of St Francis D

Margaret Irwin (1889–1967)
Madame Fears the Dark F

Christopher Isherwood (1904–86)
Mr Norris Changes Trains F
Reprinted in *The Berlin Stories* 1946 (q.v.).

Pamela Hansford Johnson (1912–81)
This Bed Thy Centre F

T.E. Lawrence (1888–1935)
Seven Pillars of Wisdom NF
First trade edition. See *Seven Pillars of Wisdom* 1926, *Revolt in the Desert* 1927.

Rose Macaulay (1881–1958)
Personal Pleasures NF

Louis MacNeice (1907–1963)
Poems V

John Masefield (1878–1967)
The Box of Delights; or, When the Wolves Were Running F
For children

R.K. Narayan (1906–2001)
The Bachelor of Arts F

'George Orwell' [Eric Arthur Blair (1903–50)]
Burmese Days F
Published on 24 June 1935

'George Orwell' [Eric Arthur Blair (1903–50)]
A Clergyman's Daughter F
Published on 11 March 1925

John Cowper Powys (1872–1963)
Jobber Skald F
First published in the USA as *Weymouth Sands*

Llewelyn Powys (1884–1939)
Dorset Essays NF

V.S. Pritchett (1900–97)
Nothing Like Leather F

Herbert Read (1893–1968)
Poems 1914–34 V

James Reeves (1909–78)
The Natural Need V
Verse preface by Laura Riding

Dorothy M. Richardson (1873–1957)
Clear Horizon F
Pilgrimage sequence xi. See *Pilgrimage* 1938.

'Sapper' [Herman Cyril McNeile (1888–1937)]
Bull-Dog Drummond at Bay F
See *Bull-Dog Drummond* 1920

Siegfried Sassoon (1886–1967)
Vigils V

Dorothy L. Sayers (1893–1957)
Gaudy Night F

Stephen Spender (1909–95)
The Destructive Element NF
See also *The Creative Element* 1953

Frank Swinnerton (1884–1982)
The Georgian Literary Scene NF

Hugh Walpole (1884–1941)
The Inquisitor F

Sylvia Townsend Warner (1893–1978)
More Joy in Heaven, and Other Stories F

'Rebecca West' [Cicily Isabel Andrews (1892–1983)]
The Harsh Voice F
Four novelettes

Dennis Wheatley (1897–1977)
The Devil Rides Out F

Henry Williamson (1895–1977)
Salar the Salmon F

John Dover Wilson (1881–1969)
What Happens in Hamlet NF

P.G. Wodehouse (1881–1975)
Blandings Castle and Elsewhere F
Stories

Humbert Wolfe (1885–1940)
The Fourth of August V
Sonnets

Humbert Wolfe (1885–1940)
Stings and Wings V

Humbert Wolfe (1885–1940)
X at Oberammergau V

W.B. Yeats (1865–1939)
A Full Moon in March V
Published on 22 November 1935

W.B. Yeats (1865–1939)
Dramatis Personae NF
Published on 9 December 1935

1936

- Death of George V (20 Jan.)
  EDWARD VIII succeeds: abdicates 10 Dec.
  GEORGE VI succeeds 11 Dec. (–1952)
  Popular Front wins a majority in Spanish elections (Feb.)
  Germany reoccupies the Rhineland (Mar.)
  Spanish Civil War begins (17 July)
  Axis Rome-Berlin formed (26 Oct.)
  Allen Lane founds Penguin Books
  Olympic Games in Berlin: US black athlete Jesse Owens wins four gold medals
  F.D. Roosevelt begins second term as US President
- Hilary Bailey born
  A.S. Byatt born
  Nell Dunn born
  Simon Gray born
  J.H. Prynne born
  David Rudkin born
- G.K. Chesterton dies
  Edward Garnett dies
  R.B. Cunninghame Graham dies
  A.E. Housman dies
  M.R. James dies
  Rudyard Kipling dies
- Maxim Gorky dies
  'Houdini' (Erich Weiss) dies
- Margaret Mitchell, *Gone with the Wind*
- Prokofiev, *Peter and the Wolf*

Eric Ambler (1909–98)
The Dark Frontier F

W.H. Auden (1907–73) and **Christopher Isherwood** (1904–86)
The Ascent of F6 D
Published on 24 September 1936. Performed 26 February 1937.

W.H. Auden (1907–73)
Look, Stranger! V
Published 22 October 1936

John Buchan (1875–1940)
The Island of Sheep F

Roy Campbell (1901–57)
Mithraic Emblems V

Joyce Cary (1888–1957)
The African Witch F

G.K. Chesterton (1874–1936)
Autobiography NF
Published on 5 November 1936

Agatha Christie (1890–1976)
The ABC Murders F

Cyril Connolly (1903–74)
The Rock Pool F

C. Day Lewis (1904–72)
Noah and the Waters V

'Nicholas Blake' [**C. Day Lewis** (1904–72)]
Thou Shell of Death F

Walter de la Mare (1873–1956)
The Wind Blows Over F
Stories. Published in October 1936.

Daphne du Maurier (1907–89)
Jamaica Inn F

T.S. Eliot (1888–1965)
Essays Ancient and Modern NF
Published on 5 March 1936

T.S. Eliot (1888–1965)
Collected Poems 1909–1935 V
Published on 2 April 1936

E.M. Forster (1879–1970)
Abinger Harvest NF
Published on 19 March 1936

William Gerhardie (1895–1977)
Of Mortal Love F

Graham Greene (1904–91)
Journey Without Maps NF
Published in May 1936

Graham Greene (1904–91)
A Gun for Sale F
Published in July 1936

Winifred Holtby (1898–1935)
South Riding F

A.E. Housman (1859–1936)
More Poems V
Edited by Laurence Housman

Aldous Huxley (1894–1963)
Eyeless in Gaza F

Pamela Hansford Johnson (1912–81)
Blessed Above Women F

James Joyce (1882–1941)
Collected Poems V

James Joyce (1882–1941)
Ulysses F
The first British edition printed in Britain. See also *Ulysses* 1922, 1986.

Patrick Kavanagh (1904–67)
Ploughman, and Other Poems V

Ronald Knox (1888–1957) (ed.)
The Holy Bible BIB

D.H. Lawrence (1885–1930)
Phoenix NF
Posthumous papers. Published in November 1936.

F.R. Leavis (1895–1978)
Revaluation: Tradition and development in English poetry NF

C.S. Lewis (1898–1963)
The Allegory of Love NF

Wyndham Lewis (1882–1957)
The Roaring Queen F

Arthur Machen (1863–1947)
The Children of the Pool, and Other Stories F

Louis MacNeice (1907–63) (tr.)
The Agamemnon of Aechylus V

A.E.W. Mason (1865–1948)
Fire Over England F

Somerset Maugham (1874–1965)
Cosmopolitans F
Stories. Published on 30 March 1936.

Charles Morgan (1894–1958)
Sparkenbroke F

Robert Nichols (1893–1944)
A Spanish Triptych V

Kate O'Brien (1897–1974)
Mary Lavelle F
Banned by the Irish Censorship Board

'Frank O'Connor' [**Michael Francis O'Donovan** (1903–1966)]
Bones of Contention, and Other Stories F

Sean O'Faolain (1900–91)
Bird Alone F

'George Orwell' [**Eric Arthur Blair** (1903–50)]
Keep the Aspidistra Flying F
Published on 20 April 1936

Nikolaus Pevsner (1902–83)
Pioneers of the Modern Movement NF

Ruth Pitter (1897–1992)
A Trophy of Arms V
Preface by James Stephens. Omits *A Mad Lady's Garland* 1934 (q.v.).

Anthony Powell (1905–2000)
Agents and Patients F

Arthur Ransome (1884–1967)
Pigeon Post F
For children. Illustrated by Ransome.

Siegfried Sassoon (1886–1967)
Sherston's Progress F
Fictionalized autobiography. See also *Memoirs of a Fox-Hunting Man* 1928, *Memoirs of an Infantry-Officer* 1930, *The Complete Memoirs of George Sherston* 1937.

Bernard Shaw (1856–1950)
The Simpleton; The Six; and The Millionairess D
Published on 4 March 1936

Sacheverell Sitwell (1897–1988)
Collected Poems V
Published in November 1936. Introductory essay by Edith Sitwell.

Stevie Smith (1902–71)
Novel on Yellow Paper F

William Soutar (1898–1943)
A Handful of Earth V

Stephen Spender (1909–95)
The Burning Cactus F
Stories

Freya Stark (1893–1993)
The Southern Gates of Arabia NF

'Michael Innes' [J.I.M. Stewart (1906–94)]
Death at the President's Lodging F

Noel Streatfeild (1895–1986)
Ballet Shoes F

Dylan Thomas (1914–53)
Twenty-five Poems V

J.R.R. Tolkien (1892–1973)
Beowulf: The monsters and the critics NF

Sylvia Townsend Warner (1893–1978)
Summer Will Show F

Evelyn Waugh (1903–66)
Mr Loveday's Little Outing, and Other Sad Stories F

Evelyn Waugh (1903–66)
Waugh in Abyssinia NF

T.H. White (1906–64)
England Have My Bones NF

G.M. Young (1882–1959)
Victorian England NF
Revised version of Young's introduction to *Early Victorian England* 1934 (q.v.)

1937

- German bombers destroy the town of Guernica in Spain (26 Apr.)
  Neville Chamberlain becomes British Prime Minister (May)
  The Duke of Windsor marries Mrs Wallis Simpson (June)
  Japanese forces take Nanking (Dec.)
- Paul Bailey born
  Steven Berkoff born
  Jilly Cooper born
  Anita Desai born
  Victoria Glendinning born
  Tony Harrison born
  Roger McGough born
  Tom Stoppard born
  Jill Paton Walsh born
- Sir J.M. Barrie dies
  Julian Bell dies
  Ella D'Arcy dies
  John Drinkwater dies
  Ivor Gurney dies
  Herman Cyril McNeile ('Sapper') dies
- David Hockney born
- Maurice Ravel dies
  Edith Wharton dies
- Ernest Hemingway, *To Have and Have Not*
  John Steinbeck, *Of Mice and Men*

W.H. Auden (1907–73)
Spain V
Published on 20 May 1937

W.H. Auden (1907–73) and **Louis MacNeice** (1907–63)
Letters From Iceland NF/V
Published on 8 July 1937

George Barker (1913–91)
Calamiterror V

Sir J.M. Barrie (1860–1937)
The Greenwood Hat MISC
Published in November 1937. Mostly autobiographical newspaper articles.

John Betjeman (1906–1984)
Continual Dew: A little book of bourgeois verse V

Edmund Blunden (1896–1974)
An Elegy, and Other Poems V
Published in November 1937

Robert Byron (1905–41)
The Road to Oxiana NF

Agatha Christie (1890–1976)
Death on the Nile F

I. Compton-Burnett (1884–1969)
Daughters and Sons F

Noël Coward (1899–1973)
Present Indicative NF
Autobiography. See also *Future Indefinite* 1954.

A.J. Cronin (1896–1981)
The Citadel F

'C.S. Forester' [Cecil Louis Troughton Smith (1899–1966)]
The Happy Return F
The first of the Hornblower novels

Stella Gibbons (1902–89)
Roaring Tower, and Other Short Stories F

Oliver St John Gogarty (1878–1957)
As I Was Going Down Sackville Street NF

Geoffrey Household (1900–88)
The Third Hour F

Christopher Isherwood (1904–86)
Sally Bowles F
Reprinted in *The Berlin Stories* 1946 (q.v.)

Rudyard Kipling (1865–1936)
Something of Myself NF
Kipling died in January 1936

Wyndham Lewis (1882–1957)
Blasting and Bombarding NF
Autobiography

Wyndham Lewis (1882–1957)
The Revenge for Love F

Charles Madge (1912–96)
The Disappearing Castle V

Charles Madge (1912–96)
Mass-Observation NF
With Tom Harrisson (1911–76). Foreword by Julian Huxley. (Mass-Observation series, no. 1.)

Olivia Manning (1915–80)
The Wind Changes F

Somerset Maugham (1874–1965)
Theatre F
Published 22 March 1937

Edwin Muir (1887–1959)
Journeys and Places V

Kate O'Brien (1897–1974)
Farewell Spain NF

Sean O'Faolain (1900–91)
A Purse of Coppers F
Stories

'George Orwell' [Eric Arthur Blair (1903–50)]
The Road to Wigan Pier NF
Published on 8 March 1937

Eric Partridge (1894–1979)
A Dictionary of Slang and Unconventional English DICT

Stephen Potter (1900–69)
The Muse in Chains NF

John Cowper Powys (1872–1963)
Maiden Castle F

John Cowper Powys (1872–1963)
Morwyn; or, The Vengeance of God F

J.B. Priestley (1894–1984)
I Have Been Here Before D
Performed 22 September 1937

J.B. Priestley (1894–1984)
Midnight on the Desert NF
Autobiography. See also *Rain Upon Godshill* 1939.

J.B. Priestley (1894–1984)
Time and the Conways D
Performed 26 August 1937

V.S. Pritchett (1900–97)
Dead Man Leading F

Terence Rattigan (1911–77)
French Without Tears D
Performed 6 November 1936

Herbert Read (1893–1968)
Art and Society NF

Isaac Rosenberg (1890–1918)
Collected Works WKS
Foreword by Siegfried Sassoon

Siegfried Sassoon (1886–1967)
The Complete Memoirs of George Sherston F
Fictionalized autobiography. See also *Memoirs of a Fox-Hunting Man* 1928, *Memoirs of an Infantry-Officer* 1930, *Sherston's Progress* 1936.

Bernard Shaw (1856–1950)
London Music in 1888–89 NF
Published on 23 September 1937

Stevie Smith (1902–71)
A Good Time Was Had By All V

Stephen Spender (1909–95)
Forward From Liberalism NF

J.R.R. Tolkien (1892–1973)
The Hobbit; or, There and Back Again F

Charles Williams (1886–1945)
Descent into Hell F

P.G. Wodehouse (1881–1975)
Lord Emsworth and Others F
Stories

Virginia Woolf (1882–1941)
The Years F
Published on 15 March 1937

W.B. Yeats (1865–1939)
Essays 1931 to 1936 NF
Published on 14 December 1937

W.B. Yeats (1865–1939)
A Vision NF
Published on 7 October 1937. A heavily revised edition of *A Vision* 1925 (q.v.). Final revised edition published in 1956.

1938

- *Anschluss* of Austria to Germany (Mar.)
  Munich agreement gives the Sudetenland to Germany (30 Sept.)
  Kristallnacht—widespread anti-Jewish rioting in Germany (9–10 Nov.)
- Caryl Churchill born
  Margaret Forster born
  Frederick Forsyth born
  Ian Hamilton born
  Allan Massie born
- Lascelles Abercrombie dies
  E.V. Lucas dies
  Sir Henry Newbolt dies
- Thornton Wilder, *Our Town*
- Walt Disney, *Snow White and the Seven Dwarfs*
  Eisenstein, *Alexander Nevsky*

Walter Allen (1911–95)
Innocence is Drowned F

Margery Allingham (1904–66)
The Fashion in Shrouds F

Eric Ambler (1909–98)
Epitaph for a Spy F

W.H. Auden (1907–73) and **Christopher Isherwood** (1904–86)
On the Frontier: A melodrama D
Published on 27 October 1938. Performed in Cambridge on 14 November 1938, with music by Benjamin Britten.

Samuel Beckett (1906–89)
Murphy F
Beckett's first published novel

Elizabeth Bowen (1899–1973)
The Death of the Heart F

Joyce Cary (1888–1957)
Castle Corner F

'Christopher Caudwell' [**Christopher St John Sprigg** (1907–1937)]
Studies in a Dying Culture NF
See also *Further Studies in a Dying Culture* 1949

Cyril Connolly (1903–74)
Enemies of Promise NF

Lettice Cooper (1897–1994)
National Provincial F

Elizabeth Daryush (1887–1977)
Verses: Sixth Book V

'Nicholas Blake' [**C. Day Lewis** (1904–72)]
The Beast Must Die F

C. Day Lewis (1904–72)
Overtures to Death, and Other Poems V

Walter de la Mare (1873–1956)
Memory, and Other Poems V
Published in May 1938

Daphne du Maurier (1907–89)
Rebecca F

Lawrence Durrell (1912–90)
The Black Book F

David Gascoyne (1916)
Hölderlin's Madness V

William Gerhardie (1895–1977)
My Wife's the Least of It F

Stella Gibbons (1902–89)
The Lowland Venus, and Other Poems V

Oliver St John Gogarty (1878–1957)
Others to Adorn V
Preface by W.B. Yeats

Robert Graves (1895–1985)
Collected Poems V

Robert Graves (1895–1985)
Count Belisarius F

Graham Greene (1904–91)
Brighton Rock F
Published in July 1938

[Basil] Liddell Hart (1895–1970)
Through the Fog of War NF

James Hilton (1900–54)
To You, Mr Chips F
See *Good-bye Mr Chips* 1934

Christopher Isherwood (1904–86)
Lions and Shadows NF
Autobiography

Osbert Lancaster (1908–86)
Pillar to Post NF
Illustrated by Osbert Lancaster

C.S. Lewis (1898–1963)
Out of the Silent Planet F
Volume i of trilogy. See also *Perelandra* 1943, *That Hideous Strength* 1945.

Wyndham Lewis (1882–1957)
The Mysterious Mr Bull NF

A.G. Macdonell (1895–1941)
Autobiography of a Cad F

Louis MacNeice (1907–63)
The Earth Compels V

Louis MacNeice (1907–63)
I Crossed the Minch NF/V
Prose, with verse

Louis MacNeice (1907–63)
Modern Poetry NF

'George Orwell' [Eric Arthur Blair (1903–50)]
Homage to Catalonia NF
Published on 25 April 1938

J.B. Priestley (1894–1984)
The Doomsday Men F

J.B. Priestley (1894–1984)
When We Are Married: A Yorkshire farcical comedy D
Performed on 11 October 1938

V.S. Pritchett (1900–97)
You Make Your Own Life F
Stories

Herbert Read (1893–1968)
Poetry and Anarchism NF

Dorothy M. Richardson (1873–1957)
Pilgrimage F
Collected edition with final section, 'Dimple Hill', and foreword by the author. Comprising *Pointed Roofs* 1915, *Backwater* 1916, *Honeycomb* 1917, *Interim* 1919, *The Tunnel* 1919, *Deadlock* 1921, *Revolving Lights* 1923, *The Trap* 1925, *Oberland* 1927, *Dawn's Left Hand* 1931, *Clear Horizon* 1935 (qq.v.).

Siegfried Sassoon (1886–1967)
The Old Century and Seven More Years NF
Autobiography. See also *The Weald of Youth* 1942 and *Siegfried's Journey* 1945.

Osbert Sitwell (1892–1969)
Those Were the Days NF
Published on 1 March 1938

Dodie Smith (1896–1990)
Dear Octopus: A comedy D
Performed on 14 September 1938

Stevie Smith (1902–71)
Tender Only to One V

Stephen Spender (1909–95)
Trial of a Judge: A tragedy D
Performed 18 March 1938

Howard Spring (1889–1965)
O Abasalom! F

Edward Upward (1903)
Journey to the Border F

Sylvia Townsend Warner (1893–1978)
After the Death of Don Juan F

Evelyn Waugh (1903–66)
Scoop F

T.H. White (1906–64)
The Sword in the Stone F
Reprinted with *The Witch in the Wood* 1940 and *The Ill-Made Knight* 1941 (qq.v.) in *The Once and Future King* 1958 (q.v.)

Charles Williams (1886–1945)
Taliessen Through Logres V

Virginia Woolf (1882–1941)
Three Guineas NF

W.B. Yeats (1865–1939)
Autobiography NF
Published on 30 August 1938. Includes *Reveries Over Childhood and Youth* 1914, *The Trembling of the Veil* 1922, *Dramatis Personae* 1935, *The Death of Synge* 1928, and other pieces. See also *Autobiographies* 1926.

W.B. Yeats (1865–1939)
The Herne's Egg D
Published on 21 January 1938

W.B. Yeats (1865–1939)
New Poems V
Published on 18 May 1938

1939

- Final collapse of Republican resistance in the Spanish Civil War
  Germany occupies rest of Czechoslovakia (Mar.)
  Italy invades Albania (Apr.)
  Molotov-Ribbentrop pact (23 Aug.)
  Germany invades Poland (1 Sept.)
  Britain and France declare war on Germany (3 Sept.)
- Alan Ayckbourn born
  Melvyn Bragg born
  Shelagh Delaney born
  Margaret Drabble born
  Germaine Greer born
  Seamus Heaney born
  Clive James born
  E.A. Markham born
  Michael Moorcock born
  Robert Nye born
  Colin Thubron born
- Ethel M. Dell dies
  Charlotte Despard dies
  Havelock Ellis dies
  Ford Madox Ford (Ford Hermann Hueffer) dies
  Llewelyn Powys dies
  W.B. Yeats dies
- Sigmund Freud dies
- John Steinbeck, *The Grapes of Wrath*
- *Gone with the Wind*

Eric Ambler (1909–98)
The Mask of Dimitrios F

W.H. Auden (1907–73) and **Christopher Isherwood** (1904–86)
Journey to a War V/NF
Published on 16 March 1939. Includes 'In Time of War', a sonnet sequence with verse commentary, by Auden; diary and prose by Isherwood.

George Barker (1913–91)
Elegy on Spain V

Roy Campbell (1901–57)
Flowering Rifle: A poem from the battlefield of Spain V

Joyce Cary (1888–1957)
Mister Johnson F

Agatha Christie (1890–1976)
Ten Little Niggers F

I. Compton-Burnett (1884–1969)
A Family and a Fortune F

W.H. Davies (1871–1940)
The Loneliest Mountain, and Other Poems V

Monica Dickens (1915–92)
One Pair of Hands NF
Autobiography. See also *One Pair of Feet* 1942, *My Turn to Make the Tea* 1951.

T.S. Eliot (1888–1965)
The Family Reunion D
Published on 21 March 1939. Performed March 1939.

T.S. Eliot (1888–1965)
Old Possum's Book of Practical Cats V
Published on 5 October 1939. Reprinted in 1940 with illustrations by Nicholas Bentley.

T.S. Eliot (1888–1965)
The Idea of a Christian Society NF
Published on 26 October 1939

Gavin Ewart (1916)
Poems and Songs V

E.M. Forster (1879–1970)
What I Believe NF
Published in May 1939

Christopher Fry (1907)
The Boy With a Cart—Cuthman, Saint of Sussex D
Performed 1937

Rumer Godden (1907–98)
Black Narcissus F

'Henry Green' [**Henry Vincent Yorke** (1905–73)]
Party Going F

Graham Greene (1904–91)
The Lawless Roads NF
Published in March 1939

Graham Greene (1904–91)
The Confidential Agent: An entertainment F
Published in September 1939

Geoffrey Grigson (1905–85) (ed.)
New Verse ANTH
Poems from the magazine *New Verse*

Patrick Hamilton (1904–62)
Impromptu in Moribundia F

Rayner Heppenstall (1911–81)
The Blaze of Noon F

Geoffrey Household (1900–88)
Rogue Male F
See also *Rogue Justice* 1982

A.E. Housman (1859–1936)
Collected Poems V

Aldous Huxley (1894–1963)
After Many a Summer F

Christopher Isherwood (1904–86)
Goodbye to Berlin F
Reprinted in *The Berlin Stories* 1946 (q.v.)

L.P. Jacks (1860–1955)
The Last Legend of Smokeover F
See also *Heroes of Smokeover* 1926

Pamela Hansford Johnson (1912–81)
Girdle of Venus F

James Joyce (1882–1941)
Finnegans Wake F
Second edition, 1946 (with list of corrections); third edition, 1950 (incorporating majority of corrections)

Ronald Knox (1888–1957)
Let Dons Delight F

Osbert Lancaster (1908–86)
Homes, Sweet Homes NF
Illustrated by by Osbert Lancaster

C.S. Lewis (1898–1963)
Rehabilitations, and Other Essays NF

'Richard Llewellyn' [Richard Llewellyn Lloyd (1906–83)]
How Green Was My Valley F
See also *Up, Into the Singing Mountain* 1963, *Down Where the Moon is Small* 1966, *Green, Green My Valley Now* 1975

Louis MacNeice (1907–63)
Autumn Journal V
See also *Autumn Sequel* 1954

Nicholas Monsarrat (1910–79)
This is the Schoolroom F

'Flann O'Brien' [Brian O'Nolan (1911–66)]
At Swim-Two-Birds F

Sean O'Casey (1880–1964)
I Knock at the Door NF
First volume of autobiography. See also *Pictures in the Hallway* 1942, *Drums Under the Windows* 1945, *Inishfallen, Fare Thee Well* 1949, *Rose and Crown* 1952.

'George Orwell' [Eric Arthur Blair (1903–50)]
Coming Up For Air F
Published on 12 June 1939

Ruth Pitter (1897–1992)
The Spirit Watches V

Anthony Powell (1905–2000)
What's Become of Waring? F

Llewelyn Powys (1884–1939)
Love and Death F

J.B. Priestley (1894–1984)
Rain Upon Godshill NF
Autobiography. See also *Midnight on the Desert* 1937.

Terence Rattigan (1911–77)
After the Dance D
Performed 21 June 1939

'Mary Renault' [Eileen Mary Challans (1905–83)]
Purposes of Love F

Anne Ridler (1912–2001)
Poems V

Osbert Sitwell (1892–1969)
Open the Door! F
Published on 7 November 1941

Stevie Smith (1902–71)
Over the Frontier F

William Soutar (1898–1943)
In the Time of Tyrants V

Stephen Spender (1909–95)
The Still Centre V

Julian Symons (1912–95)
Confusions About X V

Angela Thirkell (1890–1961)
The Brandons F

Dylan Thomas (1914–53)
The Map of Love V/F

Flora Thompson (1877–1947)
Lark Rise F
See also *Over to Candleford* 1941, *Candleford Green* 1943, *Lark Rise to Candleford* 1945

Charles Williams (1886–1945)
The Descent of the Dove NF

Leonard Woolf (1880–1969)
Barbarians at the Gate NF

W.B. Yeats (1865–1939)
Last Poems and Two Plays V/D
Published posthumously on 10 July 1939

W.B. Yeats (1865–1939)
On the Boiler MISC
Published posthumously, autumn 1939. Essays, poems, play.

1940

- Germany invades Norway and Denmark (Apr.) and the Netherlands (May)
  WInston Churchill becomes Prime Minister (10 May)
  Germany invades France (12 May)
  British begin evacuation of Dunkirk (29 May)
  Germans enter Paris (14 June): French sign armistice with Germany (22 June)
  Battle of Britain (July–Sept.)
  The London Blitz
  Italians defeated in North Africa
  F.D. Roosevelt begins third term as US President
- Maeve Binchy born
  Angela Carter born
  Bruce Chatwin born
  Susan Howatch born
- E.F. Benson dies
  John Buchan dies
  W.H. Davies dies
  Humbert Wolfe dies
- Eric Gill dies
- Trotsky assassinated
- *Cambridge Bibliography of English Literature*, ed. F.W. Bateson
  Ernest Hemingway, *For Whom the Bell Tolls*
  Upton Sinclair, *Between Two Worlds*
- Charlie Chaplin, *The Great Dictator*
  Walt Disney, *Fantasia*

Eric Ambler (1909–98)
Journey into Fear F

W.H. Auden (1907–73)
Some Poems V
Published on 14 March 1940

W.H. Auden (1907–73)
Another Time V
Published on 20 June 1940

George Barker (1913–91)
Lament and Triumph V

John Betjeman (1906–84)
Old Lights for New Chancels V

'James Bridie' [Osborne Henry Mavor (1888–1951)]
Susannah and the Elders, and Other Plays D
Contains *Susannah and the Elders, What Say They?, The Golden Legend of Shults, The Kitchen Comedy*

Vera Brittain (1893–1970)
Testament of Friendship NF
Autobiography. See also *Testament of Youth* 1933, *Testament of Experience* 1957.

John Buchan (1875–1940)
Memory-Hold-the-Door NF
Autobiography

Joyce Cary (1888–1957)
Charley is My Darling F

C. Day Lewis (1904–72) (tr.)
The Georgics of Virgil V
See also *The Aeneid of Virgil* 1952, *The Eclogues of Virgil* 1963

C. Day Lewis (1904–72)
Poems in Wartime V

T.S. Eliot (1888–1965)
The Waste Land, and Other Poems V
Published in February 1940. *The Waste Land* first published in 1923 (q.v.).

T.S. Eliot (1888–1965)
East Coker V
Published in June 1940. First published in *The New English Weekly* (Easter Number, 1940). Republished in *Four Quartets* 1944 (q.v.).

William Empson (1906–84)
The Gathering Storm V

Roy Fuller (1912–91)
Poems V

'Robert Garioch' [Robert Garioch Sutherland (1909–81)] and **Sorley MacLean [Somhairle MacGill-Eain]** (1911)
17 Poems for 6d. in Gaelic, Lowland Scots and English V

Stella Gibbons (1902–89)
Christmas at Cold Comfort Farm, and Other Stories F
See *Cold Comfort Farm* 1932, *Conference at Cold Comfort Farm* 1949

Rumer Godden (1907–98)
Gypsy, Gypsy F

'Henry Green' [Henry Vincent Yorke (1905–73)]
Pack My Bag NF

Graham Greene (1904–91)
The Power and the Glory: An entertainment F
Published in March 1940

J.F. Hendry (1912–86) and **Henry Treece** (1911–66) (eds)
The New Apocalypse ANTH
Anthology of criticism, poems, and stories. See also *The White Horseman* 1941, *The Crown and Sickle* 1944.

Rayner Heppenstall (1911–81)
Blind Men's Flowers are Green V

Pamela Hansford Johnson (1912–81)
Too Dear For My Possessing F
First volume of trilogy with *An Avenue of Stone* 1947 (q.v.) and *A Summer to Decide* 1948

'Anna Kavan' [Helen Emily Woods (1901–68)]
Asylum Piece, and Other Stories F

Arthur Koestler (1905–83)
Darkness at Noon NF

C.S. Lewis (1898–1963)
The Problem of Pain NF

Louis MacNeice (1907–63)
The Last Ditch V

Somerset Maugham (1874–1965)
The Mixture as Before F
Stories. Published on 6 June 1940.

Edwin Muir (1887–1959)
The Story and the Fable NF
Autobiography

Sean O'Casey (1880–1964)
Purple Dust D
Performed in Newcastle-on-Tyne, 16 December 1943

Sean O'Casey (1880–1964)
The Star Turns Red D
Performed 12 March 1940

'Frank O'Connor' [Michael Francis O'Donovan (1903–66)]
Dutch Interior F

Sean O'Faolain (1900–91)
Come Back to Erin F

'George Orwell' [Eric Arthur Blair (1903–50)]
Inside the Whale, and Other Essays NF
Published on 11 March 1940

Herbert Read (1893–1968)
Annals of Innocence and Experience NF

Michael Sadleir (1888–1957)
Fanny by Gaslight F

C.P. Snow (1905–80)
Strangers and Brothers F
First of the Strangers and Brothers sequence

Stephen Spender (1909–95)
The Backward Son F

Stephen Spender (1909–95)
Selected Poems V

Howard Spring (1889–1965)
Fame is the Spur F

Angela Thirkell (1890–1961)
Cheerfulness Breaks In: A Barsetshire war survey F

Dylan Thomas (1914–53)
Portrait of the Artist as a Young Dog F

Henry Treece (1911–66)
38 Poems V

Sir Hugh Walpole (1884–1941)
The Bright Pavilions F
Volume v of The Herries Chronicle. See *Rogue Herries* 1930, *Judith Paris* 1931, *The Fortress* 1932, *Vanessa* 1933.

H.G. Wells (1866–1946)
All Aboard for Ararat F

T.H. White (1906–64)
The Witch in the Wood F
Reprinted with *The Sword in the Stone* 1938 and *The Ill-Made Knight* 1941 (qq.v.) in *The Once and Future King* 1958 (q.v.).

W.B. Yeats (1865–1939)
Last Poems and Plays V/D
Published in January 1940

1941

- Germany invades Yugoslavia and Greece (Apr.) and Crete (May)
  Rudolf Hess lands in Scotland (10 May)
  Germany invades Russia (22 June)
  Siege of Leningrad begins (8 Sept.)
  The Japanese bomb Pearl Harbor (7 Dec.)
  Hitler declares war on the USA (11 Dec.)
- Derek Mahon born
  Piers Paul Read born
  Paul Theroux born
  Barbara Trapido born
- Robert Byron dies
  Sir J.G. Frazer dies

James Joyce dies
A.J.A. Symons dies
Evelyn Underhill dies
Sir Hugh Walpole dies
Virginia Woolf commits suicide (28 Mar.)
P.C. Wren dies
- Sherwood Anderson dies
Rabindranath Tagore dies
- Brecht, *Mutter Courage*
F. Scott Fitzgerald, *The Last Tycoon*
- Orson Welles, *Citizen Kane*

Harold Acton (1904–94)
Peonies and Ponies F

W.H. Auden (1907–73)
New Year Letter V
Published on 29 May 1941

H.E. Bates (1905–74)
The Modern Short Story NF
Published in July 1941

Hilaire Belloc (1870–1953)
The Silence of the Sea, and Other Essays NF

Laurence Binyon (1869–1943)
The North Star, and Other Poems V

Edmund Blunden (1896–1974)
Poems 1930–1940 V
Published on 21 January 1941, dated 1940

Phyllis Bottome (1884–1963)
London Pride F

John Buchan (1875–1940)
Sick Heart River F

Joyce Cary (1888–1957)
Herself Surprised F
First volume of trilogy with *To Be a Pilgrim* 1942 and *The Horse's Mouth* 1944 (qq.v.)

Winston Spencer Churchill (1874–1965)
Into Battle NF
See also *The Unrelenting Struggle* 1942, *The End of the Beginning* 1943, *Onwards to Victory* 1944, *The Dawn of Liberation* 1945, *Victory* 1946

I. Compton-Burnett (1884–1969)
Parents and Children F

Daphne du Maurier (1907–89)
Frenchman's Creek F

T.S. Eliot (1888–1965)
Burnt Norton V
Published on 20 February 1941. First published in *Collected Poems* 1936 (q.v.). Republished in *Four Quartets* 1944 (q.v.).

T.S. Eliot (1888–1965)
The Dry Salvages V
Published on 4 September 1941. Republished in *Four Quartets* 1944.

J.F. Hendry (1912–86) and **Henry Treece** (1911–66) (eds)
The White Horseman ANTH
See also *The New Apocalypse* 1939, and *The Crown and the Sickle* 1944

James Hilton (1900–54)
Random Harvest F

W.E. Johns (1893–1968)
Worrals of the WAAF F
The female counterpart of Biggles, created by Johns at the request of the Air Ministry to promote the Women's Auxiliary Air Force. See also *The Camels Are Coming* 1932.

G. Wilson Knight (1897–1985)
The Starlit Dome NF
2nd edition 1959

Wyndham Lewis (1882–1957)
The Vulgar Streak F

Louis MacNeice (1907–63)
Plant and Phantom V
Published in April 1941

Somerset Maugham (1874–1965)
Up at the Villa F
Published on 12 May 1941

Kate O'Brien (1897–1974)
The Land of Spices F

'George Orwell' [Eric Arthur Blair (1903–50)]
The Lion and the Unicorn: Socialism and the English genius NF
Published on 19 February 1941

W.R. Rodgers (1909–69)
Awake! and Other Poems V

Alan Ross (1922)
Summer Thunder V

A.L. Rowse (1903–97)
Poems of a Decade V

Bernard Shaw (1856–1950)
Pygmalion D
Published on 19 September 1941. Screen version: the original play with added scenes from the film. See *Androcles and the Lion* 1916.

Sydney Goodsir Smith (1915–75)
Skail Wind V
In Scots and English

'Michael Innes' [J.I.M. Stewart (1906–94)]
Appleby on Ararat F

Flora Thompson (1877–1947)
Over to Candleford F
See also *Lark Rise* 1939, *Candleford Green* 1943, *Lark Rise to Candleford* 1945

Terence Tiller (1916–87)
Poems V
New Hogarth Library 5

Rex Warner (1905–86)
The Aerodrome F

Vernon Watkins (1906–67)
The Ballad of the Mari Lwyd, and Other Poems V

'Rebecca West' [Cicily Isabel Andrews (1892–1983)]
Black Lamb and Grey Falcon NF

T.H. White (1906–64)
The Ill-Made Knight F
Reprinted with *The Sword in the Stone* 1938 and *The Witch in the Wood* 1940 (qq.v.) in *The Once and Future King* 1958 (q.v.)

Virginia Woolf (1882–1941)
Between the Acts F
Published on 17 July 1941. Virginia Woolf committed suicide in March 1941.

1942

- Singapore surrenders to the Japanese (15 Feb.)
  British victory at El Alamein (4 Nov.)
  Anglo-American landings in North Africa
- Howard Brenton born
  Douglas Dunn born
  Susan Hill born
  Howard Jacobson born
  Bernard MacLaverty born
  Jonathan Raban born
  Hugo Williams born
- Ernest Bramah (Ernest Bramah Smith) dies
  Violet Hunt dies
- Anouilh, *Antigone*
  Albert Camus, *L'Étranger*

'Flying Officer X' [H.E. Bates (1905–74)]
The Greatest People in the World, and Other Stories F
Published in September 1942

H.E. Bates (1905–74)
In the Heart of the Country NF

D.K. Broster (1878–1950)
Couching at the Door F
Stories

Joyce Cary (1888–1957)
To Be a Pilgrim F
Second volume of trilogy with *Herself Surprised* 1941 and *The Horse's Mouth* 1944 (qq.v.)

Winston Spencer Churchill (1874–1965)
The Unrelenting Struggle NF
See also *Into Battle* 1941, *The End of the Beginning* 1943, *Onwards to Victory* 1944, *The Dawn of Liberation* 1945, *Victory* 1946

Noël Coward (1899–1973)
Blithe Spirit: An improbable farce D
Performed in Manchester 16 June 1941, and in London on 2 July 1941

A.J. Cronin (1896–1981)
The Keys of the Kingdom F

Monica Dickens (1915–92)
One Pair of Feet NF
Autobiography. See also *One Pair of Hands* 1939, *My Turn to Make the Tea* 1951.

T.S. Eliot (1888–1965)
Little Gidding V
Published on 1 December 1942. Republished in *Four Quartets* 1944 (q.v.).

Roy Fuller (1912–91)
The Middle of a War V

W.S. Graham (1918–86)
Cage Without Grievance V

'Cyril Hare' [A.A.G. Clark (1900–58)]
Tragedy at Law F

[Basil] Liddell Hart (1895–1970)
This Expanding War NF

John Heath-Stubbs (1918)
Wounded Thammuz V

J.F. Hendry (1912–86)
The Bombed Happiness V

Patrick Kavanagh (1904–67)
The Great Hunger V

Sidney Keyes (1922–43)
The Iron Laurel V

Alun Lewis (1915–44)
The Last Inspection F

Alun Lewis (1915–44)
Raiders' Dawn, and Other Poems V

C.S. Lewis (1898–1963)
Broadcast Talks NF

C.S. Lewis (1898–1963)
A Preface to Paradise Lost NF

C.S. Lewis (1898–1963)
The Screwtape Letters F
See also *Screwtape Proposes a Toast* 1965

Sir Lewis Namier (1888–1960)
Conflicts NF

Robert Nichols (1893–1944)
Such Was My Singing V

Sean O'Casey (1880–1964)
Pictures in the Hallway NF
Autobiography. See also *I Knock at the Door* 1939, *Drums Under the Window* 1945, *Inishfallen, Fare Thee Well* 1949, *Rose and Crown* 1952.

Sean O'Casey (1880–1964)
Red Roses for Me D
Performed 15 March 1943

V.S. Pritchett (1900–97)
In My Good Books NF

John Pudney (1909–77)
Dispersal Point, and Other Air Poems V
Contains the famous 'For Johnny'

Terence Rattigan (1911–77)
Flare Path D
Performed 13 August 1942

A.L. Rowse (1903–97)
A Cornish Childhood NF

Siegfried Sassoon (1886–1967)
The Weald of Youth NF
Autobiography. See also *The Old Century and Seven More Years* 1938 and *Siegfried's Journey* 1945.

Sir Sacheverell Sitwell (1897–1988)
The Homing of the Winds, and Other Passages in Prose NF
Published on 9 September 1942

Stevie Smith (1902–71)
Mother, What is Man? V

Stephen Spender (1909–95)
Life and the Poet NF
Published in March 1942

Stephen Spender (1909–95)
Ruins and Visions V

Freya Stark (1893–1993)
Letters From Syria NF

G.M. Trevelyan (1876–1962)
English Social History NF

Evelyn Waugh (1903–66)
Put Out More Flags F

Evelyn Waugh (1903–66)
Work Suspended: Two chapters of an unfinished novel F

Dorothy Wellesley (1889–1956)
Lost Planet, and Other Poems V

Virginia Woolf (1882–1941)
The Death of the Moth, and Other Essays NF
Published on 9 June 1942

1943

- German army surrenders at Stalingrad (31 Jan.)
  Surrender of Axis forces in North Africa (May)
  Soviet forces defeat the Germans at the Battle of Kursk (July)
  Allied invasion of Sicily (10 July)
  Italy surrenders (3 Sept.)
- Pat Barker born
  Terry Eagleton born
  Lorna Sage born
  Rose Tremain born
  Joanna Trollope born
- Laurence Binyon dies
  R.G. Collingwood dies
  E.M. Delafield (Edmée Elizabeth Monica de la Pasture) dies
  R. Austin Freeman dies
  Elinor Glyn dies
  Sarah Grand (Frances Elizabeth McFall) dies
  Radclyffe Hall (Marguerite Antonia Radclyffe-Hall) dies
  W.W. Jacobs dies
  Beatrix Potter dies
  Beatrice Webb dies
- Sergei Rachmaninov dies

Kenneth Allott (1912–73)
The Ventriloquist's Doll V

'Flying Officer X' [**H.E. Bates** (1905–74)]
How Sleep the Brave, and Other Stories F
Published in August 1943

Gerald Brenan (1894–1987)
The Spanish Labyrinth NF

Winston Spencer Churchill (1874–1965)
The End of the Beginning NF
See also *Into Battle* 1941, *The Unrelenting Struggle* 1942, *Onwards to Victory* 1944, *The Dawn of Liberation* 1945, *Victory* 1946

Noël Coward (1899–1973)
Present Laughter D
Performed in Blackpool 20 September 1942, and in London on 29 April 1943

Noël Coward (1899–1973)
This Happy Breed D
Performed in Blackpool 21 September 1942, and in London on 30 April 1943

C. Day Lewis (1904–72)
Word Over All V

Keith Douglas (1920–44)
Selected Poems V

Lawrence Durrell (1912–90)
A Private Country V

David Gascoyne (1916)
Poems 1937–1942 V

Robert Graves (1895–1985)
The Story of Marie Powell, Wife to Mr Milton F

'Henry Green' [Henry Vincent Yorke (1905–73)]
Caught F

Graham Greene (1904–91)
The Ministry of Fear F
Published in May 1943

Geoffrey Grigson (1905–85)
Under the Cliff, and Other Poems V

Michael Hamburger (1924) (tr.)
Friedrich Hölderlin: Poems V

J.F. Hendry (1912–86)
The Orchestral Mountain V

Aldous Huxley (1894–1963)
The Art of Seeing NF

Sidney Keyes (1922–43)
The Cruel Solstice V

Mary Lavin (1912–96)
Tales From Bective Bridge F

C.S. Lewis (1898–1963)
Christian Behaviour NF
Revised and reprinted in *Mere Christianity* 1952 (q.v.). See also *Beyond Personality* 1944.

C.S. Lewis (1898–1963)
Perelandra F
Volume ii of trilogy. See also *Out of the Silent Planet* 1938, *That Hideous Strength* 1945.

'Richard Llewellyn' [Richard Llewellyn Lloyd (1906–83)]
None But the Lonely Heart F

Norman MacCaig (1910–96)
Far Cry V

'Hugh MacDiarmid' [Christopher Murray Grieve (1892–1978)]
Lucky Poet NF

Norman Nicholson (1914–87)
Man and Literature NF

J.B. Priestley (1894–1984)
Daylight on Saturday F

John Pudney (1909–77)
Beyond This Disregard V

Kathleen Raine (1908–2003)
Stone and Flower V
Drawings by Barbara Hepworth

Anne Ridler (1912–2001)
The Nine Bright Shiners V

Dorothy L. Sayers (1893–1957)
The Man Born To Be King D
Broadcast by the BBC December 1941–October 1942, produced by Val Gielgud

Edith Sitwell (1887–1964)
A Poet's Notebook NF
Published on 30 April 1943

William Soutar (1898–1943)
But the Earth Abideth V

Dylan Thomas (1914–53)
New Poems V

Flora Thompson (1877–1947)
Candleford Green F
See also *Lark Rise* 1939, *Over to Candleford* 1941, *Lark Rise to Candleford* 1945

Terence Tiller (1916–87)
The Inward Animal V

Rex Warner (1905–86)
Why Was I Killed? D

Sylvia Townsend Warner (1893–1978)
A Garland of Straw, and Other Stories F

1944

- The Allies land at Anzio (22 Jan.)
  Siege of Leningrad ends (27 Jan.)
  D-Day (4 June): Allied landings begin in Normandy
  First V-bombs land on London (June)
  Bretton Woods meeting (1 July)
  Failed attempt to assassinate Hitler (20 July)
  Warsaw rising (Aug.)

Dumbarton Oaks conference (Aug.)
Liberation of Paris (25 Aug.)
Battle of the Bulge begins in the Ardennes (16 Dec.)
Education Act introduced in Britain by R.A. Butler
Beveridge Report on full employment

- Eavan Boland born
David Constantine born
Bernard Cornwell (Bernard Wiggins) born
Alison Fell born
Craig Raine born
Carol Rumens born
- Joseph Campbell dies
Keith Douglas dies
Philip Guedalla dies
Alun Lewis dies
Thomas Sturge Moore dies
Robert Nichols dies
Sir Arthur Quiller-Couch dies
William Temple, archbishop of Canterbury, dies
- Jean Giraudoux dies
Lucien Pissarro dies
Antoine de Saint-Exupéry dies
- Jean-Paul Sartre, *Huis-Clos*
- Laurence Olivier, *Henry V*

George Barker (1913–91)
Eros in Dogma V

H.E. Bates (1905–74)
Fair Stood the Wind for France F
Published in November 1944

Laurence Binyon (1869–1943)
The Burning of the Leaves, and Other Poems V

Edmund Blunden (1896–1974)
Shells by a Stream V
Published on 27 October 1944

'James Bridie' [Osborne Henry Mavor (1888–1951)]
Plays for Plain People D
Contains *Lancelot*; *Holy Isle*; *Mr Bolfry* (co-written with Alastair Sim); *Jonah 3*; *The Sign of the Prophet Jonah*; *The Dragon and the Dove*

Vera Brittain (1893–1970)
Seed of Chaos NF

Joyce Cary (1888–1957)
The Horse's Mouth F
Third volume of trilogy with *Herself Surprised* 1941 and *To Be a Pilgrim* 1942 (qq.v.)

Winston Spencer Churchill (1874–1965)
Onwards to Victory NF
See also *Into Battle* 1941, *The Unrelenting Struggle* 1942, *The End of the Beginning* 1943, *The Dawn of Liberation* 1945, *Victory* 1946

Alex Comfort (1920–2000)
Elegies V

I. Compton-Burnett (1884–1969)
Elders and Betters F

'Edmund Crispin' [Robert Bruce Montgomery (1921–78)]
The Case of the Gilded Fly F

Patric Dickinson (1914–94)
The Seven Days of Jericho V

Clifford Dyment (1914–71)
The Axe in the Wood V

T.S. Eliot (1888–1965)
Four Quartets V
Published on 31 October 1944. First published in the USA in May 1943. Contains *Burnt Norton* 1936/1941 (qq.v.), *East Coker* 1940 (q.v.), *The Dry Salvages* 1941 (q.v.), *Little Gidding* 1942 (q.v.).

Roy Fuller (1912–91)
A Lost Season V

W.S. Graham (1918–86)
The Seven Journeys V

Robert Graves (1895–1985)
The Golden Fleece F

L.P. Hartley (1895–1972)
The Shrimp and the Anemone F
Eustace and Hilda Trilogy i. See also *The Sixth Heaven* 1946, *Eustace and Hilda* 1947.

J.F. Hendry (1912–86) and **Henry Treece** (1911–66) (eds)
The Crown and Sickle ANTH
See also *The New Apocalypse* 1939, *The White Horseman* 1941

Aldous Huxley (1894–1963)
Time Must Have a Stop F

James Joyce (1882–1941)
Stephen Hero F
Part of the first draft of *Portrait of the Artist as a Young Man* 1916 (q.v.)

Marghanita Laski (1915–88)
Love on the Supertax F

Mary Lavin (1912–96)
The Long Ago F

Laurie Lee (1914–97)
The Sun My Monument V

John Lehmann (1907–87)
The Sphere of Glass, and Other Poems V

Rosamond Lehmann (1901–90)
The Ballad and the Source F

C.S. Lewis (1898–1963)
Beyond Personality NF
Revised and reprinted in *Mere Christianity* 1952 (q.v.). See also *Broadcast Talks* 1942, *Christian Behaviour* 1943.

J. Maclaren-Ross (1912–64)
The Stuff to Give the Troops F

Louis MacNeice (1907–63)
Christopher Columbus D
Broadcast by the BBC on 12 October 1942

Louis MacNeice (1907–63)
Springboard V

Somerset Maugham (1874–1965)
The Razor's Edge F
Published on 17 July 1944

Charles Morgan (1894–1958)
Reflections in a Mirror [1st ser.] NF
Second series published in 1946

Harold Nicolson (1886–1968)
Friday Mornings 1941–4 NF

'Frank O'Connor' [Michael Francis O'Donovan (1903–66)]
Crab Apple Jelly F
Stories

Mervyn Peake (1911–68)
Rhymes Without Reason V

John Pudney (1909–77)
Almanack of Hope V

Terence Rattigan (1911–77)
While the Sun Shines: A comedy D
Performed on 24 December 1943

Herbert Read (1893–1968)
A World Within a War V

William Sansom (1912–76)
Fireman Flower, and Other Stories F

E.J. Scovell (1907–99)
Shadows of Chrysanthemums, and Other Poems V

Bernard Shaw (1856–1950)
Everybody's Political What's What NF
Published on 15 September 1944

William Soutar (1898–1943)
The Expectant Silence V

Alec Waugh (1898–1981)
His Second War F

Charles Williams (1886–1945)
The Region of the Summer Stars V

Virginia Woolf (1882–1941)
A Haunted House, and Other Short Stories F
Published on 31 January 1944, dated 1943

1945

- Roosevelt, Churchill, and Stalin meet at Yalta (4 Feb.)
  Allied bombing of Dresden (13 Feb.)
  Death of F.D. Roosevelt (12 Apr.): Harry S. Truman becomes US President
  The Russians reach Berlin (20 Apr.)
  Mussolini executed by partisans (28 Apr.)
  Hitler commits suicide (30 Apr.)
  Fall of Berlin (2 May)
  End of the war in Europe (8 May)
  Stalin, Truman, and Churchill meet at Potsdam (July)
  Labour victory in British general election: Clement Attlee replaces Churchill as Prime Minister (26 July)
  Atomic bombs dropped on Hiroshima and Nagasaki (6–9 Aug.)
  Japan surrenders (14 Aug.)
  UNESCO founded
  United Nations Organization Charter
  Nuremberg war trials open (Nov.)
- John Banville born
  Wendy Cope born
  Selima Hill born
  Shiva Naipaul born
- Maurice Baring dies
  Lord Alfred Douglas dies
  George Egerton (Mary Chavelita Dunne) dies
  Arthur Symons dies
  Charles Williams dies
- Béla Bartók dies
  Theodore Dreiser dies
  Paul Valéry dies
- Benjamin Britten, *Peter Grimes*
  Oxford History of English Literature begins publication
- Eisenstein, *Ivan the Terrible*

W.H. Auden (1907–73)
For the Time Being V
Published on 2 March 1945

John Betjeman (1906–84)
New Bats in Old Belfries V

Elizabeth Bowen (1899–1973)
The Demon Lover, and Other Stories F

Winston Spencer Churchill (1874–1965)
The Dawn of Liberation NF
See also *Into Battle* 1941, *The Unrelenting Struggle* 1942, *The End of the Beginning* 1943, *Onwards to Victory* 1943, *Victory* 1946

Walter de la Mare (1873–1956)
The Burning-Glass, and Other Poems V
Published on November 1945

Lawrence Durrell (1912–90)
Prospero's Cell NF

Rumer Godden (1907–98)
A Fugue in Time F

W.S. Graham (1918–86)
Second Poems V

Winston Graham (1910–2003)
Ross Poldark F
First of the Poldark novels

'Henry Green' [Henry Vincent Yorke (1905–73)]
Loving F

Michael Hamburger (1924)
Later Hogarth V

A.P. Herbert (1890–1971)
Light the Lights V

'Jean Plaidy' [Eleanor Hibbert] (1906–93)
Together They Ride F
The first of Hibbert's novels as 'Jean Plaidy'

'Anna Kavan' [Helen Emily Woods (1901–68)]
I am Lazarus F

Ronald Knox (1888–1957)
God and the Atom NF

Ronald Knox (1888–1957) (tr.)
The New Testament of Our Lord and Saviour Jesus Christ BIB
See also *The Old Testament* 1949, *The Holy Bible* 1955

Philip Larkin (1922–85)
The North Ship V

Alun Lewis (1915–44)
Ha! Ha! Among the Trumpets V
Foreword by Robert Graves

C.S. Lewis (1898–1963)
That Hideous Strength F
Volume iii of trilogy. See also *Out of the Silent Planet* 1938, *Perelandra* 1943.

J. Maclaren-Ross (1912–64)
Better Than a Kick in the Pants F

Nancy Mitford (1904–73)
The Pursuit of Love F

R.K. Narayan (1906–2001)
The English Teacher F
US title: *Grateful to Life and Death*

P.H. Newby (1918–97)
A Journey to the Interior F

Mary Norton (1903–92)
The Magic Bed-Knob F
First published in the USA in 1943

Sean O'Casey (1880–1964)
Drums Under the Window NF
Third volume of autobiography. See also *I Knock at the Door* 1939, *Pictures in the Hallway* 1942, *Inishfallen, Fare Thee Well* 1949, *Rose and Crown* 1952.

Oliver Onions (1873–1961)
The Story of Ragged Robyn F
Published in February 1945

'George Orwell' [Eric Arthur Blair (1903–50)]
Animal Farm F
Published on 17 August 1945

Ruth Pitter (1897–1992)
The Bridge V

William Plomer (1903–73)
The Dorking Thigh, and Other Satires V

F.T. Prince (1912–2003)
Soldiers Bathing, and Other Poems V

V.S. Pritchett (1900–97)
It May Never Happen, and Other Stories F

Terence Rattigan (1911–77)
Love in Idleness D
Performed 20 December 1944

Bertrand Russell (1872–1970)
A History of Western Philosophy NF

Siegfried Sassoon (1886–1967)
Siegfried's Journey 1916–20 NF

Autobiography. See also *The Old Century and Seven More Years* 1938 and *The Weald of Youth* 1942.

Sir Osbert Sitwell (1892–1969)
Left Hand, Right Hand! NF
Published on 27 March 1945. First published in the USA, May 1944. See also *The Scarlet Tree* 1946, *Great Morning* 1948, *Laughter in the Next Room* 1949, *Noble Essences* 1950.

Stephen Spender (1909–95)
Citizens in War—and After NF

Elizabeth Taylor (1912–75)
At Mrs Lippincote's F

Flora Thompson (1877–1947)
Lark Rise to Candleford F
See also *Lark Rise* 1939, *Over to Candleford* 1941, *Candleford Green* 1943

Henry Treece (1911–66)
The Black Seasons V

Vernon Watkins (1906–67)
The Lamp and the Veil V

Evelyn Waugh (1903–66)
Brideshead Revisited: The sacred and profane memories of Captain Charles Ryder F

H.G. Wells (1866–1946)
The Happy Turning NF

H.G. Wells (1866–1946)
Mind at the End of its Tether NF

Charles Williams (1886–1945)
All Hallows' Eve F

1946

- First meeting of the United Nations General Assembly (10 Jan.)
  Nationalization of the Bank of England
  Churchill's Iron Curtain speech at Fulton, Missouri (6 Mar.)
  Italy becomes a republic
  Fourth Republic established in France
  National Health Act
- Howard Barker born
  Julian Barnes born
  Alan Bleasdale born
  Jim Crace born
  Christopher Hampton born
  Alan Judd born
  James Kelman born
  Brian Patten born
  Philip Pullman born
  Peter Reading born
  Marina Warner born
- Helen Bannerman (creator of Little Black Sambo) dies
  Harley Granville Barker dies
  John Maynard Keynes dies
  Sir Charles Oman dies
  Ernest Rhys dies
  May Sinclair dies
  Logan Pearsall Smith dies
  H.G. Wells dies
- Damon Runyan dies
  Gertrude Stein dies
- Simone de Beauvoir, *Tous les hommes sont mortels*
  Eugene O'Neill, *The Iceman Cometh*
  Robert Penn Warren, *All the King's Men*

Edmund Blunden (1896–1974)
Shelley NF
Published on 29 April 1946

Rupert Brooke (1887–1915)
The Poetical Works of Rupert Brooke V
Adds twenty-six poems to the 1928 edition of Collected Poems

Winston Spencer Churchill (1874–1965)
Victory NF
See also *Into Battle* 1941, *The Unrelenting Struggle* 1942, *The End of the Beginning* 1943, *Onwards to Victory* 1943, *The Dawn of Liberation* 1945

R.G. Collingwood (1889–1943)
The Idea of History NF

John Stewart Collis (1900–84)
While Following the Plough NF
See also *Down to Earth* 1947

A.E. Coppard (1878–1957)
Fearful Pleasures F
Stories

Jim Corbett (1875–1955)
The Man-Eaters of Kumaon NF

Roald Dahl (1916–90)
Over to You F

Walter de la Mare (1873–1956)
The Traveller V
Published in December 1946

Keith Douglas (1920–44)
Alamein to Zem Zem NF
Prose account with incidental poems

Norman Douglas (1868–1952)
Late Harvest NF

Ronald Duncan (1914–82)
This Way to the Tomb D
Performed 11 October 1945. Music by Benjamin Britten.

Lawrence Durrell (1912–90)
Cities, Plains and People V

Christopher Fry (1907)
The Firstborn D
Broadcast by the BBC on 3 September 1947

Christopher Fry (1907)
A Phoenix Too Frequent: A comedy D
Performed 25 April 1946

Rumer Godden (1907–98)
The River F

Robert Graves (1895–1985)
King Jesus F

Robert Graves (1895–1985)
Poems 1938–1945 V

'Henry Green' [Henry Vincent Yorke (1905–73)]
Back F

Geoffrey Grigson (1905–85)
The Isles of Scilly, and Other Poems V

L.P. Hartley (1895–1972)
The Sixth Heaven F
Eustace and Hilda Trilogy ii. See also *The Shrimp and the Anemone* 1944, *Eustace and Hilda* 1947.

Christopher Isherwood (1904–86)
The Berlin Stories F
Contains *Mr Norris Changes Trains* 1935, *Sally Bowles* 1937, *Goodbye to Berlin* 1939 (qq.v.)

Christopher Isherwood (1904–86)
Prater Violet F

L.C. Knights (1906–97)
Explorations NF
See also *Further Explorations* 1965

Philip Larkin (1922–85)
Jill F

Mary Lavin (1912–96)
The Becker Wives F

Rose Macaulay (1881–1958)
They Went to Portugal NF

Norman MacCaig (1910–96)
The Inward Eye V

'Hugh MacDiarmid' [Christopher Murray Grieve (1892–1978)]
Poems of the East-West Synthesis V

Kate O'Brien (1897–1974)
That Lady F

Oliver Onions (1873–1961)
Poor Man's Tapestry F

'George Orwell' [Eric Arthur Blair (1903–50)]
Critical Essays NF
Published on 14 February 1946

Mervyn Peake (1911–68)
Titus Groan F
See also *Gormenghast* 1950, *Titus Alone* 1959

J.B. Priestley (1894–1984)
Bright Day F

V.S. Pritchett (1900–97)
The Living Novel NF

Kathleen Raine (1908–2003)
Living in Time V

Terence Rattigan (1911–77)
The Winslow Boy D
Performed 23 May 1946

Herbert Read (1893–1968)
Collected Poems V

Henry Reed (1914–86)
A Map of Verona V
Includes 'Naming of Parts'

Vita Sackville-West (1892–1962)
The Garden V

William Sansom (1912–76)
Three F
Stories

E.J. Scovell (1907–99)
Midsummer Meadows, and Other Poems V

Bernard Shaw (1856–1950)
Major Barbara: A Screen Version D
Published on 26 July 1946. Original play (1907, q.v.) with additional scenes from the scenario of the film version.

Sir Osbert Sitwell (1892–1969)
The Scarlet Tree NF
Autobiography. Published on 26 July 1946. See also *Left Hand, Right Hand!* 1945, *Great Morning* 1948, *Laughter in the Next Room* 1949, *Noble Essences* 1950.

Sydney Goodsir Smith (1915–75)
The Deevil's Waltz V

Stephen Spender (1909–95)
European Witness NF

Angela Thirkell (1890–1961)
Peace Breaks Out F

Dylan Thomas (1914–53)
Deaths and Entrances V

R.S. Thomas (1913–2000)
The Stones of the Fields V

1947

- Partition of India announced (June): establishment of Pakistan under premiership of Ali Khan
  Marshall Plan proposed
  Discovery of the Dead Sea Scrolls at Qumran
- Jenny Diski born
  David Hare born
  Liz Lochhead born
  Salman Rushdie born
  Willy Russell born
- James Agate dies
  Angela Brazil dies
  G.G. Coulton dies
  Richard Le Gallienne dies
  Hugh Lofting dies
  Marie Belloc Lowndes dies
  Arthur Machen dies
  Baroness Orczy dies
  Forrest Reid dies
  Flora Thompson dies
  Sidney Webb dies
  A.N. Whitehead dies
- Albert Camus, *La Peste*

Kingsley Amis (1922–95)
Bright November V

A.L. Barker (1918–2002)
Innocents F
Stories

H.E. Bates (1905–74)
The Purple Plain F
Published on 27 November 1947

John Stewart Collis (1900–84)
Down to Earth NF
See also *While Following the Plough* 1946

I. Compton-Burnett (1884–1969)
Manservant and Maidservant F

Lettice Cooper (1897–1994)
Black Bethlehem F

C. Day Lewis (1904–72)
The Poetic Image NF

Lawrence Durrell (1912–90)
Cefalù F
Second edition, 1958, published as *The Dark Labyrinth*

Graham Greene (1904–91)
Nineteen Stories F
Published in July 1947. Includes the contents of *The Basement Room* 1935 (q.v.) plus eleven new stories.

L.P. Hartley (1895–1972)
Eustace and Hilda F
Eustace and Hilda Trilogy iii. See also *The Shrimp and the Anemone* 1944, *The Sixth Heaven* 1946.

Pamela Hansford Johnson (1912–81)
An Avenue of Stone F
Second volume of trilogy with *Too Dear For My Possessing* 1940 (q.v.) and *A Summer to Decide* 1948

Patrick Kavanagh (1904–67)
A Soul For Sale V

James Kirkup (1918)
The Drowned Sailor, and Other Poems V

G. Wilson Knight (1897–1985)
The Crown of Life NF
See also *The Wheel of Fire* 1930, *The Imperial Theme* 1931, *The Mutual Flame* 1955

Osbert Lancaster (1908–86)
Classical Landscape with Figures NF
Illustrated by Osbert Lancaster

Philip Larkin (1922–85)
A Girl in Winter F

Laurie Lee (1914–97)
The Bloom of Candles V

C.S. Lewis (1898–1963)
Miracles NF

Malcolm Lowry (1909–57)
Under the Volcano F

Compton Mackenzie (1883–1972)
Whisky Galore F

Louis MacNeice (1907–63)
The Dark Tower, and Other Radio Scripts D
Title play broadcast by the BBC on 1 January 1946

Somerset Maugham (1874–1965)
Creatures of Circumstance F
Stories. Published on 17 July 1947.

'Frank O'Connor' [Michael Francis O'Donovan (1903–66)]
The Common Chord F
Stories

Sean O'Faolain (1900–91)
Teresa, and Other Stories F

Eric Partridge (1894–1979)
Shakespeare's Bawdy DICT

Stephen Potter (1900–69)
The Theory and Practice of Gamesmanship NF
See also *Some Notes on Lifemanship* 1950, *One-Upmanship* 1952, *Supermanship* 1958

T.F. Powys (1875–1953)
God's Eyes a-Twinkle F
Stories

J.B. Priestley (1894–1984)
The Arts Under Socialism NF

J.B. Priestley (1894–1984)
An Inspector Calls D
Performed 1 October 1946

John Pudney (1909–77)
Low Life V

'Frank Richards' [Charles Hamilton (1876–1961)]
Billy Bunter of Greyfriars School F
The first Billy Bunter book

Alan Ross (1922)
The Derelict Day V

C.P. Snow (1905–80)
The Light and the Dark F
Strangers and Brothers sequence ii

Stephen Spender (1909–95)
Poems of Dedication V

Angela Thirkell (1890–1961)
Private Enterprise F

Terence Tiller (1916–87)
Unarm, Eros V

Henry Treece (1911–66)
The Haunted Garden V

Sylvia Townsend Warner (1893–1978)
The Museum of Cheats, and Other Stories F

T.H. White (1906–64)
Mistress Masham's Repose F

Virginia Woolf (1882–1941)
The Moment, and Other Essays NF
Published on 5 December 1947

1948

- US Congress adopts Marshall Plan (Mar.)
  Organisation for European Economic Co-operation (OEEC) established
  Communists take over Czechoslovakia (May)
  End of British Mandate in Palestine: state of Israel created (May)
  Berlin airlift begins (June)
- Clare Boylan born
  David Edgar born
  Zoë Fairbairns born
  Maggie Gee born
  Ian McEwan born
  Deborah Moggach born
  Terry Pratchett born
  Nigel Williams born
- Gordon Bottomley dies
  Sir Paul Harvey (first editor of *The Oxford Companion to English Literature*) dies
  A.E.W. Mason dies
  Mary Tourtel (creator of Rupert the Bear) dies
- Prince Charles born
- A.C. Kinsey, *Sexual Behaviour in the Human Male*
  Norman Mailer, *The Naked and the Dead*
  Alan Paton, *Cry, the Beloved Country*

Harold Acton (1904–94)
Memoirs of an Aesthete NF
See also *More Memoirs of an Aesthete* 1970

Richard Aldington (1892–1962)
Complete Poems V

W.H. Auden (1907–73)
The Age of Anxiety V
Published on 17 September 1948. First published in the USA, July 1947. Auden was awarded a Pulitzer Prize for 1947 for this work.

Gordon Bottomley (1874–1948)
A Stage for Poetry NF

Elizabeth Bowen (1899–1973), **Graham Greene** (1904–91), and **V.S. Pritchett** (1900–97)
Why Do I Write? NF
Published in November 1948. Broadcast by the BBC on 7 October 1948.

Jocelyn Brooke (1908–66)
The Military Orchid F
Orchid Trilogy i. See also *A Mine of Serpents* 1949, *The Goose Cathedral* 1950.

Jocelyn Brooke (1908–66)
The Scapegoat F

Winston Spencer Churchill (1874–1965)
The Second World War NF
Published in 6 volumes (1948–53)

Jack Clemo (1916–94)
Wilding Graft F

Lawrence Durrell (1912–90)
On Seeming to Presume V

T.S. Eliot (1888–1965)
Notes Towards the Definition of Culture NF
Published on 5 November 1948

D.J. Enright (1920–2002)
Season Ticket V

Rumer Godden (1907–98)
A Candle for St Jude F

Sir Ernest Gowers (1880–1966)
Plain Words NF

Robert Graves (1895–1985)
Collected Poems 1914–1947 V

Robert Graves (1895–1985)
The White Goddess: A historical grammar of poetic myth NF

'Henry Green' [Henry Vincent Yorke (1905–73)]
Concluding F

Graham Greene (1904–91)
The Heart of the Matter F
Published in May 1948

Roy Harrod (1900–78)
Towards a Dynamic Economics NF

Aldous Huxley (1894–1963)
The Gioconda Smile D
Performed 3 June 1948. Based on Huxley's short story of the same name, first published in *Mortal Coils* 1922 (q.v.).

F.R. Leavis (1895–1978)
The Great Tradition NF

C.S. Lewis (1898–1963) and **Charles Williams** (1886–1945)
Arthurian Torso MISC
Contains the posthumous fragment 'The Figure of Arthur' by Williams, and a commentary on Williams's Arthurian poems by Lewis

Wyndham Lewis (1882–1957)
America and Cosmic Man NF

Louis MacNeice (1907–63)
Holes in the Sky V

'Robin Maugham' [Robert Cecil Maugham (1916–81)]
The Servant F

Somerset Maugham (1874–1965)
Catalina F
Published on 19 August 1948

Norman Nicholson (1914–87)
Rock Face V

Sean O'Faolain (1900–91)
The Short Story NF

Eden Phillpotts (1862–1960)
The Fall of the House of Heron F

William Sansom (1912–76)
Something Terrible, Something Lovely F

Vernon Scannell (1922)
Graves and Resurrections V

Sir Osbert Sitwell (1892–1969)
Great Morning NF
Autobiography. Published on 27 April 1948. See also *Left Hand, Right Hand!* 1945, *The Scarlet Tree* 1946, *Laughter in the Next Room* 1949, *Noble Essences* 1950.

Freya Stark (1893–1993)
Perseus in the Wind NF

Angela Thirkell (1890–1961)
Love Among the Ruins F

Arnold Toynbee (1889–1975)
Civilization on Trial NF

Sylvia Townsend Warner (1893–1978)
The Corner That Held Them F

Vernon Watkins (1906–67)
The Lady with the Unicorn V

Evelyn Waugh (1903–66)
The Loved One F

Beatrice Webb (1858–1943)
Our Partnership NF
Autobiography

Charles Williams (1886–1945)
Seed of Adam, and Other Plays D
Introduction by Anne Ridler. Contains *Seed of Adam*; *The Death of Good Fortune*; *The House by the Stable*; *Grab and Grace.*

P.G. Wodehouse (1881–1975)
Uncle Dynamite F

1949

- North Atlantic Treaty signed (Apr.): NATO created (23 Aug.)
  Republic of Eire formally proclaimed (Apr.)
  End of the Berlin blockade (May)
  Communists take power in Hungary
  Federal Republic of Germany established (Sept.)
  German Democratic Republic established (Oct.)
  Communist People's Republic of China proclaimed (Oct.)
  Harry S. Truman starts second term as US President
- Peter Ackroyd born
  Martin Amis born
  James Fenton born
  Tom Paulin born
  Michèle Roberts born
  Minette Walters born
  Graham Swift born
- J.W. Dunne dies
  Douglas Hyde dies
  Hugh Kingsmill (Hugh Kingsmill Lunn) dies
  Edith Anna Œnone Somerville dies
- Richard Strauss dies
- Simone de Beauvoir, *The Second Sex*
  Enid Blyton publishes the first Noddy books

Dannie Abse (1923)
After Every Green Thing V

H.E. Bates (1905–74)
The Jacaranda Tree F
Published in January 1949

Edmund Blunden (1896–1974)
After the Bombing, and Other Short Poems V
Published on 14 October 1949

Maurice Bowra (1898–1971)
The Creative Experiment NF

'James Bridie' [Osborne Henry Mavor (1888–1951)]
John Knox, and Other Plays D
Contains *The Forrigan Reed*, *Dr Angelus*, and *John Knox*

Jocelyn Brooke (1908–66)
A Mine of Serpents F
Orchid Trilogy ii. See also *The Military Orchid* 1948, *The Goose Cathedral* 1950.

'Olivia' [Dorothy Bussy (1866–1960)]
Olivia F

Roy Campbell (1901–57)
Collected Poems [vol. i] V
Volume ii, 1957; volume iii (translations), 1960

'Christopher Caudwell' [Christopher St John Sprigg (1907–37)]
Further Studies in a Dying Culture NF
See *Studies in a Dying Culture* 1938

Kenneth Clark (1903–83)
Landscape into Art NF

Jack Clemo (1916–94)
Confession of a Rebel NF
See also *The Marriage of a Rebel* 1980

I. Compton-Burnett (1884–1969)
Two Worlds and their Ways F

C. Day Lewis (1904–72)
Collected Poems 1929–36 V
Published in March 1949, dated 1948. See also *Collected Poems* 1954.

Nigel Dennis (1912–89)
Boys and Girls Come Out to Play F

Christopher Fry (1907)
The Lady's Not for Burning: A comedy D
Performed 10 March 1948

Roy Fuller (1912–91)
Epitaphs and Occasions V

'Robert Garioch' [Robert Garioch Sutherland (1909–81)]
Chuckles on the Cairn V

Stella Gibbons (1902–89)
Conference at Cold Comfort Farm F
See *Cold Comfort Farm* 1932, *Christmas at Cold Comfort Farm* 1940

Robert Graves (1895–1985)
The Common Asphodel NF
Essays on poetry

Geoffrey Grigson (1905–85) (ed.)
Poetry of the Present ANTH

L.P. Hartley (1895–1972)
The Boat F

Christopher Hassall (1912–63)
The Slow Night, and Other Poems 1940–8 V

Aldous Huxley (1894–1963)
Ape and Essence F

Christopher Isherwood (1904–86)
The Condor and the Cows NF
South American travel diary

Ronald Knox (1888–1957) (tr.)
The Old Testament BIB
See also *The New Testament* 1945; *The Holy Bible* 1955

Osbert Lancaster (1908–86)
Drayneflete Revealed NF
Illustrated by by Osbert Lancaster

Alun Lewis (1915–44)
In the Green Tree F
Stories. Published in 1949, dated 1948.

Rose Macaulay (1881–1958)
Fabled Shore NF

Louis MacNeice (1907–63)
Collected Poems 1925–48 V

Olivia Manning (1915–80)
Artist Among the Missing F

Somerset Maugham (1874–1965)
A Writer's Notebook NF
Published on 3 October 1949

Nancy Mitford (1904–73)
Love in a Cold Climate F

Edwin Muir (1887–1959)
The Labyrinth V

John Middleton Murry (1889–1957)
Katherine Mansfield, and Other Literary Portraits NF

R.K. Narayan (1906–2001)
Mr Sampath F

Sean O'Casey (1880–1964)
Cock-a-Doodle Dandy D
Performed 10 December 1949

Sean O'Casey (1880–1964)
Inishfallen, Fare Thee Well NF
Fourth volume of autobiography. See also *I Knock at the Door* 1939, *Pictures in the Hallway* 1942, *Drums Under the Windows* 1945, *Rose and Crown* 1952.

'George Orwell' [**Eric Arthur Blair** (1903–50)]
Nineteen Eighty-Four F
Published on 8 June 1949

Kathleen Raine (1908–2003)
The Pythoness, and Other Poems V

Terence Rattigan (1911–77)
The Browning Version D
Performed in Liverpool 26 July 1948, and in London on 8 September 1948

Terence Rattigan (1911–77)
Harlequinade D
Performed 8 September 1948

James Reeves (1909–78)
The Imprisoned Sea V

William Sansom (1912–76)
The Body F

Dorothy L. Sayers (1893–1957) (tr.)
The Comedy of Dante Alighieri, the Florentine D
Cantica 2 (*Purgatorio*) published in 1955; cantica 3 (*Paradiso*), 1962 (qq.v.)

Sir Osbert Sitwell (1892–1969)
Laughter in the Next Room NF
Autobiography. Published on 27 May 1949. See also *Left Hand, Right Hand!* 1945, *The Scarlet Tree* 1946, *Great Morning* 1948, *Noble Essences* 1950.

Dodie Smith (1896–1990)
I Capture the Castle F

Stevie Smith (1902–71)
The Holiday F

C.P. Snow (1905–80)
Time of Hope F
Strangers and Brothers sequence iii

Stephen Spender (1909–95)
The Edge of Being V

J.R.R. Tolkien (1892–1973)
Farmer Giles of Ham F

'Rebecca West' [**Cicily Isabel Andrews** (1892–1983)]
The Meaning of Treason NF

Angus Wilson (1913–91)
The Wrong Set, and Other Stories F

W.B. Yeats (1865–1939)
Poems V
The Definitive Edition

1950

- Schuman plan
  Korean War begins (6 June)
- Neil Jordan born
  Sara Maitland born
  Timothy Mo born
  Blake Morrison born

- Grace Nichols born
  A.N. Wilson born
- Warwick Deeping dies
  George Orwell (Eric Arthur Blair) dies
  Rafael Sabatini dies
  George Sampson dies
  George Bernard Shaw dies
  James Stephens dies
- Ezra Pound, *Seventy Cantos*

W.H. Auden (1907–73)
Collected Shorter Poems 1930–44 V
Published on 9 March 1950

A.L. Barker (1918–2002)
Apology for a Hero F

George Barker (1913–91)
News of the World V

George Barker (1913–91)
The True Confession of George Barker V

Maurice Bowra (1898–1971)
The Romantic Imagination NF

Gerald Brenan (1894–1987)
The Face of Spain NF

Jocelyn Brooke (1908–66)
The Goose Cathedral F
Orchid Trilogy iii. See also *The Military Orchid* 1948, *A Mine of Serpents* 1950.

Anthony Buckeridge (1912–2004)
Jennings Goes to School F
First of the Jennings series

Basil Bunting (1900–85)
Poems: 1950 V

Norman Cameron (1905–53)
Forgive Me, Sire, and Other Poems V

E.H. Carr (1892–1982)
A History of Soviet Russia NF
Published in 14 volumes (1950–78)

Agatha Christie (1890–1976)
A Murder is Announced F

Catherine Cookson (1906–98)
Kate Hannigan F
Catherine Cookson's first novel

'William Cooper' [Harry Summerfield Hoff (1910–2002)]
Scenes from Provincial Life F
See also *Scenes from Married Life* 1961, *Scenes from Metropolitan Life* 1982, *Scenes from Later Life* 1983

Walter de la Mare (1873–1956)
Inward Companion V
Published in October 1950

Ronald Duncan (1914–82)
The Mongrel, and Other Poems V

T.S. Eliot (1888–1965)
The Cocktail Party: A comedy D
Published on 9 March 1950. Performed at the Edinburgh Festival 22–7 August 1949.

Patrick Leigh Fermor (1915)
The Traveller's Tree NF

Christopher Fry (1907) (tr.)
Ring Round the Moon D
Translation of Jean Anouilh's *L'invitation au château*. Performed in London 26 January 1950.

Christopher Fry (1907)
Venus Observed D
Performed 18 January 1950)

David Gascoyne (1916)
A Vagrant, and Other Poems V

Rumer Godden (1907–98)
A Breath of Air F

E.H. Gombrich (1909–2001)
The Story of Art NF

'Henry Green' [Henry Vincent Yorke (1905–73)]
Nothing F

Graham Greene (1904–91)
The Third Man and The Fallen Idol F
Published in July 1950. *The Third Man* first published as a story in the *American Magazine* (March 1949).

Geoffrey Grigson (1905–85)
The Crest on the Silver NF
Autobiography

John Heath-Stubbs (1918)
The Darkling Plain NF

John Heath-Stubbs (1918)
The Swarming of the Bees V

Elizabeth Jane Howard (1923)
The Beautiful Visit F

Aldous Huxley (1894–1963)
Themes and Variations NF

Mary Lavin (1912–96)
Mary O'Grady F

Doris Lessing (1919)
The Grass is Singing F

C.S. Lewis (1898–1963)
The Lion, the Witch, and the Wardrobe F
Chronicles of Narnia i. See also *Prince Caspian* 1951; *The Voyage of the Dawn Treader* 1952; *The Silver Chair* 1953; *The Horse and His Boy* 1954; *The Magician's Nephew* 1955; *The Last Battle* 1956.

Norman Lewis (1908–2003)
Within the Labyrinth F

Wyndham Lewis (1882–1957)
Rude Assignment NF
Autobiograqphy

Sir Lewis Namier (1888–1960)
Europe in Decay NF

'George Orwell' [Eric Arthur Blair (1903–50)]
Shooting an Elephant, and Other Essays NF
Published posthumously on 5 October 1950

Mervyn Peake (1911–68)
The Glassblowers V

Mervyn Peake (1911–68)
Gormenghast F
See also *Titus Groan* 1946, *Titus Alone* 1959

Stephen Potter (1900–69)
Some Notes on Lifemanship NF
See also *The Theory and Practice of Gamesmanship* 1947, *One-Upmanship* 1952, *Supermanship* 1958

Barbara Pym (1913–80)
Some Tame Gazelle F

Terence Rattigan (1911–77)
Adventure Story D
Performed in Brighton 11 January 1949, and in London on 17 March 1949

James Reeves (1909–78)
The Wandering Moon V

Anne Ridler (1912–2001)
Henry Bly, and Other Plays D

Alan Ross (1922)
The Forties NF

William Sansom (1912–76)
The Passionate North F

Bernard Shaw (1856–1950)
Buoyant Billions D
Published on 15 May 1950. Performed in Zurich 21 October 1948, and in London on 10 October 1949.

'Nevil Shute' [Nevil Shute Norway (1899–1960)]
A Town Like Alice F

Jon Silkin (1930–97)
The Portrait, and Other Poems V

Sir Osbert Sitwell (1892–1969)
Noble Essences; or, Courteous Revelations NF
Autobiography. Published on 29 September 1950. See also *Left Hand, Right Hand!* 1945, *The Scarlet Tree* 1946, *Great Morning* 1948, *Laughter in the Next Room* 1949.

Stevie Smith (1902–71)
Harold's Leap V

Freya Stark (1893–1993)
Traveller's Prelude NF
Autobiography 1893–1927. See also *Beyond Euphrates* 1951, *The Coast of Incense* 1953, *Dust in the Lion's Paw* 1961.

'Antonia White' [Eirene Botting (1899–1980)]
The Lost Traveller F
Frost in May Quartet ii. See also *Frost in May* 1933, *The Sugar House* 1952, *Beyond the Glass* 1954.

Angus Wilson (1913–91)
Such Darling Dodos, and Other Stories F

Cecil Woodham-Smith (1896–1977)
Florence Nightingale NF

Virginia Woolf (1882–1941)
The Captain's Death Bed, and Other Essays NF
Published on 11 May 1950

1951

- Treaty of Paris establishes a 'common market' in coal and steel for the Benelux countries (Apr.)
  Winston Churchill becomes Prime Minister for the third time (Oct.)
  Festival of Britain
- Kate Atkinson born
  Paul Muldoon born
- Algernon Blackwood dies
  Henry de Vere Stacpoole dies
- Constant Lambert dies
- André Gide dies
- Benjamin Britten, *Billy Budd*
  J.D. Salinger, *The Catcher in the Rye*
  Herman Wouk, *The Caine Mutiny*
- John Huston, *The African Queen*

W.H. Auden (1907–73)
The Enchafèd Flood; or, The Romantic Iconography of the Sea NF
Published on 26 January 1951. First published in the USA, March 1950.

W.H. Auden (1907–73)
The Rake's Progress D
Published on 17 August 1951. An opera with libretto by Auden and Chester Kallman and music by Igor Stravinsky.

A.L. Barker (1918–2002)
Novelette, with Other Stories F

E.C. Bentley (1875–1956)
Clerihews Complete V

Roy Campbell (1901–57)
Light on a Dark Horse NF
Autobiography

Charles Causley (1917–2003)
Farewell, Aggie Weston V

Charles Causley (1917–2003)
Hands to Dance V

Jack Clemo (1916–94)
The Clay Verge V

I. Compton-Burnett (1884–1969)
Darkness and Day F

Kay Dick (1915)
Young Man F

Monica Dickens (1915–92)
My Turn to Make the Tea NF
Autobiography. See also *One Pair of Hands* 1939, *One Pair of Feet* 1942.

Keith Douglas (1920–44)
Collected Poems V

Daphne du Maurier (1907–89)
My Cousin Rachel F

E.M. Forster (1879–1970)
Two Cheers for Democracy NF
Published on 1 November 1951

E.M. Forster (1879–1970)
Billy Budd OP
Published on 1 December 1951. Opera with libretto by Forster and E. Crozier, adapted from the story by Herman Melville. Music by Benjamin Britten.

Christopher Fry (1907)
A Sleep of Prisoners D
Performed in Oxford 23 April 1951

Sir Ernest Gowers (1880–1966)
ABC of Plain Words NF
Sequel to *Plain Words* 1948 (q.v.)

Robert Graves (1895–1985)
Poems and Satires V

Graham Greene (1904–91)
The Lost Childhood, and Other Essays NF
Published in March 1951

Graham Greene (1904–91)
The End of the Affair F
Published in September 1951

Roy Harrod (1900–78)
The Life of John Maynard Keynes NF

L.P. Hartley (1895–1972)
My Fellow Devils F

L.P. Hartley (1895–1972)
The Travelling Grave, and Other Stories F
First published in the USA, 1948

Francis King (1923)
The Dividing Stream F

James Kirkup (1918)
The Submerged Village, and Other Poems V

John Lehmann (1907–87)
The Age of the Dragon V

Doris Lessing (1919)
This Was the Old Chief's Country F

C.S. Lewis (1898–1963)
Prince Caspian F
Chronicles of Narnia ii. See also *The Lion, the Witch, and the Wardrobe* 1950; *The Voyage of the Dawn Treader* 1952; *The Silver Chair* 1953; *The Horse and His Boy* 1954; *The Magician's Nephew* 1955; *The Last Battle* 1956.

Norman Lewis (1908–2003)
A Dragon Apparent NF

Wyndham Lewis (1882–1957)
Rotting Hill F
Stories

John Masters (1914–73)
Nightrunners of Bengal F
Indian Trilogy i. See also *The Deceivers* 1952, *Bhowani Junction* 1954.

Nicholas Monsarrat (1910–79)
The Cruel Sea F

Nicholas Mosley (1923)
Spaces of the Dark F

'Frank O'Connor' [Michael Francis O'Donovan (1903–66)]
Traveller's Samples F
Stories

Nikolaus Pevsner (1902–83)
The Buildings of England NF
Published in 46 volumes (1951–74)

Anthony Powell (1905–2000)
A Question of Upbringing F
Dance to the Music of Time i. See also *A Buyer's Market* 1952; *The Acceptance World* 1955; *At Lady Molly's* 1957; *Casanova's Chinese Restaurant* 1960; *The Kindly Ones* 1962; *The Valley of Bones* 1964; *The Soldier's Art* 1966; *The Military Philosophers* 1968; *Books Do Furnish a Room* 1971; *Temporary Kings* 1973; *Hearing Secret Harmonies* 1975.

V.S. Pritchett (1900–97)
Mr Beluncle F

Terence Rattigan (1911–77)
Who is Sylvia? A light comedy D
Performed in Cambridge 9 October 1950, and in London on 24 October 1950

Anne Ridler (1912–2001)
The Golden Bird, and Other Poems V

Alan Ross (1922)
Poetry, 1945–1950 V

Bernard Shaw (1856–1950)
Buoyant Billions; Farfetched Fables; and Shakes Versus Shav D
Published on 15 March 1951. *Buoyant Billions* performed in 1948 and first published in English 1950 (q.v.)

C.P. Snow (1905–80)
The Masters F
Strangers and Brothers sequence iv

Stephen Spender (1909–95)
World Within World NF
Autobiography

Freya Stark (1893–1993)
Beyond Euphrates NF
Autobiography. See also *Traveller's Prelude* 1950, *The Coast of Incense* 1953, *Dust in the Lion's Paw* 1961.

Elizabeth Taylor (1912–75)
A Game of Hide-and-Seek F

'Josephine Tey' [Elizabeth Mackintosh (1897–1952)]
The Daughter of Time F

John Wain (1925–94)
Mixed Feelings V

T.H. White (1906–64)
The Goshawk NF

Henry Williamson (1895–1977)
The Dark Lantern F
First of the 15-novel Chronicle of Ancient Sunlight sequence, ending with *The Gale of the World* 1969 (q.v.)

'John Wyndham' [J.B. Harris (1903–69)]
The Day of the Triffids F

1952

- Death of George VI (6 Feb.)
  ELIZABETH II
  Mau Mau disturbances in Kenya
  Britain becomes a nuclear power
- Douglas Adams born
  William Boyd born
  Helen Dunmore born
  Linton Kwesi Johnson born
  Hilary Mantel born
  Andrew Motion born
  Sean O'Brien born
  Stephen Poliakoff born
  Vikram Seth born
- Marjorie Bowen dies
  Norman Douglas dies
  Jeffrey Farnol dies
  Sir Desmond McCarthy dies
- Eva Perón dies
- Ray Bradbury, *The Illustrated Man*
  Agatha Christie, *The Mousetrap*

A. Alvarez (1929)
Poems V

W.H. Auden (1907–73)
Nones V
Published on 22 February 1952. First published in the USA, February 1951.

H.E. Bates (1905–74)
Love for Lydia F

John Betjeman (1906–84)
First and Last Loves NF

Alan Bullock (1914)
Hitler: a Study in Tyranny NF

Joyce Cary (1888–1957)
Prisoner of Grace F
First volume of trilogy with *Except the Lord* 1953 and *Not Honour More* 1955 (qq.v.)

C. Day Lewis (1904–72) (tr.)
The Aeneid of Virgil V
See also *The Georgics of Virgil* 1940, *The Eclogues of Virgil* 1963

Patric Dickinson (1914–94)
The Sailing Race, and Other Poems V

Daphne du Maurier (1907–89)
The Apple Tree F
Novella and stories

'Henry Green' [Henry Vincent Yorke (1905–73)]
Doting F

Aldous Huxley (1894–1963)
The Devils of Loudon F

Thomas Kinsella (1928)
The Starlit Eye V

James Kirkup (1918)
A Correct Compassion, and Other Poems V

Arthur Koestler (1905–83)
Arrow in the Blue NF
Autobiography. See also *The Invisible Writing* 1954.

F.R. Leavis (1895–1978)
The Common Pursuit NF

Doris Lessing (1919)
Martha Quest F
Children of Violence quintet i. See also *A Proper Marriage* 1954, *A Ripple From the Storm* 1958, *Landlocked* 1965, *The Four-Gated City* 1969.

C.S. Lewis (1898–1963)
Mere Christianity NF
Revised and enlarged edition of *Broadcast Talks* 1942, *Christian Behaviour* 1943, and *Beyond Personality* 1944 (qq.v.)

C.S. Lewis (1898–1963)
The Voyage of the Dawn Treader F
Chronicles of Narnia iii. See also *The Lion, the Witch, and the Wardrobe* 1950; *Prince Caspian* 1951; *The Silver Chair* 1953; *The Horse and His Boy* 1954; *The Magician's Nephew* 1955; *The Last Battle* 1956.

Wyndham Lewis (1882–1957)
The Writer and the Absolute NF

Louis MacNeice (1907–63)
Ten Burnt Offerings V

John Masefield (1878–1967)
So Long to Learn NF
Autobiography. See also *Grace Before Ploughing* 1966.

John Masters (1914–73)
The Deceivers F
Indian Trilogy ii. See also *Nightrunners of Bengal* 1951, *Bhowani Junction* 1954.

Somerset Maugham (1874–1965)
The Vagrant Mood NF
Essays. Published on 27 October 1952.

Edwin Muir (1887–1959)
Collected Poems 1921–51 V

R.K. Narayan (1906–2001)
The Financial Expert F

Mary Norton (1903–92)
The Borrowers F

Sean O'Casey (1880–1964)
Rose and Crown NF
Fifth volume of autobiography. See also *I Knock at the Door* 1939, *Pictures in the Hallway* 1942, *Drums Under the Windows* 1945, *Inishfallen, Fare Thee Well* 1949.

William Plomer (1903–73)
Museum Pieces F

Stephen Potter (1900–69)
One-Upmanship NF
See also *The Theory and Practice of Gamesmanship* 1947, *Some Notes on Lifemanship* 1950, *Supermanship* 1958

Anthony Powell (1905–2000)
A Buyer's Market F
Dance to the Music of Time ii. See also *A Question of Upbringing* 1951; *The Acceptance World* 1955; *At Lady Molly's* 1957; *Casanova's Chinese Restaurant* 1960; *The Kindly Ones* 1962; *The Valley of Bones* 1964; *The Soldier's Art* 1966; *The Military Philosophers* 1968; *Books Do Furnish a Room* 1971; *Temporary Kings* 1973; *Hearing Secret Harmonies* 1975.

Barbara Pym (1913–80)
Excellent Women F

Terence Rattigan (1911–77)
The Deep Blue Sea D
Performed in Brighton 4 February 1952, and in London on 6 March 1952

Gwen Raverat (1885–1957)
Period Piece NF

Herbert Read (1893–1968)
The Philosophy of Modern Art NF

James Reeves (1909–78)
The Password, and Other Poems V

William Sansom (1912–76)
A Touch of the Sun F

Paul Scott (1920–78)
Johnnie Sahib F

Sir Osbert Sitwell (1892–1969)
Wrack at Tidesend V
Published on 16 May 1952. Sequel to *England Reclaimed* 1927 (q.v.). See also *On the Continent* 1958.

Dylan Thomas (1914–53)
Collected Poems 1934–1952 V

Dylan Thomas (1914–53)
In Country Sleep V

Evelyn Waugh (1903–66)
Men at Arms F
Continued in *Officers and Gentlemen* 1955 and concluded in *Unconditional Surrender* 1961 (qq.v.). See also *Sword of Honour* 1965.

'Antonia White' [Eirene Botting (1899–1980)]
The Sugar House F
Frost in May Quartet iii. See also *Frost in May* 1933, *The Lost Traveller* 1950, *Beyond the Glass* 1954.

Angus Wilson (1913–91)
Hemlock and After F

1953

- Khrushchev becomes first secretary of the Communist party
  Dwight D. Eisenhower becomes President of the USA
  Edmund Hillary and Tenzing Norgay reach the summit of Mount Everest (29 May)
  Coronation of Queen Elizabeth II (2 June)
  Republic proclaimed in Egypt
- Sebastian Faulkes born
  Ronald Frame born
  Frank McGuinness born
  Tony Parsons born
  Lisa St Aubin de Terán born
  Jo Shapcott born
- Hilaire Belloc dies
  Theodore Powys dies
  Dylan Thomas dies
- Queen Mary dies
  Joseph Stalin dies (5 Mar.)
- William Faulkner, *Requiem for a Nun*
  Arthur Miller, *The Crucible*

Joan Aiken (1924–2004)
All You've Ever Wanted, and Other Stories F
For children

Kingsley Amis (1922–95)
Lucky Jim F

'Evelyn Anthony' [Evelyn Ward-Thomas (1928)]
Imperial Highness F

Nina Bawden (1925)
Who Calls the Tune F

Sybille Bedford (1911)
The Sudden View: A Mexican journey NF

Elizabeth Berridge (1921)
Upon Several Occasions F

Brigid Brophy (1929)
Hackenfeller's Ape F

Joyce Cary (1888–1957)
Except the Lord F
Second volume of trilogy with *Prisoner of Grace* 1952 and *Not Honour More* 1955 (qq.v.)

Charles Causley (1917–2003)
Survivor's Leave V

I. Compton-Burnett (1884–1969)
The Present and the Past F

'William Cooper' [Harry Summerfield Hoff (1910–2002)]
The Ever-Interesting Topic F

C. Day Lewis (1904–72)
An Italian Visit V

Walter de la Mare (1873–1956)
O Lovely England, and Other Poems V

Walter de la Mare (1873–1956)
Private View NF
Published in June 1953. Essays on literature. Introduction by David Cecil.

Patrick Leigh Fermor (1915)
The Violins of Saint-Jacques F

Ian Fleming (1908–64)
Casino Royale F
The first James Bond novel

Robert Graves (1895–1985)
Poems 1953 V

Graham Greene (1904–91)
The Living Room D
Published on 18 May 1953. Performed 16 April 1953.

Thom Gunn (1929–2004)
Poems V

L.P. Hartley (1895–1972)
The Go-Between F

John Heath-Stubbs (1918) and **David Wright** (1920–94) (eds)
The Faber Book of Twentieth-Century Verse ANTH

Margaret Kennedy (1896–1967)
Troy Chimneys F

Marghanita Laski (1915–88)
The Victorian Chaise-Longue F

Rosamond Lehmann (1901–90)
The Echoing Grove F

C.S. Lewis (1898–1963)
The Silver Chair F
Chronicles of Narnia iv. See also *The Lion, the Witch, and the Wardrobe* 1950; *Prince Caspian* 1951; *The Voyage of the Dawn Treader* 1952; *The Horse and His Boy* 1954; *The Magician's Nephew* 1955; *The Last Battle* 1956.

Norman Lewis (1908–2003)
A Single Pilgrim F

Christopher Logue (1926)
Wand and Quadrant V

'George Orwell' [**Eric Arthur Blair** (1903–50)]
England Your England, and Other Essays NF
Published on 12 November 1953

Mervyn Peake (1911–68)
Mr Pye F

Ruth Pitter (1897–1992)
The Ermine V

V.S. Pritchett (1900–97)
Books in General NF

Sir Herbert Read (1893–1968)
The True Voice of Feeling NF
Read was knighted in this year

'Mary Renault' [**Eileen Mary Challans** (1905–83)]
The Charioteer F

Paul Scott (1920–78)
The Alien Sky F

C.H. Sisson (1914–2003)
An Asiatic Romance F

R.W. Southern (1912–2001)
The Making of the Middle Ages NF

Stephen Spender (1909–95)
The Creative Element NF
See also *The Destructive Element* 1935

Freya Stark (1893–1993)
The Coast of Incense NF
Autobiography. See also *Traveller's Prelude* 1950, *Beyond Euphrates* 1951, *Dust in the Lion's Paw* 1961.

John Wain (1925–94)
Hurry On Down F

Evelyn Waugh (1903–66)
Love Among the Ruins F

P.G. Wodehouse (1881–1975)
Ring for Jeeves F

Cecil Woodham-Smith (1896–1977)
The Reason Why NF

Virginia Woolf (1882–1941)
A Writer's Diary NF
Published on 2 November 1953. Edited by Leonard Woolf.

'John Wyndham' [**J.B. Harris** (1903–69)]
The Kraken Wakes F

1954

- Colonel Nasser takes power in Egypt (Apr.)
  French forces defeated by Vietnamese communists at Dien Bien Phu (May)
  Communist forces occupy Hanoi (Oct.)
  Terrorism in Algeria: France sends troops
- Iain Banks born
  Louis de Bernières born
  Alan Holinghurst born
  Kazuo Ishiguro born
  Hanif Kureishi born
  Adam Mars-Jones born
  Tim Parks born
  Fiona Pitt-Kethley born
- Sir E.K. Chambers dies
  James Hinton dies
  W.R. Inge dies
  Francis Brett Young dies
- Henri Matisse dies

Dannie Abse (1923)
Ash on a Young Man's Sleeve F

Walter Allen (1911–95)
The English Novel NF

W.H. Auden (1907–73)
Mountains V
Published on 26 October 1954

John Betjeman (1906–84)
A Few Late Chrysanthemums V

John Betjeman (1906–84)
Poems in the Porch V

Lucy Boston (1892–1990)
The Children of Green Knowe F
First of the Green Knowe series of children's books

Christy Brown (1932–81)
My Left Foot NF

Alan Brownjohn (1931)
Travellers Alone V

Arthur C. Clarke (1917)
Childhood's End F

Noël Coward (1899–1973)
Future Indefinite NF
Autobiography. See also *Present Indicative* 1937.

Roald Dahl (1916–90)
Someone Like You F
Stories

C. Day Lewis (1904–72)
Collected Poems V
See also *Collected Poems* 1948

T.S. Eliot (1888–1965)
The Confidential Clerk D
Performed 5 March 1954

Ian Fleming (1908–64)
Live and Let Die F

Christopher Fry (1907)
The Dark is Light Enough D
Performed in Edinburgh 22 February 1954, and in London on 30 April 1954

Roy Fuller (1912–91)
Counterparts V

Roy Fuller (1912–91)
Fantasy and Fugue F

Oliver St John Gogarty (1878–1957)
It Isn't This Time of Year at All! NF
Autobiography

William Golding (1911–93)
Lord of the Flies F

Graham Greene (1904–91)
Twenty-One Stories F
Published on 8 November 1954. Includes four stories not in *Nineteen Stories* 1947 (q.v.). Two items from *Nineteen Stories* withdrawn ('The Lottery Ticket', 'The Other Side of the Border').

Thom Gunn (1929–2004)
Fighting Terms V

John Heath-Stubbs (1918)
A Charm Against the Toothache V

Aldous Huxley (1894–1963)
The Doors of Perception NF

Margaret Irwin (1889–1967)
Bloodstock, and Other Stories F

Christopher Isherwood (1904–86)
The World in the Evening F

Elizabeth Jenkins (1905)
The Tortoise and the Hare F

Pamela Hansford Johnson (1912–81)
An Impossible Marriage F

Francis King (1923)
The Dark Glasses F

Arthur Koestler (1905–83)
The Invisible Writing NF
Sequel to *Arrow in the Blue* 1952 (q.v.)

Doris Lessing (1919)
A Proper Marriage F
Children of Violence quintet ii. See also *Martha Quest* 1952, *A Ripple From the Storm* 1958, *Landlocked* 1965, *The Four-Gated City* 1969.

C.S. Lewis (1898–1963)
The Horse and His Boy F
Chronicles of Narnia v. See also *The Lion, the Witch, and the Wardrobe* 1950; *Prince Caspian* 1951; *The Voyage of the Dawn Treader* 1952; *The Silver Chair* 1953; *The Magician's Nephew* 1955; *The Last Battle* 1956.

Wyndham Lewis (1882–1957)
The Demon of Progress in the Arts NF

Wyndham Lewis (1882–1957)
Self-Condemned F
Semi-autobiographical

Louis MacNeice (1907–63)
Autumn Sequel V
Sequel to *Autumn Journal* 1939 (q.v.)

John Masters (1914–73)
Bhowani Junction F
Indian Trilogy iii. See also *Nightrunners of Bengal* 1951, *The Deceivers* 1952.

Nancy Mitford (1904–73)
Madame de Pompadour NF

Penelope Mortimer (1918–99)
A Villa in Summer F

Iris Murdoch (1919–99)
Under the Net F

Joseph Needham (1900–95)
Science and Civilisation in China NF
Published in 7 volumes (1954–88)

Norman Nicholson (1914–87)
The Pot Geranium V

J.B. Priestley (1894–1984)
The Magicians F

V.S. Pritchett (1900–97)
The Spanish Temper NF

Terence Rattigan (1911–77)
The Sleeping Prince D
Performed in Manchester 28 September 1953, and in London on 5 November 1953

Sir Herbert Read (1893–1968)
Anarchy and Order NF
See also *Poetry and Anarchism* 1938

Alan Ross (1922)
Something of the Sea V

Jon Silkin (1930–97)
The Peaceable Kingdom V

C.P. Snow (1905–80)
The New Men F
Strangers and Brothers sequence v

Rosemary Sutcliff (1920–92)
The Eagle of the Ninth F
For children

A.J.P. Taylor (1906–90)
The Struggle for Mastery in Europe NF

Dylan Thomas (1914–53)
Quite Early One Morning MISC
Broadcasts

Dylan Thomas (1914–53)
Under Milk Wood D
Preface and musical setting by Daniel Jones. First version published as *Llareggub: A piece for radio perhaps*, in *Botteghe Oscure 9* (1952). First broadcast by the BBC on 25 January 1954.

J.R.R. Tolkien (1892–1973)
The Fellowship of the Ring F
The first part of The Lord of the Rings trilogy. See also *The Two Towers* 1954 (below), *The Return of the King* 1955, *The Lord of the Rings* 1966.

J.R.R. Tolkien (1892–1973)
The Two Towers F
Second part of The Lord of the Rings trilogy. See also *The Fellowship of the Ring* 1954 (above), *The Return of the King* 1955, *The Lord of the Rings* 1966.

Sylvia Townsend Warner (1893–1978)
The Flint Anchor F

Vernon Watkins (1906–67)
The Death Bell V

'Antonia White' [Eirene Botting (1899–1980)]
Beyond the Glass F
Frost in May Quartet iv. See also *Frost in May* 1933, *The Lost Traveller* 1950, *The Sugar House* 1952.

P.G. Wodehouse (1881–1975)
Jeeves and the Feudal Spirit F

1955

- West Germany joins NATO
  Sir Anthony Eden becomes British Prime Minister
  Hugh Gaitskell becomes leader of the British Labour Party
  Execution of Ruth Ellis
  State of emergency declared in Cyprus
- Carol Ann Duffy born
  Patrick McCabe born
  Candia McWilliam born
- Ruby M. Ayres dies
  Gilbert Cannan dies
  Constance Holme dies
  L.P. Jacks dies
- Alexander Fleming dies
- Albert Einstein dies
  Thomas Mann dies
- Vladimir Nabokov, *Lolita*

Brian Aldiss (1925)
The Brightfount Diaries F

Margery Allingham (1904–66)
The Beckoning Lady F

Kingsley Amis (1922–95)
That Uncertain Feeling F

W.H. Auden (1907–73)
The Shield of Achilles V
Published on 11 November 1955. First published in the USA.

John Bayley (1925)
In Another Country F

Samuel Beckett (1906–89)
Molloy F
First published in French in 1951

Joyce Cary (1888–1957)
Not Honour More F
Third volume of trilogy with *Prisoner of Grace* 1952 and *Except the Lord* 1953 (qq.v.)

Austin Clarke (1896–1974)
Ancient Lights V

See also *Too Great a Vine* 1957, *The Horse-Eaters* 1960

I. Compton-Burnett (1884–1969)
Mother and Son F

Robert Conquest (1917)
Poems V

Robert Conquest (1917)
A World of Difference F

Walter de la Mare (1873–1956)
A Beginning, and Other Stories F

Patric Dickinson (1914–94)
The Scale of Things V

J.P. Donleavy (1926)
The Ginger Man F

Lawrence Durrell (1912–90)
The Tree of Idleness, and Other Poems V

Ian Fleming (1908–64)
Moonraker F

Christopher Fry (1907) (tr.)
The Lark D
Translation of Jean Anouilh's *L'alouette*. Performed 11 May 1955.

Christopher Fry (1907) (tr.)
Tiger at the Gates D
Translation of Jean Giraudoux's *La guerre de Troie n'aura pas lieu*. Performed 2 June 1955.

David Garnett (1892–1981)
Aspects of Love F

William Golding (1911–93)
The Inheritors F

Robert Graves (1895–1985)
The Greek Myths F

Robert Graves (1895–1985)
Homer's Daughter F

Graham Greene (1904–91)
Loser Takes All: An entertainment F
Published on 31 January 1955. Serialized in the USA in *Harper's Magazine* (October 1955–January 1956).

Graham Greene (1904–91)
The Quiet American F
Published on 5 December 1955

Aldous Huxley (1894–1963)
The Genius and the Goddess F

Elizabeth Jennings (1926–2001)
A Way of Looking V

Ruth Prawer Jhabvala (1927)
To Whom She Will F

G. Wilson Knight (1897–1985)
The Mutual Flame NF
See also *The Wheel of Fire* 1930, *The Imperial Theme* 1931, *The Crown of Life* 1947

Ronald Knox (1888–1957) (tr.)
The Holy Bible BIB
One-volume edition of Knox's translations of *The New Testament* 1945 (q.v.) and *The Old Testament* 1949 (q.v.)

Philip Larkin (1922–85)
The Less Deceived V

Laurie Lee (1914–97)
My Many-Coated Man V

Laurie Lee (1914–97)
A Rose for Winter NF

John Lehmann (1907–87)
The Whispering Gallery NF
Autobiography. See also *I Am My Brother* 1960, *The Ample Proposition* 1966.

C.S. Lewis (1898–1963)
The Magician's Nephew F
Chronicles of Narnia vi. See also *The Lion, the Witch, and the Wardrobe* 1950; *Prince Caspian* 1951; *The Voyage of the Dawn Treader* 1952; *The Silver Chair* 1953; *The Horse and His Boy* 1954; *The Last Battle* 1956.

C.S. Lewis (1898–1963)
Surprised by Joy NF
Autobiography

Wyndham Lewis (1882–1957)
Monstre Gai. Malign Fiesta F
The Human Age books ii and iii; book i, *The Childermass*, first published in 1928 (q.v.)

Norman MacCaig (1910–96)
Riding Lights V

'Hugh MacDiarmid' [Christopher Murray Grieve (1892–1978)]
In Memoriam James Joyce V

Brian Moore (1921–99)
Judith Hearne F

Nicholas Mosley (1923)
The Rainbearers F

P.H. Newby (1918–97)
The Picnic at Sakkara F

Sean O'Casey (1880–1964)
The Bishop's Bonfire D
Performed in Dublin 28 February 1955

Philippa Pearce (1920)
A Minnow on the Say F
For children

Anthony Powell (1905–2000)
The Acceptance World F
Dance to the Music of Time iii. See also *A Question of Upbringing* 1951; *A Buyer's Market* 1952; *At Lady Molly's* 1957; *Casanova's Chinese Restaurant* 1960; *The Kindly Ones* 1962; *The Valley of Bones* 1964; *The Soldier's Art* 1966; *The Military Philosophers* 1968; *Books Do Furnish a Room* 1971; *Temporary Kings* 1973; *Hearing Secret Harmonies* 1975.

Terence Rattigan (1911–77)
Separate Tables D
Performed in Liverpool 23 August 1954, and in London on 22 September 1954

'Miss Read' [Dora Jessie Saint (1913)**]**
Village School F

Dorothy L. Sayers (1893–1957) (tr.)
The Comedy of Dante Alighieri, the Florentine D
Cantica 1 (*Inferno*) published in 1949 (q.v.); cantica 3 (*Paradiso*), 1962 (q.v.)

Iain Crichton Smith (1928)
The Long River V

Stephen Spender (1909–95)
Collected Poems 1928–1953 V

Stephen Spender (1909–95)
The Making of a Poem NF

Dylan Thomas (1914–53)
A Prospect of the Sea, and Other Stories and Prose Writings F

R.S. Thomas (1913–2000)
Song at the Year's Turning V
Introduction by John Betjeman

J.R.R. Tolkien (1892–1973)
The Return of the King F
Third volume in The Lord of the Rings trilogy. See also *The Fellowship of the Ring* 1954, *The Two Towers* 1954, *The Lord of the Rings* 1966.

Charles Tomlinson (1927)
The Necklace V

John Wain (1925–94)
Living in the Present F

Evelyn Waugh (1903–66)
Officers and Gentlemen F
Preceded by *Men at Arms* 1952 (q.v.); concluded in *Unconditional Surrender* 1961 (q.v.). See also *Sword of Honour* 1965.

C.V. Wedgwood (1910)
The King's Peace 1637–1641 NF
The Great Rebellion volume i. See also *The King's War* 1958.

'Rebecca West' [Cicily Isabel Andrews (1892–1983)**]**
A Train of Powder NF
On the Nuremberg war trials; based on articles published in the *Daily Telegraph*, *Evening Standard*, *New Yorker*, and elsewhere

'John Wyndham' [J.B. Harris (1903–69)**]**
The Chrysalids F

1956

- Suez crisis (July–Nov.)
  Abortive Hungarian revolution begins (Oct.)
- Janice Galloway born
- Michael Arlen (Dikran Kouyoumdjian) dies
  Sir Max Beerbohm dies
  E.C. Bentley dies
  Walter de la Mare dies
  A.A. Milne dies
- Bertolt Brecht dies
- John Berryman, *Homage to Mistress Bradstreet*
- *A Town Like Alice*
  Ingmar Bergman, *The Seventh Seal*

J.R. Ackerley (1896–1967)
My Dog Tulip NF

Nina Bawden (1925)
The Solitary Child F

Samuel Beckett (1906–89)
Waiting for Godot D
First British publication. First published in French as *En attendant Godot* 1952 and in English in the USA in August 1955. Performed in English 3 August 1955.

Brendan Behan (1923–64)
The Quare Fellow D
Performed 1954

Brigid Brophy (1929)
The King of a Rainy Country F

'Anthony Burgess' [John Anthony Burgess Wilson (1917–93)**]**
Time for a Tiger F
Malayan Trilogy i. See also *The Enemy in the Blanket* 1958, *Beds in the East* 1959.

Agatha Christie (1890–1976)
The Mousetrap D

Adaptation of Christie's story 'Three Blind Mice' (broadcast in 1952). Performed 25 November 1952.

Sir Winston Spencer Churchill (1874–1965)
A History of the English-Speaking Peoples NF
Published in 4 volumes (1956–8)

Kenneth Clark (1903–83)
The Nude NF

Gerald Durrell (1925–95)
My Family and Other Animals NF

Ian Fleming (1908–64)
Diamonds are Forever F

Peter Fleming (1907–71)
My Aunt's Rhinoceros, and Other Reflections NF

Roy Fuller (1912–91)
Image of a Society F

David Gascoyne (1916)
Night Thoughts V

William Golding (1911–93)
Pincher Martin F

Aldous Huxley (1894–1963)
Adonis and the Alphabet, and Other Essays NF

Aldous Huxley (1894–1963)
Heaven and Hell NF

Ruth Prawer Jhabvala (1927)
The Nature of Passion F

Thomas Kinsella (1928)
Poems V

C.S. Lewis (1898–1963)
The Last Battle F
Chronicles of Narnia vii. See also *The Lion, the Witch, and the Wardrobe* 1950; *Prince Caspian* 1951; *The Voyage of the Dawn Treader* 1952; *The Silver Chair* 1953; *The Horse and His Boy* 1954; *The Magician's Nephew* 1955.

Wyndham Lewis (1882–1957)
The Red Priest F

Christopher Logue (1926)
Devil, Maggot and Son V

Rose Macaulay (1881–1958)
The Towers of Trebizond F

Nancy Mitford (1904–73), **A.S.C. Ross** (1907–80), and others
Noblesse Oblige NF
Illustrated by Osbert Lancaster. Includes contributions from Evelyn Waugh and John Betjeman.

Edwin Muir (1887–1959)
One Foot in Eden V

Iris Murdoch (1919–99)
The Flight From the Enchanter F

'Patrick O'Brian' [Richard Patrick Russ (1914–2000)]
The Golden Ocean F

V.S. Pritchett (1900–97)
Collected Stories F

James Reeves (1909–78)
Pigeons and Princesses F
For children

William Sansom (1912–76)
A Contest of Ladies F

William Sansom (1912–76)
The Loving Eye F

E.J. Scovell (1907–99)
The River Steamer, and Other Poems V

Dodie Smith (1896–1990)
One Hundred and One Dalmatians F

C.P. Snow (1905–80)
Homecomings F
Strangers and Brothers sequence vi

Alec Waugh (1898–1981)
Island in the Sun F

Angus Wilson (1913–91)
Anglo-Saxon Attitudes F

Colin Wilson (1931)
The Outsider NF

1957

- Resignation of Anthony Eden: Harold Macmillan becomes British Prime Minister
  The Treaty of Rome (25 Mar.): European Economic Community (EEC) established
  The USSR launches *Sputnik I*
- Nick Hornby born
  Irvine Welsh born
- Roy Campbell dies
  Joyce Cary dies
  A.E. Coppard dies
  Lord Dunsany dies
- Oliver St John Gogarty dies
  Ronald Knox dies

Wyndham Lewis dies
Malcolm Lowry dies
John Middleton Murry dies
Michael Sadleir dies
Dorothy L. Sayers dies

- Jean Sibelius dies
- Jack Kerouac, *On the Road*
- *My Fair Lady*

Dannie Abse (1923)
Tenants of the House V

Brian Aldiss (1925)
Space, Time, and Nathaniel F
Stories

George Barker (1913–91)
Collected Poems 1930–1955 V

Samuel Beckett (1906–89)
All That Fall D
Broadcast by the BBC on 13 January 1957

Edmund Blunden (1896–1974)
Poems of Many Years V
Published on 17 June 1957

John Braine (1922–86)
Room at the Top F
See also *Life at the Top* 1962

Vera Brittain (1893–1970)
Testament of Experience NF
Autobiography. See also *Testament of Youth* 1933, *Testament of Friendship* 1940.

Christine Brooke-Rose (1923)
The Languages of Love F

Charles Causley (1917–2003)
Union Street V

Austin Clarke (1896–1974)
Too Great a Vine V
See also *Ancient Lights* 1955, *The Horse-Eaters* 1960

I. Compton-Burnett (1884–1969)
A Father and His Fate F

Donald Davie (1922–95)
A Winter Talent, and Other Poems V

C. Day Lewis (1904–72)
Pegasus, and Other Poems V

Lawrence Durrell (1912–90)
Bitter Lemons NF

Lawrence Durrell (1912–90)
Esprit de Corps F
First of the Antrobus Trilogy. See also *Stiff Upper Lip* 1958, *Suave Qui Peut* 1966.

Lawrence Durrell (1912–90)
Justine F
Alexandrian Quartet volume i. See also *Balthazar* 1958, *Mountolive* 1958, *Clea* 1960; *Alexandrian Quartet* 1962.

T.S. Eliot (1888–1965)
On Poetry and Poets NF
Published on 13 September 1957

Ian Fleming (1908–64)
From Russia With Love F

Roy Fuller (1912–91)
Brutus's Orchard V

Thom Gunn (1929–2004)
The Sense of Movement V

Richard Hoggart (1918)
The Uses of Literacy NF

Ted Hughes (1930–98)
The Hawk in the Rain V
Published on 13 September 1957

James Joyce (1882–1941)
The Letters of James Joyce [vol. i] NF
Volumes ii and iii (edited by Richard Ellmann) published in 1966

M.M. Kaye (1908–2004)
Shadow of the Moon F

Frank Kermode (1919)
The Romantic Image NF

Francis King (1923)
The Man on the Rock F

James Kirkup (1918)
The Descent into the Cave, and Other Poems V

James Kirkup (1918)
The Prodigal Son V

Norman Lewis (1908–2003)
The Volcanoes Above Us F

Norman MacCaig (1910–96)
The Sinai Sort V

Colin MacInnes (1914–76)
City of Spades F
London Trilogy i. See also *Absolute Beginners* 1959, *Mr Love and Justice* 1960.

Alistair Maclean (1923–87)
The Guns of Navarone F

Louis MacNeice (1907–63)
Visitations V

Richard Mason (1919–97)
The World of Suzie Wong F

Iris Murdoch (1919–99)
The Sandcastle F

V.S. Naipaul (1932)
The Mystic Masseur F

P.H. Newby (1918–97)
Revolution and Roses F

Sean O'Casey (1880–1964)
The Green Crow MISC
Essays and stories. First published in the USA, 1956.

'Frank O'Connor' [Michael Francis O'Donovan (1903–66)]
Domestic Relations F

John Osborne (1929–94)
Look Back in Anger D
Performed 8 May 1956

John Osborne (1929–94)
The Entertainer D
Performed 1957 (with Laurence Olivier as Archie Rice)

Anthony Powell (1905–2000)
At Lady Molly's F
Dance to the Music of Time iv. See also *A Question of Upbringing* 1951; *A Buyer's Market* 1952; *The Acceptance World* 1955; *Casanova's Chinese Restaurant* 1960; *The Kindly Ones* 1962; *The Valley of Bones* 1964; *The Soldier's Art* 1966; *The Military Philosophers* 1968; *Books Do Furnish a Room* 1971; *Temporary Kings* 1973; *Hearing Secret Harmonies* 1975.

'Nevil Shute' [Nevil Shute Norway (1899–1960)]
On the Beach F

Stevie Smith (1902–71)
Not Waving but Drowning V

Muriel Spark (1918)
The Comforters F

Anthony Thwaite (1930)
Home Truths V

Terence Tiller (1916–87)
Reading a Medal V

Keith Waterhouse (1929)
There is a Happy Land F

Evelyn Waugh (1903–66)
The Ordeal of Gilbert Pinfold F

Angus Wilson (1913–91)
A Bit Off the Map, and Other Stories F

'John Wyndham' [J.B. Harris (1903–69)]
The Midwich Cuckoos F

1958

- Algerian crisis (May)
  General de Gaulle elected president of the Fifth French Republic (Dec.)
  Victorian Society founded
- Roddy Doyle born
  Helen Fielding born
  Caryl Phillips born
  Benjamin Zephaniah born
- F. Tennyson Jesse dies
  Rose Macaulay dies
  G.E. Moore dies
  Charles Morgan dies
  Alfred Noyes dies
  Lennox Robinson dies
  Sir John Collings Squire dies
  Marie Stopes dies
  H.M. Tomlinson dies
- Ralph Vaughan Williams dies
- Boris Pasternak, *Dr Zhivago*

A. Alvarez (1929)
The End of It V

A. Alvarez (1929)
The Shaping Spirit NF

Kingsley Amis (1922–95)
I Like it Here F

H.E. Bates (1905–74)
The Darling Buds of May F
First of the four Larkins books. See also *A Breath of French Air* 1959, *When the Green Woods Laugh* 1960, *Oh! To Be in England* 1963.

Samuel Beckett (1906–89)
Endgame D
World premiere in French (*Fin de Partie*) in London on 3 April 1957. Performed in English in New York 28 January 1958, and in London on 28 October 1958. Also includes *Act Without Words*.

Samuel Beckett (1906–89)
Malone Dies F
First published in French, 1951. English translation first published in the USA, 1956.

Brendan Behan (1923–64)
Borstal Boy NF

Brendan Behan (1923–64)
The Hostage D

John Berger (1926)
A Painter of Our Time F

John Betjeman (1906–84)
Collected Poems V

Robert Bolt (1924–95)
Flowering Cherry D
Performed 1957

Christine Brooke-Rose (1923)
Remake F

Christine Brooke-Rose (1923)
The Sycamore Tree F

'Anthony Burgess' [John Anthony Burgess Wilson (1917–93)]
The Enemy in the Blanket F
Malayan Trilogy ii. See also *Time for a Tiger* 1956, *Beds in the East* 1959.

Isabel Colegate (1931)
The Blackmailer F

'William Cooper' [Harry Summerfield Hoff (1910–2002)]
Young People F

R. F. Delderfield (1912–72)
The Dreaming Suburb F
See also *The Avenue Goes to War*, below

R.F. Delderfield (1912–72)
The Avenue Goes to War F
Sequel to *The Dreaming Suburb*, above

Lawrence Durrell (1912–90)
Balthazar F
Alexandrian Quartet volume ii. See also *Justine* 1957, *Mountolive* 1958 (below), *Clea* 1960; *Alexandrian Quartet* 1962.

Lawrence Durrell (1912–90)
Mountolive F
Alexandrian Quartet volume iii. See also *Justine* 1957, *Balthazar* 1958 (above), *Clea* 1960; *Alexandrian Quartet* 1962.

Lawrence Durrell (1912–90)
Stiff Upper Lip F
Second of the Antrobus Trilogy. See also *Esprit de Corps* 1957, *Sauve Qui Peut* 1966.

Patrick Leigh Fermor (1915)
Mani NF

Ian Fleming (1908–64)
Dr No F

Christopher Fry (1907) (tr.)
Duel of Angels D
Translation of J. Giraudoux's *Pour Lucrece*. Performed in Newcastle 3 March 1958.

Rumer Godden (1907–98)
The Greengage Summer F

William Golding (1911–93)
The Brass Butterfly D

Graham Greene (1904–91)
The Potting Shed D
Published on 3 February 1958. First published in the USA, February 1957. Performed New York 29 January 1957, and in London on 5 February 1958.

Graham Greene (1904–91)
Our Man in Havana F
Published on 6 October 1958

John Heath-Stubbs (1918)
Helen in Egypt, and Other Plays D

John Heath-Stubbs (1918)
The Triumph of the Muse, and Other Poems V

Christopher Hill (1912–2003)
Puritanism and Revolution NF

Elizabeth Jennings (1926–2001)
A Sense of the World V

Ruth Prawer Jhabvala (1927)
Esmond in India F

Thomas Kinsella (1928)
Another September V

Doris Lessing (1919)
A Ripple From the Storm F
Children of Violence quintet iii. See also *Martha Quest* 1952, *A Proper Marriage* 1954, *Landlocked* 1965, *The Four-Gated City* 1969.

Somerset Maugham (1874–1965)
Points of View NF
Essays. Published on 3 November 1958.

Stanley Middleton (1919)
A Short Answer F

Brian Moore (1921–99)
The Feast of Lupercal F

Penelope Mortimer (1918–99)
Daddy's Gone-a-Hunting F

Iris Murdoch (1919–99)
The Bell F

V.S. Naipaul (1932)
The Suffrage of Elvira F

Eric Newby (1919)
A Short Walk in the Hindu Kush NF

Philippa Pearce (1920)
Tom's Midnight Garden F
For children

Stephen Potter (1900–69)
Supermanship NF
See also *The Theory and Practice of Gamesmanship* 1947, *Some Notes on Lifemanship* 1950, *One-Upmanship* 1952

Terence Rattigan (1911–77)
Variation on a Theme D
Performed in Manchester 31 March 1958, and in London on 8 May 1958

'Mary Renault' [Eileen Mary Challans (1905–83)]
The King Must Die F

Alan Ross (1922)
To Whom It May Concern V

William Sansom (1912–76)
The Cautious Heart F

Jon Silkin (1930–97)
The Two Freedoms V

Alan Sillitoe (1928)
Saturday Night and Sunday Morning F

N.F. Simpson (1919)
A Resounding Tinkle D
Performed 2 April 1958

Sir Osbert Sitwell (1892–1969)
On the Continent V
Published on 20 March 1958. See also *England Reclaimed* 1927, *Wrack at Tidesend* 1952.

C.P. Snow (1905–80)
The Conscience of the Rich F
Strangers and Brothers sequence vii

Muriel Spark (1918)
The Go-Away Bird, and Other Stories F

Muriel Spark (1918)
Robinson F

R.S. Thomas (1913–2000)
Poetry for Supper V

'William Trevor' [William Trevor Cox (1928)]
A Standard of Behaviour F

John Wain (1925–94)
The Contenders F

C.V. Wedgwood (1910)
The King's War 1641–1647 NF
The Great Rebellion volume ii. See also *The King's Peace* 1955.

T.H. White (1906–64)
The Once and Future King F
Comprises *The Sword in the Stone* 1938, *The Witch in the Wood* 1940 (retitled 'The Queen of Air and Darkness'), and *The Ill-Made Knight* 1941 (qq.v.) but expanded and revised and with a new narrative, 'The Candle in the Wind', published for the first time

Raymond Williams (1921–88)
Culture and Society 1780–1950 NF

Angus Wilson (1913–91)
The Middle Age of Mrs Eliot F

Virginia Woolf (1882–1941)
Granite and Rainbow NF
Published on 16 June 1958

1959

- Fidel Castro takes power in Cuba (Feb.)
  European Free Trade Association (EFTA) established (Nov.)
- Dermot Bolger born
  Ben Okri born
  Jeanette Winterson born
- G.D.H. Cole dies
  Sir Walter Wilson Greg dies
  Laurence Housman dies
  Edwin Muir dies
  G.M. Young dies
- Jacob Epstein dies
  Stanley Spencer dies
- Saul Bellow, *Henderson the Rain King*
  William Faulkner, *The Mansion*
  Norman Mailer, *Advertisement for Myself*
- *Gigi*

Eric Ambler (1909–98)
Passage of Arms F

H.E. Bates (1905–74)
A Breath of French Air F
Second of the four Larkins books. See also *The Darling Buds of May* 1958, *When the Green Woods Laugh* 1960, *Oh! To Be in England* 1963.

Samuel Beckett (1906–89)
Krapp's Last Tape; Embers D
Krapp's Last Tape performed 28 October 1958; *Embers* broadcast by the BBC on 24 June 1959

Patricia Beer (1924–99)
Loss of the Magyar, and Other Poems V

Malcolm Bradbury (1932–2000)
Eating People is Wrong F

George Mackay Brown (1921–96)
Loaves and Fishes V

'Anthony Burgess' [John Anthony Burgess Wilson (1917–93)]
Beds in the East F
Malayan Trilogy iii. See also *Time for a Tiger* 1956, *The Enemy in the Blanket* 1958.

I. Compton-Burnett (1884–1969)
A Heritage and its History F

Shelagh Delaney (1939)
A Taste of Honey D
Performed 1958

Daphne du Maurier (1907–89)
The Breaking Point F
Includes 'The Birds'

T.S. Eliot (1888–1965)
The Elder Statesman D
Published on 10 April 1959. Performed at the Edinburgh Festival, 25–30 August 1958.

Ian Fleming (1908–64)
Goldfinger F

William Golding (1911–93)
Free Fall F

Robert Graves (1895–1985)
Collected Poems V

Graham Greene (1904–91)
The Complaisant Lover: A comedy D
Published on 29 June 1959. Performed 18 June 1959.

Geoffrey Hill (1932)
For the Unfallen V

Eric Hobsbawm (1917)
Primitive Rebels NF

Aldous Huxley (1894–1963)
Brave New World Revisited NF
First published in the USA, 1958. See also *Brave New World* 1932.

Elspeth Huxley (1907)
The Flame Trees of Thika NF

Pamela Hansford Johnson (1912–81)
The Unspeakable Skipton F
Dorothy Merlin Trilogy i. See also *Night and Silence* 1963 and *Cork Street, Next to the Hatter's* 1965.

P.J. Kavanagh (1931)
One and One V

Laurie Lee (1914–97)
Cider With Rosie NF
Autobiography

Christopher Logue (1926)
Songs V

Colin MacInnes (1914–76)
Absolute Beginners F
London Trilogy ii. See also *City of Spades* 1957, *Mr Love and Justice* 1960.

Louis MacNeice (1907–63)
Eighty-Five Poems V

Mervyn Peake (1911–68)
Titus Alone F
See also *Titus Groan* 1946, *Gormenghast* 1950

Simon Raven (1927–2001)
The Feathers of Death F

Anne Ridler (1912–2001)
A Matter of Life and Death V

Alan Sillitoe (1928)
The Loneliness of the Long-Distance Runner F

Andrew Sinclair (1935)
The Breaking of Bumbo F

C.P. Snow (1905–80)
The Two Cultures and the Scientific Revolution NF
See also *The Two Cultures; and A Second Look* 1964

Muriel Spark (1918)
Memento Mori F

George Steiner (1929)
Tolstoy or Dostoevsky NF

Sir Wilfred Thesiger (1910–2003)
Arabian Sands NF

John Wain (1925–94)
A Travelling Woman F

Keith Waterhouse (1929)
Billy Liar F
See also *Billy Liar on the Moon* 1975

Vernon Watkins (1906–67)
Cypress and Acacia V

Arnold Wesker (1932)
Chicken Soup with Barley D
The Wesker Trilogy i. Performed 1958. See also *Roots* 1959 (below), *I'm Talking About Jerusalem* 1960.

Arnold Wesker (1932)
Roots D
The Wesker Trilogy ii. Performed 1959, New York 1961. See also *Chicken Soup with Barley* 1959 (above), *I'm Talking About Jerusalem* 1960.

W.B. Yeats (1865–1939)
Mythologies NF

Includes *The Celtic Twilight* (1893), *The Secret Rose* (1897), *Stories of Red Hanrahan* (1897), *The Adoration of the Magi* (1897), and other pieces

1960

- Sharpeville massacre (21 Mar.)
  A US U-2 aircraft piloted by Gary Powers shot down by the USSR (May)
  Princess Margaret marries Anthony Armstrong-Jones
  Leonid Brezhnev becomes President of the USSR
  Former Gestapo chief Adolf Eichmann arrested
  France becomes a nuclear power
- Ian Rankin born
- Sir Herbert Grierson dies
  Sir Lewis Namier dies
  Eden Phillpotts dies
  Sir Leonard Woolley dies
  Dornford Yates (Cecil William Mercer) dies
- Prince Andrew born
- Aneurin Bevan dies
  Sylvia Pankhurst dies
- Boris Pasternak dies
- John Updike, *Rabbit Run*
- Alfred Hitchcock, *Psycho*

J.R. Ackerley (1896–1967)
We Think the World of You F

Kingsley Amis (1922–95)
Take a Girl Like You F

John Arden (1930)
Serjeant Musgrave's Dance: An unhistorical parable D
Performed 1959

W.H. Auden (1907–73)
Homage to Clio V

Lynne Reid Banks (1929)
The L-Shaped Room F
First of trilogy with *The Backward Shadow* 1970 and *Two is Lonely* 1974 (qq.v.)

Stan Barstow (1928)
A Kind of Loving F
Vic Brown Trilogy i. See also *The Watchers on the Shore* 1966, *The Right True End* 1976.

H.E. Bates (1905–74)
When the Green Woods Laugh F
Third of the four Larkins books. See also *The Darling Buds of May* 1958, *A Breath of French Air* 1959, *Oh! To Be in England* 1963.

John Betjeman (1906–84)
Summoned by Bells V

Christine Brooke-Rose (1923)
The Dear Deceit F

'Anthony Burgess' [John Anthony Burgess Wilson (1917–93)]
The Doctor is Sick F

'Anthony Burgess' [John Anthony Burgess Wilson (1917–93)]
The Right to an Answer F

Austin Clarke (1896–1974)
The Horse-Eaters V
See also *Ancient Lights* 1955, *Too Great a Vine* 1957

Noël Coward (1899–1973)
Waiting in the Wings D
Performed in Dublin 8 August 1960, and in London on 7 September 1960

C. Day Lewis (1904–72)
The Buried Day NF
Autobiography

Patric Dickinson (1914–94)
The World I See V

Lawrence Durrell (1912–90)
Clea F
Alexandrian Quartet iv. See also *Justine* 1957, *Balthazar* 1958, *Mountolive* 1958; *Alexandrian Quartet* 1962.

Lawrence Durrell (1912–90)
Collected Poems V

D.J. Enright (1920–2002)
Some Men are Brothers V

Ian Fleming (1908–64)
For Your Eyes Only F

Ted Hughes (1930–98)
Lupercal V
Published on 18 March 1960

Ruth Prawer Jhabvala (1927)
The Householder F

R.D. Laing (1927–89)
The Divided Self NF

D.H. Lawrence (1885–1930)
Lady Chatterley's Lover F
Published on 10 November 1960. The first unexpurgated British edition (preceded by the unexpurgated US edition in May 1959). See also *Lady Chatterley's Lover* 1928, 1929, 1932, 1933.

John Lehmann (1907–87)
I Am My Brother NF

See also *The Whispering Gallery* 1955, *The Ample Proposition* 1966

Doris Lessing (1919)
In Pursuit of the English NF
Autobiographical

Peter Levi (1931)
The Gravel Ponds V

David Lodge (1935)
The Picturegoers F

Norman MacCaig (1910–96)
A Common Grace V

Colin MacInnes (1914–76)
Mr Love and Justice F
London Trilogy iii. See also *City of Spades* 1957, *Absolute Beginners* 1959.

Olivia Manning (1915–80)
The Great Fortune F
Balkan Trilogy i. See also *The Spoilt City* 1962, *Friends and Heroes* 1965.

Gavin Maxwell (1914–69)
Ring of Bright Water NF
First of trilogy. See also *The Rocks Remain* 1963, *Raven Seek Thy Brother* 1968.

Jessica Mitford (1917–76)
Hons and Rebels NF

Brian Moore (1921–99)
The Luck of Ginger Coffey F

Edwin Muir (1887–1959)
Collected Poems 1921–58 V

Edna O'Brien (1932)
The Country Girls F
The Country Girls Trilogy i. See also *The Lonely Girl* 1962, *Girls in Their Married Bliss* 1964.

Harold Pinter (1930)
The Birthday Party, and Other Plays D
The Birthday Party performed in Cambridge 28 April 1958; revised version performed in London, 18 June 1964. Also includes *The Dumb Waiter* and *The Room*.

Harold Pinter (1930)
The Caretaker D
Performed 27 April 1960

Sylvia Plath (1932–63)
The Colossus, and Other Poems V

William Plomer (1903–73)
Collected Poems V

Dennis Potter (1935–94)
The Glittering Coffin D

Anthony Powell (1905–2000)
Casanova's Chinese Restaurant F
Dance to the Music of Time v. See also *A Question of Upbringing* 1951; *A Buyer's Market* 1952; *The Acceptance World* 1955; *At Lady Molly's* 1957; *The Kindly Ones* 1962; *The Valley of Bones* 1964; *The Soldier's Art* 1966; *The Military Philosophers* 1968; *Books Do Furnish a Room* 1971; *Temporary Kings* 1973; *Hearing Secret Harmonies* 1975.

J.B. Priestley (1894–1984)
Literature and Western Man NF

Frederic Raphael (1931)
The Limits of Love F

Terence Rattigan (1911–77)
Ross D
Performed in Liverpool 29 April 1960, and in London on 12 May 1960

Simon Raven (1927–2001)
Doctors Wear Scarlet F

Peter Redgrove (1932–2003)
The Collector, and Other Poems V
Published in 1960, dated 1959

James Reeves (1909–78)
Collected Poems 1929–59 V

Paul Scott (1920–78)
The Chinese Love Pavilion F

Alan Sillitoe (1928)
The General F

C.P. Snow (1905–80)
The Affair F
Strangers and Brothers sequence viii

Muriel Spark (1918)
The Bachelors F

Muriel Spark (1918)
The Ballad of Peckham Rye F

David Storey (1933)
This Sporting Life F

Julian Symons (1912–95)
The Thirties NF

Alec Waugh (1898–1981)
Fuel for the Flame F

Arnold Wesker (1932)
I'm Talking About Jerusalem D
The Wesker Trilogy iii. Performed 1960. See also *Chicken Soup with Barley*, and *Roots* 1959; published together as *The Wesker Trilogy* 1960.

P.G. Wodehouse (1881–1975)
Jeeves in the Offing F

Leonard Woolf (1880–1969)
Sowing NF
Autobiography. See also *Growing* 1961, *Beginning Again* 1964, *Downhill all the Way* 1967, *The Journey Not the Arrival Matters* 1969.

1961

- John F. Kennedy becomes President of the USA
  Yuri Gagarin is the first man in space (Apr.)
  Construction of the Berlin Wall (Aug.)
  UN Secretary-General Dag Hammarskjöld killed in an air crash (Sept.)
- Jonathan Coe born
  Arundhati Roy born
  Will Self born
- H.C. Bailey dies
  Oliver Onions dies
  Frank Richards (Charles Hamilton) dies
  Angela Thirkell dies
- Ernest Hemingway dies
  Carl Jung dies
- J.D. Salinger, *Franny and Zooey*
- François Truffaut, *Jules et Jim*
  Breakfast at Tiffany's

The New English Bible: The New Testament BIB

Samuel Beckett (1906–89)
Poems in English D

Robert Bolt (1924–95)
A Man for All Seasons D
Broadcast in 1954; performed 1960; film 1966

Christine Brooke-Rose (1923)
The Middlemen F

Alan Brownjohn (1931)
The Railings V

'Anthony Burgess' [John Anthony Burgess Wilson (1917–93)]
Devil of a State F

Charles Causley (1917–2003)
Johnny Alleluia V

Jack Clemo (1916–94)
The Map of Clay V

Padraic Colum (1881–1972)
Irish Elegies V

I. Compton-Burnett (1884–1969)
The Mighty and their Fall F

'William Cooper' [Harry Summerfield Hoff (1910–2002)]
Scenes from Married Life F
See also *Scenes from Provincial Life* 1950, *Scenes from Metropolitan Life* 1982, *Scenes from Later Life* 1983

William Empson (1906–84)
Milton's God NF

Roy Fisher (1930)
City V

Ian Fleming (1908–64)
Thunderball F

John Fuller (1937)
Fairground Music V

Roy Fuller (1912–91)
The Father's Comedy F

Winston Graham (1910–2003)
Marnie F
Filmed by Alfred Hitchcock in 1964

Robert Graves (1895–1985)
More Poems V

Graham Greene (1904–91)
A Burnt-Out Case F
Published on 16 January 1961

Graham Greene (1904–91)
In Search of a Character: Two African journals NF
Published on 26 October 1961

Thom Gunn (1929–2004)
My Sad Captains, and Other Poems V

Susan Hill (1942)
The Enclosure F

Elizabeth Jennings (1926–2001)
Song For a Birth or a Death, and Other Poems V

R.D. Laing (1927–89)
The Self and Others NF

'John le Carré' [David John Moore Cornwell (1931)]
Call for the Dead F

C.S. Lewis (1898–1963)
An Experiment in Criticism NF

'N.W. Clerk' [C.S. Lewis (1898–1963)]
A Grief Observed NF
Reprinted in 1964 under Lewis's own name

Edward Lucie-Smith (1933)
A Tropical Childhood, and Other Poems V

'Hugh MacDiarmid' [Christopher Murray Grieve (1892–1978)]
The Kind of Poetry I Want V

Louis MacNeice (1907–63)
Solstices V

John Masefield (1878–1967)
Bluebells, and Other Verse V

Julian Mitchell (1935)
Imaginary Toys F

Iris Murdoch (1919–99)
A Severed Head F

V.S. Naipaul (1932)
A House For Mr Biswas F

R.K. Narayan (1906–2001)
The Man-Eater of Malgudi F

'Flann O'Brien' [Brian O'Nolan (1911–66)]
The Hard Life F

'George Orwell' [Eric Arthur Blair (1903–50)]
Collected Essays NF

Harold Pinter (1930)
Night School D
Televised on 21 July 1960

Harold Pinter (1930)
A Slight Ache, and Other Plays D
A Slight Ache performed 18 January 1961. Also includes *A Night Out, The Dwarfs,* and sketches.

Peter Porter (1929)
Once Bitten, Twice Bitten V

V.S. Pritchett (1900–97)
When My Girl Comes Home F
Stories

William Sansom (1912–76)
The Last Hours of Sandra Lee F

Siegfried Sassoon (1886–1967)
Collected Poems 1908–56 V

Vernon Scannell (1922)
The Face of the Enemy F

Jon Silkin (1930–97)
The Re-Ordering of the Stones V

Alan Sillitoe (1928)
Key to the Door F

C.H. Sisson (1914–2003)
The London Zoo V

Muriel Spark (1918)
The Prime of Miss Jean Brodie F

Jon Stallworthy (1935)
The Astronomy of Love V

Freya Stark (1893–1993)
Dust in the Lion's Paw NF
Autobiography. See also *Traveller's Prelude* 1950, *Beyond Euphrates* 1951, *The Coast of Incense* 1953.

George Steiner (1929)
The Death of Tragedy NF

David Storey (1933)
Flight into Camden F

A.J.P. Taylor (1906–90)
The Origins of the Second World War NF

R.S. Thomas (1913–2000)
Tares V

Philip Toynbee (1916–81)
Pantaloon; or, The Valediction F
A novel in prose and verse. See also *Two Brothers* 1964, *A Learned City* 1966, *Views From a Lake* 1968.

Kenneth Tynan (1927–80)
Curtains NF

John Wain (1925–94)
Weep Before God V

Evelyn Waugh (1903–66)
Unconditional Surrender F
See also *Men at Arms* 1952, *Officers and Gentlemen* 1955, *Sword of Honour* 1965

Angus Wilson (1913–91)
The Old Men at the Zoo F

Leonard Woolf (1880–1969)
Growing NF
Autobiography. See also *Sowing* 1960, *Beginning Again* 1964, *Downhill all the Way* 1967, *The Journey Not the Arrival Matters* 1969.

W.B. Yeats (1865–1939)
Essays and Introductions NF
Published 16 February 1961

1962

- Execution of Adolf Eichmann
  Algerian independence (July)
  Telstar satellite launched
  Cuban missile crisis (Oct.)
  First issue of *Private Eye*
- Richard Aldington dies
  Clifford Bax dies

Wilfrid Gibson dies
Patrick Hamilton dies
Vita Sackville-West dies
R.H. Tawney dies
G.M. Trevelyan dies

- Henry Miller, *Tropic of Capricorn*
  Alexander Solzhenitsyn, *One Day in the Life of Ivan Denisovich*
- Alfred Hitchcock, *The Birds*
  David Lean, *Lawrence of Arabia*

Dannie Abse (1923)
Poems, Golders Green V

Joan Aiken (1924–2004)
The Wolves of Willoughby Chase F
For children

A. Alvarez (1929) (ed.)
The New Poetry ANTH

George Barker (1913–91)
The View From a Blind I V

Stan Barstow (1928)
Ask Me Tomorrow F

Samuel Beckett (1906–89)
Happy Days D
First published in the USA, 1961. Performed in New York 17 September 1961.

Alan Bennett (1934) and others
Beyond the Fringe D
With Peter Cook, Dudley Moore, and Jonathan Miller. Performed in Edinburgh in 1960, London 1961.

Edmund Blunden (1896–1974)
A Hong Kong House V
Published on 3 September 1962

John Braine (1922–86)
Life at the Top F
See *Room at the Top* 1957

Brigid Brophy (1929)
Flesh F

'Anthony Burgess' [John Anthony Burgess Wilson (1917–93)]
A Clockwork Orange F

'Anthony Burgess' [John Anthony Burgess Wilson (1917–93)]
The Wanting Seed F

Barbara Comyns (1909–92)
The Skin Chairs F

C. Day Lewis (1904–72)
The Gate, and Other Poems V

Len Deighton (1929)
The Ipcress File F

Kay Dick (1915)
Sunday F

Maureen Duffy (1933)
That's How It Was F

Dorothy Dunnett (1923–2001)
Game of Kings F
First of the Lymond Chronicles

Lawrence Durrell (1912–90)
The Alexandrian Quartet F
Comprising *Justine* 1957, *Balthazar* 1958, *Mountolive* 1958, *Clea* 1960 (qq.v)

T.S. Eliot (1888–1965)
Collected Plays D
Published on 31 August 1962

Janice Elliott (1931–95)
Cave with Echoes F

D.J. Enright (1920–2002)
Addictions V

Ian Fleming (1908–64)
The Spy Who Loved Me F

Dick Francis (1920)
Dead Cert F
The first Dick Francis novel

Michael Frayn (1933)
The Day of the Dog NF
Articles

Nicholas Freeling (1927–2003)
Love in Amsterdam F
First of the Van der Valk novels

Brian Friel (1929)
The Saucer of Larks F

Roy Fuller (1912–91)
Collected Poems 1936–1961 V
See also *New and Collected Poems* 1985

Robert Graves (1895–1985)
New Poems V

Robert Graves (1895–1985)
Oxford Addresses on Poetry NF

Eric Hobsbawm (1917)
The Age of Revolution: Europe 1789–1848 NF
See also *The Age of Capital* 1975, *The Age of Empire* 1987

Aldous Huxley (1894–1963)
Island F

Christopher Isherwood (1904–86)
Down There on a Visit F

P.D. James (1920)
Cover Her Face F
The first Inspector Dalgliesh novel

Ann Jellicoe (1927)
The Knack D
Performed in Cambridge, 1961

Pamela Hansford Johnson (1912–81)
An Error of Judgement F

Thomas Kinsella (1928)
Downstream V

Doris Lessing (1919)
The Golden Notebook F

Peter Levi (1931)
Water, Rock and Sand V

David Lodge (1935)
Ginger, You're Barmy F

Norman MacCaig (1910–96)
A Round of Applause V

Olivia Manning (1915–80)
The Spoilt City F
Balkan Trilogy ii. See also *The Great Fortune* 1960, *Friends and Heroes* 1965.

Christopher Middleton (1926)
Torse 3 V

Naomi Mitchison (1897–1999)
Memoirs of a Spacewoman F

Penelope Mortimer (1918–99)
The Pumpkin Eater F

Nicholas Mosley (1923)
Meeting Place F

Iris Murdoch (1919–99)
An Unofficial Rose F

V.S. Naipaul (1932)
The Middle Passage NF

P.H. Newby (1918–97)
The Barbary Light F

Edna O'Brien (1932)
The Lonely Girl F
Republished in 1964 as *The Girl with Green Eyes*. The Country Girls Trilogy ii. See also *The Country Girls* 1960, *Girls in Their Married Bliss* 1964.

Philippa Pearce (1920)
A Dog So Small F
For children

Anthony Powell (1905–2000)
The Kindly Ones F
Dance to the Music of Time vi. See also *A Question of Upbringing* 1951; *A Buyer's Market* 1952; *The Acceptance World* 1955; *At Lady Molly's* 1957; *Casanova's Chinese Restaurant* 1960; *The Valley of Bones* 1964; *The Soldier's Art* 1966; *The Military Philosophers* 1968; *Books Do Furnish a Room* 1971; *Temporary Kings* 1973; *Hearing Secret Harmonies* 1975.

Frederic Raphael (1931)
The Trouble with England F

Simon Raven (1927–2001)
Close of Play F

'Mary Renault' [**Eileen Mary Challans** (1905–83)]
The Bull From the Sea F

Bernice Rubens (1928–2004)
Madame Sousatzka F

Dorothy L. Sayers (1893–1957) (tr.)
The Comedy of Dante Alighieri, the Florentine D
Translated by Sayers and Barbara Reynolds. Cantica 1 (*Inferno*) published in 1949 (q.v.); cantica 2 (*Purgatorio*), 1955 (q.v.).

Vernon Scannell (1922)
A Sense of Danger V

J.R.R. Tolkien (1892–1973)
The Adventures of Tom Bombadil, and Other Verses from the 'Red Book' V

Edward Upward (1903)
In the Thirties F
The Spiral Ascent Trilogy i. See also *The Rotten Elements* 1969, *The Spiral Ascent* 1977.

John Wain (1925–94)
Strike the Father Dead F

Sylvia Townsend Warner (1893–1978)
A Spirit Rises F

Vernon Watkins (1906–67)
Affinities V

Arnold Wesker (1932)
Chips With Everything D
Performed 1962

1963

- General de Gaulle vetos British membership of the EEC (Jan.)
The Profumo scandal

Sir Alec Douglas-Home becomes British Prime Minister
John F. Kennedy assassinated (22 Nov.): Lyndon B. Johnson becomes President of the USA
Beeching Report on British railway system

- Simon Armitage born
  Don Paterson born
  Meera Syal born
- Phyllis Bottome dies
  Christopher Hassall dies
  Aldous Huxley dies
  C.S. Lewis dies
  Louis MacNeice dies
  Sylvia Plath dies
  John Cowper Powys dies
- Jean Cocteau dies
  Robert Frost dies
- Mary McCarthy, *The Group*
  John Robinson, *Honest to God*

Kingsley Amis (1922–95)
One Fat Englishman F

W.H. Auden (1907–73)
The Dyer's Hand, and Other Essays NF
First published in the USA, 1962

J.G. Ballard (1930)
The Drowned World F
First published in the USA, 1962

J.G. Ballard (1930)
The Four-Dimensional Nightmare F

A.L. Barker (1918–2002)
The Joy-Ride and After F

H.E. Bates (1905–74)
Oh! To Be in England F
Fourth of the four Larkins books. See also *The Darling Buds of May* 1958, *A Breath of French Air* 1959, *When the Green Woods Laugh* 1960.

Samuel Beckett (1906–89)
Watt F
First published in Paris, 1953, and in the USA, 1959

Patricia Beer (1924–99)
The Survivors V

Brigid Brophy (1929)
The Finishing Touch F

'Anthony Burgess' [**John Anthony Burgess Wilson** (1917–93)]
Honey for the Bears F

'Joseph Kell' [**John Anthony Burgess Wilson** (1917–93)]
Inside Mr Enderby F
Published under the name 'Anthony Burgess' in 1966. See also *Enderby Outside* 1968, *The Clockwork Testament* 1974, *Enderby's Dark Lady* 1984.

'Anthony Burgess' [**John Anthony Burgess Wilson** (1917–93)]
The Novel Today NF

J.L. Carr (1912–94)
A Day in Summer F

I. Compton-Burnett (1884–1969)
A God and His Gifts F

C. Day Lewis (1904–1972) (tr.)
The Eclogues of Virgil V
See also *The Georgics of Virgil* 1940, *The Aeneid of Virgil* 1952

Margaret Drabble (1939)
A Summer Bird-Cage F

Nell Dunn (1936)
Up the Junction F
Interlinked stories

T.S. Eliot (1888–1965)
Collected Poems 1909–1962 V
Published on 25 September 1963

J.G. Farrell (1935–79)
A Man From Elsewhere F

Ian Fleming (1908–64)
On Her Majesty's Secret Service F

John Fowles (1926)
The Collector F

Rumer Godden (1907–98)
The Battle of the Villa Fiorita F

Simon Gray (1936)
Colmain F

Graham Greene (1904–91)
A Sense of Reality F
Stories. Published on 20 June 1963.

Susan Hill (1942)
Do Me a Favour F

Philip Hobsbaum (1932) and **Edward Lucie-Smith** (1933) (eds)
A Group Anthology ANTH

B.S. Johnson (1933–73)
Travelling People F

Pamela Hansford Johnson (1912–81)
Night and Silence, Who is Here? F

Dorothy Merlin Trilogy ii. See also *The Unspeakable Skipton* 1959 and *Cork Street, Next to the Hatter's* 1965.

James Kirkup (1918)
Refusal to Conform V

'John le Carré' [David John Moore Cornwell (1931)]
The Spy Who Came in From the Cold F

'Richard Llewellyn' [Richard Llewellyn Lloyd (1906–83)]
Up, Into the Singing Mountain F
Sequel to *How Green Was My Valley* 1939 (q.v.); see also *Down Where the Moon is Small* 1966, *Green, Green My Valley Now* 1975

George MacBeth (1932–92)
The Broken Places V

Alistair Maclean (1923–87)
Ice Station Zebra F

Louis MacNeice (1907–63)
The Burning Perch V

Gavin Maxwell (1914–69)
The Rocks Remain NF
Second of trilogy. See also *Ring of Bright Water* 1960, *Raven Seek Thy Brother* 1968.

Brian Moore (1921–99)
An Answer From Limbo F

Iris Murdoch (1919–99)
The Unicorn F

John Osborne (1929–94)
Plays For England D
Contains *The Blood of the Bambergs*, and *Under Plain Cover*

Wilfred Owen (1893–1918)
Collected Poems V
Edited by Cecil Day Lewis

'Victoria Lucas' [Sylvia Plath (1932–63)]
The Bell Jar F
Published in January 1963. Plath committed suicide in February 1963.

F.T. Prince (1912–2003)
The Doors of Stone V

Peter Redgrove (1932–2003)
At the White Monument, and Other Poems V

Christopher Ricks (1933)
Milton's Grand Style NF

David Rudkin (1936)
Afore Night Come D
Performed 1960

Alan Sillitoe (1928)
The Ragman's Daughter F

Muriel Spark (1918)
The Girls of Slender Means F

Stephen Spender (1909–95)
The Struggle of the Modern NF

Jon Stallworthy (1935)
Out of Bounds V

David Storey (1933)
Radcliffe F

R.S. Thomas (1913–2000)
The Bread of Truth V

E.P. Thompson (1924–93)
The Making of the English Working Class NF

Anthony Thwaite (1930)
The Owl in the Tree V

Charles Tomlinson (1927)
A Peopled Landscape V

Evelyn Waugh (1903–66)
Basil Seal Rides Again; or, The Rake's Regress F

P.G. Wodehouse (1881–1975)
Stiff Upper Lip, Jeeves F

1964

- Brezhnev replaces Khrushchev as first secretary of the Communist party
  Nelson Mandela sentenced to life imprisonment
  US Civil Rights Bill
  Labour government in Britain (Oct.): Harold Wilson becomes Prime Minister
  China explodes an atomic bomb
- Alan Warner born
- Brendan Behan dies
  Clive Bell dies
  Daniel Corkery dies
  Ian Fleming dies
  J.B.S. Haldane dies
  Naomi Jacob dies
  Julian Maclaren-Ross dies
  Sean O'Casey dies
  Edith Sitwell dies
  T.H. White dies
- Pandit Nehru dies
  Cole Porter dies

- Saul Bellow, *Herzog*
  William Burroughs, *The Naked Lunch*
- The Beatles, *A Hard Day's Night* (film)
  Stanley Kubrick, *Dr Strangelove*
  Goldfinger

Joan Aiken (1924–2004)
Black Hearts in Battersea F
For children

John Arden (1930)
Three Plays D
Contains *The Waters of Babylon, Live Like Pigs,* and *The Happy Haven* (co-written with Margaretta D'Arcy)

John Arden (1930)
The Workhouse Donkey D
Performed 1963

J.G. Ballard (1930)
The Terminal Beach F

A.L. Barker (1918–2002)
Lost Upon the Roundabouts F

Samuel Beckett (1906–89)
How It Is F
A translation by Beckett of *Comment C'est* (Paris, 1961)

Samuel Beckett (1906–89)
Play and Two Short Pieces for Radio D
Play first performed in German 14 June 1963; first performed in English in New York (January 1964) and London (April 1964). Also contains *Words and Music* and *Cascando.*

John Braine (1922–86)
The Jealous God F

Christine Brooke-Rose (1923)
Out F

Brigid Brophy (1929)
The Snow Ball F

'Anthony Burgess' [John Anthony Burgess Wilson (1917–93)]
The Eve of St Venus F

'Anthony Burgess' [John Anthony Burgess Wilson (1917–93)]
Nothing Like the Sun F

A.S. Byatt (1936)
Shadow of a Sun F

Isabel Colegate (1931)
Statues in a Garden F

Donald Davie (1922–95)
Events and Wisdoms V

Len Deighton (1929)
Funeral in Berlin F

Patric Dickinson (1914–94)
This Cold Universe V

J.P. Donleavy (1926)
A Singular Man F
First published in the USA, 1963

Margaret Drabble (1939)
The Garrick Year F

Maureen Duffy (1933)
The Single Eye F

Gavin Ewart (1916)
Londoners V

Ian Fleming (1908–64)
Chitty-Chitty-Bang-Bang: The Magical Car F

Ian Fleming (1908–64)
You Only Live Twice F

Margaret Forster (1938)
Dame's Delight F

Leon Garfield (1921)
Jack Holborn F

William Golding (1911–93)
The Spire F

Robert Graves (1895–1985)
Man Does, Woman Is V

Graham Greene (1904–91)
Carving a Statue D
Published on 11 November 1964. Performed 17 September 1964.

Ian Hamilton (1938–2001)
Pretending Not to Sleep V

Tony Harrison (1937)
Earthworks V

L.P. Hartley (1895–1972)
The Brickfield F
Contd in *The Betrayal* 1966 (q.v.)

Christopher Hassall (1912–63)
Rupert Brooke NF

Eric Hobsbawm (1917)
Labouring Men NF

Jane Aiken Hodge (1917)
Maulever Hall F

Christopher Isherwood (1904–86)
A Single Man F

Elizabeth Jennings (1926–2001)
Recoveries v

B.S. Johnson (1933–73)
Albert Angelo F

Patrick Kavanagh (1904–67)
Collected Poems v

Francis King (1923)
The Japanese Umbrella, and Other Stories F

Philip Larkin (1922–85)
The Whitsun Weddings v

Doris Lessing (1919)
African Stories F
See also *Nine African Stories* 1968

C.S. Lewis (1898–1963)
Letters to Malcolm, Chiefly on Prayer NF

C.S. Lewis (1898–1963)
Poems v

Edward Lucie-Smith (1933)
Confessions and Histories v

John Masefield (1878–1967)
Old Raiger, and Other Verse v

Adrian Mitchell (1932)
Poems v

Julian Mitchell (1935)
The White Father F

Iris Murdoch (1919–99)
The Italian Girl F
Dramatized 1969

V.S. Naipaul (1932)
An Area of Darkness NF

'Flann O'Brien' [Brian O'Nolan (1911–66)**]**
The Dalkey Archive F

Edna O'Brien (1932)
Girls in Their Married Bliss F
The Country Girls Trilogy iii. See also *The Country Girls* 1960, *The Lonely Girl* 1962. Published together with Epilogue 1986.

Joe Orton (1933–67)
Entertaining Mr Sloane D
Performed 1964

Peter Porter (1929)
Poems Ancient & Modern v

Anthony Powell (1905–2000)
The Valley of Bones F
Dance to the Music of Time vii. See also *A Question of Upbringing* 1951; *A Buyer's Market* 1952; *The Acceptance World* 1955; *At Lady Molly's* 1957; *Casanova's Chinese Restaurant* 1960; *The Kindly Ones* 1962; *The Soldier's Art* 1966; *The Military Philosophers* 1968; *Books Do Furnish a Room* 1971; *Temporary Kings* 1973; *Hearing Secret Harmonies* 1975.

Simon Raven (1927–2001)
The Rich Pay Late F
Alms for Oblivion series i. See also *Friends in Low Places* 1965, *The Sabre Squadron* 1966, *Fielding Gray* 1967, *The Judas Boy* 1968, *Places Where They Sing* 1970, *Sound the Retreat* 1971, *Come Like Shadows* 1972, *Bring Forth the Body* 1974, *The Survivors* 1976.

Ruth Rendell (1930)
From Doon With Death F
Her first novel and the first of the Inspector Wexford novels

Peter Shaffer (1926)
The Royal Hunt of the Sun D
Performed 1964

C.P. Snow (1905–80)
Corridors of Power F
Strangers and Brothers sequence ix

C.P. Snow (1905–80)
The Two Cultures; and A Second Look NF
Expanded version of *The Two Cultures* 1959 (q.v.)

Sir Wilfred Thesiger (1910–2003)
The Marsh Arabs NF

J.R.R. Tolkien (1892–1973)
Tree and Leaf MISC
Contains 'On Fairy Stories' and 'Leaf by Niggle' (story)

Philip Toynbee (1916–81)
Two Brothers F
Sequel to *Pantaloon* 1961; see also *A Learned City* 1966, *Views From a Lake* 1968

'William Trevor' [William Trevor Cox (1928)**]**
The Old Boys F

Evelyn Waugh (1903–66)
A Little Learning NF
Autobiography

Angus Wilson (1913–91)
Late Call F

Leonard Woolf (1880–1969)
Beginning Again NF
Autobiography. See also *Sowing* 1960, *Growing* 1961, *Downhill all the Way* 1967, *The Journey Not the Arrival Matters* 1969.

1965

- Assassination of Malcolm X (Feb.)
  US marines land in South Vietnam (Mar.): start of the Vietnam War
  Martin Luther King heads civil rights march from Selma, to Montgomery, Alabama
  Rhodesian Declaration of Independence by Ian Smith (Nov.)
  Post Office Tower, London, opened
- A.L. Kennedy born
  J.K. Rowling born
- Sir Winston Churchill dies (24 Jan.)
  Clemence Dane (Winifred Ashton) dies
  T.S. Eliot dies
  Eleanor Farjeon dies
  Somerset Maugham dies
- Nat 'King' Cole dies
  Albert Schweitzer dies
- Norman Mailer, *An American Dream*
- The Beatles, *Help!* (film)

A.L. Barker (1918–2002)
A Case Examined F

Samuel Beckett (1906–89)
Imagination Dead Imagine F

Brendan Behan (1923–64)
Confessions of an Irish Rebel NF

Alan Bold (1943)
Society Inebrious V

Malcolm Bradbury (1932–2000)
Stepping Westward F

Melvyn Bragg (1939)
For Want of a Nail F

George Mackay Brown (1921–96)
The Year of the Whale V

'Anthony Burgess' [John Anthony Burgess Wilson (1917–93)]
Here Comes Everybody NF
An introduction to James Joyce

'Anthony Burgess' [John Anthony Burgess Wilson (1917–93)]
A Vision of Battlements F

C. Day Lewis (1904–72)
The Room, and Other Poems V

Anita Desai (1937)
Voices in the City F

J.P. Donleavy (1926)
Meet My Maker the Mad Molecule F

Margaret Drabble (1939)
The Millstone F

T.S. Eliot (1888–1965)
To Criticize the Critic, and Other Writings NF
Published posthumously on 11 November 1965

J.G. Farrell (1935–79)
The Lung F

Ian Fleming (1908–64)
The Man with the Golden Gun F

Margaret Forster (1938)
Georgy Girl F

Michael Frayn (1933)
The Tin Men F

Roy Fuller (1912–91)
Buff V

David Gascoyne (1916)
Collected Poems V

Penelope Gilliatt (1932–93)
One by One F

Robert Graves (1895–1985)
Collected Poems V

Robert Graves (1895–1985)
Collected Short Stories F
First published in the USA, 1964

Robert Graves (1895–1985)
Majorca Observed NF
Illustrated by Paul Hogarth

Robert Graves (1895–1985)
Mammon and the Black Goddess NF

Michael Hamburger (1924)
In Flashlight V

Seamus Heaney (1939)
Eleven Poems V

Christopher Hill (1912–2003)
The Intellectual Origins of the English Revolution NF

Elizabeth Jane Howard (1923)
After Julius F

Pamela Hansford Johnson (1912–81)
Cork Street, Next to the Hatter's F
Dorothy Merlin Trilogy iii. See also *The Unspeakable Skipton* 1959 and *Night and Silence* 1963.

L.C. Knights (1906–97)
Further Explorations NF
See *Explorations* 1946

'John le Carré' [David John Moore Cornwell (1931)**]**
The Looking-Glass War F

Doris Lessing (1919)
Landlocked F
Children of Violence quintet iv. See also *Martha Quest* 1952, *A Proper Marriage* 1954, *A Ripple From the Storm* 1958, *The Four-Gated City* 1969.

C.S. Lewis (1898–1963)
Screwtape Proposes a Toast, and Other Pieces MISC

David Lodge (1935)
The British Museum is Falling Down F

George MacBeth (1932–92)
A Doomsday Book V

Louis MacNeice (1907–63)
The Strings are False NF
Unfinished autobiography

Olivia Manning (1915–80)
Friends and Heroes F
Balkan Trilogy iii. See also *The Great Fortune* 1960, *The Spoilt City* 1962.

Nicholas Mosley (1923)
Accident F

Iris Murdoch (1919–99)
The Red and the Green F

Edna O'Brien (1932)
August is a Wicked Month F

'George Orwell' [Eric Arthur Blair (1903–50)**]**
Decline of the English Murder, and Other Essays NF

John Osborne (1929–94)
Inadmissible Evidence D
Performed 1964

Harold Pinter (1930)
The Homecoming D
Performed 3 June 1965

Sylvia Plath (1932–63)
Ariel F

J.B. Priestley (1894–1984)
Lost Empires F

V.S. Pritchett (1900–97)
The Working Novelist NF

Kathleen Raine (1908–2003)
The Hollow Hill, and Other Poems 1960–4 V

Simon Raven (1927–2001)
Friends in Low Places F
Alms for Oblivion series ii. See also *The Rich Pay Late* 1964, *The Sabre Squadron* 1966, *Fielding Gray* 1967, *The Judas Boy* 1968, *Places Where They Sing* 1970, *Sound the Retreat* 1971, *Come Like Shadows* 1972, *Bring Forth the Body* 1974, *The Survivors* 1976.

Alan Ross (1922)
North From Sicily V

Vernon Scannell (1922)
Walking Wounded V

Jon Silkin (1930–97)
Nature With Man V

Alan Sillitoe (1928)
The Death of William Posters F

C.H. Sisson (1914–2003)
Numbers V

Muriel Spark (1918)
The Mandelbaum Gate F

'William Trevor' [William Trevor Cox (1928)**]**
The Boarding House F

Evelyn Waugh (1903–66)
Sword of Honour F
Reduction into a single narrative of *Men at Arms* 1952, *Officers and Gentlemen* 1955, and *Unconditional Surrender* 1961 (qq.v.)

Hugo Williams (1942)
Symptoms of Loss V

P.G. Wodehouse (1881–1975)
Galahad at Blandings F

1966

- Civil rights rally in Jackson, Mississippi (June)
  US bombs Hanoi
  France withdraws from NATO
  The Cultural Revolution in China begins
  The Aberfan disaster (Oct.)
- Margery Allingham dies
  C.S. Forester (Cecil Troughton Smith) dies
  Sir Ernest Gowers dies
  Flann O'Brien (Brian O'Nolan) dies
  Frank O'Connor (Michael O'Donovan) dies
  Henry Treece dies
  Arthur Waley dies
  Evelyn Waugh dies
- Walt Disney dies

- Thomas Pynchon, *The Crying of Lot 49*
- Bob Dylan, *Blonde on Blonde*

Robert Aickman (1914–81)
Powers of Darkness F

Brian Aldiss (1925)
The Saliva Tree, and Other Strange Growths F
Stories

Kingsley Amis (1922–95)
The Anti-Death League F

W.H. Auden (1907–73)
About the House V
First published in the USA, 1965

W.H. Auden (1907–73)
Collected Shorter Poems 1927–57 V

J.G. Ballard (1930)
The Crystal World F

Stan Barstow (1928)
The Watchers on the Shore F
Vic Brown Trilogy ii. See also *A Kind of Loving* 1960, *The Right True End* 1976.

Brendan Behan (1923–64)
The Scarperer F

John Betjeman (1906–84)
High and Low V

Robert Bolt (1924–95)
Doctor Zhivago D
Screnplay of the film (1965)

Basil Bunting (1900–85)
Briggflatts V

'Anthony Burgess' [John Anthony Burgess Wilson (1917–93)]
Tremor of Intent F

Angela Carter (1940–92)
Shadow Dance F

David Caute (1936)
The Decline of the West F

R. F. Delderfield (1912–72)
A Horseman Riding By F

Lawrence Durrell (1912–90)
The Ikons, and Other Poems V

Lawrence Durrell (1912–90)
Sauve Qui Peut F
Third of the Antrobus Trilogy. See also *Esprit de Corps* 1957, *Stiff Upper Lip* 1958.

Gavin Ewart (1916)
Pleasures of the Flesh V

Elaine Feinstein (1930)
In a Green Eye V

Patrick Leigh Fermor (1915)
Roumeli NF

Eva Figes (1932)
Equinox F

John Fowles (1926)
The Magus F

Michael Frayn (1933)
The Russian Interpreter F

Leon Garfield (1921)
Devil-in-the-Fog F

Graham Greene (1904–91)
The Comedians F
Published in January 1966

L.P. Hartley (1895–1972)
The Betrayal F
Sequel to *The Brickfield* 1964 (q.v.)

Seamus Heaney (1939)
Death of a Naturalist V

Christopher Isherwood (1904–86)
Exhumations MISC
Stories, articles, and poetry

Elizabeth Jennings (1926–2001)
The Mind has Mountains V

B.S. Johnson (1933–73)
Trawl F

P.J. Kavanagh (1931)
The Perfect Stranger NF
Autobiography

Thomas Kinsella (1928)
Wormwood V

John Lehmann (1907–87)
The Ample Proposition NF
Autobiography. See also *The Whispering Gallery* 1955, *I Am My Brother* 1960.

'Richard Llewellyn' [Richard Llewellyn Lloyd (1906–83)]
Down Where the Moon is Small F
Sequel to *How Green Was My Valley* 1939 (q.v.). See also *Up, Into the Singing Mountain* 1963, *Green, Green My Valley Now* 1975.

David Lodge (1935)
Language of Fiction NF

Christopher Logue (1926)
Logue's ABC V

Norman MacCaig (1910–96)
Surroundings V

'Hugh MacDiarmid' [Christopher Murray Grieve (1892–1978)]
The Company I've Kept NF
Autobiography

Louis MacNeice (1907–63)
Collected Poems V

John Masefield (1878–1967)
Grace Before Ploughing NF
Autobiography. See also *So Long to Learn* 1952.

David Mercer (1928–80)
Three T.V. Comedies D
Contains *A Suitable Case for Treatment* (televised 1962; filmed 1966 as *Morgan*); *For Tea on Sunday* (televised 1963), and *And Did Those Feet?* (televised 1965)

Nancy Mitford (1904–73)
The Sun King NF
Celebrated biography of Louis XIV

Brian Moore (1921–99)
The Emperor of Ice-Cream F

Iris Murdoch (1919–99)
The Time of the Angels F

Bill Naughton (1910–92)
Alfie F
Based on the play of the same name (performed in 1963)

Sir Harold Nicolson (1886–1968)
Diaries and Letters 1930–62 NF

Edna O'Brien (1932)
Casualties of Peace F

Sean O'Faolain (1900–91)
The Heat of the Sun F

John Osborne (1929–94)
A Patriot for Me D
Performed 1965

Ruth Pitter (1897–1992)
Still by Choice V

Anthony Powell (1905–2000)
The Soldier's Art F
Dance to the Music of Time viii. See also *A Question of Upbringing* 1951; *A Buyer's Market* 1952; *The Acceptance World* 1955; *At Lady Molly's* 1957; *Casanova's Chinese Restaurant* 1960; *The Kindly Ones* 1962; *The Valley of Bones* 1964; *The Military Philosophers* 1968; *Books Do Furnish a Room* 1971; *Temporary Kings* 1973; *Hearing Secret Harmonies* 1975.

Simon Raven (1927–2001)
The Sabre Squadron F
Alms for Oblivion series iii. See also *The Rich Pay Late* 1964, *Friends in Low Places* 1965, *Fielding Gray* 1967, *The Judas Boy* 1968, *Places Where They Sing* 1970, *Sound the Retreat* 1971, *Come Like Shadows* 1972, *Bring Forth the Body* 1974, *The Survivors* 1976.

Sir Herbert Read (1893–1968)
Collected Poems V

Piers Paul Read (1941)
Game in Heaven with Tussy Marx F

Peter Redgrove (1932–2003)
The Force, and Other Poems V

'Mary Renault' [Eileen Mary Challans (1905–83)]
The Mask of Apollo F

'Jean Rhys' [Ella Gwendolen Rhys Williams (1890–1979)]
Wide Sargasso Sea F

Paul Scott (1920–78)
The Jewel in the Crown F
The Raj Quartet i. See also *The Day of the Scorpion* 1968, *The Towers of Silence* 1971, *A Division of the Spoils* 1975.

N.F. Simpson (1919)
The Cresta Run D
Performed 1965

Stevie Smith (1902–71)
The Frog Prince, and Other Poems V

Tom Stoppard (1937)
Lord Malquist and Mr Moon F

R.S. Thomas (1913–2000)
Pietà V

J.R.R. Tolkien (1892–1973)
The Lord of the Rings F
The complete trilogy comprising *The Fellowship of the Ring* 1954, *The Two Towers* 1954, and *The Return of the King* 1955 (qq.v.)

Charles Tomlinson (1927)
American Scenes, and Other Poems V

Philip Toynbee (1916–81)
A Learned City F
See also *Pantaloon* 1961, *Two Brothers* 1964, *Views From a Lake* 1968

'William Trevor' [William Trevor Cox (1928)]
The Love Department F

Jill Paton Walsh (1937)
Hengest's Tale F

Sylvia Townsend Warner (1893–1978)
A Stranger With a Bag, and Other Stories F
US title: *Swans on an Autumn River*

Arnold Wesker (1932)
The Four Seasons D
Performed 1965

Virginia Woolf (1882–1941)
Collected Essays NF
Published on 20 October 1966. Two further volumes published in 1967.

1967

- Jeremy Thorpe succeeds Jo Grimond as leader of the British Liberal Party
  The *Torrey Canyon* disaster (Mar.)
  China explodes a hydrogen bomb
  Arab-Israeli Six Day war (June)
  Execution of Che Guevara (Oct.)
- J.R. Ackerley dies
  Pamela Frankau dies
  Margaret Irwin dies
  Patrick Joseph Kavanagh dies
  Margaret Kennedy dies
  John Masefield dies
  Joe Orton dies
  Arthur Ransome dies
  Siegfried Sassoon dies
  Vernon Watkins dies
- *Bonnie and Clyde*
- The Beatles, *Sergeant Pepper's Lonely Hearts Club Band*
  Jimi Hendrix, *Are You Experienced?*

Dannie Abse (1923)
Three Questor Plays D
Contains *House of Cowards, Gone, In the Cage*

Fleur Adcock (1934)
Tigers V

Brian Aldiss (1925)
An Age F

Kingsley Amis (1922–95)
A Look Round the Estate V

Paul Bailey (1937)
At the Jerusalem F

Beryl Bainbridge (1934)
A Weekend with Claude F

J.G. Ballard (1930)
The Disaster Area F

Samuel Beckett (1906–89)
Come and Go D
Performed in Berlin, 14 January 1966, in German. First London production, 9 December 1968.

Samuel Beckett (1906–89)
Eh Joe, and Other Writings D
Eh Joe televised by the BBC on 4 July 1966. Also contains *Act Without Words 2*, and *Film*.

Samuel Beckett (1906–89)
No's Knife F
Includes *Stories and Texts for Nothing, The Expelled, The End, The Calmative, Enough, Ping*, and *Imagination Dead Imagine* 1965 (q.v.)

George Mackay Brown (1921–96)
A Calendar of Love, and Other Stories F

Alan Brownjohn (1931)
The Lions' Mouths V

'Anthony Burgess' [John Anthony Burgess Wilson (1917–93)]
The Novel Now NF

A.S. Byatt (1936)
The Game F

Angela Carter (1940–92)
The Magic Toyshop F

Roald Dahl (1916–90)
Charlie and the Chocolate Factory F
First published in the USA, 1964

Roald Dahl (1916–90)
James and the Giant Peach F
First published in the USA, 1961

J.P. Donleavy (1926)
The Saddest Summer of Samuel S. F
First published in the USA, 1966

Margaret Drabble (1939)
Jerusalem the Golden F

Maureen Duffy (1933)
The Paradox Players F

Nell Dunn (1936)
Poor Cow F

Eva Figes (1932)
Winter Journey F

Michael Frayn (1933)
Towards the End of the Morning F

Penelope Gilliatt (1932–93)
A State of Change F

William Golding (1911–93)
The Pyramid F

Robert Graves (1895–1985)
Poetic Craft and Principle NF

Graham Greene (1904–91)
May We Borrow Your Husband? and Other Comedies of the Sexual Life F
Published in March 1967. Contains twelve stories.

Geoffrey Grigson (1905–85)
A Skull in Salop, and Other Poems V

Thom Gunn (1929–2004)
Touch V

Christopher Hampton (1946)
When Did You Last See My Mother? D
Performed 1966

Adrian Henri (1932–2001), **Roger McGough** (1937), and **Brian Patten** (1946)
Penguin Modern Poets 10: The Mersey Sound ANTH

Michael Holroyd (1935)
Lytton Strachey: The Unknown Years NF
See also *The Years of Achievement* 1968, *Lytton Strachey* 1994

Ted Hughes (1930–98)
Woodwo MISC
Published on 18 May 1967. Poems and prose.

Christopher Isherwood (1904–86)
A Meeting by the River F

P.D. James (1920)
Unnatural Causes F

'Anna Kavan' [Helen Emily Woods (1901–68)]
Ice F

Patrick Kavanagh (1904–67)
Collected Pruse [sic] NF

P.J. Kavanagh (1931)
On the Way to the Depot V

Thomas Kinsella (1928)
Nightwalker, and Other Poems V

Arthur Koestler (1905–83)
The Ghost in the Machine NF

'Hugh MacDiarmid' [Christopher Murray Grieve (1892–1978)]
A Lap of Honour V

Roger McGough (1937)
Frinck; A Day in the Life Of; and Summer with Monica F/V

Alistair Maclean (1923–87)
Where Eagles Dare F

V.S. Naipaul (1932)
The Mimic Men NF

R.K. Narayan (1906–2001)
The Vendor of Sweets F

Peter Nichols (1927)
A Day in the Death of Joe Egg D
Performed 1967

Joe Orton (1933–67)
Crimes of Passion D
Contains *The Ruffian on the Stair*, and *The Erpingham Camp*

Joe Orton (1933–67)
Loot D

Brian Patten (1946)
Little Johnny's Confession V

K.M. Peyton (1929)
Flambards F

Harold Pinter (1930)
Tea Party, and Other Plays D
Tea Party performed 17 September 1970. Also includes *The Basement.*

Kathleen Raine (1908–2003)
Defending Ancient Springs NF

Simon Raven (1927–2001)
Fielding Gray F
Alms for Oblivion series iv. See also *The Rich Pay Late* 1964, *Friends in Low Places* 1965, *The Sabre Squadron* 1966, *The Judas Boy* 1968, *Places Where They Sing* 1970, *Sound the Retreat* 1971, *Come Like Shadows* 1972, *Bring Forth the Body* 1974, *The Survivors* 1976.

Alan Ross (1922)
Poems 1942–67 V

Bertrand Russell (1872–1970)
Autobiography NF
Published in 3 volumes (1967–9)

Alan Sillitoe (1928)
A Tree on Fire F

Andrew Sinclair (1935)
Gog F
The Albion Triptych i. See also *Magog* 1972, *King Ludd* 1988.

George Steiner (1929)
Language and Silence NF

Tom Stoppard (1937)
Rosencrantz and Guildenstern are Dead D
Performed in Edinburgh 24 August 1966, and in London on 11 April 1967

David Storey (1933)
The Restoration of Arnold Middleton D
Performed 1966

Colin Thubron (1939)
Mirror to Damascus NF

Anthony Thwaite (1930)
The Stones of Emptiness V

'William Trevor' [William Trevor Cox (1928)]
The Day We Got Drunk on Cake F

Barry Unsworth (1930)
The Greeks Have a Word For It F

John Wain (1925–94)
The Smaller Sky F

Vernon Watkins (1906–67)
Selected Poems 1930–60 V

Alec Waugh (1898–1981)
My Brother Evelyn, and Other Profiles NF

Fay Weldon (1931)
The Fat Woman's Joke F

Angus Wilson (1913–91)
No Laughing Matter F

Leonard Woolf (1880–1969)
Downhill all the Way NF
Autobiography. See also *Sowing* 1960, *Growing* 1961, *Beginning Again* 1964, *The Journey Not the Arrival Matters* 1969.

1968

- My Lai massacre in Vietnam (Mar.)
  Assassination of Martin Luther King (4 Apr.)
  Student unrest in France
  Senator Robert Kennedy dies after being shot (6 June)
  Warsaw Pact forces invade Czechoslovakia (Aug.)
  Civil rights march in Londonderry, Northern Ireland
- Valentine Ackland dies
  Enid Blyton dies
  W.E. Johns dies
  Anna Kavan (Helen Emily Woods) dies
  Sir Harold Nicolson dies
  Mervyn Peake dies
  Sir Herbert Read dies
- Tony Hancock dies
- John Steinbeck dies
- Allan Ginsberg, *Airplane Dreams*
  Gore Vidal, *Myra Breckinridge*
- *The Graduate*
  Stanley Kubrick, *2001, a Space Odyssey*
- Van Morrison, *Astral Weeks*

J.R. Ackerley (1896–1967)
My Father and Myself NF

Kingsley Amis (1922–95)
I Want it Now F

W.H. Auden (1907–73)
Collected Longer Poems V

W.H. Auden (1907–73)
Secondary Worlds NF
Lecture given in October 1967

W.H. Auden (1907–73)
Selected Poems V

Alan Ayckbourn (1939)
Relatively Speaking: A comedy D
Performed (as *Meet My Father*) 1965

Stan Barstow (1928)
A Raging Calm F

Sybille Bedford (1911)
A Compass Error F

Edward Bond (1934)
Early Morning D
Performed 1968

Edward Bond (1934)
Narrow Road to the Deep North D
Performed 1968

John Braine (1922–86)
The Crying Game F

Basil Bunting (1900–85)
Collected Poems V

'Anthony Burgess' [John Anthony Burgess Wilson (1917–93)]
Enderby Outside F
See also *Inside Mr Enderby* 1963, *The Clockwork Testament* 1974, *Enderby's Dark Lady* 1984

'Anthony Burgess' [John Anthony Burgess Wilson (1917–93)]
Urgent Copy NF

Angela Carter (1940–92)
Several Perceptions F

Charles Causley (1917–2003)
Underneath the Water V

Arthur C. Clarke (1917)
2001: A space odyssey F

Based on the screenplay by Clarke and Stanley Kubrick

Isabel Colegate (1931)
Orlando King F
Orlando Trilogy i. See also *Orlando at the Brazen Threshold* 1971, *Agatha* 1973.

Robert Conquest (1917)
The Great Terror NF

Maureen Duffy (1933)
Lyrics for the Dog Hour V

Lawrence Durrell (1912–90)
Tunc F
First of the Revolt of Aphrodite duet. See also *Nunquam* 1970.

D.J. Enright (1920–2002)
Unlawful Assembly V

Gavin Ewart (1916)
The Deceptive Grin of the Gravel Porters V

James Fenton (1949)
Our Western Furniture V

Michael Frayn (1933)
A Very Private Life F

Brian Friel (1929)
Lovers D
Performed 1967

Roy Fuller (1912–91)
New Poems V

Robert Graves (1895–1985)
Poems 1965–1968 V

John Heath-Stubbs (1918)
Satires and Epigrams V

Adrian Henri (1932–2001)
Tonight at Noon V

Geoffrey Hill (1932)
King Log V

Susan Hill (1942)
Gentleman and Ladies F

Barry Hines (1939)
A Kestrel for a Knave F
Republished in 1974 as *Kes*; film 1974

Michael Holroyd (1935)
Lytton Strachey: The Years of Achievement NF
See also *The Unknown Years* 1967, *Lytton Strachey* 1994

Ted Hughes (1930–98)
The Iron Man F
For children. Published on 26 February 1968.

James Kirkup (1918)
Paper Windows V

Doris Lessing (1919)
Nine African Stories F
See also *African Stories* 1964

George MacBeth (1932–92)
The Night of Stones V

Norman MacCaig (1910–96)
Rings on a Tree V

Derek Mahon (1941)
Night-Crossing V

Gavin Maxwell (1914–69)
Raven Seek Thy Brother NF
Third of trilogy. See also *Ring of Bright Water* 1960, *The Rocks Remain* 1963.

Julian Mitchell (1935)
The Undiscovered Country F

Brian Moore (1921–99)
I am Mary Dunne F

Iris Murdoch (1919–99)
The Nice and the Good F

P.H. Newby (1918–97)
Something to Answer For F
Winner of the first Booker Prize for Fiction, 1969

Robert Nye (1939)
Doubtfire F

Edna O'Brien (1932)
The Love Object F

Ruth Pitter (1897–1992)
Poems 1926–1966 V

Dennis Potter (1935–94)
The Nigel Barton Plays D
Contains *Stand Up, Nigel Barton* (televised 1965) and *Vote, Vote, Vote for Nigel Barton* (televised 1965)

Anthony Powell (1905–2000)
The Military Philosophers F
Dance to the Music of Time ix. See also *A Question of Upbringing* 1951; *A Buyer's Market* 1952; *The Acceptance World* 1955; *At Lady Molly's* 1957; *Casanova's Chinese Restaurant* 1960; *The Kindly Ones* 1962; *The Valley of Bones* 1964; *The Soldier's Art* 1966; *Books Do Furnish a Room* 1971; *Temporary Kings* 1973; *Hearing Secret Harmonies* 1975.

V.S. Pritchett (1900–97)
A Cab at the Door NF
First volume of autobiography. See also *Midnight Oil* 1971.

J.H. Prynne (1936)
Kitchen Poems V

Simon Raven (1927–2001)
The Judas Boy F
Alms for Oblivion series v. See also *The Rich Pay Late* 1964, *Friends in Low Places* 1965, *The Sabre Squadron* 1966, *Fielding Gray* 1967, *Places Where They Sing* 1970, *Sound the Retreat* 1971, *Come Like Shadows* 1972, *Bring Forth the Body* 1974, *The Survivors* 1976.

Paul Scott (1920–78)
The Day of the Scorpion F
The Raj Quartet ii. See also *The Jewel in the Crown* 1966, *The Towers of Silence* 1971, *A Division of the Spoils* 1975.

Peter Shaffer (1926)
The White Liars; Black Comedy D

C.P. Snow (1905–80)
The Sleep of Reason F
Strangers and Brothers sequence X

Muriel Spark (1918)
The Public Image F

Tom Stoppard (1937)
The Real Inspector Hound D
Performed 17 June 1968

Elizabeth Taylor (1912–75)
The Wedding Group F

R.S. Thomas (1913–2000)
Not That He Brought Flowers V

J.R.R. Tolkien (1892–1973)
The Road Goes Ever On V
First published in the USA, 1967

Philip Toynbee (1916–81)
Views from a Lake F
See also *Pantaloon* 1961, *Two Brothers* 1964, *A Learned City* 1966

Vernon Watkins (1906–67)
Fidelities V

1969

- Richard Nixon becomes President of the USA
  First flight of Concorde 001 from Toulouse (2 Mar.) and Concorde 002 from Bristol
  General de Gaulle resigns (Apr.)
  Investiture of Prince Charles as Prince of Wales at Caernarvon Castle (1 July)
  First moon landing (20 July)
  British troops sent to Northern Ireland (Aug.)
  Willy Brandt becomes German Chancellor
- Ivy Compton-Burnett dies
  Richmal Crompton dies
  Gavin Maxwell dies
  Stephen Potter dies
  Sir Osbert Sitwell dies
  John Dover Wilson dies
  Leonard Woolf dies
  John Wyndham dies
- Dwight D. Eisenhower dies
- P.H. Newby wins the first Booker Prize for *Something to Answer For*
- Philip Roth, *Portnoy's Complaint*
  Kurt Vonnegut, *Slaughterhouse Five*
- Federico Fellini, *Satyricon*
  John Schlesinger, *Midnight Cowboy*
- The Who, *Tommy*

Kingsley Amis (1922–95)
The Green Man F

W.H. Auden (1907–73)
City Without Walls V

Beryl Bainbridge (1934)
Another Part of the Wood F

H.E. Bates (1905–74)
The Vanished World NF
Autobiography.

Alan Bennett (1934)
Forty Years On D
Performed 1968

Ronald Blythe (1922)
Akenfield NF

Alan Bold (1943)
A Perpetual Motion Machine V

Elizabeth Bowen (1899)
Eva Trout; or, Changing Scenes F
First published in the USA, 1968

Malcolm Bradbury (1932–2000)
What is a Novel? NF

Melvyn Bragg (1939)
The Hired Man F
Cumbrian Trilogy i. See also *A Place in England* 1970, *Kingdom Come* 1980.

Brigid Brophy (1929)
In Transit F

George Mackay Brown (1921–96)
A Time to Keep, and Other Stories F

Alan Brownjohn (1931)
Sandgrains on a Tray V

Angela Carter (1940–92)
Heroes and Villains F

Charles Causley (1917–2003)
Figure of 8 V

Kenneth Clark (1903–83)
Civilisation NF

Richard Cobb (1917–96)
A Second Identity NF

Donald Davie (1922–95)
Essex Poems 1963–67 V

J.P. Donleavy (1926)
The Beastly Beatitudes of Balthasar B. F
First published in the USA, 1968

Margaret Drabble (1939)
The Waterfall F

Douglas Dunn (1942)
Terry Street V

Janice Elliott (1931–95)
Angels Falling F

Eva Figes (1932)
Konek Landing F

John Fowles (1926)
The French Lieutenant's Woman F

George MacDonald Fraser (1925)
Flashman F
The first of the Flashman novels

Rumer Godden (1907–98)
In This House of Brede F

Robert Graves (1895–1985)
The Crane Bag and Other Disputed Subjects NF

Graham Greene (1904–91)
Collected Essays NF
Published in March 1969

Graham Greene (1904–91)
Travels with my Aunt F
Published in November 1969

Geoffrey Grigson (1905–85)
Ingestion of Ice-Cream, and Other Poems V

Geoffrey Grigson (1905–85)
Poems and Poets NF

Thom Gunn (1929–2004)
Poems 1950–1966 V

Christopher Hampton (1946)
Total Eclipse D
Performed 1968

Seamus Heaney (1939)
Door into the Dark V

Susan Hill (1942)
A Change for the Better F

Michael Horovitz (1935) (ed.)
Children of Albion: Poetry of the 'Underground' in Britain ANTH

Ted Hughes (1930–98) (tr.)
Oedipus D
Published on 8 December 1969

Laurie Lee (1914–97)
As I Walked Out One Midsummer Morning NF
Autobiography

Doris Lessing (1919)
The Four-Gated City F
Children of Violence quintet v. See also *Martha Quest* 1952, *A Proper Marriage* 1954, *A Ripple From the Storm* 1958, *Landlocked* 1965.

Michael Longley (1939)
No Continuing City V

'Hugh MacDiarmid' [Christopher Murray Grieve (1892–1978)]
A Clyack-Sheaf V

Roger McGough (1937)
Watchwords V

Louis MacNeice (1907–63)
Persons From Porlock, and Other Plays for Radio D
Introduction by W.H. Auden. Title play broadcast by the BBC 30 August 1963.

Michael Moorcock (1939)
Behold the Man F

Michael Moorcock (1939)
The Final Programme F
Cornelius Chronicle i. See also *A Cure for Cancer* 1971, *The English Assassin* 1972, *The Condition of Muzak* 1977.

Nicholas Mosley (1923)
Impossible Object F

Iris Murdoch (1919–99)
Bruno's Dream F

Joe Orton (1933–67)
What the Butler Saw D

Brian Patten (1946)
Notes to the Hurrying Man V

Harold Pinter (1930)
Landscape, and Silence D
Both plays performed 2 July 1969

Alan Plater (1935)
Close the Coalhouse Door D
Performed 1968

V.S. Pritchett (1900–97)
Blind Love, and Other Stories F

Piers Paul Read (1941)
Monk Dawson F

Bernice Rubens (1928–2004)
The Elected Member F

Stephen Spender (1909–95)
The Year of the Young Rebels NF

Jon Stallworthy (1935)
Root and Branch V

Tom Stoppard (1937)
Albert's Bridge; If You're Glad I'll Be Frank D
Albert's Bridge broadcast 1967, performed in Edinburgh 1969. *If You're Glad I'll Be Frank* broadcast 1966, performed in Edinburgh 1969.

David Storey (1933)
In Celebration D
Performed 1969

Colin Thubron (1939)
Jerusalem NF

Charles Tomlinson (1927)
The Way of a World V

'William Trevor' [William Trevor Cox (1928)]
Mrs Eckdorf in O'Neill's Hotel F

Edward Upward (1903)
The Rotten Elements F
The Spiral Ascent Trilogy ii. See also *In the Thirties* 1962, *The Spiral Ascent* 1977.

Vernon Watkins (1906–67)
Uncollected Poems V
Introduction by Kathleen Raine

'Mary Wesley' [Mary Aline Mynors Farmar (1912–2002)]
The Sixth Seal F

Henry Williamson (1895–1977)
The Gale of the World F
Last of the 15-novel Chronicle of Ancient Sunlight sequence: see *The Dark Lantern* 1951.

Leonard Woolf (1880–1969)
The Journey Not the Arrival Matters NF
Autobiography. See also *Sowing* 1960, *Growing* 1961, *Beginning Again* 1964, *Downhill all the Way* 1967.

1970

- US resumes bombing of North Vietnam
  Anti-war demonstrators shot dead at Kent State University
  Harold Wilson resigns as British Prime Minister: Edward Heath forms Conservative government
  Cambodia declares itself the Khmer Republic
  The Beatles split up
- Tobias Hill born
- Vera Brittain dies
  E.M. Forster dies
  Sir Basil Liddell Hart dies
  Bertrand Russell dies
- Charles de Gaulle dies
  François Mauriac dies
  John Dos Passos dies
  Jimi Hendrix dies
- Bernice Rubens wins the Booker Prize for *The Elected Member*
- Maya Angelou, *I Know Why the Caged Bird Sings*
  Germaine Greer, *The Female Eunuch*
  Richard Bach, *Jonathan Livingston Seagull*
- Simon and Garfunkel, *Bridge Over Troubled Water*

Dannie Abse (1923)
O Jones, O Jones F

Harold Acton (1904–94)
More Memoirs of an Aesthete NF
See *Memoirs of an Aesthete* 1948

Brian Aldiss (1925)
The Hand-Reared Boy F
First of three Horatio Stubbs novels. See also *A Soldier Erect* 1971, *A Rude Awakening* 1978.

'Evelyn Anthony' [Evelyn Ward-Thomas (1928)]
The Assassin F

Paul Bailey (1937)
Trespasses F

J.G. Ballard (1930)
The Atrocity Exhibition F

Lynne Reid Banks (1929)
The Backward Shadow F
Second of trilogy. See also *The L-Shaped Room* 1960 and *Two is Lonely* 1974.

John Banville (1945)
Long Lankin F

Peter Barnes (1931)
Leonardo's Last Supper; Noonday Demons D
Double bill, performed 1969

Melvyn Bragg (1939)
A Place in England F
Cumbrian Trilogy ii. See also *The Hired Man* 1969, *Kingdom Come* 1980.

John Braine (1922–86)
Stay With Me Till Morning F

Howard Brenton (1942)
Christie in Love, and Other Plays D
Title play performed 1969. Also includes *Heads.*

Christy Brown (1932–81)
Down all the Days F

Roald Dahl (1916–90)
Fantastic Mr Fox F

C. Day Lewis (1904–72)
The Whispering Roots V
Day-Lewis was appointed Poet Laureate in 1968

Patric Dickinson (1914–94)
More Than Time V

Lawrence Durrell (1912–90)
Nunquam F
Second of the Revolt of Aphrodite duet. See also *Tunc* 1968.

J.G. Farrell (1935–79)
Troubles F
Empire Trilogy i. See also *The Siege of Krishnapur* 1973, *The Singapore Grip* 1978.

Elaine Feinstein (1930)
The Circle F

Michael Frayn (1933)
The Two of Us D
Performed 1970. Also includes *Black and Silver, The New Quixote, Mr Foot, Chinamen.*

Brian Friel (1929)
Crystal and Fox D
Performed 1968

Christopher Fry (1907)
A Yard of Sun: A summer comedy D
Performed 1970

Christopher Hampton (1946)
The Philanthropist: A bourgeois tragedy D
Performed 1970

Tony Harrison (1937)
The Loiners V

Reginald Hill (1936)
A Clubbable Woman F
The first Dalziel and Pascoe novel

Susan Hill (1942)
I'm the King of the Castle F

Ted Hughes (1930–98)
The Coming of the Kings, and Other Plays D
For children. Published on 1 September 1970.

Ted Hughes (1930–98)
Crow V
Published on 12 October 1970

Francis King (1923)
A Domestic Animal F

Penelope Lively (1933)
Astercote F
For children

David Lodge (1935)
Out of the Shelter F

George MacBeth (1932–92)
The Burning Cone V

Derek Mahon (1941)
Beyond Howth Head V

David Mercer (1928–80)
After Haggerty D
Performed 26 February 1970

Iris Murdoch (1919–99)
The Sovereignty of Good NF

Shiva Naipaul (1945–85)
Fireflies F

Peter Nichols (1927)
The National Health; or, Nurse Norton's Affair D
Performed 1969

'Patrick O'Brian' [Richard Patrick Russ (1914–2000)]
Master and Commander F
First of the Aubrey-Maturin series

Edna O'Brien (1932)
A Pagan Place F

Joe Orton (1933–67)
Funeral Games; The Good and Faithful Servants D

Brian Patten (1946)
The Homecoming V

Peter Porter (1929)
The Last of England V

Dennis Potter (1935–94)
Son of Man D
Televised 1969

Simon Raven (1927–2001)
Places Where They Sing F
Alms for Oblivion series vi. See also *The Rich Pay Late* 1964, *Friends in Low Places* 1965, *The Sabre Squadron* 1966, *Fielding Gray* 1967, *The Judas Boy* 1968, *Sound the Retreat* 1971, *Come Like Shadows* 1972, *Bring Forth the Body* 1974, *The Survivors* 1976.

'Mary Renault' [Eileen Mary Challans (1905–83)**]**
Fire From Heaven F
Alexander Trilogy i. See also *The Persian Boy* 1972, *Funeral Games* 1981.

Alan Sillitoe (1928)
A Start in Life F

C.P. Snow (1905–80)
Last Things F
Final novel (xi) in the Strangers and Brothers sequence

Muriel Spark (1918)
The Driver's Seat F

David Storey (1933)
The Contractor D
Performed 1969

John Wain (1925–94)
A Winter in the Hills F

Arnold Wesker (1932)
The Friends D
Performed 1970

Hugo Williams (1942)
Sugar Daddy V

1971

- First British soldier killed in Northern Ireland (Feb.)
  Death of François Duvalier of Haiti ('Papa Doc'): succeeded by Jean-Claude Duvalier
  Richard Nixon announces end of US offensive operations in Vietnam (Nov.)
  War in Pakistan: East Pakistan becomes independent Bangladesh
- Sir Maurice Bowra dies
  C.D. Broad dies
  Anthony Berkeley Cox dies
  Peter Fleming dies
  Sir Alan Patrick Herbert dies
  E.V. Knox dies
  Stevie Smith dies
- Coco Chanel dies
  Igor Stravinsky dies
- V.S. Naipaul wins the Booker Prize for *In a Free State*
- Alexander Solzhenitsyn, *August, 1914*
- Stanley Kubrick, *A Clockwork Orange*
  Luchino Visconti, *Death in Venice*

Fleur Adcock (1934)
High Tide in the Garden V

Brian Aldiss (1925)
The Moment of Eclipse F

Brian Aldiss (1925)
A Soldier Erect F
Second of three Horatio Stubbs novels. See also *The Hand-Reared Boy* 1970, *A Rude Awakening* 1978.

Kingsley Amis (1922–95)
Girl, 20 F

John Banville (1945)
Nightspawn F

A.L. Barker (1918–2002)
Femina Real F

George Barker (1913–91)
Poems of Places and People V

Samuel Beckett (1906–89)
Lessness F
First published in French (*Sans*), 1969

Robert Bolt (1924–95)
Vivat! Vivat Regina! D
Performed 1970

George Mackay Brown (1921–96)
Fishermen with Ploughs V

'Anthony Burgess' [John Anthony Burgess Wilson (1917–93)**]**
MF F

Angela Carter (1940–92)
Love F

Isabel Colegate (1931)
Orlando at the Brazen Threshold F
Orlando Trilogy ii. See also *Orlando King* 1968, *Agatha* 1973.

I. Compton-Burnett (1892–1969)
The Last and the First F

Kay Dick (1915)
Ivy and Stevie NF

J.P. Donleavy (1926)
The Onion Eaters F

Maureen Duffy (1933)
Love Child F

Maureen Duffy (1933)
The Venus Touch V

Janice Elliott (1931–95)
A State of Peace F
England Trilogy i. See also *Private Life* 1972, *Heaven on Earth* 1975.

Elaine Feinstein (1930)
The Magic Apple Tree V

E.M. Forster (1879–1970)
Maurice F
Published on 7 October 1971. First publication of Forster's homosexual novel, written in 1914 and previously only circulated privately.

Frederick Forsyth (1938)
The Day of the Jackal F
Film 1973

Jane Gardam (1928)
A Few Fair Days F

'Robert Garioch' [Robert Garioch Sutherland (1909–81)]
The Big Music, and Other Poems V

William Golding (1911–93)
The Scorpion God F

Graham Greene (1904–91)
A Sort of Life NF
Autobiography. Published in September 1971. See also *Ways of Escape* 1980.

Thom Gunn (1929–2004)
Moly V

David Hare (1947)
Slag D
Performed 1970

Adrian Henri (1932–2001)
Autobiography V

Geoffrey Hill (1932)
Mercian Hymns V
Prose poems

Michael Horovitz (1935)
The Wolverhampton Wanderer: An epic of Britannia V
Illustrated by Peter Blake

Susan Howatch (1940)
Penmarric F

P.D. James (1920)
Shroud for a Nightingale F

James Kirkup (1918)
The Body Servant V

Doris Lessing (1919)
Briefing For a Descent into Hell F

Michael Moorcock (1939)
A Cure for Cancer F
Cornelius Chronicle ii. See also *The Final Programme* 1969, *The English Assassin* 1972, *The Condition of Muzak* 1977.

Brian Moore (1921–99)
Fergus F
First published in the USA, 1970

John Mortimer (1923)
A Voyage Round My Father D
Broadcast in 1963; performed 1970

Paul Muldoon (1951)
Knowing My Place V

Iris Murdoch (1919–99)
An Accidental Man F

V.S. Naipaul (1932)
In a Free State F
Booker Prize 1971

John Osborne (1929–94)
West of Suez D

Harold Pinter (1930)
Five Screenplays D
Contains *The Caretaker* 1960 (q.v.), *The Servant, The Pumpkin Eater, Accident, The Quiller Memorandum*

Sylvia Plath (1932–63)
Crossing the Water V

Sylvia Plath (1932–63)
Winter Trees V

Anthony Powell (1905–2000)
Books Do Furnish a Room F
Dance to the Music of Time x. See also *A Question of Upbringing* 1951; *A Buyer's Market* 1952; *The*

Acceptance World 1955; *At Lady Molly's* 1957; *Casanova's Chinese Restaurant* 1960; *The Kindly Ones* 1962; *The Valley of Bones* 1964; *The Soldier's Art* 1966; *The Military Philosophers* 1968; *Temporary Kings* 1973; *Hearing Secret Harmonies* 1975.

V.S. Pritchett (1900–97)
Midnight Oil NF
Second volume of autobiography. See also *A Cab at the Door* 1969.

Simon Raven (1927–2001)
Sound the Retreat F
Alms for Oblivion series vii. See also *The Rich Pay Late* 1964, *Friends in Low Places* 1965, *The Sabre Squadron* 1966, *Fielding Gray* 1967, *The Judas Boy* 1968, *Places Where They Sing* 1970, *Come Like Shadows* 1972, *Bring Forth the Body* 1974, *The Survivors* 1976.

Paul Scott (1920–78)
The Towers of Silence F
The Raj Quartet iii. See also *The Jewel in the Crown* 1966, *The Day of the Scorpion* 1968, *A Division of the Spoils* 1975.

Tom Sharpe (1928)
Riotous Assembly F

Jon Silkin (1930–97)
Amana Grass V

Muriel Spark (1918)
Not to Disturb F

Stephen Spender (1909–95)
The Generous Days V

'William Trevor' [William Trevor Cox (1928)]
Miss Gomez and the Brethren F

Fay Weldon (1931)
Down Among the Women F

Arnold Wesker (1932)
Six Sundays in January F

1972

- 'Bloody Sunday' shootings in Londonderry (30 Jan.)
  President Nixon visits China (Feb.)
  Strategic Arms Limitation Treaty (SALT) signed in Moscow (Apr.)
  Arab terrorists kill 11 members of the Israeli Olympic team in Munich (Sept.)
  'Treasures of Tutankhamun' exhibition at the British Museum
  The last 'Goon Show' broadcast
- Daisy Ashford dies
  Padraic Colum dies
  C. Day Lewis dies
  R.F. Delderfield dies
  L.P. Hartley dies
  Sir Compton Mackenzie dies
- The Duke of Windsor dies
- John Berryman dies
  J. Edgar Hoover dies
  Ezra Pound dies
- John Berger wins the Booker Prize for *G*
- Bernado Bertolucci, *Last Tango in Paris*
  Francis Ford Coppola, *The Godfather*
- *Jesus Christ Superstar* (musical)

Richard Adams (1920)
Watership Down F

Alan Ayckbourn (1939)
How the Other Half Loves D
Performed in Scarborough 1969, London 1970

Beryl Bainbridge (1934)
Harriet Said . . . F

Howard Barker (1946)
Cheek D
Performed 1970

Nina Bawden (1925)
Anna Apparent F

Samuel Beckett (1906–89)
The Lost Ones F
First published in French (*Le dépeupleur*), 1971

John Berger (1926)
G F
Booker Prize 1972

John Berger (1926)
Ways of Seeing NF

John Braine (1922–86)
The Queen of a Distant Country F

Howard Brenton (1942)
Plays for Public Places: Gum and Goo; Wesley; Scott of the Antarctic D
Gum and Goo performed 1969

George Mackay Brown (1921–96)
Greenvoe F

Alan Brownjohn (1931)
Warrior's Career V

Angela Carter (1940–92)
The Infernal Desire Machines of Doctor Hoffman F

David Cook (1940)
Albert's Memorial F

R. F. Delderfield (1912–72)
To Serve Them All My Days F

Margaret Drabble (1939)
The Needle's Eye F

Douglas Dunn (1942)
The Happier Life V

Janice Elliott (1931–95)
Private Life F
England Trilogy ii. See also *A State of Peace* 1971, *Heaven on Earth* 1975.

D.J. Enright (1920–2002)
Daughters of Earth V

Elaine Feinstein (1930)
At the Edge V

James Fenton (1949)
Terminal Moraine V

Frederick Forsyth (1938)
The Odessa File F
Film 1974

Helen Gardner (1908–86) (ed.)
The New Oxford Book of English Verse 1250–1950 ANTH
See *The Oxford Book of English Verse* 1900

Graham Greene (1904–91)
The Pleasure Dome NF
Published in October 1972

David Hare (1947)
The Great Exhibition D
Performed 1972

Seamus Heaney (1939)
Wintering Out V

Susan Hill (1942)
The Bird of Night F

Ted Hughes (1930–98)
Selected Poems 1957–1967 V
Published on 23 October 1972. See also *Selected Poems* 1982, *New Selected Poems* 1995.

P.D. James (1920)
An Unsuitable Job for a Woman F
The first Cordelia Gray novel

Ruth Prawer Jhabvala (1927)
A New Dominion F

Thomas Kinsella (1928)
Notes From the Land of the Dead V

Doris Lessing (1919)
The Story of a Non-Marrying Man F

Liz Lochhead (1947)
Memo for Spring V

Michael Moorcock (1939)
The English Assassin F
Cornelius Chronicle iii. See also *The Final Programme* 1969, *A Cure for Cancer* 1971, *The Condition of Muzak* 1977.

Brian Moore (1921–99)
Catholics F

Edwin Morgan (1920)
Glasgow Sonnets V

Norman Nicholson (1914–87)
A Local Habitation V

Conor Cruise O'Brien (1917)
States of Ireland NF

Edna O'Brien (1932)
Night F

Brian Patten (1946)
And Sometimes It Happens V

Peter Porter (1929)
Preaching to the Converted V

Simon Raven (1927–2001)
Come Like Shadows F
Alms for Oblivion series viii. See also *The Rich Pay Late* 1964, *Friends in Low Places* 1965, *The Sabre Squadron* 1966, *Fielding Gray* 1967, *The Judas Boy* 1968, *Places Where They Sing* 1970, *Sound the Retreat* 1971, *Bring Forth the Body* 1974, *The Survivors* 1976.

Peter Redgrove (1932–2003)
Dr Faust's Sea-Spiral Spirit, and Other Poems V

'Mary Renault' [Eileen Mary Challans (1905)]
The Persian Boy F
Alexander Trilogy ii. See also *Fire From Heaven* 1970, *Funeral Games* 1981.

Peter Scupham (1933)
The Snowing Globe V

Andrew Sinclair (1935)
Magog F
The Albion Triptych ii. See also *Gog* 1967, *King Ludd* 1988.

Stevie Smith (1902–71)
Scorpion, and Other Poems V

C.P. Snow (1905–80)
The Malcontents F

Muriel Spark (1918)
The Hothouse by the River F

Tom Stoppard (1937)
Jumpers D
Performed 2 February 1972

David Storey (1933)
The Changing Room D
Performed 1971

Julian Symons (1912–95)
Bloody Murder: From the Detective Story to the Crime Novel NF
Revised in 1985 and 1992

'William Trevor' [William Trevor Cox (1928)]
The Ballroom of Romance F

1973

- Britain, Ireland, and Denmark join the EEC (1 Jan.)
  The US, North and South Vietnam sign ceasefire in Paris (Jan.)
  Last US troops leave Vietnam (Mar.)
  Watergate hearings begin (May)
  Henry Kissinger becomes US Secretary of State
  Arab–Israeli Yom Kippur war (Oct.), followed by oil crisis
  Princess Anne marries Captain Mark Phillips
- Kenneth Allott dies
  W.H. Auden dies
  Elizabeth Bowen dies
  Sir Noël Coward dies
  Henry Green (Henry Vincent Yorke) dies
  B.S. Johnson dies
  John Masters dies
  Nancy Mitford dies
  William Plomer dies
  Gladys Stern dies
  J.R.R. Tolkien dies
- Lyndon Baines Johnson dies
  Pablo Picasso dies
- J.G. Farrell wins the Booker Prize for *The Siege of Krishnapur*
- Alexander Solzhenitsyn, *The Gulag Archipelago* (1973–6)
- Pink Floyd, *The Dark Side of the Moon*

Dannie Abse (1923)
Funland, and Other Poems V

Peter Ackroyd (1949)
London Lickpenny V

Brian Aldiss (1925)
Billion Year Spree NF
Revised (with David Wingrove) as *Trillion Year Spree*, 1986

Ted Allbeury (1917)
A Choice of Enemies F

Kingsley Amis (1922–95)
The Riverside Villas Murder F

Martin Amis (1949)
The Rachel Papers F

Paul Bailey (1937)
A Distant Likeness F

Beryl Bainbridge (1934)
The Dressmaker F

J.G. Ballard (1930)
Crash! F

John Banville (1945)
Birchwood F

Nina Bawden (1925)
Carrie's War F

Samuel Beckett (1906–89)
First Love F
First published in French (*Premier Amour*), 1970

Alan Bennett (1934)
Habeas Corpus D

George Mackay Brown (1921–96)
Magnus F

Caryl Churchill (1938)
Owners D
Performed 1972

Arthur C. Clarke (1917)
Rendezvous with Rama F

Isabel Colegate (1931)
Agatha F
Orlando Trilogy iii. See also *Orlando King* 1968, *Orlando at the Brazen Threshold* 1971.

'William Cooper' [Harry Summerfield Hoff (1910–2002)]
Love on the Coast F

Patric Dickinson (1914–94)
A Wintering Tree V

J.P. Donleavy (1926)
A Fairy Tale of New York F

Carol Ann Duffy (1955)
Fleshweathercock V

Maureen Duffy (1933)
I Want To Go To Moscow F

Lawrence Durrell (1912–90)
Vega, and Other Poems V

J.G. Farrell (1935–79)
The Siege of Krishnapur F
Booker Prize 1973. Empire Trilogy ii. See also *Troubles* 1970; *The Singapore Grip* 1978.

Elaine Feinstein (1930)
The Celebrants, and Other Poems V

Michael Frayn (1933)
Sweet Dreams F

Roy Fuller (1912–91)
Tiny Tears V

Jane Gardam (1928)
The Summer After the Funeral F

'Robert Garioch' [Robert Garioch Sutherland (1909–81)]
Doktor Faust in Rose Street V

Graham Greene (1904–91)
The Honorary Consul F
Published in September 1973

Geoffrey Grigson (1905–85)
Sad Grave of an Imperial Mongoose V

Michael Hamburger (1924)
Ownerless Earth V

Ian Hamilton (1938–2001)
A Poetry Chronicle NF

Richard Hughes (1900–76)
The Wooden Shepherdess F
Second of the projected Human Predicament sequence

Ted Hughes (1930–98)
Prometheus on his Crag V
Published in November 1973

Philip Larkin (1922–85) (ed.)
The Oxford Book of Twentieth-Century Verse ANTH

Doris Lessing (1919)
The Summer Before the Dark F

Penelope Lively (1933)
The Ghost of Thomas Kempe F
For children

Michael Longley (1939)
An Exploded View V

George MacBeth (1932–92)
Shrapnel V

Edwin Morgan (1920)
From Glasgow to Saturn V

Paul Muldoon (1951)
New Weather V

Iris Murdoch (1919–99)
The Black Prince F

Shiva Naipaul (1945–85)
The Chip-Chip Gatherers F

John Osborne (1929–94)
A Sense of Detachment D

Brian Patten (1946)
The Unreliable Nightingale V

Anthony Powell (1905–2000)
Temporary Kings F
Dance to the Music of Time xi. See also *A Question of Upbringing* 1951; *A Buyer's Market* 1952; *The Acceptance World* 1955; *At Lady Molly's* 1957; *Casanova's Chinese Restaurant* 1960; *The Kindly Ones* 1962; *The Valley of Bones* 1964; *The Soldier's Art* 1966; *The Military Philosophers* 1968; *Books Do Furnish a Room* 1971; *Hearing Secret Harmonies* 1975.

Piers Paul Read (1941)
The Upstart F

Peter Redgrove (1932–2003)
In the Country of the Skin F

Alan Ross (1922)
The Taj Express V

Carol Rumens (1944)
A Strange Girl in Bright Colours V

Vernon Scannell (1922)
The Winter Man V

Peter Shaffer (1926)
Equus D
Performed 1973

Tom Sharpe (1928)
Indecent Exposure F

Penelope Shuttle (1947)
Wailing Monkey Embracing a Tree F

Tom Stoppard (1937)
Artist Descending a Staircase; Where Are They Now? D
Artist Descending a Staircase broadcast 1972, performed 1988. *Where Are They Now?* broadcast 1970.

David Storey (1933)
A Temporary Life F

Emma Tennant (1937)
The Time of the Crack F

'William Trevor' [William Trevor Cox (1928)]
Elizabeth Alone F

Harriet Waugh (1944)
Mirror, Mirror F

Angus Wilson (1913–91)
As If By Magic F

1974

- Harold Wilson becomes British Prime Minister for the second time
  Turkey invades Cyprus (July)
  Richard Nixon resigns (9 Aug.): succeeded as US president by Gerald Ford
  Helmut Schmidt is German Chancellor
  The 'terracotta army' discovered in China
  Deportation of Alexander Solzhenitsyn
- H.E. Bates dies
  Edmund Blunden dies
  Cyril Connolly dies
  Georgette Heyer dies
  Eric Linklater dies
- Duke Ellington dies
  Juan Perón dies
- Booker Prize shared by Nadine Gordimer for *The Conservationist* and Stanley Middleton for *Holiday*
- Erica Jong, *Fear of Flying*
- Mike Oldfield, *Tubular Bells*

Dannie Abse (1923)
A Poet in the Family NF
Autobiography. See also *A Strong Dose of Myself* 1983, *There Was a Young Man From Cardiff* 1991.

Richard Adams (1920)
Shardik F

Fleur Adcock (1934)
The Scenic Route V

Brian Aldiss (1925)
Frankenstein Unbound F
See also *Dracula Unbound* 1991

Kingsley Amis (1922–95)
Ending Up F

Beryl Bainbridge (1934)
The Bottle Factory Outing F

J.G. Ballard (1930)
Concrete Island F

Lynne Reid Banks (1929)
Two is Lonely F
Third of trilogy. See also *The L-Shaped Room* 1960 and *The Backward Shadow* 1970.

Samuel Beckett (1906–89)
Mercier and Camier F
First published in French, 1970

Sir John Betjeman (1906–84)
A Nip in the Air V
Betjeman was knighted in 1969 and appointed Poet Laureate in 1972

Edward Bond (1934)
Bingo: Scenes of money and death (and passion) D
Performed in Exeter 1973, London 1974

Howard Brenton (1942) and **David Hare** (1947)
Brassneck D
Performed in Nottingham, 1973

George Mackay Brown (1921–96)
Hawkfall, and Other Stories F

'Anthony Burgess' [John Anthony Burgess Wilson (1917–93)]
The Clockwork Testament; or, Enderby's End F
See also *Inside Enderby* 1963, *Enderby Outside* 1968, *Enderby's Dark Lady* 1984

'Anthony Burgess' [John Anthony Burgess Wilson (1917–93)]
Napoleon Symphony F

Angela Carter (1940–92)
Fireworks F
Stories

David Cook (1940)
Happy Endings F

Roald Dahl (1916–90)
Switch Bitch F
Stories

Donald Davie (1922–95)
The Shires V

Douglas Dunn (1942)
Love or Nothing V

Lawrence Durrell (1912–90)
Monsieur; or, The Prince of Darkness F
First of the Avignon quintet. See also *Livia* 1978, *Constance* 1982, *Sebastian* 1983, and *Quinx* 1985. Published together in 1992.

David Edgar (1948)
Dick Deterred D
Performed 1974

Padraic Fallon (1906–74)
Poems V
See also *Poems and Versions* 1983, *Collected Poems* 1990

Frederick Forsyth (1938)
The Dogs of War F
Film 1980

John Fowles (1926)
The Ebony Tower F

Leon Garfield (1921)
The Sound of Coaches F

Trevor Griffiths (1935)
The Party D
Performed 1973

Christopher Hampton (1946)
Savages D
Performed 1973

David Hare (1947)
Knuckle D
Performed 1974

Richard Holmes (1945)
Shelley: The Pursuit NF

Michael Holroyd (1935)
Augustus John: The Years of Innocence NF
See also *The Years of Experience* 1975

Linton Kwesi Johnson (1952)
Voices of the Living and the Dead V

Jenny Joseph (1932)
Rose in the Afternoon, and Other Poems V

Philip Larkin (1922–85)
High Windows V

'John le Carré' [David John Moore Cornwell (1931)**]**
Tinker, Tailor, Soldier, Spy F

Laurence Lerner (1925)
A.R.T.H.U.R. V
See also *A.R.T.H.U.R. & M.A.R.T.H.A.* 1980

Doris Lessing (1919)
The Memoirs of a Survivor F

Norman MacCaig (1910–96)
The World's Room V

Stanley Middleton (1919)
Holiday F
Booker Prize (shared with Nadine Gordimer for *The Conservationist*)

Iris Murdoch (1919–99)
The Sacred and Profane Love Machine F

Edna O'Brien (1932)
A Scandalous Woman F

V.S. Pritchett (1900–97)
The Camberwell Beauty, and Other Stories F

Jonathan Raban (1942)
Soft City NF

Simon Raven (1927–2001)
Bring Forth the Body F
Alms for Oblivion series ix. See also *The Rich Pay Late* 1964, *Friends in Low Places* 1965, *The Sabre Squadron* 1966, *Fielding Gray* 1967, *The Judas Boy* 1968, *Places Where They Sing* 1970, *Sound the Retreat* 1971, *Come Like Shadows* 1972, *The Survivors* 1976.

Peter Reading (1946)
For the Municipality's Elderly V

Tom Sharpe (1928)
Porterhouse Blue F

Jon Silkin (1930–97)
The Principle of Water V

Muriel Spark (1918)
The Abbess of Crewe F

J.I.M. Stewart (1906–94)
The Gaudy F
'A Staircase in Surrey' sequence. See also *Young Patullo* 1975, *A Memorial Service* 1976, *The Madonna of the Astrolabe* 1977, *Full Term* 1978.

Anthony Thwaite (1930)
New Confessions V

Claire Tomalin (1933)
The Life and Death of Mary Wollstonecraft NF

1975

- Margaret Thatcher wins Conservative leadership election (Feb.)
  Turks in Northern Cyprus declare independence
  Death of Chiang Kai-shek
  Khmer Rouge forces capture Phnom Penh (Apr.)
  Evacuation of US personnel from Saigon (Apr.)
  Helsinki agreement on human rights and security (Aug.)

The 'Guildford Four' sentenced to life imprisonment on IRA bombing charges (Oct.)
British doctor Sheila Cassidy imprisoned and tortured in Chile
Death of Franco (20 Nov.): restoration of the Spanish monarchy

- Zadie Smith born
- Sir Julian Huxley dies
  R.C. Sheriff dies
  Elizabeth Taylor dies
  Arnold Toynbee dies
  P.G. Wodehouse dies
- Barbara Hepworth dies
  Aristotle Onassis dies
  Haile Selassie dies
- Ruth Prawer Jhabvala wins the Booker Prize for *Heat and Dust*
- Saul Bellow, *Humboldt's Gift*
  Jorge Luis Borges, *The Book of Sand*
  Primo Levi, *The Periodic Table*
- Milos Forman, *One Flew Over the Cuckoo's Nest*
  Steven Spielberg, *Jaws*
- Queen, 'Bohemian Rhapsody'

Martin Amis (1949)
Dead Babies F

Alan Ayckbourn (1939)
The Norman Conquests: Table Manners; Living Together; Round and Round the Garden D
Performed in Scarborough 1973, London 1974

Hilary Bailey (1936)
Polly Put the Kettle On F

Beryl Bainbridge (1934)
Sweet William F

J.G. Ballard (1930)
High Rise F

Nina Bawden (1925)
The Peppermint Pig F

Alan Bleasdale (1946)
Scully F
Stage play 1965, televised 1984

Eavan Boland (1944)
The War Horse V

Malcolm Bradbury (1932–2000)
The History Man F

Christine Brooke-Rose (1923)
Thru F

George Mackay Brown (1921–96)
Letters from Hamnavoe NF

Alan Brownjohn (1931)
A Song of Good Life V

Charles Causley (1917–2003)
Collected Poems 1951–1975 V
See also *Collected Poems* 1997

James Clavell (1924–94)
Shogun F

Margaret Drabble (1939)
The Realms of Gold F

Maureen Duffy (1933)
Evesong V

Paul Durcan (1944)
O Westport in the Light of Asia Minor V

Janice Elliott (1931–95)
Heaven on Earth F
England Trilogy iii. See also *A State of Peace* 1971, *Private Life* 1972.

Elaine Feinstein (1930)
Children of the Rose F

Roy Fuller (1912–91)
From the Joke Shop V

Jane Gardam (1928)
Black Faces, White Faces F
Stories

Rumer Godden (1907–98)
The Peacock Spring F

Simon Gray (1936)
Otherwise Engaged, and Other Plays D
Title play performed 1975

Graham Greene (1904–91)
The Return of A.J. Raffles D
Published in December 1975. Performed 4 December 1975. Based on E.W. Hornung, *The Amateur Cracksman* 1899 (q.v.).

Seamus Heaney (1939)
North V

John Heath-Stubbs (1918)
A Parliament of Birds V

Geoffrey Hill (1932)
Somewhere is Such a Kingdom V

Eric Hobsbawm (1917)
The Age of Capital, 1848–1875 NF
See also *The Age of Revolution* 1962, *The Age of Empire* 1987

Michael Holroyd (1935)
Augustus John: The Years of Experience NF
See also *The Years of Inocence* 1974

Elizabeth Jennings (1926–2001)
Growing Points V

Ruth Prawer Jhabvala (1927)
Heat and Dust F
Booker Prize 1975

Linton Kwesi Johnson (1952)
Dread, Beat and' Blood V

Francis King (1923)
The Needle F

Laurie Lee (1914–97)
I Can't Stay Long NF
Autobiography

Norman Lewis (1908–2003)
The Sicilian Specialist F

'Richard Llewellyn' [Richard Llewellyn Lloyd (1906–83)]
Green, Green My Valley Now F
Sequel to *How Green Was My Valley* 1939 (q.v.). See also *Up, Into the Singing Mountain* 1963, *Down Where the Moon is Small* 1966.

David Lodge (1935)
Changing Places NF

Ian McEwan (1948)
First Love, Last Rites F
Stories

William McIlvanney (1936)
Docherty F

Adrian Mitchell (1932)
The Apeman Cometh V

Brian Moore (1921–99)
The Great Victorian Collection F

Iris Murdoch (1919–99)
A World Child F

V.S. Naipaul (1932)
Guerillas F

R.K. Narayan (1906–2001)
My Days NF
First published in the USA, 1974

Norman Nicholson (1914–87)
Cloud on Black Combe V

Harold Pinter (1930)
No Man's Land D
Performed 23 April 1975

Ruth Pitter (1897–1992)
End of Drought V

Sylvia Plath (1932–63)
Letters Home: Correspondence 1950–1963 NF

Peter Porter (1929)
Living in a Calm Country V

Anthony Powell (1905–2000)
Hearing Secret Harmonies F
Dance to the Music of Time xii. See also *A Question of Upbringing* 1951; *A Buyer's Market* 1952; *The Acceptance World* 1955; *At Lady Molly's* 1957; *Casanova's Chinese Restaurant* 1960; *The Kindly Ones* 1962; *The Valley of Bones* 1964; *The Soldier's Art* 1966; *The Military Philosophers* 1968; *Books Do Furnish a Room* 1971; *Temporary Kings* 1973.

J.H. Prynne (1936)
High Pink on Chrome V

Alan Ross (1922)
Open Sea V

Salman Rushdie (1947)
Grimus F

Paul Scott (1920–78)
A Division of the Spoils F
The Raj Quartet iv. See also *The Jewel in the Crown* 1966, *The Day of the Scorpion* 1968, *The Towers of Silence* 1971.

Peter Scupham (1933)
Prehistories V

Tom Sharpe (1928)
Blott on the Landscape F

Iain Sinclair (1943)
Lud Heat V

George Steiner (1929)
After Babel: Aspects of language and translation NF

J.I.M. Stewart (1906–94)
Young Patullo F
'A Staircase in Surrey' sequence. See also *The Gaudy* 1974, *A Memorial Service* 1976, *The Madonna of the Astrolabe* 1977, *Full Term* 1978.

Tom Stoppard (1937)
Travesties D
Performed 10 June 1974

Paul Theroux (1941)
The Great Railway Bazaar NF

R.S. Thomas (1913–2000)
Laboratories of the Spirit V

'William Trevor' [William Trevor Cox (1928)]
Angels at the Ritz, and Other Stories F

Kenneth Tynan (1927–80)
A View of the English Stage 1944–63 NF

Keith Waterhouse (1929)
Billy Liar on the Moon F
See *Billy Liar* 1959

Fay Weldon (1931)
Female Friends F

Hugo Williams (1942)
Some Sweet Day V

Virginia Woolf (1882–1941)
The Flight of the Mind: The letters of Virginia Woolf volume i: 1888–1912 NF
Published on18 September 1975. Edited by Nigel Nicolson. See also *The Question of Things Happening* 1976, *A Change of Perspective* 1977, *A Reflection of the Other Person* 1978, *The Sickle Side of the Moon* 1979, *Leave the Letters Till We're Dead* 1980.

1976

- Concorde enters commerical service with British Airways
  Military coup in Argentina deposes Isabel Perón (Mar.)
  Margaret Thatcher branded the 'Iron Lady' after an anti-Communist speech
  James Callaghan wins Labour leadership election and becomes Prime Minister
  Jeremy Thorpe resigns as leader of the Liberal Party: eventually succeeded (July) by David Steel
  IMF crisis in Britain
- Agatha Christie dies
  Richard Hughes dies
  Jessica Mitford dies
  William Sansom dies
  Alison Uttley dies
- Benjamin Britten dies
- Paul Robeson dies
  Max Ernst dies
  Howard Hughes dies
  Man Ray dies
  Mao Tse-tung dies
- David Storey wins the Booker Prize for *Saville*
- Alex Haley, *Roots*
- The Eagles, *Hotel California*

Peter Ackroyd (1949)
Notes for a New Culture NF

Brian Aldiss (1925)
The Malacia Tapestry F

Kingsley Amis (1922–95)
The Alteration F

Beryl Bainbridge (1934)
A Quiet Life F

John Banville (1945)
Doctor Copernicus F

Stan Barstow (1928)
The Right True End F
Vic Brown Trilogy iii. See also *A Kind of Loving* 1960, *The Watchers on the Shore* 1966. Published together as *A Kind of Loving: The Vic Brown Trilogy* 1981.

Nina Bawden (1925)
Afternoon of a Good Woman F

Samuel Beckett (1906–89)
For To End Yet Again, and Other Fizzles F

Caroline Blackwood (1931–96)
The Stepdaughter F

Malcolm Bradbury (1932–2000)
Who Do You Think You Are? F
Stories

Howard Brenton (1942)
Weapons of Happiness D
Performed 1976

George Mackay Brown (1921–96)
The Sun's Net F

George Mackay Brown (1921–96)
Winterfold V

Len Deighton (1929)
Twinkle, Twinkle Little Spy F

Gavin Ewart (1916)
No Fool Like an Old Fool V

Elaine Feinstein (1930)
The Ecstasy of Dr Miriam Garner F

Michael Frayn (1933)
Alphabetical Order D
Performed 1975

Thom Gunn (1929–2004)
Jack Straw's Castle, and Other Poems V

David Hare (1947)
Teeth 'n' Smiles D
Performed 1975

Adrian Henri (1932–2001)
One Year V

William Douglas Home (1912–92)
The Dame of Sark D
Performed 1974

Ruth Prawer Jhabvala (1927)
How I Became a Holy Mother, and Other Stories F

Neil Jordan (1950)
Night in Tunisia, and Other Stories F

Penelope Lively (1933)
A Stitch in Time F
For children

Michael Longley (1939)
Man Lying on a Wall V

Michael McLaverty (1904–92)
The Road to the Shore F
Stories

Michael Moorcock (1939)
The End of All Songs F
The Dancers at the End of Time Trilogy iii

Brian Moore (1921–99)
The Doctor's Wife F

Robert Nye (1939)
Falstaff F

Sean O'Faolain (1900–91)
Foreign Affairs, and Other Stories F

Brian Patten (1946)
Vanishing Trick V

Stephen Poliakoff (1952)
Hitting Town; City Sugar D
Hitting Town performed 1975

Anthony Powell (1905–2000)
Infants of the Spring NF
First volume of autobiography. See also *Messengers of Day* 1978, *Faces In My Time* 1980, *The Strangers All Are Gone* 1982 (collectively: *To Keep the Ball Rolling*).

Frederic Raphael (1931)
The Glittering Prizes F
Adapted from a sequence of television plays, screened 1976

Simon Raven (1927–2001)
The Survivors F
Alms for Oblivion series x. See also *The Rich Pay Late* 1964, *Friends in Low Places* 1965, *The Sabre Squadron* 1966, *Fielding Gray* 1967, *The Judas Boy* 1968, *Places Where They Sing* 1970, *Sound the Retreat* 1971, *Come Like Shadows* 1972, *Bring Forth the Body* 1974.

Piers Paul Read (1941)
Polonaise F

Peter Reading (1946)
The Prison Cell and Barrel Mystery V

Tom Sharpe (1928)
Wilt F
Sequels: *The Wilt Alternative* (1979), *Wilt on High* (1984)

Jon Silkin (1930–97)
The Little Time-Keeper V

Carolyn Slaughter (1946)
The Story of the Weasel F

Muriel Spark (1918)
The Takeover F

J.I.M. Stewart (1906–94)
A Memorial Service F
'A Staircase in Surrey' sequence. See also *The Gaudy* 1974, *Young Patullo* 1975, *The Madonna of the Astrolabe* 1977, *Full Term* 1978.

David Storey (1933)
Saville F
Booker Prize 1976

Paul Theroux (1941)
The Family Arsenal F

Rose Tremain (1943)
Sadler's Birthday F

'William Trevor' [William Trevor Cox (1928)]
The Children of Dynmouth F

Marina Warner (1946)
Alone of All Her Sex NF

Fay Weldon (1931)
Remember Me F

Virginia Woolf (1882–1941)
The Question of Things Happening: The letters of Virginia Woolf volume ii: 1912–1922 NF
Published on 23 September 1976. Edited by Nigel Nicolson. See also *The Flight of the Mind* 1975, *A Change of Perspective* 1977, *A Reflection of the Other Person* 1978, *The Sickle Side of the Moon* 1979, *Leave the Letters Till We're Dead* 1980.

1977

- Gary Gilmore executed in the US (Jan.)
  Jimmy Carter becomes President of the USA
  The 'Lib-Lab pact' between the British Liberal and Labour parties
  Uganda excluded from the Commonwealth
  'Gang of Four' expelled from the Chinese Communist Party
  Brezhnev becomes President of the USSR
- Phyllis Bentley dies
  Elizabeth Daryush dies
  John Pudney dies
  Sir Terence Rattigan dies
  Dennis Wheatley dies
  Henry Williamson dies
- Anthony Eden dies
- Maria Callas dies
  Charlie Chaplin dies
  Bing Crosby dies
  Robert Lowell dies
  Vladimir Nabokov dies
  Elvis Presley dies
- Paul Scott wins the Booker Prize for *Staying On*
- George Lucas, *Star Wars*
  Steven Spielberg, *Close Encounters of the Third Kind*

Richard Adams (1920)
The Plague Dogs F

John Arden (1930) and **Margaretta D'Arcy** (1934)
The Non-Stop Connolly Show D
Parts i and ii: *Boyhood 1868–1889*, *Apprenticeship 1889–1896*. Based on the life of the Irish patriot James Connolly. See also *The Non-Stop Connolly Show* 1978.

Paul Bailey (1937)
Peter Smart's Confessions F

Beryl Bainbridge (1934)
Injury Time F

Samuel Beckett (1906–89)
Collected Poems in English and French V

Samuel Beckett (1906–89)
Four Novellas F

Steven Berkoff (1937)
East; Agamemnon; The Fall of the House of Usher D

Howard Brenton (1942)
Epsom Downs D
Performed 1977

'Anthony Burgess' [John Anthony Burgess Wilson (1917–93)]
Abba Abba F

'Anthony Burgess' [John Anthony Burgess Wilson (1917–93)]
Beard's Roman Women F
First published in the USA, 1976

Angela Carter (1940–92)
The Passion of New Eve F

Bruce Chatwin (1940–89)
In Patagonia NF

Anita Desai (1937)
Fire on the Mountain F

Kay Dick (1915)
They F

Margaret Drabble (1939)
The Ice Age F

'Alice Thomas Ellis' [Anna Margaret Haycraft (1932)]
The Sin Eater F

Elaine Feinstein (1930)
Some Unease and Angels V

Patrick Leigh Fermor (1915)
A Time of Gifts NF

Eva Figes (1932)
Nelly's Version F

Penelope Fitzgerald (1916–2000)
The Golden Child F

John Fowles (1926)
Daniel Martin F

Michael Frayn (1933)
Clouds D
Performed 1976

Michael Frayn (1933)
Donkeys' Years D
Performed 1976

Penelope Gilliatt (1932–93)
Splendid Lives F

Trevor Griffiths (1935)
All Good Men; and, Absolute Beginners D
Televised 1974

Adrian Henri (1932–2001)
City Hedges V

Ted Hughes (1930–98)
Gaudete V
Published on 18 May 1977

Christopher Isherwood (1904–86)
Christopher and his Kind 1929–39 NF
Autobiography

P.D. James (1920)
Death of an Expert Witness F

Elizabeth Jennings (1926–2001)
Consequently I Rejoice V

Mary Lavin (1912–96)
The Shrine, and Other Stories F

'John le Carré' [David John Moore Cornwell (1931)]
The Honourable Schoolboy F

Penelope Lively (1933)
The Road to Lichfield F

Norman MacCaig (1910–96)
Tree of Strings V

Bernard MacLaverty (1942)
Secrets, and Other Stories F

Sorley MacLean [Somhairle MacGill-Eain] (1911)
Spring Tide and Neap Tide [Reothairt is Contraigh] V
In Gaelic and English

Derek Mahon (1941)
Light Music V

Olivia Manning (1915–80)
The Danger Tree F
Levant Trilogy i. See also *The Battle Lost and Won* 1978, *The Sum of Things* 1980.

Michael Moorcock (1939)
The Condition of Muzak F
Cornelius Chronicle iv. See also *The Final Programme* 1969, *A Cure for Cancer* 1971, *The English Assassin* 1972.

Paul Muldoon (1951)
Mules V

Iris Murdoch (1919–99)
The Fire and the Sun NF

V.S. Naipaul (1932)
India NF

R.K. Narayan (1906–2001)
The Painter of Signs F
First published in the USA, 1976

Peter Nichols (1927)
Privates on Parade D

Edna O'Brien (1932)
Johnnie, I Hardly Knew You F

Tom Paulin (1949)
A State of Justice V

'Ellis Peters' [Edith Mary Pargeter (1913)]
A Morbid Taste for Bones F
First of the popular Brother Cadfael series of medieval detective stories

Sylvia Plath (1932–63)
Johnny Panic and the Bible of Dreams, and Other Prose Writings MISC
Edited by Ted Hughes

Barbara Pym (1913–80)
Quartet in Autumn F

Kathleen Raine (1908–2003)
The Oval Portrait, and Other Poems V

Paul Scott (1920–78)
Staying On F
Booker Prize 1977

Peter Scupham (1933)
The Hinterland V

J.I.M. Stewart (1906–94)
The Madonna of the Astrolabe F
'A Staircase in Surrey' sequence. See also *The Gaudy* 1974, *Young Patullo* 1975, *A Memorial Service* 1976, *Full Term* 1978.

Colin Thubron (1939)
The God in the Mountain F

Anthony Thwaite (1930)
A Portion for Foxes V

J.R.R. Tolkien (1892–1973)
The Silmarillion F

Edward Upward (1903)
The Spiral Ascent F
The Spiral Ascent Trilogy iii. See also *In the Thirties* 1962, *The Rotten Elements* 1969. The third volume, entitled *No Home But the Struggle*, published here for the first time.

Tom Wakefield (1935)
Trixie Trash, Star Ascending F
Isobel Quirk Trilogy i. See also *Isobel Quirk in Orbit* 1978, *The Love Siege* 1979.

Marina Warner (1946)
In a Dark Wood F

Nigel Williams (1948)
My Life Closed Twice F

A.N. Wilson (1950)
The Sweets of Pimlico F

Virginia Woolf (1882–1941)
A Change of Perspective: The letters of Virginia Woolf volume iii: 1923–1928 NF
Published on 22 September 1977. Edited by Nigel Nicolson. See also *The Flight of the Mind* 1975, *The Question of Things Happening* 1976, *A Reflection of the Other Person* 1978, *The Sickle Side of the Moon* 1979, *Leave the Letters Till We're Dead* 1980.

Virginia Woolf (1882–1941)
The Diary of Virginia Woolf: Volume i: 1915–1919 NF
Published on 11 November 1977. See also *Diary* 1978, 1980, 1982, 1984.

1978

- Israel invades southern Lebanon
  Birth of first 'test tube' baby, Louise Brown
  Death of Pope Paul VI (Aug.): election of Karol Wojtyla as John Paul II, the first non-Italian pope for 400 years
  Camp David summit (Sept.)
  Vietnam invades Cambodia (Dec.)
- F.N.W. Bateson dies
  Edmund Crispin (Robert Montgomery) dies
  Sir Roy Harrod dies
  F.R. Leavis dies
  Hugh MacDiarmid (Christopher Murray Grieve) dies
  James Reeves dies
  Berta Ruck dies
  Paul Scott dies
  Sylvia Townsend Warner dies
- Jomo Kenyatta dies
  Golda Meir dies
- Iris Murdoch wins the Booker Prize for *The Sea, the Sea*
- Armistead Maupin, *Tales of the City*
- *The Deer Hunter*
- *Dallas* (TV series)

Peter Ackroyd (1949)
Country Life V

Brian Aldiss (1925)
Enemies of the System F

Brian Aldiss (1925)
A Rude Awakening F
Third of the three Horatio Stubbs novels. See also *The Hand-Reared Boy* 1970, *A Soldier Erect* 1971.

A. Alvarez (1929)
Autumn to Autumn and Selected Poems 1953–1976 V

Kingsley Amis (1922–95)
Jake's Thing F

Martin Amis (1949)
Success F

John Arden (1930) and **Margaretta D'Arcy** (1934)
The Non-Stop Connolly Show D
Part iii: *Professionals, 1896–1903*. Parts iv (*The New World, 1903–1910*), v (*The Great Lockout, 1910–1914*), and vi (*World War and the Rising, 1914–1916*) also published in 1978. See also *The Non-Stop Connolly Show* 1977. All six parts published together in 1986.

Beryl Bainbridge (1934)
Young Adolf F

Edward Bond (1934)
The Bundle; or, New Narrow Road to the Deep North D

Brigid Brophy (1929)
Palace Without Chairs F

'Anthony Burgess' [John Anthony Burgess Wilson (1917–93)]
1985 F

A.S. Byatt (1936)
The Virgin in the Garden F
See also *Still Life* 1985, *Babel Tower* 1996

Caryl Churchill (1938)
Light Shining in Buckinghamshire D
Performed 1976

Gillian Clarke (1937)
The Sundial V

David Cook (1940)
Walter F
See also *Winter Doves* 1979

J.P. Donleavy (1926)
The Destinies of Darcy Dancer, Gentleman F
First published in the USA, 1977. See also *Leila* 1983, *That Darcy, That Dancer, That Gentleman* 1990.

Maureen Duffy (1933)
Housespy F

Lawrence Durrell (1912–90)
Livia; or, Buried Alive F
Second of the Avignon quintet. See also *Monsieur* 1974, *Constance* 1982, *Sebastian* 1983, and *Quinx* 1985. Published together 1992.

D.J. Enright (1920–2002)
Paradise Illustrated V

Gavin Ewart (1916)
All My Little Ones v
See also *More Little Ones* 1982

J.G. Farrell (1935–79)
The Singapore Grip F
Empire Trilogy iii. See also *Troubles* 1970; *The Siege of Krishnapur* 1973.

James Fenton (1949)
A Vacant Possession v

Roy Fisher (1930)
The Thing About Joe Sullivan v

Penelope Fitzgerald (1916–2000)
The Bookshop F

Ken Follett (1949)
Eye of the Needle F

Simon Gray (1936)
The Rear Column, and Other Plays D

Graham Greene (1904–91)
The Human Factor F
Published in March 1978

Geoffrey Grigson (1905–85)
The Fiesta, and Other Poems v

David Hare (1947)
Licking Hitler D
Televised 1978

David Hare (1947)
Plenty D

Tony Harrison (1937)
From the School of Eloquence, and Other Poems v

Geoffrey Hill (1932)
Tenebrae v

Ted Hughes (1930–98)
Cave Birds v

Ted Hughes (1930–98)
Moon-Bells, and Other Poems v
For children. Published on 2 February 1978.

Jenny Joseph (1932)
The Thinking Heart v

M.M. Kaye (1908–2004)
The Far Pavilions F

Philip Larkin (1922–85)
Femmes Damnées v

Penelope Lively (1933)
Nothing Missing But the Samovar, and Other Stories F

Liz Lochhead (1947)
Islands v

George MacBeth (1932–92)
Buying a Heart v
First published in the USA, 1977

Eugene McCabe (1930)
Heritage, and Other Stories F

'Hugh MacDiarmid' [**Christopher Murray Grieve** (1892–1978)]
Complete Poems 1920–76 v

Ian McEwan (1948)
The Cement Garden F

Ian McEwan (1948)
In Between the Sheets F
Stories

Sara Maitland (1950)
Daughter of Jerusalem F

Olivia Manning (1915–80)
The Battle Lost and Won F
Levant Trilogy ii. See also *The Danger Tree* 1977, *The Sum of Things* 1980.

Allan Massie (1938)
Change and Decay in All Around I See F

Timothy Mo (1950)
The Monkey King F

John Mortimer (1923)
Rumpole of the Bailey F
The first collection of Rumpole stories

Andrew Motion (1952)
The Pleasure Steamers v

Iris Murdoch (1919–99)
The Sea, the Sea F
Booker Prize 1978

Shiva Naipaul (1945–85)
North of South NF

Norman Nicholson (1914–87)
The Shadow of Black Combe v

Tom Paulin (1949)
Personal Column v

Harold Pinter (1930)
Betrayal D
Performed in November 1978

Dennis Potter (1935–94)
Brimstone and Treacle D
Performed 1978; televised 1987

Anthony Powell (1905–2000)
Messengers of Day NF

Second volume of autobiography. See also *Infants of the Spring* 1976, *Faces In My Time* 1980, *The Strangers All Are Gone* 1982 (collectively: *To Keep the Ball Rolling*).

Barbara Pym (1913–80)
The Sweet Dove Died F

Craig Raine (1944)
The Onion, Memory V

Terence Rattigan (1911–77)
Cause Célèbre D
Broadcast 1975; performed 1977

Michèle Roberts (1949)
A Piece of the Night F

Bernice Rubens (1928–2004)
A Five Year Sentence F

David Rudkin (1936)
Ashes D
Performed 1974

Carol Rumens (1944)
A Necklace of Mirrors V

Stephen Spender (1909–95)
The Thirties and After NF

Jon Stallworthy (1935)
A Familiar Tree V

J.I.M. Stewart (1906–94)
Full Term F
'A Staircase in Surrey' sequence. See also *The Gaudy* 1974, *Young Patullo* 1975, *A Memorial Service* 1976, *The Madonna of the Astrolabe* 1977.

Tom Stoppard (1937)
Every Good Boy Deserves Favour; Professional Foul D
Every Good Boy Deserves Favour performed 1 July 1977. *Professional Foul* televised September 1977.

Tom Stoppard (1937)
Night and Day D
Performed 1978

Paul Theroux (1941)
Picture Palace F

D.M. Thomas (1935)
The Honeymoon Voyage V

R.S. Thomas (1913–2000)
Frequencies V

Colin Thubron (1939)
Emperor F

Rose Tremain (1943)
Letter to Sister Benedicta F

'William Trevor' [William Trevor Cox (1928)]
Lovers of Their Time, and Other Stories F

Tom Wakefield (1935)
Isobel Quirk in Orbit F
Isobel Quirk Trilogy ii. See also *Trixie Trash, Star Ascending* 1977, *The Love Siege* 1979.

Fay Weldon (1931)
Praxis F

Virginia Woolf (1882–1941)
The Diary of Virginia Woolf: Volume ii: 1920–1924 NF
Published on 24 August 1978. See also *Diary* 1977, 1980, 1982, 1984.

Virginia Woolf (1882–1941)
A Reflection of the Other Person: The letters of Virginia Woolf volume iv: 1929–193 NF
Published on 19 October 1978. Edited by Nigel Nicolson. See also *The Flight of the Mind* 1975, *The Question of Things Happening* 1976, *A Change of Perspective* 1977, *The Sickle Side of the Moon* 1979, *Leave the Letters Till We're Dead* 1980.

1979

- Iranian Revolution: the Shah and his family flee the country (Jan.)
  Widespread industrial action in Britain (the 'winter of discontent')
  Khmer Rouge driven out of Phnom Penh
  Margaret Thatcher becomes British Prime Minister (3 May)
  Saddam Hussein becomes President of Iraq (July)
  IRA terrorists murder Lord Mountbatten (Aug.)
  Russians invade Afghanistan (Dec.)
- J.G. Farrell dies
  Nicholas Monsarrat dies
  Eric Partridge dies
  Jean Rhys (Ella Williams) dies
  Ivor Richards dies
  Julia Strachey dies
- Mary Pickford dies
  John Wayne dies
- Penelope Fitzgerald wins the Booker Prize for *Offshore*
- The Clash, *London Calling*
- Norman Mailer, *The Executioner's Song*
  William Styron, *Sophie's Choice*
- Ridley Scott, *Alien*

Peter Ackroyd (1949)
Dressing Up: Transvestism and Drag NF

Douglas Adams (1952–2001)
The Hitch-Hiker's Guide to the Galaxy F

Fleur Adcock (1934)
Below Loughrigg V

Fleur Adcock (1934)
The Inner Harbour V

Kingsley Amis (1922–95)
Collected Poems 1944–1979 V

Alan Ayckbourn (1939)
Joking Apart; Ten Times Table; Just Between Ourselves D
Joking Apart performed in Scarborough 1978; *Ten Times Table* performed in Scarborough 1977; *Just Between Ourselves* performed in Scarborough 1976

J.G. Ballard (1930)
The Unlimited Dream Company F

Nina Bawden (1925)
Familiar Passions F

Samuel Beckett (1906–89)
All Strange Away F
First published in the USA, 1976

John Berger (1926)
Pig Earth F

James Berry (1924)
Fractured Circles V

George Mackay Brown (1921–96)
Under Brinkie's Brae NF

Angela Carter (1940–92)
The Bloody Chamber, and Other Stories F
Includes 'The Company of Wolves' (film 1984)

Angela Carter (1940–92)
The Sadeian Woman NF

Caryl Churchill (1938)
Cloud Nine D
Performed 14 February 1979

David Cook (1940)
Winter Doves F
Sequel to *Walter* 1978 (q.v.)

Roald Dahl (1916–90)
My Uncle Oswald F

Roald Dahl (1916–90)
Tales of the Unexpected F
See also *More Tales of the Unexpected* 1980

Patric Dickinson (1914–94)
Our Living John, and Other Poems V

Maureen Duffy (1933)
Memorials of the Quick and the Dead V

Douglas Dunn (1942)
Barbarians V

David Edgar (1948)
Teendreams D
Written with Susan Todd

D.J. Enright (1920–2002)
A Faust Book V

Zoë Fairbairns (1948)
Benefits F

Penelope Fitzgerald (1916–2000)
Offshore F
Booker Prize 1979

John Fuller (1937)
Lies and Secrets V

William Golding (1911–93)
Darkness Visible F

W.S. Graham (1918–86)
Collected Poems 1942–1977 V

Thom Gunn (1929–2004)
Selected Poems 1950–1975 V
See also *Poems* 1969, *Collected Poems* 1993

Seamus Heaney (1939)
Field Work V

Ted Hughes (1930–98)
Moortown V
Published on 22 October 1979

Ted Hughes (1930–98)
Remains of Elmet V

Elizabeth Jennings (1926–2001)
Moments of Grace V

Jennifer Johnston (1930)
The Old Jest F

P.J. Kavanagh (1931)
Life Before Death V

Doris Lessing (1919)
Shikasta F
Canopus in Argos: Archives i. See also *The Marriages Between Zones Three, Four and Five* 1980, *The Sirian Experiments* 1981, *The Making of the Representative for Planet 8* 1982, *The Sentimental Agents in the Volyen Empire* 1983.

Penelope Lively (1933)
Treasures of Time F

Michael Longley (1939)
The Echo Gate V

John McGahern (1934)
The Pornographer F

Roger McGough (1937)
Holiday on Death Row V

Brian Moore (1921–99)
The Mangan Inheritance F

Nicholas Mosley (1923)
Catastrophe Practice F
First of an uncompleted 7-novel sequence. See also *Imago Bird* 1980, *Serpent* 1981, *Judith* 1986, *Hopeful Monsters* 1990.

V.S. Naipaul (1932)
A Bend in the River F

Brian Patten (1946)
Grave Gossip V

Stephen Poliakoff (1952)
Shout Across the River D
Performed 1978

Jonathan Raban (1942)
Arabia Through the Looking-Glass NF

Craig Raine (1944)
A Martian Sends a Postcard Home V

Peter Reading (1946)
Fiction V

Peter Redgrove (1932–2003)
The God of Glass F

Bernice Rubens (1928–2004)
Spring Sonata F

Clive Sinclair (1948)
Hearts of Gold F
Stories

Muriel Spark (1918)
Territorial Rights F

Paul Theroux (1941)
The Old Patagonian Express NF

D.M. Thomas (1935)
The Flute-Player F

Joanna Trollope (1943)
Parson Harding's Daughter F

Tom Wakefield (1935)
The Love Siege F
Isobel Quirk Trilogy iii. See also *Trixie Trash, Star Ascending* 1977, *Isobel Quirk in Orbit* 1978.

A.N. Wilson (1950)
Kindly Light F

Virginia Woolf (1882–1941)
The Sickle Side of the Moon: The letters of Virginia Woolf volume v: 1932–1935 NF
Published on 20 September 1979. Edited by Nigel Nicolson. See also *The Flight of the Mind* 1975, *The Question of Things Happening* 1976, *A Change of Perspective* 1977, *A Reflection of the Other Person* 1978, *Leave the Letters Till We're Dead* 1980.

1980

- Rhodesia gains independence as Zimbabwe (Apr.)
  Failed attempt to rescue US hostages in Iran
  Iranian embassy siege in London (Apr.–May)
  Death of President Tito of Yugoslavia (May)
  Iraq invades Iran (Sept.): start of the Iran–Iraq war (–1988)
  Mrs Thatcher's 'U-turn' speech (Oct.)
  James Callaghan resigns as leader of the British Labour Party
  Solidarity formed in Gdansk under leadership of Lech Walesa
- Adrian Bell dies
  Olivia Manning dies
  David Mercer dies
  Barbara Pym dies
  C.P. Snow dies
  Ben Travers dies
  Kenneth Tynan dies
  Antonia White (Eirene Botting) dies
- Cecil Beaton dies
  Alfred Hitchcock dies
  John Lennon dies
  Peter Sellers dies
- Marshall McLuhan dies
  Jean-Paul Sartre dies
- William Golding wins the Booker Prize for *Rites of Passage*
- Umberto Eco, *The Name of the Rose*

Richard Adams (1920)
The Girl in a Swing F

Brian Aldiss (1925)
Moreau's Other Island F

Kingsley Amis (1922–95)
Collected Short Stories F

Kingsley Amis (1922–95)
Russian Hide-and-Seek F

Paul Bailey (1937)
Old Soldiers F

Beryl Bainbridge (1934)
Winter Garden F

J.G. Ballard (1930)
The Venus Hunters F

Lynne Reid Banks (1929)
The Indian in the Cupboard F
For children

'Dan Kavanagh' [Julian Barnes (1946)**]**
Duffy F

Julian Barnes (1946)
Metroland F

Samuel Beckett (1906–89)
Company F

John Berger (1926)
About Looking NF

Thomas Blackburn (1916–77)
Bread for the Winter Birds V

Eavan Boland (1944)
In Her Own Image V

Melvyn Bragg (1939)
Kingdom Come F
Cumbrian Trilogy iii. See also *The Hired Man* 1969, *A Place in England* 1970.

Howard Brenton (1942)
The Romans in Britain D

Alan Brownjohn (1931)
A Night in the Gazebo V

'Anthony Burgess' [John Anthony Burgess Wilson (1917–93)**]**
Earthly Powers F

J.L. Carr (1912–94)
A Month in the Country F

Bruce Chatwin (1940–89)
The Viceroy of Ouidah F

Jack Clemo (1916–94)
The Marriage of a Rebel NF
See also *Confession of a Rebel* 1949

David Constantine (1944)
A Brightness to Cast Shadows V

Catherine Cookson (1906–98)
Tilly Trotter F
The first of the Tilly Trotter saga

Wendy Cope (1945)
Across the City V

Roald Dahl (1916–90)
More Tales of the Unexpected F
See *Tales of the Unexpected* 1979

Donald Davie (1922–95)
In the Stopping Train, and Other Poems V

Anita Desai (1937)
Clear Light of Day F

J.P. Donleavy (1926)
Schultz F
First published in the USA, 1979

Margaret Drabble (1939)
The Middle Ground F

'Alice Thomas Ellis' [Anna Margaret Haycraft (1932)**]**
The Birds of the Air F

Gavin Ewart (1916)
The Collected Ewart 1933–1980 V
See also *Collected Poems* 1991

Elaine Feinstein (1930)
The Feast of Euridice V

Roy Fisher (1930)
Poems 1955–1980 V

Penelope Fitzgerald (1916–2000)
Human Voices F

Ken Follett (1949)
The Key to Rebecca F

Michael Frayn (1933)
Make and Break D

John Fuller (1937)
The January Divan V

Roy Fuller (1912–91)
The Reign of Sparrows V

William Golding (1911–93)
Rites of Passage F
Booker Prize 1980. To the Ends of the Earth Trilogy i. See also *Close Quarters* 1987 and *Fire Down Below 1989*. Published together in 1991.

Graham Greene (1904–91)
Dr Fischer of Geneva; or, The Bomb Party F

Graham Greene (1904–91)
Ways of Escape NF
Autobiography. See also *A Sort of Life* 1971.

Geoffrey Grigson (1905–85)
History of Him V

Seamus Heaney (1939)
Preoccupations NF

Seamus Heaney (1939)
Selected Poems 1965–1975 V
See also *New Selected Poems* 1990

Adrian Henri (1932–2001)
From the Loveless Matel V

Frances Horovitz (1938–83)
Water Over Stone V

Elizabeth Jennings (1926–2001)
A Dream of Spring V

Linton Kwesi Johnson (1952)
Inglan is a Bitch V

Thomas Kinsella (1928)
Poems 1956–1973 V

'John le Carré' [David John Moore Cornwell (1931)**]**
Smiley's People F

Laurence Lerner (1925)
A.R.T.H.U.R. & M.A.R.T.H.A.; or, The Loves of the Computers V
See also *A.R.T.H.U.R.* 1974

Doris Lessing (1919)
The Marriages Between Zones Three, Four and Five F
Canopus in Argos: Archives ii. See also *Shikasta* 1979, *The Sirian Experiments* 1981, *The Making of the Representative for Planet 8* 1982, *The Sentimental Agents in the Volyen Empire* 1983.

Penelope Lively (1933)
Judgement Day F

David Lodge (1935)
How Far Can You Go? F

George MacBeth (1932–92)
Poems of Love and Death V

Norman MacCaig (1910–96)
The Equal Skies V

Bernard MacLaverty (1942)
Lamb F

Olivia Manning (1915–80)
The Sum of Things F
Levant Trilogy iii. See also *The Danger Tree* 1977, *The Battle Lost and Won* 1978.

Nicholas Mosley (1923)
Imago Bird F
Second of an uncompleted 7-novel sequence. See also *Catastrophe Practice* 1979, *Serpent* 1981, *Judith* 1986, *Hopeful Monsters* 1990.

Paul Muldoon (1951)
Why Brownlee Left V

Iris Murdoch (1919–99)
Nuns and Soldiers F

Peter Nichols (1927)
Born in the Gardens D
Performed 1979

Robert Nye (1939)
Faust F

Julia O'Faolain (1932)
No Country for Young Men F

Tom Paulin (1949)
The Strange Museum V

Harold Pinter (1930)
The Hothouse D
Performed 24 April 1980

Anthony Powell (1905–2000)
Faces In My Time NF
Third volume of autobiography. See also *Infants of the Spring* 1976, *Messengers of Day* 1978, *The Strangers All Are Gone* 1982 (collectively: *To Keep the Ball Rolling*).

V.S. Pritchett (1900–97)
On the Edge of the Cliff F
Stories. First published in the USA, 1979.

Barbara Pym (1913–80)
A Few Green Leaves F

Kathleen Raine (1908–2003)
The Oracle in the Heart, and Other Poems 1975–1978 V

Frederic Raphael (1931)
Oxbridge Blues, and Other Stories F
See also *Oxbridge Blues* 1984

Jeremy Reed (1954)
Bleecker Street V

Peter Shaffer (1926)
Amadeus D
Performed 1979. Subsequently adapted by Shaffer for the film version directed by Milos Forman, 1984.

Jon Silkin (1930–97)
The Psalms With Their Spoils V

Graham Swift (1949)
The Sweet-Shop Owner F

Emma Tennant (1937)
Alice Fell F

Paul Theroux (1941)
World's End, and Other Stories F

Anthony Thwaite (1930)
Victorian Voices V

J.R.R. Tolkien (1892–1973)
Unfinished Tales of Numenor and Middle Earth F

'William Trevor' [William Trevor Cox (1928)]
Other People's Worlds F

Joanna Trollope (1943)
Leaves From the Valley F

John Wain (1925–94)
Poems, 1949–1979 V

Fay Weldon (1931)
Puffball F

Nigel Williams (1948)
Jack Be Nimble F

A.N. Wilson (1950)
The Healing Art F

Angus Wilson (1913–91)
Setting the World on Fire F

Virginia Woolf (1882–1941)
The Diary of Virginia Woolf: Volume iii: 1925–1930 NF
Published on 27 March 1980. See also *Diary* 1977, 1978, 1982, 1984.

Virginia Woolf (1882–1941)
Leave the Letters Till We're Dead: The letters of Virginia Woolf volume vi: 1936–1941 NF
Published on 18 September 1980. Edited by Nigel Nicolson. See also *The Flight of the Mind* 1975, *The Question of Things Happening* 1976, *A Change of Perspective* 1977, *A Reflection of the Other Person* 1978, *The Sickle Side of the Moon* 1979.

1981

- Greece joins the EEC
  Ronald Reagan becomes President of the USA (Jan.)
  British Social Democratic Party founded by Roy Jenkins, David Owen, William Rodgers, and Shirley Williams
  President Reagan wounded in assassination attempt (Mar.)
  Riots in Brixton, south London (Apr.)
  IRA hunger-striker Bobby Sands dies in the Maze prison (May)
  Riots in Toxteth, Liverpool (July)
  Assassination of President Sadat of Egypt: succeeded by Hosni Mubarak
  Israel annexes the Golan heights (Dec.)
- Robert Aickman dies
  Enid Bagnold dies
  Christy Brown dies
  A.J. Cronin dies
  Robert Garioch dies
  David Garnett dies
  Pamela Hansford Johnson dies
  Alec Waugh dies
- Samuel Barber dies
- Salman Rushdie wins the Booker Prize for *Midnight's Children*
- *Chariots of Fire*

Dannie Abse (1923)
Way Out in the Centre V

Martin Amis (1949)
Other People F

J.G. Ballard (1930)
Hello America F

John Banville (1945)
Kepler F

A.L. Barker (1918–2002)
Life Stories F

'Dan Kavanagh' [Julian Barnes (1946)]
Fiddle City F

Peter Barnes (1931)
Collected Plays D

Nina Bawden (1925)
Walking Naked F

Sir John Betjeman (1906–84)
Church Poems V

Elizabeth Bowen (1899–1973)
Collected Stories F

William Boyd (1952)
A Good Man in Africa F

William Boyd (1952)
On the Yankee Station, and Other Stories F

Alison Brackenbury (1953)
Dreams of Power V

John Braine (1922–86)
One and Last Love F

Anita Brookner (1928)
A Start in Life F

Isabel Colegate (1931)
The Shooting Party F

'Bernard Cornwell' [**Bernard Wiggins** (1944)]
Sharpe's Eagle F
First of the Richard Sharpe historical novels

Roald Dahl (1916–90)
George's Marvellous Medicine F
Illustrated by Quentin Blake

Maureen Duffy (1933)
Gor Saga F

Daphne du Maurier (1907–89)
The Rebecca Notebook, and Other Memories MISC
Includes short stories

Douglas Dunn (1942)
St Kilda's Parliament V

Nell Dunn (1936)
Steaming D

Janice Elliott (1931–95)
Secret Places F

D.J. Enright (1920–2002)
Collected Poems V

J.G. Farrell (1935–79)
The Hill Station F

James Fenton (1949)
Dead Soldiers V

James Fenton (1949)
A German Requiem V

Roy Fisher (1930)
Consolidated Comedies V

John Gardner (1926)
Licence Renewed F
First of a series of novels continuing and updating the adventures of Ian Fleming's James Bond character

Maggie Gee (1948)
Dying, in Other Words F

Alasdair Gray (1934)
Lanark F

Thom Gunn (1929–2004)
Talbot Road V

Tony Harrison (1937)
Continuous V

Tony Harrison (1937)
A Kumquat for John Keats V

John Heath-Stubbs (1918)
Buzz Buzz V

Ted Hughes (1930–98)
Under the North Star V

Alan Judd (1946)
A Breed of Heroes F

Molly Keane (1904–96)
Good Behaviour F
The first novel to appear under Keane's own name

Doris Lessing (1919)
The Sirian Experiments F
Canopus in Argos: Archives iii. See also *Shikasta* 1979, *The Marriages Between Zones Three, Four and Five* 1980, *The Making of the Representative for Planet 8* 1982, *The Sentimental Agents in the Volyen Empire* 1983.

Peter Levi (1931)
Private Ground V

Liz Lochhead (1947)
The Grimm Sisters V

Christopher Logue (1926)
Ode to the Dodo V

Christopher Logue (1926)
War Music D
Adapted from Homer's *Iliad*, books xvi–xix. Performed 1977. See also *Kings* 1990, *The Husbands* 1994.

Michael Longley (1939)
Patchwork V

Ian McEwan (1948)
The Comfort of Strangers F

Derek Mahon (1941)
Courtyards in Delft V

Derek Mahon (1941)
The Hunt by Night V

Adam Mars-Jones (1954)
Lantern Lecture F

Allan Massie (1938)
The Death of Men F

Michael Moorcock (1939)
Byzantium Endures F
Pyat series i. See also *The Laughter of Carthage* 1984, *Jerusalem Commands* 1992.

Nicholas Mosley (1923)
Serpent F
Third of an uncompleted 7-novel sequence. See also *Catastrophe Practice* 1979, *Imago* 1980, *Judith* 1986, *Hopeful Monsters* 1990.

Andrew Motion (1952)
Independence V

Norman Nicholson (1914–87)
Sea to the West V

John Osborne (1929–94)
A Better Class of Person NF
Autobiography. See also *Almost a Gentleman* 1991.

Brian Patten (1946)
Love Poems V

Tom Paulin (1949)
The Book of Juniper V

Caryl Phillips (1958)
Strange Fruit D
Performed 1980

Sylvia Plath (1932–63)
Collected Poems V
Edited by Ted Hughes

Peter Porter (1929)
English Subtitles V

Dennis Potter (1935–94)
Pennies From Heaven F
Novelization of 6-part serial (televised 1978)

Piers Paul Read (1941)
The Villa Golitsyn F

Peter Reading (1946)
Tom O' Bedlam's Beauties V

Peter Redgrove (1932–2003)
The Apple Broadcast, and Other New Poems V

'Mary Renault' [Eileen Mary Challans (1905)]
Funeral Games F
Alexander Trilogy iii. See also *Fire From Heaven* 1970, *The Persian Boy* 1972.

Carol Rumens (1944)
Unplayed Music V

Salman Rushdie (1947)
Midnight's Children F
Published in April 1981. Booker Prize 1981.

Willy Russell (1947)
Educating Rita D
Performed June 1980; film 1983

Muriel Spark (1918)
Loitering With Intent F

Graham Swift (1949)
Shuttlecock F

Paul Theroux (1941)
The Mosquito Coast F

D.M. Thomas (1935)
Dreaming in Bronze V

D.M. Thomas (1935)
The White Hotel F

R.S. Thomas (1913–2000)
Between Here and Now V

Rose Tremain (1943)
The Cupboard F

'William Trevor' [William Trevor Cox (1928)]
Beyond the Pale F

Fay Weldon (1931)
Watching Me, Watching You; and other stories F

Arnold Wesker (1932)
Caritas D
Performed 7 October 1981

1982

- Martial law imposed in Poland
  Argentine flag raised on the island of South Georgia (19 Mar.)
  Argentine forces invade the Falkland Islands (2 Apr.): British task force sets sail (4 Apr.)
  British forces recapture South Georgia (25 Apr.)
  Sinking of the Argentine cruiser *General Belgrano* by the British submarine HMS *Conqueror* (2 May)
  Argentine forces surrender at Port Stanley (14 June), ending the Falklands war
  Massacre of Palestinians by Christian Phalangists in Beirut
  Helmut Kohl becomes German Chancellor
- E.H. Carr dies
  Ronald Duncan dies
  Sir Geoffrey Keynes dies
  Frank Swinnerton dies
- Grace Kelly dies
- Thomas Keneally wins the Booker Prize for *Schindler's Ark*
- Isabel Allende, *The House of the Spirits*
  Carlos Fuentes, *Distant Relations*
  John Updike, *Rabbit is Rich*
- Richard Attenborough, *Gandhi*
  Ridley Scott, *Bladerunner*
  Steven Spielberg, *E.T.*

Peter Ackroyd (1949)
The Great Fire of London F

Brian Aldiss (1925)
Helliconia Spring F

Helliconia Trilogy i. See also *Helliconia Summer* 1983, *Helliconia Winter* 1985.

J.G. Ballard (1930)
Myths of the Near Future F

John Banville (1945)
The Newton Letter F

Pat Barker (1943)
Union Street F

Julian Barnes (1946)
Before She Met Me F

Samuel Beckett (1906–89)
Ill Seen Ill Said F
Translation of *Mal vu mal dit Minuit* (1981). First published in the USA, 1981.

Samuel Beckett (1906–89)
Three Occasional Pieces D
Contains *A Piece of Monologue*; *Rockaby*; *Ohio Impromptu*

Steven Berkoff (1937)
Decadence D
Performed 1981

James Berry (1924)
Lucy's Letters and Loving V

Sir John Betjeman (1906–84)
Uncollected Poems V

Maeve Binchy (1940)
Light a Penny Candle F

William Boyd (1952)
An Ice-Cream War F

Anita Brookner (1928)
Providence F

'Anthony Burgess' [John Anthony Burgess Wilson (1917–93)]
The End of the World News F

Angela Carter (1940–92)
Nothing Sacred NF

Bruce Chatwin (1940–89)
On the Black Hill F

Caryl Churchill (1938)
Top Girls D
Performed 1982

'William Cooper' [Harry Summerfield Hoff (1910–2002)]
Scenes from Metropolitan Life F
See also *Scenes from Provincial Life* 1950, *Scenes from Married Life* 1961, *Scenes from Later Life* 1983

Roald Dahl (1916–90)
The BFG F

Anita Desai (1937)
The Village by the Sea F

Patric Dickinson (1914–94)
A Rift in Time V

Douglas Dunn (1942)
Europa's Lover V

Lawrence Durrell (1912–90)
Constance; or, Solitary Practices F
Third of the Avignon quintet. See also *Monsieur* 1974, *Livia* 1978, *Sebastian* 1983, and *Quinx* 1985. Published together 1992.

'Alice Thomas Ellis' [Anna Margaret Haycraft (1932)]
The 27th Kingdom F

Gavin Ewart (1916)
More Little Ones V
See *All My Little Ones* 1978

U.A. Fanthorpe (1929)
Standing To V

Elaine Feinstein (1930)
The Survivors F

Penelope Fitzgerald (1916–2000)
At Freddie's F

John Fowles (1926)
Mantissa F

Michael Frayn (1933)
Noises Off D

Leon Garfield (1921)
Garfield's Apprentices F
Collected edition of 12 short novels, beginning with *The Lamplighter's Funeral* (1976) and concluding with *The Enemy* (1978). First published in the USA 1978.

William Golding (1911–93)
A Moving Target NF
Essays

Graham Greene (1904–91)
J'accuse: The darker side of Nice NF

Graham Greene (1904–91)
Monsieur Quixote F

Trevor Griffiths (1935)
Oi for England D
Performed and televised 1982

Geoffrey Grigson (1905–85)
Collected Poems, 1963–1980 V

Geoffrey Grigson (1905–85)
The Cornish Dancer, and Other Poems V

Thom Gunn (1929–2004)
The Passages of Joy V

Seamus Heaney (1939) and **Ted Hughes** (1930–98) (eds)
The Rattle-Bag ANTH

Alan Hollinghurst (1954)
Confidential Chats with Boys V

Geoffrey Household (1900–88)
Rogue Justice F
Sequel to *Rogue Male* 1939 (q.v.)

Elizabeth Jane Howard (1923)
Getting it Right F

Ted Hughes (1930–98)
Selected Poems 1957–1981 V
See also *Selected Poems* 1972, *New Selected Poems* 1995

Kazuo Ishiguro (1954)
A Pale View of Hills F

P.D. James (1920)
The Skull Beneath the Skin F

Kathleen Jamie (1962)
Black Spiders V

Francis King (1923)
Act of Darkness F

James Kirkup (1918)
No More Hiroshimas V

Doris Lessing (1919)
The Making of the Representative for Planet 8 F
Canopus in Argos: Archives iv. See also *Shikasta* 1979, *The Marriages Between Zones Three, Four and Five* 1980, *The Sirian Experiments* 1981, *The Sentimental Agents in the Volyen Empire* 1983.

Penelope Lively (1933)
Next to Nature, Art F

Liz Lochhead (1947)
Blood and Ice D
Performed 1982

Roger McGough (1937)
Waving at Trains V

Bernard MacLaverty (1942)
A Time to Dance, and Other Stories F

Julian Mitchell (1935)
Another Country D
Performed 1981; film 1984

Timothy Mo (1950)
Sour Sweet F

Deborah Moggach (1948)
Hot Water Man F

Michael Moorcock (1939)
The Brothel in Rosenstrasse F

John Mortimer (1923)
Clinging to the Wreckage NF
Autobiography

Paul Muldoon (1951)
Out of Siberia V

R.K. Narayan (1906–2001)
Malgudi Days F

Norman Nicholson (1914–87)
Selected Poems 1940–82 V

Edna O'Brien (1932)
Returning F

Caryl Phillips (1958)
Where There is Darkness D

Harold Pinter (1930)
Other Places D
Comprises *Family Voices*, *Victoria Station*, and *A Kind of Alaska*. Performed October 1982.

Sylvia Plath (1932–63)
The Journals of Sylvia Plath NF

Anthony Powell (1905–2000)
The Strangers All Are Gone NF
Fourth volume of autobiography. See also *Infants of the Spring* 1976, *Messengers of Day* 1978, *Faces In My Time* 1980 (collectively: *To Keep the Ball Rolling*).

Jeremy Reed (1954)
A Man Afraid V

Lisa St Aubin de Terán (1953)
Keepers of the House F

E.J. Scovell (1907–99)
The Space Between V

Muriel Spark (1918)
Bang-Bang You're Dead, and Other Stories F

Muriel Spark (1918)
Going Up to Sotheby's, and Other Poems V

David Storey (1933)
A Prodigal Child F

Graham Swift (1949)
Learning to Swim F

Emma Tennant (1937)
Queen of Stones F

Sue Townsend (1946)
The Secret Diary of Adrian Mole Aged 13¾ F

Barbara Trapido (1941)
Brother of the More Famous Jack F

Marina Warner (1946)
The Skating Party F

A.N. Wilson (1950)
Wise Virgin F

Virginia Woolf (1882–1941)
The Diary of Virginia Woolf: Volume iv: 1931–1935 NF
Published on 11 March 1982. See also *Diary* 1977, 1978, 1980, 1984.

1983

- Cruise missiles deployed in Britain
  Sally Ride is the first woman in space (July)
  Neil Kinnock elected leader of British Labour Party (Oct.)
  US invasion of Grenada (Oct.)
- Kenneth Clark dies
  Arthur Koestler dies
  Richard Llewellyn dies
  Norah Lofts dies
  Gladys Mitchell dies
  Sir Nikolaus Pevsner dies
  Mary Renault (Eileen Challans) dies
  Rebecca West (Cicily Andrews) dies
- Sir William Walton dies
- Luis Buñuel dies
  Jack Dempsey dies
  Joan Miró dies
  Tennessee Williams dies
- J.M. Coetzee wins the Booker Prize for *Life and Times of Michael K*
- Gabriel Garcia Márquez, *Chronicle of a Death Foretold*
  Alice Walker, *The Color Purple*

Dannie Abse (1923)
A Strong Dose of Myself NF
Autobiography. See also *A Poet in the Family* 1974, *There Was a Young Man From Cardiff* 1991.

Peter Ackroyd (1949)
The Last Testament of Oscar Wilde F

Brian Aldiss (1925)
Helliconia Summer F
Helliconia Trilogy ii. See also *Helliconia Spring* 1982, *Helliconia Winter* 1985.

George Barker (1913–91)
Anno Domino V

Nigel Barley (1947)
The Innocent Anthropologist NF

Nina Bawden (1925)
The Ice House F

Samuel Beckett (1906–89)
Disjecta MISC

Samuel Beckett (1906–89)
Worstward Ho F

Clare Boylan (1948)
Holy Pictures F

Clare Boylan (1948)
A Nail in the Head F

Malcolm Bradbury (1932–2000)
The Modern American Novel NF

Malcolm Bradbury (1932–2000)
Rates of Exchange F

Anita Brookner (1928)
Look at Me F

George Mackay Brown (1921–96)
Voyages V

Alan Brownjohn (1931)
Collected Poems 1952–1983 V
See also *Collected Poems* 1988

Caryl Churchill (1938)
Fen D

David Constantine (1944)
Watching For Dolphins V

'William Cooper' [Harry Summerfield Hoff (1910–2002)]
Scenes from Later Life F
See also *Scenes from Provincial Life* 1950, *Scenes from Married Life* 1961, *Scenes from Metropolitan Life* 1982

Roald Dahl (1916–90)
The Witches F
Illustrated by Quentin Blake

Len Deighton (1929)
Berlin Game F
See also *Mexico Set* 1984, *London Match* 1985

J.P. Donleavy (1926)
Leila F

Sequel to *The Destinies of Darcy Dancer, Gentleman* 1978 (q.v.)

Maureen Duffy (1933)
Londoners F

Helen Dunmore (1952)
The Apple Fall V

Lawrence Durrell (1912–90)
Sebastian; or, Ruling Passions F
Fourth of the Avignon quintet. See also *Monsieur* 1974, *Livia* 1978, *Constance* 1982, and *Quinx* 1985. Published together 1992.

Terry Eagleton (1943)
Literary Theory NF

'Alice Thomas Ellis' [Anna Margaret Haycraft (1932)**]**
The Other Side of the Fire F

Gavin Ewart (1916)
Capital Letters V

Padraic Fallon (1906–74)
Poems and Versions V
See also *Poems* 1974, *Collected Poems* 1990

James Fenton (1949)
Memory of War and Children in Exile V

George MacDonald Fraser (1925)
The Pyrates F

Roy Fuller (1912–91)
As From the Thirties V

Jane Gardam (1928)
The Pangs of Love, and Other Stories F

Maggie Gee (1948)
The Burning Book F

Penelope Gilliatt (1932–93)
Mortal Matters F

Victoria Glendinning (1937)
Vita NF

Alasdair Gray (1934)
Unlikely Stories, Mostly F

Christopher Hampton (1946)
Tales from Hollywood D

Adrian Henri (1932–2001)
Penny Arcade V

Geoffrey Hill (1932)
The Mystery of the Charity of Charles Péguy V

Susan Hill (1942)
The Woman in Black F

Frances Horovitz (1938–83)
Snow Light, Water Light V

Ted Hughes (1930–98)
River V
Hughes was appointed Poet Laureate in 1984

Howard Jacobson (1942)
Coming From Behind F

Ruth Prawer Jhabvala (1927)
In Search of Love and Beauty F

Jenny Joseph (1932)
Beyond Descartes V

James Kelman (1946)
Not Not While the Giro F

Philip Larkin (1922–85)
Required Writing NF

'John le Carré' [David John Moore Cornwell (1931)**]**
The Little Drummer Girl F

'Jane Somers' [Doris Lessing (1919)**]**
The Diary of a Good Neighbour F
See also *If the Old Could* 1984

Doris Lessing (1919)
The Sentimental Agents in the Volyen Empire F
Canopus in Argos: Archives v. See also *Shikasta* 1979, *The Marriages Between Zones Three, Four and Five* 1980, *The Sirian Experiments* 1981, *The Making of the Representative for Planet 8* 1982.

Peter Levi (1931)
The Echoing Green V

Penelope Lively (1933)
Perfect Happiness F

Bernard MacLaverty (1942)
Cal F

Sara Maitland (1950)
Telling Tales F

Deborah Moggach (1948)
Porky F

Brian Moore (1921–99)
Cold Heaven F

Penelope Mortimer (1918–99)
The Handyman F

Andrew Motion (1952)
Secret Narratives V

Paul Muldoon (1951)
Quoof V

Iris Murdoch (1919–99)
The Philosopher's Pupil F

Shiva Naipaul (1945–85)
A Hot Country F

R.K. Narayan (1906–2001)
A Tiger for Malgudi F

Grace Nichols (1950)
I is a Long-Memoried Woman V

Sean O'Brien (1952)
The Indoor Park V

Tom Paulin (1949)
Liberty Tree V

Anthony Powell (1905–2000)
O, How the Wheel Becomes It! F

Terry Pratchett (1948)
The Colour of Magic F
The first Discworld novel, published on 23 November 1983

J.H. Prynne (1936)
The Oval Window V

Michèle Roberts (1949)
The Visitation F

Carol Rumens (1944)
Star Whisper V

Salman Rushdie (1947)
Shame F

Lisa St Aubin de Terán (1953)
The Slow Train to Milan F

Peter Scupham (1933)
Winter Quarters V

Tom Stoppard (1937)
The Dog It Was That Died, and Other Plays D
Also includes *The Dissolution of Dominic Boot, 'M' is for Moon Among Other Things, Teeth, Another Moon Called Earth, Neutral Ground,* and *A Separate Peace*

Tom Stoppard (1937)
The Real Thing D
Performed 16 November 1982

Graham Swift (1949)
Waterland F

D.M. Thomas (1935)
Ararat F
Russian Nights sequence i. See also *Swallow* 1984, *Sphinx* 1986, *Summit* 1987, *Lying Together* 1990.

Colin Thubron (1939)
Among the Russians NF

J.R.R. Tolkien (1892–1973)
The Book of Lost Tales Part 1 F
Part 2 1984, Part 3 1985 (qq.v.)

'William Trevor' [William Trevor Cox (1928)]
Fools of Fortune F

Fay Weldon (1931)
The Life and Loves of a She-Devil F
Adapted for television 1986

'Mary Wesley' [Mary Aline Mynors Farmar (1912–2002)]
Jumping the Queue F

A.N. Wilson (1950)
Scandal F

1984

- USSR president Andropov dies: succeeded as first secretary by Konstantin Chernenko
  Miners' Strike in Britain
  Indian troops storm the Golden Temple at Amritsar (June)
  IRA bomb at the Grand Hotel, Brighton, during the Conservative Party conference (Oct.)
  Assassination of Indian Prime Minister Indira Gandhi (31 Oct.)
  'Do They Know It's Christmas?' single released in aid of famine relief (see 1985)
- Sir John Betjeman dies: Ted Hughes appointed Poet Laureate
  Sir William Empson dies
  Liam O'Flaherty dies
  J.B. Priestley dies
- Anita Brookner wins the Booker Prize for *Hotel du Lac*
- Milan Kundera, *The Unbearable Lightness of Being*
- Wim Wenders, *Paris, Texas*
- Madonna, 'Like a Virgin'

Peter Ackroyd (1949)
T.S. Eliot NF

Richard Adams (1920)
Maia F

Kingsley Amis (1922–95)
Stanley and the Women F

Martin Amis (1949)
Money F

Hilary Bailey (1936)
All the Days of My Life F

Beryl Bainbridge (1934)
Watson's Apology F

J.G. Ballard (1930)
Empire of the Sun F

Iain Banks (1954)
The Wasp Factory F

Lynne Reid Banks (1929)
The Warning Bell F

A.L. Barker (1918–2002)
Relative Successes F

Pat Barker (1943)
Blow Your House Down F

Julian Barnes (1946)
Flaubert's Parrot F

Samuel Beckett (1906–89)
Collected Poems 1930–78 V

Samuel Beckett (1906–89)
Collected Shorter Plays D
Includes the first publication of *Quad, Catastrophe, Nacht und Traume,* and *What Where*

Samuel Beckett (1906–89)
Collected Shorter Prose 1945–80 F

William Boyd (1952)
Stars and Bars F

Clare Boylan (1948)
Last Resorts F

Alison Brackenbury (1953)
Breaking Ground V

John Braine (1922–86)
The Two of Us F

Christine Brooke-Rose (1923)
Amalgamemnon F

Anita Brookner (1928)
Hotel du Lac F
Booker Prize 1984

George Mackay Brown (1921–96)
Christmas Poems V

George Mackay Brown (1921–96)
Three Plays D
Contains *The Loom of Light, The Voyage of St Brandon, The Well*

George Mackay Brown (1921–96)
Time in a Red Coast F
Short stories

'Anthony Burgess' [John Anthony Burgess Wilson (1917–93)]
Enderby's Dark Lady F
See also *Inside Mr Enderby* 1963, *Enderby Outside* 1968, *The Clockwork Testament* 1974

Angela Carter (1940–92)
Nights at the Circus F

Charles Causley (1917–2003)
Secret Destinations V

Caryl Churchill (1938)
Softcops D

David Constantine (1944)
Mappa Mundi V

Len Deighton (1929)
Mexico Set F
See also *Berlin Game* 1983, *London Match* 1985

Anita Desai (1937)
In Custody F

Gavin Ewart (1916)
The Ewart Quarto V

Gavin Ewart (1916)
Festival Nights V

U.A. Fanthorpe (1929)
Voices Off V

Sebastian Faulks (1953)
A Trick of the Light F

Elaine Feinstein (1930)
The Border F

Alison Fell (1944)
Kisses for Mayakovsky V

Frederick Forsyth (1938)
The Fourth Protocol F
Film 1987

Michael Frayn (1933)
Benefactors D

Roy Fuller (1912–91)
Mianserin Sonnets V

Rumer Godden (1907–98)
Thursday's Children F

William Golding (1911–93)
The Paper Men F

Alasdair Gray (1934)
1982, Janine F

Simon Gray (1936)
The Common Pursuit D

Geoffrey Grigson (1905–85)
Montaigne's Tower, and Other Poems V

Michael Hamburger (1924)
Collected Poems 1941–1983 V

Michael Hastings (1938)
Tom and Viv D

Seamus Heaney (1939)
Station Island V

Seamus Heaney (1939)
Sweeney Astray V
See also *Sweeney's Flight* 1992

Selima Hill (1945)
Saying Hello at the Station V

David Hughes (1930)
The Pork Butcher F

Howard Jacobson (1942)
Peeping Tom F

Alan Judd (1946)
Short of Glory F

James Kelman (1946)
The Busconductor Hines F

'Jane Somers' [**Doris Lessing** (1919)]
If the Old Could F
See also *The Diary of a Good Neighbour* 1983

Penelope Lively (1933)
According to Mark F

Penelope Lively (1933)
Corruption F

Liz Lochhead (1947)
Dreaming Frankenstein and Collected Poems V
Includes *Memo for Spring* 1972, *Islands* 1978, *The Grimm Sisters* 1981 (qq.v.)

David Lodge (1935)
Small World F

Medbh McGuckian (1950)
Venus and the Rain V

Derek Mahon (1941)
A Kensington Notebook V

Sara Maitland (1950)
Virgin Territory F

E.A. Markham (1939)
Human Rites V

Christopher Middleton (1926)
Serpentine V

Michael Moorcock (1939)
The Laughter of Carthage F
Pyat series ii. See also *Byzantium Endures* 1981, *Jerusalem Commands* 1992.

Edwin Morgan (1920)
Sonnets From Scotland V

Blake Morrison (1950)
Dark Glasses V

Andrew Motion (1952)
Dangerous Play V

Grace Nichols (1950)
The Fat Black Woman's Poems V

Caryl Phillips (1958)
The Shelter D
Performed 1983

Harold Pinter (1930)
One For the Road D
Performed March 1984

Fiona Pitt-Kethley (1954)
London V

Peter Porter (1929)
Fast Forward V

Dennis Potter (1935–94)
Waiting for the Boat D
Includes *Joe's Ark* (televised 1974), *Blue Remembered Hills* (televised 1979), and *Cream in My Coffee* (televised 1980)

Craig Raine (1944)
Rich V

Frederic Raphael (1931)
Oxbridge Blues, and Other Plays for Television D
Contains *Oxbridge Blues, That was Tory, Similar Triangles, He'll See You Now, The Muse, Cheap Day, Sleeps Six.* See also *Oxbridge Blues* 1980.

Simon Raven (1927–2001)
Morning Star F
The First-Born of Egypt sequence i. See also *The Face of the Waters* 1985, *Before the Cock Crow* 1986, *New Seed for Old* 1988, *Blood of My Bone* 1989, *In the Image of God* 1990, *The Troubadour* 1992.

Peter Reading (1946)
C V

Jeremy Reed (1954)
By the Fisheries V

Jeremy Reed (1954)
The Lipstick Boys F

Michèle Roberts (1949)
The Wild Girl F

Lisa St Aubin de Terán (1953)
The Tiger F

Muriel Spark (1918)
The Only Problem F

Paul Theroux (1941)
Doctor Slaughter F

D.M. Thomas (1935)
Swallow F
Russian Nights sequence ii. See also *Ararat* 1983, *Sphinx* 1986, *Summit* 1987, *Lying Together* 1990.

Colin Thubron (1939)
A Cruel Madness F

J.R.R. Tolkien (1892–1973)
The Book of Lost Tales Part 2 F
Part 1 1983, Part 3 1985 (qq.v.)

Charles Tomlinson (1927)
Notes From New York, and Other Poems V

Barbara Trapido (1941)
Noah's Ark F

Rose Tremain (1943)
The Colonel's Daughter, and Other Stories F

'Mary Wesley' [Mary Aline Mynors Farmar (1912–2002)**]**
The Camomile Lawn F

Virginia Woolf (1882–1941)
The Diary of Virginia Woolf: Volume v: 1936–1941 NF
Published on 21 June 1984. See also *Diary* 1977, 1978, 1980, 1982.

1985

- Mrs Thatcher refused honorary degree by Oxford University
  Mikhail Gorbachev becomes first secretary of the Soviet Communist Party: *Glasnost* and *Perestroika* programmes launched
  Sinking of the Greenpeace ship *Rainbow Warrior*
  Anglo-Irish agreement signed at Hillsborough Castle (15 Nov.)
  Famine in Ethiopia
  Live-Aid concerts
- Basil Bunting dies
  Robert Graves dies
  Geoffrey Grigson dies
  James Hanley dies
  G. Wilson Knight dies
  Philip Larkin dies
  Shiva Naipaul dies
- Laura Ashley dies
- Marc Chagall dies
  Rock Hudson dies of AIDS
- Keri Hulme wins the Booker Prize for *The Bone People*
- Patrick Suskind, *Perfume*
- *Back to the Future*
  Out of Africa

Peter Ackroyd (1949)
Hawksmoor F

Brian Aldiss (1925)
Helliconia Winter F
Helliconia Trilogy iii. See also *Helliconia Spring* 1982, *Helliconia Summer* 1983.

Beryl Bainbridge (1934)
Mum and Mr Armitage F

Iain Banks (1954)
Walking on Glass F

Howard Barker (1946)
Scenes From an Execution D
Broadcast and staged 1984

'Dan Kavanagh' [Julian Barnes (1946)**]**
Putting the Boot In F

Alan Bennett (1934)
A Private Function D

James Berry (1924)
Chain of Days V

Alan Bleasdale (1946)
The Boys from the Black Stuff D
Televised 1982

Dermot Bolger (1959)
Night Shift F

Edward Bond (1934)
The War Plays D
Contains *Red, Black, and Ignorant, The Tin Can People, Great Peace*

Martin Booth (1944–2004)
Hiroshima Joe F

John Braine (1922–86)
These Golden Days F

Howard Brenton (1942) and **David Hare** (1947)
Pravda: A Fleet Street comedy D

Published in May 1985. Performed 2 May 1985.

Anita Brookner (1928)
Family and Friends F

'Anthony Burgess' [John Anthony Burgess Wilson (1917–93)]
Homage to QWERTYUIOP: Selected journalism NF

'Anthony Burgess' [John Anthony Burgess Wilson (1917–93)]
The Kingdom of the Wicked F

A.S. Byatt (1936)
Still Life F
Continues *The Virgin in the Garden* 1978 (q.v.); continued in *Babel Tower* 1996 (q.v.)

J.L. Carr (1912–94)
The Battle of Pollocks Crossing F

Angela Carter (1940–92)
Black Venus F
Short stories

Jilly Cooper (1937)
Riders F

Len Deighton (1929)
London Match F
See also *Berlin Game* 1983, *Mexico Set* 1984

Carol Ann Duffy (1955)
Standing Female Nude V

Douglas Dunn (1942)
Elegies V

Paul Durcan (1944)
The Berlin Wall Café V

Lawrence Durrell (1912–90)
Quinx; or, The Ripper's Tale F
Fifth of the Avignon quintet. See also *Monsieur* 1974, *Livia* 1978, *Constance* 1982, and *Sebastian* 1983. Published together in 1992.

D.J. Enright (1920–2002)
Instant Chronicles V

John Fowles (1926)
A Maggot F

Roy Fuller (1912–91)
New and Collected Poems 1934–1984 V
See also *Collected Poems* 1962

Roy Fuller (1912–91)
Subsequent to Summer V

Jane Gardam (1928)
Crusoe's Daughter F

John Gardner (1926)
The Secret Generations F
Generations Trilogy i. See also *The Secret Houses* 1988, *The Secret Families* 1989.

Maggie Gee (1948)
Light Years F

Penelope Gilliatt (1932–93)
They Sleep Without Dreaming F

William Golding (1911–93)
An Egyptian Journal NF

Alasdair Gray (1934)
The Fall of Kelvin Walker F
Adapted from Gray's television play (1968, staged 1972)

Alasdair Gray (1934) and others
Lean Tales F
With James Kelman and Agnes Owens

Graham Greene (1904–91)
The Tenth Man F

Tony Harrison (1937)
The Fire-Gap V

Tony Harrison (1937)
V V

John Heath-Stubbs (1918)
The Immolation of Aleph V

Adrian Henri (1932–2001)
Holiday Snaps V

Geoffrey Hill (1932)
Collected Poems V

David Hughes (1930)
But for Bunter F

Elizabeth Jennings (1926–2001)
Extending the Territory V

James Kelman (1946)
A Chancer F

Thomas Kinsella (1928)
Songs of the Psyche V

Mary Lavin (1912–96)
A Family Likeness F

Doris Lessing (1919)
The Good Terrorist F

Liz Lochhead (1947)
True Confessions and New Clichés V

Michael Longley (1939)
Poems 1963–1983 V

Norman MacCaig (1910–96)
Collected Poems V

Derek Mahon (1941)
Antarctica V

Hilary Mantel (1952)
Every Day is Mother's Day F
See also *Vacant Possession* 1986

Brian Moore (1921–99)
Black Robe F

John Mortimer (1923)
Paradise Postponed F
See also *Titmuss Regained* 1990

Iris Murdoch (1919–99)
The Good Apprentice F

Tim Parks (1954)
Tongues of Flame F

Caryl Phillips (1958)
The Final Passage F

Alan Plater (1935)
The Beiderbecke Affair F

V.S. Pritchett (1900–97)
A Man of Letters NF

Simon Raven (1927–2001)
The Face of the Waters F
The First-Born of Egypt sequence ii. See also *Morning Star* 1984, *Before the Cock Crow* 1986, *New Seed for Old* 1988, *Blood of My Bone* 1989, *In the Image of God* 1990, *The Troubadour* 1992.

Peter Reading (1946)
Ukelele Music V

Peter Redgrove (1932–2003)
The Man Named East, and Other New Poems V

Jeremy Reed (1954)
Nero V

Bernice Rubens (1928–2004)
Mr Wakefield's Crusade F

Carol Rumens (1944)
Direct Dialling V

Lisa St Aubin de Terán (1953)
The High Place V

Sir Stephen Spender (1909–95)
Collected Poems 1928–1985 V

Sir Stephen Spender (1909–95)
The Journals of Stephen Spender, 1939–83 NF

J.R.R. Tolkien (1892–1973)
The Book of Lost Tales Part 3 F
Part 1 1983, Part 2 1984 (qq.v.)

Rose Tremain (1943)
The Swimming-Pool Season F

Barry Unsworth (1930)
Stone Virgin F

Fay Weldon (1931)
Polaris, and Other Stories F

Hugo Williams (1942)
Writing Home V

Nigel Williams (1948)
Star Turn F

A.N. Wilson (1950)
Gentlemen in England F

Jeanette Winterson (1959)
Boating for Beginners F

Jeanette Winterson (1959)
Oranges Are Not the Only Fruit F
Adapted for television 1989

Benjamin Zephaniah (1958)
The Dread Affair V

1986

- Michael Heseltine resigns as British Defence Secretary over the Westland affair (Jan.)
  US space shuttle *Challenger* explodes during take-off (Feb.)
  Britain and France sign Channel Tunnel treaty
  Brian Keenan and, later, John McCarthy taken hostage in Beirut (Apr.)
  US aircraft attack Libya
  Chernobyl nuclear disaster (26 Apr.)
  Iran-Contra scandal breaks in the US
- John Braine dies
  Lord David Cecil dies
  Dame Helen Gardner dies
  Christopher Isherwood dies
  Storm Jameson dies
  Sir Osbert Lancaster dies
  Noel Streatfeild dies
  Rex Warner dies
- Harold Macmillan dies
  Henry Moore dies
- Jorge Luis Borges dies
  Simone de Beauvoir dies
- Kingsley Amis wins the Booker Prize for *The Old Devils*

- Garrison Keillor, *Lake Wobegon Days*
- Woody Allen, *Hannah and her Sisters*
  Oliver Stone, *Platoon*
- *The Phantom of the Opera* (musical)
- Paul Simon, *Graceland*

Dannie Abse (1923)
Ask the Bloody Horse V
US title: *Sky in Narrow Streets*

Fleur Adcock (1934)
The Incident Book V

Kingsley Amis (1922–95)
The Old Devils F
Booker Prize 1986

Martin Amis (1949)
The Moronic Inferno, and Other Visits to America NF

Alan Ayckbourn (1939)
A Chorus of Disapproval D
Performed in Scarborough 1984, London 1985

Paul Bailey (1937)
Gabriel's Lament F

Beryl Bainbridge (1934)
Filthy Lucre F

John Banville (1945)
Mefisto F

Pat Barker (1943)
The Century's Daughter F

Julian Barnes (1946)
Staring at the Sun F

Stan Barstow (1928)
Just You Wait and See F
First of trilogy with *Give Us This Day* 1989 and *Next of Kin* 1991 (qq.v.)

Eavan Boland (1944)
The Journey, and Other Poems V

Howard Brenton (1942)
Plays 1 D
Includes *Christie in Love* (performed 1969); *Magnificence* (performed 1973); *The Churchill Play* (performed 1974); *Weapons of Happiness* (performed 1976); *Epsom Downs* (performed 1977); *Sore Throats* (performed 1979)

Christine Brooke-Rose (1923)
Xorandor F

Anita Brookner (1928)
A Misalliance F

'Anthony Burgess' [**John Anthony Burgess Wilson** (1917–93)]
The Pianoplayers F

Charles Causley (1917–2003)
Early in the Morning V

Jack Clemo (1916–94)
A Different Drummer V

Jack Clemo (1916–94)
The Shadowed Bed F

Tony Connor (1930)
Spirits of Place V

Robert Conquest (1917)
The Harvest of Sorrow NF

Wendy Cope (1945)
Making Cocoa for Kingsley Amis V

Jim Crace (1946)
Continent F

Kevin Crossley-Holland (1941)
Waterslain V

Jenny Diski (1947)
Nothing Natural F

Carol Ann Duffy (1955)
Thrown Voices V

Helen Dunmore (1952)
The Sea Skater V

Dorothy Dunnett (1923–2001)
Niccolò Rising F
First of 'The House of Niccolò' series

Janice Elliott (1931–95)
Dr Gruber's Daughter F

Elaine Feinstein (1930)
Badlands V

Patrick Leigh Fermor (1915)
Between the Woods and the Water NF

Eva Figes (1932)
The Seven Ages F

Penelope Fitzgerald (1916–2000)
Innocence F

Roy Fuller (1912–91)
Outside the Canon V

Adrian Henri (1932–2001)
Collected Poems V

Kazuo Ishiguro (1954)
An Artist of the Floating World F

Howard Jacobson (1942)
Redback F

P.D. James (1920)
A Taste for Death F

Elizabeth Jennings (1926–2001)
Collected Poems 1953–1985 V

James Joyce (1882–1941)
Ulysses F
Definitive text. See also *Ulysses* 1922, 1936.

P.J. Kavanagh (1931)
Only By Mistake F

Hanif Kureishi (1954)
My Beautiful Launderette D

'John le Carré' [David John Moore Cornwell (1931)]
A Perfect Spy F

David Lodge (1935)
Write On NF
Essays

George MacBeth (1932–92)
The Cleaver Garden V

Patrick McCabe (1955)
Music on Clinton Street F

Frank McGuinness (1953)
Observe the Sons of Ulster Marching Towards the Somme D

Hilary Mantel (1952)
Vacant Possession F
Sequel to *Every Day is Mother's Day* 1985 (q.v.)

Allan Massie (1938)
Augustus F
See also *Tiberius* 1991, *Caesar* 1993

Timothy Mo (1950)
An Insular Possession F

Deborah Moggach (1948)
To Have and to Hold F

Edwin Morgan (1920)
From the Video Box V

Nicholas Mosley (1923)
Judith F
Fourth of an uncompleted 7-novel sequence. See also *Catastrophe Practice* 1979, *Imago* 1980, *Serpent* 1981, *Hopeful Monsters* 1990.

Grace Nichols (1950)
Whole of a Morning Sky V

Ben Okri (1959)
Incidents at the Shrine F

Tim Parks (1954)
Loving Roger F

Caryl Phillips (1958)
Higher Ground F

Caryl Phillips (1958)
A State of Independence F

Fiona Pitt-Kethley (1954)
Sky Ray Lolly V

Dennis Potter (1935–94)
The Singing Detective D
Televised 1986

Anthony Powell (1905–2000)
The Fisher King F

Ian Rankin (1960)
The Flood F

Simon Raven (1927–2001)
Before the Cock Crow F
The First-Born of Egypt sequence iii. See also *Morning Star* 1984, *The Face of the Waters* 1985, *New Seed for Old* 1988, *Blood of My Bone* 1989, *In the Image of God* 1990, *The Troubadour* 1992.

Peter Reading (1946)
Stet V

'Barbara Vine' [Ruth Rendell (1930)]
A Dark Adapted Eye F

Willy Russell (1947)
Blood Brothers D
Performed 1981

Lisa St Aubin de Terán (1953)
The Bay of Silence F

E.J. Scovell (1907–99)
Listening to Collared Doves V

Peter Scupham (1933)
Out Late V

Penelope Shuttle (1947)
The Lion From Rio V

Jon Silkin (1930–97)
The Ship's Pasture V

Iain Crichton Smith (1928)
A Life V

Jon Stallworthy (1935)
The Anzac Sonata V

Paul Theroux (1941)
O-Zone F

D.M. Thomas (1935)
Sphinx F

Russian Nights sequence iii. See also *Ararat* 1983, *Swallow* 1984, *Summit* 1987, *Lying Together* 1990.

R.S. Thomas (1913–2000)
Experimenting with an Amen V

'William Trevor' [William Trevor Cox (1928)]
The News From Ireland, and Other Stories F

A.N. Wilson (1950)
Love Unknown F

Virginia Woolf (1882–1941)
The Essays of Virginia Woolf: Volume i: 1904–1912 NF
Published on 17 November 1986. See also *Essays* 1987, 1988, 1994.

1987

- The archbishop of Canterbury's envoy Terry Waite taken hostage in Beirut (Jan.)
  The 'Great Storm' devastates large areas of south-east England
  IRA bomb explodes during Remembrance Day service at Enniskillen (8 Nov.)
  Construction of the Channel Tunnel starts (Nov.)
- Richard Ellmann dies
  John Lehmann dies
  Alistair Maclean dies
  Norman Nicholson dies
  Terence Tiller dies
  Emlyn Williams dies
- Jean Anouilh dies
  Fred Astaire dies
  James Baldwin dies
  Danny Kaye dies
  Primo Levi dies
  Liberace dies
  Andrés Segovia dies
- Penelope Lively wins the Booker Prize for *Moon Tiger*
- Margaret Atwood, *The Handmaid's Tale*
  Toni Morrison, *Beloved*
- Bernardo Bertolucci, *The Last Emperor*
  Fatal Attraction
  Wall Street

Peter Ackroyd (1949)
Chatterton F

Peter Ackroyd (1949)
The Diversions of Purley, and Other Poems V

Brian Aldiss (1925)
Ruins F

Martin Amis (1949)
Einstein's Monsters F

J.G. Ballard (1930)
The Day of Creation F

Iain M. Banks (1954)
Consider Phlebas F

A.L. Barker (1918–2002)
The Gooseboy F

'Dan Kavanagh' [Julian Barnes (1946)]
Going to the Dogs F

Nina Bawden (1925)
Circles of Deceit F

Alan Bennett (1934)
Prick Up Your Ears D

Steven Berkoff (1937)
Sink the Belgrano! D
Performed 1986

James Berry (1924)
The Girls and Yanga Marshall F

Maeve Binchy (1940)
Firefly Summer F

William Boyd (1952)
The New Confessions F

Malcolm Bradbury (1932–2000)
Cuts F
Novella

Malcolm Bradbury (1932–2000)
My Strange Search for Mensonge NF

Malcolm Bradbury (1932–2000)
No, Not Bloomsbury NF

Melvyn Bragg (1939)
The Maid of Buttermere F

Howard Brenton (1942)
Dead Head D
Televised 1986

Anita Brookner (1928)
A Friend From England F

George Mackay Brown (1921–96)
The Keepers of the House F

Alan Brownjohn (1931)
The Old Flea-Pit V

'Anthony Burgess' [John Anthony Burgess Wilson (1917–93)]

Little Wilson and Big God NF
See also *You've Had Your Time* 1990

A.S. Byatt (1936)
Sugar, and Other Stories F

Bruce Chatwin (1940–89)
The Songlines F

Caryl Churchill (1938)
Serious Money: A City comedy D

Jonathan Coe (1961)
The Accidental Woman F

David Constantine (1944)
Madder V

Jenny Diski (1947)
Rainforest F

J.P. Donleavy (1926)
Are You Listening, Rabbi Löw F

Roddy Doyle (1958)
The Commitments F

Margaret Drabble (1939)
The Radiant Way F
First of trilogy with *A Natural Curiosity* 1989, *The Gates of Ivory* 1991 (qq.v.)

Carol Ann Duffy (1955)
Selling Manhattan V

Paul Durcan (1944)
Going Home to Russia V

David Edgar (1948)
Plays: One D
Includes *The Jail Diary of Albie Sachs* (performed 1978), *Mary Barnes* (performed 1979), *Saigon Rose* (performed 1976), and *Destiny* (performed 1976). See also *Plays: Two* 1989, *Plays: Three* 1991.

Janice Elliott (1931–95)
The Sadness of Witches F

'Alice Thomas Ellis' [Anna Margaret Haycraft (1932)**]**
The Clothes in the Wardrobe F
Summerhouse Trilogy i. See also *The Skeleton in the Cupboard* 1988, *The Fly in the Ointment* 1989.

Gavin Ewart (1916)
Late Pickings V

U.A. Fanthorpe (1929)
A Watching Brief V

Alison Fell (1944)
The Bad Box F

Rumer Godden (1907–98)
A Time to Dance, No Time to Weep NF
Autobiography. See also *A House With Four Rooms* 1989.

William Golding (1911–93)
Close Quarters F
To the Ends of the Earth Trilogy ii. See also *Rites of Passage* 1980, *Fire Down Below* 1989. Published together in 1991.

Philip Gross (1952)
Cat's Whisker V

Georgina Hammick (1939)
People for Lunch F

Tony Harrison (1937)
Anno Forty-Two V

Seamus Heaney (1939)
The Haw Lantern V

Eric Hobsbawm (1917)
The Age of Empire, 1875–1914 NF
See also *The Age of Revolution* 1962, *The Age of Capital* 1975

Susan Howatch (1940)
Glittering Images F

Kathleen Jamie (1962)
The Way We Live V

Ruth Prawer Jhabvala (1927)
Three Continents F

Jennifer Johnston (1930)
Fool's Sanctuary F

P.J. Kavanagh (1931)
Presence V

James Kelman (1946)
Greyhound for Breakfast F

Thomas Kinsella (1928)
Out of Ireland V

Penelope Lively (1933)
Moon Tiger F
Booker Prize 1987

Ian McEwan (1948)
The Child in Time F

Shena Mackay (1944)
Dreams of Dead Women's Handbags F
Stories

Bernard MacLaverty (1942)
The Great Profundo, and Other Stories F

Brian Moore (1921–99)
The Colour of Blood F

Blake Morrison (1950)
The Ballad of the Yorkshire Ripper V

Andrew Motion (1952)
Natural Causes V

Paul Muldoon (1951)
Meeting the British V

Iris Murdoch (1919–99)
The Book and the Brotherhood F

V.S. Naipaul (1932)
The Enigma of Arrival F

Tom Paulin (1949)
Fivemiletown V

Fiona Pitt-Kethley (1954)
Private Parts V

Ruth Pitter (1897–1992)
A Heaven to Find V

Peter Porter (1929)
The Automatic Oracle V

Dennis Potter (1935–94)
Blackeyes F
Dramatized for television 1989

Ian Rankin (1960)
Knots and Crosses F

Peter Redgrove (1932–2003)
The Moon Disposes V

Jeremy Reed (1954)
Blue Rock F

Michèle Roberts (1949)
The Book of Mrs Noah F

Carol Rumens (1944)
Plato Park V

Lisa St Aubin de Terán (1953)
Black Idol F

Iain Sinclair (1943)
White Chappell, Scarlet Tracings F

C.H. Sisson (1914–2003)
God Bless Karl Marx V

D.M. Thomas (1935)
Summit F
Russian Nights sequence iv. See also *Ararat* 1983, *Swallow* 1984, *Sphinx* 1986, *Lying Together* 1990.

Colin Thubron (1939)
Behind the Wall NF

Anthony Thwaite (1930)
Letter from Tokyo V

Charles Tomlinson (1927)
The Return V

Rose Tremain (1943)
The Garden of the Villa Mollini, and Other Stories F

John Wain (1925–94)
Open Country V

Fay Weldon (1931)
Heart of the Country F
Adapted for television 1987

'Mary Wesley' [Mary Aline Mynors Farmar (1912–2002)]
Not That Sort of Girl F

Nigel Williams (1948)
Witchcraft F

A.N. Wilson (1950)
Stray F

Jeanette Winterson (1959)
The Passion F

Virginia Woolf (1882–1941)
The Essays of Virginia Woolf: Volume ii: 1912–1918 NF
Published on 15 October 1987. See also *Essays* 1986, 1988, 1994.

1988

- Soviet withdrawal from Afghanistan (May)
  Iranian airliner shot down by the US warship *Vincennes* (July)
  Iran and Iraq announce ceasefire (Aug.)
  Mikhail Gorbachev elected President of the USSR
  Lockerbie disaster (21 Dec.)
  Margaret Thatcher becomes longest-serving 20th-century Prime Minister
- Geoffrey Household dies
  Marghanita Laski dies
  Sir Sacheverell Sitwell dies
  Raymond Williams dies
- Enzo Ferrari dies
- Peter Carey wins the Booker Prize for *Oscar and Lucinda*
- Gabriel García Márquez, *Love in the Time of Cholera*
  Anatoli Rybakov, *Children of the Arbat*
- Martin Scorsese, *The Last Temptation of Christ*
  Rain Man

Fleur Adcock (1934)
Meeting the Comet v

Brian Aldiss (1925)
Forgotten Life F

Kingsley Amis (1922–95)
Difficulties With Girls F

Hilary Bailey (1936)
As Time Goes By F

Iain M. Banks (1954)
The Player of Games F

Patricia Beer (1924–99)
Collected Poems v

Clare Boylan (1948)
Black Baby F

Alison Brackenbury (1953)
Christmas Roses v

Malcolm Bradbury (1932–2000)
The Modern World NF

Asa Briggs (1921)
Victorian Things NF

Anita Brookner (1928)
Latecomers F

Alan Brownjohn (1931)
Collected Poems 1952–1988 v
See also *Collected Poems* 1983

Justin Cartwright (1943)
Interior F

Charles Causley (1917–2003)
A Field of Vision v

Bruce Chatwin (1940–89)
Utz F

Jack Clemo (1916–94)
Selected Poems v

Isabel Colegate (1931)
Deceits of Time F

Wendy Cope (1945)
Does She Like Word-Games? v

Wendy Cope (1945)
Men and their Boring Arguments v

Jim Crace (1946)
The Gift of Stones F

Roald Dahl (1916–90)
Matilda F

Len Deighton (1929)
Spy Hook F
See also *Spy Line* 1989, *Spy Sinker* 1990

Anita Desai (1937)
Baumgartner's Bombay F

Michael Dibdin (1947)
Ratking F
First of Dibdin's novels featuring the Italian police detective Aurelio Zen

Jenny Diski (1947)
Like Mother F

Helen Dunmore (1952)
The Raw Garden v

Douglas Dunn (1942)
Northlight v

Paul Durcan (1944)
Jesus and Angela v

'Alice Thomas Ellis' [Anna Margaret Haycraft (1932)**]**
The Skeleton in the Cupboard F
Summerhouse Trilogy ii. See also *The Clothes in the Wardrobe* 1987, *The Fly in the Ointment* 1989.

Elaine Feinstein (1930)
Mother's Girl F

Eva Figes (1932)
Ghosts F

Penelope Fitzgerald (1916–2000)
The Beginning of Spring F

John Gardner (1926)
The Secret Houses F
Generations Trilogy ii. See also *The Secret Generations* 1985, *The Secret Families* 1989.

David Gascoyne (1916)
Collected Poems v

Maggie Gee (1948)
Grace F

Penelope Gilliatt (1932–93)
A Woman of Singular Occupation F

Graham Greene (1904–91)
The Captain and the Enemy F

Ian Hamilton (1938–2001)
Fifty Poems v

Ian Hamilton (1938–2001)
In Search of J.D. Salinger NF

Seamus Heaney (1939)
The Government of the Tongue NF

John Heath-Stubbs (1918)
A Partridge in a Pear Tree V

Selima Hill (1945)
My Darling Camel V

Richard Hoggart (1918)
A Local Habitation NF
Autobiographical. See also *A Sort of Clowning* 1990, *An Imagined Life* 1992.

Alan Hollinghurst (1954)
The Swimming-Pool Library F

Michael Holroyd (1935)
George Bernard Shaw: The Search for Love NF
See also *The Pursuit of Power* 1989, *The Lure of Fantasy* 1991, *The Last Laugh* 1992

Libby Houston (1941)
Necessity V

Susan Howatch (1940)
Glamorous Powers F

Ted Hughes (1930–98)
Moon-Whales V
The first British edition, published in June 1988. First published in the USA, 1976.

Ted Hughes (1930–98)
Tales of the Early World V

Alan Jenkins (1955)
In the Hot-House V

Philip Larkin (1922–85)
Collected Poems V
Editd by Anthony Thwaite

Doris Lessing (1919)
The Fifth Child F

Norman Lewis (1908–2003)
The Missionaries NF

David Lodge (1935)
Nice Work F

George MacBeth (1932–92)
Anatomy of Divorce V

Norman MacCaig (1910–96)
Voice-Over V

Medbh McGuckian (1950)
On Ballycastle Beach V

Candia McWilliam (1955)
A Case of Knives F

Deidre Madden (1960)
Birds of the Innocent Wood F
Somerset Maugham Prize

Deborah Moggach (1948)
Driving in the Dark F

Edwin Morgan (1920)
Themes on a Variation V

John Mortimer (1923)
Summer's Lease F

Edna O'Brien (1932)
The High Road F

Brian Patten (1946)
Storm Damage V

Harold Pinter (1930)
Mountain Language D
Performed 20 October 1988

Kathleen Raine (1908–2003)
To the Sun V

Simon Raven (1927–2001)
New Seed for Old F
The First-Born of Egypt sequence iv. See also *Morning Star* 1984, *The Face of the Waters* 1985, *Before the Cock Crow* 1986, *Blood of My Bone* 1989, *In the Image of God* 1990, *The Troubadour* 1992.

Piers Paul Read (1941)
A Season in the West F

Peter Reading (1946)
Final Demands V

Jeremy Reed (1954)
Engaging Form V

Carol Rumens (1944)
The Greening of the Snow Beach V

Salman Rushdie (1947)
The Satanic Verses F
Published in September 1988. The novel that occasioned the *fatwa*, or death sentence, invoked by Ayatollah Khomeni in February 1989.

Willy Russell (1947)
Shirley Valentine D
Performed 1986, film 1990

E.J. Scovell (1907–99)
Collected Poems V

Peter Scupham (1933)
The Air Show V

Peter Shaffer (1926)
Lettice and Lovage: A comedy D
Performed 1987

Jo Shapcott (1953)
Electroplating the Baby V

Andrew Sinclair (1935)
King Ludd F
The Albion Triptych iii. See also *Gog* 1967, *Magog* 1972.

Muriel Spark (1918)
A Far Cry From Kensington F

Sir Stephen Spender (1909–95)
The Temple F

Tom Stoppard (1937)
Hapgood D
Performed 8 March 1988

Graham Swift (1949)
Out of This World F

Paul Theroux (1941)
Riding the Iron Rooster NF

'William Trevor' [William Trevor Cox (1928)]
The Silence in the Garden F

Joanna Trollope (1943)
The Choir F

Barry Unsworth (1930)
Sugar and Rum F

John Wain (1925–94)
Where the Rivers Meet F
Oxford Trilogy i. See also *Comedies* 1990, *Hungry Generations* 1994.

Marina Warner (1946)
The Lost Father F

Fay Weldon (1931)
Leader of the Band F

Heathcote Williams (1941)
Whale Nation V

A.N. Wilson (1950)
Incline Our Hearts F
First of the Lampitt Papers sequence. See also *A Bottle in the Smoke* 1990, *Daughters of Albion* 1991, *Hearing Voices* 1995, *Watch in the Night* 1996.

Virginia Woolf (1882–1941)
The Essays of Virginia Woolf: Volume iii: 1919–1924 NF
Published on 5 December 1988. See also *Essays* 1986, 1987, 1994.

1989

- George Bush becomes President of the USA
  Trial of Oliver North for his part in the Iran-Contra affair (Jan.)
  Ayatollah Khomeni of Iran issues *fatwa* against British author Salman Rushdie (14 Feb.)
  Free elections in Poland: landslide victory for Solidarity
  Ti'en-An Men Square massacre (3 June)
  Erich Honecker replaced as President of East Germany by Egon Krenz
  Berlin Wall opened (Nov.)
  Cold War declared over by Presidents Bush and Gorbachev (Dec.)
  Ceaucescu regime overthrown in Romania (Dec.)
- Sir A.J. Ayer dies
  Samuel Beckett dies
  Bruce Chatwin dies
  Nigel Dennis dies
  Dame Daphne du Maurier dies
  Stella Gibbons dies
  R.D. Laing dies
- Sir Laurence Olivier dies
- Irving Berlin dies
  Emperor Hirohito of Japan dies
- Kazuo Ishiguro wins the Booker Prize for *The Remains of the Day*
- John Irving, *A Prayer for Owen Meany*
- John Taverner, *The Protecting Veil*
- *Batman*
  Sex, Lies and Videotape

Dannie Abse (1923)
White Coat, Purple Coat V

Peter Ackroyd (1949)
First Light F

Martin Amis (1949)
London Fields F

Simon Armitage (1963)
Zoom! V

Beryl Bainbridge (1934)
An Awfully Big Adventure F

John Banville (1945)
The Book of Evidence F
Continued in *Ghosts* 1993 and *Athena* 1995 (qq.v.)

A.L. Barker (1918–2002)
The Woman Who Talked to Herself F

Pat Barker (1943)
The Man Who Wasn't There F

Julian Barnes (1946)
A History of the World in 10½ Chapters F

Stan Barstow (1928)
Give Us This Day F
Sequel to *Just You Wait and See* 1986 (q.v.), continued in *Next of Kin* 1991 (q.v.)

Alan Bennett (1934)
Single Spies D
Double bill comprising *An Englishman Abroad* and *A Question of Attribution*. Performed 1988.

Dermot Bolger (1959)
Leinster Street Ghosts V

Clare Boylan (1948)
Concerning Virgins F

Howard Brenton (1942) and **Tariq Ali** (1943)
Iranian Nights D

Anita Brookner (1928)
Lewis Percy F

George Mackay Brown (1921–96)
The Wreck of the Archangel V

'Anthony Burgess' [**John Anthony Burgess Wilson** (1917–93)]
Any Old Iron F

'Anthony Burgess' [**John Anthony Burgess Wilson** (1917–93)]
The Devil's Mode, and Other Stories F

Bruce Chatwin (1940–89)
What Am I Doing Here? NF

Caryl Churchill (1938)
Ice Cream D
Performed 1989

Gillian Clarke (1937)
Letting in the Rumour V

Jonathan Coe (1961)
A Touch of Love F

Donald Davie (1922–95)
To Scorch or Freeze V

Donald Davie (1922–95)
Under Briggflats: A history of poetry in Great Britain 1960–1988 NF

Len Deighton (1929)
Spy Line F
See also *Spy Hook* 1988, *Spy Sinker* 1990

Margaret Drabble (1939)
A Natural Curiosity F
Second of trilogy. See also *The Radiant Way* 1987, *The Gates of Ivory* 1991.

David Edgar (1948)
Edgar: Shorts D
Includes *Baby Love* (performed 1973), *The National Theatre* (performed 1975), and *The Shape of the Table*

David Edgar (1948)
Heartlanders D

David Edgar (1948)
Plays: Two D
Includes *Ecclesiastes*; *The Life and Adventures of Nicholas Nickleby* (performed 1980); *Entertaining Strangers*. See also *Plays: One* 1987, *Plays: Three* 1991.

'Alice Thomas Ellis' [**Anna Margaret Haycraft** (1932)]
The Fly in the Ointment F
Summerhouse Trilogy iii. See also *The Clothes in the Wardrobe* 1987, *The Skeleton in the Cupboard* 1988.

Gavin Ewart (1916)
Penultimate Poems V

Elaine Feinstein (1930)
All You Need F

James Fenton (1949)
Manila Envelope V

Michael Frayn (1933)
The Trick of It F

Roy Fuller (1912–91)
Available for Dreams V

Janice Galloway (1956)
The Trick is to Keep Breathing F

Jane Gardam (1928)
Showing the Flag F

John Gardner (1926)
The Secret Families F
Generations Trilogy iii. See also *The Secret Generations* 1985, *The Secret Houses* 1988.

Victoria Glendinning (1937)
The Grown Ups F

Rumer Godden (1907)
A House with Four Rooms NF
Autobiography. See also *A Time to Dance* 1987.

William Golding (1911–93)
Fire Down Below F
To the Ends of the Earth Trilogy ii. See also *Rites of Passage* 1980, *Close Quarters* 1987. Published together in 1991.

Alasdair Gray (1934)
Old Negatives V

Tony Harrison (1937)
The Mother of the Muses V

Selima Hill (1945)
The Accumulation of Small Acts of Kindness V

Michael Holroyd (1935)
George Bernard Shaw: The Pursuit of Power NF
See also *The Search for Love* 1988, *The Lure of Fantasy* 1991, *The Last Laugh* 1992

Susan Howatch (1940)
Ultimate Prizes F

Ted Hughes (1930–98)
Wolfwatching V

Kazuo Ishiguro (1954)
The Remains of the Day F
Booker Prize 1989. Film 1993.

P.D. James (1920)
Devices and Desires F

James Kelman (1946)
A Disaffection F

'John le Carré' [David John Moore Cornwell (1931)**]**
The Russia House F

Peter Levi (1931)
Shadow and Bone V

Penelope Lively (1933)
Passing On F

Liz Lochhead (1947)
Mary Queen of Scots Got Her Head Chopped Off. Dracula D
Mary Queen of Scots performed 1987; *Dracula* performed 1985

George MacBeth (1932–92)
Collected Poems 1958–1982 V

Patrick McCabe (1955)
Carn F

Hilary Mantel (1952)
Fludd F

Allan Massie (1938)
A Question of Loyalties F

Iris Murdoch (1919–99)
The Message to the Planet F

Grace Nichols (1950)
Lazy Thoughts of a Lazy Woman, and Other Poems V

Tim Parks (1954)
Family Planning F

Fiona Pitt-Kethley (1954)
The Perfect Man V

Peter Porter (1929)
Possible Worlds V

V.S. Pritchett (1900–97)
A Careless Widow, and Other Stories F

J.H. Prynne (1936)
Word Order V

Simon Raven (1927–2001)
Blood of My Bone F
The First-Born of Egypt sequence v. See also *Morning Star* 1984, *The Face of the Waters* 1985, *Before the Cock Crow* 1986, *New Seed for Old* 1988, *In the Image of God* 1990, *The Troubadour* 1992.

Peter Reading (1946)
Perduta Gente V

Peter Redgrove (1932–2003)
The One Who Set Out to Study Fear F

Jeremy Reed (1954)
Red Eclipse F

Vernon Scannell (1922)
Soldiering On V

Iain Crichton Smith (1928)
The Village, and Other Poems V

Paul Theroux (1941)
My Secret History F

Charles Tomlinson (1927)
Annunciations V

Rose Tremain (1943)
Restoration F

Joanna Trollope (1943)
A Village Affair F

Fay Weldon (1931)
The Cloning of Joanna May F
Adapted for television 1992

Jeanette Winterson (1959)
Sexing the Cherry F

1990

- Nelson Mandela released from prison after 27 years (11 Feb.)
  Lithuania declares independence (Mar.)
  Anti-poll tax riots in London (Mar.)

Estonia declares independence (May)
Uzbekistan declares indepence (June)
Iraq invades Kuwait (2 Aug.)
Reunification of Germany (3 Oct.)
Margaret Thatcher resigns (22 Nov.): John Major becomes Prime Minister
Lech Walesa elected President of Poland (Dec.)

- Lucy Boston dies
Roald Dahl dies
Dan Davin dies
Lawrence Durrell dies
Rosamond Lehmann dies
Dodie Smith dies
A.J.P. Taylor dies
- Aaron Copland dies
Leonard Bernstein dies
Greta Garbo dies
- A.S. Byatt wins the Booker Prize for *Possession*
- Thomas Pynchon, *Vineland*

Dannie Abse (1923)
Remembrance of Crimes Past V

Peter Ackroyd (1949)
Dickens NF

Brian Aldiss (1925)
Bury My Heart at W.H. Smith's NF
Autobiography

Kingsley Amis (1922–95)
The Folks That Live on the Hill F

Kingsley Amis (1922–95)
Memoirs NF

J.G. Ballard (1930)
War Fever F

Samuel Beckett (1906–89)
As the Story Was Told F
Contains title piece plus 'The Capital of the Ruins'; 'The Image'; 'All Strange Away'; 'Heard in the Dark 1 and 11'; 'One Evening'; 'Neither'; 'Stirrings Still'; 'what is the word' [sic]

Alan Bennett (1934)
The Lady in the Van NF

Maeve Binchy (1940)
Circle of Friends F

Eavan Boland (1944)
Outside History V

Edward Bond (1934)
Two Post-Modern Plays D
Contains *September* and *In the Company of Men*

William Boyd (1952)
Brazzaville Beach F

Melvyn Bragg (1939)
A Time to Dance F

Howard Brenton (1942) and **Tariq Ali** (1943)
Moscow Gold D

Christine Brooke-Rose (1923)
Verbivore F

Anita Brookner (1928)
Brief Lives F

Alan Brownjohn (1931)
The Observation Car V

'Anthony Burgess' [John Anthony Burgess Wilson (1917–93)**]**
You've Had Your Time NF
See *Little Wilson and Big God* 1987

A.S. Byatt (1936)
Possession F
Booker Prize 1990

Justin Cartwright (1943)
Look At It This Way F

Caryl Churchill (1938)
Hot Fudge D
Performed 1989

Caryl Churchill (1938)
Mad Forest D
Performed 1990

Jonathan Coe (1961)
The Dwarves of Death F

Donald Davie (1922–95)
Collected Poems V

Louis de Bernières (1954)
The War of Don Emmanuel's Nether Parts F

Len Deighton (1929)
Spy Sinker F
See also *Spy Hook* 1988, *Spy Line* 1989

Jenny Diski (1947)
Then Again F

J.P. Donleavy (1926)
That Darcy, That Dancer, That Gentleman F
See also *The Destinies of D'Arcy Dancer, Gentleman* 1978

Roddy Doyle (1958)
The Snapper F

Paul Durcan (1944)
Daddy, Daddy V

Janice Elliott (1931–95)
Necessary Rites F

'Alice Thomas Ellis' [Anna Margaret Haycraft (1932)]
The Inn at the Edge of the World F

Padraic Fallon (1906–74)
Collected Poems V
Introduction by Seamus Heaney. See also *Poems* 1974, *Poems and Versions* 1983.

Elaine Feinstein (1930)
City Music V

Penelope Fitzgerald (1916–2000)
The Gate of Angels F

Margaret Forster (1938)
Lady's Maid F

Michael Frayn (1933)
Look Look D

Brian Friel (1929)
Dancing at Lughnasa D

Penelope Gilliatt (1932–93)
Lingo F

Alasdair Gray (1934)
Something Leather F

Simon Gray (1936)
Hidden Laughter D

Graham Greene (1904–91)
The Last Word, and Other Stories F

Graham Greene (1904–91)
Reflections 1923–1988 NF

David Hare (1947)
Racing Demon D
'The Hare Trilogy' i, examining the Church of England. See also *Murmuring Judges* 1991, *Absence of War* 1993.

Tony Harrison (1937)
Losing Touch V

Seamus Heaney (1939)
New Selected Poems 1966–1987 V
See also *Selected Poems* 1980

Seamus Heaney (1939)
The Redress of Poetry NF

Seamus Heaney (1939)
The Tree Clock V

John Heath-Stubbs (1918)
The Game of Love and Death V

Adrian Henri (1932–2001)
Box, and Other Poems V

Richard Hoggart (1918)
A Sort of Clowning NF
Autobiographical. See also *A Local Habitation* 1988, *An Imagined Life* 1992.

Elizabeth Jane Howard (1923)
The Light Years F
Cazalet Chronicle i. See also *Marking Time* 1991, *Confusion* 1993, *Casting Off* 1995.

Susan Howatch (1940)
Scandalous Risks F

Alan Jenkins (1955)
Greenheart V

A.L. Kennedy (1965)
Night Geometry and the Garscadden Trains F

Francis King (1923)
Visiting Cards F

Hanif Kureishi (1954)
The Buddha of Suburbia F
Televised 1993

Doris Lessing (1919)
London Observed F

David Lodge (1935)
After Bakhtin NF

Christopher Logue (1926)
Kings D
Adapted from Homer's *Iliad*, books i–ii. See also *War Music* 1981, *The Husbands* 1994.

Ian McEwan (1948)
The Innocent; or, The Special Relationship F

Sara Maitland (1950)
Three Times Table F

Allan Massie (1938)
The Hanging Tree F

Glyn Maxwell (1962)
Tale of the Mayor's Son V

Brian Moore (1921–99)
Lies of Silence F

Edwin Morgan (1920)
Collected Poems V

John Mortimer (1923)
Titmuss Regained F
Sequel to *Paradise Postponed* 1985

Nicholas Mosley (1923)
Hopeful Monsters F
Fifth (and last) of an uncompleted 7-novel sequence. See also *Catastrophe Practice* 1979, *Imago* 1980, *Serpent* 1981, *Judith* 1986.

Paul Muldoon (1951)
Madoc V

R.K. Narayan (1906–2001)
The World of Nagaraj F

Edna O'Brien (1932)
Lantern Slides F
Stories

'John MacDowell' [Tim Parks (1954)**]**
Cara Massimina F
See also *Mimi's Ghost* 1995

Brian Patten (1946)
Grinning Jack V

Ruth Pitter (1897–1992)
Collected Poems V
Introduction by Elizabeth Jennings

Anthony Powell (1905–2000)
Miscellaneous Verdicts NF

Anthony Powell (1905–2000)
A Writer's Notebook NF

V.S. Pritchett (1900–97)
Complete Short Stories F

Jonathan Raban (1942)
Hunting Mr Heartbreak NF

Craig Raine (1944)
Haydn and the Valve Trumpet NF
Essays

Simon Raven (1927–2001)
In the Image of God F
The First-Born of Egypt sequence vi. See also *Morning Star* 1984, *The Face of the Waters* 1985, *Before the Cock Crow* 1986, *New Seed for Old* 1988, *Blood of My Bone* 1989, *The Troubadour* 1992.

Piers Paul Read (1941)
On the Third Day F

Peter Redgrove (1932–2003)
Dressed as for a Tarot Pack V

Jeremy Reed (1954)
Inhabiting Shadows F

Jeremy Reed (1954)
Nineties V

'Barbara Vine' [Ruth Rendell (1930)**]**
Gallowglass F

Michèle Roberts (1949)
In the Red Kitchen F

Bernice Rubens (1928–2004)
Kingdom Come F

Carol Rumens (1944)
From Berlin to Heaven V

Salman Rushdie (1947)
Haroun and the Sea of Stories F

Lisa St Aubin de Terán (1953)
Joanna F

Peter Scupham (1933)
Watching the Perseids V

Muriel Spark (1918)
Symposium F

Emma Tennant (1937)
Sisters and Strangers F

Paul Theroux (1941)
Chicago Loop F

D.M. Thomas (1935)
Lying Together F
Russian Nights sequence v. See also *Ararat* 1983, *Swallow* 1984, *Sphinx* 1986, *Summit* 1987.

R.S. Thomas (1913–2000)
Counterpoint V

Barbara Trapido (1941)
Temples of Delight F

'William Trevor' [William Trevor Cox (1928)**]**
Family Sins, and Other Stories F

John Wain (1925–94)
Comedies F
Oxford Trilogy ii. See also *Where the Rivers Meet* 1988, *Hungry Generations* 1994.

Fay Weldon (1931)
Darcy's Utopia F

Hugo Williams (1942)
Self-Portrait With a Slide V

Nigel Williams (1948)
The Wimbledon Poisoner F
Adapted for television 1995

A.N. Wilson (1950)
A Bottle in the Smoke F
Second of the Lampitt Papers sequence. See also *Incline Our Hearts* 1988, *Daughters of Albion* 1991, *Hearing Voices* 1995, *Watch in the Night* 1996.

1991

- Gulf War (Jan.–Mar.) begins with air offensive (16 Jan.)
  Dissolution of the Warsaw Pact (Feb.)
  Release of the 'Birmingham Six'
  Disintegration of the former Yugoslavia
  Civil war in Yugoslavia begins (May)
  South Africa repeals apartheid legislation
  Failed *coup d'état* in Moscow (Aug.): Communist Party of the USSR dissolved
  Mikhail Gorbachev placed under house arrest and resigns (Aug.)
- Roy Fuller dies
  Graham Greene dies
  Sean O'Faolain dies
  Laura Riding dies
  Sir Angus Wilson dies
- Ben Okri wins the Booker Prize for *The Famished Road*
- Bret Easton Ellis, *American Psycho*
  John Updike, *Rabbit at Rest*
- *Thelma and Louise*
  The Silence of the Lambs

Dannie Abse (1923)
There Was a Young Man From Cardiff NF
Autobiography. See also *A Poet in the Family* 1974, *A Strong Dose of Myself* 1983.

Fleur Adcock (1934)
Time-Zones V

Brian Aldiss (1925)
Dracula Unbound F
See also *Frankenstein Unbound* 1974

Martin Amis (1949)
Time's Arrow F

Alan Ayckbourn (1939)
The Revenger's Comedies D
Performed 1989

Beryl Bainbridge (1934)
The Birthday Boys F

J.G. Ballard (1930)
The Kindness of Women F

A.L. Barker (1918–2002)
Any Excuse for a Party F

Pat Barker (1943)
Regeneration F
First of Barker's First World War trilogy. See also *The Eye in the Door* 1993, *The Ghost Road* 1995.

Julian Barnes (1946)
Talking It Over F

Stan Barstow (1928)
Next of Kin F
Concludes *Just You Wait and See* 1986 and *Give Us This Day* 1989 (qq.v.)

Nina Bawden (1925)
Family Money F

Christine Brooke-Rose (1923)
Textermination F

Anita Brookner (1928)
A Closed Eye F

George Mackay Brown (1921–96)
The Sea King's Daughter F

George Mackay Brown (1921–96)
Selected Poems 1954–1983 V

'Anthony Burgess' [John Anthony Burgess Wilson (1917–93)**]**
Mozart and the Wolf Gang F
Imaginary conversations

Angela Carter (1940–92)
Wise Children F

Isabel Colegate (1931)
The Summer of the Royal Visit F

'William Cooper' [Harry Summerfield Hoff (1910–2002)**]**
Immortality at Any Price F

Louis de Bernières (1954)
Senor Vivo and the Coca Lord F

Jenny Diski (1947)
Happily Ever After F

Roddy Doyle (1958)
The Van F

Margaret Drabble (1939)
The Gates of Ivory F
Third of trilogy. See also *The Radiant Way* 1987, *A Natural Curiosity* 1989.

Paul Durcan (1944)
Crazy About Women V

David Edgar (1948)
Plays: Three D
Contains *Teendreams*; *Our Own People* (performed 1977); *That Summer*; *Maydays*. See also *Plays: One* 1987, *Plays: Two* 1989.

Janice Elliott (1931–95)
The Noise From the Zoo F

Gavin Ewart (1916)
Collected Poems 1980–1991 V

Alison Fell (1944)
Mer de Glace F

Michael Frayn (1933)
Audience D

Michael Frayn (1933)
A Landing on the Sun F

John Fuller (1937)
The Mechanical Body V

Janice Galloway (1956)
Blood F

Jane Gardam (1928)
The Queen of the Tambourine F

Rumer Godden (1907–98)
Coromandel Sea Change F

Lavinia Greenlaw (1962)
The Cost of Getting Lost in Space V

Philip Gross (1952)
The Son of the Duke of Nowhere V

Michael Hamburger (1924)
Roots in the Air V

Christopher Hampton (1946)
White Chameleon D

David Hare (1947)
Murmuring Judges D
'The Hare Trilogy' ii, examining the British legal system. See also *Racing Demon* 1990, *Absence of War* 1993.

Tony Harrison (1937)
A Cold Coming V

Susan Hill (1942)
Air and Angels F

Michael Holroyd (1935)
George Bernard Shaw: The Lure of Fantasy NF
See also *The Search for Love* 1988, *The Pursuit of Power* 1989, *The Last Laugh* 1992

Elizabeth Jane Howard (1923)
Marking Time F
Cazalet Chronicle ii. See also *The Light Years* 1990, *Confusion* 1993, *Casting Off* 1995.

Linton Kwesi Johnson (1952)
Tings an' Times V

Jennifer Johnston (1930)
The Invisible Worm F

P.J. Kavanagh (1931)
An Enchantment V

Jackie Kay (1961)
The Adoption Papers V

James Kelman (1946)
The Burn F

Thomas Kinsella (1928)
Madonna, and Other Poems V

'John le Carré' [David John Moore Cornwell (1931)]
The Secret Pilgrim F

Laurie Lee (1914–97)
A Moment of War NF

Penelope Lively (1933)
City of the Mind F

Liz Lochhead (1947)
Bagpipe Muzak V

David Lodge (1935)
Paradise News F

Michael Longley (1939)
Gorse Fires V

George MacBeth (1932–92)
Trespassing V

Medbh McGuckian (1950)
Marconi's Cottage V

Jamie McKendrick (1955)
The Sirocco Room V

Allan Massie (1938)
The Sins of the Father F

Allan Massie (1938)
Tiberius F
See also *Augustus* 1986, *Caesar* 1993

Timothy Mo (1950)
The Redundancy of Courage F
E.M. Forster Award

Edwin Morgan (1920)
Hold Hands Among the Atoms V

Andrew Motion (1952)
Love in a Life V

Sean O'Brien (1952)
HMS Glasshouse V

Ben Okri (1959)
The Famished Road F
Booker Prize 1991

John Osborne (1929–94)
Almost a Gentleman NF
Sequel to *A Better Class of Person* 1981 (q.v.)

Tim Parks (1954)
Goodness F

Caryl Phillips (1958)
Cambridge F

Harold Pinter (1930)
Party Time D
Performed 31 October 1991

V.S. Pritchett (1900–97)
Complete Essays NF

Ian Rankin (1960)
Hide and Seek F

Christopher Reid (1949)
In the Echoey Tunnel V

Michèle Roberts (1949)
Psyche and the Hurricane F

Jane Rogers (1952)
Mr Wroe's Virgins F

Vernon Scannell (1922)
A Time for Fires V

Will Self (1961)
The Quantity Theory of Insanity F

Iain Sinclair (1943)
Downriver; or, The Vessels of Wrath F

C.H. Sisson (1914–2003)
Antidotes V

Colin Thubron (1939)
Turning Back the Sun F

'William Trevor' [William Trevor Cox (1928)]
Two Lives F
Contains 'Reading Turgenev', and 'My House in Umbria'

Keith Waterhouse (1929)
Jeffrey Bernard is Unwell D
Performed 1989

Fay Weldon (1931)
Moon Over Minneapolis; or, Why She Couldn't Stay F

A.N. Wilson (1950)
Daughters of Albion F
Third of the Lampitt Papers sequence. See also *Incline Our Hearts* 1988, *A Bottle in the Smoke* 1990, *Hearing Voices* 1995, *Watch in the Night* 1996.

1992

- British Conservatives under John Major returned for a fourth term
  Neil Kinnock resigns as leader of the Labour Party: succeeded by John Smith
  Sterling crisis: sterling withdrawn from the European Exchange Rate Mechanism
  Riots in Los Angeles
- Arthur Calder-Marshall dies
  Angela Carter dies
  Barbara Comyns dies
  Monica Dickens dies
  William Douglas Home dies
  George MacBeth dies
  Mary Norton dies
  Ruth Pitter dies
- Francis Bacon dies
  John Piper dies
- Isaac Asimov dies
  Willy Brandt dies
  John Cage dies
  Marlene Dietrich dies
- Booker Prize shared by Michael Ondaatje for *The English Patient* and Barry Unsworth for *Sacred Hunger*

Peter Ackroyd (1949)
English Music NF

Kingsley Amis (1922–95)
The Russian Girl F

Simon Armitage (1963)
Kid V

Simon Armitage (1963)
Xanadu V

Iain Banks (1954)
The Crow Road F

A.L. Barker (1918–2002)
Element of Doubt F
Ghost stories

Julian Barnes (1946)
The Porcupine F
Novella

Samuel Beckett (1906–89)
Dream of Fair to Middling Women F

Alan Bennett (1934)
The Madness of George III D
Performed 1991; film 1995

Clare Boylan (1948)
Home Rule F

Malcolm Bradbury (1932–2000)
Dr Criminale F

Anita Brookner (1928)
Fraud F

George Mackay Brown (1921–96)
Brodgar Poems V

George Mackay Brown (1921–96)
The Lost Village V

George Mackay Brown (1921–96)
Vinland F
Stories

'Anthony Burgess' [John Anthony Burgess Wilson (1917–93)]
A Mouthful of Air: Language and languages NF

A.S. Byatt (1936)
Angels and Insects F
Two novellas, 'Morpho Eugenia' and 'The Conjugial Angel'

Angela Carter (1940–92)
Expletives Deleted NF

Wendy Cope (1945)
Serious Concerns V

Jim Crace (1946)
Arcadia F

Louis de Bernières (1954)
The Troublesome Offspring of Cardinal Guzman F

Carol Ann Duffy (1955)
William and the Ex-Prime Minister V

Helen Dunmore (1952)
Going to Egypt F

'Alice Thomas Ellis' [Anna Margaret Haycraft (1932)]
Pillars of Gold F

Gavin Ewart (1916)
Like It Or Not V

U.A. Fanthorpe (1929)
Neck-Verse V

Sebastian Faulks (1953)
A Fool's Alphabet F

Elaine Feinstein (1930)
Loving Brecht F

Alasdair Gray (1934)
Poor Things F

Thom Gunn (1929–2004)
The Man with Night Sweats V

Thom Gunn (1929–2004)
Old Stories V

Ian Hamilton (1938–2001)
Keepers of the Flame NF

Georgina Hammick (1939)
Spoilt F

Tony Harrison (1937)
The Gaze of the Gorgon V

Seamus Heaney (1939)
Sweeney's Flight V
See also *Sweeney Astray* 1984

Adrian Henri (1932–2001)
The Cerise Swimsuit V

Richard Hoggart (1918)
An Imagined Life NF
Autobiographical. See also *A Local Habitation* 1988, *A Sort of Clowning* 1990.

Michael Holroyd (1935)
George Bernard Shaw: The Last Laugh NF
See also *The Search for Love* 1988, *The Pursuit of Power* 1989, *The Lure of Fantasy* 1991

Nick Hornby (1957)
Fever Pitch F

Susan Howatch (1940)
Mystical Paths F

Ted Hughes (1930–98)
Rain-Charm for the Duchy V

Ted Hughes (1930–98)
Shakespeare and the Goddess of Complete Being NF

Howard Jacobson (1942)
The Very Model of a Man F

Elizabeth Jennings (1926–2001)
Times and Seasons V

James Kirkup (1918)
Shooting Stars V

Philip Larkin (1922–1985)
Selected Letters NF
Edited by Anthony Thwaite

George MacBeth (1932–92)
The Patient V

Patrick McCabe (1955)
The Butcher Boy F

Film 1996. The novel formed the basis of McCabe's play *Frank Pig Says Hello* (performed 1992).

Ian McEwan (1948)
Black Dogs F

Roger McGough (1937)
Defying Gravity V

Frank McGuinness (1953)
Someone Who'll Watch Over Me D
Based on the experiences of Western hostages in Beirut, notably Brian Keenan

Hilary Mantel (1952)
A Place of Greater Safety F

Adam Mars-Jones (1954)
Monopolies of Loss F

Michael Moorcock (1939)
Jerusalem Commands F
Pyat series iii. See also *Byzantium Endures* 1981, *The Laughter of Carthage* 1984.

John Mortimer (1923)
Dunster F

Iris Murdoch (1919–99)
Metaphysics as a Guide to Morals NF

Edna O'Brien (1932)
Time and Tide F

John Osborne (1929–94)
Déja Vu D
Performed 1991

Peter Porter (1929)
The Chair of Babel V

Kathleen Raine (1908–2003)
Living With Mystery V

Ian Rankin (1960)
Strip Jack F

Ian Rankin (1960)
Wolfman F
Later published as *Tooth and Nail*

Simon Raven (1927–2001)
The Troubadour F
The First-Born of Egypt sequence vii. See also *Morning Star* 1984, *The Face of the Waters* 1985, *Before the Cock Crow* 1986, *New Seed for Old* 1988, *Blood of My Bone* 1989, *In the Image of God* 1990.

Peter Reading (1946)
Evagatory V

Peter Reading (1946)
3 in 1 V

Peter Redgrove (1932–2003)
Under the Reservoir V

Jeremy Reed (1954)
Black Sugar V
Illustrated by Jean Cocteau

Michèle Roberts (1949)
Daughters of the House F

Lisa St Aubin de Terán (1953)
Nocturne F

William Scammell (1939–2000)
Bleeding Heart Yard V

Will Self (1961)
Cock & Bull F

Jo Shapcott (1953)
Phrase Book V

Penelope Shuttle (1947)
Taxing the Rain V

Jon Silkin (1930–97)
The Lens-Breakers V

Muriel Spark (1918)
Curriculum Vitae NF
Autobiography

David Storey (1933)
Storey's Lives V

Graham Swift (1949)
Ever After F

Adam Thorpe (1956)
Ulverton F

D.M. Thomas (1935)
Flying in to Love F

R.S. Thomas (1913–2000)
Mass for Hard Times V

Charles Tomlinson (1927)
The Door in the Wall V

Rose Tremain (1943)
Sacred Country F

Barry Unsworth (1930)
Sacred Hunger F
Booker Prize 1992 (shared with Michael Ondaatje for *The English Patient*)

Minette Walters (1949)
The Ice House F

Marina Warner (1946)
Indigo; or, Mapping the Waters F

Fay Weldon (1931)
Growing Rich F

Nigel Williams (1948)
They Came From SW19 F

Jeanette Winterson (1959)
Written on the Body F

Benjamin Zephaniah (1958)
City Psalms V

1993

- Czechoslovakia divides into separate Czech and Slovakian republics (1 Jan.)
  European Community renamed European Union
  BIll Clinton becomes President of the USA
  Bombing of the World Trade Center in New York
  Siege of the Branch Davidian compound near Waco, Texas, ends
  Yasser Arafat and Yitzhak Rabin shake hands in Washington
  Occupation of the Russian parliament
- M.C. Bradbrook dies
  Anthony Burgess dies
  Penelope Gilliatt dies
  Sir William Golding dies
  Peter Quennell dies
  Dame Freya Stark dies
  E.P. Thompson dies
  Robert Westall dies
- Arthur Ashe dies
  Dizzy Gillespie dies
  Audrey Hepburn dies
- Rudolf Nureyev dies
- Roddy Doyle wins the Booker Prize for *Paddy Clarke Ha Ha Ha*
- *Schindler's List*
  Jurassic Park
  The Piano

Peter Ackroyd (1949)
The House of Doctor Dee F

Brian Aldiss (1925)
Remembrance Day F

Moniza Alvi (1954)
The Country at my Shoulder V

Kingsley Amis (1922–95)
Mr Barrett's Secret, and Other Stories F

Martin Amis (1949)
Visiting Mrs Nabokov NF

Simon Armitage (1963)
Book of Matches V

Paul Bailey (1937)
Sugar Cane F

John Banville (1945)
Ghosts F
Sequel to *The Book of Evidence* 1989 and continued in *Athena* 1995 (qq.v.)

Pat Barker (1943)
The Eye in the Door F
Second of Barker's First World War trilogy. See also *Regeneration* 1991, *The Ghost Road* 1995.

William Boyd (1952)
The Blue Afternoon F

Anita Brookner (1928)
A Family Romance F

'Anthony Burgess' [John Anthony Burgess Wilson (1917–93)]
A Dead Man in Deptford F

A.S. Byatt (1936)
The Matisse Stories F

Angela Carter (1940–92)
American Ghosts and Old World Wonders F
Stories

Justin Cartwright (1943)
Masai Dreaming F

Gillian Clarke (1937)
The King of Britain's Daughter V

Roddy Doyle (1958)
Paddy Clarke Ha Ha Ha F
Booker Prize 1993

Carol Ann Duffy (1955)
Mean Time V

Maureen Duffy (1933)
Occam's Razor F

Helen Dunmore (1952)
Zennor in Darkness F

Douglas Dunn (1942)
Dante's Drum-Kit V

Paul Durcan (1944)
A Snail in my Prime V

D.J. Enright (1920–2002)
Old Men and Comets V

James Fenton (1949)
Out of Danger V

Eva Figes (1932)
The Tenancy F

Michael Frayn (1933)
Here D

Roy Fuller (1912–91)
Last Poems V

Alasdair Gray (1934)
Ten Tales Tall and True F

Lavinia Greenlaw (1962)
Night Photograph V

Thom Gunn (1929–2004)
Collected Poems V

David Hare (1947)
Absence of War D
'The Hare Trilogy' iii, examing the British Labour Party. See also *Racing Demon* 1990, *Murmuring Judges* 1991.

Tony Harrison (1937)
Black Daisies for the Bride V

Susan Hill (1942)
Mrs De Winter F
Sequel to Daphne du Maurier's *Rebecca* 1938 (q.v.)

Elizabeth Jane Howard (1923)
Confusion F
Cazalet Chronicle iii. See also *The Light Years* 1990, *Marking Time* 1991, *Casting Off* 1995.

Ruth Prawer Jhabvala (1927)
Poet and Dancer F

Jackie Kay (1961)
Other Lovers V

A.L. Kennedy (1965)
Looking For the Possible Dance F

James Kirkup (1918)
Blue Bamboo V

Norman Lewis (1908–2003)
An Empire in the East NF

Penelope Lively (1933)
Cleopatra's Sister F

Eugene McCabe (1930)
Christ in the Fields F
Three novellas

Jamie McKendrick (1955)
The Kiosk on the Brink V

Sara Maitland (1950)
Home Truths F

Sara Maitland (1950)
Women Fly When Men Aren't Watching F
Stories

E.A. Markham (1939)
Letter From Ulster and the Hugo Poems V

Adam Mars-Jones (1954)
The Waters of Thirst F

Allan Massie (1938)
Caesar F
See also *Augustus* 1986, *Tiberius* 1991

Brian Moore (1921–99)
No Other Life F

Blake Morrison (1950)
And When Did You Last See Your Father? NF

Andrew Motion (1952)
Philip Larkin NF

Iris Murdoch (1919–99)
The Green Knight F

Robert Nye (1939)
Mrs Shakespeare F

Ben Okri (1959)
Songs of Enchantment F

Caryl Phillips (1958)
Crossing the River F

Harold Pinter (1930)
Moonlight D
Performed 7 September 1993

Fiona Pitt-Kethley (1954)
Dogs V

Dennis Potter (1935–94)
Lipstick on Your Collar D
Televised 1993

Ian Rankin (1960)
The Black Book F

Michèle Roberts (1949)
During Mother's Absence F

Carol Rumens (1944)
Thinking of Skins V

Will Self (1961)
My Idea of Fun F

Vikram Seth (1952)
A Suitable Boy F

Peter Shaffer (1926)
The Gift of the Gorgon D
Performed 1992

Alan Sillitoe (1928)
Snow Stop F

Tom Stoppard (1937)
Arcadia D
Performed 13 April 1993

Paul Theroux (1941)
Millroy the Magician F

R.S. Thomas (1913–2000)
Collected Poems, 1945–1990 V

Minette Walters (1949)
The Sculptress F

Marina Warner (1946)
Mermaids in the Basement F
Stories

Fay Weldon (1931)
Affliction F

Irvine Welsh (1957)
Trainspotting F

A.N. Wilson (1950)
The Vicar of Sorrows F

1994

- Mortar shell kills 68 in a Sarajevo marketplace
  Nelson Mandela becomes the first black President of South Africa (Feb.)
  Civil war in Rwanda
  Unexpected death of British Labour Party leader John Smith: succeeded by Tony Blair (July)
  Channel Tunnel opened (May)
  O.J. Simpson arrested
- Sir Harold Acton dies
  Jack Clemo dies
  Lettice Cooper dies
  Patric Dickinson dies
  Geoffrey Elton dies
  John Osborne dies
  Dennis Potter dies
  J.I.M. Stewart dies
  John Wain dies
- Erich Honecker dies
  Eugene Ionesco dies
  Jacqueline Kennedy Onassis dies
  Richard Nixon dies
  Kim Il Sung, North Korean dictator, dies
- James Kelman wins the Booker Prize for *How Late It Was, How Late*
- Harold Bloom, *The Western Canon*
- *Pulp Fiction*
  The Shawshank Redemption
  Forrest Gump

Peter Ackroyd (1949)
Dan Leno and the Limehouse Golem F

Kingsley Amis (1922–95)
You Can't Do Both F

Alan Ayckbourn (1939)
Wildest Dreams D
Performed 1991

J.G. Ballard (1930)
Rushing to Paradise F

Alan Bennett (1934)
Writing Home NF

Maeve Binchy (1940)
The Glass Lake F

Eavan Boland (1944)
In a Time of Violence V

Dermot Bolger (1959)
A Second Life F

Anita Brookner (1928)
A Private View F

George Mackay Brown (1921–96)
Beside the Ocean of Time F

Alan Brownjohn (1931)
In the Cruel Arcade V

A.S. Byatt (1936)
The Djinn in the Nightingale's Eye F
Original fairy tales

Caryl Churchill (1938)
The Skriker D

Jonathan Coe (1961)
What a Carve Up! F

Jim Crace (1946)
Signals of Distress F

Louis de Bernières (1954)
Captain Corelli's Mandolin F

Jenny Diski (1947)
Monkey's Uncle F

Helen Dunmore (1952)
Burning Bright F

Helen Dunmore (1952)
Recovering a Body V

Paul Durcan (1944)
Give Me Your Hand V

'Alice Thomas Ellis' [Anna Margaret Haycraft (1932)**]**
The Evening of Adam F

Roy Fisher (1930)
Birmingham River V

Janice Galloway (1956)
Foreign Parts F

Jane Gardam (1928)
Going into a Dark House, and Other Stories F

Maggie Gee (1948)
Lost Children F

Rumer Godden (1907–98)
Pippa Passes F

Alasdair Gray (1934)
A History Maker F

Trevor Griffiths (1935)
Thatcher's Children D

Philip Gross (1952)
I.D. V

Ian Hamilton (1938–2001)
Walking Possession NF
Essays and reviews

Adrian Henri (1932–2001)
Not Fade Away V

Selima Hill (1945)
Trembling Hearts in the Bodies of Dogs V

Alan Hollinghurst (1954)
The Folding Star F

Michael Holroyd (1935)
Lytton Strachey: The New Biography NF
Revised version of *The Unknown Years* 1967 and *The Years of Achievement* 1968 (qq.v.)

Susan Howatch (1940)
Absolute Truths F

Ted Hughes (1930–98)
Winter Pollen: Occasional prose NF

P.D. James (1920)
Original Sin F

Kathleen Jamie (1962)
The Queen of Sheba V

Alan Jenkins (1955)
Harm V

Elizabeth Jennings (1926–2001)
Familiar Spirits V

James Kelman (1946)
How Late it Was, How Late F
Booker Prize 1994

A.L. Kennedy (1965)
Now That You're Back F

Thomas Kinsella (1928)
From Centre City V

Doris Lessing (1919)
Under My Skin NF
See also *Walking in the Shade* 1997

Peter Levi (1931)
The Rags of Time V

Penelope Lively (1933)
Oleander, Jacaranda NF
Autobiography

Christopher Logue (1926)
The Husbands D
See also *War Music* 1981, *Kings* 1990

Ian McEwan (1948)
The Daydreamer F

Medbh McGuckian (1950)
Captain Lavender V

Bernard MacLaverty (1942)
Walking the Dog, and Other Stories F

Candia McWilliam (1955)
Debatable Land F

Derek Mahon (1941)
The Yaddo Letter V

Hilary Mantel (1952)
A Change of Climate F

Andrew Motion (1952)
The Price of Everything V

Paul Muldoon (1951)
The Annals of Chile V

Paul Muldoon (1951)
The Prince of Quotidian V

V.S. Naipaul (1932)
A Way in the World F

Edna O'Brien (1932)
The House of Splendid Isolation F

Tom Paulin (1949)
Walking a Line V

Peter Porter (1929)
Millennial Fables V

Craig Raine (1944)
History: The Home Movie V

Ian Rankin (1960)
Mortal Causes F

Peter Redgrove (1932–2003)
My Father's Trapdoors V

Jeremy Reed (1954)
Chasing Black Rainbows F

Ruth Rendell (1930)
Simisola F

Michèle Roberts (1949)
Flesh and Blood F

Salman Rushdie (1947)
East, West F
Stories

Peter Scupham (1933)
The Ark V

Will Self (1961)
Grey Area, and Other Stories F

Jon Silkin (1930–97)
Watersmeet V

Iain Sinclair (1943)
Radon Daughters F

C.H. Sisson (1914–2003)
What and Who V

Sir Stephen Spender (1909–95)
Dolphins V

Colin Thubron (1939)
The Lost Heart of Asia NF

Anthony Thwaite (1930)
The Dust of the World V

Barbara Trapido (1941)
Juggling F

Rose Tremain (1943)
Evangelista's Fan, and Other Stories F

'William Trevor' [William Trevor Cox (1928)]
Felicia's Journey F

John Wain (1925–94)
Hungry Generations F
Oxford Trilogy iii. See also *Where the Rivers Meet* 1988, *Comedies* 1990.

Minette Walters (1949)
The Scold's Bridle F

Marina Warner (1946)
From the Beast to the Blonde NF

Keith Waterhouse (1929)
City Lights NF
Autobiography. Continued in *Streets Ahead* 1995 (q.v.).

Irvine Welsh (1957)
The Acid House F

Nigel Williams (1948)
Scenes From a Poisoner's Life F

Jeanette Winterson (1959)
Art and Lies F

Virginia Woolf (1882–1941)
The Essays of Virginia Woolf: Volume iv: 1925–1928 NF
Published on 19 May 1994. See also *Essays* 1986, 1987, 1988.

1995

- Bombing of the Federal Building in Oklahoma City (Apr.)
  Jacques Chirac elected President of France
  UN safe area of Srebrenica attacked by Bosnian Serbs; massacre ensues (July)
  David Trimble becomes leader of the Ulster Unionist Party
  Seamus Heaney wins the Nobel Prize for literature
  Yitzhak Rabin assassinated (Oct.)
  Execution of Ken Saro-Wiwa in Nigeria
  Agreement for peace in Bosnia signed in Dayton, Ohio (Dec.)
- Walter Allen dies
  Sir Kingsley Amis dies
  Robert Bolt dies
  Donald Davie dies
  Gerald Durrell dies
  Janice Elliott dies
  Sir Stephen Spender dies
  Julian Symons dies
- Peter Cook dies
  Harold Wilson dies
- Robertson Davies dies
  Louis Malle dies
  Dean Martin dies
  Ginger Rogers dies
- Pat Barker wins the Booker Prize for *The Ghost Road*
- *Braveheart*

Peter Ackroyd (1949)
Blake NF

Kingsley Amis (1922–95)
The Biographer's Moustache F

Martin Amis (1949)
The Information F

Kate Atkinson (1951)
Behind the Scenes at the Museum F

John Banville (1945)
Athena F
Sequel to *The Book of Evidence* 1989 and *Ghosts* 1993 (qq.v.)

Pat Barker (1943)
The Ghost Road F
Booker Prize 1995. The third of Barker's First World War trilogy. See also *Regeneration* 1991, *The Eye in the Door* 1993.

Julian Barnes (1946)
Letters From London NF

James Berry (1924)
Hot Earth, Cold Earth V

William Boyd (1952)
The Destiny of Nathalie 'X', and Other Stories F

Clare Boylan (1948)
That Bad Woman F

Malcolm Bradbury (1932–2000)
Dangerous Pilgrimages NF

Anita Brookner (1928)
Incidents in the Rue Laugier F

Angela Carter (1940–92)
Burning Your Boats F
Collected short stories. Introduction by Salman Rushdie.

Justin Cartwright (1943)
In Every Face I Meet F

Isabel Colegate (1931)
Winter Journey F

Anita Desai (1937)
Journey to Ithaca F

Helen Dunmore (1952)
A Spell of Winter F

David Edgar (1948)
Pentecost D
Performed 12 October 1994

Penelope Fitzgerald (1916–2000)
The Blue Flower F

Victoria Glendinning (1937)
Electricity F

William Golding (1911–93)
The Double Tongue NF
Published in June 1995. Golding's last novel, left in draft at his death.

Simon Gray (1936)
Cell Mates D

David Hare (1947)
Skylight D

Robert Harris (1957)
Enigma F

Tony Harrison (1937)
The Shadow of Hiroshima V

Nick Hornby (1957)
High Fidelity F

Elizabeth Jane Howard (1923)
Casting Off F
Cazalet Chronicle iv. See also *The Light Years* 1990, *Marking Time* 1991, *Confusion* 1993.

Ted Hughes (1930–98)
New Selected Poems 1957–1994 V
See also *Selected Poems* 1972, 1982

Kazuo Ishiguro (1954)
The Unconsoled F

Ruth Prawer Jhabvala (1927)
Shards of Memory F

A.L. Kennedy (1965)
So I Am Glad F

'John le Carré' [David John Moore Cornwell (1931)]
Our Game F

David Lodge (1935)
Therapy F

Michael Longley (1939)
The Ghost Orchid V

Patrick McCabe (1955)
The Dead School F

Ian McEwan (1948)
Collected Stories F
Comprises *First Love, Last Rites* 1975 (q.v.) and *In Between the Sheets* 1978 (q.v.)

Hilary Mantel (1952)
An Experiment in Love F

Allan Massie (1938)
King David F

Timothy Mo (1950)
Brownout on Breadfruit Boulevard F

Deborah Moggach (1948)
Changing Babies F

Michael Moorcock (1939)
Blood F

P.H. Newby (1918–97)
Something About Women F

Sean O'Brien (1952)
Ghost Train V

Ben Okri (1959)
Astonishing the Gods F

Tim Parks (1954)
Mimi's Ghost F
Sequel to *Cara Massimina* 1990 (q.v.)

Anthony Powell (1905–2000)
Journals, 1982–1986 NF

Philip Pullman (1946)
Northern Lights F
His Dark Materials trilogy i. See also *The Subtle Knife* 1998, *The Amber Spyglass* 2000.

Peter Reading (1946)
Collected Poems 1970–1984 V

Bernice Rubens (1928–2004)
Yesterday in the Back Lane F

Carol Rumens (1944)
Best China Sky V

Salman Rushdie (1947)
The Moor's Last Sigh F

Tom Stoppard (1937)
Indian Ink D
Performed 27 February 1995. Expanded version of his 1991 radio play, *In the Native State*.

Charles Tomlinson (1927)
Jubilation V

Joanna Trollope (1943)
The Best of Friends F

Barry Unsworth (1930)
Morality Play F

Minette Walters (1949)
The Dark Room F

Alan Warner (1964)
Morvern Callar F

Keith Waterhouse (1929)
Streets Ahead NF
Autobiography. See *City Lights* 1994.

Fay Weldon (1931)
Splitting F

A.N. Wilson (1950)
Hearing Voices F
Fourth of the Lampitt Papers sequence. See also *Incline Our Hearts* 1988, *A Bottle in the Smoke* 1990, *Daughters of Albion* 1991, *Watch in the Night* 1996.

1996

- 'Mad Cow Disease' crisis in Britain
  Benjamin Netanyahu becomes Israeli Prime Minister
  IRA bomb destroys the Arndale Centre in Manchester
  Terrorist attack on the US base at Dhahran
  The Taliban take power in Afghanistan
  Bill Clinton re-elected as US President
- George Mackay Brown dies
  Richard Cobb dies
  Jacquetta Hawkes dies
  Molly Keane dies
  Mary Lavin dies
  Norman MacCaig dies
  Jessica Mitford dies
  P.L. Travers dies
- Ella Fitzgerald dies
  Gene Kelly dies
  Timothy Leary dies
  François Mitterrand dies
- Graham Swift wins the Booker Prize for *Last Orders*
- *The English Patient*
  Trainspotting

Beryl Bainbridge (1934)
Every Man for Himself F

Julian Barnes (1946)
Cross Channel F
Stories

Samuel Beckett (1906–89)
Eleutheria D

James Berry (1924)
Playing a Dazzler V

Melvyn Bragg (1939)
Credo F

Anita Brookner (1928)
Altered States F

A.S. Byatt (1936)
Babel Tower F
Continues *The Virgin in the Garden* 1978 and *Still Life* 1985 (qq.v.)

Roddy Doyle (1958)
The Woman Who Walked into Doors F

Margaret Drabble (1939)
The Witch of Exmoor F

Carol Ann Duffy (1955)
Stopping for Death V
With Trisha Rafferty

Patricia Duncker (1951)
Hallucinating Foucault F

Helen Dunmore (1952)
Talking to the Dead F

T.S. Eliot (1888–1965)
Inventions of the March Hare V
Edited by Christopher Ricks. Early unpublished verse.

Helen Fielding (1958)
Bridget Jones's Diary F

Eva Figes (1932)
The Knot F

Jane Gardam (1928)
Faith Fox F

Alasdair Gray (1934)
Mavis Belfrage F
Stories

David Hare (1947)
Plays: One D
Contains *Slag*; *Teeth 'n' Smiles*; *Knuckle*; *Licking Hitler*; *Plenty*. See also *Plays 2* 1997.

Seamus Heaney (1939)
The Spirit Level V

Tobias Hill (1970)
Midnight in the City of Clocks V

David Hughes (1930)
The Little Book F

Sarah Kane (1971–99)
Blasted; and, Phaedra's Love D
Blasted first published in 1994 and performed January 1995

Doris Lessing (1919)
Love, Again F

Penelope Lively (1933)
Heat Wave NF
Autobiography

Nicholas Mosley (1923)
Children of Darkness and Light F

Grace Nichols (1950)
Sunris V

Tom Paulin (1949)
Writing to the Moment NF

Harold Pinter (1930)
Ashes to Ashes D
Performed 12 September 1996

Craig Raine (1944)
Clay: Whereabouts Unknown V

Ian Rankin (1960)
Let It Bleed F

Peter Reading (1946)
Collected Poems 1985–1996 V

Ruth Rendell (1930)
The Keys to the Street F

Will Self (1961)
The Sweet Smell of Psychosis F

Graham Swift (1949)
Last Orders F

Meera Syal (1963)
Anita and Me F

Irvine Welsh (1957)
Ecstasy F
Stories

A.N. Wilson (1950)
Watch in the Night F
Fifth of the Lampitt Papers sequence. See also *Incline Our Hearts* 1988, *A Bottle in the Smoke* 1990, *Daughters of Albion* 1991, *Hearing Voices* 1995.

1997

- Tony Blair becomes British Prime Minister (May)
  Diana, Princess of Wales, dies in car crash (31 Aug.)
  Britain transfers Hong Kong back to China
  Scottish geneticists announce the successful cloning of a sheep (Dolly, born July 1996)
  Gunmen kill tourists at the Hatshepsut Temple in Luxor
  Thabo Mbeki succeeds Nelson Mandela as leader of the African National Congress
  Scotland Act receives royal assent, bringing the Scottish Parliament into being
  Paul McCartney is knighted
- Sir Isaiah Berlin dies
  L.C. Knights dies
  Laurie Lee dies
  James Lees-Milne dies
  P.H. Newby dies
  Sir V.S. Pritchett dies
  A.L. Rowse dies

Jon Silkin dies

- Sir James Goldsmith dies
- Kathy Acker dies

William S. Burroughs dies
Allen Ginsberg dies
Chaim Herzog dies
James Michener dies
Harold Robbins dies
Sir Georg Solti dies
Mother Teresa dies
Gianni Versace murdered

- Arundhati Roy wins the Booker Prize for *The God of Small Things*
- *Titanic*

Fleur Adcock (1934)
Looking Back V

Martin Amis (1949)
Night Train F
Novella

Simon Armitage (1963)
CloudCuckooLand V

Kate Atkinson (1951)
Human Croquet F

W.H. Auden (1907–73)
Prose 1926–38, Essays and Reviews, and Travel Books in Prose and Verse MISC
Published on 17 March 1997

Iain Banks (1954)
A Song of Stone F

John Banville (1945)
The Untouchable F

Clare Boylan (1948)
Another Family Christmas F
Stories

Clare Boylan (1948)
Room For a Single Lady F

Anita Brookner (1928)
Visitors F

George Mackay Brown (1921–96)
For the Islands I Sing NF
Autobiography

Charles Causley (1917–2003)
Collected Poems V
See also *Collected Poems* 1975

Jonathan Coe (1961)
The House of Sleep F

Jim Crace (1946)
Quarantine F

Patricia Duncker (1951)
Monsieur Shoushana's Lemon Trees F
Stories

Jane Gardam (1928)
Missing the Midnight F

Rumer Godden (1907–98)
Cromartie v the God Shiva F

Lavinia Greenlaw (1962)
A World Where News Travelled Slowly V

David Hare (1947)
Plays: Two D
Contains *Fanshen*; *Saigon*; *A Map of the World*; *The Bay at Nice*. See also *Plays: One* 1996.

David Hare (1947)
Amy's View D
Performed 20 June 1997

Tobias Hill (1970)
Skin, and Other Stories F

Ted Hughes (1930–98) (tr.)
Tales from Ovid V
Published in May 1997

Elizabeth Jennings (1926–2001)
In the Meantime V

A.L. Kennedy (1965)
Original Bliss F

Francis King (1923)
Dead Letters F

Doris Lessing (1919)
Walking in the Shade NF
Autobiography. See also *Under My Skin* 1994.

Ian McEwan (1948)
Enduring Love F

Jamie McKendrick (1955)
The Marble Fly V

Bernard MacLaverty (1942)
Grace Notes F

Candia McWilliam (1955)
Wait Till I Tell You F
Stories

Allan Massie (1938)
Shadows of Empire F

Allan Massie (1938)
Antony F

Brian Moore (1921–99)
The Magician's Wife F

Andrew Motion (1952)
Salt Water V

Andrew Motion (1952)
Keats NF

Don Paterson (1963)
God's Gift to Women V

Iain Pears (1955)
An Instance of the Fingerpost F

Ian Rankin (1960)
Black and Blue F

Peter Reading (1946)
Work in Regress V

Ruth Rendell (1930)
Road Rage F

Michèle Roberts (1949)
Impossible Saints F

J.K. Rowling (1965)
Harry Potter and the Philosopher's Stone F
Published in July 1997

Arundhati Roy (1961)
The God of Small Things F
Booker Prize 1997

Bernice Rubens (1928–2004)
The Waiting Game F

Will Self (1961)
Great Apes F

Alan Sillitoe (1928)
Alligator Playground F
Stories

Tom Stoppard (1937)
The Invention of Love D
Performed 1 October 1997

Anthony Thwaite (1930)
Selected Poems 1956–1996 V

Charles Tomlinson (1927)
Selected Poems 1955–1997 V

Minette Walters (1949)
The Echo F

Alan Warner (1964)
These Demented Lands F

Fay Weldon (1931)
Big Women F

1998

- Monica Lewinsky testifies to a sexual affair with President Bill Clinton
  David Trimble becomes First Minister of the Northern Ireland Assembly
  Terrorist bombs explode at US embassies in Nairobi and Dar es Salaam
  Cruise missile attacks on Sudan and Afghanistan
  John Hume and David Trimble awarded the Nobel Peace Prize
  Augusto Pinochet arrested in London
  Legislation passed establishing the Welsh Assembly
- Eric Ambler dies
  Catherine Cookson dies
  Rumer Godden dies
  Ted Hughes dies
- Martha Gellhorn dies
  Akira Kurosawa dies
  Pol Pot dies
  Frank Sinatra dies
  Dr Benjamin Spock dies
- Ian McEwan wins the Booker Prize for *Amsterdam*
- *Shakespeare in Love*

Peter Ackroyd (1949)
The Life of Thomas More NF

Martin Amis (1949)
Heavy Water, and Other Stories F

Andrea Ashworth (1969)
Once in a House on Fire NF
Autobiography

Paul Bailey (1937)
Kitty and Virgil F

Beryl Bainbridge (1934)
Master Georgie F

Pat Barker (1943)
Another World F

Julian Barnes (1946)
England, England F

John Bayley (1925)
Iris NF

Maeve Binchy (1940)
Tara Road F

William Boyd (1952)
Armadillo F

George Mackay Brown (1921–96)
The Island of the Women, and Other Stories F

A.S. Byatt (1936)
Elementals F
Stories

Carol Ann Duffy (1955)
The Pamphlet V

Maureen Duffy (1933)
Restitution F

Helen Dunmore (1952)
Your Blue-Eyed Boy F

D.J. Enright (1920–2002)
Collected Poems: 1948–1998 V

Sebastian Faulks (1953)
Charlotte Gray F

Michael Frayn (1933)
Alarms & Excursions D

Michael Frayn (1933)
Copenhagen D

David Hare (1947)
The Judas Kiss D
Performed 19 March 1998. On the relationship between Oscar Wilde and Lord Alfred Douglas.

David Hare (1947)
Via Dolorosa D
Performed 8 September 1998

Seamus Heaney (1939) (tr.)
Beowulf V

Seamus Heaney (1939)
Opened Ground V

Susan Hill (1942)
The Service of Clouds F

Tobias Hill (1970)
Zoo V

Alan Hollinghurst (1954)
The Spell F

Nick Hornby (1957)
About a Boy F
Film 2002

Ted Hughes (1930–98)
Birthday Letters V
Published on 29 January 1998. A verse chronicle of Hughes's relationship with Sylvia Plath.

Ted Hughes (1930–98) (tr.)
Phedre V

Howard Jacobson (1942)
No More Mister Nice Guy F

Ruth Prawer Jhabvala (1927)
East into Upper East F
Stories

Sarah Kane (1971–99)
Cleansed D
Performed 30 April 1998

Jackie Kay (1961)
Off Colour V

Jackie Kay (1961)
Trumpet F

Peter Levi (1931)
Reed Music V

Penelope Lively (1933)
Spiderweb F

Patrick McCabe (1955)
Breakfast on Pluto F

Ian McEwan (1948)
Amsterdam F

Hilary Mantel (1952)
The Giant, O'Brien F

John Mortimer (1923)
The Sound of Trumpets F

Andrew Motion (1952)
Selected Poems 1976–1997 V

Paul Muldoon (1951)
Hay V

Robert Nye (1939)
The Late Mr Shakespeare F

'Patrick O'Brian' [Richard Patrick Russ (1914–2000)**]**
The Hundred Days F
Aubrey-Maturin series, 19

Sean O'Brien (1952)
The Deregulated Muse NF

Ben Okri (1959)
Infinite Riches F

Joe Orton (1933–67)
Between Us Girls F

Harold Pinter (1930)
Various Voices MISC

Terry Pratchett (1948)
Carpe Jugulum F

Terry Pratchett (1948)
The Last Continent F

Philip Pullman (1946)
The Subtle Knife F
His Dark Materials trilogy ii. See also *Northern Lights* 1995, *The Amber Spyglass* 2000.

'Barbara Vine' [Ruth Rendell (1930)**]**
The Chimney-Sweeper's Boy F

J.K. Rowling (1965)
Harry Potter and the Chamber of Secrets F
Published in July 1998

Carol Rumens (1944)
Holding Pattern V

Will Self (1961)
Tough, Tough Toys for Tough, Tough Boys F
Stories

Jo Shapcott (1953)
My Life Asleep V

Alan Sillitoe (1928)
The Broken Chariot F

Jon Stallworthy (1935)
Rounding the Horn V

'William Trevor' [William Trevor Cox (1928)**]**
Death in Summer F

Joanna Trollope (1943)
Other People's Children F

Minette Walters (1949)
The Breaker F

Alan Warner (1964)
The Sopranos F

Irvine Welsh (1957)
Filth F

A.N. Wilson (1950)
Dream Children F

Jeanette Winterson (1959)
The World and Other Places F

1999

- The Maastricht Treaty on European monetary union comes into force (1 Jan.)
  Impeachment trial of President Clinton begins
  British Defence Secretary George Robertson becomes Secretary General of NATO
  President Mugabi announces policy of land seizure from white farmers in Zimbabwe
  Official opening of the Scottish Parliament
  World population officially reaches 6 billion
- Patricia Beer dies
  Naomi Mitchison dies
  Brian Moore dies
  Penelope Mortimer dies
  Iris Murdoch dies
  Edith Scovell dies
- Quentin Crisp dies
  Yehudi Menuhin dies
- Joseph Heller dies
  King Hussein of Jordan dies
  John F. Kennedy Jr dies (in plane crash)
  Stanley Kubrick dies
  Paul Mellon dies
  Mario Puzo dies
- J.M. Coetzee wins the Booker Prize for *Disgrace*
- *American Beauty*
  The Blair Witch Project
  Star Wars: Episode 1: The Phantom Menace

Peter Ackroyd (1949)
The Plato Papers F

Iain Banks (1954)
The Business F

John Bayley (1925)
Iris and the Friends NF

Clare Boylan (1948)
Beloved Stranger F

Melvyn Bragg (1939)
The Soldier's Return F

Anita Brookner (1928)
Undue Influence F

Jim Crace (1946)
Being Dead F

Anita Desai (1937)
Fasting, Feasting F

Roddy Doyle (1958)
A Star Called Henry F

Carol Ann Duffy (1955)
The World's Wife V

Patricia Duncker (1951)
James Miranda Barry F

Alison Fell (1944)
The Mistress of Lilliput; or, The Pursuit F

Helen Fielding (1958)
Bridget Jones: The Edge of Reason F

Michael Frayn (1933)
Headlong F

Philip Hensher (1965)
The Bedroom of the Mister's Wife F

Tobias Hill (1970)
Underground F

Ted Hughes (1930–98) (tr.)
Aeschylus: The Oresteia V

Ted Hughes (1930–98) (tr.)
Alcestis V
From Euripides

Howard Jacobson (1942)
Getting Licked F

Kathleen Jamie (1962)
Jizzen V

A.L. Kennedy (1965)
Everything You Need F

'John le Carré' [David John Moore Cornwell (1931)]
Single & Single F

Doris Lessing (1919)
Mara and Daun F

Tim Lott (1956)
White City Blue F

Patrick McCabe (1955)
Mondo Desperado F
Inter-linked stories

Derek Mahon (1941)
Collected Poems V

Magnus Mills (1954)
The Restraint of Beasts F

David Mitchell (1969)
Ghostwritten F

Deborah Moggach (1948)
Tulip Fever F

Andrew O'Hagan (1968)
Our Fathers F

Tim Parks (1954)
Destiny F

Tony Parsons (1953)
Man and Boy F

Don Paterson (1963)
The Eyes V

Tom Paulin (1949)
The Wind Dog V

J.H. Prynne (1936)
Poems V

Ian Rankin (1960)
Dead Souls F

Peter Reading (1946)
Apophthegmatic V

Peter Reading (1946)
Ob V

J.K. Rowling (1965)
Harry Potter and the Prisoner of Azkaban F
Published in June 1999

Bernice Rubens (1928–2004)
I, Dreyfus F

Salman Rushdie (1947)
The Ground Beneath Her Feet F

Vikram Seth (1952)
An Equal Music F

Jon Stallworthy (1935)
Singing School NF

Meera Syal (1963)
Life isn't all Ha Ha Hee Hee F

Colm Tóibín (1955)
The Blackwater Lighthouse F

Rose Tremain (1943)
Music and Silence F
Stories

Sarah Waters (1966)
Tipping the Velvet F

Fay Weldon (1931)
Godless in Eden NF

Nigel Williams (1948)
Fortysomething F

2000

2000

- Vladimir Putin elected President of Russia
  An Air France Concorde en route from Paris to New York crashes soon after take off
  Terrorist attack on the USS *Cole* off Yemen
  Results of the US presidential election postponed due to problems with the Florida count
- Sir Malcolm Bradbury dies
  Barbara Cartland dies
  Alex Comfort dies
  Penelope Fitzgerald dies
  Patrick O'Brian dies
  Anthony Powell dies
  Sir Steven Runciman dies
  R.S. Thomas dies
- Sir John Gielgud dies
  Sir Alec Guinness dies
- Ring Lardner dies
  Charles Schultz, cartoonist, dies
- Margaret Atwood wins the Booker Prize for *The Blind Assassin*
- *Gladiator*

Peter Ackroyd (1949)
London F

Fleur Adcock (1934)
Poems 1960–2000 V

Martin Amis (1949)
Experience NF
Memoirs of Amis and his father

Kate Atkinson (1951)
Emotionally Weird F

J.G. Ballard (1930)
Super-Cannes F

Iain Banks (1954)
Look to Windward F

John Banville (1945)
Eclipse F

Julian Barnes (1946)
Love Etc F

Maeve Binchy (1940)
Scarlet Feather F

Anita Brookner (1928)
The Bay of Angels F

A.S. Byatt (1936)
The Biographer's Tale F

Anita Desai (1937)
Diamond Dust, and Other Stories F

Dorothy Dunnett (1923–2001)
Gemini F
Last of 'The House of Niccolò' series

U.A. Fanthorpe (1929)
Consequences V

Jane Gardam (1928)
The Flight of the Maidens F

Alasdair Gray (1934)
The Book of Prefaces ANTH

Thom Gunn (1929–2004)
Boss Cupid V

David Hare (1947)
My Zinc Bed D
Performed 14 September 2000

Sarah Kane (1971–99)
4:48 Psychosis D
Performed June 2000

'John le Carré' [**David John Moore Cornwell** (1931)]
The Constant Gardener F

Doris Lessing (1919)
The Old Age of El Magnifico F

Patrick McCabe (1955)
Emerald Germs of Ireland F

Jamie McKendrick (1955)
Sky Nails V

Glyn Maxwell (1962)
The Boys at Twilight V

Michael Moorcock (1939)
King of the City F

Harold Pinter (1930)
Celebration D
Performed 16 March 2000

Harold Pinter (1930)
Collected Screenplays D

Harold Pinter (1930)
Remembrance of Things Past D
Performed 23 November 2000

Terry Pratchett (1948)
The Truth F

Philip Pullman (1946)
The Amber Spyglass F
His Dark Materials trilogy iii. See also *Northern Lights* 1995, *The Subtle Knife* 1998.

Craig Raine (1944)
A la Recherche du Temps Perdu V

Ian Rankin (1960)
Set in Darkness F

Peter Reading (1946)
Marfan V

Ruth Rendell (1930)
Piranha to Scurfy, and Others F
Stories

Michèle Roberts (1949)
The Looking Glass F

J.K. Rowling (1965)
Harry Potter and the Goblet of Fire F
Published in July 2000

Lorna Sage (1943–2001)
Bad Blood

Jo Shapcott (1953)
Her Book V

Zadie Smith (1975)
White Teeth F

Muriel Spark (1918)
Aiding and Abetting F
Fictionalized account of the Lord Lucan affair

Paul Theroux (1941)
Fresh-Air Fiend NF

'William Trevor' [William Trevor Cox (1928)]
The Hill Bachelors F

Joanna Trollope (1943)
Marrying the Mistress F

Minette Walters (1949)
The Shape of Snakes F

Keith Waterhouse (1929)
Soho F

Fay Weldon (1931)
Rhode Island Blues F

Jeanette Winterson (1959)
The.PowerBook F

2001

- George W. Bush becomes President of the USA
  The Taliban destroy giant statues of the Buddha at Bamiyan in Afghanistan
  Slobodan Milosevic arrested for war crimes
  The Labour Party under Tony Blair wins a second term
  Race riots in Bradford
  Terrorist attacks on the World Trade Center in New York (11 Sept.)
  Anthrax attacks begin in the US
  US and British forces launch air attacks on Afghanistan (7 Oct.)
  Kabul liberated (Nov.)
  The US Enron Corporation files for bankruptcy (Dec.)
- Douglas Adams dies
  Dorothy Dunnett dies
  Sir Ernst Gombrich dies
  Adrian Henri dies
  Elizabeth Jennings dies
  R.K. Narayan dies
  Simon Raven dies
  Anne Ridler dies
  Lorna Sage dies
  Sir Richard Southern dies
  Kathleen Tillotson dies
  Auberon Waugh dies
- W.G. Sebald dies
- Peter Carey wins the Booker Prize for *True History of the Kelly Gang*
  V.S. Naipaul wins the Nobel Prize for Literature
- *The Lord of the Rings* (film version, pt i)
  Harry Potter and the Philosopher's/Sorcerer's Stone (film version)

Brian Aldiss (1925)
The Cretan Teat F

Martin Amis (1949)
The War Against Clich NF

Simon Armitage (1963)
Little Green Man F

Beryl Bainbridge (1934)
According to Queeney F

J.G. Ballard (1930)
Complete Short Stories F

Pat Barker (1943)
Border Crossing F

Nina Bawden (1925)
The Ruffian on the Stair F

Alan Bennett (1934)
The Laying On of Hands F

Eavan Boland (1944)
Code V

Dermot Bolger (1959)
The Valparaiso Voyage F

Charles Boyle (1951)
The Age of Cardboard and String V

Melvyn Bragg (1939)
A Son of War F

A.S. Byatt (1936)
On Histories and Stories NF

Jonathan Coe (1961)
The Rotters' Club F

Catherine Cookson (1906–98)
Silent Lady F

Wendy Cope (1945) (ed.)
Heaven on Earth: 101 Happy Poems V

Wendy Cope (1945)
If I Don't Know V

Jim Crace (1946)
The Devil's Larder F

Louis de Bernières (1954)
Red Dog F

Margaret Drabble (1939)
The Peppered Moth F

Helen Dunmore (1952)
Out of the Blue: Poems, 1975–2001 V

Helen Dunmore (1952)
The Siege F

D.J. Enright (1920–2002)
Signs and Wonders: Selected essays NF

Sebastian Faulks (1953)
On Green Dolphin Street F

Elaine Feinstein (1930)
Dark Inheritance F

Frederick Forsyth (1938)
The Veteran F

Lavinia Greenlaw (1962)
Mary George of Allnorthover F

Niall Griffiths (1966)
Sheepshagger F

Seamus Heaney (1939)
Electric Light V

Geoffrey Hill (1932)
Speech! Speech! V

Selima Hill (1945)
Bunny V

Tobias Hill (1970)
The Love of Stones F

Nick Hornby (1957)
How to be Good F

Susan Howatch (1940)
The High Flyer F

P.D. James (1920)
Death in Holy Orders F

Elizabeth Jennings (1926–2001)
Timely Issues V

Alan Judd (1946)
Legacy F

Hanif Kureishi (1954)
Gabriel's Gift F

Philip Larkin (1922–85)
Further Requirements NF

Doris Lessing (1919)
The Sweetest Dream F

David Lodge (1935)
Thinks . . . F

Bernard MacLaverty (1942)
The Anatomy School F

Ian McEwan (1948)
Atonement F

Allan Massie (1938)
The Evening of the World F

Andrew Miller (1960)
Oxygen F

Magnus Mills (1954)
Three to See the King F

David Mitchell (1969)
Number9dream F

Deborah Moggach (1948)
Final Demand F

Michael Moorcock (1939)
London Bone F
Stories

John Mortimer (1923)
Rumpole Rests His Case F

Andrew Motion (1952)
Here to Eternity V

Paul Muldoon (1951)
Vera of Las Vegas V

V.S. Naipaul (1932)
Half a Life F

Patrick Neate
Twelve Bar Blues F

Sean O' Brien (1952)
Downriver V

Tony Parsons (1953)
One for my Baby F

Peter Porter (1929)
Max is Missing V

Terry Pratchett (1948)
The Last Hero F

Terry Pratchett (1948)
Thief of Time F

Craig Raine (1944)
Collected Poems 1978–1999 V

Ian Rankin (1960)
The Falls F

Piers Paul Read (1941)
Alice in Exile F

Peter Reading (1946)
[untitled] V

Michèle Roberts (1949)
Playing Sardines F
Stories

Bernice Rubens (1928–2004)
Milwaukee F

Salman Rushdie (1947)
Fury F

Lorna Sage (1943–2001)
Moments of Truth: 12 essays on 20th-century writers NF

Rachel Seiffert (1971)
The Dark Room F

Will Self (1961)
Feeding Frenzy NF

Will Self (1961)
Junk Mail NF

Will Self (1961)
Sore Sites NF

Jo Shapcott (1953)
Tender Taxes V

Alan Sillitoe (1928)
Birthday F

Ali Smith (1962)
Hotel World F

Muriel Spark (1918)
Complete Short Stories F

Paul Theroux (1941)
Hotel Honolulu NF

'William Trevor' [William Trevor Cox (1928)]
Nights at the Alexandra F

Minette Walters (1949)
Acid Row F

Marina Warner (1946)
The Leto Bundle F

Fay Weldon (1931)
The Bulgari Connection F

Irvine Welsh (1957)
Glue F

Benjamin Zephaniah (1958)
Too Black, Too Strong V

2002

- Trial of Slobodan Milosevic opens in The Hague (12 Feb.)
  British Government publishes dossier on Iraq's weapons of mass destruction (24 September)
  Terrorist bomb in Bali (12 Oct.)
  Chechen rebels take 763 hostages in a Moscow theatre (23 Oct.)
  UN arms inspectors return to Iraq (Nov.)
- A.L. Barker dies
  'William Cooper' (Harry Summerfield Hoff) dies
  D.J. Enright dies
  Elizabeth Pakenham, Countess of Longford, dies
  Mary Wesley dies

- Queen Elizabeth the Queen Mother dies
  John Entwistle (The Who) dies
  Professor Roy Porter dies
  John Thaw dies
- Stephen Jay Gould dies
  Billy Wilder dies
- Jan Martel wins the Man Booker Prize for *Life of Pi*
  Richard Russo wins Pulitzer Prize for Fiction for *Empire Falls*
- *Harry Potter and the Chamber of Secrets*
  Lord of the Rings: The Two Towers
  Gangs of New York
- Coldplay: *A Rush of Blood to the Head*

Dannie Abse (1923)
The Strange Case of Dr Simmonds and Dr Glas F

Peter Ackroyd (1949)
Albion: The Origins of the English Imagination NF

Douglas Adams (1952–2001)
The Salmon of Doubt F

Brian Aldiss (1925)
Super-State: A Novel of a Future Europe F

Moniza Alvi (1954)
Souls V

Simon Armitage (1963)
The Universal Home Doctor V

Kate Atkinson (1951)
Not the End of the World F

Alan Ayckbourn (1939)
The Crafty Art of Playmaking NF

Iain Banks (1954)
Dead Air F

John Banville (1945)
Shroud F

A.L. Barker (1918–2002)
Submerged F
Introduction by Jane Gardam

Nicola Barker (1966)
Behindlings F

William Boyd (1952)
Any Human Heart F

Anita Brookner (1928)
The Next Big Thing F

A.S. Byatt (1936)
A Whistling Woman F

Justin Cartwright (1943)
White Lightning F

David Constantine (1944)
Something for the Ghosts V

Jenny Diski (1947)
Stranger on a Train NF

Margaret Drabble (1939)
The Seven Sisters F

Carol Ann Duffy (1955)
Feminine Gospels V

Roddy Doyle (1958)
Rory & Ita NF

Michel Faber
The Crimson Petal and the White F

U.A. Fanthorpe (1929)
Christmas Poems V

Paul Farley (1965)
The Ice Age V

Michael Frayn (1933)
Spies F

Maggie Gee (1948)
The White Family F

Niall Griffiths (1966)
Kelly & Victor F

Seamus Heaney (1939)
Finders Keepers: Selected Prose, 1971–2001 NF

Philip Hensher (1965)
The Mulberry Empire; or, The Two Virtuous Journeys of the Amir Dost Mohammed Khan F

Howard Jacobson (1942)
Who's Sorry Now? F

Kathleen Jamie (1962)
Mr and Mrs Scotland Are Dead: Poems 1980–1994 V

Elizabeth Jennings (1926–2001)
New Collected Poems V

James Kelman (1946)
'And the Judges Said': Essays NF

A.L. Kennedy (1965)
Indelible Acts F

Hari Kunzru (1969)
The Impressionist F

Hanif Kureishi (1954)
The Body; and Seven Stories F

Hanif Kureishi (1954)
Dreaming and Scheming NF

Philip Larkin (1922–85)
Trouble at Willow Gables, and Other Fictions F

Toby Litt (1968)
Exhibitionism F

David Lodge (1935)
Consciousness and the Novel NF

Tim Lott (1956)
Rumours of a Hurricane F

Glyn Maxwell (1962)
The Nerve V

Blake Morrison (1950)
Things My Mother Never Told Me NF

Andrew Motion (1952)
Public Property V

Tom Paulin (1949)
The Invasion Handbook V

Paul Muldoon (1951)
Moy Sand and Gravel V

Sean O' Brien (1952)
Cousin Coat: Selected Poems 1976–2001 V

Alice Oswald (1966)
Dart V

Ian Rankin (1960)
Beggar's Banquet F

Peter Reading (1946)
Faunal V

'Barbara Vine' [Ruth Rendell (1930)**]**
The Blood Doctor F

Bernice Rubens (1928)
Nine Lives F

Will Self (1961)
Dorian: An Imitation F

Henry Shukman (1962)
In Dr No's Garden V

Zadie Smith (1975)
The Autograph Man F

Colm Tóibín (1955)
Lady Gregory's Toothbrush NF

Colm Tóibín (1955)
Love in a Dark Time: Gay Lives from Wilde to Almodóvar NF

Claire Tomalin (1933)
Pepys: The Unequalled Self NF

Colin Thubron (1939)
To the Last City F

William Trevor (1928)
The Story of Lucy Gault F

Minette Walters (1949)
Fox Evil F

Alan Warner (1964)
The Man Who Walks F

Marina Warner (1946)
Murderers I Have Known and Other Stories F

Sarah Waters (1966)
Fingersmith F

Fay Weldon (1931)
Auto da Fay NF
Autobiography

Fay Weldon (1931)
Nothing to Wear and Nowhere to Hide: Stories F

Irvine Welsh (1957)
Porno F

Louise Welsh (1965)
The Cutting Room F

A.N. Wilson (1950)
Victorians NF

2003

- Space shuttle *Columbia* explodes killing all seven astronauts (1 Feb.)
  USA and UK launch war on Iraq (19 Mar.)
  Andrew Gilligan's report on the *Today* programme concerning the reliability of the UK Government's September 2002 dossier on Iraq's weapons of mass destruction
  Baghdad falls to US troops (9 Apr.)
  Death of UK weapons expert Dr David Kelly (18 July)
  Hutton Inquiry on death of Dr David Kelly opens (1 Aug.)
  Suicide bombing destroys UN headquarters in Baghdad (19 Aug.)

Saddam Hussein captured by US troops (13 Dec.)

- Charles Causley dies
  Nicholas Freeling dies
  Winston Graham dies
  Christopher Hill dies
  Norman Lewis dies
  Frank Templeton Prince dies
  Kathleen Raine dies
  Peter Redgrove dies
  C.H. Sisson dies
  Sir Wilfred Thesiger dies
- Maurice Gibb (the Bee Gees) dies
  Roy Jenkins dies
  Lady Diana Mosley dies
  Robert Palmer, rock singer, dies
  J.M. Roberts dies
  Sir Denis Thatcher dies
  John Terraine dies
  Hugh Trevor-Roper (Lord Dacre) dies
  Sir Bernard Williams dies
- Johnny Cash dies
  J. Paul Getty dies
  Katharine Hepburn dies
  Bob Hope dies
  Elia Kazan dies
  Gregory Peck dies
  Leni Riefenstahl dies
  Edward Said dies
  Carol Shields dies
- DBC Pierre wins Man Booker Prize for *Vernon God Little*
  Jefferey Eugenides wins Pulitzer Prize for Fiction for *Middlesex*
- Dan Brown, *The Da Vinci Code* published
- *The Lord of the Rings: The Return of the King*
  Master and Commander: The Far Side of the World

Peter Ackroyd (1949)
The Clerkenwell Tales F

Monica Ali (1967)
Brick Lane F

Martin Amis (1949)
Yellow Dog F

J.G. Ballard (1930)
Millennium People F

Nicola Barker (1966)
The Three Button Trick F

Pat Barker (1943)
Double Vision F

Tim Binding (1947)
Anthem F

Clare Boylan (1948)
Emma Brown F
Based on an unfinished MS by Charlotte Brontë

Melvyn Bragg (1939)
Crossing the Lines F

Anita Brookner (1928)
The Rules of Engagement F

Ciaran Carson (1948)
Breaking News V

Jim Crace (1946)
Six F

Rachel Cusk (1967)
The Lucky Ones F

Helen Dunmore (1952)
Mourning Ruby F

Douglas Dunn (1942)
New Selected Poems, 1964–2000 V

U.A. Fanthorpe (1929)
Queuing for the Sun V

Alison Fell (1944)
Tricks of the Light F

Helen Fielding (1958)
Olivia Joules and the Overactive Imagination F

Lavinia Greenlaw (1962)
Minsk V

Niall Griffiths (1966)
Stump F

Mark Haddon (1962)
The Curious Incident of the Dog in the Night-Time F

Tobias Hill (1970)
The Cryptographer F

Toby Litt (1968)
Finding Myself F

Tim Lott (1956)
The Love Secrets of Don Juan F

Patrick McCabe (1955)
Call Me the Breeze F

Jamie McKendrick (1955)
Ink Stone V

Hilary Mantel (1952)
Giving Up the Ghost: A Memoir NF

Magnus Mills (1954)
The Scheme for Full Employment F

Magnus Mills (1954)
Once in a Blue Moon F

Andrew Motion (1952)
The Invention of Dr Cake F

Patrick Neate
The London Pigeon Wars F

Bernard O'Donoghue (1945)
Outliving V

Andrew O'Hagan (1968)
Personality F

Tim Parks (1954)
Judge Savage F

Tim Parks (1954)
A Season in Verona NF

Don Paterson (1963)
Landing Light V

DBC Pierre (1961)
Vernon God Little F

Ian Rankin (1960)
A Question of Blood F

Peter Reading (1946)
Collected Poems 3: 1997–2003 V

Michèle Roberts (1949)
The Mistressclass F

J.K. Rowling (1965)
Harry Potter and the Order of the Phoenix F

Bernice Rubens (1928–2004)
The Sergeants' Tale F

Ali Smith (1962)
The Whole Story and Other Stories F

Jean Sprackland
Hard Water V

Graham Swift (1949)
The Light of Day F

Andrew Taylor (1951)
The American Boy F

Adam Thorpe (1956)
Nine Lessons from the Dark V

Barbara Trapido (1941)
Frankie & Stankie F

Rose Tremain (1943)
The Colour F

Minette Walters (1949)
Disordered Minds F

Author Index

Abbot, George (1562–1633)
archbishop of Canterbury
A Briefe Description of the Whole Worlde (1599)
A Treatise of the Perpetuall Visibilitie and Succession of the True Church in All Ages (1624)
Abbot, George (1604–49)
religious writer
The Whole Booke of Job Paraphrased (1640)
Abbot, John (1588?–1650)
poet
Jesus Praefigured; or, A Poëm of the Holy Name of Jesus in Five Bookes (1623)
À Beckett, Arthur William (1844–1909)
humorist
Fallen Among Thieves (1870)
À Beckett, Gilbert Abbott (1811–56)
humorist and dramatist
The Revolt of the Workhouse (1834)
The Comic Blackstone (1846)
The Comic History of England (1847)
A Comic History of Rome (1851)
À Beckett, Gilbert Arthur (1837–91)
journalist and dramatist
The Happy Land (1873)
Abercrombie, Lascelles (1881–1938)
poet, dramatist, and critic
Interludes and Poems (1908)
Speculative Dialogues (1913)
Abse, Dannie (1923–)
poet, novelist, and playwright
After Every Green Thing (1949)
Ash on a Young Man's Sleeve (1954)
Tenants of the House (1957)
Poems, Golders Green (1962)
Three Questor Plays (1967)
O Jones, O Jones (1970)
Funland, and Other Poems (1973)
A Poet in the Family (1974)
Way Out in the Centre (1981)
A Strong Dose of Myself (1983)
Ask the Bloody Horse (1986)
White Coat, Purple Coat (1989)
Remembrance of Crimes Past (1990)
There Was a Young Man From Cardiff (1991)
The Strange Case of Dr Simmonds and Dr Glas (2002)
Achelly, Thomas (*fl.* 1568–95)
poet and translator
A Most Lamentable and Tragicall Historie (1576)
Ackerley, Joseph Randolph (1896–1967)
dramatist and author
The Prisoners of War (1925)
My Dog Tulip (1956)
We Think the World of You (1960)
My Father and Myself (1968)
Ackland, Rodney (1908–91)
dramatist
Improper People (1930)
Ackroyd, Peter (1949–)
novelist, biographer, and poet
London Lickpenny (1973)
Notes for a New Culture (1976)
Country Life (1978)
Dressing Up: Transvestism and Drag (1979)
The Great Fire of London (1982)
The Last Testament of Oscar Wilde (1983)
T.S. Eliot (1984)
Hawksmoor (1985)
Chatterton (1987)
The Diversions of Purley, and Other Poems (1987)
First Light (1989)
Dickens (1990)
English Music (1992)
The House of Doctor Dee (1993)
Dan Leno and the Limehouse Golem (1994)
Blake (1995)
The Life of Thomas More (1998)
The Plato Papers (1999)
London (2000)
Albion (2002)
The Clerkenwell Tales (2003)
Acton, Eliza (1799–1859)
cookery writer
Modern Cookery, in all its Branches (1845)
Acton, Sir Harold Mario Mitchell (1904–94)
writer and aesthete
Aquarium (1923)
Peonies and Ponies (1941)
Memoirs of an Aesthete (1948)
More Memoirs of an Aesthete (1970)
Acton, John Emerich Edward Dalberg, 1st Baron Acton (1834–1902)
historian
The War of 1870 (1871)
A Lecture on the Study of History (1895)
Historical Essays and Studies (1907)
The History of Freedom, and Other Essays (1907)
Adams, Douglas (1952–2001)
novelist and scriptwriter
The Hitch-Hiker's Guide to the Galaxy (1979)
The Salmon of Doubt (2002)
Adams, Jane (1710–65)
Scottish poet

Miscellany Poems (1734)
Adams, Richard George (1920–)
novelist
Watership Down (1972)
Shardik (1974)
The Plague Dogs (1977)
The Girl in a Swing (1980)
Maia (1984)
Adams, Sarah Fuller, *née* Flower (1805–48)
poet and hymn-writer
Vivia Perpetua: A dramatic poem (1841)
Adams, Thomas (*c.*1583–*c.*1660)
Puritan divine
The Gallants Burden (1612)
The White Devil; or, The Hypocrite Uncased (1613)
The Divells Banket [i.e. Banquet] (1614)
A Divine Herball (1616)
The Workes of Thomas Adams (1629)
Adcock, Arthur St John (1864–1930)
critic and novelist
An Unfinished Martyrdom, and Other Stories (1894)
East End Idylls (1897)
In the Image of God (1898)
Adcock, [Kareen] Fleur (1934–)
New Zealand-born poet
Tigers (1967)
High Tide in the Garden (1971)
The Scenic Route (1974)
Below Loughrigg (1979)
The Inner Harbour (1979)
The Incident Book (1986)
Meeting the Comet (1988)
Time-Zones (1991)
Looking Back (1997)
Poems 1960–2000 (2000)
Adderley, James Granville (1861–1942)
clergyman and novelist
Stephen Remarx (1893)
Addison, Joseph (1672–1719)
poet, essayist, and statesman
A Poem to His Majesty (1695)
A Letter from Italy, to the Right Honourable Charles Lord Halifax (1703)
The Campaign (1704)
Remarks on Several Parts of Italy (1705)
Rosamund: An opera (1707)
The Present State of the War (1708)
The Whig Examiner (1710)
Cato: A tragedy (1713)
The Free-Holder; or, Political Essays (1715)
The Drummer; or, The Haunted House: A comedy (1716)
Poems on Several Occasions (1718)
The Resurrection (1718)
Maxims, Observations, and Reflections, Moral, Political, and Divine (1719)
Notes upon the Twelve Books of Paradise Lost (1719)
The Old Whig. Numb. I (1719)
The Old Whig. Numb. II (1719)
The Works of Joseph Addison (1721)
Miscellanies, in Verse and Prose (1725)
The Christian Poet: A miscellany of divine poems (1728)
The Evidences of the Christian Religion (1730)
A Discourse on Antient and Modern Learning (1734)
Adlington, William
translator
The Golden Asse (1566)
Adolphus, John Leycester (1795–1862)
barrister and author
Letters to Richard Heber (1821)
Letters from Spain in 1856 and 1857 (1858)
Agate, James Evershed (1877–1947)
journalist, drama critic, and novelist
Ego: The autobiography of Agate (1935)
Aguilar, Grace (1816–47)
novelist, poet and Jewish historian
Records of Israel (1844)
The Women of Israel; or, Characters and Sketches from the Holy Scripture (1845)
Home Influence (1847)
A Mother's Recompense (1850)
The Vale of Cedars; or, The Martyr (1850)
Woman's Friendship (1850)
Home Scenes and Heart Studies (1853)
Aickman, Robert Fordyce (1914–81)
supernatural fiction writer
Powers of Darkness (1966)
Aïdé, Charles Hamilton (1826–1906)
novelist, poet, and musician
Rita (1858)
Aiken, Joan Delano (1924–2004)
children's author and novelist
All You've Ever Wanted, and Other Stories (1953)
The Wolves of Willoughby Chase (1962)
Black Hearts in Battersea (1964)
Aikin, John (1747–1822)
physician and author
Poems (1791)
Aikin, Lucy (1781–1864)
poet, biographer, and children's author
Poetry for Children (1801)
Epistles on Women (1810)
Lorimer (1814)
Ainsworth, Henry (1569?–1623?)
leader of the Separatist congregation at Amsterdam
An Apologie or Defence of such True Christians as are Commonly (but unjustly) called Brownists (1604)
Annotations upon the Five Bookes of Moses, and the Booke of Psalmes (1622)
Ainsworth, William Harrison (1805–82)
novelist and editor
Rookwood (1834)
Crichton (1837)
Jack Sheppard (1839)
The Tower of London (1840)

Guy Fawkes; or, The Gunpowder Treason (1841)
Old Saint Paul's (1841)
Windsor Castle (1843)
Saint James's; or, The Court of Queen Anne (1844)
James the Second; or, The Revolution of 1688 (1848)
The Lancashire Witches (1849)
Auriol (1850)
The Life and Adventures of Mervyn Clitheroe (1858)
Ovingdean Grange (1860)
The Constable of the Tower (1861)
Myddleton Pomfret (1868)
Stanley Brereton (1881)

Aird, Thomas (1802–76)
Scottish poet
Murtzoufle: A tragedy (1826)
The Captive of Fez (1830)
Orthuriel, and Other Poems (1840)

Akenside, Mark (1721–70)
poet and physician
A British Philippic (1738)
The Pleasures of Imagination (1744)
An Epistle to Curio (1744)
Odes on Several Subjects (1745)
An Ode to the Earl of Huntingdon (1748)
An Ode to the Country Gentlemen of England (1758)
An Ode to the Late Thomas Edwards (1766)
The Poems of Mark Akenside (1772)

Alcock, Deborah (1835–1913)
Irish children's novelist
The Spanish Brothers (1870)

Alcock, Mary, *née* Cumberland (*c*.1742–98)
poet
The Air Balloon (1784)
Poems (1799)

Aldington, Richard [Edward Godfree Aldington] (1892–1962)
poet, critic, and novelist
Images 1910–15 (1915)
Images of Desire (1919)
Images of War (1919)
Death of a Hero (1929)
Complete Poems (1948)

Aldiss, Brian Wilson (1925–)
novelist and short-story writer
The Brightfount Diaries (1955)
Space, Time, and Nathaniel (1957)
The Saliva Tree, and Other Strange Growths (1966)
An Age (1967)
The Hand-Reared Boy (1970)
The Moment of Eclipse (1971)
A Soldier Erect (1971)
Billion Year Spree (1973)
Frankenstein Unbound (1974)
The Malacia Tapestry (1976)
Enemies of the System (1978)
A Rude Awakening (1978)
Moreau's Other Island (1980)
Helliconia Spring (1982)
Helliconia Summer (1983)
Helliconia Winter (1985)
Ruins (1987)
Forgotten Life (1988)
Bury My Heart at W.H. Smith's (1990)
Dracula Unbound (1991)
Remembrance Day (1993)
The Cretan Teat (2001)
Super-State (2002)

Alexander, Cecil Frances, *née* Humphreys, Mrs C.F. Alexander (1818–95)
poet and hymn-writer
The Baron's Little Daughter, and Other Tales in Prose and Verse (1848)
Hymns for Little Children (1848)
Moral Songs (1849)
Narrative Hymns for Village Schools (1853)
Hymns Descriptive and Devotional for the Use of Schools (1858)

Alexander, Sir William, earl of Stirling (1567?–1640)
poet
Darius (1603)
Aurora (1604)
The Monarchick Tragedies (1604)
A Paraenesis to the Prince (1604)
An Elegie on the Death of Prince Henrie (1612)
Doomes-day; or, The Great Day of the Lords Judgement (1614)
An Encouragement to Colonies (1624)
Recreations with the Muses (1637)

Alexander, William (1824–1911)
theologian and poet
St Augustine's Holiday, and Other Poems (1886)

Alexander, William (1826–94)
Scottish novelist
Johnny Gibb of Gushetneuk in the Parish of Pyketillim (1871)

Aleyn, Charles (*d.* 1640)
poet
The Battailes of Crescey, and Poctiers (1631)
The History of Henry the Seventh (1638)

Ali, Monica (1967)
novelist
Brick Lane (2003)

Alison, Archibald (1757–1839)
clergyman and author
Essays on the Nature and Principles of Taste (1790)

Allbeury, Ted [Theodore Edward Le Bouthillier Allbeury] ['Richard Butler', 'Patrick Kelly'] (1917–)
thriller writer
A Choice of Enemies (1973)

Alleine, Joseph (1634–68)
Nonconformist divine
An Alarme to Unconverted Sinners (1672)

Alleine, Theodosia (*fl.* 1671)
daughter of Richard Alleine, wife and memorialist of Joseph Alleine
The Life and Death of Joseph Alleine (1671)

Allen, [Charles] Grant Blairfindie ['J. Arbuthnot Wilson', 'Cecil Power', 'Olive Pratt Rayner'] (1848–99)
novelist and short-story writer
Philistia (1884)
For Mamie's Sake: A tale of love and dynamite (1886)
The British Barbarians: A hill-top novel (1895)
The Woman Who Did (1895)
The Type-Writer Girl (1897)

Allen, Walter Ernest (1911–95)
novelist and critic
Innocence is Drowned (1938)
The English Novel (1954)

Allen, William (1532–94)
cardinal
A Defense and Declaration of the Catholike Churchies [sic] *Doctrine, Touching Purgatory* (1565)
A Briefe Historie of the Glorious Martyrdom of XII Priests (1582)

Allestree, Richard (1619–81)
royalist divine
The Practice of Christian Graces; or, The Whole Duty of Man (1658)
The Gentlemans Calling (1660)
The Causes of the Decay of Christian Piety (1667)
Eighteen Sermons (1669)
The Ladies Calling (1673)
The Government of the Tongue (1674)
The Art of Contentment (1675)
The Lively Oracle Given to Us (1678)
Forty Sermons (1684)

Allingham, Margery Louise (1904–66)
crime writer
The Crime at Black Dudley (1929)
The Fashion in Shrouds (1938)
The Beckoning Lady (1955)

Allingham, William ['Giraldus', 'Patricius Walker'] (1824–89)
poet and anthologist
Poems (1850)
Day and Night Songs (1854)
The Music-Master (1855)
Laurence Bloomfield in Ireland (1864)
The Ballad Book (1864)
Songs, Ballads, and Stories (1877)
Evil May-Day (1882)
The Fairies (1883)
Rhymes for Young Folk (1887)
Flower Pieces, and Other Poems (1888)

Allott, Kenneth (1912–73)
poet
The Ventriloquist's Doll (1943)

Allott or Allot, Robert (*fl.* 1600)
editor
Wits Theater of the Little World (1599)
Englands Parnassus; or, The Choysest Flowers of our Moderne Poets, with their Poeticall Comparisons (1600)

Alvarez, Alfred (1929–)
critic, poet, and novelist
Poems (1952)
The End of It (1958)
The Shaping Spirit (1958)
The New Poetry (1962)
Autumn to Autumn and Selected Poems 1953–1976 (1978)

Alvi, Moniza (1954–)
Pakistan-born poet
The Country at my Shoulder (1993)
Souls (2002)

Ambler, Eric ['Eliot Reed'] (1909–98)
thriller writer
The Dark Frontier (1936)
Epitaph for a Spy (1938)
The Mask of Dimitrios (1939)
Journey into Fear (1940)
Passage of Arms (1959)

Ames, Joseph (1689–1759)
bibliographer and antiquary
Typographical Antiquities (1749)

Ames, Richard (*d.* 1693)
poet
Sylvia's Revenge; or, A Satyr Against Man (1688)
The Female Fire-Ships: A satyr against whoring (1691)
Islington-Wells; or, The Threepenny-academy (1691)
The Double Descent (1692)
The Jacobite Coventicle (1692)
Sylvia's Complaint, of Her Sexes Unhappiness (1692)
Fatal Friendship; or, The Drunkards Misery (1693)

Ames, William (1576–1633)
Puritan divine
The Marrow of Sacred Divinity (1642)
The Workes of the Reverend and Faithfull Minister of Christ William Ames (1643)

Amhurst, Nicholas ['Caleb D'Anvers'] (1697–1742)
poet and political writer
Protestant Popery; or, The Convocation (1718)
A Collection of Poems on Several Occasions (1731)

Amis, Sir Kingsley William ['Robert Markham'] (1922–95)
novelist, poet, and short-story writer
Bright November (1947)
Lucky Jim (1953)
That Uncertain Feeling (1955)
I Like it Here (1958)
Take a Girl Like You (1960)
One Fat Englishman (1963)
The Anti-Death League (1966)
A Look Round the Estate (1967)
I Want it Now (1968)
The Green Man (1969)

Girl, 20 (1971)
The Riverside Villas Murder (1973)
Ending Up (1974)
The Alteration (1976)
Jake's Thing (1978)
Collected Poems 1944–1979 (1979)
Collected Short Stories (1980)
Russian Hide-and-Seek (1980)
Stanley and the Women (1984)
The Old Devils (1986)
Difficulties With Girls (1988)
The Folks That Live on the Hill (1990)
Memoirs (1990)
The Russian Girl (1992)
Mr Barrett's Secret, and Other Stories (1993)
You Can't Do Both (1994)
The Biographer's Moustache (1995)

Amis, Martin Louis (1949–)
novelist
The Rachel Papers (1973)
Dead Babies (1975)
Success (1978)
Other People (1981)
Money (1984)
The Moronic Inferno, and Other Visits to America (1986)
Einstein's Monsters (1987)
London Fields (1989)
Time's Arrow (1991)
Visiting Mrs Nabokov (1993)
The Information (1995)
Night Train (1997)
Heavy Water, and Other Stories (1998)
Experience (2000)
The War Against Cliché (2001)
Yellow Dog (2003)

Amory, Thomas (1691?–1788)
author
Memoirs: Containing the Lives of Several Ladies of Great Britain (1755)
The Life of John Buncle, Esq. (1756)
Danish Fairy Legends and Tales (1846)

Anderson, Alexander ['Surfaceman'] (1845–1909)
Scottish poet
A Song of Labour, and Other Poems (1873)

Anderson, Robert (1750–1830)
editor and biographer
A Complete Edition of the Poets of Great Britain (1792)

Anderson, Robert (1770–1833)
Cumbrian poet
Poems on Various Subjects (1798)
Ballads in the Cumberland Dialect (1805)

Andrewes or Andrews, John (*fl.* 1615)
poet
The Anatomie of Basenesse; or, The Foure Quarters of a Knave (1615)

Andrewes, Lancelot (1555–1626)
prelate and scholar
The Wonderfull Combate (for Gods Glorie and Mans Salvation) Betweene Christ and Satan (1592)
Scala Coeli (1611)
XCVI Sermons (1629)
Institutiones Piae; or, Directions to Pray (1630)
A Patterne of Catechisticall Doctrine (1630)
The Morall Law Expounded (1642)
Of Episcopacy (1647)
The Private Devotions [Preces Privatae] (1647)
A Manual of the Private Devotions of the Right Reverend Father in God, Lancelot Andrews (1648)

Andrews, Miles Peter ['Arley'] (*d.* 1814)
dramatist
The Election (1774)
Dissipation: A comedy (1781)

Andrews, Robert (1723–66)
poet and translator of Virgil
Eidyllia; or, Miscellaneous Poems (1757)

Angell, Sir [Ralph] Norman (1872–1967)
newspaper editor, MP, and publicist
The Great Illusion (1910)

Anger, Jane (*fl.* 1589)
author
Jane Anger Her Protection for Women (1589)

Anslay, Brian (*fl.* 1521)
yeoman of the wine cellar to Henry VIII and translator
The City of Ladies (1521)

Anson, Sir George, Baron Anson (1697–1762)
circumnavigator
A Voyage Round the World (1748)

Anstey, Christopher (1724–1805)
poet and satirist
The New Bath Guide; or, Memoirs of the B[lunde]R[hea]D Family in a Series of Poetical Epistles (1766)
Contentment; or, Hints to Servants on the Present Scarcity (1800)
The Poetical Works of the Late Christopher Anstey (1808)

'Anstey, F.' [Thomas Anstey Guthrie] (1856–1934)
novelist and humorist
Vice Versa; or, A Lesson to Fathers (1882)
Voces Populi [1st ser.] (1890)
Mr Punch's Pocket Ibsen (1893)
The Brass Bottle (1900)
In Brief Authority (1915)

'Anthony, Evelyn' [Evelyn Bridget Patricia Ward-Thomas] (1928–)
novelist
Imperial Highness (1953)
The Assassin (1970)

Apperley, Charles James ['Nimrod'] (1779–1843)
sporting writer
Memoirs of the Life of John Mytton (1835)
Nimrod's Hunting Tours (1835)
Nimrod's Northern Tour (1838)

[Appleby], Simon, the Anker of London Wall
The Fruyte of Redempcyon (1514)
Arbuthnot, John (1667–1735)
medical writer, essayist, dramatist, and miscellaneous writer
'The History of John Bull' (1712)
A Continuation of the History of the Crown-Inn (1714)
A Postscript to John Bull (1714)
Gnothi Seauton: Know Yourself (1734)
Miscellanies (1746)
Miscellaneous Works of the Late Dr Arbuthnot (1751)
Archer, William (1856–1924)
dramatic critic and journalist
English Dramatists of Today (1882)
Masks or Faces? A study in the psychology of acting (1888)
Ibsen's Prose Dramas (1890)
Play-Making (1912)
Arden, John (1930–)
playwright and novelist
Serjeant Musgrave's Dance: An unhistorical parable (1960)
Three Plays (1964)
The Workhouse Donkey (1964)
The Non-Stop Connolly Show (1977)
The Non-Stop Connolly Show (1978)
'Arlen, Michael' [Dikran Kouyoumdjian] (1895–1956)
novelist and short-story writer
The London Venture (1920)
These Charming People (1923)
The Green Hat (1924)
May Fair (1925)
Armin, Robert ['C. de C. Snuffe'] (1565?–1610)
actor and dramatist
Foole upon Foole; or, Six Sortes of Sottes (1600)
Quips upon Questions; or, A Clownes Conceite on Occasion Offered (1600)
A Nest of Ninnies (1608)
The Italian Taylor, and his Boy (1609)
The Two Maids of More-clacke (1609)
Armitage, Robert (1805–52)
novelist
Doctor Hookwell; or, The Anglo-Catholic Family (1842)
Armitage, Simon (1963–)
poet
Zoom! (1989)
Kid (1992)
Xanadu (1992)
Book of Matches (1993)
CloudCuckooLand (1997)
Little Green Man (2001)
The Universal Home Doctor (2002)
Armstrong, John ['Launcelot Temple'] (1709–79)
physician and poet
The Oeconomy of Love (1736)
The Art of Preserving Health (1744)
Taste: An epistle to a young critic (1753)
Sketches; or, Essays on Various Subjects (1758)
A Day: An epistle to John Wilkes (1761)
Miscellanies (1770)
Arnim-Schlagenthin, Mary Annette Gräfin von, later Countess Russell, *née* Beauchamp ['Elizabeth'] (1866–1941)
New Zealand-born novelist
Elizabeth and her German Garden (1898)
Arnold, Cornelius (1711–57)
poet and dramatist
Poems on Several Occasions (1757)
Arnold, Sir Edwin (1832–1904)
poet and translator
The Light of Asia; or, The Great Renunciation (1879)
With Sa'di in the Garden; or, The Book of Love (1888)
The Light of the World; or, The Great Consummation (1891)
Arnold, Edwin Lester Linden (1857–1935)
novelist
The Wonderful Adventures of Phra the Phonecian (1890)
Arnold, Matthew (1822–88)
poet and critic
Alaric at Rome (1840)
The Strayed Reveller, and Other Poems (1849)
Empedocles on Etna, and Other Poems (1852)
Poems: a New Edition (1853)
Poems: Second Series (1855)
Merope (1858)
On Translating Homer (1861)
On Translating Homer: Last Words (1862)
Essays in Criticism [1st ser.] (1865)
New Poems (1867)
On the Study of Celtic Literature (1867)
Culture and Anarchy (1869)
St Paul and Protestantism (1870)
Literature and Dogma (1873)
God and the Bible (1875)
Last Essays on Church and Religion (1877)
Mixed Essays (1879)
Discourses in America (1885)
Essays in Criticism [2nd ser.] (1888)
Essays in Criticism: Third Series (1910)
Arnold, Richard (*d.* 1521?)
chronicler
Arnold's Chronicle (1503?)
Arnold, Dr Thomas (1795–1842)
schoolmaster, religious writer, and historian
Sermons (1829)
Arnold, William Delafield ['Punjabee'] (1828–59)
Anglo-Indian official and novelist
Oakfield; or, Fellowship in the East (1853)
Arwaker, Edmund, the younger (*c.*1655–1730)
poet
The Vision (1685)

The Second Part of The Vision, a Pindarick Ode (1685)
Pia Desideria; or, Divine Addresses (1686)
An Epistle to Monsieur Boileau (1694)
An Embassy from Heav'n; or, The Ghost of Queen Mary (1704)
Truth in Fiction; or, Morality in Masquerade (1708)

Ascham, Roger (1515–68)
author
Toxophilus (1545)
The Scholemaster; or, Plaine and Perfite Way of Teachying Children, to Understand, Write, and Speake, the Latin Tong (1570)

Ash, John (1724?–79)
lexicographer
Grammatical Institutes (1763)

Ashford, Daisy [Margaret Mary Julia, later Mrs James Devlin] (1881–1972)
child author
The Young Visiters (1919)

Ashmole, Elias (1617–92)
antiquary
Theatrum Chemicum Britannicum (1652)
Sol in Ascendente; or, The Glorious Appearance of Charles the Second, upon the Horizon of London, in her Horoscopicall Sign, Gemini (1660)
The Institution, Laws and Ceremonies of the Most Noble Order of the Garter (1672)
Memoirs of the Life of Elias Ashmole, Drawn up by Himself by Way of a Diary (1717)

Ashmore, John (*fl.* 1621)
poet and translator
Certain Selected Odes of Horace, Englished; and their Arguments Annexed (1621)

Ashworth, Andrea (1969–)
academic and author
Once in a House on Fire (1998)

Askew, Anne (c.1521–46)
Protestant martyr
The First Examination (1546)
The Later Examination (1547)

Astell, Mary (1666–1731)
feminist and polemicist
A Serious Proposal to the Ladies (1694)
A Serious Proposal to the Ladies, Part II (1697)
Some Reflections upon Marriage (1700)
A Fair Way with Dissenters and their Patrons (1704)
An Impartial Enquiry into the Causes of Rebellion and Civil War in this Kingdom (1704)
The Christian Religion as Profess'd by a Daughter of the Church (1705)
Bart'lemy Fair; or, An Inquiry After Wit (1709)

Astle, Thomas (1735–1803)
bibliographer and palaeographer
The Origin and Progress of Writing (1784)

Atherstone, Edwin (1788–1872)
poet
The Last Days of Herculaneum (1821)
A Midsummer Day's Dream (1824)
The Fall of Nineveh (1828)
The Sea-Kings in England (1830)
The Fall of Nineveh (1847)

Atkinson, Kate (1951–)
novelist and playwright
Behind the Scenes at the Museum (1995)
Human Croquet (1997)
Emotionally Weird (2000)
Not the End of the World (2002)

Atkinson, William (*d.* 1509)
translator of Thomas à Kempis
Imitation of Christ (1503)

Atterbury, Francis (1662–1732)
divine
A Discourse Occasion'd by the Death of the Right Honourable the Lady Cutts (1698)
Fourteen Sermons Preach'd on Several Occasions (1708)
The Mitre and the Crown; or, A Real Distinction Between Them (1711)
Sermons on Several Occasions (1734)

Aubin, Penelope (c.1685–1731)
novelist
The Life of Madam de Beaumont (1721)
The Strange Adventures of the Count de Vinevil and his Family (1721)
The Life and Amorous Adventures of Lucinda, an English Lady (1722)
The Noble Slaves; or, The Lives and Adventures of Two Lords and Two Ladies (1722)
The Life of Charlotta du Pont, an English Lady (1723)
The Life and Adventures of the Lady Lucy (1726)
The Life and Adventures of the Young Count Albertus (1728)
A Collection of Entertaining Histories and Novels (1739)

Aubrey, John (1626–97)
antiquary
Miscellanies (1696)
Lives of Eminent Men (1813)

Auden, Wystan Hugh (1907–73)
poet, playwright, and critic
Poems (1930)
The Orators: An English study (1932)
Poems: Second Edition (1933)
The Dance of Death (1933)
The Dog Beneath the Skin; or, Where is Francis? (1935)
The Ascent of F6 (1936)
Look, Stranger! (1936)
Spain (1937)
Letters From Iceland (1937)
On the Frontier: A melodrama (1938)
Journey to a War (1939)
Some Poems (1940)
Another Time (1940)

New Year Letter (1941)
For the Time Being (1945)
The Age of Anxiety (1948)
Collected Shorter Poems 1930–44 (1950)
The Enchafèd Flood; or, The Romantic Iconography of the Sea (1951)
The Rake's Progress (1951)
Nones (1952)
Mountains (1954)
The Shield of Achilles (1955)
Homage to Clio (1960)
The Dyer's Hand, and Other Essays (1963)
About the House (1966)
Collected Shorter Poems 1927–57 (1966)
Collected Longer Poems (1968)
Secondary Worlds (1968)
Selected Poems (1968)
City Without Walls (1969)
Prose 1926–38, Essays and Reviews, and Travel Books in Prose and Verse (1997)

Austen, Jane (1775–1817)
novelist
Sense and Sensibility (1811)
Pride and Prejudice (1813)
Mansfield Park (1814)
Emma (1815)
Northanger Abbey; and Persuasion (1817)
Love & Freindship [sic] *and Other Early Works* (1922)
Lady Susan (1925)
Sanditon (1925)

Austen-Leigh, James Edward (1798–1874)
biographer of Jane Austen
A Memoir of Jane Austen (1869)
A Memoir of Jane Austen (1871)

Austin, Alfred (1835–1913)
poet, novelist, and Poet Laureate
The Poetry of the Period (1870)
Interludes (1872)
The Tower of Babel (1874)
At the Gate of the Convent, and Other Poems (1885)
Lyrical Poems (1891)
The Garden That I Love (1894)
The Conversion of Winckelmann, and Other Poems (1897)
Lamia's Winter-Quarters (1898)
Songs of England (1898)
A Tale of True Love, and Other Poems (1902)

Austin, William (1587–1634)
barrister, poet, and miscellaneous author
Haec Homo: Wherein the excellency of the creation of woman is described (1637)

Averell, William (*fl.* 1584)
author
A Dyall for Dainty Darlings, Rockt in the Cradle of Securitie (1584)

Awdely or Awdlay, John (*fl.* 1559–77)
printer and miscellaneous author
The Wonders of England (1559)
The Fraternitie of Vacabondes (1565)

Ayckbourn, Alan (1939–)
playwright and children's author
Relatively Speaking: A comedy (1968)
How the Other Half Loves (1972)
The Norman Conquests: Table Manners; Living Together; Round and Round the Garden (1975)
Joking Apart; Ten Times Table; Just Between Ourselves (1979)
A Chorus of Disapproval (1986)
The Revenger's Comedies (1991)
Wildest Dreams (1994)
The Crafty Art of Playmaking (2002)

Aylet or Aylett, Robert (1583–1655?)
poet
Peace with Her Foure Garders: Five morall meditations (1622)
Thrifts Equipage: Five divine and morall meditations (1622)
Joseph; or, Pharoah's Favourite (1623)
Divine, and Moral Speculations in Metrical Numbers, Upon Various Subjects (1654)

Aylmer, John (1521–94)
bishop of London
An Harborowe for Faithfull and Trewe Subjectes, Agaynst the Late Blowne Blaste, Concerninge the Government of Wemen (1559)

Ayres, Philip (1638–1712)
poet and miscellaneous author
The Count of Gabalis; or, The Extravagant Mysteries of the Cabalists (1680)
Emblems of Love (1683)
Lyric Poems: Made in imitation of the Italians (1687)
Mythologia Ethica; or, Three Centuries of Aesopian Fables, in English Prose (1689)
The Revengeful Mistress (1696)

Aytoun, William Edmonstoune ['T. Percy Jones', 'Bon Gaultier'] (1813–65)
poet, parodist, and novelist
Poland, Homer, and Other Poems (1832)
The Book of Ballads (1845)
Lays of the Scottish Cavaliers, and Other Poems (1849)
Firmilian; or, The Student of Badajoz (1854)

Babbage, Charles (1792–1871)
mathematician
On the Economy of Machinery and Manufactures (1832)
The Exposition of 1851 (1851)

Bacon, Anne, Lady Bacon, *née* Cooke (1528–1610)
translator
An Apologie or Answere in Defence of the Churche of Englande (1564)

Bacon, Francis, first Baron Verulam, Viscount St Albans (1561–1626)
statesman and philosopher
Essayes (1597)

A Declaration of the Practises & Treasons Attempted and Committed by Robert Late Earle of Essex and his Complices (1601)
A Briefe Discourse, Touching the Happie Union of the Kingdomes of England, and Scotland (1603)
Apologie (1604)
Certaine Considerations Touching the Better Pacification and Edification of the Church of England (1604)
The Advancement of Learning, Divine and Humane (1605)
Essayes (1612)
The Wisedome of the Ancients (1619)
Novum Organum (1620)
The Historie of the Raigne of King Henry the Seventh (1622)
De Dignitate & Augmentis Scientiarum (1623)
Apophthegmes New and Old (1625)
The Essayes or Counsels, Civill and Morall (1625)
The Translation of Certaine Psalmes into English Verse (1625)
Sylva Sylvarum; or, A Naturall Historie (1627)
Certaine Miscellany Works (1629)
The Elements of the Common Lawes of England (1630)
The Historie of Life and Death: With observations naturall and experimentall for the prolonging of life (1638)
Of the Advancement and Proficiencie of Learning or the Partitions of Sciences (1640)
Three Speeches: Concerning the post-nati, naturalization of the Scotch in England, Union of the lawes of the kingdomes of England and Scotland (1641)
The Remaines of the Right Honorable Francis Lord Verulam Viscount of St Albanes (1648)
The Felicity of Queen Elizabeth: and Her Times (1651)
Resuscitatio (1657)
The Second Part of the Resuscitatio (1670)
Baconiana (1679)

Bacon, Phanuel (1700–83)
clergyman, poet, and dramatist
The Kite: An heroi-comical poem (1722)

Bage, Robert (1728–1801)
novelist
Mount Henneth (1781)
Barham Downs (1784)
The Fair Syrian (1787)
James Wallace (1788)
Man as He Is (1792)
Hermsprong; or, Man as He is Not (1796)

Bagehot, Walter (1826–77)
economist, historian, and critic
Estimates of Some Englishmen and Scotchmen (1858)
Parliamentary Reform (1859)
The History of the Unreformed Parliament and its Lessons (1860)
Count Your Enemies and Economise Your Expenditure (1862)
The English Constitution (1867)
Physics and Politics (1872)
Literary Studies (1879)
Economic Studies (1880)
Biographical Studies (1881)

Bagnold, Enid Algerine, Lady Jones (1889–1981)
dramatist and novelist
A Diary Without Dates (1918)
'National Velvet' (1935)

Bailey, Henry Christopher (1878–1961)
novelist
My Lady of Orange (1901)
Call Mr Fortune (1920)
Mr Fortune Objects (1935)

Bailey, Hilary (1936–)
novelist, short-story writer, and critic
Polly Put the Kettle On (1975)
All the Days of My Life (1984)
As Time Goes By (1988)

Bailey, Nathan or Nathaniel (*d.c.*1742)
dictionary compiler
An Universal Etymological Dictionary (1721)

Bailey, Paul [Peter Harry Bailey] (1937–)
novelist and critic
At the Jerusalem (1967)
Trespasses (1970)
A Distant Likeness (1973)
Peter Smart's Confessions (1977)
Old Soldiers (1980)
Gabriel's Lament (1986)
Sugar Cane (1993)
Kitty and Virgil (1998)

Bailey, Philip James (1816–1902)
poet
Festus (1839)
The Angel World, and Other Poems (1850)
The Mystic, and Other Poems (1855)
Universal Hymn (1867)

Baillie, Joanna (1762–1851)
poet and dramatist
Poems (1790)
A Series of Plays [vol. i] (1798)
A Series of Plays [vol. ii] (1802)
Miscellaneous Plays (1804)
De Montfort: A tragedy (1807)
The Family Legend: A tragedy (1810)
A Series of Plays [vol. iii] (1812)
Metrical Legends of Exalted Characters (1821)
A Series of Plays [vols i–iii] (1821)
The Martyr (1826)
The Bride (1828)

Bain, Alexander (1818–1903)
Scottish philosopher and founder-editor of *Mind*
The Senses and the Intellect (1855)

Bainbridge, Beryl Margaret (1934–)
novelist
A Weekend with Claude (1967)

Another Part of the Wood (1969)
Harriet Said . . . (1972)
The Dressmaker (1973)
The Bottle Factory Outing (1974)
Sweet William (1975)
A Quiet Life (1976)
Injury Time (1977)
Young Adolf (1978)
Winter Garden (1980)
Watson's Apology (1984)
Mum and Mr Armitage (1985)
Filthy Lucre (1986)
An Awfully Big Adventure (1989)
The Birthday Boys (1991)
Every Man for Himself (1996)
Master Georgie (1998)
According to Queeney (2001)

Baker, Augustine [originally David] (1575–1641)
mystic
Sancta Sophia; or, Directions for the Prayer of Contemplation &c (1657)

Baker, Daniel (1654?–1723)
poet
The History of Job (1706)

Baker, David Erskine (1730–67)
literary historian
The Companion to the Play-house; or, An Historical Account of all the Dramatic Writers (and their Works) that have Appeared in Great Britain and Ireland (1764)

Baker, Henry (1698–1774)
poet
An Invocation of Health (1723)
Original Poems: Serious and Humorous (1725)
The Second Part of Original Poems: Serious and Humorous (1726)

Baker, Humphrey (*fl.* 1562–87)
arithmetician and astrologer
The Well Sprynge of Sciences (1562)

Baker, Sir Richard (1568?–1645)
historical and religious writer
A Chronicle of the Kings of England (1643)
Theatrum Redivivum; or, The Theatre Vindicated (1662)

Baker, Sir Samuel White (1821–93)
traveller and sportsman
The Albert N'yanza, Great Basin of the Nile, and Explorations of the Nile Sources (1866)
The Nile Tributaries of Abyssinia (1867)

Baldwin, William (*c.*1515–63)
poet
A Treatise of Morall Phylosophie (1547)
The Canticles or Balades of Salomon (1549)
A Myrroure for Magistrates (1559)
The Funeralles of King Edward the Sixt (1560)
Beware the Cat (1570)

Bale, John (1495–1563)
bishop of Ossory and dramatist
The Examinacyon and Death of the Martyr Syr John Oldecastell (1544?)
The Actes of Englysh Votaryes (1546)
God's Promises (1547?)
The Temptation of our Lord (1547?)
The Three Laws (1548?)
The Pageant of Popes (1574)

Balfour, Alexander (1767–1829)
Scottish poet and novelist
Campbell; or, The Scottish Probationer (1819)
Contemplation (1820)

Balfour, Arthur James, 1st earl of Balfour (1848–1930)
statesman and philosopher
A Defence of Philosophic Doubt (1879)

Balfour, Clara Lucas, *née* Liddell, Mrs C.L. Balfour (1808–78)
novelist and temperance activist
'Scrub'; or, The Workhouse Boy's First Start in Life (1860)

Ballantine, James (1808–77)
Scottish novelist, poet, and artist
The Gaberlunzie's Wallet (1843)
The Miller of Deanhaugh (1844)

Ballantyne, Robert Michael (1825–94)
novelist and writer for boys
Hudson's Bay; or, Every-day Life in the Wilds of North America (1848)
The Coral Island (1857)
Martin Rattler; or, A Boy's Adventures in the Forests of Brazil (1858)
Ungava (1858)
The Walrus Hunters (1893)

Ballard, George (1706–55)
antiquary
Memoirs of Several Ladies of Great Britain (1752)

Ballard, James Graham (1930–)
novelist and short-story writer
The Drowned World (1963)
The Four-Dimensional Nightmare (1963)
The Terminal Beach (1964)
The Crystal World (1966)
The Disaster Area (1967)
The Atrocity Exhibition (1970)
Crash! (1973)
Concrete Island (1974)
High Rise (1975)
The Unlimited Dream Company (1979)
The Venus Hunters (1980)
Hello America (1981)
Myths of the Near Future (1982)
Empire of the Sun (1984)
The Day of Creation (1987)
War Fever (1990)
The Kindness of Women (1991)
Rushing to Paradise (1994)
Super-Cannes (2000)
Complete Short Stories (2001)
Millennium People (2003)

Bampfylde, John Codrington (1754–*c.*1796)
poet

Sixteen Sonnets (1778)
Bancroft, John (*d.* 1696)
dramatist
The Tragedy of Sertorius (1679)
King Edward the Third, with the Fall of the Earl of March (1691)
Henry the Second, King of England: With the death of Rosamond, a tragedy (1693)
Bancroft, Richard (1544–1610)
archbishop of Canterbury
A Sermon Preached at Paules Crosse (1588)
Daungerous Positions and Proceedings: Published and practised within this iland of Brytaine, under pretence of Reformation, and for the Presbiteriall discipline (1593)
Banim, John (1798–1842)
Irish novelist
The Celt's Paradise (1821)
Damon and Pythias: A tragedy (1821)
Revelations of the Dead-Alive (1824)
Tales, by the O'Hara Family [with Michael Banim] (1825)
The Boyne Water (1826)
Tales by the O'Hara Family: Second series [with Michael Banim] (1826)
The Anglo-Irish of the Nineteenth Century (1828)
The Croppy [with Michael Banim] (1828)
The Chaunt of the Cholera [with Michael Banim] (1831)
The Smuggler (1831)
The Bit o' Writin', and Other Tales (1838)
Banim, Michael (1796–1874)
Irish novelist and short-story writer
The Ghost-Hunter and His Family (1833)
The Mayor of Windgap (1835)
Father Connell (1842)
The Town of the Cascades (1864)
Banks, Iain Menzies (1954–)
novelist
The Wasp Factory (1984)
Walking on Glass (1985)
Consider Phlebas (1987)
The Player of Games (1988)
The Crow Road (1992)
A Song of Stone (1997)
The Business (1999)
Look to Windward (2000)
Dead Air (2002)
Banks, Isabella Linnaeus, *née* Varley, Mrs G[eorge] Linnaeus Banks (1821–97)
novelist and poet
The Manchester Man (1876)
Banks, John (*c.*1650–*c.*1700)
dramatist
The Rival Kings; or, The Loves of Oroondates and Statira: A tragœdy (1677)
The Destruction of Troy: A tragedy (1679)
The Unhappy Favourite; or, The Earl of Essex: A tragedy (1682)
Vertue Betray'd; or, Anna Bullen: A tragedy (1682)
The Island Queens; or, The Death of Mary, Queen of Scotland (1684)
The Innocent Usurper; or, The Death of the Lady Jane Grey: A tragedy (1694)
Cyrus the Great; or, The Tragedy of Love (1696)
Banks or Bancks, John (1709–51)
miscellaneous author
The Weaver's Miscellany (1730)
Poems on Several Occasions (1733)
Miscellaneous Works in Verse and Prose (1738)
Banks, Lynne Reid (1929–)
novelist, playwright, and children's writer
The L-Shaped Room (1960)
The Backward Shadow (1970)
Two is Lonely (1974)
The Indian in the Cupboard (1980)
The Warning Bell (1984)
Bannerman, Helen (1863–1946)
children's writer
The Story of Little Black Sambo (1899)
Bansley, Charles (*fl.* 1550)
poet
The Pride of Women (1550)
Banville, John (1945–)
Irish novelist and short-story writer
Long Lankin (1970)
Nightspawn (1971)
Birchwood (1973)
Doctor Copernicus (1976)
Kepler (1981)
The Newton Letter (1982)
Mefisto (1986)
The Book of Evidence (1989)
Ghosts (1993)
Athena (1995)
The Untouchable (1997)
Eclipse (2000)
Shroud (2002)
Barbauld, Anna Laetitia, *née* Aikin (1743–1825)
poet
Miscellaneous Pieces in Prose (1773)
Poems (1773)
Lessons for Children of Two to Three Years Old (1778)
Lessons for Children from Three to Four Years Old (1779)
Hymns in Prose for Children (1781)
Epistle to William Wilberforce (1791)
Evenings at Home; or, The Juvenile Budget Opened (1792)
The British Novelists (1810)
Eighteen Hundred and Eleven (1812)
The Works of Anna Laetitia Barbauld (1825)
A Legacy for Young Ladies (1826)
Barber, Margaret Fairless ['Michael Fairless'] (1869–1901)
novelist and author
The Gathering of Brother Hilarius (1901)
The Roadmender, and Other Papers (1902)
Barber, Mary (1690?–1757)
Irish poet

Poems on Several Occasions (1734)
Barbour, John (*c.*1320–1395)
Scottish poet, churchman, and scholar
The Bruce (1571?)
Barclay, Alexander (1475–1552)
poet, scholar, and monk
The Castle of Labour (1505?)
The Ship of Fools (1509)
Saint George (1515)
Fifth Eclogue (1518?)
The Boke of Codrus and Mynalcas (1521?)
The Introductory to Wryte and to Pronounce Frenche (1521)
Cronycle of the Warre agaynst Jugurth (1522?)
The Mirror of Good Manners (1523?)
Eclogues (1530?)
Barclay, Florence Louisa, *née* Charlesworth ['Brandon Roy'] (1862–1921)
novelist
Guy Mervyn (1891)
The Rosary (1909)
Barclay, John (1582–1621)
author
Barclay his Argenis; or, The Loves of Poliarchus and Argenis (1625)
The Mirrour of Mindes; or, Barclay's Icon Animorum (1631)
Barclay, Robert (1648–90)
Quaker apologist
A Catechism and Confession of Faith (1673)
The Anarchy of the Ranters and Other Libertines (1676)
Quakerism Confirmed (1676)
An Apology for the True Christian Divinity (1678)
Robert Barclay's Apology for the True Christian Divinity Vindicated (1679)
Truth Triumphant through the Spiritual Warfare, Christian Labours, and Writings of Robert Barclay (1692)
Barham, Richard Harris ['Thomas Ingoldsby'] (1788–1845)
humorist and poet
Baldwin; or, A Miser's Heir (1820)
The Ingoldsby Legends; or, Mirth and Marvels [1st ser.] (1840)
Some Account of My Cousin Nicholas (1841)
The Ingoldsby Legends; or, Mirth and Marvels: Second series (1842)
The Ingoldsby Legends; or, Mirth and Marvels (1847)
Baring, Maurice (1874–1945)
novelist, short-story writer, playwright, and poet
The Black Prince, and Other Poems (1902)
Orpheus in Mayfair, and Other Stories and Sketches (1909)
Poems 1914–1919 (1920)
Barker, Audrey Lilian (1918–2002)
novelist and short-story writer
Innocents (1947)
Apology for a Hero (1950)
Novelette, with Other Stories (1951)
The Joy-Ride and After (1963)
Lost Upon the Roundabouts (1964)
A Case Examined (1965)
Femina Real (1971)
Life Stories (1981)
Relative Successes (1984)
The Gooseboy (1987)
The Woman Who Talked to Herself (1989)
Any Excuse for a Party (1991)
Element of Doubt (1992)
Submerged (2002)
Barker, George Granville (1913–91)
poet
Thirty Preliminary Poems (1933)
Poems (1935)
Calamiterror (1937)
Elegy on Spain (1939)
Lament and Triumph (1940)
Eros in Dogma (1944)
News of the World (1950)
The True Confession of George Barker (1950)
Collected Poems 1930–1955 (1957)
The View From a Blind I (1962)
Poems of Places and People (1971)
Anno Domino (1983)
Barker, Howard (1946–)
playwright
Cheek (1972)
Scenes From an Execution (1985)
Barker, Jane ['Galesia', 'Fidelia'] (1652–1732)
poet and novelist
Poetical Recreations (1688)
Love Intrigues; or, The History of the Amours of Bosvil and Galesia (1713)
Exilius; or, The Banish'd Roman (1715)
A Patch-Work Screen for the Ladies; or, Love and Virtue Recommended (1723)
The Lining of the Patch-Work Screen (1726)
Barker, Nicola (1966)
novelist
Behindlings (2002)
The Three Button Trick (2003)
Barker, Pat (1943–)
novelist
Union Street (1982)
Blow Your House Down (1984)
The Century's Daughter (1986)
The Man Who Wasn't There (1989)
Regeneration (1991)
The Eye in the Door (1993)
The Ghost Road (1995)
Another World (1998)
Border Crossing (2001)
Double Vision (2003)
Barker, William (*fl.* 1572)
translator
Cyropædia (1552?)

Barley, Nigel (1947–)
writer on anthropology and travel
The Innocent Anthropologist (1983)
Barlow, George (1847–1913)
poet
Under the Dawn (1875)
Barlow, Jane (1857–1917)
Irish novelist, short-story writer, and poet
Bog-Land Studies (1892)
Irish Idylls (1892)
Kerrigan's Quality (1893)
Strangers at Lisconnel (1895)
Ghost-Bereft, with Other Stories and Studies in Verse (1901)
Barlowe, William (*d.* 1568)
Protestant polemicist, later bishop of St Asaph and of Chichester
Read Me and Be Not Wroth/The Burial of the Mass (1528)
Barnes, Barnabe (1571–1609)
poet and dramatist
Parthenophil and Parthenophe (1593)
A Divine Centurie of Spirituall Sonnets (1595)
The Divils Charter: A tragedie (1607)
Barnes, Joshua (1654–1712)
Greek scholar, poet, fiction writer, and antiquary
Gerania: A new discovery of a little sort of people anciently discoursed of, called pygmies (1675)
The History of that Most Victorious Monarch, Edward III (1688)
Barnes, Julian Patrick ['Dan Kavanagh'] (1946–)
novelist
Duffy (1980)
Metroland (1980)
Fiddle City (1981)
Before She Met Me (1982)
Flaubert's Parrot (1984)
Putting the Boot In (1985)
Staring at the Sun (1986)
Going to the Dogs (1987)
A History of the World in 10½ Chapters (1989)
Talking It Over (1991)
The Porcupine (1992)
Letters From London (1995)
Cross Channel (1996)
England, England (1998)
Love Etc (2000)
Barnes, Peter (1931–)
dramatist
Leonardo's Last Supper; Noonday Demons (1970)
Collected Plays (1981)
Barnes, William (1801–86)
poet
Poetical Pieces (1820)
Orra: A Lapland tale (1822)
Poems of Rural Life in the Dorset Dialect (1844)
Poems, Partly of Rural Life (1846)
Hwomely Rhymes (1859)
The Song of Solomon in the Dorset Dialect (1859)
Poems of Rural Life in the Dorset Dialect: Third Collection (1862)
Poems of Rural Life in Common English (1868)
Barnfield, Richard (1574–1627)
poet
The Affectionate Shepheard (1594)
Cynthia (1595)
The Encomion of Lady Pecunia; or, The Praise of Money (1598)
Baron, Robert, of Gray's Inn (1630–58)
poet and plagiarist
Erotopaignion; or, The Cyprian Academy (1647)
An Apologie for Paris: For rejecting of Juno, and Pallas, and presenting of Ate's golden ball to Venus (1649)
Pocula Castalia (1650)
Mirza: A tragedie (1655?)
Barr, Amelia Edith, *née* Huddleston (1831–1919)
novelist
Jan Vedder's Wife (1885)
The Bow of Orange Ribbon (1886)
Barr, Robert ['Luke Sharp'] (1850–1912)
novelist and short-story writer
In a Steamer Chair, and Other Shipboard Stories (1892)
Jennie Baxter, Journalist (1899)
The Triumphs of Eugène Valmont (1906)
Barrett, Eaton Stannard ['Cervantes Hogg', 'Polypus'] (1786–1820)
novelist
All the Talents: A satirical poem (1807)
The Metropolis; or, A Cure for Gaming (1811)
The Heroine; or, Adventures of a Fair Romance Reader (1813)
The Talents Run Mad; or, Eighteen Hundred and Sixteen (1816)
Six Weeks at Long's (1817)
Barrie, Sir James Matthew ['Gavin Ogilvy'] (1860–1937)
novelist and dramatist
Better Dead (1887)
Auld Licht Idylls (1888)
When a Man's Single (1888)
A Window in Thrums (1889)
My Lady Nicotine (1890)
The Little Minister (1891)
Margaret Ogilvy (1896)
Sentimental Tommy (1896)
Tommy and Grizel (1900)
The Little White Bird (1902)
Peter Pan in Kensington Gardens (1906)
Walker London: A farcical comedy (1907)
Peter and Wendy (1911)
Quality Street (1913)
The Admirable Crichton (1914)
What Every Woman Knows: A comedy (1918)
Dear Brutus: A comedy (1922)
Mary Rose (1924)
The Plays of J.M. Barrie (1928)
The Greenwood Hat (1937)

Barrow, Isaac (1630–77)
divine, mathematician, and classical scholar
The Duty and Reward of Bounty to the Poor (1671)
Sermons Preached Upon Several Occasions (1678)
A Treatise of the Pope's Supremacy (1680)
The Works of the Learned Isaac Barrow (1683)
Of Contentment, Patience and Resignation to the Will of God (1685)

Barrow, Sir John (1764–1848)
naval administrator and traveller
An Account of Travels into the Interior of Southern Africa (1801)
Travels in China (1804)
A Voyage to Cochin-China (1806)
A Chronological History of Voyages into the Arctic Regions (1818)
The Eventful History of the Mutiny and Piratical Seizure of HMS Bounty (1831)

Barry or Barrey, Lording or Lodowick (1580–1629)
dramatist
Ram-Alley; or, Merrie-Trickes (1611)

Barstow, Stan[ley] (1928–)
novelist, short-story writer, and playwright
A Kind of Loving (1960)
Ask Me Tomorrow (1962)
The Watchers on the Shore (1966)
A Raging Calm (1968)
The Right True End (1976)
Just You Wait and See (1986)
Give Us This Day (1989)
Next of Kin (1991)

Barton, Bernard (1784–1849)
Quaker poet
Metrical Effusions; or, Verses on Various Occasions (1812)
The Convict's Appeal (1818)
Poems (1818)
A Day in Autumn (1820)
Poems (1820)
Napoleon, and Other Poems (1822)
Verses on the Death of Percy Bysshe Shelley (1822)
Poetic Vigils (1824)
A Widow's Tale, and Other Poems (1827)
A New Year's Eve, and Other Poems (1828)
The Reliquary (1836)
Household Verses (1845)

Basse, William (1583–1654)
poet
Sword and Buckler; or, Serving-Mans Defence (1602)
Three Pastoral Elegies (1602)

Bastard, Thomas (1566–1618)
satirist and divine
Chrestoleros: Seven bookes of epigrammes (1598)

Bateman or Batman, Stephen (*d.* 1584)
author and translator
A Christall Glasse of Christian Reformation (1569)
The Travayled Pylgrime (1569)

Bates, Henry Walter (1825–92)
naturalist
The Naturalist on the River Amazon (1863)

Bates, Herbert Ernest ['Flying Officer X'] (1905–74)
novelist and short-story writer
The Two Sisters (1926)
The Modern Short Story (1941)
The Greatest People in the World, and Other Stories (1942)
In the Heart of the Country (1942)
How Sleep the Brave, and Other Stories (1943)
Fair Stood the Wind for France (1944)
The Purple Plain (1947)
The Jacaranda Tree (1949)
Love for Lydia (1952)
The Darling Buds of May (1958)
A Breath of French Air (1959)
When the Green Woods Laugh (1960)
Oh! To Be in England (1963)
The Vanished World (1969)

Bauthumley, Jacob (1629–60)
Ranter
The Light and Dark Sides of God (1650)

Bawden, Nina Mary, *née* Mabey (1925–)
adult and children's novelist
Who Calls the Tune (1953)
The Solitary Child (1956)
Anna Apparent (1972)
Carrie's War (1973)
The Peppermint Pig (1975)
Afternoon of a Good Woman (1976)
Familiar Passions (1979)
Walking Naked (1981)
The Ice House (1983)
Circles of Deceit (1987)
Family Money (1991)
The Ruffian on the Stair (2001)

Bax, Clifford (1886–1962)
playwright, poet, and biographer
Antique Pageantry (1921)

Baxter, Richard (1615–91)
divine and devotional author
The Saints Everlasting Rest; or, A Treatise of the Blessed State of the Saints in their Enjoyment of God in Glory (1650)
The Right Method for a Settled Peace of Conscience, and Spiritual Comfort (1653)
The Unreasonableness of Infidelity (1655)
Gildas Salvianus: The Reformed Pastor (1656)
A Call to the Unconverted to Turn and Live and Accept of Mercy While Mercy May Be Had (1658)
The Crucifying of the World, by the Cross of Christ (1658)
The Grotian Religion Discovered (1658)
Five Disputations of Church-Government and Worship (1659)
A Holy Commonwealth, or Political Aphorisms (1659)

Catholick Unity: or the Only Way to Bring Us All To Be of One Religion (1660)
The Life of Faith, as it is the Evidence of Things Unseen (1660)
Now or Never (1662)
The Divine Life, in Three Treatises (1664)
The Cure of Church-Divisions (1670)
The Life of Faith. In Three Parts (1670)
A Christian Directory: or, A Summ of Practical Theologie, and Cases of Conscience (1673)
The Poor Man's Family Book (1674)
Richard Baxter's Catholick Theologie (1675)
Church-History of the Government of Bishops and their Councils Abbreviated (1680)
A Breviate of the Life of Margaret Baxter (1681)
Compassionate Counsel to all Young-Men (1681)
Poetical Fragments (1681)
Richard Baxter's Dying Thoughts upon Phil. I.23 (1683)
A Paraphrase on the New Testament (1685)
Richard Baxter's Penitent Confession, and his Necessary Vindication (1691)
Paraphrase on the Psalms of David (1692)
Reliquiae Baxterianae (1696)
The Practical Works of the Late Richard Baxter (1707)

Bayley, John (1925–)
literary critic and author
In Another Country (1955)
Iris (1998)
Iris and the Friends (1999)

Bayly, Lewis, bishop of Bangor (1565–1631)
The Practise of Piety (1612)

Bayly, Thomas (*d.* 1657?)
royalist divine and controversialist
Herba Parietis; or, The Wall-Flower (1650)

Bayly, [Nathaniel] Thomas Haynes ['Q in the Corner'] (1797–1839)
songwriter, novelist, and dramatist
Parliamentary Letters, and Other Poems (1818)
Erin, and Other Poems (1822)
Perfection; or, The Lady of Munster (1836)

Baynes, Thomas Spencer (1823–87)
philosopher and literary critic
An Essay on the New Analytic of Logical Forms (1850)

Beard, Thomas (*d.* 1632)
Puritan divine
The Theatre of Gods Judgements: or, A Collection of Histories out of Sacred, Ecclesiasticall, and Prophane Authours (1597)

Beardsley, Aubrey Vincent (1872–98)
illustrator and author
Last Letters of Aubrey Beardsley (1904)
Under the Hill, and Other Essays in Prose and Verse (1904)
The Story of Venus and Tannhäuser (1907)

Beattie, James (1735–1803)
poet and philosophical writer
Original Poems and Translations (1760)
The Judgment of Paris (1765)
Verses Occasioned by the Death of Charles Churchill (1765)
Poems on Several Subjects (1766)
An Essay on the Nature and Immutability of Truth (1770)
The Minstrel; or, The Progress of Genius (1771)
The Minstrel; or, The Progress of Genius (1774)
Essays (1776)
Poems on Several Occasions (1776)
Dissertations Moral and Critical (1783)
Evidences of the Christian Religion Briefly Stated (1786)
Scoticisms (1787)
Elements of Moral Science (1790)

Beaufort, Margaret, countess of Richmond and Derby (1443–1509)
The Mirroure of Golde for the Synfull Soule (1506?)

Beaumont, Francis (1584–1616)
poet and dramatist
Salamacis and Hermaphroditus (1602)
The Woman Hater (1607)
The Knight of the Burning Pestle (1613)
The Masque of the Inner Temple and Grayes Inne (1613)
The Scornful Ladie (1616)
A King and No King (1619)
The Maides Tragedy (1619)
Phylaster; or, Love Lyes a Bleeding (1620)
Poems (1640)
Wit Without Money: A comedie (1640)
Comedies and Tragedies (1647)
The Wild-Goose Chase: A comedie (1652)
The Beggars Bush (1661)
Fifty Comedies and Tragedies (1679)

Beaumont, Sir John (1583–1627)
poet
The Metamorphosis of Tabacco (1602)
Bosworth-field: With a taste of the variety of other poems (1629)

Beaumont, Joseph (1616–99)
divine and poet
Psyche; or, Loves Mysterie. In XX Canto's (1648)

Beckett, Samuel Barclay (1906–89)
Irish playwright, poet, and novelist
Whoroscope (1930)
Proust (1931)
More Pricks Than Kicks (1934)
Echo's Bones and Other Precipitates (1935)
Murphy (1938)
Molloy (1955)
Waiting for Godot (1956)
All That Fall (1957)
Endgame (1958)
Malone Dies (1958)
Krapp's Last Tape; Embers (1959)
Poems in English (1961)
Happy Days (1962)
Watt (1963)

How It Is (1964)
Play and Two Short Pieces for Radio (1964)
Imagination Dead Imagine (1965)
Come and Go (1967)
Eh Joe, and Other Writings (1967)
No's Knife (1967)
Lessness (1971)
The Lost Ones (1972)
First Love (1973)
Mercier and Camier (1974)
For To End Yet Again, and Other Fizzles (1976)
Collected Poems in English and French (1977)
Four Novellas (1977)
All Strange Away (1979)
Company (1980)
Ill Seen Ill Said (1982)
Three Occasional Pieces (1982)
Disjecta (1983)
Worstward Ho (1983)
Collected Poems 1930–78 (1984)
Collected Shorter Plays (1984)
Collected Shorter Prose 1945–80 (1984)
As the Story Was Told (1990)
Dream of Fair to Middling Women (1992)
Eleutheria (1996)

Beckford, William ['The Right Hon. Lady Harriet Marlow', 'Jaquetta Agneta Mariana Jenks'] (1760–1844)
novelist and author
Biographical Memoirs of Extraordinary Painters (1780)
Dreams, Waking Thoughts and Incidents (1783)
Vathek (1786)
Modern Novel Writing (1796)
Azemia (1797)
Italy; with Sketches of Spain and Portugal (1834)
Recollections of an Excursion to the Monasteries of Alcobaça and Batalha (1835)

Beckingham, Charles (1699–1731)
dramatist
Scipio Africanus: A tragedy (1718)
The Tragedy of King Henry IV of France (1720)

Becon, Thomas (1512–67)
Protestant divine
The Pomander of Prayer (1558)
The Sycke Mans Salve (1561)

Beddoes, Thomas Lovell (1803–49)
poet and dramatist
The Improvisatore, in Three Fyttes, with Other Poems (1821)
The Bride's Tragedy (1822)
Death's Jest-Book; or, The Fool's Tragedy (1850)
Poems Posthumous and Collected (1851)

'Bede, Cuthbert' [Edward Bradley] (1827–89)
humorist
The Adventures of Mr Verdant Green, an Oxford Freshman (1853)
The Further Adventures of Mr Verdant Green, an Oxford Undergraduate (1854)
Mr Verdant Green, Married and Done For (1857)
Little Mr Bouncer and His Friend, Verdant Green (1873)

Bedford, Arthur (1668–1745)
miscellaneous writer
The Evil and Dangers of Stage-Plays (1706)

Bedford, Sybille [Sybille von Schoenebeck] (1911–)
German-born novelist and essayist
The Sudden View: A Mexican journey (1953)
A Compass Error (1968)

Bedingfield, Thomas (*d.* 1613)
translator
The Florentine Historie (1595)

Beedome, Thomas (*d.* 1641?)
poet
Poems Divine, and Humane (1641)

Beer, Patricia (1924–99)
poet, playwright, and critic
Loss of the Magyar, and Other Poems (1959)
The Survivors (1963)
Collected Poems (1988)

Beerbohm, [Sir Henry] Max[imilian] (1872–1956)
essayist, caricaturist, and novelist
Caricatures of Twenty-Five Gentlemen (1896)
A Book of Caricatures (1907)
Zuleika Dobson: An Oxford love story (1911)
A Christmas Garland (1912)
Fifty Caricatures (1913)
Seven Men (1919)

Beeton, Isabella Mary, *née* Mayson (1836–65)
journalist and domestic writer
The Book of Household Management (1861)
The Englishwoman's Cooking-Book (1862)
Mrs Beeton's Dictionary of Every-day Cookery (1865)

Behan, Brendan Francis (1923–64)
Irish playwright
The Quare Fellow (1956)
Borstal Boy (1958)
The Hostage (1958)
Confessions of an Irish Rebel (1965)
The Scarperer (1966)

Behn, Aphra (1640?–89)
dramatist, poet, and novelist
The Forc'd Marriage; or, The Jealous Bridegroom: A tragi-comedy (1671)
The Amorous Prince; or, The Curious Husband: A comedy (1671)
The Dutch Lover: A comedy (1673)
Abdelazer; or, The Moor's Revenge: A tragedy (1677)
The Rover. Or, The Banish't Cavaliers: A comedy (1677)
The Town-Fopp; or, Sir Timothy Tawdrey: A comedy (1677)
The Lives of Sundry Notorious Villains (1678)
Sir Patient Fancy: A comedy (1678)
The Feign'd Curtizans; or, A Night's Intrigue: A comedy (1679)

The Revenge; or, A Match in Newgate: A comedy (1680)
The Second Part of The Rover (1681)
The City-Heiress; or, Sir Timothy Treat-All: A comedy (1682)
The False Count; or, A New Way to Play an Old Game (1682)
The Roundheads or, The Good Old Cause: A comedy (1682)
The Young King; or, The Mistake (1683)
Love-Letters Between a Noble-man and his Sister (1684)
Poems Upon Several Occasions (1684)
Love-Letters From a Noble Man and His Sister (1685)
A Pindarick on the Death of Our Late Sovereign (1685)
A Pindarick Poem on the Happy Coronation of His Most Sacred Majesty James II (1685)
The Amours of Philander and Silvia (1687)
The Emperor of the Moon: A farce (1687)
The Luckey Chance; or, An Alderman's Bargain: A comedy (1687)
A Congratulatory Poem to Her Most Sacred Majesty (1688)
The Fair Jilt; or, The History of Prince Tarquin and Miranda (1688)
Oroonoko; or, The Royal Slave: A true history (1688)
Three Histories (1688)
The History of the Nun; or, The Fair Vow-Breaker (1689)
A Pindaric Poem to the Reverend Doctor Burnet (1689)
The Widdow Ranter; or, The History of Bacon in Virginia: A tragi-comedy (1690)
The Histories and Novels of the Late Ingenious Mrs Behn (1696)
The Younger Brother; or, The Amorous Jilt: A comedy (1696)
All the Histories and Novels Written by the late ingenious Mrs Behn (1698)
Histories, Novels, and Translations (1700)

Bell, Gertrude Margaret Lowthian (1868–1926)
traveller and author
The Desert and the Sown (1907)
The Thousand and One Churches (1909)
Amurath to Amurath (1911)

Bell, Henry Glassford (1803–74)
Scottish poet
Summer and Winter Hours (1831)
My Old Portfolio; or, Tales and Sketches (1832)

Bellamy, Daniel, the elder (*b.* 1687)
miscellaneous writer
The Cambro-Britannic Engineer; or, The Original Mouse-Trapp Maker (1722)

Bellenden, John (*c.*1500–before Nov. 1548)
translator
The Chronicles of Scotland (1540?)

Belloc, [Joseph] Hilaire Pierre René (1870–1953)
historian, poet, and critic
The Bad Child's Book of Beasts (1896)
Verses and Sonnets (1896)
More Beasts (for Worse Children) (1897)
A Moral Alphabet (1899)
Cautionary Tales for Children (1908)
Verses (1910)
New Cautionary Tales (1930)
The Silence of the Sea, and Other Essays (1941)

Benlowes, Edward (1603?–76)
poet
Theophila; or, Loves Sacrifice (1652)

Bennett, Alan (1934–)
playwright
Beyond the Fringe (1962)
Forty Years On (1969)
Habeas Corpus (1973)
A Private Function (1985)
Prick Up Your Ears (1987)
Single Spies (1989)
The Lady in the Van (1990)
The Madness of George III (1992)
Writing Home (1994)
The Laying On of Hands (2001)

Bennett, Anna [or, incorrectly, Agnes] Maria (*c.*1750–1808)
novelist
Anna; or, Memoirs of a Welch Heiress (1785)
Juvenile Indiscretions (1786)
Agnes De-Courci (1789)
Ellen, Countess of Castle Howel (1794)
The Beggar Girl and Her Benefactors (1797)
Vicissitudes Abroad; or, The Ghost of my Father (1806)

Bennett, [Enoch] Arnold (1867–1931)
novelist
A Man From the North (1898)
Polite Farces for the Drawing-Room (1899)
Anna of the Five Towns (1902)
The Grand Babylon Hotel (1902)
Teresa of Watling Street (1904)
The Loot of Cities (1905)
Tales of the Five Towns (1905)
The Grim Smile of the Five Towns (1907)
Buried Alive (1908)
The Old Wives' Tale (1908)
What the Public Wants (1909)
Clayhanger (1910)
The Card (1911)
Hilda Lessways (1911)
The Matador of the Five Towns, and Other Stories (1912)
Milestones (1912)
The Great Adventure (1913)
The Regent: A five towns story of adventure in London (1913)
These Twain (1916)
Mr Prohack (1922)
Riceyman Steps (1923)
Imperial Palace (1930)

Journal, 1929 (1930)
The Journals of Arnold Bennett (1932)
Bennett, William Cox (1820–95)
poet and songwriter
Anti-Maud (1855)
War Songs (1855)
Benson, Arthur Christopher (1862–1925)
essayist, biographer, poet, and short-story writer
Le Cahier Jaune (1892)
The House of Quiet (1904)
The Upton Letters (1905)
From a College Window (1906)
Beside Still Waters (1907)
Benson, Edward Frederic (1867–1940)
novelist, short-story writer, and biographer
Dodo: A detail of the day (1893)
The Babe, B.A. (1897)
The Room in the Tower, and Other Stories (1912)
Dodo the Second (1914)
David Blaize (1916)
David Blaize and the Blue Door (1918)
Queen Lucia (1920)
Dodo Wonders (1921)
Miss Mapp (1922)
David of King's (1924)
Lucia in London (1927)
Mapp and Lucia (1931)
Lucia's Progress (1935)
Benson, Robert Hugh (1871–1914)
novelist and short-story writer
The King's Achievement (1905)
Benson, Stella (1892–1933)
novelist and short-story writer
I Pose (1915)
Bentham, Jeremy (1748–1832)
writer on jurisprudence
The White Bull: An oriental history (1774)
A Fragment on Government (1776)
Defence of Usury (1787)
An Introduction to the Principles of Morals and Legislation (1789)
Panopticon; or, The Inspection-House (1791)
Chrestomathia (1815)
Papers Relative to Codification and Public Instruction (1817)
The Analysis of the Influence of Natural Religion upon the Temporal Happiness of Mankind (1822)
The Book of Fallacies (1824)
The Rationale of Judicial Evidence (1827)
Deontology; or, Science of Morality (1834)
Bentley, Edmund Clerihew (1875–1956)
inventor of the clerihew and detective novelist
Biography for Beginners (1905)
Trent's Last Case (1913)
Clerihews Complete (1951)
Bentley, Phyllis Eleanor (1894–1977)
novelist
Environment (1922)
Cat-in-the-Manger (1923)
Bentley, Richard (1662–1742)
classical scholar
The Folly of Atheism, and (what is now called) Deism (1692)
Matter and Motion Cannot Think; or, A Confutation of Atheism from the Faculties of the Soul (1692)
A Confutation of Atheism from the Structure and Origin of Humane Bodies (1692)
A Confutation of Atheism from the Origin and Frame of the World (1692)
A Dissertation upon the Epistles of Phalaris (1699)
Remarks upon a Late Discourse of Free-thinking (1713)
A Sermon upon Popery (1715)
Bentley, Richard, the younger (1708–82)
dramatist, poet, and miscellaneous writer
Designs by Mr R. Bentley, for Six Poems by Mr T. Gray (1753)
Patriotism (1763)
Philodamus (1767)
Bentley, Thomas, of Gray's Inn
anthologist
The Monument of Matrones (1582)
The Sixt Lampe of Virginitie (1582)
Beresford, James (1764–1840)
clergyman and satirist
The Miseries of Human Life; or, The Groans of Timothy Testy, and Samuel Sensitive (1806)
Beresford, John Davys (1873–1947)
novelist and short-story writer
Nineteen Impressions (1918)
Berger, John Peter (1926–)
critic, novelist, and artist
A Painter of Our Time (1958)
G (1972)
Ways of Seeing (1972)
Pig Earth (1979)
About Looking (1980)
Berkeley, George (1685–1753)
philosopher and bishop of Cloyne
An Essay Towards a New Theory of Vision (1709)
A Treatise Concerning the Principles of Human Knowledge (1710)
Passive Obedience; or, The Christian Doctrine of Not Resisting the Supreme Power (1712)
Three Dialogues Between Hylas and Philonous (1713)
An Essay Towards Preventing the Ruine of Great Britain (1721)
Alciphron; or, The Minute Philosopher, in Seven Dialogues (1732)
The Theory of Vision: or Visual Language (1733)
The Querist [pt i] (1735)
Siris (1744)
A Word to the Wise; or, An Exhortation to the Roman Catholic Clergy of Ireland (1749)
A Miscellany (1752)
The Works of George Berkeley (1784)

Berkoff, Steven (1937-)
actor and playwright
East; Agamemnon; The Fall of the House of Usher (1977)
Decadence (1982)
Sink the Belgrano! (1987)
Bernard, Richard (1568–1642)
Puritan divine
Terence in English (1598)
The Faithfull Shepherd: The Shepheards Faithfulnesse (1607)
The Isle of Man; or, The Legal Proceedings in Man-shire against Sinne (1626)
The Common Catechisme (1630)
Berners, Juliana (*d.* 1388?)
writer
The Book of St Albans (1486)
The Manere of Hawkynge and Huntynge (1496)
Berridge, Elizabeth (1921-)
novelist and short-story writer
Upon Several Occasions (1953)
Berry, James (1924-)
Jamaican poet and novelist
Fractured Circles (1979)
Lucy's Letters and Loving (1982)
Chain of Days (1985)
The Girls and Yanga Marshall (1987)
Hot Earth, Cold Earth (1995)
Playing a Dazzler (1996)
Besant, Annie, *née* Wood (1847–1933)
theosophist and educationist
An Autobiography (1893)
Esoteric Christianity (1901)
Besant, Sir Walter (1836–1901)
novelist
Studies in Early French Poetry (1868)
All Sorts and Conditions of Men (1882)
The Revolt of Man (1882)
Autobiography (1902)
Besant, Sir Walter (1836–1901), and Rice, James (1843–82)
novelists
Ready-Money Mortiboy (1872)
The Case of Mr Lucraft, and Other Tales (1876)
The Golden Butterfly (1876)
The Chaplain of the Fleet (1881)
Best, George (*d.* 1584)
navigator
A True Discourse of the Late Voyages of Discoverie Under M. Frobisher (1578)
Betham, Mary Matilda (1776–1852)
poet and author
Elegies, and Other Small Poems (1796)
A Biographical Dictionary of the Celebrated Women of Every Age and Country (1804)
Poems (1808)
The Lay of Marie (1816)
Vignettes (1818)
Betham-Edwards, Matilda Barbara (1836–1919)
novelist, poet, and woman of letters
The White House by the Sea (1857)
Doctor Jacob (1864)
Bethune, Alexander (1804–43)
Scottish poet
Tales and Sketches of the Scottish Peasantry (1838)
Betjeman, Sir John (1906–84)
poet, writer on architecture, and broadcaster
Mount Zion; or, In Touch with the Infinite (1931)
Ghastly Good Taste; or, A Depressing Story of the Rise and Fall of English Architecture (1933)
Continual Dew: A little book of bourgeois verse (1937)
Old Lights for New Chancels (1940)
New Bats in Old Belfries (1945)
First and Last Loves (1952)
A Few Late Chrysanthemums (1954)
Poems in the Porch (1954)
Collected Poems (1958)
Summoned by Bells (1960)
High and Low (1966)
A Nip in the Air (1974)
Church Poems (1981)
Uncollected Poems (1982)
Betterton, Thomas (1635?–1710)
actor and dramatist
The Prophetess; or, The History of Dioclesian (1690)
The Amorous Widow; or, The Wanton Wife (1706)
The Bond-Man; or, Love and Liberty: A tragi-comedy (1719)
The History of the English Stage, From the Restauration to the Present Time (1741)
Bevington, Louisa Sarah (1845–95)
poet
Key-Notes (1879)
Bickerstaffe, Isaac (1735?–1812?)
Irish playwright
Leucothoe (1756)
Thomas and Sally; or, The Sailor's Return (1761)
Love in a Village: A comic opera (1763)
Daphne and Amintor: A comic opera (1765)
The Maid of the Mill: A comic opera (1765)
Love in the City: A comic opera (1767)
Lionel and Clarissa: A comic opera (1768)
The Padlock: A comic opera (1768)
The Recruiting Serjeant (1770)
He Wou'd If He Cou'd; or, An Old Fool Worse Than Any (1771)
Bickersteth, Edward (1786–1850)
Evangelical divine
Christian Psalmody (1833)
Bickersteth, Edward Henry (1825–1906)
Evangelical divine and author
Nineveh (1851)
Bieston, Roger (*fl.* 1554)
poet
The Bayte and Snare of Fortune (1556)
Bigg, John Stanyan (1828–65)
The Sea-King (1848)
Billingsley, Nicholas (1633–1709)
poet and divine

Brachy-Martyrologia (1657)
Kosmobrephia; or, The Infancy of the World (1658)
Thesauro-Phulakion; or, A Treasury of Divine Raptures (1667)
Binchy, Maeve (1940–)
Irish romantic novelist
Light a Penny Candle (1982)
Firefly Summer (1987)
Circle of Friends (1990)
The Glass Lake (1994)
Tara Road (1998)
Scarlet Feather (2000)
Binding, Tim (1947)
novelist and TV dramatist
Anthem (2003)
Bingham, John (*fl.* 1623)
translator of Xenophon
Anabasis: The historie of Xenophon (1623)
Bingham, Joseph (1668–1723)
ecclesiastical historian
Origines Ecclesiae; or, The Antiquities of the Christian Church [vols i, ii] (1708)
Binyon, [Robert] Laurence (1869–1943)
poet, dramatist, and art historian
Lyric Poems (1894)
First Book of London Visions (1896)
Porphyrion, and Other Poems (1898)
Second Book of London Visions (1899)
The Death of Adam, and Other Poems (1903)
England, and Other Poems (1909)
Auguries (1913)
The Winnowing-Fan (1914)
The Anvil, and Other Poems (1916)
The New World (1918)
Collected Poems (1931)
The North Star, and Other Poems (1941)
The Burning of the Leaves, and Other Poems (1944)
Birch, Thomas (1705–66)
antiquary, editor, and biographer
The Life of John Tillotson (1752)
Memoirs of the Reign of Queen Elizabeth (1754)
The History of the Royal Society of London (1756)
Bird, Isabella Lucy, later Bishop (1831–1904)
traveller and author
An Englishwoman in America (1856)
Journeys in Persia and Kurdistan (1891)
Birrell, Augustine (1850–1933)
statesman and essayist
Obiter Dicta [1st ser.] (1884)
Obiter Dicta [2nd ser.] (1887)
More Obiter Dicta (1924)
Black, William (1841–98)
Scottish novelist
A Daughter of Heth (1871)
The Monarch of Mincing Lane (1871)
The Strange Adventures of a Phaeton (1872)
A Princess of Thule (1874)
Madcap Violet (1876)
White Wings (1880)
Blackamore, Arthur (*b.* 1679)
novelist
The Perfidious Brethren; or, The Religious Triumvirate (1720)
Luck at Last; or, The Happy Unfortunate (1723)
Blackburn, Thomas Eliel Fenwick (1916–77)
poet and novelist
Bread for the Winter Birds (1980)
Blackburne, Francis (1705–87)
divine
A Serious Inquiry into the Use and Importance of External Religion (1752)
The Confessional; or, A Full and Free Inquiry into Establishing Systematical Confessions of Faith and Doctrine in Protestant Churches (1766)
Blackie, John Stuart (1809–95)
scholar, poet, and translator
Faust: a Tragedy (1834)
Blacklock, Thomas (1721–91)
poet
Poems on Several Occasions (1746)
Blackmore, Sir Richard (1654–1729)
physician and author
Prince Arthur (1695)
King Arthur (1697)
A Satyr Against Wit (1700)
Advice to the Poets (1706)
The Kit-Cats (1708)
Instructions to Vander Bank (1709)
The Nature of Man (1711)
Creation (1712)
Essays upon Several Subjects [vol. i] (1716)
A New Version of the Psalms of David (1721)
Alfred: An epick poem (1723)
Blackmore, Richard Doddridge ('Melanter', 1825–1900)
novelist and poet
Poems by Melanter (1853)
Clara Vaughan (1864)
Cradock Nowell (1866)
Lorna Doone (1869)
The Maid of Sker (1872)
Christowell (1882)
Springhaven (1887)
Tales from the Telling House (1896)
Blackstone, Sir William (1723–80)
jurist and author
The Pantheon (1747)
An Essay on Collateral Consanguinity (1750)
An Analysis of the Laws of England (1756)
A Discourse on the Study of Law (1758)
Commentaries on the Laws of England (1765)
A Reply to Dr Priestley's Remarks on the Fourth Volume of the Commentaries on the Laws of England (1769)
Blackwood, Algernon Henry (1869–1951)
supernatural fiction writer
The Empty House, and Other Ghost Stories (1906)
The Listener, and Other Stories (1907)

John Silence: Physician Extraordinary (1908)

Blackwood, Caroline Maureen [Caroline Hamilton-Temple-Blackwood] (1931–96)
novelist
The Stepdaughter (1976)

Blair, Hugh (1718–1800)
scholar and critic
A Critical Dissertation on the Poems of Ossian, the Son of Fingal (1763)
Sermons [vol. i] (1777)
Lectures on Rhetoric and Belles Lettres (1783)

Blair, Robert (1699–1746)
poet
The Grave (1743)

Blake, William (1757–1827)
poet and artist
Poetical Sketches (1783)
All Religions Are One (1788?)
There is No Natural Religion (1788?)
Songs of Innocence (1789)
The Book of Thel (1789)
The Marriage of Heaven and Hell (1790?)
The French Revolution (1791)
America: A prophecy (1793)
For Children (1793)
Visions of the Daughters of Albion (1793)
Europe: A prophecy (1794)
The First Book of Urizen (1794)
Songs of Innocence and of Experience: Shewing the two contrary states of the human soul (1794)
The Book of Ahania (1795)
The Book of Los (1795)
The Song of Los (1795)
Milton (1808?)
A Descriptive Catalogue of Pictures, Poetical and Historical Inventions (1809)
Jerusalem: The emanation of the giant Albion (1818?)

Blanchard, Edward Litt Laman (1820–89)
dramatist and author
The Life of George Barnwell; or, The London Apprentice of the Last Century (1841)
Adams's Illustrated Descriptive Guide to the Watering-Places of England (1848)
Adams's Illustrated Guide to the Lake District (1852)

Blanchard, [Samuel] Laman (1804–45)
poet, essayist, and journalist
Lyric Offerings (1828)

Bleasdale, Alan (1946–)
playwright and novelist
Scully (1975)
The Boys from the Black Stuff (1985)

Blenerhasset, Thomas (1550?–1624/5?)
poet
The Seconde Part of the Mirrour for Magistrates (1578)
A Revelation of the True Minerva (1582)

Blessington, Marguerite Gardiner, *née* Power, countess of Blessington (1789–1849)
novelist and editor
The Magic Lantern; or, Sketches and Scenes in the Metropolis (1822)
The Repealers (1833)
Conversations of Lord Byron with the Countess of Blessington (1834)
The Confessions of an Elderly Gentleman (1836)
The Confessions of an Elderly Lady (1838)
The Governess (1839)
The Idler in Italy (1839)
Strathern; or, Life at Home and Abroad (1845)

Bligh, William (1754–1817)
admiral
A Narrative of the Mutiny, on Board His Britannic Majesty's Ship Bounty (1790)
A Voyage to the South Sea (1792)

Blind, Mathilde ['Claude Lake'] (1841–96)
poet
Poems (1867)

Bloomfield, Robert (1766–1823)
Suffolk poet
The Farmer's Boy (1800)
Rural Tales, Ballads and Songs (1802)
Good Tidings; or, News from the Farm (1804)
Wild Flowers; or, Pastoral and Local Poetry (1806)
The Banks of Wye (1811)
May Day with the Muses (1822)
Hazelwood Hall (1823)
The Remains of Robert Bloomfield (1824)
The Poems of Robert Bloomfield (1827)

Blount, Charles (1654–93)
deist
Mr Dreyden Vindicated (1673)
Great is Diana of the Ephesians; or, The Original of Idolatry (1680)
The Two First Books of Philostratus Concerning the Life of Apollonius Tyaneus (1680)
Miscellaneous Works (1695)

Blount, Sir Henry (1602–82)
traveller
A Voyage into the Levant (1636)

Blount, Sir Thomas Pope (1649–97)
politician and author
Essays on Several Subjects (1691)
De Re Poetica; or, Remarks upon Poetry (1694)

Blower, Elizabeth (*b.* 1763–post 1816)
novelist
The Parsonage House (1780)
George Bateman (1782)
Maria (1785)
Features from Life; or, A Summer Visit (1788)

Blunden, Edmund Charles (1896–1974)
poet and critic
Pastorals (1916)
The Waggoner, and Other Poems (1920)
The Shepherd, and Other Poems of Peace and War (1922)
To Nature (1923)
Masks of Time (1925)

English Poems (1926)
Undertones of War (1928)
Near and Far (1929)
The Poems of Edmund Blunden (1930)
Themis (1931)
Halfway House (1932)
The Mind's Eye (1934)
Choice or Chance (1934)
An Elegy, and Other Poems (1937)
Poems 1930–1940 (1941)
Shells by a Stream (1944)
Shelley (1946)
After the Bombing, and Other Short Poems (1949)
Poems of Many Years (1957)
A Hong Kong House (1962)

Blundeville, Thomas (*fl.* 1558–61)
writer on horsemanship and translator
Three Morall Treatises (1561)
Exercises (1594)
The Art of Logike (1599)

Blunt, Wilfrid Scawen ['Proteus'] (1840–1922)
poet, traveller, and Arabist
Sonnets and Songs (1875)
Proteus and Amadeus (1878)
The Love Sonnets of Proteus (1881)
The Wind and the Whirlwind (1883)
A New Pilgrimage, and Other Poems (1889)
Esther, Love Lyrics, and Natalia's Resurrection (1892)
Griselda (1893)
Satan Absolved (1899)
Poetical Works (1914)

Blythe, Ronald George (1922–)
novelist and author
Akenfield (1969)

Boaden, James (1762–1839)
dramatist and novelist
Fontainville Forest (1794)
The Italian Monk (1797)
Aurelio and Miranda (1799)

Bodenham, John (*fl.* 1600)
editor
Bel-vedére; or, The Garden of the Muses (1600)

Bodichon, Barbara Leigh, *née* Smith (1827–91)
feminist and journalist
A Brief Summary in Plain Language, of the Most Important Laws Concerning Women (1854)
Objections to the Enfranchisement of Women Considered (1866)

Boland, Eavan Aisling (1944–)
Irish poet and translator
The War Horse (1975)
In Her Own Image (1980)
The Journey, and Other Poems (1986)
Outside History (1990)
In a Time of Violence (1994)
Code (2001)

Bold, Alan Norman (1943–)
Scottish poet, critic, editor, and novelist
Society Inebrious (1965)
A Perpetual Motion Machine (1969)

Bold, Henry (1627–83)
poet
Wit a Sporting in a Pleasant Grove of New Fancies (1657)
Poems Lyrique Macaronique Heroique (1664)
Latine Songs, with their English: and Poems (1685)

'Boldrewood, Rolf' [Thomas Alexander Browne] (1826–1915)
British-born Australian novelist
Robbery Under Arms (1888)

Bolger, Dermot (1959–)
Irish novelist, playwright, and publisher
Night Shift (1985)
Leinster Street Ghosts (1989)
A Second Life (1994)
The Valparaiso Voyage (2001)

Bolt, Robert Oxton (1924–95)
playwright and screenwriter
Flowering Cherry (1958)
A Man for All Seasons (1961)
Doctor Zhivago (1966)
Vivat! Vivat Regina! (1971)

Bolton, Edmund ['Philanactophil'] (1575?–post 1634)
poet and historian
The Roman Histories of Lucius Julius Florus (1619)
Nero Caesar; or, Monarchie Depraved (1624)

Bonar, Horatius (1808–89)
poet and hymn writer
The Bible Hymn-Book (1845)

Bond, [Thomas] Edward (1934–)
playwright, poet, and translator
Early Morning (1968)
Narrow Road to the Deep North (1968)
Bingo: Scenes of money and death (and passion) (1974)
The Bundle; or, New Narrow Road to the Deep North (1978)
The War Plays (1985)
Two Post-Modern Plays (1990)

Boner, Charles (1815–70)
translator of Hans Andersen, poet, and journalist
A Danish Story-Book (1846)
The Nightingale, and Other Tales (1846)
The Dream of Little Tuk, and Other Tales (1848)

Bonhote, Elizabeth, *née* Mapes (1744–1818)
novelist
Hortensia (1769)
The Rambles of Mr Frankly (1772)
The Fashionable Friend (1773)
Olivia; or, Deserted Bride (1787)
Darnley Vale; or, Emelia Fitzroy (1789)
Ellen Woodley (1790)
Bungay Castle (1797)

Boole, George (1815–64)
mathematician

The Mathematical Analysis of Logic (1847)
Booth, Barton (1681–1733)
actor and author
The Death of Dido: A masque (1716)
Booth, Charles (1840–1916)
shipowner and writer on social questions
Life and Labour of the People in London (1892)
Booth, Martin (1944–2004)
novelist, poet, and critic
Hiroshima Joe (1985)
Booth, William (1829–1912)
founder of the Salvation Army
In Darkest England, and the Way Out (1890)
Boothby, Guy Newell (1867–1905)
novelist and short-story writer
A Bid for Fortune; or, Dr Nikola's Vendetta (1895)
Doctor Nikola (1896)
'Farewell, Nikola' (1901)
Borde or Boorde, Andrew (1490?–1549)
physician and traveller
Dyetary of Helth (1542)
The Breviary of Helthe (1547)
The Fyrst Boke of the Introduction of Knowledge (1555)
Borrow, George Henry (1803–81)
author and translator
Faustus: His Life, Death and Descent into Hell (1825)
Romantic Ballads (1826)
The Zincali; or, An Account of the Gypsies of Spain (1841)
The Bible in Spain (1843)
Lavengro: The scholar—the gypsy—the priest (1851)
The Romany Rye (1857)
Wild Wales (1862)
Boston, Lucy Maria (1892–1990)
children's writer
The Children of Green Knowe (1954)
Boston, Thomas, the elder (1677–1732)
Scottish divine
Human Nature in its Four-fold State (1720)
Boswell, Sir Alexander ['Simon Gray'] (1775–1822)
poet and antiquary
Songs, Chiefly in the Scottish Dialect (1802)
The Spirit of Tintoc; or, Johnny Bell and the Kelpie (1803)
Edinburgh; or, The Ancient Royalty (1810)
Boswell, James (1740–95)
biographer and author
The Cub at Newmarket (1762)
Dorando: A Spanish tale (1767)
An Account of Corsica (1768)
The Journal of a Tour to the Hebrides with Samuel Johnson (1785)
The Life of Samuel Johnson (1791)
Bosworth, William (1607–50?)
poet
The Chast and Lost Lovers (1651)
Bottome, Phyllis (1884–1963)
novelist
The Master Hope (1904)
London Pride (1941)
Bottomley, Gordon (1874–1948)
poet and dramatist
Poems at White-Nights (1899)
Chambers of Imagery [1st ser.] (1907)
Poems of Thirty Years (1925)
Scenes and Plays (1929)
A Stage for Poetry (1948)
Boucicault, Dion[ysius] Lardner (1820?–90)
dramatist
London Assurance: A comedy (1841)
Old Heads and Young Hearts: A comedy (1849)
The Corsican Brothers: A dramatic romance (1852)
The Colleen Bawn; or, The Brides of Garryowen (1860)
Bourchier, John, 2nd Baron Berners (1467–1533)
statesman and author
Huon of Bordeaux (1515?)
Froissart's Chronicles (1523)
Froissart's Chronicles (1525)
The Golden Boke of Marcus Aurelius (1535)
The Castell of Love (1548?)
Arthur of Little Britain (1560?)
Bowden, Samuel (*fl.* 1726–71)
physician and poet
Poetical Essays on Several Occasions [vol. i] (1733)
Bowdler, Henrietta (1754–1830)
expurgator of Shakespeare
The Family Shakespeare (1807)
Bowdler, Jane (1743–84)
author
Poems and Essays (1786)
Bowdler, Thomas (1754–1825)
expurgator of Shakespeare
The Family Shakespeare (1818)
Bowen, Elizabeth Dorothea Cole (1899–1973)
novelist, essayist, and short-story writer
Encounters (1923)
Joining Charles, and Other Stories (1929)
The Last September (1929)
The Cat Jumps, and Other Stories (1934)
The Death of the Heart (1938)
The Demon Lover, and Other Stories (1945)
Why Do I Write? (1948)
Eva Trout; or, Changing Scenes (1969)
Collected Stories (1981)
'Bowen, Marjorie' [Gabrielle Margaret Vere Campbell, later Long] ['George R. Preedy', 'Joseph Shearing'] (1886–1952)
novelist
The Viper of Milan (1906)
The Last Bouquet (1933)
Bowes, Thomas (*fl.* 1586)
translator
The French Academie (1586)

The Second Part of the French Academie (1594)
Bowles, Caroline Anne, later Southey (1786–1854)
poet
Ellen Fitzarthur (1820)
The Widow's Tale, and Other Poems (1822)
Solitary Hours (1826)
Chapters on Churchyards (1829)
Tales of the Factories (1833)
Bowles, William Lisle (1762–1850)
poet and antiquary
Fourteen Sonnets, Elegaic and Descriptive (1789)
Verses to John Howard (1789)
Hope (1796)
St Michael's Mount (1798)
Song of the Battle of the Nile (1799)
The Sorrows of Switzerland (1801)
The Picture (1803)
The Spirit of Discovery; or, The Conquest of Ocean (1804)
The Missionary (1813)
The Invariable Principles of Poetry (1819)
Two Letters to the Right Honourable Lord Byron (1821)
The Grave of the Last Saxon; or, The Legend of the Curfew (1822)
Ellen Gray; or, The Dead Maiden's Curse (1823)
A Final Appeal to the Literary Public, Relative to Pope (1825)
Lessons in Criticism to William Roscoe (1826)
Days Departed; or, Banwell Hill (1828)
St John in Patmos (1832)
Bowra, [Sir] [Cecil] Maurice (1898–1971)
scholar and critic
The Creative Experiment (1949)
The Romantic Imagination (1950)
Boyce, Samuel (*d.* 1775)
poet and dramatist
Poems on Several Occasions (1757)
Boyd, Andrew Kennedy Hutchinson (1825–99)
clergyman and essayist
Recreations of a Country Parson [1st ser.] (1859)
Boyd, Elizabeth ['Louisa'] (*fl.* 1727–45)
poet and novelist
Variety (1727)
The Happy-Unfortunate; or, The Female-Page (1732)
Boyd, William Andrew Murray (1952–)
novelist, short-story writer, and playwright
A Good Man in Africa (1981)
On the Yankee Station, and Other Stories (1981)
An Ice-Cream War (1982)
Stars and Bars (1984)
The New Confessions (1987)
Brazzaville Beach (1990)
The Blue Afternoon (1993)
The Destiny of Nathalie 'X', and Other Stories (1995)
Armadillo (1998)
Any Human Heart (2002)
Boyer, Abel (1667–1729)
historian and dramatist
Achilles; or, Iphigenia in Aulis: A tragedy (1700)
The History of the Reign of Queen Anne (1703)
The Political State of Great Britain (1711)
Boylan, Clare (1948–)
Irish novelist and short-story writer
Holy Pictures (1983)
A Nail in the Head (1983)
Last Resorts (1984)
Black Baby (1988)
Concerning Virgins (1989)
Home Rule (1992)
That Bad Woman (1995)
Another Family Christmas (1997)
Room For a Single Lady (1997)
Beloved Stranger (1999)
Emma Brown (2003)
Boyle, Charles, 4th earl of Orrery and first Baron Marston (1676–1731)
soldier, privy councillor, and author
Dr Bentley's Dissertations on the Epistles of Phalaris, and the Fables of Aesop (1698)
Boyle, Charles (1951)
poet
The Age of Cardboard and String (2001)
Boyle, [Hon.] Robert (1627–91)
scientist
Some Motives and Incentives to the Love of God (1659)
New Experiments Physico-Mechanicall, Touching the Spring of the Air, and its Effects (1660)
The Sceptical Chymist; or, Chymico-Physical Doubts & Paradoxes (1661)
Some Considerations Touching the Usefulnesse of Experimentall Naturall Philosophy (1663)
Experiments and Considerations Touching Colours (1664)
Hydrostatical Paradoxes (1666)
The Origine of Forms and Qualities (1666)
The Excellency of Theology, compar'd with Natural Philosophy (1674)
A Disquisition About the Final Causes of Natural Things (1688)
Boyle, Roger, Baron Broghill and 1st earl of Orrery (1621–79)
statesman and author
Parthenissa That Most Fam'd Romance (1651)
The History of Henry the Fifth; The Tragedy of Mustapha, Son of Solyman the Magnificent (1668)
Two New Tragedies: The Black Prince, and Tryphon (1669)
English Adventures (1676)
Parthenissa, that Most Fam'd Romance: The six volumes compleat (1676)
Mr Anthony: A comedy (1690)
Guzman: A comedy (1693)
Herod the Great: A tragedy (1694)

Boyse, Samuel (1708–49)
poet
Translations and Poems Written on Several Subjects (1731)
Deity (1739)
Albion's Triumph (1743)
Brackenbury, Alison (1953–)
poet
Dreams of Power (1981)
Breaking Ground (1984)
Christmas Roses (1988)
Bradbury, Sir Malcolm Stanley (1932–2000)
novelist and critic
Eating People is Wrong (1959)
Stepping Westward (1965)
What is a Novel? (1969)
The History Man (1975)
Who Do You Think You Are? (1976)
The Modern American Novel (1983)
Rates of Exchange (1983)
Cuts (1987)
My Strange Search for Mensonge (1987)
No, Not Bloomsbury (1987)
The Modern World (1988)
Dr Criminale (1992)
Dangerous Pilgrimages (1995)
Braddon, Mary Elizabeth, later Maxwell ['Babington White'] (1835–1915)
novelist, short-story writer, and editor
Three Times Dead; or, The Secret of the Heath (1854)
Lady Audley's Secret (1862)
Aurora Floyd (1863)
John Marchmont's Legacy (1863)
Henry Dunbar (1864)
Sons of Fire (1895)
Bradley, Andrew Cecil (1851–1935)
critic and scholar
Shakespearean Tragedy (1904)
Oxford Lectures on Poetry (1909)
Bradley, Francis Herbert (1846–1924)
philosopher
Ethical Studies (1876)
Appearance and Reality (1893)
Bradley, Henry (1845–1923)
philologist and lexicographer
The Making of English (1904)
Bradley, Katherine Harris (1846–1914), and Cooper, Edith Emma (1862–1913) ['Arran and Isla Leigh' and 'Michael Field']
poets and playwrights
Bellerophon, and Other Poems (1881)
Canute the Great; The Cup of Water (1887)
Underneath the Bough (1893)
Bradshaw, Henry (*d.* 1513)
Benedictine monk and hagiographer
The Life of St Werburgh (1521)
Bradstreet, Anne, *née* Dudley (1612–72)
poet
The Tenth Muse Lately Sprung Up in America (1650)
Brady, Nicholas (1659–1726)
poet
The Rape; or, The Innocent Impostors: A tragedy (1692)
Bragg, Melvyn (1939–)
novelist and broadcaster
For Want of a Nail (1965)
The Hired Man (1969)
A Place in England (1970)
Kingdom Come (1980)
The Maid of Buttermere (1987)
A Time to Dance (1990)
Credo (1996)
The Soldier's Return (1999)
A Son of War (2001)
Crossing the Lines (2003)
Braine, John Gerard (1922–86)
novelist
Room at the Top (1957)
Life at the Top (1962)
The Jealous God (1964)
The Crying Game (1968)
Stay With Me Till Morning (1970)
The Queen of a Distant Country (1972)
One and Last Love (1981)
The Two of Us (1984)
These Golden Days (1985)
'Bramah, Ernest' [Ernest Bramah Smith] (1868–1942)
detective story writer
The Wallet of Kai Lung (1900)
Max Carrados (1914)
Kai Lung Unrolls his Mat (1928)
Bramhall, John (1594–1663)
archbishop of Armagh
The Serpent Salve, or, A Remedie for the Biting of an Aspe (1643)
Castigations of Mr Hobbes and his Last Animadversions in the Case Concerning Liberty and Universal Necessity (1657)
Bishop Bramhall's Vindication of Himself and the Episcopal Clergy (1672)
Bramston, James (1694?–1744)
poet and satirist
The Art of Politicks (1729)
The Man of Taste (1733)
The Crooked Six-pence (1743)
Brand, Barbarina, *née* Ogle, Lady Dacre (1768–1854)
poet and dramatist
Ina: A tragedy (1815)
Brathwaite or Braithwait, Richard ['Corymboeus'] (1588?–1673)
poet
The Golden Fleece (1611)
The Poets Willow; or, The Passionate Shepheard (1614)
The Schollers Medley; or, An Intermixt Discourse Upon Historicall and Poeticall Relations (1614)
A Strappado for the Divell (1615)

A New Spring Shadowed in Sundry Pithie Poems (1619)
Essaies Upon the Five Senses, with a Pithie One upon Detraction (1620)
Natures Embassie; or, The Wilde-Mans Measures (1621)
Times Curtaine Drawne; or, The Anatomie of Vanitie (1621)
The English Gentleman (1630)
The English Gentlewoman (1631)
Whimzies; or, A New Cast of Characters (1631)
Anniversaries upon his Panarete (1634)
A Strange Metamorphosis of Man: Deciphered in characters (1634)
Anniversaries upon his Panarete; Continued (1635)
The Arcadian Princesse; or, The Triumph of Justice (1635)
The Fatall Nuptiall; or, Mournefull Marriage (1636)
Barnabees Journall, under the Names of Mirtilus & Faustulus Shadowed (1638)
The Psalmes of David the King and Prophet, and of Other Holy Prophets (1638)
A Spiritual Spicerie (1638)
Ar't Asleepe Husband?: A boulster lecture (1640)
The Two Lancashire Lovers; or, The Excellent History of Philocles and Doriclea (1640)
The English Gentleman; and The English Gentlewoman (1641)
The Honest Ghost; or, A Voice from the Vault (1658)
Capitall Hereticks; or, The Evill Angels Embattel'd against S. Michael (1659)
A Comment Upon the Two Tales of Our Ancient, Renowned, and Ever-Living Poet Sr Jeffray Chaucer, Knight (1665)

Bray, Anna Eliza, *née* Kempe, later Stothard (1790–1883)
novelist
De Foix; or, Sketches of the Manners and Customs of the Fourteenth Century (1826)
The White Hoods (1828)
Trials of Domestic Life (1834)
Trials of the Heart (1839)

Brazil, Angela (1869–1947)
writer of school stories for girls
A Terrible Tomboy (1904)

Brenan, Gerald [Edward Fitzgerald Brenan] ['George Beaton'] (1894–1987)
writer on Spain and Spanish culture
The Spanish Labyrinth (1943)
The Face of Spain (1950)

Brent-Dyer, Elinor M. (1894–1969)
writer of school stories
The School at the Chalet (1925)

Brenton, Howard (1942–)
playwright, poet, and novelist
Christie in Love, and Other Plays (1970)
Plays for Public Places: Gum and Goo; Wesley; Scott of the Antarctic (1972)
Brassneck (1974)
Weapons of Happiness (1976)
Epsom Downs (1977)
The Romans in Britain (1980)
Pravda: A Fleet Street comedy (1985)
Plays 1 (1986)
Dead Head (1987)
Iranian Nights (1989)
Moscow Gold (1990)

Brereton, Jane, *née* Hughes (1685–1740)
poet
The Fifth Ode of the Fourth Book of Horace, Imitated (1716)
An Expostulatory Epistle to Sir Richard Steele upon the Death of Mr Addison (1720)
Merlin (1735)
Poems on Several Occasions (1744)

Breton, Nicholas (1545?–1626?)
poet
A Smale Handfull of Fragrant Flowers (1575)
A Floorish upon Fancie (1577)
The Workes of a Young Wyt (1577)
A Discourse in Commendation of the Valiant Gentleman, Maister Frauncis Drake (1581)
Brittons Bowre of Delights (1591)
The Pilgrimage to Paradise (1592)
Marie Magdalens Love; A Solemne Passion of the Soules Love (1595)
The Arbor of Amorous Devises (1597)
Auspicante Jehova (1597)
The Wil of Wit, Wits Wil, or Wils Wit, Chuse You Whether (1597)
Wits Trenchmour (1597)
A Solemne Passion of the Soules Love (1598)
The Passions of the Spirit (1599)
Melancholike Humours (1600)
Pasquils Mad-cap and his Message (1600)
Pasquils Mistresse; or, The Worthie and Unworthie Woman (1600)
Pasquils Passe, and Passeth Not (1600)
The Second Part of Pasquils Mad-cap intituled: The Fooles-cap (1600)
The Strange Fortunes of Two Excellent Princes (1600)
A Divine Poeme (1601)
The Mother's Blessing (1602)
Olde Mad-Cappes New Gally-Mawfrey (1602)
A Poste with a Madde Packet of Letters [pt i] (1602)
The Soules Harmony (1602)
A True Description of Unthankfulnesse; or, An Enemie to Ingratitude (1602)
Wonders Worth the Hearing (1602)
A Merrie Dialogue Betwixt the Taker and Mistaker (1603)
Grimellos Fortunes, with His Entertainment in his Travaile (1604)
The Passionate Shepheard; or, The Shepheardes Love (1604)

The Honour of Valour (1605)
I Pray You Be Not Angrie: A pleasant and merry dialogue, betweene two travellers (1605)
An Olde Mans Lesson, and a Young Mans Love (1605)
The Soules Immortall Crowne (1605)
Wits Private Wealth (1607)
Divine Considerations of the Soule (1608)
The Uncasing of Machivils Instructions to his Sonne (1613)
Characters Upon Essaies Morall, and Divine (1615)
Conceyted Letters, Newly Layde Open (1618)
The Court and Country; or, A Briefe Discourse Betweene the Courtier and Country-Man (1618)
Strange Newes Out of Divers Countries (1622)
Fantasticks: Serving for a Perpetuall Prognostication (1626)
The Figure of Foure; or, A Handful of Sweet Flowers (1631)

Breval, John Durant ['Joseph Gay'] (1680?–1738)
miscellaneous writer
The Art of Dress (1717)
The Confederates: A farce (1717)
Mac-Dermot; or, The Irish Fortune-Hunter (1719)
Ovid in Masquerade (1719)
Morality in Vice: An heroi-comical poem (1733)

Brewer, Ebenezer Cobham (1810–97)
miscellaneous writer
A Dictionary of Phrase and Fable (1870)

Brewer, Thomas (*fl.* 1624)
miscellaneous writer
The Life and Death of the Merry Devill of Edmonton (1631)

Brewster, Sir David (1781–1868)
natural philosopher
A Treatise on New Philosophical Instruments (1813)
The Life of Sir Isaac Newton (1831)
A Treatise on Optics (1831)
Letters on Natural Magic (1832)

Brice, Thomas (*d.* 1570)
martyrologist
A Compendious Register in Metre, Conteining the Names, and Pacient Suffryngs of the Membres of Jesus Christ (1559)
Against Filthy Writing, and Such Like Delighting (1562)

Bridges, John (*d.* 1618)
dean of Salisbury and bishop of Oxford
A Sermon, Preached at Paules Crosse (1571)
The Supremacie of Christian Princes (1573)
A Defence of the Government Established in the Church of Englande for Ecclesiasticall Matters (1587)

Bridges, Robert Seymour (1844–1930)
Poet Laureate, critic, and playwright
Poems by Robert Bridges (1873)
The Growth of Love (1876)
Poems (1879)
Poems (1880)
Prometheus the Firegiver (1883)
Eros and Psyche (1885)
Nero: Part 1 (1885)
The Feast of Bacchus (1889)
Palicio: A romantic drama in the Elizabethan manner (1890)
The Return of Ulysses: A drama in a mixed manner (1890)
The Christian Captives: A tragedy in a mixed manner (1890)
Achilles in Scyros: A drama in a mixed manner (1890)
The Humours of the Court: a Comedy; and Other Poems (1893)
Nero: Part 2 (1894)
Invocation to Music (1895)
Poetical Works [vol. i] (1898)
Now in Wintry Delights (1903)
Demeter (1905)
Poetical Works Excluding the Eight Dramas (1912)
October, and Other Poems (1920)
New Verse Written in 1921 (1925)
The Testament of Beauty (1929)
Shorter Poems (1931)

'Bridie, James' [Osborne Henry Mavor] (1888–1951)
playwright
The Switchback; The Pardoner's Tale; The Sunlight Sonata (1930)
The Anatomist, and Other Plays (1931)
Susannah and the Elders, and Other Plays (1940)
Plays for Plain People (1944)
John Knox, and Other Plays (1949)

Briggs, Asa, Lord Briggs (1921–)
social historian
Victorian Things (1988)

Brighouse, Harold (1882–1958)
playwright
Hobson's Choice (1916)

Bright, Timothy (1551?–1615)
physician and inventor of shorthand
Characterie (1588)

Bright, William (1824–1901)
church historian
A History of the Church from the Edict of Milan to the Council of Chalcedon (1860)

Brinkelow, Henry ['Roderigo Mors'] (*d.* 1546)
satirist
The Lamentacion of a Christian, Against the Citie of London (1542)

Brinsley, John, the elder (*fl.* 1633)
Puritan divine, educational writer, and translator of Ovid
Ludus Literarius; or, The Grammar Schoole (1612)
Ovids Metamorphosis Translated Grammatically (1618)

Briscoe, Sophia (*fl.* 1771–2)
novelist
The Fine Lady (1772)
Brittain, Vera Mary (1893–1970)
author, pacifist, and feminist
The Dark Tide (1923)
Testament of Youth (1933)
Testament of Friendship (1940)
Seed of Chaos (1944)
Testament of Experience (1957)
Broad, Charlie Dunbar (1887–1971)
philosopher
Perception, Physics and Reality (1914)
Brome, Alexander (1620–66)
poet
The Cunning Lovers: A comedy (1654)
Songs and Other Poems (1661)
Brome, Richard (1590?–1652?)
dramatist
The Northern Lasse: A comoedie (1632)
The Sparagus Garden: A comedie (1640)
Lachrymae Musarum: The Tears of the Muses (1649)
A Joviall Crew; or, The Merry Beggars (1652)
Five New Playes (1653)
The Queenes Exchange: A comedy (1657)
Five New Plays (1659)
Brontë, Anne ['Acton Bell'] (1820–49)
novelist
Poems by Currer, Ellis and Acton Bell (1846)
Wuthering Heights; Agnes Grey (1847)
The Tenant of Wildfell Hall (1848)
Brontë, Charlotte, later Nicholls ['Currer Bell'] (1816–55)
novelist
Poems by Currer, Ellis and Acton Bell (1846)
Jane Eyre: An autobiography (1847)
Shirley (1849)
Villette (1853)
The Professor (1857)
Brontë, Emily Jane ['Ellis Bell'] (1818–48)
novelist and poet
Poems by Currer, Ellis and Acton Bell (1846)
Wuthering Heights; Agnes Grey (1847)
Brooke or Broke, Arthur (*d.* 1563)
translator
The Tragicall Historye of Romeus and Juliet (1562)
Brooke, [Bernard] Jocelyn (1908–66)
novelist and poet
The Military Orchid (1948)
The Scapegoat (1948)
A Mine of Serpents (1949)
The Goose Cathedral (1950)
Brooke, Charlotte (1740?–93)
translator and anthologist
Reliques of Irish Poetry (1789)
Brooke, Frances, *née* Moore ['Mary Singleton'] (1724–89)
novelist and playwright
Virginia: A tragedy (1756)
Letters from Juliet, Lady Catesby (1760)
The History of Lady Julia Mandeville (1763)
The History of Emily Montague (1769)
Memoirs of the Marquis de St Forlaix (1770)
The Excursion (1777)
The Siege of Sinope: A tragedy (1781)
Rosina: A comic opera (1783)
The History of Charles Mandeville (1790)
Marian: A comic opera (1800)
Brooke, Henry (1703–83)
poet, novelist, and dramatist
Universal Beauty (1735)
A New Collection of Fairy Tales (1750)
The Earl of Essex: A tragedy (1761)
The Fool of Quality; or, The History of Henry Earl of Moreland (1766)
Juliet Grenville; or, The History of the Human Heart (1774)
Brooke, Rupert Chawner (1887–1915)
poet
Poems (1911)
1914, and Other Poems (1915)
Letters From America (1916)
Selected Poems (1917)
The Collected Poems of Rupert Brooke (1918)
The Poetical Works of Rupert Brooke (1946)
Brooke-Rose, Christine (1923–)
novelist, critic, and translator
The Languages of Love (1957)
Remake (1958)
The Sycamore Tree (1958)
The Dear Deceit (1960)
The Middlemen (1961)
Out (1964)
Thru (1975)
Amalgamemnon (1984)
Xorandor (1986)
Verbivore (1990)
Textermination (1991)
Brookfield, Jane Octavia, *née* Elton (1821–96)
novelist
Only George (1866)
Brookner, Anita (1928–)
novelist and art historian
A Start in Life (1981)
Providence (1982)
Look at Me (1983)
Hotel du Lac (1984)
Family and Friends (1985)
A Misalliance (1986)
A Friend From England (1987)
Latecomers (1988)
Lewis Percy (1989)
Brief Lives (1990)
A Closed Eye (1991)
Fraud (1992)
A Family Romance (1993)
A Private View (1994)
Incidents in the Rue Laugier (1995)
Altered States (1996)
Visitors (1997)

Undue Influence (1999)
The Bay of Angels (2000)
The Next Big Thing (2002)
The Rules of Engagement (2003)

Brooks, [Charles William] Shirley [writing also as Charles W. Brooks, C. Shirley Brooks] (1816–74)
novelist, dramatist, and journalist
Timour the Tartar! An extravaganza (1850)

Brophy, Brigid Antonia Susan (1929–)
novelist, biographer, and critic
Hackenfeller's Ape (1953)
The King of a Rainy Country (1956)
Flesh (1962)
The Finishing Touch (1963)
The Snow Ball (1964)
In Transit (1969)
Palace Without Chairs (1978)

Broster, Dorothy Kathleen (1878–1950)
novelist
Couching at the Door (1942)

Brough, Robert Barnabas (1828–60)
novelist, poet, and dramatist
Marston Lynch (1860)

Brougham, Henry Peter, Baron Brougham and Vaux (1778–1868)
statesman and historian
An Inquiry into the Colonial Policy of the European Powers (1803)
Practical Observations upon the Education of the People (1825)
Thoughts on Negro Slavery (1826)
Thoughts upon the Aristocracy of England (1835)
'We Can't Afford It!' (1835)
Political Philosophy (1842)
Albert Lunel; or, The Chateau of Languedoc (1844)
The British Constitution (1844)

Broughton, Rhoda (1840–1920)
novelist
Cometh Up as a Flower (1867)
Not Wisely But Too Well (1867)
Red as a Rose is She (1870)

Broughton, Thomas (1704–74)
divine, biographer, and miscellaneous writer
Hercules: A musical drama (1745)

Brown, Christy (1932–81)
Irish novelist and poet
My Left Foot (1954)
Down all the Days (1970)

Brown, George Douglas ['George Douglas', 'Kennedy King'] (1869–1902)
novelist
Love and a Sword (1899)
The House With the Green Shutters (1901)

Brown, George Mackay (1921–96)
Scottish poet, novelist, and short-story writer
Loaves and Fishes (1959)
The Year of the Whale (1965)
A Calendar of Love, and Other Stories (1967)
A Time to Keep, and Other Stories (1969)
Fishermen with Ploughs (1971)
Greenvoe (1972)
Magnus (1973)
Hawkfall, and Other Stories (1974)
Letters from Hamnavoe (1975)
The Sun's Net (1976)
Winterfold (1976)
Under Brinkie's Brae (1979)
Voyages (1983)
Christmas Poems (1984)
Three Plays (1984)
Time in a Red Coast (1984)
The Keepers of the House (1987)
The Wreck of the Archangel (1989)
The Sea King's Daughter (1991)
Selected Poems 1954–1983 (1991)
Brodgar Poems (1992)
The Lost Village (1992)
Vinland (1992)
Beside the Ocean of Time (1994)
For the Islands I Sing (1997)
The Island of the Women, and Other Stories (1998)

Brown, John ['Estimate'] (1715–66)
clergyman, poet, and dramatist
Honour (1743)
An Essay on Satire: Occasion'd by the death of Mr Pope (1745)
On Liberty (1749)
Barbarossa: A tragedy (1755)
Athelstan: A tragedy (1756)
An Estimate of the Manners and Principles of the Times (1757)
An Explanatory Defence of the Estimate of the Manners and Principles of the Times (1758)
A Dissertation on Poetry and Music (1763)
Description of the Lake of Keswick (1771)

Brown, Dr John (1810–82)
essayist
Horae Subsecivae (1858)
Rab and His Friends (1859)

Brown, Oliver Madox (1855–74)
novelist
Gabriel Denver (1873)
The Dwale Bluth, Hebditch's Legacy, and Other Literary Remains (1876)

Brown, Thomas (1663–1704)
poet and novelist
The Reasons of Mr Bays Changing his Religion (1688)
The Late Converts Exposed (1690)
A Collection of Miscellany Poems, Letters, etc. (1699)
Amusements Serious and Comical (1700)
A Description of Mr Dryden's Funeral (1700)
Letters From the Dead to the Living (1702)
The Works of Mr Thomas Brown, in Prose and Verse (1707)
The Remains of Mr Thomas Brown, Serious and Comical (1720)

Brown, Thomas (1778–1820)
philosopher and poet
Observations on the Zoonomia of Erasmus Darwin (1798)
Poems (1804)
Observations on the Nature and Tendency of the Doctrine of Mr Hume (1805)
The Paradise of Coquettes (1814)
The Wanderer in Norway (1816)
Lectures on the Philosophy of the Human Mind (1820)

Brown, Thomas Edward (1830–97)
Manx poet
The Doctor, and Other Poems (1887)
The Manx Witch, and Other Poems (1889)

Browne, Frances (1816–79)
novelist, poet, and children's writer
The Star of Attéghéi; The Vision of Schwartz, and Other Poems (1844)
Granny's Wonderful Chair, and Its Tales of Fairy Times (1857)

Browne, Isaac Hawkins, the elder (1705–60)
wit and poet
On Design and Beauty (1734)
A Pipe of Tobacco (1736)
Poems Upon Various Subjects, Latin and English (1768)

Browne, Mary Ann (1812–44)
poet
Ada, and Other Poems (1828)

Browne, Moses (1704–87)
poet
Piscatory Eclogues (1729)
Poems on Various Subjects (1739)
The Works and Rest of the Creation (1752)
The Excellency of the Knowledge of Jesus Christ (1772)

Browne, Peter (*c*.1665–1735)
divine
The Procedure, Extent, and Limits of Human Understanding (1728)
Things Supernatural and Divine Conceived by Analogy with things Natural and Human (1733)

Browne, Sir Thomas (1605–82)
physician and author
Religio Medici (1642)
Religio Medici (1643)
Pseudodoxia Epidemica; or, Enquiries into Very Many Received Tenets, and Commonly Presumed Truths (1646)
Hydriotaphia, Urne-Buriall; or, A Discourse of the Sepulchrall Urnes Lately Found in Norfolk (1658)
Certain Miscellany Tracts (1683)
The Works of the Learned Sir Thomas Brown (1686)
A Letter to a Friend (1690)
Posthumous Works of the Learned Sir Thomas Browne, (1712)
Christian Morals (1716)

Browne, William, of Tavistock (1591–1643)
Britannia's Pastorals [bk i] (1613)
The Shepheard's Pipe (1614)
Britannia's Pastorals. The Second Booke (1616)

Browning, Elizabeth Barrett, *née* Barrett (1806–61)
poet
The Battle of Marathon (1820)
An Essay on Mind, with Other Poems (1826)
Prometheus Bound (1833)
The Seraphim, and Other Poems (1838)
Poems (1844)
Poems (1850)
Casa Guidi Windows (1851)
Poems (1853)
Two Poems (1854)
Poems (1856)
Aurora Leigh (1856)
Poems Before Congress (1860)
Last Poems (1862)
The Greek Christian Poets and the English Poets (1863)

Browning, Robert (1812–89)
poet
Pauline: A fragment of a confession (1833)
Paracelsus (1835)
Strafford: An historical tragedy (1837)
Sordello (1840)
Pippa Passes [*Bells and Pomegranates* i] (1841)
King Victor and King Charles [*Bells and Pomegranates* ii] (1842)
Dramatic Lyrics [*Bells and Pomegranates* iii] (1842)
The Return of the Druses [*Bells and Pomegranates* iv] (1843)
A Blot in the 'Scutcheon [*Bells and Pomegranates* v] (1843)
Colombe's Birthday [*Bells and Pomegranates* vi] (1844)
Dramatic Romances and Lyrics [*Bells and Pomegranates* vii] (1845)
Luria: a Tragedy; A Soul's Tragedy [*Bells and Pomegranates* viii] (1846)
Poems (1849)
Christmas-Eve and Easter-Day (1850)
Men and Women (1855)
Poetical Works (1863)
Dramatis Personae (1864)
Poetical Works: Fourth edition (1865)
Poetical Works (1868)
The Ring and the Book [vols i, ii] (1868)
The Ring and the Book [vols iii, iv] (1869)
Balaustion's Adventure (1871)
Prince Hohenstiel-Schwangau, Saviour of Society (1871)
Fifine at the Fair (1872)
Red Cotton Night-Cap Country; or, Turf and Towers (1873)
Aristophanes' Apology (1875)
Pacchiarotto and How He Worked in Distemper; with Other Poems (1876)

La Saisiaz; The Two Poets of Croisic (1878)
Dramatic Idyls [1st ser.] (1879)
Dramatic Idyls [2nd ser.] (1880)
Jocoseria (1883)
Ferishtah's Fancies (1884)
Parleyings with Certain People of Importance in their Day (1887)
Asolando: Fancies and facts (1889)

Brownjohn, Alan [Charles] (1931–)
poet
Travellers Alone (1954)
The Railings (1961)
The Lions' Mouths (1967)
Sandgrains on a Tray (1969)
Warrior's Career (1972)
A Song of Good Life (1975)
A Night in the Gazebo (1980)
Collected Poems 1952–1983 (1983)
The Old Flea-Pit (1987)
Collected Poems 1952–1988 (1988)
The Observation Car (1990)
In the Cruel Arcade (1994)

Bruce, James (1730–94)
explorer and author
Travels to Discover the Source of the Nile (1790)

Bruce, Michael (1746–67)
poet
Poems on Several Occasions (1770)

Brunton, Mary, *née* Balfour (1778–1818)
novelist
Self-Control (1811)
Discipline (1814)
Emmeline (1819)

Bryan, Sir Francis (*d.* 1550)
poet, translator, soldier, and diplomatist
A Dispraise of the Life of a Courtier, and a Commendacion of the Life of the Labouryng Man (1548)

Bryant, Jacob (1715–1804)
scholar
An Address to Dr Priestley (1780)

Brydges, Sir Samuel Egerton (1762–1837)
poet, novelist, and bibliographer
Sonnets and Other Poems (1785)
Mary de-Clifford (1792)
Arthur Fitz-Albini (1798)
Le Forester (1802)
Censura Literaria (1805)
Poems (1807)
The British Bibliographer (1810)
Bertram (1816)
Letters on the Character and Poetical Genius of Lord Byron (1824)
An Impartial Portrait of Lord Byron as a Poet and a Man (1825)
Autobiography (1834)

Brydone, Patrick (1736–1818)
traveller and author
A Tour Through Sicily and Malta (1773)

Buchan, John, 1st Baron Tweedsmuir (1875–1940)
novelist, biographer, and statesman
Sir Quixote of the Moors (1895)
The Watcher by the Threshold, and Other Tales (1902)
Prester John (1910)
The Moon Endureth (1912)
The Thirty-Nine Steps (1915)
Greenmantle (1916)
The Power-House (1916)
Mr Standfast (1919)
Huntingtower (1922)
Midwinter (1923)
John Macnab (1925)
Witch Wood (1927)
The Runagates Club (1928)
The Gap in the Curtain (1932)
The Island of Sheep (1936)
Memory-Hold-the-Door (1940)
Sick Heart River (1941)

Buchan, William (1729–1805)
physician
Domestic Medicine; or, The Family Physician (1769)

Buchanan, George (1506–82)
historian, scholar, and poet
The Admonitioun (1571)
Ane Detectioun of the Duinges of Marie Quene of Scottes (1571)
Baptistes (1577)
De jure regno apud scotos, dialogus (1579)
Paraphrasis psalmorum Davidis (1580)
Rerum Scoticarum historia (1582)
An Assay; or, Buchanan his Paraphrase on the First Twentie Psalmes (1627)

Buchanan, Robert Williams (1841–1901)
poet, dramatist, novelist, and critic
The Fleshly School of Poetry, and Other Phenomena of the Day (1872)
Poetical Works (1878)
The New Rome: Poems and ballads of our empire (1899)

Bucke, Charles (1781–1846)
poet and author
The Fall of the Leaf, and Other Poems (1819)

Buckeridge, Anthony (1912–2004)
writer of school stories and creator of Jennings
Jennings Goes to School (1950)

Buckle, Henry Thomas (1821–62)
historian
History of Civilization in England (1857)

Bullein, William (*d.* 1576)
physician
A Newe Booke Entituled the Governement of Healthe (1558)
Bulleins Bulwarke of Defence Againste all Sicknes, Sornes, and Woundes (1562)
A Dialogue Both Pleasant and Piety-full, Against the Fever Pestilence (1564)

Bullock, Alan Louis Charles, Lord Bullock (1914–)
historian
Hitler: a Study in Tyranny (1952)
Bullock, Christopher (1690?–1724)
comedian and dramatist
A Woman's Revenge; or, A Match in Newgate: A comedy (1715)
Bullock, Shan Fadh [John William Bullock] (1865–1935)
novelist
Irish Pastorals (1901)
Bullokar, John (*fl.* 1622)
lexicographer
An English Expositor (1616)
Bullokar, William (*fl.* 1586)
phonetist
Bullokars Booke at Large, For the Amendment of Orthographie for English Speech (1580)
A Short Introduction or Guiding to Print, Write, and Reade Inglish Speech (1580)
William Bullokarz Pamphlet for Grammar (1586)
Bulteel, John, the younger (*fl.* 1683)
translator and miscellaneous writer
Birinthea: A romance (1664)
Amorous Orontus; or, The Love in Fashion: A comedy (1665)
The Comical Romance; or, A Facetious History of a Company of Stage-players (1665)
Bulwer, John (*fl.* 1648–54)
physician and author
Chirologia; or, The Naturall Language of the Hand (1644)
Anthropometamorphosis, Man Transform'd, or, The Artificial Changeling (1650)
Bulwer-Lytton, Edward George Earle Lytton, 1st Baron Lytton (1803–73)
novelist and dramatist
Ismael: An Oriental Tale, with Other Poems (1820)
Delmour; or, A Tale of a Sylphid, and Other Poems (1823)
Falkland (1827)
O'Neill; or, The Rebel (1827)
Pelham; or, The Adventures of a Gentleman (1828)
Devereux (1829)
The Disowned (1829)
Paul Clifford (1830)
Eugene Aram (1832)
England and the English (1833)
Godolphin (1833)
The Last Days of Pompeii (1834)
The Pilgrims of the Rhine (1834)
Rienzi, the Last of the Tribunes (1835)
The Duchess de la Vallière (1836)
Ernest Maltravers (1837)
Alice; or, The Mysteries (1838)
The Lady of Lyons; or, Love and Pride (1838)
Leila; Calderon the Courtier (1838)
Richelieu; or, The Conspiracy (1839)
Money (1840)
Eva; The Ill-Omened Marriage; and Other Tales and Poems (1842)
Zanoni (1842)
The Last of the Barons (1843)
Harold, the Last of the Saxon Kings (1848)
The Caxtons (1849)
King Arthur (1849)
'My Novel'; or, Varieties in English Life (1853)
A Strange Story (1862)
Caxtoniana: A series of essays on life, literature and manners (1863)
The Coming Race (1871)
Bulwer-Lytton, Rosina Doyle, *née* Wheeler, Lady Bulwer-Lytton (1802–82)
novelist
Cheveley; or, The Man of Honour (1839)
The Budget of the Bubble Family (1840)
The Peer's Daughters (1849)
Bunbury, Selina (1802–82)
Irish novelist
The Pastor's Tales (1826)
Cabin Conversations and Castle Scenes (1827)
The Abbey of Innismoyle (1828)
Retrospections (1829)
Tales of My Country (1833)
Bunting, Basil (1900–85)
poet
Poems: 1950 (1950)
Briggflatts (1966)
Collected Poems (1968)
Bunyan, John (1628–88)
religious writer
Some Gospel-Truths Opened According to the Scriptures (1656)
A Vindication of the Book Called Some Gospel-Truths Opened (1657)
A Few Sighs from Hell; or, The Groans of a Damned Soul (1658)
The Doctrine of the Law and Grace Unfolded (1659)
Profitable Meditations Fitted to Mans Different Condition (1661)
Christian Behaviour; or, The Fruits of True Christianity (1663)
The Holy City; or, The New Jerusalem (1665)
The Resurrection of the Dead, and Eternall Judgement (1665)
Grace Abounding to the Chief of Sinners (1666)
A Confession of My Faith, and a Reason of My Practice (1672)
A Defence of the Doctrine of Justification, by Faith in Jesus Christ (1672)
The Barren Fig-Tree; or, The Doom and Downfall of the Fruitless Professor (1673)
Differences in Judgment About Water-Baptism, No Bar to Communion (1673)
Instruction for the Ignorant (1675)
Light for Them That Sit in Darkness; or, A Discourse of Jesus Christ (1675)

The Strait Gate; or, Great Difficulty of Going to Heaven (1676)
Come, & Welcome, to Jesus Christ (1678)
The Pilgrim's Progress From This World, To That Which is To Come (1678)
A Treatise of the Fear of God (1679)
The Life and Death of Mr Badman (1680)
The Holy War, Made by Shaddai Upon Diabolus, for the Regaining of the Metropolis of the World (1682)
A Case of Conscience Resolved (1683)
The Greatness of the Soul, and Unspeakableness of the Loss Thereof (1683)
A Holy Life, the Beauty of Christianity; or, An Exhortation to Christians to be Holy (1684)
The Pilgrim's Progress From This World to That Which is To Come: The Second Part (1684)
Seasonable Counsel; or, Advice to Sufferers (1684)
A Discourse upon the Pharisee and the Publicane (1685)
Questions About the Nature and Perpetuity of the Seventh-Day-Sabbath (1685)
A Book for Boys and Girls; or, Country Rhimes for Children (1686)
A Discourse of the Building, Nature, Excellency, and Government of the House of God (1688)
Good News for the Vilest of Men (1688)
Solomon's Temple Spiritualized (1688)
The Water of Life (1688)
The Acceptable Sacrifice; or, The Excellency of a Broken Heart (1689)
Mr John Bunyan's Last Sermon (1689)
The Works of That Eminent Servant of Christ, Mr John Bunyan (1692)
The Heavenly Foot-Man; or, A Description of the Man that Gets to Heaven (1698)
A Relation of [*the*] Imprisonment of Mr John Bunyan (1765)

Burell, Lady Sophia, *née* Raymond, later Clay (1750?–1802)
poet
Poems (1793)

Burges, Sir James Bland [after 1821 known as Sir James Lamb] (1752–1824)
politician and author
The Birth and Triumph of Love (1796)
Richard the First (1801)
Dramas (1817)
The Dragon Knight (1818)

'Burgess, Anthony' [John Anthony Burgess Wilson] ['Joseph Kell'] (1917–93)
novelist, critic, and translator
Time for a Tiger (1956)
The Enemy in the Blanket (1958)
Beds in the East (1959)
The Doctor is Sick (1960)
The Right to an Answer (1960)
Devil of a State (1961)
A Clockwork Orange (1962)
The Wanting Seed (1962)
Honey for the Bears (1963)
Inside Mr Enderby (1963)
The Novel Today (1963)
The Eve of St Venus (1964)
Nothing Like the Sun (1964)
Here Comes Everybody (1965)
A Vision of Battlements (1965)
Tremor of Intent (1966)
The Novel Now (1967)
Enderby Outside (1968)
Urgent Copy (1968)
MF (1971)
The Clockwork Testament; or, Enderby's End (1974)
Napoleon Symphony (1974)
Abba Abba (1977)
Beard's Roman Women (1977)
1985 (1978)
Earthly Powers (1980)
The End of the World News (1982)
Enderby's Dark Lady (1984)
Homage to QWERTYUIOP: Selected journalism (1985)
The Kingdom of the Wicked (1985)
The Pianoplayers (1986)
Little Wilson and Big God (1987)
Any Old Iron (1989)
The Devil's Mode, and Other Stories (1989)
You've Had Your Time (1990)
Mozart and the Wolf Gang (1991)
A Mouthful of Air: Language and languages (1992)
A Dead Man in Deptford (1993)

Burgh, Benet (*d.* 1483)
translator
Parvus Cato; Magnus Cato (1476)

Burgoyne, John (1722–92)
soldier and dramatist
The Maid of the Oaks (1774)
The Heiress: A comedy (1786)
Richard Coeur de Lion (1786)

Burke, Edmund (1729–97)
statesman and philosopher
A Vindication of Natural Society (1756)
A Philosophical Enquiry into the Origin of Our Ideas of the Sublime and Beautiful (1757)
The Annual Register (1759)
A Short Account of a Late Short Administration (1766)
Observations on a Late State of the Nation (1769)
Thoughts on the Cause of the Present Discontents (1770)
Speech on American Taxation, April 19, 1774 (1775)
Speech on Conciliation with the Colonies, March 22, 1775 (1775)
Letter to the Sheriffs of Bristol, on the Affairs of America (1777)
Two Letters on the Trade of Ireland (1778)
Speech on Oeconomical Reformation (1780)
Letter on the Penal Laws Against Irish Catholics (1783)

Speech on the East India Bill (1784)
Speech on the Nabob of Arcot's Debts (1785)
A Letter to Philip Francis (1788)
Reflections on the Revolution in France (1790)
Speech on the Army Estimates (1790)
An Appeal from the New to the Old Whigs (1791)
Letter to a Member of the National Assembly (1791)
Two Letters on the Revolution in France (1791)
The Works of the Right Honourable Edmund Burke (1792)
A Letter to a Noble Lord (1796)
Two Letters Addressed on the Proposals for Peace with the Regicide Directory of France (1796)
Letter on the Conduct of the Minority in Parliament (1797)
A Third Letter on the Proposals for Peace with the Regicide Directory of France (1797)
Three Memorials on French Affairs (1797)
Two Letters on the Conduct of Our Domestick Parties (1797)

Burke, John (1787–1848)
genealogical and heraldic writer
A General and Heraldic Dictionary of the Peerage and Baronetage of the United Kingdom (1826)

Burnaby, Frederick Gustavus (1842–85)
cavalry officer and traveller
On Horseback Through Asia Minor (1876)

Burnand, Sir Francis Cowley (1836–1917)
dramatist, novelist, and editor of *Punch*
Happy Thoughts (1866)
The New History of Sandford and Merton (1872)

Burnet, Gilbert (1643–1715)
bishop of Salisbury, historian, and polemicist
The Mystery of Iniquity Unvailed (1673)
The History of the Reformation of the Church of England. The First Part (1679)
Some Passages of the Life and Death of the Earl of Rochester (1680)
The Life and Death of Sir Matthew Hale (1682)
Utopia (1684)
A Collection of Several Tracts and Discourses Written in the Years 1677–85 (1685)
Some Letters: Containing an account of . . . Switzerland, Italy, etc. (1686)
A Second Collection of Several Tracts and Discourses (1689)
A Discourse of the Pastoral Care (1692)
Four Discourses (1694)
An Essay on the Memory of the Late Queen (1695)
A Third Collection of Several Tracts and Discourses (1703)
Bishop Burnet's History of His Own Time [vol. i] (1724)

Burnet, Thomas (1635?–1715)
philosopher and cosmologist
The Theory of the Earth (1684)
The Theory of the Earth (1690)
Remarks upon An Essay Concerning Humane Understanding (1697)

Burnett, Frances Eliza, *née* Hodgson (1849–1924)
novelist and children's writer
Little Lord Fauntleroy (1886)
A Little Princess (1905)
The Secret Garden (1911)

Burnett, James, Lord Monboddo (1714–99)
Scottish judge and author
Of the Origin and Progress of Language (1773)
Antient Metaphysics; or, The Science of Universals (1779)

Burney, Charles (1726–1814)
musician and author
An Essay Towards a History of the Principal Comets that have Appeared Since 1742 (1769)
The Present State of Music in France and Italy (1771)
The Present State of Music in Germany, the Netherlands, and United Provinces (1773)
A General History of Music (1776)
Memoirs of the Life and Writings of the Abate Metastasio (1796)

Burney, Frances, later D'Arblay (1752–1840)
novelist and diarist
Evelina; or, a Young Lady's Entrance into the World (1778)
Cecilia; or, Memoirs of an Heiress (1782)
Brief Reflections Relative to the Emigrant French Clergy (1793)
Camilla; or, A Picture of Youth (1796)
The Wanderer; or, Female Difficulties (1814)
Memoirs of Dr Burney (1832)
Diary and Letters of Madame D'Arblay (1842)
The Early Diary of Frances Burney 1768–78 (1889)

Burns, Robert (1759–96)
Scottish poet
Poems Chiefly in the Scottish Dialect (1786)
Poems Chiefly in the Scottish Dialect (1787)
'Tam O'Shanter' (1791)
Poems Chiefly in the Scottish Dialect (1793)
The Works of Robert Burns (1800)
Poems Ascribed to Robert Burns (1801)
Reliques of Robert Burns (1808)
The Prose Works of Robert Burns (1839)
Life and Works of Robert Burns (1851)

Burrant, Robert (*fl.* 1553)
translator
Preceptes of Cato with Annotacions of D. Erasmus (1545)

Burthogge, Richard (1638?–94?)
theologian
Causa Dei; or, An Apology for God (1675)
An Essay Upon Reason and the Nature of Spirits (1694)

Burton, Isabel, *née* Arundell, Lady Burton (1831–96)
traveller and author

The Inner Life of Syria, Palestine, and the Holy Land (1875)
Arabia, Egypt, India (1879)
The Life of Captain Sir Richard F. Burton (1893)
The Romance of Isabel, Lady Burton (1897)

Burton, Sir Richard Francis (1821–90)
explorer and translator
Personal Narrative of a Pilgrimage to El-Medinah and Meccah (1855)
Book of the Sword (1884)
A Plain and Literal Translation of the Arabian Nights' Entertainments (1885)

Burton, Robert (1577–1640)
author
The Anatomy of Melancholy (1621)

Burton, William (*d.* 1616)
Puritan and translator of Erasmus
Seven Dialogues Both Pithie and Profitable (1606)

Burton, William (1575–1645)
antiquary and translator
Clitophon and Leucippe (1597)

Bury, Lady Charlotte Susan Maria, *née* Campbell (1775–1861)
diarist, novelist, and poet
Self-Indulgence (1812)
Flirtation (1827)
The History of a Flirt, Related by Herself (1840)

Bushe, Paul (1490–1558)
first bishop of Bristol
The Extirpation of Ignorance (1526?)

Bussy, Dorothy, *née* Strachey ['Olivia'] (1866–1960)
novelist and translator
Olivia (1949)

Butler, Alban (1711–73)
Catholic priest and hagiographer
The Lives of the Fathers, Martyrs, and Other Principal Saints (1756)

Butler, Joseph (1692–1752)
theologian
Fifteen Sermons Preached at the Rolls Chapel (1726)
The Analogy of Religion, Natural and Revealed, to the Constitution and Course of Nature (1736)

Butler, Samuel (1612–80)
satirist
Hudibras. The First Part: Written in the time of the late wars (1663)
Hudibras. The Second Part: By the authour of the First (1664)
Hudibras. The First and Second Parts (1674)
Hudibras. The Third and Last Part (1678)
Mercurius Menippeus. The Loyal Satirist; or, Hudibras in Prose (1682)
Hudibras. In Three Parts (1684)
The Genuine Remains in Verse and Prose (1759)

Butler, Samuel ['John Pickard Owen', 'William Bickersteth Owen'] (1835–1902)
philosopher and author
A First Year in Canterbury Settlement (1863)
Erewhon; or, Over the Range (1872)
Life and Habit (1878)
Evolution, Old and New (1879)
Erewhon Revisited Twenty Years Later (1901)
The Way of All Flesh (1903)

Byatt, Antonia Susan, *née* Drabble (1936–)
novelist, short-story writer, and critic
Shadow of a Sun (1964)
The Game (1967)
The Virgin in the Garden (1978)
Still Life (1985)
Sugar, and Other Stories (1987)
Possession (1990)
Angels and Insects (1992)
The Matisse Stories (1993)
The Djinn in the Nightingale's Eye (1994)
Babel Tower (1996)
Elementals (1998)
The Biographer's Tale (2000)
On Histories and Stories (2001)
A Whistling Woman (2002)

Byrd, William (1543–1623)
composer
Psalmes, Sonets, & Songs of Sadnes and Pietie, Made into Musicke of Five Parts (1588)
Songs of Sundrie Natures (1589)
Psalmes, Songs, and Sonnets; Some Solemne, Others Joyfull (1611)

Byrom, John (1692–1763)
poet and stenographer
Enthusiasm: A poetical essay (1752)
Epistle in Defence of Rhyme (1755)
The Universal English Short-hand (1767)

Byron, George Gordon, Lord (1788–1824)
poet
Fugitive Pieces (1806)
Poems on Various Occasions (1807)
Hours of Idleness (1807)
Poems Original and Translated (1808)
English Bards, and Scotch Reviewers (1809)
Childe Harold's Pilgrimage [cantos i–ii] (1812)
The Curse of Minerva (1812)
Waltz (1813)
The Giaour: A fragment of a Turkish tale (1813)
The Bride of Abydos: A Turkish tale (1813)
The Corsair (1814)
Ode to Napoleon Buonaparte (1814)
Lara, a Tale; Jacqueline, a Tale (1814)
Hebrew Melodies (1815)
The Siege of Corinth: a Poem; Parisina: a Poem (1816)
A Sketch From Private Life (1816)
Fare Thee Well (1816)
Monody on the Death of the Right Honourable R.B. Sheridan (1816)
Childe Harold's Pilgrimage: Canto the Third (1816)
The Prisoner of Chillon, and Other Poems (1816)
Poems (1816)
Manfred (1817)
The Lament of Tasso (1817)
Beppo: A Venetian story (1818)

Childe Harold's Pilgrimage: Canto the Fourth (1818)
Mazeppa (1819)
Don Juan [cantos i–ii] (1819)
Marino Faliero, Doge of Venice; The Prophecy of Dante (1821)
Don Juan [cantos iii–v] (1821)
Sardanapalus; The Two Foscari; Cain (1821)
The Vision of Judgment (1822)
The Age of Bronze; or, Carmen Seculare et Annus Haud Mirabilis (1823)
Don Juan [cantos vi–viii; ix–xi; xii–xiv] (1823)
The Island; or, Christian and His Comrades (1823)
Werner: A tragedy (1823)
The Deformed Transformed: A drama (1824)
Don Juan [cantos xv–xvi] (1824)
Letters and Journals of Lord Byron (1830)
Dramas (1837)

Byron, Robert (1905–41)
traveller, art critic, and historian
Europe in the Looking-Glass (1926)
The Road to Oxiana (1937)

Cadiou, Andrew (*fl.* 1472?)
translator
The Porteous of Nobleness (1508)

Caffyn, Kathleen Mannington ['Iota'] (1853–1926)
novelist and short-story writer
A Yellow Aster (1894)
Anne Mauleverer (1899)

Caine, [Sir] [Thomas Henry] Hall (1853–1931)
novelist
Recollections of Dante Gabriel Rossetti (1882)
The Deemster (1887)
A Son of Hagar (1887)
The Bondman (1890)
The Scapegoat (1891)
The Manxman (1894)
The Christian (1897)
The Eternal City (1901)

Caird, Edward (1835–1908)
philosopher
Essays on Literature and Philosophy (1892)

Caird, [Alice] Mona Henryson, *née* Alison ['G. Noel Hatton'] (1858–1932)
novelist, journalist, and essayist
The Daughters of Danaus (1894)

Calamy, Edmund (1671–1732)
Nonconformist biographer
An Abridgement of Mr [Richard] *Baxter's History of His Life and Times* (1702)
A Defence of Moderate Non-Conformity (1703)

Callcott, Maria, formerly Graham, *née* Dundas (1785–1842)
author
Journal of a Residence in India (1812)
Little Arthur's History of England (1835)

Calverley, Charles Stuart, formerly Blayds (1831–84)
poet and translator
Verses and Translations (1862)
Theocritus Translated into English Verse (1869)
Fly Leaves (1872)
Literary Remains (1885)
Complete Works (1901)

Cambridge, Ada, Mrs George Frederick Cross (1844–1926)
novelist and poet
The Two Surplices (1865)

Cambridge, Richard Owen (1717–1802)
poet
The Scribleriad (1751)
A Dialogue Between a Member of Parliament and His Servant (1752)
An Elegy Written in an Empty Assembly Room (1756)

Camden, William (1551–1623)
antiquary
Britannia Sive Florentissimorum Regnorum Angliae, Scotiae, Hiberniae Chorographica Descriptio (1586)
Remaines of a Greater Worke, Concerning Britaine (1605)
Britain; or, A Chorographicall Description of the Most Flourishing Kingdomes, England, Scotland, and Ireland, and the Ilands Adjoyning (1610)
Annales: The true and royall history of the famous Empresse Elizabeth Queene of England France and Ireland (1625)

Cameron, Caroline Emily, *née* Sharp, Mrs Lovett Cameron (1844–1921)
popular novelist
The Man Who Didn't; or, The Triumph of a Snipe Pie (1895)

Cameron, [John] Norman (1905–53)
poet and translator
The Winter House (1935)
Forgive Me, Sire, and Other Poems (1950)

Campbell, George (1719–96)
theologian
A Dissertation on Miracles (1762)
The Philosophy of Rhetoric (1776)

Campbell, Gertrude Elizabeth, *née* Blood, Lady Colin Campbell ['G.E. Brunefille'] (1861–1911)
novelist
Darell Blake (1889)

Campbell, John (1708–75)
miscellaneous author
The Present State of Europe (1750)

Campbell, John (1766–1840)
philanthropist and traveller
Travels in South Africa (1815)

Campbell, Joseph (1879–1944)
Irish poet and man of letters
The Garden of Bees (1905)
The Rushlight (1906)
The Gilly of Christ (1907)

The Mountainy Singer (1909)
Irishry (1913)
Campbell, [Ignatius] Roy[ston] Dunnachie (1901–57)
poet and translator
The Flaming Terrapin (1924)
The Wayzgoose (1928)
Adamastor (1930)
The Georgiad (1931)
Pomegranates (1932)
Flowering Reeds (1933)
Broken Record (1934)
Mithraic Emblems (1936)
Flowering Rifle: A poem from the battlefield of Spain (1939)
Collected Poems [vol. i] (1949)
Light on a Dark Horse (1951)
Campbell, Thomas (1777–1844)
poet, historian, and biographer
The Pleasures of Hope, with Other Poems (1799)
Poems (1803)
Gertrude of Wyoming: A Pennsylvanian Tale, and Other Poems (1809)
Specimens of the British Poets (1819)
Miscellaneous Poems (1824)
Theodric, and Other Poems (1824)
The Poetical Works of Thomas Campbell (1828)
Poland: A Poem. Lines on the View from St Leonard's (1831)
Letters From the South (1837)
The Pilgrim of Glencoe, with Other Poems (1842)
The Pleasures of Hope, with Other Poems (1855)
Gertrude of Wyoming; or, The Pennsylvanian Cottage (1857)
Campion, Thomas (1567–1620)
poet and musician
Observations in the Art of English Poesie (1602)
The First Booke of Ayres (1613?)
A Relation of the Late Royall Entertainment Given by the Lord Knowles (1613)
Songs of Mourning: Bewailing the Untimely Death of Prince Henry (1613)
Two Bookes of Ayres (1613?)
The Description of a Maske: Presented at the Mariage of the Earle of Somerset (1614)
The Third and Fourth Booke of Ayres ([1617])
Cannan, Gilbert (1884–1955)
novelist and playwright
Peter Homunculus (1909)
Devious Ways (1910)
Little Brother (1912)
Round the Corner (1913)
Mendel (1916)
Three Pretty Men (1916)
The Stucco House (1917)
Time and Eternity (1919)
Annette and Bennett (1922)
Capell, Edward (1713–81)
Shakespearian commentator
Prolusions; or, Select Pieces of Antient Poetry (1759)
Notes and Various Readings to Shakespeare (1779)
Carew, Richard, of Antony (1555–1620)
translator and antiquary
Examen de Ingenios. The Examination of Mens Wits (1594)
Godfrey of Bulloigne; or, The Recouverie of Hierusalem (1594)
A Herrings Tale (1598)
Carew, Thomas (1595–1639?)
poet
Coelum Brittanicum: A masque (1634)
Poems (1640)
Carey, Henry (1687?–1743)
poet, musician, and dramatist
Poems on Several Occasions (1713)
The Contrivances; or, More Ways Than One (1715)
Poems on Several Occasions (1729)
Amelia: A new English opera (1732)
Teraminta: An opera (1732)
The Tragedy of Chrononhotonthologos (1734)
The Honest Yorkshireman: A ballad farce (1735)
The Dragon of Wantley: A burlesque opera (1737)
The Musical Century, in One Hundred English Ballads (1737)
Nancy; or, The Parting Lovers (1739)
Carey, Rosa Nouchette (1840–1909)
novelist
Nellie's Memories (1868)
Only the Governess (1888)
Carlell, Lodowick (1601/2–75)
dramatist
The Deserving Favourite (1629)
Arviragus and Philicia (1639)
The Passionate Lovers: A tragi-comedy. The first and second parts (1655)
The Fool Would Be a Favourit; or, The Discreet Lover: A trage-comedy (1657)
Osmond the Great Turk (1657)
'Carleton, Captain George'
unidentified author
The Memoirs of an English Officer (1728)
Carleton, William (1794–1869)
Irish novelist
Father Butler; The Lough Dearg Pilgrim (1829)
Traits and Stories of the Irish Peasantry [1st ser.] (1830)
Traits and Stories of the Irish Peasantry [2nd ser.] (1833)
Fardorougha the Miser; or, The Convicts of Lisnamona (1839)
Parra Sashta; or, The History of Paddy Go-Easy and His Wife, Nancy (1845)
Tales and Sketches (1845)
The Black Prophet: A tale of Irish famine (1847)
The Emigrants of Ahadarra (1848)
The Tithe-Proctor (1849)
Redmond Count O'Hanlon, the Irish Rapparee (1862)

Carlile, Richard (1790–1843)
rationalist philosopher and dissenter
The Political Litany, Diligently Revised (1817)
Every Man's Book; or, What is God? (1826)
The Philosophy of the Sexes; or, Every Woman's Book (1826)
The Gospel According to Richard Carlile (1827)
Church Reform (1835)
Carlyle, Jane Welsh (1801–66)
author
Letters and Memorials of Jane Welsh Carlyle (1883)
Carlyle, Thomas (1795–1881)
critic, historian, and biographer
Wilhelm Meister's Apprenticeship (1824)
The Life of Friedrich Schiller (1825)
German Romance (1827)
Sartor Resartus (1834)
The French Revolution (1837)
Sartor Resartus (1838)
Critical and Miscellaneous Essays (1839)
Chartism (1839)
On Heroes, Hero-Worship, and the Heroic in History (1841)
Past and Present (1843)
Latter-Day Pamphlets (1850)
The Life of John Sterling (1851)
History of Frederick II of Prussia, called Frederick the Great [vols i–iv] (1858)
History of Frederick II of Prussia [vols v–vi] (1865)
Characteristics (1877)
Reminiscences (1881)
The Correspondence of Thomas Carlyle and Ralph Waldo Emerson (1883)
Letters of Thomas Carlyle 1826–1836 (1888)
Last Words of Thomas Carlyle (1892)
Carpenter, Edward (1844–1929)
poet, essayist, and social reformer
Narcissus, and Other Poems (1873)
Homogenic Love and its Place in a Free Society (1894)
Woman, and Her Place in a Free Society (1894)
Carpenter, Nathanael (1589–1628?)
author
Geography Delineated Forth in Two Bookes (1625)
Carr, Edward Hallett (1892–1982)
historian
A History of Soviet Russia (1950)
Carr, James Joseph Lloyd (1912–94)
novelist, children's writer, and publisher
A Day in Summer (1963)
A Month in the Country (1980)
The Battle of Pollocks Crossing (1985)
'Carroll, Lewis' [Charles Lutwidge Dodgson] (1832–98)
children's writer and mathematician
Alice's Adventures in Wonderland (1865)
Phantasmagoria, and Other Poems (1869)
Through the Looking-Glass, and What Alice Found There (1871)
The Hunting of the Snark (1876)
Sylvie and Bruno (1889)
Sylvie and Bruno Concluded (1893)
Life and Letters (1898)
Carson, Ciaran (1948)
poet and novelist
Breaking News (2003)
Carte, Thomas (1686–1754)
historian
A History of the Life of James, Duke of Ormond (1736)
A General History of England (1747)
Carter, Angela Olive, *née* Stalker (1940–92)
novelist, short-story writer, essayist, and translator
Shadow Dance (1966)
The Magic Toyshop (1967)
Several Perceptions (1968)
Heroes and Villains (1969)
Love (1971)
The Infernal Desire Machines of Doctor Hoffman (1972)
Fireworks (1974)
The Passion of New Eve (1977)
The Bloody Chamber, and Other Stories (1979)
The Sadeian Woman (1979)
Nothing Sacred (1982)
Nights at the Circus (1984)
Black Venus (1985)
Wise Children (1991)
Expletives Deleted (1992)
American Ghosts and Old World Wonders (1993)
Burning Your Boats (1995)
Carter, Elizabeth (1717–1806)
poet, classical scholar, and translator
Poems Upon Particular Occasions (1738)
Examination of Mr Pope's Essay on Man (1739)
Sir Isaac Newton's Philosophy Explain'd for the Use of Ladies (1739)
All the Works of Epictetus (1758)
Poems on Several Occasions (1762)
Memoirs of the Life of Mrs Elizabeth Carter (1807)
Cartwright, Justin (1943–)
South African-born novelist
Interior (1988)
Look At It This Way (1990)
Masai Dreaming (1993)
In Every Face I Meet (1995)
White Lightning (2002)
Cartwright, Thomas (1535–1603)
Puritan
A Replye to An Answere Made of M. Doctor Whitgifte (1573?)
Christian Religion (1611)
Cartwright, William (1611–43)
poet and dramatist

The Royall Slave: A tragi-comedy (1639)
Comedies, Tragi-Comedies, with Other Poems (1651)

Cary, Elizabeth, *née* Tanfield, Viscountess Falkland (1585–1639)
dramatist and translator
The Tragedie of Mariam, the Faire Queene of Jewry (1613)
The Reply of the Most Illustrious Cardinall of Perron (1630)

Cary, Henry Francis (1772–1844)
poet and translator
Sonnets and Odes (1788)
The Inferno of Dante Alighieri (1805)
The Vision; or, Hell, Purgatory and Paradise of Dante Alighieri (1814)
Lives of English Poets, from Johnson to Kirke White (1846)

Cary, [Arthur] Joyce Lunel (1888–1957)
novelist
Aissa Saved (1932)
An American Visitor (1933)
The African Witch (1936)
Castle Corner (1938)
Mister Johnson (1939)
Charley is My Darling (1940)
Herself Surprised (1941)
To Be a Pilgrim (1942)
The Horse's Mouth (1944)
Prisoner of Grace (1952)
Except the Lord (1953)
Not Honour More (1955)

Cary, Lucius, Viscount Falkland (1610?–43)
politician and author
Discourse of Infallibility (1646)

Cary, Mary (*fl.* 1636–53)
Fifth Monarchist
The Little Horns Doom and Downfall (1651)

Cassels, Walter Richard (1826–1907)
theological critic
Supernatural Religion [vols i–ii] (1874)

Caswall, Edward (1814–78)
hymn-writer
Lyra Catholica (1849)

'Caudwell, Christopher' [Christopher St John Sprigg] (1907–37)
Marxist critic, aeronautical author, and writer of detective fiction
Studies in a Dying Culture (1938)
Further Studies in a Dying Culture (1949)

Causley, Charles Stanley (1917–2003)
poet
Farewell, Aggie Weston (1951)
Hands to Dance (1951)
Survivor's Leave (1953)
Union Street (1957)
Johnny Alleluia (1961)
Underneath the Water (1968)
Figure of 8 (1969)
Collected Poems 1951–1975 (1975)
Secret Destinations (1984)
Early in the Morning (1986)
A Field of Vision (1988)
Collected Poems (1997)

Caute, [John] David (1936–)
novelist, historian, and journalist
The Decline of the West (1966)

Cave, Jane, later Winscom (*c*.1754–1813)
poet
Poems on Various Subjects, Entertaining, Elegiac, and Religious (1783)

Cave, William (1637–1713)
Anglican divine
Primitive Christianity; or, The Religion of the Ancient Christians (1673)

Cavendish, Margaret, *née* Lucas, duchess of Newcastle (1624?–74)
dramatist and poet
Philosophicall Fancies (1653)
Poems, and Fancies (1653)
The Philosophical and Physical Opinions (1655)
The Worlds Olio (1655)
Natures Pictures Drawn by Fancies Pencil to the Life (1656)
Playes (1662)
Philosophicall Letters (1664)
CCXI Sociable Letters (1664)
The Description of a New World, called the Blazing World (1666)
Life of William Cavendish (1667)
Plays, Never Before Printed (1668)

Cavendish, William, 2nd earl of Devonshire (1591?–1628)
essayist
Horæ Subseciae: Observations and discourses (1620)

Cavendish, William, 1st duke of Newcastle (1592–1676)
soldier, dramatist, and poet
The Country Captaine, and The Varietie (1649)
The Humorous Lovers: A comedy (1677)
The Triumphant Widow; or, The Medley of Humours: A comedy (1677)

Cawdry, Robert (*fl.* 1604)
compiler
A Table Alphabeticall (1604)

Cawthorn, James (1719–61)
poet
Poems (1771)

Caxton, William (1422?–91)
printer and author
The Recuyell of the Historyes of Troye (1474?)
The Game and Playe of the Chesse (1474)
History of Jason (1477?)
Godfrey of Boulogne (1481)
The Mirror of the World (1481)
Reynard the Fox (1481)
The Curial (1483)
Aesop's Fables (1484)
Caton (1484)
The Knight of the Tower (1484)

The Order of Chivalry (1484)
Charles the Great King of France (1485)
Paris and Vienne (1485)
The Book of Good Manners (1487)
Royal Book (1488?)
The Book of Feats of Arms (1489)
The Art and Craft to Know Well to Die (1490)
Blanchardine and Eglantine (1490)
Eneydos (1490)
The Four Sons of Aymon (1490)
Ars Moriendi (1491)

Cayley, George John (1826–78)
author
Las Alforjas; or, The Bridle Roads of Spain (1853)

Cecil, [Edward Christian] David Gascoyne, Lord David Cecil (1902–86)
biographer and critic
The Stricken Deer; or, The Life of Cowper (1929)

Cecil, William, Lord Burghley (1520–98)
statesman
Certaine Precepts, or Directions, for the Well-Ordering and Carriage of a Mans Life . . . (1617)

Centlivre, Susanna, *née* Freeman [sometimes called Susanna Carroll] (1669?–1723)
dramatist
The Perjur'd Husband; or, The Adventures of Venice: A tragedy (1700)
The Beau's Duel; or, A Soldier for the Ladies: A comedy (1702)
Love's Contrivance; or, Le Médecin malgré lui: A comedy (1703)
The Stolen Heiress; or, The Salamanca Doctor Outplotted: A comedy (1703)
The Gamester (1705)
The Basset-Table: A comedy (1705)
Love at a Venture: A comedy (1706)
The Platonick Lady: A comedy (1707)
The Busie Body: A comedy (1709)
The Man's Bewitch'd; or, The Devil to Do About Her: A comedy (1709)
A Bickerstaff's Burying; or, Work for the Upholders: A farce (1710)
Mar-Plot; or, The Second Part of the Busie-Body (1711)
The Perplex'd Lovers: A comedy (1712)
The Wonder! A Woman Keeps a Secret: A comedy (1714)
The Gotham Election: A farce (1715)
The Cruel Gift: A tragedy (1717)
An Epistle to the King of Sweden (1717)
A Bold Stroke for a Wife: A comedy (1718)
The Artifice: A comedy (1723)

Chalkhill, John (*c.*1594–1642)
poet
Thealma and Clearchus: A pastoral history (1683)

Chalmers, George (1742–1825)
historian and biographer
Political Annals of the Present United Colonies (1779)
Caledonia; or, An Account, Historical and Topographic, of North Britain (1807)
The Life of Mary, Queen of Scots (1818)

Chalmers, Thomas (1780–1847)
theologian and philanthropist
Astronomical Discourses (1817)
Commercial Discourses (1820)

Chaloner, Sir Thomas (1521–65)
diplomatist and author
The Praise of Folly (1549)

Chamberlain, Robert (1607?–60)
poet and dramatist
Nocturnall Lucubrations; or, Meditations Divine and Morall (1638)
The Swaggering Damsell: A comedy (1640)

Chamberlayne, Edward (1616–1703)
author
Angliae Notitiae; or, The Present State of England (1669)

Chamberlayne, William (1619–89)
physician, poet, and dramatist
Loves Victory: A tragi-comedy (1658)
Pharonnida: A heroick poem (1659)

Chambers, Sir Edmund Kerchever (1866–1954)
literary scholar
The Mediaeval Stage (1903)

Chambers, Robert (1802–71)
historian, antiquary, and publisher
Vestiges of the Natural History of Creation (1844)
Explanations (1845)

Chambers, Sir William (1726–96)
architect
A Dissertation on Oriental Gardening (1772)

Chamier, Captain Frederick (1796–1870)
nautical novelist
The Life of a Sailor (1832)
Ben Brace (1836)
The Arethusa (1837)
The Spitfire (1840)
Tom Bowling (1841)

Chandler, Mary (1687–1745)
poet
A Description of Bath (1733)

Chapman, George (1559?–1634)
poet, dramatist, and translator
Skia Nyktos. The Shadow of Night (1594)
Ovids Banquet of Sence (1595)
The Blinde Begger of Alexandria (1598)
Seaven Bookes of the Iliades of Homere, Prince of Poets (1598)
Achilles Shield (1598)
An Humerous Dayes Myrth (1599)
All Fooles (1605)
Eastward Hoe (1605)
The Gentleman Usher (1606)
Monsieur D'Olive: A comedie (1606)
Sir Gyles Goosecappe Knight: A comedie (1606)
Bussy D'Ambois (1607)
The Conspiracie, and Tragedie of Charles Duke of Byron, Marshall of France (1608)

Homer Prince of Poets (1609)
The Iliads of Homer, Prince of Poets (1611?)
May-Day: A witty comedie (1611)
Petrarchs Seven Penitentiall Psalms, Paraphrastically Translated (1612)
The Widdowes Teares: A comedie (1612)
An Epicede or Funerall Song (1613)
The Memorable Maske of the Two Honorable Houses or Inns of Courte; the Middle Temple and Lyncolns Inne (1613?)
The Revenge of Bussy D'Ambois: A tragedie (1613)
Andromeda Liberata; or, The Nuptials of Perseus and Andromeda (1614)
Homers Odysses (1614)
Twenty-four Bookes of Homers Odisses (1615?)
The Divine Poem of Musæus. First of all Books (1616)
The Whole Workes of Homer; Prince of Poetts (1616)
The Georgicks of Hesiod (1618)
Batrachomyomachia (1624?)
A Justification of a Strange Action of Nero (1629)
Caesar and Pompey: A Roman tragedy, declaring their warres (1631)
The Ball: A comedy (1639)
Chabot Admirall of France (1639)
The Tragedy of Alphonsus Emperour of Germany (1654)

Chapone, Hester, *née* Mulso, Mrs John Chapone (1727–1801)
author
Letters on the Improvement of the Mind (1773)
Miscellanies in Prose and Verse (1775)

Chappell, Bartholomew (*fl.* 1595)
poet
The Garden of Prudence (1595)

Charles, Elizabeth, *née* Rundle (1821–89)
novelist and poet
The Voice of Christian Life in Song (1858)
The Chronicles of the Schönberg-Cotta Family (1863)
Diary of Mrs Kitty Trevylyan (1864)

Charlesworth, Maria Louisa (1819–80)
author of improving fiction
A Book for the Cottage; or, The History of Mary and Her Family (1848)

Charleton, Walter (1619–1707)
philosopher and antiquarian
Epicurus's Morals (1656)

Chatterton, Henrietta Georgiana, Lady Chatterton [Marcia Lascelles, *née* Iremonger, later Dering] (1806–76)
novelist and poet
Aunt Dorothy's Tale; or, Geraldine Morton (1837)

Chatterton, Thomas (1752–70)
poet
The Execution of Sir Charles Bawdin (1772)
Poems, Supposed to Have Been Written at Bristol, by Thomas Rowley, and Others, in the Fifteenth Century (1777)
Miscellanies in Prose and Verse (1778)
A Supplement to the Miscellanies of Thomas Chatterton (1784)
The Revenge: A burletta (1795)
The Works of Thomas Chatterton (1803)

Chatwin, Bruce Charles (1940–89)
novelist and travel writer
In Patagonia (1977)
The Viceroy of Ouidah (1980)
On the Black Hill (1982)
The Songlines (1987)
Utz (1988)
What Am I Doing Here? (1989)

Chaucer, Geoffrey (1340–1400)
poet
Anelida and Arcite (1477?)
Canterbury Tales (1477)
The Parliament of Fowls (1477?)
The Consolation of Philosophy (1478?)
The House of Fame (1483)
Troilus and Criseyde (1483?)
Mars and Venus (1500?)
The Canterbury Tales (1526)
The House of Fame (1526?)
Troilus and Criseyde (1526?)
The Workes of Geffray Chaucer (1532)
The Woorkes of Geffrey Chaucer (1561)
The Workes of Our Antient and Lerned English Poet, Geffrey Chaucer (1598)
The Canterbury Tales of Chaucer (1741)
The Canterbury Tales of Chaucer (1775)

Cheke, Sir John (1514–57)
Greek scholar
The Hurt of Sedicion (1549)

Cherry, Andrew (1762–1812)
actor and dramatist
The Soldier's Daughter: A comedy (1804)

Chertsey, Andrew (*fl.* 1508–32)
translator
The Crafte to Lyve Well and to Dye Well (1505)
The Passyon of Our Lorde (1521)

Chesney, [Sir] George Tomkyns (1830–95)
novelist
The Battle of Dorking (1871)

Chester, Robert (1566–1640?)
poet
Loves Martyr; or, Rosalins Complaint (1601)

Chesterton, Gilbert Keith (1874–1936)
essayist, novelist, poet, and critic
Greybeards at Play (1900)
The Wild Knight, and Other Poems (1900)
The Defendant (1901)
The Napoleon of Notting Hill (1904)
The Club of Queer Trades (1905)
Heretics (1905)
The Man Who Was Thursday: A nightmare (1908)

Orthodoxy (1909)
The Ball and the Cross (1910)
Alarms and Discursions (1910)
The Innocence of Father Brown (1911)
The Ballad of the White Horse (1911)
The Flying Inn (1914)
The Wisdom of Father Brown (1914)
Poems (1915)
Eugenics, and Other Evils (1922)
The Man Who Knew Too Much, and Other Stories (1922)
The Everlasting Man (1925)
The Incredulity of Father Brown (1926)
Collected Poems (1927)
The Secret of Father Brown (1927)
The Scandal of Father Brown (1935)
Autobiography (1936)
Chettle, Henry (1560?–1607)
dramatist
Kind-Harts Dreame (1593)
Piers Plainnes Seaven Yeres Prentiship (1595)
Englandes Mourning Garment (1603)
Patient Grissill (1603)
The Tragedy of Hoffman; or, A Revenge for a Father (1631)
Chetwood, William Rufus (*d.* 1766)
bookseller, dramatist, and miscellaneous author
The Voyages, Dangerous Adventures, and Miraculous Escapes of Capt. Richard Falconer (1720)
The Voyages and Adventures of Captain Robert Boyle (1726)
The Voyages, Travels and Adventures of William Owen Gwin Vaughan (1736)
The Twins; or, The Female Traveller (1743)
A General History of the Stage (1749)
Cheyne, George (1671–1743)
physician, mathematician, and vegetarian
Philosophical Principles of Natural Religion (1705)
Chichester, Frederick Richard, styled by courtesy earl of Belfast ['Lord B****'] (1827–53)**
novelist
Masters and Workmen (1851)
Chidley, Katherine (*fl.* 1641–5)
radical pamphleteer and religious separatist
The Justification of the Independant Churches of Christ (1641)
A New-Yeares-Gift (1645)
Childers, [Robert] Erskine (1870–1922)
author and politician
The Riddle of the Sands: A record of secret service recently achieved (1903)
Chillingworth, William (1602–44)
theologian
The Religion of Protestants a Safe Way to Salvation (1638)
The Works of William Chillingworth (1704)
Cholmondeley, Mary ['Pax'] (1859–1925)
novelist
The Danvers Jewels (1887)
Sir Charles Danvers (1889)
Red Pottage (1899)
Moth and Rust (1902)
Prisoners (Fast Bound in Misery and Iron) (1906)
Christie, Dame Agatha Mary Clarissa, *née* Miller ['Mary Westmacott'] (1890–1976)
detective novelist and playwright
The Mysterious Affair at Styles (1921)
Poirot Investigates (1924)
The Murder of Roger Ackroyd (1926)
Murder on the Orient Express (1934)
The ABC Murders (1936)
Death on the Nile (1937)
Ten Little Niggers (1939)
A Murder is Announced (1950)
The Mousetrap (1956)
Chudleigh, Mary, *née* Lee, Lady Chudleigh (1656–1710)
poet
The Ladies Defence; or, The Bride-woman's Counsellor Answer'd (1701)
Poems on Several Occasions (1703)
Essays upon Several Subjects in Verse and Prose (1710)
Church, Richard Thomas (1893–1972)
poet and novelist
The Flood of Life (1917)
Churchill, Caryl (1938–)
playwright
Owners (1973)
Light Shining in Buckinghamshire (1978)
Cloud Nine (1979)
Top Girls (1982)
Fen (1983)
Softcops (1984)
Serious Money: A City comedy (1987)
Ice Cream (1989)
Hot Fudge (1990)
Mad Forest (1990)
The Skriker (1994)
Churchill, Charles (1731–64)
clergyman and satirist
The Apology (1761)
Night: An epistle to Robert Lloyd (1761)
The Rosciad (1761)
The Ghost [bks i, ii] (1762)
The Author (1763)
The Conference (1763)
An Epistle to William Hogarth (1763)
Poems (1763)
The Prophecy of Famine (1763)
The Candidate (1764)
The Duellist (1764)
The Farewell (1764)
Gotham [bk i] (1764)
Independence (1764)
The Times (1764)

Churchill, Sir Winston Leonard Spencer (1874–1965)
statesman, historian, and novelist
The Story of the Malakand Field Force (1898)
London to Ladysmith via Pretoria (1900)
My Early Life (1930)
Into Battle (1941)
The Unrelenting Struggle (1942)
The End of the Beginning (1943)
Onwards to Victory (1944)
The Dawn of Liberation (1945)
Victory (1946)
The Second World War (1948)
A History of the English-Speaking Peoples (1956)

Churchyard, Thomas (1520?–1604)
poet and miscellaneous writer
A Myrrour for Man (1552)
The Contention Betwyxte Churchyeard and Camell, upon David Dycers Dreame (1560)
Churchyard's Round (1566)
Churchyardes Farewell (1566)
Churchyardes Lamentacion of Freyndshyp (1566)
A Discourse of Rebellion (1570)
The Firste Parte of Churchyardes Chippes (1575)
A Lamentable, and Pitifull Description, of the Wofull Warres in Flaunders (1578)
A Prayse, and Reporte of Maister Martyne Forboishers Voyage to Meta Incognita (1578)
The Miserie of Flaunders, Calamitie of Fraunce, Misfortune of Portugall, Unquietnes of Ireland, Troubles of Scotlande: and the Blessed State of Englande (1579)
A Pleasaunte Laborinth Called Churchyardes Chance (1580)
A Warning for the Wise, a Feare to the Fond, a Bridle to the Lewde, and a Glasse to the Good (1580)
A Scourge for Rebels (1584)
The Epitaph of Sir Phillip Sidney (1586)
The Worthines of Wales (1587)
A Handful of Gladsome Verses: Given to the Queenes Majesty at Woodstocke (1592)
Churchyard's Challenge (1593)
A Musicall Consort of Heavenly Harmonie (Compounded Out of Manie Parts of Musicke) Called Churchyards Charitie (1595)
A Pleasant Discourse of Court and Wars (1596)
A Wished Reformacion of Wicked Rebellion (1598)
The Fortunate Farewel to the Most Forward and Noble Earle of Essex (1599)
The Wonders of the Ayre, the Trembling of the Earth, and the Warnings of the World Before the Judgement Day (1602)
Churchyards Good Will (1604)

Chute or Chewt, Anthony (*d.* 1595?)
poet
Shore's Wife (1593)

Chute, Francis (*d.* 1745)
poet
The Petticoat: An heroi-comical poem (1716)

Cibber, Colley (1671–1757)
Poet Laureate, actor, and dramatist
A Poem on the Death of Our Late Sovereign Lady, Queen Mary (1695)
Love's Last Shift; or, The Fool in Fashion: A comedy (1696)
Womans Wit; or, The Lady in Fashion: A comedy (1697)
Xerxes: A tragedy (1699)
The Tragical History of King Richard III (1700)
Love Makes a Man; or, The Fop's Fortune: A comedy (1701)
She Wou'd and She Wou'd Not; or, The Kind Impostor (1702)
The Careless Husband: A comedy (1705)
Perolla and Izadora: A tragedy (1706)
The Double Gallant; or, The Sick Lady's Cure: A comedy (1707)
The Lady's Last Stake; or, The Wife's Resentment: A comedy (1707)
The Secret History of Arlus and Odolphus (1710)
The Non-Juror: A comedy (1718)
Ximena; or, The Heroick Daughter: A tragedy (1719)
The Refusal; or, The Ladies Philosophy: A comedy (1721)
Caesar in Aegypt: A tragedy (1725)
Love in a Riddle: A pastoral (1729)
An Apology for the Life of Mr Colley Cibber (1740)
A Letter from Mr Cibber, to Mr Pope (1742)
The Egotist; or, Colley Upon Cibber (1743)
A Second Letter from Mr Cibber to Mr Pope (1743)
Another Occasional Letter from Mr Cibber to Mr Pope (1744)

Cibber, Theophilus (1703–58)
actor and dramatist
Patie and Peggy; or, The Fair Foundling: A Scottish ballad opera (1730)
The Lives and Characters of the Most Eminent Actors and Actresses (1753)
The Lives of the Poets of Great Britain and Ireland (1753)
An Epistle to David Garrick (1755)
Dissertations on Theatrical Subjects (1756)

Clapham, Henoch (*d.* 1614)
theological writer
A Briefe of the Bible (1596)
Aelohim-triune (1601)
An Epistle Discoursing Upon the Present Pestilence (1603)
Errour on the Left Hand, through a Frozen Securitie (1608)
Errour on the Right Hand, through a Preposterous Zeal (1608)

Clare, John (1793–1864)
poet
Poems Descriptive of Rural Life and Scenery (1820)

The Village Minstrel, and Other Poems (1821)
The Shepherd's Calendar; with Village Stories and Other Poems (1827)
The Rural Muse (1835)

Clark, Kenneth Mackenzie, Baron Clark (1903–83)
art historian and critic
The Gothic Revival (1928)
Landscape into Art (1949)
The Nude (1956)
Civilisation (1969)

Clarke, Arthur Charles (1917–)
science fiction novelist and short-story writer
Childhood's End (1954)
2001: A space odyssey (1968)
Rendezvous with Rama (1973)

Clarke, Austin (1896–1974)
Irish poet and dramatist
Ancient Lights (1955)
Too Great a Vine (1957)
The Horse-Eaters (1960)

Clarke, Charles Cowden (1787–1877)
critic and author
Tales From Chaucer, in Prose (1833)

Clarke, Gillian (1937–)
poet
The Sundial (1978)
Letting in the Rumour (1989)
The King of Britain's Daughter (1993)

Clarke, Marcus Andrew Hislop (1846–81)
novelist
His Natural Life (1875)

Clarke, Mary Victoria Cowden, *née* Novello (1809–98)
novelist, short-story writer, and Shakespeare scholar
The Complete Concordance to Shakespeare (1845)

Clarke, Samuel, of St Bennet Fink (1599–1683)
biographer and historian
A Martyrologie (1652)
England's Remembrancer (1657)

Clarke, Samuel (1675–1729)
theologian
A Demonstration of the Being and Attributes of God (1705)
A Discourse Concerning the Unchangeable Obligations of Natural Religion (1706)
The Scripture-Doctrine of the Trinity (1712)

Clarkson, Thomas (1760–1846)
pioneer anti-slavery campaigner and author
An Essay on the Slavery and Commerce of the Human Species, Particularly the African (1786)
The History of the Rise, Progress and Accomplishment of the Abolition of the African Slave-Trade (1808)

Clavell, James (1924–94)
novelist, film director, and producer
Shogun (1975)

Clavell or Clavel, John (1603–42)
highwayman
A Recantation of an Ill Led Life; or, A Discoverie of the High-way Law (1628)

Clay, Stephen (*b.* 1672)
lawyer and poet
An Epistle from the Elector of Bavaria to the French King: After the Battel of Ramilles (1706)

'Cleeve, Lucas' [Adelina Georgina Kingscote, *née* Wolff] (1860–1908)
novelist
The Woman Who Wouldn't (1895)

Cleland, John (1709–89)
novelist
Memoirs of a Woman of Pleasure (1748)
The Case of the Unfortunate Bosavern Penlez (1749)
Memoirs of Fanny Hill (1750)
Memoirs of a Coxcomb; or, The History of Sir William Delamere (1751)
Titus Vespasian: A tragedy (1755)
The Romance of a Day; or, An Adventure in Greenwich-Park (1760)
The Romance of a Night; or, The Covent-Garden Adventure (1762)
The Woman of Honor (1768)

Cleland, William (1661?–89)
covenanting colonel and poet
A Collection of Several Poems and Verses (1697)

Clemo, Jack [Reginald John Clemo] (1916–94)
poet and novelist
Wilding Graft (1948)
Confession of a Rebel (1949)
The Clay Verge (1951)
The Map of Clay (1961)
The Marriage of a Rebel (1980)
A Different Drummer (1986)
The Shadowed Bed (1986)
Selected Poems (1988)

Clerke, Bartholomew (1537?–90)
translator of Castiglione
The Courtier (1571)

Cleveland, John (1613–58)
poet
The Character of a London Diurnall (1644)
Poems (1651)
The Idol of the Clownes; or, Insurrection of Wat the Tyler (1654)
J. Cleaveland Revived: Poems, orations, epistles . . . (1659)
Clievelandi Vindiciae; or, Clieveland's Genuine Poems, Orations, Epistles (1677)

Clifford, [Sophia] Lucy, *née* Lane, Mrs W[illiam] K[ingdon] Clifford (1849–1929)
novelist, short-story writer, and dramatist
Anyhow Stories (1882)
Mrs Keith's Crime (1885)

Clifford, Martin (*d.* 1677)
Master of the Charterhouse and author
Notes Upon Mr Dryden's Poems in Four Letters (1687)

Clive, Caroline, *née* Meysey-Wigley, Mrs Archer-Clive ['V'] (1801–73)

poet and novelist
IX Poems by 'V' (1840)
The Queen's Ball (1847)
The Valley of the Rea (1851)
The Morlas (1853)
Paul Ferroll (1855)
Why Paul Ferroll Killed His Wife (1860)
Clive, Catherine ['Kitty' Clive] (1711–85)
actress and playwright
The Rehearsal; or, Bays in Petticoats: A comedy (1753)
Clough, Arthur Hugh (1819–61)
educationist and poet
The Bothie of Toper-na-Fuosich (1848)
Ambarvalia (1849)
'Amours de Voyage' (1858)
Poems (1862)
Letters and Remains of Arthur Hugh Clough (1865)
Poems and Prose Remains (1869)
Cobb, Richard Charles (1917–96)
historian and author
A Second Identity (1969)
Cobb, Samuel (1675–1713)
translator and versifier
Poetae Britannici (1700)
Poems on Several Occasions (1707)
The Female Reign (1709)
Cobbe, Frances Power (1822–1904)
writer on religion, philosophy, and women's rights
Darwinism in Morals and Other Essays (1872)
Cobbett, William ['Peter Porcupine'] (1763–1835)
essayist, politician, and agriculturalist
The Life and Adventures of Peter Porcupine (1797)
The Porcupine (1800)
Cobbett's Political Register (1802)
Cobbett's Parliamentary Debates (1804)
The Political Proteus (1804)
The Life of William Cobbett (1809)
A Grammar of the English Language, in a Series of Letters (1818)
A Year's Residence in the United States of America (1819)
The American Gardener (1821)
Cottage Economy (1821)
Cobbett's Sermons (1822)
Cobbett's Poor Man's Friend (1826)
The English Gardener (1828)
A Treatise on Cobbett's Corn (1828)
The Emigrant's Guide (1829)
Advice to Young Men (1830)
Eleven Lectures on the French and Belgian Revolutions (1830)
History of the Regency and Reign of King George the Fourth (1830)
Rural Rides (1830)
Cobbett's Two-Penny Trash; or, Politics for the Poor (1831)
A Spelling Book (1831)
Cobbett's Manchester Lectures (1832)
A Geographical Dictionary of England and Wales (1832)
Cobbett's Tour in Scotland (1833)
Cobbett's Legacy to Labourers (1835)
Cobbett's Legacy to Parsons (1835)
Cobbold, Richard (1797–1877)
clergyman, novelist, and poet
The History of Margaret Catchpole, a Suffolk Girl (1845)
Cobden, Richard (1804–65)
statesman and author
England, Ireland, and America (1835)
The Political Writings of Richard Cobden (1867)
Coe, Jonathan (1961–)
novelist
The Accidental Woman (1987)
A Touch of Love (1989)
The Dwarves of Death (1990)
What a Carve Up! (1994)
The House of Sleep (1997)
The Rotters' Club (2001)
Cogan, Henry (*fl.* 1652)
translator
Ibrahim; or, The Illustrious Bassa: An excellent new romance (1652)
Cokayne, Sir Aston (1608–84)
poet and dramatist
Small Poems of Divers Sorts (1658)
Poems (1662)
Coke, Sir Edward (1552–1634)
judge and law writer
Coke upon Littleton (1628)
Colclough, George (*fl.* 1571)
poet
The Spectacle to Repentance (1571)
Cole, George Douglas Howard (1889–1959)
Fabian economist and novelist
The World of Labour (1913)
Cole, Thomas (1726?–96)
clergyman, poet, and religious writer
The Arbour; or, The Rural Philosopher (1756)
Discourses on Luxury, Infidelity, and Enthusiasm (1761)
Colegate, Isabel (1931–)
novelist
The Blackmailer (1958)
Statues in a Garden (1964)
Orlando King (1968)
Orlando at the Brazen Threshold (1971)
Agatha (1973)
The Shooting Party (1981)
Deceits of Time (1988)
The Summer of the Royal Visit (1991)
Winter Journey (1995)
Coleridge, Christabel Rose (1843–1921)
novelist
Lady Betty (1870)
Coleridge, [David] Hartley (1796–1849)
poet and author

Biographia Borealis; or, Lives of Distinguished Northerns (1833)
Poems (1833)
Essays and Marginilia (1851)
Poems by Hartley Coleridge (1851)
Coleridge, Henry Nelson (1798–1843)
author and editor
Six Months in the West Indies in 1825 (1826)
Coleridge, Mary Elizabeth ['Anodos'] (1861–1907)
poet and novelist
The Seven Sleepers of Ephesus (1893)
Fancy's Following (1896)
Fancy's Guerdon (1897)
Coleridge, Samuel Taylor (1772–1834)
poet and critic
The Fall of Robespierre (1794)
Conciones ad Populum; or, Addresses to the People (1795)
A Moral and Political Lecture (1795)
The Plot Discovered; or, An Address to the People, Against Ministerial Treason (1795)
Ode on the Departing Year (1796)
Poems on Various Subjects (1796)
The Watchman (1796)
Poems . . . Second Edition (1797)
Fears in Solitude (1798)
Wallenstein (1800)
Poems: Third Edition (1803)
The Friend (1809)
Omniana; or, Horae Otiosiores (1812)
Remorse: A tragedy (1813)
Christabel; Kubla Khan: A Vision; The Pains of Sleep (1816)
The Statesman's Manual (1816)
Biographia Literaria; or, Biographical Sketches of my Literary Life and Opinions (1817)
Sybilline Leaves (1817)
Zapolya: A Christmas tale (1817)
Aids to Reflection (1825)
The Poetical Works of S.T. Coleridge (1828)
The Devil's Walk (1830)
On the Constitution of the Church and State (1830)
Specimens of the Table Talk of the Late Samuel Taylor Coleridge (1835)
Letters, Conversations and Recollections of S.T. Coleridge (1836)
The Literary Remains of Samuel Taylor Coleridge [vols i, ii] (1836)
The Literary Remains of Samuel Taylor Coleridge [vol. iii] (1838)
The Literary Remains of Samuel Taylor Coleridge [vol. iv] (1839)
Confessions of an Inquiring Spirit (1840)
Notes and Lectures Upon Shakespeare and Some of the Old Poets and Dramatists (1849)
Essays on His Own Times (1850)
Hints Towards the Formation of a More Comprehensive Theory of Life (1853)
Notes, Theological, Poetical, and Miscellaneous (1853)
Coleridge, Sara (1802–52)
poet
The History of the Chevalier Bayard (1825)
Pretty Lessons in Verse for Good Children (1834)
Phantasmion (1837)
Colet, John (1467–1519)
dean of St Paul's
The Æditio (1527)
The Sermon of Doctor Colete (1530)
The Ordre of a Good Chrysten Mannes Lyfe (1534)
Collier, Jeremy (1650–1726)
nonjuror and historian
Miscellanies (1694)
Miscellanies upon Moral Subjects: The second part (1695)
A Short View of the Immorality, and Profaneness of the English Stage (1698)
A Defence of the Short View of the Profaneness and Immorality of the English Stage (1699)
A Second Defence of the Short View of the Profaneness and Immorality of the English Stage, &c (1700)
The Great Historical, Geographical, Genealogical and Poetical Dictionary (1701)
Mr Collier's Dissuasive from the Play-House (1703)
An Ecclesiastical History of Great Britain, Chiefly of England [vol. i] (1708)
A Farther Vindication of the Short View of the Profaneness and Immorality of the English Stage (1708)
Collier, John, of Urmston ['Tim Bobbin'] (1708–86)
author and painter
A View of the Lancashire Dialect (1746)
Tim Bobbin's Toy-shop; or, His Whimsical Amusements (1763)
Collier, John Henry Noyes (1901–80)
short-story writer and novelist
His Monkey Wife; or, Married to a Chimp (1930)
Collier, John Payne ['Amicus Curiae'] (1789–1883)
literary scholar, poet, and forger
The Poetical Decameron (1820)
Collier, Mary ['The Washerwoman of Petersfield'] (1690?–1762)
plebeian poet
The Woman's Labour: An epistle to Mr Stephen Duck (1739)
Poems, on Several Occasions (1762)
Collingwood, Robin George (1889–1943)
philosopher and historian
Religion and Philosophy (1916)
The Idea of History (1946)
Collins, Anne (*fl.* 1653)
poet
Divine Songs and Meditacions (1653)
Collins, Anthony (1676–1729)
deist

An Essay Concerning the Use of Reason (1707)
A Vindication of the Divine Attributes (1710)
A Discourse of Free-thinking (1713)
A Philosophical Inquiry Concerning Human Liberty (1717)
A Discourse of the Grounds and Reasons of the Christian Religion (1724)
The Scheme of Literal Prophecy Considered (1726)

Collins, John (1742?–1808)
actor and poet
Scripscrapologia; or Collins's Doggerel Dish of all Sorts (1804)

Collins, John Churton (1848–1908)
essayist, biographer, and critic
The Study of English Literature (1891)

Collins, [Edward James] Mortimer ['Robert Turner Cotton'] (1827–76)
poet and novelist
Who is the Heir? (1865)

Collins, Samuel (1619–70)
physician and author
The Present State of Russia (1671)

Collins, Thomas (*fl.* 1610–15)
poet
The Penitent Publican (1610)
The Teares of Love; or, Cupids Progresse (1615)

Collins, [William] Wilkie (1824–89)
novelist and short-story writer
Memoirs of the Life of William Collins (1848)
Antonina; or, The Fall of Rome (1850)
Rambles Beyond Railways; or, Notes in Cornwall Taken A-Foot (1851)
Basil: A story of modern life (1852)
Mr Wray's Cash Box; or, The Mask and the Mystery (1852)
Hide and Seek (1854)
After Dark (1856)
The Dead Secret (1857)
The Queen of Hearts (1859)
The Woman in White (1860)
No Name (1862)
Armadale (1866)
The Moonstone: A romance (1868)
Man and Wife (1870)
Poor Miss Finch (1872)
Miss or Mrs? and Other Stories in Outline (1873)
The Frozen Deep, and Other Stories (1874)
The Law and the Lady (1875)
The Two Destinies (1876)
The Haunted Hotel (1878)
The Fallen Leaves (1879)
Jezebel's Daughter (1880)
The Black Robe (1881)
Little Novels (1887)
Blind Love (1890)
The Lazy Tour of Two Idle Apprentices; No Thoroughfare; The Perils of Certain English Prisoners (1890)

Collins, William (1721–59)
poet
Persian Eclogues (1742)
Verses Humbly Address'd to Sir Thomas Hanmer on his Edition of Shakespear's Works (1743)
Odes on Several Descriptive and Allegoric Subjects (1746)
Ode Occasion'd by the Death of Mr Thomson (1749)
The Passions: An ode (1750)
The Poetical Works of William Collins (1765)
Ode on the Popular Superstitions of the Highlands of Scotland (1788)

Collis, John Stewart (1900–84)
Irish ecologist and author
While Following the Plough (1946)
Down to Earth (1947)

Collyer, Mary, *née* Mitchell (*d.* 1763)
novelist and translator
Felicia to Charlotte (1744)

Colman, George, the elder (1732–94)
dramatist
Poems by Eminent Ladies (1755)
Polly Honeycombe: A dramatick novel of one act (1760)
Two Odes (1760)
Critical Reflections on the Old English Dramatick Writers (1761)
The Jealous Wife: A comedy (1761)
The Deuce is in Him: A farce (1763)
The Comedies of Terence (1765)
The Clandestine Marriage: A comedy (1766)
The English Merchant: A comedy (1767)
The Oxonian in Town: A comedy (1769)
Man and Wife; or, The Shakespeare Jubilee: A comedy (1770)
The Man of Business: A comedy (1774)
Prose on Several Occasions (1787)
Ut Pictura Poesis!; or, The Enraged Musician: A musical entertainment (1789)
Some Particulars of the Life of the Late George Colman (1795)

Colman, George, the younger (1762–1836)
dramatist
Two to One: A comic opera (1785)
Inkle and Yarico: An opera (1787)
Ways and Means; or, A Trip to Dover: A comedy (1788)
The Battle of Hexham: A comedy (1790)
The Surrender of Calais (1790)
The Mountaineers (1794)
The Iron Chest (1796)
The Poor Gentleman: A comedy (1802)
John Bull; or, The Englishman's Fireside: A comedy (1805)
The Heir at Law: A comedy (1808)

Colse, Peter (*fl.* 1596)
poet
Penelopes Complaint; or, A Mirrour for Wanton Minions (1596)

Colum, Padraic (1881–1972)
Irish dramatist and poet
The Land (1905)

The Fiddler's House (1907)
Wild Earth (1907)
Thomas Muskerry (1910)
Irish Elegies (1961)

Colvile or Coldewel, George (*fl.* 1556)
translator
The Consolation of Philosophy (1556)

Colvill, Robert (*d.* 1788)
Scottish poet
Britain (1757)

Colville, Elizabeth, *née* Melville, Lady Colville of Culros (*fl.* 1603)
poet
Ane Godlie Dreame (1603)

Combe, George (1788–1858)
moral philosopher and phrenologist
Elements of Phrenology (1819)
Essays on Phrenology (1819)
The Constitution of Man Considered in Relation to External Objects (1828)

Combe, William (1742–1823)
poet
Letters from Eliza to Yorick (1775)
The Diaboliad (1777)
The First of April; or, The Triumphs of Folly (1777)
The Auction (1778)
Letters of the Late Lord Lyttelton (1780)
Letters of an Italian Nun and an English Gentleman (1781)
Original Love-letters, Between a Lady of Quality and a Person of Inferior Station (1784)
The Royal Dream; or, The P[rince] *in a Panic* (1785)
The Devil upon Two Sticks in England (1790)
The Tour of Dr Syntax, in Search of the Picturesque (1812)
The Dance of Life (1817)
The Second Tour of Doctor Syntax, in Search of Consolation (1820)
The Third Tour of Doctor Syntax, in Search of a Wife (1821)

Comfort, Alex[ander] (1920–2000)
poet and author
Elegies (1944)

Compton-Burnett, Dame Ivy (1884–1969)
novelist
Dolores (1911)
Pastors and Masters (1925)
Brothers and Sisters (1929)
Men and Wives (1931)
More Women Than Men (1933)
A House and its Head (1935)
Daughters and Sons (1937)
A Family and a Fortune (1939)
Parents and Children (1941)
Elders and Betters (1944)
Manservant and Maidservant (1947)
Two Worlds and their Ways (1949)
Darkness and Day (1951)
The Present and the Past (1953)
Mother and Son (1955)
A Father and His Fate (1957)
A Heritage and its History (1959)
The Mighty and their Fall (1961)
A God and His Gifts (1963)
The Last and the First (1971)

Comyns, Barbara, *née* Bailey (1909–92)
novelist
The Skin Chairs (1962)

Concanen, Matthew (1701–49)
miscellaneous writer
Miscellaneous Poems, Original and Translated (1724)

Congreve, William ['Cleophil'] (1670–1729)
dramatist and poet
Incognita; or, Love and Duty Reconcil'd: A novel (1692)
The Old Batchelour: A comedy (1693)
The Double-Dealer: A comedy (1694)
Love for Love: A comedy (1695)
The Mourning Muse of Alexas: A pastoral (1695)
The Birth of the Muse (1697)
The Mourning Bride: A tragedy (1697)
Amendments of Mr Collier's False and Imperfect Citations, &c. (1698)
The Way of the World: A comedy (1700)
The Judgment of Paris: A masque (1701)
A Hymn to Harmony (1703)
The Tears of Amaryllis for Amyntas (1703)
A Pindarique Ode . . . on the Victorious Progress of Her Majesties Arms, Under the Conduct of the Duke of Marlborough (1706)

Connolly, Cyril Vernon ['Palinurus'] (1903–74)
essayist, editor, and critic
The Rock Pool (1936)
Enemies of Promise (1938)

Connor, Tony [John Anthony Augustus Connor] (1930–)
poet
Spirits of Place (1986)

Conquest, [George] Robert Acworth (1917–)
poet and historian
Poems (1955)
A World of Difference (1955)
The Great Terror (1968)
The Harvest of Sorrow (1986)

Conrad, Joseph [Józef Teodor Konrad Nalecz Korzeniowski] (1857–1924)
novelist and short-story writer
Almayer's Folly: A story of an eastern river (1895)
An Outcast of the Islands (1896)
The Nigger of the 'Narcissus' (1897)
Tales of Unrest (1898)
Lord Jim (1900)
The Inheritors (1901)
Youth (1902)
Typhoon, and Other Stories (1903)
Nostromo: A tale of the seaboard (1904)
The Mirror of the Sea (1906)

The Secret Agent (1907)
A Set of Six (1908)
Under Western Eyes (1911)
'Twixt Land and Sea: Three tales (1912)
Chance (1914)
Within the Tides (1915)
Victory (1915)
The Shadow-Line (1917)
The Arrow of Gold (1919)
The Rescue (1920)
The Rover (1923)
The Nature of a Crime (1924)
Tales of Hearsay (1925)
Suspense (1925)

Constable, Henry (1562–1613)
poet and author
Diana (1592)
Diana; or, The Excellent Conceitful Sonnets of H.C. (1594)
The Catholike Moderator; or, A Moderate Examination of the Doctrine of the Protestants (1623)

Constable, John (*fl.* 1520)
epigrammatist
Epigrammata (1520)

Constantine, David John (1944–)
poet, novelist, and translator
A Brightness to Cast Shadows (1980)
Watching For Dolphins (1983)
Mappa Mundi (1984)
Madder (1987)
Something for the Ghosts (2002)

Conway, Anne, *née* Finch, Viscountess Conway (1631–79)
metaphysician
The Principles of the Most Ancient and Modern Philosophy (1692)

Cook, David (1940–)
novelist and playwright
Albert's Memorial (1972)
Happy Endings (1974)
Walter (1978)
Winter Doves (1979)

Cook, Eliza (1818–89)
poet and journalist
Lays of a Wild Harp (1835)

Cook, Captain James (1728–79)
naval officer and circumnavigator
A Voyage Towards the South Pole, and Round the World (1777)
A Voyage to the Pacific Ocean (1784)

Cooke, John (*fl.* 1614)
poet and dramatist
Epigrames (1604)
Greene's Tu quoque; or, The Cittie Gallant (1614)

Cooke, Thomas, known as Hesiod Cooke ['Scriblerus Tertius'] (1703–56)
translator, poet, and dramatist
Marlborough (1722)
The Battle of the Poets (1725)
The Works of Hesiod (1728)
Tales, Epistles, Odes, Fables, &c. (1729)
The Candidates for the Bays (1730)
The Triumphs of Love and Honour (1731)
The Mournful Nuptials; or, Love the Cure of all Woes: A tragedy (1739)
Mr Cooke's Original Poems (1742)
An Epistle to the Countess of Shaftesbury (1743)
Love the Cause and Cure of Grief; or, The Innocent Murderer (1744)
A Hymn to Liberty (1746)
An Ode on Beauty (1749)
An Ode on Martial Virtue (1750)
An Ode on the Powers of Poetry (1751)
Pythagoras: An ode (1752)
An Ode on Benevolence (1753)
An Ode on Poetry, Painting, and Sculpture (1754)

Cookson, Catherine Ann, *née* McMullen (1906–98)
historical novelist
Kate Hannigan (1950)
Tilly Trotter (1980)
Silent Lady (2001)

Cooper, Anthony Ashley, 3rd earl of Shaftesbury (1671–1713)
moral philosopher
A Letter Concerning Enthusiasm (1708)
Sensus Communis (1709)
Soliloquy; or, Advice to an Author (1710)
Characteristicks of Men, Manners, Opinions, Times (1711)
Several Letters Written by a Noble Lord to a Young Man at the University (1716)
Letters from the Late Earl of Shaftesbury, to Robert Molesworth (1721)

Cooper, Jilly, *née* Sallitt (1937–)
popular novelist
Riders (1985)

Cooper, John Gilbert (1723–69)
poet and miscellaneous writer
The Power of Harmony (1745)
The Life of Socrates (1749)
Cursory Remarks on Mr Warburton's New Edition of Mr Pope's Works (1751)
Letters Concerning Taste (1754)
The Tomb of Shakespear (1755)
Epistles to the Great (1757)
The Call of Aristippus (1758)
Ver-Vert; or, The Nunnery Parrot (1759)
Poems on Several Subjects (1764)

Cooper, Lettice Ulpha (1897–1994)
novelist
National Provincial (1938)
Black Bethlehem (1947)

Cooper or Couper, Thomas (1517?–94)
bishop of Winchester
An Epitome of Cronicles of England Continued to the Reigne of Edwarde the Sixt (1549)
Cooper's Chronicle (1560)
Thesaurus linguae Romanae Britannicae (1565)

Certaine Sermons (1580)
An Admonition to the People of England (1589)
Cooper, Thomas ['The Chartist', 'Adam Hornbrook'] (1805–92)
poet and novelist
The Purgatory of Suicides (1845)
The Family Feud (1855)
The Life of Thomas Cooper (1872)
'Cooper, William' [Harry Sumerfield Hoff] (1910–2002)
novelist
Scenes from Provincial Life (1950)
The Ever-Interesting Topic (1953)
Young People (1958)
Scenes from Married Life (1961)
Love on the Coast (1973)
Scenes from Metropolitan Life (1982)
Scenes from Later Life (1983)
Immortality at Any Price (1991)
Cope, Wendy (1945–)
poet
Across the City (1980)
Making Cocoa for Kingsley Amis (1986)
Does She Like Word-Games? (1988)
Men and their Boring Arguments (1988)
Serious Concerns (1992)
Heaven on Earth: 101 Happy Poems (2001)
If I Don't Know (2001)
Copland, Robert (*fl.* 1508–47)
author, translator, and printer
Apollonius of Tyre (1510)
The Knight of the Swan (1512)
Ipomadon (1522?)
The Rutter of the See (1528)
Secreta secretorum (1528)
The Hye Way to the Spyttell Hous (1536)
The Seven Sorrows That Women Have When Theyr Husbandes Be Deade (1565?)
Copley, Anthony (1567–1607)
poet
Wits Fittes and Fancies . . . Also: Loves Owl (1595)
A Fig for Fortune (1596)
Coppard, Alfred Edgar (1878–1957)
short-story writer and poet
Adam and Eve and Pinch Me (1921)
Clorinda Walks in Heaven (1922)
Nixey's Harlequin (1931)
Crotty Shinkwin (1932)
Dunky Fitlow (1933)
Polly Oliver (1935)
Fearful Pleasures (1946)
Coppinger, Matthew (*fl.* 1682)
poet
Poems, Songs and Lover-Verses, upon Several Subjects (1682)
Corbet or Corbett, Richard (1582–1635)
bishop of Oxford and Norwich, and poet
Certain Elegant Poems (1647)
Poetica Stromata; or, A Collection of Sundry Peices [sic] *in Poetry* (1648)
Corbett, Jim [James Edward Corbett] (1875–1955)
author and conservationist
The Man-Eaters of Kumaon (1946)
Corelli, Marie [Isabella Mary Corelli, *née* Mills, later Mackay] (1855–1924)
novelist
A Romance of Two Worlds (1886)
Ardath (1889)
Barabbas (1893)
The Sorrows of Satan; or, The Strange Experience of One Geoffrey Tempest, Millionaire (1895)
The Master-Christian (1900)
Corkery, Daniel (1878–1964)
Irish critic, dramatist, novelist, and short-story writer
A Munster Twilight (1916)
The Threshold of Quiet (1917)
Cornford, Frances Crofts, *née* Darwin (1886–1960)
poet
Poems (1910)
'Cornwall, Barry' [Bryan Waller Procter] (1787–1874)
poet
Dramatic Scenes, and Other Poems (1819)
Marcian Colonna (1820)
A Sicilian Story, with Diego de Montilla, and Other Poems (1820)
Mirandola: A tragedy (1821)
The Flood of Thessaly, The Girl of Provence, and Other Poems (1823)
English Songs (1832)
Cornwallis, Sir William (1579?–1614)
essayist
Essayes [pt i] (1600)
Discourses Upon Seneca the Tragedian (1601)
Essayes [pt ii] (1601)
Essayes or Rather, Encomions, Prayses of Sadnesse (1616)
Essayes of Certaine Paradoxes (1616)
'Cornwell, Bernard' [Bernard Wiggins] (1944–)
popular historical novelist
Sharpe's Eagle (1981)
Cory, William Johnson (1823–92)
poet, classicist, and schoolmaster
Ionica (1858)
Ionica II (1877)
Coryate, Thomas (1577?–1617)
traveller and author
Coryats Crambe; or, His Colwort Twise Sodden (1611)
Coryats Crudities (1611)
From the Court of the Great Mogul (1616)
Mr Thomas Coriat to his Friends in England . . . From Agra (1618)

Cosin, John (1595–1672)
bishop of Durham
A Scholastical History of the Canon of the Holy Scriptures (1657)

Costello, Louisa Stuart (1799–1879)
painter and poet
The Maid of the Cyprus Isle, and Other Poems (1815)
Redwald: A Tale of Mona; and Other Poems (1819)
Songs of a Stranger (1825)
The Rose Garden of Persia (1845)

Cotgrave, John (*fl.* 1655)
editor
The English Treasury of Wit and Language (1655)
Wits Interpreter (1655)

Cotta or Cottey, John (1575?–1650?)
physician and author
The Triall of Witch-craft (1616)

Cottle, Joseph (1770–1853)
poet and bookseller
Poems (1795)
Malvern Hills (1798)
Alfred (1800)
Early Recollections: Chiefly relating to the late Samuel Taylor Coleridge (1837)

Cotton, Charles (1630–87)
poet, translator, and miscellaneous author
A Panegyrick to the King's Most Excellent Majesty (1660)
The Morall Philosophy of the Stoicks (1664)
Scarronides; or, Virgile Travestie (1664)
Scarronides; or, Virgile Travestie (1665)
Scarronides; or, Virgile Travestie (1667)
Horace (1671)
The Compleat Gamester; or, Instructions How to Play at Billiards, Trucks, Bowls, and Chess (1674)
Burlesque upon Burlesque; or, The Scoffer Scoft (1675)
The Wonders of the Peake (1681)
Essays of Montaigne (1685)
Poems on Several Occasions (1689)
The Genuine Works of Charles Cotton (1715)

Cotton, John (1584–1652)
Nonconformist divine
A Briefe Exposition with Practicall Observations upon the Whole Book of Ecclesiastes (1654)

Cotton, Nathaniel (1705–88)
physician and poet
Visions in Verse (1751)

Cotton, Roger (*fl.* 1590–6)
poet
A Direction to the Waters of Lyfe (1590)
An Armour of Proofe: Brought from the tower of David, to fight against Spannyardes, and all enimies of the trueth (1596)
A Spirituall Song: Conteining an historicall discourse from the infancie of the world, until this present time (1596)

Coventry, Francis (1725–54)
satirical novelist
The History of Pompey the Little; or, The Life and Adventures of a Lap-dog (1751)

Coverdale, Miles (1488–1568)
translator of the Bible
The Bible (1535)
Goostly Psalmes and Spirituall Songes (1535?)
The Byble in Englyshe (1539)
The Byble in Englyshe (1540)
Certain Most Godly, Fruitful, and Comfortable Letters of Such True Saintes and Holy Martyrs as in the Late Bloodye Persecution Gave their Lyves (1564)

Coward, Sir Noël Pierce (1899–1973)
playwright and songwriter
The Young Idea (1924)
The Rat Trap (1924)
The Vortex (1925)
Hay Fever: A comedy (1925)
Bitter Sweet (1929)
Private Lives: An intimate comedy (1930)
Cavalcade (1932)
Present Indicative (1937)
Blithe Spirit: An improbable farce (1942)
Present Laughter (1943)
This Happy Breed (1943)
Future Indefinite (1954)
Waiting in the Wings (1960)

Cowley, Abraham (1618–67)
poet
Poetical Blossomes (1633)
Loves Riddle: A pastorall comaedie (1638)
The Mistresse; or, Severall Copies of Love-Verses (1647)
The Guardian: A comedie (1650)
Poems (1656)
Ode, Upon the Blessed Restoration and Returne of His Sacred Majestie, Charls [sic] *the Second* (1660)
The Visions and Prophecies Concerning England, Scotland, and Ireland of Ezekiel Grebner (1660)
Cutter of Coleman-Street: A comedy (1663)
Verses, Lately Written Upon Several Occasions (1663)
The Works of Mr Abraham Cowley (1668)
A Poem on the Late Civil War (1679)

Cowley, Hannah ['Anna Matilda'] (1743–1809)
dramatist and poet
The Runaway: A comedy (1776)
Albina, Countess Raimond: A tragedy (1779)
Who's the Dupe? (1779)
The Maid of Arragon (1780)
The Belle's Stratagem: A comedy (1782)
Which is the Man? (1783)
A Bold Stroke for a Husband: A comedy (1784)
More Ways Than One: A comedy (1784)
A School for Greybeards; or, The Mourning Bride: A comedy (1786)
The Scottish Village; or, Pitcairn Green (1786)

The Fate of Sparta; or, The Rival Kings: A tragedy (1788)
The Town Before You: A comedy (1795)
The Siege of Acre (1801)
Cowper, Judith, later Madan (1702–81)
poet and friend of Pope
The Progress of Poetry (1783)
Cowper, Maria Frances Cecilia, *née* Madan (1726–97)
poet
Original Poems on Various Occasions (1792)
Cowper, William (1731–1800)
poet
Olney Hymns (1779)
Anti-Thelyphthora (1781)
'The Diverting History of John Gilpin' (1782)
Poems (1782)
The Task (1785)
The Iliad and the Odyssey (1791)
Latin and Italian Poems of Milton Translated into English Verse (1808)
Poems Translated from the French of Mme de la Mothe Guion (1808)
Poems, by William Cowper (1815)
Memoir of the Early Life of William Cowper (1816)
Private Correspondence of William Cowper (1824)
The Works of William Cowper (1835)
Cox, Anthony Berkeley ['Anthony Berkeley', 'Francis Iles'] (1893–1971)
crime writer
The Layton Court Mystery (1925)
The Poisoned Chocolates Case (1929)
Cox, Leonard (*fl.* 1572)
schoolmaster
The Arte or Crafte of Rhetoryke (1532)
Crabbe, George (1754–1832)
poet
Inebriety (1775)
The Candidate (1780)
The Library (1781)
The Village (1783)
The News-Paper (1785)
Poems (1807)
The Borough (1810)
Tales (1812)
The Works of the Reverend George Crabbe (1816)
Tales of the Hall (1819)
The Poetical Works of George Crabbe (1829)
The Poetical Works of George Crabbe (1834)
Crace, Jim (1946–)
novelist, short-story writer, and playwright
Continent (1986)
The Gift of Stones (1988)
Arcadia (1992)
Signals of Distress (1994)
Quarantine (1997)
Being Dead (1999)
The Devil's Larder (2001)
Six (2003)
Crackanthorpe, Hubert Montague, born Cookson (1870–96)
short-story writer
Wreckage (1893)
Sentimental Studies (1895)
Vignettes (1896)
Last Studies (1897)
Cradock, Joseph (1742–1826)
dramatist and author
Zobeide: A tragedy (1771)
Village Memoirs (1774)
The Czar: An historical tragedy (1824)
Craik, Dinah Maria, *née* Mulock (1826–87)
novelist and essayist
The Ogilvies (1849)
Olive (1850)
Bread Upon the Waters: A governess's life (1852)
John Halifax, Gentleman (1856)
Craik, George Lillie (1798–1866)
historian and critic
The Pursuit of Knowledge Under Difficulties (1830)
The Pursuit of Knowledge Under Difficulties, Illustrated by Female Examples (1847)
Cranmer, Thomas (1489–1556)
archbishop of Canterbury
Catechismus (1548)
A Defence of the True and Catholike Doctrine of the Sacrament of the Body and Bloud of Christ (1550)
An Answer Unto a Crafty Cavillation by Stephen Gardiner (1551)
The Recantation of Thomas Cranmer (1556)
Submissions and Recantations (1556)
Crashaw, Richard (1612/13–49)
poet
Steps to the Temple: Sacred poems, with other delights of the muses (1646)
Carmen Deo Nostro, Te Decet Hymnus: Sacred poems (1652)
Creasy, Sir Edward Shepherd (1812–78)
historian
Fifteen Decisive Battles of the World (1851)
Creech, Thomas (1659–1700)
poet and translator
De Natura Rerum (1682)
The Idylliums of Theocritus, with Rapin's Discourse of Pastorals Done into English (1684)
The Odes, Satyrs, and Epistles of Horace (1684)
Creighton, Mandell (1843–1901)
historian
History of the Papacy [vols i, ii] (1882)
History of the Papacy [vols iii, iv] (1887)
History of the Papacy [vol. v] (1894)
'Crispin, Edmund' [Robert Bruce Montgomery] (1921–78)
detective novelist
The Case of the Gilded Fly (1944)
Cristall, Anne Batten (*b.* 1769)
poet

Poetical Sketches (1795)
Crockett, Samuel Rutherford (1860–1914)
Scottish novelist
The Stickit Minister and Some Common Men (1893)
The Raiders (1894)
The Men of the Moss-Hags (1895)
The Red Axe (1898)
Joan of the Sword Hand (1900)
The Stickit Minister's Wooing, and Other Galloway Stories (1900)
The Moss Troopers (1912)
Croese, Gerard (1642–1710)
historian of the Quakers
The General History of the Quakers (1696)
Croft, Sir Herbert (1751–1816)
novelist and poet
The Abbey of Kilkhampton; or, Monumental Records for the Year 1980 (1780)
Love and Madness (1780)
Crofts, Freeman Wills (1879–1957)
detective novelist
The Cask (1920)
Inspector French's Greatest Case (1925)
Crofts, Robert (*fl.* 1638)
romance writer
The Lover; or, Nuptiall Love (1638)
Croker, John Wilson (1780–1857)
statesman and man of letters
An Intercepted Letter from J- T-, Esq. (1804)
The Amazoniad; or, Figure and Fashion (1806)
The Croker Papers (1884)
Croker, Thomas Crofton (1798–1854)
author and antiquary
Fairy Legends and Traditions of the South of Ireland [vol. i] (1826)
Fairy Legends and Traditions of the South of Ireland [vols ii, iii] (1828)
Croly, George (1780–1860)
clergyman, poet, and novelist
Paris in 1815 (1817)
The Angel of the World; Sebastion; with Other Poems (1820)
Catiline: A tragedy (1822)
Salathiel (1828)
Poetical Works (1830)
'Crompton, Richmal' [Richmal Crompton Lamburn] (1890–1969)
children's writer and novelist
Just—William (1922)
Cronin, Archibald Joseph (1896–1981)
Scottish novelist
Hatter's Castle (1931)
The Stars Look Down (1935)
The Citadel (1937)
The Keys of the Kingdom (1942)
'Cross, Victoria' [Annie Sophy Cory, also known as Vivian] (1868–1952)
novelist
The Woman Who Didn't (1895)
Crossley-Holland, Kevin John William (1941–)
poet and translator
Waterslain (1986)
Crowe, Catherine Ann, *née* Stevens (1790–1876)
novelist, essayist, and short-story writer
Adventures of Susan Hopley; or, Circumstantial Evidence (1841)
The Seeress of Prevorst (1845)
The Night-Side of Nature; or, Ghosts and Ghost-Seers (1848)
Spiritualism, and the Age We Live In (1859)
Crowe, William (1745–1829)
clergyman and poet
Lewesdon Hill (1788)
Crowley, Crole, or Croleus, Robert (1518–88)
author, printer, and divine
An Informacion and Peticion Agaynst the Oppressours of the Pore Commons of this Realme (1548)
The Voyce of the Laste Trumpet Blowen bi the Seventh Angel (1549)
One and Thyrtye Epigrammes (1550)
Philargyrie of Greate Britayne; or, The Fable of the Great Giant (1551)
Crowne, John (*d.* 1703)
dramatist
Pandion and Amphigenia; or, The History of the Coy Lady of Thessalia (1665)
Juliana; or, The Princess of Poland: A tragicomedy (1671)
The History of Charles the Eighth of France; or, The Invasion of Naples by the French (1672)
Andromache: A tragedy (1675)
Calisto; or, The Chaste Nimph: The late masque at court (1675)
The Countrey Wit: A comedy (1675)
The Destruction of Jerusalem by Titus Vespasian (1677)
The Ambitious Statesman; or, The Loyal Favourite (1679)
Thyestes: A tragedy (1681)
City Politiques: A comedy (1683)
Sir Courtly Nice; or, It Cannot Be: A comedy (1685)
Darius, King of Persia: A tragedy (1688)
The English Frier; or, The Town Sparks: A comedy (1690)
The Married Beau; or, The Curious Impertinent: A comedy (1694)
Caligula: A tragedy (1698)
Croxall, Samuel (1690?–1752)
miscellaneous writer
The Vision (1715)
The Fair Circassian (1720)
Fables of Aesop and Others (1722)
Cruden, Alexander (1701–70)
compiler
A Complete Concordance to the Holy Scriptures of the Old and New Testament (1738)
Cudworth, Ralph (1617–88)
divine

The True Notion of the Lords Supper (1642)
The Union of Christ and the Church, in a Shadow (1642)
A Sermon Preached Before the Honourable House of Commons, March 31 1647 (1647)
A Sermon Preached to the Honourable Society of Lincolnes-Inne (1664)
The True Intellectual System of the Universe (1678)
A Treatise Concerning Eternal and Immutable Morality (1731)

Cugoano, Ottabah
former slave
Thoughts and Sentiments on the Evil and Wicked Traffic of the Slavery and Commerce of the Human Species (1787)

Culpeper, Nicholas (1616–54)
herbalist and astrologer
The English Physitian Enlarged (1653)

Culpeper, Sir Thomas, the elder (1578–1662)
lawyer, M.P., and author
A Tract Against Usurie (1621)

Cumberland, Richard (1732–1811)
dramatist, novelist, and poet
The Brothers: A comedy (1770)
The West Indian: A comedy (1771)
The Fashionable Lover: A comedy (1772)
The Choleric Man: A comedy (1775)
Calypso: A masque (1779)
The Carmelite: A tragedy (1784)
The Natural Son: A comedy (1785)
Arundel (1789)
The Jew: A comedy (1794)
Henry (1795)
The Wheel of Fortune: A comedy (1795)
The Sailor's Daughter: A comedy (1804)
The Victory and Death of Lord Viscount Nelson (1805)
A Hint to Husbands: A comedy (1806)
The Exodiad (1807)
Memoirs of Richard Cumberland (1807)
John de Lancaster (1809)
Retrospection (1811)
Posthumous Dramatick Works (1813)

Cunningham, Allan (1784–1842)
poet, novelist, and man of letters
Songs (1813)
Sir Marmaduke Maxwell; The Mermaid of Galloway; The Legend of Richard Faulder; and Twenty Scottish Songs (1822)
Traditional Tales of the English and Scottish Peasantry (1822)
The Songs of Scotland, Ancient and Modern (1825)
Paul Jones (1826)
Lives of the Most Eminent British Painters, Sculptors and Architects (1829)
The Maid of Elvar (1833)

Cunningham, Sir Henry Stewart (1832–1920)
barrister and author
Wheat and Tares (1861)

Cunningham, John (1729–73)
poet and dramatist
Love in a Mist: A farce (1747)
The Contemplatist (1762)
Poems, Chiefly Pastoral (1766)

Curzon, George Nathaniel, Marquess Curzon of Kedleston (1859–1925)
statesman and author
Russia in Central Asia in 1889 (1889)

Curzon, Robert, Lord de la Zouche (1810–73)
travel writer
Visits to Monasteries in the Levant (1849)

Cusk, Rachel (1967)
novelist
The Lucky Ones (2003)

Cutts, John, Baron Cutts of Gowran (1661?–1707)
soldier and author
La Muse de Cavalier (1685)

Daborne or Daborn, Robert (1578?–1628)
dramatist and divine
A Christian Turn'd Turke; or, The Tragicall Lives and Deaths of the Two Famous Pyrates, Ward and Dansiker (1612)

Dacre, Charlotte, later Byrne ['Rosa Matilda'] (1782?–1841?)
novelist and poet
The Confessions of the Nun of St Omer (1805)
Hours of Solitude (1805)
Zofloya; or, The Moor (1806)
The Libertine (1807)
The Passions (1811)

Dacres, Edward (*fl.* 1636–40)
translator
Machiavels Discourses, upon the First Decade of T. Livius (1636)
The Prince (1640)

Dahl, Roald (1916–90)
children's author and short-story writer
Over to You (1946)
Someone Like You (1954)
Charlie and the Chocolate Factory (1967)
James and the Giant Peach (1967)
Fantastic Mr Fox (1970)
Switch Bitch (1974)
My Uncle Oswald (1979)
Tales of the Unexpected (1979)
More Tales of the Unexpected (1980)
George's Marvellous Medicine (1981)
The BFG (1982)
The Witches (1983)
Matilda (1988)

Dale, Robert William (1829–95)
Congregational theologian
The English Hymn Book (1874)

Dallas, Eneas Sweetland (1828–79)
journalist and author
The Gay Science (1866)

Dallas, Robert Charles (1754–1824)
miscellaneous writer

Percival; or, Nature Vindicated (1801)
Aubrey (1804)
The Morlands (1805)
Recollections of the Life of Lord Byron (1814)
Dallington, Sir Robert (1561–1637)
Master of the Charterhouse and author
Hypnerotomachia Poliphili (1592)
A Method for Travell: Shewed by taking the view of France (1605?)
Dalrymple, Sir David, Lord Hailes (1726–92)
Scottish jurist and historian
Edom of Gordon: An Ancient Scottish Poem (1755)
Ancient Scottish Poems (1770)
Remarks on the History of Scotland (1773)
Annals of Scotland [vol. i] (1776)
Dalrymple, Sir John, 4th baronet of Cranstoun (1726–1810)
Scottish judge and historian
An Essay Towards a General History of Feudal Property in Great Britain (1757)
Memoirs of Great Britain and Ireland (1771)
Dalton, John (1766–1844)
chemist and natural philosopher
A New System of Chemical Philosophy (1808)
Dampier, William (1652–1715)
explorer, buccaneer, and author
A New Voyage Round the World (1697)
Voyages and Descriptions (1699)
A Voyage to New Holland, &c in the Year 1699 (1703)
Dancer, John (*fl.* 1675)
translator and dramatist
Aminta: The Famous Pastoral (1660)
Nicomede: A tragi-comedy (1671)
'Dane, Clemence' [Winifred Ashton] (1888–1965)
novelist and playwright
Regiment of Women (1917)
A Bill of Divorcement (1921)
Daniel, George (1789–1864)
stockbroker, satirist, and book-collector
The Modern Dunciad (1814)
Daniel, Samuel (1562–1619)
poet and dramatist
The Worthy Tract of Paulus Jovius (1585)
Delia (1592)
Delia and Rosamond Augmented; [with] *Cleopatra* (1594)
The First Fowre Bookes of the Civile Warres Betweene the Two Houses of Lancaster and Yorke (1595)
The Poeticall Essayes of Sam. Danyel (1599)
The Works of Samuel Daniel Newly Augmented (1601)
A Panegyrike Congratulatory Delivered to the Kings Most Excellent Majesty . . . With a Defence of Ryme (1603)
Certaine Small Poems Lately Printed (1605)
The Queenes Arcadia: A pastoral trage-comedie (1606)
Certaine Small Workes (1607)
The Civile Wares Betweene the Howses of Lancaster and Yorke Corrected and Continued (1609)
Tethys Festival (1610)
The First Part of the Historie of England (1612)
Hymens Triumph: A pastorall tragicomaedie (1615)
The Whole Workes of Samuel Daniel Esquire in Poetrie (1623)
D'Arcy, Ella (1851–1937?)
short-story writer and novelist
Monochromes (1895)
The Bishop's Dilemma (1898)
Modern Instances (1898)
Darley, George ['Guy Penseval', 'Geoffrey Crayon jun.'] (1795–1846)
poet, mathematician, and author
The Errors of Ecstasie: A dramatic poem (1822)
The Labours of Idleness; or, Seven Nights Entertainments (1826)
Sylvia; or, The May Queen (1827)
The New Sketch Book (1829)
Nepenthe (1835)
Darwin, Charles Robert (1809–82)
naturalist
The Zoology of the Voyage of HMS Beagle (1838)
The Structure and Distribution of Coral Reefs (1842)
Geological Observations on the Volcanic Islands, Visited During the Voyage of HMS Beagle (1844)
Geological Observations on South America (1846)
On the Origin of Species by Natural Selection (1859)
Darwin, Erasmus (1731–1802)
physician, poet, and author
The Botanic Garden (1789)
The Loves of the Plants (1789)
The Golden Age (1794)
Zoonomia; or, The Laws of Organic Life (1794)
Phytologia; or, The Philosophy of Agriculture and Gardening (1800)
The Temple of Nature; or, The Origin of Society (1803)
Daryush, Elizabeth, *née* Bridges (1887–1977)
poet
Charitesse (1911)
Verses (1916)
Verses: Sixth Book (1938)
Davenant, Charles (1656–1714)
political economist and dramatist
Circe: A tragedy (1677)
Davenant or D'Avenant, Sir William (1606–68)
poet and dramatist
The Tragedy of Albovine, King of the Lombards (1629)
The Cruell Brother: A tragedy (1630)
The Just Italian (1630)
The Platonick Lovers: A tragaecomedy (1636)

The Triumphs of the Prince d'Amour: A masque (1636)
The Witts: A comedie (1636)
Madagascar; with Other Poems (1638)
Salmacida Spolia: A masque (1640)
The Unfortunate Lovers: A tragedie (1643)
Love and Honour (1649)
Gondibert: An heroick poem (1651)
The Siege of Rhodes (1656)
The Cruelty of the Spaniards in Peru (1658)
Poem, Upon His Sacred Majesties Most Happy Return to His Dominions (1660)
Poem, to the King's Most Sacred Majesty (1663)
The Rivals: A comedy (1668)
The Works of Sr William D'avenant (1673)
Macbeth: A tragedy (1674)
The Seventh and Last Canto of the Third Book of Gondibert (1685)

Davenport, Robert (*fl.* 1624–40)
poet and dramatist
A Crowne for a Conquerour; and Too Late to Call Backe Yesterday (1639)
A New Tricke to Cheat the Divill (1639)
King John and Matilda: A tragedy (1655)
The City-Night-Cap; or, Crede Quod Habes, & Habes: A tragi-comedy (1661)

Davenport, Selina
novelist
The Sons of the Viscount, and the Daughters of the Earl (1813)
The Hypocrite; or, The Modern Janus (1814)

Davidson, John (1857–1909)
poet, dramatist, and novelist
Perfervid (1890)
In a Music-Hall, and Other Poems (1891)
Fleet Street Eclogues [1st ser.] (1893)
Ballads and Songs (1894)
Fleet Street Eclogues [2nd ser.] (1895)
New Ballads (1897)
The Last Ballad, and Other Poems (1899)
Self's the Man: A tragi-comedy (1901)
The Testament of a Man Forbid (1901)
The Testament of a Vivisector (1901)
The Testament of an Empire-Builder (1902)
A Rosary (1903)
The Testament of a Prime Minister (1904)
The Theatrocrat: A tragic play of Church and stage (1905)
Holiday, and Other Poems (1906)
God and Mammon (1907)
The Testament of John Davidson (1908)
Fleet Street, and Other Poems (1909)

Davie, Donald Alfred (1922–95)
academic, poet, and critic
A Winter Talent, and Other Poems (1957)
Events and Wisdoms (1964)
Essex Poems 1963–67 (1969)
The Shires (1974)
In the Stopping Train, and Other Poems (1980)
To Scorch or Freeze (1989)
Under Briggflats: A history of poetry in Great Britain 1960–1988 (1989)
Collected Poems (1990)

Davies, Charles Maurice (1829–85)
clergyman and author
Philip Paternoster: A Tractarian love-story (1858)
Unorthodox London (1873)
Orthodox London (1874)

Davies, Lady Eleanor, later Douglas (*c.*1590–1652)
pamphleteer
A Warning to the Dragon and all his Angels (1625)

Davies, John, of Hereford (1565–1618)
poet
Mirum in Modum (1602)
Microcosmos (1603)
Wittes Pilgrimage (by Poeticall Essaies) (1605)
Bien Venu: Greate Britaines welcome to hir greate friendes, and deere breathren the Danes (1606)
Yehovah Summa Totalis; or, All in All, and, the Same for Ever; or, An Addition to Mirum in Modum (1607)
The Holy Roode; or, Christs Crosse (1609)
Humours Heav'n on Earth: With the civile warres of death and fortune (1609)
The Scourge of Folly (1611)
The Muses Sacrifice (1612)
The Muses-Teares for the Losse of their Hope (1613)
A Select Second Husband for Sir Thomas Overburies Wife, Now a Matchlesse Widow (1616)
Wits Bedlam (1617)

Davies, Sir John (1569–1626)
lawyer, poet, and historian
Orchestra; or, A Poeme of Dauncing (1596)
Hymns of Astraea, in Acrosticke Verse (1599)
Nosce Teipsum (1599)
A Discoverie of the True Causes why Ireland was Never Entirely Subdued (1612)
Nosce Teipsum (1619)
Nosce Teipsum (1622)

Davies, William Henry (1871–1940)
Welsh poet
The Soul's Destroyer (1905)
New Poems (1907)
The Autobiography of a Super-Tramp (1908)
Nature Poems and Others (1908)
Farewell to Poesy, and Other Pieces (1910)
Songs of Joy and Others (1911)
Foliage (1913)
The Bird of Paradise, and Other Poems (1914)
Child Lovers, and Other Poems (1916)
Collected Poems (1916)
The Song of Life, and Other Poems (1920)
The Hour of Magic, and Other Poems (1922)
Collected Poems [2nd ser.] (1923)
A Poet's Alphabet (1925)
The Birth of Song (1926)

A Poet's Calendar (1927)
Collected Poems (1928)
Ambition, and Other Poems (1929)
Poems, 1930–31 (1932)
Poems (1934)
Love Poems (1935)
The Loneliest Mountain, and Other Poems (1939)

Davison, John (1777–1834)
theological writer
Discourses on Prophecy (1824)

Davy, Sir Humphry (1778–1829)
natural philosopher
Researches, Chemical and Philosophical (1800)

Davys, Mary (1674–1732)
novelist, dramatist, and poet
The Amours of Alcippus and Leucippe (1704)
The Fugitive (1705)
The Northern Heiress; or, The Humors of York: A comedy (1716)
The Reform'd Coquet (1724)
The Works of Mrs Davys (1725)
The Accomplish'd Rake; or, Modern Fine Gentleman (1727)
The False Friend; or, The Treacherous Portugueze (1732)

Day, Angel (*fl.* 1575–95)
miscellaneous writer
The English Secretorie (1586)
Daphnis and Chloe (1587)

Day, John (1574–1640)
dramatist
The Ile of Guls (1606)
The Travailes of the Three English Brothers, Sir Thomas, Sir Anthony, Mr Robert Shirley (1607)
Humour Out of Breath (1608)
Law-Trickes; or, Who Woul'd Have Thought It (1608)
The Blind-Beggar of Bednal-Green (1659)

Day, Thomas (1748–89)
poet, novelist, and author
The Dying Negro (1773)
The Desolation of America (1777)
Reflections upon the Present State of England, and the Independence of America (1782)
The History of Sandford and Merton (1783)
The History of Sandford and Merton (1786)
The History of Little Jack (1788)
The History of Sandford and Merton (1789)

Day Lewis, C. [Cecil Day-Lewis] ['Nicholas Blake'] (1904–72)
poet and writer of detective fiction
Beechen Vigil, and Other Poems (1925)
Transitional Poem (1929)
From Feathers to Iron (1931)
The Magnetic Mountain (1933)
Collected Poems 1929–1933 (1935)
A Time to Dance, and Other Poems (1935)
Noah and the Waters (1936)
Thou Shell of Death (1936)
The Beast Must Die (1938)
Overtures to Death, and Other Poems (1938)
The Georgics of Virgil (1940)
Poems in Wartime (1940)
Word Over All (1943)
The Poetic Image (1947)
Collected Poems 1929–36 (1949)
The Aeneid of Virgil (1952)
An Italian Visit (1953)
Collected Poems (1954)
Pegasus, and Other Poems (1957)
The Buried Day (1960)
The Gate, and Other Poems (1962)
The Eclogues of Virgil (1963)
The Room, and Other Poems (1965)
The Whispering Roots (1970)

De Bernières, Louis (1954–)
novelist
The War of Don Emmanuel's Nether Parts (1990)
Senor Vivo and the Coca Lord (1991)
The Troublesome Offspring of Cardinal Guzman (1992)
Captain Corelli's Mandolin (1994)

Deeping, [George] Warwick (1877–1950)
novelist
Uther & Igraine (1903)
Love Among the Ruins (1904)
Sorrell and Son (1925)

Defoe, Daniel (1660–1731)
journalist, pamphleteer, poet, and novelist
An Essay Upon Projects (1697)
An Enquiry into the Occasional Conformity of Dissenters, in Cases of Preferment (1698)
The Poor Man's Plea (1698)
The Pacificator (1700)
The Original Power of the Collective Body of the People of England (1701)
The True-Born Englishman: A satyr (1701)
An Enquiry into Occasional Conformity (1702)
The Mock-Mourners: A satyr, by way of an elegy on King William (1702)
A New Test of the Church of England's Loyalty (1702)
Reformation of Manners: A satyr (1702)
The Shortest Way with the Dissenters (1702)
The Spanish Descent (1702)
A Brief Explanation of a Late Pamphlet, entituled, The Shortest Way with the Dissenters (1703)
A Collection of the Writings of the Author of the True-Born English-Man (1703)
A Dialogue Between a Dissenter and the Observator, Concerning The Shortest Way with the Dissenters (1703)
A Hymn to the Funeral Sermon (1703)
A Hymn to the Pillory (1703)
More Reformation: A satyr upon himself (1703)
The Shortest Way to Peace and Union (1703)
A True Collection of the Writings of the Author of the True-Born English-man (1703)
The Address (1704)

The Dissenters Answer to the High-Church Challenge (1704)
An Elegy on the Author of the True-Born Englishman (1704)
An Essay on the Regulation of the Press (1704)
Giving Alms No Charity, and Employing the Poor a Grievance to the Nation (1704)
A Hymn to Victory (1704)
The Lay-Man's Sermon upon the Late Storm (1704)
More Short-Ways with the Dissenters (1704)
A Review of the Affairs of France: and of All Europe (1704)
The Consolidator; or, Memoirs of Sundry Transactions from the World in the Moon (1705)
The Double Welcome: A poem to the Duke of Marlbro' (1705)
The Dyet of Poland (1705)
A Second Volume of the Writings of the Author of the True-Born Englishman (1705)
Caledonia (1706)
An Essay at Removing National Prejudices Against a Union with Scotland (1706)
A Hymn to Peace (1706)
Jure Divino (1706)
A True Relation of the Apparition of one Mrs Veal, the Next Day after her Death (1706)
The Vision (1706)
The History of the Union of Great Britain (1709)
Atalantis Major (1710)
An Essay Upon Publick Credit (1710)
The British Visions; or, Isaac Bickerstaff, Sen. (1711)
An Essay on the History of Parties, and Persecution in Britain (1711)
An Essay on the South-Sea Trade (1711)
The Present State of the Parties in Great Britain (1711)
The Secret History of the October Club (1711)
A Further Search into the Conduct of the Allies (1712)
And What if the Pretender Should Come? (1713)
A General History of Trade (1713)
Reasons Against the Succession of the House of Hanover (1713)
The Secret History of the White-Staff (1714)
An Appeal to Honour and Justice (1715)
The Family Instructor (1715)
A Hymn to the Mob (1715)
The Manufacturer; or, The British Trade Truly Stated (1719)
Robinson Crusoe (1719)
The Farther Adventures of Robinson Crusoe (1719)
The Life, Adventures, and Pyracies, of the Famous Captain Singleton (1720)
Memoirs of a Cavalier; or, A Military Journal of the Wars in Germany, and the Wars in England; from the Year 1632 to the Year 1648 (1720)
Serious Reflections During the Life and Surprising Adventures of Robinson Crusoe (1720)
Colonel Jack (1722)
Due Preparations for the Plague (1722)
A Journal of the Plague Year (1722)
Moll Flanders (1722)
Religious Courtship (1722)
A New Voyage Round the World (1724)
Roxana (1724)
A Tour Thro' the Whole Island of Great Britain, Divided into Circuits or Journies (1724)
The Complete English Tradesman, in Familiar Letters (1725)
An Essay Upon Literature; or, An Enquiry into the Antiquity and Original of Letters (1726)
The Political History of the Devil, as well Ancient as Modern (1726)
A System of Magick; or, A History of the Black Art (1726)
Conjugal Lewdness; or, Matrimonial Whoredom (1727)
An Essay on the History and Reality of Apparitions (1727)
A New Family Instructor (1727)

Deighton, Len [Leonard Cyril Deighton] (1929–)
thriller writer
The Ipcress File (1962)
Funeral in Berlin (1964)
Twinkle, Twinkle Little Spy (1976)
Berlin Game (1983)
Mexico Set (1984)
London Match (1985)
Spy Hook (1988)
Spy Line (1989)
Spy Sinker (1990)

Dekker, Thomas (1572?–1632)
dramatist and pamphleteer
Old Fortunatus (1600)
The Shoemakers Holiday; or, The Gentle Craft, with the Humorous Life of Simon Eyre, Shoomaker and Lord Mayor of London (1600)
Satiro-Mastix; or, The Untrussing of the Humorous Poet (1602)
The Wonderfull Yeare: Wherein is shewed the picture of London, lying sicke of the plague (1603)
The Honest Whore; with The Humours of the Patient Man, and The Longing Wife (1604)
The Meeting of Gallants at an Ordinarie; or, The Walkes in Powles (1604)
Newes from Graves-end: Sent to Nobody (1604)
The Double PP: a Papist in Armes (1606)
Newes from Hell (1606)
The Seven Deadly Sinnes of London (1606)
The Famous History of Sir Thomas Wyat (1607)
Jests to Make You Merie (1607)
A Knights Conjuring (1607)
North-ward Hoe (1607)
West-ward Hoe (1607)

The Whore of Babylon (1607)
The Belman of London: Bringing to light the most notorious villanies that are now practised in the kingdome (1608)
Lanthorne and Candle-light; or, The Bellmans Second Nights Walke (1608)
Foure Birds of Noahs Arke (1609)
The Guls Horne-book (1609)
Worke for Armourours; or, The Peace is Broken (1609)
If It Be Not Good, the Divel is in It (1612)
Troia-Nova Triumphans, London Triumphing (1612)
Dekker his Dreame (1620)
The Second Part of The Honest Whore (1630)
Match Mee in London (1631)

'Delafield, E.M.' [Edmée Elizabeth Monica de la Pasture] (1890–1943)
novelist, short-story writer, and playwright
Zella Sees Herself (1917)
Diary of a Provincial Lady (1930)

De la Mare, Walter John ['Walter Ramal'] (1873–1956)
poet and short-story writer
Songs of Childhood (1902)
Henry Brocken (1904)
Poems (1906)
The Return (1910)
The Three Mulla-Mulgars (1910)
The Listeners, and Other Poems (1912)
Peacock Pie (1913)
The Sunken Garden, and Other Poems (1917)
Motley, and Other Poems (1918)
Poems 1901 to 1918 (1920)
Memoirs of a Midget (1921)
The Veil, and Other Poems (1921)
The Riddle, and Other Stories (1923)
Broomsticks, and Other Tales (1925)
The Connoisseur, and Other Stories (1926)
On the Edge (1930)
The Fleeting, and Other Poems (1933)
Poems 1919 to 1934 (1935)
The Wind Blows Over (1936)
Memory, and Other Poems (1938)
The Burning-Glass, and Other Poems (1945)
The Traveller (1946)
Inward Companion (1950)
O Lovely England, and Other Poems (1953)
Private View (1953)
A Beginning, and Other Stories (1955)

Delaney, Shelagh (1939–)
playwright
A Taste of Honey (1959)

Delap, John (1725–1812)
dramatist and poet
Elegies (1760)
Hecuba: A tragedy (1762)
The Royal Suppliants: A tragedy (1781)

Delderfield, Ronald Frederick (1912–72)
popular novelist
The Dreaming Suburb (1958)
The Avenue Goes to War (1958)
A Horseman Riding By (1966)
To Serve Them All My Days (1972)

Dell, Ethel Mary (1881–1939)
popular novelist
The Way of an Eagle (1912)
The Keeper of the Door (1915)
By Request (1927)

Dell, William (*c*.1607–70)
devotional writer
The Way of True Peace and Unity among the Faithful and Churches of Christ (1649)

Deloney, Thomas (1543?–1600)
ballad-maker and pamphleteer
The Lamentation of Beckles (1586)
A Most Joyfull Songe (1586)
A New Ballet of the Straunge and Most Cruell Whippes which the Spanyards Had Prepared to Whippe and Torment English Men and Women (1588)
The Queenes Visiting of the Campe at Tilsburie with her Entertainment there (1588)
Patient Grissell (1600)
Strange Histories, of Kings, Princes, Dukes, Earles, Lords, Ladies, Knights, and Gentlemen (1602)
Thomas of Reading; or, The Sixe Worthy Yeomen of the West (1612)
The Pleasant History of John Winchcomb: In his younger yeares called Jack of Newberie (1619)
The Gentle Craft (1627)
The Garland of Good Will (1628)

De Morgan, William Frend (1839–1917)
novelist and designer
Joseph Vance (1906)
Alice-For-Short (1907)
It Never Can Happen Again (1909)
An Affair of Dishonour (1910)
A Likely Story (1911)
When Ghost Meets Ghost (1914)

Denham, Sir John (1615–69)
poet
Coopers Hill: A poëme (1642)
The Sophy (1642)
The Anatomy of Play (1651)
Coopers Hill (1655)
The Destruction of Troy (1656)
On Mr Abraham Cowley His Death, and Burial Amongst the Ancient Poets (1667)
Poems and Translations: With The Sophy (1668)
Cato Major of Old Age (1669)

Dennis, John (1657–1734)
critic, poet, and dramatist
Poems in Burlesque (1692)
The Impartial Critick (1693)
The Court of Death (1695)
A Plot and No Plot: A comedy (1697)
The Usefulness of the Stage, to the Happiness of Mankind, to Government and to Religion (1698)

Rinaldo and Armida: A tragedy (1699)
Iphigenia: A tragedy (1700)
The Advancement and Reformation of Modern Poetry (1701)
The Monument (1702)
The Grounds of Criticism in Poetry (1704)
Liberty Asserted: A tragedy (1704)
The Person of Quality's Answer to Mr Collier's Letter (1704)
Gibraltar; or, The Spanish Adventure: A comedy (1705)
The Battle of Ramillia; or, the Power of Union (1706)
An Essay on the Opera's after the Italian Manner (1706)
Appius and Virginia: A tragedy (1709)
An Essay Upon Publick Spirit (1711)
Reflections Critical and Satyrical, Upon a Late Rhapsody call'd, An Essay upon Criticism (1711)
An Essay upon the Genius and Writings of Shakespear (1712)
Remarks upon Cato, a Tragedy (1713)
A True Character of Mr Pope, and his Writings (1716)
Remarks upon Mr Pope's Translation of Homer (1717)
The Invader of His Country; or, The Fatal Resentment: A tragedy (1720)
A Defence of Sir Fopling Flutter (1722)
Vice and Luxury Publick Mischiefs; or, Remarks on a Book intitul'd, the Fable of the Bees (1724)
The Stage Defended (1726)
Remarks on Mr Pope's Rape of the Lock (1728)

Dennis, Nigel Forbes (1912–89)
novelist, playwright, and critic
Boys and Girls Come Out to Play (1949)

Dent, Arthur (1553–1603)
Puritan divine
The Plaine Mans Path-way to Heaven (1601)

Denton, Thomas (1724–77)
clergyman and miscellaneous writer
Immortality; or, The Consolation of Human Life (1754)
The House of Superstition (1762)

De Quincey, Thomas (1785–1859)
essayist and prose writer
Confessions of an English Opium Eater (1822)
Walladmor (1825)
Klosterheim; or, The Masque (1832)
The Logic of Political Economy (1844)
Autobiographic Sketches (1853)
Autobiographic Sketches (1854)
Miscellanies [i] (1854)
Miscellanies [ii] (1854)
Confessions of an English Opium Eater (1856)
Sketches, Critical and Biographic (1857)
Studies on Secret Records, Personal and Historic (1858)
Essays Sceptical and Anti-sceptical, on Problems Neglected or Misconceived (1858)
Leaders in Literature, with a Notice of Traditional Errors Affecting Them (1858)
Classic Records Reviewed or Deciphered (1859)
Critical Suggestions on Style and Rhetoric (1859)
Speculations, Literary and Philosophic (1859)
Letters to a Young Man whose Education has been Neglected (1860)

Desai, Anita (1937–)
Indian novelist
Voices in the City (1965)
Fire on the Mountain (1977)
Clear Light of Day (1980)
The Village by the Sea (1982)
In Custody (1984)
Baumgartner's Bombay (1988)
Journey to Ithaca (1995)
Fasting, Feasting (1999)
Diamond Dust, and Other Stories (2000)

Despard, Charlotte, *née* French (1844–1939)
novelist
Chaste as Ice, Pure as Snow (1874)
A Modern Iago (1879)

De Vere, Sir Aubrey (1788–1846)
poet
Julian the Apostate (1822)
The Duke of Mercia; The Lamentation of Ireland; and Other Poems (1823)

De Vere, Aubrey Thomas (1814–1902)
poet and author
The Search after Proserpine; Recollections of Greece, and Other Poems (1843)
English Misrule and Irish Deeds (1848)

D'Ewes, Sir Simonds (1602–50)
antiquary
The Journals of all the Parliaments During the Reign of Queen Elizabeth (1682)

Diaper, William (1685–1717)
poet
Dryaides; or, The Nymphs Prophecy (1712)
Nereides; or, Sea-Eclogues (1712)
An Imitation of the Seventeenth Epistle of the First Book of Horace (1714)

Dibdin, Charles (1745–1814)
actor, dramatist, and songwriter
The Shepherd's Artifice: A dramatic pastoral (1765)
The Deserter: A new musical drama (1773)
The Waterman; or, The First of August (1774)
The Quaker: A comic opera (1777)
Poor Vulcan: A burletta (1778)
The Younger Brother (1793)
A Complete History of the English Stage (1797)
The Professional Life of Mr Dibdin (1803)

Dibdin, Charles Isaac Mungo (1768–1833)
poet and playwright
Young Arthur; or, The Child of Mystery (1819)
Life in London; or, The Larks of Logic, Tom, & Jerry: An extravaganza (1822)
Comic Tales and Lyrical Fancies (1825)

Dibdin, Michael (1947–)
novelist

Ratking (1988)
Dibdin, Thomas Frognall (1776–1847)
bibliographer and author
The Bibliomania, or Book Madness (1809)
Bibliography (1812)
The Bibliographical Decameron (1817)
Bibliophobia (1832)
Dibdin, Thomas John (1771–1841)
actor, dramatist, and songwriter
The Mouth of the Nile; or, The Glorious First of August (1798)
The Cabinet: A comic opera (1802)
The Lady of the Lake; or, Roderick vich Alpine (1811)
A Metrical History of England (1813)
Ivanhoe; or, The Jew's Daughter: A melo dramatic romance (1820)
The Pirate; or, The Wild Woman of Zetland: A melo dramatic romance (1822)
The Reminiscences of Thomas Dibdin (1827)
Dick, Kay (1915–)
novelist and editor
Young Man (1951)
Sunday (1962)
Ivy and Stevie (1971)
They (1977)
Dickens, Charles John Huffham ['Boz'] (1812–70)
novelist and editor
Sketches by 'Boz' [1st ser.] (1836)
Sketches by 'Boz' [2nd ser.] (1836)
The Posthumous Papers of the Pickwick Club (1837)
Oliver Twist; or, The Parish Boy's Progress (1838)
Nicholas Nickleby (1839)
Master Humphrey's Clock [vol. i] (1840)
Master Humphrey's Clock [vols ii, iii] (1841)
Barnaby Rudge: A tale of the riots of 'eighty (1841)
The Old Curiosity Shop (1841)
American Notes for General Circulation (1842)
A Christmas Carol in Prose (1843)
Martin Chuzzlewit (1844)
The Chimes (1844)
The Cricket on the Hearth (1845)
Pictures from Italy (1846)
The Battle of Life (1846)
Dombey and Son (1848)
The Haunted Man and the Ghost's Bargain (1848)
David Copperfield (1850)
Bleak House (1853)
A Child's History of England (1853)
Hard Times, For These Times (1854)
Little Dorrit (1857)
A Tale of Two Cities (1859)
The Uncommercial Traveller (1860)
Great Expectations (1861)
Our Mutual Friend (1865)
The Mystery of Edwin Drood (1870)
The Mudfog Papers (1880)
Dickens, Monica Enid (1915–92)
novelist
One Pair of Hands (1939)
One Pair of Feet (1942)
My Turn to Make the Tea (1951)
Dickenson, John (*fl.* 1594)
romance writer
Arisbas, Euphues Amidst his Slumbers; or, Cupids Journey to Hell (1594)
The Shepheardes Complaint (1596)
Greene in Conceipt (1598)
Dickinson, Goldsworthy Lowes (1862–1932)
philosophical writer
The Greek View of Life (1896)
A Modern Symposium (1905)
Dickinson, Patric Thomas (1914–94)
poet
The Seven Days of Jericho (1944)
The Sailing Race, and Other Poems (1952)
The Scale of Things (1955)
The World I See (1960)
This Cold Universe (1964)
More Than Time (1970)
A Wintering Tree (1973)
Our Living John, and Other Poems (1979)
A Rift in Time (1982)
Digby, Sir Kenelm (1603–65)
diplomat and author
Observations on the 22 stanza in the 9th canto of the 2d book of Spencers Faery Queen (1643)
Observations upon Religio Medici (1643)
Two Treatises: In the one of which, the nature of bodies; in the other the nature of mans soule, is looked into (1644)
A Discourse Concerning the Vegetation of Plants (1661)
Digges, Leonard (1588–1635)
poet and translator
The Rape of Proserpine (1617)
Dilke, Emilia Frances, *née* Strong, later Pattison, Lady Dilke (1840–1904)
art historian, campaigner for working women, and short-story writer
The Shrine of Death, and Other Stories (1886)
The Shrine of Love, and Other Stories (1891)
Dillon, Wentworth, 4th earl of Roscommon (1633–85)
poet and translator
Horace's Art of Poetry (1680)
An Essay on Translated Verse (1684)
Poems by the Earl of Roscomon [sic] (1717)
Diski, Jenny [born Jenny Simmonds] (1947–)
novelist
Nothing Natural (1986)
Rainforest (1987)
Like Mother (1988)
Then Again (1990)
Happily Ever After (1991)
Monkey's Uncle (1994)
Stranger on a Train (2002)
Disraeli, Benjamin, 1st earl of Beaconsfield (1804–81)
statesman and novelist

Vivian Grey [vols i, ii] (1826)
Vivian Grey [vols iii, iv, v] (1827)
The Young Duke (1831)
Contarini Fleming (1832)
Ixion in Heaven (1833)
The Wondrous Tale of Alroy. The Rise of Iskander (1833)
Henrietta Temple (1836)
The Letters of Runnymede (1836)
Venetia; or, The Poet's Daughter (1837)
Coningsby; or, The New Generation (1844)
Sybil; or, The Two Nations (1845)
Tancred; or, The New Crusade (1847)
Lothair (1870)
Endymion (1880)

D'Israeli, Isaac (1766–1848)
poet and miscellaneous writer
Curiosities of Literature [1st ser., vol. i] (1791)
Curiosities of Literature [1st ser., vol. ii] (1793)
An Essay on the Manners and Genius of the Literary Character (1795)
Miscellanies; or, Literary Recreations (1796)
Vaurien; or, Sketches of the Times (1797)
Romances (1799)
Narrative Poems (1803)
Flim-flams!; or, The Life and Errors of My Uncle, and the Amours of My Aunt! (1805)
Calamities of Authors (1812)
Quarrels of Authors; or, Some Memoirs for Our Literary History (1814)
Curiosities of Literature [1st ser., vol. iii] (1817)
A Second Series of Curiosities of Literature (1823)
Curiosities of Literature (1834)
Amenities of Literature (1841)

Dixon, Ella Nora Hepworth ['Margaret Wynman'] (1855–1932)
journalist, novelist, and short-story writer
The Story of a Modern Woman (1894)

Dixon, Richard Watson (1833–1900)
poet and ecclesiastical historian
Christ's Company, and Other Poems (1861)
Last Poems (1905)

Dixon, William Hepworth (1821–79)
historian and traveller
John Howard and the Prison-World of Europe (1849)

Dobell, Sydney Thompson ['Sydney Yendys'] (1824–74)
poet and critic
The Roman (1850)
Balder (1853)
Sonnets on the War (1855)
England in Time of War (1856)

Dobson, [Henry] Austin (1840–1921)
poet and critic
Vignettes in Rhyme (1873)
Proverbs in Porcelain (1877)
The Ballad of Beau Brocade, and Other Poems of the XVIIIth Century (1892)
Eighteenth Century Vignettes [1st ser.] (1892)
Eighteenth Century Vignettes [2nd ser.] (1894)
The Story of Rosina, and Other Verses (1895)
Eighteenth Century Vignettes [3rd ser.] (1896)

Dodd, William (1729–77)
clergyman, anthologist, and forger
The Beauties of Shakespeare (1752)
Thoughts in Prison (1777)

Doddridge, Philip (1702–51)
Nonconformist divine, author, and hymn-writer
Free Thoughts on the Most Probable Means of Reviving the Dissenting Interest (1730)
Sermons on the Religious Education of Children (1732)
Submission to Divine Providence in the Death of Children (1737)
The Family Expositor; or, A Paraphrase and Version of the New Testament (1739)
Evidences of Christianity (1742)
The Principles of the Christian Religion (1743)
The Rise and Progress of Religion in the Soul (1745)
Hymns Founded on Various Texts in the Holy Scripture (1755)
A Course of Lectures on the Principal Subjects in Pneumatology, Ethics, and Divinity (1763)

Dodington, George Bubb, Baron Melcombe (1691–1762)
politician and literary patron
An Epistle to Sir Robert Walpole (1725)
The Diary of the Late George Bubb Dodington (1784)

Dodsley, Robert (1703–64)
poet, dramatist, anthologist, and bookseller
An Epistle from a Footman in London to the Celebrated Stephen Duck (1731)
A Sketch of the Miseries of Poverty (1731)
A Muse in Livery; or, The Footman's Miscellany (1732)
An Epistle to Mr Pope (1734)
Beauty; or, The Art of Charming (1735)
The Toy-Shop: A dramatick satire (1735)
The King and the Miller of Mansfield (1737)
The Art of Preaching (1738)
Sir John Cockle at Court (1738)
The Blind Beggar of Bethnal Green (1741)
Pain and Patience (1743)
A Select Collection of Old Plays (1744)
Rex et Pontifex (1745)
A Collection of Poems (1748)
The Oeconomy of Human Life (1750)
Public Virtue (1753)
Cleone: A tragedy (1758)
Select Fables of Esop and Other Fabulists (1761)

Donleavy, James Patrick (1926–)
novelist and playwright
The Ginger Man (1955)
A Singular Man (1964)
Meet My Maker the Mad Molecule (1965)
The Saddest Summer of Samuel S. (1967)
The Beastly Beatitudes of Balthasar B. (1969)
The Onion Eaters (1971)
A Fairy Tale of New York (1973)

The Destinies of Darcy Dancer, Gentleman (1978)
Schultz (1980)
Leila (1983)
Are You Listening, Rabbi Löw (1987)
That Darcy, That Dancer, That Gentleman (1990)

Donne, John (1572–1631)
poet and prose writer
Pseudo-Martyr (1610)
An Anatomy of the World: Wherein, by occasion of the untimely death of Mistris Elizabeth Drury the frailty and the decay of this whole world is represented (1611)
Ignatius his Conclave: or His Inthronisation in a Late Election in Hell (1611)
The First Anniversarie. An Anatomie of the World . . . The Second Anniversarie. Of the Progres of the Soule (1612)
Sermon on Acts 1:8 (1622)
Sermon on Judges 20: 15 (1622)
Encaenia (1623)
Three Sermons upon Speciall Occasions (1623)
Devotions Upon Emergent Occasions, and Severall Steps in my Sickness (1624)
The First Sermon Preached to King Charles, at Saint James (1625)
Foure Sermons Upon Speciall Occasions (1625)
Five Sermons Upon Speciall Occasions (1626)
A Sermon, Preached to the Kings Majestie at Whitehall (1626)
A Sermon of Commemoration of the Lady Danvers (1627)
Deaths Duell; or, A Consolation to the Soule, Against the Dying Life, and Living Death of the Body (1632)
Juvenilia; or, Certaine Paradoxes, and Problemes (1633)
Poems, by J.D.: With elegies on the authors death (1633)
Six Sermons Upon Severall Occasions (1634)
Sapienta Clamitans (1638)
LXXX Sermons (1640)
Biathanatos: A declaration of that paradoxe, or thesis, that selfe-homicide is not so naturally sinne, that it may never be otherwise (1644)
Fifty Sermons (1649)
Essayes in Divinity (1651)
Letters to Severall Persons of Honour (1651)
Paradoxes, Problemes, Essayes, Characters (1652)

Dorset, Catherine Ann (1750?–1817?)
children's poet
The Peacock 'At Home' (1807)

Doubleday, Thomas (1790–1870)
poet, dramatist, and radical politician
Sixty-Five Sonnets (1818)
Babington: A tragedy (1825)
Dioclesian (1829)

Doughty, Charles Montagu (1843–1926)
traveller, poet, and advocate of purified English
Travels in Arabia Deserta (1888)

Douglas, Lord Alfred Bruce (1870–1945)
poet and friend of Oscar Wilde
The City of the Soul (1899)
Sonnets (1909)
Oscar Wilde and Myself (1914)

Douglas, Gavin or Gawin (1474?–1522)
Scottish poet and bishop
The Palice of Honour (1535?)
Aeneid (1553)
The Palis of Honoure (1553?)

Douglas, Keith Castellain (1920–44)
poet
Selected Poems (1943)
Alamein to Zem Zem (1946)
Collected Poems (1951)

Douglas, [George] Norman (1868–1952)
travel writer and novelist
Siren Land (1911)
South Wind (1917)
They Went (1920)
Looking Back (1933)
Late Harvest (1946)

Dow, Alexander (*d.* 1779)
author and dramatist
Tales Translated from the Persian of Inatulla of Delhi (1768)
Zingis: A tragedy (1769)

Dowden, Edward (1843–1913)
critic and poet
Mr Tennyson and Mr Browning (1863)
Poems (1876)
The Life of Percy Bysshe Shelley (1886)

Dowie, Ménie Muriel, later Norman, then Fitzgerald (1867–1945)
novelist
Some Whims of Fate (1896)

Dowland, John (1563–1626)
lutenist and composer
The First Booke of Songes or Ayres of Fowre Partes (1597)
The Second Booke of Songs or Ayres (1600)
The Third and Last Booke of Songs or Aires (1603)
A Pilgrimes Solace (1612)

Dowland, Robert (*c.*1586–1641)
musician
A Musicall Banquet (1610)

Downman, Hugh (1740–1809)
physician, poet, and dramatist
The Drama (1775)
Lucius Junius Brutus; or, The Expulsion of the Tarquins (1779)

Dowson, Ernest Christopher (1867–1900)
poet and novelist
A Comedy of Masks (1893)
Dilemmas (1895)
Verses (1896)
The Pierrot of the Minute: A dramatic phantasy (1897)
Decorations: In Verse and Prose (1899)
The Poems of Ernest Dowson (1905)

Doyle, Sir Arthur Conan (1859–1930)
novelist and short-story writer

A Study in Scarlet (1888)
Micah Clarke (1889)
The Sign of Four (1890)
The White Company (1891)
The Adventures of Sherlock Holmes (1892)
The Memoirs of Sherlock Holmes (1893)
The Exploits of Brigadier Gerard (1896)
Rodney Stone (1896)
Uncle Bernac (1897)
The Tragedy of the Korosko (1898)
The Hound of the Baskervilles (1902)
Adventures of Gerard (1903)
The Return of Sherlock Holmes (1905)
Sir Nigel (1906)
Through the Magic Door (1907)
The Lost World (1912)
The Poison Belt (1913)
The Valley of Fear (1915)
His Last Bow: Some reminiscences of Sherlock Holmes (1917)
The Land of Mist (1926)
The Case-Book of Sherlock Holmes (1927)

Doyle, Sir Francis Hastings Charles, 2nd baronet (1810–88)
poet
The Two Destinies (1844)
The Return of the Guards, and Other Poems (1866)

Doyle, Roddy (1958–)
Irish novelist and playwright
The Commitments (1987)
The Snapper (1990)
The Van (1991)
Paddy Clarke Ha Ha Ha (1993)
The Woman Who Walked into Doors (1996)
A Star Called Henry (1999)
Rory & Ita (2002)

Drabble, Margaret (1939–)
novelist and biographer
A Summer Bird-Cage (1963)
The Garrick Year (1964)
The Millstone (1965)
Jerusalem the Golden (1967)
The Waterfall (1969)
The Needle's Eye (1972)
The Realms of Gold (1975)
The Ice Age (1977)
The Middle Ground (1980)
The Radiant Way (1987)
A Natural Curiosity (1989)
The Gates of Ivory (1991)
The Witch of Exmoor (1996)
The Peppered Moth (2001)
The Seven Sisters (2002)

Drake, Sir Francis (*d.* 1637)
nephew of Sir Francis Drake the circumnavigator
The World Encompassed by Sir Francis Drake (1628)

Drake, Nathan (1766–1836)
physician and literary essayist
Literary Hours; or, Sketches Critical and Narrative (1798)
Shakespeare and his Times (1817)
Memorials of Shakespeare (1828)

Drant, Thomas (*d.* 1578?)
poet and translator
A Medicinable Morall (1566)
Horace his Arte of Poetrie, Pistles, and Satyrs Englished (1567)
Epigrams and Sentences Spirituall in Vers (1568)

Drayton, Michael (1563–1631)
poet
The Harmonie of the Church (1591)
Idea: The shepheards garland. Fashioned in nine eglogs (1593)
Ideas Mirrour (1594)
Matilda (1594)
Peirs Gaveston Earle of Cornwall (1594)
Endimion and Phoebe: Ideas Latmus (1595)
Mortimeriados (1596)
The Tragicall Legend of Robert Duke of Normandy: [with] *The legend of Matilda; The legend of Piers Gaveston* (1596)
Englands Heroicall Epistles (1597)
The Barrons Wars in the Raigne of Edward the Second (1603)
To the Majestie of King James (1603)
Moyses in a Map of his Miracles (1604)
The Owle (1604)
A Paean Triumphall (1604)
Poems (1605)
Poemes Lyrick and Pastorall (1606)
The Legend of Great Cromwel (1607)
Poly-Olbion [pt i] (1612)
The Second Part, or a Continuance of Poly-Olbion from the Eighteenth Song (1622)
The Battaile of Agincourt (1627)
The Muses Elizium (1630)

Drinkwater, John (1882–1937)
poet and playwright
The Death of Leander, and Other Poems (1906)
Cophetua (1911)
Poems of Men and Hours (1911)
Poems of Love and Earth (1912)
Cromwell, and Other Poems (1913)
Swords and Ploughshares (1915)
Tides (1917)
Loyalties (1919)
Preludes 1921–1922 (1922)
Collected Poems (1923)
Collected Plays (1925)
Summer Harvest (1933)

Drue, Thomas (*fl.* 1631)
dramatist
The Life of the Dutches of Suffolke (1631)

Drummond, William, of Hawthornden (1585–1649)
poet, dramatist, and critic
Teares on the Death of Meliades (1613)
Poems by William Drummond. Of Hawthornden (1614)

Forth Feasting (1617)
A Midnights Trance: Wherein is discoursed of death, the nature of soules, and estate of immortalitie (1619)
Flowres of Sion (1623)
The History of Scotland: From the year 1423 until the year 1542 (1655)
Poems (1656)

Dryden, John (1631–1700)
poet, dramatist, and critic
Three Poems Upon the Death of His Late Highnesse Oliver Lord Protector of England, Scotland, and Ireland (1659)
Astraea Redux: A poem on the happy restoration & return of Charles the Second (1660)
To His Sacred Majesty, a Panegyrick on his Coronation (1661)
To My Lord Chancellor, Presented on New-Years-Day (1662)
The Rival Ladies: A tragi-comedy (1664)
Annus Mirabilis: The Year of Wonders, 1666 (1667)
The Indian Emperour; or, The Conquest of Mexico by the Spaniards (1667)
Of Dramatick Poesie (1668)
Secret-Love; or, The Maiden-Queen (1668)
Sir Martin Mar-all; or, The Feign'd Innocence: A comedy (1668)
The Wild Gallant: A comedy (1669)
The Tempest; or, The Enchanted Island: A comedy (1670)
Tyrannick Love; or, The Royal Martyr: A tragedy (1670)
An Evening's Love; or, The Mock-Astrologer (1671)
The Conquest of Granada by the Spaniards (1672)
Amboyna: A tragedy (1673)
The Assignation; or, Love in a Nunnery (1673)
Marriage-a-la-Mode: A comedy (1673)
The Tempest; or, The Enchanted Island: A comedy (1674)
Aureng-Zebe: A tragedy (1676)
The State of Innocence, and the Fall of Man: An opera (1677)
All for Love; or, The World Well Lost: A tragedy (1678)
Oedipus: A tragedy (1679)
Troilus and Cressida; or, Truth Found Too Late: A tragedy (1679)
The Kind Keeper; or, Mr Limberham: A comedy (1680)
Ovid's Epistles (1680)
Absalom and Achitophel [pt i] (1681)
The Spanish Fryar; or, The Double Discovery (1681)
Mac Flecknoe; or, A Satyr upon the True-Blew-Protestant Poet, T.S. (1682)
The Medall: A satyre against sedition (1682)
Religio Laici; or, A Laymans Faith (1682)
The Duke of Guise: A tragedy (1683)
The Vindication: Or, the parallel of the French Holy-League, and the English League and Covenant (1683)
The History of the League (1684)
Miscellany Poems (1684)
Albion and Albanius: An opera (1685)
Sylvae; or, The Second Part of Poetical Miscellanies (1685)
Threnodia Augustalis (1685)
The Hind and the Panther (1687)
A Song for St Cecilia's Day (1687)
Britannia Rediviva (1688)
Amphitryon; or, The Two Socia's: A comedy (1690)
Don Sebastian, King of Portugal: A tragedy (1690)
King Arthur; or, The British Worthy: A dramatick opera (1691)
Cleomenes, the Spartan Hero: A tragedy (1692)
Eleonora (1692)
Examen Poeticum: Being the Third Part of Miscellany Poems (1693)
The Satires of Decimus Junius Juvenalis (1693)
The Annual Miscellany: for the Year 1694 (1694)
Love Triumphant; or, Nature Will Prevail: A tragi-comedy (1694)
De Arte Graphica (1695)
An Ode on the Death of Mr Henry Purcell (1696)
Alexander's Feast; or, The Power of Musique (1697)
The Works of Virgil (1697)
Fables Ancient and Modern (1700)
Poems on Various Occasions; and Translations from Several Authors (1701)

Duck, Stephen (1705–56)
poet
Poems on Several Subjects (1730)
Truth and Falsehood (1734)
Poems on Several Occasions (1736)
The Vision (1737)
Every Man in his Own Way (1741)
Caesar's Camp; or, St George's Hill (1755)

Duff, William (1732–1815)
author
An Essay on Original Genius (1767)
Critical Observations on the Writings of the Most Celebrated Geniuses in Poetry (1770)

Duffet, Thomas (*fl.* 1674–8)
dramatist
The Spanish Rogue (1674)
Psyche Debauch'd: A comedy (1678)

Duffy, Carol Ann (1955–)
poet
Fleshweathercock (1973)
Standing Female Nude (1985)
Thrown Voices (1986)
Selling Manhattan (1987)
William and the Ex-Prime Minister (1992)
Mean Time (1993)
Stopping for Death (1996)

The Pamphlet (1998)
The World's Wife (1999)
Feminine Gospels (2002)

Duffy, Maureen Patricia (1933–)
novelist, poet, and playwright
That's How It Was (1962)
The Single Eye (1964)
The Paradox Players (1967)
Lyrics for the Dog Hour (1968)
Love Child (1971)
The Venus Touch (1971)
I Want To Go To Moscow (1973)
Evesong (1975)
Housespy (1978)
Memorials of the Quick and the Dead (1979)
Gor Saga (1981)
Londoners (1983)
Occam's Razor (1993)
Restitution (1998)

Dugdale, Sir William (1605–86)
antiquary
The Antiquities of Warwickshire Illustrated (1656)
The History of Imbanking and Drayning of Divers Fenns and Marshes (1662)
A Short View of the Late Troubles in England (1681)

Du Maurier, Dame Daphne (1907–89)
novelist and short-story writer
The Loving Spirit (1931)
Jamaica Inn (1936)
Rebecca (1938)
Frenchman's Creek (1941)
My Cousin Rachel (1951)
The Apple Tree (1952)
The Breaking Point (1959)
The Rebecca Notebook, and Other Memories (1981)

Du Maurier, George Louis Palmella Busson (1834–96)
artist and novelist
Peter Ibbetson (1892)
Trilby (1894)
The Martian (1897)

Dunbar, William (1460?–1513?)
Scottish poet
The Tua Mariit Wemen and the Wedo (1507?)
The Ballade of Lord Barnard Stewart (1508)
The Flyting of Dunbar and Kennedy, and Other Poems (1508)
The Golden Targe (1508)

Duncan, Ronald Frederick Henry (1914–82)
dramatist, poet, and novelist
This Way to the Tomb (1946)
The Mongrel, and Other Poems (1950)

Duncan, Sara Jeannette, Mrs Everard Cotes (1861–1922)
Canadian-born novelist
A Social Departure (1890)
An American Girl in London (1891)
A Daughter of To-day (1894)

Duncker, Patricia (1951–)
novelist
Hallucinating Foucault (1996)
Monsieur Shoushana's Lemon Trees (1997)
James Miranda Barry (1999)

Duncombe, John (1729–86)
poet
The Feminiad (1754)
The Feminead; or, Female Genius (1757)

Duncombe, William (1690–1769)
miscellaneous writer and editor of Horace
Junius Brutus: A tragedy (1735)
The Works of Horace in English Verse (1757)

Dunkin, William (1709?–65)
clergyman, poet, and friend of Swift and Chesterfield
The Lover's Web (1734)
The Poet's Prayer (1734)
Boeotia (1747)
The Poetical Works of the Late William Dunkin (1774)

Dunmore, Helen (1952–)
poet and novelist
The Apple Fall (1983)
The Sea Skater (1986)
The Raw Garden (1988)
Going to Egypt (1992)
Zennor in Darkness (1993)
Burning Bright (1994)
Recovering a Body (1994)
A Spell of Winter (1995)
Talking to the Dead (1996)
Your Blue-Eyed Boy (1998)
Out of the Blue: Poems, 1975–2001 (2001)
The Siege (2001)
Mourning Ruby (2003)

Dunn, Douglas Eaglesham (1942–)
poet, short-story writer, and editor
Terry Street (1969)
The Happier Life (1972)
Love or Nothing (1974)
Barbarians (1979)
St Kilda's Parliament (1981)
Europa's Lover (1982)
Elegies (1985)
Northlight (1988)
Dante's Drum-Kit (1993)
New Selected Poems, 1964–2000 (2003)

Dunn, Nell Mary (1936–)
novelist and playwright
Up the Junction (1963)
Poor Cow (1967)
Steaming (1981)

Dunne, John William (1875–1949)
philosopher
An Experiment with Time (1927)
The Serial Universe (1934)

Dunnett, Dorothy, *née* Halliday (1923–2001)
historical novelist and painter
Game of Kings (1962)

Niccolò Rising (1986)
Gemini (2000)
Dunsany, Edward John Moreton Drax Plunkett, 18th Baron Dunsany (1878–1957)
fantasy novelist, short-story writer, and playwright
Time and the Gods (1906)
The King of Elfland's Daughter (1924)
Dunton, John (1659–1733)
poet and author
The Athenian Gazette (1691)
The Ladies Mercury (1693)
The Dublin Scuffle (1699)
The Shortest Way with Whores and Rogues (1703)
The Life and Errors of John Dunton Late Citizen of London (1705)
Durcan, Paul (1944–)
Irish poet
O Westport in the Light of Asia Minor (1975)
The Berlin Wall Café (1985)
Going Home to Russia (1987)
Jesus and Angela (1988)
Daddy, Daddy (1990)
Crazy About Women (1991)
A Snail in my Prime (1993)
Give Me Your Hand (1994)
D'Urfey, Thomas (1653–1723)
poet and dramatist
The Siege of Memphis; or, The Ambitious Queen: A tragedy (1676)
A Fond Husband; or, The Plotting Sisters: A comedy (1677)
Madam Fickle; or, The Witty False One: A comedy (1677)
The Fool Turn'd Critick: A comedy (1678)
Trick for Trick; or, The Debauch'd Hypocrite: A comedy (1678)
Squire Oldsapp; or, The Night-Adventurers: A comedy (1679)
The Virtuous Wife; or, Good Luck at Last: A comedy (1680)
The Progress of Honesty; or, A View of a Court and City (1681)
Sir Barnaby Whigg; or, No Wit Like a Womans: A comedy (1681)
Butler's Ghost; or, Hudibras. The Fourth Part (1682)
The Royalist: A comedy (1682)
A New Collection of Songs and Poems (1683)
Choice New Songs (1684)
The Malecontent: a Satyr (1684)
The Banditti; or, A Ladies Distress (1686)
A Common-wealth of Women (1686)
A Compleat Collection of Mr D'Urfey's Songs and Odes (1687)
A Fool's Preferment; or, The Three Dukes of Dunstable (1688)
Collin's Walk Through London and Westminster (1690)
New Poems (1690)
Love for Money; or, The Boarding School: A comedy (1691)
The Marriage-Hater Match'd: A comedy (1692)
The Richmond Heiress; or, A Woman Once in the Right: A comedy (1693)
The Comical History of Don Quixote (1694)
The Comical History of Don Quixote (1694)
The Comical History of Don Quixote. The Third Part (1696)
Cinthia and Endimion (1697)
The Intrigues at Versailles; or, A Jilt in all Humours: A comedy (1697)
The Campaigners; or, The Pleasant Adventures at Brussels (1698)
A Choice Collection of New Songs and Ballads (1699)
The Bath; or, The Western Lass: A comedy (1701)
Wonders in the Sun; or, The Kingdom of the Birds: A comick opera (1706)
Stories, Moral and Comical (1707)
Durham, [Mary] Edith (1863–1944)
traveller and writer on East European affairs
Through the Lands of the Serbs (1904)
High Albania (1909)
Durrell, Gerald Malcolm (1925–95)
zoologist and author
My Family and Other Animals (1956)
Durrell, Lawrence George ['Charles Norden'] (1912–90)
novelist, poet, and travel writer
Ten Poems (1932)
Transition (1934)
The Black Book (1938)
A Private Country (1943)
Prospero's Cell (1945)
Cities, Plains and People (1946)
Cefalù (1947)
On Seeming to Presume (1948)
The Tree of Idleness, and Other Poems (1955)
Bitter Lemons (1957)
Esprit de Corps (1957)
Justine (1957)
Balthazar (1958)
Mountolive (1958)
Stiff Upper Lip (1958)
Clea (1960)
Collected Poems (1960)
The Alexandrian Quartet (1962)
The Ikons, and Other Poems (1966)
Sauve Qui Peut (1966)
Tunc (1968)
Nunquam (1970)
Vega, and Other Poems (1973)
Monsieur; or, The Prince of Darkness (1974)
Livia; or, Buried Alive (1978)
Constance; or, Solitary Practices (1982)
Sebastian; or, Ruling Passions (1983)
Quinx; or, The Ripper's Tale (1985)
Duwes or Dewes, Giles (*fl.* 1535)
writer on the French language
An Introductorie for to Lerne Frenche (1533?)

Dyce, Alexander (1798–1869)
literary scholar
Specimens of British Poetesses (1825)
Dyer, George (1755–1841)
poet and author
Poems (1792)
The Poet's Fate (1797)
Poems (1801)
Poems (1802)
Dyer, John (1699–1757)
poet
A New Miscellany (1725)
The Ruins of Rome (1740)
The Fleece (1757)
Dyment, Clifford (1914–71)
poet
The Axe in the Wood (1944)

Eachard, John (1636?–97)
Master of St Catharine's College, Cambridge
The Grounds and Occasions of the Contempt of the Clergy and Religion Enquired into (1670)
Mr Hobbs's State of Nature Considered (1672)
Some Opinions of Mr Hobbs Considered in a Second Dialogue between Philautus and Timothy (1673)
Eagleton, Terry (1943–)
literary critic
Literary Theory (1983)
Earle, John (1601?–65)
bishop, character writer, and poet
Micro-cosmographie; or, A Peece of the World Discovered; in Essayes and Characters (1628)
Eastlake, Elizabeth, *née* Rigby, Lady Eastlake (1809–93)
journalist and story writer
A Residence on the Shores of the Baltic (1841)
The Jewess (1843)
Livonian Tales (1846)
Echard or Eachard, Laurence (*c.*1670–1730)
historian and translator
An Exact Description of Ireland (1691)
Plautus's Comedies: Amphytrion, Epidicus, and Rudens (1694)
Terence's Comedies (1694)
The Roman History (1695)
A General Ecclesiastical History (1702)
The History of England [vol. i] (1707)
The History of the Revolution, and the Establishment of England in 1688 (1725)
Eden, Emily ['Lady Theresa Lewis'] (1797–1869)
novelist and traveller
The Semi-Detached House (1859)
The Semi-Attached Couple (1860)
Eden, Richard (1521?–76)
translator
A Treatyse of the Newe India (1553)
The Decades of the New Worlde or West India (1555)
The Arte of Navigation (1561)

Edgar, David (1948–)
playwright
Dick Deterred (1974)
Teendreams (1979)
Plays: One (1987)
Edgar: Shorts (1989)
Heartlanders (1989)
Plays: Two (1989)
Plays: Three (1991)
Pentecost (1995)
Edgeworth, Maria (1767–1849)
novelist and children's author
Letters for Literary Ladies (1795)
The Parent's Assistant; or, Stories for Children (1796)
Practical Education (1798)
A Rational Primer (1799)
Castle Rackrent: An Hibernian tale (1800)
Belinda (1801)
Early Lessons (1801)
Moral Tales for Young People (1801)
Popular Tales (1804)
The Modern Griselda (1805)
Leonora (1806)
Tales of Fashionable Life [vols i–iii] (1809)
Tales of Fashionable Life [vols iv, v, vi] (1812)
Continuation of Early Lessons (1814)
Patronage (1814)
Comic Dramas (1817)
Harrington, a Tale; and Ormond, a Tale (1817)
Memoirs of Richard Lovell Edgeworth (1820)
Rosamond (1821)
Frank (1822)
Harry and Lucy Concluded (1825)
Tales and Miscellaneous Pieces (1825)
Little Plays for Children (1827)
Garry Owen; or, The Snow-Woman; and Poor Bob, the Chimney-Sweeper (1832)
Helen (1834)
Edgeworth, Richard Lovell (1744–1817)
author
Essay on Irish Bulls (1802)
Essays on Professional Education (1809)
Readings on Poetry (1810)
Edwards, Amelia Ann Blanford (1831–92)
novelist, short-story writer, and travel writer
Barbara's History (1864)
Debenham's Vow (1870)
Edwards, Richard (1523?–66)
poet and dramatist
Damon and Pithias (1571)
The Paradyse of Daynty Devises (1576)
Edwards, Thomas (1699–1757)
poet and author
A Supplement to Mr Warburton's Edition of Shakespear (1747)
Egan, Pierce, the elder (1772–1849)
sporting journalist and author
Sporting Anecdotes, Original and Select (1804)
Boxiana; or, Sketches of Ancient and Modern Pugilism (1812)

The Mistress of Royalty; or, The Loves of Florizel and Perdita (1814)
Life in London; Or, the day and night scenes of Jerry Hawthorn, and his elegant friend Corinthian Tom (1821)
Real Life in London; Or, the rambles and adventures of Bob Tallyho, and his cousin, the Hon. Tom Dashall (1821)

'Egerton, George' [Mary Chavelita Dunne, later Higginson, then Clairmonte, then Bright] (1859–1945)
short-story writer, novelist, and playwright
Keynotes (1893)
Discords (1894)
Symphonies (1897)
Fantasies (1898)
The Wheel of God (1898)
Rosa Amorosa (1901)
Flies in Amber (1905)

Egerton, Sarah, *née* Fyge, later Field (1670–1723)
poet
The Female Advocate (1686)
Poems on Several Occasions (1703)

'Eliot, George' [Mary Ann (later Marian) Evans] (1819–80)
novelist
The Life of Jesus (1846)
The Essence of Christianity (1854)
Scenes of Clerical Life (1858)
Adam Bede (1859)
'The Lifted Veil' (1859)
The Mill on the Floss (1860)
Silas Marner, the Weaver of Raveloe (1861)
Romola (1863)
'Brother Jacob' (1864)
Felix Holt, the Radical (1866)
The Spanish Gypsy (1868)
Middlemarch (1872)
The Legend of Jubal, and Other Poems (1874)
Daniel Deronda (1876)
Impresssions of Theophrastus Such (1879)
George Eliot's Life, as Related in Her Letters and Journals (1885)

Eliot, Thomas Stearns (1888–1965)
poet, dramatist, and critic
Prufrock and Other Observations (1917)
Poems (1919)
The Sacred Wood (1920)
The Waste Land (1923)
Homage to John Dryden (1924)
Journey of the Magi (1927)
For Lancelot Andrewes (1928)
Animula (1929)
Ash-Wednesday (1930)
Marina (1930)
Triumphal March (1931)
Selected Essays 1917–1932 (1932)
Sweeney Agonistes: Fragments of an Aristophanic melodrama (1932)
The Use of Poetry and the Use of Criticism (1933)
After Strange Gods (1934)
The Rock (1934)
Murder in the Cathedral (1935)
Essays Ancient and Modern (1936)
Collected Poems 1909–1935 (1936)
The Family Reunion (1939)
Old Possum's Book of Practical Cats (1939)
The Idea of a Christian Society (1939)
The Waste Land, and Other Poems (1940)
East Coker (1940)
Burnt Norton (1941)
The Dry Salvages (1941)
Little Gidding (1942)
Four Quartets (1944)
Notes Towards the Definition of Culture (1948)
The Cocktail Party: A comedy (1950)
The Confidential Clerk (1954)
On Poetry and Poets (1957)
The Elder Statesman (1959)
Collected Plays (1962)
Collected Poems 1909–1962 (1963)
To Criticize the Critic, and Other Writings (1965)
Inventions of the March Hare (1996)

Elizabeth I, Queen of England (1533–1603)
A Godly Medytacyon of the Christen Sowle (1548)

Elliott, Charlotte (1789–1871)
hymn-writer and poet
The Invalid's Hymn Book (1834)

Elliott, Ebenezer ['Britannicus'] (1781–1849)
poet
Night (1810)
Peter Faultless to his Brother Simon, and Other Poems (1820)
Love (1823)
The Village Patriarch (1829)
Corn Law Rhymes: The Ranter (1830)
The Splendid Village; Corn Law Rhymes; and Other Poems (1833)

Elliott, Janice (1931–95)
novelist
Cave with Echoes (1962)
Angels Falling (1969)
A State of Peace (1971)
Private Life (1972)
Heaven on Earth (1975)
Secret Places (1981)
Dr Gruber's Daughter (1986)
The Sadness of Witches (1987)
Necessary Rites (1990)
The Noise From the Zoo (1991)

Elliott, Mary, *née* Belson (1794?–1870)
poet
The Mice, and the Pic Nic (1810)
Simple Truths in Verse (1812)

'Ellis, Alice Thomas' [Anna Margaret Haycraft, *née* Lindholm] (1932–)
novelist
The Sin Eater (1977)
The Birds of the Air (1980)
The 27th Kingdom (1982)
The Other Side of the Fire (1983)

The Clothes in the Wardrobe (1987)
The Skeleton in the Cupboard (1988)
The Fly in the Ointment (1989)
The Inn at the Edge of the World (1990)
Pillars of Gold (1992)
The Evening of Adam (1994)
Ellis, George (1753–1815)
literary scholar and satirist
Poetical Tales (1778)
Specimens of Early English Metrical Romances (1805)
Ellis, [Henry] Havelock (1859–1939)
psychologist and essayist
The New Spirit (1890)
Man and Woman (1894)
Sexual Inversion (1897)
Psychology of Sex (1933)
Ellis, Sarah, *née* Stickney, Mrs William Ellis (1812–72)
novelist and didactic writer
The Women of England (1839)
The Daughters of England (1842)
Ellwood, Thomas (1639–1713)
Quaker, poet, and friend of Milton
Davideis: The Life of King David of Israel (1712)
The History of the Life of Thomas Ellwood (1714)
Elstob, Elizabeth (1683–1758)
Anglo-Saxon scholar
The Rudiments of Grammar for the English-Saxon Tongue (1715)
Elton, Oliver (1861–1945)
literary scholar
A Survey of English Literature 1780–1830 (1912)
A Survey of English Literature 1830–80 (1920)
Elyot, Sir Thomas (1490?–1546)
diplomat and author
The Educacion or Bringinge up of Children (1530)
The Governor (1531)
Pasquil the Playne (1532)
The Doctrinall of Princis (1533?)
Of the Knowledge whiche Maketh a Wise Man (1533)
The Mortalitie of Man (1534)
The Castell of Helthe (1537?)
The Dictionary of Syr Thomas Eliot (1538)
The Bankette of Sapience (1539)
The Defence of Good Women (1540)
The Image of Governance (1540)
A Preservative Agaynste Deth (1545)
Empson, Sir William (1906–84)
poet and critic
Seven Types of Ambiguity (1930)
Poems (1935)
Some Versions of Pastoral (1935)
The Gathering Storm (1940)
Milton's God (1961)
Enright, Denis Joseph (1920–2002)
poet, novelist, critic, and editor
Season Ticket (1948)
Some Men are Brothers (1960)
Addictions (1962)
Unlawful Assembly (1968)
Daughters of Earth (1972)
Paradise Illustrated (1978)
A Faust Book (1979)
Collected Poems (1981)
Instant Chronicles (1985)
Old Men and Comets (1993)
Collected Poems: 1948–1998 (1998)
Signs and Wonders: Selected essays (2001)
'Ephelia' [possibly Joan Philips, *fl.* 1678–82]
royalist poet
A Poem to His Sacred Majesty, on the Plot (1678)
Female Poems on Several Occasions (1679)
'Errym, Malcolm J.' [James Malcolm Rymer] (1804–82?)
writer of popular fiction
Varney the Vampire; or, The Feast of Blood (1847)
Erskine, Thomas, Baron Erskine of Restormel (1750–1823)
statesman and author
A View of the Causes and Consequences of the Present War with France (1797)
Armata (1817)
Erskine, Thomas (1788–1870)
advocate and theologian
Remarks on the Internal Evidence for the Truth of Revealed Religion (1820)
An Essay on Faith (1822)
The Unconditional Freeness of the Gospel (1828)
Ervine, [John] St John Greer (1883–1971)
playwright, novelist, and drama critic
Mixed Marriage (1911)
Etherege, Sir George (1635–91)
dramatist
The Comical Revenge; or, Love in a Tub (1664)
She Wou'd if She Cou'd: A comedy (1668)
The Man of Mode; or, Sir Fopling Flutter: A comedy (1676)
Eusden, Laurence (1688–1739)
Poet Laureate
A Letter to Mr Addison, on the King's Accession to the Throne (1714)
Evans, Abel (1679–1737)
clergyman and epigrammatist
Vertumnus (1713)
Prae-existence: A poem, in imitation of Milton (1714)
Evelyn, John (1620–1706)
diarist, author, and translator
Of Liberty and Servitude (1649)
The State of France (1652)
An Essay on the First Book of T. Lucretius Carus (1656)
The French Gardiner (1658)
An Apologie for the Royal Party (1659)
A Character of England (1659)
The Golden Book of St John Chrysostom (1659)
Fumifugium; or, The Inconvenience of the Aer and Smoak of London Dissipated (1661)
A Panegyric to Charles the Second (1661)

Sculptura; or, The History, and Art of Chalcography and Engraving in Copper (1662)
Sylva; or, A Discourse of Forest-Trees, and the Propagation of Timber in His Majesties Dominions (1664)
An Idea of the Perfection of Painting (1668)
The Compleat Gard'ner (1693)
Numismata: A discourse of medals (1697)
Memoirs of John Evelyn (1818)

Evelyn, John, the younger (1655–99)
translator
Of Gardens (1672)

Ewart, Gavin Buchanan (1916–)
poet and editor
Poems and Songs (1939)
Londoners (1964)
Pleasures of the Flesh (1966)
The Deceptive Grin of the Gravel Porters (1968)
No Fool Like an Old Fool (1976)
All My Little Ones (1978)
The Collected Ewart 1933–1980 (1980)
More Little Ones (1982)
Capital Letters (1983)
The Ewart Quarto (1984)
Festival Nights (1984)
Late Pickings (1987)
Penultimate Poems (1989)
Collected Poems 1980–1991 (1991)
Like It Or Not (1992)

Ewing, Juliana Horatia, *née* Gatty, Mrs J.H. Ewing, (1841–85)
children's writer
Melchior's Dream, and Other Tales (1862)
Mrs Overtheway's Remembrances (1869)
The Brownies and Other Tales (1870)
Old Fashioned Fairy Tales (1882)

Faber, Frederick William (1814–63)
poet and hymn-writer
The Cherwell Water-Lily, and Other Poems (1840)
The Styrian Lake, and Other Poems (1842)
Sir Lancelot (1844)
The Rosary, and Other Poems (1845)

Faber, Michel
novelist
The Crimson Petal and the White (2002)

Fabyan, Robert (*d.* 1513)
chronicler
The New Cronycles of Englande and of Fraunce (1516)

Fairbairns, Zoë (1948–)
novelist and short-story writer
Benefits (1979)

Fairfax, Edward (*c.*1580–1635)
poet and translator
Godfrey of Bulloigne; or, The Recoverie of Jerusalem (1600)

Faithfull, Emily (1835–95)
feminist, publisher, and novelist
Change Upon Change (1868)

Falconar, Maria (*b.* 1771?) and Harriet (*b.* 1774?)
poets
Poems (1788)
Poems on Slavery (1788)

'Falconer, Lanoe' [Mary Elizabeth Morwenna Pauline Hawker] (1848–1908)
novelist and short-story writer
Cecilia de Noël (1891)
Mademoiselle Ixe (1891)
The Hôtel d'Angleterre, and Other Stories (1891)

Falkner, John Meade (1858–1932)
antiquarian and novelist
The Lost Stradivarius (1895)
Moonfleet (1898)
The Nebuly Coat (1903)

Fallon, Padraic (1906–74)
poet, dramatist, and short-story writer
Poems (1974)
Poems and Versions (1983)
Collected Poems (1990)

Fane, Sir Francis (*d.* 1689?)
dramatist
Love in the Dark; or, The Man of Bus'ness: A comedy (1675)
The Sacrifice: A tragedy (1686)

Fane, Mildmay, 2nd earl of Westmorland (1602–66)
poet
Otia Sacra Optima Fides (1648)

Fanshawe, Sir Richard (1608–66)
diplomat, translator, and poet
Il Pastor Fido, the Faithfull Shepherd (1647)
Il Pastor Fido the Faithfull Shepherd (1648)
Selected Parts of Horace, Prince of Lyricks (1652)
The Lusiad; or, Portugals Historicall Poem (1655)
Querer por soló querer: To love only for love sake (1670)

Fanthorpe, Ursula Askham (1929–)
poet
Standing To (1982)
Voices Off (1984)
A Watching Brief (1987)
Neck-Verse (1992)
Consequences (2000)
Christmas Poems (2002)
Queuing for the Sun (2003)

Faraday, Michael (1791–1867)
natural philosopher
Experimental Researches in Electricity (1839)

Farjeon, Benjamin Leopold (1838–1903)
novelist
Grif (1870)

Farjeon, Eleanor (1881–1965)
children's writer
Nursery Rhymes of London Town (1916)
Over the Garden Wall (1933)

Farley, Paul (1965)
poet
The Ice Age (2002)

Farmer, Richard (1735–97)
literary scholar
An Essay on the Learning of Shakespeare (1767)
Farnol, [John] Jeffery (1878–1952)
novelist
My Lady Caprice (1907)
The Broad Highway (1910)
The Amateur Gentleman (1913)
Farquhar, George (1678–1707)
dramatist
Love and a Bottle: A comedy (1698)
The Adventures of Covent-Garden (1699)
The Constant Couple; or, A Trip to the Jubilee: A comedy (1699)
Sir Harry Wildair (1701)
The Inconstant; or, The Way to Win Him: A comedy (1702)
Love and Business (1702)
The Twin-Rivals: A comedy (1702)
The Stage-Coach: A farce (1704)
The Recruiting Officer: A comedy (1706)
The Beaux' Stratagem: A comedy (1707)
Barcellona (1710)
Farrar, Frederic William ['F.T.L. Hope'] (1831–1903)
schoolmaster and author
Eric; or, Little by Little (1858)
The Life of Christ (1874)
Farrell, James Gordon (1935–79)
Anglo-Irish novelist
A Man From Elsewhere (1963)
The Lung (1965)
Troubles (1970)
The Siege of Krishnapur (1973)
The Singapore Grip (1978)
The Hill Station (1981)
Faulks, Sebastian (1953–)
novelist
A Trick of the Light (1984)
A Fool's Alphabet (1992)
Charlotte Gray (1998)
On Green Dolphin Street (2001)
Fawkes, Francis (1720–77)
clergyman and poet
Original Poems and Translations (1761)
Partridge-Shooting: An eclogue (1767)
Feinstein, Elaine (1930–)
poet, novelist, playwright, translator, and biographer
In a Green Eye (1966)
The Circle (1970)
The Magic Apple Tree (1971)
At the Edge (1972)
The Celebrants, and Other Poems (1973)
Children of the Rose (1975)
The Ecstasy of Dr Miriam Garner (1976)
Some Unease and Angels (1977)
The Feast of Euridice (1980)
The Survivors (1982)
The Border (1984)
Badlands (1986)
Mother's Girl (1988)
All You Need (1989)
City Music (1990)
Loving Brecht (1992)
Dark Inheritance (2001)
Fell, Alison (1944–)
Scottish novelist and poet
Kisses for Mayakovsky (1984)
The Bad Box (1987)
Mer de Glace (1991)
The Mistress of Lilliput (1999)
Tricks of the Light (2003)
Felltham, Owen (1602?–68)
essayist and poet
Resolves, Divine, Morall, Politicall (1623?)
Resolves, a Duple Century (1628)
Fenn, Lady Eleanor, *née* Frere ['Mrs Teachwell', 'Mrs Lovechild'] (1743–1813)
children's author
Fables by Mrs Teachwell (1783)
Fairy Spectator (1789)
Juvenile Tatler (1789)
Fenn, George Manville (1831–1909)
novelist
The Sapphire Cross (1871)
Fenton, Elijah (1683–1730)
poet and translator
Oxford and Cambridge Miscellany Poems (1708)
Poems on Several Occasions (1717)
Mariamne: A tragedy (1723)
Fenton, Sir Geoffrey (1539?–1608)
translator and statesman
Certaine Tragicall Discourses (1567)
A Discourse of the Civile Warres and Late Troubles in Fraunce (1570)
Monophylo (1572)
Golden Epistles (1575)
The Historie of Guicciardin, Conteining the Warres of Italie, and Other Partes (1579)
Fenton, James Martin (1949–)
poet
Our Western Furniture (1968)
Terminal Moraine (1972)
A Vacant Possession (1978)
Dead Soldiers (1981)
A German Requiem (1981)
Memory of War and Children in Exile (1983)
Manila Envelope (1989)
Out of Danger (1993)
Fenton, Roger (1565–1616)
divine
A Perfume Against the Noysome Pestilence (1603)
A Treatise of Usurie (1611)
Ferguson, Adam (1723–1816)
philosopher and historian
The Morality of Stage-Plays Seriously Considered (1757)
An Essay on the History of Civil Society (1767)
Institutes of Moral Philosophy (1769)

The History of the Progress and Termination of the Roman Republic (1783)
Principles of Moral and Political Science (1792)

Fergusson, Robert (1750–74)
Scottish poet
Auld Reikie (1773)
Poems (1773)
Poems on Various Subjects (1779)

Fermor, Patrick Michael Leigh (1915–)
travel writer, novelist, and translator
The Traveller's Tree (1950)
The Violins of Saint-Jacques (1953)
Mani (1958)
Roumeli (1966)
A Time of Gifts (1977)
Between the Woods and the Water (1986)

Ferrar, Nicholas (1592–1637)
theologian and translator
The Hundred and Ten Considerations of Signior John Valdesso (1638)

Ferrier, Susan Edmonstone (1782–1854)
novelist
Marriage (1818)
The Inheritance (1824)
Destiny; or, The Chief's Daughter (1831)

Fiddes, Richard (1671–1725)
divine and historian
A General Treatise of Morality (1724)
The Life of Cardinal Wolsey (1724)

Field, Nathaniel (1587–1633)
actor and dramatist
A Woman is a Weather-cocke: A new comedy (1612)
Amends for Ladies: A comedie (1618)

Fielding, Helen (1958–)
novelist
Bridget Jones's Diary (1996)
Bridget Jones: The Edge of Reason (1999)
Olivia Joules and the Overactive Imagination (2003)

Fielding, Henry ['Conny Keyber'] (1707–54)
novelist and dramatist
Love in Several Masques: A comedy (1728)
The Masquerade (1728)
The Author's Farce; and The Pleasures of the Town (1730)
Rape upon Rape; or, The Justice Caught in his own Trap: A comedy (1730)
The Temple Beau: A comedy (1730)
Tom Thumb: A tragedy (1730)
The Letter-Writers; or, A New Way to Keep a Wife at Home: A farce (1731)
The Lottery: A farce (1732)
The Modern Husband: A comedy (1732)
The Covent-Garden Tragedy (1732)
The Old Debauchees: A comedy (1732)
The Mock Doctor; or, The Dumb Lady Cur'd: A comedy (1732)
The Miser: A comedy (1733)
Don Quixote in England: A comedy (1734)
The Intriguing Chambermaid: A comedy (1734)
An Old Man Taught Wisdom; or, The Virgin Unmask'd: A farce (1735)
The Universal Gallant; or, The Different Husbands: A comedy (1735)
Pasquin: A dramatick satire on the times (1736)
The Historical Register for the Year 1736 (1737)
The Champion; or, British Mercury (1739)
An Apology for the Life of Mrs Shamela Andrews (1741)
Joseph Andrews (1742)
Miscellanies (1743)
The Wedding-Day: A comedy (1743)
A Serious Address to the People of Great Britain (1745)
The True Patriot; and The History of Our Own Times (1745)
The Jacobite's Journal (1747)
The History of Tom Jones, a Foundling (1749)
A True State of the Case of Bosavern Penlez (1749)
Amelia (1751)
An Enquiry into the Causes of the Late Increase of Robbers (1751)
The Covent-Garden Journal (1752)
The Life of Mr Jonathan Wild the Great (1754)
The Journal of a Voyage to Lisbon (1755)
The Works of Henry Fielding (1762)

Fielding, Sarah (1710–68)
novelist
The Adventures of David Simple (1744)
Familiar Letters Between the Principal Characters in David Simple, and Some Others (1747)
The Governess; or, Little Female Academy (1749)
Remarks on 'Clarissa' (1749)
The Adventures of David Simple: Volume the Last (1753)
The Cry: A new dramatic fable (1754)
The Lives of Cleopatra and Octavia (1757)
The History of the Countess of Dellwyn (1759)
The History of Ophelia (1760)

Figes, Eva (1932–)
novelist, cultural critic, and playwright
Equinox (1966)
Winter Journey (1967)
Konek Landing (1969)
Nelly's Version (1977)
The Seven Ages (1986)
Ghosts (1988)
The Tenancy (1993)
The Knot (1996)

Filmer, Sir Robert (1588?–1653)
political writer
The Anarchy of a Limited or Mixed Monarchy (1648)
The Necessity of the Absolute Power of Kings (1648)
Observations Concerning the Originall of Government (1652)

Observations Upon Aristotles Politiques Touching Forms of Government (1652)
An Advertisement to the Jury-Men of England, Touching Witches (1653)
Patriarcha; or, The Natural Power of Kings (1680)

Finch, Anne, *née* Kingsmill, countess of Winchilsea (1661–1720)
poet
Miscellany Poems on Several Occasions (1713)

Firbank, [Arthur Annesley] Ronald (1886–1926)
novelist
Odette d'Antrevernes; and A Study in Temperament (1905)
Vainglory (1915)
Inclinations (1916)
Caprice (1917)
Valmouth (1919)
Sorrow in Sunlight (1924)
Concerning the Eccentricities of Cardinal Pirelli (1926)
The Artificial Princess (1934)

Firminger, Marjorie McLean, *née* Hiscox (1899–1976)
novelist
Jam To-Day (1930)

Fish, Simon (*d.* 1531)
theologian and pamphleteer
A Supplicacyon for the Beggers (1529)

Fisher, John (1459?–1535)
saint and cardinal
The Fruitful Sayings of David (1508)
A Mourning Remembrance (1509)
The Sermon of John the Bysshop of Rochester (1521?)
Psalmes or Prayers Taken Out of Holie Scripture (1544)
A Godlie Treatisse Declaryng the Benefites of Prayer (1563?)
A Spirituall Consolation (1578?)

Fisher, Roy (1930–)
poet
City (1961)
The Thing About Joe Sullivan (1978)
Poems 1955–1980 (1980)
Consolidated Comedies (1981)
Birmingham River (1994)

FitzGerald, Edward (1809–83)
poet and translator
Euphranor (1851)
Salámán and Absál (1856)
The Rubáiyát of Omar Khayyám (1859)

Fitzgerald, Penelope Mary (1916–2000)
novelist and biographer
The Golden Child (1977)
The Bookshop (1978)
Offshore (1979)
Human Voices (1980)
At Freddie's (1982)
Innocence (1986)
The Beginning of Spring (1988)
The Gate of Angels (1990)
The Blue Flower (1995)

Fitzgerald, Thomas (1695?–1752)
poet
Poems on Several Occasions (1733)

Flatman, Thomas (1637–88)
poet and miniaturist
Poems and Songs (1674)
On the Death of the Illustrious Prince Rupert (1683)
A Song for St Caecilia's Day (1686)

Flavel, John (1630?–91)
Presbyterian divine
Husbandry Spiritualized: Or, the heavenly use of earthly things (1669)
Navigation Spiritualized; or, A New Compass for Seamen (1677)

Flecker, James [born Herman] Elroy (1884–1915)
poet and novelist
The Bridge of Fire (1907)
Thirty-Six Poems (1910)
The Golden Journey to Samarkand (1913)
Hassan (1922)

Flecknoe, Richard (*c.*1620–78)
poet and dramatist
The Affections of a Pious Soule, unto our Saviour-Christ (1640)
Miscellania; or, Poems of all Sorts (1653)
Love's Dominion (1654)
The Diarium, or Journall (1656)
Enigmaticall Characters (1658)
The Idea of His Highness Oliver, Late Lord Protector (1659)
Erminia; or, The Fair and Vertuous Lady: A trage-comedy (1661)
Love's Kingdom: A pastoral trage-comedy (1664)
The Damoiselles a la Mode: A comedy (1667)
Sir William D'Avenant's Voyage to the Other World: with his Adventures in the Poets Elizium: A poetical fiction (1668)
Epigrams of All Sorts (1669)

Fleming, Abraham (1552?–1607)
poet, translator, and antiquary
The Bucolikes of Publius Virgilius Maro (1575)
A Panoplie of Epistles; or, A Looking-glasse for the Unlearned (1576)

Fleming, Ian Lancaster (1908–64)
novelist and creator of James Bond
Casino Royale (1953)
Live and Let Die (1954)
Moonraker (1955)
Diamonds are Forever (1956)
From Russia With Love (1957)
Dr No (1958)
Goldfinger (1959)
For Your Eyes Only (1960)
Thunderball (1961)
The Spy Who Loved Me (1962)
On Her Majesty's Secret Service (1963)

Chitty-Chitty-Bang-Bang: The Magical Car (1964)
You Only Live Twice (1964)
The Man with the Golden Gun (1965)
Fleming, [Robert] Peter (1907–71)
traveller and author
My Aunt's Rhinoceros, and Other Reflections (1956)
Fletcher, Andrew (1655–1716)
Scottish patriot
A Discourse of Government with Relation to Militia's (1698)
An Account of a Conversation Concerning a Right Regulation of Governments for the Good of Mankind (1704)
Fletcher, Giles, the elder (1549?–1611)
ambassador and poet
Of the Russe Common Wealth; or, Maner of Government by the Russe Emperour (1591)
Licia, or Poemes of Love (1593)
Fletcher, Giles, the younger (1588?–1623)
poet
Christs Victorie, and Triumph in Heaven, and Earth, Over, and After Death (1610)
The Reward of the Faithfull. The Labour of the Faithfull. The Grounds of Our Faith (1623)
Fletcher, John (1579–1625)
dramatist
The Faithfull Shepheardesse (1610?)
Cupids Revenge (1615)
The Tragedy of Thierry King of France, and his Brother Theodoret (1621)
The Two Noble Kinsmen (1634)
The Elder Brother: A comedie (1637)
The Bloody Brother: A tragedy (1639)
Monsieur Thomas: A comedy (1639)
The Night-Walker; or, The Little Theife: A comedy (1640)
Rule a Wife and Have a Wife: A comoedy (1640)
Fletcher, Phineas (1582–1650)
poet
Locustae (1627)
Brittain's Ida (1628)
Sicelides a Piscatory (1631)
Joy in Tribulation; or, Consolations for Afflicted Spirits (1632)
The Purple Island; or, The Isle of Man (1633)
Fletcher, Thomas (1666–1713)
poet
Poems on Several Occasions, and Translations (1692)
Flint, Frank Stuart (1885–1960)
poet
In the Net of the Stars (1909)
Cadences (1915)
Florio, John (1553–1625?)
translator
Florio His Firste Fruites (1578)
Florios Second Frutes (1591)
A Worlde of Wordes, or Most Copious, Dictionarie in Italian and English (1598)
The Essayes or Morall Politicke and Millitaire Discourses of Michaell de Montaigne (1603)
Floyd, John [in religion: Daniel à Jesu] (1572–1649)
Jesuit
The Church Conquerant Over Humane Wit (1638)
The Totall Summe: Or, No danger of damnation unto Roman Catholiques for any errour in faith (1639)
Follett, Ken[neth] Martin (1949–)
thriller writer
Eye of the Needle (1978)
The Key to Rebecca (1980)
Foote, Samuel (1720–77)
actor and dramatist
The Roman and English Comedy Consider'd and Compar'd (1747)
Taste: A comedy (1752)
The Englishman in Paris: A comedy (1753)
The Englishman Return'd from Paris (1756)
The Author: A comedy (1757)
The Minor: A comedy (1760)
The Orators (1762)
The Patron: A comedy (1764)
The Lame Lover: A comedy (1770)
The Bankrupt: A comedy (1776)
The Devil upon Two Sticks: A comedy (1778)
The Nabob: A comedy (1778)
The Taylors: A tragedy for warm weather (1778)
Ford, Ford Madox [Ford Hermann Hueffer] (1873–1939)
novelist and poet
The Shifting of the Fire (1892)
Poems for Pictures and for Notes of Music (1900)
The Face of the Night (1904)
The Benefactor (1905)
The Fifth Queen and How She Came to Court (1906)
An English Girl (1907)
From Inland, and Other Poems (1907)
Privy Seal (1907)
The Fifth Queen Crowned (1908)
Mr Apollo (1908)
The 'Half Moon' (1909)
A Call (1910)
The Portrait (1910)
Songs from London (1910)
Ladies Whose Bright Eyes (1911)
The Panel (1912)
Collected Poems (1913)
Mr Fleight (1913)
The Young Lovell (1913)
The Good Soldier (1915)
Some Do Not (1924)
No More Parades (1925)
A Man Could Stand Up (1926)
Last Post (1928)
Ford, John (1586–1640?)
dramatist and poet

Fames Memoriall; or, The Earle of Devonshire Deceased (1606)
A Line of Life: Pointing at the immortalitie of a vertuous name (1620)
The Lovers Melancholy (1629)
The Broken Heart: A tragedy (1633)
Loves Sacrifice: A tragedie (1633)
'Tis Pitty Shee's a Whore (1633)
Perkin Warbeck (1634)
The Fancies, Chast and Noble (1638)
The Ladies Triall (1639)

Ford, Richard (1796–1858)
travel author
A Hand-Book for Travellers in Spain, and Readers at Home (1845)

Forde or Ford, Emanuel (*fl.* 1607)
romance writer
Parismus, the Renoumed [sic] *Prince of Bohemia* (1598)
Ornatus and Artesis (1599?)
Parismenos (1599)
Montelyon, Knight of the Oracle (1633)

'Forester, C.S.' [Cecil Louis Troughton Smith] (1899–1966)
novelist and creator of Hornblower
Payment Deferred (1926)
The African Queen (1935)
The Happy Return (1937)

Forster, Edward Morgan (1879–1970)
novelist, short-story writer, and critic
Where Angels Fear to Tread (1905)
The Longest Journey (1907)
A Room With a View (1908)
Howards End (1910)
The Celestial Omnibus, and Other Stories (1911)
A Passage to India (1924)
Aspects of the Novel (1927)
The Eternal Moment, and Other Stories (1928)
Abinger Harvest (1936)
What I Believe (1939)
Two Cheers for Democracy (1951)
Billy Budd (1951)
Maurice (1971)

Forster, John (1812–76)
journalist and biographer
Historical and Biographical Essays (1858)
The Life of Charles Dickens (1872)

Forster, Margaret (1938–)
novelist and biographer
Dame's Delight (1964)
Georgy Girl (1965)
Lady's Maid (1990)

Forsyth, Frederick (1938–)
thriller writer
The Day of the Jackal (1971)
The Odessa File (1972)
The Dogs of War (1974)
The Fourth Protocol (1984)
The Veteran (2001)

Fortescue, Sir John William (1859–1933)
military historian and children's writer
The History of the British Army (1899)

Fowler, Ellen Thorneycroft, later Felkin (1860–1929)
novelist and poet
Concerning Isabel Carnaby (1898)

Fowler, Henry Watson (1858–1933), and Francis George (1870–1918)
lexicographers and grammarians
The King's English (1906)
The Concise Oxford Dictionary of Current English (1911)
A Dictionary of Modern English Usage (1926)

Fowles, John Robert (1926–)
novelist and essayist
The Collector (1963)
The Magus (1966)
The French Lieutenant's Woman (1969)
The Ebony Tower (1974)
Daniel Martin (1977)
Mantissa (1982)
A Maggot (1985)

Fox, George, the elder (1624–91)
founder of the Society of Friends and author
The Vialls of the Wrath of God (1654)
The Great Mistery of the Great Whore Unfolded (1659)
An Answer to the Arguments of the Jewes (1661)
Some Principles of the Elect People of God, who in Scorn Are Called Quakers (1661)
Three General Epistles to be Read in all the Congregations of the Righteous (1664)
The Arraignment of Popery (1667)
Concerning Revelation, Prophecy, Measure and Rule, and the Inspiration and Sufficiency of the Spirit (1676)
Concerning the Living God of Truth and the World's God (1680)
Journal (1694)
A Collection of Many Select and Christian Epistles, Letters and Testimonials (1698)

Fox, William Johnson (1786–1864)
hymn compiler
Hymns and Anthems (1841)

Foxe, John (1516–87)
martyrologist
A Brief Exhortation, Fruitfull and Meete to be Read, in This Heavy Tyme of Gods Visitation in London (1563)
Foxe's Book of Martyrs (1563)
A Sermon of Christ Crucified (1570)
A Sermon Preached at the Christening of a Certaine Jew (1578)
Christ Jesus Triumphant (1579)
The Pope Confuted (1580)
A Most Breefe Manner of Instruction, to the Principles of Christian Religion (1587?)

Francis, Anne, *née* Gittins (1738–1800)
poet and translator
A Poetical Translation of the Song of Solomon (1781)

Charlotte to Werter (1787)
Miscellaneous Poems (1790)
Francis, Dick [Richard Stanley Francis] (1920–)
crime writer
Dead Cert (1962)
Francis, Philip (1708?–73)
translator, poet, and dramatist
The Odes, Epodes, and Carmen Seculare of Horace (1743)
A Poetical Translation of the Works of Horace (1747)
Francis, Sir Philip [probably 'Junius'] (1740–1818)
politician and author
The Political Contest [pt i] (1769)
The Political Contest [pt ii] (1769)
*Two Letters from Junius to the D*** of G******* (1769)
Junius: Stat Nominis Umbra (1772)
Francklin, Thomas (1721–84)
poet, dramatist, and translator
Of the Nature of the Gods (1741)
Translation: A poem (1753)
The Orphan of China (1755)
The Earl of Warwick: A tragedy (1766)
Matilda: A tragedy (1775)
Frankau, Gilbert (1884–1952)
novelist
The Woman of the Horizon (1917)
Frankau, Pamela (1908–67)
novelist and short-story writer
The Marriage of Harlequin (1927)
Franklin, Sir John (1786–1847)
Arctic explorer
Narrative of a Journey to the Shores of the Polar Sea (1823)
Narrative of a Second Expedition to the Shores of the Polar Sea (1828)
Fraser, George MacDonald (1925–)
novelist
Flashman (1969)
The Pyrates (1983)
Fraser, James Baillie (1783–1856)
novelist
The Kuzzilbash (1828)
The Persian Adventurer (1830)
Fraunce, Abraham (*fl.* 1587–1633)
poet and translator
The Arcadian Rhetorike; or, The Praecepts of Rhetorike Made Plaine by Examples, Greeke, Latin, English (1588)
The Lawiers Logike (1588)
The Countesse of Pembrokes Emanuel (1591)
The Countesse of Pembrokes Yvychurch (1591)
The Third Part of the Countesse of Pembrokes Yvychurch: entituled Amintas Dale (1592)
Frayn, Michael (1933–)
novelist, playwright, and journalist
The Day of the Dog (1962)
The Tin Men (1965)
The Russian Interpreter (1966)
Towards the End of the Morning (1967)
A Very Private Life (1968)
The Two of Us (1970)
Sweet Dreams (1973)
Alphabetical Order (1976)
Clouds (1977)
Donkeys' Years (1977)
Make and Break (1980)
Noises Off (1982)
Benefactors (1984)
The Trick of It (1989)
Look Look (1990)
Audience (1991)
A Landing on the Sun (1991)
Here (1993)
Alarms & Excursions (1998)
Copenhagen (1998)
Headlong (1999)
Spies (2002)
Frazer, Sir James George (1854–1941)
social anthropologist
The Golden Bough (1890)
Freeling, Nicholas (1927–2003)
crime writer
Love in Amsterdam (1962)
Freeman, Edward Augustus (1823–92)
historian
The History of the Norman Conquest of England (1867)
Historical Essays [1st ser.] (1871)
Historical Essays: Second Series (1873)
Historical Essays: Third Series (1879)
The Historical Geography of Europe (1881)
The Reign of William Rufus and the Accession of Henry the First (1882)
The Methods of Historical Study (1886)
Historical Essays: Fourth Series (1892)
Freeman, Richard Austin ['Clifford Ashdown'] (1862–1943)
detective novelist and short-story writer
The Red Thumb Mark (1907)
Freeth, John (1731?–1808)
the 'Birmingham Poet'
The Political Songster (1766)
Modern Songs, on Various Subjects (1782)
Frere, John Hookham (1769–1846)
diplomat, translator, and poet
Prospectus and Specimen of an Intended National Work by William and Robert Whistlecraft Relating to King Arthur and his Round Table [cantos i, ii] (1817)
Friel, Brian [Bernard Patrick Friel] (1929–)
Northern Irish playwright and short-story writer
The Saucer of Larks (1962)
Lovers (1968)
Crystal and Fox (1970)
Dancing at Lughnasa (1990)
Froude, James Anthony ['Zeta'] (1818–94)
historian, biographer, and novelist
Shadows of the Clouds (1847)

The Nemesis of Faith (1849)
Thomas Carlyle (1882)
Thomas Carlyle (1884)
Froude, Richard Hurrell (1803–36)
poet and Tractarian
Remains of the late Richard Hurrell Froude (1838)
Frowde, Philip (*d.* 1738)
dramatist and poet
The Fall of Saguntum: A tragedy (1727)
Philotas: A tragedy (1731)
Fry, Caroline, later Wilson (1787–1846)
author
Serious Poetry (1822)
The Listener (1830)
Fry, Christopher [Christopher Fry Harris] (1907–)
dramatist and poet
The Boy With a Cart—Cuthman, Saint of Sussex (1939)
The Firstborn (1946)
A Phoenix Too Frequent: A comedy (1946)
The Lady's Not for Burning: A comedy (1949)
Ring Round the Moon (1950)
Venus Observed (1950)
A Sleep of Prisoners (1951)
The Dark is Light Enough (1954)
The Lark (1955)
Tiger at the Gates (1955)
Duel of Angels (1958)
A Yard of Sun: A summer comedy (1970)
Fry, Roger Eliot (1866–1934)
art critic
Vision and Design (1920)
Fuller, John Leopold (1937–)
poet, novelist, playwright, and children's writer
Fairground Music (1961)
Lies and Secrets (1979)
The January Divan (1980)
The Mechanical Body (1991)
Fuller, Roy Broadbent (1912–91)
poet, novelist, children's writer, and editor
Poems (1940)
The Middle of a War (1942)
A Lost Season (1944)
Epitaphs and Occasions (1949)
Counterparts (1954)
Fantasy and Fugue (1954)
Image of a Society (1956)
Brutus's Orchard (1957)
The Father's Comedy (1961)
Collected Poems 1936–1961 (1962)
Buff (1965)
New Poems (1968)
Tiny Tears (1973)
From the Joke Shop (1975)
The Reign of Sparrows (1980)
As From the Thirties (1983)
Mianserin Sonnets (1984)
New and Collected Poems 1934–1984 (1985)
Subsequent to Summer (1985)
Outside the Canon (1986)
Available for Dreams (1989)
Last Poems (1993)
Fuller, Thomas (1608–61)
antiquarian and divine
The Historie of the Holy Warre (1639)
Joseph's Party-colored Coat (1640)
The Holy State (1642)
Good Thoughts in Bad Times (1645)
Andronicus; or, The Unfortunate Politician (1646)
Feare of Losing the Old Light; or, A Sermon Preached in Exeter (1646)
The Cause and Cure of a Wounded Conscience (1647)
Good Thoughts in Worse Times (1647)
Good Thoughts in Bad Times, Together with Good Thoughts in Worse Times (1649)
A Pisgah-Sight of Palestine and the Confines Thereof (1650)
Abel Redevivus; or, The Dead Yet Speaking: The lives and deaths of the moderne divines (1651)
A Collection of Sermons (1656)
Mixt Contemplations in Better Times (1660)
The History of the Worthies of England (1662)
Fullerton, Lady Georgiana Charlotte, *née* Leveson Gower (1812–85)
novelist and poet
Ellen Middleton (1844)
Fulwell, Ulpian (*d.* 1586)
poet
Like Will to Like (1568)
The Flower of Fame (1575)
The Art of Flattery (1576)
Fuseli, Henry (1741–1825)
artist and author
Reflections on the Painting and Sculpture of the Greeks (1765)

Gage, Thomas (1603?–56)
traveller
The English-American his Travail by Sea and Land; or, A New Survey of the West India's (1648)
Gainsford, Thomas (1566–1624?)
author and editor
The Vision and Discourse of Henry the Seventh (1610)
The Historie of Trebizond (1616)
The Glory of England; or, A True Description of Blessings Whereby She Triumpheth Over all Nations (1618)
Galloway, Janice (1956–)
Scottish novelist and short-story writer
The Trick is to Keep Breathing (1989)
Blood (1991)
Foreign Parts (1994)
Galsworthy, John ['John Sinjohn'] (1867–1933)
novelist, dramatist, and short-story writer
From the Four Winds (1897)
Jocelyn (1898)

A Man of Devon (1901)
The Island Pharisees (1904)
The Man of Property (1906)
The Country House (1907)
Fraternity (1909)
Justice: A tragedy (1910)
Strife (1910)
The Patrician (1911)
The Dark Flower (1913)
The Fugitive (1913)
The Mob (1914)
Five Tales (1918)
Awakening (1920)
In Chancery (1920)
To Let (1921)
The Forsyte Saga (1922)
Two Forsyte Interludes (1927)
Four Forsyte Stories (1929)
A Modern Comedy (1929)
On Forsyte 'Change (1930)
Soames and the Flag (1930)

Galt, John ['Revd T. Clarke', 'Samuel Prior'] (1779–1839)
novelist, biographer, and poet
The Battle of Largs (1804)
Letters from the Levant (1813)
The Majolo (1815)
The Earthquake (1820)
Glenfell; or, Macdonalds and Campbells (1820)
The Wandering Jew; or, The Travels and Observations of Hareach the Prolonged (1820)
Annals of the Parish; or, The Chronicle of Dalmailing (1821)
The Ayrshire Legatees; or, The Pringle Family (1821)
Sir Andrew Wylie of that Ilk (1822)
The Provost (1822)
The Steam-Boat (1822)
The Entail; or, The Lairds of Grippy (1823)
The Gathering of the West (1823)
Ringan Gilhaize; or, The Covenanters (1823)
The Spaewife (1823)
The Bachelor's Wife (1824)
Rothelan (1824)
The Omen (1825)
The Last of the Lairds; or, The Life and Opinions and Malachi Mailings (1826)
Lawrie Todd; or, The Settlers in the Woods (1830)
The Life of Lord Byron (1830)
Bogle Corbet; or The Emigrants (1831)
The Lives of the Players (1831)
The Member (1832)
The Autobiography of John Galt (1833)
Eben Erskine; or, The Traveller (1833)

Galton, Sir Francis (1822–1911)
scientist
The Narrative of an Explorer in Tropical Southern Africa (1853)
Hereditary Genius (1869)
English Men of Science (1874)
Eugenics (1905)

Gardam, Jane Mary, *née* Pearson (1928–)
novelist and short-story writer
A Few Fair Days (1971)
The Summer After the Funeral (1973)
Black Faces, White Faces (1975)
The Pangs of Love, and Other Stories (1983)
Crusoe's Daughter (1985)
Showing the Flag (1989)
The Queen of the Tambourine (1991)
Going into a Dark House, and Other Stories (1994)
Faith Fox (1996)
Missing the Midnight (1997)
The Flight of the Maidens (2000)

Gardiner, Samuel Rawson (1829–1902)
historian
History of England 1603–16 (1863)
Prince Charles and the Spanish Marriage 1617–23 (1869)
A History of England Under the Duke of Buckingham and Charles I (1875)
The Personal Government of Charles I (1877)
Introduction to the Study of English History (1881)
The Fall of the Monarchy of Charles I, 1637–1649 (1882)
History of England 1603–42 (1883)

Gardiner, Stephen (1483?–1555)
bishop of Winchester
A Detection of the Devils Sophistre (1546)
An Explication and Assertion of the True Catholique Fayth (1551)
De vera obediencia (1553)

Gardner, Dame Helen Louise (1908–86)
scholar, critic, and editor
The New Oxford Book of English Verse 1250–1950 (1972)

Gardner, John Edmund (1926–)
thriller writer
Licence Renewed (1981)
The Secret Generations (1985)
The Secret Houses (1988)
The Secret Families (1989)

Garfield, Leon (1921–)
children's writer
Jack Holborn (1964)
Devil-in-the-Fog (1966)
The Sound of Coaches (1974)
Garfield's Apprentices (1982)

'Garioch, Robert' [Robert Garioch Sutherland] (1909–81)
Scottish poet
17 Poems for 6d. in Gaelic, Lowland Scots and English (1940)
Chuckles on the Cairn (1949)
The Big Music, and Other Poems (1971)
Doktor Faust in Rose Street (1973)

Garnett, David (1892–1981)
novelist and critic
Lady into Fox (1922)
Aspects of Love (1955)

Garnett, Edward (1868–1936)
critic, satirist, and playwright
The Breaking Point (1907)
Garnett, Richard (1835–1906)
biographer, poet, and short-story writer
Relics of Shelley (1862)
The Twilight of the Gods, and Other Tales (1888)
Iphigenia in Delphi (1890)
Garrick, David (1717–79)
actor and dramatist
The Lying Valet (1741)
An Essay on Acting (1744)
Romeo and Juliet (1750)
The Fairies: An opera (1755)
Catherine and Petruchio: A comedy (1756)
The Tempest: An opera (1756)
Lilliput: A dramatic entertainment (1757)
Florizel and Perdita: A dramatic pastoral (1758)
Cymbeline: A tragedy (1762)
Cymon: A dramatic romance (1767)
The Irish Widow (1772)
Bon Ton; or, High Life Above Stairs: A comedy (1775)
Garter, Thomas (*fl.* 1562–89?)
dramatist
The Commody of the Moste Vertuous and Godlye Susanna (1578)
Garth, Sir Samuel (1661–1719)
physician and poet
The Dispensary (1699)
Gascoigne, George (1534?–77)
poet
A Hundreth Sundrie Flowres Bounde up in One Small Poesie (1573)
The Glasse of Governement (1575)
The Posies of George Gascoigne Esquire (1575)
The Droomme of Doomes Day (1576)
The Spoyle of Antwerpe (1576?)
The Steele Glas: a Satyre; Togither with The Complainte of Phylomene (1576)
The Whole Woorkes of George Gascoigne Esquyre (1587)
Gascoyne, David Emery (1916–)
poet, translator, and novelist
Roman Balcony, and Other Poems (1932)
Opening Day (1933)
Hölderlin's Madness (1938)
Poems 1937–1942 (1943)
A Vagrant, and Other Poems (1950)
Night Thoughts (1956)
Collected Poems (1965)
Collected Poems (1988)
Gaskell, Elizabeth Cleghorn ['Cotton Mather Mills'] (1810–65)
novelist and short-story writer
Mary Barton (1848)
Libbie Marsh's Three Eras (1850)
The Moorland Cottage (1850)
Cranford (1853)
Ruth (1853)
Lizzie Leigh, and Other Tales (1854)
North and South (1855)
The Life of Charlotte Brontë (1857)
Round the Sofa (1859)
Right at Last, and Other Tales (1860)
Lois the Witch, and Other Tales (1861)
Sylvia's Lovers (1863)
A Dark Night's Work (1863)
The Grey Woman, and Other Tales (1865)
Cousin Phillis, and Other Tales (1865)
Wives and Daughters (1866)
Gatty, Margaret, *née* Scott, Mrs Alfred Gatty (1809–73)
children's writer, poet, and editor
The Fairy Godmothers, and Other Tales (1851)
Aunt Judy's Tales (1859)
Parables from Nature (1861)
Aunt Judy's Letters (1862)
'Gawsworth, John' [Terence Ian Fytton Armstrong] (1912–71)
poet and editor
Poems 1930–32 (1933)
Gay, John (1685–1732)
poet and dramatist
Wine (1708)
The Present State of Wit (1711)
The Mohocks: A tragi-comical farce (1712)
Rural Sports (1713)
The Wife of Bath: A comedy (1713)
The Fan (1713)
The Shepherd's Week (1714)
The What D' Ye Call It: A tragi-comi-pastoral farce (1715)
Trivia; or, The Art of Walking the Street (1716)
Three Hours After Marriage: A comedy (1717)
Poems on Several Occasions (1720)
The Captives: A tragedy (1724)
Fables (1727)
The Beggar's Opera (1728)
Polly: An opera (1729)
Acis and Galatea: An English pastoral opera (1732)
Achilles: An opera (1733)
Fables: Volume the Second (1738)
The Distress'd Wife: A comedy (1743)
The Rehearsal at Goatham (1754)
Gee, Maggie [i.e. Mary] (1948–)
novelist and playwright
Dying, in Other Words (1981)
The Burning Book (1983)
Light Years (1985)
Grace (1988)
Lost Children (1994)
The White Family (2002)
Gentleman, Francis (1728–84)
poet and dramatist
The Sultan; or, Love and Fame (1770)
Gerard, Alexander (1728–95)
philosophical writer
An Essay on Taste (1759)
Gerard, John (1545–1612)
herbalist

The Herball or Generall Historie of Plantes (1597)
Gerhardie [originally Gaerhardi], William Alexander (1895–1977)
novelist
Futility (1922)
The Polyglots (1925)
Pretty Creatures (1927)
Jazz and Jasper (1928)
Pending Heaven (1930)
Memoirs of a Polyglot (1931)
Resurrection (1934)
Of Mortal Love (1936)
My Wife's the Least of It (1938)
Gibbes, Phebe or Phoebe (*fl.* 1777–89)
novelist
The History of Lady Louisa Stroud, and the Honourable Miss Caroline Stretton (1764)
The Woman of Fashion; or, The History of Lady Diana Dormer (1767)
Modern Seduction; or, Innocence Betrayed (1777)
Gibbon, Edward (1737–94)
historian
Critical Observations on the Sixth Book of the Aeneid (1770)
The History of the Decline and Fall of the Roman Empire: Volume the First (1776)
A Vindication of Some Passages in the History of the Decline and Fall of the Roman Empire (1779)
The History of the Decline and Fall of the Roman Empire: Volume the Second/Volume the Third (1781)
The History of the Decline and Fall of the Roman Empire [vols iv, v, vi] (1788)
Miscellaneous Works (1796)
'Gibbon, Lewis Grassic' [James Leslie Mitchell] (1901–35)
Scottish novelist and short-story writer
Stained Radiance (1930)
Sunset Song (1932)
Gibbons, Orlando (1583–1625)
composer
The First Set of Madrigals and Mottets of 5 Parts (1612)
Gibbons, Stella Dorothea (1902–89)
novelist, short-story writer, and poet
The Mountain Beast, and Other Poems (1930)
Cold Comfort Farm (1932)
Roaring Tower, and Other Short Stories (1937)
The Lowland Venus, and Other Poems (1938)
Christmas at Cold Comfort Farm, and Other Stories (1940)
Conference at Cold Comfort Farm (1949)
Gibbs, James (1682–1754)
architect
A Book of Architecture (1728)
Gibson, Edmund (1669–1748)
prelate and antiquary
Synodus Anglicana; or, The Constitution and Proceedings of an English Convocation (1702)
Family-Devotion; or, A Plain Exhortation to Morning and Evening Prayer in Families (1705)
Codex Juris Ecclesiastici Anglicani (1713)
Gibson, Wilfrid [Wilson] (1878–1962)
poet
The Stonefolds (1907)
Daily Bread (1910)
Fires (1912)
Borderlands (1914)
Battle (1915)
Whin (1918)
Krindlesdyke (1922)
Gifford, George (*d.* 1620)
divine
A Discourse of the Subtill Practises of Devilles by Witches and Sorcerers (1587)
A Dialogue Concerning Witches and Witchcraftes (1593)
Gifford, Humphrey (*fl.* 1580)
poet
A Posie of Gilloflowers (1580)
Gifford, Richard (1725–1807)
clergyman and poet
Contemplation: A poem (1753)
Gifford, William (1756–1826)
critic and satirist
The Baviad (1791)
The Maeviad (1795)
The Anti-Jacobin; or, Weekly Examiner (1797)
Epistle to Peter Pindar (1800)
The Satires of Decimus Junius Juvenalis (1802)
The Satires of Aulus Persius Flaccus (1821)
Gilbert, Sir Humphrey (1539?–83)
navigator
A Discourse of a Discoverie for a New Passage to Cataia (1576)
Gilbert, William (1540–1603)
physician and scientist
De magnete, magneticisque corporibus, et de magno magnete tellure (1600)
Gilbert, William (1804–90)
journalist and novelist
Shirley Hall Asylum; or, The Memoirs of a Monomaniac (1863)
Gilbert, Sir William Schwenck (1836–1911)
playwright, librettist, and lyricist
The 'Bab' Ballads (1869)
More 'Bab' Ballads (1872)
Trial by Jury: A novel original dramatic cantata (1875)
Original Plays (1876)
HMS Pinafore; or, The Lass That Loved a Sailor (1878)
The Pirates of Penzance; or, The Slave of Duty (1880)
Patience; or, Bunthorne's Bride (1881)
Princess Ida; or, Castle Adamant (1884)
Iolanthe; or, The Peer and the Peri (1885)
The Mikado; or, The Town of Titipu (1885)
Ruddygore; or, The Witch's Curse (1887)

The Gondoliers; or, The King of Barataria (1889)
Songs of a Savoyard (1890)
Gilchrist, Alexander (1828–61)
biographer
Life of William Blake (1863)
Gildon, Charles (1665–1724)
dramatist, critic, and poet
Miscellany Poems upon Several Occasions (1692)
Chorus Poetarum; or, Poems on Several Occasions (1694)
The Roman Brides Revenge: A tragedy (1697)
Phaeton; or, The Fatal Divorce (1698)
Measure for Measure; or, Beauty the Best Advocate (1700)
Love's Victim; or, the Queen of Wales: A tragedy (1701)
A New Miscellany of Original Poems (1701)
A Comparison Between the Two Stages (1702)
Examen Miscellaneum (1702)
The Patriot; or, The Italian Conspiracy: A tragedy (1703)
The Deist's Manual; or, A Rational Enquiry into the Christian Religion (1705)
Libertas Triumphans (1708)
The New Metamorphosis (1708)
The Golden Spy; or, A Political Journal of the British Nights Entertainments of War and Peace, and Love and Politics (1709)
A New Rehearsal; or, Bays the Younger (1714)
The Complete Art of Poetry (1718)
The Life and Strange Surprizing Adventures of Mr D[aniel] DeF[oe], of London, Hosier (1719)
All for the Better; or, The World Turn'd Upside Down (1720)
The Laws of Poetry (1721)
Gilfillan, George (1813–78)
poet and critic
A Gallery of Literary Portraits [1st ser.] (1845)
Gilliatt, Penelope Ann Douglass (1932–93)
novelist, short-story writer, playwright, and film critic
One by One (1965)
A State of Change (1967)
Splendid Lives (1977)
Mortal Matters (1983)
They Sleep Without Dreaming (1985)
A Woman of Singular Occupation (1988)
Lingo (1990)
Gillies, John (1712–96)
theological writer
Historical Collections Relating to Remarkable Periods of the Success of the Gospel (1754)
Gillies, Robert Pearse (1788–1858)
novelist, translator, and autobiographer
The Devil's Elixir (1824)
Gilpin, William (1724–1804)
topographical author
Observations on the River Wye, and Several Parts of South Wales (1782)
Observations, Relative Chiefly to Picturesque Beauty . . . Particularly the Mountains, and Lakes of Cumberland, and Westmoreland (1786)
Observations, Relative Chiefly to Picturesque Beauty . . . Particularly the High-lands of Scotland (1789)
Remarks on Forest Scenery (1791)
Three Essays on Picturesque Beauty (1792)
Picturesque Remarks on Western Parts of England and the Isle of Wight (1798)
Gisborne, Thomas, the elder (1758–1846)
theologian and poet
Walks in a Forest (1794)
Poems, Sacred and Moral (1798)
Gissing, George Robert (1857–1903)
novelist
Workers in the Dawn (1880)
The Unclassed (1884)
Demos: A story of English Socialism (1886)
Isabel Clarendon (1886)
Thyrza (1887)
A Life's Morning (1888)
The Nether World (1889)
The Emancipated (1890)
New Grub Street (1891)
Denzil Quarrier (1892)
Born in Exile (1892)
The Odd Women (1893)
In the Year of the Jubilee (1894)
Eve's Ransom (1895)
The Paying Guest (1895)
Sleeping Fires (1895)
The Whirlpool (1897)
The Town Traveller (1898)
The Crown of Life (1899)
Our Friend the Charlatan (1901)
The Private Papers of Henry Ryecroft (1903)
Veranilda (1904)
Will Warburton (1905)
The House of Cobwebs, and Other Stories (1906)
Gladstone, William Ewart (1809–98)
statesman and author
The State in its Relations with the Church (1838)
Studies on Homer and the Homeric Age (1858)
Glanvill, John (1664?–1735)
poet and translator
Some Odes of Horace Imitated with Relation to His Majesty and the Times (1690)
Poems (1725)
Glanvill, Joseph (1636–80)
philosopher
The Vanity of Dogmatizing: or Confidence in Opinions (1661)
Lux Orientalis: Or an enquiry into the opinion of the Eastern sages, concerning the praeexistence of souls (1662)
Plus Ultra; or, The Progress and Advancement of Knowledge Since the Days of Aristotle (1668)
Logou Threskeia (1670)
Philosophia Pia: Or, a discourse of the religious temper of the experimental philosophy which is profest by the Royal Society (1671)

An Earnest Invitation to the Sacrament of the Lords Supper (1673)
Essays on Several Important Subjects in Philosophy and Religion (1676)
An Essay Concerning Preaching (1678)
Saducismus Triumphatus; or, Full and Plain Evidence Concerning Witches and Apparitions (1681)

Glapthorne, Henry (1610–43?)
dramatist and poet
Albertus Wallenstein (1639)
Argalus and Parthenia (1639)
Poëms (1639)
The Hollander: A comedy written 1635 (1640)
The Ladies Priviledge (1640)
Wit in a Constable: A comedy written 1639 (1640)

Glasse, Hannah (1708–70)
writer on cookery
The Art of Cookery, Made Plain and Easy (1747)

Gleig, George Robert (1796–1888)
chaplain-general of the forces and author
The Subaltern (1825)

Glendinning, Victoria (1937–)
biographer and novelist
Vita (1983)
The Grown Ups (1989)
Electricity (1995)

Glover, Richard (1712–85)
poet and dramatist
Leonidas (1737)
London; or, The Progress of Commerce (1739)
Admiral Hosier's Ghost (1740?)
Boadicea: A tragedy (1753)
Medea: A tragedy (1761)
The Athenaid (1787)

Glyn, Elinor, *née* Sutherland (1864–1943)
novelist
The Visits of Elizabeth (1900)
Three Weeks (1907)
Elizabeth Visits America (1909)
Man and Maid (1922)

Godden, [Margaret] Rumer (1907–98)
novelist and children's writer
Black Narcissus (1939)
Gypsy, Gypsy (1940)
A Fugue in Time (1945)
The River (1946)
A Candle for St Jude (1948)
A Breath of Air (1950)
The Greengage Summer (1958)
The Battle of the Villa Fiorita (1963)
In This House of Brede (1969)
The Peacock Spring (1975)
Thursday's Children (1984)
A Time to Dance, No Time to Weep (1987)
A House with Four Rooms (1989)
Coromandel Sea Change (1991)
Pippa Passes (1994)
Cromartie v the God Shiva (1997)

Godwin, Catherine Grace, *née* Garnett (1798–1845)
poet
The Night Before the Bridal; Sappho; and Other Poems (1824)

Godwin, Francis (1562–1633)
bishop successively of Llandaff and Hereford
A Catalogue of the Bishops of England (1601)
The Man in the Moone (1638)

Godwin, William ['Edward Baldwin', 'Verax'] (1756–1836)
philosopher and novelist
Damon and Delia (1784)
Italian Letters; or, The History of the Count de St Julian (1784)
An Enquiry Concerning Political Justice (1793)
Things as They Are; or, The Adventures of Caleb Williams (1794)
The Enquirer (1797)
Memoirs of the Author of A Vindication of the Rights of Women (1798)
St Leon: A tale of the sixteenth century (1799)
Antonio: A tragedy (1800)
Thoughts Occasioned by Dr Parr's Spital Sermon (1801)
Life of Geoffrey Chaucer, the Early English Poet (1803)
Fables Ancient and Modern (1805)
Fleetwood; or, The New Man of Feeling (1805)
Faulkener: A tragedy (1807)
Essay on Sepulchres (1809)
Letters of Verax, to the Editor of the Morning Chronicle (1815)
Mandeville (1817)
Letters of Advice to a Young American (1818)
Of Population (1820)
History of the Commonwealth of England (1824)
Cloudesley (1830)
Thoughts on Man, his Nature, Productions and Discoveries (1831)
Deloraine (1833)

Goffe, Thomas (1591–1629)
dramatist
The Raging Turke; or, Bajazet the Second: A tragedie (1631)
The Couragious Turke; or, Amurath the First: A tragedie (1632)
The Tragedy of Orestes (1633)
The Careless Shepherdess: A tragi-comedy (1656)

Gogarty, Oliver St John (1878–1957)
Irish poet and author
The Ship, and Other Poems (1918)
As I Was Going Down Sackville Street (1937)
Others to Adorn (1938)
It Isn't This Time of Year at All! (1954)

Golding, Arthur (1536?–1606)
translator
The Historie of Leonard Aretine (1563)
The Abridgment of the Histories of Trogus Pompeius (1564)

Gallic Wars (1565)
Metamorphoses (1565)
Metamorphosis [books i–xv] (1567)
Sermons . . . upon the Booke of Job (1574)
Abraham's Sacrifice (1577)
The Trueness of the Christian Religion (1587)
Golding, Sir William Gerald (1911–93)
novelist, playwright, and poet
Lord of the Flies (1954)
The Inheritors (1955)
Pincher Martin (1956)
The Brass Butterfly (1958)
Free Fall (1959)
The Spire (1964)
The Pyramid (1967)
The Scorpion God (1971)
Darkness Visible (1979)
Rites of Passage (1980)
A Moving Target (1982)
The Paper Men (1984)
An Egyptian Journal (1985)
Close Quarters (1987)
Fire Down Below (1989)
The Double Tongue (1995)
Goldsmith, Oliver ['James Willington'] (1728–74)
poet, dramatist, novelist, and essayist
The Memoirs of a Protestant, Condemned to the Galleys of France, For his Religion (1758)
The Bee (1759)
An Enquiry into the Present State of Polite Learning in Europe (1759)
The Citizen of the World; or, Letters From a Chinese Philosopher Residing in London to his Friends in the East (1762)
The Life of Richard Nash, of Bath (1762)
The Mystery Revealed (1762)
An History of England (1764)
The Traveller; or, A Prospect of Society (1764)
Essays by Mr Goldsmith (1765)
Poems for Young Ladies (1766)
The Vicar of Wakefield: A tale, supposed to be written by himself (1766)
The Beauties of English Poesy (1767)
The Good Natur'd Man: A comedy (1768)
The Present State of the British Empire in Europe, America, Africa, and Asia (1768)
The Roman History (1769)
The Deserted Village (1770)
The Life of Thomas Parnell (1770)
Life of Henry St John, Lord Viscount Bolingbroke (1770)
The History of England (1771)
She Stoops to Conquer; or, The Mistakes of a Night: A comedy (1773)
Retaliation (1774)
The Grecian History (1774)
An History of the Earth and Animated Nature (1774)
A Survey of Experimental Philosophy (1776)
Gombrich, Sir Ernst Hans Josef (1909–2001)
art historian
The Story of Art (1950)
Gomersall, Robert (1602–46?)
poet and dramatist
The Levites Revenge (1628)
The Tragedie of Lodovick Sforza Duke of Milan (1628)
Poems by Robert Gomersall (1633)
Goodman, Godfrey (1583–1656)
bishop of Gloucester
The Fall of Man; or, The Corruption of Nature (1616)
Goodman, Nicholas (*fl.* 1632)
romance writer
Hollands Leaguer; or, An Historical Discourse of the Life and Actions of Dona Britanica Hollandia the Arch-Mistris of the Wicked Women of Ethiopia (1632)
Goodwin, John (1594?–1665)
republican divine
Anti-Cavalierisme (1642)
Theomaxia; or, the Grand Imprudence of Men Running the Hazard of Fighting against God (1644)
Goodwin or Goodwine, Thomas Pope (*fl.* 1595?)
romance writer
Blanchardine and Eglantine (1595)
Googe, Barnabe (1540–94)
poet and translator
The Zodiac of Life [books i–iii] (1560)
The Zodiac of Life [books i–vi] (1561)
Eglogs, Epytaphes, and Sonettes (1563)
The Zodiac of Life [books i–xii] (1565)
The Ship of Safeguard (1569)
Gore, Catherine Grace Frances, *née* Moody (1799–1861)
novelist and playwright
Theresa Marchmont; or, The Maid of Honour (1824)
The Lettre de Cachet; a Tale. The Reign of Terror; a Tale (1827)
Romances of Real Life (1829)
Women As They Are; or, The Manners of the Day (1830)
Mothers and Daughters: A tale of the year 1830 (1831)
The Hamiltons; or, The New Era (1834)
Mrs Armytage; or, Female Domination (1836)
Stokeshill Place; or, The Man of Business (1837)
The Woman of the World (1838)
The Cabinet Minister (1839)
Cecil; or, The Adventures of a Coxcomb (1841)
Cecil a Peer (1841)
Greville; or, A Season in Paris (1841)
The Banker's Wife; or, Court and City (1843)
Sketches of English Character (1846)
Gorges, Sir Arthur (1577?–1625)
poet and translator

Lucans Pharsalia: Containing the Civill Warres Betweene Caesar and Pompey (1614)
Gosse, Sir Edmund William (1849–1928)
critic, biographer, and poet
New Poems (1879)
The Life of Philip Henry Gosse (1890)
In Russet and Silver (1894)
Father and Son (1907)
The Autumn Garden (1908)
Gosse, Philip Henry (1810–88)
zoologist
The Romance of Natural History (1860)
Gosson, Stephen (1554–1624)
pamphleteer
The Schoole of Abuse (1579)
Playes Confuted in Five Actions (1582)
Gosynhyll, Edward (*fl.* 1560)
poet
The Prayse of all Women (1542?)
Gouge, William (1578–1653)
Puritan divine
Of Domesticall Duties Eight Treatises (1622)
Gough, John (1610–61)
dramatist
The Strange Discovery: A tragi-comedy (1640)
Gough, Richard (1735–1809)
antiquary
Anecdotes of British Topography (1768)
Gould, Robert (*d.* 1709)
satirist and dramatist
Love Given O're; or, A Satyr Against the Pride, Lust and Inconstancy of Woman (1682)
Presbytery Rough-Drawn (1683)
Poems (1689)
The Corruption of the Times by Money (1693)
The Rival Sisters; or, The Violence of Love: A tragedy (1696)
A Satyr Against Wooing (1698)
Innocence Distress'd; or, The Royal Penitents: A tragedy (1737)
Gower, John (1325?–1408)
poet
Confessio Amantis (1483)
Gowers, Sir Ernest Arthur (1880–1966)
civil servant and grammarian
Plain Words (1948)
ABC of Plain Words (1951)
Grafton, Richard (*d.* 1572?)
chronicler and printer
An Abridgement of the Chronicles of England (1562)
A Chronicle at Large (1569)
Graham, William Sydney (1918–86)
poet
Cage Without Grievance (1942)
The Seven Journeys (1944)
Second Poems (1945)
Collected Poems 1942–1977 (1979)
Graham, Winston Mawdsley (1910–2003)
novelist
Ross Poldark (1945)
Marnie (1961)
Grahame, James (1765–1811)
Scottish poet
Poems in English, Scotch and Latin (1794)
The Sabbath (1804)
Poems (1807)
The Siege of Copenhagen (1808)
Grahame, Kenneth (1859–1932)
children's author and essayist
Pagan Papers (1893)
The Golden Age (1895)
Dream Days (1898)
The Wind in the Willows (1908)
Grainger, James (1721–66)
Scottish physician and poet
The Sugar-Cane (1764)
'Grand, Sarah' [Frances Elizabeth McFall, *née* Clarke] (1854–1943)
novelist
Ideala (1888)
The Heavenly Twins (1893)
The Beth Book (1897)
Grange, John (*c.*1577–1611)
poet
The Golden Aphroditis (1577)
Granger, James (1723–76)
biographer and print collector
Biographical History of England from Egbert the Great to the Revolution (1769)
Grant, James (1822–87)
novelist
Adventures of an Aide-de-Camp; or, A Campaign in Calabria (1848)
The Scottish Cavalier (1850)
Grantham or Granthan, Henry (*fl.* 1571–87)
translator
Filocolo (1567)
Granville, George, Lord Lansdowne (1667–1735)
dramatist and poet
The She-Gallants: A comedy (1696)
Heroick Love: A tragedy (1698)
The Jew of Venice: A comedy (1701)
The British Enchanters; or, No Magick Like Love: A tragedy (1706)
Poems Upon Several Occasions (1712)
The Genuine Works in Verse and Prose (1732)
Granville-Barker, Harley (1877–1946)
playwright, critic, and actor
The Marrying of Ann Leete: A comedy (1909)
The Voysey Inheritance (1909)
Waste: A tragedy (1909)
The Madras House: A comedy (1911)
Prefaces to the Players' Shakespeare (1923)
Prefaces to Shakespeare (1927)
Graunt, John (1620–74)
statistician
Natural and Political Observations (1662)
Graves, Clotilde Inez Mary ['Richard Dehan'] (1863–1932)

novelist, journalist, and playwright
Dragon's Teeth (1891)
Graves, Richard (1715–1804)
poet and novelist
The Love of Order (1773)
The Spiritual Quixote; or, The Summer's Ramble of Mr Geoffrey Wildgoose (1773)
The Progress of Gallantry (1774)
Euphrosyne; or, Amusements on the Road of Life (1776)
Columella; or, The Distressed Anchoret (1779)
Eugenius; or, Anecdotes of the Golden Vale (1785)
Lucubrations (1786)
Plexippus; or, The Aspiring Plebeian (1790)
Graves, Robert von Ranke (1895–1985)
poet, novelist, critic, and translator
Over the Brazier (1916)
Fairies and Fusiliers (1917)
Country Sentiment (1920)
The Pier-Glass (1921)
Whipperginny (1923)
Welchman's Hose (1925)
Lars Porsena; or, The Future of Swearing and Improper Language (1927)
Poems 1914–26 (1927)
A Survey of Modernist Poetry (1927)
Mrs Fisher; or, The Future of Humour (1928)
Goodbye to All That (1929)
But It Still Goes On (1930)
Poems 1926–1930 (1931)
Poems 1930–1933 (1933)
Claudius the God and his Wife Messalina (1934)
I, Claudius (1934)
Collected Poems (1938)
Count Belisarius (1938)
The Story of Marie Powell, Wife to Mr Milton (1943)
The Golden Fleece (1944)
King Jesus (1946)
Poems 1938–1945 (1946)
Collected Poems 1914–1947 (1948)
The White Goddess: A historical grammar of poetic myth (1948)
The Common Asphodel (1949)
Poems and Satires (1951)
Poems 1953 (1953)
The Greek Myths (1955)
Homer's Daughter (1955)
Collected Poems (1959)
More Poems (1961)
New Poems (1962)
Oxford Addresses on Poetry (1962)
Man Does, Woman Is (1964)
Collected Poems (1965)
Collected Short Stories (1965)
Majorca Observed (1965)
Mammon and the Black Goddess (1965)
Poetic Craft and Principle (1967)
Poems 1965–1968 (1968)
The Crane Bag and Other Disputed Subjects (1969)
Gray, Alasdair James (1934–)
Scottish novelist, short-story writer, and playwright
Lanark (1981)
Unlikely Stories, Mostly (1983)
1982, Janine (1984)
The Fall of Kelvin Walker (1985)
Lean Tales (1985)
Old Negatives (1989)
Something Leather (1990)
Poor Things (1992)
Ten Tales Tall and True (1993)
A History Maker (1994)
Mavis Belfrage (1996)
The Book of Prefaces (2000)
'Gray, Maxwell' [Mary Gleed Tuttiett] (1847–1923)
novelist
The Silence of Dean Maitland (1886)
Gray, Simon James Holliday (1936–)
playwright and novelist
Colmain (1963)
Otherwise Engaged, and Other Plays (1975)
The Rear Column, and Other Plays (1978)
The Common Pursuit (1984)
Hidden Laughter (1990)
Cell Mates (1995)
Gray, Thomas (1716–71)
poet
Ode on a Distant Prospect of Eton College (1747)
An Elegy Wrote in a Country Church Yard (1751)
Odes by Mr Gray (1757)
Poems, by Mr Gray (1768)
Ode Performed in the Senate-House at Cambridge, July 1, 1769 (1769)
Poems of Mr Gray (1775)
'Green, Henry' [Henry Vincent Yorke] (1905–73)
novelist
Blindness (1926)
Living (1929)
Party Going (1939)
Pack My Bag (1940)
Caught (1943)
Loving (1945)
Back (1946)
Concluding (1948)
Nothing (1950)
Doting (1952)
Green, John Richard (1837–83)
historian
A Short History of the English People (1874)
Green, Matthew ('Peter Drake', 1696–1737)
poet and Quaker
The Grotto (1733)
The Spleen (1737)
Greenaway, Kate [i.e. Catherine] (1846–1901)
illustrator
Under the Window: Pictures & rhymes for children (1879)

Greene, [Henry] Graham (1904–91)
novelist and short-story writer
Babbling April (1925)
The Man Within (1929)
The Name of Action (1930)
Rumour at Nightfall (1931)
Stamboul Train (1932)
It's a Battlefield (1934)
England Made Me (1935)
The Basement Room, and Other Stories (1935)
Journey Without Maps (1936)
A Gun for Sale (1936)
Brighton Rock (1938)
The Lawless Roads (1939)
The Confidential Agent: An entertainment (1939)
The Power and the Glory: An entertainment (1940)
The Ministry of Fear (1943)
Nineteen Stories (1947)
The Heart of the Matter (1948)
The Third Man and The Fallen Idol (1950)
The Lost Childhood, and Other Essays (1951)
The End of the Affair (1951)
The Living Room (1953)
Twenty-One Stories (1954)
Loser Takes All: An entertainment (1955)
The Quiet American (1955)
The Potting Shed (1958)
Our Man in Havana (1958)
The Complaisant Lover: A comedy (1959)
A Burnt-Out Case (1961)
In Search of a Character: Two African journals (1961)
A Sense of Reality (1963)
Carving a Statue (1964)
The Comedians (1966)
May We Borrow Your Husband? and Other Comedies of the Sexual Life (1967)
Collected Essays (1969)
Travels with my Aunt (1969)
A Sort of Life (1971)
The Pleasure Dome (1972)
The Honorary Consul (1973)
The Return of A.J. Raffles (1975)
The Human Factor (1978)
Dr Fischer of Geneva; or, The Bomb Party (1980)
Ways of Escape (1980)
J'accuse: The darker side of Nice (1982)
Monsieur Quixote (1982)
The Tenth Man (1985)
The Captain and the Enemy (1988)
The Last Word, and Other Stories (1990)
Reflections 1923–1988 (1990)
Greene, Robert (1558–92)
poet, dramatist, and pamphleteer
Mamillia (1583)
Arbasto (1584)
Gwydonius (1584)
Morando the Tritameron of Love (1584)
The Myrrour of Modestie (1584)
Planetomachia; or, The First Parte of the Generall Opposition of the Seven Planets (1585)
Euphues his Censure to Philautus (1587)
Penelopes Web (1587)
Pandosto (1588)
Perimedes the Blacke-Smith (1588)
Ciceronis Amor: Tullies Love (1589)
Menaphon (1589)
The Spanish Masquerado (1589)
Greenes Mourning Garment (1590)
Greenes Never Too Late; or, A Powder of Experience (1590)
The Royal Exchange (1590)
Greenes Farewell to Folly (1591)
A Notable Discovery of Coosenage (1591)
The Second Part of Conny-Catching (1591)
The Third and Last Part of Conny-Catching (1592)
Philomela (1592)
A Quip for an Upstart Courtier: or, A Quaint Dispute Between Velvet Breeches and Cloth-Breeches (1592)
The Blacke Bookes Messenger: Laying open the life and death of Ned Browne one of the most notable cutpurses, crosbiters, and conny-catchers that ever lived in England (1592)
A Disputation, Betweene a Hee Conny-Catcher, and a Shee Conny-Catcher (1592)
Greenes, Groats-worth of Witte, Bought with a Million of Repentance (1592)
The Repentance of Robert Greene Maister of Artes (1592)
Friar Bacon, and Friar Bungay (1594)
Orlando Furioso (1594)
The Scottish Historie of James the Fourth, Slaine at Flodden (1598)
The Comicall Historie of Alphonsus, King of Aragon (1599)
Greenes Orpharion (1599)
Alcida Greenes Metamorphosis (1617)
Greenlaw, Lavinia (1962–)
poet and novelist
The Cost of Getting Lost in Space (1991)
Night Photograph (1993)
A World Where News Travelled Slowly (1997)
Mary George of Allnorthover (2001)
Minsk (2003)
Greenwell, Dora (1821–82)
poet
Poems (1848)
Stories That Might Be True, with Other Poems (1850)
Songs of Salvation (1873)
Camera Obscura (1876)
Greenwood, Walter (1903–74)
novelist and playwright
Love on the Dole (1933)
Gregory, Lady Isabella Augusta, Lady Gregory (1852–1932)
dramatist and translator

Poets and Dreamers (1903)
Seven Short Plays (1909)
Our Irish Theatre (1913)

Grenewey, Richard (*fl.* 1591–8)
translator
The Annales of Cornelius Tacitus (1598)

Greville, Fulke, 1st Lord Brooke (1554–1628)
statesman and poet
The Tragedy of Mustapha (1609)
Certaine Learned and Elegant Workes (1633)
The Life of the Renowned Sr Philip Sidney (1652)
The Remains of Sir Fulk Grevill Lord Brooke (1670)

Grey, Zachary (1688–1766)
literary scholar
A Defence of Our Antient and Modern Historians (1725)
A Word or Two of Advice to William Warburton (1746)
A Free and Familiar Letter to William Warburton (1750)
Critical, Historical, and Explanatory Notes on Shakespeare (1754)

Griffin, Benjamin (1680–1740)
dramatist
Injured Virtue; or, The Virgin Martyr: A tragedy (1715)

Griffith, Elizabeth (1720?–93)
novelist and playwright
The Platonic Wife: A comedy (1765)
The Double Mistake: A comedy (1766)
The School for Rakes: A comedy (1769)
The History of Lady Barton (1771)
The Story of Lady Juliana Harley (1776)

Griffiths, Niall (1966)
novelist
Sheepshagger (2001)
Kelly & Victor (2002)
Stump (2003)

Griffith, Richard (1714?–88), and Elizabeth (1720?–93)
novelists
A Series of Genuine Letters Between Henry and Frances [vols i, ii] (1757)
Two Novels: in Letters (1769)

Griffiths, Trevor (1935–)
playwright
The Party (1974)
All Good Men; and, Absolute Beginners (1977)
Oi for England (1982)
Thatcher's Children (1994)

Grigson, Geoffrey Edward Harvey (1905–85)
poet, critic, editor, and topographical author
New Verse (1939)
Under the Cliff, and Other Poems (1943)
The Isles of Scilly, and Other Poems (1946)
Poetry of the Present (1949)
The Crest on the Silver (1950)
A Skull in Salop, and Other Poems (1967)
Ingestion of Ice-Cream, and Other Poems (1969)
Poems and Poets (1969)
Sad Grave of an Imperial Mongoose (1973)
The Fiesta, and Other Poems (1978)
History of Him (1980)
Collected Poems, 1963–1980 (1982)
The Cornish Dancer, and Other Poems (1982)
Montaigne's Tower, and Other Poems (1984)

Grimald, Nicholas (1519?–62)
poet and translator
Christus Redivivus (1543)
Marcus Tullius Ciceroes Thre Bokes of Duties (1556)

Grimeston or Grimestone, Edward (*fl.* 1607)
translator
Admirable and Memorable Histories Containing the Wonders of Our Time (1607)
A Generall Historie of the Netherlands: Continued unto this present yeare of our Lord 1608 (1608)

Grimston or Grymeston, Elizabeth (*d.* 1603)
author
Miscelanea. Meditations. Memoratives (1604)

Gronniosaw, [James Albert] Ukawsaw
former slave
A Narrative of the Most Remarkable Particulars in the Life of Ukawsaw Gronniosaw, an African Prince (1770)

Grose, Francis (1731–91)
antiquary, lexicographer, and draughtsman
The Antiquities of England and Wales (1772)
A Classical Dictionary of the Vulgar Tongue (1785)
The Antiquities of Scotland [vol. ii] (1791)

Gross, Philip (1952–)
poet
Cat's Whisker (1987)
The Son of the Duke of Nowhere (1991)
I.D. (1994)

Grossmith, George (1847–1912), and [Walter] Weedon (1854–1919)
humorous novelists
The Diary of a Nobody (1892)

Grote, George ['Philip Beauchamp'] (1794–1871)
historian
A History of Greece (1846)

Grove, Sir George (1820–1900)
music scholar and editor
A Dictionary of Music and Musicians (1879)

Guest, Lady Charlotte, *née* Bertie (1812–95)
translator and diarist
The Mabinogion (1838)
The Mabinogion (1877)

Guilpin, Everard or Edward (*fl.* 1598)
poet
Skialetheia. Or, A Shadow of Truth, in Certaine Epigrams or Satyres (1598)

Gunn, Thom[son] William (1929–2004)
poet and editor
Poems (1953)
Fighting Terms (1954)
The Sense of Movement (1957)
My Sad Captains, and Other Poems (1961)

Touch (1967)
Poems 1950–1966 (1969)
Moly (1971)
Jack Straw's Castle, and Other Poems (1976)
Selected Poems 1950–1975 (1979)
Talbot Road (1981)
The Passages of Joy (1982)
The Man with Night Sweats (1992)
Old Stories (1992)
Collected Poems (1993)
Boss Cupid (2000)

Gunning, Elizabeth, later Plunkett (1769–1823)
novelist
Lord Fitzhenry (1794)
The Packet (1794)
The Orphans of Snowdon (1797)
The Gipsy Countess (1799)

Gunning, Susannah, *née* Minifie (1740?–1800)
novelist
The Histories of Lady Frances S----- and Lady Caroline S----- (1763)
Family Pictures (1764)
The Picture (1766)
Barford Abbey (1767)
The Cottage (1769)
Anecdotes of the Delborough Family (1792)
Memoirs of Mary (1793)
Love at First Sight (1797)
Fashionable Involvements (1800)

Gurney, Ivor Bertie (1890–1937)
poet and composer
Severn and Somme (1917)
War's Embers (1919)

Habington, William (1605–54)
poet
Castara (1634)
The Historie of Edward the Fourth, King of England (1640)
The Queene of Arragon: A tragi-comedie (1640)
Observations upon Historie (1641)

Haddon, Mark (1962)
novelist and TV writer
The Curious Incident of the Dog in the Night-Time (2003)

Haggard, Sir Henry Rider (1856–1925)
novelist
Cetawayo and His White Neighbours (1882)
King Solomon's Mines (1885)
She: A history of adventure (1887)
Allan Quatermain (1887)
Maiwa's Revenge; or, The War of the Little Hand (1888)
Colonel Quaritch, V.C. (1888)
Cleopatra (1889)
Allan's Wife, and Other Tales (1889)
The World's Desire (1890)
Eric Brighteyes (1891)
Nada the Lily (1892)
The People of the Mist (1894)
Joan Haste (1895)
Ayesha (1905)
She and Allan (1921)
Wisdom's Daughter: The life and love story of She-Who-Must-Be-Obeyed (1923)

Hagthorpe, John (*fl.* 1622–7)
poet
Divine Meditations, and Elegies (1622)

Hakewill, George (1578–1649)
divine
An Apologie of the Power and Providence of God in the Government of the World (1627)

Hakluyt, Richard (1552?–1615)
geographer
Divers Voyages Touching the Discoverie of America, and the Lands Adjacent (1582)
The Principall Navigations, Voiages and Discoveries of the English Nation Made by Sea or Over Land, to the Most Remote and Farthest Distant Quarters of the Earth (1589)

Hale, Sir Matthew (1609–76)
judge
Contemplations, Moral and Divine (1676)

Hales, John (1584–1656)
author
A Tract Concerning Schisme and Schismaticks (1642)
Golden Remaines of the Ever Memorable Mr John Hales (1659)

Hall, Anna Maria, *née* Fielding, Mrs S[amuel] C[arter] Hall (1800–81)
novelist and woman of letters
Sketches of Irish Character (1829)
The Whiteboy (1845)
A Woman's Story (1857)

Hall, Basil (1788–1844)
naval officer and author
Fragments of Voyages and Travels [1st ser.] (1823)
Travels in North America in the Years 1827 and 1828 (1829)

Hall, John, of Durham (1627–56)
poet and pamphleteer
Horae Vacivae; or, Essays (1646)
Poems (1647)
An Humble Motion to the Parliament of England Concerning the Advancement of Learning: and Reformation of the Universities (1649)
Paradoxes (1650)

Hall, Joseph (1574–1656)
bishop of Norwich
Virgidemiarum, Sixe Bookes (1597)
Virgidemiarum (1598)
The Kings Prophecie; or, Weeping Joy (1603)
Meditations and Vowes Divine and Morall (1605)
The Arte of Divine Meditation (1606)
Heaven Upon Earth; or, Of True Peace and Tranquillitie of Minde (1606)
Holy Observations (1607)
Characters of Vertues and Vices (1608)
Epistles the First Volume (1608)

The Discovery of a New World; or, A Description of the South Indies, Hethero Unknowne (1609)
Salomon's Divine Arts, of 1. Ethickes, 2. Politickes, 3. Oeconomickes (1609)
A Common Apologie of the Church of England (1610)
Contemplations upon the Principall Passages of the Holy Storie: The first volume (1612)
Works (1614)
Contemplations upon the Historicall Part of the Old Testament (1626)
The Olde Religion: Wherin is laid downe the difference betwixt the reformed, and Romane church (1628)
Occasionall Meditations (1630)
Christian Moderation (1640)
Episcopacie by Divine Right (1640)
An Humble Remonstrance to the High Court of Parliament (1641)
A Defence of the Humble Remonstrance: Against the frivolous and false exceptions of Smectymnuus (1641)
A Short Answer to the Tedious Vindication of Smectymnuus (1641)
The Devout Soul; or, Rules of Heavenly Devotion (1644)
The Balme of Gilead; or, Comforts for the Distressed, both Morall and Divine (1646)
Select Thoughts, One Century (1648)
Resolutions and Decisions of Divers Practicall Cases of Conscienc (1649)
The Great Mysterie of Godliness (1651)
Susurrium Cum Deo: Soliloquies (1651)
Holy Raptures; or, Patheticall Meditations of the Love of Christ (1652)

'Hall, Radclyffe' [Marguerite Antonia Radclyffe-Hall] (1880–1943)
novelist and poet
'Twixt Earth and Stars (1906)
Songs of Three Counties, and Other Poems (1913)
The Well of Loneliness (1928)

Hallam, Arthur Henry (1811–33)
friend of Tennyson
Remains in Verse and Prose (1834)

Hallam, Henry (1777–1859)
historian
View of the State of Europe During the Middle Ages (1818)
The Constitutional History of England (1827)

Halle or Hall, Edward (*c.*1498–1547)
chronicler
Halle's Chronicle (1548)

Halliwell-Phillipps [originally Halliwell], James Orchard (1820–89)
literary scholar
Shakesperiana (1841)
The Nursery Rhymes of England (1842)
A Dictionary of Old English Plays (1860)

Hamburger, Michael Peter Leopold (1924–)
poet, translator, and critic
Friedrich Hölderlin: Poems (1943)
Later Hogarth (1945)
In Flashlight (1965)
Ownerless Earth (1973)
Collected Poems 1941–1983 (1984)
Roots in the Air (1991)

Hamilton, Lady Anne (1766–1846)
poet
The Epics of the Ton; or, The Glories of the Great World (1807)

Hamilton, Anthony (1646?–1720)
soldier, poet, and author
Memoirs of the Life of the Count de Grammont (1714)

Hamilton, Elizabeth (1758–1816)
novelist and writer on education
Translation of the Letters of a Hindoo Rajah (1796)
The Cottagers of Glenburnie (1808)

Hamilton, [Robert] Ian (1938–2001)
poet, critic, biographer, and editor
Pretending Not to Sleep (1964)
A Poetry Chronicle (1973)
Fifty Poems (1988)
In Search of J.D. Salinger (1988)
Keepers of the Flame (1992)
Walking Possession (1994)

Hamilton, Patrick Anthony Walter (1904–62)
novelist and playwright
Craven House (1926)
Twenty Thousand Streets Under the Sky (1935)
Impromptu in Moribundia (1939)

Hamilton, William, of Gilbertfield (1665?–1751)
poet
The Life and Heroick Actions of the Renoun'd Sir William Wallace (1722)

Hammick, Georgina (1939–)
short-story writer
People for Lunch (1987)
Spoilt (1992)

Hammond, Henry (1605–60)
divine
A Practicall Catechisme (1645)
A Paraphrase, and Annotations upon all the Books of the New Testament (1653)
The Workes of the Reverend and Learned Henry Hammond (1674)

Hammond, James (1710–42)
poet and politician
An Elegy to a Young Lady, in the Manner of Ovid (1733)
Love Elegies (1742)

Hampton, Christopher James (1946–)
playwright
When Did You Last See My Mother? (1967)
Total Eclipse (1969)
The Philanthropist: A bourgeois tragedy (1970)
Savages (1974)
Tales from Hollywood (1983)
White Chameleon (1991)

Hanley, James (1901–85)
Irish novelist, short-story writer, and playwright
Drift (1930)
Boy (1931)
The Furys (1935)
Hannay, James (1827–73)
Irish novelist
Biscuits and Grog (1848)
Hannay, Patrick (*d.* 1629?)
poet
The Nightingale. Sheretine and Mariana. A Happy Husband. Eligies on the Death of Queene Anne. Songs and Sonnets (1622)
Hardy, Thomas (1840–1928)
novelist, poet, and short-story writer
Desperate Remedies (1871)
Under the Greenwood Tree: A rural painting of the Dutch School (1872)
A Pair of Blue Eyes (1873)
Far From the Madding Crowd (1874)
The Hand of Ethelberta (1876)
The Return of the Native (1878)
The Trumpet-Major (1880)
A Laodicean; or, The Castle of the De Stancys (1881)
Two on a Tower (1882)
The Mayor of Casterbridge: The life and death of a man of character (1886)
The Woodlanders (1887)
Wessex Tales (1888)
A Group of Noble Dames (1891)
Tess of the d'Urbervilles: A pure woman faithfully presented (1891)
Life's Little Ironies (1894)
Jude the Obscure (1895)
The Wessex Novels (1895)
The Well-Beloved: A sketch of a temperament (1897)
Wessex Poems, and Other Verses (1898)
Poems of the Past and the Present (1901)
The Dynasts: A drama of the Napoleonic Wars (1904)
The Dynasts (1906)
The Dynasts (1908)
Time's Laughingstocks, and Other Verses (1909)
Wessex Edition (1912)
A Changed Man; The Waiting Supper; and Other Tales (1913)
Satires of Circumstance (1914)
Selected Poems (1916)
Collected Poems (1917)
Moments of Vision and Miscellanous Verses (1917)
Late Lyrics and Earlier, with Many Other Verses (1922)
The Famous Tragedy of the Queen of Cornwall at Tintagel in Lyonesse (1923)
Human Shows, Far Phantasies, Songs and Trifles (1925)
The Short Stories of Thomas Hardy (1928)
Winter Words in Various Moods and Metres (1928)
The Early Life of Thomas Hardy 1840–1891 (1928)
The Later Years of Thomas Hardy 1892–1928 (1930)
Hardyng, John (1378–c.1464)
chronicler
Chronicle (1543)
'Hare, Cyril' [Alfred Alexander Gordon Clark] (1900–58)
judge and detective fiction writer
Tragedy at Law (1942)
Hare, Sir David (1947–)
playwright
Slag (1971)
The Great Exhibition (1972)
Knuckle (1974)
Teeth 'n' Smiles (1976)
Licking Hitler (1978)
Plenty (1978)
Racing Demon (1990)
Murmuring Judges (1991)
Absence of War (1993)
Skylight (1995)
Plays: One (1996)
Plays: Two (1997)
Amy's View (1997)
The Judas Kiss (1998)
Via Dolorosa (1998)
My Zinc Bed (2000)
Hare, Julius Charles (1795–1855)
clergyman and author
Guesses at Truth [1st ser.] (1827)
Harington, Sir John (1560–1612)
poet and translator
Orlando Furioso in English Heroical Verse (1591)
The Metamorphosis of Ajax (1596)
The Englishmans Docter; or, The Schoole of Salerne (1607)
Epigrams Both Pleasant and Serious (1615)
The Most Elegant and Witty Epigrams of Sir John Harrington (1618)
Harington, John (1627–1700)
poet and translator
The Grecian Story (1684)
Harison, William (1685–1713)
poet and diplomat
Woodstock Park (1706)
Harland, Henry ['Sidney Luska'] (1861–1905)
novelist and short-story writer
The Cardinal's Snuff-Box (1900)
Harraden, Beatrice (1864–1936)
novelist and suffragette
In Varying Moods (1894)
Harrington or Harington, James (1611–77)
political theorist and author
The Common-wealth of Oceana (1656)
The Prerogative of Popular Government (1657)
Aphorisms Political (1659)

Virgil's Aeneis: The Third, Fourth, Fifth and Sixth Books (1659)
Political Discourses (1660)

Harriot or Hariot, Thomas (1560–1621)
mathematician and astronomer
A Briefe and True Report of the New Found Land of Virginia (1588)

Harris, Frank [James Thomas Harris] (1856–1931)
journalist, novelist, short-story writer, and biographer
Oscar Wilde (1918)
My Life and Loves (1922)

Harris, James (1709–80)
grammarian
Hermes; or, A Philosophical Inquiry Concerning Language and Universal Grammar (1751)

Harris, Joseph (*c.*1650–*c.*1715)
dramatist
The Mistakes; or, The False Report: A tragi-comedy (1691)
The City Bride; or, The Merry Cuckold: A comedy (1696)

Harris, Robert (1957–)
novelist
Enigma (1995)

Harrison, Frederic (1831–1923)
lawyer, critic, and philosopher
Order and Progress (1875)
The Present and the Future (1880)
The Philosophy of Common Sense (1907)
Novissima Verba (1920)
De Senectute (1923)

Harrison, Mary St Leger, *née* Kingsley ['Lucas Malet'] (1852–1931)
novelist
Mrs Lorimer (1882)

Harrison, Susanna (1752–84)
poet
Songs in the Night (1780)

Harrison, Tony (1937–)
poet, playwright, and translator
Earthworks (1964)
The Loiners (1970)
From the School of Eloquence, and Other Poems (1978)
Continuous (1981)
A Kumquat for John Keats (1981)
The Fire-Gap (1985)
V (1985)
Anno Forty-Two (1987)
The Mother of the Muses (1989)
Losing Touch (1990)
A Cold Coming (1991)
The Gaze of the Gorgon (1992)
Black Daisies for the Bride (1993)
The Shadow of Hiroshima (1995)

Harrod, Sir [Henry] Roy Forbes (1900–78)
economist and biographer
Towards a Dynamic Economics (1948)
The Life of John Maynard Keynes (1951)

Harsnett or Harsnet, Samuel (1561–1631)
archbishop of Canterbury
A Declaration of Egregious Popish Impostures (1603)

Hart, Sir Basil Henry Liddell (1895–1970)
military historian and strategist
The British Way in Warfare (1932)
Through the Fog of War (1938)
This Expanding War (1942)

Hartley, David (1705–57)
philosopher
Observations on Man, his Frame, his Duty, and his Expectations (1749)

Hartley, Leslie Poles (1895–1972)
novelist and short-story writer
Night Fears, and Other Stories (1924)
The Killing Bottle (1932)
The Shrimp and the Anemone (1944)
The Sixth Heaven (1946)
Eustace and Hilda (1947)
The Boat (1949)
My Fellow Devils (1951)
The Travelling Grave, and Other Stories (1951)
The Go-Between (1953)
The Brickfield (1964)
The Betrayal (1966)

Hartlib, Samuel (1600?–62)
pamphleteer and author
A Description of the Famous Kingdome of Macaria (1641)

Hartson, Hall (*d.* 1773)
poet and dramatist
The Countess of Salisbury: A tragedy (1767)

Harvey, Christopher (1597–1663)
poet
The Synagogue; or, The Shadow of the Temple (1640)
Schola Cordis . . . in 47 Emblems (1647)

Harvey, Gabriel (1550–1631)
scholar and poet
Gabrielis Harveii Ciceronianus (1577)
Rhetor (1577)
Three Letters, and Certaine Sonnets: Especially touching Robert Greene, and other parties, by him abused (1592)
A New Letter of Notable Contents: With a straunge sonet, intituled Gorgon (1593)
Pierces Supererogation; or A New Prayse of the Old Asse (1593)

Hassall, Christopher Vernon (1912–63)
poet, librettist, and biographer
Poems of Two Years (1935)
The Slow Night, and Other Poems 1940–8 (1949)
Rupert Brooke (1964)

Hastings, James (1862–1922)
biblical scholar and editor
A Dictionary of the Bible (1898)

Hastings, Michael Gerald (1938–)
playwright and novelist
Tom and Viv (1984)

Haughton, William (1575–1605)
dramatist
English-men for my Money; or, A Pleasant Comedy, called, A Woman Will Have Her Will (1616)
Havard, William (1710?–78)
dramatist
Regulus: A tragedy (1744)
Hawes, Stephen (*d.* 1523?)
poet
The Example of Virtue (1504?)
The Convercyon of Swerers (1509)
A Joyfull Medytacyon to all Englonde (1509)
The Pastyme of Pleasure (1509)
The Comforte of Lovers (1515?)
Hawker, Robert Stephen (1803–75)
poet and antiquary
Records of the Western Shore (1834)
Reeds Shaken with the Wind (1843)
Hawkesworth, John (1715?–73)
dramatist and editor
The Adventurer (1752)
Almoran and Hamet: An oriental tale (1761)
An Account of the Voyages for Making Discoveries in the Southern Hemisphere (1773)
Hawkins or Hawkyns, Sir John (1532–95)
naval commander
A True Declaration of the Troublesome Voyadge of J. Haukins to the Parties of Guynea and the West Indies (1569)
Hawkins, Sir John (1719–89)
lawyer, biographer, and editor
A General History of the Science and Practice of Music (1776)
The Life of Samuel Johnson (1787)
Hawkins, Sir Richard (*c.*1562–1622)
The Observations of Sir Richard Hawkins Knight in his Voiage into the South Sea (1622)
Hawkins, William (1722–1801)
poet and dramatist
Henry and Rosamund: A tragedy (1749)
Tracts in Divinity (1758)
Cymbeline: A tragedy (1759)
Haydon, Benjamin Robert (1786–1846)
painter
Lectures on Painting and Design (1844)
The Life of Benjamin Robert Haydon (1853)
Correspondence and Table-Talk (1876)
Hayley, William (1745–1820)
poet and biographer
A Poetical Epistle to an Eminent Painter (1778)
Epistle to Admiral Keppel (1779)
An Essay on History (1780)
The Triumphs of Temper (1781)
An Essay on Epic Poetry in Five Epistles to Mason (1782)
A Philosophical, Historical and Moral Essay on Old Maids (1785)
The National Advocates (1795)
The Life of Milton (1796)
An Essay on Sculpture (1800)
The Life and Posthumous Writings of William Cowper (1803)
The Triumph of Music (1804)
Ballads (1805)
Memoirs (1823)
Haynes, James (1788–1851)
dramatist
Conscience; or, The Bridal Night: A tragedy (1821)
Durazzo: A tragedy (1823)
Hays, Mary (1760–1843)
novelist and feminist
Letters and Essays (1793)
Memoirs of Emma Courtney (1796)
An Appeal to the Men of Great Britain in Behalf of Women (1798)
The Victim of Prejudice (1799)
Female Biography (1803)
Hayward, Sir John (1564?–1627)
historian
The First Part of the Life and Raigne of King Henrie the IIII (1599)
The Sanctuarie of a Troubled Soule [pt i] (1601)
The Lives of the III Normans, Kings of England (1613)
Davids Teares (1622)
The Life, and Raigne of King Edward the Sixt (1630)
Haywood, Eliza (*c.*1693–1756)
novelist, dramatist, and journalist
Love in Excess; or, The Fatal Enquiry (1719)
The Fair Captive: A tragedy (1721)
Letters From a Lady of Quality to a Chevalier (1721)
The British Recluse; or, The Secret History of Cleomira, Suppos'd Dead (1722)
Idalia; or, The Unfortunate Mistress (1723)
La Belle Assemblé; or, The Adventures of Six Days (1724)
The Fatal Secret; or, Constancy in Distress (1724)
Lasselia; or, The Self-abandon'd (1724)
The Masqueraders; or, Fatal Curiosity (1724)
Poems on Several Occasions (1724)
A Wife to be Lett: A comedy (1724)
Bath-Intrigues (1725)
Fantomina; or, Love in a Maze (1725)
Memoirs of a Certain Island Adjacent to the Kingdom of Utopia (1725)
Secret Histories, Novels and Poems (1725)
The City Jilt; or, The Alderman Turn'd Beau (1726)
The Mercenary Lover; or, The Unfortunate Heiress (1726)
Cleomelia; or, The Generous Mistress (1727)
The Fruitless Enquiry (1727)
The Perplex'd Dutchess; or, Treachery Rewarded (1727)
Philidore and Placentia; or, L'amour trop delicat (1727)

The Secret History of the Present Intrigues of the Court of Caramania (1727)
The Agreeable Caledonian; or, Memoirs of Signiora di Morella (1728)
Frederick, Duke of Brunswick-Lunenburgh: A tragedy (1729)
The Opera of Operas; or, Tom Thumb the Great (1733)
Adventures of Eovaai, Princess of Ijaveo (1736)
Anti-Pamela; or, Feign'd Innocence Detected; in a Series of Syrena's Adventures (1741)
The Virtuous Villager, or Virgin's Victory (1742)
A Present for a Servant-Maid; or, The Sure Means of Gaining Love and Esteem (1743)
The Female Spectator (1744)
The Fortunate Foundlings (1744)
Life's Progress through the Passions; or, The Adventures of Natura (1748)
Dalinda; or, The Double Marriage (1749)
A Present for Women Addicted to Drinking (1750)
The History of Miss Betsy Thoughtless (1751)
The History of Jemmy and Jenny Jessamy (1753)
The Invisible Spy (1755)
The Wife (1756)

Hazlitt, William (1778–1830)
critic and essayist
An Essay on the Principles of Human Action (1805)
Free Thoughts on Public Affairs; or, Advice to a Patriot (1806)
An Abridgement of the Light of Nature Pursued (1807)
The Eloquence of the British Senate (1807)
A Reply to the Essay on Population (1807)
A New and Improved Grammar of the English Tongue (1810)
The Round Table (1817)
Characters of Shakespear's Plays (1817)
Lectures on the English Poets (1818)
A View of the English Stage; or, A Series of Dramatic Criticisms (1818)
Lectures on the English Comic Writers (1819)
Political Essays, with Sketches of Public Characters (1819)
Lectures Chiefly on the Dramatic Literature of the Age of Elizabeth (1820)
Table-Talk; or, Original Essays (1821)
Table-Talk; or, Original Essays [vol. ii] (1822)
Characteristics (1823)
Liber Amoris; or, The New Pygmalion (1823)
Select British Poets (1824)
Sketches of the Principal Picture-Galleries in England (1824)
The Spirit of the Age; or, Contemporary Portraits (1825)
Notes of a Journey Through France and Italy (1826)
The Plain Speaker (1826)
The Life of Napoleon Buonaparte [vols i, ii] (1828)
Conversations of James Northcote (1830)
The Life of Napoleon Buonaparte [vols iii, iv] (1830)
Essays on the Principles of Human Action (1836)
Literary Remains of the Late William Hazlitt (1836)
Sketches and Essays (1839)

Head, Richard (1637?–86?)
fiction writer
The English Rogue Described: In the life of Meriton Latroon, a witty extravagant (1665)
The Floating Island; or, A New Discovery (1673)
The Western Wonder; or, O Brazeel (1674)
The Life and Death of Mother Shipton (1677)

Heaney, Seamus Justin (1939–)
Irish poet and critic
Eleven Poems (1965)
Death of a Naturalist (1966)
Door into the Dark (1969)
Wintering Out (1972)
North (1975)
Field Work (1979)
Preoccupations (1980)
Selected Poems 1965–1975 (1980)
The Rattle-Bag (1982)
Station Island (1984)
Sweeney Astray (1984)
The Haw Lantern (1987)
The Government of the Tongue (1988)
New Selected Poems 1966–1987 (1990)
The Redress of Poetry (1990)
The Tree Clock (1990)
Sweeney's Flight (1992)
The Spirit Level (1996)
Beowulf (1998)
Opened Ground (1998)
Electric Light (2001)
Finders Keepers (2002)

Hearne, Mary
novelist
The Lover's Week; or, The Six Days Adventures of Philander and Amaryllis (1718)

Hearne, Thomas (1678–1735)
antiquary
Reliquiae Bodleianae; or, Some Genuine Remains of Sir Thomas Bodley (1703)
A Collection of Curious Discourses (1720)
Robert of Gloucester's Chronicle (1724)

Heath, John (*fl.* 1615)
epigrammatist and translator
Two Centuries of Epigrammes (1610)

Heath, Robert (*fl.* 1650)
poet
Clarastella: Together with poems occasional, elegies, epigrams, satyrs (1650)

Heath-Stubbs, John Francis Alexander (1918–)
poet and critic
Wounded Thammuz (1942)
The Darkling Plain (1950)
The Swarming of the Bees (1950)

The Faber Book of Twentieth-Century Verse (1953)
A Charm Against the Toothache (1954)
Helen in Egypt, and Other Plays (1958)
The Triumph of the Muse, and Other Poems (1958)
Satires and Epigrams (1968)
A Parliament of Birds (1975)
Buzz Buzz (1981)
The Immolation of Aleph (1985)
A Partridge in a Pear Tree (1988)
The Game of Love and Death (1990)

Heber, Reginald (1783–1826)
bishop of Calcutta and hymn-writer
Poems and Translations (1812)
Hymns (1827)
Narrative of a Journey Through India 1824–5 (1828)
Sermons Preached in England (1829)

Hector, Annie, *née* French ['Mrs Alexander'] (1825–1902)
novelist
Kate Vernon (1854)
Look Before You Leap (1865)
The Wooing O't (1873)
Her Dearest Foe (1876)

Helme, Elizabeth (*d.* 1816)
novelist and educationalist
Louisa; or, The Cottage on the Moor (1787)
The Farmer of Inglewood Forest (1796)
St Clair of the Isles; or, The Outlaws of Barra (1803)

Hemans, Felicia Dorothea, *née* Browne, Mrs Alfred Hemans (1793–1835)
poet
Poems (1808)
England and Spain; or, Valour and Patriotism (1808)
The Domestic Affections, and Other Poems (1812)
Modern Greece (1817)
Translations from Camoens and Other Poets, with Original Poetry (1818)
Tales and Historic Scenes, in Verse (1819)
Wallace's Invocation to Bruce (1819)
The Sceptic (1820)
Dartmoor (1821)
The Siege of Valencia; The Last Constantine; with Other Poems (1823)
The Vespers of Palermo: A tragedy (1823)
The Forest Sanctuary, and Other Poems (1825)
Records of Woman, with Other Poems (1828)
Songs of the Affections, with Other Poems (1830)
Hymns on the Works of Nature (1833)
National Lyrics, and Songs for Music (1834)
Scenes and Hymns of Life (1834)
Poetical Remains (1835)

Heminges or Heming, William (1602–53)
dramatist
The Fatal Contract: A French tragedy (1653)
The Jewes Tragedy; or, Their Fatal and Final Overthrow by Vespatian and Titus his Son (1662)

Hendred, William
translator
The Pilgrimage of Mankind (1520?)

Hendry, James Findlay (1912–86)
Scottish poet, editor, and novelist
The New Apocalypse (1940)
The White Horseman (1941)
The Bombed Happiness (1942)
The Orchestral Mountain (1943)
The Crown and Sickle (1944)

Henley, William Ernest (1849–1903)
poet, critic, and journalist
Admiral Guinea (1884)
Beau Austin (1884)
A Book of Verses (1888)
Deacon Brodie; or, The Double Life (1888)
The Song of the Sword, and Other Verses (1892)
London Voluntaries; The Song of the Sword; and Other Verses (1893)
Poems (1898)
For England's Sake (1900)
A Song of Speed (1903)

Hennell, Charles Christian (1809–50)
theological writer
An Inquiry Concerning the Origin of Christianity (1838)

Henri, Adrian Maurice (1932–2001)
poet, playwright, novelist, painter, and children's writer
Penguin Modern Poets 10: The Mersey Sound (1967)
Tonight at Noon (1968)
Autobiography (1971)
One Year (1976)
City Hedges (1977)
From the Loveless Matel (1980)
Penny Arcade (1983)
Holiday Snaps (1985)
Collected Poems (1986)
Box, and Other Poems (1990)
The Cerise Swimsuit (1992)
Not Fade Away (1994)

'Henry, the Minstrel', also known as 'Blind Harry'
Scots poet
Acts and Deeds of Wallace (1508?)

Henryson, Robert (*c.*1430–*c.*1505)
Scots poet
Orpheus and Eurydice (1508?)
The Morall Fabillis of Esope the Phrygian (1570)
The Testament of Cresseid (1593)

Hensher, Philip (1965)
novelist
The Bedroom of the Mister's Wife (1999)
The Mulberry Empire (2002)

Henty, George Alfred (1832–1902)
boys' novelist

Out on the Pampas; or, The Young Settlers (1870)
Under Drake's Flag (1883)
The Dash for Khartoum (1892)
With Buller to Natal (1900)
With Roberts to Pretoria (1901)
Heppenstall, [John] Rayner (1911–81)
novelist, poet, and translator
The Blaze of Noon (1939)
Blind Men's Flowers are Green (1940)
Heraud, John Abraham (1799–1887)
poet and dramatist
The Legend of St Loy, with Other Poems (1820)
Tottenham (1820)
The Descent into Hell (1830)
Uxmal; Macée de Léodepart (1877)
Herbert, Sir Alan Patrick (1890–1971)
author and wit
The Bomber Gipsy, and Other Poems (1918)
Light the Lights (1945)
Herbert, Edward, 1st Baron Herbert of Cherbury (1583–1648)
philosopher, historian, and poet
The Life and Raigne of King Henry the Eighth (1649)
Occasional Verses of Edward Lord Herbert, Baron of Cherbury and Castle-Island (1665)
The Life of Edward Lord Herbert of Cherbury (1764)
Herbert, George (1593–1633)
poet
The Temple: Sacred poems and private ejaculations (1633)
Hygiasticon; or, The Right Course of Preserving Life and Health unto Extream Old Age (1634)
Outlandish Proverbs (1640)
Herbert's Remains (1652)
A Priest to the Temple; or, The Country Parson his Character, and Rule of Holy Life (1671)
Herbert, Mary, *née* Sidney, countess of Pembroke (1561–1621)
patroness and author
A Discourse of Life and Death . . . [with] *Antonius: A Tragoedie* (1592)
Herbert, Sir Thomas (1606–82)
traveller and author
A Relation of Some Yeares Travaile, Begunne Anno 1626 (1634)
Herbert, William, 3rd earl of Pembroke (1580–1630)
poet
Poems (1660)
Herd, David (1732–1810)
collector and editor
Ancient and Modern Scottish Songs (1776)
Herrick, Robert (1591–1674)
poet
Hesperides; or, The Works both Humane and Divine of Robert Herrick Esq. (1648)
Herschel, Sir John Frederick William (1792–1871)
astronomer
A Preliminary Discourse on the Study of Natural Philosophy (1830)
Hervey, James (1714–58)
devotional writer
Meditations Among the Tombs (1746)
Meditations and Contemplations (1748)
Theron and Aspasio; or, A Series of Dialogues and Letters (1755)
Hervey, John, 2nd Baron Hervey of Ickworth (1696–1743)
pamphleteer and memoir writer
Observations on the Writings of the Craftsman (1730)
An Epistle from a Nobleman to a Doctor of Divinity (1733)
Hewlett, Maurice Henry (1861–1923)
novelist and poet
A Masque of Dead Florentines (1895)
The Forest Lovers (1898)
Little Novels of Italy (1899)
Halfway House (1908)
Open Country (1909)
Rest Harrow (1910)
Heyer, Georgette ['Stella Martin'] (1902–74)
historical and detective fiction novelist
The Black Moth (1921)
Regency Buck (1935)
Heylyn, Peter (1600–62)
ecclesiastical writer
Microcosmus: or, A Little Description of the Great World (1621)
The History of the Sabbath (1636)
Cosmographie in Four Bookes (1652)
Ecclesia Vindicata; or, The Church of England Justified (1657)
Examen Historicum: Or, a discovery and examination of the mistakes, falsities, and defects in some modern histories (1659)
Ecclesia Restaurata; or, History of the Reformation of the Church of England (1661)
Cyprianus Anglicanus (1668)
Aerius Redivivus; or, The History of the Presbyterians (1670)
Heywood, Jasper (1535–98)
Jesuit, poet, and translator
The Sixt Tragedie of . . . Lucius Anneus Seneca, entituled Troas (1559)
The Seconde Tragedie of Seneca Entituled Thyestes (1560)
Hercules Furens (1561)
Heywood, John (1497?–1580?)
dramatist
Johan Johan (1533)
The Pardoner and the Friar (1533)
The Play of the Wether (1533)
A Play of Love (1534)
The Foure PP (1544?)
A Dialogue Conteinyng the Nomber in Effect of all the Proverbes in the Englishe Tongue (1546)
An Hundred Epigrammes (1550)
Two Hundred Epigrammes (1555)

The Spider and the Flie (1556)
A Breefe Balet Touching the Traytorous Takynge of Scarborow Castell (1557)
A Fourth [i.e. fifth] *Hundred of Epygrams* (1560)
A Ballad Against Slander and Detraction (1562)
Works (1562)

Heywood, Thomas (1574?–1641)
dramatist
The First and Second Partes of King Edward the Fourth (1599)
A Good Wife from a Bad (1602)
If You Know Not Me, You Know No Bodie; or, The Troubles of Queene Elizabeth (1605)
If You Know Not Me, You Know No Bodie [pt ii] (1606)
A Woman Kilde with Kindnesse (1607)
The Rape of Lucrece: A true Roman tragedie (1608)
Troia Britanica; or, Great Britaines Troy (1609)
The Golden Age; or, The Lives of Jupiter and Saturne, with the Defining of the Heathen Gods (1611)
An Apology for Actors (1612)
The Brazen Age (1613)
The Silver Age (1613)
The Foure Prentises of London. With the Conquest of Jerusalem (1615)
Gynaikeion; or, Nine Bookes of Various History. Concerninge Women (1624)
Art of Love (1625?)
A Funeral Elegie: Upon the much lamented death of . . . King James (1625)
Englands Elizabeth her Life and Troubles, During her Minoritie, from the Cradle to the Crowne (1631)
The Fair Maid of the West; or, A Girle Worth Gold (1631)
The Iron Age (1632)
The English Traveller (1633)
The Late Lancashire Witches: A well received comedy (1634)
A Mayden-head Well Lost (1634)
The Hierarchie of the Blessed Angells (1635)
Philocothonista; or, The Drunkard, Opened, Dissected, and Anatomized (1635)
A Challenge for Beautie (1636)
Loves Maistresse; or, The Queens Masque (1636)
A True Discourse of the Two Infamous Upstart Prophets, Richard Farnham Weaver of White-Chappell, and John Bull Weaver of Saint Butolphs Algate, now Prisoners (1636)
Pleasant Dialogues and Dramma's (1637)
The Royall King, and the Loyall Subject (1637)
A True Description of His Majesties Royall Ship (1637)
The Wise-Woman of Hogsdon: A comedie (1638)
The Exemplary Lives and Memorable Acts of Nine the Most Worthy Women of the World (1640)
The Life of Merlin, Sirnamed Ambrosius (1641)
Fortune by Land and Sea: A tragi-comedy (1655)

Hibbert, Eleanor Alice, *née* Burford ['Jean Plaidy', 'Victoria Holt', Philippa Carr'] (1906–93)
historical and romantic novelist
Together They Ride (1945)

Hichens, Robert Smythe (1864–1950)
novelist and short-story writer
The Green Carnation (1894)
The Garden of Allah (1904)

Higden, Ranulf (*d.* 1364)
Benedictine monk
Polycronicon (1482)

Higginson or Higgeson, Francis (1587–1630)
Puritan divine
New-Englands Plantation; or, A Short and True Description of the Commodities and Discommodities of that Countrey (1630)

Higgons, Bevil (1670–1735)
poet and dramatist
The Generous Conqueror; or, The Timely Discovery: A tragedy (1702)

Hill, Aaron (1685–1750)
poet and dramatist
The Celebrated Speeches of Ajax and Ulysses, for the Armour of Achilles (1708)
Elfrid; or, The Fair Inconstant: A tragedy (1710)
The Fatal Vision; or, The Fall of Siam: A tragedy (1716)
The Creation (1720)
The Fatal Extravagance: A tragedy . . . By Joseph Mitchell (1726)
Advice to the Poets (1731)
Athelwold: A tragedy (1731)
The Tragedy of Zara (1736)
Alzira: A tragedy (1736)
The Fanciad: An heroic poem (1743)
Gideon; or, The Patriot (1749)
Meropé: A tragedy (1749)

Hill, [John Edward] Christopher (1912–2003)
historian
Puritanism and Revolution (1958)
The Intellectual Origins of the English Revolution (1965)

Hill, Geoffrey (1932–)
poet and critic
For the Unfallen (1959)
King Log (1968)
Mercian Hymns (1971)
Somewhere is Such a Kingdom (1975)
Tenebrae (1978)
The Mystery of the Charity of Charles Péguy (1983)
Collected Poems (1985)
Speech! Speech! (2001)

Hill, Reginald (1936–)
crime writer
A Clubbable Woman (1970)

Hill, Rowland (1744–1833)
preacher and hymn-writer

Village Dialogues (1801)

Hill, Selima (1945–)
poet
Saying Hello at the Station (1984)
My Darling Camel (1988)
The Accumulation of Small Acts of Kindness (1989)
Trembling Hearts in the Bodies of Dogs (1994)
Bunny (2001)

Hill, Susan Elizabeth (1942–)
novelist, short-story writer, playwright, and children's writer
The Enclosure (1961)
Do Me a Favour (1963)
Gentleman and Ladies (1968)
A Change for the Better (1969)
I'm the King of the Castle (1970)
The Bird of Night (1972)
The Woman in Black (1983)
Air and Angels (1991)
Mrs De Winter (1993)
The Service of Clouds (1998)

Hill, Tobias (1970–)
poet and novelist
Midnight in the City of Clocks (1996)
Skin, and Other Stories (1997)
Zoo (1998)
Underground (1999)
The Love of Stones (2001)
The Cryptographer (2003)

Hilton, James (1900–54)
novelist
Catherine Herself (1920)
And Now Good-bye (1931)
Lost Horizon (1933)
Good-bye Mr Chips (1934)
To You, Mr Chips (1938)
Random Harvest (1941)

Hind or Hynd, John (*fl.* 1606)
romance writer
Lysimachus and Varrona (1604)
Eliosto Libidinoso (1606)

Hines, [Melvin] Barry (1939–)
novelist
A Kestrel for a Knave (1968)

Hoadly, Benjamin (1676–1761)
bishop successively of Bangor, Hereford, Salisbury, and Winchester
The Reasonableness of Conformity to the Church of England (1703)
The Happiness of the Present Establishment, and the Unhappiness of Absolute Monarchy (1708)
The Nature of the Kingdom, or Church of Christ (1717)
The Common Rights of Subjects, Defended (1719)
A Plain Account of the Nature and End of the Sacrament of the Lord's-Supper (1735)
Sixteen Sermons (1754)
Twenty Sermons (1755)

Hoadly, Benjamin, the younger (1706–57)
physician and dramatist
The Suspicious Husband: A comedy (1747)

'Hobbes, John Oliver' [Pearl Mary Teresa Craigie, *née* Richards] (1867–1906)
novelist and dramatist
The Sinner's Comedy (1892)
The School for Saints (1897)
Robert Orange (1900)

Hobbes, Thomas (1588–1679)
philosopher
Eight Books of the Peloponnesian Warre (1629)
A Briefe of the Art of Rhetorique (1637)
Humane Nature; or, The Fundamental Elements of Policie (1650)
De Corpore Politico; or, The Elements of Law, Moral & Politick (1650)
Leviathan; or, The Matter, Forme, & Power of a Common-Wealth Ecclesiasticall and Civill (1651)
Philosophicall Rudiments Concerning Government and Society (1651)
Of Libertie and Necessitie (1654)
Elements of Philosophy (1656)
The Questions Concerning Liberty, Necessity and Chance (1656)
Three Papers Presented to the Royal Society Against Dr Wallis (1671)
Homer's Iliads in English: To which may be added Homer's Odysses (1676)
A Letter About Liberty and Necessity (1676)
Decameron Physiologicum; or, Ten Dialogues of Natural Philosophy (1678)
Behemoth; or, An Epitome of the Civil Wars of England (1679)
An Historical Narration Concerning Heresie, and the Punishment Thereof (1680)
A Dialogue Between a Philosopher and a Student of the Common Laws of England (1681)
Tracts of Thomas Hobb's (1681)
Tracts of Mr Thomas Hobbs of Malmsbury (1682)

Hobhouse, John Cam (1786–1869)
politician, author, and friend of Byron
Imitations and Translations from the Ancient and Modern Classics (1809)
A Journey Through Albania (1813)
Some Account of a Long Life (1865)

Hobsbaum, Philip [Dennis] (1932–)
poet and critic
A Group Anthology (1963)

Hobsbawm, Eric John Ernest (1917–)
historian
Primitive Rebels (1959)
The Age of Revolution: Europe 1789–1848 (1962)
Labouring Men (1964)
The Age of Capital, 1848–1875 (1975)
The Age of Empire, 1875–1914 (1987)

Hoby, Sir Thomas (1530–66)
diplomat and translator
The Book of the Courtier (1561)

Hockley, W.B. (1792–1860)
novelist
Pandurang Hari; or, Memoirs of a Hindoo (1826)
Hodge, Jane Aiken (1917–)
historical novelist and biographer
Maulever Hall (1964)
Hogarde or Huggarde, Miles (*fl.* 1557)
shoemaker or hosier and poet
The Assault of the Sacrament of the Altar (1554)
Hogarth, William (1697–1764)
artist
The Analysis of Beauty (1753)
Hogg, James (1770–1835)
poet and author
Scottish Pastorals, Poems, Songs (1801)
The Forest Minstrel (1807)
The Mountain Bard (1807)
The Spy (1810)
The Queen's Wake (1813)
The Hunting of Badlewe (1814)
The Pilgrims of the Sun (1815)
Mador of the Moor (1816)
The Poetic Mirror; or, The Living Bards of Britain (1816)
Dramatic Tales (1817)
The Brownie of Bodsbeck, and Other Tales (1818)
Winter Evening Tales (1820)
The Poetical Works of James Hogg (1822)
The Royal Jubilee: A Scottish mask (1822)
The Three Perils of Man; or, War, Women and Witchcraft (1822)
The Three Perils of Woman; or, Love, Leasing and Jealousy (1823)
The Private Memoirs and Confessions of a Justified Sinner (1824)
Queen Hynde (1826)
The Shepherd's Calendar (1829)
Songs, by the Ettrick Shepherd (1831)
Altrive Tales (1832)
The Domestic Manners and Private Life of Sir Walter Scott (1834)
Tales of the Wars of Montrose (1835)
Hogg, Thomas Jefferson ['John Brown'] (1792–1862)
friend and biographer of Shelley
Memoirs of Prince Alexy Haimatoff (1813)
The Life of Percy Bysshe Shelley (1858)
Hoggart, Richard (1918–)
scholar and critic
The Uses of Literacy (1957)
A Local Habitation (1988)
A Sort of Clowning (1990)
An Imagined Life (1992)
Holcroft, Thomas (1745–1809)
novelist, poet, and dramatist
Alwyn; or, The Gentleman Comedian (1780)
Duplicity: A comedy (1781)
The Family Picture; or, Domestic Dialogues on Amiable and Interesting Subjects (1783)
Tales of the Castle; or, Stories of Instruction and Delight (1784)
Caroline of Lichtfield (1786)
Seduction: A comedy (1787)
Anna St Ives (1792)
The Road to Ruin: A comedy (1792)
The Adventures of Hugh Trevor [vols i–iii] (1794)
The Man of Ten Thousand: A comedy (1796)
The Adventures of Hugh Trevor [vols iv–vi] (1797)
He's Much to Blame: A comedy (1798)
A Tale of Mystery: A melodrama (1802)
Hear Both Sides: A comedy (1803)
The Lady of the Rock: A melo-drama (1805)
Memoirs of Bryan Perdue (1805)
Tales in Verse (1806)
Memoirs of the Late Thomas Holcroft (1816)
Holford, Margaret, later Mrs Septimus Hodson (1778–1852)
poet
Wallace; or, The Fight of Falkirk (1809)
Holinshed, Raphael or Ralph (*d.* 1580?)
chronicler
Chronicles (1577)
The First and Second Volumes of Chronicles (1587)
Holland, Philemon (1552–1637)
translator
The Romane Historie (1600)
The Historie of the World (1601)
Moralia (1603)
The History of Twelve Caesars, Emperours of Rome (1606)
The Roman Historie (1609)
Cyropaedia (1632)
Holland, Richard (*fl.* 1450)
poet
Buke of the Howlat (1508?)
Holland, Saba, *née* Smith, Lady Holland (1802–66)
biographer of her father, the Revd Sydney Smith
A Memoir of the Reverend Sydney Smith (1855)
Hollinghurst, Alan (1954–)
poet and novelist
Confidential Chats with Boys (1982)
The Swimming-Pool Library (1988)
The Folding Star (1994)
The Spell (1998)
Holme, Constance (1881–1955)
regional novelist
Crump Folk Going Home (1913)
The Lonely Plough (1914)
The Old Road From Spain (1916)
Holmes, Richard (1945–)
biographer
Shelley: The Pursuit (1974)
Holroyd, Michael de Courcy Fraser (1935–)
biographer and novelist
Lytton Strachey: The Unknown Years (1967)
Lytton Strachey: The Years of Achievement (1968)
Augustus John: The Years of Innocence (1974)
Augustus John: The Years of Experience (1975)
George Bernard Shaw: The Search for Love (1988)

George Bernard Shaw: The Pursuit of Power (1989)
George Bernard Shaw: The Lure of Fantasy (1991)
George Bernard Shaw: The Last Laugh (1992)
Lytton Strachey: The New Biography (1994)
Holt, Jane, *née* Wiseman (*fl.* 1701–17)
dramatist and poet
A Fairy Tale (1717)
Holtby, Winifred (1898–1935)
novelist and journalist
Anderby Wold (1923)
The Land of Green Ginger (1927)
South Riding (1936)
Home, Henry, Lord Kames (1696–1782)
Scottish judge and author
Essays Upon Several Subjects Concerning British Antiquities (1747)
Essays on the Principles of Morality and Natural Religion (1751)
Historical Law-Tracts (1758)
Introduction to the Art of Thinking (1761)
Elements of Criticism (1762)
Sketches of the History of Man (1774)
Loose Hints Upon Education (1781)
Home, John (1722–1808)
dramatist
Douglas: A tragedy (1757)
Agis: A tragedy (1758)
The Siege of Aquileia: A tragedy (1760)
The Fatal Discovery (1769)
Alonzo: A tragedy (1773)
Alfred: A tragedy (1778)
Home, William Douglas (1912–92)
playwright
The Dame of Sark (1976)
Hone, William (1780–1842)
political satirist and bookseller
The Political House that Jack Built (1819)
The Man in the Moon (1820)
The Queen's Matrimonial Ladder (1820)
The Political Showman—At Home! (1821)
Hood, Thomas (1799–1845)
poet and journalist
Odes and Addresses to Great People (1825)
Whims and Oddities (1826)
National Tales (1827)
The Plea of the Midsummer Fairies; Hero and Leander; Lycus the Centaur; and Other Poems (1827)
Whims and Oddities in Prose and Verse [2nd ser.] (1827)
The Epping Hunt (1829)
The Gem (1829)
The Comic Annual (1830)
The Dream of Eugene Aram: the Murderer (1831)
Tylney Hall (1834)
'The Song of the Shirt' (1843)
Whimsicalities (1844)
Poems (1846)
Hood, Thomas [known as Tom] (1835–74)
journalist, poet, and novelist
Pen and Pencil Pictures (1856)
Hook, Theodore Edward ['Alfred Allendale', 'Vicesimus Blinkinsop'] (1788–1841)
novelist and wit
The Man of Sorrow (1808)
Sayings and Doings (1824)
Sayings and Doings; or, Sketches from Life (1825)
Sayings and Doings; or, Sketches from Life (1828)
Maxwell (1830)
Gilbert Gurney (1836)
Jack Brag (1837)
Gurney Married (1838)
Precepts and Practice (1840)
Peregrine Bunce; or, Settled at Last (1842)
Hooker, Richard (1554–1600)
theologian
Of the Lawes of Ecclesiasticall Politie (1593)
[*Laws of Ecclesiastical Policy*] *The Fift Booke* (1597)
The Answere of Mr Richard Hooker to a Supplication Preferred by Mr Walter Travers to the Lords of the Privie Counsell (1612)
A Learned and Comfortable Sermon of the Certaintie and Perpetuitie of Faith in the Elect (1612)
A Learned Discourse of Justification, Workes, and How the Foundation of Faith is Overthrowne (1612)
A Learned Sermon of the Nature of Pride (1612)
A Remedie Against Sorrow and Feare (1612)
Two Sermons Upon Part of S. Judes Epistle (1614)
Hoole, John (1727–1803)
poet and dramatist
Cyrus: A tragedy (1768)
Timanthes: A tragedy (1770)
Hooper, John (*d.* 1555)
bishop of Gloucester and Worcester
A Godly Confession and Protestacion of the Christian Fayth (1550)
'Hope, Anthony' [Sir Anthony Hope Hawkins] (1863–1933)
novelist
A Man of Mark (1890)
The Dolly Dialogues (1894)
The Prisoner of Zenda (1894)
Rupert of Hentzau (1898)
Hope, Thomas (1770?–1831)
author and collector
Anastasius; or, Memoirs of a Greek (1819)
Hopkins, Charles (1664?–1700)
poet and dramatist
Epistolary Poems (1694)
Pyrrhus King of Epirus: A tragedy (1695)
Neglected Virtue; or, The Unhappy Conquerour (1696)
Boadicea Queen of Britain: A tragedy (1697)
White-hall; or, The Court of England (1698)
Friendship Improv'd; or, The Female Warriour: A tragedy (1700)

Hopkins, Gerard Manley (1844–89)
poet
Poems of Gerard Manley Hopkins (1918)
Poems of Gerard Manley Hopkins (1930)
Hornby, Nick (1957–)
novelist
Fever Pitch (1992)
High Fidelity (1995)
About a Boy (1998)
How to be Good (2001)
Horne, Richard Henry or Hengist ['Mrs Fairstar'] (1803–84)
poet
Exposition of the False Medium and Barriers Excluding Men of Genius From the Public (1833)
Orion: An epic poem (1843)
A New Spirit of the Age (1844)
The Dreamer and the Worker (1851)
Hornung, Ernest William (1866–1921)
novelist and short-story writer
A Bride from the Bush (1890)
The Amateur Cracksman (1899)
The Black Mask (1901)
A Thief in the Night (1905)
Mr Justice Raffles (1909)
Horovitz, Frances Margaret, *née* Hooker (1938–83)
poet
Water Over Stone (1980)
Snow Light, Water Light (1983)
Horovitz, Michael (1935–)
poet, translator, and editor
Children of Albion: Poetry of the 'Underground' in Britain (1969)
The Wolverhampton Wanderer: An epic of Britannia (1971)
Horsley, Samuel (1733–1806)
bishop of St Asaph and controversialist
Letters from the Archdeacon of St Albans, in Reply to Dr Priestley (1784)
Houghton, [William] Stanley (1881–1913)
playwright
Hindle Wakes (1912)
Household, Geofrey Edward West (1900–88)
novelist and short-story writer
The Third Hour (1937)
Rogue Male (1939)
Rogue Justice (1982)
Housman, Alfred Edward (1859–1936)
poet and classical scholar
A Shropshire Lad (1896)
Last Poems (1922)
The Name and Nature of Poetry (1933)
More Poems (1936)
Collected Poems (1939)
Housman, Laurence (1865–1959)
poet, novelist, and dramatist
Green Arras (1896)
Followers of St Francis (1923)
Little Plays of St Francis (1935)
Houston, Libby (1941–)
poet
Necessity (1988)
Howard, Edward (1624–c.1700)
dramatist and poet, brother of Sir Robert Howard
The Usurper: A tragedy (1668)
The Womens Conquest: A tragi-comedy (1671)
Howard, Edward (1793?–1841)
nautical novelist
Rattlin the Reefer (1836)
The Old Commodore (1837)
Outward Bound; or, A Merchant's Adventures (1838)
Howard, Elizabeth Jane, *née* Liddon (1923–)
novelist and short-story writer
The Beautiful Visit (1950)
After Julius (1965)
Getting it Right (1982)
The Light Years (1990)
Marking Time (1991)
Confusion (1993)
Casting Off (1995)
Howard, Henry, earl of Surrey (1517?–47)
poet
An Excellent Epitaffe of Syr Thomas Wyat (1545?)
The Fourth Boke of Virgill, Intreating of the Love Betwene Aeneas & Dido (1554)
Tottel's Miscellany (1557)
Certain Bokes of Virgiles Aeneis (1557)
Howard, James (*b.* 1630?)
dramatist
All Mistaken; or, The Mad Couple: A comedy (1672)
The English Monsieur: A comedy (1674)
Howard, John (1726–90)
philanthropist and penal reformer
The State of the Prisons in England and Wales (1777)
Howard, Philip, earl of Arundel (1557–95)
first earl of Arundel
A Foure-Fould Meditation, of the Foure Last Things (1606)
Howard, Sir Robert (1626–98)
dramatist, poet, and brother-in-law of John Dryden
Poems (1660)
Four New Plays (1665)
The Duell of the Staggs (1668)
The Great Favourite; or, The Duke of Lerma (1668)
Howard, Thomas (*fl.* 1663)
fiction writer
The History of the Seven Wise Mistrisses of Rome (1663)
Howatch, Susan Elizabeth, *née* Sturt (1940–)
novelist
Penmarric (1971)
Glittering Images (1987)
Glamorous Powers (1988)

Ultimate Prizes (1989)
Scandalous Risks (1990)
Mystical Paths (1992)
Absolute Truths (1994)
The High Flyer (2001)

Howell, Ann, *née* Hilditch (*fl.* 1787–97)
novelist
Rosa de Montmorien (1787)

Howell, James (1594?–1666)
pamphleteer and poet
Dendrologia: Dodona's grove; or, The vocall forrest (1640)
Epistolae Ho-Elianae: Familiar letters domestic and forren (1645)
A Fourth Volume of Familiar Letters (1655)
Londinopolis: An historicall discourse or perlustration of the City of London (1657)
Lexicon Tetraglotton: An English–French–Italian–Spanish dictionary (1660)

Howell, Thomas (*fl.* 1568)
poet
The Arbor of Amitie (1568)

Howie, John (1735–93)
biographer
Biographia Scoticana (1775)

Howitt, Mary, *née* Botham (1799–1888)
author and translator
The Forest Minstrel, and Other Poems (1823)
The Desolation of Eyam; The Emigrant: A Tale of the American Woods, and Other Poems (1827)
The Seven Temptations (1834)
Wood Leighton; or, A Year in the Country (1836)

Hubert, Sir Francis (*c.*1568–1629)
poet
The Historie of Edward the Second Surnamed Carnarvan (1629)

Huddesford, George (1749–1809)
satirical poet
Salmagundi: A miscellaneous combination of original poetry (1791)
Bubble and Squeak (1799)

Hudson, William Henry ['Henry Harford'] (1841–1922)
novelist and nature writer
The Purple Land that England Lost (1885)
The Naturalist in La Plata (1892)
Idle Days in Patagonia (1893)
Nature in Downland (1900)
El Ombú, and Other Tales (1902)
Green Mansions (1904)
A Shepherd's Life (1910)

Hughes, Anne (*fl.* 1787–95)
novelist
Caroline; or, The Diversities of Fortune (1787)

Hughes, David John (1930–)
novelist
The Pork Butcher (1984)
But for Bunter (1985)
The Little Book (1996)

Hughes, John (1677–1720)
poet and dramatist
The Triumph of Peace (1698)
The Court of Neptune (1699)
Calypso and Telemachus: An opera (1712)
Letters of Abelard and Heloise (1713)
Apollo and Daphne: A masque (1716)
The Siege of Damascus: A tragedy (1720)
Poems on Several Occasions (1735)

Hughes, Richard Arthur Warren (1900–76)
novelist, playwright, and poet
A High Wind in Jamaica (1929)
The Wooden Shepherdess (1973)

Hughes, Ted [Edward James Hughes] (1930–98)
Poet Laureate, playwright, editor, and translator
The Hawk in the Rain (1957)
Lupercal (1960)
Woodwo (1967)
The Iron Man (1968)
Oedipus (1969)
The Coming of the Kings, and Other Plays (1970)
Crow (1970)
Selected Poems 1957–1967 (1972)
Prometheus on his Crag (1973)
Gaudete (1977)
Cave Birds (1978)
Moon-Bells, and Other Poems (1978)
Moortown (1979)
Remains of Elmet (1979)
Under the North Star (1981)
Selected Poems 1957–1981 (1982)
River (1983)
Moon-Whales (1988)
Tales of the Early World (1988)
Wolfwatching (1989)
Rain-Charm for the Duchy (1992)
Shakespeare and the Goddess of Complete Being (1992)
Winter Pollen: Occasional prose (1994)
New Selected Poems 1957–1994 (1995)
Tales from Ovid (1997)
Birthday Letters (1998)
Phedre (1998)
Aeschylus: The Oresteia (1999)
Alcestis (1999)

Hughes, Thomas (1822–96)
novelist and biographer
Tom Brown's Schooldays (1857)
Tom Brown at Oxford (1861)

Huish, Robert (1777–1850)
novelist
The Sorcerer (1795)

Hull, Thomas (1728–1808)
actor, dramatist, and author
Pharnaces: An opera (1765)
The Fairy Favour: A masque (1766)
The Royal Merchant: An opera (1768)
Henry the Second; or, The Fall of Rosamond: A tragedy (1774)
Edward and Eleonora: A tragedy (1775)
Elisha; or, The Woman of Shunem (1801)

Hulme, Thomas Ernest (1883–1917)
philosopher, poet, and aesthetician
The Complete Poetical Works (1912)
An Introduction to Metaphysics (1913)
Hume or Home, Alexander (1560?–1609)
Scottish poet
Ane Treatise of Conscience (1594)
Hymnes, or Sacred Songs (1599)
Hume, David (1711–76)
philosopher and historian
A Treatise of Human Nature (1739)
An Abstract of a Book Lately Published; Entituled, A Treatise of Human Nature (1740)
Essays Moral and Political [vol. i] (1741)
Essays Moral and Political [vol. ii] (1742)
Philosophical Essays Concerning Human Understanding (1748)
Three Essays, Moral and Political (1748)
An Enquiry Concerning the Principles of Morals (1751)
Political Discourses (1752)
Essays and Treatises on Several Subjects (1753)
The History of Great Britain (1754)
The History of Great Britain [vol. ii] (1756)
Four Dissertations (1757)
The History of England, Under the House of Tudor (1759)
The History of England, from the Invasion of Julius Caesar to the Accession of Henry VII (1761)
The Life of David Hume (1777)
Dialogues Concerning Natural Religion (1779)
Hume, Fergus[on] Wright (1859–1932)
novelist
The Mystery of a Hansom Cab (1886)
Humphreys, Eliza Margaret Jane, later von Booth, *née* Gollan ['Rita'] (1856–1938)
novelist
Sheba (1889)
A Husband of No Importance (1894)
Souls (1903)
Hunt, [James Henry] Leigh (1784–1859)
poet, essayist, and journalist
Juvenilia (1801)
Classic Tales, Serious and Lively (1807)
Critical Essays on the Performers of the London Theatres (1807)
The Prince of Wales v The Examiner (1812)
The Feast of the Poets (1814)
The Descent of Liberty: A masque (1815)
The Story of Rimini (1816)
Foliage; or, Poems Original and Translated (1818)
Literary Pocket-Book (1818)
Hero and Leander, and Bacchus and Ariadne (1819)
Amyntas (1820)
The Months (1821)
Ultra-Crepidarius (1823)
Bacchus in Tuscany (1825)
Lord Byron and Some of his Contemporaries (1828)
Christianism; or, Belief and Unbelief Reconciled (1832)
The Poetical Works of Leigh Hunt (1832)
Captain Sword and Captain Pen (1835)
The Palfrey (1842)
Imagination and Fancy (1844)
Men, Women, and Books (1847)
A Jar of Honey from Mount Hybla (1848)
The Town (1848)
Readings for Railways (1849)
The Autobiography of Leigh Hunt (1850)
Table Talk (1851)
Stories in Verse (1855)
Hunt, [Isobel] Violet (1866–1942)
society hostess and author
The Maiden's Progress (1894)
A Hard Woman (1895)
Zeppelin Nights (1916)
Hunton, Philip (1604?–82)
political author
A Treatise of Monarchie (1643)
Hurd, Richard (1720–1808)
prelate and author
Moral and Political Dialogues (1759)
Letters on Chivalry and Romance (1762)
An Introduction to the Study of Prophecies Concerning the Christian Church (1772)
Hurdis, James (1763–1801)
poet and dramatist
The Village Curate (1788)
Sir Thomas More: A tragedy (1792)
Hutcheson, Francis (1695–1747)
philosopher
An Inquiry into the Original of Our Ideas of Beauty and Virtue (1725)
An Essay on the Nature and Conduct of the Passions and Affections (1728)
Reflections Upon Laughter (1750)
A System of Moral Philosophy (1755)
Hutchinson, Lucy (1620–76?)
biographer
Memoirs of the Life of Colonel Hutchinson (1806)
Hutton, Henry (*fl.* 1619)
satirical poet
Follie's Anatomie; or, Satyres and Satiricall Epigrams (1619)
Hutton, Richard Holt (1826–97)
theologian, journalist, and critic
Essays Theological and Literary (1871)
Huxley, Aldous Leonard (1894–1963)
novelist, short-story writer, poet, and essayist
The Burning Wheel (1916)
The Defeat of Youth, and Other Poems (1918)
Leda (1920)
Limbo (1920)
Crome Yellow (1921)
Mortal Coils (1922)
Antic Hay (1923)
Little Mexican, and Other Stories (1924)

Those Barren Leaves (1925)
Point Counter Point (1928)
Arabia Infelix, and Other Poems (1929)
Holy Face, and Other Essays (1929)
Brief Candles (1930)
The Cicadas, and Other Poems (1931)
The World of Light: A comedy (1931)
Brave New World (1932)
Eyeless in Gaza (1936)
After Many a Summer (1939)
The Art of Seeing (1943)
Time Must Have a Stop (1944)
The Gioconda Smile (1948)
Ape and Essence (1949)
Themes and Variations (1950)
The Devils of Loudon (1952)
The Doors of Perception (1954)
The Genius and the Goddess (1955)
Adonis and the Alphabet, and Other Essays (1956)
Heaven and Hell (1956)
Brave New World Revisited (1959)
Island (1962)

Huxley, Elspeth Josceline (1907–)
author
The Flame Trees of Thika (1959)

Huxley, Thomas Henry (1825–95)
scientist and author
On the Educational Value of the Natural History Sciences (1854)
Evidence as to Man's Place in Nature (1863)
On Our Knowledge of the Causes of the Phenomena of Organic Nature (1863)
Science and Culture, and Other Essays (1881)
Evolution and Ethics (1893)

Hyde, Douglas (1860–1949)
poet, literary historian, and statesman
Beside the Fire: A collection of Irish and Gaelic folk stories (1890)
A Literary History of Ireland (1899)

Hyde, Edward, 1st earl of Clarendon (1609–74)
statesman and historian
Transcendent and Multiplied Rebellion and Treason Discovered by the Laws of the Land (1645)
Animadversions upon a Book intituled, Fanaticism Fanatically Imputed to the Catholick Church (1673)
A Brief View and Survey of the Dangerous and Pernicious Errors to Church and State, in Mr Hobbes's book, entitled Leviathan (1676)
Two Letters Written by the Right Honourable Edward Earl of Clarendon (1680?)
The History of the Rebellion and Civil Wars in England (1702)
The History of the Rebellion and Civil Wars in Ireland (1720)
An Appendix to the History of the Grand Rebellion (1724)
A Collection of Several Tracts (1727)
The Life of Edward Earl of Clarendon Written by Himself (1759)

Image, Selwyn (1849–1930)
artist and poet
Poems and Carols (1894)

Imlay, Gilbert (*fl.* 1793)
author and soldier
The Emigrants; or, The History of an Expatriated Family (1793)

Inchbald, Elizabeth, *née* Simpson (1753–1821)
novelist, dramatist, and actress
Appearance is Against Them: A farce (1785)
I'll Tell You What: A comedy (1786)
A Mogul Tale; or, The Descent of the Balloon (1788)
Such Things Are (1788)
A Simple Story (1791)
Every One Has His Fault: A comedy (1793)
Nature and Art (1796)
Wives as They Were, and Maids as They Are: A comedy (1797)
Lovers' Vows (1798)
The Wise Man of the East (1799)
To Marry or not to Marry: A comedy (1805)
The British Theatre (1808)
The Modern Theatre (1811)

Inge, William Ralph (1860–1954)
theologian and author
Christian Mysticism (1899)
Outspoken Essays [1st ser.] (1919)
Outspoken Essays [2nd ser.] (1922)

Ingelend, Thomas (*fl.* 1560)
interlude writer
The Disobedient Child (1570?)

Ingelow, Jean (1820–97)
poet, novelist, short-story writer, and children's writer
A Rhyming Chronicle of Incidents and Feelings (1850)
Poems (1863)
A Story of Doom, and Other Poems (1867)
Mopsa the Fairy (1869)
Off the Skelligs (1872)
Fated to be Free (1875)
Poems (1880)
Poems: Third Series (1885)

Ireland, Samuel (*d.* 1800)
engraver and author
Miscellaneous Papers and Legal Instruments Under the Hand and Seal of William Shakespeare (1795)
Mr Ireland's Vindication . . . of the Supposed Shakspeare MSS (1796)

Ireland, [Samuel] William Henry (1777–1835)
forger
An Authentic Account of the Shaksperian Manuscripts (1796)
Vortigern: An historical tragedy (1799)
The Confessions of William Henry Ireland (1805)

Irwin, Henry Crossly ['Mark Time'] (1848–1924)
Indian civil servant and author
A Derelict Empire (1912)
Irwin, Margaret Emma Faith (1889–1967)
historical novelist and short-story writer
Still She Wished For Company (1924)
Madame Fears the Dark (1935)
Bloodstock, and Other Stories (1954)
Isherwood, Christopher William Bradshaw (1904–86)
novelist and playwright
All the Conspirators (1928)
The Memorial (1932)
Mr Norris Changes Trains (1935)
Sally Bowles (1937)
Lions and Shadows (1938)
Goodbye to Berlin (1939)
The Berlin Stories (1946)
Prater Violet (1946)
The Condor and the Cows (1949)
The World in the Evening (1954)
Down There on a Visit (1962)
A Single Man (1964)
Exhumations (1966)
A Meeting by the River (1967)
Christopher and his Kind 1929–39 (1977)
Ishiguro, Kazuo (1954–)
novelist
A Pale View of Hills (1982)
An Artist of the Floating World (1986)
The Remains of the Day (1989)
The Unconsoled (1995)

Jacks, Lawrence Pearsall (1860–1955)
philosopher, theological writer, and author
All Men are Ghosts (1913)
The Heroes of Smokeover (1926)
The Last Legend of Smokeover (1939)
Jackson, Holbrook (1874–1948)
literary historian and critic
Bernard Shaw (1907)
The Eighteen Nineties (1913)
Jacob, Giles (1686–1744)
compiler of the *Poetical Register*
The Poetical Register; or, The Lives and Characters of the English Dramatick Poets (1719)
Jacob, Hildebrand (1693–1739)
poet and dramatist
The Curious Maid (1720)
Bedlam (1722)
Brutus the Trojan, Founder of the British Empire (1735)
The Works of Hildebrand Jacob (1735)
Jacobs, William Wymark (1863–1943)
short-story writer, novelist, and playwright
Many Cargoes (1896)
The Lady of the Barge, and Other Stories (1902)
Jacobson, Howard Eric (1942–)
novelist
Coming From Behind (1983)
Peeping Tom (1984)
Redback (1986)
The Very Model of a Man (1992)
No More Mister Nice Guy (1998)
Getting Licked (1999)
Who's Sorry Now? (2002)
Jago, Richard (1715–81)
poet
Edge-Hill; or, The Rural Prospect Delineated and Moralised (1767)
Labour and Genius; or, The Mill-Stream, and the Cascade (1768)
Poems, Moral and Descriptive (1784)
James, George Payne Rainsford (1799–1860)
novelist
Richelieu (1829)
Darnley; or, The Field of the Cloth of Gold (1830)
De l'Orme (1830)
Philip Augustus; or, The Brothers in Arms (1831)
Henry Masterton; or, The Adventures of a Young Cavalier (1832)
The Robber (1838)
The Smuggler (1845)
The Castle of Ehrenstein (1847)
James, Henry (1843–1916)
novelist, short-story writer, and essayist
A Passionate Pilgrim, and Other Tales (1875)
The Europeans (1878)
Daisy Miller; An International Episode; Four Meetings (1879)
The American (1879)
Roderick Hudson (1879)
The Madonna of the Future, and Other Tales (1879)
Confidence (1879)
Washington Square; The Pension Beaurepas; A Bundle of Letters (1881)
The Portrait of a Lady (1881)
The Bostonians (1886)
The Princess Casamassima (1886)
The Reverberator (1888)
The Aspern Papers (1888)
A London Life (1889)
The Tragic Muse (1890)
The Lesson of the Master (1892)
The Real Thing, and Other Tales (1893)
The Private Life (1893)
Terminations (1895)
Embarrassments (1896)
The Other House (1896)
The Spoils of Poynton (1897)
What Maisie Knew (1897)
The Two Magics ['The Turn of the Screw', 'Covering End'] (1898)
The Awkward Age (1899)
The Soft Side (1900)
The Wings of the Dove (1902)
The Better Sort (1903)
The Ambassadors (1903)

The Golden Bowl (1905)
The Finer Grain (1910)
The Outcry (1911)
The Sense of the Past (1917)
The Ivory Tower (1917)

James VI, King of Scotland, afterwards James I, King of England (1566–1625)
The Essayes of a Prentise, in the Divine Art of Poesie (1584)
His Majesties Poeticall Exercises at Vacant Houres (1591)
Daemonologie (1597)
The True Lawe of Free Monarchies; or, The Reciprock and Mutuall Dutie Betwixt a Free King, and his Naturall Subjects (1598)
Basilikon Doron (1599)
His Majesties Lepanto: or, Heroicall Song (1603)
The True Lawe of Free Monarchies; or, The Reciprock and Mutuall Dutie Betwixt a Free King, and his Naturall Subjects (1603)
A Counter-blaste to Tobacco (1604)
Triplici Nodo, Triplex Cuneus; or, An Apologie for the Oath of Allegiance (1607)
Works (1616)
The Psalmes of King David (1631)

James, Montague Rhodes (1862–1936)
scholar and ghost-story writer
Ghost Stories of an Antiquary (1904)
More Ghost Stories of an Antiquary (1911)
A Thin Ghost, and Others (1919)
A Warning to the Curious, and Other Ghost Stories (1925)

James, Phyllis Dorothy, *née* White, Baroness James of Holland Park (1920–)
crime novelist
Cover Her Face (1962)
Unnatural Causes (1967)
Shroud for a Nightingale (1971)
An Unsuitable Job for a Woman (1972)
Death of an Expert Witness (1977)
The Skull Beneath the Skin (1982)
A Taste for Death (1986)
Devices and Desires (1989)
Original Sin (1994)
Death in Holy Orders (2001)

Jameson, Anna Brownell, *née* Murphy (1794–1860)
author, art critic, and feminist
Characteristics of Women, Moral, Poetical and Historical (1832)

Jameson, [Margaret] Storm (1897–1986)
novelist, poet, and critic
The Pot Boils (1919)
The Lovely Ship (1927)
Company Parade (1934)

Jamie, Kathleen (1962–)
poet
Black Spiders (1982)
The Way We Live (1987)
The Queen of Sheba (1994)
Jizzen (1999)
Mr and Mrs Scotland Are Dead (2002)

Janeway, James (1636?–74)
non-conformist divine
A Token for Children (1672)

Jea, John (*b.* 1773)
former slave
The Life, History and Unparalleled Sufferings of John Jea, the African Preacher (1814)

Jefferies, [John] Richard (1848–87)
naturalist and novelist
The Scarlet Shawl (1874)
The World's End (1877)
The Gamekeeper at Home (1878)
The Amateur Poacher (1879)
Wild Life in a Southern County (1879)
Hodge and his Masters (1880)
Bevis: The story of a boy (1882)
The Story of My Heart (1883)
Red Deer (1884)
The Life of the Fields (1884)
After London; or, Wild England (1885)
Amaryllis at the Fair (1887)
Field and Hedgerow (1889)

Jeffrey, Francis, Lord Jeffrey (1773–1850)
critic and political writer
Contributions to the Edinburgh Review (1844)

Jellicoe, [Patricia] Ann (1927–)
playwright and director
The Knack (1962)

Jemmat, Catherine, *née* Yeo (1714–66)
poet
Miscellanies in Prose and Verse (1766)

Jenkins, Alan Fitzgerald (1955–)
poet and editor
In the Hot-House (1988)
Greenheart (1990)
Harm (1994)

Jenkins, [Margaret] Elizabeth Heald (1905–)
novelist and biographer
Harriet (1933)
The Tortoise and the Hare (1954)

Jennens, Charles (1700–73)
librettist, dramatist, and editor
Messiah (1742)
Belshazzar: An oratorio (1745)

Jenner, Charles (1736–74)
poet and novelist
Poems (1766)
The Placid Man; or, Memoirs of Sir Charles Beville (1769)
Town Eclogues (1772)

Jennings, Elizabeth Joan Cecil (1926–2001)
poet
A Way of Looking (1955)
A Sense of the World (1958)
Song For a Birth or a Death, and Other Poems (1961)
Recoveries (1964)
The Mind has Mountains (1966)
Growing Points (1975)

Consequently I Rejoice (1977)
Moments of Grace (1979)
A Dream of Spring (1980)
Extending the Territory (1985)
Collected Poems 1953–1985 (1986)
Times and Seasons (1992)
Familiar Spirits (1994)
In the Meantime (1997)
Timely Issues (2001)
New Collected Poems (2002)

Jenyns, Soame (1704–87)
poet and author
The Art of Dancing (1729)
The Modern Fine Gentleman (1746)
The Modern Fine Lady (1751)
A Free Inquiry into the Nature and Origin of Evil (1757)
A View of the Internal Evidence of the Christian Religion (1776)

Jephson, Robert (1736–1803)
dramatist and poet
Braganza: A tragedy (1775)
The Law of Lombardy: A tragedy (1779)
The Count of Narbonne: A tragedy (1781)
Julia; or, The Italian Lover: A tragedy (1787)
Conspiracy: A tragedy (1796)

Jerningham, Edward (1737–1812)
poet and dramatist
Andromache to Pyrrhus: An heroick epistle (1761)
The Nunnery: An elegy in imitation of the Elegy in a Churchyard (1762)
The Nun (1764)
An Elegy Written Among the Ruins of an Abbey (1765)
Amabella (1768)
Faldoni and Teresa (1773)
The Fall of Mexico (1775)
Stone Henge (1792)
The Siege of Berwick: A tragedy (1794)

Jerome, Jerome Klapka (1859–1927)
novelist, playwright, and journalist
The Idle Thoughts of an Idle Fellow (1886)
Three Men in a Boat (To Say Nothing of the Dog) (1889)
Diary of a Pilgrimage (and Six Essays) (1891)
Told After Supper (1891)
Sketches in Lavender, Blue, and Green (1897)
The Second Thoughts of an Idle Fellow (1898)
Three Men on the Bummel (1900)
The Passing of the Third Floor Back, and Other Stories (1907)

Jerrold, Douglas William ['John Jackdaw'] (1803–57)
dramatist, humorist, and journalist
Black-Eyed Susan; or, All in the Downs (1829)
Cakes and Ale (1842)
Punch's Letters to His Son (1843)
Mrs Caudle's Curtain Lectures (1846)
A Man Made of Money (1849)

Jesse, Fryniwyd Margaret Tennyson (1888–1958)
novelist and playwright
The Lacquer Lady (1929)
A Pin to See the Peepshow (1934)

Jewel, John (1522–71)
bishop of Salisbury
Apologia ecclesiae anglicanae (1562)
A Defence of the Apologie of the Churche of Englande (1567)

Jewsbury, Geraldine Endsor (1812–80)
novelist and woman of letters
Zoe: The history of two lives (1845)
The Half-Sisters (1848)
Marian Withers (1851)
The History of an Adopted Child (1853)
Constance Herbert (1855)
The Sorrows of Gentility (1856)
Right or Wrong (1859)

Jhabvala, Ruth Prawer (1927–)
novelist, screenwriter, and short-story writer
To Whom She Will (1955)
The Nature of Passion (1956)
Esmond in India (1958)
The Householder (1960)
A New Dominion (1972)
Heat and Dust (1975)
How I Became a Holy Mother, and Other Stories (1976)
In Search of Love and Beauty (1983)
Three Continents (1987)
Poet and Dancer (1993)
Shards of Memory (1995)
East into Upper East (1998)

Joad, Cyril Edwin Mitchinson (1891–1953)
philosopher
Essays in Common Sense Philosophy (1919)

Joceline or Jocelin, Elizabeth (1596–1622)
author
The Mothers Legacie, to her Unborne Childe (1624)

Johns, William Earle (1893–1968)
creator of Biggles
The Camels Are Coming (1932)
Worrals of the WAAF (1941)

Johnson, Bryan Stanley William (1933–73)
novelist, playwright, and poet
Travelling People (1963)
Albert Angelo (1964)
Trawl (1966)

Johnson, Charles (1679–1748)
dramatist
Love and Liberty: A tragedy (1709)
The Force of Friendship: A tragedy (1710)
The Successful Pyrate (1713)
The Victim: A tragedy (1714)
The Country Lasses; or, The Custom of the Manor (1715)
The Cobler of Preston (1716)
The Sultaness: A tragedy (1717)
Love in a Forest: A comedy (1723)
The Village Opera (1729)
The Tragedy of Medea (1731)

Johnson, Edward (1599?–1672)
historian of New England
A History of New-England (1653)
Johnson, James (c.1750–1811)
Scottish engraver and publisher
The Scots Musical Museum (1787)
Johnson, John (*fl.* 1641)
romance writer
The Academy of Love (1641)
Johnson, Linton Kwesi (1952–)
Jamaican-born dub poet
Voices of the Living and the Dead (1974)
Dread, Beat and' Blood (1975)
Inglan is a Bitch (1980)
Tings an' Times (1991)
Johnson, Lionel Pigot (1867–1902)
poet and author
The Art of Thomas Hardy (1894)
Poems (1895)
Ireland, with Other Poems (1897)
Post Liminium (1911)
Johnson, Pamela Hansford (1912–81)
novelist, playwright, and critic
This Bed Thy Centre (1935)
Blessed Above Women (1936)
Girdle of Venus (1939)
Too Dear For My Possessing (1940)
An Avenue of Stone (1947)
An Impossible Marriage (1954)
The Unspeakable Skipton (1959)
An Error of Judgement (1962)
Night and Silence, Who is Here? (1963)
Cork Street, Next to the Hatter's (1965)
Johnson, Richard (1573–1659?)
poet and romance writer
The Nine Worthies of London (1592)
The Seven Champions of Christendom (1596)
The Second Part of the Famous History of the Seaven Champions of Christendome (1597)
A Crowne-Garland of Goulden Roses, Gathered Out of Englands Royal Garden (1612)
The History of Tom Thumbe, the Little (1621)
Johnson, Samuel (1649–1702)
Whig divine
Julian the Apostate (1682)
Johnson, Samuel (1709–84)
lexicographer, poet, novelist, and critic
A Voyage to Abyssinia (1735)
London (1738)
An Account of the Life of John Philip Barretier (1744)
An Account of the Life of Mr Richard Savage (1744)
Miscellaneous Observations on the Tragedy of Macbeth (1745)
Proposals for Printing a New Edition of the Plays of William Shakespear (1745)
The Plan of a Dictionary of the English Language (1747)
Irene: A tragedy (1749)
The Vanity of Human Wishes: The tenth satire of Juvenal, imitated (1749)
A Dictionary of the English Language (1755)
The Idler (1758)
The Prince of Abissinia (1759)
The False Alarm (1770)
Thoughts on the Late Transactions Respecting Falkland's Islands (1771)
The Patriot (1774)
A Journey to the Western Islands of Scotland (1775)
Taxation No Tyranny (1775)
Prefaces, Biographical and Critical, to the Works of the English Poets (1779)
The Beauties of Johnson [pt i] (1781)
The Poetical Works of Samuel Johnson (1785)
Prayers and Meditations (1785)
The Works of Samuel Johnson (1785)
Letters To and From the Late Samuel Johnson (1788)
The Celebrated Letter from Samuel Johnson to Philip Dormer Stanhope (1790)
An Account of the Life of Dr Samuel Johnson, Written by Himself (1805)
Johnston, Jennifer Prudence (1930–)
novelist and playwright
The Old Jest (1979)
Fool's Sanctuary (1987)
The Invisible Worm (1991)
Johnstone, Charles (1719?–1800?)
novelist
Chrysal; or, The Adventures of a Guinea [vols i, ii] (1760)
The Reverie; or, A Flight to the Paradise of Fools (1762)
The History of Arsaces, Prince of Betlis (1774)
The Pilgrim; or, A Picture of Life (1775)
The History of John Juniper, Esq, alias Juniper Jack (1781)
The Adventures of Anthony Varnish; or, A Peep at the Manners of Society (1786)
Jones, Henry (1721–70)
poet and dramatist
Poems on Several Occasions (1749)
The Earl of Essex: A tragedy (1753)
Merit: A poem (1753)
The Relief; or, Day Thoughts (1754)
Kew Garden (1767)
Jones, Henry Arthur (1851–1929)
dramatist
The Silver King (1882)
Jones, Inigo (1573–1652)
architect and stage designer
Britannia Triumphans: A masque (1638)
Jones, Mary (1707–78)
poet
Miscellanies in Prose and Verse (1750)
Jones, Robert (*fl.* 1616)
composer, poet, and lutenist
The First Booke of Songes or Ayres of Foure Parts (1601)

The Second Booke of Songes and Ayres (1601)
Ultimum Vale (1605)
The First Set of Madrigals (1607)
A Musicall Dreame; or, The Fourth Booke of Ayres (1609)
The Muses Gardin for Delights; or, The Fift Book of Ayres (1610)

Jones, Samuel (*d.* 1732)
poet
Poetical Miscellanies on Several Occasions (1714)

Jones, Sir William (1746–94)
poet, orientalist, and jurist
Poems (1772)

Jonson, Ben[jamin] (1572–1637)
dramatist and poet
Every Man Out of his Humor (1600)
Every Man in His Humor (1601)
The Fountaine of Selfe-love. Or Cynthias Revels (1601)
Poetaster or The Arraignment (1602)
Sejanus his Fall (1605)
Hymenaei; or, The Solemnities of Masque, and Barriers (1606)
Volpone (1607)
The Characters of Two Royall Masques. The One of Blacknesse, the Other of Beautie (1608)
The Case is Altered (1609)
The Masque of Queenes (1609)
Catiline his Conspiracy (1611)
The Alchemist (1612)
Works (1616)
Epicoene; or, The Silent Woman: A comedie (1620)
The Masque of Augures (1622)
Neptunes Triumph for the Returne of Albion (1624)
The Fortunate Isles and their Union (1625)
Bartholomew Fayre; The Divell is an Asse; The Staple of Newes (1631)
Chloridia: Rites to Chloris and Her Nymphs: Performed in a masque, at Court (1631)
Loves Triumph Through Callipolis: Performed in a masque at Court (1631)
The New Inne; or, The Light Heart (1631)
Art of Poetry (1640)
The Workes of Benjamin Jonson (1640)

Jordan, Neil (1950–)
Irish short-story writer, novelist, and film director
Night in Tunisia, and Other Stories (1976)

Jordan, Thomas (1612?–85)
poet and dramatist
Poeticall Varieties; or, Varietie of Fancies (1637)
A Royal Arbor of Loyal Poesie (1663)
Money is an Asse: A comedy (1668)

Jortin, John (1698–1770)
ecclesiastical historian and critic
Remarks on Spenser's Poems (1734)
Remarks on Ecclesiastical History (1751)

Joseph, Jenny [Jenefer Ruth Joseph] (1932–)
poet
Rose in the Afternoon, and Other Poems (1974)
The Thinking Heart (1978)
Beyond Descartes (1983)

Josselyn, John (*fl.* 1630–75)
traveller
New-Englands Rarities (1672)

Jourdain or Jourdan, Silvester (*d.* 1650)
author
A Discovery of the Barmudas, otherwise called the Ile of Divels (1610)

Joyce, James Augustine Aloysius (1882–1941)
novelist and poet
Chamber Music (1907)
Dubliners (1914)
Portrait of the Artist as a Young Man (1916)
Exiles (1918)
Ulysses (1922)
Pomes Penyeach (1927)
Anna Livia Plurabelle (1930)
Collected Poems (1936)
Ulysses (1936)
Finnegans Wake (1939)
Stephen Hero (1944)
The Letters of James Joyce [vol. i] (1957)
Ulysses (1986)

Joye, George (*d.* 1553)
Protestant controversialist and translator of the Bible
The Psalter of David in Englishe (1530)
An Apologye Made to Satisfye W. Tindale (1535)
A Compendyouse Somme of the Very Christen Relygyon (1535)
The Unitie and Scisme of the Olde Chirche (1543)
A Present Consolacion for the Sufferers of Persecution (1544)

Judd, Alan (1946–)
novelist and biographer
A Breed of Heroes (1981)
Short of Glory (1984)
Legacy (2001)

Kane, Sarah (1971–99)
playwright
Blasted; and, Phaedra's Love (1996)
Cleansed (1998)
4:48 Psychosis (2000)

'Kavan, Anna' [Helen Emily Woods] (1901–68)
novelist and short-story writer
Asylum Piece, and Other Stories (1940)
I am Lazarus (1945)
Ice (1967)

Kavanagh, Julia (1824–77)
novelist and essayist
Madeleine (1848)

Kavanagh, Patrick Joseph (1904–67)
Irish poet and novelist
Ploughman, and Other Poems (1936)
The Great Hunger (1942)
A Soul For Sale (1947)
Collected Poems (1964)
Collected Pruse [sic] (1967)

Kay, Jackie (1961–)
poet, novelist, and playwright
The Adoption Papers (1991)
Other Lovers (1993)
Off Colour (1998)
Trumpet (1998)

Kaye, Mary Margaret (1908–2004)
novelist
Shadow of the Moon (1957)
The Far Pavilions (1978)

Kaye-Smith, Sheila (1887–1956)
novelist
The Tramping Methodist (1908)
Joanna Godden (1921)
The End of the House of Alard (1923)

Keach, Benjamin (1640–1704)
Baptist divine
War with the Devil; or, The Young Mans Conflict with the Powers of Darkness (1673)
The Glorious Lover: A divine poem (1679)
The Travels of True Godliness (1683)
The Progress of Sin (1684)
Spiritual Melody (1691)

Keane, Molly [Mary Nesta Keane] ['M.J. Farrell'] (1904–96)
Irish novelist and playwright
Good Behaviour (1981)

Keary, Annie (1825–79)
novelist and children's author
The Heroes of Asgard (1857)

Keate, George (1729–97)
miscellaneous author
The Alps (1763)
The Ruins of Netley Abbey (1764)
The Monument in Arcadia (1773)
An Epistle to Angelica Kauffmann (1781)
Poetical Works (1781)
The Distressed Poet (1787)

Keats, John (1795–1821)
poet
Poems (1817)
Endymion: A poetic romance (1818)
Lamia, Isabella, The Eve of St Agnes, and Other Poems (1820)
The Poetical Works of John Keats (1854)

Keble, John (1792–1866)
clergyman and poet
The Christian Year (1827)
National Apostasy (1833)
Tracts for the Times [Nos 4, 13, 40, 52, 54, 57, 60] (1834)
Tracts for the Times [No. 89] (1841)
Lyra Innocentium: Thoughts in verse on Christian children (1846)
Sermons, Academical and Occasional (1847)
Sermons, Occasional and Parochial (1868)
Miscellaneous Poems (1869)
Sermons for the Christian Year (1875)

Keith, George (1639?–1716)
'Christian Quaker' and missionary
The Deism of William Penn, and his Brethren (1699)
The Standard of the Quakers Examined; or, An Answer to the Apology of Robert Barclay (1702)

Kelly, Hugh (1739–77)
Irish dramatist and author
Memoirs of a Magdalen; or, The History of Louisa Mildmay (1766)
False Delicacy: A comedy (1768)
A Word to the Wise: A comedy (1770)
Clementina: A tragedy (1771)
The School for Wives: A comedy (1774)

Kelly, Isabella, later Hedgeland (*c.*1759–1857)
novelist and poet
Madeleine; or, The Castle of Montgomery (1794)
The Ruins of Avondale Priory (1796)

Kelly, John (*b. c.*1684)
novelist
Pamela's Conduct in High Life (1741)

Kelman, James (1946–)
Scottish novelist and short-story writer
Not Not While the Giro (1983)
The Busconductor Hines (1984)
A Chancer (1985)
Greyhound for Breakfast (1987)
A Disaffection (1989)
The Burn (1991)
How Late it Was, How Late (1994)
'And the Judges Said' (2002)

Kemble, Frances Anne, later Butler (1809–93)
actress, dramatist, and poet
Francis the First: An historical drama (1832)
Journal (1835)
Plays (1863)
Records of Later Life (1882)
Further Records (1890)

Kemble, John Philip (1757–1823)
actor and dramatic adaptor
King Henry V; or, The Conquest of France: A tragedy (1789)

Kemp, William (*fl.* 1600)
comic actor and dancer
Kemps Nine Daies Wonder: Performed in a daunce from London to Norwich (1600)

Kempe, Margery (*c.*1373–*c.*1439)
mystic
The Book of Margery Kempe (1501)

Ken, Thomas (1637–1711)
bishop of Bath and Wells
A Manual of Prayers for the Use of Scholars of Winchester College (1674)
An Exposition on the Church-Catechism (1685)

Kennedy, Alison Louise (1965–)
Scottish novelist and short-story writer
Night Geometry and the Garscadden Trains (1990)
Looking For the Possible Dance (1993)
Now That You're Back (1994)
So I Am Glad (1995)
Original Bliss (1997)

Everything You Need (1999)
Indelible Acts (2002)
Kennedy, John (*fl.* 1626)
romance writer
Calanthrop and Lucilla (1626)
Kennedy, Margaret Moore (1896–1967)
novelist
The Constant Nymph (1924)
The Fool of the Family (1930)
Troy Chimneys (1953)
Kennett, White (1660–1728)
prelate and author
A Dialogue Between Two Friends: Occasioned by the late revolution (1689)
The Christian Scholar (1704)
The History of England from the Commencement of the Reign of Charles I to the End of William III (1706)
A Vindication of the Church and Clergy of England (1709)
Kenrick, William ['Mary Midnight'] (1725?–79)
poet and dramatist
The Town (1748)
The Whole Duty of Woman (1753)
Epistles to Lorenzo (1756)
Eloisa; or, A Series of Original Letters (1761)
Emilius and Sophia; or A New System of Education (1762)
A Review of Doctor Johnson's New Edition of Shakespeare (1765)
Love in the Suds: A Town Eclogue (1772)
The Duellist: A comedy (1773)
Ker, William Paton (1855–1923)
literary scholar and critic
Epic and Romance (1897)
Kermode, Sir [John] Frank (1919–)
literary scholar and critic
The Romantic Image (1957)
Kerr, Robert (1755–1813)
scientific writer and translator
A General History and Collection of Voyages and Travels (1811)
Keyes, Sidney Arthur Kilworth (1922–43)
poet
The Iron Laurel (1942)
The Cruel Solstice (1943)
Keynes, John Maynard, 1st Baron Keynes (1883–1946)
economist
The Economic Consequences of the Peace (1919)
A Revision of the Treaty (1922)
A Treatise on Money (1930)
Killigrew, Anne (1660–85)
poet
Poems by Mrs Anne Killigrew (1686)
Killigrew, Henry (1613–1700)
divine and author
The Conspiracy: A tragedy (1638)
Killigrew, Thomas (1612–83)
dramatist
The Prisoners, and Claracilla: Two tragae-comedies (1641)
Comedies, and Tragedies (1664)
Killigrew, Sir William (1606–95)
dramatist and author
Pandora: A comedy (1664)
Three Playes (1665)
The Imperial Tragedy (1669)
Mid-night Thoughts (1681)
Mid-night and Daily Thoughts (1694)
Kimber, Edward (1719–69)
novelist and compiler
The Life and Adventures of Joe Thompson (1750)
King, Francis Henry ['Frank Cauldwell'] (1923–)
novelist, short-story writer, playwright, and editor
The Dividing Stream (1951)
The Dark Glasses (1954)
The Man on the Rock (1957)
The Japanese Umbrella, and Other Stories (1964)
A Domestic Animal (1970)
The Needle (1975)
Act of Darkness (1982)
Visiting Cards (1990)
Dead Letters (1997)
King, Henry (1592–1669)
bishop of Chichester
A Groane at the Funerall of that Incomparable and Glorious Monarch, Charles the First (1649)
The Psalmes of David (1651)
Poems, Elegies, Paradoxes, and Sonnets (1657)
An Elegy Upon the Most Incomparable K. Charls the I (1659)
A Sermon Preached the 30th of January at White-Hall 1664 [i.e. 1665] (1665)
King, William (1650–1729)
archbishop of Dublin
De Origine Mali (1702)
An Essay on the Origin of Evil (1731)
King, William (1663–1712)
poet and miscellaneous writer
Dialogues of the Dead (1699)
The Furmetary (1699)
The Transactioneer With Some of his Philosophical Fancies (1700)
The Art of Cookery (1708)
Miscellanies in Prose and Verse (1709)
An Historical Account of the Heathen Gods and Heroes (1711)
The Persian and the Turkish Tales, Compleat (1714)
King, William (1685–1763)
principal of St Mary Hall, Oxford, and satirical author
The Toast: An epic poem (1732)
Kinglake, Alexander William (1809–91)
historian

Eothen; or, Traces of Travel Brought Home from the East (1844)
The Invasion of the Crimea (1863)
Kingsley, Charles (1819–75)
poet, novelist, and controversialist
The Saint's Tragedy (1848)
Alton Locke, Tailor and Poet (1850)
Yeast: A problem (1851)
Sermons on National Subjects (1852)
Hypatia; or, New Foes with an Old Face (1853)
Sermons on National Subjects (1854)
Glaucus; or, The Wonders of the Shore (1855)
Westward Ho!; or, The Voyages and Adventures of Sir Amyas Leigh (1855)
The Heroes; or, Greek Fairy Tales for My Children (1856)
Two Years Ago (1857)
Andromeda, and Other Poems (1858)
The Water-Babies (1863)
'What, Then, Does Dr Newman Mean?' (1864)
Hereward the Wake (1866)
Kingsley, Henry (1830–76)
novelist
The Recollections of Geoffrey Hamlyn (1859)
Ravenshoe (1862)
Kingsley, Mary Henrietta (1862–1900)
travel writer
Travels in West Africa (1897)
'Kingsmill, Hugh' [Hugh Kingsmill Lunn] (1889–1949)
anthologist, biographer, novelist, critic, and parodist
The Will to Love (1919)
Kingston, William Henry Giles (1814–80)
boys' novelist
Peter the Whaler (1851)
The Cruise of the 'Frolic'; or, Yachting Adventures of Barnaby Brine, Esq. (1860)
Kinsella, Thomas (1928–)
Irish poet, translator, and editor
The Starlit Eye (1952)
Poems (1956)
Another September (1958)
Downstream (1962)
Wormwood (1966)
Nightwalker, and Other Poems (1967)
Notes From the Land of the Dead (1972)
Poems 1956–1973 (1980)
Songs of the Psyche (1985)
Out of Ireland (1987)
Madonna, and Other Poems (1991)
From Centre City (1994)
Kipling, [Joseph] Rudyard (1865–1936)
novelist, short-story writer, and poet
Departmental Ditties, and Other Verses (1886)
Soldiers Three (1888)
The Story of the Gadsbys (1888)
In Black and White (1888)
Under the Deodars (1888)
The Phantom 'Rickshaw, and Other Tales (1888)
Wee Willie Winkie, and Other Child Stories (1888)
Plain Tales From the Hills (1888)
Life's Handicap (1891)
The Light That Failed (1891)
Barrack-Room Ballads, and Other Verses (1892)
Many Inventions (1893)
The Jungle Book (1894)
The Second Jungle Book (1895)
Soldiers Three; The Story of the Gadsbys; In Black and White (1895)
Wee Willie Winkie; Under the Deodars; The Phantom 'Rickshaw (1895)
The Seven Seas (1896)
'Captains Courageous': A story of the Grand Banks (1897)
The Day's Work (1898)
Stalky & Co. (1899)
From Sea to Sea, and Other Sketches (1900)
Kim (1901)
Just So Stories for Little Children (1902)
The Five Nations (1903)
Traffics and Discoveries (1904)
Puck of Pook's Hill (1906)
Actions and Reactions (1909)
Rewards and Fairies (1910)
Collected Verse (1912)
A Diversity of Creatures (1917)
The Years Between (1919)
Debits and Credits (1926)
Limits and Renewals (1932)
Something of Myself (1937)
Kirke, John (*d.* 1643)
dramatist
The Seven Champions of Christendome (1638)
Kirkman, Francis (1632–*c.*1680)
bookseller and author
An Exact Catalogue of all the Comedies, Tragedies, Tragi-Comedies, Opera's, Masks, Pastorals and Interludes Printed or Published, Till 1680 (1680)
Kirkup, James Falconer (1918–)
poet, playwright, and travel writer
The Drowned Sailor, and Other Poems (1947)
The Submerged Village, and Other Poems (1951)
A Correct Compassion, and Other Poems (1952)
The Descent into the Cave, and Other Poems (1957)
The Prodigal Son (1957)
Refusal to Conform (1963)
Paper Windows (1968)
The Body Servant (1971)
No More Hiroshimas (1982)
Shooting Stars (1992)
Blue Bamboo (1993)
Knevet, Ralph (1602–72)
poet and author
Rhodon and Isis: A pastorall (1631)
Funerall Elegies (1637)
Knight, Ellis Cornelia (1758–1837)
author

Dinarbas (1790)
Marcus Flaminius; or, A View of the Military, Political and Social Life of the Romans (1792)
Knight, George Richard Wilson (1897–1985)
Shakespeare scholar and critic
The Wheel of Fire (1930)
The Imperial Theme (1931)
The Starlit Dome (1941)
The Crown of Life (1947)
The Mutual Flame (1955)
Knight, Henrietta St John, Lady Luxborough (1699–1756)
poet, landscape designer, and correspondent
Letters Written to William Shenstone (1775)
Knight, Richard Payne (1750–1824)
numismatist
The Landscape (1794)
An Analytical Enquiry into the Principles of Taste (1805)
Knights, Lionel Charles (1906–97)
Shakespeare critic
How Many Children Had Lady Macbeth? (1933)
Explorations (1946)
Further Explorations (1965)
Knolles, Richard (1550?–1610)
historian
The Generall Historie of the Turkes (1603)
Knott, Edward, name assumed after 1602 by Matthew Wilson (1582–1656)
Jesuit
Mercy & Truth; or, Charity Maintayned by Catholiques (1634)
Knowles, James Sheridan (1784–1862)
dramatist and novelist
Virginius; or, The Liberation of Rome (1820)
Caius Gracchus: A tragedy (1823)
William Tell (1825)
The Hunchback (1832)
The Love-Chase: A comedy (1837)
Dramatic Works (1841)
The Secretary (1843)
Knox, Edmund George Valpy ['Evoe'] (1881–1971)
humorist
The Brazen Lyre (1911)
Knox, John (1505–72)
Scottish reformer and historian
An Admonition or Warning (1554)
A Percel of the VI Psalme Expounded (1554)
The First Blast of the Trumpet Against the Monstruous Regiment of Women (1558)
A Fort for the Afflicted (1580)
A Notable and Comfortable Exposition Upon the Fourth of Mathew (1583)
History of the Reformation of Religion Within the Realm of Scotland (1587)
Knox, [the Rt Revd Monsignor] Ronald Arbuthnott (1888–1957)
priest and author
Naboth's Vineyard in Pawn (1913)
Absolute and Abitofhell (1915)
Broadcast Minds (1932)
The Holy Bible (1936)
Let Dons Delight (1939)
God and the Atom (1945)
The New Testament of Our Lord and Saviour Jesus Christ (1945)
The Old Testament (1949)
The Holy Bible (1955)
Knox, Vicesimus (1752–1821)
essayist
Essays, Moral and Literary (1779)
Elegant Extracts; or, Useful and Entertaining Passages in Prose (1783)
Winter Evenings; or, Lucubrations on Life and Letters (1788)
Koestler, Arthur (1905–83)
Anglo-Hungarian novelist and journalist
Darkness at Noon (1940)
Arrow in the Blue (1952)
The Invisible Writing (1954)
The Ghost in the Machine (1967)
Kunzru, Hari (1969)
novelist
The Impressionist (2002)
Kureishi, Hanif (1954–)
screenwriter and novelist
My Beautiful Launderette (1986)
The Buddha of Suburbia (1990)
Gabriel's Gift (2001)
The Body (2002)
Dreaming and Scheming (2002)
Kyd, Thomas (1558–94)
dramatist
The Spanish Tragedie (1592)
Cornelia (1594)
Kyffin, Maurice (*d.* 1599)
translator
Andria (1588)
Kynaston, Sir Francis (1587–1642)
poet
Leoline and Sydanis (1642)

Lacy, John (1615–81)
dramatist
The Dumb Lady; or, The Farrier Made Physician (1672)
The Old Troop; or, Monsieur Raggou (1672)
Sir Hercules Buffoon; or, The Poetical Squire (1684)
Sauny the Scot; or, The Taming of the Shrew: A comedy (1698)
Laing, Ronald David (1927–89)
psychiatrist and author
The Divided Self (1960)
The Self and Others (1961)
Lamb, Lady Caroline (1785–1828)
novelist and poet
Glenarvon (1816)
Verses from Glenarvon (1819)
Graham Hamilton (1822)
Ada Reis (1823)

Lamb, Charles ['Elia'] (1775–1834)
poet, dramatist, critic, and essayist
Blank Verse (1798)
A Tale of Rosamund Gray and Old Blind Margaret (1798)
John Woodvil: A tragedy (1802)
The King and Queen of Hearts (1805)
Tales from Shakespear (1807)
The Adventures of Ulysses (1808)
Specimens of English Dramatic Poets, who Lived about the Time of Shakespeare (1808)
Mrs Leicester's School (1808)
Poetry for Children, Entirely Original (1809)
The First Book of Poetry (1810)
Prince Dorus; or, Flattery Put Out of Countenance (1811)
The Works of Charles Lamb (1818)
Elia [1st ser.] (1823)
Elia: Second series (1828)
Satan in Search of a Wife (1831)
The Last Essays of Elia (1833)
Recollections of Christ's Hospital (1835)
The Letters of Charles Lamb (1837)
Eliana (1864)

Lambarde, William (1536–1601)
historian of Kent
A Perambulation of Kent (1576)

Lancaster, Sir Osbert (1908–86)
cartoonist and author
Pillar to Post (1938)
Homes, Sweet Homes (1939)
Classical Landscape with Figures (1947)
Drayneflete Revealed (1949)

Landon, Letitia Elizabeth ['L.E.L.'] (1802–38)
poet and novelist
The Fate of Adelaide, and Other Poems (1821)
The Improvisatrice, and Other Poems (1824)
The Troubador, Catalogue of Pictures, and Historical Sketches (1825)
The Golden Violet, and Other Poems (1827)
The Venetian Bracelet; The Lost Pleiad; A History of the Lyre; and Other Poems (1828)
Romance and Reality (1831)
The Vow of the Peacock, and Other Poems (1835)
Traits and Trials of Early Life (1836)
Ethel Churchill; or, The Two Brides (1837)
Duty and Inclination (1838)
Lady Anne Granard; or, Keeping Up Appearances (1842)

Landor, Walter Savage ['Calvus'] (1775–1864)
poet and author
Moral Epistle to Earl Stanhope (1795)
The Poems of Walter Savage Landor (1795)
Gebir (1798)
Poems from the Arabic and Persian (1800)
Poetry by the author of Gebir (1802)
Simonidea (1806)
Count Julian: A tragedy (1812)
Letters Addressed to Lord Liverpool, and the Parliament (1814)
Imaginary Conversations of Literary Men and Statesmen [vols i, ii] (1824)
Imaginary Conversations of Literary Men and Statesmen [vol. iii] (1828)
Imaginary Conversations of Literary Men and Statesmen: Second Series [vols iv, v] (1829)
Gebir, Count Julian and Other Poems (1831)
Citation and Examination of Wil. Shakespeare, (1834)
The Letters of a Conservative (1836)
Pericles and Aspasia (1836)
A Satire on Satirists, and Admonition to Detractors (1836)
The Pentameron and Pentalogia (1837)
Andrea of Hungary, and Giovanna of Naples (1839)
Fra Rupert (1840)
The Hellenics of Walter Savage Landor (1847)
Imaginary Conversation of King Carlo-Alberto and the Duchess Belgioso (1848)
The Italics of Walter Savage Landor (1848)
Imaginary Conversations of Greeks and Romans (1853)
The Last Fruit off an Old Tree (1853)
Antony and Octavius (1856)
Dry Sticks, Fagoted (1858)
Heroic Idyls with Additional Poems (1863)

Laneham, Robert (*fl.* 1575)
author (and actor?)
A Letter (1575)

Lang, Andrew (1844–1912)
poet, scholar, and folklorist
Ballads and Lyrics of Old France, with Other Poems (1872)
XXII Ballades in Blue China (1880)
Custom and Myth (1884)
Rhymes à la Mode (1884)
Myth, Ritual and Religion (1887)
Grass of Parnassus (1888)
The Blue Fairy Book (1889)
Letters on Literature (1889)
Cock Lane and Common Sense (1894)

Langbaine, Gerard, the younger (1656–92)
dramatic critic and biographer
A New Catalogue of English Plays (1687)
An Account of the English Dramatick Poets (1691)
The Lives and Characters of the English Dramatick Poets (1699)

Langhorne, John (1735–79)
poet and novelist
Letters on Religious Retirement, Melancholy and Enthusiasm (1762)
Solyman and Almena: An oriental tale (1762)
The Letters that Passed Between Theodosius and Constantia (1763)
The Fables of Flora (1771)
Letters to Eleonora (1771)

Langland, William (1330?–1400?)
poet
Piers Plowman (1550)

Langley, Thomas (*d.* 1581)
canon of Winchester
An Abridgement of the Notable Worke of Polidore Vergile (1546)
Lanyer or Lanier, Aemelia, *née* Bassano (1569–1645)
poet
Salve Deus Rex Judaeorum (1611)
Larkin, Philip Arthur (1922–85)
poet, novelist, and editor
The North Ship (1945)
Jill (1946)
A Girl in Winter (1947)
The Less Deceived (1955)
The Whitsun Weddings (1964)
The Oxford Book of Twentieth-Century Verse (1973)
High Windows (1974)
Femmes Damnées (1978)
Required Writing (1983)
Collected Poems (1988)
Selected Letters (1992)
Further Requirements (2001)
Trouble at Willow Gables, and Other Fictions (2002)
Laski, Harold Joseph (1893–1950)
political scientist
A Grammar of Politics (1925)
Laski, Marghanita (1915–88)
novelist and critic
Love on the Supertax (1944)
The Victorian Chaise-Longue (1953)
Lathom, Francis (1777–1832)
novelist and dramatist
The Castle of Ollada (1795)
Latimer, Hugh (1485?–1555)
bishop of Worcester
A Notable Sermon [on the plough] *of Maister Hughe Latemer* (1548)
The Fyrste Sermon of Mayster Hughe Latimer (1549)
Twenty-seven Sermons Preached by the Ryght Reverende . . . Maister Hugh Latimer (1562)
Latter, Mary (1725–77)
poet and miscellaneous author
The Miscellaneous Works (1759)
The Siege of Jerusalem, by Titus Vespasian: A tragedy (1763)
Liberty and Interest (1764)
Laud, William (1573–1645)
archbishop of Canterbury
A Relation of the Conference betweene William Lawd . . . and Mr Fisher the Jesuite (1639)
Seven Sermons Preached upon Severall Occasions (1651)
A Summarie of Devotions (1667)
The History of the Troubles and Tryal of William Laud (1695)
Lavin, Mary (1912–96)
Irish short-story writer and novelist
Tales From Bective Bridge (1943)
The Long Ago (1944)
The Becker Wives (1946)
Mary O'Grady (1950)
The Shrine, and Other Stories (1977)
A Family Likeness (1985)
Law, William (1686–1761)
theological and mystical writer
The Bishop of Bangor's Late Sermon (1717)
Remarks Upon a Late Book, entituled, The Fable of the Bees (1724)
The Absolute Unlawfulness of the Stage-Entertainment Fully Demonstrated (1726)
A Practical Treatise upon Christian Perfection (1726)
A Serious Call to a Devout and Holy Life (1729)
The Case of Reason; or, Natural Religion, Fairly Stated (1731)
A Demonstration of the Gross and Fundamental Errors of a Late Book (1737)
The Grounds and Reasons of Christian Regeneration (1739)
An Earnest and Serious Answer to Dr Trapp's Discourse (1740)
An Appeal to all that Doubt, or Disbelieve the Truths of the Gospel (1740)
The Spirit of Prayer (1749)
The Spirit of Love (1752)
The Way to Divine Knowledge (1752)
The Second Part of the Spirit of Love (1754)
Of Justification by Faith and Works (1760)
Lawes, Henry (1596–1662)
musician
Ayres and Dialogues, for One, Two, and Three Voyces (1653)
The Second Book of Ayres, and Dialogues, for One, Two, and Three Voyces (1655)
Ayres, and Dialogues, for One, Two, and Three Voyces (1658)
Lawless, Emily (1845–1913)
Irish novelist and poet
A Chelsea Householder (1882)
Hurrish (1886)
Lawrence, David Herbert (1885–1930)
novelist, poet, and short-story writer
The White Peacock (1911)
The Trespasser (1912)
Love Poems and Others (1913)
Sons and Lovers (1913)
The Prussian Officer, and Other Stories (1914)
The Rainbow (1915)
Amores (1916)
New Poems (1918)
The Lost Girl (1920)
Women in Love (1921)
Aaron's Rod (1922)
The Ladybird; The Fox; The Captain's Doll (1923)
Psychoanalysis and the Unconscious (1923)
Fantasia of the Unconscious (1923)
Kangaroo (1923)

Birds, Beasts and Flowers (1923)
England, My England (1924)
The Plumed Serpent (Quetzalcoatl) (1926)
Mornings in Mexico (1927)
The Woman Who Rode Away, and Other Stories (1928)
Lady Chatterley's Lover (1928)
Collected Poems (1928)
Lady Chatterley's Lover (1929)
Pansies (1929)
Pornography and Obscenity (1929)
Nettles (1930)
A Propos of Lady Chatterley's Lover (1930)
The Triumph of the Machine (1930)
The Virgin and the Gypsy (1930)
Love Among the Haystacks (1930)
The Man Who Died (1931)
Lady Chatterley's Lover (1932)
Etruscan Places (1932)
The Letters of D.H. Lawrence (1932)
The Lovely Lady (1933)
Last Poems (1933)
The Plays of D.H. Lawrence (1933)
Lady Chatterley's Lover (1933)
Reflections on the Death of a Porcupine, and Other Essays (1934)
Phoenix (1936)
Lady Chatterley's Lover (1960)

Lawrence, George Alfred (1827–76)
novelist
Guy Livingstone; or, Thorough (1857)

Lawrence, Thomas Edward ['J.H. Ross', 'T.E. Shaw'] (1888–1935)
soldier and author
Seven Pillars of Wisdom (1926)
Revolt in the Desert (1927)
Seven Pillars of Wisdom (1935)

Lead or Leade, Jane, *née* Ward (1623–1704)
mystic and autobiographer
The Heavenly Cloud Now Breaking (1681)
The Revelation of Revelations (1683)
The Enochian Walks with God (1694)
A Fountain of Gardens (1697)

Leapor, Mary (1722–46)
poet
Poems upon Several Occasions (1748)
Poems Upon Several Occasions (1751)

Lear, Edward ['Derry Down Derry'] (1812–88)
artist and nonsense poet
A Book of Nonsense (1846)
Journals of a Landscape Painter in Albania, Illyria etc (1851)
Journals of a Landscape Painter in Southern Calabria (1852)
Journal of a Landscape Painter in Corsica (1870)
Nonsense Songs, Stories, Botany, and Alphabets (1870)
More Nonsense, Pictures, Rhymes, Botany, etc. (1871)
Laughable Lyrics (1877)

Leavis, Frank Raymond (1895–1978)
literary critic, teacher, and educationist
New Bearings in English Poetry (1932)
Revaluation: Tradition and development in English poetry (1936)
The Great Tradition (1948)
The Common Pursuit (1952)

'Le Carré, John' [David John Moore Cornwell] (1931–)
writer of spy fiction
Call for the Dead (1961)
The Spy Who Came in From the Cold (1963)
The Looking-Glass War (1965)
Tinker, Tailor, Soldier, Spy (1974)
The Honourable Schoolboy (1977)
Smiley's People (1980)
The Little Drummer Girl (1983)
A Perfect Spy (1986)
The Russia House (1989)
The Secret Pilgrim (1991)
Our Game (1995)
Single & Single (1999)
The Constant Gardener (2000)

Lecky, William Edward Hartpole (1838–1903)
historian
The Religious Tendencies of the Age (1860)
History of the Rise and Influence of the Spirit of Rationalism in Europe (1865)
A History of England in the Eighteenth Century (1878)

Lee, Harriet (1756–1851)
novelist
The Errors of Innocence (1786)
Canterbury Tales for the Year 1797 (1797)

'Lee, Holme' [Harriet Parr] (1828–1900)
novelist
Gilbert Massenger (1855)

Lee, Laurie (1914–97)
poet and author
The Sun My Monument (1944)
The Bloom of Candles (1947)
My Many-Coated Man (1955)
A Rose for Winter (1955)
Cider With Rosie (1959)
As I Walked Out One Midsummer Morning (1969)
I Can't Stay Long (1975)
A Moment of War (1991)

Lee, Nathaniel (1649?–92)
dramatist
The Tragedy of Nero, Emperour of Rome (1675)
Gloriana; or, The Court of Augustus Cæsar (1676)
Sophonisba; or, Hannibal's Overthrow: A tragedy (1676)
The Rival Queens; or, The Death of Alexander the Great (1677)
Mithridates King of Pontus: A tragedy (1678)
Cæsar Borgia; Son of Pope Alexander the Sixth: A tragedy (1680)
Theodosius; or, The Force of Love: A tragedy (1680)

Lucius Junius Brutus, Father of his Country: A tragedy (1681)
Constantine the Great: A tragedy (1684)
On the Death of Mrs Behn (1689)
The Princess of Cleve (1689)
The Massacre of Paris: A tragedy (1690)

Lee, Sir Sidney (1859–1926)
biographer and literary historian
Queen Victoria (1902)

Lee, Sophia (1750–1824)
poet, novelist, and dramatist
The Chapter of Accidents: A comedy (1780)
The Recess; or, A Tale of Other Times [vol. i] (1783)
A Hermit's Tale (1787)
Almeyda, Queen of Granada: A tragedy (1796)
The Life of a Lover (1804)

'Lee, Vernon' [Violet Paget] (1856–1935)
critic, novelist, and short-story writer
Studies of the Eighteenth Century in Italy (1880)
Hauntings (1890)
Pope Jacynth, and Other Fantastic Tales (1904)

Le Fanu, Joseph Sheridan ['Charles de Cresseron'] (1814–73)
novelist, and short-story writer
The Cock and Anchor (1845)
The Fortunes of Colonel Torlogh O'Brien (1847)
Ghost Stories and Tales of Mystery (1851)
The House by the Churchyard (1863)
Uncle Silas (1864)
Wylder's Hand (1864)
Guy Deverell (1865)
All in the Dark (1866)
The Tenants of Malory (1867)
Haunted Lives (1868)
A Lost Name (1868)
The Wyvern Mystery (1869)
Checkmate (1871)
Chronicles of Golden Friars (1871)
The Rose and the Key (1871)
In a Glass Darkly (1872)
Willing to Die (1873)
The Purcell Papers (1880)
Madam Crowl's Ghost, and Other Tales of Mystery (1923)

Le Gallienne, Richard (1866–1947)
poet and essayist
My Lady's Sonnets (1887)
English Poems (1892)
The Religion of a Literary Man (1893)
Robert Louis Stevenson, and Other Poems (1895)
The Quest of the Golden Girl (1896)
Young Lives (1899)
Sleeping Beauty, and Other Prose Fancies (1900)
The Life Romantic (1901)
New Poems (1910)
The Lonely Dancer, and Other Poems (1913)
The Silk-Hat Soldier, and Other Poems (1915)
Vanishing Roads, and Other Essays (1915)

Lehmann, [Rudolph] John Frederick (1907–87)
poet and editor
A Garden Revisited, and Other Poems (1931)
The Noise of History (1934)
The Sphere of Glass, and Other Poems (1944)
The Age of the Dragon (1951)
The Whispering Gallery (1955)
I Am My Brother (1960)
The Ample Proposition (1966)

Lehmann, Rosamond Nina (1901–90)
novelist
Dusty Answer (1927)
Invitation to the Waltz (1932)
The Ballad and the Source (1944)
The Echoing Grove (1953)

Leigh, Richard (1649 or 50–1728)
poet and author
The Censure of the Rota: On Mr Driden's Conquest of Granada (1673)
The Transproser Rehears'd (1673)
Poems, upon Several Occasions, and, to Several Persons (1675)

Leighton, Marie Flora Barbara, *née* Connor, Mrs Robert Leighton (1869–1941)
popular novelist
Convict 99 (1898)

Leland, John (1506?–52)
antiquary
Naeniae in mortem Thomae Viati (1542)
Assertio inclytissimi Arturii regis Britanniæ (1544)
The New Year's Gift (1549)
The Assertion of Arthur (1582)
The Itinerary of John Leland the Antiquary (1710)

Leland, Thomas (1722–85)
historian
The History of Ireland (1773)

Lemon, Mark (1809–70)
journalist, humorist, dramatist, and novelist
Falkner Lyle; or, The Story of Two Wives (1866)

Lennox, Charlotte, *née* Ramsay (1729?–1804)
novelist, poet, and dramatist
Poems on Several Occasions (1747)
The Life of Harriot Stuart, Written by Herself (1750)
The Female Quixote; or, The Adventures of Arabella (1752)
Shakespear Illustrated (1753)
The Memoirs of the Countess of Berci (1756)
Henrietta (1758)
Philander: A dramatic pastoral (1758)
Sophia (1762)
The History of Eliza (1766)
The Sister: A comedy (1769)
Old City Manners: A comedy (1775)
Euphemia (1790)
Hermione; or, The Orphan Sisters (1791)

Lenton, Francis (*fl.* 1630–40)
court poet and anagrammatist

Characterismi; or, Lentons Leasures: Expressed in essayes and characters (1631)

Le Queux, William Tufnell (1864–1927)
popular novelist
The Great War in England in 1897 (1894)
England's Peril (1899)
The Invasion of 1910 (1906)
Spies of the Kaiser (1909)

Lerner, Laurence David (1925–)
poet, critic, and novelist
A.R.T.H.U.R. (1974)
A.R.T.H.U.R. & M.A.R.T.H.A.; or, The Loves of the Computers (1980)

Leslie, Charles (1650–1722)
nonjuror and controversialist
The Snake in the Grass (1696)
A Short and Easie Method with the Deists (1698)
The Wolf Stript of his Shepherd's Cloathing (1704)

Lessing, Doris May, *née* Tayler ['Jane Somers'] (1919–)
novelist, short-story writer, and playwright
The Grass is Singing (1950)
This Was the Old Chief's Country (1951)
Martha Quest (1952)
A Proper Marriage (1954)
A Ripple From the Storm (1958)
In Pursuit of the English (1960)
The Golden Notebook (1962)
African Stories (1964)
Landlocked (1965)
Nine African Stories (1968)
The Four-Gated City (1969)
Briefing For a Descent into Hell (1971)
The Story of a Non-Marrying Man (1972)
The Summer Before the Dark (1973)
The Memoirs of a Survivor (1974)
Shikasta (1979)
The Marriages Between Zones Three, Four and Five (1980)
The Sirian Experiments (1981)
The Making of the Representative for Planet 8 (1982)
The Diary of a Good Neighbour (1983)
The Sentimental Agents in the Volyen Empire (1983)
If the Old Could (1984)
The Good Terrorist (1985)
The Fifth Child (1988)
London Observed (1990)
Under My Skin (1994)
Love, Again (1996)
Walking in the Shade (1997)
Mara and Daun (1999)
The Old Age of El Magnifico (2000)
The Sweetest Dream (2001)

L'Estrange, Sir Roger (1616–1704)
journalist and pamphleteer
The Intelligencer (1663)
The Visions of Dom Francisco de Quevedo Villagas (1667)
Five Love-letters from a Nun to a Cavalier (1678)
Seneca's Morals by Way of Abstract (1678)
The Casuist Uncas'd (1680)
Citt and Bumpkin: In a dialogue over a pot of ale (1680)
A Compendious History of the Most Remarkable Passages of the Last Fourteen Years (1680)
Twenty Select Colloquies Out of Erasmus Roterodamus (1680)
The Observator. In Question and Answer (1681)
The Spanish Decameron; or, Ten Novels (1687)
Fables, of Aesop and other Eminent Mythologists (1692)
Fables and Storyes Moralized (1699)

Lever, Charles James ['Tilbury Tramp'] (1806–72)
novelist
The Confessions of Harry Lorrequer (1839)
Charles O'Malley, the Irish Dragoon (1841)
Jack Hinton, the Guardsman (1843)
Arthur O'Leary (1844)
Tom Burke, of 'Ours' (1844)
The O'Donoghue (1845)
Confessions of Con. Cregan, the Irish Gil Blas (1849)
Roland Cashel (1850)
Maurice Tiernay, The Soldier of Fortune (1852)
The Martins of Cro' Martin (1856)
The Fortunes of Glencore (1857)
Davenport Dunn; or, The Man of the Day (1859)
Barrington (1863)
Sir Brooke Fossbrooke (1866)
Lord Kilgobbin (1872)

Leverson, Ada Esther, *née* Beddington (1862–1933)
novelist, short-story writer, and journalist
The Twelfth Hour (1907)
Love's Shadow (1908)
Tenterhooks (1912)
Bird of Paradise (1914)
Love at Second Sight (1916)

Levi, Peter Chad Tigar (1931–)
poet and biographer
The Gravel Ponds (1960)
Water, Rock and Sand (1962)
Private Ground (1981)
The Echoing Green (1983)
Shadow and Bone (1989)
The Rags of Time (1994)
Reed Music (1998)

Levy, Amy (1861–89)
poet and novelist
Xantippe, and Other Verse (1881)
A Minor Poet, and Other Verse (1884)
The Romance of a Shop (1888)
A London Plane-Tree, and Other Verse (1889)
Miss Meredith (1889)

Lewes, George Henry (1817–78)
author, critic, and journalist
A Biographical History of Philosophy (1845)

Ranthorpe (1847)
Rose, Blanche, and Violet (1848)
Lewis, Alun (1915–44)
Welsh poet, novelist, and short-story writer
The Last Inspection (1942)
Raiders' Dawn, and Other Poems (1942)
Ha! Ha! Among the Trumpets (1945)
In the Green Tree (1949)
Lewis, Clive Staples ['N.W. Clerk'] (1898–1963)
literary scholar, critic, and novelist
The Pilgrim's Regress (1933)
The Allegory of Love (1936)
Out of the Silent Planet (1938)
Rehabilitations, and Other Essays (1939)
The Problem of Pain (1940)
Broadcast Talks (1942)
A Preface to Paradise Lost (1942)
The Screwtape Letters (1942)
Christian Behaviour (1943)
Perelandra (1943)
Beyond Personality (1944)
That Hideous Strength (1945)
Miracles (1947)
Arthurian Torso (1948)
The Lion, the Witch, and the Wardrobe (1950)
Prince Caspian (1951)
Mere Christianity (1952)
The Voyage of the Dawn Treader (1952)
The Silver Chair (1953)
The Horse and His Boy (1954)
The Magician's Nephew (1955)
Surprised by Joy (1955)
The Last Battle (1956)
An Experiment in Criticism (1961)
A Grief Observed (1961)
Letters to Malcolm, Chiefly on Prayer (1964)
Poems (1964)
Screwtape Proposes a Toast, and Other Pieces (1965)
Lewis, Matthew Gregory (1775–1818)
novelist, poet, and dramatist
The Monk: A romance (1796)
Village Virtues (1796)
The Minister: A tragedy (1797)
The Castle Spectre (1798)
Rolla; or, The Peruvian Hero: A tragedy (1799)
Tales of Terror (1799)
The East Indian: A comedy (1800)
Tales of Wonder (1800)
Adelmorn the Outlaw (1801)
Alfonso, King of Castile: A tragedy (1801)
The Bravo of Venice (1805)
Adelgitha; or, The Fruits of a Single Error: A tragedy (1806)
Feudal Tyrants; or, The Counts of Carlshein and Sargans (1806)
Romantic Tales (1808)
Monody on the Death of Sir John Moore (1809)
Poems (1812)
Lewis, Norman (1908–2003)
travel writer and novelist
Within the Labyrinth (1950)
A Dragon Apparent (1951)
A Single Pilgrim (1953)
The Volcanoes Above Us (1957)
The Sicilian Specialist (1975)
The Missionaries (1988)
An Empire in the East (1993)
Lewis, [Percy] Wyndham (1882–1957)
author and artist
Blast: Review of the great English vortex (1914)
Tarr (1918)
Time and Western Man (1927)
The Childermass (1928)
Paleface: The philosophy of the 'melting pot' (1929)
The Apes of God (1930)
Enemy of the Stars (1932)
Snooty Baronet (1932)
Men Without Art (1934)
The Roaring Queen (1936)
Blasting and Bombarding (1937)
The Revenge for Love (1937)
The Mysterious Mr Bull (1938)
The Vulgar Streak (1941)
America and Cosmic Man (1948)
Rude Assignment (1950)
Rotting Hill (1951)
The Writer and the Absolute (1952)
The Demon of Progress in the Arts (1954)
Self-Condemned (1954)
Monstre Gai. Malign Fiesta (1955)
The Red Priest (1956)
Lickbarrow, Isabella (1784–1847)
Lakeland Quaker poet
Poetical Effusions (1814)
Lilburne, John (1615–57)
anti-episcopalian activist, Leveller, and later Quaker
The Christian Mans Triall (1641)
The Resurrection of John Lilburne (1656)
Lillo, George (1693–1739)
dramatist
Silvia; or, The Country Burial: An opera (1730)
The London Merchant; or, The History of George Barnwell (1731)
The Christian Hero: A tragedy (1735)
Fatal Curiosity: A true tragedy (1737)
Marina (1738)
Britannia and Batavia: A masque (1740)
Elmerick; or, Justice Triumphant: A tragedy (1740)
Lilly, William (1602–81)
astrologer
Merlinus Anglicus Junior: The English Merlin Revived; or, A Mathematicall Prediction (1644)
The Starry Messenger (1645)
Christian Astrology Modestly Treated of in Three Books (1647)

Monarchy or No Monarchy in England (1651)
Annus Tenebrosus; or, The Dark Year (1652)
Lily, William (1468?–1522)
schoolmaster and grammarian
An Introduction of the Eyght Partes of Speche (1542)
Lindsay, Lindesay, Lyndsay, or Lyndesay, Sir David (1490–1555)
Scottish poet and Lyon king of arms
The Complaynte and Testament of a Popinjay (1538)
The Tragical Death of David Beaton Bishoppe of Sainct Andrews (1548?)
The Monarche (1554)
Works (1568)
Squire Meldrum (1594)
Ane Satyre of the Thrie Estaits in Commendation of Vertew and Vituperation of Vyce (1602)
Lindsay, David (1876–1945)
novelist
A Voyage to Arcturus (1920)
Ling, Nicholas (*fl.* 1580–1604)
publisher and editor
Politeuphuia Wits Common Wealth (1597)
Lingard, John (1771–1851)
historian
The Antiquities of the Anglo-Saxon Church (1806)
The History of England [vols i, ii, iii] (1819)
Linklater, Eric Robert Russell (1899–1974)
Scottish novelist and short-story writer
White-Maa's Saga (1929)
Linton, Eliza, *née* Lynn (1822–98)
novelist and journalist
Azeth the Egyptian (1847)
Lizzie Lorton of Greyrigg (1866)
The Girl of the Period (1868)
Ourselves: A series of essays on women (1869)
The Girl of the Period, and Other Social Essays (1883)
Lisle or L'Isle, William (1579?–1637)
scholar and translator
A Saxon Treatise Concerning the Old and New Testament (1623)
The Faire Aethiopian (1631)
Lithgow, William (1582–1645?)
traveller
A Most Delectable, and True Discourse, of an Admired and Painefull Peregrination in Europe, Asia and Affricke (1614)
Rare Adventures, and Painefull Peregrinations (1632)
Litt, Toby (1968)
novelist
Exhibitionism (2002)
Finding Myself (2003)
Little, Janet (1759–1813)
poet
The Poetical Works of Janet Little, the Scotch Milkmaid (1792)
Lively, Penelope Margaret, *née* Greer (1933–)
novelist, short-story writer, and children's writer
Astercote (1970)
The Ghost of Thomas Kempe (1973)
A Stitch in Time (1976)
The Road to Lichfield (1977)
Nothing Missing But the Samovar, and Other Stories (1978)
Treasures of Time (1979)
Judgement Day (1980)
Next to Nature, Art (1982)
Perfect Happiness (1983)
According to Mark (1984)
Corruption (1984)
Moon Tiger (1987)
Passing On (1989)
City of the Mind (1991)
Cleopatra's Sister (1993)
Oleander, Jacaranda (1994)
Heat Wave (1996)
Spiderweb (1998)
Livingstone, David (1813–73)
African missionary and explorer
Missionary Travels and Researches in South Africa (1857)
Narrative of an Expedition to the Zambesi and its Tributaries (1865)
'Llewellyn, Richard' [Richard Daffyd Vivian Llewellyn Lloyd] (1906–83)
Welsh novelist and playwright
How Green Was My Valley (1939)
None But the Lonely Heart (1943)
Up, Into the Singing Mountain (1963)
Down Where the Moon is Small (1966)
Green, Green My Valley Now (1975)
Lloyd, Charles (1775–1839)
poet
Poems on Various Subjects (1795)
Edmund Oliver (1798)
The Tragedies of Vittorio Alfieri (1815)
Nugae Canorae (1819)
Desultory Thoughts in London; Titus and Gisippus, with Other Poems (1821)
The Duke d'Ormond; and Beritola (1822)
Poems (1823)
Lloyd, David (1597–1663)
author
The Legend of Captaine Jones [pt i] (1631)
Lloyd, David (1635–92)
biographer
The States-men and Favourites of England since the Reformation (1665)
Memoires of the Lives of Those Personages that Suffered for the Protestant Religion (1668)
Lloyd, Robert (1733–64)
poet
The Actor (1760)
The Tears and Triumphs of Parnassus (1760)
An Epistle to Charles Churchill (1761)
Poems by Robert Lloyd (1762)
The Death of Adam: A tragedy (1763)
Lluelyn or Llewellyn, Martin (1616–82)
physician and poet

Men-Miracles: With other poemes (1646)
Lochhead, Liz (1947–)
Scottish poet and playwright
Memo for Spring (1972)
Islands (1978)
The Grimm Sisters (1981)
Blood and Ice (1982)
Dreaming Frankenstein and Collected Poems (1984)
True Confessions and New Clichés (1985)
Mary Queen of Scots Got Her Head Chopped Off. Dracula (1989)
Bagpipe Muzak (1991)
Locke, John (1632–1704)
philosopher
A Letter Concerning Toleration (1689)
An Essay Concerning Humane Understanding (1690)
A Second Letter Concerning Toleration (1690)
Two Treatises of Government (1690)
Some Considerations of the Consequences of the Lowering of Interest and Raising the Value of Money (1692)
A Third Letter for Toleration (1692)
Some Thoughts Concerning Education (1693)
Further Considerations Concerning Raising the Value of Money (1695)
The Reasonableness of Christianity as Delivered in the Scriptures (1695)
A Vindication of the Reasonableness of Christianity (1695)
A Letter to the Right Reverend Edward Ld Bishop of Worcester (1697)
Mr Locke's Reply to the Right Reverend the Lord Bishop of Worcester's Answer to his Letter (1697)
A Second Vindication of the Reasonableness of Christianity (1697)
Mr Locke's Reply to the Right Reverend the Lord Bishop of Worcester's Answer to his Second Letter (1699)
Posthumous Works of Mr John Locke (1706)
Some Familiar Letters (1708)
The Works of John Locke (1714)
Lockhart, John Gibson ['Peter Morris'] (1794–1854)
biographer and novelist
Peter's Letters to His Kinfolk (1819)
Valerius: A Roman story (1821)
Some Passages in the Life of Mr Adam Blair (1822)
Ancient Spanish Ballads, Historical and Romantic (1823)
Reginald Dalton (1823)
The History of Matthew Wald (1824)
Janus; or, The Edinburgh Literary Almanack (1826)
Life of Robert Burns (1828)
The History of Napoleon Buonaparte (1829)
Memoirs of the Life of Sir Walter Scott (1837)
Lodge, David John (1935–)
novelist and critic
The Picturegoers (1960)
Ginger, You're Barmy (1962)
The British Museum is Falling Down (1965)
Language of Fiction (1966)
Out of the Shelter (1970)
Changing Places (1975)
How Far Can You Go? (1980)
Small World (1984)
Write On (1986)
Nice Work (1988)
After Bakhtin (1990)
Paradise News (1991)
Therapy (1995)
Thinks . . . (2001)
Consciousness and the Novel (2002)
Lodge, Thomas (1558–1625)
poet, dramatist, romance-writer, pamphleteer, and translator
An Alarum Against Usurers (1584)
Scillaes Metamorphosis: Enterlaced with the Unfortunate Love of Glaucus (1589)
Rosalynde: Euphues Golden Legacie (1590)
Catharos: Diogenes in his Singularitie (1591)
Robert, Duke of Normandy (1591)
Euphues Shadow, the Battaile of the Sences (1592)
The Life and Death of William Long Beard (1593)
Phillis: Honoured with pastorall sonnets, elegies and amorous delights (1593)
A Looking Glasse, for London and Englande (1594)
The Wounds of Civill War, Lively Set Forth in the True Tragedies of Marius and Scilla (1594)
A Fig for Momus (1595)
The Divel Conjured (1596)
A Margarite of America (1596)
Wits Miserie, and the Worlds Madnesse (1596)
The Flowers of Lodowicke of Granado (1601)
The Famous and Memorable Workes of Josephus (1602)
A Treatise of the Plague (1603)
The Workes of Lucius Annaeus Seneca, both Morrall and Natural (1614)
A Learned Summary upon the Famous Poeme of William of Saluste Lord of Bartas (1621)
Lofting, Hugh (1886–1947)
children's writer
The Story of Dr Dolittle (1920)
Logue, Christopher (1926–)
poet and playwright
Wand and Quadrant (1953)
Devil, Maggot and Son (1956)
Songs (1959)
Logue's ABC (1966)
Ode to the Dodo (1981)
War Music (1981)
Kings (1990)
The Husbands (1994)

Lok, Lock, or Locke, Ann (*fl.* 1560)
poet and translator
Sermons of John Calvin (1560)
Lok, Lock, or Locke, Henry (1553?–1608?)
poet
Sundry Christian Passions Contained in Two Hundred Sonnets (1593)
Ecclesiastes, Otherwise Called the Preacher (1597)
Longley, Michael George (1939–)
Ulster poet
No Continuing City (1969)
An Exploded View (1973)
Man Lying on a Wall (1976)
The Echo Gate (1979)
Patchwork (1981)
Poems 1963–1983 (1985)
Gorse Fires (1991)
The Ghost Orchid (1995)
Lott, Tim (1956)
novelist
White City Blue (1999)
Rumours of a Hurricane (2002)
The Love Secrets of Don Juan (2003)
Love, Nicholas (*d.* 1424)
translator
The Mirror of the Life of Christ (1484)
Lovelace, Richard (1618–58)
poet
Lucasta: Epodes, Odes, Sonnets, Songs, &c (1649)
Lucasta: Posthume poems (1659)
Lover, Samuel (1797–1868)
novelist, songwriter, and portrait painter
Rory O'More (1837)
Handy Andy (1842)
Treasure Trove (1844)
Metrical Tales, and Other Poems (1860)
Lovibond, Edward (1724–75)
poet
Poems on Several Occasions (1785)
Lower, Sir William (1600?–62)
dramatist
The Phaenix in Her Flames: A tragedy (1639)
Polyeuctes; or, The Martyr: A tragedy (1655)
Horatius: A Roman tragedie (1656)
Lowndes, Marie Adelaide Julie Elizabeth Renée Belloc, Mrs Belloc Lowndes (1868–1947)
novelist
The Heart of Penelope (1904)
The Uttermost Farthing (1908)
The Lodger (1913)
Lowry, [Clarence] Malcolm Boden (1909–57)
novelist
Ultramarine (1933)
Under the Volcano (1947)
Lowth or Louth, Robert (1710–87)
bishop of London, author, scholar, and grammarian
The Life of William of Wykeham, Bishop of Winchester (1758)
A Short Introduction to English Grammar (1762)
Lubbock, Percy (1879–1965)
editor, biographer, and critic
The Letters of Henry James (1920)
The Craft of Fiction (1921)
Lucas, Charles (1769–1854)
clergyman and novelist
The Infernal Quixote (1801)
The Abissinian Reformer; or, The Bible and Sabre (1808)
Lucas, Edward Verrall (1868–1938)
essayist and topographical writer
The War of the Wenuses (1898)
A Wanderer in Holland (1905)
Lucie-Smith, [John] Edward McKenzie (1933–)
poet, art historian, anthologist, translator, and novelist
A Tropical Childhood, and Other Poems (1961)
Confessions and Histories (1964)
Ludlow, Edmund (1617?–92)
regicide
Memoirs of Edmund Ludlow Esq. (1698)
Lupset, Thomas (1495–1530)
divine
A Treatise of Charitie (1533)
The Counsailes of Saint Isidore (1534)
The Waye of Dyenge Well (1534)
Lupton, Donald (*d.* 1676)
miscellaneous writer
London and the Countrey Carbonadoed and Quartered into Severall Characters (1632)
Lupton, Thomas (*fl.* 1583)
miscellaneous writer
All for Money (1578)
A Thousand Notable Things, of Sundry Sortes (1579)
A Persuasion from Papistrie (1581)
A Dream of the Devill, and Dives (1584)
'Lyall, Edna' [Ada Ellen Bayly] (1857–1903)
novelist
The Autobiography of a Slander (1887)
The Autobiography of a Truth (1896)
Lydgate, John (1370?–1449)
poet
The Chorle and the Birde (1476)
The Horse, the Goose, and the Sheep (1476?)
Stans Puer ad Mensam (1476?)
The Temple of Glas (1477?)
The Book of the Lyf of Our Lady (1483)
The Fall of Princes (1494)
The Siege of Thebes (1497?)
The Virtue of the Mass (1500?)
The Complaint of the Black Knight (1508)
Proverbs (1510?)
The Governance of Kings (1511)
Troy Book (1513)
Testament (1520?)
Life of St Alban and St Amphibalus (1534)

The Serpent of Division (1535?)
Lyell, Sir Charles (1797–1875)
geologist
Principles of Geology (1830)
Elements of Geology (1838)
Lyly, John (1554–1606)
dramatist and author
Euphues (1578)
Euphues and his England (1580)
Alexander, Campaspe, and Diogenes (1584)
Sapho and Phao (1584)
Pappe with an Hatchet (1589)
A Whip for an Ape; or, Martin Displaied (1589)
Endimion, the Man in the Moone (1591)
Gallathea (1592)
Midas (1592)
Mother Bombie (1594)
The Woman in the Moone (1597)
Loves Metamorphosis: A wittie and courtly pastorall (1601)
Euphues the Anatomy of Wit (1617)
Lyttelton, George, 1st Baron Lyttelton (1709–73)
statesman and poet
An Epistle to Mr Pope (1730)
The Progress of Love (1732)
Advice to a Lady (1733)
Letters from a Persian in England, to his Friend at Isphahan (1735)
Dialogues of the Dead (1760)
Lytton, Edward Robert Bulwer, 1st earl of Lytton ['Owen Meredith'] (1831–91)
statesman and poet
Clytemnestra; The Earl's Return; The Artist, and Other Poems (1855)
The Wanderer (1857)
Fables in Song (1874)

Mabbe or Mab, James ['Don Diego Puede-Ser'] (1572–1642?)
translator
The Rogue; or, The Life of Guzman de Alfarache (1623)
The Spanish Bawd (1631)
Exemplarie Novells (1640)
Macaulay, Catherine *née* Sawbridge, later Graham (1731–91)
republican historian
The History of England from the Accession of James I to that of the Brunswick Line (1763)
Loose Remarks on Mr Hobbes's Philosophical Rudiments of Government and Society (1767)
Observations on a Pamphlet Entitled, Thoughts on the Present Discontents (1770)
Letters on Education (1790)
Macaulay, Dame [Emilie] Rose (1881–1958)
novelist, essayist, and travel writer
Abbots Verney (1906)
Potterism (1920)
They Were Defeated (1932)
Personal Pleasures (1935)
They Went to Portugal (1946)
Fabled Shore (1949)
The Towers of Trebizond (1956)
Macaulay, Thomas Babington, 1st Baron Macaulay (1800–59)
statesman, historian, essayist, and poet
Pompeii (1819)
Lays of Ancient Rome (1842)
Critical and Historical Essays (1843)
The History of England from the Accession of James II [vols i, ii] (1849)
Speeches (1854)
The History of England from the Accession of James II [vols iii, iv] (1855)
Macauley, Elizabeth Wright (1785?–1837)
poet
Effusions of Fancy (1812)
MacBeth, George Mann (1932–92)
poet, novelist, and editor
The Broken Places (1963)
A Doomsday Book (1965)
The Night of Stones (1968)
The Burning Cone (1970)
Shrapnel (1973)
Buying a Heart (1978)
Poems of Love and Death (1980)
The Cleaver Garden (1986)
Anatomy of Divorce (1988)
Collected Poems 1958–1982 (1989)
Trespassing (1991)
The Patient (1992)
McCabe, Eugene (1930–)
Irish playwright, novelist, and short-story writer
Heritage, and Other Stories (1978)
Christ in the Fields (1993)
McCabe, Patrick (1955–)
Irish novelist
Music on Clinton Street (1986)
Carn (1989)
The Butcher Boy (1992)
The Dead School (1995)
Breakfast on Pluto (1998)
Mondo Desperado (1999)
Emerald Germs of Ireland (2000)
Call Me the Breeze (2003)
MacCaig, Norman Alexander (1910–96)
Scottish poet
Far Cry (1943)
The Inward Eye (1946)
Riding Lights (1955)
The Sinai Sort (1957)
A Common Grace (1960)
A Round of Applause (1962)
Surroundings (1966)
Rings on a Tree (1968)
The World's Room (1974)
Tree of Strings (1977)
The Equal Skies (1980)
Collected Poems (1985)
Voice-Over (1988)

MacCarthy, Denis Florence (1817–1882)
poet and translator
Dramas of Calderón (1853)
Underglimpses, and Other Poems (1857)
The Two Lovers of Heaven: Chrysanthus and Daria (1870)
MacCarthy, Sir [Charles Otto] Desmond (1877–1952)
journalist and dramatic critic
Remnants (1918)
McCarthy, Justin (1830–1912)
politician, historian, and novelist
A History of Our Own Times [vols i, ii] (1879)
McCosh, James (1811–94)
philosopher
The Method of the Divine Government, Physical and Moral (1850)
The Supernatural in Relation to the Natural (1862)
An Examination of Mill's Philosophy (1866)
'MacDiarmid, Hugh' [Christopher Murray Grieve] (1892–1978)
Scottish poet
Annals of the Five Senses (1923)
Sangshaw (1925)
A Drunk Man Looks at the Thistle (1926)
Penny Wheep (1926)
To Circumjack Cencrastus; or, The Curly Snake (1930)
First Hymn to Lenin, and Other Poems (1931)
At the Sign of the Thistle (1934)
Stony Limits, and Other Poems (1934)
Second Hymn to Lenin, and Other Poems (1935)
Lucky Poet (1943)
Poems of the East-West Synthesis (1946)
In Memoriam James Joyce (1955)
The Kind of Poetry I Want (1961)
The Company I've Kept (1966)
A Lap of Honour (1967)
A Clyack-Sheaf (1969)
Complete Poems 1920–76 (1978)
MacDonald, George (1824–1905)
Scottish poet and novelist
Within and Without (1855)
Poems (1857)
Phantastes: A faerie romance for men and women (1858)
David Elginbrod (1863)
Adela Cathcart (1864)
Alec Forbes of Howglen (1865)
Dealings with the Faeries (1867)
Robert Falconer (1868)
At the Back of the North Wind (1870)
The Princess and the Goblin (1871)
The Marquis of Lossie (1877)
The Princess and Curdie (1882)
There and Back (1891)
Poetical Works (1893)
Macdonell, Archibald Gordon ['Neil Gordon'] (1895–1941)
novelist
England, their England (1933)
Autobiography of a Cad (1938)
Mace, Daniel (*d.* 1753)
textual critic and translator of the Bible
The New Testament in Greek and English (1729)
McEwan, Ian Russell (1948–)
novelist and playwright
First Love, Last Rites (1975)
The Cement Garden (1978)
In Between the Sheets (1978)
The Comfort of Strangers (1981)
The Child in Time (1987)
The Innocent; or, The Special Relationship (1990)
Black Dogs (1992)
The Daydreamer (1994)
Collected Stories (1995)
Enduring Love (1997)
Amsterdam (1998)
Atonement (2001)
McGahern, John (1934–)
Irish novelist and short-story writer
The Pornographer (1979)
MacGill, Patrick ['The Navvy Poet'] (1889–1963)
Irish poet and novelist
Songs of a Navvy (1911)
Children of the Dead End (1914)
McGough, Roger (1937–)
poet and playwright
Frinck; A Day in the Life Of; and Summer with Monica (1967)
Watchwords (1969)
Holiday on Death Row (1979)
Waving at Trains (1982)
Defying Gravity (1992)
McGuckian, Medbh (1950–)
Irish poet
Venus and the Rain (1984)
On Ballycastle Beach (1988)
Marconi's Cottage (1991)
Captain Lavender (1994)
McGuinness, Frank (1953–)
Irish playwright
Observe the Sons of Ulster Marching Towards the Somme (1986)
Someone Who'll Watch Over Me (1992)
Machen, Arthur [Arthur Llewellyn Jones] ['Leolinus Siluriensis'] (1863–1947)
novelist and short-story writer
The Anatomy of Tobacco; or, Smoking Methodised (1884)
The Great God Pan, and The Inmost Light (1894)
The Three Impostors; or, The Transmutations (1895)
The House of Souls (1906)
The Hill of Dreams (1907)

The Angels of Mons; The Bowmen; and Other Legends of the War (1915)
The Great Return (1915)
The Shining Pyramid (1925)
The Children of the Pool, and Other Stories (1936)

McIlvanney, William Angus (1936–)
Scottish novelist
Docherty (1975)

MacInnes, Colin (1914–76)
novelist
City of Spades (1957)
Absolute Beginners (1959)
Mr Love and Justice (1960)

Mackay, Shena (1944–)
Scottish novelist and short-story writer
Dreams of Dead Women's Handbags (1987)

McKendrick, Jamie (1955–)
poet
The Sirocco Room (1991)
The Kiosk on the Brink (1993)
The Marble Fly (1997)
Sky Nails (2000)
Ink Stone (2003)

Mackenzie, Anna Maria, *née* Wight, formerly Mrs Cox, then Mrs Johnson ['Ellen of Exeter'] (*fl.* 1783–98)
novelist
Burton-Wood (1783)
The Gamesters (1786)
Retribution (1788)
Slavery; or, The Times (1792)
The Neapolitan; or, The Test of Integrity (1796)
Dusseldorf; or, The Fratricide (1798)

Mackenzie, Sir [Edward Montague] Compton (1883–1972)
novelist
The Passionate Elopement (1911)
Carnival (1912)
Sinister Street [vol. i] (1913)
Sinister Street [vol. ii] (1914)
The Altar Steps (1922)
The Parson's Progress (1923)
The Seven Ages of Woman (1923)
Coral (1925)
Whisky Galore (1947)

Mackenzie, George, 1st Viscount Tarbat, 1st earl of Cromarty (1630–1714)
statesman and author
Several Proposals Conducting to a Further Union of Britain (1711)

Mackenzie, Sir George (1636–91)
lawyer and miscellaneous writer
Aretina; or, The Serious Romance (1660)
Religio Stoici (1663)
Reason (1690)

Mackenzie, Henry (1745–1831)
novelist and essayist
The Man of Feeling (1771)
The Man of the World (1773)
The Prince of Tunis (1773)
Julia de Roubigné (1777)

Mackintosh, Sir James (1765–1832)
philosopher and historian
Vindiciae Gallicae (1791)

Macklin, Charles (1697?–1797)
actor and dramatist
Love à la Mode: A farce (1793)
The Man of the World: A comedy (1793)

Maclaren-Ross, Julian (1912–64)
novelist and short-story writer
The Stuff to Give the Troops (1944)
Better Than a Kick in the Pants (1945)

MacLaverty, Bernard (1942–)
Northern Irish novelist and short-story writer
Secrets, and Other Stories (1977)
Lamb (1980)
A Time to Dance, and Other Stories (1982)
Cal (1983)
The Great Profundo, and Other Stories (1987)
Walking the Dog, and Other Stories (1994)
Grace Notes (1997)
The Anatomy School (2001)

McLaverty, Michael (1904–92)
Irish novelist and short-story writer
The Road to the Shore (1976)

Maclean, Allstair Stuart (1923–87)
thriller writer
The Guns of Navarone (1957)
Ice Station Zebra (1963)
Where Eagles Dare (1967)

MacLean, Sorley [Somhairle MacGill-Eain] (1911–)
Gaelic poet
Spring Tide and Neap Tide [*Reothairt is Contraigh*] (1977)

MacNeice, [Frederick] Louis (1907–63)
poet and dramatist
Blind Fireworks (1929)
Poems (1935)
The Agamemnon of Aechylus (1936)
The Earth Compels (1938)
I Crossed the Minch (1938)
Modern Poetry (1938)
Autumn Journal (1939)
The Last Ditch (1940)
Plant and Phantom (1941)
Christopher Columbus (1944)
Springboard (1944)
The Dark Tower, and Other Radio Scripts (1947)
Holes in the Sky (1948)
Collected Poems 1925–48 (1949)
Ten Burnt Offerings (1952)
Autumn Sequel (1954)
Visitations (1957)
Eighty-Five Poems (1959)
Solstices (1961)
The Burning Perch (1963)
The Strings are False (1965)
Collected Poems (1966)

Persons From Porlock, and Other Plays for Radio (1969)
Macpherson, James (1736–96)
poet
The Highlander (1758)
Fragments of Ancient Poetry (1760)
Fingal: An ancient epic poem . . . Together with several other poems translated from the Galic language (1762)
Temora: An ancient epic poem (1763)
The Works of Ossian (1765)
The Iliad (1773)
The History of Great Britain (1775)
McWilliam, Candia (1955–)
Scottish novelist
A Case of Knives (1988)
Debatable Land (1994)
Wait Till I Tell You (1997)
Madan, Martin (1726–90)
barrister, Methodist, and author
Thelyphthora; or, A Treatise on Female Ruin (1780)
Madden, Deirdre (1960–)
Irish novelist
Birds of the Innocent Wood (1988)
Madden, Samuel (1686–1765)
poet, dramatist, and pamphleteer
Memoirs of the Twentieth Century (1733)
Boulter's Monument (1745)
Madge, Charles Henry (1912–96)
poet and sociologist
The Disappearing Castle (1937)
Mass-Observation (1937)
Mahon, Derek (1941–)
Northern Irish poet and playwright
Night-Crossing (1968)
Beyond Howth Head (1970)
Light Music (1977)
Courtyards in Delft (1981)
The Hunt by Night (1981)
A Kensington Notebook (1984)
Antarctica (1985)
The Yaddo Letter (1994)
Collected Poems (1999)
Maitland, Sara (1950–)
novelist and short-story writer
Daughter of Jerusalem (1978)
Telling Tales (1983)
Virgin Territory (1984)
Three Times Table (1990)
Home Truths (1993)
Women Fly When Men Aren't Watching (1993)
Mallet, David [originally David Malloch] (1705?–65)
poet and dramatist
The Excursion (1728)
Eurydice: A tragedy (1731)
Of Verbal Criticism: An epistle to Mr Pope (1733)
Mustapha: A tragedy (1739)
Poems on Several Occasions (1743)
Amyntor and Theodora; or, The Hermit (1747)
Alfred: A masque (1751)
Britannia: A masque (1755)
Elvira: A tragedy (1763)
Mallock, William Hurrell (1849–1923)
novelist and writer on philosophy and politics
The New Republic; or, Culture, Faith, and Philosophy in an English Country House (1877)
The New Paul and Virginia; or, Positivism on an Island (1878)
A Romance of the Nineteenth Century (1881)
The Old Order Changes (1886)
Malone, Edmond (1741–1812)
critic and editor of Shakespeare
Cursory Observations on the Poems Attributed to Thomas Rowley (1782)
A Letter to Richard Farmer (1792)
An Inquiry into the Authenticity of Certain Miscellaneous Papers Attributed to Shakspeare (1796)
Malory, Sir Thomas (*fl.* 1470)
author of Le Morte DArthur
Le Morte DArthur (1485)
Malthus, Thomas Robert (1766–1834)
economist
An Essay on the Principle of Population (1798)
An Investigation of the Cause of the Present High Price of Provisions (1800)
Observations on the Effects of the Corn Laws (1814)
An Inquiry into the Nature and Progress of Rent (1815)
Principles of Political Economy (1820)
The Measure of Value Stated and Illustrated (1823)
Definitions in Political Economy (1827)
Mandeville, Bernard (1670?–1733)
satirist
Some Fables After the Easie and Familiar Method of Monsieur de la Fontaine (1703)
Typhon; or, The Wars Between the Gods and Giants (1704)
The Grumbling Hive; or, Knaves Turn'd Honest (1705)
Typhon; or, The Wars Between the Gods and Giants (1712)
The Fable of the Bees; or, Private Vices Publick Benefits (1714)
Mandeville, Sir John (*d.* 1342?)
traveller
Mandeville's Travels (1496)
Manley, [Mary] Delarivière (1663–1724)
dramatist and author
Letters Writen [sic] *by Mrs Manley* (1696)
The Lost Lover; or, The Jealous Husband: A comedy (1696)
The Royal Mischief: A tragedy (1696)
The Secret History, of Queen Zarah, and the Zarazians (1705)
Almyna; or, The Arabian Vow: A tragedy (1706)

The Lady's Pacquet of Letters (1707)
Secret Memoirs and Manners of Several Persons of Quality, of Both Sexes (1709)
Memoirs of Europe, Towards the Close of the Eighth Century (1710)
The Adventures of Rivella; or, The History of the Author of the Atalantis (1714)
Lucius, the First Christian King of Britain: A tragedy (1717)
The Power of Love (1720)

Manning, Anne (1807–79)
miscellaneous writer
Cherry and Violet (1849)
The Maiden and Married Life of Mary Powell, Afterwards Mistress Milton (1849)

Manning, Henry Edward (1808–92)
cardinal-priest and author
Sermons (1842)
The Unity of the Church (1842)
The Grounds of Faith (1852)
The Temporal Mission of the Holy Ghost; or, Reason and Revelation (1865)

Manning, Olivia Mary (1915–80)
novelist
The Wind Changes (1937)
Artist Among the Missing (1949)
The Great Fortune (1960)
The Spoilt City (1962)
Friends and Heroes (1965)
The Danger Tree (1977)
The Battle Lost and Won (1978)
The Sum of Things (1980)

Mansell, Sir Robert (1573–1636)
admiral
A True Report of the Service Done Upon Certaine Gallies Passing through the Narrow Seas (1602)

'Mansfield, Katherine' [Kathleen Mansfield Beauchamp, later Murry] (1888–1923)
New Zealand-born short-story writer
In a German Pension (1911)
Prelude (1918)
Bliss, and Other Stories (1920)
The Garden-Party, and Other Stories (1922)
The Dove's Nest (1923)
Something Childish, and Other Stories (1924)
Journal (1927)

Mantel, Hilary Mary (1952–)
novelist
Every Day is Mother's Day (1985)
Vacant Possession (1986)
Fludd (1989)
A Place of Greater Safety (1992)
A Change of Climate (1994)
An Experiment in Love (1995)
The Giant, O'Brien (1998)
Giving Up the Ghost (2003)

Manuche or Manucci, Cosmo (*fl.* 1642–64)
dramatist, of Italian origin
The Bastard: A tragedy (1652)
The Just General: A tragi-comedy (1652)
The Loyal Lovers: A tragi-comedy (1652)

Markham, Edward Archibald (1939–)
Caribbean British poet
Human Rites (1984)
Letter From Ulster and the Hugo Poems (1993)

Markham, Gervase or Jervis (1568?–1637)
miscellaneous author
A Discource of Horsmanshippe (1593)
The Most Honorable Tragedie of Sir Richard Grinvile, Knight (1595)
The Poem of Poems; or, Sions Muse (1596)
Devoreux (1597)
The Teares of the Beloved; or, The Lamentation of Saint John, Concerning the Death and Passion of Christ Jesus our Saviour (1600)
Marie Magdalens Lamentations for the Losse of Her Master Jesus (1601)
Cavelarice; or, The English Horseman (1607)
The English Arcadia [pt i] (1607)
Rodomonths Infernall; or, The Divell Conquered (1607)
The Dumbe Knight: A historicall comedy (1608)
The Famous Whore, or Noble Curtizan (1609)
Markhams Maister-peece; or, What Doth a Horseman Lacke (1610)
The English Husbandman: The first part (1613)
Cheape and Good Husbandry (1614)
Herod and Antipater (1622)
The Souldiers Accidence; or, An Introduction into Military Discipline (1625)
Markhams Faithful Farrier (1629)

Marlowe, Christopher (1564–93)
poet and dramatist
Tamburlane the Great (1590)
Dido Queene of Carthage (1594)
Edward the Second (1594)
The Massacre at Paris: with the Death of the Duke of Guise (1594?)
Hero and Leander (1598)
Hero and Leander: Begun by Christopher Marloe; and finished by George Chapman (1598)
All Ovids Elegies: 3 Bookes (1599?)
Pharsalia (1600)
Dr Faustus (1604)
The Jew of Malta (1633)

Marmion, Shackerley (1603–39)
dramatist
Hollands Leaguer: An excellent comedy (1632)
A Fine Companion (1633)
The Legend of Cupid and Psyche (1637)
The Antiquary: A comedy (1641)

'Marprelate, Martin' (pseudonym)
The Epistle (1588)
The Epitome (1588)
The Poem Mineralls (1589)
Hay Any Worke for Cooper (1589)
Martin Junior (1589)

Martin Senior (1589)
The Protestatyon of Martin Marprelat (1589)
Marryat, Frederick (1792–1848)
novelist
The Naval Officer; or, Scenes and Adventures in the Life of Frank Mildmay (1829)
The King's Own (1830)
Newton Forster; or, The Merchant Service (1831)
Peter Simple (1833)
Jacob Faithful (1834)
The Pacha of Many Tales (1835)
The Pirate and the Three Cutters (1835)
Japhet in Search of a Father (1836)
Mr Midshipman Easy (1836)
Snarleyyow; or, The Dog Fiend (1837)
A Diary in America, with Remarks on its Institutions (1839)
The Phantom Ship (1839)
Olla Podrida (1840)
Masterman Ready; or, The Wreck of the Pacific (1841)
Percival Keene (1842)
Narrative of the Travels and Adventures of Monsieur Violet (1843)
The Mission; or, Scenes in Africa (1845)
The Privateer's-Man (1846)
The Children of the New Forest (1847)
Marshall, Emma, *née* Martin (1828–99)
novelist
Life's Aftermath (1876)
Mars-Jones, Adam (1954–)
novelist and short-story writer
Lantern Lecture (1981)
Monopolies of Loss (1992)
The Waters of Thirst (1993)
Marston, John ['William Kinsayder'] (1576–1634)
dramatist and poet
The Metamorphosis of Pigmalions Image (1598)
The Scourge of Villanie (1598)
Jacke Drums Entertainment; or, The Comedie of Pasquill and Katherine (1601)
Antonio and Mellida (1602)
Antonio's Revenge (1602)
The Malcontent (1604)
The Dutch Courtezan (1605)
Parasitaster, or The Fawne (1606)
The Wonder of Women or The Tragedie of Sophonisba (1606)
What You Will (1607)
Histrio-Mastix; or, The Player Whipt (1610)
The Insatiate Countesse: A tragedie (1613)
The Workes of Mr John Marston (1633)
Martin, Catherine Edith Macauley, *née* Mackay ['Mrs Alick Macleod'] (1848?–1937)
Scottish-born Australian novelist
An Australian Girl (1890)
The Silent Sea (1892)
Martin, Gregory (*d.* 1582)
biblical translator
The New Testament of Jesus Christ (1582)
The Holie Bible (1609)
Martin, Sir Theodore (1816–1909)
poet, translator, and biographer of Prince Albert
Aladdin; or, The Wonderful Lamp (1857)
The Life of His Royal Highness the Prince Consort (1857)
Martineau, Harriet (1802–76)
novelist, economist, and woman of letters
Traditions of Palestine (1830)
Five Years of Youth; or, Sense and Sentiment (1831)
Illustrations of Political Economy (1832)
Society in America (1837)
Deerbrook (1839)
The Hour and the Man (1841)
Life in the Sick-Room; or, Essays by an Invalid (1844)
Dawn Island (1845)
Forest and Game-Law Tales (1845)
Letters on Mesmerism (1845)
Household Education (1849)
Letters from Ireland (1852)
The Positive Philosophy of August Comte (1853)
England and her Soldiers (1859)
Harriet Martineau's Autobiography (1877)
Martineau, James (1805–1900)
Unitarian theologian
The Rationale of Religious Enquiry (1836)
Endeavours After the Christian Life [1st ser.] (1843)
Marvell, Andrew (1621–78)
poet
The First Anniversary of the Government Under His Highness the Lord Protector (1655)
The Character of Holland (1665)
The Rehearsal Transpros'd (1672)
The Rehearsall Transpros'd. The Second Part (1673)
Miscellaneous Poems (1681)
Masefield, John Edward (1878–1967)
Poet Laureate, novelist, and children's writer
Salt-Water Ballads (1902)
Ballads (1903)
A Mainsail Haul (1905)
Ballads and Poems (1910)
Martin Hyde, the Duke's Messenger (1910)
The Everlasting Mercy (1911)
Jim Davis; or, The Captive of Smugglers (1911)
Dauber (1913)
Philip the King, and Other Poems (1914)
Good Friday (1916)
Lollingdon Downs, and Other Poems (1917)
Enslaved, and Other Poems (1920)
Collected Poems (1923)
King Cole, and Other Poems (1923)
Sard Harker (1924)
Midsummer Night, and Other Tales in Verse (1928)
The Box of Delights; or, When the Wolves Were Running (1935)

So Long to Learn (1952)
Bluebells, and Other Verse (1961)
Old Raiger, and Other Verse (1964)
Grace Before Ploughing (1966)

Mason, Alfred Edward Woodley (1865–1948)
novelist and short-story writer
A Romance of Wastdale (1895)
The Four Feathers (1902)
At the Villa Rose (1910)
Fire Over England (1936)

Mason, John (1645?–94)
religious writer and poet
Spiritual Songs; or, Songs of Praise to Almighty God upon Several Occasions (1683)

Mason, Richard (1919–97)
novelist
The World of Suzie Wong (1957)

Mason, William (*fl.* 1621)
essayist
A Handful of Essaies or Imperfect Offers (1621)

Mason, William (1725–97)
poet, dramatist, and musician
Musaeus: A monody to the memory of Pope (1747)
Isis: An elegy (1749)
Elfrida: A dramatic poem (1752)
Odes (1756)
Caractacus (1759)
Elegies (1763)
Poems (1764)
The English Garden (1772)
An Heroic Postscript to the Public (1774)
An Archaeological Epistle to Jeremiah Milles . . . Editor of a Superb Edition of the Poems of Thomas Rowley (1782)
King Stephen's Watch (1782)

Massie, Allan Johnstone (1938–)
novelist, biographer, and critic
Change and Decay in All Around I See (1978)
The Death of Men (1981)
Augustus (1986)
A Question of Loyalties (1989)
The Hanging Tree (1990)
The Sins of the Father (1991)
Tiberius (1991)
Caesar (1993)
King David (1995)
Shadows of Empire (1997)
Antony (1997)
The Evening of the World (2001)

Massinger, Philip (1583–1640)
dramatist
The Virgin Martir: A tragedie (1622)
The Duke of Millaine: A tragaedie (1623)
The Bond-Man (1624)
The Roman Actor: A tragaedie (1629)
The Picture: A tragaecomedie (1630)
The Renegado: A tragaecomedie (1630)
The Emperour of the East: A tragae-comoedie (1632)
The Fatall Dowry: A tragedy (1632)
The Maid of Honour (1632)
A New Way to Pay Old Debts: A comoedie (1633)
The Great Duke of Florence: A comicall historie (1636)
The Unnaturall Combat: A tragedie (1639)
Three New Playes (1655)
The Old Law (1656)
The City-Madam: A comedie (1658)

Masson, David (1822–1907)
literary scholar and biographer and founder of *Macmillan's Magazine*
Essays Biographical and Critical (1856)

Masterman, Charles Frederick Gurney (1874–1927)
politician, author, and journalist
The Condition of England (1909)

Masters, John (1914–73)
novelist and author
Nightrunners of Bengal (1951)
The Deceivers (1952)
Bhowani Junction (1954)

Masters, Mary (1694?–1771)
poet
Poems on Several Occasions (1733)

'Mathers, Helen' [Ellen Buckingham Mathews, later Reeves] (1853–1920)
novelist
Comin' Thro' the Rye (1875)
Cherry Ripe! (1878)

Mathias, Thomas James (1754?–1835)
translator and satirist
The Pursuits of Literature (1794)

Maturin, Charles Robert ['Dennis Jasper Murphy'] (1782–1824)
clergyman, novelist, and dramatist
Fatal Revenge; or, The Family of Montorio (1807)
The Wild Irish Boy (1808)
The Milesian Chief (1812)
Bertram; or, The Castle of St Aldobrand (1816)
Manuel: A tragedy (1817)
Fredolfo: A tragedy (1819)
Melmoth the Wanderer (1820)
The Albigenses (1824)

'Maugham, Robin' [Robert Cecil Romer, Viscount Maugham] (1916–81)
novelist, playwright, and author
The Servant (1948)

Maugham, William Somerset (1874–1965)
novelist, short-story writer, and playwright
Liza of Lambeth (1897)
The Making of a Saint (1898)
Orientations (1899)
The Hero (1901)
Mrs Craddock (1902)
A Man of Honour (1903)
The Merry-Go-Round (1904)
The Bishop's Apron (1906)
The Magician (1908)
Lady Frederick (1911)

The Tenth Man: A tragic comedy (1913)
Landed Gentry: A comedy (1913)
The Land of Promise: A comedy (1913)
Of Human Bondage (1915)
The Moon and Sixpence (1919)
The Trembling of a Leaf (1921)
On a Chinese Screen (1922)
Loaves and Fishes: A comedy (1924)
The Painted Veil (1925)
The Casuarina Tree (1926)
Ashenden; or, The British Agent (1928)
The Sacred Flame (1928)
Cakes and Ale; or, The Skeleton in the Cupboard (1930)
The Bread-Winner: A comedy (1930)
Six Stories Written in the First Person Singular (1931)
The Narrow Corner (1932)
For Services Rendered (1932)
Cosmopolitans (1936)
Theatre (1937)
The Mixture as Before (1940)
Up at the Villa (1941)
The Razor's Edge (1944)
Creatures of Circumstance (1947)
Catalina (1948)
A Writer's Notebook (1949)
The Vagrant Mood (1952)
Points of View (1958)

Maurice, [John] Frederick Denison (1805–72)
theologian and author
Eustace Conway; or, The Brother and Sister (1834)
Theological Essays (1853)
The Claims of the Bible and of Science (1863)
Social Morality (1869)

Max Müller, Friedrich (1823–1900)
German-born orientalist and philologist
Lectures on the Science of Language (1861)

Maxwell, Gavin (1914–69)
travel and natural history writer
Ring of Bright Water (1960)
The Rocks Remain (1963)
Raven Seek Thy Brother (1968)

Maxwell, Glyn (1962–)
poet
Tale of the Mayor's Son (1990)
The Boys at Twilight (2000)
The Nerve (2002)

May, Thomas (1595–1650)
poet, dramatist, and historian
The Heire: An excellent comedie (1622)
Pharsalia (1626)
Lucan's Pharsalia; or, The Civill Warres of Rome, betweene Pompey the Great, and Julius Caesar (1627)
Virgil's Georgicks Englished (1628)
Selected Epigrams of Martial (1629)
A Continuation of Lucan's Historicall Poem Till the Death of Julius Caesar (1630)
The Mirrour of Mindes; or, Barclays Icon Animarum (1631)
The Tragedy of Antigone, the Theban Princesse (1631)
The Reigne of King Henry the Second (1633)
The Victorious Reigne of King Edward the Third (1635)
Cleopatra Queen of Aegypt (1639)
Julia Agrippina (1639)
The Old Couple: A comedy (1658)

May, Sir Thomas Erskine, 1st Baron Farnborough (1815–86)
jurist and historian
A Treatise upon the Law, Privileges, Proceedings and Usage of Parliament (1844)
The Constitutional History of England (1861)

Mayhew, Augustus Septimus (1826–75)
novelist and dramatist
Kitty Lamere; or, A Dark Page in London Life (1855)
Paved with Gold; or, The Romance and Reality of London Streets (1858)

Mayhew, Augustus Septimus (1826–75), novelist and dramatist, **and Henry (1812–87)**
novelist, journalist, and philanthropist
The Greatest Plague of Life; or, The Adventures of a Lady in Search of a Good Servant (1847)

Mayhew, Henry (1812–87)
novelist, journalist, and philanthropist
1851; or, The Adventures of Mr and Mrs Sandboys and Family (1851)
London Labour and the London Poor (1851)

Mayne, Jasper (1604–72)
archdeacon of Chichester and dramatist
The Citye Match: A comoedye (1639)
The Amorous Warre: A tragi-comoedy (1648)

Mayor, Flora Macdonald ['Mary Strafford'] (1872–1932)
novelist and short-story writer
The Third Miss Symons (1913)

Mead, Robert (1616–53)
poet and dramatist
The Combat of Love and Friendship: A comedy (1654)

Medwall, Henry (*b. c.*1462)
dramatist
Fulgens and Lucrece (1515?)
Nature (1530)

Medwin, Thomas (1788–1869)
biographer of Byron and Shelley
Sketches in Hindoostan, with Other Poems (1821)
Journal of the Conversations of Lord Byron (1824)
The Shelley Papers (1833)
The Life of Percy Bysshe Shelley (1847)

Meeke or Meek, Mary ('Gabrielli', *d.* 1818)
novelist
Count St Blanchard; or, The Prejudiced Judge (1795)

The Mysterious Wife (1797)
The Sicilian (1798)
Anecdotes of the Altamont Family (1800)
Melbancke, Brian (*fl.* 1583)
euphuistic writer
Philotimus (1582)
Melmoth, William, the younger ['Sir Thomas Fitzosborne'] (1710–99)
author, translator, and classical scholar
Of Active and Retired Life (1735)
Two Epistles of Horace Imitated (1736)
The Letters of Pliny the Consul (1747)
Letters on Several Subjects (1748)
The Letters of Marcus Tullius Cicero to Several of his Friends (1753)
Cato; or, An Essay on Old-Age (1773)
Mendes or Mendez, Moses (*d.* 1758)
poet and dramatist
Henry and Blanche; or, The Revengeful Marriage (1745)
The Chaplet: A musical entertainment (1749)
Robin Hood: A new musical entertainment (1751)
The Seasons (1751)
A Collection of the Most Esteemed Pieces of Poetry (1767)
Mercer, David (1928–80)
playwright
Three T.V. Comedies (1966)
After Haggerty (1970)
Meredith, George (1828–1909)
novelist and poet
Poems (1851)
The Shaving of Shagpat: An Arabian entertainment (1855)
Farina (1857)
The Ordeal of Richard Feverel (1859)
Evan Harrington (1861)
Modern Love and Poems of the English Roadside (1862)
Emilia in England (1864)
Rhoda Fleming (1865)
Vittoria (1867)
The Adventures of Harry Richmond (1871)
Beauchamp's Career (1875)
The Egoist (1879)
The Tragic Comedians (1880)
Poems and Lyrics of the Joy of Earth (1883)
Diana of the Crossways (1885)
Sandra Belloni (1886)
Ballads and Poems of Tragic Life (1887)
A Reading of Earth (1888)
One of Our Conquerors (1891)
Modern Love: a Reprint (1892)
Poems (1892)
Lord Ormont and His Aminta (1894)
The Tale of Chloe, and Other Stories (1895)
The Amazing Marriage (1895)
An Essay on Comedy and the Uses of the Comic Spirit (1897)
A Reading of Life, with Other Poems (1901)
Meres, Francis (1565–1647)
divine and author
Palladis Tamia. Wits Treasury (1598)
Meriton, Thomas (*b.* 1638)
dramatist
Love and War (1658)
Merrick, James (1720–69)
poet and scholar
The Destruction of Troy (1742)
Poems on Sacred Subjects (1763)
'Merriman, Henry Seton' [Hugh Stowell Scott] (1862–1903)
novelist
The Phantom Future (1888)
The Sowers (1896)
Merry, Robert ['Della Crusca'] (1755–98)
poet and dramatist
Paulina; or, The Russian Daughter (1787)
Diversity (1788)
The Laurel of Liberty (1790)
Lorenzo: A tragedy (1791)
Mew, Charlotte Mary (1869–1928)
poet and short-story writer
The Farmer's Bride (1916)
The Rambling Sailor (1929)
Meynell, Alice Christiana Gertrude, *née* Thompson (1847–1922)
poet and essayist
Preludes (1875)
Poems (1893)
Other Poems (1896)
Later Poems (1902)
Poems on the War (1915)
A Father of Women, and Other Poems (1917)
Last Poems (1923)
Mickle, William Julius (1735–88)
Scottish poet and translator
The Concubine (1767)
Voltaire in the Shades; or, Dialogues on the Deistical Controversy (1770)
The Lusiad; or, The Discovery of India (1776)
Middleton, Christopher (1560?–1628)
romance writer, translator, and poet
The Historie of Heaven (1596)
The Famous Historie of Chinon of England (1597)
The Legend of Humphrey Duke of Glocester (1600)
Middleton, [John] Christopher (1926–)
poet, translator, and editor
Torse 3 (1962)
Serpentine (1984)
Middleton, Stanley (1919–)
novelist
A Short Answer (1958)
Holiday (1974)
Middleton, Thomas (1580–1627)
dramatist
The Wisdome of Solomon Paraphrased (1597)
Micro-Cynicon (1599)
The Ghost of Lucrece (1600)

Blurt Master-Constable; or, The Spaniards Night-Walke (1602)
The Ant, and the Nightingale; or, Father Hubburds Tales (1604)
The Black Booke (1604)
Michaelmas Terme (1607)
The Phoenix (1607)
The Famelie of Love (1608)
A Mad World, My Masters (1608)
A Tricke to Catch the Old-One (1608)
Your Five Gallants (1608?)
Sir Robert Sherley, Sent Ambassadour in the Name of the King of Persia, to Sigismond the Third, King of Poland (1609)
The Roaring Girle; or, Moll Cut-Purse (1611)
A Faire Quarrell (1617)
The Inner-Temple Masque: or Masque of Heroes (1619)
The Triumphs of Love and Antiquity (1619)
The World Tost at Tennis (1620)
The Sunne in Aries: A noble solemnity performed through the Citie (1621)
A Game at Chess (1625)
A Chast Mayd in Cheape-side: A pleasant conceited comedy (1630)
The Widdow: A comedie (1652)
The Changeling (1653)
The Spanish Gipsie (1653)
No Wit, Help Like a Womans: A comedy (1657)
Two New Playes (1657)
The Mayor of Quinborough: A comedy (1661)
Any Thing for a Quiet Life: A comedy (1662)

Mill, James (1773–1836)
Utilitarian philosopher and historian
Commerce Defended (1808)
Elements of Political Economy (1821)
Essays on Government, Jurisprudence, Liberty of the Press, Prisons and Prison Discipline, Law of Nations, Education (1825)
Analysis of the Phenomena of the Human Mind (1829)

Mill, John Stuart (1806–73)
philosopher and economist
A System of Logic, Ratiocinative and Inductive (1843)
Essays on Some Unsettled Questions of Political Economy (1844)
Principles of Political Economy (1848)
Dissertations and Discussions (1859)
On Liberty (1859)
Thoughts on Parliamentary Reform (1859)
Considerations on Representative Government (1861)
Utilitarianism (1863)
Auguste Comte and Positivism (1865)
England and Ireland (1868)
The Subjection of Women (1869)
Autobiography (1873)

Miller, Andrew (1960)
novelist
Oxygen (2001)

Miller, James (1706–44)
dramatist, poet, and satirist
The Humours of Oxford: A comedy (1730)
The Man of Taste: A comedy (1735)
Joseph and his Brethren: A sacred drama (1744)
Mahomet the Imposter: A tragedy (1744)

Miller, Thomas ['The Basket-Maker'] (1807–74)
poet and novelist
Songs of the Sea Nymphs (1832)
Godfrey Malvern; or, The Life of an Author (1842)

Mills, Magnus (1954)
novelist
The Restraint of Beasts (1999)
Three to See the King (2001)
The Scheme for Full Employment (2003)
Once in a Blue Moon (2003)

Milman, Henry Hart (1791–1868)
historian and poet
Fazio: A tragedy (1815)
Samor: Lord of the bright city (1818)
The Fall of Jerusalem (1820)
Belshazzar (1822)
The Martyr of Antioch (1822)
Anne Boleyn (1826)
The History of the Jews (1829)
Poetical Works (1839)
The History of Christianity (1840)
History of Latin Christianity, Including that of the Popes to Nicolas V (1854)

Milne, Alan Alexander (1882–1956)
novelist, playwright, essayist, poet, and children's writer
Lovers in London (1905)
The Red House Mystery (1922)
When We Were Very Young (1924)
Winnie-the-Pooh (1926)
Now We Are Six (1927)
The House at Pooh Corner (1928)
Toad of Toad Hall (1929)

Milnes, Richard Monckton, 1st Baron Houghton (1809–85)
poet and biographer
Memorials of a Tour in Some Parts of Greece, Chiefly Poetical (1834)
The Life, Letters and Literary Remains of John Keats (1848)

Milton, John (1608–74)
poet
Comus (1637)
Justa Edouardo King naufrago, ab amicus moerentibus, amoris & mneias charin (1638)
Of Reformation Touching Church-Discipline in England: and the Causes that Hitherto Have Hindred It (1641)
Of Prelatical Episcopacy (1641)
Animadversions Upon the Remonstrants Defence, Against Smectymnuus (1641)
The Reason of Church-government Urg'd Against Prelaty (1642)

An Apology against a Pamphlet call'd A modest confutation of the Animadversions upon the Remonstrant against Smectymnuus (1642)
The Doctrine and Discipline of Divorce (1643)
Of Education (1644)
The Judgement of Martin Bucer, Concerning Divorce (1644)
Areopagitica: A speech . . . for the liberty of unlicenc'd printing (1644)
Colasterion: A reply to a nameles answer against The Doctrine and Discipline of Divorce (1645)
Tetrachordon (1645)
Poems of Mr John Milton, Both English and Latin (1646)
The Tenure of Kings and Magistrates (1649)
Eikonoklastes: In answer to a book intitl'd Eikon Basilike (1649)
Pro Populo Anglicano Defensio, Contra Claudii Anonymi, alias Salmasii, Defensionem Regiam (1651)
Pro Populo Anglicano Defensio Secunda (1654)
Considerations Touching the Likeliest Means to Remove Hirelings Out of the Church (1659)
A Treatise of Civil Power in Ecclestiastical Causes (1659)
The Readie & Easie Way to Establish a Free Commonwealth (1660)
Brief Notes Upon a Late Sermon, Titl'd, The Fear of God and the King (1660)
Paradise Lost: A poem written in ten books (1667)
Accedence Commenc't Grammar (1669)
The History of Britain, That Part Especially Now Call'd England (1670)
Paradise Regain'd: A poem . . . To which is added Samson Agonistes (1671)
Of True Religion, Haeresie, Schism, Toleration (1673)
Poems, &c. Upon Several Occasions (1673)
Paradise Lost: A poem in twelve books (1674)
Mr John Miltons Character of the Long Parliament and Assembly of Divines (1681)
A Brief History of Moscovia (1682)
Letters of State (1694)
The Poetical Works of Mr John Milton (1695)
Milton's Paradise Lost (1732)

Minifie, Margaret (*fl.* 1768–83)
novelist
The Hermit (1769)
The Count de Poland (1780)

Mirk, John (*fl.* 1403)
prior of Lilleshall in Shropshire
Festial (1483)

Misselden, Edward (*fl.* 1608–54)
merchant and writer on economics
The Circle of Commerce; or, The Balance of Trade (1623)

Mitchell, Adrian (1932–)
poet, playwright, children's writer, and novelist
Poems (1964)
The Apeman Cometh (1975)

Mitchell, [Charles] Julian (1935–)
novelist and playwright
Imaginary Toys (1961)
The White Father (1964)
The Undiscovered Country (1968)
Another Country (1982)

Mitchell, David (1969)
novelist
Ghostwritten (1999)
Number9dream (2001)

Mitchell, Gladys Maude Winifred (1901–83)
detective novelist
Speedy Death (1929)

Mitchison, Naomi Mary Margaret, *née* Haldane (1897–1999)
novelist, short-story writer, children's author, and biographer
The Conquered (1923)
Cloud Cuckoo Land (1925)
Black Sparta (1928)
The Corn King and the Spring Queen (1931)
Memoirs of a Spacewoman (1962)

Mitford, Jessica Lucy (1917–76)
memoirist, journalist, and social critic
Hons and Rebels (1960)

Mitford, Mary Russell (1787–1855)
novelist, poet, and dramatist
Poems (1810)
Christina, the Maid of the South Seas (1811)
Watlington Hill (1812)
Narrative Poems on the Female Character (1813)
Julian: A tragedy (1823)
Our Village [vol. i] (1824)
Foscari: A tragedy (1826)
Dramatic Scenes, Sonnets, and Other Poems (1827)
Rienzi: A tragedy (1828)
Charles the First: An historical tragedy (1834)
Belford Regis; or, Sketches of a Country Town (1835)
Country Stories (1837)
Recollections of a Literary Life (1852)
Atherton, and Other Tales (1854)
Dramatic Works (1854)

Mitford, Nancy Freeman (1904–73)
novelist and biographer
Highland Fling (1931)
The Pursuit of Love (1945)
Love in a Cold Climate (1949)
Madame de Pompadour (1954)
Noblesse Oblige (1956)
The Sun King (1966)

Mitford, William (1744–1827)
historian
The History of Greece [vol. i] (1784)

Mo, Timothy (1950–)
Anglo-Chinese novelist
The Monkey King (1978)
Sour Sweet (1982)
An Insular Possession (1986)

The Redundancy of Courage (1991)
Brownout on Breadfruit Boulevard (1995)
Moffatt, James (1870–1944)
theologian, translator of the Bible, and author
The Historical New Testament (1901)
The New Testament (1913)
The Old Testament (1924)
The Bible (1926)
Moggach, Deborah (1948–)
novelist, short-story writer, and screenwriter
Hot Water Man (1982)
Porky (1983)
To Have and to Hold (1986)
Driving in the Dark (1988)
Changing Babies (1995)
Tulip Fever (1999)
Final Demand (2001)
Molesworth, Mary Louisa, *née* Stewart ['Ennis Graham'] (1839–1921)
novelist, short-story writer, and children's author
Lover and Husband (1869)
Cicely (1874)
'Carrots': Just a little boy (1876)
A Christmas Child (1880)
Miss Bouverie (1880)
Mollineux, Mary, later Southworth (1651–95)
poet
Fruits of Retirement; or, Miscellaneous Poems, Moral and Divine (1702)
'Moncrieff, William Thomas' [William Thomas Thomas] (1794–1857)
dramatist
The Lear of Private Life; or, Father and Daughter (1820)
Monsarrat, Nicholas John Turney (1910–79)
novelist
This is the Schoolroom (1939)
The Cruel Sea (1951)
Montagu, Charles, earl of Halifax (1661–1715)
poet
An Epistle to the Right Honourable Charles Earl of Dorset and Middlesex (1690)
The Works and Life of the Late Earl of Halifax (1715)
Montagu, Elizabeth, *née* Robinson (1720–1800)
society hostess and author
An Essay on the Writings and Genius of Shakespear (1769)
Letters of Mrs Elizabeth Montagu (1809)
Montagu, Lady Mary Wortley, *née* Pierrepont (1689–1762)
traveller and author
Court Poems: i. The basset-table. ii. The drawing-room. iii. The toilet. (1716)
The Dean's Provocation for Writing the Lady's Dressing-Room (1734)
Six Town Eclogues (1747)
Letters Written, During her Travels in Europe, Asia and Africa, to Persons of Distinction (1763)
Poetical Works (1768)
The Works of the Right Honorable Lady Mary Wortley Montagu (1803)
Letters and Works (1837)
Montgomerie or Montgomery, Alexander (1556?–1610?)
Scottish poet
The Cherrie and the Slaye (1597)
Montgomery, James (1771–1854)
poet
The Wanderer of Switzerland, and Other Poems (1806)
The West Indies, and Other Poems (1810)
The World Before the Flood (1813)
Greenland, and Other Poems (1819)
The Pelican Island, and Other Poems (1827)
Montgomery, Robert (1807–55)
poet
The Omnipresence of the Deity (1828)
Satan (1830)
Woman: The Angel of Life (1833)
Luther (1842)
Moorcock, Michael (1939–)
'New Wave' science fiction writer and fantasy novelist
Behold the Man (1969)
The Final Programme (1969)
A Cure for Cancer (1971)
The English Assassin (1972)
The End of All Songs (1976)
The Condition of Muzak (1977)
Byzantium Endures (1981)
The Brothel in Rosenstrasse (1982)
The Laughter of Carthage (1984)
Jerusalem Commands (1992)
Blood (1995)
King of the City (2000)
London Bone (2001)
Moore, Brian ['Michael Bryan'] (1921–99)
Irish novelist and playwright
Judith Hearne (1955)
The Feast of Lupercal (1958)
The Luck of Ginger Coffey (1960)
An Answer From Limbo (1963)
The Emperor of Ice-Cream (1966)
I am Mary Dunne (1968)
Fergus (1971)
Catholics (1972)
The Great Victorian Collection (1975)
The Doctor's Wife (1976)
The Mangan Inheritance (1979)
Cold Heaven (1983)
Black Robe (1985)
The Colour of Blood (1987)
Lies of Silence (1990)
No Other Life (1993)
The Magician's Wife (1997)
Moore, Edward (1712–57)
fabulist and dramatist
Fables for the Female Sex (1744)
The Foundling: A comedy (1748)

The Gamester: A tragedy (1753)
Moore, Francis ['Old Moore'] (1657–1714)
astrologer and physician
Vox Stellarum: An almanac for 1701 (1700)
Moore, George Augustus (1852–1933)
novelist, poet, and playwright
Flowers of Passion (1877)
Pagan Poems (1881)
A Modern Lover (1883)
A Mummer's Wife (1884)
A Drama in Muslin (1886)
A Mere Accident (1887)
Confessions of a Young Man (1888)
Spring Days (1888)
Mike Fletcher (1889)
Impressions and Opinions (1891)
Vain Fortune (1891)
Modern Painting (1893)
Esther Waters (1894)
Celibates (1895)
Evelyn Innes (1898)
The Bending of the Bough: A comedy (1900)
Sister Teresa (1901)
The Untilled Field (1903)
The Lake (1905)
Memoirs of My Dead Life (1906)
Reminiscences of the Impressionist Painters (1906)
The Apostle (1911)
Ave (1911)
Salve (1912)
Elizabeth Cooper: A comedy (1913)
Vale (1914)
The Brook Kerith (1916)
Lewis Seymour and Some Women (1917)
Conversations in Ebury Street (1924)
The Pastoral Loves of Daphnis and Chloe (1924)
Avowals (1924)
Héloise and Abelard (1925)
Celibate Lives (1927)
The Making of an Immortal (1928)
The Passing of the Essenes (1930)
Aphrodite in Aulis (1930)
Moore, George Edward (1873–1958)
philosopher
Principia Ethica (1903)
Moore, John (1729–1802)
physician, novelist, and author
A View of Society and Manners in France, Switzerland, and Germany (1779)
A View of Society and Manners in Italy (1781)
Zeluco (1789)
A Journal During a Residence in France (1792)
A View of the Causes and Progress of the French Revolution (1795)
Mordaunt (1800)
Moore, Thomas ['Thomas Brown the Younger'] (1779–1852)
poet
Odes of Anacreon (1800)
Corruption, and Intolerance (1801)
The Poetical Works of the Late Thomas Little (1801)
Epistles, Odes and Other Poems (1806)
A Selection of Irish Melodies [pts i, ii] (1808)
The Sceptic (1809)
Intercepted Letters; or, The Twopenny Post-Bag (1813)
Lines on the Death of [*R.B. Sheridan*] (1816)
Lalla Rookh: An oriental romance (1817)
The Fudge Family in Paris (1818)
Tom Crib's Memorial to Congress (1819)
Irish Melodies (1821)
Fables for the Holy Alliance; Rhymes on the Road (1823)
The Loves of the Angels (1823)
Memoirs of Captain Rock, the Celebrated Irish Chieftain (1824)
Memoirs of the Life of Richard Brinsley Sheridan (1825)
The Epicurean (1827)
Travels of an Irish Gentleman in Search of a Religion (1833)
The Fudges in England (1835)
Alciphron (1839)
The Poetical Works of Thomas Moore (1840)
Memoirs, Journal, and Correspondence of Thomas Moore (1853)
More, Hannah ['Will Chip'] (1745–1833)
poet and author
A Search After Happiness (1773)
The Inflexible Captive: A tragedy (1774)
Sir Eldred of the Bower, and The Bleeding Rock (1776)
Essays on Various Subjects (1777)
Percy: A tragedy (1778)
The Fatal Falsehood: A tragedy (1779)
Sacred Dramas, Chiefly Intended for Young Persons (1782)
Slavery (1788)
Thoughts on the Importance of the Manners of the Great to General Society (1788)
An Estimate of the Religion of the Fashionable World (1791)
Strictures on the Modern System of Female Education (1799)
Coelebs in Search of a Wife (1809)
Practical Piety; or, The Influence of the Religion of the Heart on the Conduct of Life (1811)
Christian Morals (1813)
Poems (1816)
Tragedies (1818)
Moral Sketches of Prevailing Opinions and Manners (1819)
Bible Rhymes (1821)
More, Henry (1614–87)
philosopher and poet
Psychodia Platonica; or, A Platonicall Song of the Soul (1642)

Democritus Platonissans; or, An Essay Upon the Infinity of Worlds out of Platonick Principles (1646)
Philosophicall Poems (1647)
Conjectura Cabbalistica (1653)
The Immortality of the Soul (1659)
A Modest Enquiry into the Mystery of Iniquity (1664)

More, Sir Thomas (1478–1535)
Lord Chancellor of England
The Lyfe of Johan Picus Erle of Myrandula (1510?)
Utopia (1516)
Epigrammata (1518)
A Dialogue Concernynge Heresyes & Matters of Religion (1529)
The Supplycacyon of Soulys (1529)
The Confutacyon of Tyndales Answere (1532)
The Apologye of Syr Thomas More Knyght (1533)
The Debellacyon of Salem and Bizance (1533)
A Letter of Syr Tho. More Knyght (1533)
The Second Parte of the Confutacyon of Tyndales Answere (1533)
The Answere to the Poysened Booke Named The Souper of the Lorde (1534)
Lady Fortune (1540?)
Utopia (1551)
A Dialoge of Comfort Against Tribulacion (1553)
The Workes of Sir Thomas More Knyght, Sometime Lorde Chauncellour of England (1557)

Morgan, Charles Langbridge (1894–1958)
novelist and playwright
The Gunroom (1919)
Portrait in a Mirror (1929)
The Fountain (1932)
Sparkenbroke (1936)
Reflections in a Mirror [1st ser.] (1944)

Morgan, Edwin George (1920–)
Scottish poet, critic, and translator
Glasgow Sonnets (1972)
From Glasgow to Saturn (1973)
Sonnets From Scotland (1984)
From the Video Box (1986)
Themes on a Variation (1988)
Collected Poems (1990)
Hold Hands Among the Atoms (1991)

Morgan, Lady Sydney, *née* Owenson (1783?–1859)
Irish novelist and poet
St Clair; or, The Heiress of Desmond (1803)
The Novice of St Dominick (1806)
The Wild Irish Girl (1806)
The Lay of an Irish Harp; or, Metrical Fragments (1807)
Woman; or, Ida of Athens (1809)
The Missionary: An Indian tale (1811)
O'Donnel (1814)
Florence Macarthy (1818)
The O'Briens and the O'Flahertys (1827)
The Princess; or, The Beguine (1835)

Morgann, Maurice (1726–1802)
author
An Essay on the Dramatic Character of Sir John Falstaff (1777)

Morier, David Richard (1784–1877)
traveller and novelist
Photo the Suliote (1857)

Morier, James Justinian (1780–1849)
diplomat, traveller, and novelist
A Journey Through Persia, Armenia, and Asia Minor, to Constantinople, in the Years 1808 and 1809 (1812)
A Second Journey Through Persia, Armenia and Asia Minor (1818)
The Adventures of Hajji Baba, of Ispahan (1824)
The Adventures of Hajji Baba, of Ispahan, in England (1828)
Zohrab the Hostage (1832)
Ayesha, the Maid of Kars (1834)
The Mirza (1841)
Misselmah: A Persian tale (1847)

Morison, Sir Richard (1510?–56)
civil servant and polemicist
A Remedy for Sedition (1536)
An Exhortation to Styrre all Englysshe Men to the Defence of theyr Countreye (1539)
An Introduction to Wisdom (1539)
An Invective Ayenste the Greate and Detestable Vice, Treason (1539)

Morley, John, 1st Viscount Morley of Blackburn (1838–1923)
statesman, critic, and biographer
Critical Miscellanies [1st ser.] (1871)

Morley, Thomas (1557–1602?)
musician
Canzonets; or, Little Short Songs to Three Voyces (1593)
Madrigalls to Foure Voyces (1594)
Canzonets; or, Little Short Songs to Foure Voyces (1597)
A Plaine and Easie Introduction to Practicall Musicke (1597)
The First Booke of Ayres; or, Little Short Songs, to Sing and Play to the Lute (1600)
The Triumphes of Oriana (1601)

Morris, William (1834–96)
poet, artist, and craftsman
The Defence of Guenevere, and Other Poems (1858)
The Life and Death of Jason (1867)
The Earthly Paradise [pts i & ii] (1868)
The Earthly Paradise [pt iii] (1869)
Grettis Saga: the Story of Grettir the Strong (1869)
The Earthly Paradise [pt iv] (1870)
Völsunga Saga: the Story of the Volsungs and Niblungs (1870)
Love is Enough; or, The Freeing of Pharamond (1873)

Three Northern Love Stories, and Other Tales (1875)
The Story of Sigurd the Volsung, and the Fall of the Niblungs (1877)
The Decorative Arts (1878)
A Summary of the Principles of Socialism (1884)
Chants for Socialists (1885)
The Manifesto of the Socialist League (1885)
Useful Work Versus Useless Toil (1886)
The Aims of Art (1887)
A Dream of John Ball; and A King's Lesson (1888)
Signs of Change (1888)
A Tale of the House of the Wolfings and All the Kindreds of the Mark (1889)
The Roots of the Mountains (1890)
News from Nowhere; or, An Epoch of Rest (1891)
The Story of the Glittering Plain (1891)
Poems By the Way (1891)
The Story of Gunnlaug the Worm-Tongue and Raven the Scald (1891)
Gothic Architecture (1893)
Socialism (1893)
The Wood Beyond the World (1894)
Child Christopher and Goldilind the Fair (1895)
The Tale of Beowulf (1895)
The Well at the World's End (1896)
Art and the Beauty of the Earth (1898)

Morrison, Arthur (1863–1945)
novelist and short-story writer
Martin Hewitt, Investigator (1894)
Chronicles of Martin Hewitt (1895)
A Child of the Jago (1896)

Morrison, [Philip] Blake (1950–)
poet and critic
Dark Glasses (1984)
The Ballad of the Yorkshire Ripper (1987)
And When Did You Last See Your Father? (1993)
Things My Mother Never Told Me (2002)

Mortimer, John Clifford (1923–)
novelist, short-story writer, and playwright
A Voyage Round My Father (1971)
Rumpole of the Bailey (1978)
Clinging to the Wreckage (1982)
Paradise Postponed (1985)
Summer's Lease (1988)
Titmuss Regained (1990)
Dunster (1992)
The Sound of Trumpets (1998)
Rumpole Rests His Case (2001)

Mortimer, Penelope Ruth, *née* Fletcher (1918–99)
novelist, biographer, and film critic
A Villa in Summer (1954)
Daddy's Gone-a-Hunting (1958)
The Pumpkin Eater (1962)
The Handyman (1983)

Morton, Henry Canova Vollam (1892–1979)
topographical writer
In Search of England (1927)

Morton, John Maddison (1811–91)
dramatist
Box and Cox: A romance of real life (1847)

Morton, Thomas (1764?–1838)
dramatist
The Way to Get Married: A comedy (1796)
Speed the Plough: A comedy (1800)
The School of Reform; or, How to Rule a Husband: A comedy (1805)
Town and Country (1807)
The Knight of Snowdoun (1811)

Moryson, Fynes (1566–1630)
traveller
An Itinerary Written by Fynes Moryson Gent. (1617)

Moser, Joseph (1748–1819)
artist, author, and magistrate
Turkish Tales (1794)
The Hermit of Caucasus: An oriental romance (1796)

Mosley, Nicholas, 3rd Baron Ravensdale (1923–)
novelist and biographer
Spaces of the Dark (1951)
The Rainbearers (1955)
Meeting Place (1962)
Accident (1965)
Impossible Object (1969)
Catastrophe Practice (1979)
Imago Bird (1980)
Serpent (1981)
Judith (1986)
Hopeful Monsters (1990)
Children of Darkness and Light (1996)

Motion, Andrew Peter (1952–)
Poet Laureate, biographer, critic, and novelist
The Pleasure Steamers (1978)
Independence (1981)
Secret Narratives (1983)
Dangerous Play (1984)
Natural Causes (1987)
Love in a Life (1991)
Philip Larkin (1993)
The Price of Everything (1994)
Salt Water (1997)
Keats (1997)
Selected Poems 1976–1997 (1998)
Here to Eternity (2001)
Public Property (2002)
The Invention of Dr Cake (2003)

Motteux, Peter Anthony (1663–1718)
translator and dramatist
Love's a Jest: A comedy (1696)
Beauty in Distress: A tragedy (1698)
The Island Princess; or, The Generous Portuguese (1699)
The History of the Renown'd Don-Quixote de la Mancha (1700)
The Masque of Acis and Galatea (1701)
Arsinoe, Queen of Cyprus: An opera (1705)
Thomyris, Queen of Scythia: An opera (1707)

Love's Triumph: An opera (1708)
A Poem Upon Tea (1712)
Mottley, John ['Elijah Jenkins'] (1692–1750)
dramatist and biographer
The Imperial Captives: A tragedy (1720)
Antiochus: A tragedy (1721)
Penelope: A dramatic opera (1728)
The Widow Bewitch'd: A comedy (1730)
Joe Miller's Jests; or, The Wits Vade-Mecum (1739)
Mottram, Ralph Hale (1883–1971)
novelist and author
The Spanish Farm (1924)
Sixty-Four, Ninety-Four! (1925)
The Crime at Vanderlynden's (1926)
Mountfort, William (1664–92)
actor and dramatist
The Injur'd Lovers; or, The Ambitious Father: A tragedy (1688)
The Successfull Straingers: A tragi-comedy (1690)
Zelmane; or, The Corinthian Queen (1705)
Mudford, William (1782–1848)
journalist and novelist
Augustus and Mary; or, The Maid of Buttermere (1803)
Muir, Edwin ['Edward Moore'] (1887–1959)
poet, critic, translator, and novelist
We Moderns (1918)
First Poems (1925)
Chorus of the Newly Dead (1926)
The Structure of the Novel (1928)
Journeys and Places (1937)
The Story and the Fable (1940)
The Labyrinth (1949)
Collected Poems 1921–51 (1952)
One Foot in Eden (1956)
Collected Poems 1921–58 (1960)
Mulcaster, Richard (1530?–1611)
schoolmaster and author
Positions Necessarie for the Training Up of Children (1581)
Muldoon, Paul (1951–)
Northern Irish poet
Knowing My Place (1971)
New Weather (1973)
Mules (1977)
Why Brownlee Left (1980)
Out of Siberia (1982)
Quoof (1983)
Meeting the British (1987)
Madoc (1990)
The Annals of Chile (1994)
The Prince of Quotidian (1994)
Hay (1998)
Vera of Las Vegas (2001)
Moy Sand and Gravel (2002)
Mulholland, Rosa, Lady Gilbert ['Ruth Murray'] (1841–1921)
Irish novelist, short-story writer, and poet
Hester's History (1869)

Mun, Thomas (1571–1641)
writer on economics
A Discourse of Trade, from England unto the East-Indies (1621)
England's Treasure by Forraign Trade (1664)
'Munda, Constantia' (*fl.* 1617)
pseudonymous female author
The Worming of a Mad Dogge; or, A Soppe for Cerberus the Jaylor of Hell (1617)
Munday, Anthony (1553–1633)
poet and dramatist
The Mirrour of Mutabilitie, or Principall Part of the Mirrour for Magistrates (1579)
The Paine of Pleasure (1580)
Zelauto: The Fountaine of Fame (1580)
A Breefe Discourse of the Taking of Edmund Campion (1581)
A Courtly Controversie, betweene Loove and Learning (1581)
A Breefe Aunswer Made Unto Two Seditious Pamphlets (1582)
The English Romayne Lyfe (1582)
Fedele and Fortunio (1585)
A Banquet of Daintie Conceits (1588)
Palladine of England (1588)
Palmerin D'Oliva: The Mirrour of Nobilitie (1588)
Palmendos (1589)
The First Book of Amadis of Gaule (1590)
Palmerin of England (1596)
Sir John Old-castle (1600)
The Downfall of Robert, Earle of Huntington, afterward Called Robin Hood of Merrie Sherwodde (1601)
The Death of Robert, Earle of Huntington. Otherwise Called Robin Hood of Merrie Sherwodde (1601)
The True Knowledge of a Mans Owne Selfe (1602)
Murdoch, Dame Iris Jean (1919–99)
novelist and philosopher
Under the Net (1954)
The Flight From the Enchanter (1956)
The Sandcastle (1957)
The Bell (1958)
A Severed Head (1961)
An Unofficial Rose (1962)
The Unicorn (1963)
The Italian Girl (1964)
The Red and the Green (1965)
The Time of the Angels (1966)
The Nice and the Good (1968)
Bruno's Dream (1969)
The Sovereignty of Good (1970)
An Accidental Man (1971)
The Black Prince (1973)
The Sacred and Profane Love Machine (1974)
A World Child (1975)
The Fire and the Sun (1977)
The Sea, the Sea (1978)
Nuns and Soldiers (1980)

The Philosopher's Pupil (1983)
The Good Apprentice (1985)
The Book and the Brotherhood (1987)
The Message to the Planet (1989)
Metaphysics as a Guide to Morals (1992)
The Green Knight (1993)

Murphy, Arthur (1727–1805)
barrister, actor, and dramatist
The Upholsterer; or, What News? (1758)
The Orphan of China: A tragedy (1759)
The Desert Island (1760)
The Way to Keep Him (1760)
All in the Wrong (1761)
The Old Maid (1761)
The Citizen (1763)
No One's Enemy But His Own: A comedy (1764)
What We Must All Come To: A comedy (1764)
The School for Guardians (1767)
Zenobia: A tragedy (1768)
The Grecian Daughter: A tragedy (1772)
Alzuma: A tragedy (1773)
The Life of David Garrick (1801)

Murray, David Christie (1847–1907)
journalist and novelist
Joseph's Coat (1881)

Murry, Ann (c.1755–post 1812)
poet
Mentoria; or, The Young Lady's Instructor in Familiar Conversations (1778)
Poems on Various Subjects (1779)

Murry, John Middleton (1889–1957)
critic, editor, novelist, and poet
Fyodor Dostoevsky (1916)
The Evolution of an Intellectual (1920)
Countries of the Mind (1922)
The Problem of Style (1922)
Keats and Shakespeare (1925)
Katherine Mansfield, and Other Literary Portraits (1949)

Minshull or Mynshul, Geffray (1594?–1668)
author
Certaine Characters and Essayes of Prison and Prisoners (1618)

Nabbes, Thomas (1605?–45?)
dramatist
Hannibal and Scipio: An historicall tragedy (1637)
Microcosmus: A morall maske (1637)
Covent Garden: A pleasant comedie (1638)
The Springs Glorie (1638)
Totenham Court: A pleasant comedie (1638)
The Bride: A comedie (1640)
The Unfortunate Mother: A tragedie (1640)

Naipaul, Shiva[dhar] Srinivasa (1945–85)
Trinidadian novelist and travel writer
Fireflies (1970)
The Chip-Chip Gatherers (1973)
North of South (1978)
A Hot Country (1983)

Naipaul, Sir Vidiadhar Surajprasad (1932–)
Trinidadian novelist and travel writer
The Mystic Masseur (1957)
The Suffrage of Elvira (1958)
A House For Mr Biswas (1961)
The Middle Passage (1962)
An Area of Darkness (1964)
The Mimic Men (1967)
In a Free State (1971)
Guerillas (1975)
India (1977)
A Bend in the River (1979)
The Enigma of Arrival (1987)
A Way in the World (1994)
Half a Life (2001)

Namier, Sir Lewis Bernstein (1888–1960)
historian
Conflicts (1942)
Europe in Decay (1950)

Napier, Sir William Francis Patrick (1785–1860)
historian
History of the War in the Peninsula and the South of France (1828)

Narayan, Rasipuram Krishnaswami (1906–2001)
Indian novelist
The Bachelor of Arts (1935)
The English Teacher (1945)
Mr Sampath (1949)
The Financial Expert (1952)
The Man-Eater of Malgudi (1961)
The Vendor of Sweets (1967)
My Days (1975)
The Painter of Signs (1977)
Malgudi Days (1982)
A Tiger for Malgudi (1983)
The World of Nagaraj (1990)

Nashe, Thomas (1567–1601)
satirist, dramatist, and pamphleteer
An Almond for a Parrat; or, Cutbert Curry-Knaves Almes (1589)
The Anatomie of Absurditie (1589)
Pierce Penilesse his Supplication to the Divell (1592)
Strange Newes, of the Intercepting Certaine Letters (1592)
Christs Teares Over Jerusalem (1593)
The Terrors of the Night; or, A Discourse of Apparitions (1594)
The Unfortunate Traveller; or, The Life of Jacke Wilton (1594)
Have With You to Saffron-walden (1596)
Nashes Lenten Stuffe (1599)
Summers Last Will and Testament (1600)

Naughton, Bill (1910–92)
playwright, novelist, and short-story writer
Alfie (1966)

Naunton, Sir Robert (1563–1635)
politician and author

Fragmenta Regalia: Or observations on the late Queen Elizabeth, her times and favorits (1641)
Neal, Daniel (1678–1743)
historian of the Puritans
The History of the Puritans or Protestant Non-Conformists (1732)
Neale, William Johnson Nelson (1812–93)
novelist
Cavendish; or, The Patrician at Sea (1831)
The Port Admiral (1833)
Gentleman Jack (1837)
The Flying Dutchman (1839)
The Naval Surgeon (1841)
Paul Periwinkle; or, The Press Gang (1841)
Neate, Patrick
novelist
Twelve Bar Blues (2001)
The London Pigeon Wars (2003)
Nedham or Needham, Marchamont (1620–78)
journalist and author
Mercurius Britanicus: Communicating the affaires of Great Britaine (1643)
Mercurius Pragmaticus: Communicating intelligence from all parts (1647)
Mercurius Pragmaticus, (for King Charles II) (1647)
The Case of the Common-Wealth of England, Stated (1650)
Mercurius Politicus: Comprising the summ of all intelligence (1650)
The Publick Intelligencer: Communicating the chief occurrences and proceedings (1655)
The Excellencie of a Free-State; or, The Right Constitution of a Common-wealth (1656)
The Publick Adviser (1657)
Interest Will Not Lie (1659)
Needham, [Noel] Joseph Terence Montgomery (1900–95)
zoologist and historian of China
Science and Civilisation in China (1954)
Nesbit, Edith, later Bland, then Tucker (1858–1924)
novelist, children's author, and poet
Lays and Legends [1st ser.] (1886)
Grim Tales (1893)
The Story of the Treasure Seekers (1899)
The Book of Dragons (1900)
The Wouldbegoods (1901)
Five Children and It (1902)
The New Treasure Seekers (1904)
The Phoenix and the Carpet (1904)
Oswald Bastable and Others (1905)
The Railway Children (1906)
Ballads and Lyrics of Socialism (1908)
The Complete History of the Bastable Family (1928)
Neville, Henry (1620–94)
political and miscellaneous writer
The Parliament of Ladies (1647)
The Ladies, a Second Time, Assembled in Parliament (1647)
Newes From the New Exchange; or, The Commonwealth of Ladies (1650)
The Isle of Pines; or, A Late Discovery of a Fourth Island in Terra Australis, Incognita (1668)
A New and Further Discovery of the Islle of Pines (1668)
Nevyle or Neville, Alexander (1544–1614)
scholar and translator
The Lamentable Tragedie of Œdipus the Sonne of Laius Kyng of Thebes out of Seneca (1563)
Newbolt, Sir Henry John (1862–1938)
poet and novelist
Admirals All, and Other Verses (1897)
The Island Race (1898)
The Sailing of the Long Ships, and Other Poems (1902)
Songs of the Sea (1904)
St George's Day, and Other Poems (1918)
Newby, [George] Eric (1919–)
travel writer
A Short Walk in the Hindu Kush (1958)
Newby, Percy Howard (1918–97)
novelist
A Journey to the Interior (1945)
The Picnic at Sakkara (1955)
Revolution and Roses (1957)
The Barbary Light (1962)
Something to Answer For (1968)
Something About Women (1995)
Newcomb, Thomas (1682?–1765)
poet
The Woman of Taste (1733)
Newman, Francis William (1805–97)
theological writer
The Soul (1849)
Phases of Faith; or, Passages from the History of my Creed (1850)
Homeric Translation in Theory and Practice (1861)
Newman, John Henry (1801–90)
cardinal, poet, and theological writer
St Bartholomew's Eve (1821)
The Arians of the Fourth Century (1833)
Lyra Apostolica (1836)
Plain Sermons by Contributors to the 'Tracts for the Times' (1839)
Remarks on Certain Passages in the Thirty-Nine Articles (1841)
Lives of the English Saints (1844)
Loss and Gain (1848)
Callista (1856)
Apologia Pro Vita Sua (1864)
Mr Kingsley and Dr Newman (1864)
The Dream of Gerontius (1866)
Essays Critical and Historical (1872)
The Idea of a University (1873)
Tracts Theological and Ecclesiastical (1874)
The Via Media of the Anglican Church (1877)

Newman, Thomas (*fl.* 1627)
translator
The Two First Comedies of Terence Called Andria, and The Eunuch (1627)
Newton, Sir Isaac (1642–1727)
mathematician and scientist
Philosophiae Naturalis Principia Mathematica (1687)
Opticks; or, A Treatise of the Reflexions, Refractions, Inflexions and Colours of Light (1704)
The Mathematical Principles of Natural Philosophy (1729)
The Method of Fluxions and Infinite Series (1736)
Newton, John (1725–1807)
Evangelical divine, poet, and hymn-writer
An Authentic Narrative of Some Remarkable and Interesting Particulars in the Life of [Newton] (1764)
Cardiphonia; or, The Utterance of the Heart (1781)
Messiah (1786)
Thoughts Upon the African Slave Trade (1788)
Letters to a Wife (1793)
Newton, Thomas (1542?–1607)
physician, poet, and translator
Seneca his Tenne Tragedies (1581)
Atropoion Delion; or, The Death of Delia (1603)
Niccols, Richard (1584–1616)
poet
The Furies. With Vertues Encomium; or, The Image of Honour (1614)
Sir Thomas Overburies Vision (1616)
The Beggers Ape (1627)
Nichols, Grace (1950–)
Guyana-born poet
I is a Long-Memoried Woman (1983)
The Fat Black Woman's Poems (1984)
Whole of a Morning Sky (1986)
Lazy Thoughts of a Lazy Woman, and Other Poems (1989)
Sunris (1996)
Nichols, John (1745–1826)
printer, antiquary, poet, and author
A Select Collection of Poems (1780)
Biographical Anecdotes of William Hogarth (1781)
Biographical and Literary Anecdotes of William Bowyer (1782)
The Epistolary Correspondence of Sir Richard Steele (1787)
Brief Memoirs of John Nichols (1804)
Literary Anecdotes of the Eighteenth Century (1812)
Illustrations of the Literary History of the Eighteenth Century (1817)
Nichols, Peter Richard (1927–)
playwright
A Day in the Death of Joe Egg (1967)
The National Health; or, Nurse Norton's Affair (1970)
Privates on Parade (1977)
Born in the Gardens (1980)
Nichols, Robert Malise Bowyer (1893–1944)
poet, playwright, and novelist
Invocation (1915)
A Spanish Triptych (1936)
Such Was My Singing (1942)
Nicholson, Norman Cornthwaite (1914–87)
poet
Man and Literature (1943)
Rock Face (1948)
The Pot Geranium (1954)
A Local Habitation (1972)
Cloud on Black Combe (1975)
The Shadow of Black Combe (1978)
Sea to the West (1981)
Selected Poems 1940–82 (1982)
Nicolson, Sir Harold George (1886–1968)
diplomatist and author
Sweet Waters (1921)
Friday Mornings 1941–4 (1944)
Diaries and Letters 1930–62 (1966)
Noonan, Robert P. ['Robert Tressall'] (1870–1911)
Irish novelist
The Ragged Trousered Philanthropists (1914)
Norden, John (1548–1625?)
topographer, cartographer, and religious writer
A Pensive Mans Practise Very Profitable for all Personnes (1584)
A Sinfull Mans Solace: Most Sweete and Comfortable, for the Sicke and Sorrowful Soule (1585)
Speculum Britanniæ the First Parte: An historicall discription of Middlesex (1593)
The Pensive Mans Practise. The Second Part; or, The Pensive Mans Complaint and Comfort (1594)
The Description of Hertfordshire (1598)
A Progresse of Pietie (1598)
Civita Londini (1600)
Vicissitudo Rerum: An elegaicall poeme, of the interchangeable courses and varietie of things in this world (1600)
A Pensive Soules Delight (1603)
The Labyrinth of Mans Life; or, Vertues Delight and Envies Opposite (1614)
Norris, John (1657–1711)
philosopher and poet
Poems and Discourses. Occasionally Written (1684)
A Collection of Miscellanies (1687)
The Theory and Regulation of Love (1688)
Christian Blessedness (1690)
Letters Concerning the Love of God (1695)
An Essay Towards the Theory of the Ideal or Intelligible World (1701)

North, Sir Dudley (1641–91)
financier and economist
Discourses Upon Trade (1691)

North, Sir Thomas (1535–1601?)
translator
The Diall of Princes (1557)
The Morall Philosophie of Doni (1570)
The Lives of the Noble Grecians and Romanes (1579)

Northcote, James (1746–1831)
painter and author
Memoirs of Sir Joshua Reynolds (1813)

Norton, Caroline Elizabeth Sarah, *née* Sheridan, later Lady Stirling-Maxwell (1808–77)
poet, novelist, and polemicist
The Sorrows of Rosalie: A Tale; with Other Poems (1829)
The Wife, and Woman's Reward (1835)
A Voice From the Factories (1836)
Lost and Saved (1863)

Norton, Mary (1903–92)
children's writer
The Magic Bed-Knob (1945)
The Borrowers (1952)

Norton, Thomas (1532–84)
statesman, poet, and dramatist
The Institution of the Christian Religion (1561)
Gorboduc (1565)
A Catechisme, or First Instruction of Christian Religion (1570)
A Declaration of the Favourable Dealing of Her Majesties Commissioners Appointed for the Examination of Certaine Traitours (1583)

Noyes, Alfred (1880–1958)
poet, novelist, and critic
The Loom of Years (1902)
The Flower of Old Japan (1903)
Poems (1904)
Drake [vol. i] (1906)
Forty Singing Seamen, and Other Poems (1907)
The Enchanted Island, and Other Poems (1909)
Tales of the Mermaid Tavern (1913)
The Watchers of the Sky (1922)

Nugent, Robert Craggs, earl Nugent (1709–88)
poet and politician
An Epistle to the Right Honourable, Sir Robert Walpole (1739)
An Ode on Mr Pulteney (1739)
An Ode, to His Royal Highness on His Birthday (1739)
Odes and Epistles (1739)
An Ode to Mankind (1741)

Nye, Robert Thomas (1939–)
novelist, poet, editor, and children's writer
Doubtfire (1968)
Falstaff (1976)
Faust (1980)
Mrs Shakespeare (1993)
The Late Mr Shakespeare (1998)

O'Brian, Patrick [originally Richard Patrick Russ] (1914–2000)
novelist
The Golden Ocean (1956)
Master and Commander (1970)
The Hundred Days (1998)

O'Brien, Conor Cruise (1917–)
Irish critic and political commentator
States of Ireland (1972)

'O'Brien, Flann' [Brian O'Nolan] (1911–66)
Irish novelist and humorist
At Swim-Two-Birds (1939)
The Hard Life (1961)
The Dalkey Archive (1964)

O'Brien, [Josephine] Edna (1932–)
Irish novelist and short-story writer
The Country Girls (1960)
The Lonely Girl (1962)
Girls in Their Married Bliss (1964)
August is a Wicked Month (1965)
Casualties of Peace (1966)
The Love Object (1968)
A Pagan Place (1970)
Night (1972)
A Scandalous Woman (1974)
Johnnie, I Hardly Knew You (1977)
Returning (1982)
The High Road (1988)
Lantern Slides (1990)
Time and Tide (1992)
The House of Splendid Isolation (1994)

O'Brien, Kate (1897–1974)
Irish novelist and playwright
Without my Cloak (1931)
The Ante-Room (1934)
Mary Lavelle (1936)
Farewell Spain (1937)
The Land of Spices (1941)
That Lady (1946)

O'Brien, Sean (1952–)
poet and critic
The Indoor Park (1983)
HMS Glasshouse (1991)
Ghost Train (1995)
The Deregulated Muse (1998)
Downriver (2001)
Cousin Coat (2002)

O'Casey, Sean [born John Casey] (1880–1964)
Irish playwright
Two Plays (1925)
The Plough and the Stars (1926)
The Silver Tassie: A tragi-comedy (1928)
Within the Gates (1933)
Windfalls: Stories, poems, and plays (1934)
I Knock at the Door (1939)
Purple Dust (1940)
The Star Turns Red (1940)
Pictures in the Hallway (1942)
Red Roses for Me (1942)
Drums Under the Window (1945)
Cock-a-Doodle Dandy (1949)

Inishfallen, Fare Thee Well (1949)
Rose and Crown (1952)
The Bishop's Bonfire (1955)
The Green Crow (1957)
Ockley, Simon (1678–1720)
orientalist
The Conquest of Syria, Persia, and Aegypt by the Saracens (1708)
'O'Connor, Frank' [Michael Francis O'Donovan] (1903–66)
Irish short-story writer, critic, and novelist
Guests of the Nation (1931)
The Saint and Mary Kate (1932)
Bones of Contention, and Other Stories (1936)
Dutch Interior (1940)
Crab Apple Jelly (1944)
The Common Chord (1947)
Traveller's Samples (1951)
Domestic Relations (1957)
O'Donoghue, Bernard (1945)
poet and academic
Outliving (2003)
O'Faolain, Julia (1932–)
Irish novelist and short-story writer
No Country for Young Men (1980)
O'Faolain, Sean [born John Francis Whelan] (1900–91)
Irish short-story writer and novelist
Midsummer Night Madness, and Other Stories (1932)
A Nest of Simple Folk (1933)
Bird Alone (1936)
A Purse of Coppers (1937)
Come Back to Erin (1940)
Teresa, and Other Stories (1947)
The Short Story (1948)
The Heat of the Sun (1966)
Foreign Affairs, and Other Stories (1976)
Ogden, Charles Kay (1889–1957)
linguistic psychologist and originator of Basic English
The Foundations of Aesthetics (1922)
The Meaning of Meaning (1923)
The ABC of Psychology (1929)
Basic English (1930)
The Basic Dictionary (1932)
Ogilby, John (1600–76)
translator and printer
The Works of Publius Virgilius Maro (1649)
Ogilvie, John (1732–1813)
Presbyterian divine, author, and poet
The Day of Judgment (1753)
Poems on Various Subjects (1762)
Paradise (1769)
The Fane of the Druids (1787)
The Fane of the Druids (1789)
The Theology of Plato (1793)
O'Hagan, Andrew (1968)
novelist
Our Fathers (1999)
Personality (2003)
O'Hara, Kane (1714?–82)
burlesque writer
Midas: An English burletta (1764)
O'Keeffe, John (1747–1833)
Irish poet, actor, and dramatist
Tony Lumpkin in Town (1780)
The Poor Soldier: A comic opera (1785)
Patrick in Prussia; or, Love in a Camp: A comic opera (1786)
Okri, Ben[jamin] (1959–)
Nigerian-born novelist, poet, and short-story writer
Incidents at the Shrine (1986)
The Famished Road (1991)
Songs of Enchantment (1993)
Astonishing the Gods (1995)
Infinite Riches (1998)
Oldham, John (1653–83)
miscellaneous author
Upon the Marriage of the Prince of Orange with the Lady Mary (1677)
Garnets Ghost (1679)
A Satyr Against Vertue (1679)
Satyrs upon the Jesuits (1681)
Poems, and Translations (1683)
The Works of Mr John Oldham (1684)
Oldmixon, John (1673–1742)
historian, pamphleteer, poet, and critic
Poems on Several Occasions (1696)
Amintas: A pastoral (1698)
Reflections on the Stage, and Mr Collier's Defence of the Short View (1699)
The Governour of Cyprus: A tragedy (1703)
The Muses Mercury; or, The Monthly Miscellany (1707)
The Dutch Barrier Our's; or, The Interest of England and Holland Inseparable (1712)
Reflections on Dr Swift's Letter to the Earl of Oxford, About the English Tongue (1712)
The Secret History of Europe (1712)
Memoirs of Ireland from the Restoration, to the Present Times (1716)
The Critical History of England, Ecclesiastical and Civil (1724)
A Review of Dr Zachary Grey's Defence of Our Ancient and Modern Historians (1725)
Clarendon and Whitlock Compar'd (1727)
The Arts of Logick and Rhetorick (1728)
An Essay on Criticism (1728)
The History of England, During the Reigns of the Royal House of Stuart (1729)
The History of England, During the Reigns of William and Mary, Anne, George I (1735)
The History of England During the Reigns of Henry VIII. Edward VI. Queen Mary. Queen Elizabeth (1739)
Memoirs of the Press, Historical and Political (1742)
Oldys, William (1696–1761)
Norroy king-of-arms and antiquary

A Dissertation Upon Pamphlets (1731)
The British Librarian (1737)
The Life of Sir Walter Ralegh (1740)
The Harleian Miscellany (1744)

Oliphant, Laurence (1829–88)
novelist
A Journey to Katmandu with the Camp of Jung Bahadoor (1852)
Piccadilly (1870)

Oliphant, Margaret Oliphant, *née* Wilson, Mrs M.O.W. Oliphant (1828–97)
novelist and short-story writer
Passages in the Life of Mrs Margaret Maitland (1849)
John Drayton (1851)
Magdalen Hepburn (1854)
Lilliesleaf (1855)
Zaidee (1855)
The Rector; and The Doctor's Family (1863)
Salem Chapel (1863)
The Perpetual Curate (1864)
Miss Marjoribanks (1866)
The Curate in Charge (1876)
Phoebe Junior (1876)
A Beleaguered City (1879)
A Little Pilgrim in the Unseen (1882)
The Land of Darkness (1888)

Onions, [George] Oliver (1873–1961)
novelist and short-story writer
Widdershins (1911)
The Story of Ragged Robyn (1945)
Poor Man's Tapestry (1946)

Opie, Amelia, *née* Alderson (1769–1853)
novelist and poet
Dangers of Coquetry (1790)
The Father and Daughter (1801)
Poems (1802)
Adeline Mowbray; or, The Mother and Daughter (1805)
Simple Tales (1806)
The Warrior's Return, and Other Poems (1808)
Temper; or, Domestic Scenes (1812)
Tales of Real Life (1813)
Valentine's Eve (1816)
New Tales (1818)
Tales of the Heart (1820)
Madeline (1822)
The Negro Boy's Tale (1824)
Tales of the Pemberton Family (1825)
The Black Man's Lament; or, How to Make Sugar (1826)
Lays for the Dead (1834)

Oppenheim, Edward Phillips (1866–1946)
popular novelist and short-story writer
The Mysterious Mr Sabin (1898)

Orage, Alfred Richard (1873–1934)
social critic and editor
Friedrich Nietzsche: The Dionysian spirit of the age (1906)
An Alphabet of Economics (1917)

Orczy, Emma Magdalena Rosalia Maria Josefa Barbara, Baroness Orczy, later Mrs Montagu Barstow (1865–1947)
novelist and short-story writer
The Scarlet Pimpernel (1905)
The Old Man in the Corner (1909)

Orme, Robert (1728–1801)
historian
A History of the Military Transactions of the British Nation in Indostan from the Year 1745 (1763)

Orton, Joe [John Kingsley Orton] (1933–67)
playwright
Entertaining Mr Sloane (1964)
Crimes of Passion (1967)
Loot (1967)
What the Butler Saw (1969)
Funeral Games; The Good and Faithful Servants (1970)
Between Us Girls (1998)

'Orwell, George' [Eric Arthur Blair] (1903–50)
novelist and social critic
Down and Out in Paris and London (1933)
Burmese Days (1935)
A Clergyman's Daughter (1935)
Keep the Aspidistra Flying (1936)
The Road to Wigan Pier (1937)
Homage to Catalonia (1938)
Coming Up For Air (1939)
Inside the Whale, and Other Essays (1940)
The Lion and the Unicorn: Socialism and the English genius (1941)
Animal Farm (1945)
Critical Essays (1946)
Nineteen Eighty-Four (1949)
Shooting an Elephant, and Other Essays (1950)
England Your England, and Other Essays (1953)
Collected Essays (1961)
Decline of the English Murder, and Other Essays (1965)

Osborne, John James (1929–94)
playwright
Look Back in Anger (1957)
The Entertainer (1957)
Plays For England (1963)
Inadmissible Evidence (1965)
A Patriot for Me (1966)
West of Suez (1971)
A Sense of Detachment (1973)
A Better Class of Person (1981)
Almost a Gentleman (1991)
Déja Vu (1992)

O'Shaughnessy, Arthur William Edgar (1844–81)
poet
An Epic of Women, and Other Poems (1870)
Music and Moonlight (1874)

Oswald, Alice (1966)
poet
Dart (2002)

Otway, Thomas (1652–85)
dramatist and poet
Alcibiades: A tragedy (1675)
Don Carlos, Prince of Spain: A tragedy (1676)
Titus and Berenice: A tragedy (1677)
Friendship in Fashion: A comedy (1678)
The History and Fall of Caius Marius: A tragedy (1680)
The Orphan; or, The Unhappy Marriage: A tragedy (1680)
The Poet's Complaint of his Muse; or, A Satyr Against Libells (1680)
The Souldiers Fortune: A comedy (1681)
Venice Preserv'd; or, A Plot Discover'd: A tragedy (1682)
The Atheist; or, The Second Part of the Souldiers Fortune (1684)
Windsor Castle (1685)
The History of the Triumvirates (1686)
The Works of Mr Thomas Otway (1712)
'Ouida' [Marie Louise de la Ramée, originally Louise Ramé] (1839–1908)
novelist and short-story writer
Held in Bondage (1863)
Stratmore (1865)
Chandos (1866)
Under Two Flags (1867)
Folle-Farine (1871)
Overbury, Sir Thomas (1581–1613)
poet and victim of court intrigue
A Wife, Now a Widdowe (1614)
The First and Second Part of the Remedy of Love (1620)
Overton, Richard (*fl.* 1642–63)
pamphleteer and satirist
Mans Mortallitie (1643)
Owen, Robert (1771–1858)
social reformer
A Statement Regarding the New Lanark Establishment (1812)
A New View of Society (1813)
Observations on the Effect of the Manufacturing System (1815)
An Exploration of the Cause of the Distress which Pervades the Civilized Parts of the World (1823)
Manifesto of Robert Owen (1840)
The Social Bible (1840)
Life, Written by Himself (1857)
Owen, Wilfred Edward Salter (1893–1918)
poet
Poems (1920)
Collected Poems (1963)
Oxenford, John (1812–77)
dramatist, critic, and translator
My Fellow Clerk: A farce (1835)

Pack, Richardson (1682–1728)
miscellaneous writer
Miscellanies in Verse and Prose (1718)
A New Collection of Miscellanies in Verse and Prose (1725)
'Pain, Barry' [Eric Odell] (1864–1928)
journalist, humorist, novelist, and short-story writer
Eliza (1900)
Eliza Getting On (1911)
Exit Eliza (1912)
Eliza's Son (1913)
Paine, Thomas (1737–1809)
political writer
The American Crisis (1776)
Common Sense (1776)
Rights of Man (1791)
The Age of Reason (1794)
Dissertation on First Principles of Government (1795)
Painter, William (1540?–94)
translator
The Palace of Pleasure (1566)
The Second Tome of the Palace of Pleasure (1567)
Paley, William (1743–1805)
theological and philosophical writer
The Principles of Moral and Political Philosophy (1785)
Horae Paulinae; or, The Truth of the Scripture History of St Paul Evinced (1790)
A View of the Evidences of Christianity (1794)
Natural Theology (1802)
Palgrave, Francis Turner ['Henry J. Thurstan'] (1824–97)
poet, novelist, and anthologist
Preciosa (1852)
The Golden Treasury of Songs and Lyrics (1861)
The Children's Treasury of English Song (1875)
Palmer, Charlotte (*fl.* 1790–1800)
novelist
Integrity and Content (1792)
It is, and it is not a Novel (1792)
Paltock, Robert (1697–1767)
novelist
The Life and Adventures of Peter Wilkins, a Cornish Man (1750)
Park, Mungo (1771–1806)
explorer and author
Travels in the Interior Districts of Africa (1799)
Parke, Robert (*fl.* 1588)
translator
The Historie of the Great and Mighty Kingdome of China, and the Situation Thereof (1588)
Parker, Henry, 8th Baron Morley (1476–1556)
translator
The Tryumphes of Fraunces Petrarcke (1555?)
Parker, Martin (*d.* 1656?)
poet and ballad-maker
The Poet's Blind Mans Bough; or, Have Among You My Blind Harpers (1641)
Parker, Matthew (1504–75)
archbishop of Canterbury
An Admonition . . . (1560)
A Godly and Necessarye Admonition of the Decrees and Canons of the Counsel of Trent (1564)

The Whole Psalter Translated into English Metre (1567?)
The Holie Bible (1568)
The Holi Bible (1569)

Parker, Samuel (1640–88)
bishop of Oxford
A Free and Impartial Censure of the Platonick Philosophie (1666)
A Discourse of Ecclesiastical Politie (1670)
A Defence and Continuation of the Ecclesiastical Politie (1671)
Religion and Loyalty; or, A Demonstration of the Power of the Christian Church Within It Self (1684)
Religion and Loyalty. The Second Part (1685)

Parkinson, John (1567–1650)
apothecary and herbalist
Paradisi in sole Paradisus terrestris: Or a garden of all sorts of pleasant flowers (1629)
Theatrum Botanicum: The Theater of Plants (1640)

Parks, Tim [Timothy Harold Parks] ['John MacDowell'] (1954–)
novelist and translator
Tongues of Flame (1985)
Loving Roger (1986)
Family Planning (1989)
Cara Massimina (1990)
Goodness (1991)
Mimi's Ghost (1995)
Destiny (1999)
Judge Savage (2003)
A Season in Verona (2003)

Parnell, Thomas (1679–1718)
poet
An Essay on the Different Stiles of Poetry (1713)
Homer's Battle of the Frogs and Mice (1717)
Poems on Several Occasions (1722)
Posthumous Works (1758)

Parr, Catherine (1512–48)
queen consort of Henry VIII
Prayers Stirrying the Mynd unto Heavenlye Medytacions (1545)
The Lamentacion of a Synner (1547)

Parr, Richard (1617–91)
divine
The Life of James Usher (1686)

Parr, Samuel (1747–1825)
scholar and author
A Spital Sermon (1801)

Parrot or Perrot, Henry (*fl.* 1606–26)
epigrammatist
Laquei Ridiculosi; or, Springes for Woodcocks (1613)

Parry, Robert (*fl.* 1595–7)
translator and poet
Moderatus, the Most Delectable & Famous Historie of the Blacke Knight (1595)
Sinetes Passion Uppon his Fortunes (1597)

Parry, Sir William Edward (1790–1855)
admiral and explorer
Journal of a Second Voyage for the Discovery of a North-West Passage (1824)
Journal of a Third Voyage for the Discovery of a North-West Passage (1826)
Narrative of an Attempt to Reach the North Pole (1828)

Parsons, Eliza, *née* Phelp (1748–1811)
novelist
The Errors of Education (1791)
Castle of Wolfenbach: A German story (1793)
Ellen and Julia (1793)
Woman as She Should Be; or, Memoirs of Mrs Menville (1793)
Lucy (1794)
The Mysterious Warning (1796)
Women as They Are (1796)
The Valley of St Gothard (1799)
The Miser and his Family (1800)
The Peasant of Ardenne Forest (1801)

Parsons or Persons, Robert, SJ (1546–1610)
Jesuit missionary and controversialist
The First Booke of the Christian Exercise, Appertayning to Resolution (1582)

Parsons, Tony (1953–)
journalist and author
Man and Boy (1999)
One for my Baby (2001)

'Paston, George' [Emily Morse Symonds] (1860–1936)
novelist, biographer, and author
A Modern Amazon (1894)

Pater, Walter Horatio (1839–94)
scholar and critic
Studies in the History of the Renaissance (1873)
Marius the Epicurean: His sensations and ideas (1885)
Imaginary Portraits (1887)
Appreciations (1889)
Greek Studies (1895)
Miscellaneous Studies (1895)

Paterson, Don (1963–)
poet
God's Gift to Women (1997)
The Eyes (1999)
Landing Light (2003)

Patmore, Coventry Kersey Dighton (1823–96)
poet
Poems (1844)
Tamerton Church-Tower, and Other Poems (1853)
The Betrothal [*The Angel in the House* i] (1854)
The Espousals [*The Angel in the House* ii] (1856)
Faithful for Ever [*The Angel in the House* iii] (1860)
The Victories of Love [*The Angel in the House* iv] (1863)
The Unknown Eros, and Other Odes (1877)
Amelia; Tamerton Church-Tower (1878)

Religio Poetae (1893)
The Rod, the Root, and the Flower (1895)
Patmore, Peter George (1786–1855)
author and editor of the *New Monthly Magazine*
Rejected Articles (1826)
Patrick or Patricke, Simon (*d.* 1613)
translator
A Discourse Upon the Means of Wel Governing a Kingdome (1602)
Patrick, Simon (1626–1707)
successively bishop of Chichester and Ely
A Brief Account of the New Sect of Latitude-Men (1662)
The Parable of the Pilgrim (1665)
A Friendly Debate Between a Conformist and a Non-Conformist (1669)
Partridge, Eric Honeywood (1894–1979)
lexicographer, etymologist, and historian of slang
A Dictionary of Slang and Unconventional English (1937)
Shakespeare's Bawdy (1947)
Patten, Brian (1946–)
poet, playwright, and children's writer
Little Johnny's Confession (1967)
Notes to the Hurrying Man (1969)
The Homecoming (1970)
And Sometimes It Happens (1972)
The Unreliable Nightingale (1973)
Vanishing Trick (1976)
Grave Gossip (1979)
Love Poems (1981)
Storm Damage (1988)
Grinning Jack (1990)
Pattison, Mark (1813–84)
scholar and biographer
Memoirs (1885)
Essays by the Late Mark Pattison (1889)
Paulin, Tom [Thomas Neilson Paulin] (1949–)
Northern Irish poet, critic, and playwright
A State of Justice (1977)
Personal Column (1978)
The Strange Museum (1980)
The Book of Juniper (1981)
Liberty Tree (1983)
Fivemiletown (1987)
Walking a Line (1994)
Writing to the Moment (1996)
The Wind Dog (1999)
The Invasion Handbook (2002)
Payn, James (1830–98)
journalist and novelist
Lost Sir Massingberd (1864)
Payne, Henry Nevil (*d. c.*1710)
conspirator and author
The Fatal Jealousie: A tragedy (1673)
The Morning Ramble: A comedy (1673)
The Siege of Constantinople: A tragedy (1675)
Paynell, Thomas (*fl.* 1528–67)
translator
This Boke Techyng al People to Governe them in Helthe (1528)
De contemptu mundi (1532?)
The Conspiracie of Lucius Catiline (1541)
The Faythfull and True Storye of the Destruction of Troye (1553)
The Treasurie of Amadis de Fraunce (1572)
Peacham, Henry, the elder (*fl.* 1577)
author
The Garden of Eloquence (1577)
Peacham or Peachum, Henry, the younger (1578?–1642?)
author
The Art of Drawing with the Pen, and Limming in Water Colours (1606)
The More the Merrier: Containing: threescore and odde head-lesse epigrams (1608)
Minerva Britanna; or, A Garden of Heroical Devises (1612)
Thalias Banquet: Furnished with an hundred and odde dishes of newly devised epigrammes (1620)
The Compleat Gentleman (1622)
Peacock, Thomas Love ['P.M. O'Donovan'] (1785–1866)
novelist, poet, and critic
The Monks of St Mark (1804)
Palmyra, and Other Poems (1806)
The Genius of the Thames (1810)
The Genius of the Thames, Palmyra, and Other Poems (1812)
The Philosophy of Melancholy (1812)
Sir Hornbrook; or, Childe Launcelot's Expedition (1814)
Sir Proteus: A satirical ballad (1814)
Headlong Hall (1816)
Melincourt (1817)
Nightmare Abbey (1818)
Rhododaphne; or, The Thessalian Spell (1818)
'The Four Ages of Poetry' (1820)
Maid Marian (1822)
The Misfortunes of Elphin (1829)
Crotchet Castle (1831)
Headlong Hall, Nightmare Abbey, Maid Marian, Crotchet Castle (1849)
'Memoirs of Percy Bysshe Shelley' (1858)
'Memoirs of Percy Bysshe Shelley, Part II' (1860)
Gryll Grange (1861)
Peake, Mervyn Laurence (1911–68)
fantasy writer, children's author, poet, and illustrator
Rhymes Without Reason (1944)
Titus Groan (1946)
The Glassblowers (1950)
Gormenghast (1950)
Mr Pye (1953)
Titus Alone (1959)
Pearce, Philippa Ann (1920–)
children's writer
A Minnow on the Say (1955)

Tom's Midnight Garden (1958)
A Dog So Small (1962)

Pears, Iain (1955–)
novelist
An Instance of the Fingerpost (1997)

Pearson, John (1613–86)
bishop of Chester
Exposition of the Apostles Creed (1659)

Peele, George (1556–96)
dramatist
The Araygnement of Paris (1584)
An Eglogue Gratulatorie (1589)
A Farewell (1589)
Polyhymnia (1590)
Descensus Astrææ (1591)
The Famous Chronicle of King Edward the First, Sirnamed Edward Longshankes, with his Returne from the Holy Land (1593)
The Honour of the Garter (1593)
The Battell of Alcazar (1594)
The Old Wives Tale: A pleasant conceited comedie (1595)
The Love of King David and Fair Bethsabe. With the Tragedie of Absalon (1599)

Penn, William (1644–1718)
Quaker and founder of Pennsylvania
The Sandy Foundations Shaken (1668)
Truth Exalted (1668)
Innocency with her Open Face (1669)
No Cross, No Crown (1669)
The Spirit of Truth Vindicated (1672)
A Brief Account of the Province of Pennsylvania in America (1681)
Some Fruits of Solitude (1693)
Primitive Christianity Revived in the Faith and Practice of the People called Quakers (1696)
A Collection of the Works of William Penn (1726)
Fruits of a Father's Love (1726)

Pennant, Thomas (1726–98)
naturalist and traveller
The British Zoology (1766)
A Tour in Scotland (1771)
A Tour in Wales (1778)
The Journey from Chester to London (1782)
Of London (1790)
Literary Life of the Late Thomas Pennant (1793)

Pennecuik, Alexander (*d.* 1730)
Scottish poet
Streams From Helicon; or, Poems on Various Subjects (1720)
An Ancient Prophecy Concerning Stock-Jobbing, and the Conduct of the Directors of the South-Sea-Company (1721)

Perceval, Arthur Philip (1799–1853)
clergyman and tractarian
A Vindication of the Principles of the Authors of the Tracts for the Times (1841)

Perceval, Richard (1550–1620)
colonist and politician
Bibliotheca Hispanica (1591)

Percy, Thomas (1729–1811)
bishop of Dromore, antiquary, and poet
Hau Kiou Choaan; or, The Pleasing History (1761)
Reliques of Ancient English Poetry (1765)
Northern Antiquities; or, A Description of the Manners, Customs, Religion and Laws of the Ancient Danes, and Other Northern Nations . . . (1770)
The Hermit of Warkworth (1771)

Percy, William (1575–1648)
poet
Sonnets to the Fairest Cœlia (1594)

Perkins, William (1558–1602)
Puritan theologian
The Foundation of Christian Religion (1590)
A Golden Chaine; or, The Description of Theologie (1591)
An Exposition of the Lords Prayer, in the Way of Catechising (1592)
A Salve for a Sicke Man; or, The Right Manner of Dying Well (1595)
A Declaration of the True Manner of Knowing Christ Crucified (1596)
The First Part of the Cases of Conscience (1604)
A Christian and Plaine Treatise of the Manner and Order of Pre-Destination (1606)
The Whole Treatise of the Cases of Conscience (1606)
A Discourse of the Damned Art of Witchcraft (1608)

'Peters, Ellis' [Edith Mary Pargeter] (1913–)
crime writer and historical novelist
A Morbid Taste for Bones (1977)

Pettie, George (1548–89)
poet
A Petite Pallace of Pettie his Pleasure (1576)
The Civile Conversation of M. Steeven Guazzo (1581)

Petty, Sir William (1623–87)
political economist
A Treatise of Taxes and Contributions (1662)
Another Essay in Political Arithmetick: Concerning the growth of the city of London (1683)
Two Essays in Political Arithmetick (1687)
Political Arithmetick (1690)

Pevsner, Sir Nikolaus Bernhard Leon (1902–83)
German-born historian of art and architecture
Pioneers of the Modern Movement (1936)
The Buildings of England (1951)

Peyton, Kathleen Wendy, *née* Herald (1929–)
children's writer
Flambards (1967)

Pfeiffer, Emily Jane (1827–90)
poet
Valisneria; or, A Midsummer Night's Dream (1857)
Gerard's Monument, and Other Poems (1873)
Poems (1876)

Quarterman's Grace, and Other Poems (1879)
Sonnets and Songs (1880)
Flowers of the Night (1889)

Phaer, Thomas (1510?–60)
translator and lawyer
The Seven First Bookes of the Eneidos (1558)
The Nyne First Bookes of the Eneidos of Virgil (1562)
The Whole Twelve Bookes of the Æneidos (1573)
The Thirteen Books of Æneidos (1584)

Philips, Ambrose (1674–1749)
poet and dramatist
Pastorals (1710)
The Distrest Mother: A tragedy (1712)
The Free-Thinker (1718)
The Briton: A tragedy (1722)
Humfrey, Duke of Gloucester: A tragedy (1723)
Ode on the Death of William, Earl Cowper (1723)
Pastorals, Epistles, Odes and Other Original Poems (1748)

Philips, John (1676–1709)
poet
The Sylvan Dream; or, The Mourning Muses (1701)
Blenheim (1705)
The Splendid Shilling: An imitation of Milton (1705)
Cerealia: An imitation of Milton (1706)
Poems (1712)

Philips, Katherine ['Orinda'] (1631–64)
poet
Pompey: A tragoedy (1663)
Poems by the Incomparable, Mrs K.P. (1664)
Poems: By the most deservedly admired Mrs Katherine Philips the Matchless Orinda (1667)
Letters from Orinda to Poliarchus (1705)

Philips, William (*d.* 1734)
dramatist
The Revengeful Queen: A tragedy (1698)
Belisarius: A tragedy (1724)

Phillips, Caryl (1958–)
West Indian-born playwright and novelist
Strange Fruit (1981)
Where There is Darkness (1982)
The Shelter (1984)
The Final Passage (1985)
Higher Ground (1986)
A State of Independence (1986)
Cambridge (1991)
Crossing the River (1993)

Phillips, Edward (1630–96?)
author
The New World of English Words; or, A General Dictionary (1658)
Theatrum Poetarum; or, A Compleat Collection of the Poets of all Ages (1675)

Phillips, John (*fl.* 1564–94)
poet and dramatist
Patient and Meek Griselda (1566?)
The Life and Death of Sir Philip Sidney (1587)

Phillips, John (1631–1706)
poet and satirist
A Satyr Against Hypocrites (1655)
Montelion, 1660; or, The Propheticall Almanack (1660)
Typhon; or, The Gyants War with the Gods: A mock poem (1665)
Maronides or, Virgil Travestie (1672)
Almahide; or, The Captive Queen: An excellent new romance (1677)
Jockey's Downfall: A poem on the late total defeat given to the Scottish Covenanters (1679)
Dr Oates's Narrative of the Popish Plot Vindicated (1680)
A Reflection on Our Modern Poetry (1695)
Augustus Britannicus (1697)

Phillips, Stephen (1864–1915)
poet and verse-dramatist
Poems (1898)
Herod: A tragedy (1901)
Ulysses (1902)
New Poems (1908)
The New Inferno (1911)
Armageddon (1915)

Phillpotts, Eden (1862–1960)
novelist, playwright, and poet
The End of a Life (1891)
Children of the Mist (1898)
Sons of the Morning (1900)
The River (1902)
The Secret Woman (1905)
The Mother (1908)
The Thief of Virtue (1910)
Widecombe Fair (1913)
The Fall of the House of Heron (1948)

Pickering or Pikeryng, John (1544–96)
interlude writer
Horestes; or, The New Interlude of Vice (1567)

'Pierre, DBC' [Peter Finlay, 1961]
Australian-born novelist
Vernon God Little (2003)

Pilkington, Laetitia, *née* van Lewen (1708?–50)
poet and dramatist
The Statues; or, The Trial of Constancy (1739)
The Memoirs of Mrs Laetitia Pilkington (1748)

Pilkington, Mary (1766–1839)
novelist
Tales of the Cottage; or, Stories, Moral and Amusing for Young Persons (1798)

Pilkington, Matthew (c.1700–74)
poet
Poems on Several Occasions (1730)

Pinero, Sir Arthur Wing (1855–1934)
actor and playwright
The Times: A comedy (1891)
The Cabinet Minister: A farce (1892)
The Notorious Mrs Ebbsmith (1895)
The Second Mrs Tanqueray (1895)
The Princess and the Butterfly; or, The Fantastics (1897)
Trelawny of the 'Wells': A comedietta (1898)

The Gay Lord Quex: An original comedy (1899)
Iris (1902)
The Thunderbolt (1909)
Mid-Channel (1910)

Pinter, Harold (1930–)
playwright and poet
The Birthday Party, and Other Plays (1960)
The Caretaker (1960)
Night School (1961)
A Slight Ache, and Other Plays (1961)
The Homecoming (1965)
Tea Party, and Other Plays (1967)
Landscape, and Silence (1969)
Five Screenplays (1971)
No Man's Land (1975)
Betrayal (1978)
The Hothouse (1980)
Other Places (1982)
One For the Road (1984)
Mountain Language (1988)
Party Time (1991)
Moonlight (1993)
Ashes to Ashes (1996)
Various Voices (1998)
Celebration (2000)
Collected Screenplays (2000)
Remembrance of Things Past (2000)

Piozzi, Hester Lynch, Mrs Thrale (1741–1821)
author and memorialist of Johnson
Anecdotes of the Late Samuel Johnson (1786)

Pitt, Christopher (1699–1748)
poet and translator
Vida's Art of Poetry (1725)
Poems and Translations (1727)
An Essay on Virgil's Aeneid (1728)
The Aeneid of Virgil (1740)
The Works of Virgil, in Latin and English (1753)
Poems . . . Together with The Jordan (1756)

Pitt-Kethley, [Helen] Fiona (1954–)
poet and novelist
London (1984)
Sky Ray Lolly (1986)
Private Parts (1987)
The Perfect Man (1989)
Dogs (1993)

Pitter, Ruth (1897–1992)
poet
First Poems (1920)
A Mad Lady's Garland (1934)
A Trophy of Arms (1936)
The Spirit Watches (1939)
The Bridge (1945)
The Ermine (1953)
Still by Choice (1966)
Poems 1926–1966 (1968)
End of Drought (1975)
A Heaven to Find (1987)
Collected Poems (1990)

Pix, Mary (1666–1720)
dramatist
Ibrahim, the Thirteenth Emperour of the Turks: A tragedy (1696)
The Inhumane Cardinal; or, Innocence Betray'd: (1696)
The Spanish Wives: A farce (1696)
Queen Catharine; or, The Ruines of Love: A tragedy (1698)
The False Friend; or, The Fate of Disobedience: A tragedy (1699)
The Beau Defeated: or, The Lucky Younger Brother: A comedy (1700)
The Double Distress: A tragedy (1701)
Violenta; or, The Rewards of Virtue (1704)
The Conquest of Spain: A tragedy (1705)
The Adventures in Madrid: A comedy (1709)

Place, Francis (1771–1854)
radical reformer
Illustrations and Proofs of the Principle of Population (1822)
Improvement of the Working People (1822)

Plater, Alan Frederick (1935–)
playwright, scriptwriter, and novelist
Close the Coalhouse Door (1969)
The Beiderbecke Affair (1985)

Plath, Sylvia ['Victoria Lucas'] (1932–63)
American-born poet and novelist
The Colossus, and Other Poems (1960)
The Bell Jar (1963)
Ariel (1965)
Crossing the Water (1971)
Winter Trees (1971)
Letters Home: Correspondence 1950–1963 (1975)
Johnny Panic and the Bible of Dreams, and Other Prose Writings (1977)
Collected Poems (1981)
The Journals of Sylvia Plath (1982)

Playford, John (1623–86)
musician and publisher
A Breefe Introduction to the Skills of Musick for Song & Violl (1654)

Plomer, William Charles Franklyn (1903–73)
South African-born novelist, short-story writer, and poet
Turbott Wolfe (1926)
I Speak of Africa (1927)
The Family Tree (1929)
Paper Houses (1929)
The Case is Altered (1932)
The Fivefold Screen (1932)
The Invaders (1934)
The Dorking Thigh, and Other Satires (1945)
Museum Pieces (1952)
Collected Poems (1960)

Plot, Robert (1640–96)
antiquary
The Natural History of Oxford-Shire (1677)
The Natural History of Stafford-Shire (1686)

Plumer, Francis (*d.* 1794)
author
A Candid Examination of the History of Sir Charles Grandison (1754)

Plumptre, Anne or Anna (1760–1818)
miscellaneous author
Narrative of a Three Years' Residence in France (1810)
Plumptre, James (1770–1832)
dramatist, critic, and traveller
The Lakers: A comic opera (1798)
Pocock, Isaac (1782–1835)
painter and dramatist
Hit or Miss! (1810)
The Miller and his Men: A melo-drama (1813)
Rob Roy Macgregor; or, Auld Lang Syne: A musical drama (1818)
Nigel; or, The Crown Jewels (1823)
Poliakoff, Stephen (1952–)
playwright
Hitting Town; City Sugar (1976)
Shout Across the River (1979)
Polidori, John William (1795–1821)
physician, author, and secretary to Lord Byron
Ernestus Berchtold; or, The Modern Oedipus (1819)
The Vampyre (1819)
Polwhele, Richard (1760–1838)
miscellaneous writer
Poems (1791)
Pomfret, John (1667–1702)
poet
The Choice (1699=)
Reason (1700)
Miscellany Poems on Several Occasions (1702)
Quae Rara, Chara: A poem on Panthea's confinement (1707)
Ponet or Poynet, John (1514?–56)
successively bishop of Rochester and Winchester
A Shorte Treatise of Politike Power, and of the True Obedience (1556)
Poole, Joshua (c.1615–c.1656)
anthologist and writer of schoolbooks
The English Parnassus; or, A Helpe to English Poesie (1657)
Pope, Alexander (1688–1744)
poet and translator
An Essay on Criticism (1711)
Miscellaneous Poems and Translations (1712)
Windsor-Forest (1713)
Ode for Musick (1713)
The Rape of the Lock: An heroi-comical poem (1714)
The Temple of Fame (1715)
The Iliad of Homer [vol. i] (1715)
The Iliad of Homer [vol. ii] (1716)
The Iliad of Homer [vol. iii] (1717)
The Works of Mr Alexander Pope (1717)
The Iliad of Homer [vol. iv] (1718)
The Iliad of Homer [vols v, vi] (1720)
The Odyssey of Homer [vols i, ii, iii] (1725)
The Odyssey of Homer [vols iv, v] (1726)
The Dunciad: An heroic poem (1728)
The Dunciad, Variorum (1729)
An Epistle to the Right Honourable Richard Earl of Burlington (1731)
Of the Use of Riches: An Epistle to Lord Bathurst (1733)
The First Satire of the Second Book of Horace (1733)
An Essay on Man [Epistles i–iii] (1733)
The Impertinent; or, A Visit to the Court (1733)
An Epistle to Lord Cobham (1734)
An Essay on Man [Epistle iv] (1734)
The First Satire of the Second Book of Horace (1734)
Sober Advice From Horace (1734)
An Epistle from Mr Pope to Dr Arbuthnot (1735)
Of the Characters of Women (1735)
The Works of Mr Alexander Pope [vol. ii] (1735)
Letters of Mr Pope, and Several Eminent Persons (1735)
Mr Pope's Literary Correspondence for Thirty Years, 1704 to 1734 (1735)
The Works of Alexander Pope [vols iii–iv] (1736)
Horace His Ode to Venus (1737)
The Second Epistle of the Second Book of Horace, Imitated (1737)
Letters of Mr Alexander Pope, and Several of his Friends (1737)
The First Epistle of the Second Book of Horace, Imitated (1737)
The Works of Alexander Pope [vols v–vi] (1737)
The Sixth Epistle of the First Book of Horace Imitated (1738)
The First Epistle of the First Book of Horace Imitated (1738)
An Imitation of the Sixth Satire of the Second Book of Horace (1738)
One Thousand Seven Hundred and Thirty Eight (1738)
The Universal Prayer (1738)
One Thousand Seven Hundred and Thirty Eight: Dialogue II (1738)
Memoirs of the Extraordinary Life, Works, and Discoveries of Martinus Scriblerus (1741)
The Works of Alexander Pope (1751)
The Works of Alexander Pope (1797)
The Works of Alexander Pope, in Verse and Prose (1806)
Pope, Walter (1630?–1714)
poet and biographer
Moral and Political Fables, Ancient and Modern (1698)
Pordage, Samuel (1633–91?)
poet and dramatist
Poems Upon Several Occasions (1660)
Troades Englished (1660)
Herod and Mariamne: A tragedy (1673)
The Siege of Babylon (1678)
The Medal Revers'd: A satyre against persecution (1682)
Porter, Anna Maria (1780–1832)
novelist and poet

Artless Tales (1793)
Walsh Colville; or, A Young Man's First Entrance into Life (1797)
Octavia (1798)
The Lake of Killarney (1804)
The Hungarian Brothers (1807)
Don Sebastian; or, The House of Braganza (1809)
Ballad Romances, and Other Poems (1811)
The Recluse of Norway (1814)
The Knight of St John (1817)
The Feast of St Magdalen (1818)
The Village of Mariendorpt (1821)
Roche-Blanche; or, The Hunters of the Pyrenees (1822)
The Barony (1830)
The Tuileries (1831)

Porter, Henry (*d.* 1599)
dramatist
The Two Angrie Women of Abington (1599)

Porter, Jane (1776–1850)
novelist
Thaddeus of Warsaw (1803)
The Scottish Chiefs (1810)
The Pastor's Fire-side (1817)
Duke Christian of Luneburg; or, Tradition From the Harz (1824)
Tales Round a Winter Hearth (1826)

Porter, Peter Neville Frederick (1929–)
Australian-born poet
Once Bitten, Twice Bitten (1961)
Poems Ancient & Modern (1964)
The Last of England (1970)
Preaching to the Converted (1972)
Living in a Calm Country (1975)
English Subtitles (1981)
Fast Forward (1984)
The Automatic Oracle (1987)
Possible Worlds (1989)
The Chair of Babel (1992)
Millennial Fables (1994)
Max is Missing (2001)

Porter, Thomas (1636–80)
dramatist
The Carnival: A comedy (1663)
The Villain: A tragedy (1663)
The French Conjurer: A comedy (1678)

Potter, [Helen] Beatrix (1866–1943)
children's author and illustrator
The Tale of Peter Rabbit (1902)

Potter, Dennis Christopher George (1935–94)
playwright
The Glittering Coffin (1960)
The Nigel Barton Plays (1968)
Son of Man (1970)
Brimstone and Treacle (1978)
Pennies From Heaven (1981)
Waiting for the Boat (1984)
The Singing Detective (1986)
Blackeyes (1987)
Lipstick on Your Collar (1993)

Potter, Stephen Meredith (1900–69)
humorist, radio producer, and critic
The Muse in Chains (1937)
The Theory and Practice of Gamesmanship (1947)
Some Notes on Lifemanship (1950)
One-Upmanship (1952)
Supermanship (1958)

Povey, Charles (1652?–1743)
clergyman and author
The Virgin in Eden; or, The State of Innocency (1741)

Powell, Anthony Dymoke (1905–2000)
novelist, critic, and autobiographer
Afternoon Men (1931)
Venusberg (1932)
From a View to a Death (1933)
Agents and Patients (1936)
What's Become of Waring? (1939)
A Question of Upbringing (1951)
A Buyer's Market (1952)
The Acceptance World (1955)
At Lady Molly's (1957)
Casanova's Chinese Restaurant (1960)
The Kindly Ones (1962)
The Valley of Bones (1964)
The Soldier's Art (1966)
The Military Philosophers (1968)
Books Do Furnish a Room (1971)
Temporary Kings (1973)
Hearing Secret Harmonies (1975)
Infants of the Spring (1976)
Messengers of Day (1978)
Faces In My Time (1980)
The Strangers All Are Gone (1982)
O, How the Wheel Becomes It! (1983)
The Fisher King (1986)
Miscellaneous Verdicts (1990)
A Writer's Notebook (1990)
Journals, 1982–1986 (1995)

Powell, George (1658?–1714)
actor and dramatist
The Treacherous Brothers: A tragedy (1690)
Alphonso: King of Naples: A tragedy (1691)

Powell, Thomas (1572?–1635?)
lawyer and author
Tom of all Trades; or, The Plaine Path-way to Preferment (1631)

Powys, John Cowper (1872–1963)
novelist, poet, and essayist
Odes, and Other Poems (1896)
Poems (1899)
Wood and Stone (1917)
Wolf Solent (1929)
A Glastonbury Romance (1933)
Jobber Skald (1935)
Maiden Castle (1937)
Morwyn; or, The Vengeance of God (1937)

Powys, Llewelyn (1884–1939)
essayist and novelist
Black Laughter (1925)
Skin for Skin (1925)

The Cradle of God (1929)
Impassioned Clay (1931)
A Pagan's Pilgrimage (1931)
Dorset Essays (1935)
Love and Death (1939)
Powys, Theodore Francis (1875–1953)
novelist
Black Bryony (1923)
Mr Tasker's Gods (1925)
The House with the Echo (1928)
Mr Weston's Good Wine (1928)
God's Eyes a-Twinkle (1947)
Praed, Rosa Caroline, *née* Murray-Prior, Mrs Campbell Praed (1851–1935)
Australian-born novelist
Policy and Passion (1881)
The Other Mrs Jacobs (1903)
Praed, Winthrop Mackworth (1802–39)
poet
Lillian (1823)
The Ascent of Elijah (1831)
Poems (1864)
Pratchett, Terry (1948–)
fantasy novelist
The Colour of Magic (1983)
Carpe Jugulum (1998)
The Last Continent (1998)
The Truth (2000)
The Last Hero (2001)
Thief of Time (2001)
Pratt, Samuel Jackson ['Courtney Melmoth'] (1749–1814)
poet, novelist, and dramatist
Liberal Opinions, upon Animals, Man, and Providence (1775)
The Pupil of Pleasure; or, The New System Illustrated (1776)
Charles and Charlotte (1777)
Travels for the Heart (1777)
Shenstone-Green; or, The New Paradise Lost (1779)
The Tutor of Truth (1779)
Emma Corbett; or, The Miseries of Civil War (1780)
Sympathy; or, A Sketch of the Social Passion (1781)
The Fair Circassian: A tragedy (1781)
Family Secrets, Literary and Domestic (1797)
Prest, Thomas Peckett (1810?–79)
writer of popular fiction
A String of Pearls; or, The Sailor's Gift (1846)
Preston, John (1587–1628)
Puritan divine
The New Covenant; or, The Saints Portion (1629)
The Breast-Plate of Faith and Love (1630)
Life Eternall; or, A Treatise of the Divine Essence and Attributes (1631)
Preston, Thomas (1537–98)
dramatist
Cambises (1570?)
Prestwich, Edmund (*fl.* 1651)
poet and translator
Hippolitus Translated out of Seneca (1651)
Price, Laurence (*fl.* 1625–80?)
writer of ballads and political squibs
The Witch of the Woodlands; or, The Coblers New Translation (1655)
Price, Richard (1723–91)
writer on ethics, politics, and economics
A Review of the Principal Questions and Difficulties in Morals (1758)
Observations on the Nature of Civil Liberty (1776)
An Essay on the Population of England (1780)
Price, Sir Uvedale (1747–1829)
writer on the picturesque
An Essay on the Picturesque (1794)
Prichard, Thomas Jeffery Llewelyn (1790–1862)
Welsh author
The Adventures and Vagaries of Twm Shon Catti (1828)
Prideaux, Humphrey (1648–1724)
historical writer
The True Nature of Imposture Fully Display'd in the Life of Mahomet (1697)
The Old and New Testament Connected in the History of the Jews and Neighbouring Nations (1716)
Priestley, John Boynton (1894–1984)
novelist, playwright, critic, and essayist
Brief Diversions (1922)
The English Comic Characters (1925)
Adam in Moonshine (1927)
The English Novel (1927)
Apes and Angels (1928)
The Good Companions (1929)
Angel Pavement (1930)
Dangerous Corner (1932)
English Journey (1934)
I Have Been Here Before (1937)
Midnight on the Desert (1937)
Time and the Conways (1937)
The Doomsday Men (1938)
When We Are Married: A Yorkshire farcical comedy (1938)
Rain Upon Godshill (1939)
Daylight on Saturday (1943)
Bright Day (1946)
The Arts Under Socialism (1947)
An Inspector Calls (1947)
The Magicians (1954)
Literature and Western Man (1960)
Lost Empires (1965)
Priestley, Joseph (1733–1804)
theologian and scientist
The Rudiments of English Grammar (1761)
A Course of Lectures on the Theory of Language, and Universal Grammar (1762)
An Essay on a Course of Liberal Education for Civil and Active Life (1765)

The History and Present State of Electricity (1767)
An Essay on the First Principles of Government (1768)
The History and Present State of Discoveries Relating to Vision, Light, and Colours (1772)
Experiments and Observations on Different Kinds of Air (1774)
Hartley's Theory of the Human Mind (1775)
Disquisitions Relating to Matter and Spirit (1777)
The Doctrine of Philosophical Necessity Illustrated (1777)

Primrose, Diana (*fl.* 1630)
poet
A Chaine of Pearle; or a memoriall of the peerless graces, and heroick vertues of Queene Elizabeth (1630)

Prince, Frank Templeton (1912–2003)
poet and scholar
Soldiers Bathing, and Other Poems (1945)
The Doors of Stone (1963)

Prince, Mary
former slave
The History of Mary Prince, a West Indian Slave (1831)

Prior, Matthew (1664–1721)
poet and diplomat
The Hind and the Panther Transvers'd to the Story of the Country-Mouse and the City-Mouse (1687)
An Ode in Imitation of the Second Ode of the Third Book of Horace (1692)
An English Ballad: In answer to Mr Despreaux's Pindarique ode on the taking of Namure (1695)
To a Young Gentleman in Love (1702)
A Letter to Monsieur Boileau Depreaux (1704)
An English Padlock (1705)
The Squirrel (1706)
Poems on Several Occasions (1708)
Erle Robert's Mice: A tale, in imitation of Chaucer (1712)
The Dove (1717)
Poems on Several Occasions (1719)
The Conversation (1720)
Colin's Mistakes (1721)
Down-Hall (1723)
The Turtle and the Sparrow (1723)

Pritchett, Sir Victor Sawdon (1900–97)
short-story writer, novelist, critic, and essayist
Marching Spain (1928)
Clare Drummer (1929)
The Spanish Virgin, and Other Stories (1930)
Shirley Sanz (1932)
Nothing Like Leather (1935)
Dead Man Leading (1937)
You Make Your Own Life (1938)
In My Good Books (1942)
It May Never Happen, and Other Stories (1945)
The Living Novel (1946)
Mr Beluncle (1951)
Books in General (1953)
The Spanish Temper (1954)
Collected Stories (1956)
When My Girl Comes Home (1961)
The Working Novelist (1965)
A Cab at the Door (1968)
Blind Love, and Other Stories (1969)
Midnight Oil (1971)
The Camberwell Beauty, and Other Stories (1974)
On the Edge of the Cliff (1980)
A Man of Letters (1985)
A Careless Widow, and Other Stories (1989)
Complete Short Stories (1990)
Complete Essays (1991)

Procter, Adelaide Anne (1825–64)
poet and campaigner for women's rights
Legends and Lyrics [1st ser.] (1858)
The Victoria Regia (1861)
A Chaplet of Verses (1862)

Proctor, Thomas (*fl.* 1578–84)
poet
A Gorgious Gallery, of Gallant Inventions (1578)

Prynne, Jeremy Halvard (1936–)
poet
Kitchen Poems (1968)
High Pink on Chrome (1975)
The Oval Window (1983)
Word Order (1989)
Poems (1999)

Prynne, William ['Matthew White'] (1600–69)
barrister and Puritan pamphleteer
Histrio-mastix: The players scourge, or actors tragaedie (1633)
A Soveraigne Antidote to Prevent, Appease and Determine Our Unnaturall and Destructive Civill Wars (1642)
The Opening of the Great Seale of England (1643)
The Popish Royall Favourite (1643)
The Treachery and Disloyalty of Papists to their Soveraignes, in Doctrine and Practise (1643)
The Soveraigne Power of Parliaments and Kingdomes (1643)
A Breviate of the Life of William Laud (1644)
A Breife Memento to the Present Unparliamentary Junto (1649)
The Quakers Unmasked, and Clearly Detected to be But the Spawn of Romish Frogs (1655)

'Psalmanazar, George' (1679?–1763)
literary impostor
*Memoirs of ****. Commonly Known by the Name of George Psalmanazar; a Reputed Native of Formosa* (1764)

Pudney, John Sleigh (1909–77)
poet, novelist, and children's writer
Dispersal Point, and Other Air Poems (1942)
Beyond This Disregard (1943)
Almanack of Hope (1944)
Low Life (1947)

Pugin, Augustus Welby Northmore (1812–52)
architect and ecclesiologist

Gothic Furniture in the Style of the 15th Century (1835)
Contrasts. Or, a parallel between the noble edifices of the fourteenth and fifteenth centuries and similar buildings of the present day (1836)
The True Principles of Pointed or Christian Architecture (1841)
An Apology for the Revival of Christian Architecture in England (1843)

Pullman, Philip (1946–)
children's writer
Northern Lights (1995)
The Subtle Knife (1998)
The Amber Spyglass (2000)

Pulteney, William, earl of Bath (1684–1764)
statesman and author
The Discovery; or, The Squire Turn'd Ferret (1726)
The Honest Jury; or, Caleb Triumphant (1729)
An Epistle from L---- to Lord C----------d (1740)

Purchas, Samuel (1577–1626)
traveller and author
Purchas his Pilgrimage; or, Relations of the World and the Religions Observed in all Ages and Places Discovered, from the Creation unto this Present (1613)
Purchas his Pilgrim (1619)
Purchas his Pilgrimes (1625)

Purney, Thomas (1695–1730)
clergyman and poet
Pastorals (1716)
A Full Enquiry into the True Nature of Pastoral (1717)
The Chevalier de St George: An heroi-comick poem (1718)

Purver, Anthony (1702–77)
translator of the Bible
A New and Literal Translation of all the Books of the Old and New Testament (1764)

Pusey, Edward Bouverie (1800–82)
theologian and tractarian
The Doctrine of the Real Presence (1855)
An Eirenicon (1865)
An Eirenicon: Part 2 (1869)
An Eirenicon: Part 3 (1870)

Puttenham, George (1530?–90)
author
The Arte of English Poesie (1589)

Pye, Henry James (1745–1813)
poet, Poet Laureate, and dramatist
Beauty (1766)
Elegies on Different Occasions (1768)
The Triumph of Fashion (1771)
Farringdon Hill (1774)
The Democrat (1795)
Adelaide: A tragedy (1800)
Alfred (1801)
A Prior Claim: A comedy (1805)

Pym, Barbara Mary Crampton (1913–80)
novelist
Some Tame Gazelle (1950)
Excellent Women (1952)
Quartet in Autumn (1977)
The Sweet Dove Died (1978)
A Few Green Leaves (1980)

Quarles, Francis (1592–1644)
poet
A Feast for Wormes: Set forth in a poeme of the history of Jonah (1620)
Hadassa; or, The History of Queene Ester (1621)
Job Militant: With meditations divine and morall (1624)
Sions Elegies, Wept by Jeremie the Prophet (1624)
Sions Sonets (1625)
Argalus and Parthenia (1629)
Divine Poems (1630)
The Historie of Samson (1631)
Divine Fancies: Digested into epigrammes, meditations, and observations (1632)
Emblemes (1635)
Hieroglyphikes of the Life of Man (1638)
Enchyridion (1640)
Barnabas and Boanerges: Or, wine and oyle for afflicted soules (1644)
The Loyall Convert (1644)
The Shepheards Oracle (1644)
Solomons Recantation, entituled Ecclesiastes, Paraphrased (1645)
Judgement and Mercie for Afflicted Soules (1646)
Hosanna; or, Divine Poems on the Passion of Christ (1647)

Quiller-Couch, Sir Arthur Thomas ['Q'] (1863–1944)
novelist, short-story writer, and literary scholar
Dead Man's Rock (1887)
The Astonishing History of Troy Town (1888)
Wandering Heath (1895)
Adventures in Criticism (1896)
Old Fires and Profitable Ghosts (1900)
The Oxford Book of English Verse 1250–1900 (1900)
The Mayor of Troy (1906)
True Tilda (1909)
The Oxford Book of Victorian Verse (1912)
On the Art of Writing (1916)

Quillinan, Edward (1791–1851)
poet and novelist
The Sacrifice of Isabel (1816)

Raban, Jonathan (1942–)
travel writer and critic
Soft City (1974)
Arabia Through the Looking-Glass (1979)
Hunting Mr Heartbreak (1990)

Radcliffe, Ann, *née* Ward (1764–1823)
novelist and poet
The Castles of Athlin and Dunbayne (1789)

A Sicilian Romance (1790)
The Romance of the Forest (1791)
The Mysteries of Udolpho: A romance (1794)
A Journey Made in the Summer of 1794, Through Holland and the Western Frontier of Germany (1795)
The Italian; or, The Confessional of the Black Penitents (1796)
Poems (1815)
Gaston de Blondeville; Keeping Festival in Ardenne; St Alban's Abbey (1826)

Radcliffe, Mary Anne (*c.*1746–post 1810)
feminist, autobiographer, and novelist
The Female Advocate; or, An Attempt to Recover the Rights of Women from Male Usurpation (1799)
Manfroné; or, The One-Handed Monk (1809)

Raine, Craig Anthony (1944–)
poet and editor
The Onion, Memory (1978)
A Martian Sends a Postcard Home (1979)
Rich (1984)
Haydn and the Valve Trumpet (1990)
History: The Home Movie (1994)
Clay: Whereabouts Unknown (1996)
A la Recherche du Temps Perdu (2000)
Collected Poems 1978–1999 (2001)

Raine, Kathleen Jessie (1908–2003)
poet and critic
Stone and Flower (1943)
Living in Time (1946)
The Pythoness, and Other Poems (1949)
The Hollow Hill, and Other Poems 1960–4 (1965)
Defending Ancient Springs (1967)
The Oval Portrait, and Other Poems (1977)
The Oracle in the Heart, and Other Poems 1975–1978 (1980)
To the Sun (1988)
Living With Mystery (1992)

Rainold or Reynolds, Richard (*d.* 1606)
writer on rhetoric
The Foundation of Rhetoric (1563)

Ralegh or Raleigh, Sir Walter (1552?–1618)
statesman, soldier, historian, and poet
A Report of the Truth of the Fight about the Iles of the Açores, this Last Somer (1591)
The Discoverie of the Large, Rich, and Bewtiful Empyre of Guiana (1596)
The History of the World (1614)
The Prerogative of Parlaments in England (1628)
Sir Walter Raleighs Instructions to his Sonne and to Posterity (1632)
The Prince; or, Maxims of State (1642)
To day a Man, To morrow None (1644)
Judicious and Select Essayes and Observations (1650)
Sir Walter Raleigh's Sceptick, or Speculations (1651)

Ralph, James (1705?–62)
Pennsylvanian-born poet and dramatist
The Tempest; or, The Terror of Death (1727)
Night (1728)
Sawney: An heroic poem. Occasion'd by the Dunciad (1728)
Zeuma; or, The Love of Liberty (1728)
Clarinda; or, The Fair Libertine (1729)
The Fall of the Earl of Essex (1731)

Ramsay, Allan (1686–1758)
Scottish poet
Christ's Kirk on the Green (1718)
Content (1719)
A Poem on the South-Sea (1720)
Poems (1720)
Fables and Tales (1722)
The Fair Assembly (1723)
The Tea-Table Miscellany [vol. i] (1723)
The Ever Green: Being a collection of Scots poems (1724)
Health (1724)
The Gentle Shepherd: A Scots pastoral comedy (1725)
Poems by Allan Ramsay (1728)

Randolph, Thomas (1605–35)
poet and dramatist
Aristippus; or, The Joviall Philosopher (1630)
The Jealous Lovers: A comedie presented to their gracious Majesties (1632)
Poems with the Muses Looking-Glasse: and Amyntas (1638)

Rands, William Brighty ['Henry Holbeach', 'Matthew Browne'] (1823–82)
children's writer
Lilliput Levee (1864)

Rankin, Ian (1960–)
Scottish crime writer
The Flood (1986)
Knots and Crosses (1987)
Hide and Seek (1991)
Strip Jack (1992)
Wolfman (1992)
The Black Book (1993)
Mortal Causes (1994)
Let It Bleed (1996)
Black and Blue (1997)
Dead Souls (1999)
Set in Darkness (2000)
The Falls (2001)
Beggar's Banquet (2002)
Resurrection Men (2002)
A Question of Blood (2003)

Ransome, Arthur Michell (1884–1967)
author, journalist, children's writer, and illustrator
Bohemia in London (1907)
'Racundra's' First Cruise (1923)
Swallows and Amazons (1930)
Pigeon Post (1936)

Raphael, Frederic Michael (1931–)
novelist, playwright, and critic
The Limits of Love (1960)
The Trouble with England (1962)

The Glittering Prizes (1976)
Oxbridge Blues, and Other Stories (1980)
Oxbridge Blues, and Other Plays for Television (1984)

Rastell, John (1475?–1536)
barrister, printer, and author
The Nature of the Four Elements (1520?)
Celestina (1525?)
Of Gentleness and Nobility (1525?)

Rastell, William (1508?–65)
judge and elder son of the printer John Rastell
Rastell's Abridged Statutes (1557)

Rathbone, Hannah Mary, *née* Reynolds (1798–1878)
poet and novelist
So Much of the Diary of Lady Willoughby as Relates to Her Domestic History, and to the Eventful Period of the Reign of Charles I (1844)

Rattigan, Sir Terence Mervyn (1911–77)
playwright
French Without Tears (1937)
After the Dance (1939)
Flare Path (1942)
While the Sun Shines: A comedy (1944)
Love in Idleness (1945)
The Winslow Boy (1946)
The Browning Version (1949)
Harlequinade (1949)
Adventure Story (1950)
Who is Sylvia? A light comedy (1951)
The Deep Blue Sea (1952)
The Sleeping Prince (1954)
Separate Tables (1955)
Variation on a Theme (1958)
Ross (1960)
Cause Célèbre (1978)

Raven, Simon Arthur Noel (1927–2001)
novelist and playwright
The Feathers of Death (1959)
Doctors Wear Scarlet (1960)
Close of Play (1962)
The Rich Pay Late (1964)
Friends in Low Places (1965)
The Sabre Squadron (1966)
Fielding Gray (1967)
The Judas Boy (1968)
Places Where They Sing (1970)
Sound the Retreat (1971)
Come Like Shadows (1972)
Bring Forth the Body (1974)
The Survivors (1976)
Morning Star (1984)
The Face of the Waters (1985)
Before the Cock Crow (1986)
New Seed for Old (1988)
Blood of My Bone (1989)
In the Image of God (1990)
The Troubadour (1992)

Ravenscroft, Edward (1644–1704)
dramatist
The Citizen Turn'd Gentleman: A comedy (1672)
The Careless Lovers: A comedy (1673)
King Edgar and Alfreda: A tragi-comedy (1677)
Scaramouch a Philosopher, Harlequin a School-boy, Bravo, Merchant, and Magician: A comedy after the Italian manner (1677)
The Wrangling Lovers; or, The Invisible Mistress: A comedy (1677)
The English Lawyer: A comedy (1678)
The London Cuckolds: A comedy (1682)
Dame Dobson: or, The Cunning Woman (1684)
Titus Andronicus; or, The Rape of Lavinia (1687)
The Canterbury Guests; or, A Bargain Broken: A comedy (1695)
The Italian Husband: A tragedy (1698)

Raverat, Gwen[dolen] Mary (1885–1957)
autobiographer
Period Piece (1952)

Rawlins, Thomas (1620?–70)
medallist and dramatist
The Rebellion: A tragedy (1640)

Rawlinson, Richard (1690–1755)
topographer and antiquary
The English Topographer (1720)

Ray, John (1627–1705)
naturalist and author
A Collection of English Proverbs (1670)
Observations Topographical, Moral, & Physiological (1673)
A Collection of English Words Not Generally Used (1674)
The Wisdom of God Manifested in the Works of the Creation (1691)
Miscellaneous Discourses Concerning the Dissolution and Changes of the World (1692)
Philosophical Letters (1718)

Reach, Angus Bethune (1821–56)
journalist and novelist
The Natural History of 'Bores' (1848)
Clement Lorimer; or, The Book with the Iron Clasps (1849)

Read, Sir Herbert Edward (1893–1968)
poet and critic
Songs of Chaos (1915)
Mutations of the Phoenix (1923)
Reason and Romanticism (1926)
The Meaning of Art (1931)
Form in Modern Poetry (1932)
Art Now (1933)
The End of a War (1933)
Poems 1914–34 (1935)
Art and Society (1937)
Poetry and Anarchism (1938)
Annals of Innocence and Experience (1940)
A World Within a War (1944)
Collected Poems (1946)
The Philosophy of Modern Art (1952)

Read, Sir Herbert Edward (1893–1968)
poet and critic
The True Voice of Feeling (1953)
Anarchy and Order (1954)
Collected Poems (1966)

'Read, Miss' [Dora Jessie Saint] (1913–)
novelist
Village School (1955)
Read, Piers Paul (1941–)
novelist
Game in Heaven with Tussy Marx (1966)
Monk Dawson (1969)
The Upstart (1973)
Polonaise (1976)
The Villa Golitsyn (1981)
A Season in the West (1988)
On the Third Day (1990)
Alice in Exile (2001)
Reade, Charles (1814–84)
novelist and dramatist
Peg Woffington (1852)
Christie Johnstone (1853)
'It Is Never Too Late To Mend': A matter-of-fact novel (1856)
The Course of True Love Never Did Run Smooth (1857)
'Love Me Little, Love Me Long' (1859)
The Cloister and the Hearth (1861)
Hard Cash: A matter-of-fact romance (1863)
Griffith Gaunt; or, Jealousy (1866)
Put Yourself in His Place (1870)
A Simpleton (1873)
A Perilous Secret (1885)
Reade, [William] Winwood (1838–75)
poet, novelist, and controversialist
Charlotte and Myra (1859)
The Martyrdom of Man (1872)
Reading, Peter (1946–)
poet
For the Municipality's Elderly (1974)
The Prison Cell and Barrel Mystery (1976)
Fiction (1979)
Tom O' Bedlam's Beauties (1981)
C (1984)
Ukelele Music (1985)
Stet (1986)
Final Demands (1988)
Perduta Gente (1989)
Evagatory (1992)
3 in 1 (1992)
Collected Poems 1970–1984 (1995)
Collected Poems 1985–1996 (1996)
Work in Regress (1997)
Apophthegmatic (1999)
Ob (1999)
Marfan (2000)
[untitled] (2001)
Faunal (2002)
Collected Poems 3: 1997–2003 (2003)
Record or Recorde, Robert (1510?–58)
mathematician and author
The Worke and Practise of Arithmetike (1543)
The Castle of Knowledge (1556)
The Whetstone of Witte (1557)
Rede, [William] Leman (1802–47)
dramatist and journalist
The Rake's Progress (1833)
Redgrove, Peter William (1932–2003)
poet, novelist, playwright, short-story writer, and critic
The Collector, and Other Poems (1960)
At the White Monument, and Other Poems (1963)
The Force, and Other Poems (1966)
Dr Faust's Sea-Spiral Spirit, and Other Poems (1972)
In the Country of the Skin (1973)
The God of Glass (1979)
The Apple Broadcast, and Other New Poems (1981)
The Man Named East, and Other New Poems (1985)
The Moon Disposes (1987)
The One Who Set Out to Study Fear (1989)
Dressed as for a Tarot Pack (1990)
Under the Reservoir (1992)
My Father's Trapdoors (1994)
Reed, Henry (1914–86)
poet, dramatist, and critic
A Map of Verona (1946)
Reed, Isaac (1742–1807)
biographer, Shakespeare editor, and bibliophile
The Repository (1777)
[R. Dodsley] *A Select Collection of Old Plays* (1780)
Biographia Dramatica; or, A Companion to the Playhouse (1782)
Reed, Jeremy (1954–)
poet, novelist, and translator
Bleecker Street (1980)
A Man Afraid (1982)
By the Fisheries (1984)
The Lipstick Boys (1984)
Nero (1985)
Blue Rock (1987)
Engaging Form (1988)
Red Eclipse (1989)
Inhabiting Shadows (1990)
Nineties (1990)
Black Sugar (1992)
Chasing Black Rainbows (1994)
Reeve, Clara (1729–1807)
novelist and poet
Original Poems on Several Occasions (1769)
The Champion of Virtue: A gothic story (1777)
The Old English Baron: A Gothic story (1778)
The Two Mentors (1783)
The Progress of Romance (1785)
The Exiles; or, Memoirs of the Count de Cronstadt (1788)
The School for Widows (1791)
Memoirs of Sir Roger de Clarendon (1793)
Destination; or, Memoirs of a Private Family (1799)
Reeves, James (1909–78)
poet and critic
The Natural Need (1935)
The Imprisoned Sea (1949)

The Wandering Moon (1950)
The Password, and Other Poems (1952)
Pigeons and Princesses (1956)
Collected Poems 1929–59 (1960)

Reid, Christopher John (1949–)
poet
In the Echoey Tunnel (1991)

Reid, Forrest (1875–1947)
Ulster novelist
The Kingdom of Twilight (1904)
The Bracknels: A family chronicle (1911)
Uncle Stephen (1931)

Reid, Thomas Mayne ['Charles A. Beach'] (1818–83)
writer for boys
The Rifle Rangers; or Adventures of an Officer in Southern Mexico (1850)
The Desert Home; or, The Adventures of a Lost Family in the Wilderness (1852)
The Boy Hunters; or, Adventures in Search of a White Buffalo (1853)

Reid, Thomas (1710–96)
philosopher
An Inquiry into the Human Mind (1764)
Essays on the Intellectual Powers of Man (1785)

Relph, Josiah (1712–43)
Cumberland poet
A Miscellany of Poems (1747)

'Renault, Mary' [Eileen Mary Challans] (1905–83)
novelist
Purposes of Love (1939)
The Charioteer (1953)
The King Must Die (1958)
The Bull From the Sea (1962)
The Mask of Apollo (1966)
Fire From Heaven (1970)
The Persian Boy (1972)
Funeral Games (1981)

Rendell, Ruth Barbara, *née* Grasemann ['Barbara Vine'] (1930–)
writer of detective fiction and psychological thrillers
From Doon With Death (1964)
A Dark Adapted Eye (1986)
Gallowglass (1990)
Simisola (1994)
The Keys to the Street (1996)
Road Rage (1997)
The Chimney-Sweeper's Boy (1998)
Piranha to Scurfy, and Others (2000)
The Blood Doctor (2002)

Repton, Humphry (1752–1818)
landscape-gardener
Observations on the Theory and Practice of Landscape Gardening (1803)

Reynolds, Frederic (1764–1841)
dramatist
Werter: A tragedy (1786)
Better Late Than Never: A comedy (1790)
The Dramatist; or, Stop Him Who Can! A comedy (1790)
How to Grow Rich: A comedy (1793)
The Will: A comedy (1797)
Management: A comedy (1799)
Life: A comedy (1801)

Reynolds, George William Macarthur (1814–79)
novelist
Alfred de Rosann; or, The Adventures of a French Gentleman (1839)
Grace Darling; or, The Heroine of the Fern Islands (1839)
Pickwick Abroad; or, The Tour in France (1839)
The Mysteries of London [1st ser.] (1845)
Mysteries of the Court of London [1st ser.] (1849)

Reynolds, Henry (1563?–1635?)
translator and critic
Torquato Tasso's Aminta Englisht (1628)
Mythomystes: Wherein a short survay is taken of the nature and value of true poesy and depth of the Ancients above our moderne poets (1632)

Reynolds, John (1667–1727)
dissenting minister and poet
Death's Vision Represented in a Philosophical Sacred Poem (1709)

Reynolds, John Hamilton (1794–1852)
poet
The Eden of the Imagination (1814)
Safie: An eastern tale (1814)
The Naiad, with Other Poems (1816)
Benjamin the Waggoner (1819)
Peter Bell: A lyrical ballad (1819)
The Garden of Florence, and Other Poems (1821)

Reynolds, Sir Joshua (1723–92)
painter and author
A Discourse (1769)

Rhodes, William Barnes ['Cornelius Crambo'] (1772–1826)
poet and dramatist
The Satires of Juvenal (1801)

'Rhys, Jean' [Ella Gwendolyn Rees Williams] (1890–1979)
novelist
The Left Bank, and Other Stories (1927)
Postures (1928)
Wide Sargasso Sea (1966)

Ricardo, David (1772–1823)
political economist
Proposals for an Economical and Secure Currency (1816)
On the Principles of Political Economy and Taxation (1817)

Rich, Barnabe (1540?–1617)
author and soldier
Dialogue Between Mercury and an English Soldier (1574)
Allarme to England (1578)
Riche his Farewell to Militarie Profession (1581)
The Straunge and Wonderfull Adventures of Don Simonides, a Gentilman Spaniarde (1581)

The Second Tome of the Travailes and Adventures of Don Simonides (1584)
A Path-way to Military Practise (1587)
The Adventures of Brusanus, Prince of Hungaria (1592)
A Souldiers Wishe to Britons Welfare (1604)
Faultes Faults, and Nothing Else But Faultes (1606)
Roome for a Gentleman; or, The Second Part of Faultes Collected and Gathered for the True Meridian of Dublin (1609)
A New Description of Ireland (1610)
The Excellency of Good Women (1613)
Opinion Diefied [sic] (1613)
The Honestie of this Age (1614)
The Irish Hubbub; or, The English Hue and Crie (1617)

Rich, Richard (*fl.* 1610)
author
Newes from Virginia (1610)

'Richards, Frank' [Charles Hamilton] (1876–1961)
boys' writer and creator of Billy Bunter
Billy Bunter of Greyfriars School (1947)

Richards, Ivor Armstrong (1893–1979)
critic and poet
Principles of Literary Criticism (1924)
Practical Criticism (1929)

Richards, Nathaniel (1612?–54)
poet and dramatist
The Celestiall Publican (1630)
The Tragedy of Messallina, the Roman Emperesse (1640)

Richardson, Dorothy Miller (1873–1957)
novelist
Pointed Roofs (1915)
Backwater (1916)
Honeycomb (1917)
Interim (1919)
The Tunnel (1919)
Deadlock (1921)
Revolving Lights (1923)
The Trap (1925)
Oberland (1927)
Dawn's Left Hand (1931)
Clear Horizon (1935)
Pilgrimage (1938)

Richardson, Jonathan (1665–1745)
portrait painter, aesthetic theorist, and poet
An Essay on the Theory of Painting (1715)
Explanatory Notes on Milton's Paradise Lost (1734)
Morning Thoughts; or, Poetical Meditations, Moral, Divine and Miscellaneous (1776)

Richardson, Samuel (1689–1761)
novelist
A Seasonable Examination of the Pleas and Pretensions of the Proprietors of, and Subscribers to, Play-Houses (1735)
Aesop's Fables (1739)
Pamela; or, Virtue Rewarded [vols i, ii] (1740)
Letters Written to and for Particular Friends (1741)
Pamela; or, Virtue Rewarded [vols iii, iv] (1741)
Clarissa; or, The History of a Young Lady [vols i, ii] (1747)
Clarissa; or, The History of a Young Lady [vols iii, iv; v–vii] (1748)
The History of Sir Charles Grandison (1753)
A Collection of the Moral and Instructive Sentiments . . . Contained in the Histories of Pamela, Clarissa, and Sir Charles Grandison (1755)

Richardson, William (1743–1814)
literary historian
A Philosophical Analysis and Illustration of Some of Shakespeare's Remarkable Characters (1774)

Richmond, Legh (1772–1827)
Evangelical divine
Annals of the Poor (1814)

Ricks, Christopher (1933–)
literary critic and editor
Milton's Grand Style (1963)

Riddell, Charlotte Elizabeth Lawson, *née* Cowan, Mrs J.H. Riddell ['F.G. Trafford'] (1832–1906)
novelist and short-story writer
The Moors and the Fens (1858)
City and Suburb (1861)
George Geith of Fen Court (1864)
Maxwell Drewitt (1865)
Austin Friars (1870)
Frank Sinclair's Wife, and Other Stories (1874)
The Mystery in Palace Gardens (1880)
The Senior Partner (1881)
The Prince of Wales's Garden Party, and Other Stories (1882)
Weird Stories (1884)
Mitre Court (1885)

Rider, William (*fl.* 1655)
dramatist
The Twins: A tragi-comedy (1655)

Rider, William (1723–85)
miscellaneous writer and translator
Candidus; or, The Optimist (1759)

Ridge, William Pett ['Warwick Simpson'] (1860–1930)
novelist and short-story writer
Eighteen of Them (1894)
Outside the Radius (1899)

Riding, Laura (1901–91)
American-born poet and critic
The Close Chaplet (1926)
Love as Love, Death as Death (1928)
Poet: a Lying Word (1933)

Ridler, Anne Barbara, *née* Bradby (1912–2001)
poet, playwright, and anthologist
Poems (1939)
The Nine Bright Shiners (1943)
Henry Bly, and Other Plays (1950)

The Golden Bird, and Other Poems (1951)
A Matter of Life and Death (1959)
Ridley, Glocester or Gloster (1702–74)
clergyman, poet, and miscellaneous author
Jovi Eleutherio; or, An Offering to Liberty (1745)
Melampus (1781)
Ridley, James ['Sir Charles Morell'] (1736–65)
fiction writer
The History of James Lovegrove, Esquire (1761)
The Tales of the Genii (1764)
Ridley, Nicholas (1500?–55)
successively bishop of Rochester and London
A Brief Declaracion of the Lordes Supper (1555)
A Frendly Farewel, which Master Doctor Ridley . . . did write . . . unto all his true lovers and frendes in God, a litle before that he suffred (1559)
Ritchie, Anne Isabella, *née* Thackeray, Lady Ritchie (1837–1919)
novelist, biographer, and essayist
The Story of Elizabeth (1863)
The Village on the Cliff (1867)
Records of Tennyson, Ruskin, Robert and Elizabeth Browning (1892)
Ritson, Joseph (1752–1803)
literary scholar
Observations on the First Three Volumes of the History of English Poetry (1782)
A Select Collection of English Songs (1783)
Pieces of Ancient Popular Poetry (1791)
Cursory Criticisms on the Edition of Shakespeare Published by Edmond Malone (1792)
The English Anthology (1793)
Scottish Song (1794)
Bibliographia Poetica (1802)
Rivers, George (*fl.* 1639)
romance writer
The Heroinae; or, The Lives of Arria, Paulina, Lucrecia, Dido, Theutilla, Cypriana, Aretaphila (1639)
Roberts or Robarts, Henry (*fl.* 1590)
author
A Defiance to Fortune (1590)
Phaeander, the Mayden Knight (1595)
Honours Conquest (1598)
Haigh for Devonshire (1600)
Roberts, Michèle Brigitte (1949–)
novelist and poet
A Piece of the Night (1978)
The Visitation (1983)
The Wild Girl (1984)
The Book of Mrs Noah (1987)
In the Red Kitchen (1990)
Psyche and the Hurricane (1991)
Daughters of the House (1992)
During Mother's Absence (1993)
Flesh and Blood (1994)
Impossible Saints (1997)
The Looking Glass (2000)
Playing Sardines (2001)
The Mistressclass (2003)
Roberts, Morley Charles (1857–1942)
novelist and short-story writer
The Private Life of Henry Maitland (1912)
War Lyrics (1918)
Robertson, Thomas William (1829–1871)
playwright
Society: A comedy (1865)
Caste: An original comedy (1867)
Robertson, William (1721–93)
historian
The History of Scotland During the Reigns of Queen Mary and of King James VI (1759)
The History of the Reign of the Emperor Charles V (1769)
The History of America (1777)
Robins, Elizabeth Parkes ['C.E. Raimond'] (1862–1952)
American-born actress, novelist, and suffragette
George Mandeville's Husband (1894)
Robinson, Emma (1814–90)
novelist
Whitefriars; or, The Days of Charles the Second (1844)
Robinson, Henry (1605–73?)
writer on economics
Englands Safety, in Trades Encrease (1641)
Robinson, Henry Crabb (1775–1867)
diarist
Amatonda (1811)
Diary, Reminiscences, and Correspondence (1869)
Robinson, [Esmé Stuart] Lennox (1886–1958)
Irish playwright and theatre manager
The Cross-Roads (1910)
The Lost Leader (1918)
The Whiteheaded Boy: A comedy (1920)
Crabbed Youth and Age (1924)
The Big House (1928)
Robinson, Mary, *née* Darby ['Perdita', 'Anne Frances Randall'] (1758–1800)
actress, novelist, and poet
Poems (1775)
Vancenza; or, The Dangers of Credulity (1792)
The Widow; or, A Picture of Modern Times (1794)
Angelina (1796)
Hubert de Sevrac (1796)
Walsingham; or, The Pupil of Nature (1797)
The False Friend (1799)
A Letter to the Women of England, on the Injustice of Mental Subordination (1799)
The Natural Daughter (1799)
Lyrical Tales (1800)
The Poetical Works of the Late Mrs Mary Robinson (1806)
Robinson, Richard (*fl.* 1576–1600)
author and compiler
The Auncient Order, Societie, and Unitie Laudable, of Prince Arthure, and his Knightly Armory of the Round Table (1583)

Robinson, Thomas (*fl.* 1598–1603)
lutenist and composer
The Schoole of Musicke (1603)
Roche, Regina Maria, *née* Dalton (1773–1845)
novelist
The Children of the Abbey (1796)
Clermont (1798)
Rodgers, William Robert (1909–69)
Northern Irish poet, novelist, and critic
Awake! and Other Poems (1941)
Rogers, Jane (1952–)
novelist
Mr Wroe's Virgins (1991)
Rogers, John ['Thomas Matthew'] (1500?–55)
martyr and editor of the Bible
The Byble (1537)
Rogers, Samuel (1763–1855)
poet
An Ode to Superstition, with Some Other Poems (1786)
The Pleasures of Memory (1792)
An Epistle to a Friend, with Other Poems (1798)
The Voyage of Columbus (1810)
Poems by Samuel Rogers (1812)
Human Life (1819)
Italy: Part the first (1822)
Italy: a Poem. Part the Second (1828)
Recollections of the Table-Talk of Samuel Rogers (1856)
Rogers, Thomas (*d.* 1616)
translator
Of the Imitation of Christ (1580)
Roget, Peter Mark (1779–1869)
physician and lexicographer
Thesaurus of English Words and Phrases (1852)
'Rohmer, Sax' [Arthur Henry Sarsfield Ward] (1883–1959)
thriller writer
The Mystery of Dr Fu-Manchu (1913)
Rolfe, Frederick William Serafino Austin Lewis Mary ['Baron Corvo'] (1860–1913)
novelist and author
Stories Toto Told Me (1898)
In His Own Image (1901)
Hadrian the Seventh (1904)
Don Tarquinio: A kataleptic phantasmatic romance (1905)
Rolland, John (*fl.* 1560)
Scottish poet
The Court of Venus (1575)
Roper, Margaret, *née* More (1505–44)
daughter of Sir Thomas More
A Devout Treatise upon the Pater Noster (1526?)
Roper, William (1496–1578)
biographer
The Mirrour of Vertue in Worldly Greatnes; or, The Life of Syr Thomas More (1626)
Roscoe, William Stanley (1753–1831)
historian and poet
Mount Pleasant (1777)
The Wrongs of Africa (1787)
The Butterfly's Ball and the Grasshopper's Feast (1807)
Rosenberg, Isaac (1890–1918)
poet and painter
Night and Day (1912)
Youth (1915)
Moses (1916)
Collected Works (1937)
Ross, Alan John (1922–)
poet and editor
Summer Thunder (1941)
The Derelict Day (1947)
The Forties (1950)
Poetry, 1945–1950 (1951)
Something of the Sea (1954)
To Whom It May Concern (1958)
North From Sicily (1965)
Poems 1942–67 (1967)
The Taj Express (1973)
Open Sea (1975)
Ross, Alexander (1591–1654)
poet, author, and controversialist
Three Decads of Divine Meditations (1630)
Mel Heliconium; or, Poeticall Honey (1642)
The Philosophicall Touch-stone (1645)
Leviathan Drawn Out With a Hook: Or, animadversions on Mr Hobbes his Leviathan (1653)
Ross, Alexander (1699–1784)
Scottish poet
The Fortunate Shepherdess (1768)
Ross, Sir John (1777–1856)
rear-admiral and circumnavigator
A Voyage of Discovery (1819)
Rossetti, Christina Georgina (1830–94)
poet
Verses by Christina G. Rossetti (1847)
Goblin Market, and Other Poems (1862)
The Prince's Progress, and Other Poems (1866)
Commonplace, and Other Short Stories (1870)
Sing-Song (1872)
A Pageant, and Other Poems (1881)
Time Flies: A reading diary (1885)
Poems (1890)
The Face of the Deep: A devotional commentary on the Apocalypse (1892)
New Poems (1896)
Rossetti, Dante Gabriel (1828–82)
poet and artist
The Early Italian Poets (1861)
Poems (1870)
Ballads and Sonnets (1881)
Collected Works (1886)
Rossetti, William Michael (1829–1919)
critic and biographer
Swinburne's Poems and Ballads (1866)
A Memoir of Shelley (1886)
Rous, Francis (1579–1659)
Puritan divine

Thule; or, Vertues Historie (1598)
The Psalmes of David in Meeter (1643)

Rowe, Elizabeth, *née* Singer ['Philomela'] (1674–1737)
poet
Poems on Several Occasions (1696)
Friendship in Death (1728)
Letters on Various Occasions, in Prose and Verse (1729)
Letters Moral and Entertaining (1731)
Letters Moral and Entertaining, in Prose and Verse (1733)
The History of Joseph (1736)
Devout Exercises of the Heart (1737)
Miscellaneous Works in Prose and Verse (1739)

Rowe, Nicholas (1674–1718)
Poet Laureate and dramatist
The Ambitious Step-Mother (1701)
Tamerlane: A tragedy (1702)
The Fair Penitent: A tragedy (1703)
Ulysses: A tragedy (1706)
The Royal Convert: A tragedy (1708)
Callipaedia (1712)
Poems on Several Occasions (1714)
The Tragedy of Jane Shore (1714)
The Tragedy of the Lady Jane Grey (1715)
Lucan's Pharsalia, Translated into English Verse (1719)

Rowlands, Samuel (1570?–1630?)
poet and satirist
The Betraying of Christ; Judas in Despaire; The Seven Words of Our Savior on the Crosse (1598)
The Letting of Humors Blood in the Head-vaine (1600)
Greenes Ghost Haunting Conie-Catchers (1602)
'Tis Merrie When Gossips Meete (1602)
Ave Caesar: God Save the King (1603)
Looke to it: for, Ile Stabbe Ye (1604)
Hell's Broke Loose (1605)
Humors Antique Faces (1605)
A Terrible Battell Betweene the Two Consumers of the Whole World: Time and Death (1606)
Democritus; or, Doctor Merry-man his Medicines, Against Melancholy Humors (1607)
Diogines Lanthorne (1607)
Humors Looking Glasse (1608)
A Whole Crew of Kind Gossips (1609)
The Knave of Clubbes (1612)
The Knave of Harts (1612)
The Melancholie Knight (1615)
The Night-Raven (1620)
Good Newes and Bad Newes (1622)

Rowley, Samuel (*d.* 1633?)
dramatist
When You See Me, You Know Me; or, The famous chronicle historie of King Henry the Eight (1605)
The Noble Souldier; or, A Contract Broken, Justly Reveng'd (1634)

Rowley, William (1585?–1642?)
dramatist
A Search for Money (1609)
A New Wonder; a Woman Never Vext: A pleasant conceited comedy (1632)
All's Lost by Lust (1633)
A Match at Mid-night: A pleasant comoedie (1633)
A Shoo-Maker a Gentleman (1638)
The Witch of Edmonton: A known true story (1658)

Rowling, Joanne Kathleen (1965–)
children's writer
Harry Potter and the Philosopher's Stone (1997)
Harry Potter and the Chamber of Secrets (1998)
Harry Potter and the Prisoner of Azkaban (1999)
Harry Potter and the Goblet of Fire (2000)
Harry Potter and the Order of the Phoenix (2003)

Rowse, Alfred Leslie (1903–97)
historian and poet
Poems of a Decade (1941)
A Cornish Childhood (1942)

Rowson, Susanna, *née* Haswell (1762–1824)
novelist, dramatist, and actress
Victoria (1786)
Charlotte (1791)
The Fille de Chambre (1792)
Reuben and Rachel; or, Tales of Old Times (1799)

Roy, Arundhati (1961–)
Anglo-Indian novelist
The God of Small Things (1997)

Roy, William (*fl.* 1527–31)
friar and amanuensis to William Tyndale
The True Beliefe in Christ and his Sacramentes (1550)

Rubens, Bernice Ruth (1928–2004)
novelist
Madame Sousatzka (1962)
The Elected Member (1969)
A Five Year Sentence (1978)
Spring Sonata (1979)
Mr Wakefield's Crusade (1985)
Kingdom Come (1990)
Yesterday in the Back Lane (1995)
The Waiting Game (1997)
I, Dreyfus (1999)
Milwaukee (2001)
Nine Lives (2002)
The Sergeants' Tale (2003)

Ruck, [Amy] Berta [i.e Roberta] (1878–1978)
romantic novelist
His Official Fiancée (1914)

Rudkin, [James] David (1936–)
playwright
Afore Night Come (1963)
Ashes (1978)

Rumens, Carol[-Ann] (1944–)
poet, novelist, and editor
A Strange Girl in Bright Colours (1973)
A Necklace of Mirrors (1978)
Unplayed Music (1981)
Star Whisper (1983)
Direct Dialling (1985)

Plato Park (1987)
The Greening of the Snow Beach (1988)
From Berlin to Heaven (1990)
Thinking of Skins (1993)
Best China Sky (1995)
Holding Pattern (1998)

Rushdie, Ahmed Salman (1947–)
novelist
Grimus (1975)
Midnight's Children (1981)
Shame (1983)
The Satanic Verses (1988)
Haroun and the Sea of Stories (1990)
East, West (1994)
The Moor's Last Sigh (1995)
The Ground Beneath Her Feet (1999)
Fury (2001)

Rushton, Edward (1756–1814)
poet
The Dismember'd Empire (1782)
West-Indian Eclogues (1787)
Expostulatory Letter to George Washington (1797)

Ruskin, John (1819–1900)
art critic, artist, and social reformer
Modern Painters [vol. i] (1843)
Modern Painters: Volume II (1846)
The Seven Lamps of Architecture (1849)
The King of the Golden River; or, The Black Brothers (1850)
Poems (1850)
The Stones of Venice: Volume the First (1851)
Pre-Raphaelitism (1851)
The Stones of Venice: Volume the Second (1853)
The Stones of Venice: Volume the Third (1853)
Lectures on Architecture and Painting (1854)
The Opening of the Crystal Palace (1854)
Modern Painters: Volume III (1856)
Modern Painters: Volume IV (1856)
The Political Economy of Art (1857)
The Two Paths (1859)
Modern Painters: Volume V (1860)
'Unto This Last': Four essays on the first principles of political economy (1862)
The Ethics of the Dust (1865)
Sesame and Lilies (1865)
The Crown of Wild Olive (1866)
Lectures on Art (1870)
Fors Clavigera [vol. i] (1871)
The Art of England (1884)
The Pleasures of England (1884)
On the Old Road (1885)
Dilecta (1886)
Praeterita: Outlines of scenes and thoughts perhaps worthy of memory in my past life (1886)
Praeterita [vol. ii] (1887)
Praeterita [vol. iii] (1888)

Russell, Bertrand Arthur William, 3rd earl Russell (1872–1970)
philosopher
The Principles of Mathematics (1903)
Philosophical Essays (1910)
Principia Mathematica (1910)
The Analysis of Mind (1921)
A History of Western Philosophy (1945)
Autobiography (1967)

Russell, George William ['Æ'] (1867–1935)
poet and essayist
Homeward (1894)
The Earth Breath, and Other Poems (1897)
The Nuts of Knowledge (1903)
The Divine Vision, and Other Poems (1904)
The Mask of Apollo, and Other Stories (1904)
By Still Waters (1906)
Deirdre (1907)
The Renewal of Youth (1911)
Collected Poems (1913)
Gods of War, with Other Poems (1915)
Imaginations and Reveries (1915)
Salutation (1917)
The Candle of Vision (1918)
The Inner and the Outer Ireland (1921)
Enchantment, and Other Poems (1930)
Vale, and Other Poems (1931)
Song and its Fountains (1932)
The Avatars (1933)
The House of the Titans, and Other Poems (1934)

Russell, Thomas (1762–88)
poet
Sonnets and Miscellaneous Poems (1789)

Russell, Willy [William Martin Russell] (1947–)
playwright
Educating Rita (1981)
Blood Brothers (1986)
Shirley Valentine (1988)

'Rutherford, Mark' [William Hale White] (1831–1913)
novelist
The Autobiography of Mark Rutherford, Dissenting Minister (1881)
Mark Rutherford's Deliverance (1885)
The Revolution in Tanner's Lane (1887)
Miriam's Schooling, and Other Papers (1890)
Catharine Furze (1893)

Rutherford, Samuel (1600?–61)
Scottish divine
Lex, Rex: The law and the prince. A dispute for the just prerogative of King and people (1644)
Christ Dying and Drawing Sinners to Himselfe (1647)

Rutter, Joseph (*fl.* 1633–40)
dramatist
The Shepheard's Holy-Day: A pastorall tragi-comaedie (1635)

Rycaut or Ricaut, Sir Paul (1628–1700)
historian
The Present State of the Ottoman Empire (1667)
The History of the Turkish Empire from the Year 1623 to the Year 1677 (1680)

Rymer, Thomas (1641–1713)
poet, critic, archaeologist, and historiographer
Reflections on Aristotles Treatise of Poesie (1674)
Edgar; or, The English Monarch: An heroick tragedy (1678)
The Tragedies of the Last Age Consider'd and Examin'd (1678)
A Short View of Tragedy (1693)

Sabatini, Rafael (1875–1950)
historical novelist
The Tavern Knight (1904)
The Sea-Hawk (1915)
Scaramouche: A romance of the French Revolution (1921)
Captain Blood, his Odyssey (1922)

Sackville-West, Vita [Victoria Mary Sackville-West] (1892–1962)
poet and novelist
Poems of East and West (1917)
Orchard and Vineyard (1921)
The Land (1926)
The Edwardians (1930)
All Passion Spent (1931)
The Garden (1946)

Sadleir, Michael (1888–1957)
bibliographer and novelist
Excursions in Victorian Bibliography (1922)
Fanny by Gaslight (1940)

Sadler, John (1615–74)
master of Magdalene College, Cambridge
Olbia: The New Iland Lately Discovered (1660)

Sage, Lorna (1943–2001)
literary critic
Bad Blood (2000)
Moments of Truth: 12 essays on 20th-century writers (2001)

Saint-German, Christopher (1460?–1540)
lawyer
Doctor and Student (1530?)

St Aubin de Terán, Lisa (1953–)
novelist and poet
Keepers of the House (1982)
The Slow Train to Milan (1983)
The Tiger (1984)
The High Place (1985)
The Bay of Silence (1986)
Black Idol (1987)
Joanna (1990)
Nocturne (1992)

St-John, Henry, 1st Viscount Bolingbroke (1678–1751)
statesman and author
The Occasional Writer (1727)
A Dissertation upon Parties (1735)
The Idea of a Patriot King (1740)
Remarks on the History of England (1743)
Letters on the Spirit of Patriotism (1749)
Letters on the Study and Use of History (1752)
A Letter to Sir William Windham (1753)
Philosophical Works (1754)

Saintsbury, George Edward Bateman (1845–1933)
literary scholar and critic
A History of Nineteenth-Century Literature (1896)
A Short History of English Literature (1898)

St Serfe, Sir Thomas (*fl.* 1668)
dramatist
Tarugo's Wiles: or, The Coffee-House: A comedy (1668)

Saker, Austin (*fl.* 1580)
author
The Laberynth of Libertie (1580)

'Saki' [Hector Hugh Monro] (1870–1916)
novelist and short-story writer
The Westminster Alice (1902)
Reginald (1904)
Reginald in Russia, and Other Sketches (1910)
The Chronicles of Clovis (1912)
The Unbearable Bassington (1912)
Beasts and Super-Beasts (1914)
When William Came (1914)

Sala, George Augustus (1828–95)
journalist, caricaturist, and novelist
Twice Round the Clock; or, The Hours of the Day and Night in London (1859)
The Strange Adventures of Captain Dangerous (1863)

Sale, George (1697?–1736)
orientalist and translator of the Koran
The Koran (1734)

Saltmarsh, John (c.1610–47)
mystical writer
Reasons for Unitie, Peace, and Love (1646)
Sparkles of Glory; or, Some Beams of the Morning-Star (1647)

Saltonstall, Wye (*fl.* 1630–40)
translator
Tristia (1633)
Ovids Heroicall Epistles (1636)

Sampson, George (1873–1950)
scholar
English for the English (1921)

Sancho, [Charles] Ignatius (1729?–80)
Afro-British letter writer
Letters of the Late Ignatius Sancho, an African (1782)

Sanderson, Robert (1587–1663)
bishop of Lincoln
Ten Sermons Preached (1627)
Several Cases of Conscience (1660)
Episcopacy Not Prejudicial to Regal Power: A treatise written in the time of the Long Parliament (1661)

Sandys, George (1578–1644)
traveller, poet, and translator
A Relation of a Journey Begun An: Dom: 1610 (1615)

The First Five Books of Ovid's Metamorphosis (1621)
Ovid's Metamorphosis Englished (1626)
A Paraphrase upon the Psalmes of David (1636)
A Paraphrase upon the Divine Poems (1638)
Christs Passion: A tragedie (1640)

Sanford or Sandford, James (*fl.* 1569)
translator
Of the Vanitie and Uncertaintie of Artes and Sciences (1569)

Sansom, Martha, *née* Fowke (1690–1736)
poet
The Epistles of Clio and Strephon (1720)

Sansom, William [Norman Trevor Sansom] (1912–76)
short-story writer and novelist
Fireman Flower, and Other Stories (1944)
Three (1946)
Something Terrible, Something Lovely (1948)
The Body (1949)
The Passionate North (1950)
A Touch of the Sun (1952)
A Contest of Ladies (1956)
The Loving Eye (1956)
The Cautious Heart (1958)
The Last Hours of Sandra Lee (1961)

'Sapper' [Herman Cyril McNeile] (1888–1937)
thriller writer
Men, Women, and Guns (1916)
Bull-Dog Drummond (1920)
The Return of Bull-Dog Drummond (1932)
Bull-Dog Drummond at Bay (1935)

Sassoon, Siegfried Loraine (1886–1967)
poet and autobiographer
The Old Huntsman, and Other Poems (1917)
Counter-Attack, and Other Poems (1918)
The War Poems of Siegfried Sassoon (1919)
Satirical Poems (1926)
The Heart's Journey (1928)
Memoirs of a Fox-Hunting Man (1928)
In Sicily (1930)
Memoirs of an Infantry-Officer (1930)
The Road to Ruin (1933)
Vigils (1935)
Sherston's Progress (1936)
The Complete Memoirs of George Sherston (1937)
The Old Century and Seven More Years (1938)
The Weald of Youth (1942)
Siegfried's Journey 1916–20 (1945)
Collected Poems 1908–56 (1961)

Savage, Richard (1697?–1743)
poet
The Convocation; or, A Battle of Pamphlets (1717)
Love in a Veil: A comedy (1719)
The Tragedy of Sir Thomas Overbury (1724)
The Authors of the Town (1725)
Miscellaneous Poems and Translations (1726)
The Bastard (1728)
Nature in Perfection; or, The Mother Unveil'd (1728)
The Wanderer (1729)
An Epistle to the Right Honourable Sir Robert Walpole (1732)
The Progress of a Divine (1735)
The Works of Richard Savage (1775)

Savile, George, marquis of Halifax (1633–95)
politician and author
Observations Upon a Late Libel, called A letter from a person of quality to his friend, concerning the Kings declaration, &c (1681)
The Anatomy of an Equivalent (1688)
The Lady's New-Years Gift; or, Advice to a Daughter (1688)
A Rough Draft of a New Model at Sea (1694)

Savile, Sir Henry (1549–1622)
scholar and translator
The Ende of Nero and Beginning of Galba (1591)

Sayers, Dorothy Leigh (1893–1957)
writer of detective fiction, anthologist, and translator
Whose Body? (1923)
Clouds of Witness (1926)
The Unpleasantness at the Bellona Club (1928)
Murder Must Advertise (1933)
The Nine Tailors (1934)
Gaudy Night (1935)
The Man Born To Be King (1943)
The Comedy of Dante Alighieri, the Florentine (1949)
The Comedy of Dante Alighieri, the Florentine (1955)
The Comedy of Dante Alighieri, the Florentine (1962)

Scammell, William Neil (1939–2000)
poet
Bleeding Heart Yard (1992)

Scannell, Vernon (1922–)
poet, novelist, and critic
Graves and Resurrections (1948)
The Face of the Enemy (1961)
A Sense of Danger (1962)
Walking Wounded (1965)
The Winter Man (1973)
Soldiering On (1989)
A Time for Fires (1991)

Schreiner, Olive Emilie Albertina, later Cronwright ['Ralph Iron'] (1855–1920)
South African novelist and author
The Story of an African Farm (1883)

Scoggin or Scogan, John (*fl.* 1480)
court fool and suppositious author
The Jestes of Skogyn (1570?)
The First and Best Part of Scoggins Jests (1626)

Scot or Scott, Reginald (1538?–99)
writer on witchcraft
A Perfite Platforme of a Hoppe Garden; and Necessarie Instructions for the Making and Mayntenaunce Thereof (1574)
The Discoverie of Witchcraft (1584)

Scot or Scott, Thomas (*fl.* 1616)
author

Philomythie or Philomythologie: Wherein outlandish birds, beasts, and fishes, are taught to speake true English plainely (1615)
Scott, James (1733–1814)
clergyman, poet, and political writer
Heaven: A vision (1760)
Odes on Several Subjects (1761)
Scott, John (1730–83)
poet and author
Four Elegies: Descriptive and Moral (1760)
Observations on the Present State of the Parochial and Vagrant Poor (1773)
Amwell (1776)
Moral Eclogues (1778)
The Poetical Works of John Scott (1782)
Critical Essays on Some of the Poems, of Several English Poets (1785)
Scott, Jonathan (1754–1829)
orientalist
The Arabian Nights Entertainments (1811)
Scott, Mary, later Taylor (1752?–93)
poet
The Female Advocate (1774)
Scott, Paul Mark (1920–78)
novelist and playwright
Johnnie Sahib (1952)
The Alien Sky (1953)
The Chinese Love Pavilion (1960)
The Jewel in the Crown (1966)
The Day of the Scorpion (1968)
The Towers of Silence (1971)
A Division of the Spoils (1975)
Staying On (1977)
Scott, Sarah, *née* Robinson (1723–95)
novelist and historian
The History of Cornelia (1750)
Agreeable Ugliness; or, The Triumph of the Graces (1754)
A Journey Through Every Stage of Life (1754)
A Description of Millenium Hall, and the Country Adjacent (1762)
The History of Sir George Ellison (1766)
The Test of Filial Duty (1772)
Scott, Thomas, of Ipswich (1705–75)
hymn-writer and dissenting minister
England's Danger and Duty (1745)
Lyric Poems, Devotional and Moral (1773)
Scott, Sir Walter (1771–1832)
poet and novelist
The Chase, and William and Helen (1796)
Goetz of Berlichingen; with The Iron Hand (1799)
An Apology for Tales of Terror (1799)
The Eve of Saint John (1800)
Minstrelsy of the Scottish Border (1802)
The Lay of the Last Minstrel (1805)
Ballads and Lyrical Pieces (1806)
Marmion (1808)
English Minstrelsy (1810)
The Lady of the Lake (1810)
The Vision of Don Roderick (1811)
Rokeby (1813)
The Bridal of Triermain; or, The Vale of St John (1813)
Waverley; or, 'tis Sixty Years Since (1814)
The Lord of the Isles (1815)
Guy Mannering; or, The Astrologer (1815)
The Field of Waterloo (1815)
The Antiquary (1816)
Tales of My Landlord [1st ser.] (1816)
Harold the Dauntless (1817)
The Border Antiquities of England and Scotland (1817)
Rob Roy (1818)
Tales of My Landlord, Second Series (1818)
The Provincial Antiquities and Picturesque Scenery of Scotland (1819)
Tales of My Landlord, Third Series (1819)
Novels and Tales of the Author of Waverley (1819)
Ivanhoe (1819)
The Poetical Works of Sir Walter Scott (1820)
The Monastery (1820)
The Abbot (1820)
Kenilworth (1821)
The Pirate (1821)
Lives of the Novelists (1821)
The Fortunes of Nigel (1822)
Halidon Hill (1822)
Historical Romances of the Author of Waverley (1822)
Peveril of the Peak (1823)
Quentin Durward (1823)
Novels and Romances of the Author of Waverley (1823)
St Ronan's Well (1823)
Redgauntlet (1824)
Tales of the Crusaders (1825)
Woodstock; or, The Cavalier (1826)
Tales and Romances of the Author of Waverley (1827)
The Life of Napoleon Buonaparte (1827)
Chronicles of the Canongate (1827)
Tales of a Grandfather (1827)
Chronicles of the Canongate: Second series (1828)
Religious Discourses (1828)
Tales of a Grandfather. Second Series (1828)
Anne of Geierstein; or, The Maiden of the Mist (1829)
Tales of a Grandfather [3rd ser.] (1829)
Waverley Novels (1829)
The Doom of Devorgoil; Auchindrane; or, The Ayrshire Tragedy (1830)
Letters on Demonology and Witchcraft (1830)
Tales of a Grandfather [4th ser.] (1830)
Tales of My Landlord: Fourth and Last Series (1832)
Tales and Romances of the Author of Waverley (1833)
The Poetical Works of Sir Walter Scott, Bart. (1833)
The Miscellaneous Prose Works of Sir Walter Scott (1834)

Scovell, Edith Joy (1907–99)
poet
Shadows of Chrysanthemums, and Other Poems (1944)
Midsummer Meadows, and Other Poems (1946)
The River Steamer, and Other Poems (1956)
The Space Between (1982)
Listening to Collared Doves (1986)
Collected Poems (1988)
Scupham, [John] Peter (1933–)
poet
The Snowing Globe (1972)
Prehistories (1975)
The Hinterland (1977)
Winter Quarters (1983)
Out Late (1986)
The Air Show (1988)
Watching the Perseids (1990)
The Ark (1994)
Seacole, Mary (1805–81)
autobiographer
Wonderful Adventures of Mrs Seacole in Many Lands (1857)
Sedley, Sir Charles (1639–1701)
poet and dramatist
Pompey the Great: A tragedy (1664)
The Mulberry-Garden: A comedy (1668)
Antony and Cleopatra: A tragedy (1677)
Bellamira; or, The Mistress: A comedy (1687)
Seiffert, Rachel (1971)
novelist
The Dark Room (2001)
Selden, John (1584–1654)
jurist and antiquary
The Duello or Single Combat (1610)
Titles of Honor (1614)
The Historie of Tithes (1618)
A Briefe Discourse, Concerning the Power of the Peeres and Comons of Parliament, in Point of Judicature (1640)
The Priviledges of the Baronage of England, when they sit in Parliament (1642)
Table-Talk (1689)
Self, Will (1961–)
novelist
The Quantity Theory of Insanity (1991)
Cock & Bull (1992)
My Idea of Fun (1993)
Grey Area, and Other Stories (1994)
The Sweet Smell of Psychosis (1996)
Great Apes (1997)
Tough, Tough Toys for Tough, Tough Boys (1998)
Feeding Frenzy (2001)
Junk Mail (2001)
Sore Sites (2001)
Dorian (2002)
Senior, Nassau William (1790–1864)
economist and essayist
An Outline of the Science of Political Economy (1836)
A Journal Kept in Turkey and Greece (1859)
Seth, Vikram (1952–)
Anglo-Indian poet and novelist
A Suitable Boy (1993)
An Equal Music (1999)
Settle, Elkanah (1648–1724)
dramatist and poet
Mare Clausum; or, A Ransack for the Dutch (1666)
Cambyses King of Persia: A tragedy (1671)
The Empress of Morocco: A tragedy (1673)
Notes and Observations on the Empress of Morocco Revised (1674)
Love and Revenge: A tragedy (1675)
The Conquest of China, by the Tartars: A tragedy (1676)
Ibrahim the Illustrious Bassa: A tragedy (1677)
Pastor Fido; or, The Faithful Shepherd: A pastoral (1677)
Fatal Love; or, The Forc'd Inconstancy: A tragedy (1680)
The Female Prelate: Being the history of the life and death of Pope Joan. A tragedy. (1680)
Absalom Senior; or, Achitophel Transpros'd (1682)
The Heir of Morocco, with the Death of Gayland (1682)
Distress'd Innocence; or, The Princess of Persia: A tragedy (1691)
The Fairy Queen: An opera (1692)
The Ambitious Slave; or, A Generous Revenge: A tragedy (1694)
Philaster; or, Love Lies A-Bleeding: A tragi-comedy (1695)
A Defence of Dramatick Poetry (1698)
Seward, Anna (1742–1809)
poet and author
Elegy on Captain Cook (1780)
Monody on Major André (1781)
Louisa: A poetical novel (1784)
Llangollen Vale, with Other Poems (1796)
Original Sonnets on Various Subjects (1799)
Memoirs of the Life of Erasmus Darwin (1804)
Poetical Works (1810)
Sewel, William (1654–1720)
Quaker historian
The History of the Rise, Increase, and Progress of the Christian People Called Quakers (1722)
Sewell, Anna (1820–78)
novelist
Black Beauty: The autobiography of a horse, translated from the original Equine (1877)
Sewell, Elizabeth Missing (1815–1906)
novelist and children's author
Amy Herbert (1844)
Sewell, George (1690?–1726)
poet and dramatist
The Patriot (1712)
A Vindication of the English Stage (1716)
The Tragedy of Sir Walter Raleigh (1719)
Poems on Several Occasions (1719)

A New Collection of Original Poems (1720)
Posthumous Works of Dr George Sewell (1728)

Sexby, Edward ['William Allen'] (*d.* 1658)
soldier and apologist for tyrannicide
Killing Noe Murder (1657)

Seymour, Frances, *née* Thynne, countess of Hertford, later duchess of Somerset (1699–1754)
patron of letters and learning
The Story of Inkle and Yarrico (1738)

Shadwell, Thomas (1642?–92)
dramatist and Poet Laureate
The Sullen Lovers; or, The Impertinents: A comedy (1668)
The Royal Shepherdess: A tragi-comedy (1669)
The Humorists: A comedy (1671)
The Miser: A comedy (1672)
Epsom-Wells: A comedy (1673)
Psyche: A tragedy (1675)
The Libertine: A tragedy (1676)
The Virtuoso: A comedy (1676)
The History of Timon of Athens, the Man-hater (1678)
A True Widow: A comedy (1679)
The Woman-Captain: A comedy (1680)
The Lancashire-Witches, and Tegue o Divelly the Irish Priest: A comedy (1682)
The Medal of John Bayes: A satyr against folly and knavery (1682)
The Tenth Satyr of Juvenal (1687)
The Squire of Alsatia: A comedy (1688)
Bury-Fair: A comedy (1689)
The Amorous Bigotte: With the second part of Tegue o Divelly (1690)
The Scowrers (1691)
The Volunteers; or, The Stock-Jobbers: A comedy (1693)

Shaffer, Peter Levin (1926–)
playwright
The Royal Hunt of the Sun (1964)
The White Liars; Black Comedy (1968)
Equus (1973)
Amadeus (1980)
Lettice and Lovage: A comedy (1988)
The Gift of the Gorgon (1993)

Shakespeare, William (1564–1616)
dramatist and poet
Venus and Adonis (1593)
Henry VI Part 2 (1594)
Lucrece (1594)
Titus Andronicus (1594)
Henry VI Part 3 (1595)
Richard II (1597)
Richard III (1597)
Romeo and Juliet (1597)
Henry IV Part 1 (1598)
Loves Labors Lost (1598)
The Passionate Pilgrime; or, Certaine Amorous Sonnets (1599)
Romeo and Juliet (1599)
A Midsommer Nights Dreame (1600)
The Merchant of Venice (1600)
Henry IV Part 2 (1600)
Much Adoe About Nothing (1600)
Henry V (1600)
The Merrie Wives of Windsor (1602)
Hamlet (1603)
Hamlet, Prince of Denmarke (1604)
King Lear (1608)
Troilus and Cressida (1609)
Pericles, Prince of Tyre (1609)
Shake-speares Sonnets (1609)
A Midsommer Nights Dreame (1619)
Othello (1622)
Comedies, Histories and Tragedies: Published according to the true originall copies (1623, First Folio). Contains the following plays printed for the first time: *All's Well That Ends Well, Antony and Cleopatra, As You Like It, The Comedy of Errors, Coriolanus, Cymbeline, Henry VII, Henry VI Part 1, Julius Caesar, King John, Macbeth, Measure for Measure, The Taming of the Shrew, The Tempest, Timon of Athens, Twelfth Night, The Two Gentlemen of Verona, The Winter's Tale*
Comedies, Histories and Tragedies (1632, Second Folio)
Comedies, Histories and Tragedies (1633, Third Folio)
Comedies, Histories and Tragedies (1685, Fourth Folio)
The Works of Mr William Shakespear (1709)
The Works of Mr William Shakespear (1714)
The Works of Shakespear (1725)
The Works of Shakespeare (1733)
The Works of Shakespear (1743)
The Works of Shakespear (1747)
The Plays of William Shakespeare, with the Corrections and Illustrations of Various Commentators (1765)
Twenty of the Plays of Shakespeare (1766)
Mr William Shakespeare His Comedies, Histories and Tragedies (1768)
The Plays of William Shakespeare (1773)
Supplement to the Edition of Shakespeare's Plays Published in 1778 by Samuel Johnson and George Steevens (1780)
The Plays and Poems of William Shakespeare (1790)
The Plays of William Shakespeare (1803)
The Works of William Shakespeare (1842)

Shapcott, Jo (1953–)
poet
Electroplating the Baby (1988)
Phrase Book (1992)
My Life Asleep (1998)
Her Book (2000)
Tender Taxes (2001)

Sharp, Samuel (1700?–78)
author
Letters from Italy (1766)
Sharpe, Lewis (*fl.* 1640)
dramatist
The Noble Stranger (1640)
Sharpe, Roger (*fl.* 1610)
author
More Fooles Yet (1610)
Sharpe, Tom [Thomas Ridley Sharp] (1928–)
novelist
Riotous Assembly (1971)
Indecent Exposure (1973)
Porterhouse Blue (1974)
Blott on the Landscape (1975)
Wilt (1976)
Sharpham, Edward (*fl.* 1607)
dramatist
Cupids Whirligig (1607)
The Fleire (1607)
Shaw, George Bernard (1856–1950)
Irish dramatist, novelist, and social critic
Cashel Byron's Profession (1886)
An Unsocial Socialist (1887)
The Quintessence of Ibsenism (1891)
Widowers' Houses: A comedy (1893)
Plays Pleasant and Unpleasant (1898)
The Perfect Wagnerite (1898)
Fabianism and the Empire (1900)
Three Plays for Puritans (1901)
Mrs Warren's Profession (1902)
Man and Superman (1903)
The Irrational Knot (1905)
John Bull's Other Island, and Major Barbara (1907)
The Doctor's Dilemma; Getting Married; and The Shewing-Up of Blanco Posnet (1911)
Misalliance;The Dark Lady of the Sonnets; and Fanny's First Play (1914)
Love Among the Artists (1914)
Common Sense About the War (1914)
Androcles and the Lion; Overruled; Pygmalion (1916)
How to Settle the Irish Question (1917)
Heartbreak House; Great Catherine; and Playlets of the War (1919)
Back to Methuselah (1921)
Saint Joan (1924)
The Intelligent Woman's Guide to Socialism and Capitalism (1928)
Immaturity (1930)
The Apple Cart: A political extravaganza (1930)
Complete Plays (1931)
Too True to be Good; Village Wooing; and On the Rocks (1934)
Short Stories, Scraps and Shavings (1934)
Prefaces (1934)
The Simpleton; The Six; and The Millionairess (1936)
London Music in 1888–89 (1937)
Pygmalion (1941)
Everybody's Political What's What (1944)
Major Barbara: A Screen Version (1946)
Buoyant Billions (1950)
Buoyant Billions; Farfetched Fables; and Shakes Versus Shav (1951)
Shebbeare, John (1709–88)
novelist
The Marriage Act (1754)
Letters on the English Nation (1755)
The History of the Sumatrans (1760)
Sheffield, John, earl of Mulgrave, marquis of Normanby, duke of Buckingham (1648–1721)
politician and poet
An Essay upon Poetry (1682)
The Character of Charles II, King of England (1696)
Sheil, Richard Lalor (1791–1851)
politician and dramatist
Adelaide; or, The Emigrants: A tragedy (1814)
The Apostate: A tragedy (1817)
Bellamira; or, The Fall of Tunis: A tragedy (1818)
Evadne; or, The Statue: A tragedy (1819)
Damon and Pythias: A tragedy (1821)
Shelley, Mary Wollstonecraft, *née* Godwin (1797–1851)
novelist
History of a Six Weeks' Tour Through a Part of France, Switzerland, Germany, and Holland (1817)
Frankenstein; or, The Modern Prometheus (1818)
Valperga; or, The Life and Adventures of Castruccio, Prince of Lucca (1823)
The Last Man (1826)
The Fortunes of Perkin Warbeck (1830)
Lodore (1835)
Falkner (1837)
Rambles in Germany and Italy, in 1840, 1842, and 1843 (1844)
Shelley, Percy Bysshe (1792–1822)
poet
Original Poetry by Victor and Cazire (1810)
Posthumous Fragments of Margaret Nicholson (1810)
Zastrozzi (1810)
The Necessity of Atheism (1811)
St Irvyne; or, The Rosicrucian (1811)
An Address to the Irish People (1812)
Declaration of Rights (1812)
The Devil's Walk (1812)
A Letter to Lord Ellenborough (1812)
Proposals for an Association of Philanthropists (1812)
Queen Mab (1813)
A Vindication of Natural Diet (1813)
A Refutation of Deism: in a Dialogue (1814)
Alastor; or, The Spirit of Solitude: and Other Poems (1816)
Laon and Cythna; or, The Revolution of the Golden City (1817)

A Proposal for Putting Reform to the Vote Throughout the Kingdom (1817)
The Revolt of Islam (1817)
The Cenci: A tragedy (1819)
Rosalind and Helen: a Modern Eclogue; with Other Poems (1819)
Oedipus Tyrannus; or, Swellfoot the Tyrant (1820)
Prometheus Unbound: A lyrical drama (1820)
Adonais: An elegy on the death of John Keats (1821)
Epipsychidion (1821)
Hellas (1822)
Poetical Pieces by the Late Percy Bysshe Shelley (1823)
Posthumous Poems of Percy Bysshe Shelley (1824)
Miscellaneous and Posthumous Poems of Percy Bysshe Shelley (1826)
The Masque of Anarchy (1832)
The Works of Percy Bysshe Shelley, with his Life (1834)
The Poetical Works of Percy Bysshe Shelley (1839)
Essays, Letters from Abroad, Translations and Fragments (1840)
The Works of Percy Bysshe Shelley (1847)
Shelley Memorials (1859)
The Works of Percy Bysshe Shelley (1876)

Shelton, Thomas (*fl.* 1597–1629?)
translator of Cervantes
Don Quixote (1612)

Shenstone, William (1714–63)
poet and landscape gardener
Poems Upon Various Occasions (1737)
The Judgment of Hercules (1741)
The School-Mistress (1742)
Works, in Verse and Prose (1764)

Shepherd, Luke [pseudonym?] (*fl.* 1548)
poet
Antipus (1548)
Doctour Doubble Ale (1548?)
John Bon and Mast Person (1548?)
Pathos (1548?)
The Upcheering of the Mass (1548)

Sheppard, Samuel (*fl.* 1646)
royalist author
The Loves of Amandus and Sophronia (1650)

Sherburne, Sir Edward (1618–1702)
poet and translator
Salmacis. Lyrian & Sylvia. Forsaken Lydia. The Rape of Helen (1651)
The Tragedies of L. Annaeus Seneca (1701)

Sheridan, Frances, *née* Chamberlaine (1724–66)
novelist and dramatist
Memoirs of Miss Sidney Bidulph (1761)
The Discovery: A comedy (1763)
The Dupe: A comedy (1764)
Conclusion of the Memoirs of Miss Sidney Bidulph (1767)
The History of Nourjahad (1767)

Sheridan, Richard Brinsley (1751–1816)
dramatist
The Rivals: A comedy (1775)
A Trip to Scarborough: A comedy (1781)
The School for Scandal: A comedy (1781)
The Critic; or, A Tragedy Rehearsed (1781)
Pizarro (1799)

Sheridan, Thomas (1687–1738)
poet and translator
The Philoctetes of Sophocles (1725)
The Satyrs of Persius (1728)
The Satires of Juvenal Translated (1739)
The Simile; or, Woman: a Cloud (1748)

Sherley, Sir Anthony (1565–1635?)
traveller
Travels into Persia (1613)

Sherlock, Thomas (1678–1761)
prelate and author
The Tryal of the Witnesses of the Resurrection of Jesus (1729)

Sherlock, William (1641?–1707)
dean of St Paul's and controversialist
A Practical Discourse Concerning Death (1689)
The Case of the Allegiance Due to Soveraign Powers (1691)

Sherriff, Robert Cedric (1896–1975)
playwright and novelist
Journey's End (1929)

Sherwood, Mary Martha (1775–1851)
writer for children
The History of the Fairchild Family; or, The Child's Manual (1818)

Shiel, Matthew Phipps (1865–1947)
novelist
Prince Zaleski (1895)

Shipman, Thomas (1632–80)
poet
Henry the Third of France, Stabb'd by a Fryer. With the fall of the Guise (1678)
Carolina; or, Loyal Poems (1683)

Shirley, Henry (c.1594–1627)
dramatist
The Martyr'd Souldier (1638)

Shirley, James (1596–1666)
poet and dramatist
The Wedding (1629)
The Gratefull Servant: A comedie (1630)
The Schoole of Complement (1631)
Changes; or, Love in a Maze: A comedie (1632)
The Bird in a Cage: A comedie (1633)
A Contention for Honour and Riches (1633)
The Wittie Faire One: A comedie (1633)
The Triumph of Peace: A masque, presented by the foure honourable houses, or Innes of Court (1634)
The Traytor: A tragedie (1635)
Hide Parke: A comedie (1637)
The Lady of Pleasure: A comedie (1637)
The Young Admirall (1637)

The Example (1637)
The Gamester (1637)
The Dukes Mistris (1638)
The Royall Master (1638)
The Maides Revenge: A tragedy (1639)
Loves Crueltie: A tragedy (1640)
The Opportunitie: A comedy (1640)
The Coronation: A comedy (1640)
The Constant Maid: A comedy (1640)
St Patrick for Ireland (1640)
The Humorous Courtier: A comedy (1640)
The Arcadia (1640)
Poems (1646)
Six New Playes (1653)
Cupid and Death: A masque (1653)
The Gentleman of Venice: A tragi-comedie (1655)
The Politician: A tragedy (1655)

Shirley, William (*fl.* 1739–80)
dramatist
The Parricide; or, Innocence in Distress: A tragedy (1739)
Edward the Black Prince; or, The Battle of Poictiers: An historical tragedy (1750)
Electra: A tragedy (1765)

Shore, Louisa Catherine (1824–95)
poet
War Lyrics (1855)
Gemma of the Isles (1859)

Shorthouse, Joseph Henry (1834–1903)
novelist
John Inglesant (1881)

Shukman, Henry (1962)
poet
In Dr No's Garden (2002)

'Shute, Nevil' [Nevil Shute Norway] (1899–1960)
novelist
Marazan (1926)
A Town Like Alice (1950)
On the Beach (1957)

Shuttle, Penelope Diane (1947–)
poet and novelist
Wailing Monkey Embracing a Tree (1973)
The Lion From Rio (1986)
Taxing the Rain (1992)

Sibbes, Richard (1577–1635)
Puritan divine
The Bruised Reede, and Smoaking Flax (1630)
A Fountaine Sealed; or, The Duty of the Sealed to the Spirit, and the Worke of the Spirit in Sealing (1637)
Beames of Divine Light, Breaking Forth from Severall Places of Holy Scripture (1638)

Sidgwick, Henry (1838–1900)
philosopher
The Methods of Ethics (1874)

Sidnam, Jonathan (*fl.* 1630)
dramatist
Filli di Sciro; or, Phillis of Scyros: An excellent pastorall (1655)

Sidney, Algernon (1622–83)
political writer
Discourses Concerning Government (1698)

Sidney, Sir Philip (1554–86)
poet and soldier
The Countesse of Pembrokes Arcadia (1590)
Astrophel and Stella (1591)
The Countesse of Pembrokes Arcadia (1593)
The Defence of Poesie (1595)
The Countesse of Pembrokes Arcadia (1598)

Sigerson, Dora, afterwards Mrs Clement Shorter (1866–1918)
poet and short-story writer
The Fairy Changeling, and Other Poems (1897)
Ballads and Poems (1899)
The Woman Who Went to Hell, and Other Ballads and Lyrics (1902)
The Country-House Party (1905)
Collected Poems (1907)
New Poems (1912)
Madge Linsey, and Other Poems (1913)
The Sad Years, and Other Poems (1918)
Sixteen Dead Men, and Other Ballads of Easter Week (1919)

Silkin, Jon (1930–97)
poet and editor
The Portrait, and Other Poems (1950)
The Peaceable Kingdom (1954)
The Two Freedoms (1958)
The Re-Ordering of the Stones (1961)
Nature With Man (1965)
Amana Grass (1971)
The Principle of Water (1974)
The Little Time-Keeper (1976)
The Psalms With Their Spoils (1980)
The Ship's Pasture (1986)
The Lens-Breakers (1992)
Watersmeet (1994)

Sillitoe, Alan (1928–)
novelist, poet, and playwright
Saturday Night and Sunday Morning (1958)
The Loneliness of the Long-Distance Runner (1959)
The General (1960)
Key to the Door (1961)
The Ragman's Daughter (1963)
The Death of William Posters (1965)
A Tree on Fire (1967)
A Start in Life (1970)
Snow Stop (1993)
Alligator Playground (1997)
The Broken Chariot (1998)
Birthday (2001)

Simeon, Charles (1759–1836)
Evangelical divine
Horae Homilecticae; or, Discourses upon the Whole Scriptures (1819)
Memoirs of the Life of the Rev. Charles Simeon (1847)

Simpson, Norman Frederick (1919–)
playwright

A Resounding Tinkle (1958)
The Cresta Run (1966)
Sinclair, Andrew Annandale (1935–)
novelist, biographer, and cultural historian
The Breaking of Bumbo (1959)
Gog (1967)
Magog (1972)
King Ludd (1988)
Sinclair, Catherine (1800–64)
author and philanthropist
Modern Accomplishments; or, The March of Intellect (1836)
Modern Society; or, The March of Intellect (1837)
Sir Edgar Graham; or, Railway Speculators (1849)
Sinclair, Clive John (1948–)
novelist and short-story writer
Hearts of Gold (1979)
Sinclair, Iain Macgregor (1943–)
poet and novelist
Lud Heat (1975)
White Chappell, Scarlet Tracings (1987)
Downriver; or, The Vessels of Wrath (1991)
Radon Daughters (1994)
Sinclair, May [Mary Amelia St Clair] (1863–1946)
novelist, short-story writer, and poet
Essays in Verse (1891)
The Divine Fire (1904)
The Helpmate (1907)
Feminism (1912)
Sisson, Charles Hubert (1914–2003)
poet, critic, novelist, and translator
An Asiatic Romance (1953)
The London Zoo (1961)
Numbers (1965)
God Bless Karl Marx (1987)
Antidotes (1991)
What and Who (1994)
Sitwell, Dame Edith Louisa (1887–1964)
poet and author
Twentieth Century Harlequinade, and Other Poems (1916)
Façade (1922)
Bucolic Comedies (1923)
The Sleeping Beauty (1924)
Troy Park (1925)
Rustic Elegies (1927)
Collected Poems (1930)
The English Eccentrics (1933)
A Poet's Notebook (1943)
Sitwell, Sir [Francis] Osbert Sacheverell (1892–1969)
poet, novelist, and autobiographer
Argonaut and Juggernaut (1919)
Out of the Flame (1923)
England Reclaimed (1927)
The Collected Satires and Poems (1931)
Miracle on Sinai (1933)
Those Were the Days (1938)
Open the Door! (1939)
Left Hand, Right Hand! (1945)
The Scarlet Tree (1946)
Great Morning (1948)
Laughter in the Next Room (1949)
Noble Essences; or, Courteous Revelations (1950)
Wrack at Tidesend (1952)
On the Continent (1958)
Sitwell, Sir Sacheverell (1897–1988)
poet and art historian
The People's Palace (1918)
The Hundred and One Harlequins, and Other Poems (1922)
Collected Poems (1936)
The Homing of the Winds, and Other Passages in Prose (1942)
Skelton, John (1460?–1529)
priest, royal tutor, poet, and dramatist
The Bouge of Court (1499?)
A Ballade of the Scottysshe Kynge (1513)
The Tunnyng of Elynour Rummyng (1521?)
The Garland of Laurel (1523)
Skelton Laureate Agaynste a Comely Coystrowne (1527?)
Diverse Ballads (1528?)
A Replication (1528)
Magnyfycence (1530?)
Colin Clout (1531?)
Certain Books (1545)
Phillip Sparrow (1545?)
Why Come Ye Not to Court? (1545?)
Pithy Pleasaunt and Profitable Workes of Maister Skelton (1568)
Slaughter, Carolyn (1946–)
novelist
The Story of the Weasel (1976)
Sleath, Eleanor (*fl.* 1798–1811)
novelist
The Orphan of the Rhine (1798)
Smart, Christopher (1722–71)
poet and translator
Poems on Several Occasions (1752)
The Hilliad: An epic poem (1753)
Hymn to the Supreme Being (1756)
The Works of Horace (1756)
A Song to David (1763)
Hannah: An oratorio (1764)
A Poetical Translation of the Fables of Phaedrus (1764)
A Translation of the Psalms of David (1765)
The Works of Horace, Translated into Verse (1767)
The Parables of Our Lord and Saviour Jesus Christ (1768)
Hymns, for the Amusement of Children (1772)
Poems of the Late Christopher Smart (1791)
'Smectymnuus', collective pseudonym of five Protestant ministers: Stephen Marshall (1594?–1655), Edmund Calamy (1600–66),

Thomas Young (1587–1655), Matthew Newcomen (1610?–69), and William Spurstowe (1605?–66)
An Answer to a Booke entituled, An Humble Remonstrance (1641)
A Vindication of the Answer to the Humble Remonstrance (1641)
Smedley, Menella Bute (1820–77)
poet and novelist
The Story of Queen Isabel, and Other Verses (1863)
Poems Written for a Child (1868)
Smellie, William (1740–95)
printer, naturalist, antiquary, and first editor of the *Encyclopaedia Britannica*
Encyclopaedia Britannica; or, A Dictionary of Arts and Sciences (1771)
Smiles, Samuel (1812–1904)
biographer and advocate of self-improvement
The Life of George Stephenson, Railway Engineer (1857)
Self-Help (1859)
Lives of the Engineers (1867)
Character (1871)
Smith, Adam (1723–90)
political economist
The Theory of Moral Sentiments (1759)
An Inquiry into the Nature and Causes of the Wealth of Nations (1776)
Essays on Philosophical Subjects (1795)
Smith, Alexander (*fl.* 1714–26)
translator and author
The History of the Lives of the Most Noted Highway-men, Foot-pads, House-breakers, Shop-lifts and Cheats of Both Sexes . . . (1714)
The Secret History of the Lives of the Most Celebrated Beauties, Ladies of Quality, and Jilts (1715)
Smith, Ali (1962)
novelist and short-story writer
Hotel World (2001)
The Whole Story and Other Stories (2003)
Smith, Charlotte, *née* Turner (1749–1806)
poet and novelist
Elegaic Sonnets, and Other Essays (1784)
Manon Lescaut; or, The Fatal Attachment (1786)
The Romance of Real Life (1787)
Emmeline, the Orphan of the Castle (1788)
Ethelinde; or, The Recluse of the Lake (1789)
Celestina (1791)
Desmond (1792)
The Emigrants (1793)
The Old Manor House (1793)
The Banished Man (1794)
The Wanderings of Warwick (1794)
Montalbert (1795)
Marchmont (1796)
Elegaic Sonnets, and Other Poems [vol. ii] (1797)
The Young Philosopher (1798)
The Letters of a Solitary Wanderer (1800)
Beachy Head, with Other Poems (1807)
Smith, Dodie [Dorothy Gladys Smith] ['C.L. Anthony'] (1896–1990)
dramatist and novelist
Autumn Crocus (1931)
Service (1932)
Dear Octopus: A comedy (1938)
I Capture the Castle (1949)
One Hundred and One Dalmatians (1956)
Smith, Henry (1550–91)
Puritan divine
The Examination of Usury, in Two Sermons (1591)
Sermons (1592)
Smith, Horatio, known as Horace (1779–1849)
poet, novelist, and journalist
A Family Story (1799)
Trevanion; or, Matrimonial Errors (1801)
Rejected Addresses; or, The New Theatrum Poetarum (1812)
Horace in London (1813)
Amarynthus, the Nympholept (1821)
Brambletye House; or, Cavaliers and Roundheads (1826)
The Moneyed Man; or, The Lesson of a Life (1841)
Smith, Iain Crichton [Iain Mac a'Ghobhainn] (1928–)
Scottish poet, playwright, and novelist
The Long River (1955)
A Life (1986)
The Village, and Other Poems (1989)
Smith, James (1775–1839)
author and humorist
Comic Miscellanies (1840)
Smith, Captain John (1580–1631)
soldier, governor of Virginia, and author
A Description of New England; or, The Observations, and Discoveries, of Captain John Smith (1616)
The Generall Historie of Virginia, New-England, and the Summer Isles (1624)
An Accidence or the Path-way to Experience: Necessary for all young sea-men (1626)
The True Travels, Adventures, and Observations of Captaine John Smith (1630)
Smith, John (1616?–52)
Cambridge Platonist
Select Discourses (1660)
Smith, [Lloyd] Logan Pearsall (1865–1946)
American-born essayist
The Youth of Parnassus, and Other Stories (1895)
Trivia (1918)
More Trivia (1922)
Afterthoughts (1931)
Smith, Stevie [Florence Margaret Smith] (1902–71)
poet and novelist
Novel on Yellow Paper (1936)
A Good Time Was Had By All (1937)

Tender Only to One (1938)
Over the Frontier (1939)
Mother, What is Man? (1942)
The Holiday (1949)
Harold's Leap (1950)
Not Waving but Drowning (1957)
The Frog Prince, and Other Poems (1966)
Scorpion, and Other Poems (1972)

Smith, Sydney (1771–1845)
clergyman and author
Two Letters on the Subject of the Catholics (1807)
The Works of the Rev. Sydney Smith (1839)

Smith, Sydney Goodsir (1915–75)
Scottish poet
Skail Wind (1941)
The Deevil's Waltz (1946)

Smith, Sir Thomas (1513–77)
statesman, scholar, and author
De Republica Anglorum: The Maner of Government of England (1583)
The Common-welth of England, and Manner of Government Thereof (1589)

Smith, Walter (*fl.* 1523)
author
The Merry Jests of the Widow Edith (1525)

Smith, William (*fl.* 1596)
poet
Chloris; or, The Complaint of the Passionate Despised Shepheard (1596)

Smith, Zadie (1975–)
novelist
White Teeth (2000)
The Autograph Man (2002)

Smollett, Tobias George (1721–71)
novelist, poet, and dramatist
Advice (1746)
Reproof: A satire (1747)
The Adventures of Gil Blas of Santillane (1748)
The Adventures of Roderick Random (1748)
The Regicide; or, James the First, of Scotland: A tragedy (1749)
The Adventures of Peregrine Pickle (1751)
The Adventures of Ferdinand Count Fathom (1753)
The History and Adventures of the Renowned Don Quixote (1755)
A Compendium of Authentic and Entertaining Voyages (1756)
The Critical Review; or, Annals of Literature (1756)
A Complete History of England (1757)
The Reprisal; or, The Tars of Old England: A comedy (1757)
The British Magazine (1760)
The Life and Adventures of Sir Launcelot Greaves (1762)
Travels Through France and Italy (1766)
The Present State of all Nations (1768)
The History and Adventures of an Atom (1769)
The Expedition of Humphry Clinker (1771)

Snow, Charles Percy, Baron Snow of Leicester (1905–80)
novelist
Death Under Sail (1932)
Strangers and Brothers (1940)
The Light and the Dark (1947)
Time of Hope (1949)
The Masters (1951)
The New Men (1954)
Homecomings (1956)
The Conscience of the Rich (1958)
The Two Cultures and the Scientific Revolution (1959)
The Affair (1960)
Corridors of Power (1964)
The Two Cultures; and A Second Look (1964)
The Sleep of Reason (1968)
Last Things (1970)
The Malcontents (1972)

Soane, George (1790–1860)
dramatist and novelist
The Hebrew: A drama (1820)
Faustus: A romantic drama (1825)

Somervile or Somerville, William (1675–1742)
poet
Occasional Poems, Translations, Fables, Tales, &c (1726)
The Chace (1735)
Field Sports (1742)

Somerville, Edith Anna Œnone ['Somerville'] (1858–1949) and 'Martin Ross' [Violet Florence Martin] (1862–1915)
novelists
An Irish Cousin (1889)
Naboth's Vineyard (1891)
The Silver Fox (1897)
Some Experiences of an Irish R.M. (1899)
Further Experiences of an Irish R.M. (1908)
Dan Russel the Fox (1911)
In Mr Knox's Country (1915)
Mount Music (1919)
The Big House of Inver (1925)

Sorley, Charles Hamilton (1895–1915)
Scottish poet
Marlborough, and Other Poems (1916)

Sotheby, William (1757–1833)
poet and translator
Poems (1790)
Oberon (1798)
The Battle of the Nile (1799)
The Georgics of Virgil (1800)
The Siege of Cuzco: A tragedy (1800)
Julian and Agnes; or, The Monks of the Great St Bernard: A tragedy (1801)
Oberon; or, Huon de Bourdeaux (1802)
Saul (1807)
Constance of Castille (1810)
Tragedies (1814)
Farewell to Italy, and Occasional Poems (1818)

Soutar, William (1898–1943)
Scottish poet

Conflict (1931)
The Solitary Way (1934)
A Handful of Earth (1936)
In the Time of Tyrants (1939)
But the Earth Abideth (1943)
The Expectant Silence (1944)

South, Robert (1634–1716)
controversialist and preacher
Interest Deposed, and Truth Restored (1660)
Sermons Preached upon Several Occasions (1679)
Twelve Sermons Preached upon Several Occasions (1692)
Tritheism (1695)

Southern, Richard William (1912–2001)
medieval historian
The Making of the Middle Ages (1953)

Southerne, Thomas (1659–1746)
dramatist
The Loyal Brother; or, The Persian Prince: A tragedy (1682)
The Disappointment; or, The Mother in Fashion (1684)
Sir Anthony Love; or, The Rambling Lady: A comedy (1691)
The Wives Excuse; or, Cuckolds Make Themselves: A comedy (1692)
The Maids Last Prayer; or Any, Rather Than Fail: A comedy (1693)
The Fatal Marriage; or, The Innocent Adultery (1694)
Oroonoko: A tragedy (1696)
The Fate of Capua: A tragedy (1700)
The Spartan Dame: A tragedy (1719)
Money the Mistress (1726)

Southey, Robert (1774–1843)
poet, biographer, translator, and historian
Poems (1795)
Joan of Arc (1796)
Poems (1796)
Letters Written During a Short Residence in Spain and Portugal (1797)
Poems . . . The Second Volume (1799)
Thalaba the Destroyer (1801)
Amadis of Gaul (1803)
Madoc (1805)
Metrical Tales, and Other Poems (1805)
Letters from England (1807)
Palmerin of England (1807)
Specimens of the Later English Poets (1807)
Chronicles of the Cid (1808)
The Curse of Kehama (1810)
History of Brazil . . . Part the First (1810)
The Life of Nelson (1813)
Odes to the Prince Regent, the Emperor of Russia, and the King of Prussia (1814)
Roderick, the Last of the Goths (1814)
The Minor Poems of Robert Southey (1815)
The Lay of the Laureate: Carmen nuptiale (1816)
The Poet's Pilgrimage to Waterloo (1816)
History of Brazil . . . Part the Second (1817)
Wat Tyler (1817)
History of Brazil . . . Part the Third (1819)
The Life of Wesley, and the Rise and Progress of Methodism (1820)
A Vision of Judgement (1821)
History of the Peninsular War [vol. i] (1823)
The Book of the Church (1824)
A Tale of Paraguay (1825)
Vindiciae Ecclesiae Anglicanae (1826)
History of the Peninsular War [vol. ii] (1827)
Sir Thomas More; or, Colloquies on the Progress and Prospects of Society (1829)
Essays, Moral and Political (1832)
History of the Peninsular War [vol. iii] (1832)
Lives of the British Admirals [vols i, ii] (1833)
The Doctor [vols i, ii] (1834)
Lives of the British Admirals [vol. iii] (1834)
The Doctor [vol. iii] (1835)
The Doctor [vol. iv] (1837)
Lives of the British Admirals [vol. iv] (1837)
The Poetical Works of Robert Southey [vols i, ii] (1837)
The Doctor [vol. v] (1838)
The Poetical Works of Robert Southey, [vols iii–x] (1838)
Oliver Newman: A New-England tale (1845)
The Doctor [vols. vi, vii] (1847)
Robin Hood (1847)
Southey's Common-place Book: First Series (1849)
Southey's Common-place Book: Second Series (1849)
The Life and Correspondence of the Late Robert Southey (1849)
Southey's Common-place Book: Third/Fourth Series (1850)

Southwell, Robert (1561?–95)
Jesuit and poet
An Epistle of Comfort, to the Reverend Priestes, & to the Laye Sort Restrayned in Durance (1587)
Marie Magdalens Funeral Teares (1591)
Moeniae (1595)
Saint Peters Complaint, with Other Poemes (1595)
The Triumphs over Death; or, A Consolatorie Epistle (1595)
S. Peters Complaint. And Saint Mary Magdalens Funerall Teares (1616)

Spark, Muriel Sarah, *née* Camberg (1918–)
novelist, short-story writer, poet, and playwright
The Comforters (1957)
The Go-Away Bird, and Other Stories (1958)
Robinson (1958)
Memento Mori (1959)
The Bachelors (1960)
The Ballad of Peckham Rye (1960)
The Prime of Miss Jean Brodie (1961)
The Girls of Slender Means (1963)
The Mandelbaum Gate (1965)

The Public Image (1968)
The Driver's Seat (1970)
Not to Disturb (1971)
The Hothouse by the River (1972)
The Abbess of Crewe (1974)
The Takeover (1976)
Territorial Rights (1979)
Loitering With Intent (1981)
Bang-Bang You're Dead, and Other Stories (1982)
Going Up to Sotheby's, and Other Poems (1982)
The Only Problem (1984)
A Far Cry From Kensington (1988)
Symposium (1990)
Curriculum Vitae (1992)
Aiding and Abetting (2000)
Complete Short Stories (2001)

Sparke, Edward (*d.* 1692)
divine
Scintillula Altaris (1652)

Sparke, Michael (1588?–1653)
stationer and author
Crumms of Comfort, the Valley of Teares, and the Hill of Joy (1628)
Scintilla; or, A Light Broken into Dark Warehouses (1641)
The Narrative History of King James, for the First Fourteen Years (1651)
A Second Beacon Fired by Scintilla (1652)

Speed, John (1552?–1629)
antiquary and cartographer
The Genealogies Recorded in the Sacred Scriptures (1611)
The History of Great Britaine, Under the Conquests of the Romans, Saxons, Danes and Normans (1611)
The Theatre of the Empire of Great Britaine (1612)

Speght, Rachel (*b.* 1597)
polemicist and poet
A Mouzell for Melastomus, the Cynicall Bayter of, and Foule Mouthed Barker Against Evahs Sex (1617)
Mortalities Memorandum: With a dreame prefixed, imaginarie in manner, reall in matter (1621)

Speke, John Hanning (1827–64)
African explorer
Journal of the Discovery of the Source of the Nile (1863)

Spence, Joseph (1699–1768)
anecdotist and critic
An Essay on Pope's Odyssey (1726)
Polymetis; or, An Enquiry Concerning the Agreement Between the Works of the Roman Poets, and the Remains of the Antient Artists (1747)

Spencer, Herbert (1820–1903)
philosopher
The Proper Sphere of Government (1843)
Social Statics (1851)
Essays: Scientific, Political, and Speculative [1st ser.] (1858)
A System of Synthetic Philosophy (1860)
The Man Versus the State (1884)

Spender, Sir Stephen Harold (1909–95)
poet, playwright, and translator
Twenty Poems (1930)
Poems (1933)
Vienna (1934)
The Destructive Element (1935)
The Burning Cactus (1936)
Forward From Liberalism (1937)
Trial of a Judge: A tragedy (1938)
The Still Centre (1939)
The Backward Son (1940)
Selected Poems (1940)
Life and the Poet (1942)
Ruins and Visions (1942)
Citizens in War—and After (1945)
European Witness (1946)
Poems of Dedication (1947)
The Edge of Being (1949)
World Within World (1951)
The Creative Element (1953)
Collected Poems 1928–1953 (1955)
The Making of a Poem (1955)
The Struggle of the Modern (1963)
The Year of the Young Rebels (1969)
The Generous Days (1971)
The Thirties and After (1978)
Collected Poems 1928–1985 (1985)
The Journals of Stephen Spender, 1939–83 (1985)
The Temple (1988)
Dolphins (1994)

Spenser, Edmund ['Immerito'] (1552?–99)
poet
The Shepheardes Calender (1579)
Three Proper and Wittie, Familiar Letters (1580)
The Faerie Queene (1590)
Complaints (1591)
Daphnaida (1591)
Amoretti and Epithalamion (1595)
Colin Clouts Come Home Againe (1595)
Fowre Hymnes (1596)
Prothalamion; or, A Spousall Verse in Honour of the Double Marriage of Ladie Elizabeth and Ladie Katherine Somerset (1596)
The Second Part of the Faerie Queene: Containing the fourth, fifth, and sixth bookes (1596)
The Faerie Queene (1609)

Spottiswood, John (1565–1639)
archbishop of St Andrews and Scots historian
The History of the Church of Scotland (1655)

Sprackland, Jean
poet
Hard Water (2003)

Sprat, Thomas (1635–1713)
bishop of Rochester
The Plague of Athens, which Hapned in the Second Year of the Peloponnesian Warra (1659)

Observations on Monsieur de Sorbier's Voyage into England (1665)
The History of the Royal-Society of London (1667)
A True Account and Declaration of the Horrid Conspiracy Against the Late King (1685)
Sprigge, Joshua (1618–84)
divine
Anglia Rediviva: England's Recovery (1647)
Spring, [Robert] Howard (1889–1965)
novelist and playwright
Shabby Tiger (1934)
O Abasalom! (1938)
Fame is the Spur (1940)
Spurgeon, Charles Haddon (1834–92)
preacher and theologian
John Ploughman's Talk; or, Plain Advice for Plain People (1869)
John Ploughman's Pictures; or, More of his Plain Talk for Plain People (1880)
Squire, Sir John Collings ['Solomon Eagle'] (1884–1958)
poet, humorist, and editor
Imaginary Speeches, and Other Parodies in Prose and Verse (1912)
The Three Hills, and Other Poems (1913)
Books in General (1918)
Poems, First Series (1918)
The Birds, and Other Poems (1919)
Poems: Second Series (1922)
The Grub Street Nights Entertainment (1924)
Stacpoole, Henry de Vere (1863–1951)
novelist and poet
The Intended (1894)
The Blue Lagoon (1908)
Stallworthy, Jon Howie (1935–)
poet, critic, and editor
The Astronomy of Love (1961)
Out of Bounds (1963)
Root and Branch (1969)
A Familiar Tree (1978)
The Anzac Sonata (1986)
Rounding the Horn (1998)
Singing School (1999)
Stanbridge, John (1463–1510)
grammarian
Accidence (1505?)
Stanhope, Philip Dormer, 4th earl of Chesterfield (1694–1773)
statesman and letter writer
Letters to his Son (1774)
Characters of Eminent Personages of His Own Time (1777)
Stanhope, Philip Henry, 5th earl Stanhope,Viscount Mahon (1805–75)
historian
Historical Essays Contributed to the 'Quarterly Review' (1849)
Stanley, Arthur Penrhyn (1815–81)
historian and theologian
The Life and Correspondence of Thomas Arnold (1844)
Essays, Chiefly on Questions of Church and State (1870)
Stanley, Sir Henry Morton (1841–1904)
explorer, administrator, author, and journalist
How I Found Livingstone (1872)
Through the Dark Continent (1878)
In Darkest Africa (1890)
Stanley, Thomas, the elder (1625–78)
classical scholar and poet
Aurora, & The Prince. Oronta the Cyprian Virgin (1647)
Europa. Cupid Crucified. Venus Vigils (1649)
Poems (1651)
The History of Philosophy (1655)
Stannard, Henrietta Eliza Vaughan, *née* Palmer, Mrs Arthur Stannard ['John Strange Winter', 'Violet Whyte'] (1856–1911)
novelist
Bootles' Baby (1885)
Bootles' Children (1888)
Stanyhurst, Richard (1547–1618)
translator
The First Foure Bookes of Virgil his Aeneis (1582)
Stapleton, Thomas (1535–98)
Catholic controversialist and translator
The History of the Church of Englande (1565)
Stapylton, Sir Robert (1605?–69)
dramatist and translator
Erotopaignion (1645)
Juvenal's Sixteen Satyrs; or, A Survey of the Manners and Actions of Mankind (1647)
The Slighted Maid: A comedy (1663)
The Step-Mother: A tragi-comedy (1664)
The Tragedie of Hero and Leander (1669)
Stark, Dame Freya Madeline (1893–1993)
travel writer
The Valleys of the Assassins, and Other Persian Travels (1934)
The Southern Gates of Arabia (1936)
Letters From Syria (1942)
Perseus in the Wind (1948)
Traveller's Prelude (1950)
Beyond Euphrates (1951)
The Coast of Incense (1953)
Dust in the Lion's Paw (1961)
Starke, Mariana (1762?–1838)
dramatist
The Widow of Malabar: A tragedy (1791)
Starkey or Stirk, George (1627–65)
empiric
Natures Explication and Helmont's Vindication; or, A Short and Sure Way to a Long and Sound Life (1658)
The Dignity of Kingship Asserted (1660)
Steel, Flora Annie, *née* Webster (1847–1929)
novelist and short-story writer
Miss Stuart's Legacy (1893)
On the Face of the Waters (1896)

Steele, Sir Richard (1672–1729)
essayist, dramatist, and poet
The Procession: A poem on Her Majesties funeral (1695)
The Christian Hero (1701)
The Funeral; or, Grief a-la-mode: A comedy (1701)
The Lying Lover; or, The Ladies Friendship: A comedy (1704)
The Tender Husband; or, The Accomplish'd Fools: A comedy (1705)
The Tatler (1709)
The Spectator (1711)
The Englishman's Thanks to the Duke of Marlborough (1712)
The Guardian (1713)
The Englishman (1713)
The Crisis; or, A Discourse Representing the Just Causes of the Late Happy Revolution (1714)
The Englishman: Being the Close of the Paper So Called (1714)
The Lover (1714)
Mr Steele's Apology for Himself and his Writings (1714)
Poetical Miscellanies (1714)
The Publick Spirit of the Tories (1714)
The Reader (1714)
The Englishman: Second Series (1715)
Town-Talk (1715)
The Plebian (1719)
The Crisis of Property (1720)
A Nation a Family (1720)
The Conscious Lovers: A comedy (1722)
Steiner, [Francis] George (1929–)
literary and cultural critic
Tolstoy or Dostoevsky (1959)
The Death of Tragedy (1961)
Language and Silence (1967)
After Babel: Aspects of language and translation (1975)
Stennett, Joseph (1663–1713)
hymn-writer, Baptist minister, pamphleteer, and poet
A Poem to the Memory of His Late Majesty William the Third (1702)
Stephen, Sir James (1789–1859)
statesman, historian, and biographer
Essays in Ecclesiastical Biography (1849)
Stephen, Sir James Fitzjames (1829–94)
jurist
Horae Sabbaticae (1892)
Stephen, James Kenneth (1859–92)
poet
Lapsus Calami (1891)
Stephen, Sir Leslie (1832–1904)
biographer, editor, and man of letters
The Playground of Europe (1871)
Hours in a Library [1st ser.] (1874)
History of English Thought in the Eighteenth Century (1876)
Samuel Johnson (1878)
An Agnostic's Apology, and Other Essays (1893)
The English Utilitarians (1900)
Stephens, James (1882–1950)
Irish poet, novelist, and short-story writer
Insurrections (1909)
The Crock of Gold (1912)
The Hill of Vision (1912)
The Adventures of Seumas Beg; The Rocky Road to Dublin (1915)
Songs from the Clay (1915)
Deirdre (1923)
Stern, Gladys Bronwyn (1890–1973)
novelist
Tents of Israel (1924)
Sterne, Laurence (1713–68)
novelist and author
The Case of Elijah and the Widow of Zerephath, Consider'd (1747)
The Abuses of Conscience (1750)
The Life and Opinions of Tristram Shandy, Gentleman [vols i, ii] (1759)
The Sermons of Mr Yorick [vols i, ii] (1760)
The Life and Opinions of Tristram Shandy, Gentleman [vols iii, iv] (1761)
The Life and Opinions of Tristram Shandy, Gentleman [vols v, vi] (1762)
The Life and Opinions of Tristram Shandy, Gentleman [vols vii, viii] (1765)
The Sermons of Mr Yorick [vols iii, iv] (1766)
The Life and Opinions of Tristram Shandy, Gentleman [vol. ix] (1767)
A Sentimental Journey Through France and Italy (1768)
A Political Romance (1769)
Sermons by the Late Rev. Mr Sterne [*Sermons of Mr Yorick*, v, vi, vii] (1769)
Letters from Yorick to Eliza (1773)
Letters of the Late Rev Mr L. Sterne (1775)
Sterne's Letters to his Friends on Various Occasions (1775)
The Beauties of Sterne (1782)
Sterry, Peter (1613–72)
Puritan and Platonist
A Discourse of the Freedom of the Will (1675)
Stevens, George Alexander (1710–84)
poet and dramatist
Albion Restored; or, Time Turned Oculist (1758)
The Celebrated Lecture on Heads (1765)
The Court of Alexander: An opera (1770)
Songs, Comic and Satyrical (1772)
Stevenson, Robert Louis (1850–94)
poet, novelist, and essayist
Edinburgh: Picturesque Notes (1878)
An Inland Voyage (1878)
Travels with a Donkey in the Cévennes (1879)
Virginibus Puerisque, and Other Papers (1881)
Familiar Studies of Men and Books (1882)
New Arabian Nights (1882)
The Silverado Squatters (1883)
Treasure Island (1883)

A Child's Garden of Verses (1885)
More New Arabian Nights: The Dynamiter (1885)
Prince Otto (1885)
Strange Case of Dr Jekyll and Mr Hyde (1886)
Kidnapped (1886)
Memories and Portraits (1887)
The Merry Men, and Other Tales and Fables (1887)
Underwoods (1887)
The Black Arrow: A tale of two roses (1888)
The Wrong Box (1889)
The Master of Ballantrae: A winter's tale (1889)
Ballads (1890)
Across the Plains, with Other Memories and Essays (1892)
The Wrecker (1892)
Catriona (1893)
Island Nights' Entertainments (1893)
Vailima Letters (1895)
Weir of Hermiston: An unfinished romance (1896)
Songs of Travel, and Other Verses (1896)
St Ives (1898)

Stevenson, William (*fl.* 1553)
dramatist
Gammer Gurton's Needle (1575)

Stewart, Dugald (1753–1828)
philosopher
Elements of the Philosophy of the Human Mind [vol. i] (1792)
Philosophical Essays (1810)
Biographical Memoirs, of Adam Smith, W. Robertson, and Thomas Reid (1811)
The Philosophy of the Active and Moral Powers of Man (1828)

Stewart, John Innes Mackintosh ['Michael Innes'] (1906–94)
academic, critic, and novelist
Death at the President's Lodging (1936)
Appleby on Ararat (1941)
The Gaudy (1974)
Young Patullo (1975)
A Memorial Service (1976)
The Madonna of the Astrolabe (1977)
Full Term (1978)

Stillingfleet, Edward (1635–99)
theologian
Irenicum: A Weapon-salve for the Churches Wounds (1660)
Origines Sacrae: Or, a rational account of the grounds of the Christian faith (1662)
A Letter to a Deist (1677)
The Mischief of Separation (1680)
Origines Britannicae; or, The Antiquities of the British Church (1685)
The Doctrines and Practices of the Church of Rome Truly Represented (1686)

Stockdale, Percival (1736–1811)
poet and dramatist
Churchill Defended (1765)

Stoker, Bram [i.e. Abraham] (1847–1912)
Anglo-Irish theatre manager, novelist, and short-story writer
Under the Sunset (1881)
Dracula (1897)
The Lair of the White Worm (1911)

Stone, Elizabeth, *née* Wheeler (*b.* 1803)
novelist and social historian
William Langshawe, the Cotton Lord (1842)
The Young Milliner (1843)

Stopes, Marie Charlotte Carmichael (1880–1958)
scientist and sex reformer
Married Love (1918)
Wise Parenthood (1918)

Stoppard, Tom [born Tomas Straussler] (1937–)
Czechoslovakian-born playwright
Lord Malquist and Mr Moon (1966)
Rosencrantz and Guildenstern are Dead (1967)
The Real Inspector Hound (1968)
Albert's Bridge; If You're Glad I'll Be Frank (1969)
Jumpers (1972)
Artist Descending a Staircase; Where Are They Now? (1973)
Travesties (1975)
Every Good Boy Deserves Favour; Professional Foul (1978)
Night and Day (1978)
The Dog It Was That Died, and Other Plays (1983)
The Real Thing (1983)
Hapgood (1988)
Arcadia (1993)
Indian Ink (1995)
The Invention of Love (1997)

Storer, Thomas (1571–1604)
poet
The Life and Death of Thomas Wolsey Cardinall (1599)

Storey, David Malcolm (1933–)
novelist, playwright, and poet
This Sporting Life (1960)
Flight into Camden (1961)
Radcliffe (1963)
The Restoration of Arnold Middleton (1967)
In Celebration (1969)
The Contractor (1970)
The Changing Room (1972)
A Temporary Life (1973)
Saville (1976)
A Prodigal Child (1982)
Storey's Lives (1992)

Stow, John (1525–1605)
chronicler and antiquary
A Summarie of Englyshe Chronicles (1565)
The Chronicles of England, from Brute Unto this Present Yeare 1580 (1580)

The Annales of England . . . untill this Present Yeere 1592 (1592)
A Survay of London (1598)

Strachey, [Giles] Lytton (1880–1932)
critic and biographer
Landmarks in French Literature (1912)
Eminent Victorians (1918)
Queen Victoria (1921)
Books and Characters, French and English (1922)

Strachey, William (1572–1621)
colonist and author
For the Colony in Virginea Britannia (1612)

Streatfeild, Noel (1895–1986)
children's writer
Ballet Shoes (1936)

Streeter, Burnett Hillman (1874–1937)
biblical scholar
Foundations (1912)

'Stretton, Hesba' [Sarah Smith] (1832–1911)
children's writer
Jessica's First Prayer (1867)
Jessica's Mother (1868)

Strickland, Agnes (1796–1874)
poet and biographer
The Seven Ages of Woman, and Other Poems (1827)

Strode, William (1602–45)
poet and dramatist
The Floating Island: A tragi-comedy (1655)

Strype, John (1643–1737)
ecclesiastical historian
Memorials of Thomas Cranmer (1694)
Annals of the Reformation and Establishment of Religion (1709)
The Life and Acts of Matthew Parker (1711)
The Life and Acts of John Whitgift (1718)
Ecclesiastical Memorials (1721)

Stuart, Gilbert (1742–86)
historian
An Historical Dissertation Concerning the Antiquity of the English Constitution (1768)
A View of Society in Europe, in its Progress from Rudeness to Refinement (1778)

Stubbe, Stubbes, or Stubbs, Henry (1632–76)
physician and author
Campanella Revived; or, An Inquiry into the History of the Royal Society (1670)
The Plus Ultra reduced to a Non Plus (1670)
Rosemary & Bayes (1672)

Stubbes or Stubbs, Philip (*fl.* 1581–93)
Puritan pamphleteer
The Anatomie of Abuses (1583)

Stubbs, John (1543?–91)
Protestant polemicist
The Discoverie of a Gaping Gulf (1579)

Stubbs, William (1825–1901)
historian and bishop
The Constitutional History of England: in its Origin and Development [vol. i] (1873)

Studley, John (*b. c.*1547)
translator
Agamemnon (1566)
Medea (1566)

Stukeley, William (1687–1765)
antiquary
Itinerarium Curiosum; or, An Account of the Antiquitys and Remarkable Curiositys in Nature or Art (1724)
Palaeographia Sacra (1736)
Stonehenge: A temple restor'd to the British Druids (1740)
Abury: A temple of the British Druids (1743)

Sturgis, Howard Overing (1855–1920)
novelist
Tim (1891)
Belchamber (1904)

Suckling, Sir John (1609–42)
poet and dramatist
Aglaura (1638)
Fragmenta Aurea (1646)
The Last Remains of Sr John Suckling (1659)
The Works of Sir John Suckling (1696)

Surtees, Robert Smith (1805–64)
sporting novelist
Jorrocks' Jaunts and Jollities (1838)
Handley Cross; or, The Spa Hunt (1843)
Hillingdon Hall; or, The Cockney Squire (1845)
Hawbuck Grange; or, The Sporting Adventures of Thomas Scott, Esq. (1847)
Mr Sponge's Sporting Tour (1853)
'Ask Mamma'; or, The Richest Commoner in England (1858)
Plain or Ringlets? (1860)
Mr Facey Romford's Hounds (1865)

Sutcliff, Rosemary (1920–92)
children's writer
The Eagle of the Ninth (1954)

Sutcliffe, Alice (*fl.* 1634)
author
Meditations of Man's Mortalitie; or, A Way to True Blessednesse (1634)

Swan, John (1605–71)
encyclopaedist
Speculum Mundi; or, A Glasse Representing the Face of the World (1635)

Swift, Graham Colin (1949–)
novelist
The Sweet-Shop Owner (1980)
Shuttlecock (1981)
Learning to Swim (1982)
Waterland (1983)
Out of This World (1988)
Ever After (1992)
Last Orders (1996)
The Light of Day (2003)

Swift, Jonathan ['M.B. Drapier', 'T.N. Philomath'] (1667–1745)
satirist and poet

A Discourse of the Contests and Dissensions Between the Nobles and the Commons in Athens and Rome (1701)
A Tale of a Tub (1704)
Predictions for the Year 1708 (1708)
The Accomplishment of the First of Mr Bickerstaff's Predictions (1708)
Baucis and Philemon (1709)
A Famous Prediction of Merlin, the British Wizard (1709)
A Project for the Advancement of Religion, and the Reformation of Manners (1709)
A Vindication of Isaac Bickerstaff Esq. (1709)
The Examiner; or, Remarks upon Papers and Occurences (1710)
A Meditation Upon a Broom-Stick (1710)
Miscellanies in Prose and Verse (1711)
The Conduct of the Allies, and of the Late Ministry (1711)
Some Advice Humbly Offer'd to the Members of the October Club (1712)
A Proposal for Correcting, Improving and Ascertaining the English Tongue (1712)
Mr C[olli]*n's Discourse of Free-thinking, Put into Plain English* (1713)
Part of the Seventh Epistle of the First Book of Horace Imitated (1713)
The First Ode of the Second Book of Horace Paraphras'd (1714)
The Publick Spirit of the Whigs (1714)
A Proposal for the Universal Use of Irish Manufacture (1720)
The Bubble (1721)
A Letter to a Young Gentleman, Lately Enter'd into Holy Orders (1721)
A Letter to the Shop-keepers, Tradesmen, Farmers and Common-people of Ireland (1724)
A Letter to Mr Harding the Printer (1724)
Some Observations Upon a Paper Relating to Woods's Half-pence (1724)
A Letter to the Whole People of Ireland (1724)
Seasonable Advice (1724)
A Letter to the Right Honourable the Lord Viscount Molesworth (1724)
Fraud Detected; or, The Hibernian Patriot (1725)
Cadenus and Vanessa (1726)
Gulliver's Travels (1726)
Miscellanies in Prose and Verse (1727)
A Short View of the State of Ireland (1728)
The Intelligencer (1728)
The Journal of a Dublin Lady (1729)
A Modest Proposal (1729)
An Epistle Upon an Epistle From a Certain Doctor to a Certain Great Lord (1729)
A Libel on D---- D--------, and a Certain Great Lord (1730)
The Grand Question Debated (1732)
The Lady's Dressing-Room (1732)
Miscellanies: The Third Volume (1732)
The Life and Genuine Character of Doctor Swift (1733)
On Poetry (1733)
A Beautiful Young Nymph Going to Bed (1734)
Miscellanies in Prose and Verse: Volume the Fifth (1735)
The Works of Jonathan Swift (1735)
A Proposal for Giving Badges to the Beggars in all the Parishes of Dublin (1737)
The Beasts Confession to the Priest (1738)
A Complete Collection of Genteel and Ingenious Conversation (1738)
Verses on the Death of Dr Swift, Written by Himself (1739)
Dean Swift's Literary Correspondence (1741)
Some Free Thoughts on the Present State of Affairs (1741)
Three Sermons (1744)
Directions to Servants (1745)
Brotherly Love (1754)
The Works of Jonathan Swift (1754)
The History of the Last Four Years of the Queen (1758)

Swinburne, Algernon Charles (1837–1909)
poet and critic
The Queen-Mother; Rosamond (1860)
Atalanta in Calydon (1865)
Chastelard (1865)
Notes on Poems and Reviews (1866)
Poems and Ballads [1st ser.] (1866)
A Song of Italy (1867)
Siena (1868)
Songs Before Sunrise (1871)
Under the Microscope (1872)
Bothwell: A tragedy (1874)
Essays and Studies (1875)
Erechtheus: A tragedy (1876)
Poems and Ballads: Second Series (1878)
The Heptalogia; or, The Seven Against Sense (1880)
Songs of the Springtides (1880)
Studies in Song (1880)
Mary Stuart: A tragedy (1881)
Tristram of Lyonesse, and Other Poems (1882)
A Century of Roundels (1883)
A Midsummer Holiday, and Other Poems (1884)
Marino Faliero: A tragedy (1885)
The Jubilee (1887)
Locrine: A tragedy (1887)
Poems and Ballads: Third Series (1889)
The Sisters (1892)
Astrophel, and Other Poems (1894)
Studies in Prose and Poetry (1894)
The Tale of Balen (1896)
Rosamund, Queen of the Lombards (1899)
A Channel Passage, and Other Poems (1904)
Love's Cross-Currents (1905)
The Poems of Algernon Charles Swinburne (1905)
The Duke of Gandia (1908)

Swinnerton, Frank Arthur (1884–1982)
novelist and critic

The Georgian Literary Scene (1935)
Syal, Meera (1963–)
actress and author
Anita and Me (1996)
Life isn't all Ha Ha Hee Hee (1999)
Sylvester, Joshua (1563–1618)
poet and translator
The Second Weeke or Childhood of the World (1598)
Bartas: His Devine Weekes and Workes Translated (1605)
Lachrimae Lachrimarum; or, The Distillation of Teares Shede for the Untimely Death of the Incomparable Prince Panaretus (1612)
The Parliament of Vertues Royal (1614)
The Second Session of the Parliament of Vertues Reall (1615)
Symonds, John Addington (1840–93)
poet, critic, and translator
Many Moods (1878)
Shelley (1878)
Sketches and Studies in Italy (1879)
New and Old (1880)
Essays Speculative and Suggestive (1890)
In the Key of Blue, and Other Prose Essays (1893)
Symons, Alphonse James Albert (1900–41)
biographer and anthologist
An Anthology of 'Nineties' Verse (1928)
The Quest for Corvo: An experiment in biography (1934)
Symons, Arthur William (1865–1945)
poet and critic
An Introduction to the Study of Browning (1886)
Days and Nights (1889)
Silhouettes (1892)
London Nights (1895)
Amoris Victima (1897)
Images of Good and Evil (1899)
The Symbolist Movement in Literature (1899)
Cities (1903)
A Book of Twenty Songs (1905)
Spiritual Adventures (1905)
The Fool of the World, and Other Poems (1906)
The Romantic Movement in English Poetry (1909)
Tristan and Iseult (1917)
Jezebel Mort, and Other Poems (1931)
Symons, Julian Gustave (1912–95)
crime novelist, poet, and critic
Confusions About X (1939)
The Thirties (1960)
Bloody Murder: From the Detective Story to the Crime Novel (1972)
'Symson, William' (*fl.* 1715)
unidentified pseudonymous author
A New Voyage to the East Indies (1715)
Synge, [Edmund] John Millington (1871–1909)
Irish dramatist and poet
The Shadow of the Glen and Riders to the Sea (1905)
The Well of the Saints (1905)
The Aran Islands (1907)
The Playboy of the Western World (1907)
The Tinker's Wedding (1907)
Poems and Translations (1909)
Deirdre of the Sorrows (1910)

Tailor, Robert (*fl.* 1613–15)
dramatist
The Hogge Hath Lost His Pearle: A comedy (1614)
Talbot, Catherine (1721–70)
essayist, letter writer, and bluestocking
Reflections on the Seven Days of the Week (1770)
Essays on Various Subjects (1772)
Talfourd, Thomas Noon (1795–1854)
judge and author
Ion: A tragedy (1836)
Tannahill, Robert (1774–1810)
Scottish poet
Poems and Songs (1815)
Tate, Nahum (1652–1715)
dramatist and Poet Laureate
Poems (1677)
Brutus of Alba; or, The Enchanted Lovers: A tragedy (1678)
The Loyal General: A tragedy (1680)
The History of King Lear (1681)
The History of King Richard the Second (1681)
The Ingratitude of a Common-wealth; or, The Fall of Caius Martius Coriolanus (1682)
The Second Part of Absalom and Achitophel (1682)
Cuckolds-Haven: or, An Alderman no Conjurer: A farce (1685)
A Duke and No Duke: A farce (1685)
Poems by Several Hands, and on Several Occasions (1685)
The Island-Princess (1687)
Characters of Vertue and Vice (1691)
Miscellanea Sacra; or, Poems on Divine & Moral Subjects (1696)
A New Version of the Psalms of David (1696)
Elegies (1699)
Panacea: A poem upon tea (1700)
Injur'd Love; or, The Cruel Husband: A tragedy (1707)
The Triumph of Union (1707)
Tatersal, Robert (*fl.* 1734)
poet
The Bricklayer's Miscellany; or, Poems on Several Subjects (1734)
Tatham, John (*fl.* 1632–64)
dramatist and city poet
The Fancies Theater (1640)
Ostella; or, The Faction of Love and Beauty Reconcil'd (1650)
The Distracted State: A tragedy (1651)
The Scots Figgaries; or, A Knot of Knaves: A comedy (1652)

The Rump; or, The Mirrour of the Late Times: (1660)
Taverner, Richard (1505?–75)
translator, religious reformer, and editor of the Bible
The Most Sacred Bible (1539)
Proverbes or Adagies (1539)
Taverner, William (*d.* 1731)
dramatist
The Faithful Bride of Granada (1704)
Tawney, Richard Henry (1880–1962)
historian
The Agrarian Problem in the Sixteenth Century (1912)
The Acquisitive Society (1921)
Taylor, Alan John Percivale (1906–90)
historian
The Struggle for Mastery in Europe (1954)
The Origins of the Second World War (1961)
Taylor, Andrew (1951)
novelist
The American Boy (2003)
Taylor, Ann (1782–1866)
poet
Original Poems for Infant Minds (1804)
Rhymes for the Nursery (1806)
Hymns for Infant Minds (1810)
Taylor, Elizabeth (1912–75)
novelist and short-story writer
At Mrs Lippincote's (1945)
A Game of Hide-and-Seek (1951)
The Wedding Group (1968)
Taylor, Sir Henry (1800–86)
poet and author
Isaac Comnenus (1827)
Philip van Artevelde (1834)
A Sicilian Summer; St Clement's Eve; The Eve of the Conquest (1875)
Taylor, Isaac, of Stanford Rivers (1787–1865)
artist, author, and inventor
The Natural History of Enthusiasm (1829)
Fanaticism (1833)
Spiritual Despotism (1835)
Taylor, Jane (1783–1824)
children's poet and novelist
Display (1815)
Essays in Rhyme, on Morals and Manners (1816)
Taylor, Jeremy (1613–67)
bishop of Down and Connor
A Sermon Preached in Saint Maries Church in Oxford: Upon the anniversary of the Gunpowder-treason (1638)
Of the Sacred Order, and Offices of Episcopacy by Divine Institution, Apostolicall Tradition, & Catholike Practice (1642)
A Discourse Concerning Prayer ex tempore, or, by Pretence of the Spirit (1646)
The Great Exemplar of Sanctity and Holy Life According to the Christian Institution (1649)
The Rule and Exercises of Holy Living (1650)
The Rule and Exercises of Holy Dying (1651)
XXVIII Sermons Preached at Golden Grove (1651)
XXV Sermons Preached at Golden-Grove (1653)
The Golden Grove; or, A Manuall of Daily Prayers and Letanies, Fitted to the Dayes of the Weeke (1655)
Deus Justificatus: Two discourses of original sin (1656)
A Discourse of the Nature, Offices and Measures of Friendship (1657)
Ductor Dubitantium (1660)
The Worthy Communicant (1660)
A Choice Manual, Containing What is To Be Believed, Practised, and Desired or Praied For (1664)
A Dissuasive from Popery to the People of Ireland [pt i] (1664)
Antiquitates Christianae (1675)
Taylor, John ['The Water Poet', 'Mary Makepeace'] (1580–1653)
poet
The Sculler (1612)
The Pennyles Pilgrimage; or, The Money-lesse Perambulation, of John Taylor, Alias the Kings Majesties Water-Poet (1618)
The Praise, Antiquity, and Commodity, of Beggery, Beggers, and Begging (1621)
Superbiae Flagellum; or, The Whip of Pride (1621)
A Memorial of all the English Monarchs (1622)
All the Workes of John Taylor the Water-Poet (1630)
Divers Crabtree Lectures: Expressing the severall languages that shrews read to their husbands (1639)
A Juniper Lecture: With the description of all sorts of women, good and bad (1639)
Mad Fashions, Odd Fashions, All Out of Fashions; or, The Emblems of these Distracted Times (1642)
Taylor, Philip Meadows (1808–76)
Indian officer and novelist
Confessions of a Thug (1839)
Tippoo Sultaun (1841)
Taylor, Thomas ['The Platonist'] (1758–1835)
Platonist philosopher and translator
Concerning the Beautiful; (1787)
A Vindication of the Rights of Brutes (1792)
The Works of Plato (1804)
Taylor, Tom (1817–80)
dramatist
The Fool's Revenge (1850)
'Still Waters Run Deep': An original comedy (1855)
The Overland Route: A comedy (1866)
Taylor, William (1765–1836)
miscellaneous author and translator
Iphigenia in Tauris (1793)
Dialogues of the Gods (1795)
Select Fairy Tales (1795)
Ellenore (1796)
Nathan the Wise (1805)

Temple, Sir William (1628–99)
statesman and author
Upon the Death of Mrs Catherine Philips (1664)
An Essay upon the Advancement of Trade in Ireland (1673)
Observations upon the United Provinces of the Netherlands (1673)
Miscellanea (1680)
Miscellanea: the Second Part (1690)
Memoirs of What Past in Christendom: From the war begun in 1672 to the peace concluded 1679 (1692)
An Introduction to the History of England (1695)
Letters Written by Sir William Temple During his Being Ambassador at The Hague (1699)
Letters Written by Sir W. Temple, and Other Ministers of State, Both at Home and Abroad (1700)
Miscellanea: the Third Part (1701)
Memoirs: Part III (1709)
The Works of Sir William Temple (1720)

Temple, William (1881–1944)
archbishop of Canterbury
Mens Creatrix (1917)
Christus Veritas (1924)

Tennant, Emma Christina (1937–)
novelist and journalist
The Time of the Crack (1973)
Alice Fell (1980)
Queen of Stones (1982)
Sisters and Strangers (1990)

Tennyson, Alfred, 1st Baron Tennyson (1809–92)
Poet Laureate
Poems, by Two Brothers (1827)
Timbuctoo (1829)
Poems, Chiefly Lyrical (1830)
Poems (1832)
Poems (1842)
The Princess (1847)
In Memoriam A.H.H. (1850)
Ode on the Death of the Duke of Wellington (1852)
Maud, and Other Poems (1855)
Idylls of the King (1859)
Enoch Arden (1864)
The Holy Grail, and Other Poems (1869)
Idylls of the King (1870)
'The Last Tournament' (1871)
Gareth and Lynette (1872)
Queen Mary (1875)
Harold (1877)
The Lover's Tale (1879)
Ballads, and Other Poems (1880)
Becket (1884)
The Cup; and The Falcon (1884)
Tiresias, and Other Poems (1885)
Locksley Hall Sixty Years After (1886)
Carmen Saeculare: An ode in honour of the Jubilee of Queen Victoria (1887)
Demeter, and Other Poems (1889)
Idylls of the King (1889)
The Foresters (1892)
The Silent Voices (1892)
The Death of Oenone, Akbar's Dream, and Other Poems (1892)

'Tey, Josephine' [Elizabeth Mackintosh] ['Gordon Daviot'] (1897–1952)
crime writer and dramatist
The Daughter of Time (1951)

Thackeray, William Makepeace ['Michael Angelo Titmarsh'] (1811–63)
novelist
The Yellowplush Correspondence (1838)
Catherine (1839)
An Essay on the Genius of George Cruikshank (1840)
The Paris Sketch Book (1840)
Comic Tales and Sketches (1841)
The History of Samuel Titmarsh and the Great Hoggarty Diamond (1841)
The Second Funeral of Napoleon (1841)
Some Passages in the Life of Major Gahagan (1841)
The Irish Sketch-Book (1843)
Men's Wives (1843)
The Luck of Barry Lyndon (1844)
Jeames's Diary (1845)
Notes of a Journey from Cornhill to Grand Cairo (1846)
Mrs Perkins's Ball (1847)
The Book of Snobs (1848)
Vanity Fair (1848)
'Our Street' (1848)
Doctor Birch and his Young Friends (1849)
The History of Pendennis (1849)
The History of Samuel Titmarsh and the Great Hoggarty Diamond (1849)
Rebecca and Rowena (1849)
The Kickleburys on the Rhine (1850)
The Confessions of Fitz-Boodle; and Some Passages in the Life of Major Gahagan (1852)
The History of Henry Esmond, Esq. (1852)
A Shabby Genteel Story, and Other Tales (1852)
The English Humourists of the Eighteenth Century (1853)
The Newcomes (1854)
The Rose and the Ring; or, The History of Prince Giglio and Prince Bulbo (1855)
The Memoirs of Barry Lyndon (1856)
The Virginians (1858)
The Four Georges (1861)
Lovel the Widower (1861)
The Adventures of Philip on His Way Through the World (1862)
Roundabout Papers (1863)
Denis Duval (1867)

Thelwall, John ['John Beaufort'] (1764–1834)
reformer and author

Poems on Various Subjects (1787)
The Natural and Constitutional Right of Britons to Annual Parliaments (1795)
Poems Written in Close Confinement in the Tower and Newgate (1795)
The Rights of Nature, Against the Usurpations of Establishments (1796)
The Daughter of Adoption (1801)
The Trident of Albion (1805)

Theobald, Lewis (1688–1744)
poet, translator, dramatist, and editor of Shakespeare
The Perfidious Brother: A tragedy (1715)
The Odyssey of Homer (1716)
Orestes: A dramatic opera (1718)
Pan and Syrinx: An opera (1718)
Shakespeare Restored (1726)
The Rape of Proserpine (1727)
Double Falsehood; or, The Distrest Lovers . . . Written originally by W. Shakespeare (1728)
Perseus and Andromeda (1730)
The Fatal Secret: A tragedy (1735)

Theroux, Paul Edward (1941–)
American-born novelist and travel writer
The Great Railway Bazaar (1975)
The Family Arsenal (1976)
Picture Palace (1978)
The Old Patagonian Express (1979)
World's End, and Other Stories (1980)
The Mosquito Coast (1981)
Doctor Slaughter (1984)
O-Zone (1986)
Riding the Iron Rooster (1988)
My Secret History (1989)
Chicago Loop (1990)
Millroy the Magician (1993)
Fresh-Air Fiend (2000)
Hotel Honolulu (2001)

Thesiger, Sir Wilfred [Patrick] (1910–2003)
travel writer
Arabian Sands (1959)
The Marsh Arabs (1964)

Thirkell, Angela Margaret (1890–1961)
novelist
Ankle Deep (1933)
Wild Strawberries (1934)
The Brandons (1939)
Cheerfulness Breaks In: A Barsetshire war survey (1940)
Peace Breaks Out (1946)
Private Enterprise (1947)
Love Among the Ruins (1948)

Thirlwall, Connop (1797–1875)
historian and bishop
The Pictures; The Betrothing (1825)
A History of Greece (1835)

Thomas, Bertram Sidney (1892–1950)
Arabist and travel writer
Arabia Felix (1932)

Thomas, Donald Michael (1935–)
novelist, poet, and translator
The Honeymoon Voyage (1978)
The Flute-Player (1979)
Dreaming in Bronze (1981)
The White Hotel (1981)
Ararat (1983)
Swallow (1984)
Sphinx (1986)
Summit (1987)
Lying Together (1990)
Flying in to Love (1992)

Thomas, Dylan Marlais (1914–53)
poet
18 Poems (1934)
Twenty-five Poems (1936)
The Map of Love (1939)
Portrait of the Artist as a Young Dog (1940)
New Poems (1943)
Deaths and Entrances (1946)
Collected Poems 1934–1952 (1952)
In Country Sleep (1952)
Quite Early One Morning (1954)
Under Milk Wood (1954)
A Prospect of the Sea, and Other Stories and Prose Writings (1955)

Thomas, [Philip] Edward ['Edward Eastaway'] (1878–1917)
poet, critic, and topographical writer
The Woodland Life (1897)
Rest and Unrest (1910)
A Literary Pilgrim in England (1917)
Last Poems (1918)
Collected Poems (1920)

Thomas, Elizabeth ['Corinna'] (1675–1731)
poet
Miscellany Poems on Several Subjects (1722)
The Metamorphosis of the Town; or, A View of the Present Fashions (1730)

Thomas, Ronald Stuart (1913–2000)
Welsh poet
The Stones of the Fields (1946)
Song at the Year's Turning (1955)
Poetry for Supper (1958)
Tares (1961)
The Bread of Truth (1963)
Pietà (1966)
Not That He Brought Flowers (1968)
Laboratories of the Spirit (1975)
Frequencies (1978)
Between Here and Now (1981)
Experimenting with an Amen (1986)
Counterpoint (1990)
Mass for Hard Times (1992)
Collected Poems, 1945–1990 (1993)

Thomas, Thomas (1553–88)
printer and lexicographer
Dictionarium linguae latinae et anglicanae (1587)

Thomas, William (*d.* 1554)
dictionary maker
Principal Rules of the Italian Grammer (1550)

Thompson, Edward (1739?–86)
sailor and author
The Meretriciad (1761)
Thompson, Edward Palmer (1924–93)
historian
The Making of the English Working Class (1963)
Thompson, Flora Jane, *née* Timms (1877–1947)
autobiographical novelist
Bog-Myrtle and Peat (1921)
Lark Rise (1939)
Over to Candleford (1941)
Candleford Green (1943)
Lark Rise to Candleford (1945)
Thompson, Francis (1859–1907)
poet
Poems (1893)
New Poems (1897)
Shelley (1909)
The Works of Francis Thompson (1913)
Thompson, William (1712?–66)
poet
Sickness (1745)
Poems on Several Occasions (1757)
Thompson, William (1775–1833)
political economist
An Inquiry into the Principles of the Distribution of Wealth (1824)
Thomson, George (1757–1851)
song collector
A Select Collection of Original Scottish Airs for the Voice (1793)
Thomson, James (1700–48)
poet and dramatist
Winter (1726)
A Poem Sacred to the Memory of Sir Isaac Newton (1727)
Summer (1727)
Spring (1728)
Britannia (1729)
The Seasons, A Hymn, A Poem to the Memory of Sir Isaac Newton, and Britannia, a Poem (1730)
The Tragedy of Sophonisba (1730)
Antient and Modern Italy Compared (1735)
Greece (1735)
Rome (1735)
Britain (1736)
The Prospect (1736)
Agamemnon: A tragedy (1738)
The Works of Mr Thomson (1738)
Edward and Eleonora: A tragedy (1739)
Alfred: A masque (1740)
Tancred and Sigismunda: A tragedy (1745)
The Castle of Indolence (1748)
Coriolanus: A tragedy (1749)
Thomson, James ['Bysshe Vanolis', 'B.V.'] (1834–82)
poet
The City of Dreadful Night, and Other Poems (1880)
Poetical Works (1895)
Thorpe, Adam (1956)
poet, playwright, and novelist
Ulverton (1992)
Nine Lessons from the Dark (2003)
Thubron, Colin Gerald Dryden (1939–)
novelist and travel writer
Mirror to Damascus (1967)
Jerusalem (1969)
The God in the Mountain (1977)
Emperor (1978)
Among the Russians (1983)
A Cruel Madness (1984)
Behind the Wall (1987)
Turning Back the Sun (1991)
The Lost Heart of Asia (1994)
To the Last City (2002)
Thwaite, Anthony Simon (1930–)
poet, critic, and editor
Home Truths (1957)
The Owl in the Tree (1963)
The Stones of Emptiness (1967)
New Confessions (1974)
A Portion for Foxes (1977)
Victorian Voices (1980)
Letter from Tokyo (1987)
The Dust of the World (1994)
Selected Poems 1956–1996 (1997)
Tickell, Thomas (1686–1740)
poet
Oxford (1706)
A Poem, to his Excellency the Lord Privy-Seal, on the Prospect of Peace (1712)
The First Book of Homer's Iliad (1715)
An Epistle from a Lady in England; to a Gentleman at Avignon (1717)
Kensington Garden (1721)
Tighe, Mary, Mrs Henry Tighe (1772–1810)
poet
Psyche, with Other Poems (1811)
Tiller, Terence Rogers (1916–87)
poet
Poems (1941)
The Inward Animal (1943)
Unarm, Eros (1947)
Reading a Medal (1957)
Tillotson, John (1630–94)
divine
The Wisdom of Being Religious (1664)
The Rule of Faith (1666)
Sermons Preach'd Upon Several Occasions [vol. i] (1671)
Sermons Concerning the Divinity and Incarnation of Our Blessed Saviour (1693)
The Works of John Tillotson (1696)
Tilney, Edmund (*d.* 1610)
master of the revels and author
The Flower of Friendship (1568)
Tindal, Matthew (1657–1733)
deist

An Essay Concerning the Laws of Nations, and the Rights of Soveraigns (1694)
The Rights of the Christian Church Asserted (1706)
A Defence of the Rights of the Christian Church (1707)
A Defence of Our Present Happy Establishment (1722)
Christianity as Old as the Creation; or, The Gospel, a Republication of the Religion of Nature (1730)

Tofte, Robert (1562–1620)
poet and translator
Laura: The Toyes of a Traveller; or, The Feast of Fancie (1597)
Alba: The months minde of a melancholy lover (1598)
Orlando Inamorato (1598)
The Batchelars Banquet; or, A Banquet for Batchelars (1603)
Ariosto's Satyres (1608)
Honours Academie; or, The Famous Pastorall, of the Faire Shepheardess, Julietta (1610)
The Blazon of Jealousie (1615)

Tóibín, Colm (1955)
novelist, biographer, and critic
The Blackwater Lightship (1999)
Lady Gregory's Toothbrush (2002)
Love in a Dark Time (2002)

Toland, John (1670–1722)
deist
Christianity Not Mysterious (1696)
The Life of John Milton (1699)
Amyntor; or, A Defence of Milton's Life (1699)
The Art of Governing by Partys (1701)
Paradoxes of State (1702)
Reasons for Naturalizing the Jews in Great Britain and Ireland (1713)
The State-Anatomy of Great Britain [pt i] (1717)
Hypatia (1753)

Tolkien, John Ronald Reuel (1892–1973)
philologist and author
Beowulf: The monsters and the critics (1936)
The Hobbit; or, There and Back Again (1937)
Farmer Giles of Ham (1949)
The Fellowship of the Ring (1954)
The Two Towers (1954)
The Return of the King (1955)
The Adventures of Tom Bombadil, and Other Verses from the 'Red Book' (1962)
Tree and Leaf (1964)
The Lord of the Rings (1966)
The Road Goes Ever On (1968)
The Silmarillion (1977)
Unfinished Tales of Numenor and Middle Earth (1980)
The Book of Lost Tales Part 1 (1983)
The Book of Lost Tales Part 2 (1984)
The Book of Lost Tales Part 3 (1985)

Tollet, Elizabeth (1694–1754)
poet
Poems on Several Occasions (1724)

Tomalin, Claire (1933–)
biographer
The Life and Death of Mary Wollstonecraft (1974)
Pepys: The Unequalled Self (2002)

Tomkis or Tomkys, Thomas (*fl.* 1604–15)
dramatist
Lingua; or, the Combat of the Tongue, and the Five Senses for Superiority (1607)
Albumazar: A comedy (1615)

Tomlinson, [Alfred] Charles (1927–)
poet, translator, editor, and graphic artist
The Necklace (1955)
A Peopled Landscape (1963)
American Scenes, and Other Poems (1966)
The Way of a World (1969)
Notes From New York, and Other Poems (1984)
The Return (1987)
Annunciations (1989)
The Door in the Wall (1992)
Jubilation (1995)
Selected Poems 1955–1997 (1997)

Tomlinson, Henry Major (1873–1958)
travel writer and novelist
All Our Yesterdays (1930)

Tonna, Charlotte Elizabeth, *née* Browne ['Charlotte Elizabeth'] (1790–1846)
novelist
Helen Fleetwood: A tale of the factories (1841)

Tooke, John Horne (1736–1812)
radical politician and author
Epea Pteroenta; or, The Diversions of Purley (1786)
The Proceedings at Large, on the Trial of John Horne Tooke, for High Treason (1795)

Tooke, William (1744–1820)
Russian historian, editor, and miscellaneous author
The Loves of Othniel and Achsah (1769)

Toplady, Augustus Montague (1740–78)
divine and poet
Poems on Sacred Subjects (1759)
A Letter to the Rev. Mr John Wesley (1770)
Psalms and Hymns for Public and Private Worship (1776)

Topsell, Edward (1572–1625)
divine and author
The Historie of Foure-Footed Beastes (1607)

Tourneur, Cyril (1575?–1626)
dramatist and poet
The Transformed Metamorphosis (1600)
The Atheist's Tragedie; or, The Honest Man's Revenge (1611)

Tourtel, Mary (1874–1948)
creator of Rupert Bear
The Adventures of Rupert the Little Bear (1921)

Townley, James (1714–78)
dramatist
High Life Below Stairs: A farce (1759)
Townsend, Sue (1946–)
novelist and playwright
The Secret Diary of Adrian Mole Aged 13¾ (1982)
Townshend or Townsend, Aurelian (*fl.* 1601–43)
poet and dramatist
Albions Triumph: Personated in a maske at court. By the Kings Majestie and his lords (1632)
Tempe Restored: A masque presented by the Queene, and fourteene ladies (1632)
Toynbee, Arnold Joseph (1889–1975)
historian
Nationality and the War (1915)
A Study of History (1934)
Civilization on Trial (1948)
Toynbee, [Theodore] Philip (1916–81)
novelist, poet, critic, and diarist
Pantaloon; or, The Valediction (1961)
Two Brothers (1964)
A Learned City (1966)
Views from a Lake (1968)
Traherne, Thomas (1637–74)
poet and author
Roman Forgeries (1673)
Christian Ethicks; or, Divine Morality (1675)
A Serious and Pathetical Contemplation of the Mercies of God (1699)
Hexameron; or, Meditations on the Six Days of Creation (1717)
The Poetical Works of Thomas Traherne (1903)
Centuries of Meditations (1908)
Trapido, Barbara (1941–)
South African-born novelist
Brother of the More Famous Jack (1982)
Noah's Ark (1984)
Temples of Delight (1990)
Juggling (1994)
Frankie & Stankie (2003)
Trapnel, Anna (*fl.* 1642–60)
prophetic writer
A Legacy for Saints: Being several experiences of the dealings of God with Anna Trapnel (1654)
Trapp, Joseph (1679–1747)
clergyman, poet, and pamphleteer
Abra-Mule; or, Love and Empire: A tragedy (1704)
The Real Nature of the Church or Kingdom of Christ (1717)
The Works of Virgil (1731)
Thoughts Upon the Four Last Things (1734)
The Nature, Folly, Sin, and Danger, of Being Righteous Over-much (1739)
Travers, Ben[jamin] (1886–1980)
playwright and novelist
A Cuckoo in the Nest (1922)
Rookery Nook (1923)
Travers, Pamela Lyndon (1906–96)
children's writer
Mary Poppins (1934)
Treece, Henry (1911–66)
poet, novelist, children's author, and editor
38 Poems (1940)
The Black Seasons (1945)
The Haunted Garden (1947)
Trelawny, Edward John (1792–1881)
adventurer and biographer
Adventures of a Younger Son (1831)
Recollections of the Last Days of Shelley and Byron (1858)
Tremain, Rose (1943–)
novelist, short-story writer, and playwright
Sadler's Birthday (1976)
Letter to Sister Benedicta (1978)
The Cupboard (1981)
The Colonel's Daughter, and Other Stories (1984)
The Swimming-Pool Season (1985)
The Garden of the Villa Mollini, and Other Stories (1987)
Restoration (1989)
Sacred Country (1992)
Evangelista's Fan, and Other Stories (1994)
Music and Silence (1999)
The Colour (2003)
Trevelyan, George Macaulay (1876–1962)
historian
England Under the Stuarts (1904)
History of England (1926)
English Social History (1942)
Trevisa, John of (*c.*1330–1402)
author and translator
Bartholomeus de proprietatibus rerum (1495)
Trevor, William [William Trevor Cox] (1928–)
novelist, short-story writer, and playwright
A Standard of Behaviour (1958)
The Old Boys (1964)
The Boarding House (1965)
The Love Department (1966)
The Day We Got Drunk on Cake (1967)
Mrs Eckdorf in O'Neill's Hotel (1969)
Miss Gomez and the Brethren (1971)
The Ballroom of Romance (1972)
Elizabeth Alone (1973)
Angels at the Ritz, and Other Stories (1975)
The Children of Dynmouth (1976)
Lovers of Their Time, and Other Stories (1978)
Other People's Worlds (1980)
Beyond the Pale (1981)
Fools of Fortune (1983)
The News From Ireland, and Other Stories (1986)
The Silence in the Garden (1988)
Family Sins, and Other Stories (1990)
Two Lives (1991)
Felicia's Journey (1994)

Death in Summer (1998)
The Hill Bachelors (2000)
Nights at the Alexandra (2001)
The Story of Lucy Gault (2002)

Trimmer, Sarah, *née* Kirby (1741–1810)
children's writer and writer on education
An Easy Introduction to the Knowledge of Nature, and Reading the Holy Scriptures (1780)
Fabulous Histories (1786)
Reflections upon the Education of Children in Charity Schools (1792)

Trollope, Anthony (1815–82)
novelist and short-story writer
The Macdermots of Ballycloran (1847)
The Kelleys and the O'Kellys; or, Landlords and Tenants (1848)
La Vendée (1850)
The Warden (1855)
Barchester Towers (1857)
The Three Clerks (1857)
Doctor Thorne (1858)
The Bertrams (1859)
Castle Richmond (1860)
Framley Parsonage (1861)
Tales of All Countries [1st ser.] (1861)
Orley Farm (1861)
North America (1862)
Tales of All Countries [2nd ser.] (1863)
Rachel Ray (1863)
The Small House at Allington (1864)
Can You Forgive Her? (1864)
Miss Mackenzie (1865)
The Belton Estate (1866)
Nina Balatka (1867)
The Last Chronicle of Barset (1867)
The Claverings (1867)
Lotta Schmidt, and Other Stories (1867)
Linda Tressel (1868)
Phineas Finn; the Irish Member (1869)
He Knew He Was Right (1869)
The Vicar of Bullhampton (1870)
The Struggles of Brown, Jones, and Robinson (1870)
Sir Harry Hotspur of Humblethwaite (1870)
Ralph the Heir (1871)
The Golden Lion of Granpere (1872)
The Eustace Diamonds (1872)
Phineas Redux (1873)
Lady Anna (1874)
Harry Heathcote of Gangoil (1874)
The Way We Live Now (1875)
The Prime Minister (1876)
The American Senator (1877)
Is He Popenjoy? (1878)
An Eye for an Eye (1879)
John Caldigate (1879)
Cousin Henry (1879)
The Duke's Children (1880)
Dr Wortle's School (1881)
Ayala's Angel (1881)
The Fixed Period (1882)
Kept in the Dark (1882)
Marion Fay (1882)
Why Frau Frohmann Raised Her Prices, and Other Stories (1882)
Mr Scarborough's Family (1883)
The Landleaguers (1883)
An Autobiography (1883)
An Old Man's Love (1884)

Trollope, Frances, *née* Milton (1779–1863)
novelist and travel writer
Domestic Manners of the Americans (1832)
The Refugee in America (1832)
The Life and Adventures of Jonathan Jefferson Whitlaw; or, Scenes on the Mississippi (1836)
The Widow Barnaby (1839)
The Life and Adventures of Michael Armstrong: the Factory Boy (1840)
The Widow Married (1840)
The Barnabys in America; or, Adventures of the Widow Wedded (1843)
Hargrave; or, The Adventures of a Man of Fashion (1843)
The Laurringtons; or, Superior People (1844)
The Old World and the New (1849)
Petticoat Government (1850)
The Life and Adventures of a Clever Woman (1854)
Fashionable Life; or, Paris and London (1856)

Trollope, Joanna ['Caroline Harvey'] (1943–)
novelist
Parson Harding's Daughter (1979)
Leaves From the Valley (1980)
The Choir (1988)
A Village Affair (1989)
The Best of Friends (1995)
Other People's Children (1998)
Marrying the Mistress (2000)

Trollope, Thomas Adolphus (1810–92)
novelist and journalist
Filippo Strozzi (1860)
Giulio Malatesta (1863)

Trotter, Catharine, later Cockburn (1674–1749)
dramatist and author
Olinda's Adventures; or, The Amours of a Young Lady (1693)
Agnes de Castro: A tragedy (1696)
Fatal Friendship: A tragedy (1698)
Love at a Loss; or, Most Votes Carry It: A comedy (1701)
The Unhappy Penitent: A tragedy (1701)
A Defence of the Essay of Human Understanding (1702)
The Revolution of Sweden: A tragedy (1706)
A Discourse Concerning a Guide in Controversies (1707)
The Works of Mrs Catharine Cockburn (1751)

Tucker, Abraham ['Edward Search'] (1705–74)
philosopher
The Light of Nature Pursued (1768)

Tuke, Sir Samuel (*c.*1620–74)
dramatist
The Adventures of Five Hours: A tragi-comedy (1663)
Tupper, Martin Farquhar (1810–89)
versifier and dramatist
Proverbial Philosophy (1838)
Turberville or Turbervile, George (*c.*1544–*c.*1597)
poet and translator
The Eglogs of the Poet B. Mantuan Carmelitan, Turned into English Verse (1567)
Epitaphes, Epigrams, Songs and Sonets (1567)
The Heroycall Epistles of . . . Publius Ovidius Naso, in Englishe Verse (1567)
A Plaine Path to Perfect Vertue (1568)
The Booke of Faulconrie or Hauking (1575)
Tragicall Tales (1587)
Turner, Charles Tennyson [before 1835, Charles Tennyson] (1808–79)
poet
Sonnets and Fugitive Pieces (1830)
Turner, William (*d.* 1568)
herbalist
A New Herball (1551)
Tusser, Thomas (1524?–80)
agricultural author and poet
A Hundreth Good Pointes of Husbandrie (1557)
Five Hundreth Points of Good Husbandry United to as Many of Good Huswiferie (1573)
Tutchin, John (1661?–1707)
poet and pamphleteer
Poems on Several Occasions (1685)
The Bloody Assizes: Or, a compleat history of the life of George Lord Jefferies (1689)
The Foreigners (1700)
Tuvill or Touteville, Daniel (*c.*1584–1660)
essayist
Essaies Politicke, and Morall (1608)
Essayes, Morall and Theologicall (1609)
Twyne or Twine, Lawrence (*fl.* 1576)
translator
The Patterne of Painefull Adventures (1594)
Twyne, Thomas (1543–1613)
physician and translator
The Breviary of Britayne (1573)
Tyler, Margaret (*fl.* 1578)
translator
The Mirrour of Princely Deedes and Knighthood (1578)
Tynan, Katharine, *née* Hinkson (1861–1931)
Irish poet and novelist
Louise de la Vallière, and Other Poems (1885)
Shamrocks (1887)
Ballads and Lyrics (1891)
Cuckoo Songs (1894)
Innocencies (1905)
The Adventures of Alicia (1906)
The Yellow Domino, and Other Stories (1906)
Experiences (1908)
New Poems (1911)
Irish Poems (1913)
The Holy War (1916)
Tynan, Kenneth Peacock (1927–80)
drama critic and theatre producer
Curtains (1961)
A View of the English Stage 1944–63 (1975)
Tyndale, William (1494?–1536)
translator of the Bible
The New Testament (1525)
The New Testament (1526)
The Obedience of a Christen Man (1528)
The Pentateuch (1530)
The Practyse of Prelates (1530)
An Answere unto Sir Thomas Mores Dialogue (1531)
The Manuell of the Christen Knyght (1533)
The Newe Testament Corrected (1534)
The Newe Testament in Englyshe and Latyn (1538)
The Whole Workes of W. Tyndall, John Frith, and Doct. Barnes (1572)
Tyrwhit, Lady Elizabeth (*fl.* 1574)
devotional writer
Morning and Evening Prayers (1574)
Tyrwhitt, Thomas (1730–86)
classical commentator and literary scholar
Observations and Conjectures Upon Some Passages of Shakespeare (1766)
A Vindication of the Appendix to the Poems, called Rowley's (1782)
Tytler, Alexander Fraser, Lord Woodhouselee (1747–1813)
historian
Essay on the Principles of Translation (1791)
Tytler, William (1711–92)
historian and editor
An Historical and Critical Inquiry into the Evidence Against Mary Queen of Scots (1760)

Udall or Uvedale, John (1560?–92)
Puritan
A Demonstration of the Trueth of that Discipline which Christe Hath Prescribed for the Government of His Church (1588)
The State of the Churche of Englande (1588)
Udall, Nicholas (1505?–56)
dramatist and scholar
Floures for Latine Spekynge (1533)
Apophthegmes (1542)
Ralph Roister Doister (1566?)
Ullerston, Richard (*d.* 1423)
theological writer
A Compendious Olde Treatyse (1530)
Underdowne, Thomas (*fl.* 1566–87)
poet and translator
An Æthiopian Historie written in Greeke by Heliodorus (1569?)
Ovid his Invective against Ibis (1569)

Underhill, Evelyn, afterwards Mrs Stuart Moore (1875–1941)
writer on mysticism and spirituality
Mysticism (1911)
Unsworth, Barry Forster (1930–)
novelist
The Greeks Have a Word For It (1967)
Stone Virgin (1985)
Sugar and Rum (1988)
Sacred Hunger (1992)
Morality Play (1995)
Upton, John (1707–60)
literary scholar
Critical Observations on Shakespeare (1746)
Upward, Edward Falaise (1903–)
novelist and short-story writer
Journey to the Border (1938)
In the Thirties (1962)
The Rotten Elements (1969)
The Spiral Ascent (1977)
Urquhart, Sir Thomas (1611–60)
author and translator
Epigrams: Divine and Moral (1641)
Pantochronochanon; or, A Peculiar Promptuary of Time (1652)
The First Book of the Works of Mr Francis Rabelais, Doctor in Physick (1653)
Ussher, James (1581–1656)
archbishop of Armagh
A Body of Divinitie (1645)
The Annals of the World (1658)
Eighteen Sermons Preached in Oxford, 1640 (1659)
Uttley, Alison [Alice Jane Uttley] (1884–1976)
children's writer
The Squirrel, the Hare, and the Little Grey Rabbit (1929)

'Valentine, Douglas' [George Valentine Williams] (1883–1946)
thriller writer
The Man With the Club Foot (1918)

Vanbrugh, Sir John (1664–1726)
dramatist and architect
The Relapse; or, Virtue in Danger (1697)
Aesop: A comedy (1697)
The Provok'd Wife: A comedy (1697)
A Short Vindication of The Relapse and The Provok'd Wife, from Immorality and Prophaneness by the Author (1698)
The Pilgrim: A comedy (1700)
The False Friend: A comedy (1702)
The Confederacy: A comedy (1705)
The Mistake: A comedy (1706)
The Country House: A farce (1715)
The Provok'd Husband (1728)
Vancouver, George (1757–98)
naval captain
A Voyage of Discovery to the North Pacific Ocean, and Round the World (1798)

Vane, Sir Henry (1613–62)
statesman and author
The Retired Mans Meditations (1655)
A Healing Question Propounded and Resolved (1656)
Vaughan, Henry ['Silurist'] (1622–95)
poet
Poems, with the Tenth Satyre of Juvenal Englished (1646)
Silex Scintillans; or, Sacred Poems and Private Ejaculations (1650)
Olor Iscanus: A collection of some select poems, and translations (1651)
The Mount of Olives; or, Solitary Devotions (1652)
Flores Solitudinis: Certaine rare and elegant pieces (1654)
Hermetical Physick; or, The Right Way to Preserve and to Restore Health (1655)
Silex Scintillans: Sacred poems and private ejaculations (1655)
The Chymists Key to Shut and to Open (1657)
Thalia Rediviva (1678)
Vaughan, Thomas ['Eugenius Philalethes'] (1622–66)
alchemist and poet, twin brother of Henry Vaughan
Anima Magica Abscondita: Or a discourse of the universall spirit of nature (1650)
Anthroposophia Theomagica; or, A Discourse of the Nature of Man and his State After Death (1650)
Magia Adamica; or, The Antiquitie of Magic, and the Descent Thereof from Adam Downwards, Proved (1650)
The Man-Mouse Taken in a Trap (1650)
Lumen de Lumine; or, A New Magicall Light Discovered, and Communicated to the World (1651)
Aula Lucis; or, The House of Light (1652)
Euphrates; or, The Waters of the East (1655)
Vaughan, Sir William (1575–1641)
poet and colonialist
The Golden-grove (1600)
Naturall and Artificial Directions for Health (1600)
The Golden Fleece (1626)
Venn, Henry (1725–97)
divine
The Complete Duty of Man (1763)
Villiers, George, 2nd duke of Buckingham (1628–87)
dramatist
The Rehearsal (1672)
The Chances: A comedy (1682)

Wade, Thomas (1805–75)
poet and dramatist
Tasso and the Sisters: Tasso's Spirit: The Nuptials of Juno: The Skeletons: The Spirits of the Ocean (1825)

Woman's Love; or, The Triumph of Patience (1829)

Wager, Lewis (*d.* 1562)
interlude writer
The Life and Repentance of Mary Magdalene (1566)

Wager, William (*fl.* 1565–9)
interlude writer
The Cruel Debtor (1566)
The Longer Thou Livest (1569?)
Enough is as Good as a Feast (1570?)

Wain, John Barrington (1925–94)
poet, novelist, short-story writer, and critic
Mixed Feelings (1951)
Hurry On Down (1953)
Living in the Present (1955)
The Contenders (1958)
A Travelling Woman (1959)
Weep Before God (1961)
Strike the Father Dead (1962)
The Smaller Sky (1967)
A Winter in the Hills (1970)
Poems, 1949–1979 (1980)
Open Country (1987)
Where the Rivers Meet (1988)
Comedies (1990)
Hungry Generations (1994)

Wake, William (1657–1737)
archbishop of Canterbury
The Principles of the Christian Religion Explained (1699)

Wakefield, Tom (1935–)
novelist and short-story writer
Trixie Trash, Star Ascending (1977)
Isobel Quirk in Orbit (1978)
The Love Siege (1979)

Waley, Arthur David (1889–1966)
poet and translator
One Hundred & Seventy Chinese Poems (1918)

Wallace, Alfred Russel (1823–1913)
naturalist
A Narrative of Travels on the Amazon and Rio Negro (1853)
Contributions to the Theory of Natural Selection (1870)
Darwinism (1889)

Wallace, [Richard Horatio] Edgar (1875–1932)
journalist, thriller and short-story writer
The Four Just Men (1905)
Sanders of the River (1911)
The Mind of Mr J.G. Reeder (1925)

Waller, Edmund (1606–87)
poet
Poems (1645)
A Panegyrick to my Lord Protector (1655)
The Passion of Dido for Aeneas (1658)
To the King, upon His Majesties Happy Return (1660)
A Poem on St James's Park (1661)
Instructions to a Painter (1666)
Divine Poems (1685)
The Maid's Tragedy Altered (1690)

Wallis, John (1616–1703)
mathematician
A Briefe and Easie Explanation of the Shorter Catechism (1648)
Hobbius Heauton-timorumenos: Or, a consideration of Mr Hobbes his dialogues (1662)
A Defence of the Royal Society, and the Philosophical Transactions, particularly those of July, 1670 (1678)

Walpole, Horace, 4th earl of Orford (1717–97)
author and letter writer
The Lessons for the Day (1742)
The Beauties (1746)
A Letter to the Whigs (1747)
A Second and Third Letter to the Whigs (1748)
A Catalogue of the Royal and Noble Authors of England (1758)
A Dialogue Between Two Great Ladies (1758)
Fugitive Pieces in Verse and Prose (1758)
Anecdotes of Painting in England (1762)
The Castle of Otranto (1764)
Historic Doubts on the Life and Reign of King Richard III (1768)
The Mysterious Mother: A tragedy (1768)
A Description of Strawberry-Hill (1774)
A Letter to the Editor of the Miscellanies of Thomas Chatterton (1779)
Postscript to the Royal and Noble Authors (1786)
The Works of Horatio Walpole (1798)
Letters to George Montagu (1818)
Letters to William Cole, and Others (1818)
Private Correspondence of Horace Walpole (1820)
Memoirs of the Last Ten Years of the Reign of George II (1822)
Letters to Sir Horace Mann (1833)

Walpole, Sir Hugh Seymour (1884–1941)
New Zealand-born novelist and short-story writer
The Wooden Horse (1909)
Maradick at Forty (1910)
Mr Perrin and Mr Traill (1911)
The Cathedral (1922)
Harmer John (1926)
Rogue Herries (1930)
Judith Paris (1931)
The Fortress (1932)
Vanessa (1933)
The Inquisitor (1935)
The Bright Pavilions (1940)

Walsh, Jill Paton (1937–)
children's writer and novelist
Hengest's Tale (1966)

Walsh, William (1663–1708)
poet and critic
A Dialogue Concerning Women (1691)
Letters and Poems, Amorous and Gallant (1692)

Walter, William (*fl.* 1520)
translator

Titus and Gesippus (1525?)
Guistarde and Sigismonde (1532)
Walter, of Henley (*fl.* 1250)
author
Boke of Husbandry (1508?)
Walters, Minette Caroline Mary, *née* Jebb (1949–)
crime novelist
The Ice House (1992)
The Sculptress (1993)
The Scold's Bridle (1994)
The Dark Room (1995)
The Echo (1997)
The Breaker (1998)
The Shape of Snakes (2000)
Acid Row (2001)
Fox Evil (2002)
Disordered Minds (2003)
Walton, Izaak (1593–1683)
angler and biographer
'The Life of Sir Henry Wotton' (1651)
The Compleat Angler; or, The Contemplative Man's Recreation (1653)
The Life of John Donne (1658)
Life of Richard Hooker (1665)
The Lives of Dr John Donne, Sir Henry Wooton, Mr Richard Hooker, Mr George Herbert (1670)
The Life of Dr Sanderson, Late Bishop of Lincoln (1678)
Walton, John (*fl.* 1410)
poet and translator
The Consolation of Philosophy (1525)
Warburton, William (1698–1779)
theological writer, translator, and editor
Miscellaneous Translations, in Prose and Verse (1724)
A Critical and Philosophical Enquiry into the Causes of Prodigies and Miracles (1727)
The Alliance Between Church and State (1736)
The Divine Legation of Moses Demonstrated (1738)
A Vindication of the author of the Divine Legation of Moses (1738)
A Vindication of Mr Pope's Essay on Man (1740)
A Critical and Philosophical Commentary on Mr Pope's Essay on Man (1742)
The Principles of Natural and Revealed Religion (1753)
A View of Lord Bolingbroke's Philosophy (1754)
Remarks on Mr David Hume's Essay on the Natural History of Religion (1757)
The Doctrine of Grace (1763)
Sermons and Discourses on Various Subjects and Occasions (1767)
Tracts, by Warburton and a Warburtonian (1789)
Ward, Catharine George (*b.* 1787)
novelist and poet
The Cottage on the Cliff (1823)
Ward, Edward (1667–1731)
poet, humorist, and author
The School of Politicks; or, The Humours of a Coffee-House (1690)
The Poet's Ramble After Riches (1691)
Female Policy Detected; or, The Arts of a Designing Woman Laid Open (1695)
The London Spy (1698)
A Trip to Jamaica (1698)
A Trip to New-England (1699)
The Reformer (1700)
A Step to the Bath: With a character of the place (1700)
The Secret History of the Calves-head Clubb; or, The Republican Unmasqu'd (1703)
Hudibras Redivivus; or, A Burlesque Poem on the Times (1705)
The Life and Notable Adventures of that Renown'd Knight Don Quixote de la Mancha (1711)
The History of the Grand Rebellion (1713)
The Field-Spy; or, The Walking Observator (1714)
British Wonders; or, A Poetical Description of the Several Prodigies . . . That Have Happen'd in Britain Since the Death of Queen Anne (1717)
A Collection of Historical and State Poems, Satyrs, Songs, and Epigrams (1717)
The Delights of the Bottle; or, The Compleat Vintner (1720)
Nuptial Dialogues and Debates (1723)
Durgen; or, A Plain Satyr upon a Pompous Satyrist . . . (1728)
Ward, Mary Augusta, *née* Arnold, Mrs Humphry Ward (1851–1920)
novelist
Milly and Olly; or, A Holiday Among the Mountains (1881)
Miss Bretherton (1884)
Robert Elsmere (1888)
The History of David Grieve (1892)
The Case of Richard Meynell (1911)
Ward, Robert Plumer (1765–1846)
novelist
Tremaine; or, The Man of Refinement (1825)
De Vere; or, The Man of Independence (1827)
De Clifford; or, The Constant Man (1841)
Ward, William George (1812–82)
roman Catholic theologian and philosopher
The Ideal of a Christian Church (1844)
Waring, Anna Laetitia (1820–1910)
poet and hymn-writer
Hymns and Meditations (1850)
Warner, Alan (1964–)
Scottish novelist
Morvern Callar (1995)
These Demented Lands (1997)
The Sopranos (1998)
The Man Who Walks (2002)
Warner, Marina Sarah (1946–)
novelist, critic, and cultural historian

Alone of All Her Sex (1976)
In a Dark Wood (1977)
The Skating Party (1982)
The Lost Father (1988)
Indigo; or, Mapping the Waters (1992)
Mermaids in the Basement (1993)
From the Beast to the Blonde (1994)
The Leto Bundle (2001)
Murderers I Have Known (2002)

Warner, Rex Ernest (1905–86)
poet, novelist, and translator
The Aerodrome (1941)
Why Was I Killed? (1943)

Warner, Sylvia Townsend (1893–1978)
novelist, poet, and short-story writer
The Espalier (1925)
Lolly Willowes; or, The Loving Huntsman (1926)
Mr Fortune's Maggot (1927)
The True Heart (1929)
A Moral Ending, and Other Stories (1931)
The Salutation (1932)
More Joy in Heaven, and Other Stories (1935)
Summer Will Show (1936)
After the Death of Don Juan (1938)
A Garland of Straw, and Other Stories (1943)
The Museum of Cheats, and Other Stories (1947)
The Corner That Held Them (1948)
The Flint Anchor (1954)
A Spirit Rises (1962)
A Stranger With a Bag, and Other Stories (1966)

Warner, William (1558?–1609)
poet
Pan his Syrinx, or Pipe (1584)
Albions England; or, Historicall Map of the Same Island (1586)
The First and Second Parts of Albions England (1589)
Albions England: The Third Time Corrected and Augmented (1592)
Menaecmi: A pleasant and fine conceited comœdie (1595)
Albions England (1596)
Albions England (1602)
A Continuance of Albions England (1606)

Warren, John Byrne Leicester, 3rd Baron de Tabley ['George F. Preston', 'William Lancaster'] (1835–95)
poet
Ballads and Metrical Sketches (1860)

Warren, Samuel (1807–77)
novelist
Ten Thousand a-Year (1841)

Warton, Joseph (1722–1800)
poet and critic
The Enthusiast; or, The Lover of Nature (1744)
Odes on Various Subjects (1746)
Ranelagh House (1747)
An Essay on the Writings and Genius of Pope [vol. i] (1756)
An Essay on the Writings and Genius of Pope (1782)

Warton, Thomas, the elder (1688?–1745)
poet
Poems on Several Occasions (1748)

Warton, Thomas, the younger (1728–90)
poet and literary scholar
The Pleasures of Melancholy (1747)
New-market (1750)
The Triumph of Isis (1750)
The Union; or, Select Scots and English Poems (1753)
Observations on the Faerie Queene of Spenser (1754)
The Oxford Sausage; or, Select Poetical Pieces (1764)
The History of English Poetry (1774)
Poems: A new edition (1777)
An Enquiry into the Authenticity of the Poems Attributed to Thomas Rowley (1782)
Essays on Gothic Architecture (1800)

Waterhouse, Keith Spencer (1929–)
novelist, playwright, and journalist
There is a Happy Land (1957)
Billy Liar (1959)
Billy Liar on the Moon (1975)
Jeffrey Bernard is Unwell (1991)
City Lights (1994)
Streets Ahead (1995)
Soho (2000)

Waters, Sarah (1966)
novelist
Tipping the Velvet (1999)
Fingersmith (2002)

Watkins, Vernon Phillips (1906–67)
Welsh poet
The Ballad of the Mari Lwyd, and Other Poems (1941)
The Lamp and the Veil (1945)
The Lady with the Unicorn (1948)
The Death Bell (1954)
Cypress and Acacia (1959)
Affinities (1962)
Selected Poems 1930–60 (1967)
Fidelities (1968)
Uncollected Poems (1969)

Watson, Henry (*fl.* 1500–18)
translator
The Shyppe of Fooles (1509)
Valentine and Orson (1510?)
Oliver of Castille (1518)

Watson, Thomas (1557?–92)
poet and translator
Antigone (1581)
The Hecatompathia; or, Passionate Centurie of Love (1582)
The Lamentations of Amyntas for the Death of Phillis (1587)

Watson, Sir [John] William (1858–1935)
poet
The Prince's Quest, and Other Poems (1880)

Wordsworth's Grave, and Other Poems (1890)
Lachrymae Musarum, and Other Poems (1892)
Odes and Other Poems (1894)
The Father of the Forest, and Other Poems (1895)
The Purple East (1896)
The Hope of the World, and Other Poems (1898)
For England (1904)
Sable and Purple, with Other Poems (1910)
The Man Who Saw, and Other Poems Arising Out of the War (1917)
Retrogression, and Other Poems (1917)

Watts, Isaac (1674–1748)
poet, hymn-writer, and theological writer
Horae Lyricae (1705)
Hymns and Spiritual Songs (1707)
Divine Songs (1715)
A Guide to Prayer (1715)
The Psalms of David (1719)
Death and Heaven (1722)
Logick (1725)
A Short View of the Whole Scripture History (1732)
Philosophical Essays on Various Subjects (1733)
The World To Come (1739)
The Improvement of the Mind (1741)

Watts-Dunton, [Walter] Theodore (1832–1914)
critic, poet, and novelist
The Coming of Love, and Other Poems (1898)
Aylwin (1899)

Waugh, Alec [Alexander Raban Waugh] (1898–1981)
novelist and poet
The Loom of Youth (1917)
Myself When Young (1923)
Love in These Days (1926)
Three Score and Ten (1929)
'"Sir", She Said' (1930)
Wheels Within Wheels (1933)
The Balliols (1934)
His Second War (1944)
Island in the Sun (1956)
Fuel for the Flame (1960)
My Brother Evelyn, and Other Profiles (1967)

Waugh, Evelyn Arthur St John (1903–66)
novelist, essayist, and biographer
Decline and Fall (1928)
Vile Bodies (1930)
Remote People (1931)
Black Mischief (1932)
A Handful of Dust (1934)
Mr Loveday's Little Outing, and Other Sad Stories (1936)
Waugh in Abyssinia (1936)
Scoop (1938)
Put Out More Flags (1942)
Work Suspended: Two chapters of an unfinished novel (1942)
Brideshead Revisited: The sacred and profane memories of Captain Charles Ryder (1945)
The Loved One (1948)
Men at Arms (1952)
Love Among the Ruins (1953)
Officers and Gentlemen (1955)
The Ordeal of Gilbert Pinfold (1957)
Unconditional Surrender (1961)
Basil Seal Rides Again; or, The Rake's Regress (1963)
A Little Learning (1964)
Sword of Honour (1965)

Waugh, Harriet (1944–)
novelist
Mirror, Mirror (1973)

Weaver or Wever, Richard (*fl. c.*1549–53)
dramatist
Lusty Juventus (1550?)

Webb, Beatrice Martha, *née* Potter (1858–1943)
political reformer and author
The Co-operative Movement in Great Britain (1891)
My Apprenticeship (1926)
Our Partnership (1948)

Webb, Mary Gladys, *née* Meredith (1881–1927)
novelist
The Golden Arrow (1916)
Precious Bane (1924)

Webb, Sidney James, 1st Baron Passfield (1859–1947)
writer on sociology and political reform
Socialism in England (1890)

Webb, Sidney [James], 1st Baron Passfield (1859–1947), and Beatrice [Martha], *née* Potter (1858–1943)
writers on sociology and political reform
The History of Trade Unionism (1894)
Industrial Democracy (1897)

Webbe, William (*fl.* 1568–91)
author
A Discourse of English Poetrie (1586)

Webster, Augusta, *née* Davies ['Cecil Home'] (1837–94)
poet, dramatist, and translator
A Woman Sold, and Other Poems (1867)
Portraits (1870)

Webster, John (1580?–1635?)
dramatist
The White Divel; or, The Tragedy of Paulo Giordano Ursini, Duke of Brachiano (1612)
The Devils Law-Case; or, When Women Goe to Law, the Devill is Full of Business (1623)
The Duchess of Malfi (1623)
Appius and Virginia: A tragedy (1654)
A Cure for a Cuckold: A pleasant comedy (1661)

Webster, John (1610–82)
Puritan writer
The Displaying of Supposed Witchcraft (1677)

Wedderburn, Robert (*c*.1510–*c*.1557)
Scottish poet
The Complaynt of Scotland (1550)
Wedgwood, Dame Cicely Veronica (1910–)
historian
The King's Peace 1637–1641 (1955)
The King's War 1641–1647 (1958)
Weekley, Ernest (1865–1954)
lexicographer
The Romance of Words (1912)
Weever, John (1576–1632)
poet and antiquary
Epigrammes in the Oldest Cut, and Newest Fashion (1599)
Faunus and Melliflora; or, The Original of Our English Satyres (1600)
The Mirror of Martyrs; or, The Life and Death of that Thrice Valiant Captaine, and Most Godly Martyre, Sir John Old-castle Knight Lord Cobham (1601)
Weldon, Sir Anthony (*d.* 1649?)
historical writer
The Court and Character of King James (1650)
Weldon, Fay, *née* Birkinshaw (1931–)
novelist, playwright, and screenwriter
The Fat Woman's Joke (1967)
Down Among the Women (1971)
Female Friends (1975)
Remember Me (1976)
Praxis (1978)
Puffball (1980)
Watching Me, Watching You; and other stories (1981)
The Life and Loves of a She-Devil (1983)
Polaris, and Other Stories (1985)
Heart of the Country (1987)
Leader of the Band (1988)
The Cloning of Joanna May (1989)
Darcy's Utopia (1990)
Moon Over Minneapolis; or, Why She Couldn't Stay (1991)
Growing Rich (1992)
Affliction (1993)
Splitting (1995)
Big Women (1997)
Godless in Eden (1999)
Rhode Island Blues (2000)
The Bulgari Connection (2001)
Auto da Fay (2002)
Nothing to Wear and Nowhere to Hide (2002)
Wellesley, Dorothy Violet, *née* Ashton (1889–1956)
poet
Lost Planet, and Other Poems (1942)
Wells, Herbert George (1866–1946)
novelist, short-story writer, and social critic
The Stolen Bacillus, and Other Incidents (1895)
The Time Machine: An invention (1895)
The Wonderful Visit (1895)
The Island of Dr Moreau (1896)
The Wheels of Chance (1896)
Certain Personal Matters (1897)
The Invisible Man: A grotesque romance (1897)
The Plattner Story, and Others (1897)
The War of the Worlds (1898)
Tales of Space and Time (1899)
When the Sleeper Wakes (1899)
Love and Mr Lewisham (1900)
The First Men in the Moon (1901)
The Sea Lady: A tissue of moonshine (1902)
Mankind in the Making (1903)
Twelve Stories and a Dream (1903)
The Food of the Gods, and How It Came to Earth (1904)
Kipps: The story of a simple soul (1905)
A Modern Utopia (1905)
In the Days of the Comet (1906)
First and Last Things (1908)
New Worlds for Old: A plain account of modern socialism (1908)
The War in the Air (1908)
Ann Veronica (1909)
Tono-Bungay (1909)
The History of Mr Polly (1910)
The Country of the Blind, and Other Stories (1911)
The New Machiavelli (1911)
Marriage (1912)
The Passionate Friends (1913)
The War That Will End War (1914)
The Wife of Sir Isaac Harman (1914)
The World Set Free (1914)
Bealby (1915)
Mr Britling Sees It Through (1916)
What is Coming? (1916)
The Soul of a Bishop (1917)
The Outline of History (1919)
The Undying Fire (1919)
The Salvaging of Civilization (1921)
A Short History of the World (1922)
The World of William Clissold (1926)
The Science of Life (1929)
The Shape of Things to Come (1933)
Experiment in Autobiography (1934)
All Aboard for Ararat (1940)
The Happy Turning (1945)
Mind at the End of its Tether (1945)
Welsh, Irvine (1957–)
Scottish novelist and short-story writer
Trainspotting (1993)
The Acid House (1994)
Ecstasy (1996)
Filth (1998)
Glue (2001)
Porno (2002)
Welsh, Louise (1965)
novelist
The Cutting Room (2002)
Welsted, Leonard (1688–1747)
poet

The Works of Dionysius Longinus, on the Sublime (1712)
Palaemon to Caelia, at Bath; or, The Triumvirate (1717)
Epistles, Odes, &c., Written on Several Subjects (1724)
Of Dulness and Scandal (1732)
The Summum Bonum; or, Wisest Philosophy (1741)

Wesker, Arnold (1932–)
playwright and short-story writer
Chicken Soup with Barley (1959)
Roots (1959)
I'm Talking About Jerusalem (1960)
Chips With Everything (1962)
The Four Seasons (1966)
The Friends (1970)
Six Sundays in January (1971)
Caritas (1981)

Wesley, Charles (1707–88)
Methodist and hymn-writer
An Epistle to John Wesley (1755)

Wesley, John (1703–91)
clergyman, diarist, and founder of Methodism
A Collection of Psalms and Hymns (1738)
Hymns and Sacred Poems (1739)
A Collection of Psalms and Hymns (1741)
The Character of a Methodist (1742)
The Principles of a Methodist (1742)
The Principles of a Methodist Farther Explain'd (1746)
Sermons on Several Occasions (1746)
A Letter to a Person Lately Join'd with the People call'd Quakers (1748)
A Plain Account of the People Called Methodists (1749)
Serious Thoughts upon the Perseverance of Saints (1751)
An Address to the Clergy (1756)
The Doctrine of Original Sin (1757)
A Survey of the Wisdom of God in the Creation (1763)
A Plain Account of Christian Perfection (1766)
The Works of the Rev. John Wesley (1771)
Thoughts upon Slavery (1774)
A Calm Address to Our American Colonies (1775)
Reflections on the Rise and Progress of the American Rebellion (1780)
The Journal of John Wesley (1827)

'Wesley, Mary' [Mary Aline Siepmann, *née* Farmar] (1912–2002)
novelist
The Sixth Seal (1969)
Jumping the Queue (1983)
The Camomile Lawn (1984)
Not That Sort of Girl (1987)

Wesley, Samuel, the elder (1662–1735)
divine and poet
Maggots; or, Poems on Several Subjects, Never Before Handled (1685)
The Life of Our Blessed Lord (1693)

West, Gilbert (1703–56)
poet
Stowe (1732)
Odes of Pindar (1749)

West, Jane ['Prudentia Homespun'] (1758–1852)
novelist and poet
The Advantages of Education; or, The History of Maria Williams (1793)
A Gossip's Story, and A Legendary Tale (1796)
The Mother (1809)

'West, [Dame] Rebecca' [Cicily Isabel Andrews, *née* Fairfield] (1892–1983)
novelist and political essayist
The Return of the Soldier (1918)
The Judge (1922)
The Harsh Voice (1935)
Black Lamb and Grey Falcon (1941)
The Meaning of Treason (1949)
A Train of Powder (1955)

West, Richard (*fl.* 1606–19)
poet
Newes from Bartholomew Fayre (1606)

Weyman, Stanley John (1855–1928)
novelist
The House of the Wolf (1890)
A Gentleman of France (1893)
Under the Red Robe (1894)

Whalley, Peter (1722–91)
author and editor
An Enquiry into the Learning of Shakespeare (1748)

Wharton, Henry ['Anthony Harmer'] (1664–95)
divine and author
A Specimen of Some Errors and Defects in the History of the Reformation by Gilbert Burnet (1693)

Whately, Richard (1787–1863)
philosopher, political economist, and archbishop of Dublin
Elements of Logic (1826)
Elements of Rhetoric (1828)

Wheatley, Dennis (1897–1977)
popular novelist
The Devil Rides Out (1935)

Whetstone, George (*c.*1551–87)
poet and author
The Rocke of Regard (1576)
A Remembraunce of the Wel Imployed Life, of George Gaskoigne Esquire (1577)
The Right Excellent and Famous Historye, of Promos and Cassandra (1578)
An Heptameron of Civill Discourses (1582)
The English Myrror (1586)
The Censure of a Loyall Subject (1587)
Sir Philip Sidney, his Honorable Life, his Valiant Death, and his True Vertues (1587)
Aurelia (1593)

Whewell, William (1794–1866)
philosopher and scientist
The History of the Inductive Sciences (1837)
The Philosophy of the Inductive Sciences (1840)
Lectures on the History of Moral Philosophy in England (1852)

Whibley, Charles (1859–1930)
scholar, critic, and journalist
A Book of Scoundrels (1897)

Whichcote or Whichcot, Benjamin (1609–83)
provost of King's College, Cambridge
Select Sermons of Dr Whichcot (1698)
Several Discourses (1701)
Moral and Religious Aphorisms (1703)
The Works of the Learned Benjamin Whichcote (1751)

'White, Antonia' [Eirene Botting] (1899–1980)
novelist and translator
Frost in May (1933)
The Lost Traveller (1950)
The Sugar House (1952)
Beyond the Glass (1954)

White, Gilbert (1720–93)
naturalist
The Natural History and Antiquities of Selborne (1789)
A Naturalist's Calendar (1795)

White, Henry Kirke (1785–1806)
poet
Clifton Grove (1803)
The Remains of Henry Kirke White (1807)

White, James (1759?–99)
scholar and novelist
Earl Strongbow; or, The History of Richard de Clare and the Beautiful Geralda (1789)

White, Joseph Blanco [formerly José Maria Blanco] (1775–1841)
poet, novelist, and theological author
Vargas (1822)
Practical Internal Evidence Against Catholicism (1825)
Second Travels of an Irish Gentleman in Search of a Religion (1833)
Observations on Heresy and Orthodoxy (1835)
The Life of Joseph Blanco White (1845)

White, Terence Hanbury ['James Aston'] (1906–64)
novelist and poet
Loved Helen, and Other Poems (1929)
England Have My Bones (1936)
The Sword in the Stone (1938)
The Witch in the Wood (1940)
The Ill-Made Knight (1941)
Mistress Masham's Repose (1947)
The Goshawk (1951)
The Once and Future King (1958)

Whitefield, George (1714–70)
Evangelical author and hymn-writer
A Journal of a Voyage from London to Savannah in Georgia (1738)
A Continuation of the Reverend Mr Whitefield's Journal (1739)
A Short Account of God's Dealings with the Reverend George Whitefield (1740)
A Letter to the Reverend John Wesley (1741)
Nine Sermons (1742)
Hymns for Social Worship (1753)

Whitehead, Alfred North (1861–1947)
mathematician and philosopher
An Enquiry Concerning the Principles of Natural Knowledge (1919)

Whitehead, George (1636?–1723)
Quaker
A Serious Apology for the Principles and Practices of the People Call'd Quakers (1671)
The Christian Progress of George Whitehead (1725)

Whitehead, John (1740?–1804)
physician and biographer
The Life of John Wesley (1793)

Whitehead, Paul (1710–74)
satirist
Manners: A satire (1739)
The Gymnasiad; or, Boxing Match (1744)
Poems and Miscellaneous Compositions (1777)

Whitehead, William (1715–85)
dramatist and Poet Laureate
An Essay on Ridicule (1743)
The Roman Father (1750)
Poems on Several Occasions (1754)
A Charge to the Poets (1762)
Plays and Poems, by William Whitehead, Esq. Poet Laureat (1774)
Variety (1776)
Poems by William Whitehead (1788)

Whitehorne, Peter (*fl.* 1560)
translator
The Arte of Warre (1562)

Whitford, Richard (*fl.* 1495–1555?)
translator of the Rule of St Augustine
The Rule of St Augustine (1525)

Whitgift, John (1530?–1604)
archbishop of Canterbury
An Answere to a Certen Libel Intituled, An Admonition (1572)
The Defense of the Answere to the Admonition, Against the Replie (1574)

Whiting, Nathaniel (1617?–82)
poet
Le hore di recreatione; or, The Pleasant Historie of Albino and Bellama (1637)

Whitlock, Richard (*c.*1616–*c.*1672)
author
Zootomia; or, Observations of the Present Manners of the English (1654)

Whitlocke, Bulstrode, the elder (1605–75)
politician, diplomat, and author
Memorials of the English Affairs (1682)

Whitney, Geoffrey (1548?–1601?)
poet

A Choice of Emblemes and Other Devises (1586)
Whitney, Isabella (*fl.* 1567–73)
poet
The Copy of a Letter (1567?)
A Sweet Nosgay, or Pleasant Posye (1573)
Whittingham, William (1524?–79)
reformer and translator of the Bible
The Newe Testament of Our Lord Jesus Christ (1557)
The Bible and Holy Scriptures Conteyned in the Olde and Newe Testament (1560)
Whittington, Whytynton, or Whytinton, Robert (*fl.* 1520)
grammarian
The Thre Bookes of Tullyes Offyces (1534)
Whyte-Melville, George John (1821–78)
novelist
Digby Grand (1853)
The Interpreter: A tale of the war (1858)
Holmby House (1860)
Wilberforce, William (1759–1833)
philanthropist
A Practical View of the Prevailing Religious System of Professed Christians (1797)
An Appeal to the Inhabitants of the British Empire, in Behalf of the Negro Slaves of the West Indies (1823)
Wilcox, Thomas (1549?–1608)
Puritan divine
Satire Menippée (1595)
Wild or Wylde, Robert (1609–79)
poet
Iter Boreale (1660)
Wilde, Oscar Fingal O'Flahertie Wills (1854–1900)
poet, dramatist, short-story writer, and novelist
Ravenna (1878)
Vera; or, The Nihilists (1880)
Poems (1881)
The Happy Prince, and Other Tales (1888)
The Picture of Dorian Gray (1891)
Intentions (1891)
Lord Arthur Savile's Crime, and Other Stories (1891)
A House of Pomegranates (1891)
Lady Windermere's Fan: A play about a good woman (1893)
Salomé: A tragedy (1894)
The Sphinx (1894)
A Woman of No Importance (1894)
The Soul of Man (1895)
The Ballad of Reading Gaol (1898)
The Importance of Being Earnest: A trivial comedy for serious people (1899)
An Ideal Husband (1899)
De Profundis (1905)
Wilkie, William (1721–72)
Scottish poet
The Epigoniad (1757)
Fables (1768)
Wilkins, George (*fl.* 1604–8)
dramatist
The Miseries of Inforst Marriage (1607)
The Painfull Adventures of Pericles Prince of Tyre (1608)
Wilkins, John (1614–72)
bishop of Chester
The Discovery of a World in the Moone (1638)
Mathematicall Magick: Or, the wonders that may be performed by mechanicall geometry (1648)
An Essay Towards a Real Character, and a Philosophical Language (1668)
Willan, Leonard (*fl.* 1649–70)
dramatist
Astraea; or, True Love's Myrrour: A pastoral (1651)
Orgula; or, The Fatal Error: A known true story (1658)
Williams, Anna (1706–83)
editor
Miscellanies in Prose and Verse (1766)
Williams, Sir Charles Hanbury (1708–59)
diplomat and satirist
The Country Girl: An ode (1742)
Williams, Charles Walter Stansby (1886–1945)
novelist, poet, and playwright
The Silver Stair (1912)
Poems of Conformity (1917)
Divorce (1920)
War in Heaven (1930)
Many Dimensions (1931)
The Place of the Lion (1931)
The Greater Trumps (1932)
Shadows of Ecstasy (1933)
Descent into Hell (1937)
Taliessen Through Logres (1938)
The Descent of the Dove (1939)
The Region of the Summer Stars (1944)
All Hallows' Eve (1945)
Seed of Adam, and Other Plays (1948)
Williams, Heathcote (1941–)
poet, playwright, and novelist
Whale Nation (1988)
Williams, Helen Maria (1762–1827)
political writer, poet, and novelist
Edwin and Eltruda (1782)
An Ode on the Peace (1784)
Peru (1784)
Poems (1786)
Julia (1790)
Letters Written in France, in the Summer of 1790 (1790)
Letters Containing a Sketch of the Politics of France (1795)
Paul and Virginia (1795)
A Tour in Switzerland (1798)

Sketches of the State of Manners and Opinions in the French Republic (1801)
A Narrative of the Events which have Taken Place in France (1815)
Poems on Various Subjects (1823)

Williams, Hugo Mordaunt (1942–)
poet
Symptoms of Loss (1965)
Sugar Daddy (1970)
Some Sweet Day (1975)
Writing Home (1985)
Self-Portrait With a Slide (1990)

Williams, Isaac (1802–65)
poet
The Cathedral; or, The Catholic and Apostolic Church in England (1838)
The Christian Scholar (1849)
The Seven Days; or, The Old and New Creation (1850)

Williams, John ['Anthony Pasquin'] (1761–1818)
satirist and miscellaneous writer
Poems: by Anthony Pasquin (1789)

Williams, Nigel (1948–)
novelist and playwright
My Life Closed Twice (1977)
Jack Be Nimble (1980)
Star Turn (1985)
Witchcraft (1987)
The Wimbledon Poisoner (1990)
They Came From SW19 (1992)
Scenes From a Poisoner's Life (1994)
Fortysomething (1999)

Williams, Raymond Henry (1921–88)
critic and novelist
Culture and Society 1780–1950 (1958)

Williamson, Henry (1895–1977)
novelist and author
The Beautiful Years (1921)
Dandelion Days (1922)
The Dream of Fair Women (1924)
Tarka the Otter (1927)
The Pathway (1928)
Salar the Salmon (1935)
The Dark Lantern (1951)
The Gale of the World (1969)

'Willoby, Henry'
unidentified pseudonymous poet
Willobie his Avisa; or, The True Picture of a Modest Maide, and of a Chast and Constant Wife (1594)

Wilmot, John, 2nd earl of Rochester (1647–80)
poet
Corydon and Cloris; or, The Wanton Sheepherdess (1676?)
A Letter From Artemiza in the Town to Chloë in the Country (1679)
A Satyr Against Mankind (1679)
Upon Nothing (1679)
A Very Heroical Epistle From My Lord All-Pride to Dol-Common (1679)
Poems on Several Occasions (1680)
Valentinian: A tragedy (1685)
Poems on Several Occasions: with Valentinian, a Tragedy (1691)
Familiar Letters (1697)
The Miscellaneous Works of the Late Earls of Rochester and Roscommon (1707)
Remains of the Earl of Rochester (1718)

Wilson, Andrew Norman (1950–)
novelist and biographer
The Sweets of Pimlico (1977)
Kindly Light (1979)
The Healing Art (1980)
Wise Virgin (1982)
Scandal (1983)
Gentlemen in England (1985)
Love Unknown (1986)
Stray (1987)
Incline Our Hearts (1988)
A Bottle in the Smoke (1990)
Daughters of Albion (1991)
The Vicar of Sorrows (1993)
Hearing Voices (1995)
Watch in the Night (1996)
Dream Children (1998)
Victorians (2002)

Wilson, Sir Angus Frank Johnstone (1913–91)
novelist, short-story writer, and critic
The Wrong Set, and Other Stories (1949)
Such Darling Dodos, and Other Stories (1950)
Hemlock and After (1952)
Anglo-Saxon Attitudes (1956)
A Bit Off the Map, and Other Stories (1957)
The Middle Age of Mrs Eliot (1958)
The Old Men at the Zoo (1961)
Late Call (1964)
No Laughing Matter (1967)
As If By Magic (1973)
Setting the World on Fire (1980)

Wilson, Colin (1931–)
author
The Outsider (1956)

Wilson, John (1627?–96)
dramatist and recorder of Londonderry
The Cheats: A comedy (1664)

Wilson, John ['Christopher North'] (1785–1854)
poet, novelist, journalist, and essayist
The Isle of Palms, and Other Poems (1812)
The City of the Plague, and Other Poems (1816)
The Foresters (1825)
The Recreations of Christopher North (1842)

Wilson, John Dover (1881–1969)
Shakespeare scholar and editor
What Happens in Hamlet (1935)

Wilson, Robert (*fl.* 1572–1600)
dramatist
The Three Ladies of London (1584)
The Three Lords and Ladies of London (1590)
The Coblers Prophesie (1594)

Wilson, Thomas (1525?–81)
secretary of state and scholar
The Arte of Rhetorique (1553)
Winkworth, Catherine (1827–78)
poet and translator
Lyra Germanica [1st ser.] (1855)
Lyra Germanica: Second Series (1858)
Winstanley, Gerrard (1609–76?)
Digger
The Breaking of the Day of God (1648)
The Mysterie of God, Concerning the Whole Creation, Mankinde (1648)
The Saints Paradise; or, The Fathers Teaching the only Satisfaction to Waiting Souls (1648)
Winstanley, William (1628?–98)
compiler
England's Worthies (1660)
Winterson, Jeanette (1959–)
novelist
Boating for Beginners (1985)
Oranges Are Not the Only Fruit (1985)
The Passion (1987)
Sexing the Cherry (1989)
Written on the Body (1992)
Art and Lies (1994)
The World and Other Places (1998)
The.PowerBook (2000)
Winzet or Wingate, Ninian (1518–92)
Scottish controversialist
The Last Blast of the Trompet of Godis Worde Aganis the Ursurpit Auctoritie of John Knox (1562)
The Buke of Fourscoir-thre Questions (1563)
Wiseman, Nicholas Patrick Stephen (1802–65)
archbishop of Westminster, cardinal, and author
Fabiola; or, The Church of the Catacombs (1855)
Wither, George (1588–1667)
poet and pamphleteer
Prince Henries Obsequies; or, Mournefull Elegies Upon his Death (1612)
Abuses Stript, and Whipt; or, Satirical Essayes (1613)
Epithalamia; or, Nuptiall Poems (1613)
A Satyre (1614)
Fidelia (1615)
The Shepherds Hunting (1615)
A Preparation to the Psalter (1619)
The Songs of the Old Testament (1621)
Faire-Virtue, the Mistresse of Phil'arete (1622)
Juvenilia (1622)
The Hymnes and Songs of the Church (1623)
The Schollers Purgatory (1624)
Britain's Remembrancer: Containing a narration of the plague lately past (1628)
The Psalmes of David Translated into Lyrick Verse (1632)
A Collection of Emblemes, Ancient and Moderne (1635)
The Nature of Man (1636)
Haleluiah; or, Britans [sic] *Second Remembrancer* (1641)
Campo-Musae (1643)
Mercurious Rusticus; or, A Countrey Messenger (1643)
Letters of Advice: Touching the Choice of Knights and Burgesses (1644)
Vox Pacifica: A Voice Tending to the Pacification of God's Wrath (1645)
Justitiarius Justificatus: The Justice Justified (1646)
Opobalsamum Anglicanum (1646)
Amygdala Britannica, Almonds for Parrets (1647)
Carmen Expostulatorium; or, A Timely Expostulation (1647)
Prosopopoeia Britannica (1648)
Carmen Eucharisticon (1649)
The Dark Lantern (1653)
The Protector (1655)
Fides-Anglicana (1660)
Speculum Speculativum; or, A Considering-Glass (1660)
The Prisoners Plea (1661)
Tuba-Pacifica (1664)
Meditations Upon the Lords Prayer (1665)
Three Private Meditations (1665)
Sigh for the Pitchers (1666)
Divine Poems on the Ten Commandments (1688)
Wodehouse, Pelham Grenville (1881–1975)
novelist and playwright
The Pothunters (1902)
Psmith, Journalist (1915)
My Man Jeeves (1919)
The Inimitable Jeeves (1923)
Carry On, Jeeves! (1925)
Summer Lightning (1929)
Very Good, Jeeves (1930)
Right Ho, Jeeves (1934)
Blandings Castle and Elsewhere (1935)
Lord Emsworth and Others (1937)
Uncle Dynamite (1948)
Ring for Jeeves (1953)
Jeeves and the Feudal Spirit (1954)
Jeeves in the Offing (1960)
Stiff Upper Lip, Jeeves (1963)
Galahad at Blandings (1965)
Wodrow, Robert (1679–1734)
ecclesiastical historian
The History of the Sufferings of the Church of Scotland (1721)
Wolcot, John (1738–1819)
satirist and poet
Persian Love Elegies (1773)
A Poetical, Supplicating, Modest and Affecting Epistle to those Literary Colossuses the Reviewers (1778)
Lyric Odes, to the Royal Academicians (1782)
More Lyric Odes, to the Royal Academicians (1783)
The Lousiad: Canto i (1785)
Lyric Odes, for the Year 1785 (1785)

Bozzy and Piozzi; or, The British Biographers (1786)
Farewel [sic] *Odes. For the Year 1786* (1786)
A Poetical and Congratulatory Epistle to James Boswell (1786)
Ode Upon Ode; or, A Peep at St James (1787)
Tales and Fables (1788)
The Cap: A satiric poem (1795)
The Fall of Portugal; or, The Royal Exiles (1808)
Carlton House Fete; or, The Disappointed Bard (1811)

Wolfe, Humbert (1885–1940)
poet and civil servant
London Sonnets (1920)
Shylock Reasons with Mr Chesterton, and Other Poems (1920)
Kensington Gardens (1924)
The Unknown Goddess (1925)
Humoresque (1926)
News of the Devil (1926)
Cursory Rhymes (1927)
Requiem (1927)
The Silver Cat, and Other Poems (1928)
This Blind Rose (1928)
The Uncelestial City (1930)
Snow (1931)
The Fourth of August (1935)
Stings and Wings (1935)
X at Oberammergau (1935)

Wollaston, William (1660–1724)
moral philosopher
The Religion of Nature Delineated (1722)

Wolley, Hannah (*fl.* 1661–84)
cookery writer
The Queen-like Closet; or, Rich Cabinet (1670)

Wollstonecraft, Mary, later Godwin (1759–97)
novelist and essayist
Thoughts on the Education of Daughters (1787)
Mary: A fiction (1788)
Of the Importance of Religious Opinions (1788)
Original Stories, from Real Life (1788)
The Female Reader; or, Miscellaneous Pieces in Prose and Verse (1789)
Elements of Morality for the Use of Children (1790)
A Vindication of the Rights of Men (1790)
A Vindication of the Rights of Woman (1792)
An Historical and Moral View of the Origin and Progress of the French Revolution (1794)
Letters Written During a Short Residence in Sweden, Norway and Denmark (1796)
The Wrongs of Woman (1798)

Wood, Anthony à (1632–95)
antiquary
Historia et Antiquitates Universitatis Oxoniensis (1674)
Athenae Oxonienses [vol. i] (1691)
Athenae Oxonienses [vol. ii] (1692)
The History and Antiquities of the Colleges and Halls in the University of Oxford (1786)

Wood, Ellen, *née* Price, Mrs Henry Wood (1814–87)
novelist and short-story writer
Danesbury House (1860)
East Lynne (1861)
The Channings (1862)
Mrs Halliburton's Troubles (1862)
The Shadow of Ashlydyat (1863)
Roland Yorke (1869)
George Canterbury's Will (1870)
Johnny Ludlow [1st ser.] (1874)

Woodes, Nathaniell (*fl.* 1550–94)
dramatist
The Conflict of Conscience (1581)

Woodham-Smith, Cecil Blanche (1896–1977)
historian and biographer
Florence Nightingale (1950)
The Reason Why (1953)

Woodhouse or Wodehouse, Peter (*fl.* 1605)
poet
The Flea (1605)

Woodville or Wydville, Anthony (1422?–83)
Baron Scales and 2nd Earl Rivers
Dicts or Saying of the Philosophers (1477)
The Morale Proverbes of Cristyne (1478)
Cordiale, or Four Last Things (1479)

Woolf, Leonard Sidney (1880–1969)
author and publisher
The Village in the Jungle (1913)
The Wise Virgins (1914)
Barbarians at the Gate (1939)
Sowing (1960)
Growing (1961)
Beginning Again (1964)
Downhill all the Way (1967)
The Journey Not the Arrival Matters (1969)

Woolf, [Adeline] Virginia, *née* Stephen (1882–1941)
novelist and essayist
The Voyage Out (1915)
Kew Gardens (1919)
Night and Day (1919)
Monday or Tuesday (1921)
Jacob's Room (1922)
The Common Reader [1st ser.] (1925)
Mrs Dalloway (1925)
To the Lighthouse (1927)
Orlando: A biography (1928)
A Room of One's Own (1929)
The Waves (1931)
The Common Reader: Second Series (1932)
Flush: A biography (1933)
The Years (1937)
Three Guineas (1938)
Between the Acts (1941)
The Death of the Moth, and Other Essays (1942)
A Haunted House, and Other Short Stories (1944)
The Moment, and Other Essays (1947)
The Captain's Death Bed, and Other Essays (1950)

A Writer's Diary (1953)
Granite and Rainbow (1958)
Collected Essays (1966)
The Flight of the Mind: The letters of Virginia Woolf volume i: 1888–1912 (1975)
The Question of Things Happening: The letters of Virginia Woolf volume ii: 1912–1922 (1976)
A Change of Perspective: The letters of Virginia Woolf volume iii: 1923–1928 (1977)
The Diary of Virginia Woolf: Volume i: 1915–1919 (1977)
The Diary of Virginia Woolf: Volume ii: 1920–1924 (1978)
A Reflection of the Other Person: The letters of Virginia Woolf volume iv: 1929–193 (1978)
The Sickle Side of the Moon: The letters of Virginia Woolf volume v: 1932–1935 (1979)
The Diary of Virginia Woolf: Volume iii: 1925–1930 (1980)
Leave the Letters Till We're Dead: The letters of Virginia Woolf volume vi: 1936–1941 (1980)
The Diary of Virginia Woolf: Volume iv: 1931–1935 (1982)
The Diary of Virginia Woolf: Volume v: 1936–1941 (1984)
The Essays of Virginia Woolf: Volume i: 1904–1912 (1986)
The Essays of Virginia Woolf: Volume ii: 1912–1918 (1987)
The Essays of Virginia Woolf: Volume iii: 1919–1924 (1988)
The Essays of Virginia Woolf: Volume iv: 1925–1928 (1994)

Woolley, Sir [Charles] Leonard (1880–1960)
archaeologist and author
Ur of the Chaldees (1929)

Wordsworth, William (1770–1850)
Poet Laureate
Descriptive Sketches (1793)
An Evening Walk (1793)
Lyrical Ballads with a Few Other Poems (1798)
Lyrical Ballads, with Other Poems (1801)
Lyrical Ballads, with Pastoral and Other Poems (1802)
Lyrical Ballads, with Pastoral and Other Poems (1805)
Poems, in Two Volumes (1807)
Concerning the Relations of Great Britain, Spain, and Portugal . . . as Affected by the Convention of Cintra (1809)
The Excursion: Being a portion of The Recluse, a poem (1814)
Poems (1815)
The White Doe of Rylstone; or, The Fate of the Nortons (1815)
Thanksgiving Ode, January 18, 1816 (1816)
Peter Bell: A tale in verse (1819)
The Waggoner (1819)
The Miscellaneous Poems of William Wordsworth (1820)
The River Duddon (1820)
Memorials of a Tour on the Continent, 1820 (1822)
A Description of the Scenery of the Lakes in the North of England (1822)
Ecclesiastical Sonnets (1822)
The Poetical Works of William Wordsworth (1827)
A Guide Through the District of the Lakes in the North of England (1835)
Yarrow Revisited, and Other Poems (1835)
The Poetical Works of William Wordsworth (1836)
The Sonnets of William Wordsworth (1838)
The Poetical Works of William Wordsworth (1840)
Poems, Chiefly of Early and Late Years (1842)
The Poems of William Wordsworth, Poet Laureate (1845)
The Prelude; or, Growth of a Poet's Mind (1850)
The Poetical Works of William Wordsworth (1857)
The Poetical Works of William Wordsworth: The Centenary Edition (1870)
The Prose Works of William Wordsworth (1876)
The Recluse (1888)

Wotton, Sir Henry (1568–1639)
diplomat and poet
The Elements of Architecture (1624)
Reliquiae Wottonianae: Or, a collection of lives, letters, poems (1651)

Wotton, William (1666–1727)
scholar
Reflections upon Ancient and Modern Learning (1694)
Reflections upon Ancient and Modern Learning (1697)
A Discourse Concerning the Confusion of Languages at Babel (1730)

Woty, William (1731?–91)
poet
Poetical Works (1770)

Wraxall, Sir Nathaniel (1751–1831)
historical writer
Historical Memoirs of My Own Time (1815)

Wrednot, William (*fl.* 1604)
author
Palladis Palatium: Wisdomes Pallace; or, The Fourth Part of Wits Commonwealth (1604)

Wren, Percival Christopher (1885–1941)
popular novelist
Beau Geste (1924)
Beau Sabreur (1926)
Beau Ideal (1928)

Wright, James (1643–1713)
antiquary and miscellaneous writer
Country Conversations (1694)
Historia Histrionica: An historical account of the English-stage (1699)

Wright, John (*fl.* 1708–27)
poet and hymn-writer
The Best Mirth; or, The Melody of Sion (1712)
Spiritual Songs for Children (1727)

Wright, Thomas (1810–77)
antiquary
Biographia Britannica Literaria; or, Biography of Literary Characters of Great Britain and Ireland [vol. i] (1842)

Wroth, Lady Mary (1586?–post 1640)
poet
The Countesse of Mountgomeries Urania (1621)

Wyatt, Sir Thomas (1503?–42)
poet
The Quyete of Mynde (1528)
Certayne Psalmes Chosen Out of the Psalter of David (1549)

Wycherley, William (1641–1716)
dramatist and poet
Love in a Wood; or, St James's Park: A comedy (1672)
The Gentleman Dancing-Master: A comedy (1673)
The Country-Wife: A comedy (1675)
The Plain-Dealer: A comedy (1677)
Miscellany Poems (1704)
The Posthumous Works of William Wycherley (1728)
The Posthumous Works of William Wycherley [vol. ii] (1729)

Wycliffe or Wiclif, John (*d.* 1384)
religious reformer
Wycklyffes Wicket (1546)
Two Short Treatises, Against the Orders of the Begging Friars (1608)

'Wyndham, John' [John Wyndham Parkes Lucas Beynon Harris] ['John Beynon', 'Lucas Parkes', 'Johnson Harris'] (1903–1969)
novelist and short-story writer
The Day of the Triffids (1951)
The Kraken Wakes (1953)
The Chrysalids (1955)
The Midwich Cuckoos (1957)

Yalden, Thomas (1670–1736)
poet
The Temple of Fame (1700)

Yarington, Robert (*fl.* 1601)
dramatist
Two Lamentable Tragedies (1601)

'Yates, Dornford' [Cecil William Mercer] (1885–1960)
popular novelist
The Brother of Daphne (1914)
Berry and Co. (1921)

Yates, Edmund Hodgson (1831–94)
journalist, novelist, and short-story writer
My Haunts and their Frequenters (1854)
Black Sheep (1867)

Yearsley, Ann, *née* Cromartie (1752–1806)
poet, dramatist, and novelist
Poems, on Several Occasions (1785)
Poems, on Various Subjects (1787)
A Poem on the Inhumanity of the Slave-Trade (1788)
Stanzas of Woe (1790)
Earl Goodwin: An historical play (1791)
Reflections on the Death of Louis XVI (1793)
The Rural Lyre (1796)

Yeats, William Butler (1865–1939)
poet and dramatist
Mosada (1886)
The Wanderings of Oisin, and Other Poems (1889)
The Countess Kathleen, and Various Legends and Lyrics (1892)
The Celtic Twilight (1893)
The Land of Heart's Desire (1894)
A Book of Irish Verse (1895)
Poems (1895)
The Secret Rose (1897)
The Tables of the Law. The Adoration of the Magi (1897)
The Wind Among the Reeds (1899)
The Shadowy Waters (1900)
Cathleen ni Hoolihan (1902)
Ideas of Good and Evil (1903)
Where There is Nothing (1903)
In the Seven Woods (1903)
The Hour-Glass (1903)
The Hour-Glass; Cathleen ni Houlihan; The Pot of Broth (1904)
The King's Threshold: and On Baile's Strand (1904)
The Tables of the Law; The Adoration of the Magi (1904)
Stories of Red Hanrahan (1905)
Poems, 1899–1905 (1906)
Deirdre (1907)
Discoveries (1907)
The Collected Works in Verse and Prose (1908)
The Unicorn From the Stars, and Other Plays (1908)
The Green Helmet, and Other Poems (1910)
Poems: Second Series (1910)
Synge and the Ireland of his Time (1911)
Responsibilities (1914)
Easter, 1916 (1916)
Responsibilities, and Other Poems (1916)
Reveries Over Childhood and Youth (1916)
The Wild Swans at Coole, Other Verses and a Play in Verse (1917)
Per Amica Silentia Lunae (1918)
Nine Poems (1918)
Two Plays for Dancers (1919)
The Wild Swans at Coole (1919)
Michael Robartes and the Dancer (1921)
Four Plays for Dancers (1921)
The Trembling of the Veil (1922)

Later Poems (1922)
Plays in Prose and Verse (1922)
The Player Queen (1922)
Plays and Controversies (1923)
The Cat and the Moon, and Certain Poems (1924)
Essays (1924)
A Vision (1925)
Autobiographies (1926)
October Blast (1927)
Stories of Red Hanrahan and the Secret Rose (1927)
The Tower (1928)
The Death of Synge, and Other Passages from an Old Diary (1928)
A Packet for Ezra Pound (1929)
Words for Music Perhaps, and Other Poems (1932)
The Winding Stair, and Other Poems (1933)
Collected Poems (1933)
The Words Upon the Window Pane (1934)
Wheels and Butterflies (1934)
Collected Plays (1934)
The King of the Great Clock Tower (1934)
A Full Moon in March (1935)
Dramatis Personae (1935)
Essays 1931 to 1936 (1937)
A Vision (1937)
Autobiography (1938)
The Herne's Egg (1938)
New Poems (1938)
Last Poems and Two Plays (1939)
On the Boiler (1939)
Last Poems and Plays (1940)
Poems (1949)
Mythologies (1959)
Essays and Introductions (1961)

Yonge, Charlotte Mary (1823–1901)
novelist and children's author
Abbeychurch; or, Self-control and Self-conceit (1844)
Scenes and Characters; or, Eighteen Months at Beechcroft (1847)
The Heir of Redclyffe (1853)
The Little Duke; or, Richard the Fearless (1854)
Heartsease; or, The Brother's Wife (1854)
The Lances of Lynwood (1855)
The Railroad Children (1855)
The Daisy Chain; or, Aspirations (1856)
Dynevor Terrace; or, The Clue of Life (1857)
Countess Kate (1862)
The Sea Spleenwort, and Other Stories (1862)
The Trial (1864)
The Clever Woman of the Family (1865)
The Dove in the Eagle's Nest (1866)
The Chaplet of Pearls; or, The White and Black Ribaumont (1868)
The Pillars of the House; or, Under Wode, Under Rode (1873)
Stray Pearls (1883)
The Two Sides of the Shield (1885)
Beechcroft at Rockstone (1888)
The Release; or Caroline's French Kindred (1896)

Yonge, Nicholas (*d.* 1619)
musician
Musica Transalpina. Cantus (1588)
Musica Transalpina. Cantus (1597)

Young, Arthur (1741–1820)
agriculturalist and author
The Theatre of the Present War in North America (1758)
Reflections on the Present State of Affairs at Home and Abroad (1759)
The Adventures of Emmera; or, The Fair American (1767)
The Farmer's Letters to the People of England (1767)
A Six Weeks' Tour Through the Southern Counties of England and Wales (1768)
A Six Months Tour Through the North of England (1770)
The Farmer's Tour Through the East of England (1771)
A Tour in Ireland (1780)
Annals of Agriculture, and Other Useful Arts (1784)
Travels, During the Years 1787, 1788, and 1790 (1792)

Young, Edward (1683–1765)
poet
An Epistle to the Right Honourable the Lord Lansdown (1713)
A Poem on the Last Day (1713)
The Force of Religion; or, Vanquish'd Love (1714)
Busiris, King of Egypt: A tragedy (1719)
A Letter to Mr Tickell (1719)
The Revenge: A tragedy (1721)
The Universal Passion: Satire i (1725)
Ocean (1728)
A Vindication of Providence; or, A True Estimate of Human Life (1728)
Two Epistles to Mr Pope (1730)
Poetical Works of the Reverend Edward Young (1741)
The Complaint; or, Night-Thoughts on Life, Death and Immortality: Night the First (1742)
The Complaint; or, Night-Thoughts on Life, Death and Immortality (1750)
The Brothers: A tragedy (1753)
The Centaur not Fabulous (1755)
The Works of the Author of the Night Thoughts (1757)
Conjectures on Original Composition (1759)
Resignation (1762)

Young, Francis Brett (1884–1954)
novelist
Deep Sea (1914)
The Iron Age (1916)

Young, George Malcolm (1882–1959)
historian

Early Victorian England 1830–65 (1934)
Victorian England (1936)

Zangwill, Israel (1864–1926)
novelist, short-story writer, and playwright
The Big Bow Mystery (1892)
Ghetto Tragedies (1893)
The King of Schnorrers (1894)
Dreamers of the Ghetto (1898)
Ghetto Comedies (1907)

Zephaniah, Benjamin (1958–)
poet and playwright
The Dread Affair (1985)
City Psalms (1992)
Too Black, Too Strong (2001)

Zouch or Zouche, Richard (1590–1661)
lawyer and author
The Dove; or, Passages of Cosmography (1613)
The Sophister: A comedy (1639)

Index of Anonymous Titles

Aben-Hamet, the Last of the Abencerages 1826
Account of the European Settlements in America, An 1757
Adam Bell, Clim of the Clough, and William of Cloudesly 1505
Adventures of Abdalla, The 1729
Adventures of Ladie Egeria, The 1585
Albion Knight 1566?
Alexander the Great 1520?
Amours of Messalina, late Queen of Albion, The 1689
Andria [Terence] 1520?
Antidote Against Melancholy, An 1661
Apius and Virginia 1575
Apocrypha, The 1895
Arabian Nights Entertainments 1706
Arden of Feversham 1592
Aristotles Politiques, or discourses of government 1598
Ars amatoria [Ovid] 1513
Assembly of the Gods, The 1498
Belisarius 1767
Beware the Beare 1650
Boccus and Sydracke 1530?
Boke of Secretes of Albertus Magnus, The 1560
Bonduca 1696
Booke of Common Prayer, The 1549
Book of a Ghostly Father 1521?
Book of Common Prayer, The 1662
Buik of Alexander, The 1580?
Caesar and Pompey 1606
Caesar: Commentaries 1530
Castle Howard 1732
Cawwood the Rooke 1640
Celestina 1596
Christmas Carols 1521
Chronicles of England 1480
Claudius Tiberius Nero 1607
Cobler of Caunterburie, The 1590
Cock Laurel's Boat 1518?
Collection of Pieces on the Occasion of the Dunciad, A 1732
Comical History of Francion, The 1655
Common Conditions 1576
Compleat Key to the Dispensary, A 1714
Costlie Whore, The 1633
Courte of Venus, The 1563?
Court of Atalantis, The 1714
Court of Sapience, The 1480
Court of Venus, The 1538
Critical Remarks on Sir Charles Grandison, Clarissa and Pamela 1754
Dane Hew 1560?
Dangerous Connections 1784
Decameron, The [Boccaccio] 1620
Deceyte of Women, The 1557?
Demaundes Joyous, The 1511
Description of Britain 1480
Destruction of Jerusalem, The 1510?
Dialoges of Creatures Moralysed, The 1530?
Diverting Works of the Countess D'Anois [i.e. d'Aulnoy], *The* 1707
Dives and Pauper 1493
Dramatic Historiographer, The 1735
Eikon Basilike 1649
English in France, The 1828
Essay in Defence of the Female Sex, An 1696
Euordanus Prince of Denmark 1605
Euryalus and Lucretia 1515?
Everie Woman in Her Humor 1609
Everyman 1515?
Fair Em the Miller's Daughter 1591?
Fair Hebrew, The 1729
Family Robinson Crusoe, The 1814
Famous Hystory of Herodotus, The 1584
Famous Victories of Henry the Fifth, The 1598
Fayre Mayde of the Exchange, The 1607
Fissher-Mans Tale, The 1595
Forrest of Fancy, The 1579
Four Cardinal Virtues, The 1545?
Frederick of Jennen 1517?
Friar and the Boy, The 1511?
Generides 1504?
Gentleman's Study, The 1732
Genuine Memoirs of the Celebrated Miss Maria Brown 1766
George a Greene 1599
Gest of Robin Hood, A 1500?
Gesta Romanorum 1502?
Golagros and Gawain 1508
Golden Legend, The 1483
Grete Herball, The 1526
Gulliver Decyphered 1726
Guy of Warwick 1500?
Happy Slave, The 1677
Hermeticall Banquet, A 1651
Heroik Friendship: A tragedy 1719
Hickscorner 1515?
History and Adventures of Gil Blas, The 1716
History of Agathon, The 1773
History of Charlotte Summers, The 1750
History of Little Goody Twoshoes, The 1765
History of Sir William Harrington, The 1771
History of the Earl of Warwick, The 1707
Honest Lawyer, The 1616
Hundred Merry Tales, A 1526?

Image of Idleness, The 1555?
Impatient Poverty 1560
Informacyon for Pylgrymes unto the Holy Londe, The 1515
Ingenious and Diverting Letters of the Lady ---------'s Travels into Spain, The 1691
Jacke of Dover 1604
Jack Juggler 1562?
Jack Upland 1536?
Jacob and Esau 1557
Jacob and Esau 1568
Jeaste of Syr Gawayne, The 1528?
John the Evangelist 1550?
Joseph of Arimathea 1511?
Jovial Crew, The 1731
Kalender of Shepherdes, The 1506
King Alexander 1525?
King Darius 1565
King Edward the Fourth and the Tanner of Tamworth 1596
King Leir, and His Three Daughters 1605
King Ponthus 1509?
Knack to Know a Knave, A 1594
Knack to Know an Honest Man, A 1596?
Knight of Curtesy and the Fair Lady of Faguell, The 1556?
Ladies Library, The 1714
Ladies Tale, The 1714
Larum for London, A 1602
Lazarillo de Tormes. The Second Part 1596
Letter from Mrs Jane Jones, A 1737
Letters Writ by a Turkish Spy 1687
Liberalitie and Prodigalitie 1602
Life and Death of Captaine Thomas Stukeley, The 1605
Life and Death of Hector, The 1614
Life and Death of Jacke Straw, The 1594
Life and Death of Virgil, The 1518?
Life and Memoirs of Mr Ephraim Tristram Bates, The 1756
Life of Marianne, The 1736
Life of Mr Cleveland, Natural Son of Oliver Cromwell, The 1731
Life of Pamela, The 1741
Life of St Thomas 1520
Locrine 1595
London Prodigall, The 1605
Loves Garland 1624
Lusts Dominion 1657
Man in the Moone, Telling Strange Stories, The 1609
Marriage of Wit and Science, The 1570
Mary of Nemmegen 1518?
Maske of Flowers, The 1614
Maxims of the Saints Explained, The [Fenélon] 1698
Maydes Metamorphosis, The 1600
Melusine 1510
Memoirs of a Man of Quality 1738
Memoirs of the Court of England 1707
Memoirs of the Court of Lilliput 1727
Memoirs of the Life and Adventures of Signor Rozelli 1709
Merlin 1510
Merry Devill of Edmonton, The 1608
Merry Tales of Skelton, The 1567
Military Sketch-Book, The 1827
Moral Tales 1775
Morindos a King of Spaine 1609
Mucedorus and Amadine 1598
Mundus & Infans 1522
Narrative of All the Robberies, Escapes, etc. of John Sheppard, A 1724
Natchez, The 1827
New Custom 1573
Nice Wanton 1560
Noble Birth and Gallant Atchievements of Robin Hood, The 1662
Octavian 1505?
Old Christmas 1533
On Old Age [Seneca] 1481
Pamela Censured 1741
Pamela; or, Virtue Triumphant 1741
Paths of Virtue Delineated, The 1756
Paul and Virginie 1788
Peregrinations of Jeremiah Grant, The 1763
Philippes Venus 1591
Phoenix Nest, The 1593
Pierce the Ploughmans Crede 1553?
Pilgrimage of the Soul, The 1483
Ploughman's Tale, The 1535?
Princess Cloria, The 1661
Princess of Cleves, The 1679
Princess of Monpensier, The 1666
Promptorium Parvulorum 1499
Protestant Tutor, The 1679
Puritaine, The 1607
Queen Hester 1561
Rap at the Rhapsody, A 1734
Rare Triumphs of Love and Fortune, The 1589
Rauf Coilyear 1572
Reason Triumphant Over Fancy 1773
Remedy Against the Troubles of Temptations, The 1508
Revengers Tragaedie, The 1607
Richard Coeur de Lion 1509
Robert the Devil 1500?
Robin Good-Fellow 1628
Schole House of Women, The 1541
Scoggins Jestes 1613
Second Part of the Troublesome Raigne of King John, The 1591
Secret History of Queen Elizabeth, and the Earl of Essex, The 1680
Seven Sages of Rome, The 1506?
Sir Bevis of Hampton 1500
Sir Eglamour of Artois 1500
Sir Isumbras 1530
Sir Lamwell 1530?
Sir Torrent of Portingale 1505?
Sir Tryamour 1503?
Solomon and Marcolphus 1529?

Solyman and Perseda 1592
Somebody and Others 1550?
Sorrows of Werter, The 1779
Squire of Low Degree, The 1520?
Swetnam, the Woman-hater 1620
Syr Degore 1512?
Tales of Military Life 1829
Taming of a Shrew, The 1594
Tarleton's Tragical Treatises 1578
Tarltons Newes Out of Purgatorie 1590
Taxes, The 1757
Thersytes 1562?
Thomas Lord Cromwell 1602
Three Kings of Cologne 1496?
Till Eulenspiegel 1555?
Tittle-Tattle 1749
Tragedy of Marcus Tullius Cicero, The 1651
Tragedy of Nero, The 1624
Trial of Treasure, The 1567
Triumph for True Subjects, A 1581
Troublesome Raigne of John King of England, The 1591
Tunbridge-Wells 1677
Tunbridge-Wells 1678
Two Merry Milke-Maids, The 1620
Verses Addressed to the Imitator of Horace 1733
Verses on Occasion of Mr Gulliver's Travels 1727
Vindication of the Press, A 1718
Warres of Cyrus King of Persia, The 1594
Wealth and Health 1565
Westminster-Drollery 1671
Westminster Drollery, the Second Part 1672
William of Palermo 1515?
Wily Beguilde 1606
Wisdome of Doctor Dodypoll, The 1600
Yorick's Meditations upon Various Interesting and Important Subjects 1760
Yorkshire Tragedy, A 1608
Youth 1530?
Ypotis 1520?
Zulima 1719

Index of Periodicals

Adventurer, The 1752
All the Year Round 1859
Annual Register, The 1759
Anti-Jacobin, The 1797
Argosy, The 1865
Athenaeum, The 1828
Athenian Gazette, The 1691
Aunt Judy's Magazine 1866
Belgravia 1866
Bentley's Miscellany 1837
Blackwood's Edinburgh Magazine 1817
Blast 1914
Bookman, The 1891
Bow Bells 1862
Boy's Own Paper, The 1879
British Magazine, The 1760
Cassell's Family Magazine 1874
Chambers's Edinburgh Journal 1832
Champion, The 1739
Cobbett's Political Register 1802
Comic Annual, The 1830
Cornhill Magazine, The 1860
Covent-Garden Journal, The 1752
Craftsman, The 1726
Critical Review, The 1756
Dublin University Magazine, The 1833
Edinburgh Review, The 1802
Englishman, The 1713
Englishman, The 1714
Englishman: Second Series, The 1715
Examiner, The 1710
Examiner, The 1808
Female Spectator, The 1744
Female Tatler, The 1709
Figaro in London 1831
Fraser's Magazine 1830
Free-Holder, The 1715
Free-Thinker, The 1718
Friend, The 1809
Gem, The 1829
Gentleman's Magazine, The 1731
Girl's Own Paper, The 1880
Grub-Street Journal, The 1730
Guardian, The 1713
Household Words 1850
Idler, The 1758
Idler Magazine, The 1892
Illustrated London News, The 1842
Intelligencer, The 1663
Intelligencer, The 1728
Jacobite's Journal, The 1747
Keepsake, The 1828
Ladies Mercury, The 1693
Literary Magazine, The 1756
London Magazine, The 1732
London Spy, The 1698
Longman's Magazine 1882
Lover, The 1714
Macmillan's Magazine 1859
Manufacturer, The 1719
Medley, The 1710
Mercurius Britanicus 1643
Mercurius Politicus 1650
Mercurius Pragmaticus 1647
Mercurius Pragmaticus 1649
Monthly Review, The 1749
Muses Mercury, The 1707
New Monthly Magazine, The 1814
New Statesman, The 1913
Nineteenth Century, The 1877
North Briton, The 1762
Notes and Queries 1849
Observator, The 1681
Occasional Writer, The 1727
Once a Week 1859
Pall Mall Magazine, The 1893
Pearson's Magazine 1896
Plebian, The 1719
Porcupine, The 1800
Publick Adviser, The 1657
Publick Intelligencer, The 1655
Punch 1841
Quarterly Review, The 1809
Rambler, The 1750
Reader, The 1714
Relation of all Matters Passed, A 1614
Review of the Affairs of France, A 1704
Reynolds's Miscellany 1846
St James's Magazine, The 1861
Saturday Review, The 1855
Savoy, The 1896
Scots Magazine, The 1739
Scrutiny 1932
Spectator, The 1711
Spectator, The 1828
Spy, The 1810
Strand Magazine, The 1891
Tatler, The 1709
Temple Bar 1860
Tinsleys' Magazine 1867
Tit-Bits 1881
Town-Talk 1715
True Patriot, The 1745

Westminster Review, The 1824
Whig Examiner, The 1710
World, The 1874
Yellow Book, The 1894